EUROPEAN WRITERS

The Romantic Century

EUROPEAN WRITERS

The Romantic Century

JACQUES BARZUN

EDITOR

GEORGE STADE

EDITOR IN CHIEF

Volume 7

CHARLES BAUDELAIRE

TO

THE WELL-MADE PLAY

CHARLES SCRIBNER'S SONS / NEW YORK

Copyright © 1985 Charles Scribner's Sons

Library of Congress Cataloging in Publication Data
(Revised for volumes 5, 6, and 7)
Main entry under title:

European writers.

    Vols. 5–   . Jacques Barzun, editor; George Stade, editor in chief.
Includes bibliographies.
    Contents: v. 1–2. The Middle Ages and the
Renaissance: Prudentius to Medieval Drama. Petrarch to
Renaissance Short Fiction—v. 3–4. The Age of Reason
and the Enlightenment: René Descartes to Montesquieu.
Voltaire to André Chénier—v. 5–7. The Romantic
Century: Johann Wolfgang von Goethe to Alexander
Pushkin. Victor Hugo to Theodor Fontane. Charles
Baudelaire to The Well Made Play.
    1. European literature—History and criticism—
Addresses, essays, lectures. I. Jackson, W. T. H.
(William Thomas Hobdell), 1915–   . II. Stade, George.
III. Barzun, Jacques, 1907–   .
PN501.E9   1983   809'.894   83–16333
ISBN 0–684–16594–5 (v. 1–2)
ISBN 0–684–17914–8 (v. 3–4)
ISBN 0–684–17915–6 (v. 5–7)

Published simultaneously in Canada
by Collier Macmillan Canada, Inc.
Copyright under the Berne Convention.

"Feodor Dostoevsky": The publisher gratefully acknowledges the permission
granted by Columbia University Press to reprint with editions *Feodor
Dostoevsky* by Ernest J. Simmons. Copyright © 1969 Columbia University
Press. Originally published as number 40 of the Columbia Essays on Modern
Writers series.

"Émile Zola": The Publisher gratefully acknowledges the permission granted
by Columbia University Press to reprint with editions *Emile Zola* by Jean-
Albert Bédé. Copyright © 1974 Columbia University Press. Originally
published as number 69 of the Columbia Essays on Modern Writers series.

The paper in this book meets the guidelines for permanence and durability of
the Committee on Production Guidelines for Book Longevity of the Council
on Library Resources.

EDITORIAL STAFF

LIST OF SUBJECTS

Volume 5

LIST OF SUBJECTS

Volume 6

LIST OF SUBJECTS

Volume 7

viii

LIST OF SUBJECTS

CHARLES BAUDELAIRE
(1821–1867)

LIFE

BAUDELAIRE LIVED IN a world even more aware than our own of rapid transformations in every aspect of life. The term "modernity," which figures importantly in his writings, came into the French language only during his youth. By the time he published *Les fleurs du mal* (*The Flowers of Evil*, 1857) he had already lived under four political regimes. He was born on 9 April 1821 under the Bourbon monarchy that the Allies (Russia, Prussia, and Austria) had restored to the rule of France after they defeated Napoleon in 1815. In 1830 a revolution brought in a constitutional monarchy under the citizen-king Louis-Philippe. This "bourgeois monarchy" yielded in 1848 to a further revolution, and the Second Republic (the first had been under the Revolution, 1792–1804) was instituted, only to succumb to a coup d'etat by Louis Napoleon, nephew of Bonaparte, on 2 December 1851, that soon ushered in the Second Empire.

Titles like "restoration," "second" republic, "second" empire suggest repetitiveness; in fact, the term "revolution" originally characterized the planets' movements in their orbits. In contrast to these political cycles, social and economic currents ran in an irreversible course. Baudelaire's contemporaries understood that there had occurred a change from an aristocratic to a bourgeois society, from a domination by wealthy landowners to the predominance of commercial and industrial interests. A more democratic polity and more dynamic economy made available to writers vastly greater means of publication, particularly in the newly flourishing periodical press, yet it was not clear that the dominant bourgeoisie cared for the literary enterprises that writers might undertake. Baudelaire and his contemporaries therefore cast nostalgic glances back to the aristocracy yet also sympathized with the new workers' movements—for both represented alternatives to the bourgeoisie.

All these changes could be perceived as the falling away from a valued past or as progress toward an ever-improving future. One's status in life was no longer fixed. The minister Guizot, faced with complaints about the property qualification that limited voting rights under Louis-Philippe, could answer simply, "Make yourselves more money" *(enrichissez-vous)*. The power of money in a world of increasingly free markets, in which not only goods but also "free labor" was sold, destroyed traditional values. Karl Marx could characterize the bourgeois age as one in which "all that is solid melts into the air" *(verdampft*, evoking the steam power of new industries). In the 1850's, the great capital city of Paris itself dramatically exemplified this mobile fluidity. Under the direction of Baron Haussmann, old quarters of the city were torn up—especially those that had been rebellious—and grand new avenues regulated and accelerated the flow of traffic, while also facilitating the rapid deployment of troops and free lines of fire in case of an uprising.

Baudelaire's own family offers a vivid emblem of this complex historical layering. His father, Joseph-François, was an old man (born in 1758 under Louis XV) when Charles was born. His life had been shattered and remade by the course of history: he studied in a seminary and was ordained a priest, but during the Revolution he left the church. His connections included intellectually liberal aristocrats (such as Condorcet, the great projector of mankind's future, who died in the Terror), and he finally held a sinecure at the Senate under the first Napoleon's empire. Baudelaire looked back to his father as a cultured man who had practiced both poetry and painting, although with no distinction. Baudelaire's mother was born in 1793 in London, where many French families had emigrated during the Revolution. In his later life Baudelaire recalled the brief period he had enjoyed alone with his mother, after his father's death in February 1827 and before her remarriage in November 1828. The rapid transitions—from life with an elderly father to life alone with his mother to life with a stepfather—must have provoked strong and complex feelings. His stepfather, Jacques Aupick, born in 1789, the year of the Revolution, was over thirty years younger than his father. Having begun his career with Napoleon's army, Aupick managed to flourish under the newer regimes. He became head of the garrison in Lyons at the time of the workers' rebellion there, rose to general, became head of the Polytechnical Institute (France's West Point) in Paris just before the 1848 Revolution, served the new republic as ambassador in Constantinople and then in Madrid, and was named a senator under the Second Empire, dying just before the publication of *Les fleurs du mal* in 1857.

Baudelaire's two fathers represent two ages: one of religion, philosophy, and the arts; the other of the military, technology, and politics. They form a useful model for the contradictions Baudelaire felt within himself, beginning from childhood. Another contradiction also shaped Baudelaire's family life: the extreme propriety of his mother's correspondence with Charles is inconsistent with the sensual details through which his autobiographical jottings depict her. Modern research has discovered, however, that she did not herself lead a life of exemplary propriety: only weeks after her second marriage, she was delivered of a stillborn child. We may thus surmise the compensatory energy behind her expressed shock at Charles's choices in life, the mother's hidden impropriety exaggerating the son's faults.

Baudelaire's life after his mother's remarriage may be seen as a series of disasters. They do not tell the whole story, but they help us to understand his excitement when he read about the ruinous course of the life of Edgar Allan Poe (1809–1849), in which he saw a version of his own. In his last year of secondary school, Baudelaire was expelled for refusing to hand over a note from a schoolmate. While beginning a purely nominal course of legal studies, he contracted venereal disease and ran severely into debt. To keep him out of trouble, his family put him on a ship bound for India, a trip that lasted nearly a year and was intended to be longer. Shortly after his return, he began a liaison with Jeanne Duval. The two lived together much of the next decade, did not finally give up trying to do so until 1856, and remained in touch until at least 1864. A mulatto, minor actress, and prostitute, Jeanne stood outside of all bourgeois norms. She was also of limited intelligence, not passionately attached to Baudelaire, and frequently in a position to exploit him.

On his twenty-first birthday, Baudelaire inherited from his father an estate large enough to give him a comfortable income, but within two years he had reduced his capital by almost half, with further debts impending. His family, as French law allowed, named a trustee to manage the estate (September 1844). Baudelaire thus became again a legal minor. The next year, shortly after the publication of his first signed work (1845), he attempted suicide, after which a period of reasonable calm and productivity followed. In 1848 he joined the revolutionary activity—according to one witness, crying, "We must shoot General Aupick!" Napoleon III's coup d'etat so dismayed him that he was "physically depoliticized" (letter of 5 March 1852). By his middle thirties, his literary career seemed well launched, but in 1857 *Les fleurs du mal* was attacked by the state, leading to the suppression of six poems and to a fine. The remaining decade of Baudelaire's life passed in continuous financial difficulty, worsening health, and loneliness. From 1864 to 1866, he tried living in Brussels in order to escape his creditors, to work on a book, and to earn lecture fees, but all failed and he was stranded there when a stroke left him helpless. He was taken back to Paris, where he died on 31 August 1867, aphasic. It was widely believed that his premature senility resulted from syphilis, but medical debate continues. The disease was very common, often caught by schoolboys on their visits to brothels, and the available treatments were ineffective. Beyond these historical facts, it is striking that Baudelaire might have suffered from the same disease and been struck down at the same age as Adrian Leverkühn, Thomas Mann's representative modern artist in *Doctor Faustus.*

Another version of Baudelaire's life would emphasize his resiliency. On the trip to India he acted heroically during a storm, and more important, this trip gave a basis in experience for a world of poetic imagery drawn from the sea, ships, and the tropics. So too, the relationship with Jeanne Duval was not only, as Baudelaire sometimes insisted, the great love of his life; it was also fundamental to some of his greatest poems. Even the public disgrace inflicted on his poetry bore fruit. Baudelaire had considered *Les fleurs du mal* complete as pub-

lished, and he lamented the need to "artificially become a poet again" (19 February 1858), as he felt obliged to do in order to replace the poems struck from the volume. Nonetheless, the work he did for the second edition (1861) was in both quality and fecundity unmatched in his earlier career. The question of how closely one may, or should, relate the life and the work will come up again, but first a clearer sense of the work is necessary.

THE CORPUS

Baudelaire holds his place in world literature as the author of a book of poetry, *Les fleurs du mal,* yet this slim volume occupies only one out of the seven volumes in the first collected edition (1868–1870). The rest of his work greatly rewards anyone drawn to it by the poetry, and it can fascinate even readers who know nothing of the poems. Because the translation of lyric poetry is so difficult, many English-speaking readers prefer Baudelaire's prose. The assiduity of scholars, following on the devotion of friends, has produced an elaborate edition of Baudelaire's letters. Selections from these can be compelling, and they are invaluable sources for the biography, but Baudelaire is not a great letter-writer like John Keats, Gustave Flaubert, or D. H. Lawrence. His greatest prose is found in his criticism, his studies of the "artificial paradises" of intoxicants, and the *Petits poèmes en prose* (*Paris Spleen,* collected 1869).

Baudelaire's first published writings are in art criticism: he produced commentaries (in the manner of Denis Diderot and extending the insights of Stendhal) on the great annual exhibitions of current painting—the "Salons." The *Salon of 1846,* the "Salon of 1859" (published in the *Revue française*), "The Essence of Laughter" (in *La porte feuille,* 1855), and "The Painter of Modern Life" (in *Figaro,* 1863) are extraordinary works. Not only do they capture the widely various artistic energies of Baudelaire's time—the great romantic canvases of Eugène Delacroix, the mad antics of English pantomime, the journalistic illustrations of Constantin Guys—their ideas and judgments also inspire art critics to this day. He wrote less, and less notably, on literature. The high point in this genre is a review of Flaubert's *Madame Bovary* (1857) in *L'Artiste*, but the essays on his poetic contemporaries are also worth reading. His one piece of music criticism (1863) won him praise from Friedrich Nietzsche as Richard Wagner's first intelligent admirer. Baudelaire's criticism analyzes contemporaries with an acuity that gives the critical writing as firm a place in cultural history as the masterpieces it proclaims.

The bulk of Baudelaire's prose may seem anomalous to American readers; it consists of translations of the prose works of Edgar Allan Poe. The anomaly is double. First, Poe may not seem great enough to merit the labors of a master of world literature. And second, even if we agree that Baudelaire did for Poe's prose what he boasted he had done for Paris—turned into gold the mud he had to start with—there is no way of demonstrating this outside the French language. These translations, however, remain current and classic in French. They have provided an access to Poe for generations of European readers. Later French poet-critics who admired Baudelaire, especially Stéphane Mallarmé and Paul Valéry, carried forward his concern with Poe. The effect has been to make Poe an integral part of European high culture, while in the United States he is popular among relatively uncultivated readers. "Translation" is itself a crucial term in Baudelaire's thinking about the arts. Another translation makes up part of *Artificial Paradises* (*Les paradis artificiels*, collected 1860). These essays on wine, hashish, and opium include Baudelaire's version of Thomas De Quincey's *Confessions of an English Opium-Eater* (1821). Problems of "translation" even haunt Baudelaire's most innovative prose, the fifty "little poems" of *Paris Spleen* that try to achieve a style responsive to the "countless crisscrossing relations" of modern city life. Several of these prose pieces are versions of verse from *Les fleurs du mal.*

Les fleurs du mal offers a textual problem. Because Baudelaire wrote new poems for the second edition to replace those suppressed in 1857, there is no single author's edition that includes all the poems written for the volume. This would not be important, were it not that Baudelaire emphasized in 1857 that the collection had to be understood as a whole, and Barbey d'Aurevilly, with Baudelaire's encouragement, wrote of the volume's "secret architecture." In sending the 1861 edition to Alfred de Vigny, Baudelaire insisted that it was no "collection": it had "a beginning and an end" and the new poems replaced the suppressed ones within a "single framework" (*ca.* 16 December 1861). The usual French solution is to publish the 1861 text, followed by the suppressed poems, but several American translations put them back as close as possible to their original locations. This is unsatisfactory, however, because in making the second edition, Baudelaire moved a number of poems. Thus the location of a poem in 1857 is no guarantee of its same location in 1861. Most readers now discount the claim for a "secret architecture." Although there are clearly principles of resemblance and contrast that give particular poems relations to other poems, and there is some sense of progression through the volume as a whole, no one has demonstrated the necessity for every poem to occur in a particular order. (My references follow the numbering of 1861.)

The 1857 *Fleurs du mal*, after an introductory poem, "To the Reader," contains 100 poems in five sections. The longest section, "Spleen and Ideal," includes 77 poems; next comes "Flowers of Evil," comprising 12 poems; the remaining eleven are divided into "Rebellion," "Wine," and "Death." The 1861 edition contains 126 poems, plus "To the Reader," and excludes the six suppressed. The major difference between the two editions is that in 1861 after "Spleen and Ideal" comes a new section of 18 poems (making it the second largest), "Parisian Scenes." Of these, ten are new and include several of the greatest. The section "Wine" now precedes "Flowers of Evil" instead of following "Rebellion," and the concluding "Death" ends with three new poems, the final poem of the volume being its longest by far, "The Voyage." Even that poem is no longer than 144 lines, and only a handful of poems exceed 50 lines.

Baudelaire is one of the few poets to have achieved recognition as a major poet on the strength of short poems alone. Petrarch's epic, *Africa* (in Latin), not his sonnets, was long accounted his claim to greatness. Shakespeare's 154 sonnets are overshadowed by his 37 plays. For the English romantics, despite their great lyrics, the long work remained a major goal: William Wordsworth's *Prelude*, Keats's *Hyperion*, Percy Bysshe Shelley's *Prometheus Unbound*. Even in the twentieth century, William Butler Yeats and T. S. Eliot wrote plays and long poems. In France, Arthur Rimbaud, Mallarmé, and Valéry, all of whom took much from Baudelaire, nonetheless strove for longer compositions. After *Les fleurs du mal*, Baudelaire thought of writing novels and plays, but he did not. His prose is in minor or secondary genres. We shall return to Baudelaire's place in literary history, but now is the time to enter more intimately into his work.

To begin examining Baudelaire's poetry, I shall take one of the longer poems from *Les fleurs du mal.* It originally appeared in the excerpt from the volume that Baudelaire succeeded in placing in the prestigious *Revue des deux mondes* in 1855. In both editions it comes near the end, in the section "Flowers of Evil."

THE CORPSE: "A VOYAGE TO CYTHERA"

"A Voyage to Cythera" ("Un voyage à Cythère") comprises fifteen quatrains, rhymed *abba*, a pattern the French call "embracing."

The line contains twelve syllables, typically with a caesura—a break—after the sixth. In using this "alexandrine" line, Baudelaire followed the tradition of major French poetry from Ronsard in the sixteenth century, through Racine in the seventeenth, to his own older contemporary Victor Hugo. Baudelaire, however, employs fewer variations on the classic form of the line than did Hugo. As a prosodic conservative, he thus distanced himself from the romantic style.

As a "voyage," this poem has a plot, and its movement is more obvious than in other of Baudelaire's poems, which are sometimes deliberately immobilized. Here movement dominates from the beginning. In the first stanza the heart, "like a bird, flutters" and "soars," while the ship "rolls" over the waves. The first words of the poem, "my heart," suggest a poem of subjectivity, a romantic display of the first-person singular; but instead the first person is omitted from the narrative for twenty lines, for the poem's structure depends on an alternation between personal responses and external descriptions. The narrative represents the coming to terms with a series of discoveries, made visually, from a distance. After the opening, the first person recurs one-third of the way through (line 20, "I glimpsed"), which marks the beginning of the discoveries. The first person returns again just over two-thirds of the way through (lines 45–46, "Your sorrows are mine! / I felt . . ."), where the process of coming to terms begins. This balanced three-part structure is another classically conservative element.

After the buoyancy of the first stanza, the second abruptly shifts register: "What is that sad, black island?" This contrast to the radiance of the first stanza leads to another jolt, for the gloomy island is Cythera, in Greek mythology the home of the goddess of love. But its glamour is worn. No matter what "people say" and "songs" tell, its magic appeal holds only for "old boys," bachelors whose love life has become routine: "Look, after all, it's a poor piece of earth."

Suddenly in the third stanza another voice breaks in to hymn the mysteries of the island in a formal apostrophe: ''Isle of sweet secrets and the holidays of the heart!'' The happy movement of the heart and ship in the first stanza here carries over to the island's air, with the repetition of the verbs ''soar'' (lines 2 and 11) and ''roll'' (lines 3 and 16). The syntax is elevated. Modifiers are placed, contrary to usual practice in speech, before what they modify, thus delaying the appearance of subject and verb. Such ''suspended'' effects echo Latin gravity: ''De l'antique Vénus le superbe fantôme / Au-dessus de tes mers plane comme un arome'' (Of the ancient Venus the proud ghost / Above your waters floats like a scent). By the poem's end we will distrust ghost stories; when banished Venus returns as a ghost, the smell is not all ''roses.'' The invocation reaches its climax in a rolling of repeated *r* sounds, but then the second voice breaks in again, continuing the sound of *r*, but reversing its import: the ''garden of *r*oses'' becomes a ''*r*ocky dese*r*t'' (lines 16 and 19). This dramatic dialogue of two voices exemplifies what often energizes Baudelaire's work, the interplay of levels of speech, often wholly different registers of vocabulary—here the language of song against that of sight, what is heard of in old poetry against what is seen in contemporary encounters.

The narrative again resumes; a ''singular object'' has attracted attention. The next twenty lines specify what has been seen. The description begins by stating what the object is not. The sixth stanza repeats the language of ecstatic classical song, offering a glimpse of erotic intensity that the poem holds out only to deny. For what the object is, standing out in contrast to the ''white sails'' of the ship, is the ''black'' shape of a gibbet—like a ''cypress,'' traditionally the tree of death, rather than the ''myrtle'' (line 13), traditionally the tree of love. The birds too have changed. After the initial resemblances among heart, bird, and ship, in stanza 7 the ship ''troubles'' the birds, breaking the imagined harmony of man and nature, and in stanza 8 nature takes its revenge: ''ferocious birds'' are tearing apart a hanged man. Rapid shifts of language try to assert mobility against the fixating power of this spot. The understatement of calling the hanged man ''ripe'' yields to speaking of him as ''a thing all rotten''; the birds are rehumanized as full of ''anger,'' but their destructiveness is so inhumanly methodical that their beaks are like ''tools.''

The ninth stanza is held by the dreadful object: ''The eyes were two holes, and from the belly, broken open, the heavy intestines flowed down over his thighs, and his tormentors, gorged with dreadful treats, had with the blows of their beaks absolutely castrated him.''

The last movement begins with the speaker addressing the corpse, as he had earlier addressed the island, and in the same outworn vocabulary, ''Dweller of Cythera, child of so lovely a sky.'' The speaker surmises that the hanged man practiced ''disgusting rituals,'' but now—without any formal mark to indicate a second speaker—the language turns wrenchingly: ''Ridiculous hanged man, your sorrows are mine!'' From speculation about the other, the speaker turns to himself: ''Like vomit coming up to my teeth I felt the long river of gall from old sorrows.'' Are these sorrows the speaker's own, or are they a larger human sorrow, stretching back even to the times of Venus' glory? Facing this ''poor devil,'' initial horror and subsequent scorn yield to sympathy. The speaker himself now feels the ''beaks'' and ''jaws'' of ''crows'' and ''panthers'' that ''used so much to love grinding up my flesh.'' The outer scene is internalized. The ''sky'' and ''sea'' may be ''enchanting'' and ''calm,'' but ''for me everything was black and bloody,'' and ''as in a heavy shroud, my heart was wrapped in that allegory.''

Just before the end, the poem acknowledges its mode. The narrative of events in the Mediterranean Sea is redefined as ''allegory.'' The hanged man himself has no value, but is appropriated for another purpose. No connection joins the present speaker and the classical meanings of Cythera that provide the setting: "On your isle, O Venus, I found nothing standing but a symbolic gibbet, from which hung my image." The voyage to Cythera becomes a voyage into a mirror; the horror is not what one sees there, but how one sees oneself. "My image," runs the implied argument, is an image that nauseates me, but also an image I have made. Perhaps I could make another one: "Ah, Lord, give me the strength and courage to face my heart and my body without disgust."

Reading this "flower of evil" helps to define the meaning of that violently contradictory title. The "flowers" of lines 13 and 22, which are absent from the modern island, nonetheless blossom in the form of poetry, while the evil we encounter is not "unspeakable rituals" (line 43)—a literary banality like the "Eldorado" of old songs (lines 6 and 7)—but rather the pain of "old sorrows" (line 48). Wallace Stevens suggested that his poem "Esthétique du mal" was about the relations of poetry and pain, and I find this useful for Baudelaire. "Mal," "evil" or "disease," can also mean "difficulty"—like that of making poetry when all the old songs have already worn out, when even the innovations of romanticism have become clichés.

Baudelaire departs from the norms of romanticism in his management of the "I." This poem makes programmatically clear how little that "I" can be identified with the empirical existence of Charles Baudelaire. Baudelaire never voyaged in the Mediterranean. The poem's setting comes from Gérard de Nerval, who in 1844 published several journalistic pieces on his disillusion on encountering the old isle of Cythera, then barren under English rule. Here is an excerpt from Nerval:

I saw a little monument, vaguely standing out against the azure of the sky, and which . . . seemed the still standing statue of some tutelary divinity. But as we approached further, we made out clearly the object . . . which drew that coast to the attention of travelers. It was a gallows, with three branches, of which only one was decorated [occupied by a corpse].

(L'Artiste, 11 August 1844)

Baudelaire's poem translates the writing of another into his own. This is not unique in his method. The sonnet "Unluck" ("Leguignon," 11) translates stanzas from Henry Wadsworth Longfellow for its octave and from Thomas Gray for its sestet, yet the poem is both successful and as fully "Baudelaire's" as any other. Baudelaire's "I," then, is a certain way of negotiating a relationship with literature. Baudelaire felt sure that he had never plagiarized from Poe, because all he had found in Poe was himself. For Baudelaire, the process of reading or seeing was, to the extent that it succeeded, a finding of himself in what he read or saw. This may lead to the claustrophobia of "spleen" or the self-tormenting, ironic self-observation frequent in his work. Baudelaire could discover himself in very uncomfortable ways—the hanged man of Cythera, or Poe, execrated by the American bourgeoisie and driven to a shameful death—but the process could also be wonderfully satisfying. In all cases, the process is a transfer of properties; something becomes merely a sign for something else, as in allegory.

As often in Baudelaire, "A Voyage to Cythera" employs classical versification and rhetoric and yet demonstrates that the traditional understanding of the classical has no value for us; and that Venus' isle may never have been so alluring as the songs said, although it was once important to think it so. Baudelaire attacked the "Pagan School" of poets who relied on classical myth, and he relished the savage caricatures of ancient history produced by the artist Honoré Daumier. In the Salon of 1846, he mocked the classical genre of tragedy as a dead form in which inhuman restrictions are put on human motivations and appetite. "Realism of subject matter and classicism of form" is a tempting slogan, but Baudelaire never praised realism, and he

1329

always acknowledged that the romantics had "rejuvenated" and even "resuscitated" French poetry (essay on Théophile Gautier). An English example illustrates the positive side of Baudelaire's relation to romanticism. The movements of "A Voyage to Cythera" and Keats's "Ode to Psyche" are strikingly parallel. Keats laments that Psyche came too late in classical mythology to have a cult:

> . . . Temple thou hast none,
> Nor altar heap'd with flowers;
> No virgin-choir to make delicious moan
> . . . no heat
> Of pale-mouth'd prophet dreaming.
> (28–30, 34–35)

So in Baudelaire, "There was no temple with wooded shades where the young priestess, loving flowers, would go, her body aflame with secret warmth." In both cases the absence of external trappings turns the poetry inward, in Keats more hopefully: "Yes, I will be thy priest, and build a fane / In some untrodden region of my mind," and there will flourish "branched thoughts, new grown with pleasant pain."

Yet to see in Baudelaire only the nonempirical "I," the recourse to allegory, the translation of one literary work into another, is to ignore much. For his poetry clearly also relates to the experience of Paris in the Second Empire, the experience of a man with a complex erotic life in a varied social world. The sea of "A Voyage to Cythera" is not wholly alien to Paris. The city itself becomes oceanic: "Tell me, does your heart sometimes fly, Agatha, far from the black ocean of the filthy city, to another ocean where splendor shines?" (72). From a Paris garret, chimneys and bell towers seem "masts of the city" (86). The "multitude" of the city and the "solitude" of the ocean are "equal and convertible for the active poet" ("Crowds," in *Paris Spleen*). The principle of transfer that makes possible allegory and translation connects diverse elements of life. Baudelaire had traveled, but in thinking

of De Quincey, who had not, he turned to the "voyager," the "ancient mariner," as "metaphors that poets use" for a man who has struggled with life (*Artificial Paradises*). James Joyce's figure of Ulysses for the modern city-dweller already lurked in Baudelaire.

TWO BODIES ("CARRION" AND "JEWELS")

The response to seeing a corpse in a setting designed for love runs from "A Voyage to Cythera" through many other of Baudelaire's most striking poems. A dead body focuses attention from the beginning of "Carrion" ("Une charogne," 29; also translated as "A Corpse"): "Remember the object that we saw, my soul, that sweet and lovely summer morning, at the turn of a path, a foul corpse, on a bed scattered with pebbles, its legs in the air like a lewd woman." The poem's effect comes from the tension between horror and beauty, the past sight and the present address to the beloved. The initial rhyming contrast between "soul" (*âme*) and "foul" (*infâme*) is exacerbated. Both the positive and the negative are amplified, and the positive becomes an aspect of the corpse itself: "The sky watched the splendid carcass open like a flower." Rhyming with these lines is the contrasting second half of the stanza: "The stench was so strong that you thought you would faint on the grass." "Open" (*s'épanouir*) and "faint" (*évanouir*) echo each other, and the formal preterite tense of narrated action (*crûtes*, "thought") powerfully distinguishes human queasiness from natural process, described in the imperfect tense. The poem recalls medieval verse in its contempt of the flesh, and even more closely baroque poems (such as Andrew Marvell's "To His Coy Mistress") that seek to win a lover through exploitation of religious sentiments, but the end strikes a new note. The final turn contrasts the body of the beloved, whom the poem reduces from "soul" to corpse, with the achievement of the poet:

"Then, my beauty, tell the vermin who will eat you with their kisses, that I have preserved the form and divine essence of my decomposed loves."

The last word of the poem, "decomposed," is not only a term of organic decay; it is also a key term in Baudelaire's aesthetics. In the "Salon of 1859" he argues that the Imagination is "queen of the faculties" because it "decomposes all creation" and with the "amassed materials" it "creates a new world." In the poem, the process of "giving back" to Nature "all that it had joined together" produces a new flowering and a "strange music." The corpse becomes a "sketch" left for the "artist to finish . . . from memory." Baudelaire's criticism warns against directly imitating nature and urges instead recourse to "memory." The poem thus offers further insight into what "fleurs du mal" might be. Their beauty is difficult, to achieve it may be a dreadful task that takes all the writer's energy: one's soul threatens to faint along the way. This difficulty emerges again in a prose poem, "The Artist's Profession of Faith" ("Le *confiteor* de l'artiste"). A glorious day at the seashore threatens to overwhelm his capacities, provoking this final formulation: "The study of beauty is a duel in which the artist cries out in fear before he is beaten."

A comparable interplay of mastery and submission shapes the confrontation with another body and another beauty in "Jewels" ("Les bijoux," 6), one of the suppressed poems. The loved one, although naked, has yielded to her lover's "heart" and kept on her "sonorous jewels," which give her the "conquering air" that, paradoxically, "Moorish slaves" have. She calmly "let herself be loved." Here she is a "tamed tiger," but her body then "troubles" and "disorders" the speaker's repose. There is no overt violence in the scene, yet the language of power pervades it, and the poem ends ominously with the dying firelight "flooding with blood that amber-colored skin." Within this framework is set the "ecstasy" produced in the speaker by the "sparkling world of metal and stone," the jewels where "sound and light are mixed," and by the "metamorphoses" of the beloved's "poses": "And her arm and her leg, and her thigh and her loins, polished like oil and curved like a swan . . . and her belly and her breasts, those grapes of my vine."

As in "A Voyage to Cythera" and "Carrion," the eyes encounter the parts of another body, but the "decomposition," the dismemberment here, in contrast to the other poems, is registered positively. Even a mixture that might seem grotesque provides pleasure: "I thought I saw united by a new design the hips of Antiope with the chest of a boy, that is how much her pelvis stood out from her waist." Perhaps the jewels' stone and metal guard this body against decay, making it hard rather than soft—as elsewhere we see a woman whose "polished eyes are made of enchanting minerals," who is "nothing but gold, steel, light, and diamonds" (27). The "statue with jet eyes, great angel with brow of bronze" (39) figures as a paradoxical positive ("front d'airain" also has the sense of a bold front, a brazenness). The soft, vulnerable body usually associated with love is notably absent. At rare moments a fraternal feeling for "the vomit of Paris" (105) allows Baudelaire to speak as "The Soul of the Wine" (L'Âme du vin, 104) and promise to restore to the worker's son his vigor and color, to be for "that frail athlete of life the oil that strengthens again the muscles of wrestlers."

In their contrast between disgust and ecstasy, as well as between the "soft" and the "hard" body, "Carrion" and "Jewels" define extremes of Baudelaire's work, and they thus help us to understand the contrast of "Spleen" and "Ideal" in the section in which they stood only half a dozen poems apart in 1857. "Extremes" defines a major effect of Baudelaire's poetry and of his reputation. If these two poems stand in dramatic contrast with one another, they resemble each other in their divergence from the ordinary norms of love poetry and good taste. Shock is omnipresent in Baudelaire's work. He proclaimed that beauty is always strange ("bizarre") and that its effect is "astonishment." This sense of beauty is related to his life in Paris, the great capital of choked, foggy streets, where "the ghost in broad daylight accosts [the verb *raccrocher* is often used of a prostitute's solicitation] the passerby" (90). The "magic" of the city is violent, as "paving stones rise into fortresses" (sketch for epilogue to *Les fleurs du mal*) in the barricades of revolutionary days, times that fill the city with corpses at every turning.

The city forms a basic structure for experience, and it also provides a consciously felt environment. One resorts to shock to stand out from the crowd, to assert one's own life against the surrounding, ghostly wraiths. Among the crowd of all those who have ever written, to differentiate oneself requires something striking. Baudelaire found in Poe, moreover, an argument he made his own: human incapacity for attention over a prolonged period, the "interrupted reading" imposed by "needs of business," constrains the artist. Commercial culture becomes an argument for short lyrics. So too, in a city where the eye predominates over the ear, where images more than sounds are the stuff of poetry and experience, the short poem offers the advantage of a readily apprehensible, visible form.

Baudelaire's shocking effects arise from the depths of city life, and they directly respond to some of its circumstances. They also willfully outrage bourgeois decorum. Baudelaire rightly prided himself on the traditional excellence of his spelling, his grammar, his diction, and his verse-making, but none of these literary virtues carried any weight with a public indifferent to writing as a craft. Romantic emphasis on inspiration here conspired with bourgeois ignorance. Baudelaire's poetry shocked by its subject matter of prostitution and perversion. In a society that condoned the everyday exploitation of workers' bodily labor to bring wealth to others, it was considered poetically unmentionable that some women (estimated at 34,000 in Paris of the 1850's) should sell their bodies to bring pleasure to others. The "ideal" of such moralistic denial of the flesh was one target for Baudelaire. He agreed throughout his career with Stendhal's formulation that "beauty is a promise of satisfaction," not a self-sufficient object of contemplation. Therefore he could never wholly accept the post-Kantian idealist aesthetics of disinterest that for the bourgeoisie stood as a detached realm beside capitalist economics: the contemplation of forms on display for themselves alone, beside the exploitation of bodies in toil for production. The body that sells pleasure by displaying itself contradicts both bourgeois aesthetics and economics. But, viewed differently, the prostitute paradoxically fulfills bourgeois norms, for the sale of "love" completes the centuries-long process of desanctification that reduces every "value" to the market. Thus in the poem's beginning, "You'd take everyone in the world into your bed," the woman addressed has "eyes lit up like shop windows" (25).

The prostitute has a further place in Baudelaire's poetry. The prostitute not only violates bourgeois decency and criticizes its hypocrisy by taking bourgeois commercial values to an unacknowledged logical extreme, but she also images the poet. In an early manuscript poem, Baudelaire writes of his love, "To have shoes she has sold her soul, but God would laugh if I . . . put on high airs by this disgrace, I who sell my thought and want to be an author" ("Je n'ai pour maîtresse une lionne illustre"). If the prostitute sells her soul by selling her body, does not the writer do even worse by selling his thought? The journalistic market in *esprit*, wit, intelligence, made the writer deeply complicit in the bourgeois mechanisms that he opposed and that stifled him. The ideal of free thought, confronted with the necessities of the free market, created a partially paralyzing conflict marked by key terms like "ennui" and "spleen" in Baudelaire's work. As a productive writer, one contributed to the din, the traffic, that drowned out value.

Baudelaire's short poems respond to two possibilities within this situation: first, the need for a powerful form to fix, to still, the chaos; second, the need for a sudden opening, a shock that unfixes the reader's usual self. Thus Baudelaire praised the sonnet form; its constraint makes its idea "spring forth more energetically." He then develops an image drawn from urban experience: "Have you noticed that a bit of sky, seen through a cellar window, or between two chimneys . . . or through an arcade, gives a deeper idea of infinity than the grand panorama you see from the top of a mountain?" (letter of 18 February 1860). The sonnet in France as in England had fallen into disuse after the Renaissance and was explicitly revived by romanticism. Yet great romantic poets like Victor Hugo did not write in the form, so Baudelaire's use of it, while "romantic," still allowed him room for individuality.

POLARITIES

Probably Baudelaire's most famous poem is the sonnet "Correspondences" ("Correspondances," 4), which in its narrow space opens out an infinity:

> Nature is a temple, where living pillars sometimes murmur confused words. Man passes through it by forests of symbols that look at him with familiar gazes. Like long echoes that from afar mix themselves into a deep and shadowy unity, vast as night and as day, smells, colors, and sounds answer back to each other. There are smells cool as babies' flesh, sweet as oboes, green as meadows, and others corrupt, rich, and triumphant, that have the expansion of infinite things, like amber, musk, benzoin, and incense, and sing the transports of the spirit and the senses.

This poem has long been understood in relation to the subsequent literary movement called symbolism. But as we saw in "A Voyage to Cythera," Baudelaire does not make any significant distinction between the terms "symbol" and "allegory." In this he differs from such romantics as Johann Wolfgang von Goethe and Samuel Taylor Coleridge, for whom "translucence" distinguishes the symbol. Baudelaire, however, emphasizes "shadowy" confusion. No principle joins any element firmly to any other: a sensory motif returns to the primal unity, and when it comes back it may be transformed into anything else. That is, the principle of "correspondence" unmoors things from their properties. As in allegory, nothing is itself alone and for itself, but it may function as a relay for something else. In his *Intimate Journals* (*Journaux intimes*, 1887), Baudelaire writes of "prostitution" as the process by which a unity becomes a duality, that is, a unique property becomes the property of another. In this sense of the word, correspondences are not only a mode of allegory but also a mode of prostitution. The infinity opened up offers "transports of . . . the senses," a phantasmagoria of sensory transfer, a free market in the sensual.

Much later, in "Spleen and Ideal," Baudelaire offers another version of this perception. "Obsession" (79) answers back to "Correspondences." Its last words repeat "familiar gazes" from early in "Correspondences," and its opening image transforms the "temple" of Nature: "Great forests, you terrify me like cathedrals!" Only night might please the speaker, but the light of its stars "speaks a language that I know." He seeks instead "the blank, the black, and the bare"—an end to the ceaseless transports, by which one property becomes only a sign for another. But the process continues: the "shadows" become "canvases," on which there "live . . . departed beings with familiar gazes."

Both poems depend on correspondences and both might be called obsessional, though the one has the positive tone of mystical experience and the other the negative of Renaissance mad songs. The echo of "familiar gazes" suggests that each evokes "family" experience, a sense of totality that may begin in the infant's relation to its mother's body as a total and surrounding world. Such unity precedes knowledge of oneself as a separate individuality, whether painfully as in "A Voyage to Cythera" or with exhilarating liberation. Baudelaire speculated that the power of "genius" is that of "childhood, recaptured through an act of will" ("The Painter of Modern Life"). Yet as he recalled childhood, not only were there moments of sensual correspondence like that by which he "confounded" the "odor of fur" with that of womankind, he also found in his earliest experience "two contradictory sentiments" coexisting: "the horror of life and the ecstasy of life" (*Intimate Journals*.)

Some of Baudelaire's poems, like "A Voyage to Cythera," move from ecstasy to horror. Others, like "Carrion," blend the two very closely together. Yet others, like "Correspondences" and "Obsession," are strongly polarized toward one or the other extreme. Less important than Baudelaire's explicit statements of value are the continuing ambivalence of "contradictory sentiments" and the recurrent patterns that cut across any particular emphasis. One such pattern is that of disillusion, as in "A Voyage to Cythera," but this very notion is double-edged. Disillusion is "strange" (*bizarre*, like the beautiful): "half regret for the vanished phantom, half pleasant surprise at the novelty of the real fact" ("The Rope," in *Paris Spleen*). The confidence of reposing on something solid, no matter how barren and rocky, brings reassurance.

In this light we may contrast "Paris Dream" ("Rêve parisien," 102) with "The Abyss" ("Le gouttre," first published in 1862). These two late poems touch opposite extremes. The flashing limbs of "Jewels" moved Baudelaire to figures like those of the biblical Song of Songs (breasts become "grapes of my vine"). His dream of Paris elaborates the "world of metal and stone" into a vision like that of the New Jerusalem in Revelation, a city that transcends nature: "I had banished from these spectacles the vegetable, which is irregular, and proud of my genius . . .

I enjoyed . . . the intoxicating monotony of metal, marble, and water." This "terrible landscape" is both a glorious creation of will and a source of fright to its creator. It extends Ralph Waldo Emerson's fear that "things are in the saddle and ride mankind," that human creation has overreached human control, like Frankenstein's monster. The city itself was a human creation that thinkers from Wordsworth at the beginning of the century to Georg Simmel at the end believed was going beyond human control and causing human nature to change, even so fundamentally as in the balance among the senses. The eye was thought to be predominating over the ear. The end of Baudelaire's dream fulfills this tendency: over the scene there reigned "(terrible novelty! Everything for the eye and nothing for the ears!) a silence of eternity." Here the dream breaks off. Against the dream's "eternity" and "silence," the clock is "brutally striking noon"; the speaker's eyes, "full of flame" from his vision, awake to "the horror" of his shabby room.

In "The Abyss" the terrible novelty of vision offers only horror, without ecstasy, and produces constant "vertigo." In the "Paris Dream," the enclosure of the room contrasts the breadth of vision, but in "The Abyss" vision is terror, and waking provides no escape: "I'm afraid of sleep as I would be afraid of a big hole. . . . I see nothing but infinity from all the windows."

"Elevation" ("Élévation," 3) and "The Longing for Nothingness" ("Le goût du néant," 80) likewise draw different emotions from comparable situations. "Elevation" clearly celebrates a traditional understanding of the "ideal." The poet's spirit "moves with agility" above the earth, even beyond the sun and the heavenly spheres. The serene fields of light are a happy change from the fogs of existence, for those "whose thoughts like larks take free flight to the skies in the morning"— like the birds of "A Voyage to Cythera." This happy spirit gains an overview, "soars over life," and "effortlessly understands the language of flowers and dumb things." Yet this overview has little content; contrast the success of Wordsworth's "Tintern Abbey" in substantiating what it means to "see into the life of things." If one has soared beyond all life, why should one even be interested in the language of things? In the following poem, "Correspondences," we have noted that the "confused words" of nature lack the clarity promised here. The poem's energy is in the flight, not the goal; the movement itself produces value. "Elevation" prefigures the bitter wisdom of "The Voyage" ("Le voyage") that concludes *Les fleurs du mal:* "We want . . . to plumb the depths of the abyss, Hell or Heaven, what difference, to the bottom of the Unknown to find something *new!*"

Even more closely, however, "Elevation" is answered by "The Longing for Nothingness." Again the speaker is beyond the world, which no longer touches him; even "lovely spring has lost its smell." Again he takes an overview: "I observe from above the globe's roundness, and I don't even try to find there the shelter of a hut." The situation is like that of a stranded mountain-climber: "Time swallows me up minute by minute as an endless snow does a stiffened body." The only wish is to end this paralysis, which is, paradoxically, painful in its absence of feeling: "Avalanche, will you carry me down in your fall?" Against the "ideal" of "Elevation," here is "spleen." Yet the situation makes possible a new, rich story—that of the descent. If the soaring of "Elevation" and its birds no longer works, there remains the "plunging" so frequent in Baudelaire's world. Here we understand another meaning of "fleurs du mal."

The path downward has traditionally been painful and evil, but it inspires Baudelaire's most original poetry, even if that poetry must begin from the already worn trappings of romantic satanism. In helping Baudelaire think about how to defend his poetry from prosecution, the great critic Sainte-Beuve offered a line of analysis familiar to English readers from Keats's melancholy reflections on the sit-uation of the late-coming poet. As Baudelaire put it in notes for a preface to the second edition: "Illustrious poets had already divided up a long time ago the most flowery provinces of the kingdom of poetry. It seemed to me pleasant, and all the more agreeable because the task was difficult, to draw *beauty* from "mal" [evil, pain, difficulty]." Or in Sainte-Beuve's terms: "Lamartine had taken the skies. Victor Hugo had taken the earth, and more than the earth. Laprade had taken the forests. Musset had taken passion. . . . Others had taken the home, rural life, etc. . . . What was left? What Baudelaire took" ("Petits moyens de défense" for Baudelaire's trial, cited in notes to Pléiade 1. 790).

Baudelaire drew energy from doing what previous poets had left undone, no matter how difficult and painful. Even more, though, the arrangement of *Les fleurs du mal* and the chronology of Baudelaire's works (the two are not identical, but here they tend to confirm each other) suggest that his continuing poetic production depended on his reading of his work in order to renew it, bringing out unexploited aspects of situations, feelings, images, and words that he had already used. Self-reading likewise accounts for the writing in such prose poems as "A Hemisphere in a Woman's Hair," "The Invitation to the Voyage," and "The Widows," which closely correspond to poems from *Les fleurs du mal* ("Hair," 23, "The Invitation to the Voyage," 53, and "The Little Old Women," 91). We return to translation and the allegorical procedure that assigns fresh meaning to a given setting.

SPLEEN

Baudelaire's "spleen," which we touched on in "The Longing for Nothingness," is not unprecedented. Coleridge's "Dejection" ode wishes for the violence of a storm to "startle this dull pain, and make it move and live." Nonetheless, Baudelaire made this vein his own, and later poets cannot touch it without fearing his influence. His poems of the "Ideal" are admirable performances of a kind that many poets have succeeded in; his poems of the charnel house or brothel build a tension between subject and treatment that many readers even now cannot accept. Only the "Parisian Scenes," we shall see later, remain equally powerful.

Poems 75 through 79 bear the title "Spleen," and number 74, "The Cracked Bell" ("La cloche fêlée"), was first published in 1851 under the title "Spleen." The word "spleen" in French is taken directly from English and denotes a particularly modern and thus somewhat "alien" form of melancholy. It is related to the more traditional "ennui" (a word English takes from French), which in "To the Reader" ("Au lecteur") Baudelaire allegorically transformed into the deadliest of sins: "Although he does not make a big stir or a big fuss, he would willingly make the earth a ruin, and in a yawn swallow the world. . . . His eye weighted with an involuntary tear, he dreams of scaffolds while smoking his hookah." This "delicate monster" resembles the figure the speaker says he is like in the third "Spleen" (77), "the king of a rainy country, rich, but impotent, young and yet very old," who cannot be cheered by "hunting, nor hawking, nor his people dying in front of his balcony." In *The Waste Land,* T. S. Eliot drew on the opposite imagery, that of drought, to develop a similar feeling.

Spleen, as we saw in "The Longing for Nothingness," is inseparable from a distortion of time. The fourth "Spleen" (78) begins with three parallel stanzas, each invoking and prolonging the same dreary moment, "When . . . When . . . When. . . ." The sudden furious howling of bells that breaks this suspense brings only a slow, silent procession within the speaker's spirit. The mood is not dispelled but exacerbated, and the "Hope" that earlier fluttered timidly "like a bat" now "weeps" in defeat. The decor of everyday life composes the scene: "my cat, trying to make a bed on the tiles" (75); "a big chest of drawers loaded

with accounts, verses, love letters, lawsuits, romances, with heavy tresses rolled up in receipts"; "I am an old boudoir full of faded roses, where a jumble of outworn fashions lies" (76). And this scenery comes to life: "The big bell mourns, and the smoking log sings along in falsetto with the sniffling clock," while in a smelly pack of cards "the jack of hearts and the queen of spades speak forebodingly of their used-up loves" (75).

The "language of flowers" in "Elevation" seemed to promise something good, but this language of "mute things" oppresses the hearer. And in hearing it, he becomes like the things that speak it. The old desks and dressing rooms are figures for the speaker. The "I" is dispersed among things. The poem begins, "I have more *souvenirs* than if I were a thousand years old," and it takes full advantage of the ambiguity by which *souvenirs* can mean either "memories"—spiritual presences in the mind—or "memorials," "keepsakes," things by which memory may be evoked. This hovering between the material and mental, this weighting of the spirit together with a discomforting vivacity in things, begins the sequence of the four "spleen" poems, and ends it, in allegory.

The first one begins: "Pluviose [personification of a rainy month], angered against the whole city, lavishly pours from his urn a shadowy cold upon the inhabitants of the neighboring cemetery, and mortality upon the foggy suburbs." The most chilling effect is produced by the grammatical parallel that indifferently connects the dead and the living. But there is some difference: the cemeteries have "inhabitants" (the figure of speech that thus abuses reality is called catachresis), while the suburbs, through the figure of metonymy, have swallowed up their dwellers, so that the poem speaks of the place but not the people. "Mortality" is puzzling; why not simply "death?" In one way, there is a great difference between death and mortality. Since it is the liability to death, mortality can be properly attributed only to those who are living, and by this logic to "pour out mortality" is to insist on the life of those it is poured out on, as if until that moment they had been not only living but immortal. Another sense for the term, however, emerges from the newly massive and intensive statistical studies of nineteenth-century Paris, including elaborate tables of mortality drawn up neighborhood by neighborhood. To speak of "mortality," then, suggests the statistical chance of death. Even something so intimate as death can be viewed impersonally and economically. A person has a particular probability of death just as a commodity has a particular probability of being sold. What happens to the individual becomes a function of numerical accounting.

The allegorical figure of "Pluviose" requires comment. The image of the water-bearer is traditional (Aquarius in the Zodiac), but the name "Pluviose" was newly invented for the calendar designed in the French Revolution. The term was both new—existing in the language only since 1792—and discarded—since the revolutionary calendar had been put aside and was never revived. Thus the status of this figure to whom such grand power is attributed is no different from that of the "superannuated fashions" in the boudoir. They too were just invented and already defunct.

The last "Spleen" ends, "Long hearses, without drums or music, move slowly through my soul; Hope, beaten, weeps, and dreadful Anguish, despotic, on my bowed skull plants his black flag." To this allegory of the emotions, we might contrast a moment from Petrarch's sonnets: "Love, who in my thought lives and reigns and keeps his principal seat in my heart, sometimes comes armed upon my forehead and settles down there and puts up his banner" ("In vita," 91). The shift from "forehead" to "skull" suggests a graver defeat and exemplifies Baudelaire's insistence on the anatomical, as in "Carrion," which Sainte-Beuve called "petrarchizing upon the horrible." Even more striking is the shift from the triumph of love to that of anguish. This is the poetry of terminal conditions, perhaps even of a world that is ending. In notes for a preface to reissuing *Les fleurs du mal,* Baudelaire characterized his inspiration as the "Muse of the last days." Yet the worst terror of the condition is that it seems as if nothing can end; the wish for nothingness persists: if *only* it were the last days, if only the avalanche would carry me down.

The final image of the second "Spleen" transposes this sense of apocalypse to one of its privileged locations for the Western imagination, to Egypt, the land whose monumental constructions and hieroglyphic inscriptions had impressed even the ancient Greeks as signs of mysterious wisdom, but no one knew specifically what. (Only a few decades before Baudelaire wrote, Jean François Champollion had won fame for deciphering the Rosetta stone.) The condition of protracted terminality, in a mind with more memories than a millennium would bring, is evoked as "an old sphinx ignored by an indifferent world, forgotten on the map, and with a savage spirit that sings only to the rays of the setting sun." The song of sunset, the poetry of decadence, the flowers of evil, the muse of the last days— all these are suggested. But the sun sets only to rise again. Sunset brings no more relief than do the bells of the fourth "Spleen."

An impatient desire constricted—as by the sphinx's stone—paralyzed, unable to satisfy or even to terminate itself, this condition of spleen also occurs in "The Cracked Bell": "My soul is cracked, and when in its boredom it wants to people the cold night air with its songs, it often happens that its weakened voice seems the thick rasp of a wounded man, forgotten beside a lake of blood, under a great pile of the dead, and who is dying—immobile—amidst tremendous efforts." This correspondence transports the mind and senses, transforming the self into someone else and far away, but the new identification is no more gratifying than the one on Cythera. The night is "peopled" only with corpses; like Pluviose the poet pours forth something chilling.

CHARLES BAUDELAIRE

RETARDED MOVEMENT

This paralyzed voice in "The Cracked Bell" gives an image for the labored movement of Baudelaire's poems. Part of his accomplishment was to make beauty from slowness and stiffness. A number of his poems use refrains or repeated lines within a stanza form. These devices slow down the poems and make them seem more like objects in space than movements in time. "The Invitation to the Voyage" ("L'Invitation au voyage," 53) is only a prelude; the voyage never occurs but remains suspended in the optative: "My baby, my sister, think of the sweetness of going away to live together there, to love and die in the country that's like you! . . . There everything is nothing but order and beauty, luxury, calm, and sensual bliss." There the time passes happily: "Shining furniture polished by the years would decorate our rooms. . . . There everything is nothing but order and beauty, luxury, calm, and sensual bliss." Even immobility is not anguished but tranquil: "See on those canals, those ships asleep with their wayfaring spirit. . . . There everything is nothing but order and beauty, luxury, calm, and sensual bliss." If every voyage fosters hopes that the arrival will dash (see the prose poem "Already!" ["Déjà!"]), the "Invitation" is the voyage to the voyage, and thus doubly secure and happy.

Because they are a means of voyaging, ships pleased Baudelaire. He admired the beautiful complications of moving shapes produced by the lines and masts of a ship as it is under way, the metamorphoses of "imaginary figures" that its "real elements" engender (*Intimate Journals*). We have seen the attraction of the ship in "A Voyage to Cythera"; in "The Beautiful Ship" ("Le beau navire," 52), the ship epitomizes the beauty and elegance of the beloved: "When you go sweeping the air with your wide skirt, you give the effect of a beautiful ship, heading out to sea, its canvas spread, that goes rolling with a rhythm that's sweet, and lazy, and slow." This poem finds a way to hold that movement within a rhythm of its own. After the first three stanzas, the poem repeats the first stanza, then follows it with two new ones, repeats the second stanza, followed by two new ones, repeats the third stanza, and ends.

A more intricate pattern of retardatory repetition is seen in "Evening Harmony" ("Harmonie du soir," 47). The musical suggestion of its title proclaims its ambition to shape time pleasurably, while the music of its rhymes is a tour de force: the whole poem uses only two rhymes in its sixteen lines. The subject of the poem is time—both a time of day and a particular moment within the recurrence of this hour. In the second "Spleen" the sphinx's song of sunset lost its apocalyptic finality through our awareness of repetition; in "Evening Harmony" the poem moves gradually from acknowledging the multiple repetitions of sunset to focusing on one in particular.

The poem begins, "Here come the times when swinging on its stalk each flower gives off odor like a censer; sounds and smells move round in the evening air, melancholy waltz and slow swoon." In the next stanza, the second line becomes the first and the fourth line the third—thus allowing for two new lines, which in their turn are repeated in the third stanza, and so on. The persistence of the rhymes would allow for the poem's complete closure by a return to the first and third lines of the first stanza as the second and fourth lines of the last. Another possible closure would be normal in this *pantoum* form: the first line repeated as the last. Baudelaire follows neither pattern. The "times" of line 1 gradually become a particular time. The present tense of habitual repetition changes its status; in line 12 a past tense is introduced that could comport only with the normal specificity of a singular present. In itself this twelfth line, which defines the poem's temporality, could well belong to a spleen poem: "The sun has set in its blood that is congealing." The final stanza, however, sets this line, when it is repeated, in a context of hope, which speaks of a "tender heart" gathering up "every trace of the radiant past" and concludes, "Your memory shines within me like a monstrance." The monstrous sphinx at sunset arouses terror or dismay among those who behold it, but this monstrance at sunset awakens reverent awe and seems to give a light of its own.

One more poem can illustrate the variety and complexity with which Baudelaire works through the modes of repetition. "The Irreparable" ("L'Irréparable," 54) uses a five-line stanza in which the last line very closely repeats the first, most often identically. Only once in the first eight stanzas does the sense run on from the end of one stanza into the next. Thus the effect of repetition is enhanced by enclosure. Also only once in the first eight stanzas does the meaning significantly shift from the first to the last line: a single sharp reversal from "Hope that shines in the windows of the inn" to "The devil has snuffed out everything in the windows of the inn." These eight stanzas develop the notion of "the irreparable" through allusion to the plot of a fairy-drama in which, just when things seemed hopeless, a good fairy appeared to save things. Baudelaire introduces this figure in the ninth stanza, and its beneficent interpolation coincides with a double shift in versification. The tenth and final stanza both runs on in sense from the ninth and reduces the echo between last line and first to its minimum—the rhyme word alone:

—I have sometimes seen, in the midst of a
    commonplace theatre
  Stirred by its melodious orchestra,
A fairy light up in a hellish sky
  A miraculous dawn;
I have sometimes seen in the midst of a
    commonplace theatre

A being, who has nothing but light, gold and
    gauze,
  Floor dreadful Satan;
But my heart, where ecstasy never comes,

Is a theatre where one waits
Forever, forever in vain, for the Being with wings
  of gauze!

The "irreparable" lies in coming too late. Something that has indeed happened will never happen again. The verse's break from repetition, rather than freeing the soul from paralysis, seals its isolation from the past. The "theatre" loses substantial existence as a public scene and becomes an allegorical sign for the speaker's "heart."

"THE SWAN"

The allegory of the heart takes on new tones in the three "Parisian Scenes" dedicated to Victor Hugo, all written in 1859 for the second edition of *Les fleurs du mal*: "The Swan" ("Le cygne," 89) "The Seven Old Men" ("Les sept vieillards," 90), and "The Little Old Women" ("Les petites vieilles," 91). These titles sound laughably distant from the conventional subjects of great poetry, but Victor Hugo had defined the innovation of modern art as combining the sublime and the grotesque, in accord with the sense of human duality that Christianity had brought into the world (Preface to *Cromwell*, 1827). In sending Hugo the two poems on old people, Baudelaire praised Hugo's blending of "magnificent charity" with "touching familiarity" (23? September 1859). This combination of grandeur and intimacy, the high and the low, an art that aspires to greatness while taking subjects from the neglected aspects of everyday life, links Baudelaire and Hugo to Wordsworth and Coleridge, whose *Lyrical Ballads* (1798) include such poems as "The Idiot Boy" and "The Mad Mother."

Baudelaire further resembles these English romantics in the movement of "The Swan." It meditatively circles back through layers of memory in response to a present moment of excitation, to which it returns before moving outward in a final gesture of spiritual generosity. This is the pattern of Coleridge's "Frost at Midnight" and Wordsworth's "Tintern Abbey." But those poems summon a natural landscape; Baudelaire's evokes what he called "the landscape of great cities," which offers the "deep and complex fascination of a capital . . . grown old in the glories and tribulations of life" ("Salon of 1859"). In keeping with his own precise attention to dress and his "Praise of Makeup" in "The Painter of Modern Life," Baudelaire refused to provide nature poems when requested for an anthology: "I've . . . always thought that in Nature, fresh and flowering, there was something burdensome and impudent." Nature for Baudelaire had only allegorical use, as a sign to which he could attach human value: "In the depths of the woods, shut in under those vaults like those of sacristies and cathedrals, I think of our amazing cities, and the marvelous music that rolls through the treetops seems to me the translation of human lamentation" (letter to Ferdinand Desnoyers, late 1853 or early 1854).

Baudelaire's urban emphasis leads Americans to neglect his links with romanticism and emphasize those to modernism. Innumerable readers of the last forty years have first encountered Baudelaire in reading T. S. Eliot's *The Waste Land* (1922). The first section of that modernist masterpiece comes to its climax in a nightmare vision of London, beginning "Unreal City." Eliot's note to this phrase cites Baudelaire's "Seven Old Men": "Swarming city, city full of dreams, where in broad daylight the spectre accosts the passerby." The passage continues to move within the foggy world of Baudelaire's poem, and Eliot ends by quoting the last line of "To the Reader": "Hypocrite lecteur, mon semblable, mon frère!" (Hypocritical reader, my likeness, my brother!)

Marcel Proust, who read Baudelaire with a sensibility formed by the humane sympathies of George Eliot and John Ruskin, found "The Little Old Women" an unsurpassable high point. Proust was fascinated too by Baudelaire's attention to the strange singularities of experience that take a moment out of the normal flow of time. One could say that Baudelaire occupies a place in literary history that is the shortest distance between Honoré de Balzac and Proust—the slim volume of poetry between the two great novelistic bulks. In the "Parisian Scenes," Baudelaire was most attractive to Proust just where he was most fully drawing on Balzac. Baudelaire's Paris is not extensively described; Balzac had already done the work. Again and again in Baudelaire moments occur that could be copiously elaborated from pages of the *Human Comedy*. For example, the phrase, "Prostitution lights up in the streets" (95) condenses through its strong yet abstract personification many moments from *Splendors and Miseries of Courtesans* (1843). Or again, Balzac and Baudelaire both see the everyday bourgeois world of Paris given dramatic contour by Gothic shadows: "Meanwhile, dirty demons in the atmosphere wake up heavily, like businessmen" (95).

I shall return to Baudelaire and Balzac's "realism," and we have already discussed romanticism and modernism; but "The Swan" requires also a consideration of Baudelaire's relations to the classics—quite different from those in "A Voyage to Cythera." Baudelaire represents a crossroads in literary history. He has baffled all attempts to compartmentalize him safely within any period. Moreover, his elaborations of "modernity" as nonchronological, marking beauty in any age, have encouraged recent critics to rethink the basic ideas of literary history.

"The Swan" establishes relations between the classical past and the Paris of Baudelaire's time. It directly alludes to the Roman poet Vergil, and it approaches the style and subject matter of Jean Racine, the greatest of the earlier French poets who harked back to antiquity. This lyric of 52 lines manages to hold itself in the company of the epic *Aeneid* and the tragedy *Andromaque*. The poem begins after Troy's fall with the fate of the surviving Trojans: "Andromache, I think of you!" Andromache had been the wife of Hector and was taken by Achilles' son Pyrrhus, only then to be handed over to the Trojan Helenus, himself another slave. When Aeneas encounters her in the third book of the *Aeneid*, she is offering memorial observances to the empty tomb of Hector by a river that mimics the Simois, which flowed by Troy. The "lying Simois" in Baudelaire directly echoes Vergil.

But what has this to do with the swan of the title? The poem goes through four full stanzas before reaching the swan. In crossing Paris, the speaker has remembered a swan he once saw, bizarrely out of place, seeking water in the city dust, and this memory has awakened further memories, of Andromache and her river, and then thoughts of other exiles, including the poet himself, who feels exiled "in spirit." Beginning like a riddle, the poem proceeds by leaps, gaps, and contrasts, which close briefly in stanzas 9 and 10 but which then open out from the momentary conjunction in memory. The swan thus functions as a transfer point, itself absent from the present scene, yet making possible a number of meanings. The swan functions as a sign, and through its operation "new palaces, blocks, old suburbs, all for me become allegory, and my dear remembrances [*souvenirs*] are heavier than rocks."

The swan thus approaches the sphinx of the second "Spleen," but the weight of allegorical oppression comes here in the middle of the poem, and the work accumulates energy to move beyond this sticking point. It risks absurdity to hinge such a large encompassment of history and feeling on a swan, which "escaped from its cage and, its webbed feet rubbing the dry pavement, dragged its white plumage over the rough ground." Baudelaire lavishes interpretive energy on the remembered sight. He starts by looking down on it: "By a dry gutter [in French a mocking verbal echo, "ruis*seau* sans *eau*"] the beast opening its beak bathed its wings nervously in the dust." There follows a lightning escalation, as the beaked beast is given first the power of speech, then a deep inner life, and at last an impatient eloquence that rises to prophetic denunciation: "And it said, its heart full of its lovely native lake, 'Water, when will you rain? When will you rumble, thunder?' . . . as if it were addressing reproaches to God!" This apocalyptic swan-song causes nothing to happen. It is "ridiculous and sublime." The sky remains "ironic and cruelly blue," but to the swan's "mad behavior" Baudelaire has given a meaning. In the *Artificial Paradises*, he recalls a poet who on seeing Racine's *Esther* found it natural that Haman should make a passionate declaration of love—for so he interpreted Haman's falling at Esther's feet begging her to pardon his crimes. The "great beauties" that "this method" could add, "even to Racine," carry over to the swan. Baudelaire focuses on the energy of insistence rather than the proper meaning of the scene. So in our reading of Baudelaire, it is often more rewarding to respond to the power of gesture than to ask whether we are seeing love or abjection.

Baudelaire has already risked absurdity, grotesque disproportion, in initially evoking Andromache: "Andromache, I think of you! That little river, poor and sad mirror where once shone the measureless majesty of your widow's griefs, that lying Simois which by your tears grew great [*grandit*]. . . ." Will Baudelaire's echo mirror Vergil as falsely as Andromache's rivulet did the Simois? No matter how feeble a river, it cannot actually become large [*grandir*], or even significantly larger, through a person's tears. Baudelaire exaggerates [*grandir*], but through the grandeur of Andromache's sorrowing spirit, through the terrible history she bears witness to, the river she weeps in becomes important [*grandir*]. Through their reduced state of victimization, Andromache weeping, "bent" by the empty tomb of her husband, and the swan, "holding up its eager head on its twisting neck," link Paris today and the classical past. Andromache remembers the Troy that has fallen, and likewise for the speaker "Old Paris no longer exists (the shape of a city changes more quickly, alas! than a mortal's heart).'' By the poem's end, an appeal to "whoever has lost what will never be found again, never!" also alludes to the Roman history that connects Aeneas' Troy and Baudelaire's France. All those victims "have sucked at Sadness like a good she-wolf"—recalling Romulus and Remus.

Yet Rome suggests another connection between the present and the past. Neither contains only victims; there are also victors. Andromache "fell from the arms of a great husband, a mere chattel, beneath the hand of proud Pyrrhus." Likewise, the modern French empire's military and commercial energies have brought to Paris "the black woman, thin and consumptive, tramping in the mud, and with haggard eye seeking the absent coco palms of splendid Africa behind the huge wall of fog." Politics count, beginning with the poem's dedication. At the time Victor Hugo was living in exile from the empire, and the dedication to him precluded publication in any prominent journal. When Baudelaire sent "The Seven Old Men" and the "The Little Old Women" to Hugo, Louis Napoleon had just declared an amnesty, which Hugo refused to accept. Baudelaire appreciatively wrote, "Poets *are worth as much* as Napoleons [also the name of a gold coin]" (23? September 1859).

The poem conveys the misery of what is lost forever, the irreparable, yet it enacts a process of recovery. The swan returns in memory and brings back Andromache. The poet can see again "in spirit" the "rough-hewn capitals and shafts" and the "jumbled bric-a-brac" in shop windows of a vanished Paris. Victor Hugo, king of romanticism in Baudelaire's youth, now again means a great deal to him. Even some of his own earlier poetry is recaptured. The splendid lines about the absent palm trees are reworked from "To a Malabar Woman," the third poem Baudelaire had published, over thirteen years earlier. The poem offers another world that follows different laws from those of Troy or Paris.

Its recoveries mitigate their losses. Yet this escape in "spirit" is itself an "exile"; the westward translation of empire and culture brings alienation. Baudelaire's work does not allow us to rest content, any more than do "sailors forgotten on an island." The misery that joins Andromache, the swan, and "many others as well" seems to span all of history and the whole range of life. Either the human condition is inescapable, or the whole of life must be remade.

THE INDIVIDUAL

Baudelaire was not committed to remaking the world except in poetry, yet his experience was deeply marked by the violent political energies of nineteenth-century France. Scenes of confrontation run through his writings. In "The Painter of Modern Life," he argues that almost all our "originality" comes from the "trademark" that our time stamps on us. In accordance with this "historical theory of beauty," a crucial part of Baudelaire's literary character resides in these historical traces— which appear not descriptively, as direct copies, but as what he paradoxically calls "the memory of the present." Thus the description of the "duel" between the artist's wish to "see everything" and the stylizing power of memory turns into a scene from insurrectionary politics, an assault by "a riot of details, which all demand justice with the fury of a crowd panting for absolute liberty."

One trademark of Baudelaire's time was individuality. As early as the *Salon of 1846*, he analyzed individuality in relating artistic and social tendencies—the revolutionary heritage in politics and romanticism in the arts. In the arts today, everyone is an "emancipated worker," no longer willing to undergo the discipline of a "school." The "republicans of art" make the present condition of painting an "anarchic liberty that glorifies the individual . . . to the detriment of associations." In contrast to an earlier "collective originality," the current "small-holder" mentality, by glorifying the individual, "has necessitated the infinite subdivision of the territory of art." Over centuries of economic history, the enclosure of common lands and the erosion of guilds and apprenticeship freed laborers for the open market, while freeing individual owners to set their own terms. Likewise, in Baudelaire's analysis the domination of the "individual" makes it now inevitable for strong poets or painters to have unknowingly drastic effects on "disciples" whom they have never met or taught. Paradoxically, the strong individual and the impersonal market go together.

Baudelaire opposes this situation with a parable: "Have you felt, you whose strolling curiosity has often thrust you into the midst of a riot, the same joy I have at seeing a guardian of the public sleep clubbing a republican?" So too republicans of art should be treated. Returning to this vein much later, Baudelaire criticized Wagner's belief that revolutionary innovations in art required revolutionary governments to support them. Against this "essentially humane illusion," Baudelaire argued that despotism allowed advanced art to flourish: only under the empire was Wagner performed in Paris. The dubious political position that Baudelaire defined in the service of great and innovative art recalls a common question in cultural debates over the last two centuries, from the severe analysis of Shakespeare's monarchic politics of the imagination by the romantic, democratic critic William Hazlitt up through modern controversy over the reactionary positions of Yeats, Eliot, and Ezra Pound. Is great art somehow inhumane, or at least illiberal?

Baudelaire's case, however, illustrates the danger of taking a writer's explicit pronouncements at face value. He himself, we recall, joined the people in 1848, and his work was not promoted but prosecuted under the empire. Moreover, he himself subscribed to the individuality that gave each artist his unique

plot of ground. Although he often denounced the democratic, individualist tenor of his time, he wore its trademark. He could feel it as a loathsome disease, yet was compelled to acknowledge it: "We all have the republican spirit in our veins, like syphilis in our bones, we are democratized and syphilized" (this pun on "civilized" goes back at least to Byron's *Don Juan*). For Baudelaire the very circumstance of modern authorship is a destructive and guilty pleasure: "The day a young writer corrects his first proofsheet, he's as proud as a schoolboy who's just first got syphilis" *(Intimate Journals)*. We return to the question of "A Voyage to Cythera": can Baudelaire face his own body and heart without disgust?

Baudelaire argues that self-criticism is essential to a successful career; anything less will leave a poet "incomplete," dependent on the vagaries of instinct (essay on Wagner). We have already noted Baudelaire's self-reading as a basis for new writing. In thus inevitably becoming a critic, a poet will look to others as well. After uneasy contemplation of one's own image, it may be exhilarating to find oneself in another. The artist's "double character" leads him as critic to "praise and analyze the most luxuriously the qualities that he himself most needs as a creator, and that form the antitheses to those he most superabundantly possesses" (essay on Delacroix, 1863).

In practicing such "antithetical" criticism, critics stand toward the work criticized as artists do toward nature. Through this further doubling, "the best account of a painting may be a sonnet or elegy" (*Salon of 1846*), and thus also the best criticism of a poem may be another poem, perhaps in prose. A work of art for Baudelaire is less an imitation of nature than a passionate "protest" in the name of humanity against nature (*Salon of 1846*). We noted earlier that the imagination must "decompose" nature and "make a new world" ("Salon of 1859"). Baudelaire therefore criticized the premise of realism that art should see the world as if one were not there. He found in those praised for realism something wholly different:

> I have often been astonished that the great glory of Balzac was to pass for an observer; it always seemed to me that his principal merit was to be a visionary, a passionate seer. All his characters are endowed with the vital heat with which he himself was animated. All his fiction is as deeply colored as dreams. . . . Everyone in Balzac, even the doorkeepers, has genius. All their souls are guns loaded to the brim with willpower. That's Balzac himself.
>
> (essay on Gautier)

The energy of this vision drove Balzac to "darken the shadows and brighten the highlights" of his characters; he was like those etchers "who are never satisfied with the bite and turn the main lines of the plate into ravines." This tendency is generally summarized as "Balzac's faults," but Baudelaire argues that it precisely defines the quality of his genius.

Such a critical appreciation gives substance to Baudelaire's claim that poetry "constantly contradicts the facts" and therefore, whether happy or sad, always bears a "utopian character" and "everywhere negates iniquity" (essay on Pierre Dupont). It brings beauty that exists nowhere else, for if you wanted such beauty in the everyday world, you would have to destroy and remake that world as completely as the poet has done in his work. Thus poetry is both "the realest thing there is" but "completely true only in *another world*" (notes on realism). In a moment of extravagance, Baudelaire may claim, seeing a new generation that has modeled its life on the characters of Balzac, that "the visionary makes reality." Against this, however, the laws of artistic composition ensure that a Balzacian character works only in Balzac's world and is "ridiculous" in everyday life (review of *The Ridiculous Martyrs*). If art is to make a difference to life, small changes are not enough. One must not merely imitate Balzac's charac-

ters; the world must be remade completely, into "another."

The commitment to "antithetical" practices in criticism, and the claim that poetry and criticism are governed by the same principles, make the question of Baudelaire's "sincerity" difficult to evaluate. Just when he hailed Balzac in the *Salon of 1846* as the greatest exemplar of "the heroism of modern life," he was caricaturing him ruthlessly in "How One Pays Debts, When One Is a Genius": Balzac, he wrote, simply hired hack writers to do work that he then signed. In "The Painter of Modern Life," Baudelaire referred to the signature as "those few letters, easy to counterfeit, that figure a name," and he contrasted works, "signed with [the] mighty soul." Balzac won greatness with this spiritual signature, but he won financial relief with the graphic. This conflict between individual signature and mass production signals the inconsistency in Baudelaire's critical writing: a frequent emphasis on the individual temperament as the decisive element in art coexists with a frequent emphasis on impersonality.

Baudelaire held that criticism could be justified only by being "partial, passionate, and political" (*Salon of 1846*). This antithetical vocation always produces a situational, rhetorical complexity. In sending his study of Gautier to Victor Hugo, Baudelaire noted his difference from Hugo on the relation between art and morality. Hugo linked them very closely; Baudelaire often separated them utterly. "But in a time," Baudelaire continued, "when the world draws away from art with such horror, when men let themselves be brutalized by the exclusive ideal of utility, I think that there's no great evil in exaggerating a little bit the opposite idea. I have perhaps claimed too much. It was in order to get enough" (letter to Hugo, 23? September 1859). Such a rhetoric of situational discounting, however, is questionable. Baudelaire acknowledges that in dealing with the public he exaggerated "in order to get enough," but in this letter he was writing to ask a favor from

Hugo. Was it not therefore important to downplay the differences between them? In order to get enough from Hugo, might not Baudelaire again be claiming "too much," exaggerating a little bit the similarity between the two?

Such rhetorical complexity is further evident in a letter to Madame Sabatier. This mistress of a wealthy banker had attracted a notable circle of artistic personalities, many of whom corresponded with her in exceedingly bawdy terms. Baudelaire, however, conducted a lengthy, platonic correspondence, in which he sent anonymously some of the loveliest poems that were to go into *Les fleurs du mal.* With one he wrote:

> To explain to you my silences and my fervors, fervors almost religious, I will tell you that when my being is groveling in the blackness of its natural wickedness and foolishness, it dreams deeply of you. From that exciting and purifying dream there is generally born a happy accident.—You are for me not only the most attractive of women;—of all women, but also the dearest and most precious of superstitions.—I am selfish, I make use of you.—Here is my miserable ass-wipe [*torche-cul*].
>
> (8 May 1854)

The strange tone derives from the paradoxical meanings of "purification." A cathartic may be considered foul, because in purging it produces waste. One is made clean by making toilet paper dirty. In thus symbolizing the genesis of his poetry, Baudelaire revivifies the deprecatory cliché of literature as wastepaper. More largely, within the conventions of self-abasing love rhetoric, Baudelaire also effects a dramatic reversal, for he purifies himself by sullying the exalted recipient of his wastes. We need to know much more than we do in order fully to understand the letter's tone, but it is not clear even what we should know.

In another letter, Baudelaire wrote to his mother:

> You know how much I am horrified by all overstatement. I am aware of my wrongs to you; and every time that I feel something vividly, the fear of exaggerating its expression forces me to say the thing as coldly as I can. You will not be wrong then in supposing beneath my words a heat and intensity of desire that I have not perhaps entirely put there, through the reserve that is habitual to me.
>
> (20 December 1855)

On the one hand, this letter invites the reader to supply the emotional substance that Baudelaire intends but cannot himself provide. On the other hand, like much of his correspondence, it involves money: in asking for financial help from his mother, whom he had not seen in over a year, it may offer the minimal possible concession to the need to show some warmth, which he does not feel at all. We have no way of knowing, and the language of the letter is such as always to baffle sure knowledge.

In writing of *Les fleurs du mal*, Baudelaire once insisted, "No one except people of absolute bad faith will fail to understand the willed impersonality of my poems" (10 November 1858). Yet later he wrote to Ancelle, the administrator of his estate, who despite all their troubles was one of the few people that he was close to, "Must I say to you, you who have not guessed it any more than the others, that in this *dreadful* book, I've put all my *heart,* all my *tenderness,* all my *religion* (travestied), all my *hate?*" (18 February 1866). This statement alone stands in simple contradiction to the one previously cited, but Baudelaire offers to resolve such contradictions: "It's true that I'll write the opposite, that I'll swear up and down that it's a work *of pure art,* of *monkey tricks,* or *double-dealing;* and I'll be lying." First the rhetoric of sincerity is derailed by the parenthetical "travestied," and then the resolution asks for faith in a self-proclaimed liar. How can we know what to believe?

In everyday life, we judge truth by consequences. Since Immanuel Kant, the aesthetic has been deliberately inconsequential; art is supposed to exist for itself alone. We have seen, however, Baudelaire continually suggesting that he has uses for his art, and there is no doubt that his readers have. Our choices about Baudelaire are implicated in our interpretations, and consequences follow from interpretive decisions. I acknowledge that as a major correlative of romantic individuality, ''sincerity'' was a deep problem for Baudelaire. He recognized the historical causes of this problem, and he saw too that it impinged on his personal life. He felt the burden of individuality, yet he also valued its power—and in his writing on drugs explored means to increase its power.

In his antithetical wish to free himself from this burden, Baudelaire drew on alternatives to individuality that his time partly offered. He could look back to the ''classic'' norm of impersonality; he could look back to the ''medieval'' norm of collectivity; he could look ahead to a ''modern'' dispersal of the self. This ''vaporization'' would oppose the ''centralization'' of the self established by both romanticism and bourgeois life (Intimate Journals). ''All that is solid melts into the air.'' This ''going up in steam'' of the self, the hashish smoker's sudden realization that ''your pipe is smoking you,'' is allied with the industrial forces of production controlled by the bourgeoisie, and yet promises to lead beyond the bourgeois world.

''Classical'' impersonality imposed a painful, ironic self-contemplation that was too great to bear, although at times Baudelaire experimented with it and at other times it imposed itself on him. ''Medieval'' collectivity could only mean yielding to artistic clichés and to an equally intolerable social conformity. Nonetheless, from our distance, we find Baudelaire deeply marked by the ''collective originality'' of his time. These traces make him different from us, and hard to take, and marvelously fascinating.

Baudelaire followed out the ''modern'' part of dispersal through allegory, which allowed properties to be transferred in exchanges that achieved no totality but always left a pressing urgency of difference. His practice of literature and criticism as translation, the dual process of finding oneself different in another, and making others different by appropriating their works or lives to one's own, enriched this vein. Politically, the only path to remaking the world as wholly different was that of revolution, but after the possibilities of 1848, Baudelaire was ''physically depoliticized'' by Napoleon's coup and led the life of a declassed bourgeois. His art held out the dream of another world that was individually attainable by its maker, but also by its readers. It thus signals the renewed ''utopian'' possibility of an undertaking in common.

Selected Bibliography

EDITIONS

INDIVIDUAL WORKS
Salon de 1845. Paris, 1845.
Salon de 1846. Paris, 1846.
Histoires extraordinaires. Paris, 1856. Translations from Edgar Allan Poe.
Nouvelles histoires extraordinaires. Paris, 1857. Translations from Edgar Allan Poe.
Les fleurs du mal. Paris, 1857.
Adventures d'Arthur Gordon Pym. Paris, 1858. Translation from Edgar Allan Poe.
Les paradis artificiels. Paris, 1860.
Les fleurs du mal. Paris, 1861. 2nd ed., with deletions and additions.
Eureka. Paris, 1864. Translations from Edgar Allan Poe.
Histoires grotesques et sérieuses. Paris, 1856. Translations from Edgar Allan Poe.
Les épaves. Amsterdam [actually Brussels], 1866. Miscellaneous poems, including suppressed pieces from Les fleurs du mal.
Les fleurs du mal. Paris, 1868. 3rd ed. Includes more new poems.
Curiosités esthétiques. Paris, 1868. Collected writings on art.
L'Art romantique. Paris, 1868 [actually 1869]. Collected writings on literature and music.
Petits poèmes en prose. Paris, 1869. Also includes other miscellaneous prose.

CHARLES BAUDELAIRE

Oeuvres posthumes et correspondances inédites. Edited by Eugène Crépet. Paris, 1887. First publication of *Journaux intimes.*

COLLECTED WORKS

Correspondance. Edited by Claude Pichois and Jean Ziegler. 2 vols. Paris, 1973.

Oeuvres complètes. Edited by Claude Pichois. 2 vols. Paris, 1975–1976.

These four volumes are the starting point for the serious study of Baudelaire as a whole by anyone who reads French. Their apparatus refers to earlier collected editions and to the relevant specialized scholarship. Readers interested only in the poetry should consult *Les fleurs du mal,* edited by Antoine Adam, Paris, 1961.

TRANSLATIONS

Campbell, Roy. *Poems of Baudelaire.* London, 1952.

Charvet, T. E. *Charles Baudelaire: Selected Writings on Art and Artists.* Baltimore, 1972.

Howard, Richard. *Les fleurs du mal.* Boston, 1982.

Hyslop, Lois Boe, and Francis E. Hyslop, Jr. *Baudelaire: A Self-Portrait.* New York, 1957. Selected letters with biographical commentary.

————. *Baudelaire as a Literary Critic.* University Park, Pa., 1964.

Isherwood, Christopher. *Intimate Journals.* Boston, 1957.

Lowell, Robert. *Imitations.* New York, 1961. Pp. 46–73.

Mathews, Marthiel, and Jackson Mathews, eds. *The Flowers of Evil.* Selected translations by various hands. New York, 1955.

Mayne, Jonathan. *Baudelaire: Art in Paris 1845–1862. Salons and Other Exhibitions.* London, 1965.

————. *Baudelaire: The Painter of Modern Life and Other Essays.* London, 1964.

Morini, Simona, and Frederic Tuten. *Charles Baudelaire: Letters from His Youth.* Garden City, N.Y., 1970. Includes material unknown to the Hyslops.

Scarfe, Francis. *Baudelaire: Selected Verse.* Baltimore, 1961. These prose versions may be the most useful for readers who know some French.

Varèse, Louise. *Paris Spleen.* New York, 1947. Prose poems.

BACKGROUND STUDIES

Clark, T. J. *The Absolute Bourgeois: Artists and Politics in France 1848–1851.* London, 1973.

Graña, César. *Modernity and Its Discontents: French Society and the French Man of Letters in the Nineteenth Century.* New York, 1967.

Kuhn, Reinhard. *The Demon of Noontide: Ennui in Western Literature.* Princeton, N.J., 1976.

Moers, Ellen. *The Dandy: Brummell to Beerbohm.* New York, 1960.

Praz, Mario. *The Romantic Agony.* London, 1933.

Starkie, Enid. *Petrus Borel the Lycanthrope.* New York, 1954.

BIOGRAPHICAL AND CRITICAL STUDIES

TRANSLATED FROM FRENCH

Brombert, Victor. "Baudelaire: Confinement and Infinity." In *The Romantic Prison.* Princeton, N.J., 1978.

Butor, Michel. *Histoire extraordinaire: Essay on a Dream of Baudelaire's.* London, 1969.

Gide, André. "Baudelaire and M. Faguet." In *Pretexts.* New York, 1959.

————. "Preface to the *Fleurs du Mal.*" In *Pretexts.* New York, 1959.

Laforgue, Jules. "Notes on Baudelaire." In *Selected Writings.* New York, 1956.

Poulet, Georges. "Baudelaire." In *Studies in Human Time.* Baltimore, 1956.

————. "Baudelaire." In *Metamorphoses of the Circle.* Baltimore, 1966.

————. *Exploding Poetry.* Chicago, 1984.

Proust, Marcel. "Apropos of Baudelaire." In *Pleasures and Days.* New York, 1957.

————. "Sainte-Beuve and Baudelaire." In *On Art and Literature 1896–1919.* New York, 1958.

Sartre, Jean-Paul. *Baudelaire.* New York, 1950.

Valéry, Paul. "The Position of Baudelaire." In *Leonardo, Poe, Mallarmé: Collected Works,* vol. 8. Princeton, N.J., 1972.

TRANSLATED FROM GERMAN

Adorno, Theodor W. "Lyric Poetry and Society." *Telos* 20:56–71 (1974).

Auerbach, Erich. "The Aesthetic Dignity of the *Fleurs du mal.*" In *Scenes from the Drama of European Literature.* Minneapolis, Minn., 1984.

Benjamin, Walter. *Charles Baudelaire: A Lyric Poet in the Era of High Capitalism.* London, 1973.

Friedrich, Hugo. "Baudelaire." In *The Structure of Modern Poetry*. Evanston, Ill., 1974.

Jauss, Hans Robert. "La Douceur du Foyer: The Lyric of 1857 as a Pattern for the Communication of Social Norms." In *Aesthetic Experience and Literary Hermeneutics*. Minneapolis, Minn., 1982.

—————. "The Poetic Text Within the Change of Horizons of Reading: The Example of Baudelaire's 'Spleen IV.'" In *Toward an Aesthetic of Reception*. Minneapolis, Minn., 1982.

Stierle, Karlheinz. "Baudelaire and the Tradition of the *Tableau de Paris*." *New Literary History* 11:345–361 (1980).

WRITTEN IN ENGLISH

Abrams, M. H. "Coleridge, Baudelaire, and Modernist Poetics." In *New Perspectives on German Literary Criticism*. Edited by Richard E. Amacher and Victor Lange. Princeton, N.J., 1979.

Berman, Marshall. "Baudelaire: Modernisms in the Streets." In *All That Is Solid Melts into Air*. New York, 1982.

Bersani, Leo. *Baudelaire and Freud*. Berkeley and Los Angeles, 1977.

De Man, Paul. "Literary History and Literary Modernity." In *Blindness and Insight,* 2nd ed. Minneapolis, Minn., 1983.

—————. "The Rhetoric of Temporality." In *Blindness and Insight,* 2nd ed. Minneapolis, Minn., 1983.

—————. "Anthropomorphism and Trope in the Lyric." In *The Rhetoric of Romanticism*. New York, 1984.

Eliot, T. S. "Baudelaire." In *Selected Essays*. New York, 1932.

—————. "From Poe to Valéry." In *To Criticize the Critic*. London, 1965.

Fairlie, Alison. "Baudelaire's Correspondence." In *Imagination and Language*. Cambridge, 1981.

Hardy, John Edward. "Baudelaire's 'Rêve Parisien': The Silent Babel." In *The Curious Frame*. Notre Dame, Ind., 1962.

Hemmings, F. W. J. *Baudelaire the Damned*. New York, 1982. The best introductory biography.

Hubert, Judd D. "Symbolism, Correspondence, Memory." *Yale French Studies* 9:46–55 (1952).

—————. "Baudelaire's Revolutionary Poetics." *Romantic Review* 46:164–177 (1955).

Johnson, Barbara. "Poetry and Its Double: Two *Invitations au voyage*." In *The Critical Difference*. Baltimore, 1981.

Klein, Richard. "Baudelaire and Revolution: Some Notes." *Yale French Studies* 39:85–97 (1967).

—————. "Straight Lines and Arabesques: Metaphors of Metaphor." *Yale French Studies* 45:64–86 (1970).

Mehlman, Jeffrey. "Baudelaire with Freud: Theory and Pain." *Diacritics* 4:7–13 (Spring 1974).

Nelson, Lowry, Jr. "Baudelaire and Virgil: A Reading of 'Le Cygne.'" *Comparative Literature* 13:332–345 (1961).

Riffaterre, Michael. "Describing Poetic Structures: Two Approaches to Baudelaire's 'Les Chats.'" *Yale French Studies* 36–37:200–242 (1967).

Sabin, Margery. *English Romanticism and the French Tradition*. Cambridge, Mass., 1976.

Shattuck, Roger. "Vibratory Organism: Seeing Nature Whole." *Georgia Review* 31:454–470 (1977).

Wellek, René. "Charles Baudelaire." In *A History of Modern Criticism*, vol. 4. New Haven, Conn., 1965.

JONATHAN ARAC

FEODOR DOSTOEVSKY

(1821–1881)

ONE IS NOW surprised when a Soviet literary critic writes: "A great advance in our knowledge of thinking and creativity is needed to understand why, for example, Albert Einstein believed that he had obtained more from Dostoevsky than from Carl Friedrich Gauss, one of the greatest physicists, astronomers, and mathematicians." For, years ago, Lenin, when asked what he thought about Dostoevsky's novels, is reported to have replied: "I have no time for such trash." And though Maxim Gorky extolled Dostoevsky's genius and compared him to Shakespeare, he also condemned him as "petit-bourgeois and defeatist," guilty of the unpardonable sin in Soviet morality of selfish individualism, which is as certain, Gorky concluded, "as there are no goats without a smell." And the anti-Soviet Vladimir Nabokov, who is partial to the dissidence of dissent in things literary, not unexpectedly lines up on Lenin's side of the barricades when he asserts that Dostoevsky is "a much overrated sentimental and Gothic novelist of the time . . . one of those megaphones of elephantine platitudes."

Nevertheless, there has never been any question of Dostoevsky's position as a novelist and thinker among his countrymen. A staggering bibliography about every phase of his life and work has accumulated. Even Soviet critics, though they disapprove of him as a political reactionary, an admirer of czars, and a professed believer in Russian Orthodoxy, are not disposed to leave him safe and undisturbed in his prerevolutionary immortality, for he is one of the most widely read of the great nineteenth-century Russian novelists and has exercised a profound influence on some of the best Soviet writers. The wealth of Soviet critical and scholarly literature on Dostoevsky is of primary importance for our understanding of him.

Some evidence supports the notion that the upsurge of Dostoevsky's popularity in the Soviet Union since Stalin's death is simply another manifestation—in reverse so to speak—of a renewal of the historical trend of Russian "Westernization" in cultural as well as in social and economic endeavors. For between the two world wars and afterward no nineteenth-century novelist has received as much attention in western Europe and the United States as Dostoevsky, although critical appraisal has tended to concentrate on his significance as a prophet, philosopher, and psychologist, and as a political, social, and religious thinker, rather than as a literary artist. All this is perhaps understandable in our own day of hard choices in intellectual loyalties, for many political, moral, and religious problems that have disturbed generations during these years were most effectively dramatized in Dostoevsky's celebrated works.

The doctrine of Friedrich Nietzsche, who admitted indebtedness to Dostoevsky's psychology, that the creator of good or evil must first destroy all values, closely resembles that of Shigalev in *The Possessed* (1873). And by the time Thomas Masaryk's *Spirit of Russia,* which singled out Dostoevsky as the key figure in the development of Russian nineteenth-century thought, appeared in 1913, a veritable cult of Dostoevsky had begun to sweep over the intellectual world of western Europe. Before the advent of Adolf Hitler, one German critic went so far as to say that since Martin Luther's time there had been no greater spiritual influence on Germany than Dostoevsky. Later André Malraux testified that Dostoevsky had profoundly affected the whole intellectual history of his generation in France. Indeed, Jean-Paul Sartre paid tribute to Dostoevsky, whose condemnation of the tyranny of reason provided inspiration for the existentialist belief that human action becomes simply the expression of a biological urge to self-assertion. And Albert Camus also, in *L'Homme révolté* (*The Rebel,* 1951), drew heavi on the agonizing questions propounded in *The Brothers Karamazov* (1879–1880) in elaborating his thesis that the mistaken belief in reason in modern times has led to a loss of all sense of values and the cynical seizure of power by dictators.

By the time it reached the United States this European cult had dwindled somewhat, but more recently American interest in Dostoevsky has been rising. If the test of a great writer is not so much what he says but what he does to us—the extent to which he imposes his vision and transforms our own experience—in these terms Dostoevsky seems to make a special appeal today to American readers. Though the focus of our interest does not exclude aesthetic considerations, it is mainly concerned with social, political, and religious problems involved in the throbbing human dramas of his characters and with his extraordinary psychological probing of their tormented lives. It is also possible that we feel a special kinship with the "sick consciousness" of these troubled men and women as they struggle to realize their identity in a world from which they are alienated. For Dostoevsky's anti-heroes, like those in so much contemporary American fiction, are overwhelmed with the infirmity of doubt, caught on the treadmill of endless reflection, and doomed to inertia because of a lack of will.

Unlike his great contemporaries Ivan Turgenev and Leo Tolstoy, members of wealthy, cultured families of the landed gentry, Dostoevsky belonged to a family perched insecurely on the lower rung of the Moscow middle-class ladder—he called himself an "intellectual proletarian." The family had no pretensions to culture, and his father, an ex-army surgeon, harsh and rigid in domestic matters, was subsequently murdered by serfs on the small property he owned in the country. This disparity in social position and educational training influenced Dostoevsky's literary interests and the subjects of his novels, so different from those of Turgenev and Tolstoy.

At the age of seventeen Dostoevsky entered the Saint Petersburg Military Engineering School, and during five years there he devoted all the spare time he could steal from dull drill and the science of fortifications to reading belles lettres. A high degree of intellectual curiosity was part of his intense nature. Besides Russian authors, of whom his favorites were Pushkin and Gogol, he read a variety of foreign writers: Homer, Shakespeare, Corneille, Racine, Rousseau, Goethe, Byron, and Schiller, the last with an enthusiasm he never lost (Schiller and the Schlegels contributed much to his later aesthetic theorizing). His youthful delight in stories of adventure was fed by the Gothic romances of Ann Radcliffe, M. G. Lewis, Charles Maturin, and E. T. A. Hoffmann, translations of which had a vogue in Russia at that time. Their lurid trappings and scenes no doubt encouraged his taste for the melodramatic and for the plots of violence and crime that later entered into the structure of his own fiction. Nor did he neglect novelists who could lay claims to realism, such as Sir

Walter Scott, Honoré de Balzac, Victor Hugo, George Sand, and Eugène Sue.

Not much information exists about Dostoevsky's developing personality during these formative years, but there is evidence enough to suggest that the shy, secretive, lonely persona portrayed in biographies is somewhat at variance with the facts. He could be all these things when thrust into contact with official bureaucrats or social superiors, but he also enjoyed nights out with fellow cadets, good food and drink, interesting conversation, music, theater, and the company of young women. There was a plunging, all-or-nothing quality in his nature that manifested itself early in gambling bouts and grandiose plans for achieving quick financial successes, although he was nearly always improvident in money matters. It was a time for dreaming, and he was a passionate dreamer about fame, self-sacrificing deeds, and idealistic friendships.

By 1843, when Dostoevsky had finished his professional training, the career of army engineer had given way to the determination to write. He felt that he had something to say in literature and had already begun his apprenticeship by translating Balzac's *Eugénie Grandet* (1833). In the fall of the next year he wrote his brother Mikhail: "Here is my hope. I am finishing a novel of the size of *Eugénie Grandet.* The novel is rather original." At the age of twenty-three he resigned his commission in the service, revised and recopied his novel again and again, and in the spring of 1845, with many misgivings and entirely unsure of his talent, allowed a young friend to take the finished manuscript of *Poor Folk* to the leading literary critic Vissarion Belinsky for his judgment. Many years later, in *The Diary of a Writer* (1873–1881), Dostoevsky recalled with deep feeling Belinsky's ecstatic reactions. He extolled the infallible artistic instinct with which Dostoevsky had revealed the hidden nature of his hero. "That is the secret of high artistic value," Belinsky declared, "That is truth in art! That is the artist's service to truth! The truth has been revealed and an-

nounced to you as an artist, it has been brought as a gift; value this gift and remain faithful to it, and you will be a great writer!"

Though the short novel *Poor Folk* (1846) has some of the usual faults of the beginner, Belinsky's lofty praise was prophetically correct, for he realized that Dostoevsky had created something quite new in Russian fiction. This story of an impoverished, elderly copying clerk who struggles hopelessly for respectability and conceals his real love for a poor orphaned girl beneath a sentimentally expressed paternal affection was the first Russian social novel. This fact and the story's implied condemnation of society's unconcern for the underprivileged delighted the liberal reformer Belinsky and won enthusiastic response from readers. Pushkin's rather exceptional short story of lowly people, "The Station Master" (1830), and Gogol's famous "The Overcoat" (1842)—one of Gogol's works that had persuaded Belinsky to acclaim him as the founder of the "natural school"— certainly helped to inspire *Poor Folk* and led the critic to regard Dostoevsky as a disciple of the "natural school." Dostoevsky had discovered the fantastic reality of the city's humiliated and injured, and he became their poet. In part he introduced to Russia the emphasis of the humanitarian literature of the West, which at this time was supplanting socially privileged heroes and heroines with the poor and rejected, as in the novels of George Sand, Sue, and Charles Dickens. And the epistolary form of his first novel was prompted not so much by Samuel Richardson's *Clarissa* (1747–1748) or Rousseau's *Nouvelle Héloïse* (1761) as by Sand's *Jacques* (1834), whose hero has been compared with Devushkin in *Poor Folk.*

But unlike Gogol or any possible predecessors in this vein of writing, Dostoevsky added a new dimension—an intense psychological interest in which the conflict of his hero is not observed from the outside but is profoundly analyzed from within. Belinsky and others, he wrote his brother about *Poor Folk,* "find in me a new and original spirit in that I proceed by analysis and not by synthesis, that is, I plunge into the depths, and, while analyzing every atom, I search out the whole." The result was a piercing insight into the tragic futility of poor people in love, people victimized by the cruel circumstances of contemporary society. Dostoevsky's handling of the ensuing psychological drama established the fact that with *Poor Folk* he had begun his own school of Russian realistic fiction.

With literary success came social success, and both went to the head of the youthful Dostoevsky. Bumptiously he wrote his brother of endless invitations to salons and dinners by well-bred nobles and literary celebrities. But this short, fair-haired man, with small gray eyes, a sickly complexion, and nervously twitching lips, cut a sorry figure in polished society. He was awkward in his movements, ill at ease, and in conversation alternated between prolonged silences and fiery monologues. Extremely sensitive, he soon realized that he was out of place in such a milieu.

Fortunately Dostoevsky's mind was on writing and he quickly followed up his first effort with another short novel, *The Double* (1846). More confident now of his powers, he announced to his brother that the new tale was "ten times superior to *Poor Folk*. Our crowd says that since *Dead Souls* there has never been anything like it in Russia, that the work is one of genius, and what do they not say!" Despite the laughable comparison to a full-length novel and a great masterpiece, Dostoevsky, like Gogol, had striven for originality but in a much more limited sphere of narrative art. *The Double* is an amazing study (for its time) in abnormal psychology. The hero, Golyadkin, a minor civil servant afflicted by a growing persecution mania, encounters a man who looks exactly like him and bears the same name. At first Golyadkin befriends him and secures a position for him in his office. The remainder of the story relates in meticulous detail the hero's adventures with his Double. With mounting indignation Golyadkin ob-

serves him winning the praise and favor of his superiors and fellow workers that he himself had tried so vainly to achieve. In his deranged mind the Double becomes the leader of a conspiracy against him, and he makes futile efforts to denounce the insolent fellow. After a final series of events in which his rival humiliates him, the tale ends with the Double helping Golyadkin into a carriage on his way to an insane asylum.

The ability with which Dostoevsky sustains the illusion of the Double and the subtlety of his psychological insight into Golyadkin's warped mind reveal the young author's impressive artistic skill. The hero's mental disorder is not unrelated to him. This first attempt at analyzing a split personality seems to be connected with Dostoevsky's later preoccupation with various aspects of dualism in the creation of some of his most memorable characters. Though he never again pushes the pathological aspects quite so far as in the case of Golyadkin, he comes close in the famous scene in *The Brothers Karamazov* in which Ivan is confronted by his Double, who so effectively exposes his ambivalence.

Belinsky praised *The Double* when he first heard parts of it in manuscript, but his enthusiasm waned after he read it in print—he found the story incompatible with the social significance he demanded in literature. Worse still, the public pronounced it boring. In a spirit of self-criticism that contrasts admirably with his previous self-praise, Dostoevsky wrote his brother of the failure of *The Double* and then added: "I have a terrible vice: unlimited pride and ambition. The idea that I deceived expectations and spoiled something that could have been a great story has crushed me." Many years later he admitted in *The Diary of a Writer* that the form of the tale had been entirely unsuccessful, but, he insisted, "I never projected a more serious idea in literature."

Between the remainder of 1846 and 1849, when Dostoevsky's early literary period was brought to an abrupt end by his arrest, he wrote more short stories and sketches, such as "Mr. Prokharchin," "The Landlady," "A Faint Heart," and "The Honest Thief." And shortly after *Poor Folk* appeared he had also embarked on his first full-length novel. He obviously intended it to be a major work and an answer to Belinsky and his followers, who by now had dismissed him as a failure. Planned as a psychological novel in depth, *Netochka Nezvanova* began to appear in *Fatherland Notes* in 1849. But only three episodes, the third unfinished, had been published when Dostoevsky's arrest put an end to the work. He never resumed it, perhaps because he recognized its lack of compositional and stylistic unity.

Each of the episodes is in the form of a separate tale connected by the continuing presence of the narrator, Netochka, a pattern that may have been inspired by Lermontov's *Hero of Our Time* (1840). In the first Netochka tells of her childhood with her mother and stepfather, Yefimov, whose talent as a violinist is frustrated by his self-contempt, a confession of defeat that seems to reflect Dostoevsky's own artistic self-disparagement at this time. The little girl is brilliantly drawn. One is impressed by Dostoevsky's technique in the difficult matter of child psychology, employed so effectively in the later novels, especially in his treatment of Netochka's morbid love for her wayward stepfather and her guilt over her dislike for her mother. The second episode is concerned with Netochka's adoption, after the death of her parents, into a wealthy family and her passionate attachment there to Katya, the young daughter of the household. The marked contrast between the meek Netochka and the proud Katya in their love-hate relationship anticipates similar contrasts in characterizations in the great novels. In the unfinished third episode the only notable creation is the sinister, vengeful husband of Netochka's benefactress, who gives evidence of developing into a towering figure of wickedness. This unfinished novel, which Dostoevsky reprinted in his collected works in revised form, is noteworthy as an indication of rapidly maturing art and for anticipating ideas, images, characterizations, and devices, such as the philosophical dialogue or monologue, that would repeatedly appear in novels to come.

To a limited degree one may perceive the main direction of Dostoevsky's future creative development in the writing of this first literary period. Some characters are preliminary studies of later, more famous ones. They are dreamy, unpractical people or wretched clerks and poor students who live in unsavory corners of Saint Petersburg. Though they are not entirely creatures born of literary influences, neither are they in every respect the result of a young man's limited observations of life around him. His intense analysis of their feelings, however, reflects his own emotional, spiritual, and psychological self-examination. But an experience was awaiting him that would deepen his perception of human nature and develop his genius for revealing the inner struggle that goes on in the souls of suffering men and women.

Opposing views on art were the real reason for Dostoevsky's break with Belinsky. The famous critic's social and political beliefs led him to reject "pure art." His approach was a utilitarian one: literature must reveal the life of the masses and in analyzing the contemporary human condition must pass judgment on it. Dostoevsky's position at this time contained elements of an idealistic Kantian aesthetic; it stressed "pure form," the free play of the mind, art without a purpose. He emphasized the autonomy of art and the irrationality of the creative act, in which ideas, problems, questions, theories, dreams, and hypotheses lead to mental struggle and intellectual drama out of which emerges an artistically realistic vision of life. On the other hand, Dostoevsky, although a firm believer in autocracy and the Russian Orthodox faith, was powerfully affected by Belinsky's advocacy of socialism and atheism, which was aimed against a reactionary church and the oppressive rule of Nicholas I.

It is not surprising, then, that Dostoevsky, seeking new friends after his rupture with Belinsky and his disciples, should have found them among the Friday gatherings at the home of the idealistic Mikhail Petrashevsky, where discussions were held on writings of the French utopian socialists Fourier, Saint-Simon, and Proudhon, and on the need for social reforms in Russia. But he also associated himself with a smaller group of more venturesome souls in these gatherings, the so-called Durov Circle, whose members, convinced that reforms could not be achieved by peaceful methods, secretly conspired to promote revolutionary action to free the serfs. They planned to propagandize their views by printing their own writings on a clandestinely procured hand press. It is also known that Dostoevsky repeatedly and enthusiastically read to members of both circles Belinsky's famous contraband letter to Gogol, in which, among other things, he excoriated the church and praised atheism.

The czar's government, aware of these developments through police informers, and fearful of contagion from the revolutionary turmoil in the West at this time, arrested members of the Petrashevsky Circle in April 1849. After a long investigation, twenty-one prisoners, including Dostoevsky, were condemned to be shot. The memory of the horrible experience he and his comrades underwent during the grisly preparations for execution that cold December morning in Semyonev Square before the czar's commutation was announced haunts the pages of Dostoevsky's fiction. His sentence was changed to four years at hard labor in a prison at Omsk, Siberia, and thereafter four years as a soldier in the ranks.

It is important to realize, in the light of Dostoevsky's reaction to this catastrophe, that he had been involved in an illegal activity, and he drew on the experience in writing *The Possessed* in the 1870's, a novel inspired by a political murder committed by the revolutionary S. G. Nechaev and his fellow conspirators.

"Probably I could never have become a *Nechaev*," he wrote in *The Diary of a Writer*, "but a follower of Nechaev, I am not certain; it may be I could have . . . in the days of my youth." In short, he believed his severe penalty justified, and like the sinning characters in his future novels who achieve salvation by suffering, he willingly accepted punishment as an atonement for his crime.

Dostoevsky served his sentence like any of the common murderers and thieves among whom he lived in chains, stench, and hard labor. He endured profound spiritual agony during the ordeal, and he dates his first epileptic seizures from this time. Eventually he got to know well many of his rough fellow convicts and to admire them—"in one way or another, the most gifted of our people," he remarked. Though he was forbidden to write, his imagination actively worked on literary plans. "How many native types, characters, did I take with me from prison!" he later told his brother. "How many tales of vagabonds, robbers, and, in general, of the whole gloomy, wretched existence. There is enough for entire volumes. What a wonderful people! On the whole, I did not lose my time. If not Russia, then I have come to know the Russian people well, as well as only few knew them."

The New Testament was the only book allowed him in prison, and as though repenting for having embraced Belinsky's atheistic belief, he read it at every opportunity. He rediscovered Christ and found spiritual sustenance in the Gospels. Only Christ could raise up the sinner, comfort the fallen, and promise the humble of heart new life on earth. This faith brought him serenity and assuaged the bitterness of prison existence. Not long after his release he wrote a woman who had befriended him during this period of his religious change:

Here it is: to believe that there is nothing more beautiful, more profound, more sympathetic, more reasonable, more manly, and more perfect than Christ, and not only is there nothing, but, I tell myself with jealous love, there can be nothing. Besides, if anyone proved to me that Christ was outside the truth, and it *really* was so that the truth was outside Christ, then I would prefer to remain with Christ than with the truth.

The statement is important, for unbelief is implicit in his very assertion of belief. The remainder of his life was to be a holy pilgrimage, an endless search for God, but he combined in his heart the most ardent faith with the greatest disbelief. Perhaps the search itself was the end, the spiritual bread of his existence and, one may add, of his artistic powers.

Dostoevsky entered prison a young radical and unbeliever, and he left it with a heightened respect for the authority of the crown and a new faith in the teachings of Christ. His experience had taught him the doctrine of salvation by suffering, and the New Testament had fortified his belief in it. Finally, he had discovered the virtues of the Russian common people and had become convinced of their special significance in the fate of his country. In the growth of his creative art prison played not a negative but a positive role. It did not change his creative process; there was no essential break with the past in this respect. Prison defined and deepened his creative powers and provided him with rich material for the further study of the suffering individuals in whom he had been interested from the beginning. In his early works he had been concerned with the souls of the "insulted and injured"; in prison he learned to understand and to analyze them more profoundly.

The chains were struck off Dostoevsky's ankles on 23 January 1854; on release from prison he was ordered to Semipalatinsk, a Siberian garrison town, to serve as a common soldier. In keeping with the attitude of patient acceptance he had practiced in prison, he wrote his brother, "I do not complain; this is my cross and I have deserved it." He worked hard as a soldier and strove to win the approbation of his superiors. Starved for reading matter after four years of deprivation, he ea-

gerly absorbed in his spare time quantities of books and magazines he requested from his brother. And once again he began to get the feel of the pen.

This uneventful existence was suddenly complicated by his passionate love for frail, sickly, blonde Marya Isaeva. She was married to a hopeless drunkard whose opportune death hardly improved Dostoevsky's situation—a young schoolteacher promptly claimed her favors. Life seemed to imitate art, for there is nothing more fantastic in Dostoevsky's fiction than this triangular love affair in which he went to unbelievable extremes to promote the cause of his rival while protesting his undying love for this rather pretty, flighty, and somewhat hysterical woman. (The deceased drunkard of a husband and Marya reappear as Marmeladov and his spouse in *Crime and Punishment* [1867].) She married Dostoevsky in 1857, an alliance that turned out to be anything but happy.

Marriage increased his ever-present financial needs, which now intensified the desire to write. As an ex-convict he required permission to publish, but he felt it would soon come, for he had been promoted to a junior officer's rating. Various literary designs crowded his brain, ideas he had thought out in prison. Yet he feared to spoil the major work he had in mind by beginning it prematurely; the conception of the central character, he decided, would take several years to mature in his imagination. Accordingly, the first two pieces he finished after release from prison have no connection with his experience there.

The long short story "Uncle's Dream" (1859) is one of Dostoevsky's best-wrought tales, a Gogolian satire on the sniveling society of a small provincial town for which Semipalatinsk must have been the model. At times situational humor leavens the exposure of cynical human foibles. The ancient prince, whom the town's dowager schemes to marry off to her daughter Zina, is a delightful caricature. The brilliant concluding scene, where the mother's deception is revealed to assembled townsfolk when the befuddled prince insists that his engagement to Zina is simply a beautiful dream, bears comparison with the famous concluding scene in Gogol's play *The Government Inspector* (1836).

The humorous and tragic combine in the short novel *The Village of Stepanchikovo and Its Inhabitants* (1859), better known in English by the title *The Friend of the Family*. Dostoevsky thought this longer work "incomparably above" "Uncle's Dream," and at first he was most enthusiastic over its two main characters, Colonel Rostanev and Foma Opiskin, whom he described as "tremendously typical" and "faultlessly fashioned." Though the work continued the line of his early artistic development, it also opened up new perspectives of greater things to come. Rostanev's mother, a general's widow, arrives to settle on her son's estate, and with her appears Opiskin, a companion of her husband who had been degraded by him to the position of a family buffoon. Now, in altered circumstances, this vain, scheming, Russian Tartuffe, who once aspired to be an author, gains an extraordinary ascendancy over the whole household, and especially over its meek master, Rostanev. Opiskin's ambitious effort is a palpable compensation for his former degradation. Dostoevsky concentrates on the psychological portrayal of this complex, dualistic creature, and the strength of the characterization saves the novel from being a mediocre work. The analytical treatment of Opiskin goes beyond that of the ambivalent creations of the early tales. For in the conflict between self-esteem and self-abasement, Dostoevsky now suggests a kind of reciprocity that is almost psychic; the two states of mind aid and abet each other. The dominant aspect of Opiskin's dualism—the desire to suffer and make others suffer—Dostoevsky developed more cogently in later characters. Critics have pointed out, and with some justification, that the frustrated author Opiskin is a parody of Gogol in that writer's more lamentable guise as a misdirected preacher of asceticism, moral nonsense, and futile religiosity.

Dostoevsky's hope that these two works, particularly *The Friend of the Family*, would help to revive the literary reputation he had enjoyed before prison turned out to be disappointed—they went entirely unnoticed. More than ever he felt it necessary to get back to Saint Petersburg, among remembered scenes and friends who might encourage his writing. He obtained the aid of highly placed officials and wrote pleading letters and laudatory poems to members of the royal family. These expressions of patriotic sentiment and contrition for past offenses, however seemingly sycophantic, represented changed values resulting from his prison experience. He was finally permitted to resign from the army and to settle in Tver. After he had languished there for some months, a plea to the emperor that he required medical aid succeeded. Ten years after he set out for Siberia in chains, he returned, in December 1859, to his beloved Saint Petersburg, a free man.

Life took on exquisite meaning again. Revolutionary elements in the capital wanted to glorify him as a former political prisoner. Dostoevsky would have none of it. He sympathized with the reforms of the new czar, Alexander II, and the pending emancipation of the serfs in 1861, but he distrusted extremes of radicalism, especially its ridiculing of religion. What he really wanted was to start a magazine—a regular source of income if successful and an assured outlet for his own writing. With his brother Mikhail as ostensible owner and business manager (as an ex-convict he could not publicly control the magazine) and himself as editor, the first issue of *Time* appeared in 1861. It was an immediate success, not only because of Dostoevsky's editorial skills, but also because *Time*'s announced ideological position—a compromise between contending Slavophiles and Westernizers among the intelligentsia—urged both factions to join with the common people and recognize in these children of the soil the national spirit and salvation of the nation. This conviction, which had dawned on Dostoevsky in prison, now proved to be a popular approach, and he introduced various elements of it into his journalistic writings and fiction.

Old and new like-minded friends rallied around Dostoevsky and his magazine, some of whom were to have considerable influence on his political, social, and artistic views, such as the poet Apollon Maikov and the critics Apollon Grigoriev and N. N. Strakhov. They supported his renewed defense of the autonomy of art, a continuation of his old battle with the deceased Belinsky, whose utilitarian view of literature was now more rigidly advocated by the radical-democratic critics N. G. Chernyshevsky and N. A. Dobrolyubov. "Art is always contemporary and real," Dostoevsky argued, but one cannot impose various designs on it because it has "its own integral, organic life."

During these first years after his return to Saint Petersburg, Dostoevsky wrote *The House of the Dead,* an amazing work that regained for him something of the popularity he had enjoyed on the publication of *Poor Folk.* He had originally planned it as a novel based on a horrific episode he had heard about at Omsk, and he had jotted down notes for it during stays in the prison hospital. But it ultimately took the form of memoirs of a man condemned to ten years of hard labor for killing his wife. The book is really a faithful record of Dostoevsky's own experiences in prison; part of it first appeared in a newspaper, but then this and the remainder were printed in the 1861–1862 issues of *Time.* Turgenev and Alexander Herzen acclaimed it, and Tolstoy valued it as Dostoevsky's best work.

He strove for impersonality and objectivity, for he realized that these qualities would contribute artistically to the authenticity of the account. The plan of the work is carefully thought out: first a general description of prison life; then a consideration of social types among the inmates, with deeper psychological studies of the more striking convicts; and finally a kind of history of this form of penal existence illustrated by detailed realistic descriptions of certain episodes, such as the highly diverting Christmas theatricals of the convicts and the wonderful scene of the prisoners' communal bath, a pandemonium that is "simply Dantean," Turgenev declared. However, running through the whole book is the unifying motif of liberty, which these convicts had lost. It is effectively symbolized by their unconscious efforts to imitate the behavior of free men, and by the wounded eagle the prisoners catch and then happily set free. In the acute psychological studies of such unusual convicts as Gazin and Orlov, indomitable criminal types for whom ordinary morality is childish and reason completely subordinated to the unrelenting will to evil, Dostoevsky gained fresh insights that served him well in handling criminal aspects of such creations as Valkovsky, Raskolnikov, Svidrigailov, and Stavrogin. Yet there emerges from the book Dostoevsky's new conviction that among these rough and lowly convicts were many of Russia's most "extraordinary people."

While writing *The House of the Dead* Dostoevsky was also working on his novel *The Insulted and the Injured,* which likewise appeared in the pages of *Time* in 1861. It was to be "a novel with an idea," he remarked, "and it will bring me into fashion." Though critics roasted the work, the reading public applauded it. Three years later he rather lamely apologized: since the magazine urgently needed a novel, he had obliged, and hence there were in it "walking texts and not characters"; if "a crude work had emerged," there were "two most serious characters portrayed very faithfully and artistically" and "a half hundred pages of which I am proud."

Readers today would agree and perhaps add that in *The Insulted and the Injured* one can detect the authentic feel and atmosphere of the great novels. The idea he mentioned—and ideas were to become a fixed feature of later masterpieces—concerns a woman's right to offer her love to the man of her choice in defiance of convention and family control. The idea is not well sustained; it is lost in the maze of plot and sentimental melodrama inspired by Hoffmann, Sue, Hugo, and even Dickens. Vanya loves Natasha, but he does everything in his power to aid her love for Alyosha; Alyosha in turn loves both Natasha and Katya, and each woman is eager to further the suit of the other. Then this love in triplicate is confounded by little Nellie's love for Vanya.

It is not difficult to guess that Natasha is one of the "two most serious characters." Though aspects of emotional dualism in women in love had been touched on in Dostoevsky's previous writings, Natasha is the first fully portrayed representative of the type that reappears repeatedly in later novels. Dostoevsky writes of her: "She anticipated with pleasure the happiness of loving endlessly and torturing the man she loved simply because she loved him and that was why perhaps she hastened to give herself to him as a sacrifice."

Nor can there be any doubt that little Nellie is the second character, an absorbing psychological study of a child of thirteen in her initial experience with real love. She is the first of those Dostoevskian females who, as he remarks in the novel, "smothered her own impulses; sympathetic but locked up in pride and inaccessibility."

Vanya, the narrator, qualifies as one of the "walking texts" that Dostoevsky mentioned—choosing a method of narration was always a major problem for him; Dostoevsky employed, singly or in combination, the omniscient author, confession, diary, memoirs, and notes. Yet Vanya takes on a special interest, for he is a writer, and up to a point his career is a faithful transcript of Dostoevsky's before his arrest.

If the novel can be said to have a hero, it is the anti-hero Prince Valkovsky; his wicked-ness dominates all plot lines of the work. In unmotivated villainy he is a direct descendant of those fearsome convicts Gazin and Orlov in *The House of the Dead.* But unlike them, he is not instinctively amoral. Dostoevsky even attempts, unconvincingly, to provide motives for his evildoing. In the defeat of natural goodness by evil, the burden of the novel, the spiritual experience of penal servitude had not yet taught Dostoevsky how to transmute typical villains of melodrama into the artistic criminal types of his masterpieces.

"My name is worth a million," Dostoevsky told a friend after his recent popular literary successes. Leaving the magazine and his ailing wife in his brother's care, he set out in the summer of 1862 to realize an old dream—a trip to Europe. At the end of ten weeks, after visits to various European capitals, he was back in Russia, and in the fall of 1863 there appeared in *Time* his essay "Winter Notes on Summer Impressions." His observations only served to strengthen his faith in the future lofty destiny of Russia if it could be kept free from the poison of the West. The evils of bourgeois civilization he saw in Berlin, Paris, and London distressed him, and the socialist remedy advocated was worse.

In 1863 the government suppressed *Time* because of a seemingly unpatriotic article on the Polish rebellion. At this critical juncture Dostoevsky again left for Europe, to seek a cure, he said, for his epilepsy. But it is known that he hoped to repair his precarious finances at gambling resorts abroad and keep a rendezvous with a beautiful Saint Petersburg woman, Polina Suslova, with whom he was in love. His luck with both was execrable—he lost at roulette and Polina jilted him. He returned to find his wife dying of tuberculosis and his financial affairs in a desperate state. However, an opportune legacy enabled him to revive the magazine, but only if he altered its name.

Epoch began to appear early in 1864. It got off to a bad start by identifying itself with Dostoevsky's now sharply conservative position. In fact his first major contribution, *Notes from the Underground* (1864), is in part a satire of the radicals, especially Chernyshevsky. The underground man inveighs against the egoism of socialists, who believe that human beings can be governed by rational self-interest.

But this remarkable work is infinitely more than a polemic, for it reveals, among other achievements, a capacity for psychological analysis unique in literature. "I place strong hopes in it," Dostoevsky wrote his brother. "It will be a powerful and frank thing; it will be truth." If one were to separate his total production into two creative periods, the dividing date would be 1864, for *Notes from the Underground* marks a new emphasis in the more or less uniform pattern of his writings up to this point.

Previous heroes lack a deep moral consciousness of their own personalities. They seem incapable of analyzing their thoughts and feelings in relation to the world in which they live. In this respect the hero of *Notes from the Underground* represents an altered approach to characterization. The underground man is a profound analyst of himself and others. He is deeply, morbidly conscious of his personality and an astute logician in explaining its complex nature. The work highlights what had only been suggested earlier—Dostoevsky's searching dialectic, his extraordinary ability to dramatize conflicts of the human mind. And this feature distinguishes the remaining masterpieces.

Notes from the Underground is cast in the form of a "confession," but Dostoevsky adroitly suggests the presence of an unseen interlocutor whose reactions and implied gestures to what the hero says convey to his monologue the heightened impression of overhearing a telephone conversation. When the Soviet scholar M. M. Bakhtin observed that all Dostoevsky's heroes are characterized by their language, he might have added that the verbal portrait of the underground man is the most expressive of them.

In the first part the underground man, an unhappy individual of about forty, engages in a microscopic analysis of himself. It is soon apparent that he is one of those dualistic creatures of the early tales, with the important difference that he is fully aware of his dualism. In fact an irresistible urge to discuss the contradictions of his nature is the entire substance of his self-analysis. He is the supreme alienated man for whom no truth is absolute and every good is relative. His dissection leads him to the conclusion that his ambivalence is based on one fundamental opposition—a conflict between will and reason. For him the whole meaning of human existence lies in self-assertion of the irrational will.

In the second part the underground man relates experiences that illustrate his dualism, and its possible resolution is suggested in the episode with the prostitute who possesses Christian pity and love and therefore can be saved, whereas he has only reason to fall back on and is cut off from life. A more explicit resolution, deleted by the censor, indicated that his salvation was to be found in the realization of a need for faith in Christ.

At the end, however, the struggle between will and reason in the underground man is still unresolved, and Dostoevsky left it so in future editions. It is little wonder that Nietzsche's joy was "extraordinary" when he first read the work, in which he discovered "music, very strange, very un-Germanic music." Indeed, on a purely metaphysical level the first part may be regarded as an overture to existentialism. The hero would fit very well into the tragic and absurd condition of life that Sartre allots to man.

Dostoevsky's emphasis, however, is on the spiritual life of dislocated man in a real and acceptable world, and in this sense *Notes from the Underground* is the philosophical introduction to the forthcoming cycle of great novels. Their basic motifs appear in this introduction. Dostoevsky had taken a long step forward in crystallizing a favorite type character and in involving it with religious, political, and social ideas of immeasurable importance in his later fiction.

In the course of fifteen months (April 1864–June 1865) misfortunes overwhelmed Dostoevsky: his wife died, as did his brother Mikhail, the mainstay of *Epoch;* and finally the magazine expired. Burdened with debts (the magazine's and those of his brother's family, which he assumed), he accepted a trifling advance from a shyster bookdealer for a novel, with the stipulation that if the manuscript were not delivered by 1 November 1866, all rights to his published and future writings would belong to this exploiter. To escape debtors' prison he fled abroad in July 1865, and repeated the debacle of his second trip to Europe—he lost at gambling the little money he had and endured another frustrating episode in his pursuit of Polina Suslova.

While in Wiesbaden frantically trying to raise funds to pay hotel bills and return home, Dostoevsky wrote M. N. Katkov, editor of the *Russian Messenger,* to plead for an advance on a novel. The letter contains a rather detailed outline of *Crime and Punishment:* "the psychological account of a crime" of an expelled university student sunk in utter poverty. "Under the influence of strange, 'incomplete' ideas that go floating about" he decides to kill and rob a useless old woman, a moneylender, save his poor mother and sister, then finish his education and expiate his crime by good deeds. After the murder, "insoluble questions confront" him. He feels "cut off from mankind" and confesses because *"he himself experiences a moral need"* for punishment. Katkov sent the advance, and Dostoevsky went back to Russia to write the novel. It was published in the *Russian Messenger* during 1866 and aroused great popular interest.

Actually, Dostoevsky had conceived *Crime and Punishment* years before—he thought of it then as the confession of a convict. And before he left for Europe in 1865 he had vainly sought an advance for still another story he was writing, "The Drunkards," which, he told the editor, would concern not only the question of drunkenness but "all its ramifications, especially the picture of a family and the rearing of children in these circumstances." Clearly this had to do with the remarkable character Marmeladov and his equally remarkable family, which Dostoevsky now worked into the design of *Crime and Punishment.*

The tremendous effort he expended on the work is revealed in Dostoevsky's notebooks. They take us into his laboratory, as it were, and these rough drafts, preliminary sketches of characters and scenes, and above all his corrections and observations, extending to the minutest details of the material, provide a deep insight into the creative process of a literary genius and the infinite pains he took with everything that made for artistic perfection.

Crime and Punishment is closely involved with contemporary events. Dostoevsky's own poverty at the time and the financial crisis in Russia in the 1860's provide background for Raskolnikov's situation and exacerbated state of mind. Money is at the root of his difficulties and in one way or another determines the thoughts and actions also of the Marmeladovs, Sonya, Luzhin, Lebezyatnikov, and Svidrigailov. Raskolnikov's theory of the right to kill on the premise that a noble end justifies illicit means was no doubt suggested by Rastignac's theorizing in Balzac's *Père Goriot* (1835). This proposition, an outgrowth of the "incomplete ideas" of the time mentioned by Dostoevsky, amounts to a continuation of his attacks on the materialist philosophy of the radicals. The hero is one of them, a profoundly human, suffering nihilist in whose soul life and theory conflict. On one level, in fact, the work is a social novel, a satirical debunking of radical youth preaching Chernyshevsky's doctrine of revolutionary democracy.

But the novel's focus is on Raskolnikov's tormented struggle with good and evil. Dostoevsky goes well beyond the "idea of Rastignac" in dissecting the impulses that lead his dualistic hero to kill and then to repent. In these respects the complex motivation is absorbingly reflected in conflicting trial flights in the notebooks. At one point in the notes Dostoevsky warns himself: "The main anatomy of the novel: it is of crucial importance to bring the matter to a real climax and do away with this vagueness, that is, *explain the murder in one manner or another* and establish his character and attitudes clearly." Although motivation for the murder is ambiguous, the novel's central idea is unmistakable: reason cannot take the place of the living process of life. For Raskolnikov, dialectics had taken the place of life. In prison his satanic pride, which had led him to violate the moral law, gives way to the realization that happiness cannot be achieved by a reasoned plan of existence but must be earned by suffering.

Though Raskolnikov dominates the novel, in none of Dostoevsky's previous fiction had the secondary characters been so well individualized, especially the Marmeladov family, and the meek, ineffable Sonya, who is the hero's good angel as the mysterious Svidrigailov is his evil angel. In these and others, all reality, as in the case of Raskolnikov, becomes an element in their self-knowledge. Dostoevsky had given entirely new dimensions to the detective story by infusing into it compelling philosophical, psychological, and social elements. The unity and concentration of the action, with each episode advancing the development of the central theme, and all of this cast against a background of vividly described Saint Petersburg life that adds meaning and tone to the behavior of the characters, made *Crime and Punishment*, compositionally speaking, the most achieved of Dostoevsky's masterpieces.

As sheer story, however, the novel does not rest on dialectics, morality, or the central idea, although these features contribute to its total impression. It is the high seriousness of this drama of crime that attracts the reader. The intensity of the step-by-step revelation of Raskolnikov's plan, the dramatic account of the murder, and then the equally intense psychological analysis of the disintegration of all the forces that had goaded him on to kill—this is the vital story that never loses its grip on the reader's imagination and emotions. And over all radiates a spiritual glow that illumines the darkest recesses of the criminal and the morally debased, and inspires them to seek a deeper meaning in life through suffering to ultimate salvation.

While working on the last part of *Crime and Punishment*, Dostoevsky remembered his contract with the bookseller to deliver the manuscript of a novel. The date was fast approaching and postponement was denied. Fortunately three years earlier he had outlined a novel about a rebel against society who abandons Russia for Europe to devote himself entirely to gambling. He now took up this subject, hired a young stenographer, Anna Snitkina, and in twenty-six days dictated a short novel, *The Gambler* (1866). The work is plainly based on his own passion for gambling and his equally passionate love affair with Polina Suslova. The story centers on the love-hate relationship of Polina Alexandrovna, an imperious beauty, and the gambler Alexei Ivanovich. This masochistic-sadistic emotional duel is an intensified and exaggerated reflection of the relations of Dostoevsky and Polina Suslova. Created in such haste, *The Gambler* was bound to be a minor effort, but it has several powerful scenes that develop further the psychological manifestations of the love-hate syndrome that dominates the relationships of a number of Dostoevsky's men and women.

The stenographer, who was twenty-five years younger than Dostoevsky, soon married him (February 1867). She resented his in-laws' continued demands on his meager funds and wisely suggested going abroad when creditors once more threatened prosecution. They remained in Europe for four years, traveling from country to country. Anna endured long periods of abject poverty when Dostoevsky lost previous advances and money from everything he could pawn in his craze for gambling. There were also epileptic fits, a revival of his love for Polina Suslova, the tragic death of their firstborn, and attacks of sick, nervous irritability. But her devotion to him and his genius never faltered. Dostoevsky's second marriage was one of real love and the most fortunate event in his life.

Abroad he tried to keep informed of happenings in Russia and Europe by avidly reading newspapers and magazines, and by correspondence with literary friends at home. At Geneva he attended meetings of the International League for Peace and Freedom, where diatribes against Christianity, and clarion calls to bloody revolution by fiery orators such as M. A. Bakunin, horrified him. He worried over their influence on like-minded people in Russia, and it was in this disturbed state that he began, in 1867, to think about his next work.

Of all Dostoevsky's novels, *The Idiot* was the most difficult to write. The starting point is a court trial he read about in the Russian press concerning gentry parents who had tortured their children, particularly a daughter of fifteen. He not infrequently drew on newspaper accounts of domestic tragedies and criminal cases for his fiction, and he defended the practice because of its importance to his conception of realism. "I have my own special view of reality in art," he wrote to a correspondent:

> What the majority call almost fantastic and exceptional sometimes signifies for me the very essence of reality. . . . In every issue of a newspaper you meet accounts of the most real facts and amazing happenings. For our writers they are fantastic; they are not concerned with them; yet they are reality because they are facts.

Here Dostoevsky has in mind his great rivals Turgenev and Tolstoy, whose depictions of the gentry class, he believed, dealt with typical, surface features of reality. "I have an understanding of reality and realism entirely different from that of our realists and critics," he wrote another correspondent:

> My idealism is more real than theirs. Lord! To relate sensibly all that we Russians have experienced in our last ten years of spiritual growth—indeed, do not our realists cry out that this is fantasy! Nevertheless, this is primordial, real realism!

In one of his finest short stories, "A Gentle Creature" (1876), we observe him in the process of transmuting "the fantastic facts of reality" into art—a brief press release about a young wife who jumped to her death with an icon clasped to her breast is filtered through the alembic of his analytical mind as he imagines a frame of action consistent with psychological realism and the truth of tragedy.

But Dostoevsky added an important dimension to his notion of "fantastic realism." He preferred to shift the emphasis from the external world to that of the minds and hearts of his characters, for he was primarily interested in the realities of their spiritual existence. Art he regarded as a medium for conveying the wisdom of life, the emotions of the soul. Though convinced that he was fundamentally concerned with social, intellectual, and spiritual problems of average Russians, he insisted that he elevated them to universal significance in his search—as he put it—"with complete realism to find man in man." He defined his innovation as an attempt to represent in fiction spiritual phenomena above and beyond social practices, to resolve the psychological contradictions of man in terms of true and eternal "humanness." "They call me a psychologist," he wrote in his notebook. "It is not true. I'm only a realist in the higher sense; that is, I portray all the depths of the human soul."

A study of the copious notebook material on *The Idiot* shows how the "fantastic realism" of the newspaper report of the trial was eventually transformed into what can only be described as a form of "mystical realism." In the notes Dostoevsky piles up plan after plan, at least eight of them, in an effort to grasp clearly the novel's plot and characters. Family groups appear and disappear, heroes and heroines shove each other off the front stage, lineaments of one possible protagonist are transferred to another, and incidents of murder, suicide, rape, theft, and arson compete for attention. In the early plans the principal character is a typical Dostoevskian Double with traits utterly unlike those of the finished novel's meek hero.

In this bewildering mélange of plot, counterplot, and unresolved characters, what obviously frustrated Dostoevsky was an inability to hit upon a central idea and a hero who fully embodied it. Not until the sixth plan does he suddenly formulate the idea and the image of the character to represent it—the idiot, Prince Myshkin. "The chief idea of the novel," he wrote his niece at this point, "is to portray the positively beautiful man [in a moral sense]. . . . The good is an ideal, but the ideal, both ours and that of civilized Europe, is still far from having been worked out. There is only one positively beautiful man in the world—Christ." But Dostoevsky pulls away from this cul de sac, for in the novel the "divine character" of Myshkin vanishes as the radiance of his pure moral nature is stained by human weaknesses. However, there is nothing humorous in Myshkin, as some critics have maintained. "If Don Quixote and Pickwick as philanthropists are charming," Dostoevsky jotted down in his notes, "it is because they are comical. The hero of this novel, the prince, is not comical but does have another charming quality—he is *innocent!*"

In the fantastic world of the Epanchins, the Ivolgins, and their hangers-on, the main action concerns the love affairs of Rogozhin, Ganya, Nastasya, and Aglaya. From the ensuing complications emerge most of the superb scenes. But Dostoevsky carefully avoids emphasizing Myshkin's spirituality solely in relation to these love intrigues by providing a field of action for him. It is described as the

"dark forces" of the new generation given to sensuality, to the accumulation of wealth, and even to crime. All characters are drawn into this crisis of moral decline, and Myshkin alone stands opposed to the "dark forces," preaching his ineffectual doctrine of service, compassion, brotherly love, and man's salvation through the image of Christ. He tells all that the world is beautiful and life is happiness. Despite his faith, he fails. Nearly everyone looks down on him, and his experiences are symbolic of Christ's among the Pharisees. In the end the sinning people he comes in contact with or influences are rendered unhappy, and he himself lapses into idiocy.

The story of Myshkin has sometimes been regarded as Dostoevsky's own spiritual biography. But the image of the "positively beautiful" hero does not wholly succeed. Dostoevsky himself seems to have had misgivings on this score, for he wrote Strakhov: "In the novel much was composed in haste, much is prolix and has not succeeded. I do not stand behind the novel. I stand behind my idea." Nevertheless, he had written one of the great novels of world literature.

In attempting to create a morally perfect hero, Dostoevsky had gambled with popular interest. Readers were baffled by *The Idiot*, and critics regarded it as a falling-off after the tremendously successful *Crime and Punishment*. Further, publishers were not eager to buy up the book rights, and long before the last installment appeared (February 1869), Dostoevsky was in Katkov's debt for another novel. Expenses attendant upon the birth of his second child at this time took every available penny, and he eagerly accepted a small advance from Strakhov for a short story that turned into a short novel, *The Eternal Husband* (1870). Its smooth narrative style and well-constructed plot about a husband, Pavel Pavlovich, born to be cuckolded—in this case by his friend Velchaninov—contribute to a singularly fine achievement. The tale seems like a deliberate exercise piece in Dostoevsky's now finished psychological technique; concentration is mostly on analysis, whereas characters and scenes echo those in previous works. In the careful dissection of Pavel Pavlovich's ambivalent thoughts and actions after he has discovered his friend's betrayal of him, one is reminded of how much Dostoevsky's writing is identified with the history of the human consciousness in its tragic duality.

Meanwhile Dostoevsky had been contemplating a large novel, entitled "Atheism," about a Russian who loses his faith in God and through experiences with people of various intellectual, philosophical, and religious persuasions falls into an abyss of his own creation. Finally he rediscovers a stronger faith in the Russian Christ and the Russian soil.

Some months later this project merged into a still vaster one designed as five separate but connected novels, to be called "The Life of a Great Sinner." The extant notes indicate that Dostoevsky intended to portray his hero from childhood to manhood. He is involved in numerous adventures, including a blasphemous crime that compels a stay in a monastery. Having rejected God, he wanders over Russia, indulges in debauchery, and encounters real figures of a past epoch of vigorous Orthodoxy and well-known representatives among Slavophiles and Westernizers. Christ and anti-Christ, Russia and Europe are debated, and the battlefield of this Dostoevskian conflict is the hearts of the men and women of the novel. In the end the hero achieves sincere love, confesses his sins, and establishes a new life of faith in God and pious good deeds. To portray a great sinner's spiritual pilgrimage through an evil world of little faith to the distant goal of salvation, which he gains through suffering and glorifies by saintliness, was the end of Dostoevsky's creative scheme of things. "This novel is my entire hope," he wrote his niece, "and the whole expectation of my life."

Although "The Life of a Great Sinner" was to remain another of Dostoevsky's unwritten novels, it cast its shadow over nearly everything else he did write, and he pilfered scenes, incidents, and characters from its outline to piece out the imperfections of what he considered lesser works. This is true of his next novel, *The Devils* (better known in English as *The Possessed*), which he began at the end of 1869, putting aside his projected magnum opus in order to send Katkov a work long since promised. For subject he once again seized upon a "fantastic" event in the press—members of a Moscow student revolutionary cell, headed by S. G. Nechaev, a disciple of Bakunin, murdered a comrade who, they suspected, intended to betray them. Initially Dostoevsky thought of it as a short "pamphlet-novel," a frankly tendentious fictionalized treatment of the murder that would give him an opportunity to speak out more directly against radicals, who, he believed, were threatening to undermine Russia. But the work soon took on the proportions of a full-length novel and is one of his indubitable masterpieces. As in the case of *The Idiot*, notebooks for *The Possessed* provide valuable information on the labor he expended in formulating his central idea and the hero who would embody it, in defining numerous other characters in a story packed with action and drama, and in working out the intricacies of an involved plot. Various complications resulted from efforts to regard the young radicals of the newspaper accounts as direct descendants of idealistic revolutionaries of his own generation of the 1840's. The notes indicate that several characters are based upon real figures he knew about; others are composites of people in his own life.

After almost a year of work, he destroyed much of what he had written, for only facts of living reality served to inspire his imagination. Features and figures in the plan of "The Life of a Great Sinner" had begun to fuse in his mind with the Nechaev affair. For the initial hero, Pyotr Verkhovensky (Nechaev), he substituted Stavrogin, suggested by the unnamed hero of "The Life of a Great Sinner," and the novel's field of action was extended to involve, besides revolutionary conspiracy, some of those profound questions of religion and morality implicit in the design of his un-written magnum opus. He had finally hit upon his central idea. He wrote Maikov that the malady afflicting youth in the 1840's had not ended; the devils had gone out of the Russians and entered into a herd of swine, into the Ne-chaevs, had drowned, and the healed man, from whom the devils had gone out, was seated at the feet of Jesus. "The whole voca-tion of Russia," Dostoevsky continued, "is contained in Orthodoxy, in the *light from the East,* which will stream to mankind blinded in the West because it has lost Christ. . . . Well, if you want to know, this is precisely the theme of my novel. It is called 'The Devils'!"

The Possessed's first chapters appeared in Katkov's *Russian Messenger* in January 1871. At this point Dostoevsky faltered. He was ill, was out of funds again, and had become con-vinced that he could complete the novel only in Russia. Katkov sent him the fare and Dos-toevsky returned to Saint Petersburg in July in time to attend the trial of Nechaev and his co-conspirators. His enthusiasm for the novel re-vived, and by the end of 1872 the last parts were published.

Stavrogin, who dominates the work, was in-tended by Dostoevsky to integrate its two the-matic divisions, the romantic element sug-gested in part by the plan for "The Life of a Great Sinner," and the revolutionary conspir-acy inspired by the Nechaev affair. In Stavro-gin, Dostoevsky underlines in his notes, *"in the whole pathos of the novel . . . he is the hero."* His personal magnetism draws all to him, and he exerts a powerful influence, es-pecially on Pyotr Verkhovensky, Shatov, and Kirilov. If we may judge from notebooks and novel, however, Dostoevsky never freed him-self from a degree of uncertainty about Stav-rogin's image. The ambiguities of his spiritual and political contacts with various conspira-tors are matched by those reflected in his re-lations with the principal women: Liza, Darya, and crippled Marya Timofeevna, whom he marries to make a martyr of himself and to outrage people's feelings. Though this obscu-rity has convinced some critics that Dostoev-sky wished to convey a profound symbolic truth in Stavrogin, the notebooks reveal that he deliberately made him mysterious, a tacit admission perhaps of artistic defeat in por-traying a character who originally had so much potential significance for him. But the function Stavrogin ultimately fulfills is skill-fully maintained and highly effective. In his inner struggle he reaches a stage of psycholog-ical amorality in which he is unable to distin-guish between good and evil. "At Tiknon," the famous chapter concerning Stavrogin's vi-olation of the little girl that Katkov refused to print, is of primary importance for an under-standing of the characterization. There it be-comes plain that the forces of evil have taken full possession of Stavrogin; he has lost faith in God and as a consequence the innate good-ness of his nature has utterly atrophied. Only one way out remains—suicide.

The reformed radical Shatov, not Stavrogin, is the principal bearer of ideas that amount to Dostoevsky's ideological answer to the would-be revolutionists. Their amazing meeting is a travesty of the movement, and their leader, Pyotr Verkhovensky, is a half-comic, melodra-matic villain. The other conspirators, among them Virginsky and Shigalev, emerge as dolts, eccentrics, and rascals who lack their leader's courage. In his treatment of the revolutionists and their activities, Dostoevsky's powerful di-alectical method is sacrificed to a polemical purpose.

The old liberal, Stepan Trofimovich Ver-khovensky, father of the bloodthirsty Pyotr, is brilliantly depicted as a kind of Russian Don Quixote, in whose image Dostoevsky pokes fun at the political and social beliefs of his own youth. When this lovable old man is off-stage, interest in the narrative noticeably wanes. At the novel's conclusion, the last ves-tige of Stepan's liberalism vanishes before the new faith he has acquired in the religion of the common people whom he had formerly scorned.

The Possessed revived Dostoevsky's popularity, which was further enhanced, after his return from Europe, by impressive public readings from his works. He now began to frequent conservative social gatherings, where he made friends with prominent people, some of whom were close to the throne, such as the powerful senator K. P. Pobedonostsev. Such connections helped to secure Dostoevsky's appointment as editor of the conservative weekly the *Citizen*, in January 1873. But its reactionary emphasis proved too much for even him, and he resigned after a little more than a year, in April 1874. Fortunately his financial condition had improved, for his wife had undertaken the publication of his works, from which a substantial income was obtained.

During his editorship of the *Citizen*, Dostoevsky contributed to it the column "Diary of a Writer," and after his resignation he revived it, in January 1876, as a separate monthly publication. He continued it for more than a year and also published additional numbers in 1880 and 1881. The "Diary" contains reporting on current events, such as court trials, suicides, spiritualism, and conditions of children working in factories, but he also used it as a medium for expressing ideas on broad social, political, and religious questions. In its pages may also be found literary reminiscences and criticism, autobiographical matter, and short stories and sketches: "Vlas," "Bobok," "The Peasant Marei," "The Heavenly Christmas Tree," "A Gentle Creature," and "The Dream of a Ridiculous Man," which contains Dostoevsky's best presentation of "The Golden Age"—a vision of earth before the Fall—that captivates several of his heroes. Behind the "Diary," however, is a larger purpose. Journalism and literature were closely allied in his mind, for he firmly believed that the interrelation of art and reality must center in the observation of daily existence, and he draws on such material in this publication for his fiction. The "Diary" attracted numerous readers and is of major importance in any study of Dostoevsky's views as well as his remaining novels.

In the "Diary" Dostoevsky tells of the origin of his next novel, *A Raw Youth* (1875): the confession of the illegitimate, unfledged Arkady Dolgoruky about his adventures in the social world of Saint Petersburg, where he seeks the father he hates for neglecting him so long but whose affection he yearns for. There is an appealing freshness in Dolgoruky, whose thoughts, confusion, bravado, sensitiveness, and youthful idealism are portrayed with keen awareness. In the characterization, as well as in much else connected with the work, Dostoevsky once again borrowed from his plan for the unwritten "Life of a Great Sinner."

When Dolgoruky finally discovers his father, Versilov, interest shifts, and the latter virtually supplants his son as hero. There is some truth in the observation that Dostoevsky despairingly made to his wife: "There are four novels in *A Raw Youth*." For at the end of the first part, the plot is all but submerged by the excessive motivation forced on him by the introduction of a profusion of new characters. Besides the initial theme, three others are developed, and a fifth barely adumbrated. The ensuing intrigue involves several love stories, the struggle between father and son for possession of the beautiful Katerina Akhmakova, and a mysterious letter compromising her, sewn in the lining of Dolgoruky's clothes, which all the chief characters desperately strive to obtain for their own nefarious purposes. The incomplete fifth theme, only tenuously connected with the whole, concerns a group of revolutionary conspirators, again based on a newspaper account of their activities. On this occasion the surprising fact is that Dostoevsky portrays the radicals almost as heroes, at least compared with the "devils" in *The Possessed*.

Versilov is the novel's most fascinating character, and his puzzling personality recalls that of the enigmatic Stavrogin. He is developed in much the same manner—by flashbacks, hearsay, and the effect he has on other people. As with Stavrogin, the final portrait leaves an incomplete but powerful impression. As a Russian nobleman Versilov is cynical in matters political, believes that no class is so fond of idleness as the toiling masses, and maintains that the delights of labor have been invented by the idle from virtuous motives. His attachment to God is purely sentimental, but he tells his son that the idea of virtue without Christ is the idea of all modern civilization—a Dostoevskian conviction. He also echoes Dostoevsky's favorite belief that Europe stands on the brink of destruction because of its revolutionary materialism and denial of Christ, and that Russia, which lives not for itself but for the whole world, will in the end lead Europe to the kingdom of God and salvation.

In connection with the ambivalent Versilov, Dostoevsky for the first time is emphatically explicit about the underlying principles that inspired his preoccupation with dualism in the portrayal of some of his greatest characters. Its psychological manifestation as the determinant of thought, feeling, and action is demonstrably a reflection of the part that dualism played in his own nature.

A Raw Youth is usually ranked beneath the other great novels of Dostoevsky's last period. The notebooks, more nearly complete than those for any of his other novels, indicate that his intentions are unrealized in the finished work. For one thing, the notes call for an expansive attack on contemporary social evils that is lacking in *A Raw Youth*. He seems somehow to have gotten lost in the complexity of plot. The Dostoevskian quality of inwardness is noticeably absent, and the customary concern of his characters with profound moral and religious problems, while occasionally evident on the surface, never penetrates to the core of their relation to life. Action does not develop into thought but often becomes an end in itself. This failure no doubt arises from lack of a convincing central idea, which in the

masterpieces provides the dynamics of thought and contributes so much to artistic integration of the total work. Dostoevsky explained that the first stage of his creative process was that of the "poet"—an effort of imaginative inspiration that resulted in the formulation of the central idea of a novel. The next stage he described as "the activity of the artist"—concretizing from his drafts and notes the finished work itself. The notebooks for *A Raw Youth* indicate that to a considerable extent he had been less than successful in both stages.

In the last "Diary of a Writer," for December 1877, Dostoevsky tells his readers that he is discontinuing it in order to devote himself to an artistic work that had been "imperceptibly and involuntarily composing itself" in his mind during the past two years. *The Brothers Karamazov* began to appear in the *Russian Messenger* in January 1879, and the last chapter was completed in November 1880.

In a sense Dostoevsky had been preparing for this supreme effort throughout most of his creative life. The major theme—the charge of parricide against the innocent Dmitri and the judicial error that results in his conviction—was based on a convict's account that Dostoevsky had heard in his Siberian prison. The section on the boys' club, involving Kolya Krasotkin and little Ilyusha, derives from a discarded episode in notes for *The Idiot*. The "Diary of a Writer" contains much material that has a direct bearing on the subject matter and ideas of the novel. The plan of "The Life of a Great Sinner" contributes its increment, especially in the characterizations of Alyosha and Zosima. And several character types he had been developing since he began to write fiction achieve their fullest expression in this last work.

Although *The Brothers Karamazov* is Dostoevsky's longest novel, the plot's bare outline may be summarized in a few sentences: the story of a crime in which Dmitri Karamazov and his father are rivals for Grushenka's love. Prompted by the second son, Ivan, an illegitimate son, Smerdyakov, murders the father, and Dmitri is accused and convicted on circumstantial evidence.

But into this sordid tale Dostoevsky introduces a titanic struggle of love and hate with all its psychological and spiritual implications, cast against a background of the life of a town and its monastery. Throughout the work there persists a search for faith, for God—the central idea of the novel. In no other masterpiece does the white-hot intensity of his ideological world glow so brightly or does he spiritualize ideas so arrestingly and profoundly. In it are concentrated all his mature art, wisdom, and doubts. All that life meant for him—its experiences and symbols, and his vision of them—is reflected in these extraordinary characters.

Although nothing in human experience may satisfactorily explain the extreme motives and actions of old Karamazov, his sons, Zosima, Grushenka, and Katerina Ivanovna, nevertheless these characters, like symbols or personifications of ideas in a modern allegory of life, are treated so realistically that we effect a willing suspension of disbelief and accept them as living human beings. In such creations artistic reality tends to approximate spiritual reality or ideas of spiritual reality.

The father has left his mark on each son. This Karamazov taint is carnal sensuality, which, in its less vicious manifestations, Dostoevsky describes as "a zest for life." It is the father's dominating trait, ruins Dmitri, is just below the surface in Ivan, and even rears its ugly head in the saintlike Alyosha. All the Karamazovs are philosophers, Dmitri remarks, and the animal instinct in them constantly struggles with the moral and spiritual side of their natures.

Alyosha, as the notes indicate, took shape earliest in Dostoevsky's mind, and his description in the novel as "the future hero of my story" suggests that the author hoped to continue his development in one or more se-

quels. Alyosha was destined to undergo the hero's holy pilgrimage in the plan of "The Life of a Great Sinner." The only brother who loves life more than the meaning of life, Alyosha is identified with the Christian ideal. Though in the sequel Dostoevsky obviously intended him to sin in making his way through the purgatory of modern life, he carries in his heart the secret of renewal that will enable him to wrestle with the devil without losing his soul.

Dmitri loves life, but its meaning continually puzzles him. Simplicity and deep feeling are the essence of his being. "To hell with all who pry into the human heart!" he exclaims. What troubles him most is that a man of lofty mind begins with the ideal of the Madonna and ends with the ideal of Sodom. Out of a feeling of moral guilt for his father's murder—he had wished for his death—he accepts his conviction. "I want to suffer," he declares, "and by suffering I shall purify myself."

Ivan, who is more concerned with life's meaning than with life itself, is the most absorbing character and in many respects the mental image of his creator. He is the last of Dostoevsky's remarkable series of Doubles, and his ambivalence is centered in a cosmic struggle with God. Ivan begins with an act of rebellion and ends in utter metaphysical insurrection against God's world. The Karamazov taint in him takes the form of intellectual pride. In his pride he dreams of becoming a man-god, but when the submissive side of his nature predominates, he accepts the world-god, for he cannot understand the higher harmony between man and the world of God. In this inner struggle Ivan is concerned really with those factors that were at the bottom of Dostoevsky's own search for faith—the problem of sin and suffering and their relation to the existence of God.

The resolution of Ivan's struggle is concentrated in the section "Pro and Contra," one of Dostoevsky's finest artistic achievements. After recounting to Alyosha true stories about the torture of children, Ivan demands justice for these victims, and justice not in heaven or hell but on earth. If eternal harmony is to be obtained at the expense of these persecuted innocent children, he declares, then he must renounce the harmony of God's world. And when Alyosha insists that Christ, who suffered for the sake of all humankind, had the right to forgive those responsible for the suffering of the innocent, Ivan counters with the famous "Legend of the Grand Inquisitor," in which the Inquisitor condemns Christ for preaching man's freedom of choice in the knowledge of good and evil. In both the notes and a letter to the novel's editor, Dostoevsky asserts that Ivan's argument rejecting the meaning of God's world is unanswerable and that Ivan also approves the Inquisitor's reason for denying Christ.

In the next section, however, Dostoevsky attempts an answer, which he puts in the mouth of the old monk Zosima. It had already appeared in Dostoevsky's own words in the "Diary of a Writer": that equality is to be found only in the spiritual dignity of human beings; that suffering does not destroy the harmony of life but is a fulfillment, an act of Godly justice that corrects transgressions for the sake of the whole; that the secret of universal harmony is achieved not by the mind but by the heart, by feeling and faith; that if one loves all living things, this love will justify suffering, all will share in each other's guilt, and suffering for the sins of others will then become the moral duty of every true Christian. This inconclusive debate between Ivan and Zosima reflects the anguished dialogue that went on in Dostoevsky's doubting, dualistic mind in his own search for faith.

Perhaps Dostoevsky intended to elaborate on the answer in the sequel to the novel, but after his celebrated speech at the unveiling of Pushkin's statue, which electrified a distinguished audience with its ringing prophecy of Russia's world mission, he had only a few more months to live. He died on 28 January 1881, and with him died the continuation of his great work. More so than any of his other novels, *The Brothers Karamazov* faithfully mirrors the inner struggle that was the source of his art—his mind was with the reasoning of Ivan, his heart with the precepts of Zosima. This mighty conflict of mind and heart adds an element to the novel that transcends mortal experience. There is a sense of infinity in the book that reaches out beyond the earthy passions of its story to a region where the ultimate, universalized reasons for all human behavior exist. It somehow seems to justify Dostoevsky's belief that the higher realism he took as his province was like that of Shakespeare—not restricted to mere imitations of life, but concerned with the mystery of humankind and the human soul.

Selected Bibliography

EDITIONS

Poor Folk. Saint Petersburg, 1846.
The Double. Saint Petersburg, 1846.
The Friend of the Family. Saint Petersburg, 1859.
The Insulted and the Injured. Saint Petersburg, 1861.
The House of the Dead. Saint Petersburg, 1861.
Winter Notes on Summer Impressions. Saint Petersburg, 1863.
Notes from the Underground. Saint Petersburg, 1864.
The Gambler. Saint Petersburg, 1866.
Crime and Punishment. Saint Petersburg, 1867.
The Idiot. Saint Petersburg, 1869.
The Eternal Husband. Saint Petersburg, 1870.
The Diary of a Writer. Saint Petersburg, 1873–1881.
The Possessed. Saint Petersburg, 1873.
A Raw Youth. Saint Petersburg, 1875.
The Brothers Karamazov. Saint Petersburg, 1879–1880.

TRANSLATIONS

INDIVIDUAL WORKS

The Brothers Karamazov. Translated by Constance Garnett. New York, 1945.
Crime and Punishment. Translated by Jessie Coulson. New York, 1952.

The Diary of a Writer. Translated by Boris Brasol. New York, 1949.

A Disgraceful Affair. Translated by Nora Gottlieb. Philadelphia, 1963.

The Friend of the Family. Translated by Constance Garnett. New York, 1949.

The House of the Dead. Translated by Constance Garnett. New York, 1915.

The Idiot. Translated by David Magarshack. Baltimore, 1955.

The Insulted and the Injured. Translated by Constance Garnett. New York, 1955.

Letters from the Underground. Translated by C. J. Hogarth. New York, 1957.

Poor Folk. Translated by Robert Dessaix. Ann Arbor, Mich., 1982.

The Possessed. Translated by Constance Garnett. New York, 1948.

Winter Notes on Summer Impressions. Translated by Robert Lee Renfield. New York, 1955.

COLLECTED WORKS

Great Short Stories of Fyodor Dostoevsky. New York, 1968.

Occasional Writings. Edited by David Magarshack. New York, 1969.

The Short Stories of Dostoevsky. Edited by William Phillips. New York, 1957.

Works. Translated by Constance Garnett. 12 vols. New York, 1951.

CORRESPONDENCE, NOTEBOOKS

Dostoevsky: Letters and Reminiscences. Edited by S. S. Koteliansky and J. Middleton Murry. New York, 1923.

Letters. Edited by Ethel C. Mayne. New York, 1984.

Letters of Dostoevsky to His Wife. Edited by Elizabeth Hill and D. Mudie Hill. New York, 1930.

Letters of Fyodor M. Dostoevsky. Edited by Ethel C. Mayne. London, 1914.

The Notebooks for the Five Major Novels. Edited by Edward Wasiolek. Chicago, 1967–1971.

The Unpublished Dostoevsky: Diaries and Notebooks (1860–1881). Ann Arbor, Mich., 1975–1976.

BIOGRAPHICAL AND CRITICAL STUDIES

Abraham, G. *Dostoevsky.* New York, 1974.

Bakhtin, Mikhail. *Problems of Dostoevsky's Poetics.* Translated by R. W. Rotsei. Ann Arbor, Mich., 1973.

Belknap, R. L. *The Structure of* The Brothers Karamazov. The Hague, 1976.

Berdyaev, Nicholas. *The Spirit of Dostoevsky.* Translated by Donald Attwater. New York, 1957.

Camus, Albert. *The Rebel: An Essay on Man in Revolt.* Translated by Anthony Bower. New York, 1954.

Carr, Edward Hallett. *Dostoevsky, 1821–1881.* New York, 1981.

Cerny, V. *Dostoevsky and His Devils.* Ann Arbor, Mich., 1975.

Coulson, Jessie. *Dostoevsky: A Self-Portrait.* London, 1962.

Curle, Richard. *Characters of Dostoevsky: Studies from Four Novels.* London, 1950.

Dostoevskaia, A. *Fyodor Dostoevsky: A Study.* New York, 1972. (By his daughter.)

Dostoevsky, Anna. *Reminiscences.* Translated and edited by Beatrice Stillman. New York, 1975. (By his second wife.)

Fanger, Donald. *Dostoevsky and Romantic Realism.* Cambridge, Mass., 1965.

Frank, Joseph. *Dostoevsky: The Seeds of Revolt, 1821–1849.* Princeton, N.J., 1976.

————. *Dostoevsky: The Years of Ordeal, 1850-1859.* Princeton, N.J., 1983.

Gide, André. *Dostoevsky.* Translated and with an introduction by Arnold Bennett. New York, 1925.

Grossman, L. *Dostoevsky: A Biography.* Indianapolis, Ind., 1975.

Ivanov, Vyacheslav. *Freedom and the Tragic Life: A Study in Dostoevsky.* Translated by Norman Cameron. New York, 1952.

Jackson, Robert Louis. *Dostoevsky's Quest for Form: A Study of His Philosophy of Art.* New Haven, Conn., 1966.

Jones, M. *Dostoevsky: The Novel of Discord.* London, 1976.

Labrin, Janko. *Dostoevsky: A Study.* New York, 1947.

Linnér, Sven. *Dostoevskij on Realism.* Stockholm, 1967.

Lord, R. *Dostoevsky: Essays and Perspectives.* Berkeley, Calif., 1970.

Magarshack, David. *Dostoevsky.* Westport, Conn., 1976.

Matlaw, R. E. *"The Brothers Karamazov": Novelistic Technique.* The Hague, 1957.

Meier-Graefe, Julius. *Dostoevsky: The Man and His Work.* Translated by Herbert H. Marks. New York, 1928.

Merezhkovsky, D. S. *Tolstoi as Man and Artist, with an Essay on Dostoevsky.* New York, 1902.

Mochulsky, Konstantin. *Dostoevsky: His Life and Works.* Translated by Michael A. Minihan. Princeton, N.J., 1967.

Murry, John Middleton. *Fyodor Dostoevsky: A Critical Study.* New York, 1966.

Passage, Charles E. *Dostoevsky the Adapter: A Study in Dostoevsky's Use of the Tales of Hoffmann.* University of North Carolina Studies in Comparative Literature, no. 10. Chapel Hill, N.C., 1954.

Payne, Robert. *Dostoevsky: A Human Portrait.* New York, 1961.

Peace, R. *Dostoevsky.* Cambridge, Mass., 1975.

Powys, John Cowper. *Dostoevsky: A Study.* London, 1946.

Reeve, F. D. *The Russian Novel.* New York, 1966.

Roe, Ivan. *The Breath of Corruption: An Interpretation of Dostoevsky.* London, 1946.

Simmons, Ernest J. *Dostoevsky: The Making of a Novelist.* New York, 1940.

Steiner, George. *Tolstoy or Dostoevsky: An Essay in the Old Criticism.* New York, 1971.

Troyat, Henri. *Firebrand: The Life of Dostoevsky.* Translated by Norbert Guterman. New York, 1946.

Wasiolek, Edward. *Dostoevsky: The Major Fiction.* Cambridge, Mass., 1964.

Woodhouse, C. *Dostoevsky.* New York, 1974.

Yarmolinsky, Avrahm. *Dostoevsky: His Life and Art.* New York, 1957.

ERNEST J. SIMMONS

GUSTAVE FLAUBERT

(1821–1880)

GUSTAVE FLAUBERT IS a writer of contradictory qualities and great complexities. He seems to be at once a romantic and a realist, an idealist and at the same time disillusioned, a writer of great emotion and a pure formalist. He is certainly one of the great proponents of art for art's sake, yet a generation of French writers—including Émile Zola, Guy de Maupassant, and the Goncourt brothers—considered him the father of neorealism and the social novel. Flaubert detested the mediocrity of French culture, but he spent most of his career writing about the stupidity of that world. He was not interested in politics, yet his *Éducation sentimentale (Sentimental Education)* is considered one of the best social documents on the revolution of 1848.

Of course, any writer can be said to embody contradictory impulses. But Flaubert's contradictions are fascinating precisely because they are specifically a reaction to the problems of the early modern world and the rise of modern culture. More than any other writer who preceded him, Flaubert detested not merely mankind but those particular changes that he imagined had come about as a result of the rising tide of industry and democracy. Being at once a critic and a part of that world, Flaubert, as did many later writers, found himself in an untenable and insoluble position. He saw his times as the nadir of civilization. As he puts it: "'89 destroyed royalty and the nobility, '48 the bourgeoisie, and '51 the people. There is

nothing left but a bestial and imbecile rabble."[1] Although he believed that a writer should have "neither religion nor fatherland nor even any social conviction" (Steegmuller, p. 278), Flaubert still had social convictions about his own era. But though he detested his times, he was unable to suggest alternatives or how to achieve change, even in his art. His only recourse was to the power of art and description in the hope that these might make others share his beliefs and his pessimism.

Flaubert was born on 12 December 1821 at the hospital in Rouen, where his father was chief surgeon. He grew up in quiet comfort, performing plays, reading, and writing—always imagining an exotic and lush world that was the opposite of provincial Norman existence. It is hard to believe that one of the greatest writers in French sprang from this small-town life. If one tries to look for moments that led to the creation of Flaubert's genius, it is difficult if not impossible to discover anything remarkable or unusual in his childhood.

One event stood out in Flaubert's own imagination—and he wrote and rewrote this experience with such persistence that we must stop and take notice, although at first glance we seem to be dealing with a very common occurrence. At the age of of fifteen, Flaubert

---

[1]Francis Steegmuller, *Flaubert and Madame Bovary* (1977), p. 278. Further references to Steegmuller in the text are to this work.

saw a pretty woman nursing her baby on a beach. That woman—Élise Schlésinger—seized Flaubert's conscious and unconscious desires with such force that she shows up in one form or another in five novels that Flaubert wrote—*Mémoires d'un fou* (Memoirs of a Madman, written that year), *November*, the first *Sentimental Education* (all published posthumously), *Madame Bovary* (1857), and the final version of *Sentimental Education* (1869). Flaubert made friends with Élise Schlésinger and her husband and remained friends with them for most of his adult life. What this chance encounter triggered for Flaubert was an obsession with adultery and with women who were both lovers and mothers, as we will see.

A significant event, perhaps more significant than the first, took place in 1844. Flaubert was afflicted by a series of epileptic attacks when he was twenty-three years old. These attacks were a kind of visionary experience for Flaubert and were inspired by Saint Anthony, whose life Flaubert had read about and about whom he later wrote one of his major novels. In any case, these visions and attacks became the physical excuse for Flaubert to give up his law studies, which he detested, and to begin officially his career as a writer—a career in which he had previously only dabbled.

Flaubert's first significant novel was *November*, written when he was only twenty. It is a work of nostalgia for his own innocence, lost in a sexual sense only three years earlier. The novel recalls his first memorable sexual encounter. (He had apparently slept with his mother's maid earlier, but this adventure must not have struck him as particularly poignant or literary.) In the summer of 1839, when Flaubert was seventeen, his parents sent him on a trip to the south of France, Malta, and Corsica. On the trip, young Gustave met Eulalie Foucaud, a thirty-five-year-old Creole with an absent husband and a young daughter. Eulalie ran a hotel in Marseille and fell in love with the young tourist. For Flaubert, the ex-

perience was a triumphant entrance into a world of sexuality and voluptuousness that all his writing and reading had held out before him as a golden reward of life.

Flaubert's late adolescence, like that of most other people, was filled with thoughts of sexuality, but one might point to a special role that he gave to the sensual and the voluptuous that never left his work. Literature and sexuality were virtually inseparable. When Flaubert was not writing about sexuality, he was writing about superabundance, sensuality, hedonism, appetite, and depravity. His adolescent journals reveal this desperate yearning, to which he gave life in the fantasy world of Oriental courtesans, dancing girls, exotic prostitutes, as well as a world inspired by the marquis de Sade of murder, necrophilia, rape, and bestiality. Flaubert was at once attracted and repulsed by his own masturbatory vision, as a typical entry in his journal reveals:

> Oh flesh, flesh, that demon that keeps coming back incessantly, that tears the book from your hands and the cheerfulness from your heart, makes you somber, ferocious, selfish; you repel it, it returns; you surrender to it ecstatically, fling yourself at it, sprawl upon it, your nostrils flare, your muscle stiffens, your heart palpitates—and then you fall back moist-eyed, fed up, exhausted.
>
> (*Intimate Notebooks*, p. 29)

To this entry Flaubert added the comment "pitiable" in parenthesis to underscore his own repulsion for (and perhaps mastery of) his fantasies. Out of this desperation and ambivalence came *November*.

The novel derives much of its power from its youthful adoration of women and sexuality. The style is painfully intense, and words like "torment" and "yearning" are the building blocks of the book, as the following tribute to female tightrope walkers suggests: "I tormented my imagination dreaming of those strangely formed thighs so firmly encased in pink tights, those supple arms wreathed in bangles" (F. Jellinek trans., p. 8)

The novel chronicles the narrator's brief affair with a prostitute. The world created swells with polymorphous sensuality as the young narrator wanders through woods and fields—described as female and responsive. The narrator virtually makes love to the earth:

> I lay face downward on the ground in a place where there seemed to be the most shade, silence and darkness, the place that might best conceal me; and panting, I lunged into unbridled desire. The clouds hung heavy and sultry, they weighed on me, they crushed me as one breast crushes another. . . . I felt myself swooning with bliss beneath the weight of this amorous nature.
>
> (pp. 59–61)

Flaubert's youthful remaking of nature itself into his lover is important to his later work because it represents the way Flaubert ultimately saw his art as a transformation of mere reality. Obviously nature is a little more indifferent to most of us than Flaubert's narrator thinks. But writing and art can eroticize the world and in turn can eroticize the writing process so that fantasies become real, and the real can be incorporated into fantasy.

This eroticization of the world becomes so overwhelming in *November* that when the narrator enters the city from his erotic pastoral, every woman he sees wants him:

> Ladies in wraps bent from their balconies to see me and gazed at me, saying: "Love us! Love us!" . . . There was Woman everywhere: I rubbed elbows with her, I brushed against her, I inhaled Woman, for the air was redolent of her fragrance. . . . Not this woman nor that one, one no more than the other, but all of them, each of them, in the infinite variety of their forms and of my corresponding desire.
>
> (pp. 62–63)

Flaubert eroticizes every surface of reality—whether rural or urban landscape. In *November* the eros seems poignantly maternal. Nature is a huge and panting mother, and the city of women is in essence a projection of that desire for the mother. This early novel signals Flaubert's repeated obsession with the mother as sexual object. Although Marie, the prostitute who becomes the narrator's lover, frequently calls the narrator "child," she is described ambivalently as "serpentine, demonic," planting kisses in the way that "a beast of prey explores the belly of its victim" (p. 85). What is most interesting is the crossover in Flaubert's youthful mind between the mother as nurturer and the mother as predator. In Flaubert's work the erotic ultimately becomes crossed with the sadistic, and Marie's own biography sounds as though it came from a book by Sade, one of Flaubert's favorite authors. Marie, deflowered by an old nobleman, consorts with a variety of hunchbacks, dwarfs, and outcasts and is marked by perversions that "left upon her . . . the scent of a dying perfume, traces of vanished passions, that gave her a voluptuous majesty; debauch adorned her with an infernal beauty" (p. 117). In Marie, whose name must not be discounted as a reference to the Virgin Mary, Flaubert brings together for the first time the seemingly contradictory qualities he sought in women and in his female characters—the nurturing mother and the sadic lover.

November is not a fully realized novel, and one is tempted to agree with Flaubert's own assertion that the work is "a sentimental and amorous mishmash. . . . The action is nil. . . . Perhaps it is very beautiful, but I'm afraid it may be very false and rather pretentious and stilted" (p. viii). Flaubert tried to remedy this lack of action and characterization in his first version of *Sentimental Education*, written between 1843 and 1845. The word "sentimental" here is not used in our modern sense of "overly maudlin" and "melodramatic" but in the older usage denoting "of the feelings." Flaubert hoped to show how a young man's emotions were shaped and developed in an encounter with an older woman. The plot, while concerned with adulterous love and the fate of two young men, is quite different from the final version of the novel published years later. In the earlier work the story divides between two friends: Henri, who seeks romantic love and worldly power, and Jules, disappointed in love and fulfilled through suffering and art. In a sense the work is a kind of allegory about the inability of Flaubert to decide between these two ways of life, and the novel reveals this tension.

As Flaubert wrote in a letter to Louise Colet in 1852, the characters of Jules and Henri are two aspects of a vision:

> As far as literature is concerned, there are in me two distinct characters: one who is fond of declamation, of lyricism, of lofty flights, eaglelike, of the sound of sentences and the summits of thought; and the other who scrapes and digs out the truth as much as he can, who likes to stress the little facts as much as the big, and who tries to make you feel in an almost *physical* way the thing he reproduces. . . . The [first] *Sentimental Education* represented, without my knowing it, an attempt at fusing these two tendencies.

In this letter there is a deep perception of the dichotomy that haunts Flaubert's subsequent works—these two opposite views coexist and contradict one another in each of Flaubert's novels. Their unique and powerful quality springs from a tension between the lyrical descriptions of nature and life and the peculiarity of the quotidian physical details.

In the first *Sentimental Education* one sees this tension as well. Particularly, Flaubert glorifies femininity and the romantic love it offers at the outset only to tear down these ideals in the resolution of the book. The story opens when Henri Gosselin, eighteen years old, arrives in Paris to begin his study of law (as Flaubert himself had). Henri lodges at the home of Monsieur Renaud, who has an attractive wife named Émilie, with whom Henri falls in love. The first part of the book traces this infatuation and its consummation; this section prefigures the youthful longings in *November.* The characteristic contradictory themes of lyrical idealism and wallowing

physicality dominate. This split is manifested in Henri's aesthetic of sexuality set against the mediocrity of life in Renaud's boarding house. Madame Renaud herself is a kind of goddess of sensuality and the romantic, and Henri places himself at her feet assuming that his adoration will free him from the bondage of student life, just as Emma Bovary will look to passion to free her from Yonville.

Émilie Renaud is another of Flaubert's maternal heroines "whose motherly ways had a certain tender, almost amorous quality." Her husband fits into a pattern of oafish older men and father types to be defeated—Messieurs Bovary and Arnoux included. Flaubert contemptuously referred to this type as the "Garçon"—the smug, self-satisfied shopkeeper, businessman, or professional. Monsieur Renaud is aptly described in this role:

> At the first interview he gave the impression of being shrewd, at the second, rather silly; he frequently smiled in an ironical way at the most insignificant things, but when you talked to him seriously he would stare at you over the top of his gold-rimmed spectacles with such profound intensity that it might almost be mistaken for subtlety. . . . The protuberant curves of his body, which was short and stocky, were covered with flabby, whitish flesh; he had a fat belly, weak, plump hands like those of an old woman of fifty, was knock-kneed, and always managed to get horribly muddy whenever he went out.

In contrast to the oafishness of the husband, Émilie is delightful and nurturing:

> She had such fine black eyes and handsome eyebrows, her lips were still so red and moist, her hands, in every action they performed, still moved with nimble grace. . . . If her bosom, which she was at little pains to hide, was perhaps rather full, on the other hand how sweet a fragrance it distilled when you came near her!
>
> (Garman, p. 15)

In *November* there was no rival to the young male protagonist, but in *Sentimental*

Education, as in his later works, there is a kind of savage competition against the Garçon, whether he is the husband of a desirable woman or the representative of middle-class society in general. While Émilie represents a flight from the ordinary and oppressive world through sensuality and love, the husband embodies the values of the society that traps and imprisons the hero and Flaubert himself. So this book begins a trend for Flaubert in which sensuality offers the possibility of revolt against the constrictions of life, and writing about that sensuality creates a method of revolt for Flaubert himself.

The divided consciousness of Flaubert holds out two possibilities of revolt for the characters of this novel. Jules, who begins in a secondary role, represents artistic isolation and suffering. At first he falls in love and fails with the woman in question. But his retreat from the pain of love leads to the painful but valuable existence of scholar and artist. Jules seeks solace in the world of Orientalism and the exotic, reading the novels of Sade, writing scholarly works on the "Asiatics," and in composing poems. His obscure existence is made to seem more important as the novel moves on, and eventually it is Jules's aesthetic and intellectual choice that is held out as the successful revolt.

The less successful revolt is the one followed by Henri—adultery and passion. This way comes to represent another kind of failure, since Henri and Émilie, once they become lovers, can no longer live in the oafish world of Monsieur Renaud's Garçon. Ironically, they make their way to America, apparently seen by Flaubert as the place of revolution and of anonymity. There they also run into financial problems and fall out of love. Once the power of adulterous revolt is ruined, both Henri and Émilie return to France—she to her husband and Henri to begin his spiral down to the abject mediocrity that Flaubert expands on in the later version of *Sentimental Education.* We seem to be told that the road of passion and love will lead to the palace of mediocrity, and

by the end of the novel, Henri becomes a copy of the doltish Garçon. From his initial idealism he now moves to a "kind of lukewarm conviction and easygoing gusto that led him to fool himself and sometimes other people." We might see this conversion to oafhood as a statement by Flaubert that the quest for power and love will lead away from true revolt. Jules's conversion to scholarship and art thus becomes the right choice for Flaubert.

Following Henri's failed love affair, a certain formlessness in the novel signals Flaubert's abandonment of his protagonist Henri for Jules. Flaubert uses this part of the novel to make general statements about art, changes the form of the novel to a kind of theatrical dialogue, and shifts to Jules's life—but discusses it from Olympian heights of generalization. Gerhard Gerhardi has suggested that the reason for this decomposition of the narrative line is that Flaubert's famous quasi-epileptic attack near Pont L'Évêque intervened and not only changed the nature of his writing but also the artistic direction of the writer himself. This attack, in which Flaubert felt himself "carried off suddenly in a torrent of flames," is paralleled within the work by Jules's sudden insight into life that occurs after he has been hounded through the countryside by a mangy dog. Gerhardi notes that "it is hard to avoid the conclusion that Flaubert meant to dramatize his break with the world of contingency in the hallucinatory sequence . . . preceding Jules's entrance into the world of art." In his own mind, Flaubert had become, at this point, a writer to be reckoned with.

It was now that Flaubert decided to write a work he had thought about for some time—his "great Oriental tale." There was during the late eighteenth and nineteenth centuries a great fascination with the Middle East—a fascination that coincided with the European powers' exploration and colonization of the Middle and Far East. Literary intellectuals, among others, tended to think of these regions as romantic, mystical, erotic, and forbidden. Flaubert's decision to write *La tentation de*

Saint Antoine (*The Temptation of Saint Anthony*, published in revised form in 1874) was a logical consequence of this interest, which would combine his researches into ancient archaeology, his obsession with the Orient, and his reverence for mysticism. To prepare, he read widely in the sacred texts of Buddhism, Hinduism, Islam, and Confucianism, as well as Arabic, Indic, Japanese, and Persian folklore and poetry. He researched the writings of the Church fathers, the Acts of Council, the *Dictionary of Heresies*, and other religious works.

In the novel, Saint Anthony, a fourth-century monk, retires to a cave where he is tempted by a variety of demons and spirits. Flaubert's plan was to expand the list of tempters to include every mythological and heretical figure in all the civilizations of the world. Included are the Sphinx, the Queen of Sheba, the Chimera, the Marcionites, the Carpocratians, and every religious sect and religion that Flaubert had managed to study. There was no plot to speak of, and when the book was completed in September 1849, it was a huge mass of learning with little palpable interest for most readers. Maxime du Camp and Louis Bouilhet, two close friends, were called to Flaubert's home in Croisset, near Rouen, for a reading of the work, so far kept secret. As du Camp later wrote, "The hours during which Bouilhet and I, exchanging an occasional glance, sat silently listening to Flaubert . . . have remained very painful in my memory." After four days of listening to 541 large manuscript pages, du Camp concluded that he had heard

> words, words—harmonious phrases expertly put together . . . but often redundant, and containing whole passages that could have been transposed and combined without changing the effect of the book as a whole. There was no progression—the scene always remained the same. . . . We could not understand, we could not imagine, what Flaubert was driving at, and indeed he was arriving nowhere.
>
> (Steegmuller, p. 135)

Flaubert asked his friends for their opinion of his book and was told to "throw it into the fire, and never speak of it again."

After this crushing judgment Flaubert was unable or unwilling to write for several years. Yet he managed to change this failure to a kind of success. Du Camp and Bouilhet advised him to abandon his lyrical, idealistic, and romantic vision since these brought out the worst excesses of his style. They suggested that instead he write a realistic work that would anchor him to a more mundane, precise, recognizably novelistic technique. Honoré de Balzac was held up as an example of objectivity in narration to be emulated. For Flaubert, who valued the lofty and lyrical, Balzac represented among other things a descent to the cesspool of callous social climbers and aristocratic snobs.

Although Flaubert abandoned his project, he did eventually rewrite *The Temptation of Saint Anthony* twenty years later in a much abbreviated form. While du Camp and Bouilhet might have been correct about the ungainliness of the earlier draft, what they seemed to have missed was Flaubert's herculean effort to re-create the intellectual and philosophical moment of an age. This project, which seemed foolish and excessively arcane to them, was one that he repeated again and again in future works including *Madame Bovary, Sentimental Education, Salammbô* (1862), and *Bouvard and Pécuchet* (1881). Though Flaubert repeatedly emphasized that he was against politics and social novels, his interest in reproducing the ideology of a historical moment made him one of the predominant novelists we think of as cultural critics. What Flaubert realized following the debacle of *The Temptation of Saint Anthony* was that the depiction of his own time and thought, not that of the distant past, could best serve his purpose in creating art. As he later observes:

> To return to the antique in literature has been done already. To return to the Middle Ages has also been done already. The present is the only

GUSTAVE FLAUBERT

hope for literary subject matter. But the present offers an unstable foundation; at what point can one safely attach the first beams? But it is entirely on that the vitality and durability of modern literature depends; on being able to find a secure point of attachment in the present.

(Steegmuller, p. 199)

But before Flaubert could divest himself of his own second-rate romantic illusions and heal the wounds inflicted by du Camp and Bouilhet's rejection of his work, he had to have a period of wandering in the desert. Such an occasion was provided by du Camp himself. He had once traveled through Asia Minor and now decided on an extended trip to the Middle East to photograph the great monuments of Egypt. He begged Flaubert to accompany him. After Flaubert secured the permission of his own mother, he agreed to go. In October 1849 they left for Egypt, where Flaubert was finally able to experience directly the Orient he had read about so assiduously in fantastic books like the *Arabian Nights* and Victor Hugo's *Les orientales* (1829)—a world he had known only through works of Western imagination.

Flaubert had always taken the Middle East rather personally. He imagined that he himself was part of antiquity, transposed to rural France by a kind of bad joke of fate. He wrote without much sense of humility of his desire to possess Cleopatra or Sheba as his mistress. And so this trip was to be a "purge of exoticism" that would flush the mundane from his psyche. His readings burst into life—transformed into material shape:

Thus, as soon as I landed at Alexandria, I saw before me, alive, the anatomy of the Egyptian sculptures: the high shoulders, long torso, thin legs, etc. . . . Here the Bible is a picture of life today.

(*Flaubert in Egypt*, pp. 75–79)

But Flaubert cared little for the massive pyramids and sculptures that still bring tourists to the Middle East and which du Camp had come to photograph. His interest was in the living examples of Oriental sensuality, sexuality, and sensibility that were so different from the habits of his Norman, or even Parisian, neighbors and friends. Flaubert dragged along with du Camp, but noted with amusement that most of the monuments he was forced to visit were covered with bird droppings. "Birdshit is Nature's protest in Egypt. . . . Nature has said to the monuments of Egypt: 'You will have none of me? You will not nourish the seed of the lichen? *Eh bien, merde!*' (well—shit!)."

Flaubert reveled in the exotic, bizarre, sexual, and excremental aspects of life in the Middle East. This world represented a living assault on the conventionality of the Garçon. Fascination ripples through the travel notes— there one sees syphilitic beggars, a hospital for venereal disease in which the patients exhibit their sores and lesions, dissected cadavers, camel urine, bird droppings, and the thousand natural and unnatural shocks that the European might receive in this most different culture. Flaubert's fascination with prostitution and sordid sexuality was fueled by nights spent with famous courtesans like Kuchuk Hanem and days engaged in pederasty at the baths. The Orient became a cavalcade of the bizarre, as one journal entry serves to indicate:

To amuse the crowd, Mohammed Ali's jester took a woman in a Cairo bazaar one day, set her on the counter of a shop, and coupled with her publicly while the shopkeeper calmly smoked his pipe.

On the road from Cairo to Shubra some time ago, a young fellow had himself publicly buggered by a large monkey—as in the story above, to create a good opinion of himself and make people laugh.

A marabout died a while ago—an idiot—who had long passed as a saint marked by God; all the Moslem women came to see him and masturbated him—in the end he died of exhaustion.

(*Flaubert in Egypt*, p. 44)

We might want to remember that while Flaubert was living this life counter to the metropolitan vision of Paris, he was gestating, as it were, his next novel, *Madame Bovary.* What Emma Bovary was unable to achieve in the way of sensuality and revolt in Yonville, Flaubert was permitted in the colonies. What Flaubert ultimately desired in sensual and literary life was a way of combining the fantastic and the earthly, the ideal and the excremental, the revolt against the Garçon's authority and the authority of his mother. The Orient provided a way for Flaubert to reconcile these contradictions. He could make love to a prostitute who evoked images of the *Arabian Nights* while breathing in the "smell of rancid butter." The contrast, what Flaubert frequently called the "bitterness" of this contrast, is what he most desired—and here one might refer to the scene in *Madame Bovary* in which love is pledged to Emma by Rudolphe amid a display of cattle and compost at the agricultural fair. The bedbugs on Kuchuk Hanem's mattress serve the same purpose:

> [They] were the most enchanting touch of all. Their nauseating odor mingled with the scent of her skin, which was dripping with sandalwood oil. I want a touch of bitterness in everything—always a jeer in the midst of our triumphs, desolation even in the midst of enthusiasm.
>
> (*Flaubert in Egypt*, p. 220)

The tension between the beautiful and the profane led Flaubert to books of antiquity like Apuleius' *Golden Ass* that combine "incense and urine, bestiality and mysticism," or to François Rabelais, whose use of excrement Flaubert sees as "lyrical." The Orient represented a vision of sensuality merged with a literary appreciation of the exotic—it was a world in which physical experience was a lesson in artistic and aesthetic sensibility.

Although he was close to writing *Madame Bovary,* Flaubert expresses in the travel journals a lack of interest in writing at all:

> At the present moment I see no reason whatever (even from a literary point of view) to do any-

thing to get myself talked about. To live in Paris, to publish, to bestir myself—all that seems very tiresome, seen from this distance.
>
> (*Flaubert in Egypt*, p. 96)

Yet the suggestive quality of the Orient and of antiquity stood as silent lessons to Flaubert. When he saw the Parthenon, he could not help writing: "The Parthenon is one of the things that has most deeply penetrated my being in my entire life. Let people say what they will—Art is not a lie" (Steegmuller, p. 204).

Flaubert returned to Croisset in 1851, after twenty months of travel, and began to think once more of writing his realistic novel. Bouilhet suggested that he pattern the work after the life of a local health officer, Eugène Delamare, and his wife, who poisoned herself to escape a life of adultery and debt. This subject would allow Flaubert to combine his hatred for the mediocrity of contemporary life with his desire, expressed in *The Temptation of Saint Anthony*, to re-create in fiction the ideology of an era. Since Madame Delamare was reputed to have read and been corrupted by second-rate romantic novels, Flaubert would also be able to attack the inferior quality of modern literature in this new project.

Flaubert set to work with great difficulty, and in creating this great work of maturity, established certain hallmark practices and theories he would abide by most of his life. The first was a painfully slow period of composition. Unlike his writing of *The Temptation of Saint Anthony*, which proceeded rapidly, Flaubert found that the new fiction moved agonizingly slowly. It took him, on the average, four days to write one manuscript page, even though he worked between seven and twelve hours every day. He wanted a perfect style, and such perfectionism made speedy progress impossible. This painful trial of writing became the only way that Flaubert could ever write, suffering through art as did Jules in the first *Sentimental Education.* His frequent outbursts of frustration and rage became typical:

> I'm tormenting myself, scarifying myself. . . . My novel is having a frightful time getting started. I have abscesses of style, I itch with sentences that never appear. What a heavy oar the pen is, and what a difficult current ideas are to row in.
>
> (Steegmuller, p. 237)

He felt that writing was like "playing the piano with leaden balls attached to his fingers" (Steegmuller, p. 255).

This pain was a necessary counterpart to Flaubert's rather impossible aim of trying to create a style that would be objective, almost scientific, and that would eliminate any sense of an authorial presence in a novel. His style would eschew the language of romance and would present life as barely and sordidly as it could:

> I am trying to be impeccable, to follow a straight geometric line. No lyricism, no observations, personality of the author absent. It will be dismal to read: there will be atrocities in it—wretchedness, fetidness.
>
> (Steegmuller, p. 249)

In attempting this scientific style, Flaubert hoped to make his book focus more on method and style itself than on the story—which he hoped to make wretched and fetid. That is, his aim was to keep our sympathies away from the characters and focused on the *way* the story was told. In his view this method of narrating would elevate the project of novel-writing out of the trough of mere storytelling and into the higher realm of true art. Rather than using lyricism as a decoration, he would create a style so perfectly written and purely aesthetic that it would be lyrical and transcendent in and of itself.

In distancing his reader from the story, Flaubert thought he had done something rather new. He writes of *Madame Bovary*, "It will be the first time in any book, I think, that the young hero and the young heroine are made mock of. . . ." The point is not that the novel is a satire or a farce; it is among the first of a genre of writing that is now called the "anti-novel," in which our hopes and aspirations are not allied with those of the main characters. In this sense the reader is outside, looking in at the dissection of an aberrant and diseased human soul. Flaubert saw this distancing as part of the "scientific" nature of writing and reading that his work demanded.

Flaubert seems to be re-creating in words the dissections of cadavers that he watched his father perform at the Rouen Infirmary. Like the scalpel, writing was a scientific tool for observation—perhaps a better tool for understanding life than science could ever provide. Flaubert prided himself that his fiction was as accurate as science, and the following incident seemed to confirm this belief to him:

> I had great success today. You know that yesterday Rouen was "honored" by a visit from the minister of war. Well, I discovered in this morning's *Journal de Rouen* a sentence in the mayor's speech of welcome that I had written the day before, word for word, in my *Bovary* (in a speech by a prefect at an agricultural show). Not only were the idea and the words the same, but even the rhythm of the style. It's things like this that give me pleasure. When literature achieves the accuracy of an exact science, that's something!
>
> (Steegmuller, p. 282)

If writing were truly scientific, then Flaubert was not simply inventing the life of imaginary characters when he wrote novels; he was describing a particular set of circumstances that might create—according to the rules of logic and science—any number of Emma Bovarys:

> Everything one invents is true, you may be sure. Poetry is as precise as geometry. Induction is as accurate as deduction; . . . My poor Bovary, with-

out a doubt, is suffering and weeping at this very
instant in twenty villages in France.

(letter to Louise Colet, 14 August 1853)

Fiction can be seen here as combining science
and art, observation and creation, aesthetics
and morality. The writer was no longer simply
a storyteller but a kind of social psychologist—a scientist whose specialty was the
human psyche and the environment that contained it. That Flaubert did not entirely accomplish this goal in attempting to fit his theories into practice is probably a saving grace.
As Henry James pointed out, "The great good
fortune of *Madame Bovary* is that the theory
seems to have been invented after the fact."

Flaubert's aesthetic view was widely misunderstood when *Madame Bovary* was published. The novel received a great deal of notoriety, considering that it was the work of an
unknown provincial. It was first published in
serial form in du Camp's own *Revue de Paris*,
but after several installments du Camp decided he had to edit the work to remove objectionable passages that might incur the Napoleonic censorship. Flaubert was furious over
this violation of artistic integrity. Yet despite
these bowdlerizations (the scene describing
the curtained cab, among other episodes, was
removed), the novel was brought to trial.
Flaubert was vindicated, however, through the
efforts of family and friends. The scandal of
course helped to sell the book, as did the reputation of the work for explicit sexuality.
What remains most remarkable is that *Madame Bovary* was widely condemned not for
its lack of morality but for its dedication to
realism.

Flaubert never thought of himself as a realist, though. As he writes: "Everyone thinks I
am in love with reality when I actually detest
it." The novelist Edmond Duranty, a professional realist, had written that the book "represents an obsession with description. Details
are counted one by one, all are given equal
value; every street, every house, every room,

every brook, every blade of grass is described
in full. . . . There is neither emotion nor feeling for life in this novel." Jules Barbey d'Aurevilly wrote that Flaubert was an "unwaver-
ing analyst . . . a describer of the minutest
subtlety," but that a machine made "in Bir-
mingham or Manchester out of good English
steel" could have done the job just as well.

How could Flaubert have been considered a
realist when he himself detested the realism
of writers like Balzac? Perhaps the general
reader simply found the inclusion of sordid
detail—the dung outside Emma's father's
farmhouse, the erotic implications of the wandering cab, the hideous, blind beggar, or the
clinical description of Emma's death—to be a
stinging reminder of what is "real" in life. Or
the lack of any "virtuous character," as
Sainte-Beuve bemoaned, might have created
the impression of a radical attempt to undermine the traditions of romance.

But Flaubert was not merely interested in
undermining tradition or poking his nose into
the sordid. What he wanted to do was to link
ideas and facts by instilling in material objects
what other authors had often presented as abstract ideas and moral addresses put directly
to the reader. Maurice Nadeau writes that
"when Flaubert declared that 'ideas are facts,'
he meant to reunite in a single whole the
planes of imagination and dream and everyday life. . . ." (*The Greatness of Flaubert*, p.
139). Nadeau goes on to say that "it is amusing that Flaubert should be accused of 'realism' when he was the first to conjure up the
total world of mingled consciousness and fact,
through sensible appearances and with the aid
of poetic language" (p. 142). What Nadeau
does not say, though, is that such a technique
could not help being considered "realistic" by
a public who was used to the accepted conventions of eighteenth- and early-nineteenth-cen-
tury novel writing. Of course Flaubert might
be said to have redefined the world "realism"
by combining the psychological and the imaginative with detailed physical descriptions of

setting. Along with Balzac and to a certain extent Denis Diderot, Flaubert wanted to be so grounded in a materialist mode of writing that his scientific style would stand the traditional moralistic and idealistic novel on its head.

Let us examine his method by reading the famous description of Charles Bovary's hat at the opening of *Madame Bovary*:

> It was one of those headgears of composite order, in which we can find traces of the bear and the coonskin, the shako, the bowler, and the cotton nightcap; one of those poor things, in fine, whose dumb ugliness has depths of expression, like an imbecile's face. Ovoid and stiffened with whalebone, it began with three circular strips; then came in succession lozenges of velvet and rabbit fur separated by a red band; after that a sort of bag that ended in a cardboard polygon covered with complicated braiding, from which hung, at the end of a long, thin cord, small twisted gold threads in the manner of a tassel. The cap was new; its peak shone.
>
> (P. de Man trans.)[2]

Such a description, although tried occasionally by Balzac, was clearly an affront to most French readers, who had not usually been required by their novels to pursue such detail in a quotidian, albeit extraordinary, object. Even minutely detailed works like Daniel Defoe's *Robinson Crusoe* (1719) do not describe any one object in such length and certainly not at the opening of the narrative. The purpose of this paragraph may well have been to demonstrate symbolically in one object the entire range and mediocrity of Charles's personality, but the casual reader could only feel this section to be strangely without purpose. As Henry James wrote:

> To many people *Madame Bovary* will always be a hard book to read and an impossible one to enjoy. They will complain of the abuse of description, of the want of spontaneity, of the hideousness of the subject, of the dryness and coldness and cynicism of the tone.
>
> (*Madame Bovary and the Critics*, B. F. Bart ed., p. 63)

In some sense Flaubert's method was objectionable not so much because it chose the sordid but because it did so by placing greater emphasis on language and description than on the setting itself, as Paul Valéry and Gérard Genette have noted. The language draws attention to itself, so that the author is actually demonstrating *how* one writes *about* someone like Emma Bovary rather than actually *just writing* about her. Style triumphs over any mere subject.

> Style, as I conceive it, style as it will be realized some day—in ten years, or ten generations! It would be rhythmical as verse itself, precise as the language of science; and with undulations—a swelling of the violin, plumage of fire! A style that would enter into the idea like the point of a lancet.
>
> (*Madame Bovary and the Critics*, p. 37)

This adulation of style places *Madame Bovary* among the first novels to treat language as something unique in itself. And it is precisely language—or rather its misuse—that causes Emma Bovary's problem. Her tragedy is brought about by her mistaking the clichés of the pseudoromantic novels she reads for truths about the world. She is a character, like Don Quixote, who learns to see the world as if it were a romance. By mistaking the world for a literary construction, she inevitably places too great a premium on language and narrative—a misperception that ultimately destroys her. However, Flaubert's use of this misperception is much more scathing and all-encompassing than that of Cervantes. Cervantes allows a real world that can judge the foolishness of Quixote's mad quest, while Flaubert sees Emma's error as endemic, so

---

[2]Further references to *Madame Bovary* are to this edition.

that the readers of *Madame Bovary* themselves are doomed to repeat the heroine's logocentric misreadings. These readers, being no better or more perceptive than Emma, are strangely unsuited to understand the novel. Flaubert felt he had "torn out a bit of . . . [his] innards to serve up to the bourgeoisie" when he wrote his novel.

As a typical novel reader, Emma's first response to most situations is to place herself in a novelistic context. For example, after taking Rudolphe as a lover, she

> recalled the heroines of the books that she had read, and the lyric legion of these adulterous women began to sing in her memory with the voice of sisters that charmed her. She became herself, as it were, an actual part of these lyrical imaginings; at long last, as she saw herself among these lovers she had so envied, she fulfilled the love-dream of her youth.
>
> (part 2, ch. 9)

Emma transforms experience into narrative—choosing the second-rate narratives that had taught her how to interpret the world.

Flaubert's distance from the characters in the novel and his concern for style and method can be observed in the well-known scene at the agricultural fair when Rudolphe reveals his desire for Emma. The clichéd language of love culled from the popular romantic novels of the day is set against the awarding of prizes for farming accomplishments:

> "Take us, for instance," he said, "how did we happen to meet? What chance willed it? It was because across infinite distances, like two streams uniting, our particular inclinations pushed us toward one another."
>
> And he seized her hand; she did not withdraw it.
>
> "First prize for general farming!" announced the president.
>
> "—Just now, for example, when I went to your home. . . ."
>
> "To Mr. Binet of Quincampoix."
>
> "—Did I know I would accompany you?"

> "Seventy francs!"
>
> "—A hundred times I tried to leave; yet I followed you and stayed. . . ."
>
> "For compost!"
>
> "—As I would stay tonight, tomorrow, all other days, all my life!" . . .
>
> "But no, tell me there can be a place for me in your thoughts, in your life, can't there?"
>
> "Hog! first prize. . . ."
>
> (part 2, ch. 8)

The scene strikes one as rather comic, but Flaubert also shows how two forms of shallow language play off against each other. The language of the provincial fair and the inflated language of pseudoromanticism are equally devoid of the lyricism and transcendence that Emma expects to find through passion. These are words without the truth of real style.

One further scene that might illustrate the way Flaubert places his narrative and method in the foreground is the notorious cab scene in which Emma and her new lover Léon make love in a horsedrawn carriage while it wanders through the streets of Rouen. Flaubert deliberately leaves out any sexual description, and the reader merely gets a kind of guided tour of the city:

> "Where to, sir?" asked the coachman.
>
> "Anywhere!" said Léon, pushing Emma into the cab.
>
> And the lumbering machine set out.
>
> It went down the Rue Grand-Pont, crossed the Place des Arts, the Quai Napoléon, the Pont Neuf, and stopped short before the statue of Pierre Corneille.
>
> "Go on," cried a voice that came from within.
>
> The cab went on again; and as soon as it reached the Carrefour Lafayette, set off downhill, and entered the railroad station at a gallop.
>
> "No, straight on!" cried the same voice.
>
> (part 3, ch. 2)

Narrative style, the trick of presentation, is the subject of this scene, while the sexual action in the cab is secondary. Flaubert's brilliant way of depicting action by not describing it all brought the author as close as he might come to his ideal of writing about "nothing at all," and in effect makes his readers focus on the line between style and story.

Emma's attempt to escape from her small world is not so different from Flaubert's attempt to escape from his own culture through art. In fact her escape is only one of many attempted flights, including Saint Anthony's retreat to his cave, *November*'s hero's escape to eroticism and then suicide, Henri's flight to Madame Renaud and America, Frédéric Moreau's move to the provinces, Bouvard and Pécuchet's rush to country life, Saint Julian's escape from his fate, and so on. None of these characters manages actually to disengage from the stagnation of his situation because no one chooses to escape through art. Flaubert offers no character the hope of the one mode that brought value to his own existence. In *Madame Bovary* escape from the world of the Garçon is impossible since all the characters are incarnations of this loutish archetype—from Monsieur Homais to the priest Bournisien. The Garçon is lauded at the end of the novel when Homais wins the Legion of Honor. The circle of entrapment is complete with Emma dead and Homais's mediocrity held aloft for commendation and memorialization.

After dwelling in the detail of provincial life, Flaubert decided finally to go ahead with his long-held wish to write a tale about the Orient. His obsession with this world, along with his practical experience, led him to create *Salammbó*, a work about as far from Yonville as he could go. The world was Carthage in the third century before Christ. As Flaubert wrote: "Few people will guess how sad one had to be to undertake to revive Carthage! It's a wilderness I was forced into out of disgust with modern life." Perhaps the choice to flee to antiquity was a mistake for Flaubert. "Hérodias" (1877), *Salammbó, The Temptation of Saint Anthony*, and "Saint Julian the Hospitaller"—all of which take place in the distant past—have failed to capture the imagination of the modern reader. They remain for the most part works that scholars will read for what they tell us about Flaubert, but are strangely stiff, remote, and bizarre. This is not to say that all these works are failures; certainly much brilliance erupts from the wealth of details, eroticism, and mystery that research and imagination produced. But these works fail to become stories so weighted are they with theory and scholarship. They are exemplary pieces, demonstration models, theoretical proofs that as experiments are fascinating but as narratives are often ponderous and leaden.

Flaubert's reasons for choosing the Orient are complex, as we have seen, but we cannot discount his cherished belief that he himself was actually reincarnated from the spirit of one long dead:

> It seems to me I've always existed, and I have memories going back to the pharaohs. I can see myself quite clearly at different ages in history, exercising different professions and with varying fortunes. . . . I have been a boatman, a *leno* [pimp] in Rome at the time of the Punic Wars, then a Greek rhetor in Suburrum eaten alive by bugs. I died in the Crusades from having eaten too many grapes on the coast of Syria. . . . Perhaps [I was] an eastern emperor. . . .
>
> (Nadeau, p. 161)

In a word, though Normandy was Flaubert's motherland, it was to the East that he traced the origins of his inspiration; though Croisset was his prison, Carthage was his land of freedom. His desire was therefore to apply to antiquity the scientific method he had evolved in writing *Madame Bovary*. Instead of the ordinariness of provincial life, he would now turn to the rich, lyrical, and superabundant world of Oriental opulence. These two novels that appear at first glance so different seem to come out of a similar desire: "I wanted to fix a mirage by applying to antiquity the methods of the modern novel."

The method of *Salammbó* is staggering.

Where in earlier works the profusion of sordid detail led to an oversupply of ordinary objects—in essence providing a counterbalance to the lyrical side of the narrative—in *Salammbô* the details themselves swell to a lurid and lyrical superfluity of lion skins, incense, jewels, flesh, spices, perfumes, tattoos, necklaces, rings, vermilion, and antinomy, piled on with the heavy strokes of a nineteenth-century harem painting. One thinks of the description of Hanno partaking of his favorite drink of weasel ashes and asparagus boiled in vinegar, or of the suggestive details of Salammbô's terrace:

> In the middle of the terrace was a small ivory bed, covered with lynx skins, with cushions of parrot feathers . . . and in the four corners rose four long burners full of spikenard, incense, cinnamon, and myrrh.
>
> (Krailsheimer, p. 51)

Or of the feast given for the barbarians in which

> oblong flames wavered over the bronze breastplates. The dishes encrusted with precious stones flashed and scintillated in sparkling profusion. The drinking bowls, rimmed with convex mirrors, multiplied the magnified reflection of things around. . . . the Greek wines that come in wineskins, Campanian wines kept in amphorae, Calabrian wines brought over in casks, as well as wines of cinnamon, jujube, and lotus. The wine spilled in slippery puddles on the ground. A cloud of steam from the hot food rose up into the foliage and mingled with the vapors exhaled by the crowd. One heard, at the same time, the noise of champing jaws, conversation, song, goblets, Campanian pitchers shattering into a thousand fragments, or the clear note of some great silver dish.
>
> (p. 19)

Such a description breathes excess—not only in the scene itself but in the scholarship that went into the making of the novel. Throughout *Salammbô* one is impressed and exhausted by the attempt to place into one book so much of the ancient world. Flaubert believed that for a book to exude truth "you have to be crammed up to the ears with your subject." And following his own advice, Flaubert claimed to have read more than fifteen hundred authors, ancient and modern, in preparation for the work. He even returned midway through the novel to the Middle East to steep himself in the past.

The danger of all this background is that it eclipses the main characters and makes them mere mannequins set against a display of archaeological artifacts. The beautiful and awesome virgin Salammbô is entirely without personality. She is a sculpted embodiment of the Oriental woman—the opposite in every extreme of the motherly Madame Renaud in the first *Sentimental Education*. In the story Salammbô, the royal devotee of the goddess Tanit, offers herself to the brutal warrior Matho in exchange for the goddess' holy veil, which Matho has stolen. Ultimately, Matho is dismembered and Salammbô dies on her wedding day in punishment for touching the veil.

Flaubert defended his desire to create a character without much depth by claiming that in effect he did not want to be precise about anything. He simply wanted to give an impression of the Carthaginian world. He defied anyone to "draw a Carthaginian chair or Salammbô's robe" since he had left everything purposely "indefinite." No one could dare call him a realist in this work.

Yet what is quite definite is an unleashing of sadistic violence unlike that in any of Flaubert's other works, with the exception of some youthful imitations of Sade. In *Salammbô*, mutilations, tortures, decomposing bodies, and infanticide are signposts along the Oriental way. One scene in which thousands of children are thrown into the burning mouth of an idol caused particular consternation to contemporary readers. Descriptions like the following are typical:

> the vermin could be seen leaving the dead, who were growing cold, to run over the hot sand.

Perched on the top of boulders, crows stayed motionless, turned toward the dying.

When darkness had fallen, yellow dogs, those filthy beasts that follow armies, softly came into the midst of the barbarians. First they licked the clotted blood from still warm stumps of flesh; and soon they began to devour the corpses, ripping them open at the belly.

(p. 196)

Despite (or because of) protests against this lurid sort of description, *Salammbô* was quite a popular book and clinched Flaubert's reputation as a writer of note beyond the notoriety he had earned through a scandalous first novel. Appealing to the cult of Orientalism, Flaubert had written a work whose exoticism and morbidity sealed a pact between the readers and their escapist fantasies of harem nights and opiated days. If, as Edward Said has explained, the West had expropriated the Orient by re-creating it in the European imagination as a fantasy to be possessed, then Flaubert deliberately wrote a kind of viaticum that allowed novel readers to travel into that world collectively through an imaginative invasion and domination.

From this exotic past Flaubert moved again to the present and focused on his own generation. *Sentimental Education* is a continuation of the general project of depicting an age, an ideology, and a system of life. In *Madame Bovary*, it was provincial life; in *The Temptation of Saint Anthony* and in *Salammbô*, the mythic and religious world of antiquity; and in *Sentimental Education*, the life of young men in Paris at the time of the revolution of 1848. As Flaubert wrote:

For the past month I've been hard at it on a novel of modern manners that will be set in Paris. I want to write the moral history of the men of my generation: the "sentimental" history would be more accurate.

(Nadeau, p. 184)

In the first version of this book, written some twenty years earlier, the word "sentimental" seems to have been used fairly straightforwardly to signify "education of the feelings"; in this later work, however, one witnesses the obliteration of all sentiments, the denial of feeling, leading to the ultimate deflation and destruction of emotion.

This book is more mature and wide-ranging than the first *Sentimental Education*. In that earlier work we followed Jules and Henri as the former turned to art and the latter to disillusion. But in the second version a whole cast of characters proceeds through particular events of their time, absorbing the spirit of that age and changing their opinions as they develop. However, the net effect is that everyone becomes cynical, defeated, compromised, and without hope. While Jules was at least given the possibility of becoming an artist, his counterpart, Deslauriers, merely aims at power. No other character ever becomes even remotely admirable.

Flaubert was brutal toward his own era for many reasons, as we have seen, but this work is particularly bleak because he felt that his own generation had failed horribly through incompetence. His rage against French culture in general is made even more obvious by linking the love story of Frédéric Moreau and Madame Arnoux to the political and social convulsions of the time. The story begins during the declining reign of Louis Philippe, moves on to the revolution of 1848, and ends with the compromise and failure of that revolution in the coup d'etat of 1851. The state's trajectory of failure is mirrored in Frédéric's personal decline and ultimate failure. All the characters (with the exception of Dussardier, perhaps) are examples of compromised ideals, incompetence, inactivity, lack of imagination, and defeat.

The story of disillusion begins at the moment that Frédéric arrives in Paris to study law and fails his exams (as did Flaubert). In the beginning of Frédéric's listless drifting, he and his friend Deslauriers spin out fantasies of ideal careers. Frédéric wants to be the Sir Walter Scott of France; Deslauriers wants to be a philosopher. Frédéric changes his views and determines to become a follower of passion like Goethe's famous hero Werther; Deslauriers abandons philosophy for political economy. Frédéric then settles on painting, but immediately swerves again, deciding to write a history of aesthetics. In the same breath he fixes on the idea of dramatizing various periods of the French Revolution. This project metamorphoses immediately into a history of the Renaissance. Frédéric then tries to become a politician, promising if elected to destroy the rich. When he is defeated he concludes that the masses are cretins, and he becomes the lover of a wealthy woman, only to discover that she has no money. The movement here is from idealism to compromise and corruption. His mediocrity is manifest in his devotion to ideals and his absolute lack of interest in acting to uphold them.

In effect Frédéric is seduced by an ideology just as Emma Bovary was. Both these characters look to art as a salvation without realizing that they are incapable of living up to the ideals of even second-rate art. Aside from his artistic and scholarly aspirations, Frédéric actually has no career. "I have no profession; you are my exclusive occupation," he says to Madame Arnoux. In a novel devoted, in some sense, to the finding of a career, Frédéric proves the impossibility of his doing anything in life—and as with Emma Bovary, an obsessive passion holds out the only hope for salvation.

The decline of political ideas parallels the decline of all ideals in this work. Sénécal, the revolutionary who believes in the radical political theories of Charles Fourier and in the masses, becomes the harsh foreman in Arnoux's factory, and after that he is transformed into a policeman who kills Dussardier at a demonstration.

Art itself, Flaubert's one salvation, is also compromised in this commercial world. Monsieur Arnoux, the Garçon in yet another form, is the editor of the magazine *L'Art industriel*—an oxymoron if ever there was one for Flaubert. Arnoux's plan is to sell art at popular prices, and he accomplishes this goal by bestowing fame on second-rate artists whom he can control. Because Arnoux's view is that art is only a commodity, he delights in the market. In his next business venture, Arnoux runs a pottery factory that sells tiles with mythological designs in Renaissance style for the bathroom. Art has become merely utilitarian, and antiquity is deformed into mere decoration for that least revered of rooms. Mirroring the decline of art, the magazine *L'Art industriel* now becomes simply *L'Art*, run by a collective owned by shareholders, each of whom has the right to publish by virtue of the investment. Art for industry's sake now becomes art for money's sake. The same magazine is then transmuted into the revolutionary journal *Le flambard*, with its motto "Gunners to your cannon!" It treats "a book of poems and a pair of boots in exactly the same style."

Flaubert felt that political art was as much a travesty as industrial art. In the novel he has the artist Péllerin make revolutionary art ridiculous by painting a work showing "the Republic, or Progress, or Civilization, in the form of Christ driving a locomotive through a virgin forest"—an image all the more repulsive to Flaubert when one recalls that for him "modern stupidity and greatness are symbolized by a railroad." When Arnoux winds up setting up a patriotic music hall, and failing that a Gothic art shop specializing in religious knick-knacks, the failure of art is complete—the spiritual impulse merging with art in this world of compromised ideals can only produce worthless commodities.

The failure of projects and the compromise of ideals, of course, are not the only themes of *Sentimental Education*. There is also love. Frédéric plunges into an amorous obsession with Madame Arnoux after meeting her on a boat trip, an event paralleling Flaubert's own obsession with Madame Schlésinger. (Maurice Schlésinger, incidentally, was the prototype of Monsieur Arnoux in his various business enterprises.) Frédéric manages to find the Arnoux house and make himself a frequent visitor. Marie-Angèle Arnoux is a virtuous married woman, as her name perhaps exaggerates. Caught in this triangle, Frédéric suffers the torments of hating the husband (and liking him as well), desiring the wife, but being unable either to imagine her sexually or to exchange a word with her. The novel runs on this track for most of its plot, while Frédéric's fecklessness and paralysis reign.

Frequently Frédéric associates Madame Arnoux with his own mother, Madame Moreau. In fact the original name for Marie was supposed to be Madame Moreau, but Flaubert changed his mind and gave that name to Frédéric's mother—a fact that reminds us of Flaubert's own obsession with maternal women. The revolt through passion, a theme we have seen throughout Flaubert's writing, is not only ineffective but also is not even fully achieved. Frédéric never consummates his desire for Madame Arnoux, and his mistress is compromisingly also the lover of Monsieur Arnoux. Madame Arnoux remains chaste in body if not desire, and the final meeting of Marie and Frédéric is particularly touching and revealing because in it he realizes that her sexual aura consisted mainly of a maternal glow. When Frédéric meets her after several years have passed, enough time has elapsed to show him her true relation in his unconscious to his own mother. She removes her hat and lets him see her now-white hair, and Frédéric feels as if he were dealt "a blow full in the chest"; he also feels "repugnance akin to a dread of committing incest."

The book ends ambiguously when Frédéric and Deslauriers recall their childhood with longing and nostalgia. They remember one day in their adolescence when they naively went to the local brothel with bouquets of flowers for the whores, but had to flee from embarrassment. The men describe this act of ingenuous incompletion, incomplete as was Frédéric's passion for Madame Arnoux, as "the happiest moment of our lives." Failure to act is held aloft as a pleasure—the implication being that the adult world of sexuality is a deflation and a disappointment. Sexuality, along with art, politics, power, and ideals in general, turns out to be false.

In *Sentimental Education* sexuality is worked into the political arena in a way that no novelist before had done. The pyrrhic climax of Frédéric's infatuation with Madame Arnoux is set to take place on exactly the same day that the February revolution begins. Marie fails to appear because her son falls gravely ill, an act she sees as punishment for her adulterous desires. Frédéric, upset at her absence, plunges into the streets to "indulge in violent actions," including his first sexual encounter with his future mistress, who is Arnoux's at the moment. This development is particularly brilliant because the action of attempted adultery and then the placebo of fornication with Arnoux's mistress are linked to the overthrow of the king. The political and the erotic are set up by Flaubert to reveal a desire to replace the traditional old guard with a new order. But both attempts fail since Madame Arnoux does not show up and the revolution itself fails. The parody of Frédéric's appropriation of Arnoux's mistress rather than his wife is played out in the larger scene as the mob ransacks the royal palace:

> An obscene curiosity impelled the mob to ransack all the closets, search all the alcoves, and turn out all the drawers. Jailbirds thrust their arms into the princesses' bed, and rolled about on it as a consolation for not being able to rape them. . . . In the entrance-hall, standing on a pile of clothes, a prostitute was posing as a statue of Liberty, motionless and terrifying, with eyes wide open.
>
> (p. 289)

This pastiche of Eugène Delacroix's painting of Liberty leading the earlier revolution of 1830 is all the more telling since, as Flaubert's somewhat heavy symbolism implies, the people, like Frédéric, have accepted a prostitute for the real thing. The ideal easily becomes its opposite in this world.

Flaubert skillfully works the lives of his characters into the political world and the political world into the lives of the characters. Monsieur Dambreuse has a heart attack after the dismissal of General Changarnier; Frédéric's illegitimate child dies as the revolution fails; Monsieur Arnoux, the indomitable and indestructible father figure, easily becomes an officer in the revolutionary guard as he previously had been in the National Guard.

The complexity of this work, its attention to political and cultural history, its fatal and affecting love story, make it one of Flaubert's great works. Its special contribution to the history of the novel lies in the interconnecting of ideology, political event, psychological motivation, sexuality, and style into one seamless whole. All events are overdetermined, foreground and background are equally important, despite Flaubert's fear that he had made a work in which "backgrounds eclipse the foregrounds."

The oddity of this integration of elements is underlined by the contemporary critical response. Unlike *Madame Bovary* or *Salammbô*, *Sentimental Education* was generally reviled or ignored. It was considered too "stark," revealing an "intelligence that is all on the surface, with neither feeling, nor passion, enthusiasm, ideal, insight, thought, nor depth." One critic went so far as to say that the work was "not a novel" but merely a narrative that by being real "ceases to interest." What must have been difficult for contemporaries to accept was the strong attack on their generation and culture, the hopelessness of Flaubert's disillusionment.

But the most devastating aspect of Flaubert's critique was really structural. He implied, by linking background and foreground in this way, that the political and emotional were inseparable. This is to say, the failure of his characters was not the failure of an individual hero in a novel but of the entire social structure. France had become the character whose sentiments had not only failed to be educated but probably were never really there in

the first place. We are not surprised to read another critic who complained that the colors of Flaubert's palette were "filth." Flaubert was never more correct than when he said that "the public only wants books that encourage its illusions, whereas *Sentimental Education*" clearly does not.

Flaubert's final works are a mixed grouping of tales, short stories, and long, strangely unnovelistic pieces. Flaubert published a reworked version of *The Temptation of Saint Anthony* and three short stories, all the while working on a final novel, *Bouvard and Pécuchet*, during the 1870's. *The Temptation of Saint Anthony*, a novel he described as "the work of my whole life," was the youthful work rejected by Flaubert's friends, reworked in middle age, and finally rewritten in 1872. As in the earlier versions and in the myth itself, Saint Anthony the Hermit is assailed by a variety of tempters who try to destroy his faith. In Flaubert's work, Saint Anthony cannot summon up refutations to this cumulative and powerful attack on religion, philosophy, and basic moral beliefs. The reader is ultimately placed on the side of the tempters, and the message of the devil seems to be the same as Flaubert's own bleak outlook on the impossibility of knowing or believing:

> All is illusion. Form may be an error of your senses. Substance an invention of your mind. Are you even sure you're alive? It may be that there is nothing.
>
> (ch. 6)

The work is pervaded by a profound negativity, all the more disturbing because of its allinclusiveness. In early works Flaubert had attacked specific aspects of human life in particular epochs. Now he attacks the very enterprise of life itself, of consciousness, religion, and the necessity for morality.

In form, *The Temptation of Saint Anthony* is not a novel. It carries forward Flaubert's project of escaping the requirements of the traditional novel. There is barely a plot; the hermit merely sits in his cave and is assailed by each spirit in the manner of a medieval pageant play. The true subject of the book, as Michel Foucault points out in *Power/Knowledge,* is the history of books as repositories of cultural ideas and values. It is "a book produced from other books." In it we see the culmination of Flaubert's archaeological and scholarly modes of thought. The novel thus becomes a kind of encyclopedia or compendium that embraces all previous books, leaving aside the technology of fiction—character, plot, development—for a direct appropriation of knowledge.

Bouvard and Pécuchet was Flaubert's next project, and one he was to die before completing. It was a work intended to destroy once and for all the last remnants of the traditional novel, replacing them with the ultimate statement of encyclopedic form. *Bouvard and Pécuchet* supersedes *The Temptation of Saint Anthony* by concentrating not on the single focus of religion, but on the multitude of works that constitute all past and contemporary knowledge spewing out from "the unlimited proliferation of printed paper," as Foucault puts it. The story is simple: two middle-aged men meet by chance in a cafe in Paris and discover that they both are copyists—that is, the nineteenth-century equivalents of Xerox machines. They become fast friends, and when one of them inherits money, they decide to escape the oppression of city life to buy a country house. There they pursue nothing less than all the branches of human knowledge in a maniacally programmatic manner. They study agriculture, but fail to produce crops. They move on to another subject, devour every book, and then move on again—traversing philosophy, religion, history, science, medicine, cooking, and so on. The novel is often nothing more than a huge list of books consulted, with an occasional episode of sexual adventure or trouble with the neighbors.

Flaubert died before finishing volume 1, but the ending he envisaged would have had the two clerks renounce all learning and return to copying. The second volume of the work would be composed of all the quotations they had copied; it was to be Flaubert's grandest and final attack on human stupidity, containing verbatim the innumerable foolish things actually said or written by scholars and thinkers. This second volume was to serve "to spew out on my contemporaries the contempt they inspire in me, even if I break my ribs in the attempt." In keeping with the misanthropic tone, he adds that he wants to "exhale my resentment, spew forth my hatred, expectorate my spleen, ejaculate my anger, deterge my indignation." It seems fitting that he died in the attempt.

The third and final volume was to be a "Dictionary of Received Ideas"—the alphabetical compendium of the clichés and trite expressions of the Garçon and society in general. It would include "in alphabetical order and on every possible subject, all you need to say in public to pass for a decent, agreeable fellow." It goes without saying that Flaubert did not like decent, agreeable fellows. That third volume does exist in incomplete form and amounts to a powerfully funny satire of routinized thought, as trenchant as Jonathan Swift's *Polite Conversation* (1738).

The totality of the projected work amounted to nothing less than a cannonade on institutions, knowledge, systems, and the capacity of humans to help themselves through education. "I want to prove," Flaubert wrote to Maupassant, "that any education of whatever kind doesn't mean much, and that human nature means everything, or nearly everything." With this sweeping condemnation of education, Flaubert is left in a strange position. He still allows that the only escape from mediocrity—and mediocrity here includes the very enterprise of being human for the past two thousand years—is art.

Yet Flaubert's art by this stage had become merely a collection of lists about the mediocrity of life. The ultimate goal of his art—form—had become simply the walls of this warehouse of human stupidity. His prized form of expression—the book—could only condense and reproduce other books. Without a political critique like that of Zola, Dickens, George Eliot, or William Morris, Flaubert was unable to provide any alternative to humanity's stupidity. He was therefore caught in the paradox that his art—unless it lost itself in some Oriental reverie—was unable to create a vision of anything other than that stupidity he reviled.

Flaubert was aware of this impasse. He had heard enough criticism of his work to accept the charge that he was unable to create characters for whom one might have sympathy. His old friend George Sand made this very charge to Flaubert, and in response he wrote a short tale, "A Simple Heart," to balance out *Bouvard and Pécuchet,* which he was composing at the same time. "A Simple Heart" portrays a servant woman who lives, in Flaubert's words,

> an obscure life, the life of a poor country girl who is pious but faithful without fuss, and tender as new bread. She loves a man, her mistress's children, her nephew, an old man whom she tends, and finally her parrot. When the parrot dies she has it stuffed, and when she too dies she confuses the parrot with the Holy Ghost.
>
> (Nadeau, p. 252)

The story is written in a style that Flaubert emphasizes is "not ironical . . . it is very serious and very sad." His aim was "to move, to bring tears to the eyes of the tender-hearted; I am tender-hearted myself." This is Flaubert's genuine attempt to avoid the problem of encyclopedism and aestheticism, and it turns out to be a wonderfully moving work. However, it is so atypical of Flaubert that critics seem to have to apologize for its style or else insist on reading it in an ironic mode. In some way it is like the story of an Emma Bovary—but this one a provincial woman who has never read a novel, who accepts her lot in life, and who never has an ironic narrator to set her misery into folly.

Two other short stories of this period seem to partake of this exceptionally sympathetic writing—"Saint Julian the Hospitaller" and "Hérodias." The first story movingly recounts the legend of Saint Julian, detailing his miserable punishment for his sadistic attachment to hunting and his eventual salvation, as he floats heavenward on the body of Christ, who emerges from the body of a rotting leper. The second tale concerns the biblical episode of Salome and Saint John the Baptist. Here, in another atypical moment for Flaubert, redemption is offered at the end of the work when Herod weeps before the ghastly head of John, and the followers of Christ say, "Take heart! He has gone down to the dead to proclaim the coming of Christ." This is quite a different ending from Deslauriers and Frédéric's musings on brothels in *Sentimental Education.*

These stories, while they each pick up a thread of Flaubert's literary obsessions—provincial realism, myth, and antiquity—are essentially counterpoints to the direction of Flaubert's last major works. Those final novels reveal the truly unusual insights Flaubert had over his contemporaries. These radical experiments with narrative attempt to write about ideology, to contain within themselves the collected cultural monuments of the period, to become repositories of collected knowledge and at the same time showplaces for the futility of that knowledge.

Looking back on Flaubert's career, one notices a sweeping movement from romantic to nihilist, from lyrical to encyclopedic, from scorn for daily life to scorn for the very idea of life. In *Les romanciers naturalistes* (1893), Zola pointed out the effect of this change, attributing it in part to Flaubert's obsession with documenting through books the stupidity of humans:

> Note that his books are all there, that he had never done anything but study this imbecility, even in the splendid visions of *The Temptation of Saint Anthony.* He simply flung his admirable

style over human folly, and I mean the lowest, the most vulgar, with occasional vistas of the wounded poet.

Indeed, Flaubert's critique, ungrounded as it was in any sense of history or explanation, grew more and more centered on folly and form—folly to keep the flames of savage indignation roaring, and form to elevate the attempt to the holiness of artistic style. Perhaps Zola understood this paradox best when he wrote that Flaubert's

> desire for perfection was, in the novelist, a real sickness that exhausted and immobilized him. If we follow him carefully, from this point of view, from *Madame Bovary* to *Bouvard and Pécuchet,* we shall see him gradually become preoccupied with form, reduce his vocabulary, increasingly limit the humanity of his characters. To be sure, this endowed French literature with perfect masterpieces. But it was sad to see this powerful talent relive the ancient fable of the nymphs who were changed to stone. Slowly, from the legs to the waist, then to the head, Flaubert turned to marble.

Ironically, it was in marble that Flaubert was immortalized by the world that had been the object of his intense and lifelong indignation. It is an irony Flaubert would not have failed to miss.

Selected Bibliography

EDITIONS

INDIVIDUAL WORKS
Madame Bovary. Paris, 1857.
Salammbô. Paris, 1862.
L'Éducation sentimentale: histoire d'un jeune homme. Paris, 1869.
La tentation de Saint Antoine. Paris, 1874.
Trois contes. Paris, 1877. Contains "Un coeur simple," "La légende de Saint Julien l'Hospitalier," and "Hérodias."
Bouvard et Pécuchet. Paris, 1881.

Premières oeuvres. Paris, 1914–1920. Contains *Novembre.*
La première Éducation sentimentale. Paris, 1963.
Dictionnaire des idées reçues, suivi des Mémoires d'un fou. Edited by Claude Bonnefoy. Paris, 1964.

COLLECTED WORKS
Oeuvres complètes. 23 vols. Paris, 1910–1933. Includes thirteen vols. of letters.
Oeuvres. Edited by C. Thibaudet and R. Dumesnil. 2 vols. Paris, 1946–1948.

TRANSLATIONS

Bouvard and Pecuchet. Translated by A. J. Krailsheimer. New York, 1976.
Dictionary of Accepted Ideas. Translated by Jacques Barzun. New York, 1954.
First Sentimental Education. Translated by D. Garman. Berkeley, Calif., 1972.
Flaubert in Egypt: A Sensibility on Tour. Translated and edited by F. Steegmuller. Boston, 1973; Chicago, 1979.
Intimate Notebooks, 1840–1841. Translated by F. Steegmuller. Garden City, N.Y., 1967.
Madame Bovary. Translated by E. Marx-Aveling. New York, 1918.
————. Translated by F. Steegmuller. New York, 1957.
————. Translated by P. de Man. New York, 1965.
November. Translated by F. Jellinek, New York, 1932. The 1967 edition contains an introduction by F. Steegmuller.
Salammbô. Translated by A. J. Krailsheimer. New York, 1977.
Selected Letters. Translated and edited by F. Steegmuller. New York, 1953.
Sentimental Education. Translated by L. Hearn. New York, 1911. Edited by F. Carmody. Kentfield, Calif., 1974.
Three Tales. Translated by R. Baldick. Baltimore, 1961.

BIOGRAPHICAL AND CRITICAL STUDIES

Bart, B. F., ed. *Madame Bovary and the Critics: A Collection of Essays.* New York, 1966.

Levin, Harry. *The Gates of Horn*. Oxford, 1963.

Nadeau, Maurice. *The Greatness of Flaubert*. Translated by B. Bray. New York, 1972.

Sartre, Jean-Paul. *The Family Idiot: Gustave Flaubert*. Vol 1: 1821–1857. Chicago, 1981.

Spencer, Phillip. *Flaubert: A Biography*. New York, 1952.

Starkie, Enid. *Flaubert: The Making of the Master*. New York, 1967.

————. *Flaubert: The Master*. New York, 1971.

Steegmuller, Francis. *Flaubert and Madame Bovary: A Double Portrait*. New York, 1939. Rev. ed., New York, 1968, and Chicago, 1977.

LENNARD J. DAVIS

EDMOND LOUIS ANTOINE DE GONCOURT
(1822–1896)
JULES ALFRED HUOT DE GONCOURT
(1830–1870)

THE GONCOURT BROTHERS, Edmond Louis Antoine and Jules Alfred Hout, were two sensitive and aristocratic French men of letters famous for their remarkable literary collaboration. Their fruitful association resulted in the joint writing of more than thirty volumes of art criticism, history, novels, plays, and, above all, their *Journal*. This diary of their artistic life has been hailed as their best book and one of the great literary achievements of modern times. It is also an indispensable reference work for an intimate understanding of the literary history of their period. The unique partnership was ended by the death of Jules on 20 June 1870, at Auteuil.

After his brother's death, Edmond continued, for another twenty-six years, until his own death on 16 July 1896 at Champrosay, the diary he and Jules had started on the day their first novel, *En 18 . . .*, was published, 2 December 1851. It proved an unfortunate date for a literary debut, since it coincided with Louis Napoleon's coup d'etat. In 1885 Edmond inaugurated a literary salon that gathered in the garret of his home at Auteuil, the celebrated Grenier. There he received the world of letters, including some future members of the Académie Goncourt, which he es-

tablished in his will and funded by his estate for the purpose of awarding an annual prize, the Prix Goncourt, to an outstanding young novelist.

The Goncourts inherited their claim to noble birth from their great-grandfather, Antoine Huot, who in 1786 acquired the *seigneurie* of Goncourt, a small village in Lorraine. Their father, Marc-Pierre de Goncourt, and their mother, his second wife, Annette-Cécile Guérin, were married in 1821 and moved to Paris shortly after the birth of Edmond, the eldest of four children, in Nancy on 26 May 1822. Jules was born in Paris on 17 December 1830. The other two children born to their parents, both girls, died at an early age. A professional soldier who served with great distinction in several Napoleonic campaigns, Marc-Pierre died in 1834, leaving Madame de Goncourt solely responsible for the welfare and education of their sons. Fortunately, in addition to a substantial dowry, she owned some property in the provinces and was therefore able to ensure a proper education for her sons at the Collège Bourbon.

Madame de Goncourt, who came from a family of civil servants, opposed Edmond's announced desire to be an artist. Bowing to family and financial pressures, he became instead a solicitor's clerk and in 1847 accepted a minor position in the treasury; an inheritance from his mother, who died in September 1848, freed him from this routine clerical job, which he later described as so horribly boring that he had contemplated suicide to escape it. The modest fortune left them by their mother was sufficient to spare the two brothers the need to earn a living and enabled them to lead a life of independence in which they could indulge the passionate devotion to art and literature they came to share. Abandoning their ambition to become painters after spending the better part of two years (1849–1850) on sketching tours in southern France, Algiers, Switzerland, and Belgium and on the Normandy coast, the brothers turned to writing: their first efforts included several one-act plays, which were rejected, and the previously mentioned novel, *En 18 . . .* , on which Jules had already begun to work during their trip to Normandy. After the disastrous failure of this novel to attract favorable critical or public attention, as much because of its own shortcomings as because it was published the same day Louis Napoleon overthrew the Second Republic, the brothers devoted the years from 1851 to 1862 to research and writing on the art and history of the eighteenth century during the reigns of Louis XV and Louis XVI, as well as during the Revolution and Directory. At the same time they contributed articles on art to a number of Parisian reviews and newspapers, such as *L'Éclair*, owned by their cousin, the comte de Villedeuil.

Their activities during this period were not limited exclusively to writing. In addition to their literary collaboration, they shared a mistress named Maria (her last name is unknown). As a midwife with a wide acquaintance with the demimonde, she was able to supply them with detailed information on the world of the professional prostitute for their projected novel on this subject, *La fille Elisa*.

Commenting in their journal at the end of February 1854 on their absorption in writing one of their first historical studies, *Histoire de la société française pendant la Révolution* (History of French Society During the Revolution, 1854), they record how they devoted their days to going through hundreds of pamphlets in order to write their book at night. They followed this important work with a sequel, *Histoire de la société française pendant le Directoire* (History of French Society During the Directory, 1855). But then, for some unknown reason, instead of continuing in the same vein to write the projected monograph on French society during the Empire, they turned their considerable talents to less weighty subject matter. They produced a series of biographies of eighteenth-century women from various classes, ranging from the scandalous singer Sophie Arnould to the queen Marie Antoinette (published respectively in 1857 and 1858). Other monographs were devoted to the mistresses of Louis XV (1860) and a general study of *La femme au dix-huitième siècle* (The Eighteenth-Century Woman, 1862). Critics have speculated that the Goncourts turned to these studies of eighteenth-century women because they were discouraged by the savage attacks on their work, or by the discovery of the superior feelings they were able to experience from treating women as inferiors, a tendency that was to display itself characteristically in their novels. The Goncourts were interested not in writing the official history of the last monarchs of the ancien régime, the Revolution, or the Directory, but in creating an innovative type of social history. They wanted to capture the nuances of contemporary life as revealed in such documents as pamphlets, periodicals, and newspapers, as well as unpublished sources, such as correspondence and diaries. The scrupulous documentation and meticulous scholarship displayed by the Goncourts in their histories and biographies, as well as their attention to intimate descriptions of the minor details of everyday existence, are also characteristic of their art criticism and novels.

The Goncourts' *L'Art du dix-huitième siècle*

(Art of the Eighteenth Century, 1875) is still considered a classic, necessary reading for students of eighteenth-century painting as well as for professional art historians. (However, the Goncourts' claim to have almost single-handedly resurrected eighteenth-century French art has been proved substantially untrue by Seymour Simches in his study *Le romantisme et le goût esthétique du XVIIIe siècle*, 1964.) Originally published as a series of monographs from 1859 to 1875, *L'Art du dix-huitième siècle* includes studies of such major figures as Jean Antoine Watteau, François Boucher, Jean Honoré Fragonard, Jean Baptiste Siméon Chardin, Maurice Quentin de La Tour, Pierre-Paul Prud'hon, and Jean Baptiste Greuze; and there are also essays on such minor figures as Charles de Saint-Aubin, Philibert-Louis Debucourt, and the vignettists Hubert-François Gravelot, Charles-Nicolas Cochin, Charles-Dominique-Joseph Eisen, and Jean-Michel Moreau the younger. The best-known and most famous of these pieces, the interpretative essay on Watteau, evokes for readers by means of the quivering, vivid style of their sketch the grace, charm, and agitation they themselves had experienced under the spell of Watteau's poetic enchantments. At the same time, this work, like their histories and biographies, is zealously documented.

Anita Brookner, in her study of the Goncourts' art criticism, while acknowledging the great deal of documentary information they unearthed, points out that their attitude to the eighteenth century was heavily biased, based as it was on the romantic notion that the past is better than the present, as well as on their own particular brand of taste, in which they took, in her judgment, excessive pride. It is perhaps due to their special and limited taste that they failed to assess properly the genius of some of their contemporaries. They judged Ferdinand Delacroix and Honoré Daumier inferior to A. G. Decamps and Gavarni, and other great artists of their own day, such as Édouard Manet, Claude Monet, and Edgar

Degas, received only passing, usually slighting, mention in the *Journal.*

When these two critics and historians of art turned their talents to the novel, they created a nervous, impressionistic style called *écriture artiste*. The purpose of this style was to capture in words their impressions of reality, just as their contemporaries, the impressionist painters, were attempting to fix in color their subjective and sensory impressions of nature. Yet the Goncourts failed to perceive that the impressionists were striving to achieve in painting the same effects they sought in literature.

In fact, if one were to seek a brief summary of their work as art critics, historians, biographers, novelists, and dramatists, it would be found in Edmond's own appraisal, contained in the preface to the 1887 edition of the *Journal,* that the object of their ambition was "to show changing humanity in its *momentary reality.*"

The Goncourts' "botanizing approach" to works of art, as Robin Ironside has described it, also bears witness to their scientific habit of collecting specimens, like an eighteenth-century naturalist, for detailed analysis and description. It is also true, as Robert Ricatte has remarked on their personal choice of painters, that their favorite artists were all masters in their ability to capture the momentary and fleeting gesture. Because the works they were describing were often not well known by the public, the Goncourts were challenged to exercise their powers of evocation to make readers see works that were not before their eyes. As a result of their artistic ability and their devotion to the cult of the word picture, in Ricatte's judgment, the description of gestures and momentary actions in both their art criticism and their novels is inimitable.

Other aspects of their interest in art must also be mentioned; namely, their love of eighteenth-century Japanese art and their affection for bibelots, or small decorative objects, always of the French or Japanese eighteenth century, of which they became passionate and discriminating collectors. Both preoccupations supplied material for their novels *Manette Salomon* (1867) and *Madame Gervaisais* (1869). Another of the Goncourts' cherished beliefs, however—that the enthusiasm they had expressed for Japanese art in *Manette Salomon* merited them recognition as the originators of the wave of Japanese enthusiasm that swept France in the second half of the nineteenth century—is today considered untenable. The credit, instead, should go to the artists Félix Bracquemond, Monet, and James Abbott McNeill Whistler.

Although Jules Champfleury is generally credited with the creation of the documentary novel, the Goncourts' contributions to the development of the social documentary were more serious than his. Their descriptions of the lower classes were authentic; Champfleury's were caricatures. Each of their novels or plays is set in a different social milieu, and the scenic backdrop is based on notes taken straight from life.

Aside from their first effort at novel writing, *En 18 . . .* , Jules and Edmond wrote six novels in collaboration. *Charles Demailly* (first published in 1860 as *Les hommes de lettres* [The Men of Letters]) describes the literary and journalistic world the Goncourts had known since 1850. *Soeur Philomène* (1861) is a documentary of hospital life, as well as an analysis of a nun's mysticism. *Renée Mauperin* (1864), which the brothers had originally intended to entitle *La jeune bourgeoisie*, depicts the domestic life of a bourgeois family and its decline. *Germinie Lacerteux* (1864) is a case history of a servant's degeneration and hysteria set against a proletarian background. *Manette Salomon* (1867) is a documentary depicting the manners and problems of the artistic world. *Madame Gervaisais* (1869) is a case study of religious hysteria that presents the church in an unfavorable light. The brothers also wrote two plays together: *Henriette Maréchal* (1865), a realistic play of love and death involving the wife and daughter of a businessman, the conclusion of which borders on melodrama; and *La patrie en danger* (The Fatherland in Danger; written in 1868, produced in 1873), a patriotic drama that takes place during the French Revolution.

Edmond completed another four novels on his own: *La fille Elisa* (published in 1877, but Jules had already collaborated on this novel before his death in 1870) is a social study of crime, prostitution, and the penal system. *Les frères Zemganno* (1879) tells of two brothers (reminiscent of the brothers Goncourt) who share the circus life. *La Faustin* (1882) presents a picture in chiaroscuro of theatrical life. *Chérie* (1884) is a novel about a sophisticated young lady amid the elegance of the rich and powerful court circles of the Second Empire. A play, *À bas le progrès* (Down with Progress, 1893), summarizes Edmond's lifelong hatred of scientific progress and the commercialism of the philistine bourgeoisie.

Their achievement as novelists, although it lacks the driving genius of Honoré de Balzac's *La comédie humaine* or the massive power of Émile Zola's *Les Rougon-Macquart*, does provide an undeniably important documentary of extraordinary fidelity; it covers an exceptionally wide range of the classes and social milieus of French society during the Second Empire and the first decades of the Third Republic.

Scattered comments on the novel throughout their *Journal*, extracts of which were published as *Idées et sensations* (Ideas and Sensations, 1866), and the prefaces to their novels, gathered together and published with additional material as *Préfaces et manifestes littéraires* (Prefaces and Literary Manifestos, 1888), while not exactly constituting a systematic definition of their theory of fiction, do provide a sufficiently coherent body of statements to define adequately their conception of the novel. Contemporaries of Gustave Flaubert, the chief exemplar of realism, and Zola, the best-known representative of naturalism, the Goncourts were disciples of the first and teachers of the second. Identified by various literary historians as either realist or naturalist, associated by other scholars with the school of sick romanticism, they were among the early practitioners of the realist novel and precursors of the naturalist tradition, inaugurated by their novel *Germinie Lacerteux.*

With their strikingly different attitudes to the eighteenth century as opposed to the nineteenth century, the brothers exhibit a split aesthetic personality. In spite of all their efforts to return to a more acceptable era in their search for romantic beauty, they were intensely modern in their commitment to depict in their novels the life that was happening around them. Commenting on the evolution of the novel after Balzac (for whom they had the greatest admiration), they note in their *Journal* on 24 October 1864: "Since Balzac, the novel has had nothing in common with what our fathers understood by the word. The novel of today is based on documents related verbally or taken from nature, just as history is based on written documents."

Regardless of their aristocratic attitude, in their adherence to modernism the Goncourt brothers devoted novel after novel to descriptions of the ordinary aspects of the daily life of writers, journalists, nurses, servants, shopkeepers, painters, prostitutes, prisoners, circus performers, and actors, as well as to the upper middle class and aristocratic circles. "Historians tell the story of the past; novelists tell the story of the present," they remark in the *Journal.* In their endeavor to be true to life or nature, they relied heavily on direct observation and careful documentation. Their novels are all based on real events and experiences; they are "human documents," as Edmond called them, artistically transformed into novels by means of *écriture artiste,* or artistic style, which attempts to give beauty and life to ugliness in nature and in art.

In a very real sense, however, their descriptions of contemporary life reveal an emphasis on the dark side of romanticism, a fixation on the tragic, the ugly, and the grotesque. They exhibit, moreover, a habitual obsession with the theme of suffering and conflict in their examination of misery among the lower classes and low life of society. Guy de Maupassant in an article critical of writers who attempted to imitate what he believed to be the excessively complex style of the Goncourts nevertheless wrote with great respect of Edmond and Jules as the two modern masters of "the new type of sickly, morbid, but remarkably penetrating, subtle, and self-conscious literature."

As the Goncourts note in a journal entry of 27 March 1865: "Yes, it is true that there is an element of sickness in our talent, and a considerable element at that." But this was a voluntary sickness (as Paul Bourget called it), which they fostered to heighten their nervous sensibilities. This sickness, they point out, which "at the moment causes displeasure and irritation, will one day be regarded as our charm and strength. Sickness sensitizes man for observation, like a photographic plate." Their novels represent an effort at an accurate, truthful recording of the world around them; but their impressionistic style records the sensations that their nature and temperament led them to feel when they observed their subject matter. For this reason, their material description of things and places is not for the sake of description, but to transport the reader into "a certain setting favorable to the moral emotion which should arise from those things and places" (*Journal,* 23 July 1865).

In the preface to *Germinie Lacerteux,* one of the finest of their better-known novels, the Goncourts indicate their intention to discover whether tragedy is still alive in their day and to determine whether the fateful sufferings visited on the poor and lower classes can excite in their readers the same pity and emotions as do the misfortunes that befall fashionable members of society. In view of their clearly stated intention of casting their novel in a tragic mode, it is not surprising to find fatality stressed throughout the novel; however, such a choice reflects their own personal, fatalistic view of the world, a view nurtured by their melancholy. Pierre Sabatier, in his study *L'Esthétique des Goncourt,* has described their special kind of melancholic materialism as an artistic and aesthetic materialism that stops just short of the prevailing scientific determinism of their day. The same may be said of their view of religion, which stops just at the threshold of moral and intellectual nihilism.

Even though they systematically attempted in their fiction to make psychology into a branch of physiology, the Goncourts were less rigorously deterministic than a philosopher like Hippolyte Taine, a proponent of scientific determinism, or a novelist such as Zola, who espoused Taine's position and pretended to express a strict physiological determinism in his novels. The reason for this, Sabatier suggests, can be found in the fact that the Goncourts, although they make no mention of it themselves, accepted the eighteenth-century humanitarian idea of people's right to happiness. They believed the loss of this idea would lead to utter selfishness on the part of the masses. They concluded that it would be a grave social mistake and a serious crime against the people to deprive them entirely of the happiness they derived from their illusions, especially those of religion.

But is the gloomy portrayal the Goncourts present in their realistic novels of contemporary French society completely true? It is Albert Thibaudet's opinion that the Goncourts' realistic novels "could as well be called romanced reality," since "reality does not necessarily imply truth—and vice versa." As a case in point, one should consider that in the very midst of France's thriving and growing prosperity, the Second Empire's men of letters were disaffected from its industry and commerce. According to Henri Peyre, "Literally all the writers of talent (Baudelaire, Flaubert, Goncourt, Zola, Renan) portrayed the culture of their country as decadent, soulless, sold to speculators; the bourgeois became a perpetual butt for their sarcasms."

The Goncourts elected to portray the ugliness in the streets around them to protest the profound changes in values and life caused by the economic expansion of an increasingly democratic and industrial society that seemed to have forgotten the humanitarianism of the eighteenth century. Even so, their primary interest in making of themselves "painters of modern life," to use a phrase of Charles Baudelaire's, was first and foremost determined by their literary ambition and aesthetic aim to expand the scope of the novel into a scientific and psychological study of "contemporary moral History" (preface to *Germinie Lacerteux*). They wanted for the novel the "freedom and frankness" of science.

Paradoxical as it may seem, both Jules and Edmond held the idea of progress in contempt; and they were eager not only to capture the nuances and reality of contemporary life, but also to lay bare the failures of progress, to examine them with a clinical objectivity that would leave their readers with few illusions concerning such social realities as poverty, abortion, mental illness, prostitution, prison life, and human degradation. "The skepticism of the eighteenth century was healthy; our skepticism, however, is characterized by bitterness and suffering," they averred (*Journal,* 15 May 1866).

The fact that Edmond and Jules wrote six of their major novels in tandem makes the question of their literary collaboration one that must be examined. Reflecting on his brother's death, Edmond stated his conviction that Jules had "died from his pursuit of a perfect stylistic form," an effort to which he had devoted both his physical and his mental energies to the point of exhaustion (*Journal,* 22 June 1870). The truth is that Jules died of syphilis. Nevertheless, he was, as Edmond acknowledged, the better stylist of the two and contributed most to the development of their *écriture artiste.* Edmond viewed Jules as the "embellisher" of their novels, but classified himself as the "architect."

Alidor Delzant, the brothers' first biographer, who obtained his information from Edmond, provides one of the most reliable descriptions of their method of literary partnership:

> Once they had decided to write a novel, the two brothers, seeking inspiration in a cloud of tobacco smoke, deliberated on its plan, then agreed on the vivid descriptive passages to incorporate from their notebooks. After having envisaged the work in their minds, they soon broke the subject down into a certain number of distinct tableaus or scenes, including the beginning and end. The rest of the book was composed haphazardly in no special order, until all the threads were woven around the plot. Actual writing began with an attack on the beginning and the end as the most important parts, the brothers shut up in separate rooms, each working on the same chapter. The reading of the two different chapters was followed by long sessions in which the best parts of the different versions were blended together and the stylistic features precisely determined.
>
> (Les Goncourt, p. 316)

This technique not only contributed to the tenuousness of their plots, but also resulted in the accumulation of epithets as well as the repetition and juxtaposition of similar words and phrases, a style that met with Charles-Augustin Sainte-Beuve's strong disapproval. Both factors contributed to the gap between them and the public—a gap of which they complained frequently and bitterly.

In The Art of French Fiction, Martin Turnell indicates that three of the principal aspects of the Goncourts' impressionistic style are: "The passive spectator, the separation of attributes from their object, and the divorce of effects from their cause." The following passage, a description of landscape fading into dusk as seen by Germinie Lacerteux from the ramparts on the outskirts of Paris, not only illus-

trates the first two of these techniques, but provides as well examples of other characteristics of the Goncourts' range of stylistic devices:

> When they turned back, she wanted to climb up and sit on the ramparts again. There was no longer any sun. The sky was gray below, pink in the middle, blueish above. The horizons were darkening; the green of the leaves was deepening, dulling, the tin roofs of the wine stalls took on gleams of moonshine, fires began to pierce the dark, the crowd became grayish, the whites of laundry became blue. Little by little everything was effaced, toned down, lost in a dying, colorless remnant of daylight, and from the denser shadows began to rise, with a rattling din, the noise of people who come alive at night.
>
> (Germinie Lacerteux, ch. 12)

This passage provides fine examples of two different aspects of the Goncourts' impressionistic approach to reality. The first of these is the reproduction of the actual sequence of experiences as they strike the passive spectator's mind. In this passage, the device serves to convey a rare moment of quiescence or tranquillity in the case history of a neurotic domestic servant whose life oscillates between phases of manic energy and depressive states of complete indifference. The careful accumulation of selected details, as well as the meticulous enumeration of shapes, colors, and sounds, are all presented for one purpose: to produce on the reader the desired psychological effect. The second stylistic feature is their marked preference for representing objects in terms of color, a good example of their impressionistic method of presenting nature, a method by which "the world becomes a thing of broken patterns and conflicting colors, and uneasy movement," as Arthur Symons has so perfectly described it.

One basic stylistic device the Goncourts used to separate colors from their objects is the substantivized adjective, as in the construction "the whites of laundry" instead of the more normal phrase "the white laundry." By this means, they achieve the impressionistic effect of having us see a flash of whiteness before we perceive any specific object. Inversion is another linguistic technique they used to obtain impressionist effects, as in "from the denser shadows began to rise, with a rattling din, the noise of people who come alive at night." In this case, the device is used not for pictorial effect, but to record an impression perceived by the sense of hearing, the spectator first becoming aware of the rising noise before being able to recognize it as the sound of human voices.

In his preface to the *Journal*, Edmond remarked that if he and his brother had been somewhat cavalier in their disregard for syntax and unscholarly in their choice of vocabulary, it was because they had "invariably chosen those phrases and expressions that least blunted and *academicized* the sharpness" of their sensations and the originality of their ideas. Grammar and logic are indeed subverted by the impressionist style, to the point that the sentence, as Martin Turnell notes, "is no longer a logical progression; it follows the eye," becoming instead a record of impressions or psychological notations.

Concerning their use of color, André Billy gives credit to Max Fuchs for having identified at least one major difference in the artistic style of the two brothers: Jules tended to favor violent colors, whereas Edmond preferred halftones and chiaroscuro. Neither of these preferences, of course, is typical of impressionistic painting. Jules's use of wild, savage coloration is suggestive of the fauves. Edmond's treatment of light and shade calls to mind a more academic style. Both preferences become more fully developed in their novels. In the novels Edmond wrote on his own, such as *La fille Elisa*, *Les frères Zemganno*, and *La Faustin*, his fondness for the various shades of twilight assumes a progressively greater significance. André Billy, in fact, goes so far as to suggest that the twilight glow that pervades *Les frères Zemganno* gives the impression of

being a "projection, as it were, of Edmond's inconsolable grief." Commenting on *La Faustin's* critical reception, Edmond complained that his colleagues failed to notice he had "introduced a new poetry and fantasy into the study of reality," or that he had "tried to help realism take a step forward by endowing it with certain chiaroscuro qualities" it previously lacked. For after all, "things are surely just as real seen in moonlight as in the rays of the noonday sun" (*Journal*, 8 February 1882). In making this statement, Edmond himself appears to be ignoring just how fond he was, even before *La Faustin*, of indulging in descriptions of people, landscapes, or objects fading or disappearing in the slight or imperfect light of twilight or dusk, thus creating an impression of the dissolution of reality.

Edmond, who described in the *Journal* the physical strain Jules felt from his stylistic efforts, points out in the preface to *Les frères Zemganno* that he—Edmond—was also subject to the nervous disorders brought on by the effort to express with artistic perfection the reality of modern life:

> Readers complain of the jarring emotions that contemporary writers excite within them with their brutal realism; they hardly suspect that these same writers suffer even more than they do from the creation of that realism, and that sometimes they suffer from nervous exhaustion for several weeks because of the book to which they have so laboriously and painfully given birth.

As a result of their search for the mot juste, as well as their desire to reflect accurately the reality of the world around them, the brothers' novels abound not only in technical and scientific terms, popular expressions, and the jargon of various trades and professions, but in many neologisms of their own creation. In their tendency to nervousness, as in their penchant for neologisms, as John Porter Houston has remarked, the Goncourts show themselves to be Balzac's heirs.

Italics are a device the Goncourts frequently employed to underscore the originality of their vocabulary or to emphasize the introduction or creation of a neologism. In *Manette Salomon*, for example, they italicized their newly coined substantivized adjective "invrai" in the sentence "Il avait au suprême point le sens de *l'invrai*" (He had to the highest degree the sense of the unlikely), so as to call the reader's attention to this fact. Unfortunately, as with most of their stylistic devices, the brothers made excessive use of this one. Consequently their novels are teeming with italicized words and phrases, a practice that proves annoyingly distracting on occasion.

Given the bourgeois age in which the Goncourts lived, one might well ask: How were these artists, these aristocrats with their program for a popular or proletarian novel, as announced in the preface to *Germinie Lacerteux*, received by the public? Their works were, as Lewis Galantière has noted, nearly always received with critical vilification, greeted with such epithets as "sculptured slime," "literature of putrescence," or "brutal realism." Reflecting on this matter, the brothers commented in their *Journal* (27 June 1866): "Sickness, disease. That is the reproach that is constantly thrown at our books. But what is not sickness in this age of ours?"

Bernard Weinberg, in his *French Realism: The Critical Reaction 1830–1870*, devotes a chapter to the critical reception of the six novels Edmond and Jules wrote and published together. Restricting himself almost exclusively to the reactions of professional contemporary French literary critics, he discovered that on *Germinie Lacerteux*, *Soeur Philomène*, and *Manette Salomon* opinion was almost evenly divided; *Charles Demailly* and *Madame Gervaisais* received preponderantly unfavorable criticism; *Renée Mauperin* was greeted with almost unanimous praise. But the intransigent enemies of realism attacked them so vociferously that they succeeded in drowning out the positive opinions of the Goncourts' defenders. The critical difference centered,

Weinberg determined, on four major aspects of the Goncourts' novels: undesirable subject matter, riff-raff, low society, and a fascination for the repellent; stress on the pathological disorders exhibited by their rather exceptional heroes or heroines; distortion of reality in the name of a "truthful" realism that represents society as worse than it really was; and exaggerated emphasis on external details and exclusion of moral or spiritual considerations. Most of these faults, including the lack of plot structure and weak, careless composition, were attributed to the realistic system the collaborators championed.

A chronological review of the brothers' novels, taking into account twentieth-century reassessments of their fiction, may help us to understand not only their progress as novelists, but also what remains of value in their work for the modern reader or critic. *Charles Demailly*, which some critics call their first real novel, relates the story of a malicious wife who persecutes her husband, ruins his artistic career, and drives him insane. The work is divided into four distinct parts: a description of the social milieu of journalists and artists; Charles's hasty marriage to an actress named Marthe and his equally sudden disillusionment following their honeymoon, when he discovers his new wife to be stupid and heartless; the conspiracy of the novelist's old journalistic cronies to join the wife's vicious campaign to persecute her husband; and the tragic story of the writer's growing mental instability and final descent into madness. This is their only novel named for a male character, who, incidentally, is in many ways a self-portrait of the brothers and shares their hatred, fear, and disdain of women. Upon completing this work, the authors noted how the emotional grip it had held on them vanished on publication: "It is similar to the aftereffects of coition; your work arouses nothing in you but boredom, indifference, and disgust" (*Journal*, 28 January 1859).

The shared misogynism of the Goncourts, evident in this novel as in almost all their subsequent works, is stated explicitly in the following journal entry:

> Woman, an evil and stupid beast, unless educated and extremely civilized. Thus, the young girl never dreams, never thinks, never loves. Poetry in a woman is never natural, it is an acquisition of education. The worldly woman is the only woman; the rest, females. Inferiority of feminine intelligence to masculine intelligence.... Woman the most beautiful and most admirable of machines for reproduction.
>
> (13 October 1855)

But they seemed to be obsessed by the power of this subspecies, because the characters after whom the majority of their novels are named are indeed "females": a servant, a poor orphan girl who becomes a sister of charity, a model, a prostitute, and an actress. The admirable portrait of the young bourgeois girl Renée Mauperin proves an exception to this general trend, but it is difficult to ignore the androgynous nature of this female, who thinks and acts like a male. One of their few women characters to come close to being a woman of the world is Madame Gervaisais, but even the personality of this woman of the upper middle class is presented in physiologically unflattering terms. The young, aristocratic heroine of Edmond's novel *Chérie* can hardly be considered a woman of the world, since this novel is concerned with presenting a young female on the threshold of womanhood.

Charles Demailly aroused mostly disgust among contemporary critics, who attacked the authors for presenting only the sordid side of the journalistic and literary world. Structurally, the work was criticized for its lack of organization and unity, abuses of syntax, and affected manner of expression. Only the psychological study of Charles in the second part and the character development of Marthe Demailly drew some appreciative comments. As for modern judgments of this work, André Billy finds it to be "full of disorder and con-

fusion." In the opinion of Robert Baldick, it is nothing more than four very dissimilar books that have been joined together without any effort to create a unified or integrated narrative discourse.

Examining this work from the perspective of Northrop Frye's definition of the "anatomy," or Menippean satire, as a separate genre of fiction in which "the intellectual structure built up from the story makes for violent dislocations in the customary logic of narrative," Richard Grant argues that *Charles Demailly* is "unified and carefully elaborated on a thematic basis," which is the authors' "pessimistic view of reality that lies behind a cheery illusion." This theme, the struggle between illusion and reality, is not only the unifying factor in the story, but is, Grant maintains, the central theme of all their fiction. If the Goncourts were reread in this light, he argues, their novels would appear more successful. But however much he tries, by applying one unitary principle, to show the thematic unity of *Charles Demailly* as well as the rest of the Goncourts' fiction, Grant himself finds the novel seriously flawed by the brothers' failure to make believable characters of Charles and Marthe. No motive is given, he objects, to explain her vicious behavior toward her husband, while his personality is subordinated to the thematic purpose of the novel to such an extent that it is rendered almost abstract.

Despite all its inadequacies, most modern critics agree that *Charles Demailly* marks an important step in the Goncourts' development as novelists. Specifically, in its study of an artist's career adversely affected by a malicious wife, it foreshadows the theme of *Manette Salomon*. More generally, it prefigures several of the major themes or preoccupations in their subsequent novels: hatred of females, artistic devotion to visual descriptions, and the psychological and physiological nature of the protagonists, whose temperaments are made to depend on a nervous disorder or pathological condition influenced by their physical or social milieu.

Because of the Goncourts' restraint in depicting the on-site reality of all they had experienced during their first visits to the Paris hospital of La Charité to document *Soeur Philomène*, Robert Ricatte, in *La création romanesque chez les Goncourt, 1851–1870*, refers to it as a prenaturalist novel. The few contemporary critics who bothered to review *Soeur Philomène*, a psychological analysis of a sister-of-charity's love for a young surgeon named Barnier, set amid a detailed description of hospital life, found it irreverent, reprehensible, and repulsive. At least one critic, however, as Bernard Weinberg's research has shown, answered most of these critical objections when he praised the Goncourts for using literature not as an escape from life, but as a means of providing direct contact with it. Considered in this light, the choice of subject matter appears to him entirely appropriate.

Like so many of the Goncourts' novels, *Soeur Philomène* was based on a true incident, in this case a story told to them by the poet Louis Bouilhet: A nursing sister at a Rouen hospital had fallen in love with a medical intern, a friend of his whom he found hanged one morning. Although the novel begins with a long and tedious presentation of the main character's social background, as in *Charles Demailly*, and although the plot is tenuous at best, this second of their mature novels, perhaps because it is a shorter, less complicated piece, is remarkably well organized around the main scenes, an operation on and the subsequent death of Romaine, the young intern's first mistress.

Commenting on the Goncourts as representatives of realist tendencies in the novel, A. W. Raitt selected *Soeur Philomène* as an example of their realistic storytelling techniques. Two such aspects of their style evident in this story, in his judgment, are the description of the mental or emotional states of the characters in physiological, rather than psychological, terms, and the attention accorded to the commonplace and sordid existence of the lower classes. For instance, when Soeur Philomène witnesses death, her reaction to it is described in purely physical terms: "She felt her chest becoming constricted, her legs weakening, and a chill in her bones ran from her kneecap to the tip of her big toe." The story's setting amid the drab, poverty-stricken milieu of the lower classes, who must depend on charity for whatever medical care they can obtain, illustrates Raitt's other point. Patrick Charvet, a literary historian, is critical of the lack of definition given to the relations between the nun (whose original was named Marie Gaucher) and Barnier; too much consideration, in his opinion, is given to a programmatic description of hospital life. Robert Ricatte judges *Soeur Philomène* to be the best example of the Goncourts' fusion of documentary realism and artistic fantasy.

Renée Mauperin was received with almost unanimous praise, the character of the heroine being hailed as the novel's greatest virtue. Almost a century after her creation, Robert Baldick can still remark that "she is certainly one of the most convincing girls in the nineteenth century." In the preface to the 1875 edition of this novel, Edmond cautioned the reader that in writing *Renée Mauperin*, the authors were less interested in the creation of a novel like other novels than with the protrayal of the social evolution of the bourgeoisie. This change in social status is shown in their studies of the children of this class, represented, in Edmond's words, by Renée, "the modern girl as the artistic and mannish education of the past thirty years have made her," and her brother, Henri, such as "the doctrinaires and parliamentary government have made him since the ascension of King Louis-Philippe" to the throne in 1830. The Goncourts wished to leave no doubt that they were concerned less with the plot or story line of their novel than with the textualizing of the social reality they had observed.

Compared with some of the Goncourts' later novels, *Renée Mauperin* nevertheless remains the most faithful to traditional narrative form. The result the Goncourts achieved by a deliberate disregard for the unity of plot composition, moreover, is judged positively by Arthur Symons, who believed that this aspect of their fictional technique enabled them to capture "the sense of the passing of life, the heat and form of its moments as they pass" in their novels. But, as Richard Grant points out, the Goncourts' efforts to downgrade plot resulted in the reinforcement of the "sense of separation of the various segments of the novel." This fragmentation of narrative form was carried even further by the division of their novels into numerous short chapters. When this factor is added to the extremely visual aspect of their work, such as the impressionistic sensitivity to visual effects evident in the opening and closing chapters of *Renée Mauperin*, or in the many descriptive passages for foregrounding and backgrounding in *Germinie Lacerteux*, it is not surprising to find modern critics describing the Goncourts' narrative method in the technical language of the cinema, in studies of such novels as *Manette Salomon* and *La fille Elisa*.

But in view of the absence of a strong narrative structure, one is faced with the question of defining what it is that holds a Goncourt novel together. Furthermore, how is it possible to reconcile the obviously static quality of a great many scenes with the many references found among modern critics to the cinematographic quality of the works and the sense of movement this implies? The answer can only be suggested by the fact that the many scenes they describe are like so many frames or stills of a film, and the life or biography of the main characters is the essential unifying link. Indeed, as Pierre Sabatier observes, all their novels, with the exception of *La Faustin* and *Soeur Philomène*, are very complete biographies, following the main character's life from birth to death, passing through all its major phases. In a journal entry for 18 June 1886, Edmond,

who prided himself on being an analyst, noted with a certain self-satisfaction that his novels, while lacking action or plots, always contained "interesting characters."

In 1865 the Goncourts published what is today considered by most critics to be one of their finest novels, *Germinie Lacerteux*. In its own day, it was one of their most controversial works. The issue that brought forth the most vehement attacks was the novel's realism, or more precisely, in this case, the Goncourts' nascent naturalism. This new element in their work is evident not only in their descriptions of life's seamier aspects, but especially in their concentration on the degradation of their heroine, a female servant from the humblest social class, as well as on the pathological symptoms of her mental decline as she suffers the ravages of alcoholism, nymphomania, hysteria, and tuberculosis.

The real-life model for the character of Germinie was the Goncourts' own cook and housekeeper, Rose Malingre, who had worked for the Goncourt family since the age of seventeen. Because of her apparently total devotion and fidelity to them, the brothers were profoundly shocked when, after her rather sudden death in 1862, their mistress, Maria, revealed to them the truth about Rose's secret life of alcoholism and debauchery. The discovery of this deception in the one woman they never suspected capable of it, a woman whom they considered almost as a surrogate mother, left them profoundly disillusioned and contributed to their distrust of women. Shortly after learning about their ideal servant's secret life, they wrote in their *Journal:* "Suspicion of the entire female sex has entered into our minds for the rest of our lives; a horror of the duplicity of woman's soul, of her prodigious gift, her consummate genius, for mendacity" (21 August 1862). Once over the initial shock, the brothers forgave Rose and expressed their pity for this proud woman who had fallen prey to such a lamentable and loathsome life because of her personal and financial problems. But the lasting impact of this experience on their work, as well as their lives, is evident in the misogynistic attitude that shapes the characterization of women in their novels after this event.

In many respects, the Goncourts' attitude toward the female can be found to parallel their sentiments toward the working class, a class for which they had little real sympathy. For although they were among the first novelists in nineteenth-century France to portray the lower classes realistically, they regarded the collective behavior of workers as a threat to civilization, just as they represented the female as a danger to the artist's vocation. The Goncourts were not the only chroniclers of the late nineteenth century to share this view; as Susanna Barrows shows in a sophisticated analysis, most crowd psychologists of the period, from Taine to Zola and Gustave Le Bon, stressed the crowd's "irrationality, its primitive and savage mentality, its insatiable thirst for alcohol, its 'hypnotic' leadership, and its female character." On this point, it is worth noting that the Goncourts avoided crowd scenes and chose not to portray the collective behavior of crowds or workers, as Zola, their disciple, would do on a magnificent scale. They presented only tableaus of individual workers, such as the base and vicious Jupillon, the glovemaker, and the drunkard Gautruche, the house painter, the two men who were the objects of Germinie's sexual mania. One of the chief difficulties with the Goncourts' efforts to make of *Germinie Lacerteux* a proletarian novel was precisely its unflattering portrayal of the people who, some critics charged, were misrepresented as overcome by vice and addicted to the lowest sort of conduct, almost incapable of a moral or virtuous action.

Even more objectionable to these same critics was the exceptional character of the Goncourts' heroine, Germinie, who, because of the pathological nature of her behavior, they considered to be a gross distortion of the ordinary working-class girl. But critics sympathetic to literary realism defended the Goncourts' right to include the lowest classes in their novel, as well as to depict the evil that existed in society, although some added the proviso that if evil were to be included, it should be in such a way as to inspire a hatred of it.

From the point of view of the history of the development of prose fiction in late-nineteenth-century France, perhaps the greatest significance of *Germinie Lacerteux* was its impact on the literary career of the young Émile Zola, who was to establish himself as the chief representative of naturalism with his numerous articles on the subject and the series of novels he wrote from 1871 to 1893, to which he gave the collective title *Les Rougon-Macquart*. His first article on the Goncourts was a review of *Germinie Lacerteux* in which he defended the Goncourts' use of social determinism in the formation of Germinie's personality; it also contained, as Robert Niess points out in his study of the relationship between Zola and Edmond de Goncourt, Zola's "apologia for physiological explanations of human conduct, germs of his own later theories of the role of heredity and environment in the development of the human being, an ardent plea for freedom in art, liberty from fixed conventions and universal norms of taste"—a preliminary outline, in short, of what were to become his chief ideas in the battle for the triumph of naturalism in France.

Among modern readers and scholars who have studied the Goncourts' fiction, most agree that *Germinie Lacerteux* is their best novel, but at least one scholar, Richard Grant, goes so far as to hail it as a great novel; in his judgment, "it combines new views of personality with powerful social protest, in a milieu described to bring out the horrors that can surround the existence of a human being." He finds, in essence, that the Goncourts succeeded in making of their novel a "great, serious, passionate, living form of literary study and social inquiry," to use the definition of a modern novel they give in the preface to *Germinie Lacerteux.*

In contrast to *Germinie Lacerteux*'s controversial reception, the Goncourts' penultimate novel written in collaboration, *Manette Salomon*, was a considerable popular success, even though it met with little critical reaction. But as one of the few critics who did review it noted, the central character of this novel, a study of artistic circles in Paris from the 1840's to the mid-fifties or early sixties, was not Manette, the beautiful Jewish model, but her husband, Coriolis. A talented painter from the West Indies, he had vowed never to be caught in the trap of marriage so he could devote himself entirely to art. Unfortunately for him, however, while seeking a model worthy to complete what he expected to become his masterpiece, a painting of an Oriental seraglio entitled *Le bain turc*, he happened to catch sight of the perfect model for his work, Manette, who had become a model not because of her need to earn a living, but because she was so proud of her beautiful body.

Seduced by Manette's beauty, Coriolis finds his entire life changed: his creative energy and artistic aspirations are destroyed by Manette, who becomes his mistress, the mother of his illegitimate child, and, finally, his legally married wife. This marriage, which takes place near the end of the novel, represents the final symbolic castration of a man who was once an ambitious artist, but who is now totally subjugated to his shrewish wife, a formidable femme fatale. In this novel, however, the Goncourts are not merely satisfied to indict Manette as a dangerous female and to make her the object of this misogyny. She is especially vilified for being Jewish and for having debased her husband's artistic ambitions to the point where he is forced to produce only profitable hackwork. Her actions and behavior as a domineering Jewish mother are exaggerated to the point of caricature by the Goncourts' need to vent their anti-Semitism.

Although *Manette Salomon* repeats the theme of *Charles Demailly* and echoes that of *En 18 . . .* , in which the hero is revolted to discover that his lover is Jewish, the particular interest of this novel lies elsewhere, specifically in the stylistic transposition of "painting into literature," in the chronicle of an artist's life during the July Monarchy, and in the conflict between the neoclassicists, led by Jean Auguste Dominique Ingres, who held that drawing should be superior to color in painting, and their opponents, the romantics, who rallied around Delacroix, whose theories and brilliant paintings stressed the importance of color.

As for this last point, however, Therese Dolan Stamm, discussing the role of Gavarni in the brothers' aesthetic, argues to the contrary. The quarrel between Ingrists and colorists was far less important to them, she maintains, then their interest in the artistic achievement of their close friend and favorite artist, Gavarni. A lithographer and caricaturist of Parisian manners, he also depicted the more bitter aspects of family life. Although Coriolis is modeled largely on another of the Goncourts' friends, Paul de Saint-Victor, many of his characteristics recall those of Gavarni. Gavarni's death in 1866, the year before *Manette Salomon* was published, had a profound effect on both Goncourts, and Jules, who felt an almost filial attachment to the older artist, devoted the last years of his life to a final collaboration with Edmond on a book about Gavarni's life and work. Taken together with their biography of Gavarni and their Salon reviews for 1852 and 1855, *Manette Salomon* constitutes one of the fullest expressions of their views on the aesthetic standards of contemporary artists, as well as providing many insights into their own philosophy of art. In this novel, which begins in 1840 with a meeting at the Paris zoo of Coriolis with his good friends, the untalented Garnotelle and two bohemian artists, the Goncourts use fictional painters (most of whom are based on real-life prototypes) to denounce certain artistic trends of the times and convey their own artistic values.

The Goncourts' disdain for the official academic art of their day is displayed in the scornful remarks of Chassagnol, who embodies their ideas on art and frequently serves as their spokesman, when his friend Anatole announces that he has entered the contest for the Prix de Rome, the highest official student award in France (then and now): "Ah, the Prix de Rome! . . . You will see—let me tell you: an honorable mediocrity, that's all it will make of you . . . just like the others, to be sure!" The Goncourts' resentment against the degree of conformity to the traditions of academic art expected of a Prix de Rome winner can perhaps be traced to the fact that its recipients were generally supposed to adhere to the academy's single standard of beauty, never admitting the possibility of more than one such ideal. In the Goncourts' scale of aesthetic values, as Anita Brookner has remarked, "beauty was the antithesis of life," for the unvarnished truth and natural representation of life was what they believed art to be all about. Another reason the Goncourts, like many contemporary artists, mistrusted the academy and its standards and scorned the Prix de Rome was that—as they show in their unflattering portrayal of the untalented winner of this prize, the social climber Garnotelle—it was frequently awarded to painters totally devoid of artistic genius. Its laureates usually produced technically precise but uninspired, artificial compositions full of flattering, derivative references to the works of established academicians.

But although they were champions of anti-academic art, the brothers did not extend their approval to all forms of nonacademic art. In their judgments on the work of some of their contemporaries, the Goncourts were unable to appreciate or acknowledge the accomplishments of some of the great artists of their own time, such as Gustave Courbet. Although he is never mentioned by name in the novel, the authors manage to convey their strong disapproval of his brand of realism. Their spokesman, Chassagnol, in his discussion with Coriolis on modernity in art, pillories the vulgarity of what they considered to be the mindless ugliness of Courbet's works:

> Oh, that question, the question of modernity, everyone believes it is resolved because in our time there has been this caricature of Truth, an effort to shock the bourgeois: Realism! Because a particular gentleman has made a private religion of gross ugliness, of a choiceless, unselected pile of vulgarity and modernity . . . ugh! It should all be the same to me, but it's so common, so lacking expression, without any of the character which gives beauty and life to the Ugly in nature and art: Style!
>
> (ch. 106)

If there is any doubt that Courbet is the villain in mind, one has only to consider this entry in their *Journal* for 18 September 1867, written after they had seen a one-man show by Courbet:

> Nothing, nothing, nothing at all in this exhibition of Courbet's. Two paintings of the sea and sky at the very most. Apart from that, a striking thing for this master of realism, not a single study from nature. The body of his *Woman with a Parrot* is as far removed in its way from the real nude as almost any academic study from the eighteenth century. Ugliness, and more ugliness. And ugliness without much character, ugliness without the beauty of ugliness!

In view of their anti-academic stance and the importance they attached to the artist's original response before nature, they could scarcely have been more critical of Courbet's "vulgar" realism, as they termed it, as opposed to their own concept of a realism refined by *écriture artiste* and based on the original and direct observation of contemporary life. The Goncourts' substitution of the ugly for the beautiful, it should be noted, bears a strong resemblance to Charles Baudelaire's substitution of evil for good in his most important collection of verse, *Les fleurs du mal.*

There is also a lack of originality reflected in Chassagnol's speech in favor of modernity,

THE GONCOURTS

for many of his statements on modern art owe their inspiration to the writings of Stendhal and Théophile Gautier, as well as Baudelaire, as more than one scholar has noted. Efforts to define their contemporary realist position further occur when Chassagnol proclaims the aesthetically jarring realism of Jacques-Louis David's *The Death of Marat* the standard of truth and modernity, because of its "feeling for the contemporary, for life that pokes you with its elbows, for the present in which you feel your passions stir and a part of yourself quiver." This statement is a fair summary of their requirement that the modern artist be sensitive to his own milieu and draw his subject matter from it.

Apart from the story of Coriolis, there is within this novel of ideas and sensations another novel, that of the unsuccessful painter, Anatole, one of the most sympathetic characters the Goncourts ever created. The Paris bohemian, as Morris Bishop once observed, "is less the seed plot of young genius than the waste heap of failures." One of the most painful scenes in the novel concerns this happy-go-lucky prankster's loss of commitment to his vocation and his slide into the life of a pure bohemian who because of his misery and suffering has lost the pride he once felt in considering himself a painter. The loss of this illusion is soon followed by the discovery of still another painful fact—that he is no longer thirty-nine. Yet in contrast to the bitter conclusion of Coriolis's story, the final chapter of the novel is devoted to describing the happiness this middle-aged former artist turned assistant zookeeper has discovered amid the plants and animals of the Jardin des Plantes, where the Goncourts picture him as reliving the joys of Eden, "mercifully unafflicted with an Eve," as Robert Baldick remarks. The reader cannot help concluding, however, that Anatole's Eden, a zoological garden, is nothing more than an artificial paradise surrounded by a decadent society.

From the viewpoint of composition or structure, *Manette Salomon* is divided into at least three major themes: the conjugal drama of Coriolis, a chronicle of nineteenth-century French artistic life, and Anatole's story. It therefore lacks any clearly defined intention. Fragmented into several parts, much like *Charles Demailly*, *Manette* lacks the formal cohesion of the brothers' shorter novels, *Soeur Philomène* and *Germinie Lacerteux*, but it is nevertheless of a higher artistic quality than the earlier novel *Charles Demailly*.

Finally, although *Manette Salomon* is sometimes compared with Henry Murger's *Scènes de la vie de Bohème* (Scenes of Bohemian Life, 1848) because of the similarity in subject matter and setting, the resemblance is superficial. The Goncourts' description of the hard and disagreeable elements of bohemian life, which stands in marked constrast to Murger's more conventional celebration of the joy the bohemian artists derive from their freedom, is a more authentic and artistically superior documentary of contemporary mores.

The last novel Edmond wrote in collaboration with Jules, whose illness was beginning to get the best of him, *Madame Gervaisais*, was based on the conversion and death in Rome of their beloved aunt, Nephtalie de Gourmont. It reflects the strong influence that her excessive taste and intense enthusiasm for bric-à-brac and objets d'art, with which she had infected both of them, had on the formation of their descriptive style. It is precisely the dominance of the brothers' almost fanatical attention to the description of pictorial details that draws forth the criticism of Henry James, who summed up the Goncourts' efforts in this story as "an attempt to trace the conversion of a spirit from skepticism to Catholicism through contact with the old marbles and frescoes, the various ecclesiastical bric-à-brac of Rome," while totally failing to provide the least description of the agitations of the soul or the spiritual reality of Madame Gervaisais's mystical experience. In seeing the Goncourts predominantly as painters rather than writers in *Madame Gervaisais*, James was, of course, touching on a vital aesthetic tendency of the nineteenth century, the convergence between literature and painting.

It was against this tendency that Sainte-Beuve, like James, was reacting when he told the brothers, who were anxious to have his reaction to their novel (which had been met with a wall of silence since its publication) that in *Madame Gervaisais* they were no longer writers, but musicians or painters, much like Jean Jacques Rousseau, Bernardin de Sainte-Pierre, François-René de Chateaubriand, Victor Hugo, Gautier, and Saint-Victor, all of whom followed a similar tendency. But he did not stop there; he went on to accuse them of wishing to go even farther in this direction, of attempting to achieve the impossible, to capture the soul of things by interpreting movement in terms of color (*Journal*, 2 March 1869). As disciples of Gautier and believers in the doctrine of art for art's sake, the Goncourts readily accepted the convergence of prose fiction and painting as part of their descriptive technique.

Sainte-Beuve also attacked the authors of *Madame Gervaisais* for their lack of understanding of Christian mysticism, especially their distortion of the *Imitation of Christ*, which they misrepresented as a distressing, gloomy, and somber work of devotion, the verses of which they had described as falling like petrifying drops of cold water on Madame Gervaisais's heart until they had deadened all her natural affection and tenderness. Why did the Goncourts, who claimed that it was not their intention at the outset of *Madame Gervaisais* to attack the Catholic religion, write a book that was unmistakably hostile to the church? Their answer was that once they had begun writing their book, they were pushed by some "irresistible force" they said was in the air, a force that drove them to write the novel they did (*Journal*, 16 May 1868). Nonetheless, it is difficult to understand how they could present such an exaggeratedly negative interpretation of a work like the *Imitation*, one of the most positive and easily understood works of religious devotion for Christians, without a deliberate antireligious bias. Despite any claims on their part to the contrary, the Catholic critic Barbey d'Aurevilly attacked the brothers for having produced a surreptitiously deadly anti-Catholic work.

Structurally, *Madame Gervaisais* is unlike the previous novels, which tend to emphasize the disconnected and disjunct nature of reality and the surprises or disillusionments that fate holds for their characters. Unexpectedly, here the Goncourts reveal an obvious concern for a classically balanced form. This is evident, Robert Ricatte points out, in the balanced symmetry of the series of symbolically antithetical scenes from which the novel is constructed, such as the contrast between Madame Gervaisais's life before and after her conversion, and the cruelty of pagan Rome and the mysticism of Christian Rome. This uncharacteristic attention to formal values reveals the authors' arbitrary intention to give a classical, and therefore, by their own standards, artificial, unity to this work, which chronicles the degradation of a refined and intelligent woman of the world as she falls victim to religious hysteria, due in part to the influence of the Roman milieu upon her, as well as the physiological effects of tuberculosis and menopause. As a result of her weakened mental and physical state, she finally yields to the demand of her inhuman spiritual director, Father Sibilla, that she renounce her maternal affection for her mentally retarded child, Pierre-Charles, to prove her complete conversion to a life of religious devotion. Weak in dialogue and characterization, *Madame Gervaisais* fails to appeal to the modern reader, just as it failed to meet with acceptance by the Goncourts' contemporaries. This novel feels as though it depends solely for effect on the authors' descriptive enumeration of external details. Meanwhile the heroine has been reduced to one more hapless emotional female.

The novels Edmond wrote and published on his own after 1870 met with objections similar to those that had greeted the novels written jointly with Jules. The first of these, *La fille*

Elisa, which Jules had helped to plan before his death, is perhaps Edmond's finest novel. It is the story of a prostitute condemned to life imprisonment for murdering, in a fit of hysteria, a soldier with whom she had fallen in love. Although some critics deplored the subject matter and demanded that the author himself be prosecuted or shut up in an asylum, the novel was a moderate success with the public: 10,000 copies were sold within a few days of its publication.

In *Madame Gervaisais*, the Goncourts strongly suggested that reading can be harmful to one's mental health, especially if the reader is an emotional female subject to physiological and psychological stress. In *La fille Elisa*, the works of religious devotion have been replaced by a hundred or so novels of love and adventure, and by religiously inspired novels of the Restoration period, books in which stories of pious pilgrims in search of a mystical rose are mingled with narrative accounts of robbers and platonic love, all of which are described as resembling a collection of village Holy Week books. These novels, which Elisa discovers in a lending library, fill her imagination for months on end with dreams of heroism and devotion, to the point, the narrator tells us, that "she felt herself seized with the desire to accomplish actions resembling those she had read about, and an imperious need to sacrifice herself in her own way tormented her young girlish heart."

It is inconceivable that Edmond, when he wrote the chapter devoted to what had become for Elisa a new passion—reading novels—could not have had in mind the importance Flaubert had attached to the impact on Emma Bovary's imagination of the popular romantic books she had read, books that made her a victim of romantic ennui.

Both Emma and Elisa dream of a great romantic love or adventure like those they have read about in the cheap romances they have devoured, the one in a convent, the other in a brothel, two obviously antithetical settings. But although there are similarities in the effect of the reading on these two susceptible girls, there are also important differences, perhaps the main one being that whereas Emma's retreat from reality leads her into illicit relationships, Elisa dreams of escape from her professional life of illicit sex. Moreover, although Emma's search for her ideal lover occupies most of her life after her marriage, Elisa's relationship with the man she feels fate has sent her, since he embodies all her romantic notions, lasts just one brief chapter, until she learns he is a police informer, an agent provocateur, and as such beneath even the contempt of a prostitute.

Her romantic illusion shattered, Elisa develops a passionate hatred for men. But there remains a more enduring dream awakened in her by her reading, the "aspiration of a defiled soul toward spiritual love," a dream of chastity, which, as the narrator explains, is of the greatest importance for the prostitute. Combined with her now hostile attitude to men, it is this prolonged and lofty dream of an innocent childhood love that makes understandable to the reader, if not to the society in which she lives, Elisa's hysterical reaction to the sudden physical advances of the soldier she had loved, Jules Tanchon; she stabs him to death in an uncontrollable frenzy.

As a result of her crime, Elisa is condemned to life imprisonment at Noirlieu, where prisoners were subjected to the American Auburn system of punishment, one imposing perpetual silence on the inmates. Horrified as the Goncourts were by their observations of this system at work in the women's prison at Clermont d'Oise (the model for Noirlieu), which they visited in 1862, Edmond turned his novel into an act of social protest against this "philanthropic and moral torture," as they referred to it in their *Journal* (28 October 1862).

Stylistically, *La fille Elisa* is heavier and less intense than the novels Edmond wrote in collaboration with Jules, a master of dialogue and a brilliant colorist. But in fairness to the author, it must be noted that he states his intention in the novel's preface to give it a severe simplicity, to confront the reader with the harsh life of the prostitute and the prisoner. As for its structure, opinion among modern critics is divided over the question of whether or not Edmond overstructured his text. Some critics give him high marks for his effort to compose a well-balanced and carefully organized story replete with a narrative method that calls for the technical language of the cinema to describe it. Others, like Hubert Juin, complain of his having reduced narrative to a rigid and geometrical pattern. He offers as evidence Edmond's need to make his novel a demonstration piece for his ideas on the excellence of realism as he practiced it, in contrast to the work of the Goncourts' heirs, the naturalists, especially Zola, of whom Edmond was becoming increasingly jealous. By coincidence, Zola published one of his famous experimental novels, *L'Assommoir*, the same year *La fille Elisa* appeared. One last source of criticism was the introduction of the author himself in the novel's final chapter, an act of authorial intrusion that most commentators find unjustified.

Les frères Zemganno, with its portrayal of the daily routine of two misogynistic acrobats, Nello and Gianni, brothers (like the Goncourts themselves, their prototypes) who practice sexual abstinence out of dedication to their cult of muscular energy, apparently had little or no appeal for either the critics or the public. The reviewers who did take note of the work were shocked by its brutal language and by the introduction into the story of such a false and improbable character as La Tompkins; she is a wealthy young American bareback rider, on whom the misogynistic author casts the suspicion of being responsible for the tragic accident that causes Nello to break both his legs. Even Zola, who had frequently assisted in the campaigns to gain critical and popular acceptance of the Goncourts' novels, shared the general public's attitude that this one was too strange and fantastic to arouse any sympathetic response. But although Zola had recognized *Germinie Lacerteux* as the first

step toward a true literary naturalism, he took Edmond's antagonistic remarks on the vulgar level of reality implied by the term "realism" expressed in the preface to *Les frères Zemganno* as a first step toward betrayal of naturalism. Lacking imagination and poetic inspiration, Edmond failed to achieve the "poetic realism" he had announced as his goal in the introduction to his second novel. But because this book was inspired by great love for the brother who had predeceased him, he still succeeded, according to André Billy, in writing a "sensitive and original" novel, not only of circus life, but of brotherly love.

Despite an unprecedented advertising campaign, Edmond's third effort at solo novel writing, *La Faustin*, a sensitive psychological study based on the personality of a successful but lowborn actress, Rachel, and her life in the theater, likewise failed to stimulate much interest among the public, and the reviewers and critics were once more divided in their reactions. Most critics found the portrayal of La Faustin's lover, the English aristocrat Lord Annandale, for whom she had abandoned her first love, the theater, to be so odd and unnatural that it destroyed for them any credibility the story might have had. The appearance of *La Faustin*, in which Edmond claimed to have "introduced a new poetry and fantasy into the study of reality," prompted the critic Ferdinand Brunetière, who found little "poetry and fantasy" to praise but much realism to denounce, to suggest that Edmond could not even be considered a true naturalist; his work was in fact unnatural, no more than "the spirit of Japanese art" introduced into fiction.

The final and perhaps least significant of all Edmond's books, *Chérie*, a subtle portrayal of a young girl going through the rites of puberty, is a documentary rather than a novel. It is based on "human documents" given to him by Marie Abbatucci, whom he referred to in a *Journal* entry (30 September 1878) as a "storehouse of rare and unknown human documents" about the girls and women of his day, and by Pauline Zeller (whom, it has been suggested, he declined to marry because of his devotion to literature), who allowed him to incorporate the diary she had kept as a sixteen-year-old into his narrative of Chérie's life.

As with his previous novels, Edmond prefaced Chérie with an explanation of his views on the evolution of the novel in the nineteenth century and referred once again to his efforts to lead a literary movement that would elevate realism, would apply it not only to low life and low subjects but also to fashionable and educated people. Zola, in Le roman expérimental (1880), a formulation of his naturalistic theories, responded to the literary manifesto with which Edmond had prefaced Les frères Zemganno; Zola objected that it would be wrong for a naturalist to ignore the vulgar reality found on all levels of society. In spite of Zola's objections to his ideas on "poetic realism," Edmond, in the preface to Chérie, reiterated his original position on this matter by further declaring his intention to portray a society of wealth, power, and fine company, a society in which aristocratic behavior, lofty aspirations, and refined manners would be represented as realities as authentic as the coarse and common reality of the people, the only reality Zola recognized. This clash was but one more of a series of vicissitudes in the rather difficult relationship that linked these two men for more than thirty years.

As far as the composition of his last novel is concerned, the reviewers attacked it for its lack of plot, even though Edmond made it quite clear that he sought intentionally to render his work as devoid of plot as possible so as to approximate his ideal of a new type of literary production for which the term "novel" would no longer be appropriate. Once more, however, his efforts at innovation in the art of fiction were met with an unfavorable critical reaction. One commentator, Armand Pontmartin, remarked that the elder Goncourt's latest narrative effort was simply further evidence of the steady deterioration of his literary output since the death of Jules.

Just as he and his brother had taken the public to task for its literary preference for "false" or unrealistic novels in the preface to Germinie Lacerteux in 1864, so Edmond utilized the introduction to Chérie some twenty years later to castigate the reading public for its inability to judge properly the significance of new literary productions. As for the abyss that the Goncourts had noted between the artist and the public during Jules's lifetime, Edmond did nothing to bridge it. On the contrary, he appears to have made every effort to widen the chasm by alienating not only the public, who did not read his works, but even those who did, by the introduction into his novels of incredible characters, the final dissolution of any resemblance to plot in his stories, and the further exaggeration of an already precious style.

The history of the Goncourts' efforts to gain recognition in the theater, one of their lifelong ambitions, is similar to their efforts to overcome the hostile reactions their novels received. It constitutes another unhappy chapter in their ongoing struggle with the critics, the public, the governments of the Second Empire and the Third Republic, and other assorted enemies, ranging from common prostitutes to an empress. The brothers wrote only two plays together, Henriette Maréchal and La patrie en danger. Only Henriette was performed during Jules's lifetime; La patrie en danger, a rather poor historical drama about the French Revolution, had to wait until 1875 because of their difficulties in finding a producer. The only play Edmond wrote on his own was À bas le progrès (Down with Progress), a short, unsuccessful one-act farce presented at the theater of Menus Plaisirs in January 1893, just three years before Edmond's death in 1896.

The two very nervous and apprehensive dramatists made their debut on the evening of 5 December 1865, when Henriette Maréchal premiered at the Théâtre Français. They were overwhelmed by the tumult it caused. But the demonstrations it provoked had little or nothing to do with the fact that it was a realistic study of contemporary norms and human illusions or that it was a play almost totally devoid of dramatic quality. Most of the commotion was caused by students and others who were opposed to the imperial regime of Napoleon III. These people believed the Goncourts, well known for their anti-Republicanism, had benefited from their friendship with Princess Mathilde Bonaparte in having their play selected for presentation at the Théâtre Français. It was not these demonstrations, however, that closed the doors on their play after only six performances, but political pressure from the government, evident in newspapers like the *Gazette de France,* which questioned whether the taxpayers' money should be used to finance the production of such plays. The play was finally banned on 17 December 1865, most likely due to the influence of the empress Eugénie, who thus allowed her veiled hostility and jealousy of Princess Mathilde's rival salon to show itself.

Edmond's other work in the theater consisted entirely of dramatic adaptations by himself or others of the following novels (with their date of presentation): *Soeur Philomène* (1887), *Renée Mauperin* (1887), *Germinie Lacerteux* (1888), *Les frères Zemganno* (1890), *La fille Elisa* (1890), *Charles Demailly* (1892), and *Manette Salomon* (1896). Most of these plays were produced in Paris, at either the Odéon or the Théâtre Libre, where Edmond had the good fortune to find a sympathetic producer, the theater's founder, Monsieur Antoine, who also did much to contribute to the relative success of several of Edmond's plays by acting in them. But it seems that if any of these theatrical versions of their novels gave evidence of being a success, such as *Germinie Lacerteux* or *La fille Elisa,* the government of the Third Republic, which had replaced that of the Second Empire, intervened. The president of the republic himself, Sadi Carnot, was so shocked by *Germinie Lacerteux* that he ordered its matinee performances suspended—only because he was unable to convince the minister for fine arts to

ban it entirely. Adapted by a young disciple of Edmond's, Jean Ajalbert, *La fille Elisa* was a great success at the Théâtre Libre, but was banned as immoral by the government when it was transferred to the Théâtre Porte Saint-Martin to reach a larger public. Furthermore, almost without exception each premiere was followed by savage, insulting reviews labeling these works either immoral or boring.

In addition to having introduced realism into the theater, the Goncourts also believed strongly that the language of the theater was in need of renewal; they felt it was time to replace the formal language of the classical theater of the seventeenth and eighteenth centuries, as well as the somewhat grandiloquent language of the romantic stage, with a new form of theatrical speech. In the preface to *Henriette Maréchal,* therefore, they proposed to introduce a "langue littéraire parlée" (a spoken literary language), a realistic language they defined only as being an approximation of everyday speech, with most of its syntactical idiosyncrasies, but at the same time reflecting the dramatists' more correct use of grammar. The Goncourts never succeeded in bringing about the revolution they had hoped for in this respect, but it is undeniable that their concept of a theatrical language closer to the spoken idiom was a step in the direction followed by most of their successful contemporary dramatists.

In view of political harassment (during the Second Empire the brothers were once hauled into police court for some supposedly immoral verses that they had not written, but merely quoted in an article), public indifference to most of their early literary attempts, and a generally unsympathetic and hostile press, one may well wonder how the Goncourts were able to sustain the strength of their commitment to literature. Reflecting on the "hard and horrible struggle against anonymity" that they faced in their early efforts to gain recognition, they noted that all the "monotonous, uneventful spiritual agony" they suffered at the beginning of their career was wiped out by the taste of a "little success, the discovery of a publisher, the earning of a few hundred francs, and the smell of a little incense" (*Journal*, 6 April 1857). The slightest taste of success was sufficient to make them forget their ordeal. As they became better known, they also made the literary friendships and social connections that sustained them in their persistent efforts to achieve the recognition they believed they deserved as serious, committed men of letters.

In the summer of 1862 the aspiring young authors received a dinner invitation from Princess Mathilde Bonaparte, who had read their *Marie-Antoinette* and wished to make their acquaintance. This invitation transformed their social life; they became regular guests of the princess, either at her Paris home in the rue de Courcelles or at her estate at Saint-Gratien. Her salon was a gathering place for most of the leading artists, writers, and intellectuals of her day, including Gavarni, Gautier, Flaubert, Taine, Ernest Renan, and Sainte-Beuve, one of the most influential literary critics of his day, as well as the comte de Nieuwerkerke, superintendent of fine arts, and a host of others.

Another major event in their lives as professional writers was the organization in November of the same year of a twice-monthly dinner at the Magny restaurant, in which they played a part together with Gavarni, Sainte-Beuve, and several others. Eventually enlarged, the Magny dinners included among regulars from the princess Mathilde's salon occasional guests such as Ivan Turgenev, George Sand, Marcellin Berthelot, and many others. At these dinners, according to the Goncourts' description of them, the guests were "free to discuss any subject under the sun," although the usual subject of conversation, they noted in their *Journal*, was woman. They also recorded discussions ranging from dirty tricks in the literary profession to a debate on infinity and the existence of God, or the merits of Homer, whom they said they considered less talented than Victor Hugo, thus sparking a disagree-

able scene with the drama critic Saint-Victor. Even at these convivial gatherings, which included some of their closest friends, the Goncourts still appear to have been suffering from a sense of isolation, for on 8 June 1863 they confided in their *Journal:* "It is alarming to see how, in every discussion, we are always alone and never make converts. Perhaps that is why God made us two," as though they were two lonely prophets crying in the wilderness, whether the subject be politics, art, literature, or music.

The same sort of irritation with their friends, social acquaintances, and fellow men of letters is evident on almost every page of their *Journal*, which bears the subtitle "Memoirs of Literary Life," and in the predominantly uncharitable, frequently treacherous, portraits of these people they have left to posterity, especially in the case of the half dozen or so regulars of the Magny dinner club, Princess Mathilde, and successful rivals and disciples such as Guy de Maupassant and Zola. As Henry James put it so well in his review of the *Journal*, "As a general thing what they commemorate as workers is the simple breakdown of joy," since their diary, like most of their fictional output, is preponderantly concerned with "revelations of suffering."

With their novel *Germinie Lacerteux*, the Goncourts launched the naturalist movement as a reaction against the false and insipid novels of their times, most of which were escapist in tendency. But by concentrating their attention on Germinie's degradation, as on that of their other protagonists, they revealed their fundamentally pessimistic conception of life. By associating her pathological symptoms with a degenerating society, they accentuated the decadence of that society, as did their friends and contemporaries Gautier and Flaubert. In turn, they influenced the formation of the decadent movement, which was to shape French fiction in the closing two decades of the nineteenth century. Specifically, as Jean Pierrot notes, publication of Edmond's novel *La Faustin* in 1882, in which the bored and depressed heroine reads Thomas De Quincey's *Confessions of an English Opium Eater,* provoked a new interest in that work, which played an important role in the development of the decadent school of French literature. Their influence, furthermore, made itself felt on this movement through the work of their disciple J. K. Huysmans. He was impregnated with their writings, especially *Germinie Lacerteux,* which played an important part in his orientation toward a writing vocation, as did the sensual mysticism he found in *Madame Gervaisais,* the anatomy of which became one of the mainstays of his fiction. In one of the masterpieces of French decadent literature, Huysmans's *À rebours* (1884), the decadent aristocrat and central figure of the novel, Des Esseintes, exploits religious objects for their picturesque effect; in his *En route* (1895) the mysticism involved in the religious conversion of the hero, Durtal, has been described as the intellectual stimulation for a declining sensuality.

While the Goncourt brothers cannot be ranked as great novelists, their original and influential contribution to the development of nineteenth-century French prose fiction requires that they be regarded as worthy disciples of Flaubert. Modern critics, nevertheless, still tend to be as critical of the Goncourts' fictional technique and prose style as were some of their contemporaries, in some cases even more so. John Porter Houston, writing on decadent style, is not only critical of their heavily substantival and participial style, their tendency to complicate language for the sake of grammar, their penchant for neologisms, and their lack of fictional technique; he challenges as well the notion that a degenerate nervous system is a refined one, as the brothers so often suggested. Nor does he find any perceptual sensitivity in their curiously static novels. Still, Houston as well as other scholars who have studied the stylistic evolution of French prose fiction in the second half of the nineteenth century acknowledges the influential role the Goncourts played in the revolution in prose style that culminated in the work of Marcel Proust, one of the greatest French writers of the twentieth century.

In his lengthy masterpiece, *À la recherche du temps perdu* (*Remembrance of Things Past,* 1913–1929), Proust pays his own homage to the Goncourt brothers; he has one of his characters, Marcel, the aspiring writer, after having read a supposedly unpublished document from the Goncourts' *Journal* (which is actually a pastiche by Proust), conclude that it is impossible for him to match their powers of observation. Since this pastiche of the Goncourts contains a favorable review of the characters in his own novel, Proust cleverly pays himself the compliment of making it appear that if they had had the opportunity to read his novels, the Goncourts would have been full of praise for his talent as a novelist. Appropriately, in 1919, largely because of the insistence of the first president of the Académie Goncourt, Léon Daudet, the son of Alphonse Daudet, one of Edmond's closest friends, Proust was named the winner of the Prix Goncourt, one of the most coveted literary awards in France today.

Selected Bibliography

COLLECTED WORKS

Oeuvres d'Edmond et Jules de Goncourt. 44 vols. Paris, 1921–1936. Definitive ed. Directed by the Académie Goncourt.
Journal: Mémoires de la vie littéraire. Edited by R. Ricatte. 4 vols. Paris, 1959. Only ed. that includes entire journal. Definitive ed.

INDIVIDUAL WORKS

BY EDMOND AND JULES DE GONCOURT
En 18 . . . . Paris, 1851. Novel.
Salon de 1852. Paris, 1852. Art criticism.
La révolution dans les moeurs. Paris, 1854. Social comment.
Histoire de la société française pendant la Révolution. Paris, 1854; Geneva, 1971, repro. of orig. ed. History.

Histoire de la société française pendant le Directoire. Paris, 1855. History.

La peinture a l'Exposition de 1855. Paris, 1855. Art criticism.

Sophie Arnould. Paris, 1857. Biography.

Portraits intimes du dix-huitième siècle. 2 vols. Paris, 1857–1858. Biography.

Histoire de Marie-Antoinette. Paris, 1858. Biography.

Les hommes de lettres (later called *Charles Demailly*). Paris, 1860. Novel.

Les maîtresses de Louis XV. Paris, 1860. Biography.

Soeur Philomème. Paris, 1861. Novel.

La femme au dix-huitième siècle. Paris, 1862. Biography.

Renée Mauperin. Paris, 1864. Novel.

Germinie Lacerteux. Paris, 1864. New ed. 1979, preface by H. Juin. Novel.

Henriette Maréchal. Paris, 1866. Drama.

Idées et sensations. Paris and Brussels, 1866. Extracts from the Goncourts' unpublished journal.

Manette Salomon. Paris, 1867. New ed. 1979, preface by H. Juin. Novel.

Madame Gervaisais. Paris, 1869. Novel.

La patrie en danger. Paris, 1873. Drama.

Gavarni: L'Homme et l'oeuvre. Paris, 1873. Biography.

L'Amour au dix-huitième siècle. Paris, 1875. History.

L'Art du dix-huitième siècle. Paris, 1875. Originally published as 12 separate monographs between 1859 and 1870. Edited by J.-P. Bouillon as *L'Art du dix-huitième siècle et autres textes sur l'art*, Paris, 1967.

Journal des Goncourt: Mémoires de la vie littéraire. 9 vols. Paris, 1887–1896. More complete than *Idées et sensations* but includes only what E. de Goncourt deemed appropriate for publication in his lifetime.

Préfaces et manifestes littéraires. Paris and Brussels, 1888.

BY JULES DE GONCOURT

Lettres de Jules de Goncourt. Paris, 1885. Preface by Henry Céard.

BY EDMOND DE GONCOURT

La fille Elisa. Paris, 1877. New ed. 1979, preface by H. Juin. Novel.

Les frères Zemganno. Paris, 1879. Novel.

La maison d'un artiste. Paris, 1881. Art criticism.

La Faustin. Paris, 1882. New ed. 1979, preface by H. Juin. Novel.

Chérie. Paris, 1884. Novel.

Les actrices au dix-huitième siècle. 3 vols.: *Madame Saint-Huberty*, Paris, 1882; *Mademoiselle Clairon*, Paris, 1890; *La Guimard*, Paris, 1893. Geneva, 1973, repro. of orig. ed. Biography.

L'Art japonais du dix-huitième siècle. 2 vols.: *Outamaro*, Paris, 1891. Revised ed. 1978. *Hokousaï*, Paris, 1896. New ed. 1978. Art criticism.

À bas le progrès. Paris, 1893. Drama.

TRANSLATIONS

The Confidantes of a King: The Mistresses of Louis XV. Translated by Ernest Dowson. London and Edinburgh, 1907.

Elisa: The Story of a Prostitute. Translated by Margaret Crosland. New York and London, 1959. Reprinted 1960.

La Faustin. Translated by G. F. Monkshood and Ernest Tristan. London, 1906.

French Eighteenth-Century Painters. Translated and introduced by Robin Ironside. New York and London, 1948. Reprinted Ithaca, N.Y., 1981. Selection from original edition.

Germinie. Translator anonymous. Introduced by Martin Turnell. New York, 1955.

The Goncourt Journals, 1851–1870. Edited and translated by Lewis Galantière. New York, 1937. Reprinted 1968. Selections.

Renée Mauperin. Translated by Alys Hallard (pseud.). New York, 1902.

Pages from the Goncourt Journal. Edited and translated by Robert Baldick. New York and London, 1962.

Paris Under Siege, 1870–1871: From the Goncourt Journal. Edited and translated by G. J. Becker, introduction by P. H. Beik. Ithaca, N.Y., 1969.

Paris and the Arts, 1851–1896: From the Goncourt Journal. Edited and translated by G. J. Becker and Edith Philips. Ithaca, N.Y., 1971.

Sister Philomene. Translated by Laura Ensor. London, 1890.

The Woman of the Eighteenth Century: Her Life, Her Love, and Her Philosophy. Translated by Jacques LeClercq and Ralph Roeder. New York, 1927. London, 1928.

The Zemganno Brothers. Translated by Leonard Clark and Iris Allam. London, 1957.

BIOGRAPHICAL AND CRITICAL STUDIES

Baldick, Robert. *The Goncourts.* New York, 1960.

Barrows, Susanna, *Distorting Mirrors: Visions of the Crowd in Late Nineteenth-Century France.* New Haven, Conn., and London, 1981.

Billy, André. *The Goncourt Brothers.* New York, 1955.

Bishop, Morris. *A Survey of French Literature: The Nineteenth and Twentieth Centuries.* New York, 1965.

Bourget, Paul. *Nouveau essais de psychologie contemporaine.* Paris, 1901. Vol. 2, pp. 135–193.

Brookner, Anita. *The Genius of the Future: Studies in French Art and Art Criticism: Diderot, Stendhal, Baudelaire, Zola, the Brothers Goncourt, Huysmans.* New York and London, 1971.

Charvet, P. E. *The Nineteenth and Twentieth Centuries, 1870–1940.* New York, 1967.

Delzant, Alidor. *Les Goncourt.* Paris, 1889.

Fosca, François. *Edmond et Jules de Goncourt.* Paris, 1941.

Grant, R. B. *The Goncourt Brothers.* New York, 1972.

Houston, J. P. *The Traditions of French Prose Style.* Baton Rouge, La., 1981.

James, Henry. "The Journal of the Brothers de Goncourt." In *Selected Literary Criticism,* edited by Morris Shapira. New York, 1964.

Levin, Harry. *The Gates of Horn.* New York, 1966.

Matthews, J. H. "From Naturalism to the Absurd: Edmond de Goncourt and Albert Camus." *Symposium* (Fall 1968), pp. 241–255.

Niess, R. J. "Émile Zola and Edmond de Goncourt." *The American Legion of Honor Magazine* 41:85–105 (1970).

Peyre, Henri. *French Literary Imagination and Dostoevsky, and Other Essays.* University, Ala., 1975.

Pierrot, Jean. *The Decadent Imagination, 1880–1900.* Chicago and London, 1981.

Proust, Marcel. "Les Goncourt devant leurs cadets," in *Textes retrouvés,* edited by Philip Kolb and Larkin B. Price. Urbana, Ill., 1968.

Raitt, A. W. *Life and Letters in France: The Nineteenth Century.* New York, 1965.

Ricatte, Robert. *La création romanesque chez les Goncourt, 1851–1870.* Paris, 1953.

————. *La genèse de "La fille Elisa."* Paris, 1960.

Sabatier, Pierre. *L'Esthétique des Goncourt.* Paris, 1920. Reprinted Geneva, 1970.

Simches, S. O. *Le romantisme et le goût esthétique du XVIIIe siècle.* Paris, 1964.

Stamm, T. D. *Gavarni and the Critics.* Ann Arbor, Mich., 1981.

Sullivan, E. D. *Maupassant the Novelist.* Princeton, N.J., 1954.

Symons, Arthur. "Goncourt." In *The Encyclopaedia Britannica,* 14th ed., vol. 10.

Thibaudet, Albert. *French Literature from 1975 to Our Era.* New York, 1967.

Turnell, Martin. *The Art of French Fiction.* London, 1959.

Ullman, Stephen. *Style in the French Novel.* New York and London, 1957.

Weinberg, Bernard. *French Realism: The Critical Reaction, 1830–1870.* New York, 1937.

Zola, Émile. "Edmond et Jules de Goncourt." In *Les romanciers naturalistes.* Paris, 1881.

T. H. GOETZ

HENRIK IBSEN
(1828–1906)

IN ANY HISTORICAL account of the world's greatest dramatists, Aeschylus, Sophocles, and Euripides are followed after a long gap first by William Shakespeare, then by Jean Baptiste Racine, after whom, it seems, there is another break: for a hundred years after Racine's death no one writes tragedies of any note, and it is scarely thought proper that a man of the Enlightenment should even make the attempt. The eighteenth century, the century in which modern science began to establish itself, is untragic, and historians who take a very broad view—some would say too broad—see nemesis in this: the consolations of tragedy are denied to the world of rationalism and freethinking. We live today, the same historians continue, in an age when tragedy has died. But the skeptic, considering that the Greek dramatists are separated from the English and the French by about 2,000 years, and that however many tragedies were written in this period, only nine, all by Seneca, are extant, will not be persuaded that these speculations mean very much. And in any case, he will ask, was not the second half of the nineteenth century the age of Ibsen: is tragedy not restored to the heights in him?

Certainly Ibsen brings to a theater that was becoming more and more photographic and thus, arguably, "scientific" in its realism, themes linked with those of the Greeks. *Hedda Gabler* (1890) is Euripides' *Medea* in modern dress; Hedda is the murderer of her lover's child in a new guise. *Ghosts* (1881) translates the Fate of Greek tragedy into a scientifically verifiable equivalent, inherited disease. John Gabriel Borkman and Halvard Solness, one the owner of an ocean-steamship company, the other an architect, challenge whatever gods are available to their generation in a mood akin to what the Greeks would have called hubris, overweening pride. The form of the late plays, too, is akin to classical drama, both French and Greek, in its unity of subject, and often in its unity of time and place as well. The huge Shakespearean casts of Ibsen's earlier plays are reduced sometimes to a mere half dozen, the stage often occupied by only two characters at a time. Yet the topics could not be more modern: women's liberation in *A Doll's House* (1879); Freudian longings in *The Lady from the Sea* (1888); ruthless profiteering in *Pillars of Society* (1877); "free love" in *Rosmersholm* (1886). True, Ibsen denied any propagandist intentions or even an interest in the rights of women; but although the ideas of his characters were not identical with his own, they helped to establish his reputation, which still stands almost as high as that of any dramatist before his time.

There have always been dissenters. Even in his native Norway, Ibsen has been seen by some as too international, not sufficiently Norwegian, too vaguely general to be anything in particular. More damaging potentially has been the charge that his characters are not rounded, are mere cyphers who dance to the call of his plots. He has been called an uncompromising pessimist (despite *Little Eyolf* [1894] and *The Lady from the Sea*). His language has been called bare, featureless, without vital force, though it has also been said that all his language is poetry, even when it is printed as prose. His plots, which often follow the pattern of popular French theater of his own day, have been called by H. L. Mencken, a sympathetic critic, thumping melodramas. Mary McCarthy described his work, viewed as a whole, as "repetitive and inchoate." But all this makes him particularly interesting for anyone concerned with the history of theater. Can a dramatist with so high a reputation be as poor in quality as some critics have maintained? Does Ibsen's reputation reflect adversely on critical opinions? What does his continuing success in the theater say, if anything, about modern audiences? It may be difficult to achieve agreement on the answers to such questions, but that does not mean there are no satisfactory answers.

Born in 1828 in a remote timber port, Skien, on the Norwegian coast, the son of the owner of a general store, Ibsen was the second son in a family of six children. Early impressions went deep: when he was six years old, his father had to mortgage most of his possessions to meet his debts, and the shadow of this threatened bankruptcy still haunts the late play *John Gabriel Borkman* (1896). Again, Ibsen's suspicion that he was an illegitimate child, unjustified though it may have been, is reflected in the illegitimacy or supposed illegitimacy of Dina Dorf in *Pillars of Society,* Regine in *Ghosts,* and Hedvig in *The Wild Duck* (1884). Fires in the timber houses of Skien were a constant threat; of the many fires in Ibsen's plays, the one in *Ghosts* is the most significant, leading as it does to Oswald's dark utterance, "We are all of us burning down."

Leaving school at fifteen, Ibsen became apprenticed to an apothecary at Grimstad, further down the Oslo fjord from Skien, where two years later a maid in his master's house bore him an illegitimate son. Though he showed little interest in the boy at any time, his imagination fed once more on the theme of illegitimacy. Personal concerns were, however, already beginning to be of less importance than those of the world at large; already he was starting to feel something of the revolutionary fervor abroad in Europe. What the French Revolution had failed to achieve in 1789 was being reasserted in 1848, though now with a stronger flavor of nationalism. Norway, joined to Sweden since 1814 in an unwilling union, had good cause to assert its national identity, and was to achieve independence almost a century later, in 1915, though without violent struggle. Ibsen, admiring the patriotic fervor of the Hungarians, was dissatisfied with the peaceable attitude of Norwegians and their ideal of parliamentary democracy. His own sympathy with a total revolution beyond any spoken of at that time by politicians is perceptible in his first play, *Catiline* (written in 1848–1849), named after the conspirator who attempted to overthrow the state in ancient Rome.

Arriving in 1850 at the University of Christiania (now Oslo), Ibsen soon found friends among political radicals. His failure to pass the matriculation examination debarred him, however, from continuing his studies, while his success as a dramatist launched him early on his long career in the theater. His play *The Burial Mound* was performed that same year (though not published until 1854), and in 1851 he was appointed to the Norwegian Theater in Bergen with the task of "assisting as dramatic author"; shortly after, he went on a study tour of theaters in Denmark and Germany. Now followed plays on Norwegian history, including *Lady Inger of Østraat* (1855), *The Vikings at Helgeland* (1858), and *The Pretenders* (1864). But in all these history is less important than self-realization. The main characters are interested not so much in the fate of Rome or Norway as in the possibility of achieving greatness, ascending a throne, wielding regal power, while in *The Pretenders* there is the culmination of a strong personal element: the two pretenders to the crown of medieval Norway bear a resemblance to Ibsen himself and his rival dramatist, Bjørnstjerne Bjørnson. Ibsen is at least as much concerned with his own claim to the crown of a dramatist as with his character's historical rivalries.

The early plays, now very seldom performed, are in fact projections of a titanic impulse in Ibsen, one to which he gave rein all his life; he demanded total mastery not only over his own craft of playwriting but also over something that we can only call the universe. Like Johann Wolfgang von Goethe's Faust, Ibsen's heroes of this kind assert or attempt to assert for themselves a cosmic identity: the pretender Skule, for example, who sets himself up as a king, will be satisfied with nothing but the supremacy of a Lucifer. In romantic language he proclaims: "My kingdom? It is a dark one—like that of the angel who set himself up against God." In the same vein Ibsen provides Skule with a diabolical figure who offers to take him, as Satan took Christ, to the top of a high mountain and show him all the glory of the world, an offer he comes within an ace of accepting. This theme recurs in much later plays that seem on the surface to be entirely about social problems. There is often also in the early plays a strong-willed woman who plays a part not unlike that of a devil.

The titanic impulse and the fear are intimated in accounts of Ibsen's own personality, for though in his youth he was described as quiet and unassuming, he was conscious of his distinctive gifts, refused to accept the contry lads of Skien as his social equals, and left Grimstad followed by jeers. Timid as a suitor, he seldom expressed passion; timid in all physical matters, he usually showed his courage rather in the printed word. "This quiet, reticent, not very prepossessing, unassuming young man," wrote a member of the theater board at Bergen, "with a glance that was usually half-veiled and seldom lit up, and then only briefly, rather gave the impression of being an exceedingly withdrawn and shy per-

son. . . . He not infrequently manifested a certain helplessness." For years in his youth he was, like Løvborg in *Hedda Gabler*, a heavy drinker. With the increasing success of his plays, however, his shyness revealed its obverse face.

In 1857 Ibsen married Suzannah Thoresen, a woman of dramatic temperament who provided him with a living image of the inspiring "new woman" he so often portrayed in his plays. His confidence was strengthened by government grants in 1863 for travel in Germany, France, and Italy; from 1866 on he received an annual grant to enable him to devote himself to writing, and a large part of his time was spent abroad. His timidity would now at times turn into a petty aggressiveness; he would make brutal verbal attacks on an unoffending friend or flaunt on his chest, as part of his ordinary wear, his medals presented by governments. "He is a domineering character," wrote a Danish friend in Rome, "egocentric and unbending, with a passionate masculinity and a curious admixture of personal cowardice, compulsively idealistic yet totally indifferent to expressing his ideals in daily life, restlessly questing, confused, yet striving for clarity." The few accounts of his amiability still leave the predominant impression of an insecure man of gigantic ambition.

These extremes were reflected in his political ideas. He welcomed the autocratic regime of czarist Russia for its oppressiveness. "Only think of the glorious love of liberty it engenders," he writes to his Danish admirer Georg Brandes; on another occasion he declares, like Stockmann in *An Enemy of the People* (1882), "Society and everything else must be wiped out." He believed in the great personality who, like Stockmann in his vision of himself, could achieve everything single-handedly, although he showed in *John Gabriel Borkman* the merciless fate awaiting such pride. But knowledge of Ibsen's life is of little use in relation to the plays. Many artists of all kinds have been equally egocentric and yet sublimated the accident of character in the finest art. The lack of warmth in Ibsen's relations with men and women, the bitterness and vanity observed by many acquaintances, do nothing to affect his status as a dramatist. At most they underline the rarity of characters with generous friendly impulses: though the *Lady from the Sea* is an exception, his creations are in the main prim idealists, ruthless egoists, naively pious conformists, enthusiastic visionaries, an array that Ibsen seems vicariously to condemn through the self-denunciation of Rubek in his final work, *When We Dead Awaken* (1899).

The dilemma in which he was placed—to be or not to be oneself—is given dramatic life in what are often considered his greatest plays, *Brand* (1866) and *Peer Gynt* (1867), two poetic dramas not based on history but freely invented, though the character Brand has been taken to refer to the Danish theologian of Ibsen's day Søren Kierkegaard, who was famous at that time throughout Scandinavia. In this pair of plays the pretensions of an egoism akin to Lucifer's are thoroughly examined, though Brand at first sight is the reverse of an egoist and is ambiguously both accepted and rejected. A pastor in a lonely Norwegian fjord, he goes from one self-sacrifice to another, dragging his family with him into poverty, denying himself and them the bare necessities of life, heedless of everything except the martyr's crown that awaits him. In his way, however, he is paradoxically as assertive as Skule or Catiline. Coming to the fjord as a preacher, he hopes to remake all men, "to make them like God." Defeated by others who are burdened with feelings of guilt, he turns from converting them to his own salvation. If he cannot make gods of men he will at least make himself a god. Unlike Skule, however, he sees the path to divine likeness not in revolt but in self-renunciation. Brand believes that he can "be himself" only through the total annihilation of his personal will, that from this annihilation will grow the mastery of the world he has renounced. He hurls himself into the work, stripping away one selfish

passion after another, denying himself the sunlight that was once his source of life, sacrificing even his own child. At last, seeing that his wife still means something to him, that he still has personal desires, he climbs alone into the mountains, to worship in isolation. There, however, an avalanche sweeps down on him and destroys him, filling the valley below, as he calls out, "Is there no salvation for the Will of Man?" The reply comes from a supernatural voice sounding above the thunder: "He is the God of Love."

It is a paradoxical ending, and much of the final scene is a whirl of contradictions and double meanings from which it is difficult to derive any clear significance. But the vigor of Brand's self-abandon with its implicit self-affirmation, the use of the Norwegian landscape and climate as symbol and atmosphere, and the dramatic power of religious fanaticism give life to the play even as it depresses. By sheer intensity it makes its mark.

Paired with *Brand,* in Ibsen's career, comes another play in verse, *Peer Gynt,* often seen as his masterpiece. This time there appears a Norwegian hero of distinct personal character, and yet of such a national kind that he has been called Ibsen's Falstaff. The passages where Peer, a young peasant lad, lies daydreaming in the grass, or persuades his ailing mother that he is taking her for a fearful and exhilarating sleigh ride along the mountaintops, are among the best scenes Ibsen wrote at any time; so is the scene in which he exploits Norwegian folklore to show the home of the troll-king, made even more famous through Edvard Grieg's musical setting.

At this point in his career Ibsen could have felt himself a new Goethe—Peer has been called a "counter-Faust"—or a new Shakespeare, drawing, as they also drew, on the resources of a recently discovered national inheritance. The folklore still serves a personal purpose, however. Peer is not only a lively creation, he is a fresh embodiment of the theme that *Brand* and most of the preceding plays had taken up. Having made his fortune, he sets out to see the world and arrives in Egypt, where he is proclaimed Emperor of Self in a lunatic asylum whose inmates caricature various German philosophers of egoism much spoken of in Ibsen's time. His youthful, carefree dash becomes middle-aged ruthlessness. There is a memorable scene—daring not only in its demands on contemporary stagecraft— in which Peer is seen after a shipwreck swimming in the sea, clinging to a plank, and deliberately cutting off the fingers of a man whose need to share the plank with him will destroy his own chances of survival. Ibsen could have painted no starker picture of the selfishness that keeps the human race alive. But though Peer goes on to realize more and more of "the Gyntian Self—an army of wishes, appetites, and desires"—he discovers no more satisfaction in it than Brand did in his self-denial. At a crossroads he meets a symbolic Buttonmolder, who challenges him to show one reason why he should not be melted down at the end of his life and turned into something useful. As another stranger, the Thin Man, puts it, if Peer has been a great enough sinner, he deserves to be purified, transformed into his better self, just as a photographic negative is turned into a positive. The implication is that his evil deeds are the obverse or the counterpart of good deeds he might have done. But Peer confesses that he has taken sin lightly, merely splashed himself with mud; he can claim no more than that he has traded in slaves, shipped idols to China, pushed a man into the sea, and this is not enough.

The scene with the Thin Man is difficult to comprehend. Murder and slave trading sound wicked enough to secure Peer's salvation on the unusual terms offered; by any traditional standard they would be of no benefit to him, and some new thought seems to be involved. The explanation may well be found in the idea that, as the German dramatist Friedrich Hebbel and the philosopher G. W. F. Hegel had both argued, guilt is a matter not of good and evil actions, but rather of the condition of being alive.

All life is guilty, by virtue of being "one-sided" and individual, and of not being the Whole, which is "all-sided." Dramatic guilt, on the other hand, is concerned with the man or woman who oversteps the bounds of moderation, either in good or in evil; and—according to Hebbel—the greatest tragedy arises from a hero who is destroyed on account of an admirable undertaking, who has, in other words, been too good. This theory, which holds that guilt is "present in all human conduct" and yet that a man can be too good, was called absurd in Hebbel's time. It does not seem to be as intelligible as Martin Luther's thought when he observed that he was more fearful about his good works (as sources of pride) than about his misdeeds. It does affirm, however, that the more pronounced an individual's talent is, the more forceful its expression, the greater the tragic dissonance within the wider scheme of things, that is, within the Whole in which good and evil are transcended.

On these terms it can be argued, as James McFarlane has done, that Peer Gynt fails to be a man great enough for tragedy. He asserts himself as an individual, but there is no enduring Self present. In a famous scene, Peer peels layer after layer of an onion, seeing them as layers of his own personality, to find nothing at all at the center. McFarlane argues,

> Peer has never really been himself and has defied the purpose of his life; to be oneself is to kill oneself, or in other words to show unmistakably the Master's intention in whatever one does; right and wrong, good and evil do not enter into the calculations when it comes to escaping the casting-ladle, for a sinner counts as much as a saint provided things are done "on a grand scale."
>
> (*The Oxford Ibsen*, vol. 3, pp. 30–33)

Thus Peer is due to be melted down. His negatives are not dark enough to produce bright images of virtues he has in any case never displayed. Possibly Brand likewise fails to be a great enough sinner, though it has also been argued that his self-denial is tragic enough to satisfy Hebbel's theory.

Notwithstanding the rollicking beginning, *Peer Gynt* tends toward the end to be based more on recondite philosophizing than dramatic action, even though the symbolic Buttonmolder still belongs to the world of folklore in which the play starts. Peer's own objection to the Buttonmolder's account—"it [the theory of justification] seems incredibly complicated"—is a reasonable one. But as it appears almost at the end, however much Peer tries to make himself out a great sinner, he has been innocent all his life. In a scene that can be difficult to produce in the theater without sentimentality, he meets Solveig, who has always been in love with him. Now an old woman, she tells him, "You've done no wrong, my only boy," rocking him to sleep on her lap, singing to him that his true self has been preserved in her faith and hope and love. The effect is not unlike that at the end of *Brand*, for all this while the Buttonmolder has been lurking in the background; as he calls to Peer that they must meet at the next crossroads, where Peer must demonstrate his great sinfulness or be melted down, Solveig tells him to "sleep and dream." If the Buttonmolder's casting-ladle corresponds in its annihilating power to Brand's avalanche, Solveig corresponds to the love of God announced out of the disaster. She has the last word in the play, it is true, but we are left with the surmise that Peer may be melted down after all. A knowledge of Hegelian philosophy, especially the idea of synthesis, is useful in understanding the conclusions of both these plays.

Yet more complex, but less effective dramatically, is the unwieldy play *Emperor and Galilean* (1873), partly written before *Brand* and *Peer Gynt* but completed later, in which both self-assertion and self-denial are combined in one man, the Roman emperor Julian, who tries to fuse the untrammeled freedom and happiness of the Greeks (as nineteenth-century writers were prone to see them) with the self-sacrifice and spirituality of Christianity. But Julian's plan to beget within himself "the Messiah of the two empires, the spirit and the world," is a failure almost from the start, and the play limps on, never reaching beyond the ambiguities with which Ibsen had already felt dissatisfied in earlier works. In Hegelian terms, *Brand* and *Peer Gynt* are thesis and antithesis: the synthesis, intended in *Emperor and Galilean*, was never achieved.

It was about this time that Ibsen gave up writing not only lyric poetry but also plays in verse. After *Peer Gynt*, all his plays are in prose, and increasingly spare and plain. Verse drama had by then gone out of fashion. Robert Browning and Alfred Lord Tennyson had had no success with it, nor had Hebbel. The successes of Alexandre Dumas *fils*, Victorien Sardou, and Émile Augier in France had all been in prose and, though Stéphane Mallarmé still thought in the period 1864–1867 of writing a tragedy in verse, that was not where the future of the theater lay, at least so far as speech-drama was concerned. In opera, it was in these same years that Richard Wagner and Giuseppe Verdi were calling on the power of music to supply something akin to what poetry at its best could provide. For Ibsen, with the social themes his drama was about to deal with, there was no place for music. His intention in the later plays—as early as 1874—was to achieve complete naturalism: "It was the illusion of reality I wanted to produce," he tells Edmund Gosse. He stopped writing verse of any kind after his *Poems* appeared in 1871. As he wrote twelve years later, in reply to a request for a verse prologue, he was devoting himself by that time to "the very much more difficult art of writing in straightforward, realistic, everyday language." Many critics agree with John Northam that despite this intention all his plays, "early or late, in verse or in modern prose, are a form of poetry," and it is true that a more mystical element enters some of the last plays of all. It is true also that the themes of the earlier plays, with all their personal quality, the expression of Ibsen's struggle for self-knowledge, are often present in the last twelve. All the same, the last twelve form a group together, and it is on them that Ibsen's reputation usually rests.

By 1868 Ibsen was the best-known Scandinavian in Europe. In 1869 he was invited to be Norway's representative at the opening of the Suez Canal; two years later he was given a high Danish decoration; two years later still there was a student torchlight procession in his honor in Christiania. Translations of his plays began to appear in several languages. *The League of Youth* (1869) had made no great mark. *Pillars of Society*, published in 1877, must, however, have been surprising to readers of all countries, following as it did on *Emperor and Galilean.* Instead of a huge philosophical, "all-embracing" play, Ibsen had written about one of the scandals of his time, the practice of sending ships to sea in unseaworthy condition for the sake of collecting insurance money. Coupled with this social evil as objects of attack were Norwegian insularity, relations between workers and employers, sexual morality, and women's rights, all new themes for the stage. In addition, the form of the play had turned out, after the first act, to be almost like French classical drama in its concentration on a few characters. At the same time, there was a painstaking development of motivation and plot, with a realistic background, and a subplot connected with speculation in railway development. The skill with which all this is combined shows genius. One strand tangles with another, threats and near disasters emerge with uncommon power; as one plot sinks out of sight for a while another rises to spin the whole work forward. The craftsmanship displayed is remarkable. What is lacking is personality, individuality: nobody in the play is memorable for his or her own sake; the protagonists are rather pieces to be moved in a complex game. The most prominent are either puritanically naive, like the voice of conscience represented by Lona Hessel, or villainous hypocrites like Bernick, the man she has traveled across the sea from America to expose. In the play's conclusion, though Bernick makes a public confession and Lona declares that the spirit of truth and the spirit of freedom are the pillars of society, it is easy to see she has been duped. The naiveté and cynical opportunism of characters in all the later plays have begun to show themselves. The extremely complicated patterns are all in black and white. The life of the play comes less from the characters than from the conflict within Ibsen himself.

Bernick and his rival enact again the rivalry of the pretenders to the Norwegian throne, and by implication the rivalry of Ibsen with his fellow dramatists. Even in small details of plot, the same man is voicing his hopes and anxieties, judging himself, pardoning himself, beginning the process over again. Like every other work of Ibsen's this play is part of a single confession, a constantly thwarted desire for more than ordinary life.

But from this time on, Ibsen was master of his craft. Trained in the theater at Bergen and Christiania, he knew precisely what a play was. He had learned, to quote C. E. Montague,

that a play-goer, unlike a reader, cannot skip, and that therefore he must never be allowed to fall into the state of mind in which, if he were reading, he would skip; he learnt that dialogue is effective in the theatre only when every speech produces a distinct change in the relation of the speakers, that it must carry the hearer on over a rippled surface of small surprises to a foreseen goal, piquing curiosity in detail while meeting expectation on the whole; he learned how the characters of a play are mobilized; how their exits and entrances are brought into vital relation with the general purpose of the piece. . . . When an early act of one of the plays ends, you are left with a definite sense of being halfway up a ladder to the top of a wall beyond which there is something interesting. He plays on you like a flute, and knows every vent and stop of your attention. To those who care about the technical qualities of plays, his plays give, on this score alone, a pleasure like that of seeing an expert contrive and exploit long series of happy combinations of position with billiard balls.

(*Dramatic Values*, p. 140)

Modest though that praise becomes, in the final image, it describes the basis on which Ibsen had been building the reputation that was about to culminate in notoriety.

Compared with any other play written in the same half of the century, *Pillars of Society* has an uncommon vigor. It still has not achieved the clean lines and explosive effect of the "tragedy of modern times" Ibsen began in 1878, which turned out to be no tragedy after all, but the first dramatic bombshell in European literature. There had been plays meant to shock before this time: Pierre Augustin Beaumarchais' *The Marriage of Figaro* (1784) and Friedrich von Schiller's *The Robbers* (1781) had stirred revolutionary sentiment, and Daniel François Esprit Auber's opera *La muette de Portici* had in 1831 actually set off a revolution in Brussels. But in the whole history of modern drama there had never before been a stir like the one created by *A Doll's House*.

In some of its essentials, *A Doll's House* takes over popular themes of the previous generation in the theater. The rigid morality of Torvald Helmer and the willingness of his wife, Nora, to sacrifice herself completely for his sake are the stuff not only of Victorian melodrama but also of plays by Hebbel, whose *Maria Magdalene* (1844) and *Herodes und Mariamne* (1850) prepared the ground in some ways. The woman who has sinned and seeks reconciliation with her unbending husband is a stock figure in the repertory of the time. Not that Nora has sinned as Hebbel's Mary Magdalene has sinned—sexually: she has merely forged her dead father's signature on a security in order to raise money to take her ailing husband abroad for the sake of his health. The technicality of her legal offense

and her impulsive generosity can, in the theater, make her seem almost innocent, as stock heroines tend to be. Then there is the villain, Krogstad, who knows Nora's secret and blackmails her with it, partly to revenge himself on her husband (who once dismissed him from his job), partly in the unlikely expectation of succeeding him as manager of the local bank. Blackmailing villains are equally parts for which any repertory company of the time would have had an actor always available. Contemporary audiences would also have recognized the fatal letter, which Krogstad sends to Helmer when Nora refuses to meet his demands and which is lodged in the glass-frosted letter box behind the front door, in full view for most of act 3, adding visibly to the tension. The grotesquely lugubrious Dr. Rank, rotting with disease, and announcing that he will send a card with a black cross over his name when the final horrible disintegration has begun, contrasts with these stereotyped figures like a death's head.

There is a solemnity about them all, relieved now and then by flightiness in Nora, which has led to an interpretation of the play (by Hermann Weigand) as high comedy of the subtlest order. Ibsen, it has been argued, cannot have taken these people as seriously as they take themselves and is really treating them all with light irony. Yet the fact remains that he spoke at first of writing a tragedy, and in his preliminary notes he intended Nora to meet the catastrophic revelation of her misdeed first with despair, then with resistance, then defeat. Perhaps he did write a good deal of the play with that pattern in mind. As George Bernard Shaw wrote:

Up to a certain point in the last act, *A Doll's House* is a play that might be turned into a very ordinary French drama by the excision of a few lines, and the substitution of a sentimental happy ending for the famous last scene. . . . But at just that point in the last act, the heroine very unexpectedly . . . stops her emotional acting and says: "We must sit down and discuss all this that has been happening between us." And it was by this new technical feature, this addition of a new movement, as musicians would say, to the dramatic form, that *A Doll's House* conquered Europe and founded a new school of dramatic art. (*The Quintessence of Ibsenism*, 2nd ed., p. 192)

It is not in fact a "discussion" that Nora unexpectedly proposes. The new feature is Nora's unheard-of refusal to submit to her husband, even after the blackmailer has changed his tune, and her decision to slam the door on Helmer, abandoning her children as well, to go away and face the world on her own. That door slamming echoed soon after in all the theaters of Europe. Translations into a dozen languages appeared in a few years. The play was so much the topic of discussion that it was rumored society hostesses were marking their invitation cards with a request not to introduce it into conversation. British newspapers were scandalized: "A morbid and unwholesome play"; "Unnatural, immoral, and, in its concluding scene, essentially undramatic"; "Strained deductions, lack of wholesome human nature, pretentious inconclusiveness. . . . Cannot be allowed to pass without a word of protest against the dreary and sterilizing principle which it seeks to embody." These were among many quotations chosen by William Archer, Ibsen's translator, to demonstrate the absurd prejudices of the playwright's opponents, many of them evidently Torvald Helmers in replica.

For a middle-class woman in ordinary circumstances, Nora had done the unthinkable. The tarantella with which she concludes act 2, dancing in a frenzy like a woman bitten by a deadly spider, is a dramatic demonstration of the Dionysiac fury often latent in Ibsen's women: a sign of more than suburban unhappiness, a declaration of intent to find a new life altogether. For the first time, Ibsen gives the hint of an expression here to a theme that was to occupy him continually: the possibility of mankind transforming itself into a race of revelers. Yet Nora is also continuing the struggle for what Brand and Peer Gynt had sought, the realization of her true self, and this was the culmination of a long process in European thought. Since medieval times the right of the individual to self-realization had been more and more acknowledged; fifteenth-century Florence had asserted it explicitly and with a new force; Jean Jacques Rousseau, in his *Confessions* (1781), had announced his intention of challenging the Almighty to condemn him for being the man he had been created to be. Few women had profited by this individualism. But before Nora, no woman in fiction had made such an impact, or had combined self-realization with a desire for the dynamic revelry that Friedrich Nietzsche was beginning to see, at just about the same time, as the proper cure for overcivilized Europeans. The suffragettes and the women's liberation movements of this century, having gained in importance for several decades, received a great impetus. The questions that still hover over *A Doll's House* remain, all the same: Was Ibsen serious? Was his meaning ironical? Did the failure of Brand and Peer Gynt to realize themselves still play a part in his thought? What was the melodramatic action meant to imply?

As a married couple, Helmer and Nora are an easy target for satire, he with the prattle about his little sweet tooth, his little squirrel, she with her flaunting of macaroons, her pretty ways, answering to the image he has made for her. If a tragedy had been intended, a less stridently possessive male might have been conceived, a less obviously foolish doter and dominator. Nora is drawn more in the round: her teasing of Rank with a silk stocking is in keeping with the woman who is growing out of subservience, and her delighted games with her children are in the vein of Leo Tolstoy's *Anna Karenina*, published a few years earlier, in 1875–1876. But Tolstoy's concern both for the rigidly moral husband and for the passionate Anna puts his novel on a different plane. The husband, Karenin, is not satirized as Helmer is, however serious his neglect of his wife has been; and Anna, though she abandons her husband and ultimately kills herself, follows through her decision to live with her lover. Nora, in leaving home, is acting naively, on sudden impulse. She has no job in prospect, no man in prospect, no one to whom she can turn for comfort. Her children are likely to be well looked after by the nanny, but she has not weighed what absence from them will mean, and she may be back in a few days or weeks, with or without a new arrangement with Helmer. Ibsen's own sense that the play solved little is shown by his letter to Sophie Adlersparre of 1882: "I couldn't remain standing at *A Doll's House;* after Nora, Mrs. Alving of necessity had to come." In other words, the liberated woman who saw herself as Nora must be confronted with the consequences of liberation in his next play, *Ghosts.*

But though Ibsen was conscious after completing *A Doll's House* that he had not found the solution to Nora's troubles that his admirers might have liked, it is less probable that in the writing of the play he felt the same. The mimicry of contemporary melodrama, though it ensured some success, also made for the crudities that damage the play. It succeeded more as a propagandist piece than Ibsen had intended it should.

A dramatist needs to attend to the fashion of the day more than novelists or poets do. Once in print, they can wait for fame to come, if it is ever going to. The dramatist as a rule needs an audience and a theater to establish his work by means of a spectacular success. Ibsen both followed fashion and created it. Using the French form of the "well-made play," he gave audiences what they knew. Treating themes of political and social interest, he shocked and aroused them. With *Ghosts* he established himself as both a superb playwright and a dealer in unmentionables, for where Nora had merely slammed a door, Mrs. Alving was confronted with the scandalous fact of her son's inherited disease, apparently venereal, and the public reacted as though he had meant to infect them personally. For some years, none of the bigger Scandinavian theaters would produce the play. In Germany the police refused at first to allow public performances. In England *Ghosts* was not performed till 1891, to the accompaniment of remarks like "a dirty act done publicly," "naked loathsomeness," and even "maunderings of nookshotten Norwegians," "muck-ferreting dogs."

But unlike Eugène Brieux in his *Damaged Goods* (1902), Ibsen did not mean to go into clinical detail about syphilis or gonorrhea to shock errant young men out of sowing wild oats. The disease of Mrs. Alving's son, Oswald, is as much symbolic as real, a way of demonstrating in real terms how the dead hand of the past haunts the present. Mrs. Alving had intended to be a liberated woman. But the conventional proprieties had made her cover up her husband's depraved behavior with other women. She had sent Oswald abroad throughout his childhood, to prevent him from turning into a man such as his father had been. But as the play begins, her expectations for Oswald are quickly dashed: she hears him offstage flirting with Regine, the maid, exactly as his father had done years before with the young woman's mother.

The revelation is melodrama in the highest degree. Mrs. Alving stares wild-eyed at the half-open door, manages to bring out hoarsely the words "Ghosts! Those two in the conservatory . . . come back to haunt us," and walks unsteadily away. So at least the stage directions indicate, though a modern director is likely to underplay the whole scene. What cannot be underplayed is Mrs. Alving's prudery, and her insistence on supplying a reference to the symbolic title of the play as the first-act curtain falls. Oswald's brief flirtation in the back room is nothing out of the ordinary, and although he is imitating his father, he has done nothing to suggest the terrifying symbolism his mother perceives when she speaks shortly afterward of ghosts spreading across the whole country, "as numerous as the sands of the sea." Ibsen's later tendency to give worldwide significance to events and characters not impressive enough to bear such a weight begins to show itself more clearly here than in any of his previous works. His symbols begin to take on a life of their own, almost independent of the reality of the plays.

What has to be admired is the construction. Basically, the theme of *Ghosts* moves toward one dramatic moment: the revelation by Oswald that he is infected, and his simultaneous demand that his mother put an end to his life to spare him torment. Little development is needed to arrive at this point, but to keep the action moving Ibsen provides a subplot: the carpenter Engstrand first involves Mrs. Alving's former admirer, Pastor Manders, in the burning down of the new orphanage about to be named after Mrs. Alving's husband, then blackmails him into acquiescence in the establishment of a brothel Engstrand is planning. In the course of the dialogue, Ibsen introduces so much information about events before the curtain rose that an exact reconstruction of the relations between the Alvings can be built up, obtruding at times on the characterization: there are frequent speeches in which people remind each other of past events, more in order to inform the audience about them than to display their own forgetfulness.

On the other hand, Ibsen is able to introduce so much about the past that various contradictory explanations can be given. What is not seen onstage, but only talked about, has no firm hold on the audience's memory, and it often appears as though Mrs. Alving is paying the penalty for her attempt to stifle her husband's natural enjoyment of life. Thanks to her, it seems, he took to the company of loose women and so contracted the disease that has now been passed on to her son. That, at any rate, can be deduced from various remarks, and often is. At other times, it appears that Captain Alving was consorting with prostitutes before Mrs. Alving met him; and from still another of her accounts of the past she seems to have done very well in coping with

this man who lounged on the sofa drinking all day and expected her to provide him with women at night. It is something of a mystery how she managed not only to keep his sex life and drunkenness from public knowledge for so many years, but even to establish for him a great reputation as a charitable benefactor to society. The irony in the name of the Captain Alving Orphanage is self-evident, although it is based on an assumption that local people have been as simpleminded as Pastor Manders himself is. Yet there is nothing to show which account of the past is true, whether Mrs. Alving is guilty or merely too self-critical.

As always, Ibsen's deepest preoccupations are involved. Mrs. Alving is as much a seeker after self-realization as are Brand, Peer Gynt, and Oswald himself. The horrible moment at the final curtain, when she senses the recurrence of the brain disease that will destroy his reason, is his cry to his mother to give him the sun. This echoes a recurrent theme in the plays, which had last appeared in *Emperor and Galilean*, where the cry clearly had a mystical meaning. Oswald now calls for the supreme revelation that had tempted Ibsen all his life, the complete mastery of outflowing benevolence, or love, and ambiguously the power and scorching destructiveness that the sun symbolizes. That revelation had been darkly foreshadowed at the end of act 2, when the flames of the burning orphanage were seen across the width of the stage through the conservatory windows. It was the vision of this hell that gave Oswald occasion to say, "We are all burning down," as indeed he himself was. Now at the end of act 3 the same conservatory window, dark all through the act, gray with misty rain in act 1, is lit up by the rising sun. Oswald, sitting in his chair with his back to it, cannot see it, and there seems to be some significance in that. (Modern productions omitting both the fire and the sun flaunt their disregard of Ibsen's clear stage directions. Whatever the directions may mean, the audience has a right to see them realized.) This final moment is like the ambiguous avalanche at the end of *Brand,* a simultaneous affirmation of destructiveness and life-giving power.

The scandalized voices in the British press could not have been conscious of Ibsen's deeper intentions. The assumption that he simply meant to shock his audiences ignored the fact that he had provided in disease a credible modern equivalent to the Fate of ancient Greek drama, combining with it his pervading concern with individual freedom. Mrs. Alving would like to be completely without inhibitions. When she overhears Oswald flirting with Regine, she at once thinks they should marry, though they are as yet unaware of what she already knows, that they are half-brother and half-sister, and though as yet neither of them has spoken of marriage. To her mind, incest is no barrier if they can be happy in this way. Similarly she blames herself for restraining her husband's "joy of life," which for him meant an uninhibited sexual life that was repugnant to her. *Ghosts* ends with her self-contradicting realization both that such total freedom is the cause of her son's disease and that she herself is responsible for the disease by having tried to limit the freedom and thereby driven her husband to excesses. As with the symbolism of the rising sun, there is an unresolved paradox at the center of the play. The concept of "Emperor," or self-affirmation in this world, still conflicts with "Galilean," or total self-denial. Brand and Peer Gynt still continue their alternating dialectical dance.

The same alternation marks the next three plays, in which the position of idealists like Mrs. Alving is viewed from various points. The scandal started by *Ghosts* seemed to Ibsen like a revelation of what the play had partly been maintaining, that society was rotten to the core. He went on now to write one of his most vigorous and unified works, *An Enemy of the People,* which explores the position of a man not unlike himself (and in whom he acknowledged a certain resemblance), who experiences the hypocrisy of small-town businessmen. Dr. Stockmann arrives at a Norwegian spa, after a long absence, to discover that the water provided to visitors who drink it for their health is infected by sewage that has been allowed to seep into the spring. Announcing this fact, he expects it to be given wide publicity and to see the spring, for which he as medical adviser is responsible, properly cleaned and reestablished. Instead, local interests combine to shut him up. The profits made through the spa industry are more important to the town than the health of visitors, and even the prospect of a long-term decline in the spa's reputation is of no immediate concern. Stockmann makes impassioned demands, in vain; as his anger rises so does the violent mood in the town. His house is attacked, its windows smashed; he loses his job and is finally left isolated, sustained only by the faith placed in him by his own family. His final realization is another paradox, that the strongest man is the man who is most alone.

Stockmann's position is so like Ibsen's as to make this play, more than any other, seem like a personal statement. The continual energy of the play adds to the impression that it was a heated retort to the condemnations of *Ghosts* that Ibsen had had to endure. Society, he must have felt, was infected with a virulent disease. The idealist in him, who existed alongside the pessimist, had been outraged, for the "enemy of the people" was no enemy to Ibsen himself. The infected spring discovered by Stockmann implies, so far as Stockmann is concerned, that the whole human race is infected. Instead of looking for allies inside and outside the town or, failing that, deciding to leave this relatively minor matter for something with more political importance, Stockmann begins to rage with the demand that the whole community should be disinfected. Before long he is talking of revolution, and soon after states that "all the spiritual sources of our life" are being poisoned. He speaks of exterminating leading politicians "like any other pest." The whole community, he declares, ought to be wiped out like vermin; the population of the whole country deserves the same fate. His egoism becomes inflated to the point where only laughter can make the play tolerable.

Yet Ibsen took Stockmann seriously enough to say that although "the Doctor is more muddle-headed than I am," he has other traits that "make people more willing to hear certain things from him that, if I myself had said them, they would not perhaps have taken so well." Whether he thought Stockmann's contempt for the "damned, compact, liberal majority" would be one of his more acceptable attitudes is a moot point. Ibsen was no democrat when he told the Danish critic Georg Brandes that he would join a revolution that promoted the abolition of the state ("He is a complete anarchist, wants to wipe everything out," wrote a friend); his admiration for absolutist autocracy as an encouragement to freedom lovers suggests that he was closer to Stockmann than he realized.

The plays of this period oscillate in an almost regular movement, alternately representing attitudes of self-affirmation and self-denial, and there was something to be gained dramatically from this procedure. A character as oblivious of others as Stockmann can arouse opposition and create confrontations that suit a crude form of theater as much as they suit crude politics. To have made him more self-aware would have been to forgo a play apparently concerned with the state of the world at large, and to substitute for it a play about a small local scandal. It could be left to another play to show the shortcomings of the idealist, and this Ibsen did in *The Wild Duck*.

Symbolism now becomes more significant, and more ambiguous, than in any of the previous plays. The plot is built around a duck wounded by a huntsman after an expedition shooting wild birds; the huntsman, old Werle, has presented it to the girl Hedvig, generally believed to be his employee Hjalmar's daughter, though more probably his own daughter by Hjalmar's wife, Gina. The idealist this time is a zealous puritan, Gregers Werle, old Werle's son, whose attitude toward revealing

truth at all costs is akin to Stockmann's. Gregers is determined that Hjalmar shall realize the truth—that Hedvig is not his own child but has been foisted on him by the old man. Only when Hjalmar has faced that truth, he thinks, and forgiven his wife her adultery, can the father, mother, and daughter live together as a happy family: anything less than a truthful relationship means hypocrisy. But when the moment of truth comes, Hjalmar cannot stand it and proposes to desert his wife and child.

Without the duck, this would be a simple tale without reverberance, a newspaper story dramatized. With the duck, it becomes so complex as to lend interpretation a wide rein. On the one hand, the duck is a wild bird, a free creature from outside civilization symbolizing the world of freedom that Gregers, like Stockmann, Mrs. Alving, and Nora, wants to make real. On the other, it is a wounded creature kept in a loft also containing pigeons and hens, separated by a curtain from an attic studio. Here Hjalmar's father, Ekdal, who works in the studio, occasionally goes to shoot a rabbit. The home of the duck is at the top of the house (appropriately enough for an ideal) in a room where the clock has stopped, as though it lived in a timeless eternity. Yet it is also a suicidal bird that, when it was shot by Werle, plunged to the bottom of the water and held on to the weeds with its beak (as ducks are said to do, in the play, when menaced), meaning (like Oswald) to make sure of death rather than suffer a hampered life. Here the symbolic sense becomes more complex, for Gregers sees Hedvig as a kind of wild duck, and regards it as his mission in life to save her and old Ekdal, as well as Hjalmar Ekdal, from their suicidal tendencies by forcing them to come up from the depths of their illusions to the light of day, like a well-trained dog retrieving a bird for the huntsman. The duck must return to its wild state of natural freedom, which is as much as to say that Hjalmar and the others must be made free by truth.

This symbolism gives a wider dimension to

Gregers' zeal. He is not simply demanding that unpleasant truths be faced, but implying that by facing them Hjalmar will become transformed. Ibsen's own conviction that the age he lived in was a kind of "closure," and that a new age containing the conditions for the potential happiness of mankind was about to emerge (as he said in a speech on 24 September 1887), is perhaps involved here too. The utopian "third Empire" announced in *Emperor and Galilean* was still in his mind. But the symbol is a clumsy device, as he himself realizes when he allows characters within the play itself to comment on the awkwardness of symbolism generally. In fact the plot leads to a tragic conclusion precisely because Gregers chooses to talk in symbols. When he suggests to Hedvig that she should set her father an example by sacrificing for his sake the dearest possession she has, he means her to shoot the wild duck. But Hedvig has grown so accustomed to symbolism that she cannot take him literally, and shoots instead the symbolic wild duck that she is herself. Far from saving her from suicide, Gregers has caused her to kill herself, and precisely because he has brought into his truth-seeking a wider dimension. If he had not talked in terms of dogs and wild ducks, the confusion might have been avoided.

Truth and self-delusion, reality and appearance are weighty themes that have helped to give the play a long life on the stage. It may be that Mary McCarthy was right to say that the plays "grow more grandiose as the symbolic content inflates them," that Ibsen mechanically manipulates emotions. It is hard to defend *The Wild Duck* against the criticism that its characters are as gullible and naive as any in the plays before it. The new feature in Ibsen's work is the author's self-awareness, which shows up his symbolism even as he uses it. But this may be no more than a means of self-preservation. In the doctrine of some German romantics the perfect work of literature was the one that was completely conscious of its own limitations, and the criticism of symbolism contained within *The Wild Duck* itself could be regarded by Ibsen as a claim that the play was unassailable, being its own judge. That would account for the continuing use of symbolism of the same sort in later plays. It is as though awareness of the sometimes aesthetically disastrous effects of his symbolism granted him indulgence to use it at will.

The relevance of the symbol in *Rosmersholm* to the play as a whole is slight, though it does something to make the plot more portentous. The central character here is Johannes Rosmer, descendant of a long line of Christian clergy who have lived for generations in his family home, although he himself no longer has the faith of his forefathers. Some years before the play begins, an attractive and lively young woman, Rebecca West, came to live in his lonely house and determined to have his love for herself. Full of advanced ideas, she played on the conscience of his childless wife, Beate, urging her to see that Rosmer needed the child Beate was unable to bear him, and eventually driving her to throwing herself into the millrace outside the house. All this Rebecca reveals to Rosmer in act 3, adding that at the time she saw nothing wrong in her own actions. She had intended that she and Rosmer should "go forward together on the road toward freedom," but saw that this could never be while he was languishing in the gloom of his marriage. Salvation lay only in driving Beate to suicide. Now, after the event, she sees with Rosmer's eyes, still influenced by Christianity, that she was wrong. She is ennobled by her new vision, but downcast at the crippling of her will by conscience. Rosmer, whose mission all along has been to ennoble mankind, is downcast himself at this revelation. To reassure him, and to prove to him that men and women can act nobly, Rebecca agrees to his demand that she atone by throwing herself into the millrace exactly as Beate had done. With this understanding, Rosmer's faith in humanity revives, and he is prepared again to go on with his mission.

Paradoxically, however, he feels that he must also demonstrate to Rebecca that he shares her "unfettered view of life," and can do so only by drowning along with her. At length they both agree on this course of action, and are last seen from the window of the house, offstage, leaping into the foaming torrent.

Henry James, before he became converted to advocating Ibsen's plays, called *Rosmersholm* "dreary," "of a grey mediocrity . . . jusqu'à être bête [to the point of being silly]." Sigmund Freud took it completely seriously, writing a detailed analysis of Rebecca's character, in which he saw the Oedipus complex at work. The playgoer will certainly be struck by a baldness in the language, a mechanical note in the dialogue, especially near the end when Rosmer and Rebecca discuss whether he is going to die with her, or she with him, and decide indisputably as they move toward the stream that they are going together. Rosmer's motives, first in allowing Rebecca to atone in this way and then in destroying the purpose of it by not going on with his mission after all, are paradoxical to the point of absurdity.

Some symbolism was needed, Ibsen may have felt, to give more reverberance to this lame ending, and it is provided by the ancestral legend of the "white horses" of Rosmersholm, whose foaming manes are seen in the torrent where Rosmer and Rebecca end their lives. But the reverberance is hollow. The horses have seldom been mentioned until this moment and have no connection with the events and motives in the play; they are rather a romantic adornment, a suggestion of Fate at work that is far less appropriate than the inherited disease in *Ghosts*. *Rosmersholm* is not generally regarded as one of Ibsen's best plays. Its vaguenesses about "going forward together," "ennobling mankind," and advocating "faith in humanity" contribute to this low estimate.

By contrast, *The Lady from the Sea* is often enjoyed for its serenity, its tranquil atmosphere and untragic conclusion. It has been compared in its theme of provincial nostalgia

with the plays of Anton Chekhov, and it is true that much of the art of the play relies, to an unusual extent for Ibsen, on ensemble acting, rhythms, and apparently casual conversations very much in Chekhovian style. The "lady from the sea" herself, Ellida, is all the same recognizably an Ibsen heroine. In some ways she is a companion-figure to Rebecca, although Ellida, aware of the same fundamental demand for freedom, is the happier woman.

Like Rebecca, Ellida lives with a man, Wangel, whose wife has died; like her again, she feels a strange attraction to water, something like the "oceanic feeling" spoken of in another connection by Freud. Living near the sea, she is constantly haunted by it, to the point that she is almost identified with it: it is so apt a symbol for the quenching of all individuality that its symbolism scarcely becomes apparent. In contrast to *Rosmersholm*, however, the play begins not in a dark room in a northern parsonage, but on a warm and brilliantly clear summer morning. The relaxed atmosphere continues almost throughout; even the curtain between acts does not fall on moments of suspense.

Dramatic action is introduced through the Stranger, a seaman to whom Ellida was once betrothed and who represents the attraction to the sea that she so strongly feels even as she seems reconciled to her placid and unsatisfying marriage. It is not fast-moving action, like that in *An Enemy of the People*. Ordinary talk continues for much of the play, establishing the peaceable world from which Ellida feels herself excluded by her memories of the Stranger. Even when she rejects the Stranger and finally declares her continuing attachment to her husband, the calm surface is scarcely rippled. For the first time since *Love's Comedy* (1862), Ibsen had written a play with a happy ending.

In that earlier play the hero, the poet Falk, takes his leave in act 3 with the words:

The instrument I play is double-tongued,
a dulcimer with underlying strings

and two-fold note; one high and light in tone,
singing of happiness; and down below
another, deep and constant, answering.

The answering low note is present also in *The Lady from the Sea*. When the Stranger is first mentioned, he is spoken of as a murderer and seems meant to embody a terrifying elemental power. Ellida's earlier "marriage" to him (as he regards it) thus becomes a representation of her one-time unity with some infinite, boundless life to which she longs to return, something like the Dionysian liberty that characters in the earlier plays often crave. When he does appear, the Stranger seems to have been deliberately diminished. What he means to Ellida is not in doubt. She is terrified by him, above all by his eyes, which are more than she can endure. It seems clear, however, that Ibsen did not mean the audience to regard the Stranger in the same light. The murder mentioned earlier, if it was ever committed, seems now to be of no consequence, and the man himself is dressed (according to the stage directions) in a way that must make him look comical. Far from being elemental, he is conciliatory to the point almost of self-destruction. Producing a pistol when Ellida declines to abandon her husband and his family for the sake of joining him at sea, he threatens to shoot not her but himself, and eventually he leaves with every mark of consideration and respect for her.

Ellida seems in the end to have recognized that her longing for the elemental could lead to peace rather than destruction: her free choice is itself elemental. Unlike Rebecca, she is not impelled by her desire for freedom to drive herself and her husband to insanity. Ibsen, for his part, seems to be moving, as Shakespeare did in his later years, toward a phase of plays of reconciliation—there is, at least, one more play of his with a similarly hopeful ending, and the parallel with Shakespeare has been noted by Kenneth Muir. It is less clear why the Stranger's dangerous aspect should never receive any dramatic representation, being entirely accounted for in a few words spoken about him, or even why Ibsen wanted him to wear a tam-o'-shanter on his bushy red hair. Yet the relaxed atmosphere is a pleasing Indian summer, with no hint of the darkness gathering in Ibsen's mind for his next production.

Hedda Gabler is by general agreement the outstanding work of his later period, as it was also the play that established his fame in England. Until this time, though he had been feted in Scandinavia and Germany, he had still not been performed in France; and in England his supporters, Edmund Gosse, William Archer, and Arthur Symons, still struggled to make headway. The turning point for English-speaking audiences is marked by the change of attitude of Henry James, who until then had privately confided in Gosse that he could see nothing to admire in the plays he had read. In 1891 James published an article, "On the Occasion of *Hedda Gabler*," having seen the play performed a few weeks earlier, and the emergence on Ibsen's side of a formidable and widely respected champion effectively silenced all opposition. Shaw's book *The Quintessence of Ibsenism*, appearing in the same year, seemed to settle the matter, although the Irish poets and dramatists W. B. Yeats and J. M. Synge remained unpersuaded. In Europe as a whole, Ibsen was now the master dramatist. Within a few years James openly preferred him to Shakespeare; James Joyce wrote his now-famous review in the *Fortnightly Review* of 1900, declaring that there were few better things in all drama than Ibsen's last eleven plays; Shaw observed that the issues treated by Ibsen concerned the modern age in a way that Shakespeare's had ceased to do.

This tragedy of the times was the culmination of a development heralded by G. E. Lessing and Beaumarchais more than a hundred years earlier. The period when an audience could feel strongly for the situation of a prince or an aristocrat, Lessing had said in his *Hamburg Dramaturgy* (1767–1768), had now passed. The tragic dramatist must concern himself with characters like those in his audience, no longer the courtiers of Louis XIV or Frederick the Great, but city-dwelling merchants and other members of the middle class. The result from Lessing onward had often been sentimental. Accompanying the theory was a belief in the essential goodness of man that tended to obscure evil or to suggest that it was either redeemable by the love of a good woman or a step on the path to perfect good. With Friedrich Nietzsche's *The Birth of Tragedy* (1872), however, a new conception, congenial to Ibsen, entered the theory of tragedy. For the Greeks, Nietzsche maintained, tragedy had originated in the worship of the god Dionysus, dedicated to the darker side of human nature, to elemental passions, orgiastic revels that might end in blood lust and cruelty. Only through the experience of this exultant affirmation of all that Lessing would have regarded as inhuman, Nietzsche now asserted, did the Greeks come to learn the peace of Apollo. The true Greek tragedian worshiped in the temple of both the Apollonian and the Dionysian gods.

Ibsen's characters had from the beginning had in them something like a demand for Dionysian revelation. His earliest play, *Catiline* (1850), had included a woman called Furia, whose fury had inspired the hero to revolutionary action. Later plays included warrior women of Viking times or modern women with similar qualities. The unfettered ruthlessness of Rebecca West, cold and calculating though it is, is distantly akin to Nietzsche's amoral Dionysians. Nora's wild tarantella is a dance of fury. Ellida Wangel's love of the sea is akin in a different way. Following these two now came Hedda Gabler, a woman who, if she had any ideal at all, would have liked to see her lover coming back to her "with vine leaves in his hair," a reveler returning from a Dionysian orgy.

Hedda is a woman cast as the heroine of a middle-class tragedy, and she knows it. Her surroundings are not poor but commonplace,

her husband is not a tyrant but a booby, her prospects of escape from pettiness are nil. Nil, nothingness, perpetual annihilation of every spark of life is her experience from moment to moment. "The pale, apparently cold beauty," Ibsen writes of her. "Great demands on life and happiness . . . Hedda's desperation is a conviction that life must offer so many possibilities of happiness, but she can't catch sight of any of them. It is the want of a goal in life that torments her." With that, he states the paradox of Hedda's existence. She does from time to time seem to make, or to want to make, great demands on life. But many commentators have seen her as fairly large in her negations, and it is equally often apparent that she has no demands and cannot see any that she might make. Mean and moody, she is never magnificent.

The chance of magnificence presents itself to her when a man arrives whose love affairs used to interest her. Eilert Løvborg's return to town with Hedda's former classmate Thea Elvsted arouses in Hedda the thought of escape from the cosy platitudes of her husband, Tesman, and the sexual blandishments of a friend of the house, Judge Brack. Where Tesman can only research narrowly into the lace industry of medieval Brabant, Løvborg has written a supposedly distinguished work, a book with a wide historical sweep and a vision of the future that sounds possibly meretricious; Hedda now sees her opportunity to inspire him to still greater achievements, though it has been argued that she does so more to inflate her own ego than out of interest in him, and almost equally as much because it provides her with a new chance to torment Thea Elvsted, as she used to do in their schooldays.

The first climax of the plot occurs when Løvborg and Tesman are invited to a dinner at Judge Brack's at which Løvborg is to retire to a private room and read his new manuscript to his friends. Here Hedda sees her chance to control the destiny of another human being. Løvborg will, she believes, go to the party and return, like Dionysus himself, "with vine leaves in his hair." The great release from humdrum conventionality is about to burst open for her, and she exults in it. But it is an absurd delusion, as Ibsen makes clear. Løvborg is a reformed alcoholic who does not dare take another drink for fear he will succumb again. In urging him to risk a return to his old addiction, Hedda is not only cruelly irresponsible, but self-frustrating—no Dionysus can come from a fresh enslavement. Again, a dinner at the highly respectable home of Brack, due to last two and a half hours, some of the time being spent listening to Løvborg reading his manuscript, is unlikely to effect much of a change. Hedda's expectations sound like conscious mockery of any desire for release.

As things turn out, the highly respectable party ends up, not so very incredibly, in a brothel. Løvborg, degraded and demoralized, loses his manuscript, though for reasons of his own he tells Thea he has destroyed it. Hedda's plan, if it was a plan, has failed. But she has other and yet more ruthless plans in mind. Meeting him in his despair, she allows him to borrow one of her father's pistols so that he may make the great gesture of meeting fearlessly his own death. There is no need for her to do so, as she realizes when her husband returns home with the missing manuscript. If she wished, she could restore Løvborg's confidence. But swearing Tesman to secrecy about having found it, she burns the manuscript in the stove, page by page, ensuring that Løvborg really does have nothing to live for. Pregnant herself with Tesman's child, she sees the manuscript as Løvborg's child with Thea and aborts it as she would gladly abort her own. She waits now for news of his noble self-execution.

Disappointment comes a second time. Løvborg can neither live nor die splendidly. News comes that he has shot himself not in the temple, which Hedda would regard as the right place, but in the belly, or, according to some translators, in the sexual organs, and has died horribly, and perhaps merely by accident. Even her most obscene scheming has failed.

Hedda differs from Euripides' Medea, who destroys her lover's children, in that she has no fiery passion, and does not act out of revenge. Unlike Medea, she has not been cruelly wronged, but has chosen her husband in the expectation of living an untroubled life of luxury, and totally misjudged both him and his prospects of promotion. Even when she speaks of "lust for life" she is demolishing any hope of realizing it. An infinite perversity grinds away in her, eating her own life and the life of others.

With Løvborg dead, there now remains only one further necessity, to destroy herself. To be brought to this, however, she needs some incentive, and by means of a neat manipulation in the action she is offered one. Judge Brack returns after Løvborg's death to tell her that he has recognized the pistol Løvborg used as one of a pair that belonged to her father, and threatens to inform the police of this if Hedda does not consent to become his mistress. Like most blackmail in Ibsen's plays, this is a bait too easily swallowed. Nothing in this revelation of Brack's can point to Hedda's connivance in the suicide of Løvborg. For once, however, Hedda refuses to deceive. The idea of making love with anyone, even Løvborg, has always been repugnant to her, and to be threatened with Brack's sexual dictation is more than she can bear. Very nearly the last blow has been struck, and she will be deprived of freedom forever. In a way that provides a swift ending to the plot, Tesman himself blocks off all escape. This naive and completely conventional husband announces, surprisingly, that from now on he proposes to spend his evenings away from home with another woman, Thea Elvsted, piecing together the notes left by Løvborg in an effort to restore and publish the lost manuscript. Judge Brack, he assures Hedda, will gladly keep her company during his absences, and Brack gleefully confirms his own willingness.

There is absolutely no way out now but for Hedda to take the remaining pistol and shoot herself, as she expected Løvborg to do. Tesman, hearing the shot, rushes into the back room and shouts back, neatly making Hedda's point for her: "Shot herself! Shot herself in the temple! Think of that!" This time the correct symbolic form of suicide has been adopted. The cynic Brack lies half prostrate in his armchair as the curtain falls on his line, "But good God Almighty . . . people don't do such things!" Middle-class morality, as it is called, is shamed by this determined action.

Any notion that this is a romantically beautiful death is undermined by Ibsen's stage direction, which requires Hedda first to play a wild dance tune on the piano in the adjoining room—a reminder of Nora's tarantella—and then to put her head out between the dividing curtains and mimic Tesman's prim objection. This disembodied mockery is an unsentimental rejection of all Tesman and Brack stand for. Almost simultaneously the piano music is a fleeting affirmation of the Dionysian: the paradoxical ambiguity of earlier plays recurs again, since this is the prelude to Hedda's death, her negation. Hedda finally rejects humanity and all its works. At the same time, however, she dies, romantically speaking, a noble death. She has the courage of her conviction that her world is not worth living in.

The play is of a different order from anything else Ibsen had written. Hedda emerges with surprising force for a character so negative in every way. Where Shakespeare's Timon of Athens begins in generosity and ends disillusioned, she begins in disillusion as though she had never known any other condition. Where Iago eagerly relishes the thought of Othello's downfall, she is coldly destructive, giving the barest hint of what she would prefer to the spectacle of mediocrity all around her— a snatch of a tune, a reference to classical myth, and that is all. The limitations of her opposition to such petty villains as Brack and such innocent blunderers as Tesman, together with the ordinariness of her aspirations in marrying him, deprive her of the stature she might have if she were to confront more serious injustice. Yet although null she is not a nullity. The play has force even in its portrayal of life-denying self-regard. The part of Hedda continues to attract star actresses, who give it more fascination by the very fact that they show her as a live woman who aborts every living instinct.

There is next to no symbolism in *Hedda Gabler*. *The Master Builder* (1892) is entirely concerned with buildings as symbols of human endeavor. The architect Solness, whose career and death it shows, is once again very like a self-portrait of Ibsen, insofar as he had accustomed himself to writing plays on social problems. These inevitably come to mind when Solness regrets having given up building churches for the sake of concentrating on "houses for people to live in." Since *Emperor and Galilean* Ibsen had not written anything with what might be called a religious purpose, though his preoccupation with religious or at least metaphysical questions had gone on appearing beneath the realistic surface. From now on the sense of a mission shows itself in all the plays. Though they continue to be in prose and to be realistic in plot and setting, they correspond to Solness' ambition when he says that in the future he wants to build houses with tall steeples, reaching into the sky.

The symbolic meaning governs the play now even more than it did in *The Wild Duck*, at the same time demonstrating the difficulty of reconciling realism with symbolism. Solness is inspired by another of Ibsen's spirited women, Hilde Wangel (her name is close in sound to the name of the lady from the sea), to whom he confides his ambition. But when she asks him why he does not go on and build the house of his dreams, a house for living in with a great spire attached, his reply is made absurd by the demands of realism. Nobody, he says, would want to buy such a design, and that is evident enough. Symbolically, Solness seems to mean that spiritual or religious striving is in his times irreconcilable with living in everyday circumstances. Realistically, he states a truism.

The steeple has, however, a second, sexual significance that gains in importance as the plot progresses. The challenge to build it, presented by Hilde Wangel, is a test of Solness' virility that ultimately proves disastrous. The last occasion on which he built a steeple was years ago, when Hilde was still a girl: she saw him climb to the top to place a wreath in the traditional topping-out ceremony, and claims—though he himself has no recollection of this—to have had his promise to take her as his "princess" when she grew up. Since then, Solness has been afraid to climb steeples. He felt on that previous occasion he was confronting God, and his jocular reference to Hilde as a little devil gives a wider dimension not seen in Ibsen's plays for many years. In effect, he is reenacting the conflict of the throne-claimant Skule, who seemed to himself to have been tempted on a mountaintop by Satan, as Christ was tempted, with all the riches and glory of the world. Hilde now offers something similar to Solness, urging him (as Hedda urged Løvborg) to build high again, and, though she has little that is diabolical about her, there is an obliviousness in her urging that allows her to triumph even in his catastrophe.

In the final scene Solness has at last built himself a house with a steeple, although, since it is offstage, the oddity of it is not visible. A crowd including his wife, his friends, and Hilde has assembled onstage to witness what is for him a renewed attempt at conquering his fear of heights, though few of them realize that he half expects to be punished by the Almighty for his daring. The dramatic tension increases as the people in sight of the audience indicate his success, to the point where he is standing on the scaffolding at the tip of the spire crowning it with his wreath. Hilde declares that he is disputing with someone, that she can hear a mighty song of triumph; she is herself in an ecstasy of fulfillment.

What follows is anticlimax, not dramatically but technically. Solness is seen by all onstage falling from the tower. It seems that his nerve has failed after all, or that Hilde has brought about his fall—both interpretations have been made—or that there has been an accident. It is vital for the success of the play to know what did happen, since Solness has been presented, so far as the symbolism is concerned, in a grandiose conflict. But Ibsen's stage directions, strangely enough in a man so expert in theater, demand the impossible. He requires the producer to show "a human body and some planks and poles" indistinctly plunging down among the trees at the rear of the scene, and, though he clearly has some symbolic intention, there are no means of making the meaning of the fall comprehensible to the audience. Since no realistic explanation of the falling planks and poles is offered, we must, presumably, suppose Solness has not lost his nerve, but been brought down by some oak-riving thunderbolt from above. But symbolism and reality yawn apart more widely here than ever. For the spectator in the theater the device fails. Even a reader of the play must be left asking himself what has caused the disaster.

A younger contemporary, the German dramatist Frank Wedekind, said that what Ibsen was revealing in *The Master Builder* was his own inability to realize his ambitions. Solness' aim is vague enough to allow of that interpretation, and it would be difficult to make much of a case for the remainder of Ibsen's work. Inwardly, he may well have given up the struggle. The last three plays have nothing to match the black intensity of *Hedda Gabler*.

Little Eyolf has seldom been ranked with the best of Ibsen's work, though it has been seen, with the other last plays, as another of the several parallels with the last "reconciliatory" plays of Shakespeare. For a claim on its behalf that gives it pride of place, the account by John Northam should be read. It must be admitted, and is admitted by Northam, that the two principal characters, Alfred Allmers and his wife, Rita, are presented from the beginning as thoroughgoing egoists. Their emotion at the death of their son, Eyolf, which takes place in act 1, sounds more like the consequence of an affront than like grief. For the play to succeed it must show a process of regeneration, which perhaps, if Northam is right, begins at the moment when Rita first speaks of the hard lives led by the children who, though socially inferior, were in a sense Eyolf's companions. The main line of the action shows Rita and Allmers at length coming to a decision to replace Eyolf, not by another child of their own but with these children of others, whom they propose to invite in his place to use his room and his toys, giving the title of the play a new meaning by their common identity with him. In all this there would seem to be a humanitarian spirit completely opposed to the earlier selfishness of the couple.

But it seldom happens that Ibsen allows an absence of ambiguity. Running beneath this straightforward plot is a current of deeper personal interest to him, the account of Allmers' devotion to his sister, Asta, whom he also at times calls by the name of Eyolf. In this asexual yet extremely close relationship, Ibsen explores the ramifications of egoism in a way that traces it even into the final scene with its would-be selflessness. In a sense, Allmers identifies himself with Asta, and identifies her in turn with his lost son. The decision to welcome the village children as his own is thus, at an unconscious level, a way of preserving himself. All these little Eyolfs are Asta, who is what Carl Gustav Jung would call Allmers' anima, his complement. They are not, as he conceives of them, really distinct from him, and that is reflected in the unreality of his project. The children have not been consulted, nor have their parents; there is no reason to suppose they will fall in with the rather impractical proposals, which can be seen as mere projections of an egoism that still does not know its own bounds. Little Eyolf is Alfred Allmers writ large.

Concern with egoism is still the theme of the contrastingly pessimistic work *John Gabriel Borkman*. Ibsen had achieved worldwide fame by now, but the theme is as old as the earliest of his works, although it receives more concentrated attention here. Borkman, a speculator whose financial deals once brought him a prison sentence, is in real terms a businessman, but by implication still a man like Skule, aiming at world dominion. The steamship lines he once owned encircled the globe, and although his conduct of affairs was held by the law courts to be dishonest, he claims that had it succeeded he would have been a great benefactor to many people.

As the play opens his wife, Gunhild, and her twin sister, Ella, in love with Borkman's son, Erhart, sadly discuss his past life while he paces up and down, as he has done for years since his release from prison, in the room above their heads. Not until act 2 does he appear, a distinguished-looking man in his sixties, to explain his failure as being due to the publication of some private letters by a close friend, and to maintain his complete innocence of the crimes for which he has been punished. As happens in other of Ibsen's plays, the nature of these past events is obscure. Whether Borkman was guilty or innocent—whether, granted a few days for his plans to mature, he could have benefited millions—it is impossible to say. He dreamed of doing so at least, and the Napoleonic stance he adopts, confronting himself in the mirror, confirms the nature of his ambition. At times he seems a ruthless, condescending, pompous man, an image of what Ibsen himself, in his worst moments of glory, must have perceived in his own character, though the admiration Ibsen felt for the great individual must also be borne in mind.

It is not unreasonable to see the play as a projection of personal vanity, a public confession of the cruder emotions Ibsen must have known in his triumphal progress. But Borkman has nothing left in him except the remaining flickers of his ambition. In the final act he takes the unmotivated decision to walk out of the snowbound, lonely house where he has lived for eight years and ascend the hill outside, where he is found by the two women dying of extreme cold. He is still fired with his former vision. The mountain chain in the distance is for him a vast, infinite, inexhaustible kingdom. Though the blast of cold air from it is deathly, it comes like a greeting from subject spirits, millions of imprisoned men and women whom he longs to release as he might release veins of metal from the rocks, and as Ibsen sometimes appears to have wanted to release them through his plays. Passionately he declares his love for them, as he dies of the freezing air that is like the coldness of their response. Again paradox is the final note. A spectator may be unsure what kind of love Borkman means—whether it is not, like the love of Allmers, still pervaded by egoism—but it is certainly a love that kills him, just as Brand was killed by the avalanche that proclaimed the love of God.

That avalanche remained in Ibsen's mind as the conclusion of *When We Dead Awaken,* the play published shortly before the breakdown in health that left him unable to write or even to read. In its title, this promises what all the plays implicitly or explicitly portend, the coming of an age when the present condition of mankind shall be surpassed. Like Nietzsche, Ibsen might have said that man is something that is to be overcome; certainly he spoke of a Darwinian evolution in the spiritual world that might bring about such a change. As in all the plays, however, while the faults of people are clear—mediocrity, hypocrisy, self-deception, puritanism, cowardice, selfishness—the kind of society in which they would wither is left vague, and the remedies attempted are usually the cultivation of ruthless self-assertion, amorality, and exultant Dionysian revelry even at the cost of life and limb. Between these two poles there is never room for devoted love or loyalty, no Cordelia or Horatio, Antigone or Bérénice, though a fu-

sion of opposites often concludes the final acts, as it concludes this last play of all.

Rubek the sculptor bears an obvious resemblance to Ibsen the dramatist when he looks back at his life and accuses himself of portraying the men and women who have been his subjects as honest cart horses, simpleminded donkeys, low-browed dogs, overfed pigs, and a few thick-skulled bullnecks, "all those animals that man has corrupted in his own image, and that have corrupted man in return." That catalog, despite the curious idea that animals have corrupted man, suggests, as Robert Brustein says, what Ibsen now thought of the characters in his realistic plays. Yet the first act ends in the same spirit as before, when Rubek accepts the invitation of Irene, another Rebecca, another Hilde, another Furia, to climb the mountains near which they are staying and show her all the glory of the world. So familiar is the theme in Ibsen's mind that he portrays Rubek as embarrassed by it and makes him at first pass it off as a joke. But at last he and Irene do climb a mountain, despite warnings of bad weather on the way. Their persistence can only be symbolic of a determination to move to some nebulous higher things, which Rubek spells out a little when he says that the storm gathering over their heads is like the prelude to the day of resurrection. At length they do climb on alone, Irene welcoming the glory and splendor of the light, foreseeing their arrival at "the very top of the tower lit by the rising sun," rehearsing the by-now hackneyed symbolism and language of so many earlier plays. And the avalanche that sweeps them away as Brand was swept away reveals the mysterious figure of a nun who has, unsuspected, climbed with them, and who now pronounces words of pardon: "Peace be with you." Paradox is provided as in *Brand,* though with more contrivance now.

This possibly Christian ending is not, however, the note on which the play finishes. An underlying contrast has been contained all through in the subplot concerning another friend of Rubek's, Maia, who has none of Irene's lofty ambitions but prefers to be carried off by Ulfheim, a lusty sportsman of comic pretentiousness. She too has been on the mountainside, but she takes the sensible precaution of avoiding the avalanche. While its roar dies away, her song of freedom is still heard from below, as Ulfheim clambers down the slopes, somehow holding her in his arms. The regenerated human race may resemble her, or it may rise out of the destruction of Rubek's idealism, or it may lie with a renewed Christianity represented by the nun: the play leaves the vision of the future indeterminate.

When We Dead Awaken is not often performed. It has never had the same strength in the theater as *A Doll's House* or *Ghosts* or *Hedda Gabler*, perhaps because its characterizations are cruder, or because the symbolism is vaguer, the motivations more abruptly presented. It is best seen, no doubt, as a last attempt by an aging dramatist to rehearse the themes that had always preoccupied him, and, though the conclusions remain unchanged, the vigor that had sustained him for fifty years of composition is still recognizable. But he had reached his peak, and like the other three plays after *Hedda Gabler* this one is a stock-taking, a self-examination and self-reaffirmation, rather than a dramatic renewal.

These last years saw only the beginning of Ibsen's fame. Though he suffered a stroke in 1900 and could no longer write, he was by that time established as the greatest European playwright of his day, in some opinions one of the greatest of all time. By 1897, though there was still some dissent, the dispute about his plays in Europe was virtually over. In the United States there had been performances of *A Doll's House* (adapted as *The Child Wife*) at the Grand Opera House, Milwaukee, as early as 1882, and of *Ghosts* at Aurora Turner Hall, Chicago, in the same year, six years after the first performance of any Ibsen play outside Scandinavia. Louisville, Kentucky, followed

with *A Doll's House* in 1883. A performance in Norwegian was given in Chicago in February 1893, followed a month later by one in English. The London production by Beerbohm Tree of the same year later went on tour in America. *John Gabriel Borkman* was performed by the Criterion Independent Theatre in New York in 1897. By that time Ibsen was being championed by the highly regarded novelist W. D. Howells, as well as by the Norwegian immigrant communities, though opposition still came from New England puritans. Such opposition may have delayed full recognition in the United States, for Ezra Pound complained as late as 1916—though early in his own life—that he had had the opportunity of seeing only two Ibsen plays performed (*Hedda* and *Peer Gynt*). After World War I, the tide began to flow.

In England it had begun already, with Shaw's lighthearted borrowings, James Joyce's *Exiles* (first published in 1918), John Galsworthy's social dramas *Strife* (1909) and *Justice* (1910), and Harley Granville-Barker's *The Voysey Inheritance* (1905). Gerhart Hauptmann and Hermann Sudermann in Germany, Arthur Schnitzler in Austria, and Roberto Bracco in Italy all admired and imitated Ibsen; in France, where a naturalist theater had already existed since Émile Zola and Henry Becque, he was promoted in the 1890's with other avant-gardists by the Théâtre Libre Antoine.

Problem plays treating contemporary American life in the manner of Ibsen were being written in the early twentieth century by Augustus Thomas, Clyde Fitch, Edward Sheldon, and Rachel Crothers, forerunners of the emergence of America's greatest playwright, Eugene O'Neill. But though O'Neill's earliest one-act plays, a cycle of sea-pieces written in 1916–1918, were naturalistic, and *Ile* (1917) was both naturalistic and symbolic, his genius soon experimented with other forms, including expressionism, and his preference was for August Strindberg rather than

Ibsen. Of later American dramatists, Ibsen's greatest admirer has been Arthur Miller, especially in *All My Sons* (1947), with its echoes of *Pillars of Society*, and in *The Price* (1968). Miller's version of *An Enemy of the People* (1950) made it a play with a more direct message than the original. Tennessee Williams began, broadly speaking, in an Ibsen tradition. But to trace the influence of Ibsen in modern theater would be like writing a history of half of it. His realism has been as much imitated as it has been rejected by dramatists such as Bertolt Brecht, Federico García Lorca, W. B. Yeats, Clifford Odets, and Edward Albee.

A film version of *Peer Gynt*, with Charlton Heston in the title role, was made by David Bradley in 1941. Joseph Losey directed *A Doll's House* in 1973, with Jane Fonda and David Warner. That same year, Patrick Garland directed *A Doll's House*, with performances by Claire Bloom and Anthony Hopkins. *Hedda*, directed by Trevor Nunn and starring Glenda Jackson, was made in 1975.

Realism, not very distinct from naturalism, was part of a movement that attempted to reproduce on stage a resemblance to the perceived world akin to the one produced by photography. In the extreme form of naturalism it was even proposed that a room onstage should be exactly like a real room with "the fourth wall" removed to provide the audience with a view; plays should be "slices of life" without dramatic falls-of-curtain; language, including dialect and defects of speech, should be exactly reproduced. Ibsen's realism was never of this kind. His curtains are nearly always designed for effect in proscenium theaters. His sets are carefully thought out: the room behind the stage or above it can be as telling as anything seen by the audience, and when he requires a piece of furniture it is usually in order to add meaning. General Gabler's portrait hangs on the wall as a reminder of Hedda's family tradition; the letter box threatens to disclose Nora's secret; the rope around Ellida Wangel's garden protects her temporarily from the Stranger. The few characters in the later plays who are not middle-class speak a little differently from the rest, but not in dialect. The language becomes simpler and simpler, including words readily translated from one European language into another much more frequently than in *Brand*, which presents serious problems of translation with its characteristically Norwegian vocabulary. Increasingly, too, characters speak to each other in a way that sounds natural on the whole but at the same time expounds the past in as much complexity as is needed to understand the present.

For the distinctive mark of Ibsen's craftsmanship is his ability to write not the "narrative theater" of *Peer Gynt*, good as that is, but the play in which a dramatic moment is presented at the point at which it is about to explode. Mrs. Alving is about to celebrate the opening of the orphanage that will blot out her husband's evil memory when her son arrives to frustrate her completely. Rosmer is about to embark on his mission when Rebecca West reveals to him what she has done to make him free to do so, and he is crippled by the news. Ellida lives a not entirely unhappy life with her husband's family till the memory of her earlier "marriage" with the Stranger is revived. The past events revealed by these dialogues are sometimes extremely involved. Ibsen's mastery is shown when he conveys them while persuading the audience that they are listening to realistic conversation.

Ibsen wanted realistic sets. Theater-in-the-round does him an injustice. But he was never content with realism alone, even when he had decided, in Solness' words, to produce "houses for people to live in." Such concern with social problems made his name, but it was not his main concern. The plays most easily reducible to social problems alone still have traces of myths underlying them, myths that fitted closely to his own personal situation. Born in a culturally remote part of Europe where a national theater had barely begun, fighting his way in thirty years to preeminence, he knew what self-assertion costs, but he was not simply ambitious for himself. One of the philosophies that developed in the nineteenth century, mainly out of Hegel, was a belief in self-assertion after the achievement of complete self-knowledge, leading to a position in society of representative value: the Gyntian Self, which Ibsen subjected to such ironic scrutiny, was taken to have a more than individual value, perhaps a cosmic one. Napoleon was still widely regarded as a man who had reflected the ambitions of a whole generation. Wagner saw himself in much the same way, as more than a composer, almost as the founder of a world religion. Ibsen, whose themes and images are sometimes surprisingly close to Wagner's, was much readier to question the achievements open to the Self in this wider sense. As fast as the new world is glimpsed, as it is by Borkman and Rubek, it is destroyed again, in a sequence of oppositions and fusions and renewed oppositions that never ends.

Dialectical philosophies like those of Hegel and Nietzsche often seem to consist of recognizing and rejoicing in such cyclical repetitions, where others look for an eternal affirmation of truth, beauty, and love. Dialectical philosophies also tend to concern themselves more with the pattern than the people. The opposites revolve and clash, join and separate; the philosopher fits his realities to that knowledge as Ibsen fitted his characters to the ambiguous purposes of his plays. The stereotyping of many of his characters suggests this pattern, though this is not to say that the characters are simple. Tesman is primarily moral yet willing to leave his wife alone with Judge Brack; Rebecca West professes noble ideals but sees no wrong in hounding Rosmer's wife to suicide; Krogstad is a blackmailing villain to Nora at one moment, but reverts to benevolence in a flash. Like many other of Ibsen's creations, these are people drawn in black and white, stark contrasts in themselves, confronting equally stark contrasts in others. Tesman's naiveté makes Hedda's life unbearable. Rebecca drives the unaware Rosmer to sui-

cide. Krogstad's scheming astonishes Nora, in her complete ignorance of the niceties of the law. Through these oppositions the plays have a vigor that can look deceptively like the vigor of life, though they are more often spun by the rotations of a philosopher's wheel than by the detailed observation of a dramatist interested in the minutiae of conduct and motive. In some ways, such vigor suits the drama, which lives as a rule on clashes and climaxes, and Ibsen's reputation owes a good deal to that coincidence of thought and theater. A hundred years after his first great successes they still flourish, and it may be that most of his work will go on doing so as long as theater lasts.

The crux in all discussion of Ibsen's reputation is, however, the nature of his language. Though he gave up verse in order to allow his characters to use everyday speech, he still retained symbolism, and though he wanted to give the illusion of reality, this aim was not necessarily reconcilable with either symbolic language or symbolic action. The recent claim that all his work is poetry still holds the center of attention. The contrary view, represented by T. S. Eliot, holds that while Ibsen had greater technical ability than, say, the Jacobean playwright Cyril Tourneur, he was not a greater dramatist, since he abandoned poetry. "For the greatest drama," Eliot wrote in his *Dialogue on Dramatic Poetry*, "is poetic drama, and dramatic defects *can* be compensated by poetic excellence." No debate that ignores these opposing views can claim to be concerned with the central issues.

Selected Bibliography

EDITIONS

INDIVIDUAL WORKS

Note: The first date in the following entries indicates the first publication. The second date indicates the first translation into English.

Catiline. Christiania (Norway), 1850; New York, 1921.

The Burial Mound. Bergen (Norway), 1854; New York, 1921.

Lady Inger of Østraat. Christiania, 1858; London, 1890.

The Feast at Solhoug. Christiania, 1856; London, 1908.

The Vikings at Helgeland. Christiania, 1858; London, 1890.

Love's Comedy. Christiania, 1862; London, 1900.

The Pretenders. Christiania, 1864; London, 1890.

Brand. Copenhagen (Denmark), 1866; London, 1891.

Peer Gynt. Copenhagen, 1867; London, 1892.

The League of Youth. Copenhagen, 1869; London, 1890.

Poems. Copenhagen, 1871; London, 1902. A selection.

Emperor and Galilean. Copenhagen, 1873; London, 1876.

Pillars of Society. Copenhagen, 1877; London, 1888.

A Doll's House. Copenhagen, 1879; London, 1882.

Ghosts. Copenhagen, 1881; London, 1885.

An Enemy of the People. Copenhagen, 1882; London, 1888.

The Wild Duck. Copenhagen, 1884; London, 1890.

Rosmersholm. Copenhagen, 1886; London, 1889.

The Lady from the Sea. Copenhagen, 1888; London, 1890.

Hedda Gabler. Copenhagen, 1890; London, 1891.

The Master Builder. Copenhagen, 1892; London, 1893.

Little Eyolf. Copenhagen, 1894; London, 1895.

John Gabriel Borkman. Copenhagen, 1896; London, 1897.

When We Dead Awaken. Copenhagen, 1899; London, 1900.

Olaf Liljekrans. Copenhagen, 1902; New York, 1921.

St. John's Night. Christiania, 1909; London, 1970.

COLLECTED WORKS

Samlede Verker. 21 vols. in 22. Edited by Francis Bull, Halvdan Koht, and Didrik Arup Seip. Oslo (Norway), 1928–1957.

TRANSLATIONS

The Collected Works of Henrik Ibsen. 12 vols. Revised and edited by William Archer. London, 1906–1912. Does not include earliest plays.

The Complete Prose Plays. Translated and introduced by Rolf Fjelde. New York, 1965.

The Oxford Ibsen. 8 vols. Edited by James McFarlane, with translations by James McFarlane, Jens Arup, and others. Oxford, 1960–1977. Includes translations of first drafts and sketches.

BIOGRAPHICAL AND CRITICAL STUDIES

Andersen, Annette. "Ibsen in America." *Scandinavian Studies and Notes* 14:65–109, 115–155 (1937).

Anstey, F. *Mr Punch's Pocket Ibsen.* London, 1893.

Archer, W. *Play-Making: A Manual of Craftsmanship.* London, 1913.

Beerbohm, Max. *Around Theatres.* London, 1953.

Bentley, Eric. *The Modern Theatre.* London, 1948.

———. *In Search of Theatre.* New York, 1954.

Brandes, Georg. *Eminent Authors of the Nineteenth Century.* Translated by Ramus B. Anderson. New York, 1886.

———. *Henrik Ibsen. Bjørnstjerne Bjørnson.* London, 1899.

Brooks, Cleanth, and Robert B. Heilman. *Understanding Drama.* London, 1946.

Brustein, Robert. *Theatre of Revolt: An Approach to the Modern Drama.* Boston, 1964.

Bull, Francis. *Ibsen: The Man and the Dramatist.* Oxford, 1954.

Clurman, Harold. *Ibsen.* New York, 1977.

Cox, R. G. "Rehabilitating Ibsen." *Scrutiny* 14:211–217 (1947).

Croce, Benedetto. *European Literature in the Nineteenth Century.* London, 1924.

Dowden, Edward. *Essays Modern and Elizabethan.* London and New York, 1910.

Egan, Michael, ed. *Ibsen: The Critical Heritage.* London, 1972.

Fergusson, Francis. *The Idea of a Theater.* Princeton, N.J., 1949.

Fjelde, Rolf, ed. *Ibsen: A Collection of Critical Essays.* Englewood Cliffs, N.J., 1965.

Franc, Miriam. *Ibsen in England.* Boston, 1919.

Gosse, Edmund. *Ibsen.* London, 1907.

———. *Studies in the Literature of Northern Europe.* London, 1879.

———. *Northern Studies.* London, 1899.

Granville-Barker, Harley. *On Dramatic Method.* London, 1931; New York, 1956.

Gray, Ronald. *Ibsen: A Dissenting View.* Cambridge, 1977.

Grumman, P. H. *Henrik Ibsen.* New York, 1928.

Haakonsen, Daniel, ed. *Contemporary Approaches to Ibsen.* Oslo, 1966.

Heller, Otto. *Henrik Ibsen: Plays and Problems.* Boston and New York, 1912.

Ibsen, Bergliot. *The Three Ibsens: Memories of Henrik, Suzannah and Sigurd Ibsen.* Translated by G. Schjelderup. London, 1951.

Jaeger, Henrik. *The Life of Ibsen.* Translated by Clara Bell. London, 1890.

James, Henry. *The Scenic Art.* Edited by Allan Wade. London, 1949.

Jorgenson, Theodore. *Henrik Ibsen: A Study in Art and Personality.* Northfield, Minn., 1945.

Knight, G. Wilson. *Ibsen.* Edinburgh, 1962.

Koht, Halvdan. *The Life of Ibsen.* Translated by Ruth McMahon and Hanna Larsen. London and New York, 1931.

McCarthy, Mary. *Sights and Spectacles, 1937–1958.* London, 1959.

McFarlane, James. *Ibsen and the Temper of Norwegian Literature.* London and New York, 1960.

————, ed. *Discussions of Henrik Ibsen.* Boston, 1962.

————, ed. *Henrik Ibsen.* Harmondsworth, 1970. A critical anthology.

Meyer, Michael. *Henrik Ibsen.* 3 vols. London, 1967–1971. Abridged in one vol., 1974.

Montague, C. E. *Dramatic Values.* London, 1910.

Montrose, J. Moses. *Henrik Ibsen: The Man and His Plays.* New York, 1908.

Muir, Kenneth. *Last Periods of Shakespeare, Racine and Ibsen.* Liverpool, 1962.

Northam, John. *Ibsen's Dramatic Method: A Study of the Prose Dramas.* London, 1953.

————. *Ibsen: A Critical Study.* Cambridge, 1973.

Peacock, Ronald. *The Poet in the Theatre.* London, 1946.

————. *The Art of Drama.* London and New York, 1957.

Robertson, J. G. *Essays and Addresses on Literature.* London, 1935.

Robins, Elizabeth. *Ibsen and the Actress.* London, 1928.

Shaw, George Bernard. *The Quintessence of Ibsenism.* London and Boston, 1891; 2nd ed., London and New York, 1913; New York, 1957.

————. *Our Theatres in the Nineties.* 3 vols. London and New York, 1931.

Symons, Arthur. *Figures of Several Centuries.* London, 1916.

Tennant, P. F. D. *Ibsen's Dramatic Technique.* Cambridge, 1948.

Thompson, Alan Reynolds. *The Dry Mock: A Study of Irony in Drama.* Berkeley, Calif., 1948.

Valency, M. J. *The Flower and the Castle.* New York, 1964.

Weigand, Hermann J. *The Modern Ibsen.* New York, 1925.

Weightman, John. "Ibsen and the Absurd." *Encounter* 45:4.48–52 (October 1975).

Williams, Raymond. *Drama from Ibsen to Brecht.* London, 1968.

Zucker, A. E. *Ibsen, the Master Builder.* London, 1930.

BIBLIOGRAPHIES

Tedford, Ingrid. *Ibsen Bibliography 1928–1957.* Oslo and Bergen, 1961. See also the Bibliographies section in *The Oxford Ibsen,* edited by James McFarlane, vol. 8, p. 383.

RONALD GRAY

HIPPOLYTE TAINE
(1828–1893)

A S A PHILOSOPHER, a critic of literature and art, and a historian, Hippolyte Taine was a leading figure in French intellectual life from the mid-1860's to his death in 1893. In his time, Taine was as famous as his friends Ernest Renan and Charles Augustin Sainte-Beuve; like his great Victorian contemporaries Thomas Carlyle, John Ruskin, and Matthew Arnold, he was fearless in taking on the whole of the culture in which he found himself. He wrote a doctoral thesis on Jean de La Fontaine and his fables; he studied medicine and attended lectures on physiology and natural sciences; he made himself famous with a book of philosophy that demolished some of the leading philosophical reputations of the age. He wrote popular travel books and composed a technical psychological treatise, *De l'intelligence* (*On Intelligence*, 1870); he was a preeminent historian of English literature and a champion of the works of Stendhal, Honoré de Balzac, and Gustave Flaubert. His theoretical criticism laid the groundwork for Émile Zola's naturalism. As professor of aesthetics and art history at the École des Beaux Arts, he wrote five books on painting and sculpture. He spent the last twenty years of his life writing the immense, impassioned *Les origines de la France contemporaine* (*The Origins of Contemporary France*, 1875–1893) in eleven volumes.

At fourteen he laid down the regimen that was to set the pattern for the rest of his life: a twenty minute recess in the afternoon and an hour of music after dinner. Otherwise he spent his time reading voraciously and writing one or another of the thirty-five volumes that make up his life's work. Despite its variety of subject matter, Taine's work has an extraordinary degree of unity. By the time he was twenty, Taine was convinced that the methods of natural science could fruitfully be applied to the study of literature, art, and history. Caught up in the mid-nineteenth-century euphoria about the future of science, he conceived a sociology of culture that was to reveal the universal axioms underlying all of art and history.

Taine's ideas sit a little awkwardly with modern readers, and despite his passion, energy, and intelligence, he lacked some quality of commanding literary personality or imaginative genius that might have kept his work alive today. Taine occupies an honorable place in the history of criticism, and his *Histoire de la littérature anglaise* (*History of English Literature*, 1863–1864) is still recommended to students from time to time. But I have the impression that he is now little read. Since 1972, when Leo Weinstein's valuable study appeared, the commentary on Taine has slowed to a few scattered articles. Yet Taine writes as evocatively as Sainte-Beuve, and his place in the history of thought is equal to Renan's. Anybody who reads a few pages of Taine will recognize that he is a writer of brilliance and imaginative force. With that in mind, I have quoted generously from Taine, telling the story of his unfolding thought from his own works, as far as possible. Even in English translations, the rush and energy of his style catch one up.

Like most nineteenth-century writers, Taine was a child of the middle class. His father was an attorney, and his family had long belonged to the professional class of the town of Vouziers, in the mountains of the Ardennes, where Taine was born on 21 April 1828. He was educated at home until shortly after his father's death in 1842; he then went to Paris, where he was soon followed by his mother and two sisters, to attend classes at the Collège Bourbon. From the first Taine was a brilliant and hardworking student. In 1847 he won almost every prize the Collège Bourbon had to offer, both in letters and science. In 1848 he placed first in the qualifying examination for the École Normale, a highly competitive institution founded in 1808 for the training of future professors.

Taine later looked back on his years at the École Normale as the most fruitful of his life. He formed several lifelong friendships; he read constantly and became a fluent writer in French and Latin, in both verse and prose; he perfected his English and learned German in order to read G. W. F. Hegel; he became a student of Baruch Spinoza's philosophy. Also at this time, like many of the most thoughtful young men of his era, he lost his religious faith and substituted for it a faith in the future of science.

All of Taine's professors were deeply impressed by his learning and intellectual distinction; all were troubled by his passion for abstraction and classification. At the end of Taine's second year Étienne Vacheret, the director of studies, wrote a sketch of Taine that demonstrates that his adult character was already formed:

The most hardworking and distinguished student that I have known at the École Normale.

Prodigious learning for his age. An ardor and avidity for knowledge the like of which I have never seen. A mind remarkable for its rapidity of apprehension, for the finesse, subtlety, and force of its thought. However, he comprehends, understands, judges, and formulates too quickly. He is too fond of formulas and definitions, to which he too often sacrifices reality, without realizing it. . . . Moreover, he is not of this world. Spinoza's motto will be his: "Live in order to think."

(*H. Taine: Sa vie et sa correspondance* 1.123–124)

After being "first, by a great distance, in all the interviews and examinations" at the École Normale, Taine met the first reverse of his intellectual career in August 1851, when he failed the philosophy examination; the examiners disliked his lesson on Spinoza, finding it both iconoclastic and tiresomely presented. This failure caused a scandal, but Taine himself scarcely paused before moving on to the next step, taking a post as a substitute teacher at the Collège de Nevers. For the next three years he suffered one setback after another in his career, but he met his defeats with impressive tenacity and resilience.

Two months after his arrival at the Collège de Nevers, the coup d'etat of Louis Napoleon occurred, and all faculties were requested to sign a statement of adherence to the new regime. Alone among his faculty Taine refused to sign, because the government had come to power illegally. Once the new rule was approved by a plebiscite, he made no further objections to signing a declaration of adherence. Still, he was given a warning and transferred to the lycée of Poitiers in March 1852. Still under suspicion, he was moved again in September 1852 to the lycée of Besançon. At this point Taine had had enough and applied for a leave, which was readily given and renewed every year for the term of his ten-year appointment.

Taine had been left a modest income by his father, and he took a few private students, so that he was free to set to work on an essay in

French on the sensations and also one in Latin. When the essay on the sensations was submitted as part of his doctoral work, it was refused because of its "undesirable tendencies." At once Taine switched from psychology to literature and set to work on an essay on the fables of La Fontaine. In a few months his Latin essay, on the characters of Plato's dialogues, and his French essay on La Fontaine were both finished. The award of his doctorate in May 1853 marked the end of his university career. Henceforth he was to be known primarily as a man of letters—a critic, historian, philosopher, journalist, and travel writer.

As soon as his dissertations were accepted, Taine set to work on a book on Livy for a competition set by the French Academy. In this work he established the outlines of the four ideas that were to dominate all of his later writings. In addition to showing the importance of milieu, race, and historical moment in forming a writer, he gave his first explanation of his idea of the *master faculty:*

> The challenge to me, in research, is to find a dominant and characteristic trait from which everything can be deduced in a geometric fashion, and in a word to have the formula of the thing. . . . It seems to me that Titus Livius is the following: an orator who became a historian.
>
> (quoted in Kahn, p. 258)

The academy found the essay too "modern" in its philosophical tastes, but when Taine rewrote the piece and argued his position in a more subdued fashion, he was given the prize in 1854. His determination to import scientific methods into the study of history and literature apparently caused some scandal, but not enough to banish him from the French intellectual establishment.

By 1854, when he was twenty-six, Taine had had six arduous years, three as a hardworking student at the École Normale, and three of being buffeted about by the political and ideological winds of the early years of the Second Empire. It is hardly surprising that he broke down and had to rest and travel to restore his health. Taine, however, was not one to let even an illness go by without turning it to account. Unable to read himself, he had himself read to, and for the first time he began to study the French Revolution. He attended lectures in medicine and physiology. He took a trip through the Pyrenees and wrote *Voyage aux eaux des Pyrénées* (*A Tour Through the Pyrenees,* 1855), the first of several travel books published by Hachette.

From 1855 through 1863, Taine wrote voluminously for periodicals, chiefly the *Revue de l'instruction publique, Revue des deux mondes,* and *Journal des débats.* These were journals of limited circulation, but unlike our contemporary little magazines they paid comparatively well, and they were read by many of the most influential people in France. Taine concentrated on three subjects: the philosophy of history, contemporary French philosophy, and English literature. His volume *Nouveaux essais de critique et d'histoire* (New Critical and Historical Essays, 1865) was based primarily on his essays in the philosophy of history.

This period of traveling and mixing with people outside academic life, and the experience of writing a travel book in a popular style, made a decisive change in Taine's manner of writing. As his leading ideas were fully established by the time he wrote his book on Livy, so his literary personality emerged fullblown after his nervous illness. He stopped writing abstractly and deductively, moving in geometrical fashion from the universal to the particular. Now he worked his way from vivid particulars up to the general idea. The governing scheme of abstract ideas was still there, but it was filled in with drama, color, and movement. His prose became readable, attractive, even compelling; he became adroit in finding everywhere excitement, intensity, and contrast. Despite his demurs about positivism, a philosophy negating all metaphysical and mystical ideas in the interest of science,

Taine, because of his lively prose, became its spokesman in France more than Auguste Comte himself, the official father of positivism. Taine's writings attracted a wide audience, whereas Comte's dry and abstract style confined his works to a tiny circle of advanced thinkers.

By 1857 Taine had established a sufficient reputation and found enough self-confidence to publish a scathing attack on the eclectic and spiritualist school of French philosophy, led by Victor Cousin, who had been among those who objected to Taine's book on Livy. *Les philosophes français du XIXe siècle* (The Nineteenth-Century French Philosophers, 1857) made Taine famous, or notorious. He satirized Cousin and his followers because of their fondness for empty abstractions and their insistence on putting moral considerations before scientific fact; he justified the harsh mockery of his tone on the ground that he was discussing not private individuals but the rulers of French philosophy. From that time on he was something of a lion in Parisian literary society, moving in the circle of Renan, Sainte-Beuve, Wilhelm Scherer, Théophile Gautier, Flaubert, and the Goncourt brothers. For the rest of his life, whatever he wrote was certain to attract public attention.

It was as a well-known figure in the Parisian literary world, speaking with recognized authority, that Taine undertook his next work. The *History of English Literature* is his undoubted masterpiece, and he was engaged in writing it between 1855 and 1863. The first piece he wrote was on Thomas Macauley, and the last was the famous introductory chapter. The work was dedicated to François Guizot, the moderately conservative politician and historian who wrote a large-scale history of the English revolution and was an admirer of British gradualism and avoidance of extremes; the spirit of Guizot guides Taine's social and political views, though not his literary taste.

Two questions pose themselves about Taine's choice of English literature as a subject. First, why did he choose to turn from philosophy to literature? Second, why English literature rather than another?

Taine's first love was philosophy, but he had failed his philosophy examination because of the conservatism of the examiners. Then the fellowship in philosophy was abolished. Thus Taine was almost driven from philosophy and into the less ideologically explosive domain of letters for his doctoral dissertations. His Latin essay was halfway between literature and philosophy; his essay in French changed from a treatise on the sensations to one on La Fontaine's fables. Thus he arrived via philosophy and psychology at the domain of literature. But he did not abandon philosophy and psychology; rather he brought them along with him to provide the conceptual framework for his literary history. His notions of master faculty, milieu, race, and historical moment provide the ostensibly scientific methodology for his studies.

Taine's choice of English literature as a subject arose from a multiplicity of causes. For the nineteenth-century French, English literature was the supreme romantic literature, the literature of passion and high imagination in contrast to their own literature of wit, logic, and measured conversation. Just as Matthew Arnold saw French literature and institutions as a corrective to the excesses of British individualism, so Taine saw English literature as a corrective to the French worship of central authority, order, and reason. Taine was a spokesman for the realism and scientism that prevailed in France after 1850, but his taste was formed by the romantic literature of the earlier part of the century. He made great imaginative capital out of the contrast between his stance as the scientific, rational inquirer into literary phenomena and the wild, irregular nature of English literature. Taine was highly conscious of his part in the tradition of cultural comparison back and forth across the English Channel. In addition, he thought of English literature as uniquely suited to the demonstration of his theses about literature. It had a continuous development from the earliest Saxon times down to the present; it ultimately asserted its fundamentally Anglo-Saxon racial character despite the Norman Conquest; it revealed the evolution of the modern British gentleman out of the Anglo-Saxon savage.

The introductory chapter to the *History of English Literature* is a manifesto in the grand French manner; it is Taine's central account of his project for creating "a science of art." He assumes that the purpose of reading anything at all—a poem, work of philosophy, a system of laws—is to discover the person behind the words. Thus psychology is the master science, giving us access to the mind behind words and deeds. In Hegelian fashion, psychology is the true subject of literature, art, and history. Literary works and historical events are interesting only as revelations of the underlying mental life. But if the words on the page reveal the psychology of the individual author, his psychology in turn is a revelation of the psychology of his race, his geographical and social milieu, and his historical moment. The greater the writer, the more profoundly he expresses the national character, the times, and the leading ideas that produced him. Beyond that, the very greatest works of art reveal what is at the core of humanity itself. Taine says, "I intend to write the history of a literature, and to seek in it for the psychology of a people." So studying literature is a way of studying that half-mythical but necessary subject—"national character."

Ideally Taine would like to be able to go from the individual work to a universal axiom about human nature, for he is always seeking basic causes in works of art. He usually means by "cause" not so much "antecedent conditions" as "discovering the essence of a thing"—that which makes it what it is. His conception of causality is fundamentally Hegelian in its emphasis on essence and in its giving a secondary position to antecedents. Taine had a certain taste for stating his faith in the universal reign of causality in outrageous ways. Thus the sentence from the intro-

duction to his *History* that gave the most scandal to the pious: "Vice and virtue are products, like vitriol and sugar." In the uproar that followed, everyone forgot the explanation contained in the rest of the sentence: "every complex phenomenon arises from the more simple phenomena on which it hangs." Taine never tired of reiterating his determination to show the rule of natural law everywhere, even in the hitherto inviolate domains of ethics and art.

Taine's borrowings from science were not limited to a universal application of the laws of causality; he borrowed far more detailed conceptions. Thus Charles Darwin's notion of the survival of the fittest is the basis for Taine's view that the greatest artists best reflect the nature of their age: the survivors are the best representatives of the characteristics of a species; the same is true of writers. The principle that overdevelopment of one organ makes for the weakening of the others leads Taine to the explanation that in Germany the overemphasis on philosophy contributed to weakness in the visual arts. For Taine, these biological and zoological comparisons are not metaphors but statements of fact.

Taine also believed that the scientific method, pursued far enough, would finally lead to a total knowledge, a great hierarchy of axioms with a single governing universal at the top. Thus science would escape from the contingent and constantly surprising unfolding of history into a sphere of timeless truth. The structure of theology, minus God, would be reconstituted inside the domain of science. In the foreground is the chaos of endless change; but somewhere just beyond the horizon are the changeless tablets of scientific law.

Taine's notion of the master faculty provides him with an organizing principle in all his works from the book on Livy onward; it can be applied to a single author, to an epoch, or to a national spirit. The master faculty is the central, determining characteristic from which all the others may be derived. All of

Livy's character is derived from the fact that he was an orator turned historian; Balzac's came from his being a businessman with constant money troubles; the character of seventeenth-century France followed from its conception of the *honnête homme*—the intelligent, well-bred man of goodwill; the character of the lion follows from his being a great flesh eater. In short, the master faculty is the principle of individuation; it is the ruling passion that swallows up all the others.

Finding the master faculty involves a voyage inward or downward to the primitive root of a writer or an age. One arrives at it by successive condensations. Three paragraphs summarizing an author or an age are reduced to three sentences, and from that can be derived a single phrase that names the master faculty. Afterward one can restore the details and characteristics that were abandoned along the road to the ultimate abstraction, "deriving" them, in the spirit of geometry, from the master faculty. Taine found this internal consistency everywhere, and it was perhaps his deepest commitment both of method and belief. In comparison, his ideas of race, milieu, and moment are more lightly held.

Of Taine's four leading conceptions, it is his notion of *race* that has caused the most difficulty, largely because of the disastrous manifestations of racism in the twentieth century. Also, his idea of race contains a number of heterogeneous and ill-defined entities. Taine does not distinguish between race and ethnicity or race and nationality, so that he can refer to the English race or the French race. Race is primarily a cultural entity, but it does have a hazy biological component. In the absence of any very clear notion of heredity, Taine speaks of the transmission of characteristics by Saxon blood or French blood. Race consists of a mixture of hereditary and acquired characteristics, the latter having been stamped in by constant repetition over a long period of time. At some points he emphasizes the hereditary aspects of race:

What we call race are innate and the hereditary dispositions which man brings with him into the world, and which, as a rule, are united with the marked differences in the temperament and structure of the body. They vary with various people. There is a natural variety of men, as of oxen and horses.

(*History of English Literature*, van Laun trans., 1.10)

But he also speaks of races as a composite of acquired characteristics: "At any moment we may consider the character of a people as an abridgement of all its preceding actions and sensations."

Race also merges with national character and geography. The French race is logical and sociable; the English race is imaginative and lonely. The Latins of the clement south, on the smiling Mediterranean, tend to have sunny dispositions. The Germanic people of the cold and rainy north, facing the stormy northern seas, are moody and melancholy.

Taine is not individually responsible for this muddle, which he largely took over from the accepted anthropological thought of his age, as Jacques Barzun shows in his book *Race: A Study in Modern Superstition*. These notions of race arose and became charged with political and cultural significance in the heyday of nationalist wars in Europe and imperialist expansion in Asia and Africa; they tended to be instruments of political justification.

For Taine, however, race was a useful notion in the comparative study of culture and was remarkably free of its usual invidiousness. Following the ideas of Madame de Staël in her *Germania*, Taine makes much literary use of the differences between the Latin and Germanic peoples, two great representatives of the primitive, widely dispersed Aryan race. The Latins created classical literature:

The literatures of the Latin populations are classic and nearly or remotely allied to Greek poesy, Roman eloquence, the Italian Renaissance, and the age of Louis XIV; they refine and ennoble, they embellish and prune, they systematize and give proportion. Their latest masterpiece is the drama of Racine, who is the painter of princely ways, court proprieties, social paragons, and cultivated natures; the master of an oratorical style, skillful composition, and literary elegance.

(*Lectures on Art*, Durand trans., 2.187)

The Germanic peoples, on the other hand, created the great romantic literatures:

The Germanic literatures . . . are romantic; their primitive source is the Edda and the ancient sagas of the north: their greatest masterpiece is the drama of Shakespeare, that is to say, the crude and complete representation of actual life, with all its atrocious, ignoble, and commonplace details, its sublime and brutal instincts, the entire outgrowth of human character displayed before us, now in a familiar style bordering on the trivial, now poetic even to lyricism, always independent of rule, incoherent, excessive, but of incomparable force, and filling our souls with the warm and palpitating passion of which it is the outcry.

(*Lectures on Art* 2.187–188)

The Latin peoples are logical and analytic; the Germanic peoples are intuitive and synthetic. The Latin peoples are rhetoricians; the Germanic peoples are poets and prophets.

Thus race provides for Taine another strategy for doing what always interested him the most—depicting character, whether of an individual, a nation, or an age. In its oversimplification and blithe indifference to evidence, Taine's conception of race is intellectually unacceptable. But as a literary device it served him well, helping him give drama and contrast to his account of English literature.

Moment is the least important of Taine's triad of race, milieu, and moment, and his use of the term is slippery. At one point he speaks of it as "the acquired speed" of a stretch of time, that is, the extent to which the past is propelling the present. Moment can also mean an artist's literary generation or a whole epoch

such as the English Renaissance. It can also mean the personal influence on a writer, as distinct from the more impersonal forces of a milieu.

More important than any of these other uses of the term moment is Taine's using it to denote the place of a work of art in tradition. Generally speaking, Taine pays little attention to literary tradition or to the artistic forms that embody it. But when he does turn his attention to those matters, he is both cogent and eloquent:

Consider, for instance, two epochs of a literature or art—French tragedy under Corneille and under Voltaire, the Greek drama under Aeschylus and under Euripides, Italian painting under da Vinci and under Guido. Truly, at either of these two extreme points the general idea has not changed . . . the mould of verse, the structure of drama, the form of the body has endured. But among several differences there is this, that the one artist is the precursor, the other the successor; the first has no model, the second has; the first sees objects face to face, the second sees them through the first; that many great branches of art are lost, many details are perfected, that simplicity and grandeur of impression have diminished, pleasing and refined forms have increased—in short, that the first work has influenced the second.

(*History of English Literature* 1.12–13)

If Taine's thoughts on race are now a slightly sinister historical curiosity, and his notion of moment too wandering to be of much use, his conception of *milieu* has been thoroughly absorbed into the mainstream of literary and artistic study. After him it became commonplace to look at works of art as expressions of their age; and it became an almost universal assumption that even the greatest works are conditioned by their cultural context.

First, milieu refers to geography and climate. The Latin and Germanic "races" became differentiated largely because of climate.

The Latins, living in a warm climate on the borders of a calm sea, developed a convivial, cheerful temperament and achieved great things in mathematics, science, and the visual arts. The Germanic peoples of the north, facing the stormy seas, have a tendency to violence, melancholy, drunkenness, and imagination; they achieve greatness in poetry and ethical life. A brief reflection suffices to show the fanciful nature of this conception: to be workable it would be necessary to rearrange both climate and geography, with the English Channel running parallel to the equator directly north of France, and Paris having significantly better winter weather than London. Blaise Pascal would have had to become a British subject, and Jane Austen would have had to emigrate to France.

Second, milieu refers to the conditioning social and political facts of a culture. These facts shape the values of a people, and the values in turn inform all works of art. Taine sees the difference between Roman art and Italian Renaissance art as arising from differences in political structure:

> Sometimes the state policy has been at work, as in the two Italian civilizations: the first turned to action, conquest, government, legislation, on account of the original site of its city of refuge, its borderland emporium, its armed aristocracy, who, by importing and drilling strangers and conquered, created two hostile armies, having no escape from its internal discords and its greedy instincts but in systematic warfare; the other, shut out from unity and from any great political ambition by the stability of its municipal character, the cosmopolitan position of its pope, and the military intervention of neighboring nations, directed the whole bent of its magnificent and harmonious genius toward the worship of pleasure and beauty.
>
> (*History of English Literature* 1.11)

Even religion, to the naturalist Taine, is fathered by historical circumstance; that notion is commonplace enough now, but its state-ment in the mid-nineteenth century required a certain daring:

> Sometimes social conditions have impressed their mark, as eighteen centuries ago by Buddhism, when around the Mediterranean, as well as in Hindustan, the extreme results of aryan conquest and civilization induced intolerable oppression, the subjugation of the individual, utter despair, the thought that the world was cursed, with the development of metaphysics and myth, so that man in this dungeon of misery, feeling his heart softened, begot the idea of abnegation, charity, tender love, gentleness, humility, brother love—there, in a notion of universal nothingness, here under the fatherhood of God.
>
> (*History of English Literature* 1.12)

The philosophic underpinning of Taine's notion of milieu is the axiom of the interdependence of parts. As he says, "Art is a kind of philosophy made sensible, religion a poem taken for true, philosophy an art and a religion dried up and reduced to simple ideas." It follows, then, that "civilization forms a body, and its parts are connected with each other like the parts of an organic body."

Taine's conceptual apparatus was generally in accord with the advanced thought of his time. The higher criticism, as in Renan, was busy explaining the human origins of divine revelation and making Jesus the son of man; in a similar fashion, Taine was secularizing literature, depicting genius as growing out of its origins in nationality and history. Darwin's evolutionary theories gave immense impetus to the already flourishing interest in classification and in studies of development—both in history and in the individual. Taine's preoccupation with individual literary personalities at the expense of studying literary form, group tendencies, or tradition was perfectly consonant with the individualism of the later nineteenth century, which often echoed Carlyle's assertion that history was the biography of great men. At the time, there seemed nothing incongruous in a "scientific" history of literature that reads almost like a biographical dictionary of authors chronologically arranged. Taine's determinism was doubtless crude and doctrinaire, but it was a polemical response to much magical talk about "inspiration" in literary matters and "manifestations of God's will" in historical ones.

Turning from the ideas set forth in the introductory chapter to the main body of the *History of English Literature,* we find that Taine follows through consistently in employing his ideas; but his literary personality could never be inferred from his system of ideas. His genius as a writer lies in the creation of character—whether of a writer, a nation, or an age. As Zola said of Taine, "When M. Taine studies Balzac, he does exactly what Balzac does when he studies Père Grandet." And Taine himself said, "From the novel to criticism and from criticism to the novel, the distance at present is not very great." Alongside Taine the cool scientist of culture is Taine the impassioned poet–novelist with a melodramatic imagination that seeks out the idiosyncratic, the gigantic, the grotesque, the extravagant, the mad. Taine is enamored of scientific exactitude and of exaggeration and excitement. His stance is that of the lucid, dispassionate Frenchman examining the wild, formless, passionate literature of the English. The logical grid of his ideas holds firm under the assault of the energies and uncontrolled imagination of English literature. From the vantage of the realistic-scientific culture of the later nineteenth century, Taine looks out with amazement and admiration at the romantic literature on which his taste was formed in the first half of the century.

Taine's nature was full of yoked contraries, which were also the contraries that preoccupied his contemporaries; and he was disturbed by the warring elements of his nature. He never reconciled the artistic and scientific sides of his nature, but he made a fruitful career out of their interaction. A series of contrasted pairs is evident everywhere in Taine's work:

Scientific Law—Individual Uniqueness
Science—Literature
Realism—Romanticism
Sociology—Psychology
Reason—Passion
Order—Chaos
Decorum—Inspiration
Southern—Northern
Latin—Germanic
French—English
Oratory—Poetry
Mind—Body
The Bourgeois—The Savage
The State—The Individual

These contraries are reflected in the heavily underlined contrasts of Taine's style and in the series of personifications and literary personalities through which he tells the story of English literature. His intention is to show how "the Saxon barbarian has been transformed into the Englishman of today." One side of his character-drawing is devoted to the creation of "moral persons" suggestive of Wallace Stevens' "major men." There is "the Saxon," "the Renaissance man," "the Puritan," "the Restoration rake," "the eighteenth-century English gentleman," and so on. The very landscapes in Taine vibrate with personality. The first paragraph of the first chapter of the *History of English Literature* describes the climate and geography of the lands that border on the North Sea:

As you sail along the North Sea from the Scheldt to Jutland, you will mark in the first place that the characteristic feature is want of slope; marsh, waste, shoal; the rivers hardly drag themselves along, swollen and sluggish, with long, black-looking waves; the flooding stream oozes over the banks, and appears farther on in stagnant pools. In Holland the soil is but a sediment of mud; here and there only does earth cover it with a crust, shallow and brittle, the mere alluvium of the river, which the river seems ever about to destroy. Thick clouds hover above, being fed by ceaseless exhalations. They lazily turn their violet flanks, grow black, suddenly descend in heavy showers; the vapor, like a furnace-smoke, crawls forever on the horizon.

(1.23)

From so much rain and mud, which make for heavy forests and other uncivilized manifestations, springs a race superb in its oafishness:

Huge white bodies, cool-blooded, with fierce blue eyes, reddish flaxen hair; ravenous stomachs, filled with meat and cheese, heated by strong drinks; of a cold temperament, slow to love, home-stayers, prone to brutal drunkenness; these are to this day the features which descent and climate preserve in the race. . . . In Germany, storm-beaten, in wretched boats of hide, amid hardships and dangers of seafaring life, they were preeminently adapted for endurance and enterprise, inured to misfortune, scorners of danger.

(1.26)

The people of the Germanic north personify the climate of the north; in Taine, everything is pregnant with metaphor and personification. The form is that of scientific history, but what we actually witness is a highly colored historical pageant.

Taine delights in finding paradox everywhere: it is from their very lumpishness that the Germanic races fashion their moral seriousness and love of heroism:

Dull and congealed, his ideas cannot expand with facility and freedom. . . . But this spirit, void of the sentiment of the beautiful, is all the more apt for the sentiment of the true. The deep and incisive impression which he receives from contact with objects, and which as yet he can only express with a cry, will afterwards liberate him from Latin rhetoric, and will vent itself on things rather than words. . . . Many moral instincts have gained the empire over him; and amongst them the need for independence, the disposition for serious and strict manners, the

inclination for devotion and veneration, the worship of heroism.

(1.56)

In addition to high color and paradox, Taine has a Balzacian fluency, abundance, and intensity in his descriptions of the composite person that represents a race or an epoch. In his treatment of the pagan Renaissance, he abstracts the master faculty of "warmth of imagination" and then amplifies his formula with a wealth of eloquent detail:

. . . men no longer make themselves master of objects by bits, or isolated, or through scholastic or mechanical classifications, but as a whole, general and complete views. With the eager grasp of a sympathetic spirit . . . an extraordinary warmth of soul, a superabundant and splendid imagination, reveries, visions, artists, believers, founders, creators—that is what such a form of intellect produces; for to create we must have, as had Luther and Loyola, Michel Angelo and Shakespeare, an idea, not abstract, partial, and dry, but well defined, finished, sensible—a true creation, which acts inwardly, and struggles to appear to the light.

(1.144)

In following the course of English literature from Saxon times through to Lord Tennyson, Taine is attracted to whatever is violent or bizarre or exotic. Whatever smacks too much of common sense or ordinary life fills him with disgust, so that he can scarcely find a kind word for Samuel Johnson, whose reputation he suspects is based on the mysterious British taste for banal moralizing. He finds the literature of the Restoration a dim and vulgar copy of the French seventeenth century; Lord Byron is the only English romantic poet who really captures his imagination.

Given such tastes, it is scarcely surprising that a highly romanticized Shakespeare is the hero of Taine's *History of English Literature.* One critic has said, "No other Latin experienced Shakespeare as profoundly as Taine," and the ninety pages on Shakespeare are the most sustained performance in the *History*. Taine is totally engrossed in his subject, and remains intelligent and precise even in the midst of his raptures. Shakespeare's master faculty, says Taine, is passionate imagination, and his essay is focused on manifestations of that quality in all of Shakespeare's characters, from the brutish Caliban in *The Tempest* up to the great tragic heroes. In plays we have only the unfolding action and the speech and appearance of the characters; we have no direct knowledge of their inner thoughts and emotions. Yet Taine devotes much of his attention to making inferences about the inner lives of Shakespeare's characters, treating them as if they were characters in novels rather than plays. He also gives an account of Shakespeare's life and provides an evocative description of his various styles. But he pays little attention to Shakespeare's plots, his dramaturgy, his role in the Globe theater, or the complex of philosophical and political ideas expressed in his work. For Taine, Shakespeare's genius lay in his grasp of the passion at the center of every character. Of Shakespeare's powers of thought and construction we hear almost nothing; like the rest of English literature at its greatest, the plays have sacrificed thought and form to intensity of passion. The absence of shaping intelligence is seen as a kind of guarantee of a deeper authenticity. Here is Taine summing up the way Shakespeare's master faculty of imagination is manifested in all his characters:

> They are all united, and all marked by the same sign, void of will and reason, governed by mood, imagination, or pure passion, destitute of faculties contrary to those of the poet. . . . Go through the groups, and you will only discover in them divers forms and divers states of the same power. Here, a herd of brutes, dotards, and gossips made up of a mechanical imagination; further on, a company of men of wit, animated by a gay and foolish imagination; then, a charming swarm of women whom their delicate imagination raises so high and their self-forgetting love carries so far; elsewhere a band of villains, hardened by

unbridled passions, inspired by artistic rapture; in the center a mournful train of grand characters, whose excited brain is filled with sad or criminal visions, and whom an inner destiny urges to murder, madness, or death.

(1.350)

Figures such as Brutus and Horatio are largely edited out of Taine's cast of Shakespearean characters.

Even Shakespeare's wit is the wit of untrammeled imagination rather than the wit of reason; Taine will not permit his Shakespeare to approach the common daylight of logic and irony:

> Of wit there are many kinds. One, altogether French, which is but reason, a foe to paradox, scorner of folly, a sort of incisive common sense, having no occupation but to render truth amusing and evident, the most effective weapon with an intelligent and vain people: such was the wit of Voltaire and the drawing rooms. The other, that of improvisatores and artists, is a mere inventive rapture, paradoxical, unshackled, exuberant, a sort of self-entertainment, a phantasmagoria of images, flashes of wit, strange ideas, daring and intoxicating, like the movement and illumination in a ballroom.

(1.320)

If Shakespeare offers an ideal subject for Taine's conception of master faculty, he is more difficult to present as a pure representative of his age. Indeed Taine finds it necessary to talk out of both sides of his mouth when discussing Shakespeare and his milieu: "a nature poetical, immoral, inspired, superior to reason by the sudden revelations of its seer's madness; so extreme in joy and grief, so abrupt of gait, so agitated and impetuous in its transports, that this great age alone could have cradled such a child." Up to this point, Taine presents the genius of the age and the genius of Shakespeare as happily compatible in temper. But a little later he says, "Of Shakespeare all came from within—I mean from his soul and his genius; circumstances and the externals contributed but slightly to his development'' (1.296). Since Taine's idea of the genius of the age is largely derived from his conception of Shakespeare, it is hardly surprising that he finds the two spirits compatible. But when he turns to consider the ordinary round of life in Elizabethan London, he finds no mirror of Shakespeare's soul; his external life was ''commonplace.'' In such wavering moments, Taine reveals his usually submerged awareness that the relation of a writer to his age is not that of mirror to object, but something far more oblique and ambiguous.

Writing primarily for a French audience, Taine is full of comparisons between French and English literature. Following Stendhal rather closely, he compares Shakespeare's vision with that of classical French tragedy:

> If Racine or Corneille had framed a psychology, they would have said, with Descartes: man is an incorporeal soul, served by organs, endowed with reason and will, dwelling in palaces or porticos, made for conversation and society, whose harmonious and ideal action is developed by discourse and replies, in a world constructed by logic beyond the realms of time and space.
>
> If Shakespeare had framed a psychology, he would have said . . . Man is a nervous machine, governed by a mood, disposed to hallucinations, carried away by unbridled passions, essentially unreasoning, a mixture of animal and poet, having instead of mind rapture, instead of virtue sensibility, imagination for prompter and guide, and led at random, by the most complex and determinate circumstances, to sorrow, crime, madness, and death.
>
> (1.340)

Taine's treatment of Shakespeare provides a particularly clear illustration of how he sees the relation of a writer to his works. Very little in the way of tradition, convention, or the mechanics of composition intervenes between the writer and his works. When the writer is angry he writes angrily; when he is sad he writes sadly. He feels every passion he depicts. Every character is an extension of the writer's personality, and every speech of a character is also a speech of the author. The work of literature is significant only as a vehicle for literary personality. Thus arises Taine's sensitivity to voice and tone in literature, alongside his determination to ignore the fact that works of art exist in the world independent of their makers. The existence of a work as a ''thing-in-itself'' is of no interest whatever to Taine. Unless Shakespeare's plays can be imagined as pregnant with Shakespeare's spirit, they are mere husks of the past.

Taine closes his volumes on English literature with a comparison of Tennyson and Alfred de Musset, the favorite poet of his youth. He has little to say about the relations of the two poets to the economic and political life of the age, but characterizes them by contrasting the audiences for which they wrote. Throughout his work, some of Taine's most telling passages are accounts of the way audiences shape literary works, eliciting just those qualities in a writer that complete the audience's conception of itself. After an account of Victorian country house life, Taine says:

> Such is this elegant and commonsense society, refined in comfort, regular in conduct, whose dilettante tastes and moral principles confine it within a sort of flowery border. . . .
>
> Does any poet suit such a society better than Tennyson? Without being a pedant, he is moral; he may be read in the family circle by night; he does not rebel against society and life; he speaks of God and the soul, nobly, tenderly, without ecclesiastical prejudice; there is no need to reproach him like Lord Byron; he has no violent and abrupt words, extravagant and scandalous sentiments; he will pervert nobody.
>
> (2.537)

Tennyson is read by the privileged, the respectable, and the dull in their well-ordered country houses: Musset is read in the restless, cosmopolitan bohemia of Paris:

> In this gulf, which is like a vast sea, dreams, theories, fancies, intemperate, poetic, and sickly de-

sires, collect and chase each other like clouds. . . .

Such is the world for which Alfred de Musset wrote; in Paris he must be read. Read? We all know him by heart. He is dead, and it seems as if we daily hear him speak. A conversation among artists, as they jest in a studio, a beautiful young girl leaning over her box at the theater, a street washed by the rain, making the black pavement shine, a fresh, smiling morning in the woods of Fontainebleau, everything brings him before us, as if he were alive again. Was there ever a more vibrating and genuine accent? This man, at least, never lied. He only said what he felt, and he said it as he felt it. He thought aloud.

(2.539)

Thus Taine's account of English literature ends with a curious twist. He leaves English poetry cozily prosing away in country houses, mouthing platitudes. The spirit of romance recrosses the English Channel to become incarnate among the agile-minded French bohemians in the extravagant figure of Musset. Rational Latins and romantic Germanic peoples, passionate north and sensible south, are for the moment forgotten. The last picture is of Parisian liveliness confronting Victorian dullness. Perhaps, for all his cosmopolitanism, Taine is at the end thanking God that he is not British. Taine's favorite novel was Stendhal's La chartreuse de Parme (The Charterhouse of Parma, 1839), which he read more than forty times. Its spirit of operatic extravagance and ironic intelligence prevails in Taine's final pages. Inflamed passion and moral seriousness have been all very well for five books, but at the end Taine returns to the mobile emotions and unmoral sincerity of Paris.

In 1864, at the suggestion of Napoleon III, Taine was appointed professor of aesthetics and art history at the École des Beaux Arts, succeeding the distinguished architect Eugène Viollet-le-Duc. The conservative Viollet-le-Duc had been jeered off the platform when he tried to give his first lecture; the intellectually radical Taine was greeted with applause.

Taine's attack on the reigning philosophers had made him influential enemies, but he had become a hero to students. His first appearance on the lecture platform was a moment of high drama. Twenty years later the writer Paul Bourget remembered the occasion in this fashion:

The audience, seated in a huge semi-circular hall, faced the professor who . . . resembles a Protestant minister in his pulpit, bearded, wearing glasses, and speaking simply to men like himself. The students are more attentive than one would expect from those young, bearded, and long-haired men with their bright eyes and mocking expressions. The professor seems as young as the students. . . .

The teacher was speaking in his somewhat monotonous voice, his accent sounded vaguely foreign. This man, so modest that he seemed unaware of his European reputation and so simple that his only concern seemed to be to serve truth, became for us the apostle of a New Faith. Here was a man who had never sacrificed on the altar of official doctrines, this man had never lied.

(quoted in Weinstein, p. 21)

For the next five years Taine worked quickly and intensely on art history. Almost every year he prepared a new course of formal lectures, which were promptly revised for publication in book form. In this half decade he published five books on art: Philosophie de l'art (Philosophy of Art, 1865); Philosophie de l'art en Italie (Art in Italy, 1866), with a companion travel volume containing many fine descriptions of art works, Voyage en Italie (Trip to Italy, 1866); Philosophie de l'art dans les Pays-Bas (Art in the Netherlands, 1868); and Philosophie de l'art en Grèce (Art in Greece, 1869).

In moving so seamlessly from philosophy and literature to art history, Taine showed a generous share of the versatility of the intellectuals of his time. Of course, he was helped by the fact that knowledge was less specialized then than now, and by his conviction that his methods were as well suited to visual art as to literature. He was able to bring his scientific and literary interests forward with him into his new investigations. His art-historical books have almost as many references to literature as to works of art, and he also analyzes the subject matter of art history from the point of view of race, moment, milieu, and master faculty. The argumentative drive of his lectures is to verify the "law" of "the exact correspondence which is always seen between a work and the medium out of which it is evolved." Thus Taine argues that Rembrandt was supplied with his characteristic interplay of light and darkness by the way late afternoon light fades into obscurity in the humid air of the Netherlands. The medieval hatred of the body accounts for the feeble and emaciated figures in art from the fall of Rome to the Renaissance. As with literary works, Taine traces every artwork to its ground in nature or culture.

However, Taine also makes significant additions to the theoretical structure he had first enunciated in the introduction to the *History of English Literature*. First, he constructs a carefully argued theory of art as imitation, provisionally leaving art and music outside the structure. Here is his summary of his theory of imitation:

> At first we thought that the object of art was to *imitate sensible appearances*. Then separating material from intellectual imitation, we found that what it desired to reproduce in sensible appearances is the *relationship of parts*. Finally, remarking that relations are, and ought to be, modified in order to obtain the highest results of art, we proved that if we study the relationship of parts it is *to make predominant an essential character*.

And a little later in the same lecture:

> The end of a work of art is to manifest some essential or salient character, consequently some important idea, more clearly and more completely than is obtainable from real objects. To do this, art uses a group of connected parts, and modifies their relationships.
>
> (*Lectures on Art*, p. 57)

That is, art may begin with the representation of visible appearances, but it ends by "imitating" a governing conception in the mind of the artist. Thus Michelangelo expresses his despair over tyranny through the powerfully contorted statues on the Medici tombs, and Peter Paul Rubens celebrates the new prosperity of the Flemish in the rosy flesh of his nudes. Like a well-wrought essay, a great work of painting or sculpture has a thesis that is demonstrated in all of its parts, and understanding a work of art becomes a matter of reading backward, as it were, from its visible elements to its unstated central idea.

Everywhere in his work on art, Taine reveals the truth in this piece of self-description: "What I perceive through a work of art, as through any work, is the state of mind that produced it." This "state of mind" includes not only the artist but his society and his epoch. The sociology of culture is mirrored in the psychology of the artist, and both are encoded in the work of art that he produces. Thus the psychology of the artist is a portal through which Taine can advance to the depiction of the societies of classical Greece, Renaissance Italy, and seventeenth-century Holland; such descriptions, in fact, make up the bulk of his volumes on art, overshadowing the artworks themselves. Rather, he describes the societies he finds mirrored in the consciousness of artists of various countries and epochs.

For the first time, Taine set out to establish a scale of values for making judgments about works of art, something he had previously rejected as contrary to the scientific spirit. Two of his criteria are eminently those of tradition: a work's unity of effect and its ability to withstand the test of time. The other two criteria are the importance and beneficence of character. These are not original with Taine, but their explicitly ethical emphasis makes them surprising in the context of his thought. The first criterion—the importance of a character—is determined by whether he represents a mere fad in society, a whole movement, such as classicism, an epoch such as the Middle Ages, a national character, or all of humankind. At the bottom are ordinary best-sellers that capitalize on passing fashions, and at the top are world masterpieces such as Plato's *Dialogues* (*ca.* 400 B.C.) and Shakespeare's tragedies. This scale of importance does not upset anything in the already established aspects of Taine's thought or in the conventional judgments made by ordinary readers.

Surprisingly, Taine also proposed that the more morally edifying a work of art is, the better it is as art. But the scale of beneficence goes against his own tastes in literature, if not in visual art, and places a set of dull and blameless worthies at the top of the scale: Samuel Richardson's Pamela, Clarissa, and Sir Charles Grandison, for example. The scale of beneficence works out in a more congenial fashion with regard to visual art, since the highest place goes to Greek sculpture, with its perfectly proportioned nudes that embody the ideals of a lucid and harmonious civilization.

This bow to morality probably had something to do with Taine's advance toward middle age and a more settled way of life. At this period in his life he broke with his mistress, the novelist Camille Selden, married, became the head of a family, and acquired a house in the country. Now he may have wished, for the first time, to parry the charges of immorality that were hurled at him because of his refusal to let his scientific views give precedence to morality.

As an art historian, Taine's official position is that he is all on the side of health, beauty, plenitude, and clear light in works of art; but his imagination is still powerfully moved by strangeness, distortion, and ugliness. In the following passage, he is depicting the long transition from medieval to Renaissance art: from the undernourished, gloomy figures of Gothic stained glass to the glorious fleshliness of the Italian Renaissance:

Among the masters of the fifteenth century, you still find numerous signs which denote the ancient consumption and the immemorial fast: in Memling, at the Bruges hospital, faces quite out of the monastic pale, heads too big, brows bulging out through the exaggerations of mystic reverie, meager arms, the monotonous placidity of passive life preserved like a pale flower in the shade of the cloister; in Fra Angelico, attenuated bodies hidden beneath radiant copes and robes, reduced to beatified phantoms, no breasts, elongated heads and protuberant brows; in Albert Dürer, thighs and arms too thin, bellies too large, and ungraceful feet, anxious, wrinkled, and worn countenances, pale and wan Adams and Eves, all chilly and benumbed, to whom one would like to give clothes; among almost all, this form of the skull which recalls the fakirs or the hydrocephalous, and those hideous infants, scarcely viable, a species of tadpole, whose enormous head is prolonged by a flabby body, and then by a slender appendage of wriggled and twisted members.

(*Lectures on Art*, p. 293)

In the works Taine describes, he finds the element of meagerness and distortion is still strong, reflecting the fading medieval world. Ostensibly the passage is a piece of objective art-historical description. But underneath that appearance it is a rhapsody on the sufferings visited on the human body by a cruel spiritual idea. The hideous tadpole body of the infant of the last sentence, with its immense head and puny appendages, is an emblem of the overweening mind and despised body in the medieval world. In essence, Taine's description is an assault on medieval Christianity's hatred for the things of this world as expressed in its rejection of the body.

In his period as an art historian, Taine became somewhat more conventional. He introduced an explicitly moral element into his theory of art; he delighted in the beauty of Greek figure sculpture and Renaissance painting. He insisted again on his scholarly stance as a man of science and a disinterested observer. But the moral scale he introduced obviously bored him; the grotesque and the surreal enchanted him, while he was merely pleased by beauty. Despite his vaunted objectivity, he is often passionate, doctrinaire, and polemical. The cool language of analysis may prevail for a paragraph, but then it gives way to the overheated prose of melodrama. Taine may pause for a moment at moderation, but he soon goes on to extremes, where he is more at home.

In 1870 Taine published his long-contemplated treatise *On Intelligence*, which had its beginnings in his doctoral essay on the sensations. He planned a companion volume "On the Will," which was never written. By "intelligence" Taine meant whatever faculties enter into acts of cognition. In part his work is an epistemological treatise in which he follows Spinoza in assuming that the order and interconnections of things are the same as the order and interconnections of ideas. In part it is an empirical work that gathers all the medical and experimental knowledge available, drawing on medical journals, physiology, neurology, and linguistics.

In the preface Taine explains the connection between this treatise and his earlier work:

> Between psychology . . . and history as it is now written, the relationship is very close. For history is applied psychology, psychology applied to more complex cases. . . . Carlyle has written that of Cromwell; Sainte-Beuve that of Port Royal; Stendhal has made twenty attempts on that of the Italians; M. Renan has given us that of the semitic race . . . what historians do with respect to the past, the great novelists and dramatists do with the present. For fifteen years I have contributed to these special and concrete psychologies; I now attempt general and abstract psychology.
>
> (*De l'intelligence* 1.x)

History, then, is psychology made manifest, and consciousness and phenomena run parallel to one another. But Taine would not be himself if he let matters stand in such an untroubled symmetry. What we experience is "true hallucinations." Reason staggers precariously to its correct conclusions amid madness and encroaching dreams:

> We may compare the silent elaboration of which consciousness is the ordinary result to the progress of the slave who, after the games of the circus, crossed the length of the arena, among the wearied lions and glutted tigers, bearing in his hand an egg; if he arrived safely, he received his freedom. So passes the mind through the confusion of monstrous deliria and yelling madness, almost always with impunity, to settle itself in accurate consciousness and exact recollection.
>
> (*De l'intelligence* 1.vii)

The conclusion of *On Intelligence* is an optimistic one. Reason, however weak and vulnerable, however beset by the instincts, usually reaches its goal of accurate conceptions of things. Cognition involves a long journey through madness and error, but usually arrives at the truth surprisingly intact. The defeat of France in the Franco-Prussian War in 1870, the very year *On Intelligence* was published, gave a severe blow to this qualified optimism and caused Taine's thought to take a new turn.

With the publication of *Les philosophes français du XIXe siècle* in 1857, Taine emerged as a famous personality in French intellectual life, an enfant terrible equipped with philosophy, wit, and formidable scientific and literary learning. For the next thirteen years he wrote book after book demonstrating the application of the methods of natural science to literature, art, and psychology. Just as his great contemporary Renan gave a purely naturalistic account of Christ in his *Vie de Jésus* (*Life of Jesus*, 1888), ignoring the supernatural, so Taine gave a naturalistic account of the arts, placing them firmly in this world. He saw himself as one of a small band of independent thinkers, an ally of the future and an enemy of the morass of prescientific error and superstition. With the defeat of France and the subsequent rise of the Commune in Paris, Taine was profoundly shaken in his confidence as a Frenchman, a bourgeois, and a champion of positive science.

Until 1870 France was indisputably the leading power of continental Europe, and it was possible in France to admire Germanic art and philosophy with a confident sense of French political superiority. Until 1870 there had been no effective challenge to the supremacy of the bourgeoisie, established in power by the Revolution of 1789. The application of rational thought and scientific method to human affairs had seemed to guarantee steady progress for humanity; when the Commune brought back the Goddess of Reason of the French Revolution, her smile took on a sinister cast for Taine. The defeat of France by Bismarck's Germany appalled Taine and aroused his latent patriotism; he no longer wanted to praise the barbaric energy and poetic imagination of the Germanic peoples but to diagnose the spiritual illness that had made France vulnerable to defeat. When he saw the bourgeois government driven out of Paris by the Commune, Taine's latent class loyalty was aroused. Like most artists and thinkers, Taine had regarded his fellow bourgeois with a certain contempt, identifying himself only with the tiny intellectual elite. Now he saw the middle class as the vessel of civilization, the guardian of civil society.

Taine's crisis of confidence in his nation, his class, and his intellectual commitments led directly to his undertaking the task that was to occupy the last twenty years of his life: *The Origins of Contemporary France*. Taine directed scorching criticism first at the old regime, then at the French Revolution, and finally at Napoleon Bonaparte, thus managing to outrage every major segment of French

opinion. The work stirred passionate interest and debate as it appeared, and its longevity is attested to by a thirty-seventh French edition in 1947. The great English historian Lord Acton said of Taine's history:

> Of books that are strong enough to work a change and form an epoch in a reader's life, there are two, perhaps, on our revolutionary shelf. One is Taine, and the other is Michelet. No man feels the grandeur of the Revolution until he reads Michelet, or the horror of it without reading Taine.
>
> (quoted in Weinstein, pp. 141–142)

In his preface to the first volume, *L'Ancien Régime* (*The Ancient Regime*, 1875), Taine defines the nature of his undertaking by means of two metaphors. The first, predictably, is scientific: "A historian may be allowed the privilege of a naturalist; I have regarded my subject the same as the metamorphosis of an insect." Typically, he is claiming scientific disinterest at the same moment he is editorializing by calling France an insect. The second metaphor is medical: France is the patient, and Taine is the doctor, trying to determine how the illness could have been prevented. He discovers that France fell sick after drinking a poisonous mixture of scientific method and classical style, which produced the deadly conception of Reason that ruled during the Revolution.

Taine makes allowance for the abuses of power and the economic problems that led up to the Revolution. Indeed he even allows that its fundamental effect was to transfer property and power from one class to another. But his deepest interest is in the intellectual climate out of which the Revolution arose. In depicting the disastrous marriage of natural philosophy and classical style, Taine shows how they combined to create a rigid, timeless Goddess of Reason, dangerously ignorant of the wisdom of history and tradition. Taine was the most distinguished follower of Edmund Burke in attacking the Revolution's abstract rationalism and defending the wisdom intertwined with tradition, an odd position for a champion of positive science to find himself in.

After praising the experimental and scientific spirit of the eighteenth century, Taine says, "the same operations in the hands of closet speculators, salon amateurs, and oratorical charlatans in public places, will undoubtedly end in mischievous compounds and destructive explosions." This pseudoscience found a hospitable medium of expression in the classical style, with its pleasant blurring of specifics:

> It is the organ only of a certain species of reasoning, *la raison raisonnante* [reasoning in a vacuum], that requiring the least preparation for thought, giving itself as little trouble as possible, content with its acquisitions, taking no pains to renew them, incapable, or unwilling, to embrace the plenitude and complexity of actualities. In its purism, in its disdain of terms suited to the occasion, in its avoidance of lively sallies, in the extreme regularity of its developments, the classic style is powerless to fully portray or record the infinite and varied details of experience.
>
> (*The Ancient Regime*, Durand trans., p. 191)

Thus Taine redirects at the philosophes and their revolutionary successors the very criticisms most frequently leveled at his own work: that it was the product of a loose and polemical scientism rather than of science; and that it was so general in its focus that details inconvenient for the arguments were easily thrust aside or ignored.

Added to this over-general style of thought and merely speculative interest in science, according to Taine, was the dangerous thought of Jean Jacques Rousseau, the catalyst that rendered the mixture explosive. Rousseau thought that society was founded on the usurpation of natural right by the rise of private property and its champion, the state. Natural humanity has been corrupted by a society organized to defend privilege. Once the corruption of society is removed, natural reason will emerge and natural goodness will reassert it-

self. Taine had no patience with the theory of rule of natural reason in human affairs or the natural goodness of humanity. Of reason, he says:

> Not only is reason not natural to man nor universal to humanity, but again, in the conduct of man and of humanity, its influence is small. . . . The place obtained by reason is always restricted; the office it fulfills is generally secondary. Openly or secretly, it is only a convenient subaltern, a domestic advocate unceasingly suborned, employed by the proprietors to plead in their behalf; if they yield it precedence in public it is only through decorum.
>
> (*The Ancient Regime*, p. 240)

In Taine's distorted and hostile account, Rousseau's baseless optimism about human nature and his hatred of civilization formed the ideological basis for the Reign of Terror. The faith that the stripping away of the corruptions of civilization would liberate the naturally virtuous individual and restore the rule of reason was used to justify the crimes of Jean-Paul Marat and Maximilien de Robespierre during the Terror. Robespierre is described with a steamy virulence that shows the hatred Taine felt for the Jacobins:

> . . . all these heads, Robespierre, according to his maxims, must strike off. He is well aware of this; hostile as his intellect may be to precise ideas, he when alone in his closet, face to face with himself, sees clearly, as clearly as Marat. . . . At the end of three years, Robespierre has overtaken Marat, at the extreme point reached by Marat at the outset, and the theorist adopts the policy, the aim, the means, the work, and almost the vocabulary of the maniac: armed dictatorship of the urban mob, systematic maddening of the urban populace, war against the bourgeoisie, extermination of the rich, proscription of opposition writers, administrators, and deputies. . . . Henceforth he may in vain abstain from action, take refuge in rhetoric, stop his chaste ears, and raise his hypocritic eyes to heaven; he cannot avoid seeing or hearing under his immaculate feet the streaming gore, and the bones crashing

in the open jaws of the insatiable monster which he has fashioned and on which he must prance.
(*The French Revolution*, Durand trans., 2.251)

Not only did the Jacobins inspire Taine with fear and loathing, he also regarded them as a group of men with mediocre abilities and little experience of political responsibility. Thus they were all too likely to fall back for guidance on a half-understood philosophy of reason. Their main achievement was to facilitate the transfer of property and power from one class to another. Otherwise the Jacobins simply carried further the disastrous policy of a centralized state power that had been the constant aim of the monarchy ever since the civil wars of the Fronde.

Taine's unfriendly treatment of Napoleon cost him the friendship of the Princess Mathilde Bonaparte, whose salon he had frequented for many years. For Taine, Napoleon did not so much end the Revolution as fulfill its aim. He was the greatest egoist and the greatest genius of the modern world. He rationalized, regularized, and centralized French government and law, and thus brought to a bad fruition the work of the old regime and the Revolution. Taine saw in this centralization a stifling of individual abilities, a crushing of initiatives, and a denial of pluralism that were constantly undermining France. Overcentralized and overregulated, France was becoming more and more rigid and immobile. With a belief in laissez-faire worthy of a Manchester manufacturer, Taine attributed the fall of France in 1870 to the strangulating effects of overcentralized administration—the master flaw, as it were.

The furious debate over *The Origins of Contemporary France* as it appeared volume after volume for twenty years was in part encouraged by the fact that, as Edmund Wilson said, "it is not a history at all, but simply an enormous essay." Although there are passages of superb historical narrative, Taine's primary intent is argumentative and demonstrative, so that the narrative is always at the service of the argument. The argument itself is constantly energized by Taine's tireless indignation at the wrongheadedness of the rulers of France, virtually from Louis XIV onward. The rulers had so mismanaged affairs that France easily fell prey to the German armies, and Taine felt driven to assert their blameworthiness again and again.

However turbulent the political passions Taine poured into this history, and however turbulent the public controversies surrounding his work, the last two decades of Taine's life were full of comforts and honors. He had evolved from an enfant terrible into one of the established eminences of French intellectual life. In 1871 he received an honorary degree from Oxford; in 1878 he was at last elected to the French Academy. In 1874 the Taines bought a country house near the lake of Annecy, where they lived most of the year. During the winter in Paris, they gave Monday night dinners for friends who included most of the notables of French artistic and intellectual life.

After 1885 Taine was in increasingly poor health, and although he still continued to publish, he was forced to restrict his hours of work. He died in Paris on 5 March 1893 and was buried near his beloved home in the country.

Little is heard about Taine these days. Occasionally he is spoken of as a forebear of the present generation of structuralist critics in France, but they show no inclination to acknowledge his paternity. Perhaps he is one of those writers who disappear because part of their work has been thoroughly absorbed and part has been thoroughly abandoned. Certainly Taine's notion that works of art must be understood as expressions of their milieu has since become almost axiomatic in literary study. Marxist criticism has absorbed and transmuted the sociological study of literature, something that Taine may almost be said to have invented. Psychoanalytic criticism has taken over Taine's interest in the psychological basis of artistic creation and historical change. The intellectual position that Taine created and spent a lifetime defending has had heirs who may have used it as a point of departure. These writers have followed their own lines of development to the point of no longer remembering the original.

Taine lives on invisibly in the critical tradition rather than in his own works. Reading through Taine today, it is hard not to agree with Henry James: "As a writer . . . I enjoy Taine more almost than I do anyone; but his philosophy of things strikes me as essentially superficial." His leading ideas now seem more like powerful rhetorical stratagems than substantive philosophical ideas. His books, however, retain their vigor and fertility of metaphorical invention.

If there is to be a revival of interest in Taine, the emphasis will have to be on the energy of his imagination and the lively readability of his books. As a thinker he has passed into history; as a writer with verve and intelligence, he is still very much alive.

Selected Bibliography

EDITIONS

Place of publication is Paris.

Essai sur les fables de La Fontaine. 1853. Reissued as La Fontaine et ses fables, 1861. 17th ed., 1905.

Voyage aux eaux des Pyrénées. 1855. Reissued as Voyage aux Pyrénées. 3rd ed., 1860.

Essai sur Tite Live. 1856. 7th ed., 1904.

Les philosophes français du XIXe siècle. 1857. Reissued as Les philosophes classiques du XIXe siècle. 3rd ed., 1868.

Essais de critique et d'histoire. 1858. 10th ed., 1904.

Histoire de la littérature anglaise. 4 vols. 1863–1864. 3rd ed., 5 vols., 1873; 8th ed., 5 vols., 1892; 13th ed., 1911.

Philosophie de l'art. 1865.

Nouveaux essais de critique et d'histoire. 1865. 12th ed., 1923.

Philosophie de l'art en Italie. 1866.

Voyage en Italie. 1866.

Notes sur Paris. 1867.

De l'idéal dans l'art. 1867.

Philosophie de l'art dans les Pays-Bas. 1868.

Philosophie de l'art en Grèce. 1869.

De l'intelligence. 2 vols. 1870. 32nd ed., 1948.

Notes sur l'Angleterre. 1871.

De suffrage universel et de la manière de voter. 1871.

Les origines de la France contemporaine. 11 vols. 1875–1893. 37th ed., 1947.

    L'Ancien régime. 1875.

    La révolution. Vol. 1: L'Anarchie, 1878. Vol. 2: La conquête jacobine, 1881. Vol. 3: Le gouvernement révolutionnaire, 1884.

    Le régime moderne. Vol. 1, 1891. Vol. 2, 1894.

Derniers essais de critique et d'histoire. 1894.

Carnets de voyage: Notes sur la province (1863–1865). 1897.

H. Taine: Sa vie et sa correspondance. 4 vols. 1902–1907.

Étienne Mayran. 1910.

TRANSLATIONS

All translations published in New York.

History of English Literature. 2 vols. Translated by H. van Laun. 1872.

Italy: Rome and Naples. Translated by J. Durand. 1868.

Italy: Florence and Venice. Translated by J. Durand. 1869.

Journeys Through France. Translated anonymously. 1897.

Lectures on Art. 2 vols. Translated by J. Durand. 1875.

Life and Letters of H. Taine. 3 vols. 1902–1908. Vols. 1 and 2 translated by R. Devonshire. Vol. 3 translated by E. Sparvel-Bayly.

Notes on England. Translated by W. F. Rae. 1872.

Notes on Paris. Translated by J. A. Stevens. 1875.

On Intelligence. 2 vols. Translated by T. D. Haye. 1889.

The Origins of Contemporary France. 6 vols. Translated by J. Durand. 1876–1894.

    The Ancient Regime. 1876.

    The French Revolution. Vol. 1, 1897. Vol. 2, 1892. Vol. 3, 1885.

    The Modern Regime. 2 vols. 1890–1894.

A Tour Through the Pyrenees. Translated by J. S. Fiske. 1874.

BIOGRAPHICAL AND CRITICAL STUDIES

Aarsleff, Hans. "Taine: His Importance for Saussure and Structuralism." *Yale Review* 68:71–81 (1978).

Barzun, Jacques. *Race: A Study in Modern Superstition.* New York, 1937.

Bourget, Paul. *Essais de psychologie contemporaine: Baudelaire, M. Renan, Flaubert, M. Taine, Stendhal.* Paris, 1883. Pp. 175–330.

Butler, R. "Zola between Taine and Sainte-Beuve." *Modern Language Review* 69:279–289 (1974).

Chevrillon, André. *Taine: Formation de sa pensée.* Paris, 1932.

Cresson, André. *Hippolyte Taine: Sa vie, son oeuvre; avec un exposé de sa philosophie.* Paris, 1951.

Daugherty, S. B. "Taine, James, and Balzac: Toward an Aesthetic of Romantic Realism." *Henry James Review* 2:12–24 (1980).

Eustis, A. A. *Hippolyte Taine and the Classical Genius.* Berkeley, Calif., 1951.

Frank, F. S. "The Two Taines of Henry James." *Revue de littérature comparée* 45:350–365 (1971).

Giraud, Victor. *Essai sur Taine: Son oeuvre et son influence . . .* Paris, 1901.

Kahn, S. J. *Science and Aesthetic Judgment: A Study in Taine's Critical Method.* London and New York, 1953.

Leroy, Maxime. *Taine.* Paris, 1933.

Levin, Harry. "Literature as an Institution." Reprinted from *Accent,* 1947. In *Criticism: The Foundations of Modern Literary Judgment.* New York, 1948. Pp. 546–553.

Morawski, Stefan. "The Problem of Value and Criteria in Taine's Aesthetics." *Journal of Aesthetics and Art Criticism* 21:407–421 (1963).

Rosca, D. D. *L'Influence de Hegel sur Taine, théoricien de la connaisance et de l'art.* Paris, 1928.

Weinstein, Leo. *Hippolyte Taine.* New York, 1972.

Wellek, René. *A History of Modern Criticism, 1750–1950.* Vol. 4. New Haven, Conn., 1965. Pp. 27–57.

Wilson, Edmund. *To the Finland Station.* New York, 1953. Pp. 44–54.

MASON COOLEY

LEO TOLSTOY
(1828–1910)

IN NOVEMBER 1855 Count Leo (in Russian: Lev) Tolstoy arrived in Saint Petersburg directly from the Crimea, where he had participated in the war with the European powers and had observed the siege of Sevastopol. The disastrous war was being brought to a close. Nicholas I, after ruling despotically for thirty years, had died in February, and the heir, Alexander II, was expected to undertake long-delayed reforms, including the abolition of serfdom. Everyone felt that an era of Russian history was ending. The time was ripe for the advent of a new generation of writers. At this propitious moment Tolstoy entered the circle of literati grouped around the influential journal *Sovremennik (The Contemporary)*.

Tolstoy was already well known by reputation to the Saint Petersburg writers who welcomed him. His first work, *Childhood*, had appeared in *The Contemporary* in 1852 and had been greeted by almost unanimous praise from all the factions that made up the contentious Russian literary scene. Ivan Turgenev, whose *Sportsman's Sketches* had established him as the leading writer of the day, wrote to the editor of *The Contemporary*: "This is a sure gift. Write him and encourage him to continue. Tell him, in case he may be interested, that I welcome, hail, and applaud him." *Childhood* had been followed by *Boyhood* (1854) and several short stories, but when Tolstoy came to Saint Petersburg he was hailed as the author of *Sevastopol Sketches*, the first two of which had appeared in *The Contemporary* earlier in 1855.

Sevastopol Sketches had electrified the public with their accounts of the Russian soldiers' suffering and heroism under continual bombardment in the besieged city. "The hero of my tale is truth," Tolstoy had written, and the precision of his account, combined with an elevated and sonorous lyricism, had impressed upon his readers the tragedy of war. The second sketch, "Sevastopol in May," began: "Already six months have passed since the first shot whistled from the bastions of Sevastopol and plowed the earth at the enemy's fortifications, and since that time thousands of bombs, cannonballs, and bullets have not ceased to fly from the bastions to the trenches and from the trenches to the bastions, and the angel of death has not ceased to soar above us." In his role as war correspondent Tolstoy had gone far beyond "dispatches from the front" to evolve a style combining factuality with prophetic vision. He was greeted on his arrival in Saint Petersburg both as the hero of Sevastopol (his role in the fighting had in fact been slight) and as the hope for the future of Russian literature.

The Saint Petersburg writers expected Tolstoy to take up the career considered appropriate for a Russian literary man in the mid-nineteenth century. He would ally himself with one of the factions, announce his ideological position on the literary and social questions debated by the intelligentsia, and settle down as a regular contributor to one of the journals, probably *The Contemporary*, where all his work to date had been published. They reckoned without Tolstoy's independent character. He lost no time in establishing himself as wholly different in his habits and attitudes from members of the Russian intelligentsia. He quarreled with Turgenev, rejected the ideological positions of all the factions, and played the role of officer and aristocrat to the hilt by visiting in society, carousing at night with gypsies, and sleeping until two in the afternoon. The intellectuals reached their verdict, ''a wild man,'' and yet still they courted him, eager to acquire so much talent and energy for the service of their cause.

In subsequent decades, as in the 1850's, Russian literary men continued to regard Tolstoy as a valuable national property to be exploited for the glory of Russian literature. His life and work continued to be bound inextricably with the vicissitudes of national life and yet to express the concerns of each decade in ways peculiarly his own. The pressures of these forces, national and individual, shaped that mythical ''Tolstoy'' possessed by the modern reader. Virginia Woolf thought him the very type of the alien element in the Russian character that prevents Russian literature from ever being wholly accessible to Europeans. Yet Tolstoy seems far more the world's than Russia's, too large to be confined within a single national tradition or even a single historical period.

With Tolstoy's debut the constellation of writers whose work would make the Russian novel a powerful voice in world literature was complete. The tide of novels began by the end of the 1850's and continued with undiminished force up to 1880. In this period Tolstoy wrote two works, *War and Peace* (written 1863–1869) and *Anna Karenina* (written 1873–1876), that have become accepted into the world's common fund of literature. He is the author of other original and ingratiating works that continue to hold the reader's affection, among them *Childhood* (1852), *Family Happiness* (1859), *The Cossacks* (1863), *The Death of Ivan Ilich* (1886), *Master and Man* (1895), *Father Sergius* (1911), and *Hadji-Murad* (1912). These and a few more items compose his purely literary legacy, but he also wrote strange, powerful, polemical works— *The Kreutzer Sonata* (1891), *A Confession* (1884), *What Is Art?* (1897–1898), *Resurrection* (1899)—that are an inseparable part of our modern conception of Tolstoy.

Beyond that, Tolstoy's own life has become a part of our literary tradition. Boris Eikhenbaum observes that in another epoch Tolstoy would not have been a writer. Tolstoy entered literature because in the Russian conditions of the time, literature was the arena open to independent action. There was scarcely another possibility for setting one's own course. One could retreat and become the manager of one's estate—Tolstoy's grandfather and father had taken this path, and Tolstoy would try it in his turn—but then one lost the possibility of influencing public life. In spite of his hatred of the ideological polemics that drained Russian life of all force of action, Tolstoy entered the public arena repeatedly. His energies spread out beyond literature into pedagogy, social thought, and moral philosophy. Again and again he sought to turn the gold coin of his fame as a writer into public influence.

In the last decades of his life Tolstoy publicly repudiated his earlier literary career to devote himself to the moral betterment of humankind. He succeeded in becoming the spokesman for a great ethical position and achieved world influence and renown. His creed was based on the realization in daily life of the ethical principles of Christ—a freely chosen life of simplicity and poverty, resistance to evil through the force of one's example, and nonviolence in every sphere of life from the personal to the national. He had thirsted from youth to play the role of a great prophet. That desire was justified by his consciousness of his genuinely great powers, but the wish was sometimes so transparent that it dismayed Maxim Gorky, who wrote in his memoirs:

> I was always put off by that stubborn, despotic aspiration to turn the life of Count Leo Nikolae-vich Tolstoy into "The Life of the Saintly Father Our Blessed Boyar Leo." . . . He had been planning to "suffer" for a long time; he expressed his sorrow that he hadn't succeeded; but he wanted to suffer not simply, not from a natural wish to test the stubbornness of his will, but from a clear and, I repeat, despotic intention to strengthen the yoke of his religious ideas, the burden of his teaching, to make his prophecy irrefutable, to consecrate it in people's eyes by his suffering and to force them to accept it, you understand— force them!
>
> (*Sobranie sochinenii,* Moscow, 1963, vol. 18, p. 75)

Tolstoy's life and work are tied to a place more surely than any other Russian writer's. Yasnaya Polyana, the estate where he spent his early childhood, where he later brought his wife, where they raised a large family, and where he wrote his books and became a prophet of moral awakening, was in a profound sense his home. He once answered "Where were you born?" on a playful family questionnaire with "At Yasnaya Polyana on the leather couch." Yasnaya Polyana means "serene fields," and it is located in the central Russian heartland near Tula, some few hours' drive south of Moscow.

We can speak of a Yasnaya Polyana idyll that dominates Tolstoy's life and work to the end of the 1870's. Yasnaya Polyana was bound up in Tolstoy's thinking with the continuity of his family and its traditions, with the dream of finding a place where he could lead a life of moral integrity and productive work, and with the desire to secure a retreat from the corrupting influence of society at large. How he dreamed upon the theme of Yasnaya Polyana

is revealed in a remarkable letter he wrote from the Caucasus in 1852 to his Aunt Toinette:

> Here is how I imagine the happiness that awaits me in the future. The years pass and I find myself, already no longer young, but not yet old, at Yasnaya. My affairs are in order, I have no worries or problems. You are still living at Yasnaya. You have grown a little older, but you are still active and in good health. Life goes on as before: I work in the morning, but we are together almost all day. After dinner in the evening I read something aloud to you that you won't be bored listening to. Then conversation begins. I tell you about my life in the Caucasus, you recount your recollections of the past, of my father and mother. You tell me the horror tales that we used to listen to with frightened eyes and open mouths. We recall those who were dear to us and are no longer living. You cry and I do, too, but with reconciled tears. We talk of my brothers who come to visit us and of dear Mashenka [Tolstoy's sister], who will visit her beloved Yasnaya with the children for several months every year. We will have no acquaintances. No one will come to bother us and spread gossip. A beautiful dream, but I allow myself to dream of even more. I am married. My wife is gentle, kind, and loving and she loves you as I do. Our children call you "grandmother." You live upstairs in the big house, in that room where grandmother used to live. Everything in the house is the way it was when papa was alive, and we continue to live that life, only changing roles: you will take on the role of grandmother, I the role of papa, though I don't hope ever to deserve it, my wife, that of mama, our children, our role. Mashenka will be in the role of both the aunts, but not unhappy as they were. Even Gasha [Toinette's servant] will be in the place of Praskovya Isaevna [the former housekeeper]. The only thing missing is a person who could replace you in relationship to the whole family. We won't find such a wonderful loving soul. No, you will not have a replacement. . . . If you made me the Russian emperor, if you offered me Peru, in a word if a fairy godmother appeared with a magic wand and asked me what I want, I can say

in all honesty with hand on heart: Just one thing, to realize my dream.

(*Sobranie sochinenii*, vol. 17, p. 56)

Three generations of life at Yasnaya Polyana provided Tolstoy with material that would become the backbone of his novels. Yasnaya Polyana had been the estate of his formidable grandfather Prince Nicholas Volkonsky, who had retired there when he incurred the czar's disfavor and himself became disillusioned with public life. Prince Volkonsky had risen to prominence during the reign of Catherine the Great, attaining the rank of *général en chef* and serving as ambassador extraordinary to the king of Prussia. Tolstoy's mother, Princess Marya Volkonsky, had spent her girlhood at Yasnaya Polyana, educated there by her widowed father in the spirit of the philosophes, who were his chief reading and the major influences on his own mind and sensibilities. The figure of his grandfather loomed large in Tolstoy's imagination, as did in a very different way the figure of his mother. Yasnaya Polyana had been in his grandfather's generation a symbol of the independence of the nobility from the court and administration, a place where reason and order and the pursuits of the mind were dominant, and the place where his mother had quietly nurtured in herself the moral sentiments and spiritual aspirations that later set the tone for her family.

Princess Marya's married life at Yasnaya Polyana formed the second generation of the idyll, the one Tolstoy harks back to in his letter as the model for his own future life. Prince Volkonsky had kept his daughter with him beyond the age when she should have married, and it was only after his death that her relatives, finding her possessed of a surprising and dangerous independence, grew alarmed and sought a husband for her. They found one in the handsome, socially brilliant Count Nicholas Tolstoy, who had been forced to seek a wealthy bride because his father had squandered the family fortune.

Nicholas Tolstoy brought with him to live at Yasnaya Polyana his widowed mother, a spoiled, aristocratic grande dame with a strong sense of her rank. From time to time his sisters Alexandra and Polina, and Tatyana Ergolskaya ("Toinette"), a relative, stayed with the family. Toinette had grown up with the Tolstoy children and was in love with Nicholas, whom she hoped to marry, but in a self-sacrificing spirit native to her character she stepped aside to permit the family fortunes to be saved. Tolstoy recognized the ready-made novel in his parents' marriage and Aunt Toinette's role and incorporated it into *War and Peace.*

Marya Tolstoy won over her new relatives by her lively and gentle temperament and settled down to bear Nicholas five children, the fourth being Leo, born 28 August 1828. The family idyll was cut short by the untimely death of Marya Tolstoy soon after the birth of her last child, a daughter, when Leo was not yet two years old. Aunt Toinette took over the task of mothering the children and became, as Tolstoy was to say, the most important influence on his life.

The high spiritual ideal that came to Tolstoy from the tradition of his mother's life is central to the Yasnaya Polyana idyll. He had in his possession his mother's papers—her diaries, notebooks, and letters. They reveal that Princess Volkonsky was a highly educated, even intellectual, woman. Her reading encompassed history, travel notes, philosophy, and moral instruction. Among authors whom she read and in many cases translated were Laurence Sterne, Blaise Pascal, Voltaire, Alphonse de Lamartine, Jean Jacques Rousseau, and Georges de Buffon, as well as many now-forgotten authors of sentimental admonitions and instructive tales. Princess Marya took seriously the discipline of self-improvement that was enjoined upon her by her reading. Pious and sentimental by temper, she kept watch on her own spiritual development and was concerned as a mother that her children should develop their moral potentialities. After her marriage she read Rousseau's *Émile* together with her sister-in-law and engaged her in discussion of pedagogical theory. She kept a notebook on the methods she employed to mold the spirit of her oldest son, Nicholas.

Princess Marya also had literary aspirations. In her girlhood she had kept the other girls spellbound at balls by narrating stories to them. Her papers include her poems; accounts of trips she made; a moral fairytale, "The Forest Twins," about the transformation of simple shepherdesses into princesses; and a story, "The Russian Pamela," about the love of a prince's son for a poor girl. Her writings express the simple noble sentiments: that the meaning of life is found only in virtue, that only truth is worthy of human suffering and striving, that happiness lies in the aspiration to well-being of those around us, and that it is easier to bear poverty than to avoid becoming attached to wealth.

Along with her sincere dedication to the search for the moral life, Princess Marya also gives an impression of gaiety, thirst for experience, and appreciation of the larger life. According to one story, her mortal illness was caused by her fall from a swing when she had swung up with too much abandon. She was bitterly disappointed when Czar Alexander I passed along the road near Yasnaya Polyana in 1823 and she saw only his carriage from afar without getting a glimpse of his person. She admired the czar and took an interest in monarchs as actors in the great affairs of state. She felt herself to be a woman of the highest class, the daughter of a man who had been a participant in history. She felt at home among great aspirations. They were in some sense her own, in spite of her personal modesty.

The atmosphere of moral striving, self-examination, and the search for the good lingered on at Yasnaya Polyana after her death. It was reflected in her sister-in-law Alexandra's meek Christianity; in Aunt Toinette's preservation of the tradition of Marya's goodness and spirituality; in Toinette's self-abnegating service to the family; and in the influence of the oldest son, Nicholas, on the younger children. Tolstoy was less than two when his mother died, but the high-minded tone of Yasnaya Polyana continued to shape his development up to twelve years of age, when, after the death of his father, he went to live with his Aunt Polina in Kazan. Indeed, the rules inculcated by the Yasnaya Polyana tradition were those Tolstoy used to measure his conduct to the end of his life. There came to be a recognizable Tolstoy family tone, which made the poet Afanasy Fet say about the three of the four brothers he knew:

> I am convinced that the underlying type of all three Tolstoy brothers is identical, as identical as the type of maple leaves, in spite of all the variations of their features. And if I tried to develop that thought, I would show to what degree was characteristic of all three brothers that passionate enthusiasm, without which one of them could not have become the writer, L. Tolstoy. The difference in their relationship to life consists in the way in which each of them withdrew from an unsuccessful dream. Nicholas quenched his transports with skeptical irony, Leo left his unrealizable dream with silent remorse, and Sergey with painful misanthropy.
>
> (*Vospominanie*, Moscow, 1890, vol. 1, p. 296)

Tolstoy's life is one of the best-recorded of any writer's. He kept diaries for most of his adult life, and he inspired those around him to keep diaries, so that for many periods of his life we have multiple accounts of his daily actions and states of mind. Self-analysis was not only his habit but his pleasure. In his youth he read many of the same authors who had formed his mother's sensibility, in particular Rousseau and Sterne, from both of whom he learned to examine the immediate flow of experience. Tolstoy kept his diaries from 1846, when he was eighteen years old, to his death in 1910. He interrupted them for only one significant break, from 1865 to 1878, when he had established his own domestic idyll at Yasnaya Polyana and was occupied in composing *War and Peace* and *Anna Karenina.*

Tolstoy's diaries are his indispensable aid to following and shaping his inner life. They are both retrospective and projective. Particularly in youth he spent much time laying out programs of action for himself:

What will be the aim of my life in the country during the next two years? (1) To study the entire course of legal sciences needed for the final examination at the university. (2) To study practical medicine and some medical theory. (3) To study languages: French, Russian, German, English, Italian, and Latin. (4) To study agriculture, both theoretical and practical. (5) To study history, geography, and statistics. (6) To study mathematics—the gymnasium course. (7) To write my dissertation. (8) To attain an average level of accomplishment in music and painting. (9) To write rules. (10) To acquire a certain understanding of the natural sciences. (11) To write compositions in all the subjects that I will be studying.

(*Sobranie sochinenii*, vol. 19, p. 40)

Boris Eikhenbaum remarks that in fact the writing of rules was the main point of Tolstoy's activity. His programs of moral improvement and steps to social success were as ambitious as his programs of self-instruction. The grandiose plans were never realized. Indeed, their primary purpose seems to have been to allow Tolstoy to record in his diary all the ways in which he fell short of them, a task he undertook with gusto. Nevertheless, the programs were indispensable to Tolstoy's development as a writer. In his fiction, as in his life, a motive force was the program of moral action. His compensatory imagination caused him to remake reality, to project onto the past or the future the forms that suited his inner sense of how things should be. His work is distinguished by its documentarity: it is full of the details and events of his own observed and lived reality. Yet whatever story he took, whether from his own life or from the lives of others, he reshaped it to suit his rules, his pro-

grams. Eikhenbaum calls Tolstoy's diaries of youth the laboratory in which he worked out his craft. They were also the workshop in which he constructed the programs of values he hoped to advance through his life work.

We see Tolstoy casting about in the diaries for a role to play in the world. He is full of great ambitions: he thinks now of writing a history of Europe in the nineteenth century, now of founding a religion, now of writing a code of laws, now of becoming a famous writer. In this period from 1847 to 1852 his brothers regarded him as a failure. He dropped out of his law course at the University of Kazan; he tried to manage his estate but grew tired of the task and abandoned it; he went to Saint Petersburg planning to enlist as a cadet, but decided against it. He spent his time drinking, womanizing, gambling his inheritance away. He dreamed of bettering his lot by marrying an heiress. Finally, his brother Nicholas, in a desperate attempt to save him, took him off to the Caucasus, where by serving as a volunteer Leo won an officer's commission.

In the undemanding and isolated conditions of a Cossack border station Tolstoy began writing in earnest and produced the work that established him as a writer, *Childhood.* Yet he was not satisfied that he had found an occupation answering to his need, and the search in the diaries continued, through his stay among the Saint Petersburg intelligentsia, through his retreat once more to Yasnaya Polyana, through two trips abroad, and through a passionate involvement in pedagogy. In 1862 he married eighteen-year-old Sofya Andreevna Behrs, brought her straight to Yasnaya Polyana, and began at last to establish the domestic idyll he had elaborated with such pleasure to his Aunt Toinette. In the next decade he wrote his great novels and ceased to write his diary.

In 1878, when he once again became engaged in a search for a great and significant task that would give meaning to his life and change the world, Tolstoy returned to his diary. His spiritual crisis resulted in the repudiation of his earlier life and work and the rejection of the wealth he had accumulated through his literary efforts and the good management of his estate. His wife could not accept this new program, which contradicted the whole of their lives together and threatened to impoverish their children. The children divided into parties, some taking the side of their mother, some of their father. Thus the diaries of his last decades, begun as an aid to his inner search, became inadvertently the history of a family drama, which culminated in 1910 when Tolstoy, old and in ill health, left his home to escape his wife's importunities and to find the ideal life of spirituality and poverty that his beliefs bound him to. He died at the railway station at Astapovo on 7 November 1910.

The diaries were not only the record of but a weapon in the struggle between Tolstoy and his wife, which still seizes the popular imagination as powerfully as any of his fictions. In these last years of his life a veritable war of diaries was waged in the Tolstoy family. Not only did Sofya Andreevna keep her own diary, expressly to counter the pernicious story she suspected her husband of constructing for posterity; not only did one or another of the children keep diaries; but Tolstoy himself kept two diaries, a "public" diary, accessible to his wife and others, and a secret one for himself alone. In the battle among the members of the family for the right to tell the story, the physical possession of the diaries became a matter of concern. Tolstoy's disciple Vladimir Chertkov, the self-appointed guardian of the moral awakening that Tolstoy's name was attached to, persuaded Tolstoy to surrender the diaries to him. Sofya Andreevna took this as a profound betrayal of her role as wife, companion, and literary secretary to her husband. She suspected that Tolstoy had made a secret will depriving her and the children of the rights to his works after his death. Chertkov in fact had persuaded him to do so. The loss of the diaries instigated her desperate opposition and led to Tolstoy's final departure.

Thus Tolstoy, who had coveted the power that the written word could have if it was wholly given over to truth, found his own diaries invested with a power that he could never have anticipated. Throughout his life Tolstoy was disturbed by writing that was not ultimately serious, by writing that emphasized the aspect of pleasure and play (this was his objection to William Shakespeare, whom he found too pliant to be moral). Seeking to find a form in which truth itself would be the hero, he constantly changed his literary direction. His diaries, the searching record of his own aspirations and experiences, were in many ways the very foundation of the Tolstoyan aesthetic.

When Tolstoy sent the manuscript of his first work, *Childhood*, to N. A. Nekrasov in 1852 for publication in *The Contemporary*, he wrote to him by way of introducing the work: "This manuscript comprises the first part of a novel, *Four Epochs of Growth*." *Childhood*, and as much of the tetralogy as Tolstoy completed, is shaped by the notion of a self unfolding in time, in responsive sympathy with its surroundings and experiences. The emphasis on growth and formation, and the consequent fluid image of the self, was to become a keystone of Tolstoy's vision as artist. Though Tolstoy did not invent this view of the self, he devoted a lifetime of creative work and thought to its examination. Indeed, we might say that this vision of the self, which has lately come to be called "expressivist," was at the heart of those far-flung endeavors and generous expenses of energy, mind, and emotion that characterized this man's prodigious life.[1]

Rousseau had written of the "expanding plenitude" that "extends our being." Johann Gottfried von Herder took his cue from Rousseau and worked out a unified scheme for the relationship of self to external reality. Herder sought to find again a single center from

---

[1]The term "expressivist theory" was coined by Isaiah Berlin: see his *Vico and Herder*, New York, 1976.

which everything the individual does flows inevitably. In the thought of Herder and those who followed him, a program of life that would be conducive to the natural unfolding of the self's potentialities had been elaborated. In *Childhood* Tolstoy shows himself well aware of the program. Indeed the structure of the work is directly derived from it, and Tolstoy assiduously moves through the series of formative experiences that had become touchstones of the life of feeling: maternal love, sympathetic concern for those less fortunate than oneself, religious exaltation, responsiveness to natural beauty, desire for artistic self-expression, friendship, romantic love, death.

In his tracing of the child's awakening sense of moral responsibility, Tolstoy focuses in particular on Nikolenka's developing sense of his own fortunate position in society and the unfortunate position occupied by those of lower rank, a sense that the psychologist Robert Coles dubbed "entitlement." Turgenev's *Sportsman's Sketches*, written in the tradition of George Sand's country romances and the village stories of the German moralists, had set a new standard for depicting members of the lower classes. The unfortunate—who included tutors and governesses as well as servants and peasants—must be shown fully to be persons in the light of the new standard of selfhood. They must be shown to have aesthetic and moral sensibility, to enjoy the full play of consciousness in which the significance of life was now felt to reside. In his sketches of the tutor Karl Ivanych, the old housekeeper Natalya Savishna, the holy fool and pilgrim Grisha, Tolstoy creates portraits of members of the lower classes who have rich inner lives. The child Nikolenka develops sentiments of pity and justice in response to the full feelings he observes in them.

As the boy's capacity for self-expression flowers, Tolstoy reveals a damaging paradox in expectations of self-expression. In the programmatic chapter "Childhood" he emphasizes what is unique to early childhood, the child's pure sensations and the unfettered responses to the misfortunes of others. Later, life spoils the child's pure feeling. As the child's moral awareness is developed, his exposure to society develops a corresponding insincerity. For the first time we see the struggle between purity and the knowing consciousness that shapes so much of Tolstoy's work.

Even before the time of Rousseau the myth of the noble savage had provided one image of an untrammeled freedom in which the self could develop apart from the corrupting influence of society. Whereas European writers looked to America as the locus of their fantasies, the Russians found a promised land within their own borders, and the Russian romantic writers hastened to glorify the Caucasus, with its exotic peoples and wild, majestic scenery. Tolstoy began his novel of life in the Caucasus, *The Cossacks*, in the early 1850's during his service there, but he published it only in 1863. The Greben Cossacks, whom Tolstoy lived among and observed in his border station, were Russians belonging to the sect of Old Believer schismatics. They had retreated into the wild border area in earlier centuries to escape persecution and in modern times had taken on the duty of defending the border in return for the right to preserve their own customs and self-government. They were not exactly "noble savages," but they were simple people living in close touch with nature and with considerable freedom by Russian standards, since most peasants in Russia were bound to the land and hence to the owners of the land.

The Cossacks is filled with much closely observed ethnographic detail, but its main interest lies in Tolstoy's depiction of the psychology of his hero, Olenin, a young man from the landowning class who has come from Moscow to escape the empty life he has been leading in society and to find new purpose in the romantic Caucasus. He has formed an image of life there from books. The novel traces the gradual displacement of Olenin's romantic image with one more true to life, still noble but infused with the actual complexity of reality itself. Olenin has dreamed that he will meet and marry a beautiful Cossack girl. Soon after his arrival he settles upon the lovely and aloof daughter of his landlord, Maryanka, but discovers that she is to be betrothed to a young Cossack, Lukashka. Lukashka is for Olenin the perfect image of what he himself longs to be, a "brave," courageous and a superb horseman. He kills a hostile Chechen tribesman and feels no remorse, only triumph in his skill and bravery. For Lukashka everything is straightforward: he does his duty at the cordon, he drinks and enjoys himself on leave at the border station, and he plans to marry Maryanka and settle down to the life of his forefathers. Olenin is civilized. Self-consciousness complicates and, in the end, spoils everything. Trying to befriend Lukashka, he merely bumbles and draws Lukashka's suspicion and hostility. The proud Maryanka is curious about the lodger, but she comes to feel contempt for him and spurns him for Lukashka. Nothing is left for Olenin but to leave the station and return to his own society, unburdened of his illusion that he, a pampered, civilized man, can become a Cossack.

Much of the Cossacks' nobility derives from their immersion in simple, useful work that fills their time and gives their lives meaning. Maryanka is usually shown at her chores—milking, driving the goats to pasture, harvesting the grapes. Though the Cossacks' activities render them in some measure prosaic, they still remain beyond Olenin's reach, images of the ideal Other with whom the self cannot merge. Tolstoy has created a remarkable figure in the old Cossack Eroshka, a hunter and himself something of an outcast in the village, who lives in the old way. He is the village's storyteller, the repository of the legends of a golden age in which the Cossacks, untouched by civilization, lived like the Chechen tribesmen, truly noble savages. Eroshka also has something about him of the legendary trickster who survives through cunning. His acquisitiveness, his willingness to

manipulate Olenin for his own ends, his lack of fidelity either to Olenin or to his favorite, Lukashka, are passed over as the godlike attributes of a simple nature that has not been spoiled by the complex ethical codes of civilized society. In the ways that count, reverence for life and knowledge of nature, Eroshka is pure.

After the publication of *Childhood* and the *Sevastopol Sketches* the critic Nikolay Chernyshevsky wrote that Tolstoy was chiefly interested in "the psychological process, its forms, its laws, the dialectic of the soul." Methods of depiction of the inner life were further developed in *The Cossacks* and culminated in the great interior monologues of *War and Peace*. Chernyshevsky went on to say:

> Count Tolstoy's attention is turned most of all on how some feelings and thoughts develop out of others; he is interested in observing how a feeling, arising spontaneously from a given situation or impression and submitted to the influence of memories and the force of combinations projected by the imagination, turns into other feelings, then again returns to the starting point and again and again wanders away, being transformed along the whole chain of recollections; how a thought, born of the first sensation, leads to other thoughts, is drawn farther and farther, merges daydreams with real sensations, dreams of the future with the reflection of the present.
>
> (*Polnoe sobranie sochinenii*, Moscow, 1947, vol. 3, p. 422)

In *The Cossacks* Olenin's experience of the Caucasus and the consequent change in his own apprehension of reality constitute the story. Though the work is by no means structured according to the Jamesian "point of view," Olenin's consciousness defines the form of the novel. For long chapters we are apart from Olenin while Tolstoy tells us about the life of the station from the ethnographer's point of view, and yet the very objectivity of these passages is tied to Olenin. That the station has its independent life, of which he is not a part, is the lesson he must learn. Events find their meanings in his consciousness, as he discovers the essential truth that an objective world exists apart from himself. Thus the novel is both objective and subjective: objective in insisting on the presence of the larger world, subjective in focusing on the process of Olenin's development. It was Tolstoy's habit to diffuse his energies into many projects; some came to fruition decades after they were begun, others remained forever incomplete. His major novels crown whole decades of work, uniting in monumental, collage-like summations the themes and devices of lesser works. *War and Peace* comprehends the exploration of self worked out in the *Childhood* trilogy, the modes of consciousness and self-testing of *The Cossacks*, the domestic theme of *Family Happiness*, and the battle detail of the *Sevastopol Sketches*. At the same time it stretches the possibilities of all these thematic spheres. The nature of Tolstoy's imagination was such that combination led to new possibilities.

War and Peace belongs to the small group of literary works that seem placed beyond ordinary standards of literary judgment. It meant much personally to Tolstoy, for it demonstrated that he could realize the large ambitions that had haunted his imagination from childhood. He had the good fortune to understand the grandeur of the project as he embarked upon it. He wrote to his relative Alexandra Tolstoy:

> I have never before felt my powers of mind and even of moral force so free and so ready for work, and I do have work. That work is a novel of the period 1810–1820, which has occupied me entirely since the autumn. I am a writer now with the full force of my soul and I write and think as I have never written and thought before.
>
> (*Polnoe sobranie sochinenii*, Moscow, 1953, vol. 61, p. 23)

The work occupied seven years of Tolstoy's life—1863 to 1869. The monumentality of the task can be assessed through the novel's archive, which amounts to thousands of manuscript pages (and far from all of the drafted materials survive). Many episodes were redrafted numerous times. Other episodes were created and then found no place. Tolstoy often redrafted an episode once again when he had the page proofs in hand.

I have spoken of a Yasnaya Polyana idyll that provided a center for Tolstoy's imaginative projections of how life should be lived. *War and Peace* is saturated by the themes of the idyll. At its heart is the imagined world of Yasnaya Polyana's past during the time of Prince Volkonsky and after Marya's marriage to Nicholas. Though Tolstoy incorporates much factual material from the family tradition, he works it into his notion of how things might ideally have been had everything cohered to give his parents' lives their deepest significance. The documentary and visionary sides of Tolstoy's work come together here. We see how profoundly Yasnaya Polyana (called Bald Hills in the novel) was for him a space of the imagination in which the peculiarly Tolstoyan world could be invented. In keeping with the family history so firmly associated in Tolstoy's mind with Yasnaya Polyana, the novel is organized as the history of two families, the Rostovs and Bolkonskys. Indeed, we may speak of these families as collectively composing two of the major characters.

In the story of the Bolkonsky family Tolstoy transparently re-creates the epoch of his mother's girlhood, which was spent with her father at the country estate. The Bolkonsky family manifests collective characteristics: high-minded seeking for the good, devotion to duty, and self-denial. In Tolstoy's rich fictional world the making of discriminations among things that are like is paramount; each member of the family must be distinguished by his individual style of adherence to the general pattern of the family character. In old Prince Bolkonsky, duty and the renunciation of society are the product of cold reason and fierce pride. Princess Marya's devotion to duty is mediated by her pietism into personal humility and self-sacrifice for others. The Bolkonskys' spiritual elevation is extended to a wholly fictional character, Prince Andrey, who is attached to the family. In Prince Andrey, the Bolkonsky qualities of character are manifested on a new, ideal plane as greatness of soul and capacity to turn the intellect to the fundamental questions of the meaning of life and death.

The Rostovs are associated with Tolstoy's father's family in much the same way that the Bolkonskys are associated with his mother's family. Old Ilya Rostov, whose profligate ways land his family in penury, harks back to the spendthrift Ilya Tolstoy. Madame Rostov is a portrait of Leo's doting and proud Tolstoy grandmother. Nicholas Rostov is drawn from Tolstoy's father but incorporates much of the youthful experience of Leo himself. The marriage of Nicholas to Marya is taken from the story of his own parents' marriage, rethought and idealized. Sonya plays the role in the family of Tatyana Ergolskaya. The Rostov family character is defined by spontaneity, which gives them the ability to live in harmony with their physical natures and to escape the suffering and distortion of self caused by the analytical and self-examining mind so characteristic of the Bolkonskys. Nicholas represents the Rostov character in its mundane expression, but again Tolstoy has added a character who raises the family principles to their ideal embodiment. In Natasha Rostova, Tolstoy shows the principle of spontaneity achieving a purity of expression that elevates it to the quality of a life force. Natasha, too, has her prototypes: Tolstoy's sister-in-law, Tatyana Behrs, and his wife, Sofya. But she is tied less to the detail of a specific life than Princess Marya, and this endows her with the freedom of action Tolstoy gives to his purely fictional heroes, Andrey and Pierre.

One central character, Pierre Bezukhov, stands apart from the families. He embodies the free search for the self's most just expression. If Tolstoy projected into Andrey his own longing to be perfectly comme il faut, to be a man of aristocratic hauteur and noblesse oblige, in Pierre he embodies his own capacity for falling into error while seeking the good. In Pierre we see how the man of good character whose moral sense is intact is nevertheless turned aside from the right path by the complexities of reality, by his own baser desires, and by his failure to stand up to those of less rectitude. Significantly, the great moments in Pierre's life are rare moments of assertion of will when circumstance, desire, and action come into conjuction. Yet in the end his very passivity makes him open to a larger vision of the world than any other character can encompass.

Just as there are family heroes in *War and Peace,* so there are family villains, the Karagins and the Kuragins. They embody self-seeking worldliness and tone-deafness to the inner moral voice. Tolstoy has achieved in the Kuragin family—old Prince Vassily, Anatole, and the beautiful Hélène—a brilliant portrayal of lack of moral intuition. The very flatness in the depiction of these characters is made to seem not a result of Tolstoy's artistic decision, but the fault of their own truncated natures. The Kuragins are the chief agents of evil in the lives of the protagonists: Hélène by marrying Pierre turns him temporarily away from his pursuit of virtue; Anatole comes near to seducing Natasha, the greatest moral crisis in her life. The Kuragin viciousness is underscored by the presence of a demonic figure of evil, the sinister officer Dolokhov, friend of Anatole and agent of vice and death.

In this comprehensive design Tolstoy finds room to accommodate all the seemingly disparate values that the program of self-formation had specified as necessary to the fully expressed self: intellect and nature, spirit and body. The true expression of spontaneous feeling is discriminated from false self-indulgence, the harmonious relationship with the physical self from corrupting vice. The principle of growth itself, rather than the destiny of any character, is Tolstoy's subject, and so the destinies of this large array of characters cross and recross, not so much to form a plot as to show the vicissitudes of the self's development through time.

It is his interest in time as the medium of growth that leads Tolstoy to his interest in history. Each individual has a private life lived in the interior of the consciousness, full of meaning for him but closed to others. Social organization is introduced at the level of family life, where the potentialities of self are shaped by the pressures of family principles and interaction among members of the group. At its most abstract, time becomes history, in which the individual is situated in the flux of the human mass that bears so inexorably upon him that his acts take on new meanings, extraneous to his own understanding or his own intentions.

The historical event is produced by the confluence of innumerable wills. Kings, being subject to the same forces as others, are deceived in their illusions of power: ''The king is history's slave.'' Those whom conventional histories have glorified as the movers of human destiny share the common human condition of being subject to the flux of events that they are part of and that they cannot see from their position within the flow. Yet Tolstoy does not assert the dominance of chance. The individual wills and acts of men cohere in ways unseen by them to form a grand design. Napoleon is petty and laughable because he believes that his smallest action has great consequences. The actual forces that bring the French across Europe in 1812, that lead to a Russian victory, and that then bear the Russian and allied armies to Paris seem to Tolstoy to reflect the will of providence, but those forces are not discoverable because their multiplicity is incommensurate with our ability to know.

War and Peace brings to perfection the special Tolstoyan verisimilitude by which he is able to suggest a world infinitely expansive and therefore coterminous with our own experience of reality. It is Tolstoy's gift to see that the eternal qualities of people, objects, situations can be found in entities that appear different at first glance. He needs both documentarity—precision of factual detail, especially as observed by the eye—and abstraction—the fixed and immovable truth of things. Between these two poles the forms of cohesion, the ways in which truth indwells in the detail, are myriad, and that abundance gives Tolstoy the large freedom of discrimination and invention from which the rich fictional world of the novel is elaborated.

The final volume of *War and Peace* was published in December 1869. By January 1870 Tolstoy was casting about for a new topic. He made a number of false starts, though as early as February 1870 he thought of writing the story of the fall of a married woman of high society. It took several years for the mass of possibilities to crystallize into the structure of *Anna Karenina*. Still, the conjunction is telling: readers are still discussing the epilogue of *War and Peace*, still debating whether it is plausible that the delightful Natasha Rostova should turn into a domestic frump, and it comes into Tolstoy's head to write a novel about a fallen woman. *Anna Karenina* is related to the epilogue of *War and Peace* in a curious way. The characters of the latter meet in the epilogue as survivors in a genuine sense. Russia has undergone a grave crisis in the War of 1812. The two families at the center of the novel have undergone crises parallel to the national one. Each has lost a son. The characters who remain have regrouped their forces in strategic marriages, Pierre to Natasha, Nicholas to Marya. They have undergone much, have risked much, and have come through. The mood of the epilogue well justifies Tolstoy's original title, ''All's Well That Ends Well.'' There is behind *War and Peace* a strong compensatory force. Even death is shown to exalt the dying and to educate the living into spiritual mysteries. Everything that bears down upon humanity can be reconsidered, reformed. The novel can be a compensation for what life itself withholds from us.

Turning to *Anna Karenina,* we find the opening sentence: "Happy families are all alike; every unhappy family is unhappy in its own way." We begin with the Oblonsky household, where everything is in disorder because the wife has discovered her husband's affair with the governess. On the opening page we encounter a number of generic terms for family members: "the wife," "the husband," "the children," "the English governess," "the French governess," "the cook," "the kitchen-maid," "the coachman"; but where in *War and Peace* the epilogue shows us an array of characters all beautifully fitted into their roles as "the wife," "the husband," "the children," "the maid," here everything is awry. From the first paragraph we see the beginnings of a movement that will go directly counter to the movement of *War and Peace:* not reconciliation, flowering, compensation, but dissolution, chaos, death.

The shift in emphasis is striking in the character of Stiva Oblonsky, Anna's brother. Stiva is most full of that vital force that Tolstoy has honored in *War and Peace.* He is plump with life's juices. We have a keen sense of his fleshly presence: we constantly know where the parts of his body are and what they are feeling. In a difficult moment, Nicholas Rostov comes to the realization that "one could kill and rob and yet be happy." Stiva is such a person who can be happy out of his sheer excess of physical vitality even though he is in a painful and morally untenable situation. Pondering the difficult situation with his wife, he asks, What am I to do?

He could find no answer, except life's usual answer to the most complex and insoluble questions. That answer is: live in the needs of the day, that is, find forgetfulness. He could no longer find forgetfulness in sleep, at any rate not before night . . . consequently he must seek forgetfulness in the dream of life.

(*Sobranie sochinenii,* vol. 8, p. 10)

We have come a long way from the world of *War and Peace;* its rich affirmation of present experience has now become "the dream of life," even for so spontaneous and earthly a presence as Stiva Oblonsky. Only forgetfulness can assure happiness.

As the novel progresses, the recognition of the equivocal nature of human happiness is ever more harshly impressed on us. It is the very stuff of Anna's story, but we come to the same recognition in the situation of the chief male character, Constantine Levin, who, after achieving the marriage he wants and starting a family, suddenly finds himself hiding a piece of rope so that he won't be tempted to hang himself with it. The novel reaches its climax in a scene that powerfully evokes hatred of life. Anna has left her husband and gone to live openly with her lover, the socially brilliant officer of the guards Aleksey Vronsky. But giving in to desire brings them both unhappiness. Anna's husband refuses to allow her custody of their son. A debauched but hypocritical society refuses to accept Anna after she has openly flouted its rules of decorum. Vronsky is prevented from achieving the brilliant career that his position and capabilities should have ensured him. Anna fears the loss of his love and turns her anger and dissatisfaction against him. The relationship grows colder and colder, more full of anger and blame, until a break seems imminent.

A desperate Anna sets out to confront Vronsky, whom she suspects of going to the country for the day to court a young woman of good society. Here Tolstoy goes entirely into Anna's consciousness and shows us the world through her inner chaos, which is driving her to destruction. Through Anna's vision we see a kaleidoscope of broken images. We are situated wholly within her ugly vision of the world. Everything that she sees fills her with loathing, seems grotesque and hateful. The word "vision" is critical here. The eye is a powerful instrument for Tolstoy. He relies greatly on *seeing* in itself as the foundation of truth. Sight is the major organizing principle of Tolstoy's texts. It reveals to us what words conceal in the telltale gesture or the inadvertent expression of the face. As Anna approaches her death she attains the summit of the capacity to see—her sight is called a "searchlight." Though Tolstoy fixes us firmly within her point of view by repeating that her horrific vision is "what she thought she saw," it would be wrong to dismiss what is seen as a crazy woman's distorted vision. Her insight has its own powerful truth:

> Where did I leave off? At the point that I cannot imagine a situation in which life would not be a torment; that we all have been created in order to suffer, and that we all know this and try to invent means of deceiving ourselves. But when you see the truth, what are you to do?
>
> (*Sobranie sochinenii*, vol. 9, p. 386)

Where Stiva can find forgetfulness in "the dream of life," Anna *sees* and cannot *not see.* Anna comes to a conclusion that is fully motivated in the circumstances: "Why not put out the candle?" Where *War and Peace* affirms the power of life to make something even of pain and grief, *Anna Karenina* shows us that life has infinite capacity to harm and that we are helpless before it.

In the epilogue to *Anna Karenina* the survivors are once again gathered together, but "survivor" in this novel means a very different thing. In *War and Peace* we see a group of people who by undergoing disaster have grown fully to be themselves and have found a deserved happiness. In *Anna Karenina* the survivors are people maimed by life, diminished rather than augmented by the experience of living. Even Levin, who has saved

himself for the time being by a tenuous faith, seems vulnerable.

Anna Karenina is not all dejection. As in *War and Peace,* much of its charm comes from fresh and vivid scenes of the joy of life: Levin skating or, later, taking part with the peasants in mowing; the happy consummation of healthy and productive love in Levin and Kitty; even Anna's deep gladness and vitality before it is irreparably damaged. Nowhere else in Tolstoy do we have so full a feeling of his protean energies and vivid responsiveness combined with so intense an insight into how that very life-energy can bring on loathing of life. At bottom *Anna Karenina* does not hold out a great deal of hope, and it is understandable that Tolstoy, soon after writing it, in the tide of his great crisis, rejected it and all his past works—works that had led him to this evil intensity of vision.

In the epilogue to *Anna Karenina* Tolstoy says of his autobiographical (or, in Lidia Ginzburg's phrase, "autopsychological") hero Levin, "Thus he lived, not knowing and not foreseeing the possibility of knowing what he was and why he lived on earth, and tormented by his ignorance to such a degree that he feared suicide, and yet with all this, firmly laying down his own special defined road in life." The years of writing *Anna Karenina* had been for Tolstoy a time of what William James, using Tolstoy as an exemplary case of the kind of religious conversion that is precipitated by the loss of all sense of meaning in life, called "anhedonia."

In 1869, while on a trip to Penza province to buy land, Tolstoy had experienced during a night spent in the little town of Arzamas an inexplicable terror, which he described in a letter to his wife:

> For two days I have been tormented by anxiety. Three nights ago I spent the night at Arzamas, and something unusual happened to me. It was two o'clock in the morning, I was terribly tired, wanted to sleep and wasn't sick. But suddenly, there came over me such a depression, fear, hor-

ror as I have never experienced before, and that God grant no one to experience.

(*Sobranie sochinenii,* vol. 17, p. 322)

In 1880 he described the occasion in an unfinished, posthumously published story titled *Notes of a Madman.* In his nighttime fear the narrator asks, "What is bothering me, what am I afraid of?" and hears the answer:

"Me," inaudibly answered the voice of death. "I am here." A chill ran over me. Yes, death. It comes, it is here, and it shouldn't be. If I were really facing death, I could not be experiencing what I was experiencing. I would be afraid. But now I was not afraid, but saw, felt, that death was coming, and at the same time felt that it shouldn't be there. My whole being felt the necessity, the right, to life and at the same time that death was occurring. And that internal division was terrible.

As Tolstoy was coming out of his crisis he began to draft versions of his new creed, which resulted in *A Confession* (finished in 1882).

The answer that Tolstoy found and that made it possible for him to go on to the full, new career that stretched from 1880 to 1910 was, in James's words,

that his trouble had not been with life in general, not with the common life of common men, but with the life of the upper, intellectual, artistic classes, the life which he had personally always led, the cerebral life, the life of conventionality, artificiality and personal ambition. He had been living wrongly and must change. To work for animal needs, to abjure lies and vanities, to relieve common wants, to be simple, to believe in God, therein lay happiness.

(*Varieties of Religious Experience,* p. 180)

As James remarks, Tolstoy had drunk too deeply of the cup of bitterness ever to forget its taste, but his discovery had given him something to live by.

Tolstoy's *A Confession* inaugurates a new style in his writing, one that dominates the work of the final thirty years. This austere, aphoristic, often biblical style is both closer to conversational forms of the language and more solemn than the narrative style of his earlier literary work. Tolstoy had always preferred the omniscient, authorial narrative to the use of the point-of-view because it gave him the opportunity to unify in a Godlike perspective the many vantages of his characters and even to speak from time to time as God or as a prophet who has access to fundamental truths. In the period after *A Confession* the style of his writings, both fiction and nonfiction, is that of an author who seems at one with the deity. The time of the narrative is often retrospective: Tolstoy summarizes whole epochs of his characters' lives in a discourse that moves inexorably toward the truths he wants to unfold. At its best, in such works as *The Death of Ivan Ilich* and *Father Sergius,* the style achieves scriptural solemnity; at other times it is coercive.

Tolstoy's lifelong preoccupation with death reached its greatest intensity in the crisis that resulted in *A Confession.* Death had been a persistent theme in his work from the beginning. In *Childhood* Nikolenka's premonition of his mother's death is borne out in actuality at the end of the volume. The narrator of "Notes of a Billiard Marker" describes the elevation he expects death's nearness to bring. In the third of the *Sevastopol Sketches* Tolstoy tries his hand for the first time at the tour de force that he became master of—the description of a man's thoughts as he is dying, up to the extinction of consciousness. One of his best works in the years before *War and Peace* is "Three Deaths" (1859), in which he likens the peasant's meek acceptance of death to the natural and unconscious passing of a tree, contrasting these "proper" deaths unfavorably with the death of a landowner.

The two great novels are shaped by the deaths of pivotal characters. Tolstoy said of Prince Andrey that he had intended to have him die at Austerlitz but then "took pity on him and spared him.'' Prince Andrey is attached to the Bolkonsky family, that is, to the avatars of Tolstoy's mother's family, the Volkonskys, and hence is connected in the fabric of Tolstoy's imagination to his own dead mother. Old Prince Bolkonsky's death is described in detail in the novel; it is the means both for Marya's own recognition of the boundary between life and death and for the renewal of her capacity to live. In the epilogue we are given clues that Princess Marya herself will die young, leaving a bereft husband and young children. In spite of his initial sparing of Prince Andrey, Tolstoy discovered nevertheless that he must let him die to complete the thematic economy of his novel. So, after much of the novel was set in type, Tolstoy changed the ending he had planned; he wrote into the galley proofs the remarkable passages describing Prince Andrey's delirium at Mytishchi (the famous ''hovering fly'' scene) and then created the episode in which Prince Andrey on his deathbed discovers that death is an awakening.

The expressive philosophy that so influenced Tolstoy always had a catch in it. With its emphasis on process it tends to suggest that the person cannot be whole until the life is complete. It thus opens the way to a glorification of death. Rousseau had already given the hint in his celebrated conclusion to *La nouvelle Héloïse*, with the transfigured Julie on her deathbed. That life is process and therefore inimical to perfect love is one of the truths Prince Andrey expresses in his deathbed inner monologue. Anna Karenina's death achieves no such great philosophy; it is only a release from the torments that the conflict between physical vitality and moral purpose have imposed upon her. But for Tolstoy the question of what kind of meaning might be inherent in the experience of dying remained critical.

Soon after his crisis, as soon as he could bring himself to think again about writing fiction, Tolstoy began a story that is very likely the greatest ever written on the theme of death, *The Death of Ivan Ilich.* Tolstoy's brother Sergei teased him by saying of the story: ''They praise you because you discovered that people die. As if no one would have known it without you.'' In spare and solemn language Tolstoy recounts the story of one Ivan Ilich, a successful judge who, having fallen and struck his side while hanging drapes in his new quarters, becomes ill and begins the slow decline toward death. The first part of the story describes the reactions of his colleagues and his family after his death. We see mundane society life continuing its frivolous concerns, untouched by the mystery of extinction. The second part of the story opens with a straightforward statement of its moral: ''The story of Ivan Ilich's life was most simple and ordinary and most terrible.'' Thus from the start we know that Ivan Ilich will die and what the significance of his life has been. Tolstoy turns our attention to the process: Ivan Ilich by living an ordinary life killed his finest impulses; suffering and death redeem him.

Tolstoy was fond of the proverb ''Il faudra mourir seul'' (One dies alone), and the story brilliantly evokes the increasing isolation of the dying from the process of the living. Whereas in *War and Peace* Tolstoy had shown that it is natural for the survivors to retreat from the knowledge of death possessed by the dying, in order that they may go on living, in *The Death of Ivan Ilich* he is merciless toward those of the world who stand apart from Ivan Ilich's death. It is as though Tolstoy, seeing that he is growing old, increasingly consumed by his fear of death, resents those around him whose lives will inevitably go on once his own stops.

Like many of Tolstoy's works, the story was suggested by an incident that came to his attention: he heard about the death of Ivan Ilich Mechnikov, a judge of the Tula court who died of cancer in 1881 and was said to have expressed remorse on his deathbed for his unproductive life. Mechnikov's brother, a well-known scholar and revolutionary, commented that although his brother was a careerist,

> and I don't like careerists, how much richer his psychological register was than what Tolstoy has done with his hero! That's what enlightenment means, I thought, if even such an artist as Tolstoy found it necessary to turn the soul of his vulgarized hero into a square of poorly cleaned parquet.
> (*Vospominanie*, Moscow, 1967, vol. 2, p. 157)

That Tolstoy did reshape Mechnikov's story is clear from one detail known to us: it was to his wife that the real Ivan Ilich confided his sense of his misspent life, while in Tolstoy's story the wife is much too limited and unresponsive to be the recipient of such confidences. Nevertheless, Tolstoy has gained an artistic advantage by the simplification of his character. The painter Kramskoi remarked on the story's biblical quality. By subtracting all the things that make a man's life and character rich, by reducing Ivan Ilich to banality, Tolstoy makes him into the perfect test case of death's power to transform. In Prince Andrey we see a great nature realizing its capacities in death, but *Ivan Ilich* affirms the capacity of even the most ordinary and unheroic life to find significance in death. In spite of its solemnity *Ivan Ilich* is an optimistic story, as the Gospels are optimistic stories.

Tolstoy had taken seriously Rousseau's assertion that it is society—"high society" in particular—that corrupts. After his spiritual crisis he took on the task of making himself over as best he could into a simple man. If he could not escape the torturing consciousness of the educated man, he could, he believed, at least refrain from living the artificial and corrupting life of one. That his new view came directly out of the principles of the expressive philosophy that had formed him in his youth is clear from his late statement of his aesthetic principles, *What Is Art?* In the expressive view of Herder and others, all activities of life are expressions of self, but in particular those that have their foundations in feeling or the creative impulse. The century separating *What Is Art?* from Herder and other thinkers in the expressive vein had shown up the paradoxes in a view that bases its primary value on self and yet struggles to attain exalted ideals of service and brotherhood. Yet Tolstoy strives mightily once again to reconcile the axiom that art comes out of the artist's need for self-expression with the moral imperative that art must serve social welfare. Clearly the contradiction can be eliminated if we look to the artist's own moral health: if his soul is pure, then his self-expression will inevitably serve truth. This formulation satisfied Tolstoy, if few others.

Following his own precepts, Tolstoy determined to write only works that would be morally beneficial. To some extent this meant writing tracts, putting together daybooks of uplifting quotations, engaging in polemics with those who were embarked on an evil path (including the church and the czar), and writing educational materials for the peasantry. But Tolstoy by no means ceased to write fiction, and some of his most powerful works—works in a style different from that of his early ones—belong to the last thirty years of his life. Tolstoy was preoccupied with the temptations society puts in the way of its educated members. He was striving to find the way back to the simplicity and faith he saw in the lower classes. These preoccupations shape all his later work. They manifest themselves in two ways: the harsh exposé of society as it is and the uplifting depiction of exemplary figures who show the way to virtue.

In this last period Tolstoy seemed obsessed by the harmful consequences of relations between the sexes. In the 1850's he had examined the institution of marriage in *Family Happiness*, where he had followed the line of Jules Michelet and Pierre-Joseph Proudhon, conservatives on the "woman question." Like them he asserted that woman's destiny is to marry and have children, that romantic love is a threat to the sanctity of the family, and that tender feelings should be put aside in marriage, to be replaced by devotion to children and to the husband as the father of the children. At the time he wrote *Family Happiness* Tolstoy had not yet had any experience of marriage, and after concluding the work he became embarrassed by the "nonsense" he had indulged in. He hoped for much from his own marriage, and in many ways got much. (Victor Shklovsky is right when he says, "He chose the fate that he needed and the woman that he needed was Sofya Andreevna.") *War and Peace* reflects his domestic happiness in its good marriages, although Pierre's mistaken marriage to the debauched Hélène is a warning about the power of a bad woman. In *Anna Karenina* marriages go awry, but we still have before us the successful example of Levin and Kitty.

Beginning in the 1880's Tolstoy was at constant war with his wife over his desire to dispose of his property and lead the life of a simple man. From then on his treatment of marriage among the upper classes was merciless: marriage, he believed, concentrates the vices of society. *The Kreutzer Sonata* calls for absolute chastity within marriage. Its protagonist, Poznyshev, has murdered his wife out of jealousy over her lover, but he comes to the conclusion that he was to blame for her infidelity by introducing his wife to sensuality: "If I had known what I know now, all would have been different. On no account would I have married her. . . . I would not have married at all." Beethoven's sonata has been the spur to the wife's illicit passion, and thus corrupt art is implicated as another avenue through which base society appeals to man's evil impulses. Tolstoy's passionate indictment of marriage in *The Kreutzer Sonata* was no doubt influenced by his continuing sexual need for his wife, which, together with his sense of duty to family, prevented him from realizing the virtuous life he sought.

At the end of the 1880's and throughout the 1890's Tolstoy worked on another of his summations, the novel *Resurrection*. The family idyll disappears entirely as the organizing principle of the long work. Now attention is focused on a society in dissolution from top to bottom. The scenes of Tolstoy's new panoramic vision take place in the ruined villages, the unjust courts, the prisons, and on the road to Siberian exile. The protagonist, Nekhlyudov, while serving as a member of the court, comes across a woman of the lower classes, Katyusha Maslova, whom he had seduced and abandoned in his youth. He resolves to marry her to save her from a life of degradation. He strives to get her freed from prison, but society opposes his righteous desire at every turn. In the end Katyusha marries the virtuous revolutionary Simonson instead, but Nekhlyudov has been transformed by his exposure to Russia's poverty and injustice; as the novel ends he sits down to read the Gospels.

Resurrection has never achieved the popularity of Tolstoy's other long novels, perhaps because it lacks the underlying structure of romance that shapes the others, for all their realism. Here Tolstoy's compensatory imagination is focused on showing how society can be overcome and the path of virtue found, rather than on the attainment of personal happiness.

The good peasant had always seemed to Tolstoy to be the answer to society's corruption. He often introduces a variant of the figure at the end of a work, where, as an icon of the exemplary life, it brings the fluidity of Tolstoyan character and time to stasis. In *Childhood* the narrative is rounded off with the story of the old housekeeper, Natalya Savishna, who has sacrificed her own happiness for the mistress and children, but who remains unembittered, her declining years illuminated by her childlike faith. Riding away from the Cossack station, Olenin sees the simple life of Eroshka and Maryanka, continuing as if he did not exist. Pierre's grave doubts about the meaning of life are resolved by his acquaintance in French captivity with the peasant Platon Karataev, whose unresisting accommodation to all life shows Pierre how to overcome evil. Levin, when in such spiritual pain that he contemplates suicide, is saved by the words of faith uttered by an old peasant.

The need to show the true virtue of the peasants becomes increasingly pressing as Tolstoy repudiates the upper classes more forcefully. Thus, in *Ivan Ilich* the peasant Gerasim's calm certainty of right behavior and unselfconscious attentiveness to his master's needs show up society's false attitude toward death. Yet Tolstoy can make Gerasim an exemplary figure precisely because he holds his imagination aloof from any inquiry into Gerasim's desires, psychological processes, or circumstances of life. Falsity enters because of what is left unsaid.

Elsewhere Tolstoy had tried to fill that lack by applying his searching realistic method to the life of the peasants. As early as the 1850's he had started the novella *Polikushka* (1863), which gives an unremittingly bleak picture of village life while fixing the blame on the structure of society. In the 1880's he turned his attention to the plight of town peasants whose moral foundations had been destroyed by their uprooting from the patriarchal way of life. In his play *The Power of Darkness* (1887) he seized on an incident that came before the Tula court: a peasant had married a well-off widow, then forced the widow's daughter to have sexual relations with him. When the daughter bore a child, the peasant smothered the baby to hide the evidence of his illicit relationship. Subsequently, a marriage was arranged for the daughter, but at the betrothal the peasant was seized by guilt and confessed his crime to the assembled crowd. Tolstoy turned this sensational event into a brooding parable of fall and salvation. Keeping close to the details of the original story for the most part, he added two almost allegorical figures: Akim, a saintly peasant, and Matryona, a force of primitive evil. The parents of the weak and criminal Nikita, they struggle for possession of his soul. Nikita's confession affirms that

the power of faith is still alive in the peasants in spite of their degradation by city life.

Throughout his inquiry into peasant life, Tolstoy held to the irreducible fact on which their virtue was founded: they worked. In his short novel *Master and Man* (1895) Tolstoy lays out this opposition with stark simplicity. The "master" is now only a merchant and not even a member of the spoiled aristocratic class, but even his little bit of privilege has taken him away from the plain truths accessible to the poor. Moved by greed, he sets out in a snowstorm to acquire a piece of land. He and his driver, Nikita, are overpowered on the road by the storm's fury, and the merchant achieves enlightenment before his death, coming to realize that the true goal of human life lies in mutual concern.

Summaries of Tolstoy's work in the late period make it sound hollowly moralistic, but the great works like *Master and Man* transcend their didacticism through perfection of style. Tolstoy's late work retains the documentary precision of detail of his early work. At his best, he wrote beautiful parables that combine keen realistic observation with the inevitability of prophetic truth.

The plight of the educated man trying to find his way back to elemental virtue was close to Tolstoy, and many of his most powerful works of the last period address it. The protagonist of *Father Sergius* is an aristocratic officer, reminiscent of Prince Andrey, who retires from the world to enter a monastery. The occasion for his leaving society is his discovery that the woman of good family to whom he is betrothed has been the mistress of Czar Nicholas I. Out of pride he determines to become a monk, to set himself above the czar who has had the power to ruin his life with impunity. He excels in his career in the church as he excelled in the military, eventually becoming a famous holy man who is sought out by crowds of people for advice and cures.

Though Father Sergius achieves genuine elevation of spirit, he is still prey to pride and sexual desires. At length he leaves the monastery and makes his way to a woman whom he knew in youth. The widow Pashenka embodies Tolstoy's new sense of Christian duty. Though she does not attend church or remember to observe the rituals, she devotes herself cheerfully and wholeheartedly to the service of those around her. Sergius comes to the conclusion, "I lived for people under the pretense of living for God; she lives for God, imagining that she lives for people." Under the influence of her example, Sergius becomes a poor pilgrim and devotes his life to doing good to those he meets.

Throughout his career Tolstoy had shown a genius for projecting the lives and thoughts of the rulers of men, beginning in *War and Peace* with his depictions of Napoleon and Alexander I. In his late period he returned frequently to the czars and boldly treats them with the freedom of invention he employs with fictional characters. In his late unfinished work "The Deathbed Notes of the Elder Fyodor Kuzmich" Tolstoy deals with a persistent rumor concerning Alexander I. The story current among the people asserted that another man was buried in the czar's place and that Alexander had taken up a new life as a monk. Tolstoy had been haunted by the vision of a soldier running the military gauntlet (such episodes figure in "After the Ball" and in *Hadji-Murad*), and he makes the sight of a soldier being beaten the incident that triggers the czar's final resolve to quit his exalted life. Some parts of the story, in which Tolstoy has the czar recount his childhood memories of his brother Constantine and of life at the court of Catherine the Great, hark back to *Childhood* in their precise evocation of the child's experiences. Tolstoy's intention is to show that in the child who will be czar we find the same impulses of goodness, the same alertness to insincerity, that are in other children. The czar's story is a variant, at the uppermost reaches of society, of the common story, the corruption of the child as he is fitted for his role in society.

The lives of rulers figure largely in Tolstoy's last great work, the short novel *Hadji-Murad,* in which Tolstoy harks back to a figure who had fascinated him in his youth. During Tolstoy's stay in the Caucasus, the lieutenant of the Muslim leader Shamil's forces, Hadji-Murad, a famous warrior, had come over to the Russians. At the time it had seemed to Tolstoy that this was an act of cowardice, but in his subsequent study of the period he came to the conclusion that Hadji-Murad was a victim of the circumstances of his life. Once again Tolstoy created a panoramic view of society, incorporating his major themes into a major summary work. The difference is that he was now able to achieve that breadth in a work a fraction of the size of *War and Peace.*

From the line soldiers in the little border station who are waiting in ambush when the news comes that Hadji-Murad is about to come over, Tolstoy moves up through the ranks of society, to the governor, Vorontsov, at Tiflis and finally to Nicholas I himself. Parallel to this movement he shows the Chechens' society from bottom to top, concluding with the ruler, Shamil. In his dispassionate tone he treats every character equally, whether soldier or czar, with the exception that he has more sympathy for the forces that mold the soldiers' lives. At every level Tolstoy emphasizes that each person is mainly caught up in his private concerns, his family, his own desires. What is vital to one man is unimportant or of unequal significance to another. But the ruler's state of mind is different, for his momentary whims have far-reaching consequences that affect the lives of many men. Hadji-Murad is caught between the "policies" of Nicholas and Shamil and is in the end destroyed by them.

In his final years Tolstoy came to be called the "second czar," because the government was afraid to touch him. He was the only man in Russia besides the czar who could speak his mind forthrightly with impunity. He had earned that freedom through the power of his work and his example. When he took up his pen to speak of czars as though they were men like himself, he proved that writing can be, as he had dreamed, a real power in the world.

Selected Bibliography

FIRST EDITIONS

INDIVIDUAL WORKS

Childhood (Detstvo). Short novel. *Sovremennik (The Contemporary)* 9 (1852).

"The Raid" ("Nabeg"). Story. *Sovremennik* 3 (1853).

Boyhood (Otrochestvo). Short novel. *Sovremennik* 9 (1854).

"Sevastopol in December" ("Sevastopol v dekabre mesyatse"). Sketch. *Sovremennik* 6 (1855).

"Sevastopol in May" ("Sevastopol v mae"). Sketch. *Sovremennik* 9 (1855).

"The Woodfelling" ("Rubka lesa"). *Sovremennik* 9 (1855).

"Sevastopol in August, 1855" ("Sevastopol v avguste 1855 goda"). Sketch. *Sovremennik* 1 (1856).

"Two Hussars" ("Dva gusara"). Story. *Sovremennik* 5 (1856).

Youth (Yunost). Short novel. *Sovremennik* 1 (1857).

"Three Deaths" ("Tri smerti"). Story. *Biblioteka dlya chteniya (Library for Reading)* 1 (1859).

Family Happiness (Semeinoe schastie). Short novel. *Russkii vestnik (Russian Messenger)* 7 and 8 (1859).

"Who Teaches Whom to Write, We the Peasant Children, or They Us?" ("Komu u kogo uchitsya pisat, krestyanskim rebyatim u nas ili nam u krestyanskikh rebyat?"). Pedagogy. Yasnaya Polyana, 1862.

The Cossacks (Kazaki). Short novel. *Russkii vestnik* 1 (1863).

Polikushka. Short novel. *Russkii vestnik* 2 (1863).

War and Peace (Voina i mir). Parts 1 and 2 in *Russkii vestnik* (1865–1866). Separate publication, Moscow, 1867–1869.

Alphabet (Azbuka). Stories for children. Moscow, 1872. Revised as *New Alphabet (Novaya azbuka)* and *Russian Books for Reading (Russkie knigi dlya chteniya).* Moscow, 1874.

Anna Karenina. Novel. *Russkii vestnik* (1875–1877). Separate publication, Moscow, 1878.

A Confession (Izpoved). Written 1879–1882. First published Geneva, 1884, due to censor's forbidding publication in Russia. First Russian publication, Moscow, 1906.

"What People Live By" ("Chem lyudi zhivy"). Story. *Detskii otdykh (Children's Recreation)* 12 (1881).

"Where Love Is, God Is" ("Gde lyubov, tam i bog"). Story. Moscow, 1885.

The Death of Ivan Ilich (Smert Ivana Ilicha). Short novel. Moscow, 1886.

"How Much Land Does a Man Need?" ("Mnogo li cheloveku zemli nuzhno?"). Story. *Russkoe bogatstvo (Russian Wealth)* 4 (1886).

"Three Hermits" ("Tri startsa"). Story. *Niva (Field)* 13 (1886).

"Yardstick" ("Kholstomer"). Short novel. In *Sochineniya grafa L. N. Tolstogo.* Moscow, 1886.

"What Then Must We Do?" ("Tak chto zhe nam delat?"). Essay. Geneva, 1886. First Russian publication, Moscow, 1906.

The Power of Darkness (Vlast tmy). Play. Moscow, 1887.

The Kreutzer Sonata (Kreitserova sonata). Short novel. Moscow, 1891.

The Fruits of Enlightenment (Plody prosveshcheniya). Play. Moscow, 1891.

Master and Man (Khoziain i rabotnik). Short novel. *Severnyi vestnik (Northern Messenger)* 3 (1895).

What Is Art? (Chto takoe iskusstvo?). Essay. *Voprosy filosofii i psikhologii (Problems of Philosophy and Psychology)* (1897–1898).

Resurrection (Voskresenie). Novel. Moscow, 1899.

Father Sergius (Otets Sergei). Short novel. Written 1889–1900. Published posthumously in Moscow, 1911.

"The Living Corpse" ("Zhivoi trup"). Play. Written 1897–1900. Published posthumously in *Russkoe slovo (Russian Word)* (23 September 1911).

"After the Ball" ("Posle bala"). Story. Written 1903. Published posthumously, Moscow, 1911.

Notes of a Madman (Zapiski sumashedshego). Short novel. Written 1884–1903. Published posthumously, Moscow, 1912.

Hadji-Murad (Khadzhi-Murat). Short novel. Written 1896–1904. Published posthumously, Moscow, 1912.

"I Cannot Remain Silent" ("Ne mogu molchat"). Essay. Published simultaneously in newspapers in England, France, Germany, Italy, and Russia. 1908.

COLLECTED WORKS

Polnoe sobranie sochinenii. 90 vols. Moscow, 1928–1955. Fullest edition, but editing of some artistic texts leaves much to be desired.

Sobranie sochinenii v dvadtsati tomakh. Moscow, 1960–1965. Revised 1978–. Current standard edition for artistic texts.

TRANSLATIONS

Tolstoy Museum. *L. N. Tolstoi v perevodakh na inostrannye yazyki.* Moscow, 1961. Lists all known translations of Tolstoy's works 1862–1960; individual entries printed in language of the translation, so non-Russian readers can use this volume to find English translations.

The Works of L. Tolstoy. Translated by Louise and Aylmer Maude. New York and London, 1928–1937. Includes Aylmer Maude's biography of Tolstoy, all the major works and many of the minor ones, and a selection of the major articles.

BIOGRAPHICAL AND CRITICAL STUDIES

Bayley, John. *Tolstoy and the Novel.* London, 1966.

Canadian-American Slavic Studies (Winter 1978).

Christian, R. F. *Tolstoy: A Critical Introduction.* London, 1969.

————, ed. *Tolstoy's Letters.* 2 vols. New York, 1978.

————. *Tolstoy's "War and Peace": A Study.* Oxford, 1962.

Davie, Donald, ed. *Russian Literature and Modern English Fiction: A Collection of Critical Essays.* Chicago, 1965.

Eikhenbaum, Boris. *Tolstoi in the Seventies.* Ann Arbor, Mich., 1980.

————. *Tolstoi in the Sixties.* Ann Arbor, Mich., 1980.

————. *The Young Tolstoi.* Ann Arbor, Mich., 1972.

Gibian, George, ed. *Anna Karenina.* New York, 1970. The Maude translation; backgrounds and sources; essays in criticism. Norton Critical Edition series.

————. *War and Peace.* New York, 1966. The Maude translation; backgrounds and sources; essays in criticism. Norton Critical Edition series.

Gifford, Henry, ed. *Leo Tolstoy: A Critical Anthology.* Harmondsworth, 1971.

Goldenweizer, A. B. *Talks with Tolstoy.* Translated by S. S. Koteliansky and Virginia Woolf. New York, 1969.

Gorky, Maxim. *Literary Portraits.* Translated by Ivy Litvinov. Moscow, 1961.

Institut d'études slaves. *Tolstoi aujourd'hui. Colloque international Tolstoi.* Paris, 1980.

Jones, Malcolm, ed. *New Essays on Tolstoy.* Cambridge, 1978.

James, William. *Varieties of Religious Experience.* New York, 1902. Reprinted 1936.

Kuzminskaya, Tatyana A. *Tolstoy As I Knew Him.* New York, 1948. Translation of *My Life at Home and at Yasnaya Polyana* by Tolstoy's sister-in-law.

Lukács, Georg. "Tolstoy and the Development of Realism" and "Leo Tolstoy and Western European Literature." In *Studies in European Realism.* New York, 1974. Pp. 103–132, 133–158.

Mann, Thomas. "Goethe and Tolstoy" and "Anna Karenina." In *Essays of Three Decades.* New York, 1947. Pp. 93–175.

Matlaw, Ralph, ed. *Tolstoy: A Collection of Critical Essays.* Englewood Cliffs, N.J., 1967.

Reminiscences of Lev Tolstoi by His Contemporaries. Moscow, 1961.

Shestov, Lev. *Dostoevsky, Tolstoy and Nietzsche.* Athens, Ohio, 1969.

Shklovsky, Victor. *Lev Tolstoy.* Moscow, 1978.

Steiner, George. *Tolstoy or Dostoevsky: An Essay in the Old Criticism.* New York, 1959.

Tolstoy on Education. Translated by Leo Wiener, with an introduction by Reginald Archambault. Chicago, 1967.

Tolstoi, Lev Nikolaevich. *Last Diaries.* Translated by Lydia Weston-Kesich, edited and with an introduction by Leon Stillman. New York, 1960.

Tolstoy, Sophia. *The Final Struggle: Countess Tolstoy's Diary for 1910. With Extracts from Leo Tolstoy's Diary of the Same Period.* New York, 1980.

Troyat, Henri. *Tolstoy.* Translated by Nancy Amphoux. Garden City, N.Y., 1967.

Wasiolek, Edward. *Tolstoy's Major Fiction.* Chicago, 1978.

BIBLIOGRAPHIES

Bibliografiya literatury o L. N. Tolstoi, 1917–1973. 4 vols. Moscow, 1960–1978.

Leo Tolstoy: An Annotated Bibliography of English-Language Sources to 1978. Metuchen, N.J., and London, 1979. Lists criticism and commentaries.

PATRICIA CARDEN

GIOSUE CARDUCCI

(1835–1907)

OF ALL THE great figures who have shaped the course of Italian literature, Giosue Carducci may have suffered the most precipitous decline in popularity in recent years. Although his work still fills a respectable number of pages in school anthologies, Carducci is not widely read today by those in search of pleasure alone; and while his scholarly work is still of significance to researchers, his verse is no longer the important influence on new poetry it was in the late nineteenth and early twentieth centuries. This is a dramatic change in fortune, for during his lifetime Carducci was lionized to an extent hardly known earlier by an Italian literary figure and showered with honors both nationally and internationally. Some of the reasons for this adulation in his own time may be found in the strong desire of a newly united and still somewhat defensive Italian nation to single out figures from the world of culture and learning on whom to project its nascent values and aspirations. But Carducci was also a writer of great talent and perspicacity, able in his writings not only to express the nationalistic, and later imperialistic, aspirations of a young nation, but also to articulate its often only half-formulated misgivings about its new identity.

The second half of the nineteenth century, the period following the death of Giacomo Leopardi in 1837 and the publication of the final edition of Alessandro Manzoni's novel *I Promessi sposi* in 1840, was a time of doldrums for Italian literature. The greatest figure on the cultural scene was not a writer at all, but an opera composer, Giuseppe Verdi, whose earliest successes date from about the time of Carducci's first efforts at poetry, and whose last masterpieces are from the same period as the writings of Carducci's maturity. Although Carducci, rather surprisingly, preferred Richard Wagner's music to Verdi's, and Verdi commissioned other kinds of authors for his librettos, the two had certain characteristics in common—among them a genuine love for their country (which neither was afraid to express in the most unabashed fashion) and a certain prickliness of temperament, which both evidently cultivated in part to keep an importunate public at a suitable distance.

Carducci was also a contemporary of Giacomo Puccini, and the difference between the hearty romanticism of the early and middle Verdi and the fin de siècle decadence of Puccini is a measure of how much Italian and European tastes had changed during the course of the second half of the nineteenth century. Carducci too was influenced by these changes in taste; some critics have even identified similarities between his writings and those of such decadents as Algernon Charles Swinburne and Gabriele D'Annunzio, pointing out that Carducci was a contemporary not only of Wagner but also of Friedrich Nietzsche and even the young Sigmund Freud. Like Verdi, however, Carducci has his roots in the relatively untroubled official culture of the mid-nineteenth century and never really participated in any of the movements at the end of the century that opposed this earlier cultural dominance. Although he was an avowed opponent of romanticism, for example, Carducci never succeeded in freeing his work from a kind of romantic fervor, a warmth of expression that sets it off from the deliberately dispassionate writings of the antiromantic Parnassian group in France, for example. And unlike the decadents, with their penchant for the unusual and the exotic, Carducci's tastes were always the conventional ones of the middle-class nineteenth century burgher that he in fact remained for all of his life.

When Giosue Carducci was born on 27 July 1835, Italy was not yet united. He was born, therefore, not a citizen of Italy, but a subject of Leopold II, archduke of Tuscany: his birthplace, the little town of Valdicastello north of Lucca, was part of that Austrian prince's domain. Carducci's father was a doctor employed by a French mining company operating in Italy. While Giosue was still an infant, his father left the mining company and became a public health officer at Bolgheri, another tiny town, some miles away in the Maremma region of Tuscany, south of Leghorn and west of Siena. The Maremma is a wild and desolate area largely unsuited for cultivation, similar in many ways to the Scottish moors. Carducci always felt that there was a special affinity between this remote and untamed region and his own restless spirit. The impression made on him by the Maremma—where his boyhood pets were a young falcon and a wolf pup, and his earliest reading, the Latin and Italian classics that he borrowed from his father's library—was to remain with him for the rest of his life and inspire a number of his best-known poems.

Carducci's father, Michele, was an enthusiastic proponent of Italian unity who had spent some time in prison for his beliefs. In 1848, the year of revolutions throughout Europe, he was accused of subversive activity by his fellow townspeople (many of whom he had treated, often without pay) and subsequently driven from his home. He eventually found refuge in the more cosmopolitan and less bigoted capital city of Florence, where Giosue was able to continue his studies in an excellent school run by the Scolopi priests. He began to write poetry and, together with some of his classmates, formed a literary society, the Amici Pedanti or "pedantic friends," a group that was sharply critical of prevailing literary tastes and favored a return to the classics and the literary and ethical values associated with them. When Carducci was eighteen, his unusual intellectual promise received official recognition in the form of a scholarship to the prestigious Scuola Normale Superiore at Pisa, from which he graduated in 1856 licensed to teach in secondary institutions in Leopold's realm.

Carducci's first position was in the little town of San Miniato del Tedesco. Here he soon gained notoriety for his free-wheeling living habits and, in 1857, published his first book of verse—ostensibly to pay some debts run up in a local tavern. In the same year his brother Dante committed suicide after a violent quarrel with his father. The following year his father died—of grief at the family tragedy, according to some—leaving Carducci head of a family that before long was composed not only of his mother and younger brother, Valfredo, but also of his new wife, Elvira, née Menicucci, who had been engaged to Carducci for a number of years and whom he married in 1859. Burdened with these new financial responsibilities, the young writer accepted an invitation to join the Barbèra publishing house, for which he was to prepare a series of editions of the works of the earlier Italian poets: the beginning of what was to be a long and illustrious career as a philologist and critic.

In 1860, a time when public events leading to national unification were causing great changes in the lives of all Italians, an equally dramatic change took place in Carducci's life:

he was named professor of Italian literature at the University of Bologna, the oldest and one of the most respected universities in Europe. Twenty-five years old at the time of his appointment, Carducci was to remain at Bologna for forty-four years—in effect, the rest of his life. The professorship at Bologna meant that the young writer and scholar was now relatively free of financial worries and able to devote more of his time to the composition of poetry and learned articles; by the time of his death these writings would fill more than thirty volumes in the standard edition of his works.

His first decade as professor at Bologna was not without controversy. Some of it was sparked by the hymn "A Satana" ("To Satan"), written in 1863 and published under the pseudonym of Enotrio Romano two years later. Although this poem is a panegyric to reason and rebellion very generically conceived and not an apology for satanism, its title and anticlerical content did not fail to have the electrifying effect on the Italian reading public that the poet evidently intended. Much of the other poetry that Carducci produced in this period is harshly critical of government policies that he found either excessively subservient to the church or too namby-pamby for his liking. It is not surprising that a young man holding such views was soon in trouble with the authorities. In 1867 Carducci was threatened with a transfer from his position as professor of Italian at the University of Bologna to that of professor of Latin at the University of Naples—unless he tempered the expression of his political convictions. The threat was not carried out, partly because Carducci agreed to trim his political sails, at least in public. By the end of the decade Giosue and Elvira were comfortably settled in Bologna and the parents of four children: Bice, Laura, Libertà, and Dante.

In the first years of the next decade, however, several events took place that shook Carducci's private life. In 1870 his mother died; shortly afterward so did his only son, three-year-old Dante, named after his late uncle and his father's favorite. The following year, an admiring letter from Carolina Cristofori Piva changed the course of the poet and professor's life even more drastically. Carolina—the Lina or Lidia of the many poems and letters he wrote to her—was thirty-three years old at the time she met Carducci (though he believed she was twenty-six), the wife of an army officer, and the mother of three children. She soon became his mistress and confidante, the subject of some of his most successful and ardent poetry, and the recipient of a large number of extremely passionate love letters. His relationship with this woman uncovered new depths in the poet's character, depths that his readers and admirers were surprised to discover much later when the poet's letters were begun to be made public in 1938.

In 1877 Carducci published the first volume of his *Odi barbare (Barbarian Odes)*, poems in Italian whose forms and meters followed those of the Greek and Latin poets of antiquity rather than the Italian literary tradition. In 1878 he met the queen of Italy, Margherita of Savoy, and for the occasion wrote both an ode and an essay on the "eternally regally feminine." The former radical and republican had now become a supporter of the monarchy, much to the disgust of at least some of his followers. In 1881 Lidia died. In the same year Carducci began to write for the *Cronaca bizantina*, a flamboyant and very successful literary journal that numbered the young D'Annunzio among its contributors. Carducci's last years, many of them spent in infirm health, were marked by the publication of several more volumes, including his own editions of his collected poems and prose. He was also the recipient of abundant honors, among them, in 1890, nomination as senator of the kingdom of Italy. In 1906 Carducci was awarded the Nobel Prize for Literature, the first Italian to be so recognized. He died in Bologna in 1907.

Carducci was a moody man, quick to anger and given to violent rages all his life. His earliest letters are filled with expressions of scorn for contemporary political and literary society and sprinkled with references to the heated arguments in which he was repeatedly involved. When speaking of his contemporaries, Carducci did not hesitate to express himself in very plain terms. Writing to his friend Giuseppe Chiarini in 1862, for example, he characterizes the work of other poets of his day as "unworthy slop made by this garbage heap of verse writers inundating Italy . . . utterly insipid, miserable, sexless eunuchs without common sense or heart or even any sort of ear . . . this river of rottenness oozing from an old sore of Italy and known today as civil, patriotic, national, or call it what you will kind of poetry." He continued to express himself in this unequivocal fashion throughout his life, not only in private correspondence, but frequently in public utterances as well, almost as though it were only in this harshly antagonistic fashion that he could manage to arrive at an authentic definition of himself and his task as a writer.

Although Carducci seemed to relish his contentiousness, from time to time he was also heartily sorry for the pain he caused his friends. "I am aware," he wrote in 1867 to his publisher Barbèra, "that as the years go by I tend to grow mean, and my snarling and vicious temperament chafes at the restraints imposed on it by good manners. . . . But perhaps the cause is within me; I am not in agreement with myself." Writing again to Chiarini, he says:

> Sometimes I am afraid of myself; when I look inside myself, I find that I do not admire or love anyone, that I constantly have to pretend in order not to show the people I talk to how ridiculous and worthy of being spit on they are. . . . When I wake up in the morning [my] first sensation . . . is a ferocious desire to contend, a desire that on a physical level is precisely the instinct to tear something to pieces.
>
> (26 March 1869)

Carducci's feeling that his character was split into two parts is important both for what it tells us of his own personality and because it provides a link between him and writers elsewhere in this era who were also positing the possibility of the existence of contradictory, perhaps even violently opposed, character traits within a single individual. Feodor Dostoevsky's *Crime and Punishment*, for example, dates from 1866, Robert Louis Stevenson's *The Strange Case of Dr. Jekyll and Mr. Hyde* from 1886. For all his truculence, however, Carducci was nonetheless fond of his literary colleagues and acquaintances and kept up an extensive correspondence with them. Unlike such earlier writers as Vittorio Alfieri, Ugo Foscolo, Leopardi, and Manzoni, who did much of their work in solitude, Carducci seemed to require association with others with whom he could discuss his thoughts and work.

The person with whom he shared his most intimate thoughts, however, was Lidia—and she was much more than a friend. The extraordinary letters that he wrote to this woman—"the most penetrating, lively, and impassioned love letters in our literature," the critic Giorgio Barberi Squarotti has called them—reveal still another side of this man: his capacity for physical passion of quite astonishing intensity. Whatever feelings Lidia may have had toward Carducci, he believed that his love for her was the most important thing that had ever happened to him. His letters to her show him in a variety of moods: overcome with desire, consumed by jealousy, determined to give her up, elated at the prospect of one of their rare meetings and sentimentally reminiscent afterward, teasing and playful, confident and happy in her love, or plunged into the blackest depression. To Lidia, Carducci said things that he had never said before to anyone and perhaps not articulated even to himself. Moreover, the tone of these letters is markedly different from that of virtually all his other writing. In some ways the letters are the closest thing to literary realism that Carducci ever wrote; in this sense they might even be said to represent a sharper and more definitive break with the conventional language for passionate expression than any that had been achieved by contemporary Italian novelists. While in Carducci's poetry, expressions of personal feeling are always couched in conventional and often elaborately literary language, in his letters to Lidia he speaks straight from the heart in prose that is vivid, simple, and often quite moving as he wrestles to define his feelings and come to grips with the larger issues of his personality and existence.

Frequently frustrated and enraged by the difficulties of arranging a meeting with Lidia and often all but overcome by violent desire, Carducci gives voice in some of these letters to a despair sharply at odds with the vigor and wholesome optimism of his public pronouncements. Many are dominated by thoughts of death and a longing for physical and psychic dissolution into nothingness. "To sleep and forget about oneself is everything," he wrote in 1874. "Nothingness is the good. True, eternal, saintly nothingness." Despite his many accomplishments and the pride he justifiably took in them, Carducci was often acutely aware of the futility of his life. A man who had many friends and lived much of his life in the public eye, he also suffered from a loneliness and anxiety so profound that at times he sincerely believed he would have preferred to be dead.

A number of striking contradictions lie at the center of this writer's character. A Jacobin and revolutionary at the beginning of his life, Carducci ended it a monarchist and apologist for imperialism. Bearishly antisocial and scornful of middle-class values, he nonetheless became the spokesman and in some ways the paragon of bourgeois Italy for succeeding generations. Although a respectable family man who loved his children and was genuinely fond of his wife, he poured much of his strongest emotional energy into an illicit love affair with a woman he was able to see only at very infrequent intervals. A committed political writer who castigated the moral failings of his contemporaries, he was also tantalized by fantasies of hedonistic escape from his everyday responsibilities. Finally, although a man who lived life boisterously and savored its material pleasures to the full, Carducci was also both fascinated and horrified by the thoughts of death that accompanied him throughout his long existence.

Unlike the early work of Foscolo and Leopardi, which is often of considerable artistic merit, Carducci's earliest poetry is today of mainly historical interest. The poet himself consigned much of this work to the prehistory of his writing when he chose in 1871 to describe his verse from 1850 to 1863 as *Juvenilia* (Childish Things). The poems in that collection and the next—the *Levia gravia* or "light and serious things" of 1868—are noteworthy for the strong ethical passion and longing for freedom and heroic action that they express. Even as a very young man, Carducci fervently believed that it was through literature that the moral and political corruption he saw in the world around him could be both depicted and remedied. It was in the hope of doing just this that he entered the literary arena as a "standard-bearer of the classics," crusading against what he saw as a debased and reactionary romanticism stifling Italy's intellectual life.

Although the *Rime* (Rhymes) of 1857 had been dedicated to the archromantic Leopardi, whom Carducci admired both for his poetic excellence and the materialist philosophy he clung to through the despair and suffering of a particularly painful life, it was Leopardi's fellow romantic Manzoni, and especially Manzoni's followers, whom Carducci viewed as his antagonists. Even though by the 1850's and 1860's Manzoni had abandoned poetry and the novel to devote his energies to moral tracts and disquisitions on the Italian language, his numerous and irksome followers still formed an important part of the Italian literary scene. In rejecting what he saw as this group's hypocritical and ultimately self-serving piety and reactionary obeisance to the church, Carducci took the further step of condemning the novel itself—the literary form preferred by Manzoni and his less talented followers—as a medium for discussing contemporary issues. Carducci believed that prose should be used for writing history rather than fiction, and thought that poetry was superior to prose of whatever sort. In taking this position, however, Carducci showed his lack of awareness of the enduring contributions being made to the exploration of the human psyche by the nineteenth-century novel, both inside and outside Italy. Furthermore, his antiromanticism involved what now seems a shortsighted rejection of the realistic and populist artistic currents taking shape in Europe during this period. Carducci's disdain for this sort of romanticism and the historical novel it had spawned was a product of both his anticlerical convictions and his strong nationalistic feelings. Romanticism, after all, had had its origins in France and Germany; and in Carducci's day the presence of French- and German-speaking troops bivouacked in Italy was a major obstacle to the country's unification. What is noteworthy in all of these attitudes is the young Carducci's conviction that literature was a very serious matter, a kind of priestly calling or religion involving the most serious issues confronting humanity.

However interesting Carducci's literary and social views may have been in this period, the poetry that he wrote in the fifties and early sixties is derivative and bookish; its language is drawn from the poets of earlier centuries—Dante, Petrarch, Cino da Pistoia, Politian—though revivified by the living Tuscan dialect the young poet had always heard around him and which he spoke and wrote with considerable verve. Certain formal aspects of this poetry—for example, the preference for the ode and its tone of moral seriousness—indicate another important influence, that of the Italian neoclassical writers of the time of the French Revolution: Guiseppe Parini, Vincenzo Monti, Alfieri, and Foscolo, among others. Much of what this early poetry says is conventional, even trite, but there are interesting hints in it of what is to come. In the sonnet "Passa la nave mia" (My Ship Is Passing), for example, written when the poet was only sixteen, we can find the first expression of what will become a perennial longing for escape, as Carducci describes his desire to journey "to the shadowy port of oblivion/to the white reef of death." Other early poems are irreverent castigations of the middle classes. A famous example is the sonnet "Pietro Metastasio," with its final line stigmatizing the nineteenth century as a "vile little century that pretends to be Christian" (secoletto vil che cristianeggia). In this same period, by way of contrast, Carducci also wrote "Alla croce di Savoia" (To the Cross of Savoy), with its quite different conclusion, "Oh white Cross of Savoy,/God save you! and God save the king!" Whatever his reservations about contemporary politics, and although very much a republican later, at this point in his life Carducci was an enthusiastic supporter of the formula "Italy and Victor Emanuel," a proponent, that is, of unification under a monarch from the House of Savoy.

Some of the most readable poems from this period are the satirical ones. In them we find Carducci complaining that he is surrounded by intellectual dwarfs—uncouth poets ("Born in a milk bucket/you learned to write in a barrel") or pedants obsessively attached to footnotes ("Pietro Fanfani is in the notes/And the notes are in Fanfani:/In the beginning there were only the notes/and then the notes created Fanfani"). One of the best of these early invectives, addressed "Al beato Giovanni della Pace" (To Blessed Giovanni della Pace), consists of a scathing satire on the contemporary mania for glorifying new saints and freshly exhumed relics, bits of bone that could be turned into tiepins; on drunken clergymen and masses made meaningful only as excuses for arranging business or love affairs; and on invocations of the Madonna by hypocritical women lifting their skirts for their lovers.

It is in this context of boyish obstreperousness that the hymn "A Satana" must be considered. Certainly one of Carducci's most famous poems, it was composed "all in a rush and straight from the heart," as he said later. The work is not a philosophically rigorous inversion of conventional values of the sort that Friedrich Nietzsche was proposing in Germany at this same time, but simply uses the name Satan to praise Reason, Nature, Progress, Love, Joy, and Beauty—all certainly very conventional ideals—and to condemn obscurantism, especially as practiced by the Christian church. Predictably, what the young Carducci sees as the forces of darkness do not prevail. The final image of Satan crossing the plains in a railroad car to "conquer the priests' Jehovah" may seem a bit ridiculous today, and its anticlericalism may have been outmoded even in Carducci's own time. While the poem shocked those it was meant to offend, others raised more thoughtful objections. One such objection was that the form of the hymn was antidemocratic and comprehensible only to an educated elite; it thus undermined the revolutionary cause it was meant to promote.

How to reconcile a revolutionary message with an aristocratic notion of form worried Carducci throughout his career. The question of the proper language for poetic invective is important in the *Giambi ed epodi* (Iambics and Epodes), the poems of political and social protest he wrote mostly between 1867 and 1872, although they were not collected under this title until 1882. The name "Iambics and Epodes" was meant to indicate kinship between these often vehement poems of political protest and the satirical and political poetry of Horace and Archilocus. For the most part, these are occasional poems inspired by specific events. Several were first delivered as toasts at commemorative banquets and only later appeared in printed form; at least one— "Nel vigesimo anniversario dell'VIII agosto MDCCCLVCIII" (On the Twentieth Anniversary of the Eighth of August, 1848)—was first made known to the public as a poster on the walls of Bologna celebrating a famous uprising against the Austrians.

If, as one critic has suggested, Carducci's earlier lyrics are sometimes like clothes too big for their wearers because the erudite form overwhelms a relatively slender content, the *Giambi ed epodi* suffer from the opposite fault: the message is often so urgent, even violent, that it bursts the confines of language and form, and the result is not so much poetry as diatribe. Certainly these are not poems often read today except by those with a taste for literary invective or a special interest in political history. Although the country was now unified and, after 1870, had Rome as its capital, Carducci is harshly critical of the new nation and disappointed that Italy had not been spiritually reborn in the manner of ancient Rome or revolutionary France as hoped by the patriots who fought for its unification. The greed, timorousness, and mendacity that Carducci finds characteristic of the new order seem to him an unforgivable affront to the memories of the great Italians of the past and the recent patriots who had struggled and died for their dreams of a country both united and spiritually renewed.

This contrast between the glories of the past and a disheartening present reality is drawn very sharply in "Nostri santi e nostri morti" (Our Saints and Our Dead), written for All Saints Day 1869. In this brief poem Carducci praises the unsung heroes who have died in the struggle for national liberation; he compares them to the Christian saints and the ancient Greek heroes, even though their blood has not yet fertilized the "vengeance, justice, and liberty" that their ghosts are calling for. Instead, it nourishes only the grass cropped by the horses of foreign cavalry and the roses that adorn the tyrants' beds. In another of the poems from *Giambi ed epodi*, "Meminisse horret"—the title, "[the soul] is horrified to remember," is a tag from Vergil—the same contrast is drawn between past and present, in this case using the Italian heroes of the Renaissance—Piero Capponi, Francesco Ferrucci, Dante, and Machiavelli. The present-day counterparts of these great heroes, as Carducci says quite specifically in the metaphor that closes the poem, are eager to compromise with their oppressors, willing to prostitute even their mothers on the tombs of the past. The language grows even more violent in another poem, "Per Giuseppe Monti e Gaetano Tognetti" (1868), written in response to Pope Pius IX's execution of two patriots captured while trying to foment an insurrection to unite Rome with Italy. The pope is depicted with hands as red with blood as his face is ruddy with good health. While he thinks about the punishment the prisoners are about to suffer, the pontiff rubs his hands in glee: whereas Saint Peter was content to cut off the ears of Christ's tormentors, he will go one better and lop off his victims' heads. Outraged by the heartlessness of this attitude, the poet calls on "philosophers, soldiers, poets, and workers" to join together to raze the Vatican.

For Carducci in the *Giambi ed epodi*, virtually all celebrations by official Italy are tainted with the compromises and failures of the new regime. When he describes the traditional wedding of Venice and the sea in "Le nozze del mare" (The Wedding with the Sea, 1869), this festival reminds him only of Italy's humiliating naval defeat at Lissa in the Austrian war (1866). And at the conclusion of "In morte di Giovanni Cairoli" (On the Death of Giovanni Cairoli, 1870), he states bitterly, "la nostra patria è vile"—our fatherland is vile.

Religion, government, the military, commerce, industry ("Per il quinto anniversario della battaglia di Mentana" [On the Fifth Anniversary of the Battle of Mentana, 1872] closes with "knights of industry" filling their sacks with booty, indifferent to the imminent deluge as long as it comes "tomorrow")—no institution escapes his corrosive analysis. Nor do the family, women, or current sexual morals. "A proposito del processo Fadda" (On the Fadda Trial, 1879), for example, is a violent denunciation of the hypocrisy and morbid curiosity of respectable matrons who have flocked to a lurid murder trial in search of a titillation they are too timid to seek more openly.

In these onslaughts Carducci is responding to distressing events in his own life as well as to national disappointments. Several of these pieces were written during the years that saw the death of his mother and little son and the beginning of his stormy liaison with Lidia. His intolerance and outrage are not unconnected with his own restlessness and sense of futility. In these poems as never before in his writing, the private and the public, the lived and the literary have become tightly intermingled. The violent, scandalous language and imagery contributed a great deal to Carducci's fame, just as they increased the bewildering notions he had about himself as a literary, indeed a theatrical, creation of his own making. Although these poems meant a kind of liberation from the derivative conventionality of his earlier work, they mark no break with traditional notions of literary audience or poetic form. In an Italy where, in Carducci's own words, "the peasant and subproletarian underclass is either dying of hunger, or brutalizing itself with pellagra and superstition, or emigrating," the erudite language, classical syntax, and learned allusions clearly indicate that the audience Carducci addressed was the minuscule (though influential) educated minority who could read and appreciate what he was writing.

Of all the *Giambi ed epodi*, the poem that perhaps most clearly exhibits the poet's moral and ideological confusion is "Ripresa: Avanti! Avanti!" (Reprise: Forward! Forward!, 1872). In thumping meters, Carducci compares himself to a rider on a galloping bay horse different in kind from the prissy or bumbling mounts of his contemporaries, a steed carrying him to poetic heights that will establish him as the "new bard of a new age." Yet in this exhilarating rush toward glory, the poet suddenly becomes aware that in all he has done he has neglected an aspect of life symbolized by "virgins dancing in the May sunshine/and the flash of white shoulders beneath golden locks." Despite his efforts to change the world with his poetry, he has succeeded only in becoming famous, that is, ineffectual; he is now bitterly aware of the futility both of his poetry and of the life he has lived in its service. To counter these despairing meditations, Carducci turns to recollections of his boyhood days in the Maremma and the myths of Italy's glorious past as exemplars of the wholesome and genuine in a world of sham and disappointment. Thanks to the force of these memories, he is able to continue his journey toward the setting sun of the poem's conclusion.

At the end of this polemical poem there is a longing for repose in the uncontaminated landscape of the Maremma and the comforting myths of the past. This emotion will return in many of Carducci's other writings of the seventies and eighties—in particular the lyrics of the *Rime nuove (New Lyrics)*. Some of the poems that make up this volume were composed as early as the late 1860's, even though it was not until 1887 that the collection appeared. The differences between these poems and the invectives of the *Giambi ed epodi*, however, are not so much differences of chronology as of style and subject matter. Rather than delineating a certain period of Carducci's life and poetic production, the *Rime nuove* are representative of the poet's abiding interest in traditional forms and meters. Among these poems are some of his best-known and most admired and frequently anthologized works, in his own day and since.

All the poems of the *Rime nuove* are in conventional rhymes and meters and employ the usual language of the Italian lyric. They are "new" only in the sense that they are meant to continue the development of poetry in Italian rather than to ally themselves with the Greek and Latin tradition represented by the

Odi barbare and the *Giambi ed epodi.* In subject matter—especially in their introspective and autobiographical concerns and use of landscape as an image for emotional states—the *Rime nuove* frequently recall similar compositions by Leopardi, a writer Carducci may have been thinking of, and some of whose ontological anxieties he certainly shared. In these poems Carducci reflects on the mysteries of life and death, loneliness and memory, the universe and the place of the individual within it—perennial themes of poetry since the beginning of writing. It is perhaps because these themes are universal and are treated in traditional fashion that the poems of this collection have remained popular.

Carducci, by now a popular and active university professor and the editor of a number of scholarly editions and monographs on earlier Italian poetry, has begun to be concerned with the place of his own work in the development of his country's traditional literary forms. The book contains a large number of poems about poetry and begins with an apostrophe "Alla rima" ("To Rhyme") as practiced by both poets and the unschooled fashioners of folksong and poetry throughout Western Europe—spiritual forebears as "sacred and beloved" as the verse forms they developed. This poem is followed by a section of thirty-four sonnets; the first two describe the history of this form from Dante and Petrarch through Tasso and Shakespeare, Alfieri and Foscolo, down to Carducci himself. In "Classicismo e romanticismo" (Classicism and Romanticism, 1873) Carducci defines his position in the classicism/romanticism controversy. As usual, he gives the latter a good pasting, comparing romanticism to moonlight and describing it as a "sterile and libidinous little nun" (monacella lasciva e infeconda) with a languid predilection for churchyards, ruins, and the poor. Classicism, by contrast, is described as a virile and healthy sun, the source of life and fruitfulness, a welcome companion to wholesome work and celebration. During the time that he was writing blasts like this at romanticism, however, Carducci was also reading Charles Baudelaire and Heinrich Heine; in a poem like "Anacreontica romantica" (Romantic Anacreontic, 1873) he is not above employing such romantic devices as vampires who feast on the poet's heart—though he does so, admittedly, only to parody the poetry of love-slavery and Gothic paraphernalia that he detested.

Perhaps the fullest and most explicit statement of Carducci's poetic beliefs during this period is in the "Congedo" or farewell (1887) at the very end of the *Rime nuove*. In this description of the poet and his art, Carducci contrasts his own writing with that of certain contemporaries: the sycophants fawning on the wealthy, the dreamers constantly bumping their noses against reality, and the utilitarian poets dirtying their hands in manure to raise an occasional violet or cauliflower for society's delectation. Unlike these, the poet Carducci imagines is a kind of craftsman, a robust blacksmith with "muscles of steel" sweating in his poetic smithy as he hammers out the sword of political protest, the sacred implements of religious ritual, and the golden arrow of pure art.

It is this conception of poetry as a product of robust and disinterested energy that lies behind some of Carducci's most successful compositions, "San Martino" (St. Martin's Day) of 1883, for example:

Up the bristling hills
The fog rises in the drizzle,
And underneath the northwind
The sea is frothing and howling;

But through the streets of the village
Out of the bubbling winevats
Goes the harsh smell of the wine
To gladden the hearts it reaches.

The spit on the hardwood fire
Splutters as it turns:
The hunter stands in the doorway
Whistling while he gazes

At black birds in flocks
Among the reddish clouds
Similar to banished thoughts
That migrate in the evening.

The scene depicted in this brief text celebrating 11 November is at once simple and turbulent: the rough natural landscape, the new wine and roasting game that signal autumn for the community, and the private thoughts of the hunter come together in a single coherent impression as the motion, noise, and aromas of the poem's early stanzas subside into the silent sky and departing birds of its conclusion. In this poem, with its vivid, precise description of external reality and its carefully understated emotional message, we can see Carducci moving toward a conception of poetry that will become increasingly important for the writers of later generations.

As was the case with Leopardi's *Canti* (definitive edition 1845), many of the poems in the *Rime nuove* focus very closely on the poet's own feelings and emotions, in particular on his moodiness and sometimes uncontrollable rages. One example is the sonnet "In riva al mare" (By the Sea), completed and first published in 1885, but probably sketched out much earlier. Here, in a setting reminiscent of those often employed by the later Nobel Prize-winning Italian poet Eugenio Montale, the poet scrutinizes the Tyrrhenian Sea for clues to his inner turbulence. The agitation of the ocean—which is filled, we learn, with "stupid and filthy" predatory fish chasing equally stupid prey—is analogous to the poet's own moods, which are as resistant to rational control as the ocean is to the moon's "useless lamp" shining on the "black wrath" of its waves. This is Sturm und Drang to be sure, but tempered by a new realistic vision impatient with the conventions of the past, similar to that which will come with Montale.

In two other sonnets in the first part of this volume, Carducci uses this traditional form to treat less conventional subjects. In the first,

"Martino Lutero" (Martin Luther, 1886), he compared himself to the famous Protestant leader—like the poet, a lover of wine and of argument and a battler with God. In the second, "A un asino" (To a Jackass, 1884), he creates a kind of apotheosis of this animal replete with apostrophes, rhetorical questions in the best classical manner, and erudite allusions to the Old Testament and Homer. The slightly startling subjects of these sonnets indicate the poet's desire for a poetic content that will reflect his ebullient temperament, while his choice of form shows his determination—at least for the moment—to remain within the formal limits of the Italian literary tradition.

The dominant emotion of much of the poetry that Carducci wrote in these years is a profound melancholy, deepened by obsessive thoughts of death, an unhappiness and despair occasioned no doubt by the deaths of his son and mother, the souring of his marriage, and his growing frustration at having to live apart from the woman he loved and who (as he said over and over in his letters to her) meant everything to him. This melancholy is evident in the pessimistic "Colloqui con gli alberi" ("Conversation with Trees," 1873). In this poem the poet disclaims any affection for the oak, which in his view has too often bestowed its leaves on military conquerors who were nothing but "insane destroyers of cities," or for the laurel, which has also provided wreaths for the unworthy, whether poets or emperors. Instead, he prefers the grape, whose fruit provides him with the means for temporary oblivion, and the fir, whose wood will make up his coffin and "close in the end/my thoughts' dark tumult and their vain desire." This feeling of melancholy, "spleen," or Weltschmerz runs like a dark thread throughout many of the poems of this volume. In "Brindisi funebre" (Funereal Toast, 1874), for example, the poet gloomily asserts that only the dead and drink are of importance to him and wonders: "Do joy and beauty/Still exist in the world?/In the sunlit lands/Is there still love?" So too in "Tedio invernale" ("Winter Weariness," 1875), he can no longer believe that flowers and sunshine, youth, glory, beauty, faith, virtue, and love have existed anywhere since the time of Homer, a heroic age now reduced to ashes in the filthy fog of contemporary life engulfing him.

These poems of melancholy also include some of Carducci's most celebrated poetic achievements. In the powerful lament, "Funere mersit acerbo" (Plunged in Bitter Death, 1870—the title is again a quote from Vergil), Carducci interrogates the shade of his dead brother, Dante; in language reminiscent of the classical elegists who had written on similar themes, he begs him to receive the soul of the nephew who bears his name and has been expelled from the gaudy gardens of life and driven to the cold and lonely shores of death. "Pianto antico" ("An Ancient Lament"), which was written in 1871 just seven months after the death of little Dante, is another poem in memory of his dead son. It is perhaps the most famous poem on this theme that Carducci wrote and is considered by many a small masterpiece:

> The tree you used to stretch for
> With your tiny infantile hand
> The verdant pomegranate
> With the lovely vermillion flowers
>
> In the silent lonely garden
> Has just now burst into leaf
> As June once more revives it
> With sunshine and with warmth.
>
> You, blossom of my tree
> Blasted and withered by time,
> You, final and single flower
> Of this my futile life,
>
> Lie in the cold of the ground,
> Lie in the black of the ground,
> Where the sun no longer revives
> And love has no power to waken.

In this natural contrast sanctioned by centuries of myth and poetry, the forces of the upper world of heat, light, and life fight a losing battle with those of the lower world of cold, darkness, and death. This struggle is mediated by the brilliant red and green of the pomegranate tree of the kind that actually grew in Bologna in the poet's garden in Via Broccaindosso. For the atheist Carducci, however, the pomegranate has lost the refructifying power that it had in ancient myth and is consequently powerless before the ineluctable force that has ended his son's existence.

In the darkness and discouragement of Carducci's middle years, it was Lidia who represented the single bright spot. During the nearly ten years of his relationship with this "sweet panther," as he liked to call her, Carducci wrote a number of poems in which she plays a prominent role. Of these, the three "Primavere elleniche" (Hellenic Springtimes) of 1872 are perhaps the best known. They were also crucial in the development of Carducci's work and mark the transition between the Italian forms of the *Rime nuove* and the classicizing meters of the *Odi barbare.* The three odes in the "Aeolian," "Doric," and "Alexandrian" modes that make up this "Hellenic" cycle present an escape fantasy at once erotic and chaste. In the first, after a lengthy description of springtime in Greece (which Carducci knew only from books, most of them books of ancient poetry), he invites his mistress to set sail with him for a land where they will be welcomed by the poets and beauties of antiquity and can forget the "impure shores" of the West. In the last, in which the lovers are embracing in the rain in a Milanese cemetery, the poet's excited imagination turns this site into the faraway "fabulous fields of Elysium" he imagines to be their spiritual home.

For Carducci the desire for flight from the unpleasant realities of everyday life often takes the form of regression to childhood and childhood memories. "Nostalgia" (Nostalgia, 1871) is typical of the many poems of this sort in the *Rime nuove* and later collections. Here it is to the Maremma of his youth that the poet longs to return, a land of sparsely shaded, in-fertile soil, of bristling cork trees, wild horses, black skies and storms, where he can be swallowed up by the thunderclap, hills, and the sea and thus forget his cares. For Carducci the Maremma is an unfailing source of peace and contentment, a land that is austere and untamed, uncomplicated by urban realities, contemporary historical events, or even time itself. In a much later poem, "Traversando la maremma toscana" ("Crossing the Tuscan Maremma," 1885), this savage and uncompromising landscape is compared to the poet's moody and untamed temperament, much as the sea is in "In riva al mare." This time, however, the poet finds some emotional support from the landscape, at the very sight of which his heart leaps up and his eyes fill with tears. Even if everything that he has ever hoped for, loved, or dreamed has been in vain, and life has nothing left for him but death, the Maremma, with its "misty fogs and green meadow/Smiling in the morning rain," still has the power to soothe his grief and assuage his discouragement.

Although the Maremma that occurs in Carducci's works is usually unpopulated, the "Idillio maremmano" ("An Idyll of the Maremma," 1872) introduces into these wild spaces a human inhabitant who will find counterparts in other poems of Carducci's maturity. In this instance she is a "blond Maria" whose robust physicality has stuck in his memory since childhood. As he now thinks about her, Carducci is sure that she is happily married and the mother of "bold sons . . . leaping on the backs of half-tamed horses" while she watches with a mixture of pride and maternal apprehension. For the poet, the vigorous outdoor life this woman leads is preferable to his own "cold, dark, and worrisome" lot as an intellectual; he concludes his meditation by announcing that he would be glad to change places with Maria and spend his time pursuing a runaway buffalo rather than the line of verse that continues to elude him in his study.

Clearly, the Maria of the "Idillio maremmano," with her eyes as blue as the cornflowers in the wheat fields around her, is an entirely literary creation who has little in common with the real peasants of central Italy during this period of industrialization, expanding capitalization, disruption of the traditional patterns of life, and consequent emigration, often to America. Like the sunny and bookish Greece used as surrogate for a Bologna where the weather was often rainy and chill, and where Carducci had lectures and exams to give and a domestic life to lead with a woman he did not love, the Maremma of these idyllic poems was more a projection of the poet's own needs and dissatisfactions than a historical or geographical reality. It was a fantasy, however, that found favor with the middle-class readers of Carducci's generation. In this depiction of an uncomplicated but sturdily healthy and dignified open air existence, Carducci's readers could find both an alternative to the urban grayness of their own lives and a positive description of peasant life contradicting the grim reports on rural conditions that were beginning to reach them.

The nostalgia for a simpler sort of external reality that plays a large part in so much of Carducci's poetry can assume both autobiographical and historical shapes. "Davanti San Guido" ("Before San Guido," 1874) is an example of the former, "Il comune rustico" (The Rustic Commune, 1885) of the latter. Carducci worked on the first of these poems for more than fifteen years, and many believe that the final result is his single most important composition. "Davanti San Guido" describes a train ride through western Tuscany. Seated in a railway coach that is bringing him back to Bologna and the work and family that await him there, the poet suddenly realizes that the row of cypresses he can see from the train's window are in fact the cypresses of Bolgheri, the tiny town where he spent his childhood. When the train stops, the rustling made by the limbs of these cypresses in the wind seems to invite him not to leave this place of political and cultural preconsciousness, where Pan and the wood nymphs will soothe his cares in the "divine harmony" of nature. When the poet protests that he is no longer a naughty urchin but a respectable adult who cannot remain with them any longer, they respond by invoking the image of his dead grandmother buried in their shadow. Suddenly, memories of this woman and the folktales she used to tell rush over the poet with such force that he is now certain that everything he has been seeking throughout his life has been located all along in Bolgheri, where his life began. As the train begins to pull away from the station, the poet rouses from his reverie:

> Puffing, the train began to move on
> As I wept softly to myself;
> And a fleet herd of wild horses
> Ran whinnying at the sound.
>
> While not even glancing at all the racket
> A gray donkey kept right on munching
> Slowly and seriously
> On the blue and red of a thistle.
>
> (109–116)

The dour donkey brings to an enigmatic conclusion a poem in which the world of nature, folklore, and the family seen from a child's perspective has been set against the urban world of Bologna and the poet's role there as breadwinner and father. Although Carducci finally rejects the kind of regression the cypresses hold out to him and returns to the city and his responsibilities, his hesitation and embarrassment would seem to explain the derisive image of the donkey.

"Il comune rustico" is set in the late Middle Ages in a little town in the northeast corner of Italy near the border of today's Hungary, Austria, and Yugoslavia. In this poem Carducci once again demonstrates that his is no luridly romantic return to a Middle Ages of witches and devils, but a historical evocation of the "rustic virtues" of a simple mountain village in Italy many centuries ago. The central section of the poem consists, in fact, of a speech by the "consul" of this village, who exhorts the "senate" of his assembled countrymen not only to share the communal grazing lands equally, but also—indeed above all—to be prepared to defend their common soil against the Slavs and Hungarians who threaten their borders. As the sun sparkles on the simple scene while the women pray to the Madonna and the cattle graze in peace, the men of the village all raise their hands to swear they will abide by this covenant. When the poet was still at his grandmother's knee in the years he remembers in "Davanti San Guido," life was simple, and right and wrong easily identifiable. Similarly, during the infancy of the nation as imagined in "Il comune rustico"—a time long before unification, the political compromises of "transformism," and industrialization—political life was simple too, and important decisions could be arrived at collectively and naturally and then supported by all good men without need for dissent or discussion.

Although the action of many of the lyrics of the *Rime nuove* seems situated in a zone of fantasy or memory somewhere outside of time, "Il comune rustico" has a precise historical as well as geographical context. This attention to history is even more important for the poems of the *Odi barbare,* the poems Carducci wrote in classical rather than Italian meters, and on which his fame principally rests today. As early as 1857 Carducci had been interested in adapting the forms and meters of the poets of ancient Greece and Rome to Italian poetry and contemporary subjects. However, it was only in the 1870's and 1880's—the fruitful two decades in which he also wrote most of the *Rime nuove*—that he began to work seriously on this project. Although the definitive edition of the fifty *Odi barbare* divided into two books was not published until 1893, it had been preceded by several earlier collections of verses of this sort: the *Odi barbare* of 1877, the *Nuove odi barbare* (New Barbarian Odes) of 1882, and the *Terze odi barbare* (Third Barbarian Odes) of 1889. These collections include some of the most fa-

mous—the most admired as well as the most severely criticized—of Carducci's poems.

The formal qualities of these poems are perhaps their most important characteristic. Before Carducci, indeed beginning in the Renaissance, Italian poets such as Leon Battista Alberti and Gabriello Chiabrera had attempted to adapt the quantitative meters of classical prosody—meters based on length of syllable rather than stress or accent—to poetry in the vulgar tongue. In the nineteenth century, Friedrich Gottlieb Klopstock, Friedrich Hölderlin, and Wolfgang von Goethe in Germany, and Charles Marie Leconte de Lisle in France, had also experimented with Greek and Roman meters as a basis for poetry in modern European languages. Carducci's efforts to write Italian lyrics according to the rules of classical prosody and in the forms made famous by the Greek and Latin poets of antiquity were therefore not without precedent, although his experiments were to prove more successful than those of any of his predecessors. Carducci's method was to consider the meters of the Greek and Latin poets as if they were based on stress rather than syllable length and then to devise corresponding verses in Italian. The Latin hexameter, for example, is reproduced in his odes by a verse that consists of six stressed syllables rather than of six classical feet. Unlike the standard Italian hendecasyllable—the Italian form perhaps closest to the classical hexameter—which is eleven syllables long (though with adjoining vowels frequently elided), Carducci's "barbarian" line can vary in number of syllables from eleven to sixteen or more.

Such a poetic strategy had several important consequences. First, in Carducci's line the accents fall at different points from those in conventional Italian verse; the effect is therefore much less "musical"—or at least musical in a very different way. Second and more important still, the *Odi barbare* do not rhyme. Although unrhymed verse had been used before in Italian, most notably in Annibale Caro's sixteenth-century translation of the *Aeneid* and much of the work of Leopardi, rhyme was still an important element in Italian verse of the time. The *Odi barbare* thus represented a truly new kind of poetry, at once reminiscent of the meters and texture of ancient verse and markedly different from it, poetry that might have been written by a "barbarian" compelled by the nature of his own tongue to deviate from classical practice—which was what Carducci himself said about them. In adopting this new and unfamiliar poetic style Carducci was courting incomprehension and unpopularity with his readers, but characteristically the unconventionality of the project made it all the more attractive to him. If Italian readers, he said defiantly in one of his letters, were unable to make sense of the verses he was now writing, then so much the worse for them.

This attitude is reflected in the "Preludio" ("Prelude," 1875), which serves as a preface to the *Odi barbare* of 1877 much as "Alla rima" had for the *Rime nuove.* In this brief ode Carducci describes the poetry of his day as worn out and meretricious—all too willing to offer its "flaccid flanks" to the embraces of the vulgar. Carducci is not interested in easy conquests of this sort. He prefers the challenge of a more recalcitrant mistress, a form that is difficult, resistant like an untamed bacchante struggling to evade her lover's embrace. Later, in the "Ragioni metriche" (Metrical Reasons, 1881), he goes so far as to call the "settenario," or traditional seven-syllable Italian line, "vile" and describes the eight-syllable line as suitable only for servants. Despite these expressions of disdain for conventional forms, however, Carducci continued during this entire period, and indeed for the rest of his life, to write poems in both traditional and "barbarian" forms.

Compared to the *Rime nuove,* the *Odi barbare* are fewer in number and concerned with subjects of a less personal and occasional nature. They also tend to be longer and more formal in conception. In some ways the *Odi barbare* represent a return to the public themes of

the *Giambi ed epodi,* though the rage at contemporary events that characterizes that collection is largely absent here. In the *Odi barbare* both public and personal concerns are placed in a much broader context, projected against the vast backdrop of the history of Italy from pre-Roman times to the present day. It is this new, erudite, and serious use of history as an essential component of his poetry that marks off the *Odi barbare* in still another way from the rest of Carducci's verse.

At the center of Carducci's thoughts about Italian history was Rome, the seat not only of the Caesars and of the popes, but also the "third Rome" now finally part of Italy—"an immense ship launched on the conquest of the world," as he describes it in the 1881 ode "Roma" dedicated to the city. For Carducci, Rome was not only the symbol of a united Italy free at last from papal oppression and ignorance and thus poised expectantly toward the future, but also the matrix of that classical civilization whose values he felt were now being compromised by a new and inferior way of life. The complex view that he held of the city and the significance it had for him can be seen in the ode "Dinanzi alle terme di Caracalla" (In Front of the Baths of Caracalla, 1877).

The poem is in sapphic stanzas of three hendecasyllables plus a quinario as equivalents of the classical three sapphics plus an adonic. The hendecasyllables, however, as in verse 9 describing a flock of crows—"Continui, dènsi, nèri, crocidànti," (Continuous, dense, black, cackling)—are very different in both accent and sound from their Italian counterparts. Because of this unusual meter, the lack of rhyme, and the unfamiliar stanzaic form, the linguistic texture of this poem is quite unlike that of most other Italian verse. The poem begins on a plain outside Rome where the ruined baths mentioned in the title are located. It is a chilly spring day (Carducci wrote the poem in April): the sky is dappled with clouds, the wind "moves moistly" across the plain, and the Alban mountains in the background are white with snow. Standing in this landscape is a British woman tourist, "her green veil pulled back on her ashen locks," thumbing through a guidebook in search of information about the crumbling walls before her, structures that once challenged heaven and the passage of time itself, but now are only ruins where the crows flock in sinister augury and churchbells toll "heavy through the air from the Lateran."

In this desolate and somewhat forbidding scene, a peasant appears, but he is not an idealized figure of the sort that populated the Arcadian poetry of the previous century, or any kin to the robust rustics described elsewhere in Carducci's own poetry. Ankles wound with the rag wrapping favored by the inhabitants of the Agro Romano, unshaven and malaria ridden, he slouches by the ruins without even a glance. "Fever," Carducci exclaims, "here I invoke you." But instead of going on to inveigh against the "social question" of the unsanitary conditions of life in the Roman Campagna and its malarial marshes, Carducci turns instead to address a long prayer to Fever herself. In his apostrophe to this ancient divinity once worshipped by the Romans, he prays for the expulsion from the sacred city of the race of speculators currently despoiling it. These "new men," Carducci goes on, are intent only on their own "tiny affairs" and unaffected by the "religious awe" that Rome and its monuments ought to inspire; Rome is of as little importance to them as the Baths of Caracalla to the ignorant tourist and indifferent peasant of the poem's opening lines. Here lies the real scandal, for in this sacred city "the goddess Roma is sleeping":

> Her head resting on the august Palatine hill,
> her arms reaching from the Caelian to the
>   Aventine,
> and her strong shoulders extended through Porta
>   Capena
> and out the Appian Way.

(37–40)

A good deal of the machinery of romantic literature has been put into motion here: the taste for travel and ruins, the foreboding weather and ominous birds, a distant and superior past juxtaposed with an inferior present, the interest in peasant life. The main point is not so much the poet's indignation at social injustice as it is his expression of a deeper alienation from a present indifferent to the past and lacking dignity of its own. The erudition of the poet–professor, the modernism of an Edgar Allan Poe or Charles Baudelaire evident in the harsh colors of the poem's first lines, the outrage at contemporary political failings that had animated so many of the *Giambi ed epodi*, and the private despair that is also characteristic of Carducci's letters of this period, all come together in this classicizing but at the same time neoromantic and, finally, very modern composition.

Although the exhortation in this poem to restore to Rome the sense of religious awe it once enjoyed is rather subdued, in other odes in this volume Carducci's expression of patriotic sentiments often becomes quite strident and borders on the jingoistic. In "Alla Vittoria" (To Victory, 1877), for example, written in celebration of a statue of Victory erected at Brescia, the concluding lines praise: "Brescia the strong, Brescia the ironlike,/ Brescia the lioness of Italy/slaked with enemy blood." And at the end of "Saluto italico" (Italian Salute, 1879) Carducci calls out: "In the face of the foreigner, who armed encamps/ on our soil, O sing: Italia, Italia, Italia!"— rhetoric more suited to the opera stage or the soccer stadium than to the poetry of a man who by this time was generally recognized as Italy's greatest living poet. Especially in the years since the fall of Fascism—a movement notorious for its vociferous and empty rhetoric—patriotic utterances of this kind have been viewed with scant favor by Italian readers and critics. It is, in fact, Carducci's taste for language of this sort that at least partially accounts for his decline in popularity in recent years.

Another poem that illustrates these tendencies to rhetorical excess as well as demonstrates the scope and depth of Carducci's skill is the long ode "Alle fonti del Clitumno" ("By the Sources of Clitumnus," 1876). This poem too begins with the description of a natural setting, the Umbrian countryside near Spoleto, where the river of the title has its source. As in the "Idillio maremmano," a healthy peasant mother appears with her infant daughter in the midst of a pleasant landscape fragrant with wild sage and thyme. Nearby, her son waters his flock while her husband guides a cart pulled by the same sort of oxen that Vergil had described nearly two millennia earlier. This is the land of the Umbrians, the Etruscans, and the Romans, the land whose inhabitants rose up to fight against Hannibal just as the peasants in the Friulian Carnia had promised in "Il comune rustico" to do against the Hun and the Slav. Today, however, the clamor of these nearly forgotten wars has given way to silence. Rome no longer rings with the triumphal processions of the past. The nymphs who used to inhabit the area have fled weeping back to the rivers and the tree trunks from which they once emerged. A "red-haired Galilean," abetted by black-robed priests, has driven them away, "across the fields/resounding with human labor and the hills that remember the empire." It is these new invaders, these blasphemers of life and of love, who have destroyed what once was the glory of Italy, who "have created a desert and called it/the kingdom of God." Christ and his priests will not prevail; the dark days of their destruction of human values have now come to an end, and the human soul is ready to rise once more and take control of its destiny. The poem closes on this note of hope for a triumphantly atheistic future with an invocation to "Mother Italy": "mother of cattle/strong at turning the sod and plowing the fields left fallow,/Italy the mother/of fierce wild horses whinnying in war/mother of grain and grape and eternal laws/and illustrious arts to make life sweet."

The mountains, the woods, and the waters of green Umbria resound to the poet's song, and the steam locomotive in the distance whistles in augury of labor and industry yet to come.

Though Carducci has wedded the myths of pre-Roman Italy to his own industrializing present, he once again finds the present inferior to the past: but he is not without hope for a new race of industrious Italians finally freed from the bonds of the clergy and their life-denying religion. Carducci's ideology is on full display here, from the anticlericalism of "A Satana," to the nostalgia for an idyllic rustic life of the *Rime nuove,* to the erudition of Carducci the professor and researcher. It is significant that this poem extolling the virtues of the Italian laborer and heralding a new era of opportunity for this class was, in fact, written at a time of severe confusion and upheaval for the Italian peasant and industrial worker. The disruption of an old way of life for agricultural and factory workers alike was generated in large part by the industrialization symbolized by the locomotive.

To see where Carducci actually stands in relation to these crude realities of his day, it is helpful to consider the style of this ode. The language that it uses to describe Italian rural life is extremely stylized. The peasant's cart, for example, is a "dipinto plaustro" ("depicted wain" it might be rendered in English) instead of a simple painted "carro" or cart. The tone of the poem is consistently exalted, and the vocabulary and historical allusions are so learned as to be inaccessible to the ordinary reader without notes. So too the vocatives and frequent separation of modifiers from their objects show that this text is addressed to the cultured reader familiar with the conventions of both Latin and Italian poetry and able to recognize and appreciate literary devices and allusions. If the principal message is to praise the Italic and pre-Christian virtues of industriousness, valor, and endurance, which the laboring classes are presumed to possess, the language of this poem suggests that it is for the elite that their praise is intended. This apparently contradictory attitude was another aspect of Carducci's thought that did not fail to trouble his later readers, particularly those after the end of the war and fall of Fascism in 1945.

In other odes that juxtapose past and present, Carducci was much less hopeful than in "Alle fonti del Clitumno." One such example is "Nella Piazza di San Petronio" (In San Petronio Square, 1877), here translated in unrhymed elegiac couplets similar to those of the original:

Dark, turreted Bologna arises in the limpid
    winter,
and the hill above, all white with snow, is
    laughing.

It is the kindly hour when the dying sun salutes
your towers and your temple, lord Petronio:

the towers whose ramparts and the temple whose
    lonely top
have been so long caressed by the wings of time.

The sky is like a diamond sparkling in the cold
and the air hangs like a silvery veil

on the forum, where it softens the outlines of the
    buildings
raised on high by our forbears' valiant arms.

Tarrying on the upper reaches of these
    structures,
languid and violet, the sun smiles, seeming,

as it strikes the gray of the rock and the dark,
    vermillion brick
to awaken a soul that for centuries has lain dead,

and a sad desire is rekindled in the chilly air
for burning Mays and evenings of warmth and
    fragrance,

when highborn ladies went to dance in the city
    squares
and the consuls returned in triumph with
    conquered kings.

Just so the laughing muse eludes my trembling
    verse
and its vain desire for the beauty of time gone by.

The setting, a main square in Bologna, evokes the city where Carducci lived and worked for nearly half a century. As the last rays of the winter sun strike the brick and stone, the city's illustrious past is conjured up, and the poet feels a melancholy desire for the dancing and warmth, the beauty, and—perhaps above all—the political ascendance that Bologna enjoyed in the late Middle Ages. After a moment he realizes this happy past is irrevocably gone and his verses are powerless to bring it back. The occasion that gave rise to this poem was not a visit to some celebrated locale but the sight of a town square that Carducci passed almost every day of his life. Perhaps this is why the poet does not feel the compulsion to conclude his poem on a note of official optimism but can end it on this dying fall as darkness engulfs the square, the city, and the poet's dreams of reviving a world now gone.

The sense of failure and mild anxiety that hang over the closing lines of "Nella Piazza di San Petronio" become even more insistent in what is perhaps Carducci's most famous ode of this type: "Alla stazione in una mattina d'autunno" ("At the Station on an Autumn Morning," 1876). Here again the situation is commonplace, even banal: the departure of the poet's mistress after a brief amorous encounter. The separation of the two lovers takes place in the classic environment for such events in late-nineteenth-century literature: the railway station. In this urban landscape the street itself is affected by the same melancholy that hangs over the poet:

How sluggishly the streetlights
plod in a line behind the trees
among the branches dripping with rain
yawning their light on the mud.

                (1–4)

As the lovers arrive at the station, the train pulls in, whistling weakly at first, then more and more stridently, beneath a leaden and ghostly sky. As the poet gazes at them, the train's "dark carriages" are transformed into funereal processions out of Dante and Vergil. "Where and toward what is it going?" he asks, "to what unknown pain/what torment or distant hope?" When Lidia, in this hallucinatory landscape, hands over her ticket to the guard, she seems to be giving up even her happy memories along with the pasteboard; and the raincoat-clad brakemen testing the brakes of the train with their "bundles of iron" seem shades involved in some lugubrious rite. As the rain continues to rush in torrents down the windows of the carriages, the train becomes a strange monster, ominously "conscious of its metallic soul," snorting and puffing as it "blinks its flaming eyes" and flapping its doors like the wings of a dragon preparing to carry its prey to hell. Suddenly the poet remembers another time, when Lidia was with him in the country and the sun—"the young and luminous sun of June"—kissed her cheek and "like a halo/my dreams more beautiful than the sun/embraced her noble figure." This bright image of warmth and love and hope is only there for a moment, however. When the train moves off, it is quickly dispelled by the return of the rain and the mist in which the poet staggers drunkenly, wondering whether he too has been turned into a ghost. Even the leaves that continue to fall lie "cold, constant, silent, and heavy" on his soul, and it seems that "now, everywhere,/and forever in the world it is November." Bewildered and bereft of his "sense of being," the poet ends the poem by crying out that he wants only to fade into the mist and to rest "in a tedium that lasts forever."

Carducci's last volume, *Rime e ritmi* (Rhymes and Rhythms, 1899), consists of twenty-nine poems in both "barbarian" and conventional meters. These were written after the *Rime nuove* of 1887 and the final *Odi barbare* of 1889. Few of the poems in this volume have been treated kindly by the critics, who have noted in them the decline of the poet's inspiration. Carducci, once a fire-breathing radical, is now a firm supporter of the monarchy and of Italy's imperialist adventures in Africa under Prime Minister Francesco Crispi. Much in this collection does seem forced and emotionally empty, though the so-called Alpine Idylls and the brief lyrics written for Annie Vivanti, the young writer with whom Carducci had a rather avuncular liaison toward the end of his life, continue to attract favorable comment. The last poem in the *Rime e ritmi*, one that marks the end of all of Carducci's poetic output, is a simple "stornello"—a kind of folk epigram often used for riddles and in popular music:

> *Fior tricolore*
> *Tramontano le stelle in mezzo al mare*
> *E si spengono i canti entro il mio core.*

Tricolored flower,/The stars go down in the depths of the sea/And the songs in my heart are extinguished.

Here "core" rhymes with "tricolore" (though in an earlier version the flower was a "fior d'amore," instead of "tricolore") as the poem closes on a note at once nationalistic and populist. In the last poem of his last book, Carducci invokes the flag rather than love, in a form from folk rather than literary tradition.

After Carducci's death, the nationalistic and authoritarian tendencies that had begun under Crispi took center stage with Mussolini and Fascism. During the twenty years of this regime, the tendencies toward overblown rhetoric, vociferous celebration of the nation's history, and the truculence toward outsiders latent in some of Carducci's writing became central elements in the official "Fascist style." The new regime, however, was more interested in evoking the marching legions of the Roman past than in weighing the true significance of the ancient monuments and intellectual achievements that had occupied Carducci's imagination. Just as Manzoni's militant Christianity had degenerated into the pious sentimentality of the "manzoniani" whom Carducci detested, so Carducci's evocation of the heroic ages as an ideal against which a later time could measure its own achievements disintegrated into the self-justifying panegyrics of the Fascist state.

It is no wonder that the postwar era preferred the more laconic style of such poets as Giuseppe Ungaretti and Montale, whose understated poetry was part of their quest for personal and literary authenticity. Although the reaction against Carducci had begun long before then with the self-effacing and antiheroic works of the "crepuscular" poets active just before World War I, the poetry written during and after World War II in Italy spoke with the new moral authority that it had gained in the painful experience of the Resistance. Writers and critics of this later generation were deeply suspicious of the hedonistic evasiveness and lack of commitment that they saw in the writings of both the crepusculars and Carducci. Moreover, the virtual disappearance of social structures based on rigid class divisions so important in nineteenth-century life meant that the new age was also disinclined to view the aristocratic as a worthy ideal for either letters or life.

For readers today it is not Carducci the educator or Carducci the orator—much less the sonorous, semiofficial "poet of the third Italy"—whose writings seem most pertinent. Instead, it is Carducci the ordinary man who was frightened of death, suffered from loneliness and the weight of his responsibilities, sought his pleasures where he could, and sometimes behaved in less than admirable fashion, who seems most worthy of our attention. In his critical assessment of Carducci, Benedetto Croce complained of a lack of philosophical depth in his poetry and other writings, and it is true that Carducci was not a systematic thinker or even much interested in abstract thought. He was devoted to literature, not so much for what it reveals about human achievement or for the theoretical constructions that may be assembled from it, but for itself, as a means of giving raw and perhaps otherwise meaningless experience shape and significance. Croce also remarked that Carducci was Italy's last great classical poet. What he meant was that Carducci took his vocation very seriously, more seriously than

many poets have been able to do since. Carducci was a classical poet in another sense as well. In his most successful poetry he was able to use his mastery of the literary forms he inherited from the past to give meaning and importance to the painful or merely boring experiences of everyday life. His poetry offers consolation for the limitations of the human condition and reaffirms that sense of the continuity of experience that is the goal of all classical literature. Though his strongest ties in many ways are with romanticism, it is as a classical writer in this sense that Carducci is likely to be remembered.

Selected Bibliography

EDITIONS

INDIVIDUAL WORKS

Rime di Giosue Carducci. San Miniato, 1857.

Levia gravia di Enotrio Romano. Pistoia, 1868.

Poesie di Giosue Carducci. Florence, 1871. Includes *Decennalia, Levia gravia, Juvenilia.*

Primavere elleniche. Florence, 1872.

Nuove poesie di Enotrio Romano. Imola, 1873.

Odi barbare. Bologna, 1877.

Levia gravia di Giosue Carducci. Bologna, 1881.

Giambi ed epodi. Bologna, 1882.

Nuove odi barbare. Bologna, 1882. 2nd ed. Bologna, 1886.

Ça ira. Rome, 1883.

Rime nuove. Bologna, 1887.

Terze odi barbare. Bologna, 1889.

Delle odi barbare di Giosue Carducci, Libri II ordinati e corretti. Bologna, 1893.

Rime e ritmi. Bologna, 1899.

COLLECTED WORKS

Opere di Giosue Carducci. Edited by the author. 20 vols. Bologna, 1889–1903.

Poesie di Giosue Carducci 1850–1900. Edited by the author. Bologna, 1901.

Prose di Giosue Carducci 1859–1903. Edited by the author. Bologna, 1905.

Opere di Giosue Carducci. 30 vols. Bologna, 1935–1940. National edition in honor of the 100th anniversary of Carducci's birth.

GIOSUE CARDUCCI

Lettere di Giosue Carducci. 22 vols. Bologna, 1938–1968.

MODERN EDITIONS

Giambi ed epodi. Edited by E. Palmieri. Bologna, 1959.
Odi barbare. Edited by M. Valgimigli. Bologna, 1959.
Poesie. Edited by G. Barberi Squarotti. Milan, 1978.
Poesie scelte. Edited by L. Baldacci. Milan, 1974.
Rime e ritmi. Edited by M. Valgimigli and G. B. Salinari. Bologna, 1964.
Rime nuove. Edited by P. P. Trompeo and G. B. Salinari. Bologna, 1961.

TRANSLATIONS

The Barbarian Odes of Giosue Carducci. Translated by William Fletcher Smith. Menasha, Wis., 1939.
Carducci. Translated by G. L. Bickersteth. New York, 1913. A selection of his poems, with notes and three introductory essays.
The Lyrics and Rhythms of Giosue Carducci. Translated by William Fletcher Smith. Colorado Springs, Colo., 1942.
The New Lyrics of Giosue Carducci. Translated by William Fletcher Smith. Colorado Springs, Colo., 1942.
Poems of Giosue Carducci. Translated by Frank Sewall. New York, 1892.
Political and Satiric Verse of Giosue Carducci. Translated by William Fletcher Smith. Colorado Springs, Colo., 1942.

BIOGRAPHICAL AND CRITICAL WORKS

Barberi Squarotti, Giorgio. "Profilo storico-critico." In Giosue Carducci, *Poesie,* edited by G. Barberi Squarotti. Milan, 1978.
Biagini, Mario. *Il poeta della terza Italia: Vita di Giosue Carducci.* Milan, 1961.
Binni, Walter. "Linea e momenti della poesia carducciana." "Tre liriche del Carducchi." "Carducci politico." In his *Carducci e altri saggi.* Turin, 1960.
Bruscagli, Riccardo. *Carducci nelle lettere: Il personaggio e il prosatore.* Bologna, 1972.
Cambon, Glauco, and John Frederick Nims. "Alla stazione in una mattina d'autunno." In *The Poem Itself,* edited by Stanley Burnshaw. New York, 1962.
Chiarini, Giuseppe. *Memorie della vita di Giosue Carducci raccolte da un amico.* Florence, 1935.
Citanna, Giuseppe. "Giosue Carducci." In *Letteratura italiana: I maggiori.* Milan, 1956.
Contarino, Rosario. "Giosue Carducci." In *Il secondo ottocento.* Vol. 8, tome 2 of *La letteratura italiana: Storia e testi,* edited by Carlo Muscetta. Bari, 1975.
Contini, Gianfranco. "Giosue Carducci." In *Letteratura dell'Italia unita,* edited by Gianfranco Contini. Florence, 1968.
Croce, Benedetto. *La letteratura della nuova Italia,* vol. 2. Reprinted as vol. 6 of *Scritti di storia letteraria e politica.* Bari, 1921.
———. *Storia d'Italia dal 1871 al 1915.* In *Scritti di storia letteraria e politica,* vol. 22. Bari, 1928.
De Rienzo, Giorgio. "Il prototipo carducciano." In his *Narrativa toscana dell'ottocento.* Florence, 1975.
Devoto, Giacomo. "Giosue Carducci e la lingua italiana." *Convivium* 25, N. S. 1:524–536 (1957).
Getto, Giovanni. "Prosa e poesia di Giosue Carducci." In his *Carducci e Pascoli.* Naples, 1965.
Giannessi, Ferdinando. *Il grande Carducci.* Treviso, 1958.
Highet, Gilbert. "Parnassus and Antichrist." In *The Classical Tradition: Greek and Roman Influences on Western Literature.* New York, 1957.
Jeanroy, Alfred. *Giosue Carducci: l'homme et le poète.* Paris, 1911.
Paolucci, Anne. "Moments of the Creative Process in the Literary Criticism of Giosue Carducci." *Italica* 33:110–120 (1956).
Pighi, Giovanni Battista. "Poesia barbara e illusioni metriche." *Convivium* 25, N. S. 1:547–559 (1957).
Praz, Mario. "Giosue Carducci as a Romantic." *The University of Toronto Quarterly* 5:176–196 (1935–1936).
———. "Il 'classicismo' di Giosue Carducci." In his *Gusto neoclassico.* Milan, 1974.
Salinari, Giambattista. "Giosue Carducci." In *Storia della letteratura italiana,* edited by Emilio Cecchi and Natalino Sapegno. Vol. 8, *Dall'ottocento al novecento.* Milan, 1970.
Santangelo, Giorgio. *Carducci.* Palermo, 1960.
———. "Giosue Carducci." In *Dizionario critico della letteratura italiana,* edited by Vittore Branca. Turin, 1973.

GIOSUE CARDUCCI

Scotti, Mario. "Giosue Carducci." In *Dizionario biografico degli italiani*, vol. 20. Rome, 1977.

Serra, Renato. "Per un catalogo (Carducci e Croce)." In his *Scritti critici*. Rome, 1919. Reprinted Florence, 1958. *Scritti*, vol. 1.

Timpanaro, Sebastiano. "Giordani, Carducci e Chiarini." In his *Classicismo e illuminismo nell'ottocento italiano*. Pisa, 1965.

Williams, Orlo. *Giosue Carducci*. New York, 1914.

CHARLES KLOPP

ÉMILE ZOLA
(1840–1902)

É MILE ZOLA WAS born on 2 April 1840. His birth harks back to the days of Louis-Philippe, king of the French. So what are Zola's titles to the exceptional treatment he is receiving, in and out of France, as a living figure? Obviously, I daresay overwhelmingly, the part he played in the Dreyfus affair is a prime factor. Nowadays, to a surprising number of moderately cultured people, those exotic syllables, Zola, spell courage and decency. The paunchy, myopic man with the beribboned pince-nez, never a shining knight in his physical appearance, has achieved the recognition Anatole France promised him as "a moment of the conscience of mankind." This, be it noted, is a posthumous, indeed comparatively recent, development. No one should suppose, for instance, that the transfer of Zola's remains to the Panthéon (1908), which followed shortly upon the rehabilitation of Captain Alfred Dreyfus, united friends and foes in at least a display of esteem for the dead man's character. Far from it! Contrived as a political gesture by the then premier (none other than Zola's old comrade-in-arms, Georges Clemenceau), the ceremony was marred by vociferous protests from the rightist faction and by an attempt on the life of Dreyfus himself. It is no exaggeration to say that only the trials of World War II rid Zola's name of its former, divisive virulence.

In the United States, too, Zola was a beneficiary of World War II or of events that led to it. For a long time his American fortunes had pursued a wholly predictable course. When Honoré de Balzac ceased to be anathema to self-respecting families, Zola replaced him as the main proponent of Gallic materialism and godlessness—and as purveyor of smut extraordinary. To be sure, he, unlike Balzac, had earned a similar reputation at home: Jules Barbey d'Aurevilly dubbed him "the Michelangelo of the gutter"; François Mauriac vividly recalled how his parents referred to chamber pots as "the zolas." The French, however, proved to be lusty customers of whatever the devil had to offer, whereas the American public, such as it was, labored under a sense of guilt. As late as 1927, Ernest A. Boyd depicted Zola in the garb of the anti-Christ. Then, on the eve of the war, linked, it would seem, to a feeling of revulsion against Adolf Hitler's malevolence, especially against his persecution of Jews, a dramatic change occurred: Hollywood, mirabile dictu, was responsible for it. Woefully inaccurate in its detail, but saved by the grace of Paul Muni's performance, a screen version of Zola's life lifted him bodily from the realm of the damned into that of the heroes of thought. The Dreyfus affair supplied the necessary pathos, and, incidentally, enough "punch lines" were delivered to bruise the sensitivities of the French government, whose censors banned the film for twenty years and then insisted on substantial cuts.

Zola was not born a fighter: he molded himself into one. As a youth he had displayed escapist traits that were indicative of a thoroughly romantic makeup. Later he took his espousal of naturalism to represent a repudiation of those early tendencies. Still later, however, he himself entertained few illusions that, on escaping escapism, he had uprooted his romanticism as well.

The poet in him came from the South, unmistakably. There remained throughout, to Zola's literary stance, a wordy, almost rhetorical touch that bespoke its Mediterranean origins. Until he went to Paris—to stay and to struggle—the accident of his birth in the capital weighed but lightly against the fifteen formative years (1843–1858) that he spent, for the most part, at Aix-en-Provence. Nor do his near-Parisian roots on the maternal side alter the picture significantly. When, at the age of twenty, Émilie Aubert married forty-four-year-old François Zola, a native Dalmatian, half-Italian and half-Greek, she, to all practical purposes, entered the typically southern world of her husband.

A civil engineer of some merit, but prone to embark upon highly speculative ventures, the elder Zola died in 1847, leaving his family in dire financial straits. He was still a citizen of Venice. So was young Émile, according to French law, until he became of age and could apply for naturalization papers. Some day his political enemies would brand him a *métèque* (a foreigner, an interloper)—about the worst insult in their vocabulary.

The next ten years tell a tale of endless court battles fought by François Zola's widow to stem the tide of oncoming ruin and ensure a proper education for her son. When the boy finally entered secondary school, he was late in his studies and inordinately shy. Luck had it, however, that he came under the protective wing of two older schoolmates, the sons of well-established local families, one of whom, Paul Cézanne, was also destined for fame as an artist. For several years, on Sundays and holidays, the three companions roamed the countryside, drinking in the poetry of nature along with that of their favorite poets. Victor Hugo was their first god, soon joined, then eclipsed, by Alfred de Musset. Musset, the nonchalant roué par excellence, was already on his way to the strange destiny that made him a healer of adolescent pangs, adept at dissolving them into wisps of idealized love. Chalk him up, paradoxical though it may seem, as Zola's original master and prompter. Musset it was who "taught me how to weep"—delicious tears, of course, while waiting for bitter ones. Musset it was who peopled the sun-drenched, lavender-scented solitudes of Provence with a number of "love-fairies," all to become one, in due time, as the imaginary dedicatee of the *Contes à Ninon* (Tales for Ninon, 1864).

There is today, with increasing frequency, another, a tragic side to Provençal inspiration. The murderous sun and wind, and the primitive passions they foster, supply the underlying theme of many a novel by Jean Giono, Thyde Monnier, or Henri Bosco. Zola may have shown the way in some passages of *Les Rougon-Macquart* (1871–1893); but, as a general rule, I cannot see that he forged a specific link between the greed of his Provençal creatures and the ruggedness of their habitat. His one novel of the soil has the plenteous Beauce for its locale. The Rougons are small-town products. They, and the Macquarts, too, fall prey to the mistral, Provence's ruling wind, only in the sense that modern conditions make it, spiritually speaking, a germ carrier, laden with the miasmas of political intrigue and urban civilization. All in all, Zola's vision of Provence remained that of an earthly paradise, perhaps lost forever, which he drew from limbo on at least one occasion when he wanted to conjure up a tableau of luxuriant love amidst the complicities of nature. I refer, of course, to that fantastic creation of his—the sheltered, impossibly huge park in *La faute de l'abbé Mouret* (*The Sin of Father Mouret*,

1875), where the hero and his child-mistress play Adam and Eve, and the name of which, aptly enough, happens to be "le Paradou."

In 1858 Madame Zola moved to Paris in search of work and assistance. Émile, for his part, entered the Lycée Saint-Louis; he was a badly confused youth whose scholastic averages fell precipitously. At nineteen, in his kind of situation, there was no recourse except to quit school and look for employment. He found none, or none that mattered, until February 1862, when he became a shipping clerk in the publishing firm of Hachette & Co. A biographical sketch, written at a later date for the benefit of Alphonse Daudet, reads in part: "The years 1860 and 1861, abominable. Not a penny to my name, literally. Whole days without food. . . . Sort of happy, nevertheless. Interminable walks across Paris, especially along the quays, which I adored." Note this last: the siren had sung her song; the poor devil was hopelessly smitten.

It is not easy to measure the impact of Paris on Zola's imagination. Paris, to him personally, became the crucible of every manly experience, intellectual as well as emotional. This accounted for still another romantic relationship, though far less elemental, hence far less elementary, than had been his with Provence. Where dream meets reality, the clash is bound to have complex reverberations. It took Zola a lifetime to sort his feelings in the matter. The late novel that bears Paris' name will restore it to its pristine splendor as the City of Light. Midway through the novelist's career it will stand again and again in the image of the modern metropolis, whose brazen law crushes or degrades human values. Yet on other occasions, the perspective appears to reverse itself: Paris emerges as a victim, perhaps the most pitiable of them all, its soul and body violated by the ruffians of the Second Empire. Just now, to the famished newcomer in his garret, it appears to him as a kind of siren whose cruel whims fill him with alternate moods of despair and anger.

When chance contacts in the house of Hachette finally enabled Zola to break into print, his sparse readers were treated to a battle royal between the "Provençal," or Musset-in-pink, and the "Parisian," or Musset-in-black, brands of emotionalism. The Contes à Ninon, his maiden effort, fairly dripped with maudlin sentimentality; and surprisingly, this vein did not dry out for ten more years; Nouveaux [New] contes à Ninon appeared in 1874. Dark, drab, desolate romanticism, on the other hand, informed La confession de Claude (Claude's Confession, 1865), Zola's earliest full-length novel. This story of bohemian life, told in the first person, with strong autobiographical overtones, recounts a young man's pathetic attempts at redeeming both the prostitute who had initiated him and himself in the process. But stark though they are, and reminiscent of Musset's Confession d'un enfant du siècle (Confession of a Child of the Century, 1836), Claude's juvenile effusions end on the hopeful note—possibly an echo from Hugo's Les misérables (1862)—that whoever "tears the fabric of the night" may "hasten the slow and majestic rise of the day." Even his imperial majesty's prosecutor general, who frowned at the vividness of some of the scenes, had to concede that the book on the whole did not offend public morality.

Late in 1865, Zola—never a philanderer, by the way—entered into a serious affair with Gabrielle-Alexandrine Meley, whom he was to marry in 1870. Shortly afterward (January 1866) he resigned from his job in order to embark upon a journalistic career. This was a calculated risk. Potentially, at any rate, it meant money—the sinew of independence. It also meant a tribune, an audience, an intoxicating sense of power.

Zola left us an enormous legacy of newspaper and magazine articles. Those he collected (nine volumes in all) represent only a fraction of his output. Any but the briefest comments thereon would cause the present essay to burst at the seams. Let it be clear, however, that if poetry expressed Zola's first nature, journalism became his second. The one tended to abstract him from the world; the other brought him back with a vengeance. Literary chronicler, art critic, political columnist, social reporter, he achieved identification with his times through this journalistic ubiquity. He also discovered the advantages of prepublishing his novels in serialized form and, initially at least, was not above serving up a couple of potboilers (*Le voeu d'une morte* [A Dead Woman's Vow], 1866; *Les mystères de Marseille* [*The Mysteries of Marseilles*], 1867). All in all, nevertheless, he took his responsibilities most seriously. Unlike Gustave Flaubert or the Goncourt brothers, he did not mind "dirtying his hands" in the give-and-take of public controversy: so much so that even his fictional work may be said—not the least bit disparagingly—to be journalistic in essence. By divesting the word of its ephemeral connotations, only to retain what journalism meant to him *as a vehicle*, one arrives at a fair understanding of Zola's mental processes. Half his writings, novels included, ring in some *vérité en marche*—as did, specifically, his last campaign in Clemenceau's newspaper *L'Aurore*. And surely, *J'Accuse* would make a handsome caption for the other half.

It is fitting to remark at this point that Zola, fervent crusader though he was, never evinced an interest in active politics, never carried a "party card," never courted elective office, never spoke on the issues in anyone's name save his own. Even *J'Accuse* (*I Accuse*, 1898), with its stress on the first person, was to be the public utterance of a private citizen. Its author, in other terms, was basically the same man whose *Confession de Claude* had romantically asserted the individual's prerogative to cry out his feelings (*vivre tout haut*); the same man who, at the age of twenty-six (1866), published his first collection of critical essays as *Mes haines*—*my* hatreds—and another (on the annual art exhibition) under the title *Mon salon*—*my* salon. As his outlook steadily widened, running the gamut from emotional to aesthetic to social experience, so did his need for self-expression.

There is every reason to suppose that Zola's political sympathies, at the outset of his career, were already oriented to the left. Yet his concept of the creative artist as supreme among individuals threatened to make a shambles of whatever democratic principles he may have had. Next to the conservative pundits, whose fiats and taboos stifled the progress of art, hoi polloi—obtuse, sheeplike, fainthearted—were the target of his contempt: for it was they who recoiled at the boldness of the Goncourt brothers' *Germinie Lacerteux* (1864) or burst out laughing before a Manet canvas. But where do you draw the line between the people as common people and what is called "the public"? Zola—the young Zola—did not quite know and did not care: "Frankly," he averred, "I would sacrifice humanity to the artist." By much the same token, he rebuked the critic Hippolyte Taine himself, who submerged the artist under the mechanical forces that govern the world. As if an invention counted for anything outside the inventor; as if a work of art were not "a corner of nature reflected through the author's temperament!" This oft-quoted formula recurs three times in *Mes haines* and *Mon salon*, then rather startlingly, after a nine-year interval, in a study on Alexandre Dumas *fils*. By that time (1875) Zola was an avowed disciple of Taine and fast becoming a social-minded writer. Paradox, or contradiction? Neither, I venture to say. He was henceforth reasonably satisfied that he could reconcile a fiercely personal stance with the exigencies of humanitarian concern. He likewise saw himself as temperamentally suited to become a surveyor of temperaments.

The word "temperament" plainly belongs to the vocabulary of psychophysiology. It has always been reminiscent of Galen's old theory of humors. In the late eighteenth and early nineteenth centuries the Ideologues used it, or reasonable equivalents, to counteract and dispel the animistic implications of the word "character." When Zola happened on the scene, their influence had been running through two separate channels. The straighter current had carried far enough to produce Taine's massive, monistic-mechanistic philosophy and, of late, to receive Charles Darwin's powerful contribution. On the other hand, the more circuitous romantic route had allowed for a great deal of compromise. Romantic writers were not hardcore materialists and conceived of a spiritual world over, above, and in conjunction with that of physical necessity. The latter was not ignored, however, and claimed an ever-growing share of their attention. Jules Michelet, whose impact on the young Zola looms uncommonly large, made almost a fetish of physiological causes in his *Tableau de la France* and his disquisitions on *La femme* (*Woman*, 1860) and *L'Amour* (*Love*, 1858). Nor could it be denied that, from Balzac's *Comédie humaine* (*Human Comedy*, 1842 ff.) to the Goncourts' *Germinie Lacerteux*, by way of Flaubert's *Madame Bovary* (1857), the novel crystallized along increasingly "clinical" lines. By 1866 the gap was about to close between harder and softer determinists—and Zola seemed predestined to close it. How and how much he hovered on the threshold of decision may be gathered from the following pronouncement—wherein, incidentally, he stumbled on a future title of his: "What we do nowadays is take a *bête humaine* [human animal] and study him *within the margin of freedom* left him by his environment" (italics mine).

The protagonists of Zola's next two novels—*Thérèse Raquin* (1867) and *Madeleine Férat* (1868)—are indeed human brutes, swayed by the "fatalities" of their nerves, blood, and flesh. It matters little that Thérèse and Laurent end as criminals, whereas Madeleine and Guillaume certainly do not. Both stories are "autopsies" in Zola's words, "case studies" in our own—one verging on the exceptional and the other falling squarely into it. Case number one arises from a trite enough

"triangle" situation. Thérèse's pitifully inadequate husband seals his doom when he brings his friend, Laurent, into the family circle. In the course of a boat ride wife and lover drown him and camouflage the deed as an accident. A kind of visceral revulsion (about the only "remorse" soulless creatures can feel) grips them when the body is recovered from the Seine and they are called upon to identify it. The corpse keeps intruding, in a quasi-physical way, upon the murderers' days and nights—until, finally, they commit suicide under the very eyes of the victim's paralyzed mother, who has known their secret for some time and gloats mutely over their demise.

Case number two purported to illustrate the "law" enunciated in Michelet's *L'Amour*, to the effect that he who impregnates or even merely possesses a virgin remains her "spouse" for all time. Nothing whatever may erase the original imprint: so much so that children by a second husband are likely to resemble the first. Faithful to the script, Zola drags Madeleine through the whole harrowing experience, and makes doubly sure of the result by having her conceive in the room she once shared with her lover. The macabre denouement, as improbable as the episodes that led to it, brings death to the child, suicide to Madeleine, and insanity to the father.

There is some unfairness in pooling together the awkwardly contrived machine that is *Madeleine Férat* and a near-masterpiece such as *Thérèse Raquin*. Ideologically, however, they belong to the same transitional period and conceal a residue of caution beneath their outward boldness. True enough, the "margin of freedom" enjoyed by Zola's characters had shrunk to practically nil. True again, he now (for the first time) called himself a "naturalist writer" and flaunted, as an epigraph to the second printing of *Thérèse Raquin*, Taine's famous dictum "Vice and virtue are products, like vitriol and sugar." Yet it is symptomatic that even then he paid little heed to the *race*, or heredity, ingredient that surely, to a simon-pure physiologist, must be paramount in controlling the chemistry of temperaments. Neither story enlightens us very much as to the antecedents of the dramatis personae. Where they are concerned the word "product" does not point to a definite hereditary legacy. Slaves they are, but to the primordial instincts that rule the animal kingdom at large, and then to *moment* and *milieu* in the narrowest sense—namely, to the circumstances of time and place that throw them together.

Not until the winter months of 1868–1869 was the last piece of the puzzle allowed to fall into position. The hard-driving novelist spent part of that time poring over medical books, among them *Traité philosophique et physiologique de l'hérédité naturelle* (Philosophical and Physiological Treatise on Natural Heredity, 1847–1850) by Dr. Prosper Lucas. Its author assumed an air of authority—mostly unwarranted—that may or may not have deceived Zola into endorsing his thoroughly deterministic conclusions. That he appropriated those is, of course, a matter of record; but he permitted himself an aside or two that leave some doubt as to the depth of his conviction. One needs a hypothesis, Zola reflected, "whether or not it is accepted as indisputably true." Or again: "Let me take a philosophical prop, for the sake . . . of connecting my books with one another. Materialism may be the best bet, for it believes in forces that will require no explaining." Quite refreshing, this dash of humor (one hopes it *is* humor), as Zola braces himself for the grim, twenty-five-year exertion that will produce *Les Rougon-Macquart.*

Unlike Balzac, who began with hardly any preconceptions at all, then codified his system some twelve years and one hundred works later, Zola, the engineer's son, drew the most elaborate blueprints, only to depart from them, consciously or not, on many occasions. At least the substance of his voluminous preliminary notes may readily be found in modern editions and monographs; but whoever is unable to wade through them will find a substitute of sorts in *Le docteur Pascal* (*Doctor Pascal*, 1893), the last novel in the series, part of which comprises a recapitulation and interpretation of what has gone on before. The author achieved this perilously didactic purpose by creating one member of the Rougon tribe with whom he could identify. At his death in 1873 Dr. Pascal Rougon is supposed to have left behind him an impressive "natural and social history of his family under the Second Empire"—in other terms, right down to its subtitle, a dummy replica of *Les Rougon-Macquart.* Poetic license is involved here, whereby the good doctor, revived in print twenty years after his official demise, surveys his creator's progress over the intervening decades and, more significantly still, endorses the conscientious qualms and modified viewpoints that such a long travail necessarily entailed.

For the benefit of his niece and pupil, Clotilde, Pascal displays his pride and joy—the family tree that Zola had drawn at a very early stage, no later than 1869 or 1870, then made public, in quasi-final form, as an appendix to *Une page d'amour* (*A Love Affair*, 1878). Rooted in Plassans (that is, Aix-en-Provence), the "stump" is represented by Adélaïde Rougon née Fouque, still alive in 1872 at the age of one hundred and four, but neurotic from birth and definitely insane since 1851. She had borne three children: one, Pierre, by her husband, a hard-working gardener; two, Ursule and Antoine, by her lover, a disreputable smuggler named Macquart. The three branches had proliferated, even becoming knotted through the marriage of François Mouret, Ursule's son, to Marthe Rougon, Pierre's daughter. By 1872 Adélaïde's descendants number about thirty. All exemplify in varying degrees "the laws of nerve and blood irregularities that as the result of a primal organic lesion break out among members of a family."

An obedient disciple of Prosper Lucas, Pascal has adopted his nomenclature of hereditary components and done "as scientific a job as possible" of apportioning them in each and every case. Yet he expresses reservations that were Zola's in 1893 but may not have been his at the outset. Who can ever hope not to miss an important collateral contribution? Most of all, how much credit should be given an infant discipline that, temporarily at least, straddles the frontier between poetry and science proper?

> Poets walk as pioneers, in the vanguard; oftentimes they discover virgin territory and point to forthcoming answers. *There* lies a margin all their own—that which separates the truth already conquered, already definitive, from the unknown whence will be extracted the truth of tomorrow. . . . What an immense fresco stands to be painted, what a colossal human comedy or tragedy awaits its writer, in the form of heredity—the very genesis, you might say, of families, societies, and the entire world!

Granted, by now, that heredity provides the theme for all human manifestations, natural and instinctive, the products of which we call virtues and vices. But understood, too, that milieu and moment play the variations. Milieu and moment rise henceforth to their full stature as a spatial and temporal climate—a living stage of Darwinian proportions, made to order for the strong, treacherous to the weak: all the more so, in modern times, as it keeps shifting at an accelerated pace. The Rougon-Macquart story, Pascal muses,

> epitomizes that of the Second Empire from Louis-Napoleon's coup d'etat to the Sedan defeat. . . . Our folk issued from the people; they spread all over contemporary society; they invaded all fields, carried, as it were, on the tidal wave of present-day cravings.

Ambivalent feelings—again the later Zola's feelings—pervade this verdict. Still very much to the fore, in 1893, is his detestation of an era when materialistic principles (not bad in themselves: how could they be, to a materialist?) became perverted at the hands of

schemers, speculators, and social climbers. Yet he has the doctor contending that civilization is better than the sum of its parts—that the life current, even as it crosses a wasteland of dregs and scoria, retains its inherent majesty and will purge itself in due time.

Such buoyant hopes may have had their germ in Zola's attitude toward the Franco-Prussian War. Exempt from conscription as a widow's son, he spent most of the wartime months in unoccupied southern France. Thus he was spared the permanent scars that closer experience inflicted upon some of his future disciples (Guy de Maupassant, Joris-Karl Huysmans, and others), causing them to wallow in stark pessimism and think of themselves as a "lost generation." What is more, the swift collapse of the regime presented him with a providential finis to his contemplated saga. Until then, the fortunes of the Rougon-Macquarts stood open-ended, so to speak, and no Tarpeian rock could clearly be seen near the Capitol. As Fate took a hand, Zola shed a tear for the innocent but welcomed the punishment visited upon the guilty. Shocking or not, his concept of war—of that particular war—was in the biblical tradition of Joseph de Maistre. At the outbreak of hostilities, a violent article of his had exhorted "fifty thousand French soldiers on the bank of the Rhine" to refuse to fight for the imperial government. With the Sedan capitulation and the subsequent overthrow of that government, he viewed the catastrophe as a purifying process, still unspeakably cruel in its immediate repercussions, yet therapeutic in the long run.

Seven novels span a first period, 1871–1877, through which the author tried his formula upon a long-reluctant public. Both in form and in substance, this subcycle exhibits characteristics that faded toward the end.

Initially at least, the Rougons dominated the scene. They enjoyed, over the Macquarts, the advantage of legitimacy; and with it, a driving spirit, a native shrewdness, that their underprivileged cousins did not possess in equal proportion. *La fortune des Rougon* (*The*

Fortune of the Rougons, 1871), volume 1 of the series, written before the war, *La conquête de Plassans* (*A Priest in the House,* vol. 4, 1874), and *Son Excellence Eugène Rougon* (*His Excellency,* vol. 6, 1876) show Pierre Rougon's eldest son, Eugène, masterminding his family into a position of commanding local power and himself into the highest of state functions. In this particular group the first novel is easily the best; but no small interest attaches to Zola's recital of the excellency's career, modeled in large part after that of Eugène Rouher, Napoleon III's minister of state for seven years. Its merit lies in the small nuggets of universal truth that Zola managed to extract from his consideration of modern "machine politics" and "government by cronies."

Aristide, Pierre Rougon's second son, takes over in the second volume, *La curée* (*The Kill,* 1872). To him the lower forms of gratification: money, women, luxury. A matter of days after the coup d'etat, he "swoops down" on Paris like a vulture. Under the assumed name Saccard (it would not do to embarrass brother Eugène), he makes, loses, and recoups millions through the wild real-estate speculations that attended Baron Haussmann's program for the beautification of the capital. His second marriage to a woman much younger than himself is a purely financial transaction that leads him to tolerate an affair between her and his grown son, Maxime. The most scabrous episodes of this liaison take place in the hothouse of Saccard's mansion and introduce the reader to an early device of Zola's, symbolistic in essence, that emphasizes the mimetic influence of environment. Maxime and his stepmother literally grow into "flowers of evil," almost indistinguishable from the huge poisonous plants that witness and condone their vicious disport.

Volume 3 in the cycle (1873) interrupted the Rougon parade long enough to bring forward a major Macquart figure. *Savage Paris* is as far as English translators ever went in rendering its title, *Le ventre de Paris.* An early one passed it off as *The Flower and Market Girls of Paris.* Flower and market girls indeed! Lying and jutting out before us is the city's belly— namely, the central market (*les Halles*), a shining new structure (1854) at the time of the action. Smelly, oily, greasy, meaty, cheesy as you please, its opulence comes off, mimetically once again, on the shopkeepers who thrive in its shadow. This is the kingdom of the Fat, and Lisa Quenu, Antoine Macquart's elder daughter, stands very nearly enthroned as its queen. No Rougon would aspire to her kind of royalty, founded as it is on ungrateful chores and the practice of petit-bourgeois virtues. The Rougons own the law, sometimes make it, and gamble under its cover. Not so the Macquarts. Outsiders they are and misfits they remain for the most part; but the few among them who do not topple from various heights or drift aimlessly may be expected to learn the hard way about the exact price of security and respectability. Take honest Lisa, encamped in her delicatessen store, for a rare illustration of how a "reformed" Macquart is apt to turn into a pillar of society. When brother-in-law Florent, a political subversive, becomes a liability, she betrays him to the police and has him sent back to the penal colony whence he came.

Implicit in Zola's very premises, the theme of the fall followed closely upon that of the rise and began asserting itself with *La faute de l'abbé Mouret* (vol. 5). Mention has been made earlier of the walled Paradou, or Zola's version of a Provençal Garden of Eden, where young abbé Serge Mouret convalesces after an attack of brain fever and is nursed by sixteen-year-old Albine, the park attendant's niece. A love story unfolds, wringing from the author's pen a torrential but final outflow of the same metaphoric "correspondences" that ran through *La curée* and *Le ventre de Paris.* Albine, herself, is a flower of that paradise; from the flowers and from the trees, to whose song of songs her inner ear is attuned, she asks and receives "thunderous" encouragement as she leads Serge along the path of temptation; and when she realizes that she is a woman after all, with a balance of unfulfilled desires that no vegetable, or even unthinking animal, can possibly experience, she still wants to die as a flower among flowers, on a bed of hyacinths and tuberoses whose sweet "symphony" slowly asphyxiates her. But what of Serge's so-called transgression? It is definitely not related to the breaking of his chastity vows: for Zola views priestly celibacy as a monstrous imposition, virginity as an abnormal state, and sexual intercourse—provided it does not elude the procreative ends of nature—as the life-giving sacrament. For a clue to his meaning, one must turn once more to omniscient Dr. Pascal. The following is a portrait of Serge's uncle as he revisits the Paradou's site—long after the garden has been torn down:

> He, Pascal, was a scholar, a clear-sighted man. He did not believe in an idyllic humanity living in a land of milk and honey. He saw, instead, the evils and the taints; he had spread them out, probed, cataloged them for thirty years; and all he needed was his passion for life, his reverence for the energies of life, to throw him into a perpetual joy: whence flowed his love of others, a fraternal emotion, an empathy detectable even under his rough exterior of an anatomist and the factitious impersonality of his studies.

This is Zola describing Zola as he saw himself eighteen years after the publication of *La faute de l'abbé Mouret.* Which strands had led from it to *Germinal* (1885) and *La terre* (*Earth,* 1887), which would lead further to *Les trois villes* (*Three Cities,* 3 vols., 1894–1898) and *Fécondité* (*Fruitfulness,* 1899), were by then becoming apparent. And so was the true "error" of abbé Mouret. The Paradou had vanished like a dream. The Paradou *was* a dream. Serge, henceforth a poor parish priest slowly dying from consumption, had been doomed to fall into the realities of the world-in-exile symbolized by the communities nearby—a world in which grim, obdurate peasants, ploughing the earth and their women alike,

toiled in utter blindness for the harvests of the future.

Thus far established critics had paid scant attention to Zola's novels. *La faute de l'abbé Mouret,* for the first time, drew some lively comment—severe as a rule and most of it denouncing this "outrage" to "the noble spiritualism of Christianity" (Barbey d'Aurevilly). But it remained for *L'Assommoir* (*Drunkard,* vol. 7, 1877) to unleash a literary storm second only to the controversies that *La terre* was to arouse ten years later.

L'Assommoir carries the reader hundreds of physical and spiritual miles from the fairylike Paradou—to a Parisian faubourg ominously called "de la Goutte d'Or" (of the Golden Drop) from what, in olden days, must have been a tavern sign. In due course the scene narrows down to one of the saloons with which the neighborhood is liberally sprinkled. Old man Colombe's establishment stays nameless: we merely know that it is an *assommoir*—a "knock-out bar"—similar to others and the epitome of them all. The feeling of epic simplification becomes reinforced through further pinpointing—this time to the evil heart of the house, the "rot-gut dispenser":

> The attraction of the place was, toward the back, on the other side of an oak railing, in a glass-encased courtyard, the distilling machine working in full view of the patrons—a mess of long-necked alembics, of retorts reaching underground, a hellish kind of brewery in front of which boozing workers stood a-dreaming.

Such procedure evolved from Zola's previous uses of symbolism, but it was not the same procedure. Gone was the former sense of identification and quasi-parity between actors and surroundings. As Zola developed the pattern of failure, the logic of the system compelled him to stress the ascendancy of things. He could not become more of a materialist, but he could—and did—write "of mice and men," sometimes locked in uneven combat against the forces of nature, sometimes ensnared in traps of their own making.

The pernicious powers that issue from *l'assommoir* radiate and fester like a cancer. They shatter the comparative happiness of the Coupeau household. In the wake of a bad accident, the husband, a roofer by trade, loses his zest for work and takes to drink. The wife, Gervaise, struggles for a while and keeps her laundry shop going, but moral decay is contagious. When Coupeau brings in Lantier, a former lover of hers, by whom she had had three children before marriage; when, under the eyes of Anna (Nana), her legitimate daughter, sordid episodes follow, her will, never too strong, breaks down completely: she in turn becomes an alcoholic and dies at forty-one, "slowly, horribly, exhausted by pain and misery." A most moving creation, this sister of Lisa Macquart's—and as pathetic, as lovable, in her defenselessness as the matron of *les Halles* was sturdy and coldly aseptic.

A practical lesson (*de la morale en action*) according to its author, *L'Assommoir* hovered on the brink of didacticism. That it stayed clear of this pitfall redounds to Zola's eternal credit. However, while its predecessors (*La faute de l'abbé Mouret* excepted) were framed in the political context of the Second Empire, *L'Assommoir* broached the much larger social question and testified to the awakening of a man's social conscience. There was abundant justification for Zola's claim that he presented French readers with the first piece of fiction ever devoted to the lower classes, the first that "smelled of the common people," the first that "did not lie." One may well wonder how in heaven some leftist critics found cause to reproach him for slandering the workingman. They missed the clear implication that society at large was responsible, not only for the prosperity of public malefactors such as *père* Colombe, but for the systematic degradation and subjection of the have-nots.

The proletarian "smell" came forth by means of an unheard-of stylistic device. Not content to record conversations in the vernacular, Zola also reported the *thoughts* of his characters. Thus, through a very extraordinary blend of direct and indirect discourse, *L'Assommoir* achieved a consistent atmospheric flavor. It did so at considerable risk, if only because slang forms are notoriously ephemeral. Beginning with the title word itself, which no longer applies in that particular sense, examples of obsolescence have been garnered in an effort to discredit Zola's "philological experiment." The least this writer can say is that, on preparing, in 1937, a French-English glossary of one chapter of *L'Assommoir*, he found nine-tenths of its vocabulary to be miraculously fresh. Louis-Ferdinand Céline's *Voyage au bout de la nuit* (*Journey to the End of Night*, 1932) was five years old at the time and already showing symptoms of linguistic arteriosclerosis.

Purists grumbled, mixing their criticism with ideological objections; but the public recovered from initial shock quickly enough to send the book through thirty-five printings in a few months. Unofficially assisted by Zola himself, William Busnach converted Gervaise's story into a melodrama that ran for three hundred consecutive performances. Dance halls echoed to the rhythms of *L'Assommoir-Polka*. Decorative plates representing scenes from the novel were sold at popular prices. First-year royalties enabled the author to purchase, in the suburban village of Médan, on the banks of the Seine, the "rabbit hutch" that was to grow into a somewhat pretentious country house, a famous literary rendezvous, and, posthumously, the Émile Zola Foundation for sick children of poor families. Fame, wealth, status symbols—all those bourgeois increments abruptly and paradoxically heralded the golden age of naturalism.

The golden age of naturalism extended from *L'Assommoir* to *La terre*, a period of exactly ten years (1877–1887). This means—well, almost—that it was that of Zola, of "Zola tout seul" (Zola alone), as an opponent remarked somewhat later. Whatever following he built never boasted a concerted strategy, let alone a unified doctrine: more about this in a moment. In the last analysis, Zola's continued success stemmed from his own ways with the public (if one excepts some unimpressive forays into the theater) and his consummate skill in throwing the opposition off balance. By far the major part of his strength lay in a bold assessment of what he could accomplish, as a man of letters and would-be indoctrinator, within the frame of bourgeois reference that he felt no need and no urge to subvert. Somewhat different from the Zola of *Mes haines,* the mature Zola chose to trust to the intelligence of the average individual; and alone, it would seem, on the literary scene of his day, he wrote for wide consumption without heaping either flattery or scorn on the heads of his readers. He appointed himself physician extraordinary to a sick society, not its coddler or high executioner. This presupposed, between doctor and client, a bond of confidence and even complicity. The patient must be saved, not only from himself, but from those whose personal or political advantage it was to pronounce him in the best of health; in today's parlance, he must be dissociated from the "establishment." There was no other meaning to Zola's dictum: "The republic will be *naturaliste*—or it will not be."

The novelist's popularity reached a new peak in 1880. This, by all odds, should have been his brightest year so far. It was not. As we shall see, private woes descended upon Zola and left him a profoundly disturbed man. Yet most of the intended harvest was in before the lightning struck—quite enough to make him the master of that particular hour.

In 1880 he published *Nana.* As a follow-up to *L'Assommoir* Zola had elected to produce a novel of the "psychological" variety, classically restrained under a romantic title (*Une page d'amour,* vol. 8 of *Les Rougon-Macquart*). This, of course, put into effect the grand design he had evolved to keep the critics guessing. Could it be, after all, that Zola was no unredeemable blackguard? *Nana* rang out the

answer. *Nana* was another "leaf" taken from the book of love—but the starkest imaginable, one that divested sexual desire or intercourse of the last shreds of idealization. *Nana* raised (or lowered) Woman to the status of a mythical force, at work to corrupt and disrupt society "between her snow-white thighs." A blind force, by the way, a mere instrument, wholly unconscious of its evil destination. But the instrument of whom—or what? On the one hand, Nana's story provided the true sequel to *L'Assommoir:* not only in the literal sense that the heroine was Gervaise's and Coupeau's daughter, but insofar as she, like her parents, had been preordained from birth to become chattel for the privileged few. Yet on the other hand, any illustration of that old theme—the devil and the flesh—tends to establish man's lust, even the rich man's lust, as a law of nature; willy-nilly, it restricts to hypocrisy, to stuffy righteousness, the guilt of the upper classes. In short, the deterministic system to which Zola was beholden detracted somewhat from the value of *Nana* as a moral and social document. Such as it was, however, the book evoked from the conservative press all the boos its author confidently expected. Reviewers called him an ignoramus (which he *was,* to a large extent, in the ways of profligacy); they branded him an impotent maniac, haunted by unfulfillable erotic dreams. But the public, also as expected, took to *Nana* like fish to water. Only hours after the volume went on sale, its publisher ordered ten thousand copies added to the first printing. Throughout the years few other works from Zola's pen ever outsold *Nana* in France—and none abroad.

In 1880 *Les soirées de Médan* (Evenings at Médan) was also published. How many remember today that this collection of six short stories about the Franco-Prussian War, written by Zola and the five young habitués who gathered around his table every Thursday evening, provided the initial vehicle for Maupassant's incomparable *Boule-de-suif?* The host, for his part, offered "L'Attaque du moulin"

("The Attack on the Mill")—a contrived narrative, with romantic overtones, that barely overstepped the threshold of honest mediocrity. Nevertheless, the undertaking afforded concrete evidence that, for the time being at least, Zola had mustered the loyalties of quite a few promising neophytes. They responded, if truth must be told, to the robustness of his character far more than to his personal brand of aesthetics. Almost to a man, they eschewed complete identification with his "scientific" tenets; but long after they had gone their separate ways, one of them (Huysmans) was heard to exclaim: "Ah! quels reins [what loins he has], ce Zola!"

And 1880 was the year of *Le roman expérimental* (*The Experimental Novel*). It was yet another "Médanien," Henry Céard, who, in 1879, drew his host's attention to Dr. Claude Bernard's fourteen-year-old *Introduction à l'étude de la médecine expérimentale* (*Introduction to the Study of Experimental Medicine*, 1865). Céard came to rue his initiative, so avidly did Zola take up this little classic and begin appropriating its contents. *Le roman expérimental* stops short of being a plagiarism only because it professes to be one. The author avowed his intention to "entrench himself" behind Claude Bernard and proceeded to liken the play and interplay of his fictional characters to that of chemical compounds in a test tube. Critic after critic has underscored ever since the childishness of such mechanistic postulates as applied to the workings of literary creation. What should be said in defense of an otherwise indefensible theory is that it was good propaganda. Zola, who flattered himself that he knew how to "drive wedges" into people's minds, had deliberately calculated the impact of this heavy blow. It stamped him in the public eye as the "practical sociologist" he wanted to be.

But 1880 was also a year of mourning. Two losses in succession—that of Flaubert, whom he revered, and that of Zola's mother—threw the novelist into a state of depression. It took immense effort on his part to carry on amid signs that he was prone to morbid fears and mental disturbances. A preoccupation with death—with his own death, final, irremediable, since he no longer expected to have children—crept diffusely into his current work, never to ebb, at least in significant degree, until his liaison with Jeanne Rozerot, from 1888 on, rekindled his zest for living and gratified his paternal yearnings. Those intimate adumbrations were to lend unusual color and poignancy to several of his forthcoming novels—not inconsiderably to that entitled *La joie de vivre* (*Zest for Life*, 1884).

Conceived in the waning months of 1880, but gestated over a period of years, *La joie de vivre* did not appear till 1884. It was to have been called "La douleur" (Sadness), and the dramatic reversal of titles was neither stoically nor sardonically intended. Zola's protagonist, Pauline Quenu, does exemplify the joy of living in the very special sense that she is the lay counterpart of a sister of mercy. The daughter of Lisa, the queen of *les Halles*, she has miraculously escaped the curse of heredity or, at any rate, transferred to good deeds, to the renunciation of personal gain, the purposefulness that her mother brought to acquisitive ends. Yet Pauline, by the very nature of her mission, inhabits a vale of sorrows, just as surely as Alfred de Vigny's Eloa, the angel of compassion, inhabited a world of evil. Thus, *La joie de vivre*, unique as such in Zola's production, projects the image of a divided man and author, whose humanitarian resolves identify him with his heroine and whose broodings with the recipients of her charity.

Let no one believe that Zola, unsettled though he was, could remain silent for long. While waiting for *La joie de vivre* to mature, he added installments ten and eleven to the *Rougon-Macquart* series. Octave Mouret, abbé Serge's brother, served as a connecting link between *Pot-bouille* (Steaming Cauldron, 1882) and *Au bonheur des dames* (Ladies' De-

light, 1883). Throughout the former this ambivalent character assumes a fair share of the petty intrigues and sordid amorous encounters that take place within the walls of an apartment house; in the latter, he presides regally over the management of a department store and, on making his first million, proposes marriage to the most devoted (and least corruptible) of his saleswomen. Both works are substandard—for a Zola, that is—but show him still playing cat-and-mouse with the pundits. Whereas *Pot-bouille* resembled *Nana* in its savage depiction of bourgeois (this time lower-middle-class) appetites, its successor sounded like a hymn to free capitalistic enterprise. What kind of person was this Monsieur Zola anyway? Hardly had the "troglodytes" given their accolade to the "safe" doctrines embodied in *Au bonheur des dames,* than the irrepressible trouble-monger let go of his towering masterpiece in the form of a quasi-socialistic novel.

Germinal, Zola's epic of the coal mines, is essentially the story of a strike and of its repression at the hands of the army. The action is set in 1864—the year the First International was born; the year, too, when the government of Napoleon III granted French labor the right to strike while denying it the right to organize. This crude formula, an invitation to bloody conflict, endless litigation, or both, prevailed until March 1884, at which time the Third Republic extended de jure recognition to most labor unions.

March 1884—note the date. When Zola drew the first sketches of *Germinal,* shortly after the new year, he may have had it in mind to assert the prerogatives of an "experimental" novelist and press for quick adoption of the new law. As it happened, events robbed him of that privilege. Parliament acted under the sting of a long and bitter strike that broke out on 21 February at the mines of Anzin in northern France. The disturbance, on the other hand, provided Zola with a "live" background, far better suited to his broader pur-

poses than the documentation he had culled on the subject of labor unrest from specialized books. He rushed to Anzin, mingled with the miners, interviewed managers of the struck companies, even insisted on descending into a pit. As a result, the novel throbs with barely suppressed excitement and indignation.

Yet it is not a "socialist" novel, at least not in the modern sense of the word. The title itself, borrowed from the revolutionary calendar of 1792, strongly suggests that its ideological roots plunge all the way back into the eighteenth century. Moreover, no little symbolic significance attaches to the fact that 1885, the year of *Germinal*'s unveiling, also was that of Victor Hugo's death and apotheosis. Had Zola planned to don the old seer's mantle, his timing could not have been better; for *Germinal* was in effect an updated version of *Les misérables*—a reminder that both physically and spiritually people were born and created to breathe the open air, not the foul vapors of subterranean depths. But nowhere does the writer commit himself to the violent therapeutics of either Pierre Proudhon or Karl Marx; nowhere does he uphold the principle of class struggle and advocate a proletarian takeover. There is indeed some evidence that the Paris Commune of 1871 had left a sour taste in his mouth; that his sporadic contacts, through Ivan Turgenev, with Russian political refugees (Peter Kropotkin, Mikhail Bakunin, and Peter Lavrov, after whom he fashioned Souvarine in *Germinal*) increased his abhorrence of radical means; and that his subsequent interview (1886) with Jules Guesde, the French Marxist leader, all but confirmed him in the belief that the "pie-in-the-sky" promises of socialism were pure demagoguery.

As a warning, however, or as a prophecy, *Germinal* purported to be, and was, and remained ever after, Zola's most solemn utterance in the realm of "practical sociology." It presented the ruling classes with, according to him, an inescapable dilemma: either they would atone for their shameless exploitation of the downtrodden, of those they confined to the level of beasts, or they would sign their own death warrants. Piecemeal legislation of the "too little and too late" variety could not possibly prevent the "germination" of a "black and vengeful army" whose explosive potential was more than enough to "blow the earth to bits."

Germinal surpasses *L'Assommoir* in that it is built on a heroic scale. The spotlight no longer falls on a handful of workingmen, but on the toiling, suffering masses presented as an entity; no longer on their ill-spent idle hours, but on a lifetime bereft of idle hours—unless you count as such the moments they devote to procreating, in mechanical abandon, the galley slaves (or avengers?) of the future. The devouring monster who faces them is no longer a mere alembic, a provider of oblivion, ensconced in a neighborhood tavern; it is the consortium known as the *Régie* (governing board), whose decrees, issued in Paris and carried out by local subordinates, resemble those of a remote and implacable deity. By no means does this aggrandizement result in a lack of individual characterization; yet such is Zola's absolute mastery that personal lives appear to be—indeed are meant to be—submerged within the pulsating, swirling, random life of the whole. The mob scenes for which *Germinal* is justly famous serve to emphasize its emblematic quality. So does the invisibility of the *Régie*. So does the gnawing feeling, implanted on page after page, that both camps, however unevenly, are but the tools of a third force, call it fate if you will, tortuously engaged in leading humankind, through blood, sweat, and tears, to an unknown destination.

Germinal has all the features and—so the author hopes—the cleansing power of a Greek tragedy. When the strikers, driven into submission by hunger and rifle fire, show a disposition to resume work, Souvarine, the dreamy nihilist who until then had cloaked himself in contemptuous aloofness, blows up the mine and floods it. An ambivalent gesture—not in his eyes, to be sure, but from the lofty dialectical standpoint that Zola maintained throughout his career: a trauma is a purge; every night brings promise of the dawn.

Insofar as the wretched miners of *Germinal* have a leader, the part falls to Étienne Lantier, youngest of Gervaise Macquart's illegitimate children. He is cast in the not-too-savory role of a self-taught, youthful militant whose immature notions cannot provide inspired guidance and gradually estrange him from his followers. As he departs for Paris in a fit of enraged frustration, we are given broad hints that he will sink to the level of raw politics—perhaps become the prototype of the corrupt labor chieftain. This, in our day, might supply the kernel of a resounding, cynical success story. Not so with Zola. In true Darwinian (and puritanical) style, he dooms his inadequate hero to ultimate failure and oblivion. From the family tree one learns that Étienne will participate in the Paris Commune of 1871, be tried, and languish thereafter as a deportee in faraway New Caledonia.

This, in turn, supplies a clue to the meaning of *L'Oeuvre* (*The Masterpiece* 1886), next to appear in the series. Granted, the externals of *L'Oeuvre* thoroughly differ from those of *Germinal*. It was to be the novel of the art world—a world with which Zola was long since conversant; and it was to lay bare the dilemmas of creativity, many times removed from the so-called social question. Yet in broad philosophical terms the new book again raised the social question par excellence: where should the weary pilgrims of the century go? The change of milieu was not so abrupt as appeared at first sight: art, too, had its "establishment," its oppressive *Régie*, its angry young men, its crusaders and fumbling pioneers, its traitors and agents provocateurs. The moment remained exactly the same: a murky period precariously suspended between past and future, a time for anguish and soul-searching. Moreover, the "race" factor, in *L'Oeuvre*, looms as ominously as ever. Claude Lantier, the main character, is

Étienne's flesh-and-blood brother; and far more disinterested, far more appealing though he is, his career, mutatis mutandis, follows the same downward path.

A painter by vocation, Claude is largely self-made and plagued with a lack of intellectual discipline that causes him to squander his natural gifts. He, too, has a diseased mind: his pursuit of originality turns to frenzy and impotence and warps his sense of values, both human and artistic. He, too, will end in abject failure: not a *raté* (failure) in the mediocre sense—rather a near-genius, who either overshot or undershot the mark and, at the time of his self-inflicted death, leaves "nothing of note, absolutely nothing" behind him.

Was Claude's figure drawn in the pseudolikeness of Édouard Manet, or Cézanne, or both? Was he set up as a straw man, the better to burn them in effigy? Speculation has been rife on the subject. Quite undeniably, Zola was no longer an ardent admirer and defender of the new school of painting. He still clamored for revolutionary ways of "seeing" and "rendering," still upheld the "regenerators" as regenerators, but questioned, unwisely it now appears, the permanent value of their achievements. In due time he dubbed both Cézanne and Manet "unfulfilled geniuses," with more than a suggestion that Cézanne sinned through exuberance, and Manet through some sort of anemic deficiency. Only to that extent, however, did they (and others, no doubt) pose as models for Claude Lantier. Zola fully exercised the novelist's privilege to extract one composite character from multiple reality. He did not tax his erstwhile friends with pathological tendencies other than those of a century at large—from which he, Zola, considered himself a sufferer just as well. Actually, the more one analyzes Claude's final, abortive "masterpiece"—a nude allegory of Womanhood who rises against a bustling Parisian background, whose haunches and navel are painted a bright vermilion, whose gilded thighs resemble the pillars of an altar, whose genitals flower into a "mystical rose"—the

more one is reminded, not of anything that ever came from a contemporary brush, but of the aberrations of decadent symbolism as shown—a little later—in the literary works of fin-de-siècle illuminati.

L'Oeuvre, in fact, is above all else an autobiographical novel—the most intimate Zola ever wrote and as such quite possibly the most moving. Not only does it overflow with memories of his childhood in Provence and struggling years in Paris, but it documents the spiritual crisis that had opened in 1880 and shaken his aplomb almost to the breaking point. As late as 1886 *L'Oeuvre* instituted a manner of Don Quixote–Sancho Panza, or Eusebius–Florestan, dialogue within himself. Ever since *La confession de Claude*, that very name, Claude, sometimes used by Zola as a nom de plume, had held strange associations with the romantic and, in his eyes, erratic side of his nature. By way, it would seem, of exorcising his demons, he sent Claude Lantier to a calamitous death and camped alongside him the far steadier figure of Pierre Sandoz, a professional writer and the lifelike image of Zola the plodder, of Zola the would-be believer in the "no-nonsense" of science and the virtues of patient endeavor. Yet the book closes on a very ambiguous note. Standing over Claude's grave, Sandoz chides himself for "cheating with life" as his friend never did: in other terms, for issuing under false pretenses works that he knows in his heart of hearts are no more authentic and viable than Lantier's own compositions. Were this to be accepted literally, Sandoz's abrupt resolve (*allons travailler!* [let's get to work]) would sound very hollow indeed, and *L'Oeuvre* might be called a bleak admission of failure on the part of Zola the poet and Zola the scientist.

As it happened, the fortunes of both took an unexpected turn. The romantic demons had not been exorcised after all. They returned in full fury and, more surprisingly still, they, not Sandoz's sedate gods, pointed the way to ultimate liberation. Ostensibly *La terre* was to forge another link—the fifteenth—in a long chain of "experiments." Today, however, with the benefit of hindsight, we realize that this controversial work, in fact and in effect, broke the pseudo-scientific spell under which the novelist had been laboring for years.

The sociological intent of *La terre* is indeed obscure. Although one episodic character can be heard advocating agrarian socialism, by no means does he propound the author's views. Farmers, even the more substantial among them, are shown to suffer from a variety of economic ills; but Zola appears to be reasonably satisfied that they themselves bear a measure of responsibility for their plight. Briefly, the peasants, unlike industrial workers, were one of the oldest social classes in existence; they stood within reach of the ancestral dream—ownership of the land; yet having thrown off the shackles of serfdom, they remained slaves to the flinty qualities that had won the struggle for them—their rapaciousness, their guile, their insatiable animal hunger.

One would hesitate to say that Zola felt out of sympathy with the peasantry, but it must be admitted that his saga of the countryside breathed none of the warmth and little of the urgency that not so long before pervaded the pages of *Germinal*. Despite the fact that the novelist went through his usual paces, revisiting his mother's native Beauce for on-the-spot documentation, the suspicion arises that the end product, qua novel, was primarily a rhetorical exercise based upon literary reminiscences. It was meant to relegate to their proper place the bucolic fantasies of George Sand—and in this it succeeded admirably. It also invited comparison with Balzac, whose unfinished fresco, *Les paysans* (The Peasants, 1844), bid fair to count among his greatest: perhaps a good enough reason this direct challenge to an awesome predecessor lacked the imaginative power Zola had brought or would bring to several others. As an observer of the rural scene he contributes little that is intrinsically new and seems content to accentuate

Balzacian traits. From Fourchon to Fouan, from Courtecuisse to Bécu or Lequeu, from Mouche to Mouche (pure coincidence?), family names retain their punlike, sometimes half-obscene quality. Greed and murderous hatred, not to mention uninhibited lust, supply the main motivations, as they had done in *Les paysans*—only more so. Cunning remains the peasant's favorite weapon, but violence, already present in Balzac, is markedly on the increase. Comic relief turns to positive ribaldry. Where Balzac had made a wry jumble of human and animal life on the farm, Zola pointedly juxtaposes the insemination of cows and that of women, or again the birth of a calf and that of a child.

Harsh though it may sound, this estimate of *La terre* does not purport to exonerate its original detractors. The work should have been recognized for what it was, for what the author intuitively felt it to be: "the living poem of the soil"; or, more accurately perhaps, the poem of man's incestuous attachment to the earth; the poem of Cybele as mother and mistress: equally demanding in both roles, yet strangely sparing at times, or at least capricious, in the dispensation of her bounties. It is a poem as removed from the paradisiacal climate of the Paradou garden as reality can be from a midsummer night's dream. The poem of fecundity, yes, but of fecundity through human fecundation. The earth's womb must be penetrated, the seed sown, the fruit reaped; people must sweat and people must die, so that "the bread of life may spring from the land." In this respect at any rate, *La terre* far outdistanced Balzac's conceptions. Out of its manure-scented chapters there issues, willy-nilly, a paean to civilization: for no matter how close to the brute man is depicted to be, he is also credited with a dim sense of direction and purposefulness. But for him the planet will forever remain a desert or a jungle.

La terre proved to be another popular success—probably for the wrong reasons. It did portend, however, profound changes in Zola's status within the literary world. The first blow, a painful one no doubt, came from the ranks. Editorialized by *Figaro* on 18 August 1887, the famous "Manifeste des Cinq" (Manifesto of the Five) violently upbraided Zola's "betrayal," his "descent into unadulterated filth," and the "Hugoesque inflation" that robbed his characters of any credibility. The five young signatories were not the Médan habitués, of course, but they had been fellow travelers up to that point. They were, to be exact, followers of Daudet and Edmond de Goncourt, who, out of sheer jealousy, either inspired their diatribe or secretly chuckled over it; and it may well be that as a result of their action, the Médaniens themselves felt badly shaken. *La terre* caused to explode not only an accumulation of petty rancors, but also the intellectual differences that separated Zola from even his most loyal retinue. Always tenuous at best, naturalist unity fell to pieces within the space of a few years. Meanwhile conservative critics, ever on the lookout for a chink in Zola's armor, had pounced on their long-awaited opportunity. Less than two weeks after the publication of the "Manifeste des Cinq," Ferdinand Brunetière, official spokesman for the *Revue des deux mondes*, was blazoning the fact that "the master had finally alienated his disciples" and proclaiming *urbi et orbi* "the bankruptcy of naturalism."

It is entirely conceivable that the threatened dispersal of naturalism did not displease Zola altogether. Let his opponents cry havoc as long as the general public stayed solidly and unquestioningly behind him. (It did. Not even the utter chastity of his next book, *Le rêve* [The Dream, 1888], almost perverse in its contrast to *La terre*, could disconcert and discourage his readers.) Furthermore, let naturalism disintegrate if it must and if the net result should be a sense of emancipation he, Zola, had come to crave as much as anyone else. The day was approaching when he would assume a sanguine mood and offer himself as a valedictorian for the whole movement. The future, he prophesied to Jules Huret in 1891,

> belongs to the man or men who will plumb the soul of modern society; who, having rid themselves of excessively rigid doctrines, will prove amenable to a more plausible, softer-hearted acceptance of life. I am looking forward to a broader, more complex representation of the truth, to greater openness in our understanding of mankind, to, shall we say, a classical coming of age of naturalism.

Whereupon, the same reporter tells us, his buoyant interlocutor had blurted out: "And mind you, if I live long enough, I'll do them myself—the things *they* want!"

Whence this truculent exercise in benignity? Whence this new upsurge of self-confidence? By the time of the Huret interview, few were those among Zola's acquaintances who did not know or suspect the answer. Madame Zola herself was about to learn that ever since the last months of 1888 her husband had been carrying on an affair with her former seamstress, Jeanne Rozerot, an attractive and reasonably literate woman in her early twenties. Originally, at least, the aging novelist had fallen prey to what he himself described as a "recrudescence of life"—to what his contemporary, Paul Bourget, aptly called "the demon of twelve-noon"; but, as we know, there was nothing in him of the profligate, nor was Jeanne a sordid adventuress. Their attachment became unbreakable when she bore him a daughter and a son. Over and above his pangs of remorse Zola's paternal pride led him to profess a renewed ability to "move mountains." He weathered his wife's anger, which relented only at length and then solely for the sake of the children. Not the least of a number of ironic twists was that being a father—even out of wedlock— gave him an added sense of bourgeois respectability. He now had a stake in the future. Yesterday the ribbon of the Legion of Honor; tomorrow—why not—a seat in the French Academy: and would Monsieur Brunetière be red in the face! Membership in the academy never materialized, but what matters to posterity is that the dialogue between life and death that ran steadily through Zola's novels no longer was allowed to end on a note of despair.

As might be expected, this shift in inspirational values did not occur overnight. It was in fact, to follow a jagged course through the remaining volumes of *Les Rougon-Macquart*. *Le rêve*, a romantic idyll and perhaps something more: perhaps a spiritual purge in the aftermath of *La terre*, antedates Zola's liaison; yet it coincides with his first "dreams" of amorous rejuvenation and must have assumed, in retrospect, a premonitory character: for, of its several drafts, one took up the ancient theme of the senescent guardian falling helplessly in love with his ward. *La bête humaine* (*The Human Beast*, 1890), on the other hand, and to a lesser extent *L'Argent* (Money, 1891) testify to the stubbornness of old habits. Only in *La débâcle* (1892) and *Le docteur Pascal* (1893) did Zola's new (or renewed) gospel sound loud and clear.

With the world of railroads as its background, *La bête humaine* bid fair, and indeed purported, to be still another probe into the scope and meaning of material progress. As a devotee of science, Zola could ill afford not to celebrate the wonders of the railroad track and its contribution to "the exchange of ideas, the transformation of nations, the mingling of races, the ultimate unification of the planet." Yet he chose (Was it a choice? Was it not, rather, a kind of compulsion?) to underline the mechanical or mechanizing aspects of technological advance. There is a futuristic coloring to his vision of Jacques Lantier, the engineer, grafted, so to speak, onto his engine, *la Lison*, as one with it in a vertiginous sexual embrace. It is, however, an unequal and darkly symbolic embrace. The life of the machine suffuses that of the man, empties his mind of whatever rational processes may have

been his, restores him to his feral origins. Thus the story evolves into a recital of wanton crime and bloody murder. It goes even further than did *La terre* in stressing the animality of human beings. Whereas the epic of the fields found a layer of civilization deeply embedded within the human beast, that of the railroads exposes the human beast under a thin crust of civilization.

Through the expedient of returning Saccard, the protagonist of *La curée*, to center stage, Zola presumed to open to his readers the sanctum sanctorum of modern capitalism—namely, the stock market. A rash venture on his part, since he knew nothing of its operations, never owned a share in his life, never even possessed a bank account. The true wonder, then, is not that *L'Argent* should fall far short of being a masterpiece, but that it should be as competent a novel as it actually is. Zola's informants did their homework, with the result that, structural weaknesses notwithstanding, *L'Argent* today remains unrivaled as a portrayal of the stock exchange and would need few transpositions to evoke for us not the distant saga of speculation under the Second Empire, but that, closer to our times, of the Staviskys in France or the Insulls in America. Saccard's financial schemes, as well may be imagined, come to a crash in a kind of götterdämmerung atmosphere, with hosts of hapless victims left wailing across the night. Yet surprisingly enough, Zola does not issue a blanket indictment of his hero. Saccard's recklessness is taken to be but a malformation or misuse of the creative urge that makes the world go round. Not a little sophistry attaches to this judgment, whose devious purpose it is to bring out an analogy with love. Money has no odor; money is what money manipulators make it. Likewise—and this is a note not heard in Zola's novels since *La faute de l'abbé Mouret*—none of the filth that is being stirred in the name of love can defile love itself.

Should war, both foreign and civil, be defended, or excused, on roughly the same dialectical grounds? Should we look upon it as an illustration of Darwin's "haughty and heart-rending" law of necessity—then make a text and pretext of that very premise to assert: "War is life itself. . . . None but the warlike nations ever prospered. A nation perishes the minute it disarms"? This was the tenor of a Zola article published in *Figaro* on the twenty-first anniversary of the Sedan capitulation and generally considered to be a blurb for his forthcoming novel, *La débâcle.* A while ago, this article and the novel itself came under heavy criticism from an otherwise very sympathetic commentator, Henri Guillemin, who sees in them a damaging concession to the "establishment" (remember: Zola coveted a seat in the French Academy!) and a white-washing of the retrograde policies followed after Sedan—up to and including the savage repression of the Commune uprising. We shall, in these pages, adopt a kindlier view of Zola's motivations. We made it clear that he had a flair for publicity and was not above making opportunistic moves. We also took note of the fact that while his heart beat to the left, his head tended to lean to the right in vague fear of the "red peril" that somehow the writing of *Germinal* had conjured up before his eyes. It is no less true, however, that he had been toiling for twenty-five years on the fundamental assumption that his appointed task was to cleanse the Augean stables of the Second Empire. For twenty of those twenty-five years he had regarded Sedan as a deed of immanent justice that closed one era and opened another. What he wrote in 1891 he could have written in 1871 just as well—that Sedan was relevant, "not merely in terms of war," but also and chiefly as "the collapse of a dynasty and the tumbling down of an age."

How, then, could Zola, without tearing up the fabric of his work, without repudiating its conclusions, acknowledge publicly—whether or not he acknowledged privately—that nothing was changed and that not even the trauma of Sedan had been able to raise France from the trough of corruption? Short of becoming an out-and-out revolutionary, the author of *Les Rougon-Macquart* was bound to express temporary faith in the Third Republic and long-term confidence in the due process of evolution. Thus *La débâcle* re-intones the litanies so often encountered in earlier novels—only magnified by the euphoria of new-found love and parenthood. Over the Sedan holocaust, over Paris still ablaze in the wake of fratricidal war, an immaculate sky keeps singing "of eternal nature, of eternal humanity," of "the renewal promised to all who hope and who labor."

By no means an impeccably constructed novel, *La débâcle* stands nevertheless as one of Zola's most impressive achievements. It is a work of great scope and power, not unworthy of comparison with Leo Tolstoy's *War and Peace* (1862–1869). Sweepingly majestic in its description of the battlefields, crystal clear in its reconstruction of strategic or tactical maneuvers, masterly in its handling of enormous masses of people, it shows Zola at his narrative and epic best. Yet the emphasis appears to be on individuals, combatants and noncombatants alike. There is merit in the author's later boast that he discarded, once and for all, the trappings, the flourishes, the heroics of the conventional war tale, substituting for them the naked truth: that of the smoke, the noise, the bloodshed, the stench, the pent-up brutality, the visceral fears, the cries of the wounded, the involvement of innocent bystanders—civilians, women, children. This may be the reason, at a time when the Franco-Prussian War (and the Commune) remained very much a topical subject, when veterans were just about reaching the reminiscent age, the success of *La débâcle*—Zola's biggest best-seller—exceeded all expectations. This may also be the reason the army took a dim view of it. One prominent general averred that he was "shocked"; another chided the author for presenting reality "under noxious aspects." No better proof is needed that if perchance Zola tried appeasing the establishment, part at least of the establishment refused the bait—thus setting the stage for the open break that was to be precipitated by the Dreyfus affair.

To all practical or hopefully practical purposes, then, the debacle of the imperial regime signaled that of the Rougon-Macquart tribe, so that the nineteenth book of the series brought it to its logical end. Since, however, in keeping with Zola's philosophy, every end calls for a beginning, the twentieth and last volume would provide that beginning. We have already given proper consideration to the recapitulative aspects of *Le docteur Pascal* and should be content at this time to lay stress on the strong emotional impulse that made it a thinly veiled transposition of Zola's personal love story. Pascal Rougon "weds" his niece Clotilde (without benefit of clergy), and has a child by her. That, unlike Zola, he had been a lifelong bachelor removes from him the "stigma" of adultery; that he is at least ten years older than his creator when he becomes a father accentuates further, not indeed the incongruity of his "marriage," but on the contrary its Ruth-and-Boaz quality, the symbolic beauty, the invincible promise, the sanctity of it. To J. van Salten Kolff, on 22 February 1893, he wrote:

> It was courageous, on concluding this history of the terrible Rougon-Macquart family, to have it give birth to a last child: the unknown child, perhaps the messiah of tomorrow. A mother nursing her child, isn't that continuing the world—and redeeming it?

As it happened, Zola did not wait for the messiah of tomorrow. Almost two full years before finishing *Les Rougon-Macquart*, shortly after the Huret interview of 1891, he set out to "rid himself of excessively rigid doctrines" and achieve "greater openness in [his] understanding of mankind." This was tantamount to instituting himself the messiah of today.

In a sense he had never been anything else.

To show his true colors as a kindred spirit to the Hugos and the Michelets, all he had to do was throw away the paraphernalia of the "experimental novel" and pick up the pilgrim's staff that had lain within reach in a corner of his laboratory. What is more, *Le docteur Pascal* made it clear that this could be done without renouncing one's scientific tenets: it was just a matter of endowing modern technology and modern economics with a spirituality of their own. The conflict between science and religion, between progressive and traditional values, would be resolved through a return to fundamentals. Universal love—not only human brotherhood, but a Saint Francis–like extension of it to every living thing—would eventually lead to universal peace and harmony. In a world whose inexhaustible bounties could be rationally developed and distributed, even the Darwinian concepts upheld in *La débâcle* would lose their dire pertinence.

Zola saw no contradiction between his tolerance of war as a means of surgical purification—when the tree is diseased and the rotten branch must be cut off—and his advocacy of nonviolence in a society pure and mature enough to turn its technical knowledge into an instrument of social justice. He, not unlike Tolstoy, acquired the conviction that by divesting the New Testament of its supernatural envelope, by breaking the Church's monopoly over it, one could extract from its teachings the charter of the future. And, again not unlike Tolstoy, he saw the artist as the apostle of the new faith. As if in anticipation of André Gide's famous axiom that good feelings make for bad literature, he, in the last decade of his life, endeavored to prove exactly the opposite.

Alas, he did not succeed. There are, to be sure, passages of great force and brilliance in Zola's triptych *Les trois villes: Lourdes*, 1894, *Rome*, 1896, *Paris*, 1898; and in the unfinished *Quatre évangiles* (Four Gospels: *Fécondité*, 1899; *Travail*, 1901; *Vérité*, posthumous, 1903; and the fourth "Justice", never written). This enormous production, however, while it bears witness to the author's unflagging stamina, is decidedly anticlimactic from a literary standpoint. It takes uncommon courage to follow abbé Pierre Froment's spiritual journey from Lourdes, the shrine of "naive faith and illusion"—through Rome, the hardheaded metropolis of political Catholicism—to Paris, where he finally resolves to abandon his cassock and become a lay worker in the service of justice and human love. Of the three novels involved, the least unrewarding is probably *Paris,* if only because a certain grandeur attaches to the implicit contrast between the Paris of the Rougon-Macquart era and the new Paris of the coming century, hopefully reinstated to its former role as the capital of Thought.

But then nothing less than heroism is required to withstand the heavy rhetoric, the utopian arbitrariness, the utter unreality of Zola's *Évangiles.* Even their symbolism descends at times to sheer puerility: the "gospels" were to unfold the life story of Pierre Froment's four sons, pointedly christened Mathieu, Luc, Marc, and Jean after the four evangelists; the patronymic itself, Froment (*wheat* in French), becomes an obvious emblem of fertility; Mathieu's wife, Marianne, borrows her given name from the woman in the Phrygian cap who traditionally personifies the French republic; and that happy couple gives birth to twelve children who in turn present them, on their diamond wedding anniversary, with 134 grandchildren and great-grandchildren. Were it not for lack of space, we might be tempted to probe more deeply into the whys and wherefores of Zola's messianic intemperance; we might even reach some instructive and not altogether damning conclusions; yet, one of them would have to be that if *La débâcle* came reasonably close to emulating Tolstoy's *War and Peace,* none of Zola's subsequent works even remotely offers itself as a counterpart to Tolstoy's *Resurrection* (1899).

If we are to believe Daudet—but *is* Daudet believable?—Zola's irruption into the Dreyfus case was primarily due to his fondness for the limelight. This would be presupposing that he himself was aware of a decline in his creative powers and anxious to divert his energies into other than literary channels. The inference would also be that, for the first time in years, he grievously misjudged public reaction. As a result of his gesture, his popularity faded overnight, never to return in full panoply until long after his death.

Reasons for this are not far to seek. For many months after Captain Dreyfus was found guilty of treasonable acts (22 December 1894) and deported to Devil's Island, few if any outside his family challenged the verdict. Still stung by its defeats, the nation at large was riding a wave of jingoism that made the army—or its decisions—virtually untouchable. Then, Dreyfus was a Jew. The image of the Jews as an alien element, bent on capturing all control and subverting all traditional values—was being kept successfully in the forefront of public consciousness by the likes of Édouard Drument, the venomous author of *La France juive* (Jewish France, 1886), whose newspaper, *La libre parole* (The Free Word), had been founded for the express purpose of spreading the anti-Semitic creed. So it is that when Zola, long before becoming interested in the Dreyfus case per se, rose in defense of the Jews (*Pour les Juifs* [For the Jews], *Figaro,* 16 May 1896), he was already contradicting the prevalent mood and aligning himself with the fractious, "intellectual," minority.

Only the salient facts about Zola's intervention and subsequent trial—this affair within an affair—may be recalled here. Late in 1897, when the finger of evidence began pointing away from Dreyfus and to a fellow officer, Major Ferdinand Esterhazy; when the latter was forced to request a hearing, ostensibly to "clear his name," Zola, through a series of articles and brochures, joined in the demand for a review of the Dreyfus sentence. Esterhazy's swift acquittal by a court-martial (11 January 1898) effectively quashed this move and prompted Zola to write his impassioned *Lettre à M. Félix Faure, Président de la République.* Published 13 January in Georges Clemenceau's *L'Aurore*, known to posterity under the title *J'accuse*, which Clemenceau gave it, this "letter" inculpated the entire military hierarchy—here and there somewhat randomly for lack of adequate proof, but with unerring accuracy in its overall assumption that the army was concealing its mistakes and saving face at the expense of common justice. A libel suit instituted by the government inevitably followed, and Zola was condemned to the maximum penalty of one year in prison and a 3,000-franc fine (23 February). Having lost on appeal (18 July), he was prevailed upon by Clemenceau and others to evade the sentence—on the grounds, it would seem, that this was the only way to keep the Dreyfus case open. A reluctant Zola stole away to England and remained there until June of the following year, when he was still technically liable to arrest but the march of events made it fairly safe for him to return. In his absence the tangled truth had begun unraveling: a high officer had committed suicide; Esterhazy had fled and issued from abroad a confession of sorts; orders were going out to bring Dreyfus back for a retrial. As Dreyfus stepped on French soil, Zola called his homecoming "a rebirth" and the results of his campaign "a harvest of uprightness, equity, and infinite hope."

It did not take him long to realize how mistaken he was. Unable to exonerate Dreyfus without incriminating senior officers, the military court chose to recondemn him . . . with extenuating circumstances! He who should have been acquitted was awarded instead a magnanimous presidential "pardon." The "Dreyfus crusade" fizzled out—partly because Dreyfus himself, an army man whose mental processes did not differ basically from those of his accusers, chose to discourage it and wait six more years for his total rehabilitation (15 July 1906). Meanwhile an amnesty bill designed to liquidate the affair as expediently as possible was rammed through parliament and defended by the premier, René Waldeck-Rousseau, in the crudest terms imaginable: "Amnesty," he said, "does not judge, does not ac-

cuse, does not acquit: it ignores." Last-minute "Dreyfusists" prepared to make hay out of the labors of early "Dreyfusards." Young Charles Péguy complained mournfully that "every mystique degenerates into politics."

Zola, for his part, went on fighting. *La vérité en marche* (Truth on the March, 1901), a collection of his writings throughout the Dreyfus affair, contains—apropos of the "pardon" and on the subject of amnesty—vigorous protests against the guileful policies followed by the government. There can be no question, however, that Zola's former assertive tones ("Dreyfus is innocent. I swear it. I pledge my life. I pledge my honor. . . . I may be smitten here, [but] I shall conquer") were giving way to those of disbelief and frustration: "I stand in dread . . . in sacred terror. . . . The impossible [has] come to pass. . . . Future generations will shudder in shame," and so on. A veteran of many journalistic brawls, but a novice in the field of action, Zola was visibly shaken. Indomitable, yet shaken. Mudslinging and derision had taken their toll:

> Zola's a big pig,
> The older he gets, the stupider he is;
> Zola's a big pig,
> Let's catch and roast the silly pig.

He had earned the suffrage of part at least of the intelligentsia; a book of homage had been presented to him (1898) under the patronage of a Franco-Belgian committee that included, besides Clemenceau, Maurice Maeterlinck and Émile Verhaeren; but the first words of dedication read—all too ominously: "The people learn their lesson even as they stone those who love them."

The posturing, the prophesying, the anathematizing—and the resultant stoning—were part and parcel of the romantic heritage that Zola, wisely or not, had chosen to assume in later years. After half a century or so he was reechoing Hugo's hyperbolic claim that he would scale the heavens in order to steal the truth; that, if thunders should bark, *he* would roar. Whatever megalomania is involved here may be a character trait—it certainly was in Hugo's case; but its deeper significance must be assessed in the context of romantic vaticination. Sooner or later, with Hugo and Zola, there comes a time when the man subsumes himself into the poet; when his commitment to self-expression reaches the visionary level; when the word becomes the Word in so spontaneous a manner that even self-conceit acquires the colors of self-abnegation.

It is, I believe, extremely revealing that Zola should have sworn to Dreyfus' innocence ''by my forty years of toil, by the authority that such labor may have given me.'' This is at once romantic nonsense and the reason Zola's championship of Dreyfus is still remembered, whereas other participants in the drama are readily forgotten. Let us face it: we went, we are still going, through experiences that dwarf the Dreyfus case; Zola's involvement in the specific issues thereof has, really, no greater relevance to our times than Voltaire's effort on behalf of Calas; but what matters in modern terms is that he entered the fray, not as a high-minded politician (assuming the breed exists), not as a man of action, not even as a writer systematically *engagé* in the Sartrean sense of the word, but as a *clerc* (Julien Benda's expression), *as a man of thought*, whose devotion to principles, and to principles only, prepared, nay, designated him for this extraordinary assumption of risk and responsibility.

Zola died a strange accidental death, on 29 September 1902, when carbon monoxide fumes from a defective chimney asphyxiated him in his sleep. Talk of foul play arose immediately and is still being intermittently revived. There is little evidence to support it—the most likely explanation is that Zola fell a victim to ingrained, unhealthy habits of another age that some of us are old enough to remember: lighting coal fires in the bedroom—closing windows hermetically—bolting inside doors for added privacy. The sensational aspects of that death lay much less in its manner than in its timing at the hands of fate. In one of the most eloquent and substantial tributes that the event elicited (there were many hollow ones), Gabriel Trarieux had this to say:

> He died at the top of his strength, his faculties still unimpaired. Among all ways of dying this is one to be envied. There are those who deplore that he was denied well-earned returns, a happy old age, the inevitable apotheosis, the vast emotional outpouring that took place, on a starry spring night, around the peaceful coffin of Victor Hugo. Of small importance, however, in the face of the gestures of survivors. I, for one, am of the opinion that the style of his funeral—which was his last battle—suited best that incorrigible warrior, far too bitterly dedicated ever to become a patriarch. Clashing hurrahs and outrages are an apotheosis, too, and the proof that one still lives. This kind of an apotheosis Hugo also would have known if he had died on the morrow of his *Châtiments.*

Selected Bibliography

EDITIONS

INDIVIDUAL WORKS
Contes à Ninon. Paris, 1864.
La confession de Claude. Paris, 1865.
Mes haines. Paris, 1866.
Le voeu d'une morte. Paris, 1866.
Les mystères de Marseille. Marseilles, 1867.
Thérèse Raquin. Paris, 1867.
Madeleine Férat. Paris, 1868.
La fortune des Rougon. Paris, 1871. Vol. 1 of *Les Rougon-Macquart, histoire naturelle et sociale d'une famille sous le Second Empire* (hereafter *RM*).
La curée. Paris, 1872. Vol. 2 of *RM.*
Le ventre de Paris. Paris, 1873. Vol. 3 of *RM.*
La conquête de Plassans. Paris, 1874. Vol. 4 of *RM.*
Nouveaux contes à Ninon. Paris, 1874.
La faute de l'abbé Mouret. Paris, 1875. Vol. 5 of *RM.*
Son Excellence Eugène Rougon. Paris, 1876. Vol. 6 of *RM.*
L'Assommoir. Paris, 1877. Vol. 7 of *RM.*
Une page d'amour. Paris, 1878. Vol. 8 of *RM.*
Le roman expérimental. Paris, 1880.
Nana. Paris, 1880. Vol. 9 of *RM.*

Pot-bouille. Paris, 1882. Vol. 10 of *RM.*

Au bonheur des dames. Paris, 1883. Vol. 11 of *RM.*

La joie de vivre. Paris, 1884. Vol. 12 of *RM.*

Germinal. Paris, 1885. Vol. 13 of *RM.*

L'Oeuvre. Paris, 1886. Vol. 14 of *RM.*

La terre. Paris, 1887. Vol. 15 of *RM.*

Le rêve. Paris, 1888. Vol. 16 of *RM.*

La bête humaine. Paris, 1890. Vol. 17 of *RM.*

L'Argent. Paris, 1891. Vol. 18 of *RM.*

La débâcle. Paris, 1892. Vol. 19 of *RM.*

Le docteur Pascal. Paris, 1893. Vol. 20 of *RM.*

Les trois villes: Lourdes. Paris, 1894.

Les trois villes: Rome. Paris, 1896.

Les trois villes: Paris. Paris, 1898.

Les quatre évangiles: Fécondité. Paris, 1899.

Les quatre évangiles: Travail. Paris, 1901.

La vérité en marche. Paris, 1901.

Les quatre évangiles: Vérité. Paris, 1903.

COLLECTED WORKS

Oeuvres complètes. 48 vols. Paris, 1906.

————. Notes and commentaries by Maurice Le Blond (Zola's son-in-law). 50 vols. Paris, 1927–1929.

————. Edited by Henri Mitterand. 15 vols. Paris, 1966–1970. A far richer and more truly critical edition than Le Blond, above.

Les Rougon-Macquart, histoire naturelle et sociale d'une famille sous le Second Empire. Edited by Henri Mitterand. 5 vols. Paris, 1964–1967.

TRANSLATIONS

The Debacle. Translated by L. W. Tancock. Baltimore, 1972.

Doctor Pascal. Translated by Vladimir Kean. London, 1957.

The Dream. New York, 1888.

Earth. Translated by Ann Lindsay. New York, 1955.

The Experimental Novel. Translated by Belle M. Sherman. New York, 1964.

Germinal. Translated by Havelock Ellis. New York, 1937.

————. Translated by L. W. Tancock. Baltimore, 1961.

The Heirs of Rabourdin. Translated by Teixeira de Mattos. London, 1894.

His Excellency. Translated by Alec Brown. London, 1958.

The Human Beast. Translated by Louis Colman. New York, 1948.

The Kill. Translated by Teixeira de Mattos. London, 1958.

Ladies' Delight. Translated by April Fitzlyon. London, 1958.

A Love Affair. Translated by Jean Stewart. New York, 1957.

Madeleine Férat. Translated by Alec Brown. New York, 1957.

The Masterpiece. Translated by Thomas Walton. London, 1957.

Modern Marriage. Translated by Benjamin R. Rucker. New York, 1893.

The Mysteries of Marseilles. Translated by Edward Vizetelly. New York, 1976.

Nana. Translated by George Holden. Baltimore, 1972.

Paris. Translated by Edward Vizetelly. New York, 1898.

A Priest in the House. Translated by Brian Rhys. New York, 1957.

Restless House. Translated by Percy Pinkerton. New York, 1953.

Rome. Translated by Edward Vizetelly. New York, 1896.

Savage Paris. Translated by David Hughes and Marie-Jacqueline Mason. New York, 1955.

Shell Fish. New York, 1911.

The Sin of Father Mouret. Translated by Sandy Petry. Englewood Cliffs, N.J., 1969.

Theresa. New York, 1952.

The Three Cities. Translated by Edward Vizetelly. New York, 1894.

Three Faces of Love. Translated by Roland Gant. New York, 1968.

Truth. Translated by Edward Vizetelly. London, 1912.

Zest for Life. Translated by Jean Stewart. Bloomington, Ind., 1956.

CORRESPONDENCE

Correspondance. Edited by B. H. Bakker. Paris, 1978.

Émile Zola's Letters to J. van Salten Kolff. Edited by Robert Judson Niess. Saint Louis, 1940.

Paul Cézanne's Letters. Edited by John Rewald and translated by Marguerite Key. New York, 1976.

CRITICAL STUDIES

Barbusse, Henri. *Zola.* Translated by Mary Balairdie Green and Frederick C. Green. New York, 1932.

ÉMILE ZOLA

Bédé, Jean Albert, *Emile Zola*. New York, 1974.

Brown, Calvin Smith. *Repetition in Zola's Novels*. Athens, Ga., 1952.

Carter, Lawson A. *Zola and the Theatre*. New Haven, Conn., 1963.

Grant, Elliott Mansfield. *Émile Zola*. New York, 1966.

Hemmings, Frederick William John. *Émile Zola*. Oxford, 1966.

——————. *The Life and Times of Émile Zola*. London, 1977.

Hewitt, Winston R. *Through Those Living Pillars: Man and Nature in the Work of Émile Zola*. The Hague, 1974.

Josephson, Matthew. *Zola and His Time*. New York, 1969.

Kranowski, Nathan. *Paris in the Works of Émile Zola*. New York, 1966.

Patterson, J. G. *A Zola Dictionary*. London, 1912.

Richardson, Joanna. *Zola*. London, 1978.

Schor, Naomi. *Zola's Crowds*. Baltimore, 1975.

Vizetelly, Edward. *Émile Zola, Novelist and Reformer*. New York, 1904.

JEAN-ALBERT BÉDÉ

GIOVANNI VERGA

(1840–1922)

NO MATTER WHAT the country, its south is a special region. Southern writers, especially those of countries above the equator, tend to have similar qualities. They often have a gentility that is not necessarily gentle in their style of writing or of living. They have an inbred aristocratic flair, even when they are born on a dirt farm. Except when waging war, they tend to be pacific and above politics. They have a natural feel for the history that roots them in a glorious independent past, before northern, ideological hordes swept through and dismantled their lustrous autonomy. Their style is expansive and their way of living can be generous while their poverty is prodigious. Southern writers of most nationalities have one thing in common—they resent the North and cannot wait to go there and find out why.

Giovanni Verga came from Catania, near Mount Etna, in Sicily—the most southern province of Italy, which the Sicilians tellingly call "the Continent." He was properly southern in his haughtiness, his reticence, his highborn, low-income background; above all, he had the ambivalent attitude that sent him scurrying in 1860 to Florence and Milan, at the age of twenty, living there and in Paris, loving the intellectual ambience of these cities, their aristocratic circles and their women. ("Ladies" would be a more appropriate word, since Verga had a pronounced predilection for amatory elegance.) The literary result of the two decades he spent mostly on the sophisticated continent was three novels: *Eva* (1873), *Tigre reale* (Royal Tigress, 1875), and *Eros* (1875). D. H. Lawrence, who considered Verga the greatest Italian novelist after Alessandro Manzoni, reservedly called them "interesting, alive, bitter, somewhat unhealthy, smelling of the seventies and of Paris and the Goncourts." Verga supported himself mostly by journalism, but he also depended on his ancestral land for sustenance, often returning there to check the accounts. On these visits to the region that so influenced his personality he began to appreciate and love the land as well as the people around the seaport of Catania, where his family, to which he remained attached, still lived. When his brother became too sick to look after the holdings, Verga, at forty, returned home to stay.

At this stage of his life began his greatest love affair—with the peasants he had worked with and whom he had come to know, the people "sitting on the lowest rung of the ladder." At the same time, what he perceived as a type of spurious affection for "the Continent" had begun to wane. A story formed around this experience: "Il come, il quando, ed il perché" ("How, When, and Why," from *Vita dei campi* [Life in the Fields], 1880); it tells how, when, and why he became disillusioned. The story's elegant, lovely, snobbish heroine clearly represents the impulsive but loveless northern city to which she returns. Her Sicilian lover is

Verga, who finally says goodbye to her and her "caprice" (the name of an autobiographical sketch about the same parting lovers). He has given her his passionate all. She has given him, in exchange, an impulsive bauble of her being. He is left with nothing but the moment of love, which is gone as soon as she is out of sight. She has no real interest in him, his southern passion, or the South whose peasantry he extols. She cannot wait to leave the rustic scene of her emotional lapse to return to the continental gaiety and cynicism that she has compromised by becoming involved with such an intensely, provincially, serious lover. He, in turn, realizes that he has only himself to blame for expecting her not to find the entire affair overwhelmingly tedious. While waiting to leave Catania for the security of continental society, she is impatient for the train to start, jingling her perfume bottle anxiously—a scene Lawrence calls "one of the most amusingly biting things in the literature of love. How bored she must have been by his preaching the virtues of the humble poor!" At that point, Verga stopped preaching and began teaching not the virtues, but the nature of southern people.

Verga does not idealize them, like Vergil, nor does he take them idyllically lightly, like Theocritus, who also wrote about Sicilian rural life. He sees the Sicilian as the last outpost of a primitive, direct, unironic way of thinking. This is not only humanly attractive; it is also artistically convenient. By the predictability of their activities, by the limitation of their scope and their hopes, the peasants became ideal subjects. They could sit still for a portrait; that is, their minds could, and their minds, with their minimal convolutions, are what made the sketching special. The characters blend into the stillness of the landscape. Rosso Malpelo (from the story of the same name) is almost a mole of a man, protectively colored brown like the earth, and when he enters the tunnel, never to emerge, it is as if the animal has returned to its lair.

Literary audiences were insensitive to the kind of social issues put forth in Verga's writings. They were largely dominated by the sentimental romantic tradition, which preferred a psychological adventure story told in hemophiliac prose that gushed purple at the scratch of a pen. Verga needed to find, and ultimately succeeded in finding, a style appropriate to the type of innocent being represented by Malpelo. The style would fit his break with the sophisticated world of the North, the tyranny of fashion that demanded a revolt in his writing method. Here, he tells how he came upon it:

> I had published several of my first novels. They went well: I was preparing others. One day, I don't know how, there came into my hands a sort of broadside, a halfpenny sheet, sufficiently ungrammatical and disconnected, in which a sea-captain succinctly relates all the vicissitudes through which his sailing-ship has passed. Seaman's language, short, without an unnecessary phrase. It struck me, and I read it again; it was what I was looking for, without definitely knowing it. Sometimes, you know, just a sign, an indication is enough. It is a revelation.
>
> (D. H. Lawrence, *Phoenix*, 1936, p. 249)

Verga's great mature works show him to be not only one of the first major regional authors, but also an artist whose innovations of style and form are influential to this day in Italian letters, painting, and film. Borrowing a technique from the French naturalist authors, Verga elaborated it into the documentary poetry known as *verismo* (literally, truthfulness). Critics have been hard put to clarify the differences between *verismo*, naturalism, and realism. It is not difficult to define these terms with examples, but it is considerably more difficult to elaborate a theoretical basis for them that accounts for their many variations. Naturalism is writing that stresses the unadorned physical elements of nature—there is something romantic in its dismissal of the psychological, the subtle, something melodramatic about its forthrightness. Realism stresses the plausible, unattractively logical motivations behind a character's actions; it is essentially unromantic and aggressively unmelodramatic. *Verismo* appears to go beyond realism in its revolt against the romantic coloring of metropolitan emotions or the idyllic retouching of the truth as it is seen in the country. *Verismo* seems to strip reality even barer than naturalism and seems more psychologically oriented than naturalism. Benedetto Croce said, "Verismo when understood as an aesthetic formula is absurd, like any aesthetic formula. But in history it does not stand as a formula or as a rule; rather, it is a fact or a number of facts."

Sicily in the middle of the nineteenth century was one of the poorest, most arid regions of Europe. Verga, in his language, found a harsh, bare equivalent to the very soil he described. But this hard, angular style required the demanding regimen of Verga's early years in Florence, where so many Italian writers have gone to polish their language.

Giovanni Verga was a strikingly good-looking man. He was of medium height, with piercing eyes and a fine reddish moustache, an appearance that ensured his welcome in the cosmospolitan circles of Florence and, later, Milan, where he spent most of every year during his development and maturity as a writer. In his autobiographical short story "Di la dal mare" ("Across the Sea") in *Novelle rusticane* (*Little Novels of Sicily*, 1883), we see the ambivalence he felt for the brilliant, urbane world of the North contrasted to the arid, desolate terrain of the South; Sicily, however, was not devoid of a certain terrible beauty:

> . . . where unknown, almost mysterious lives quivered and suffered who knows what poor joys, poor sorrows, how like to those he was telling . . . all the while came the sad Sicilian folksong, telling . . . of humble hopes, amid the monotonous moaning of the sea. . . .
>
> Already Sicily was rising like a cloud out of the far horizon. Then Etna all at once lit up like a golden ruby and the paling coast broke here and there into gulfs and obscure promontories. . . . In the distance were boats, like black dots, and the coast swathed in foam; on the left

Calabria and on the right . . . Charybdis stretching her white arms toward rocky, lofty Sicily.

> (*Little Novels of Sicily*, pp. 212–213)

Verga's *verismo*, his statement of facts as they are, with no metaphoric filter, deals with expressions of human behavior beyond any personal, political, or philosophical vision. He believed that Sicily, like all that was basic, primitive, and dramatically simple, was also universal. Above all, in writing about Sicily he was dealing with what he knew best, and he proved to be a stubbornly faithful witness of life in his native region. He became the voice of the South and the first important writer of Italy as a unified country.

Verga's literary ancestry appears to have two principal lines. On one hand, there is a link to the type of agrarian society that inspired Leo Tolstoy and Ivan Goncharov. On the other hand, there is a connection with Gustave Flaubert, Honoré de Balzac, and Émile Zola, who, already involved with the consequences of the bourgeois revolution, wrote about money, possession, and the power of wealth. The Sicilian society into which Verga was born, characterized by extremes of wealth and poverty, was in many ways primitive and static, thereby giving Verga ample opportunity to contrast it with the more socially evolved bourgeois culture of his French models. This conflict reflects the geographical and social division of Italy at the turn of the century. The North, where Verga played and published, was industrialized and had attained a certain class homogeneity. Conversely, the South was still polarized between the rich and the poor, the survivors and the damned. Verga's imagination gave life to the raw, vital extremes of the South and brought them to the attention of all of Europe.

Verga was prolific and did not limit himself to writing about the poor in extreme situations; he also wrote about the less dramatic but equally marginal middle class. Ultimately Verga came into his own as a writer when he moved away from middle-class subjects to the peasants he knew so well. In doing so he transformed the literary technique of the French naturalist authors. The political implications of Verga's work result from his *verismo* (a manner of writing that lends itself to political statement) rather than from an inherently polemical nature. Verga was not antagonistic to the conquering North, but merely depicted a different Italy—a region that had been unified, but had never come to play an important role in the social and political life of the nation. A lesser author might have been condemned by this regional affinity to having a limited appeal, but in Verga's case the tragic strength of his major novels, *I Malavoglia* (The Malavoglia Family, 1881; published in English as *The House by the Medlar Tree*) and *Mastro-don Gesualdo* (1889), has ensured his eminent position.

Giovanni Verga was perhaps the last incarnation of a nearly extinct literary species—the gentleman writer. He was born on 2 September 1840. His family, which had once called itself "de Verga," indicating a noble Spanish origin, was comfortably affluent. His father's side was said to be related to the barons of Fontanabianca, a tie that the laureate poet Giosue Carducci, in a rather nasty letter to a mutual friend, vehemently disputed. Verga's mother, Caterina Di Mauro, was born of solid middle-class stock and was considered by friends "definitely an intellectual." She was an avid reader of contemporary literature, including, in particular, the controversial *Life of Jesus* by Ernest Renan—altogether unusual for a good housewife and mother in charge of her children and their education.

Verga had a fine school record and absorbed the intellectual atmosphere of his home, showing a precocious orientation toward literature. Although his parents were well off, they were not rich enough to permit him an entirely free decision regarding his future. Verga's father wanted him to become a lawyer and, perhaps, later a member of Parliament. Giovanni preferred to dedicate himself to humanist studies at the academy of Don Antonio Abate, a man of character and imagination, but not particularly gifted as a writer. It was a provincial school, but it provided a lively and stimulating environment, and Verga could make up for its academic deficiencies with his own talent and imagination.

In 1857, when he was seventeen, Verga finished his first novel, the historical *Amore e patria* (Love and Country). Showing a youthful restraint, he managed to limit it to 672 pages that would never be published. *Amore e patria* is hardly a crucial work in Verga's development as a writer of fiction, but it demonstrates a desire to extend his provincial experience to a world of the past. It also demonstrates a definite commitment to the large-scale writing required of the novel. Later, he would discover that he had been aiming for depth rather than latitude in his early novels, seeking to know and describe things in passionately reconstructed detail.

Although in obedience to his father Verga attempted to study law, his efforts were in vain, and in 1861, once and for all, he abandoned the school of law in Catania. He did not, however, return immediately to writing. Eager to take part in the adventure of the newly unified country, he served in the National Guard for four years. Documentation of this period in his life is scarce. It is known that his unit was used by the northern establishment, which was now in control, to suppress peasant insurrection in Sicily at the cost of many lives, but there is no indication that Verga took part in the suppression.

In 1861, while in service, Verga wrote his second novel, the four-volume *Carbonari della montagna* (Mountain Police), which was published with private funds. This work was inspired by the poor in Sicily, whom he had ample occasion to observe for the first time when he and his family retreated to their country villa for fear of a cholera epidemic in Catania.

The year 1865 proved an important turning point in Verga's life. The young author moved to Florence and joined a group of the leading literary figures of the time. He began to measure himself against a much larger backdrop of events, culture, and creativity. This was the first move in what would become a recurrent pattern for Verga. Each year he would spend many months in the cultural centers of Florence, Milan, London, and Paris, then return home to the rural isolation of Sicily. He usually wrote about Sicily while sojourning in the literary gathering spots of Italy and the rest of Europe. He needed distance to give himself the objectivity necessary for his burgeoning *verismo*, which brutally and simply portrayed brutal simplicity.

Verga's move to Florence was occasioned by a literary tradition. The idiom of Florence is still to some degree considered the standard against which literary writing is measured, and Verga was following a long line of eminent authors who had gone to Florence to perfect their style. Although the Sicilian accent prevails in Verga's work, there is, especially in his early efforts, a distinctly Florentine flavor to his combination of elegant and casual words and expressions.

The early Florentine period produced *Una peccatrice* (A Sinful Woman) in 1866, *La ricamatrice* (The Embroideress) in 1869, and *Storia di una capinera* (Story of a Linnet) in 1871, somewhat artificial works that emulate the Florentine bourgeoisie and ignore the strong attraction of his native soil. Works of this period dwell on a more tranquil and less dramatic society than the Sicily Verga knew so well. His tone is moderate, and although he appears close to the French realistic authors he admired, he is not as basic as he would become in his more mature works.

In 1870 Rome became the capital of Italy but Milan was already the center for publishers, agents, writers, and the theater that it remains today. Verga moved to Milan and rapidly established himself as a promising young writer with a discreet but by no means irrelevant romantic life. He became the object of an envy and hostility amplified by the fierce and open antagonism of Carducci, who, in a letter to a mutual friend, advised her not to trust "that false Sicilian baron." Some critics, in deference to Italy's most famous poet, expressed the unflattering opinion that Verga might remain no more than "a promising writer." In 1880 Roberto Sacchetti, a fellow writer, described Verga as "one of the most prominent writers in society," praising his scrupulous attendance of society events. So even during these productive years in Milan, Verga had yet to convince the public and critics alike that an important new writer had appeared on the scene. *Eva, Eros, Tigre reale,* and *Primavera e altri racconti* (*Spring and Other Stories,* 1876) vacillate in theme and locale between urban Milan and the fierce, primitive Sicily that still fascinated Verga and that he still visited. Up to this point, the upper-class circles had the greater impact. Still, he began to be noted for his determination not to spare his readers one naturalistic detail, including graphic descriptions of love that went against local standards and were poorly tolerated by both readers and most of the influential critics.

Verga, in reaction, began to deploy his native talent to depict the harsh, primitive life of the lower classes in the South. He was already working on a style that would tell the tale of the impoverished countryside and its self-brutalizing inhabitants in all its starkness. Using neither dialect nor slang, he managed to capture the quality of both local speech and the mind behind the words, achieving verisimilitude rather than editorial exactness. Dialect is, after all, a romantic technique—it has a quaintness more akin to pastoral mannerism than to Verga's expressionist slashes.

VITA DEI CAMPI

In 1880 *Vita dei campi,* a collection of short stories, was published. The protagonists of *Vita dei campi* are, on the surface, bold and extroverted. Their behavior is far more theatrical than that of characters in Verga's earlier work and it is represented by a combination of straightforward, Hemingway-like vocal and physical action and primitive reflection. The characters are rigid and one-dimensional; often they are greedy, jealous, or violent. Their intolerable lives are uncomplicated. The code of behavior is demanding, and their rigid society offers them little in return for compliance. Several elements had by this time become typical of Verga's fictional universe—most important, the overwhelming role of destiny and the inability of his characters to change their circumstances. The stories present rituals, events, and gestures as a ballet of initiatives, provocations, and reactions that, according to the code, are inevitable.

The best-known work in this collection is "Cavalleria rusticana," a title often given to the entire book in translation. This tale met with an extraordinary degree of success. Turiddu returns from military service to discover that the woman he loves, Lola, has married the coachman, Alfio. The prose shuffles along unsubtly, but as direct in its intention as Turiddu, who watched as

> on Sundays she [Lola] stood on the gallery with her hands on her stomach to show everyone the big gold rings her husband had given her as a gift. Turiddu kept on passing, again and again, on the street, with a pipe in his mouth and his hands in his pockets, with a mien of indifference, making eyes at the girls, but deep inside it gnawed at him that Lola's husband had all that gold and that she pretended not to notice him when he passed by.
>
> (*Cavalleria rusticana, and Other Stories*, p. 33)

Turiddu begins to court another woman, Santuzza, but Lola perversely draws him back. Blinded by jealousy, Santuzza reveals their affair to Alfio. The two men challenge each other to a duel. Although Turiddu appears to be winning, Alfio blinds him with a handful of earth and kills him. Significantly, it is the dry soil of the land that actually and symbolically dooms not only Turiddu, but also an entire network of Verga's subjects.

"Cavalleria rusticana" appeared in three different versions. As a short story it met with the critical esteem of Luigi Pirandello, as well as praise from authoritative critics. But not until Verga adapted the short story for the stage and it was performed in 1884 with Eleonora Duse did it become an enormous popular success and earn him instant celebrity as the poet of primitive Sicily. Many reasons have been given for the work's instant success. One, no doubt, was the presence of Duse, the greatest actress of the era. Another was that Turin was a northern city oriented toward French culture; thus it is not surprising that a story drawn from a distant, unknown southern locale caused a romantic stir. The customs of the Sicilians, who had been a part of Italy for only a few years, had a type of folkloric appeal that excited an almost colonial interest. Verga presented an exotic reality with a documentary technique that was new in the history of Italian literature. He may well have been regarded as a type of literary Christopher Columbus. Sicily held the same fascination for many Italians that the color, beauty, primitiveness, and legends of Africa and India held for English audiences of the same period.

Verga's style, or, rather, absence of style, was also relevant to this success. Although, as he often admitted, he had derived his literary method from Flaubert and Zola, his brutal *verismo* so advanced the cause of naturalism that audiences were shocked by the new technique. It presented bare facts directly, with no attempt at interpretation, no ideology, and no official aesthetics. Italian literature in general was unfamiliar with naturalism, and the volcanic tremor that Verga caused with "Cavalleria rusticana" was translated into a huge popular success—a success that was further augmented when Pietro Mascagni adapted the short story as a libretto for an opera (1890).

"La Lupa" ("The She-Wolf") later attracted the attention of several writers, including D. H. Lawrence and Pirandello. "La Lupa" is the nickname of Pina, witchlike in appearance but a brave, sensual, full woman who, "feeling the flesh afire beneath her clothes," falls in love with the young and strong Nanni. At harvest time she works furiously in the fields to be close to him. One evening she reveals herself to him, saying, "It's you I want. You who are beautiful . . . I want you!" Nanni does not want her, but rather her young daughter, Maricchia. Pina, desperate to have Nanni near her, accepts him in her house as the husband of her daughter. Her passion flares even more fiercely. The heat reaches her son-in-law. Nanni tries to resist her silent call by appealing to religion, but finally, on a summer afternoon, Pina, overwhelmed by the fire in her flesh, easily seduces him. Questioned by his wife, Maricchia, Nanni acknowledges that he was unable to ignore the afternoon call of the she-wolf. Shortly thereafter he is kicked in the chest by a mule. Although he almost dies, he later recovers. Nanni redoubles his efforts to escape the she-wolf's spell and his own guilt. Desperate, he resorts to going at her with an ax in an open field. But as she lies waiting for him in the field the story ends, and the reader is not told whether he brings his ax down or whether first he lays it down beside them.

This story is typical of Verga at that time. Events are determined and unavoidable. Nanni feels he has no choice but to try to kill Pina. Pina, whose nature it is to face danger, is bound to defy moral conventions and thus provoke violence. In the acceptance of their destinies these characters realize their tragic possibilities. Their lives, in all other respects irrelevant, are momentarily ennobled, if only in the pages of literature. It is clear that none of them will leave any other mark of their passage on earth, no matter how hard, bloody, and painful their struggle to survive. This aspect is central to Verga's poetics. Nanni, La Lupa, Turiddu, and Santuzza are all seen in an exceptional moment of their lives—that of the extreme, unavoidable gesture that will seal their fate. Verga seems to believe that revelation occurs only in these exceptional moments. His technique is to force his characters painfully and desperately toward their extreme limit—each one will either mete out destruction or be destroyed. The notion that revelation can spring only from tragedy is one that Verga shares with other writers from Feodor Dostoevsky on. (Arthur Miller's *View from the Bridge* demonstrates this concept in modern Italo-American terms; his play is about the arrival of two Sicilian immigrants who seem to step out of Verga's pages—in 1956.) But in Verga's tragedy, unlike Dostoevsky's, there is neither consolation nor redemption. According to Lawrence in *Phoenix:*

> The Sicilian—in our sense of the word—does not have any soul. He just hasn't got our sort of subjective consciousness, the soulful idea of himself.

A closer examination of the short stories in *Vita dei campi* will show that Lawrence's observation applies to some, but not all, of Verga's writing. True, no Verga character is able to change the course of his life. But there are also stories that occur predominantly in the mind of the protagonist, to whom acting and reacting mean very little, leaving Verga to describe only the primitive emotions of these people. Such is the case with "Jeli il pastore" and "Rosso Malpelo."

"Jeli il pastore" (Jeli the Shepherd) is the story of a peasant boy who lives entirely alone. He is deeply attached to the horses that he takes care of and considers them his only friends. At times during the summer months he enjoys the company of a rich boy, Don Alfonso. After the death of his father Jeli, alone and defenseless, wanders with his herd for a long time, leaving behind a little girl, Mara, whom he has befriended. When he returns he finds she has grown up to be a pretty young woman and is about to move to a distant town. While Jeli, in his solitude, continues to think of her, she becomes engaged to Massaro Neri's son. Jilted by him because she has been involved with Don Alfonso, she encourages Jeli to marry her. Once they are married everyone tells Jeli she is continuing to see Don Alfonso, but he does not believe them. At a picnic dinner while Jeli is shearing his sheep he asks Mara not to dance with Don Alfonso. She does so anyway and, as he sees her languidly abandon herself in Don Alfonso's arms, he suddenly understands their relations. He rises and cuts Don Alfonso's throat with a single stroke.

Here, tragedy occurs in Jeli's unprecedented departure from his introverted and solitary life, in his inexperienced interplay with other people. In Jeli's primitive, innocent interaction with animals and nature, there are no antagonists. Tragedy results from a sudden imbalance that his unexercised, weak will can neither resolve nor avert. Jeli is abruptly uprooted from the pastoral world he knows and can control, and is thrust by desire out into the world of the "others" and the village, a relatively complex society to which he is unable to adapt. For Jeli, like other protagonists of Verga, simplicity is both a virtue and a damnation—he is noble yet too simple to be saved.

"Rosso Malpelo" is both the title and the protagonist of another story in *Vita dei campi*. In order to protect himself, Rosso, who works in a sand quarry, must be mean and conniving. His co-workers mistreat him, saying that he is only allowed to work out of charity, since his father died there when a large sand pillar caved in. Rosso despises them all because they did nothing to rescue his father, whose death he now wishes to avenge. He befriends a lame boy and teaches him what he has learned from life. "Fortunate are the dead . . . they do not suffer any longer." After his little friend dies of tuberculosis, Rosso is truly alone. He decides that it would be best if they were both dead. When the men at the quarry decide to explore a tunnel, they enlist Rosso, whom surely no one will miss, who picks up "his father's tools" and enters the tunnel, never to return.

Unlike Jeli's, every aspect of Rosso's life is motivated by his social circumstances. The abject conditions and the intricate relations within the mine are like a net that is thrown over a captured animal, that determines its every movement, that is accepted by Rosso as neither more nor less than life. Rosso has no quarrel with his gloomy, limited universe. He knows he must struggle to survive. Feelings of solidarity or hopes of change are alien to his experience; concepts such as "class" or "group" are unfathomable. Given the circumstances Rosso Malpelo, living or dead, is neither better nor worse off than any of his colleagues. Rosso's final condition appears quietly inevitable from the beginning.

Many critics have indicated that when an author takes such pains to emphasize social conditions at the expense of the internal life of the individual, he can provide only a symbolic representation of reality. Verga, however, stalked each of his subjects with the determination of an anthropologist on the lookout for new evidence. There is no doubt that *Vita dei campi* was a step forward in Verga's literary evolution—although not necessarily of the type that critics of his time could immediately appreciate. They felt that Verga's writing was uneven in quality, that his urge to find new ways of understanding his characters forced him to experiment and consequently affected the coherence of his form. But Verga felt he had to pay the price—that is, to search for a different way of writing detached from literature, formally unpleasant, closer to the elementary condition of life—in order to lead his readers to the new territory he had discovered and wanted to explore.

NEDDA

In 1874 Verga's *Nedda* was published. The plot of the short novel is as uncomplicated as the life of its protagonist. Nedda is a humble Sicilian girl, an olive picker whose mother is gravely ill. She accepts her poverty and loneliness with fatalistic resignation; life has always taken this form and will never change. Her mother's condition worsens, and eventually she dies. Nedda meanwhile has met Janu, who prunes olive trees. They find solace in each other and soon Nedda is pregnant. In order to make more money and eventually marry, Janu decides to work some distance away. However, Janu falls victim to malaria (which at that time in Sicily was as common as influenza is today) and dies shortly thereafter. Nedda remains alone to give birth to a child, who slowly dies of malnutrition.

Verga was as yet uncertain about the long novel of the French and English tradition. His style and talent were better suited to the shorter narrative form. For his sparse depiction of southern misery, the short story proved a convenient form, allowing him to experiment with a comment-free, implied relationship between author and character. Nedda almost never speaks. Dark and silent, vulnerable yet powerful, introverted in her thought, she communicates with an unseen protagonist—"il destino," or Fate. It is the writer who, moving around her like a documentary camera, observes and eloquently draws attention to her morbid acceptance of disaster. The story is a poetic but detached anthropological study of poor womanhood and, in particular, of the poverty of women's status in the bleak landscape of the South.

Verga is coolly indifferent as he follows Nedda through a sad and tormented life of unconscious dignity. She is frozen in time, in the pages of literature as on film, facing adversity the way a tree stands in the wind, braced by an unexpressed but nevertheless stubborn determination to survive. And Verga's stoic, unapologetic style validates the steadfastness of his heroine. Nedda is the first complete character of substance that Verga created—new to his writing, new to Italian literature, and new to Verga's public. His friend and colleague, Luigi Capuana, wrote, "I think that he has discovered an almost untouched mine in our literature."

Nedda and Padron 'Ntoni (the protagonist of his first great novel, *I Malavoglia*), were born twins in the mind of their author. A Sicilian fisherman who owns a small boat, 'Ntoni is pitted in a savage battle, in which there can be neither success nor surrender, against land, sea, family, and friends. Like Nedda, 'Ntoni bears his desperate circumstances with a stubborn unspoken determination. He confronts a literal and figurative sea of troubles with an animalistic will to survive. The landscape around both characters is as unyielding as their resources are meager in an endless fight against people, nature, and time. Like Nedda, Padron 'Ntoni and his family are imbued with an immense, almost genetic fatigue that precludes any social or geographic mobility, but that also precludes surrender. To understand the nature of this family's struggle is to understand Verga's aesthetic of identity.

I MALAVOGLIA

Discussing the project of *I Malavoglia*, Verga wrote to his publisher in Milan, "What I have in my mind is . . . something like a storm of the imagination around life and existence." Verga's highest ambition was to extend, over a span of several novels, a phantasmagorical bridge from the poor to the rich, from the elementary levels of society to the sophisticated milieu of the entrenched middle class and even as far as the nobility. He thought of writing this work in five unrelated volumes: the poor fisherman (*I Malavoglia*), the worker who becomes wealthy (*Mastro-don Gesualdo*), and three novels that were never realized about a noble family and the international set of Italy and Paris.

The Malavoglia family falls into the category of "i vinti" (the defeated) to which Verga devoted his entire human comedy. The family name means "love of misfortune" or "ill will," and it is apt, although the members of this family are described with a certain affection by the novel's semi-educated, semi-detached narrator:

> Master 'Ntoni's family was set out like the fingers of a hand. First came the old man himself, the thumb, who commanded when to feast and when to fast; then his son Bastianazzo, big and burly as the St. Christopher painted under the arch of the fish market in the city of Catania. . . . Then came 'Ntoni's wife, La Longa (The Long One), a tiny woman who kept busy weaving, salting anchovies, and bearing children, like a good housewife. And last the grandchildren, in order of age. 'Ntoni, the eldest, a loafer of twenty. . . . Then Luca who, his grandfather always said, had more good sense than his older brother; . . . and Mena, short for Filomena. . . . After Mena came Alessio, or Alessi for short, who was the very image of his grandfather . . . and finally Lia, short for Rosalia, who was not yet fish, flesh, or fowl. On Sundays, when they walked into church one behind the other, it looked like a procession.
>
> (*The House by the Medlar Tree*, pp. 7–8)

The Malavoglias live in a poor Sicilian fishing village, in a house that stands next to a medlar tree, the very symbol of the roots and branches of their lineage, as the house is the symbol of family unity. They are prosperous, not rich, and are guardedly respected by the much poorer people of the town. They own a small fishing boat called *La Provvidenza (Providence)*, which introduces the ironic theme. Padron 'Ntoni, the elderly grandfather who heads the clan, buys a stock of beans on credit, to export them for what he imagines will be a tidy profit. But "on an ugly Sunday in September" the *Providence* goes under during a storm and the cargo is lost.

Mena, the second-youngest granddaughter, is left without a dowry. She can no longer marry since the family must repay its debt by selling its boat and the house all its members were born in. Luca departs for the service and eventually perishes at sea. Young 'Ntoni, the old man's grandson, leaves the village only to come home even poorer, in rags. He joins a group of smugglers and is arrested for wounding an official. Lia, the youngest and most marriageable daughter, loses all chances of a husband after her reputation is ruined at her brother's trial. She has no choice but to leave town; eventually she becomes a prostitute. Padron 'Ntoni, crushed by events, asks to be taken to the hospital, where he dies alone. The house is repurchased by Alessi, the youngest grandson, who takes Padron 'Ntoni's place in the family.

The individuality of the Malavoglia family resides in the clan rather than any one member, and the members borrow their personal traits from the clan. The language of the family is in code, an elemental, antique code—a mixture of proverbs and commonplaces filtered through the received "knowledge" of the clan. Security is minimal but well defined: a trade or a house. And when this precarious "stability" is jeopardized by old 'Ntoni's tragic whim, treacherous Destiny itself rebels. The possible benefits of such a daring gamble are so minimal, especially in view of the dismal consequences, that the entire undertaking seems all the more pathetic. When Padron 'Ntoni loses his son to the sea, he has risked and lost everything. Most sacrilegiously he has compromised the security of his family. He is a passive Old Man of the Sea, finally confronting his ever-present adversary, whose waves have roared their challenge to him in the deep darkness of the endless seaside night. But this vicarious confrontation leads to the most visceral defeat. His insubordination to the code of life is doomed from the start by a social, economic, religious, and ultimately fatal rigidity—a rigidity rooted in the arid fields that rule his destiny.

When *I Malavoglia* was finally completed, Verga was emphatic in describing his work as "a sincere and honest effort" to portray what critics have correctly identified as a Darwinian position. At the same time, the geographically schizophrenic Verga celebrated the North's industrial progress and positivist philosophy. How does he reconcile this new intellectual optimism with a determinism that views life as inevitable defeat? Verga replied:

> My job is to observe and he who observes such a spectacle [the fight for life] can barely manage to extricate himself from the story even for a moment or two, can barely succeed in offering a dispassionate representation, let alone attempt to change reality. He can only offer the attempt to keep everything in its real place, without touching up or coloring the facts.
>
> (*Phoenix*, p. 249)

In other words, unadorned reality produces a dramatic truth that in itself is sufficient to enthrall the reader. This is the essence of *verismo*. Like a painter who finds endless fascination in a monochrome landscape, Verga describes the tragically meaningless, Sisyphean task of living, and like a type of magic primitivist, reproduces the unsophisticated workings of the local mind. D. H. Lawrence put it thus: "Verga tried to convey this . . . breathless muddle of the peasant mind. When one is used to it, it is amusing, and a new movement in deliberate consciousness" (*Phoenix*, p. 250).

Verga succeeded technically in *I Malavoglia* at something he was unable to do in *Nedda*. The emotional participation of the author–narrator in *Nedda* gives way in *I Malavoglia* to a detached, narrated presentation of speech, which became the characteristic style of Verga. He called it "free indirect discourse," halfway between dialogue and narration. Traces of this technique can be found later in Cesare Pavese and Eleo Vittorini—and in James Joyce. Leo Spitzer maintained that Verga's originality lies in his way of filtering narration through the minds of his characters. Verga does not attempt to distinguish between the narrator's and the characters' points of view: the difference in mentalities can be detected in the irony that pervades the book. Thus despite his impersonal attitude, the invisible narrator infuses every word of the novel with his presence, a lyric gruffness that ensures a real empathy.

Watching the lawyer advise them about their bankruptcy, the narrator presents the family's amazement that the lawyer "talked for such a long time without even spitting once, or scratching his head" as an objective fact. He does not try to express their psychology, their subjective feelings. By not saying it directly, Verga manages to say it emphatically with the ambiguous objectivity that became his stylistic signature. In church, Verga objectively states that Mary Angel, the barkeep, "has lost no business," because she takes her customers to mass with her, but leaves her blind uncle behind because "it is no sin if he doesn't go"; and the narrator agrees by *not telling* us she felt or thought this.

On a sad, cold evening a squall is followed by a gentle rain. Here Verga manages a supreme blend of the voices of the narrator and the characters.

> Uncle Crocifisso was on his knees before the altar of Our Lady of the Sorrows with his beads in his hand, and he was reciting the verses of the rosary in a nasal voice which would have touched the heart of the devil himself. Between one Ave Maria and the next everybody talked about the lupin deal and the Provvidenza out at sea, and La Longa, who was going to be left with five children on her hands.
>
> "Nowadays," said Master Cipolla, shrugging his shoulders, "everybody is discontented with his lot and wants to take heaven by storm."
>
> "The fact is that to-day will be a bad day for the Malavoglia," Mastro Zuppiddo announced.
>
> "I shouldn't like to be in Bastianazzo's shoes," said Piedipapera.
>
> Evening came down sad and cold. From time to time a squall came from the north, followed by fine, gentle rain. It was one of those evenings when, if your boat is safely drawn up with its hull nice and dry on the sand, you enjoy sitting with the youngster on your knees, watching the steam rising from the pot and listening to your wife's slippers padding about the house behind you. That Sunday—which promised to last all

Monday as well—all the idlers preferred spending the evening at the tavern, and even the doorposts seemed to enjoy reflecting the warmth of the fire, and Uncle Santoro, who had been put outside to rest his chin on his knees and hold out his hand to beg, had moved close in, to warm his back a bit, too.

(*The House by the Medlar Tree*, p. 28)

In *I Malavoglia* Verga departs from Zola and Balzac, his acknowledged masters. He offers no subjective justification or introspective analysis of his characters. They act on the gloomy page as they do in life, in response to circumstances that they cannot control. Their grandiose obsession, to continue in spite of continuous frustration, is observed with wide open but unastonished eyes.

For this reason, in *I Malavoglia*, Verga places the action in an undefined remoteness beyond individual dates and events. In this eternal sameness, history is absent. The reader is only vaguely aware of geographic location and, in a general, indirect way, of period. The culture of the region is so constant in its tradition that we do not notice the absence of a specific era. Not that the cast of *I Malavoglia* is mankind or human destiny in general; rather, the story is a specific instance of economic Darwinism.

But Verga's drama is less scientific than poetic, and not devoid of an affectionately ironic glint. This is conveyed by a style as impoverished as the Sicilian village itself. Verga's characters, instead of communicating directly, speak in proverbs and commonplaces that have become meaningless through unending repetition. These expressions are covered with a veneer of experience but, more than anything else, they resemble a dreamlike, childlike memorization of reality. He understands that the rigors of living off a sea "which can unleash a storm as suddenly as a shot from a prickly-pear tree" produces a fog of superstitions, clichés, and inane sayings by which the villagers, not unlike the proverb

mongerers of George Orwell's *1984*, grope toward communication:

You can't sail a boat without steering.

You've got to be a priest before you can be Pope.

Work at what you know. You won't get rich, but you'll make a living.

Do what your father did before you or you'll finish badly.

(p. 8)

This stale blend of memories and platitudes has grown out of the arid soil. As undifferentiated as stalks of dry grass, the oral expressions, like the exhausted land, can barely sustain the population. It is a drained, insubstantial language that barely breathes. Of the master of the household, who inherited these proverbs from his elders, Verga's smiling, grim narrator says:

He had many other sensible sayings as well. That was why the house of the Malavoglia prospered and Master 'Ntoni was considered in town a most profound man. And he would have been made a town counselor if Don Silvestro the wily town secretary had not told everybody that 'Ntoni was a rotten reactionary, a lover of Bourbons, and a conspirator in the plot to restore King Bomba's son. So that 'Ntoni could push the village around the way he did his family. To which 'Ntoni retorted, "The head of a household can't sleep when he wants."

(p. 8)

It is surprising that while so many critics wade through philosophical, sociological, and anthropological discussions of Verga's pessimism, relatively little has been said of his ironic humor. Here, while waiting for the ship to come in, Mr. Piedipapera (Mr. Pigeontoe) makes one pronouncement after another:

"Since the revolution the fish have become spiteful."

"What's the revolution got to do with it? The

1554

anchovies have *always* known a storm is coming a day ahead of time," said Master 'Ntoni.

"I'll tell you what the trouble is," said Mr. Cipolla [Mr. Onion]. "It's those damn steamers going backwards and forwards, beating the sea with their paddle-wheels! The fish are frightened and disappear. What do you expect?"

La Locca's son, listening to the conversation, gaping and scratching his head: "If that was the case, there wouldn't be any more fish at Syracuse or Messina either, because that's where the steamers go. But they take fish away from Messina and Syracuse on the railway by the ton!"

"Idiot!" he said. "Keep quiet when your elders and betters are talking!"

The lad went off, shouting and punching himself on the head, as if to show that everyone took him for a dunce just because he was La Locca's son.

(p. 22)

Occasionally even in Greek drama there is a shaft of humor beaming into the dark plot; so Verga's chorus of local gossips have their fun at the expense of miserable neighbors. Once more we are presented with a real name that has a wackily symbolic meaning (literally, Mr. Fly), who lives with his donkey's flies.

"He cooks and washes and mends his own shirts. All he needs is a skirt and he could be a woman."

"When he gets married," Mina said, "his wife will drive the donkey cart and he'll stay at home and diaper the kids."

Nunziata said, "I wouldn't throw him out if they gave him to *me*."

(p. 21)

Even nature cannot always be taken seriously:

The gossips in the street had dispersed and, as the village gradually went to sleep, you began to hear the sea snoring away, not many yards away at the end of the little street. Every now and then the snore rose to a snort, like somebody rolling over in bed.

(p. 25)

This is the same sea that grandfather 'Ntoni's fortune was riding on deep in the distance, as he watched and muttered, "What an ugly sea!"

On the day that the news arrives of the sinking of his ship and the loss of his investment, the imagery becomes whimsically diabolical; the wind blows "as though the Devil were behind it . . . howled as if all the cats of the village were on the roof . . . the day dawned darker than the soul of Judas . . . a distant sail scudded through the mist as though the Devil were after it." But, in a quick modulation to an appropriately mournful key, the women "made the sign of the cross at the sight of the ship with the poor devils on board. . . . 'Devils are in the air today,' said the mistress of the tavern, Sister Mary Angel, crossing herself with holy water. 'A day like this can drive a person to sin.'" What begins to emerge is no longer a writer intrigued by his innovations in style and subject matter, but an artist with a mature control over his creative destiny. He has variety of tone, dynamic imagery, technique—with a sure grasp of them all.

Verga's sketches are drawn with only a few strokes, but they are bold and clear. Here is the wife of the chemist (who, in the unecumenical eyes of the town, is a radical "Protestant *and* Jew") at the funeral of Bastianazzo, who went down with 'Ntoni's cargo: "looking so stolid 'you would take her for the corpse itself. . . . That's why they called her The Lady.'" His imagery essentially unifies the work. The Malavoglia house, in jeopardy because of the sinking, suddenly becomes a "house leaking at every joint." Each image is dipped in the brine of the theme.

But it is the ending, justifiably famous in Italy, that shows what never ceases to stand out in Verga's work: his ability to distill not only the whole work, but also the unspoken sorrow that informs it and the landscape, into one short scene. Young 'Ntoni, just out of jail, returns late at night in order not to be seen by the neighbors, who would make the family miserable if they knew he had come home.

> "There's a home for you here if you want it. There's a bed for you in there."
>
> "No," 'Ntoni answered. "I must go away. Mother's bed, which she wetted with her tears when I wanted to go away, was in there. Do you remember the conversations we used to have in the evening while the anchovies were being salted? And how Nunziata asked us riddles? And Lia and mother were both there, and you could hear voices all over the village, as though we were one big family. I didn't understand then, and I wanted to go away, but now I understand, and I've got to go away."
>
> He stared at the ground as he spoke, with his head buried in his shoulders. Alessi flung his arms round him.
>
> "Good-bye!" said 'Ntoni. "You see that I'm right to go, because I can't stay here. Good-bye, and forgive me, all of you!"
>
> (p. 246)

He gobbles down a bowl of soup, which turns to poison in his stomach because he has to leave. "The others hardly dared breathe, because their hearts were caught in a vice, and they realized that what 'Ntoni said was right."

Lawrence calls *I Malavoglia* a great novel "in spite of" the flood of "savage and tragic pity he poured upon the humble fisher-folk . . . whether they asked for it or not." Verga's people "are not intellectual but neither was Hector." And is there not a Homeric quality in the parting of the younger 'Ntoni, who returns but, like Hector, must go?

In the closing pages of the novel Verga achieves a stunning irony concerning the ever present proverbs that have been the old man's excuse for thinking and communicating. As his life draws to its dismal close, old 'Ntoni, "a graveyard raven," goes about "bent over double," randomly reciting proverbs completely out of any context, as though they were a religionless litany:

> "Fetch the axe for the stricken tree!" he would say; or: "You can't fall in the water with-

out getting wet!" or: "Flies buzz round a skinny horse!" If anyone asked him why he was everlasting wandering about, he would answer: "Hunger drives the wolf from the forest!" or: "A starving dog doesn't fear the stick!"

> (p. 229)

But standing by themselves, set blankly against the landscape, these apparently vapid utterances develop a yet more complex irony. Without the cluttered primitive mind vainly trying to order them, without feeble attempts at thinking to hinder their hidden poetic sense, the commonplaces take on a meaning of their own. They even apply to old 'Ntoni's condition. *He* is the "stricken tree" that stood by the house that symbolized the family and its roots. *He* had to "fall in the water," whose wetness he forgot when the ship, his son, and the family security went under. The chorus of gossips, like "flies, buzz around" his skinny frame, which has carried the burden of his being like a horse. The hunger "that drives the wolf from the forest" is the spiritual and physical hunger that finally drives him out into the open, wandering out of the forest of his confusion and his family's tangled emotions. No wonder he stands in the street like "a starving dog" and does not fear "the stick" of outrageous fortune. Verga has subtly changed keys and shown us that there is sense in what was apparent nonsense, and he modulates into compassion for these statements that are now not nearly as empty as the belly growling in accompaniment.

It was not until 1948, when Luchino Visconti directed a film based on *I Malavoglia*, *La terra trema* (The Trembling Earth), that Verga's innovative point of view was reconfirmed in the Italian creative process. Visconti listens and records with no emotional intervention, so that the characters are compelled by other motives than those of their hungers, which they do not fathom. They act as necessity dictates and it is left to the author, or "auteur," to observe and record the events artistically, with no attempt at rationalization. The structure of Verga's narrative reminds one of the work of a talented cameraman. The frames move slowly, inexorably following sequences of events that the camera is powerless to influence. Verga's style corresponds to the lives of his characters; it is brutal and direct, forging a hard, sparse inventory of words, bare as the cupboards of the people, meant only to keep the narrative alive. It is what would become known as *scrittura povera* ("poor" writing) and is the unique, inimitable feature of Giovanni Verga's art.

When, in 1881, *I Malavoglia* was published in Milan, the popular and critical response was equally spare in its response. Verga that year was an enthusiast of the Universal Exhibition, a world's fair of industry and progress that fired intellectuals of Milan with heady optimism: the Sicily that Verga described in such abundance of harsh detail appeared remote and incomprehensible. But Verga continued to be an observer who, while not participating emotionally in events, ruthlessly went on to record the bright and the dark in the knowledge that sense could come from their interplay.

NOVELLE RUSTICANE

After *Storia di una capinera*, a semipopular romance in epistolary form that relates the sentimental adventures of two innocent schoolgirls, Verga beat an emphatic retreat from the fiction of elegant intrigue to sketches drawn from actual experience, from the landscape overshadowed by Mount Etna and its environs, still lacquered by the volcano's last eruption.

Novelle rusticane (Brief Novels of the Country) was published in Turin in 1883, two years after the appearance of *I Malavoglia*. It is a pivotal work in his development, appearing after his romantic "northern" novels and the very different collection of short stories *Vita dei campi*, written three years before and centered on the poor southern life. The *Novelle* in

turn foreshadow his later masterpiece *Mastro-don Gesualdo*. His approach is becoming less tentative. His lyricism is burlier, tougher. He distills his ever present societal notions into brief dramatic conflicts. The dozen stories in the book average about fifteen pages each. But these *novelle* are indeed novels in brief, written in the freewheeling, episodic, near-epic sprawl of the long novel. He also seems to be sketching characters he will later paint in deeper chromatic tones. His brutal observational technique works to stunning effect. Luckily for English readers the volume was excellently translated by D. H. Lawrence, as *Little Novels of Sicily.*

The *Novelle rusticane* begin around 1860, with the arrival of the king of Naples, Francis the son of Bomba (sic). In "Cos'é il re" ("So Much for the King"), Old Cosimo drives a sedan chair for royalty, returning to Sicily after Garibaldi's revolt. It is a great day for old Cosimo and his first moment of glory occurs when his neighbors pay him a visit to find out "what it was like." The years pass and he treasures his moment in the sun when the king and queen rode on his sedan chair, pulled by the donkeys who still live with him. Then, one day, the king demands the donkeys in lieu of taxes.

There is in general a heavy political content to this book. The opening story, "Il reverendo" ("His Reverence"), could well be the most devastatingly anticlerical piece ever written. The town priest swindles, connives, seduces; he upbraids the people during their confessions; he uses casuistry when they demand justice. He virtually enslaves his niece, whom he keeps in his sexual thrall. They are both living in mortal sin; the girl is terrified but the priest barely notices. The poor are resigned, in their proverb-ridden way, to the fact that they can do nothing "because the pitcher can't win against the stone, and we can't go to Law with His Reverence because he is the one who *is* the Law." His Reverence is his own lawyer and his own prosecutor. He is respected by the powerful and feared by all. If "anyone mentioned his niece," with whom he was sleeping, he would, in effect, threaten him with excommunication, by "refusing . . . Mass and confession."

But the story has the quality of a miniature epic. Time passes, Garibaldi's Thousand ride through, and the town seeks revenge on the priest, who must "hide like a rat in a hole because the peasants want to do him in." After the revolution, as more time passes, the peasants become literate and "reckon up accounts better than you could yourself" (as the narrator tells us in tones of warning). The judges begin to fear public opinion and "to dispense judgment like Solomon." The priest grows old and his bitterness turns the quantities of food he consumes to gall; while the brother he had left to lead a "hard life eating bread and onion, digested better than an ostrich." His wife-niece, still unmarried but ruling his house, torments him whenever they commit mortal sin, saying he ought to be excommunicated for betraying the pope. He is left scorned and hated, ranting, "There's no religion, no justice, no nothing left. . . . They don't want to do the will of God, that is all there is to it!"

"I galantuomini" ("The Gentry") is a strange, amoral tale about the early "gentry" who have earned the title only because they know how "to read and write. That's their trouble," says the narrator. "They hook you by your name and your family's name and those that gave you birth and raised you, all with that beak of a pen of theirs; then you'll never get out from under their books! You're crucified with debt!" But when the volcano erupts, the peasants have nothing to lose and with their hands in their pockets they watch the homes of the gentry being buried by lava. The uppity daughter of Piddu, a member of the gentry, flings herself "into the arms of the stable boy, now [that] she has lost all hope of getting married and lives way off in the lonely country in miserable poverty." When Piddu opens his heart to a benevolent confessor, the priest says, "At least *you* can let it out. The poor folks who can't read or write are afraid to tell these things for fear of jail! They can't read or write enough to defend themselves!"

"Libertà" ("Liberty") is a violent story of public vengeance in which the outraged peasants revolt during the momentary liberation of Sicily. Verga's extraordinary reluctance to weight the narrative toward a sympathy for his family interests is remarkable. In this story, the poor exact a hideous vengeance on the gentry, who have gulled, bludgeoned, and ruled them. An ironic chorus, "Hurray for Liberty," echoes with careful randomness, throughout the story. The prose becomes tense and harsh like the crowd, a turbulent sea in front of the gentry's club.

> "You first, baron, because your foreman beat us bloody!"
> "Now you, you rich glutton, who ate our lives."
> "Now you, constable, who used the law only on the poor."

And they continue to kill until "the blood smoked and went drunk. Down with landowners, Hurray for Liberty!" Then there is a cameo appearance by a fornicating priest "who used to preach hell to those who stole a crust of bread. . . . Don't kill me, I'm in mortal sin! The mortal sin being his housekeeper whose father sold her to the priest when she was fourteen during the famine and who, ever since, has been filling the streets with hungry brats." So much for the enemy. But then the tide of blood rises to pitiless levels. The crowd disembowels the vineyard owner, then, crazed with power and guilt, kills the eleven-year-old child of a lawyer, "blond as gold." Someone's lame justification is that he would have become another lawyer. A baroness is thrown off her balcony with her child in her arms. "Hurray for Liberty!" says the narrator.

And liberty is achieved for a few days. Verga syncopates time and history by condensing all the horror and cynicism of postrevolutionary confusion into two pages, which not only cover Italy's actual political turmoil but also hint at the French reign of terror. "They looked at one another suspiciously, each thinking what his neighbor had on his conscience." They did not want to go without mass on Sundays "like dogs." With the club of the gentry boarded up, "they no longer knew where to get their masters' orders." "They began to divide up the goods and the fields, counting on their fingers," calculating their shares. Liberty meant sharing, "but which of the surveyors and lawyers was left to do the job accurately?" If anyone made a mistake, if "anyone wanted to eat enough for two he was killed as if he were the gentry."

The generals arrive to mete out justice, shoot a few of the exuberantly vicious peasants, and make peace. The gentry, who cannot live without the peasants to work the land, are reconciled with the peasants, who need the literacy of the gentry. The son of the druggist killed by the peasants steals the wife of his father's killer. Life goes on much as before. All this is told in eleven pages. Verga, making up for the lapses of his continental romantic novels, was now committed to straightforward reality; he had no time to waste, no imagery to squander, no metaphors to glamorize past or present history. He was writing toward future novels that would take into more detailed account the psychology that was becoming his poetics. The characters in his great novel *Mastro-don Gesualdo* are prefigured in the *Novelle rusticane*, stories that, in their cascading surge of persons and episodes, are full-length novels in embryo. Verga examines his characters, including the priest of filth, who will resurface again and again, until he not only understands them but, by the grace of his maturing art, allows the possibility of compassion for them. We even see in the short piece called "La roba" ("Property") an illiterate laborer whose ambition and business talent bring him success and sorrow. He is no doubt a study for the subject of Verga's next and greatest novel, *Mastro-don Gesualdo*.

MASTRO-DON GESUALDO

Mastro-don Gesualdo was written by Verga between 1881 and 1889. Verga's masterpiece has been compared in scope and energy with Balzac's best works. Italian society at that time was suddenly faced with a degree of what today would be called upward mobility. Verga, acutely aware of the social and economic mechanisms that made this mobility possible, pitted the vital emerging bourgeoisie against the fading aristocracy unable to adjust to a new era. This theme has fascinated Italian authors from Pirandello to Giuseppe Tomasi Di Lampedusa, but it was Verga who pioneered it.

With *Mastro-don Gesualdo,* Verga became the first Italian author to give literary life to the emerging southern bourgeoisie. Gesualdo Motta, the protagonist of the work, is a poor bricklayer who, by dint of hard work, becomes a contractor and then a wealthy and powerful landowner. "Mastro-don" means worker-gentleman.

Gesualdo has one raison d'être—to work to increase his personal fortune. Never shedding his straightforward, crude approach to life, he seeks to become part of the ruling class by marrying the frail Bianca Trao, who belongs to the most aristocratic (but also the poorest) family in town. The marriage, however, is a pitiful mismatching of class, style, and temperament—a sad parody of the differences in birth and education between Mastro-don Gesualdo, the nearly illiterate mason, and the delicate noblewoman he has wed. Still, he urges his daughter, who is passionately in love with an impoverished man, to marry the elderly duke of Leyra. She plays her new role as a duchess with a vengeance and consumes her father's fortune. She becomes distant and hostile toward him, as well as superior in a "you asked for it" manner. Don Gesualdo, grieved by the amount of money squandered in his mansion and begrudged to his land that, like him, is being scorned and neglected, awaits his death, relegated to a secluded room. He dies alone, hardly tolerated, and is finally abandoned by all.

> Don Gesualdo was thinking how much good money must be slipping away; all that eating and drinking at his daughter's expense, devouring the dowry he had given her, the rich land he had brooded over for so long, night and day, and had measured out in his sleep, and won at last acre by acre, day by day, denying himself the very bread from his mouth; the house, everything, everything, everything would slip through their hands. Who would be there to defend his property after his death?—his poor possessions!
>
> (Cecchetti trans., p. 315)

Verga's art seems to ride apace with Italy's evolution. In *Mastro-don Gesualdo* Verga's world view becomes more complex, enriched by an awareness of Italy's new and varied social clashes. The psychology also becomes more complex and, as Verga tells us, the languages of the various classes partake of "the nuances and the ambiguities of sentiments, all the artifices of words." As different environments demand different manners, as different occasions demand different attire, so Verga's "artifice of words" is dressed up or down in tone according to the company it keeps. In his introduction Giovanni Cecchetti is very astute in allying Verga's style with his subjects:

> ... these basic principles, which came to him from *verismo* (to create works of art that are true to life), led him to the adoption of a specific language which each time was to suit a specific environment, as if born of that environment itself. The language of *Mastro-don Gesualdo* encompasses three different social levels—the common people, the wasted but still proud aristocracy, and the Sicilian bourgeoisie of the last century—and it must, therefore, be viewed as the amalgamation of three different languages.

He also sheds light on the reason Verga stopped in the middle of *Mastro-don Gesualdo* to devote himself to the writing of the short pieces in *Novelle rusticane*

> These extremely complex expressive requirements may explain why, before devoting himself to the composition of the second novel of his series, Verga felt he needed to practice and sharpen his skills on the pages of shorter narratives.

As for the mystery of why Verga never finished the other novels:

> It may also explain why he could not proceed with the writing of the other three novels, which had to be in a language full of reticent nuances on one side and of the empty words of the totally self-centered aristocratic parasites on the other.

Verga now clearly meant to imply the need for social change through his ever sharpening depiction of the primitive poor, the small agrarian landowners, the lower-class city dwellers, the merchant middle class, the upper-class professionals, and the aristocracy. Their variety fascinated him in the twofold socio-aesthetic way that was natural to the moral criticism of his time (though there is a return to this nonduality in recent Italian critical writing). While he was living in Milan, Florence, and Paris, his imagination and his affections remained tied to the Sicilian countryside. But in Mastro-don Gesualdo, Verga found an extraordinary character, one powerful enough to traverse the universe of difference that stretched between low and high society.

Don Gesualdo enabled Verga to portray the wealthy through the eyes of a newcomer, to find a new way to enter the mind of his protagonist, Gesualdo Motta, a poor man who finally becomes rich and proud; whose desire for material possessions makes him capable of violence and unscrupulous behavior. He is a man who achieves everything he sets out to do and has the dubious pleasure of getting just what he asked for without ever finding peace or happiness. This compelling ambition produces an incurable loneliness; his balance has been lost forever in the passionate struggle to get ahead.

Gesualdo Motta is the champion loser among all of Verga's defeated souls. He stands out because the harshness of the battle waged and momentarily won endows his tragedy with a dimension of grandeur. Verga succeeds most brilliantly in showing the vitality of Gesualdo's climb, his irresistible strength, and his blind allegiance to the natural law that drives him forward. Despised by the nobility even when he becomes a rich man, abandoned by the servants in the middle of a revolution, ignored by his own daughter when he falls ill, Don Gesualdo never stops fighting.

> . . . Don Gesualdo, green with anger, jumped onto the back of his mule once more, and went off while it was still raining cats and dogs, his head in his shoulders, soaked to the bone, his heart blacker than the cloudy sky before his eyes; the town gray and sad too in the rain, up on top of the mountain, the ringing of the noon hour passing by in waves, carried by the wind, and losing itself in the distance.
>
> All those who met him, knowing of the disaster that had befallen him, forgot to greet him and kept going. He gave furious glances and from time to time he grumbled to himself:
>
> "I'm still on my feet! My name is Mastro-don Gesualdo! As long as I'm on my feet, I know how to help myself!"
>
> Only one man, a poor devil, who was going the same way, offered to take him under his umbrella. He answered:
>
> "I need far more than an umbrella, my friend! Don't worry, I'm not afraid of the rain, or of the hail, not me!"
>
> He reached the town after midday. The canon-priest Lupi had just gone to lie down for his nap, right after lunch.
>
> "I'm coming, I'm coming, Don Gesualdo!" he shouted from the window as he was called.
>
> Someone going about his own business at that time, seeing him soaked through . . . said:
>
> "Eh, Don Gesualdo? . . . What a disaster! . . ."

He stood there, like a rock, a bitter smile on his pale and thin lips, and answered:

> "Eh, those are things that happen. If you walk in the rain you'll get wet, and if you ride a horse you'll fall. But as long as there is nobody dead, all the rest can be managed."

(p. 74)

The Darwinian notion that blindly man must inevitably progress is at the heart of this novel. Gesualdo, driven by the same force that grants his success, arrives at disillusion. He is like an ancient gladiator who cannot avoid his match, cannot refuse to win, and cannot taste the fruits of his victory. There are no rewards in Verga's fictional world, but then there is no divine punishment. That Don Gesualdo dies alone and in pain is not a moral statement. More than anything it is a representation of life's sublime indifference.

Verga's approach here as in all his *verismo* works, is to examine the customs of an unknown tribe. Again, no aspect of life is too irrelevant, obvious, or intolerable to note. Again, Verga makes no moral judgment on Gesualdo's financial methods or on his ruthless ambition. At the same time, he delineates with his customary ruthless clarity Gesualdo's gross mistakes and naivetés; in short, everything that will ruin him morally and psychologically. Through his carefully detached point of view, Verga is able to create a special tension between the triumph the protagonist feels and the failure the reader witnesses.

Once more, like a stubborn movie director who refuses to shift the angle of his camera, Verga never leaves his protagonist. On the other hand, there is no identification between Verga and Don Gesualdo. The author does not want to create a romantic empathy, and he does not fall in love with his creation. Don Gesualdo is not someone the reader can easily like or identify with. But the portrait is so clearly drawn and the behavior so consistent that the reader inevitably shares Don Gesualdo's bewildering mixture of feelings—antagonism, disgust, pity—as they rush through him to us in Verga's deliberately arranged avalanche of emotions and thoughts. Verga's art is on the track of an unpredictable creature—irrational man. He enters the unsophisticated mind because it has fewer categories and its motions can be plotted with comparative ease. This does not mean it is easy. D. H. Lawrence has this to say:

> Now the emotional mind, if we may be allowed to say so, is not logical. It is a psychological fact, that when we are thinking emotionally or passionately, thinking and feeling at the same time, we do not think rationally: and therefore, and therefore, and therefore. Instead, the mind makes curious swoops and circles. It touches the point of pain or interest, then sweeps away again in a cycle, coils around and approaches again the point of pain or interest. There is a curious spiral rhythm, and the mind approaches again and again the point of concern, repeats itself, goes back, destroys the time-sequence entirely, so that time ceases to exist, as the mind stoops to the quarry, then leaves it without striking, soars, hovers, turns, swoops, stoops again, still does not strike, yet is nearer, nearer, reels away again, wheels off into the air, even forgets, quite forgets, yet again turns, bends, circles slowly, swoops and stoops again, until at last there is the closing-in, and the clutch of a decision or a resolve.
>
> This activity of the mind is strictly timeless, and illogical. Afterwards you can deduce the logical sequence and the time sequence, as historians do from the past. But in the happening, the logical and the time sequence do not exist.
>
> (*Phoenix*, p. 249)

Since history is visible in the background—turmoils, revolution, social tensions—many have seen a line connecting Balzac's Père Goriot with Gesualdo Motta. They are both greedy, successful, naive, and unfortunate. They are both capable of creating wealth but unable to make anyone happy, least of all themselves. The world of Verga is more elementary, with no nuances, no ambiguities, no obliquity. No one is allowed to experience the feelings the author denies to himself. Even illness acquires, in Verga's world, a dry, unsentimental modernist image, endowed with neither mystery nor moral connotations. Death is neither bad nor good, but simply "natural."

Verga's love and fascination for the theater are at work in the spectacular opening scene of *Mastro-don Gesualdo:* two houses are burning side by side and Gesualdo Motta runs forward and identifies himself by struggling against all odds to save what belongs to him. The presentation of the protagonist is completed in a few pages. Gesualdo succeeds, his house will not burn, he is capable of controlling his territory. Now the reader knows that Don Gesualdo is ready to take on all comers.

In *Mastro-don Gesualdo*, Verga perfects his use of the chorus. The entire village accompanies the action, reverberating with voices, proverbs, conventional wisdom, archaic dreams, and fears. This is not a Greek chorus in that it is neither passive nor moral. It is but one more external force to be taken into account, seldom a favorable force, frequently an obstacle, always a consideration. The people are unintentionally cruel. Cooperation and solidarity never appear in Verga's world. These values have nothing to do with the "struggle." The individual is irrelevant to the landscape surrounding him.

Mastro-don Gesualdo and *I Malavoglia* were to be the first novels in Verga's epic tribute to Balzac and Zola, his masters in realism. But Verga's *comédie humaine* ended abruptly in the middle of the third volume. Volume 1, *I Malavoglia*, had started on the lowest rung of the social scale, etching the crude defeat of the poor fisherman's family. In volume 2, out of the elemental slime rose *Mastro-don Gesualdo*, the peasant who climbed the social rope only to find, when he reached the top, that it was a venomous snake. *La duchessa di Leyra* was the third volume in the would-be pentalogy. It dealt with groping through the crowd to the aristocratic clouds. But as if the novel itself understood the impossibility of such an ascent, it refused to go on, like the tired Sicilian mule of Verga's story, and gave out in the middle of the journey. It was as if Verga had looked too hard and too long and could no longer see the straight path. The epic stopped at the grave of Don Gesualdo.

PLAYS AND FINALE

In 1896, Verga wrote, produced, and staged a number of two-act plays in Turin. One was *La Lupa*, derived from the short story of the same title. Giacomo Puccini was apparently interested in adapting *La Lupa* as an opera libretto. Although the project never materialized, Verga, having written the "libretto" with his fellow Sicilian writer Federico De Roberto, used his script for the theater.

Caccia al lupo (Wolf Hunting) and *Caccia alla volpe* (Fox Hunting) were staged during the same period with considerable success in Milan. Once more, Verga was pursuing his original dream of portraying without comment the lives of the poor as well as of the rich. The first described the connubial jealousy of a poor farmer, and the second depicted the same situation in an aristocratic setting. But the dream eluded Verga. *Caccia al lupo* has some of the brutal and primitive force that the author successfully injected into his best writing. A betrayed husband is intent on planning his vendetta with a determination that knows no caution and allows for no second thoughts. *Caccia alla volpe*, on the other hand, which meant to offer a subtle representation of the mischievous behavior of a rich lady who is undecided between her husband and her lover, proved less satisfying. The situation appears to have been unfamiliar to Verga, and although he created a clever plot, the characters remain remote and unsympathetic.

Dal tuo al mio (From You to Me), Verga's last and most complex play, deals with a declining aristocratic family that is approaching ruin because of mismanagement of its sulfur mines. The family's financial difficulties prevent the two daughters from marrying suitors of the appropriate rank, and one of them elopes with the foreman of the mine, Luciano. At the end, because of a strike and the continuous violence at the mine, the father forgives his erring daughter.

This play has been seen as the third part of the unfinished series entitled *I vinti* (The Vanquished). Its material, as many critics have indicated, is straight from the early episodes of *Mastro-don Gesualdo*. Thomas G. Bergin underlines the "note of humanitarian propaganda" in the play, which, apparently, Verga recognized. When the play was later made into a novel, Verga defended himself halfheartedly against this charge in the preface, and even wrote of the "humanitarian mission" of literature. Bergin cites this as "an open confession of the retreat from the old impersonal attitude and confirms a tendency toward humanitarianism which we have observed cropping out sporadically in the work following *Mastro-don Gesualdo*."

For all this, *Dal tuo al mio* is the only work that approaches the grand quality of *Mastro-don Gesualdo*. Here, all is conflict, tension, and confrontation between the aristocratic interest in preserving the status quo and the new, vital, and vulgar middle class. The aristocratic landowner loses and must give way to the emerging lower class, which imposes its new brand of will and power. Here, the poor are showing a new face. No longer content merely to accept fate, they conceive the idea of a union, start to organize, and try to fight back. Once again, private lives delineate social behavior according to a pattern of betrayal and selfishness.

This work offers itself to different interpretations. Does it represent a better understanding of the working class, or does it show, instead, that workers share unpleasant character traits with the rest of society? Verga reacted to critics by claiming that his sole purpose was to create not a politics but an aesthetics. *Dal tuo al mio* may not have been a masterpiece, but it was greatly discussed in its time and achieved a huge success. It is a complex predecessor of the proletarian play.

Verga's last twenty years were not particularly productive, yet his fame continued to grow. Nationalism, the socialist seeds of fascism, the futurist movement, and D'Annunzio were near and dear to him. The last democratic government before Benito Mussolini appointed him to the Italian senate. Luigi Pirandello spoke in favor of his nomination, and Benedetto Croce signed the decree.

Giovanni Verga died in Catania on 27 January 1922. That Verga had tried to be a witness of two worlds, and had succeeded in one, was confirmed by the enormous number of poor people who showed up at his funeral. Luigi Russo, an eminent critic, wrote, "They were following in a procession, thousands of people. They were all saying: 'The poet of the poor is dead.' "

Selected Bibliography

EDITIONS

INDIVIDUAL WORKS

NOVELS
I carbonari della montagna. 4 vols. Catania, 1861–1862.
Una peccatrice. Turin, 1866.
La ricamatrice. [Milan], 1869.
Storia di una capinera. Milan, 1871.
Eva. Milan, 1873.
Nedda. Milan, 1874.
Eros. Milan, 1875.
Tigre reale. Milan, 1875.
I Malavoglia. Milan, 1881.
Il marito di Elena. Milan, 1882.
Mastro-don Gesualdo. Milan, 1889.

SHORT STORIES
"Sulle lagune." *Nuova Europa* nos. 236–277 (intermittent issues) (1863).

Primavera e altri racconti. Milan, 1876.
Vita dei campi. Milan, 1880.
"Poveri pescatori." *Nuova antologia* (1880).
Novelle rusticane. Turin, 1883.
Drammi intimi. Milan, 1884.
Vagabondaggio. Florence, 1887.
I ricordi del Capitano d'Arce. Milan, 1891.
Don Candeloro e compagni. Milan, 1894.
La Lupa. Milan, 1896.
"Una capanna e il tuo cuore." *Illustrazione Italiana.* 1:200 (1919).

PLAYS
Cavalleria rusticana. Turin, 1884.
Caccia al lupo and *Caccia alla volpe.* Milan, 1902.
Dal tuo al mio. Nuova antologia. (16 May–16 June, 1905).

COLLECTED WORKS
Opere di Giovanni Verga. Edited by Vito Perroni. Milan, 1939–1946.
Tutte le novelle. 2 vols. Milan, 1942.
Giovanni Verga, Opere. Edited by Luigi Russo. Milan, 1958.
I grandi romanzi. Edited by F. Cecco and C. Riccardi. Milan, 1972.

TRANSLATIONS

Cavalleria rusticana, and Other Stories. Translated by D. H. Lawrence. Westport, Conn., 1975.
The House by the Medlar Tree. Translated by Eric Mosbacher. New York, 1953.
Little Novels of Sicily. Translated by D. H. Lawrence. New York, 1925. Reprinted 1953, 1975.
Mastro-don Gesualdo. Translated by D. H. Lawrence. New York, 1923. Reprinted 1955, 1976.
Mastro-don Gesualdo: A Novel. Translated by Giovanni Cecchetti. Berkeley, Calif., 1979.
The She-Wolf and Other Stories. Translated by Giovanni Cecchetti. Berkeley, Calif., 1973.

BIOGRAPHICAL AND CRITICAL STUDIES

Alexander, Alfred. *Giovanni Verga: A Great Writer and His World.* London, 1972.
Asor Rosa, Alberto. *Il caso Verga.* Palermo, 1972.
Bacchelli, R. *I grandi romanzi.* Milan, 1972.
Bergin, Thomas Goddard. *Giovanni Verga.* Westport, Conn., 1969.

Bigazzi, R. *I colori del vero. Vent'anni di narrativa: 1860–80.* Pisa, 1969.

Bontempelli, M. *Verga, L'Aretino, Scarlatti, Verdi.* Milan, 1941.

Borsellino; Nino. *Storia di Verga.* Bari, 1982.

Caccia, E. "Il linguaggio dei 'Malavoglia' tra storia e poesia." In *Tecniche e valori dal Manzoni al Verga.* Florence, 1969.

Cappellani, N. *Opere di Giovanni Verga.* Florence, 1940.

Capuana, L. *Verga e D'Annunzio.* Bologna, 1972.

Cecchetti, Giovanni. *Giovanni Verga.* Boston, 1978.

Chiappelli, F., ed. *Lettere al traduttore di Giovanni Verga.* Florence, 1954.

Croce, Benedetto. *La letteratura della nuova Italia.* Vol. 3. Bari, 1922.

De Roberto, F. *Casa Verga e altri saggi Verghiani.* Florence, 1964.

Devoto, G. *Nuovi studi di stilistica.* Florence, 1962.

Garrone, D. *Giovanni Verga.* Florence, 1940.

Gaudioso, M. *Storicismo e verismo nella narrativa del mondo degli umili.* Catania, 1973.

Ghidetti, Enrico. *Verga, guida storico critica.* Rome, 1979.

Giachery, E. *Verga e D'Annunzio.* Turin, 1968.

Hempel, W. *Giovanni Vergas Roman "I Malavoglia" und die Wiederholung als erzöhlerisches Kunstmittel.* Cologne, 1959.

Lawrence, D. H. *Phoenix.* New York, 1936.

————. "Giovanni Verga." In *Selected Literary Criticism.* London, 1957.

Lugli, V. "I due Mastro Don Gesualdo." In *Dante e Balzac.* Naples, 1952.

Luperini, R. *Pessimismo e verismo in Giovanni Verga.* Padua, 1968.

Marzot, G. *L'Arte del Verga.* Vicenza, Italy, 1930.

Masiello, V. *Verga tra ideologia e realtà.* Bari, 1970.

Momigliano, A. *Dante, Manzoni, Verga.* Messina, 1955.

Navarria, A. *Lettura di poesia nell'opera di Giovanni Verga.* Messina, 1962.

Perroni, L. *Studi critici su Giovanni Verga.* Rome, 1934.

Pomilio, M. *La fortuna del Verga.* Naples, 1963.

Pullega, P. *Leggere Verga: Antologia della critica Verghiana.* Bologna, 1973.

Ragusa, Olga Maria. *Verga's Milanese Tales.* New York, 1964.

Russo, Luigi. *Giovanni Verga.* 6th ed. Bari, 1959.

Santangelo, G. "Verga." In *I classici Italiani nella storia della critica,* edited by W. Binni. Florence, 1954.

————. *Storia della critica Verghiana.* Florence, 1969.

Seroni, A. *Verga.* Palermo, 1973.

Sipala, P. M. *L'Ultimo Verga e altri scritti Verghiani.* Catania, 1969.

Sorensen, H. "Le problème du narrateur dans 'I Malavoglia' de Verga." In *Language and Society.* Copenhagen, 1961.

Spitzer, L. *L'Originalità della narrazione nei "Malavoglia."* Belfagor 11:27–53 (1956).

Torraca, F. *Studi e rassegne.* Naples, 1907.

Viti, G. *Verga verista: Guida a "I Malavoglia," a "Mastro-Don Gesualdo," e alle maggiori novelle veriste.* Florence, 1977.

Woolf, David. *The Art of Verga: A Study in Objectivity.* Sydney, 1977.

BIBLIOGRAPHIES

Raya, G. *Un secolo di bibliografia Verghiana.* Padua, 1960.

FURIO COLOMBO

STÉPHANE MALLARMÉ
(1842–1898)

STÉPHANE MALLARMÉ IS known for some fifty short, delicate, impenetrable lyrics; for one long, delicate, impenetrable tone poem, *L'Après-midi d'un faune (The Afternoon of a Faun);* and for a critical theory that makes a work of literature independent of its author and uninterpretable by its readers. The image of ethereality is incorrect and unfortunate, but it is one of Mallarmé's lasting creations. In response to a fellow poet's questionnaire in 1885, Mallarmé prepared a short autobiographical note, which begins, ''I exist only on paper.'' He claimed to live a life free of events and to write a ''pure poetry,'' irrelevant to biographical, historical, and sociological concerns. *La poésie pure,* Mallarmé said, consists of language about language (''The 'pure work' implies the elocutionary disappearance of the poet, who cedes the initiative to words''); and he indicated that such poems, ''far removed from everything,'' would exist for each future generation in the present tense of Art. Mallarmé originated the powerful trend in modern aesthetics to dissociate the art work from the artist's life and times; his poetry is a primary instance for twentieth-century aestheticist theories of a text free from meaning and reference. Mallarmé's reputation as the architect of symbolist, ivory-tower poetics has been used to bolster the belief that, as one current theorist puts it, ''literary history has little or nothing to do with literature,'' and, more radically, ''that the bases for historical knowledge are not empirical facts but written texts, even if these texts masquerade in the guise of wars or revolutions'' (Paul de Man, *Blindness and Insight,* p. 165). Hence the curious ritual with which so many books on Mallarmé commence: the firm, swift dismissal of biographical and historical context, or else, in more introductory texts, the demure apology for providing a few ''facts.''

But precisely because he denied the relevance of external criteria to his poetry, Mallarmé's work requires more psychological, historical, and sociological elucidation than the work of virtually any other writer. Take, for example, this late sonnet:

Victoriously having fled the beautiful suicide
Ember of glory, blood through foam, gold,
   tempest!
Oh to laugh if over there a purple spreads
To drape royal only my absent tomb.

What! of all that luster not even a shred
Remains, it is midnight, in the dark which fetes
   us
Except that a presumptuous treasure of the head
Pours its caressed nonchalance without
   torchlight,

Yours always such a delight! yours
Yes alone from the vanished heaven retains
A little puerile triumph in dressing your coiffure

With brilliance when on the pillows you pose it
As a martial helmet of an infant empress
Whence to emblemize you roses would fall.
     (''Victorieusement fui le suicide beau'')

The mixed metaphors and oxymoronic rhetoric; the diction, at once dark and precious; the convoluted syntax and the uncooperative punctuation—all illustrate the famous inaccessibility of Mallarmé's "mathematical language." Yet this poem is not a closed system; its words were not selected at random by an inhuman hand, and Mallarmé, in fact, defined a poem as a temporary victory over chance. The coherence of vocabulary, for instance, would suggest a reference external to the poem, though not necessarily extrinsic to it. "Victoriously," "glory," "blood," "purple drapery," "royal," "tomb," "luster," "brilliance," "torchlight," "triumph," "martial helmet," "empress"—in 1885, the year this sonnet was published, these words could hardly fail to invoke the military and political history of France in the nineteenth century, and the odd sequence in the second line ("Tison de gloire, sang par écume, or, tempête!") would doubtless seem, to Mallarmé's contemporaries, a string of battle clichés.

Mallarmé himself participated in none of the battles that France fought during his lifetime: the Crimean War, the Italian War, the Franco-Prussian War, the numerous imperial adventures in Africa, Mexico, and Indochina. And he was born too late to fight in the less inglorious wars of Napoleon's First Empire. But politics, gory as war, were inescapable in postrevolutionary France. The poet's great-great uncle, François René Auguste Mallarmé, was an extremist member of the National Convention and, in 1793, voted for the execution of Louis XVI; after which he presided over significant meetings of the Convention, encouraged the Terror, held office under Bonaparte, and died as an exiled regicide only ten years before his nephew's grandson was born. Stéphane Mallarmé appears to have been ashamed of this ancestry: he omits mention of it in his autobiographical note and, many years before, when he was a government functionary's son in a school for aristocrats, he took the name Marquis de Boulainvilliers and hid the fact from his family. (Also while in school he changed his name from the French form Étienne to the Greek Stéphane.)

Letters home testify to his early awareness of historical events, and a bit of correspondence from his fourteenth year—particularly relevant to the imperial infant of the sonnet—concerns his school's celebration of Napoleon III's newborn "bébé impérial." Mallarmé was too young in 1848 to be aware of the "accidental revolution" that replaced Louis Philippe, the citizen-king, first with the comte de Paris (another royal infant), next with a provisional republic, and finally—inevitably—with the Second Empire of an elected despot. Mallarmé, at age six, would have been too preoccupied with emotional survival to notice his elders' political conversations—his mother had died the previous year and his father remarried in 1848—but the revolution's effects would extend well into the future of French social and intellectual life. Karl Marx said that 1848 was a mere parody of 1789, but Alexis de Tocqueville thought it not only a piece of histrionics but also an agent for intensifying the already extreme class hatreds of France; Gustave Flaubert wrote that, after the experience of 1848, "men of intelligence were idiots for the rest of their lives."

Mallarmé lived mostly in the provinces or in the suburbs of Paris until he was nearly thirty, and since politics in France is the prerogative of the capital, he had no immediate involvement until the chaos of 1870–1871. He was descended from an unbroken line of lawyers and bureaucrats and was himself a lycée instructor in an era when education was a hot political issue; so it would be unwise to think of him at any point as "disengaged." But Mallarmé reacted to the Franco-Prussian War, in which his friend Henri Regnault, the painter, was killed, and to the revolt in Paris that followed it, with special vehemence: "There is in today's atmosphere an unknown dose of woe and insanity . . . modern history . . . subsists on something other than these

STÉPHANE MALLARMÉ

childish old things. I have never so completely hated Foolishness" (letter to Frédéric
Mistral, 1870).

What he meant by insanity is plain. In the
German siege of Paris, hundreds died of starvation, exposure, and falling shells—all in
order to keep a Hohenzollern from the throne
of Spain—while the luxury restaurants remained open throughout the ordeal, serving,
when necessary, such items of *nouvelle cui-
sine* as elephant, kangaroo, and cat. In the
Commune rioting and government response
that followed surrender, leftists murdered the
archbishop of Paris and the Tuileries were set
afire. More than twenty thousand Parisians
died. With the overthrow of Napoleon III,
France became once again a republic, but the
republican assembly was composed for the
most part of monarchists. This "insane" fact
is typical of politics in nineteenth-century
France, where elections were held to determine not representation but forms of government, and where the alternation between
ultramontane and bourgeois monarchies, re-
publics, terrors, military dictatorships, and
empires resulted in a system of numbered governments (Second Empire, Third Republic)
and in some incomparably comic accidents of
nomenclature (Louis Napoleon).

Yet nothing significant ever altered, or so
the French seemed to think: a change of rulers
meant merely another squandered elite. In response to this poor theater of political history,
Mallarmé evinced in public an attitude modeled on Hamlet's to Claudius. In the essay
"L'Action restreinte" ("Action Restricted,"
1895) he wrote of himself and his associates
that

> this generation seems not very concerned—even
> beyond its lack of interest in politics—with the
> desire for physical exertion. . . . Acting . . .
> yields in return the happy thought that you,
> being the cause of it, therefore exist. . . . This
> can be accomplished in two ways: either in a
> lifetime of willing and ignoring it . . . or in the

> . . . daily newspapers and their whirlwind, deter-
> mining in them, in one sense, some strength.
>
> (*Selected Poetry and Prose,* M. A. Caws ed.,
> p. 77)

This essay goes on to assert "the right to accomplish nothing exceptional, or lacking in
vulgar bustle," and by that Mallarmé means
the poet's right to compose a "timeless" book
that may "shake off the bulk of the moment."
Mallarmé thus establishes his antithesis between verse and newspaper prose, between literature and history, between eternity and the
temporal—yet his stance is anything but apo-
litical; it is from first to last an expression of
hatred for the unlovable politics of an "evil
century."

Mallarmé's sonnet "Victorieusement fui le
suicide beau" embodies and complicates this
antithesis between poetry and politics. The
images of monarchy and martial heroism per-
tain to the public world of the journalist,
while the rococo infant and her roses belong
to the poet's stock of tropes. The "presumptuous treasure of the head" may be an emblem
for poetry itself (the French word for "pours"
in line 8 is *verse*), and the comfort it provides
is the infant's delight. The "beautiful suicide"
is double edged. To die for France, whether on
a battlefield or in the Champs-Élysée, was
thought to be beautiful, a noble self-sacrifice,
and the speaker has fled this unwanted extinction with a sense of victory. On the other
hand, to walk off the stage of history is no less
suicidal—Mallarmé, in fact, calls this kind of
abdication "suicide" in the essay quoted
above. Nor is the infant empress without ambiguity: she is a figure (or figurine) of both
politics and poetics. She reduces the pretensions of monarchies and empires, which more
than once in France were "ruled" by babies
and maternal regents; moreover, as we have
seen, Mallarmé found contemporary politics
"childish." But this infant also triumphs over
the darkness of a time lacking in luster and a
place "without torchlight," of a century and a

nation that, as Alphonse de Lamartine re-marked, were sunk in ennui. The infant em-press' head ornament (some intellectual glory?) lights up the darkness; and, to honor her triumphal entry into the poem, symbolic petals fall. Poetry and politics have their own spheres of influence: "It's probably just as well for politics to get along without Litera-ture and decide its fate with guns," Mallarmé wrote in a letter to Henri Cazalis in 1871. "That puts Literature on its own." The con-descending tone of both sonnet and letter tells us that poetry and politics are not separate-but-equal: the products of imagination pro-vide light in the darkness that public life has caused. Mallarmé's sonnet proclaims the sov-ereign empire of art.

But the poem's texture is more complex than this "political" analysis would suggest. The "absent tomb" may be a Tomb of the Un-known Poet—an empty sepulcher for those who have refused, in Flaubert's phrase, to die for the bourgeoisie; or the empty tomb could be taken to complement "the vanished heaven," in which case the sonnet relates Christ's evacuation from the earth to the dis-appearance of Christianity from the modern world. Mid-century was a time of religious fer-vor—the miracle at Lourdes occurred when Mallarmé was sixteen—but not for the liberal intelligentsia of France. They were put off by the church's proximity to wealth and power, and, in any case, the church had condemned all forms of religious liberalism in 1864, shortly before the proclamation of papal infal-libility. Thus this poem, like mid-century lib-eralism, affiliates Christianity with royalty, imperialism, and battle casualties; literature, to which intellectuals turned their powers, is said to "take a triumph" from both church and state, from both vanished heaven and absent tomb.

Images of absence, however, appear obses-sively in Mallarmé's poems, and they may at root be neither political nor religious. Mal-larmé's "uneventful" life is filled with stun-ning absences, deaths, and displacements.

After his mother died when he was five, Mal-larmé was sent to live with his grandparents, and he turned for affection to his younger sis-ter, Maria, and to an American friend named Harriet. His relation to both was exceedingly close—a psychoanalytic case study—until each girl died, one year after the other, during Stéphane's adolescence. Various juvenile writings seem to show that Stéphane re-pressed the pain of his mother's death and that after Maria and Harriet died he felt guilt at living on in a world that excluded them. The sense of mental sterility, of existing under a psychic lid, never left Mallarmé, and his doubts about a society of creatures born to die are manifest in his rejection of conventional pursuits (religion, politics, commerce) as so much "vulgar bustle."

Of necessity, Mallarmé became a master of substitution. He married early, in 1863, the year his father died, a woman with his sister's name and likeness, and they produced a daughter, a new Mademoiselle Mallarmé, with admirable swiftness. Their son died in child-hood, and excerpts from his father's memo-rial, "Le tombeau d'Anatole" ("A Tomb for Anatole," 1887), may give some sense of Mal-larmé's response to the redundant tragedy of his life:

> time of the
>   empty chamber
> —
>   until one
>   opens it
> perhaps all
>   follows from this
>   (morally) . . .
>
>   no—I will not
> give up
>   nothingness
>   father - - - I
> feel nothingness
>   invade me

Substitute persons were never quite enough, and Mallarmé made a career of writing poems that project an absent anima figure—the infant empress is one example—onto a firmament of azure.

His poem "Soupir" ("Sigh"), written the year after his marriage, is the least ambiguous instance:

My soul—across your brow where there dreams,
                    O calm sister,
An autumn strewn with freckles,
And across the wandering sky of your angelic
    eye—
Mounts, as in a melancholy garden,
Faithful, a white jet of water sighs toward the
    Azure!
—Toward the Azure softened by October, pale and
    pure,
Which mirrors in great basins its infinite languor
And lets—on dead water where the tawny agony
Of leaves strays in the wind and cleaves a cold
    furrow—
The yellow sun crawl on in one long ray.

The speaker addresses the azure sky as his calm sister, in the informal second person, and he paints the sky as a pale female face with angelic eye and freckled brow. In agony, his sigh mounts toward the azure, but his reach extends no further than the basins of dead water in which the sky is reflected. He must live without his anima in the unsatisfactory world of graves ("a cold furrow") and blown leaves and partial sunlight. Reality has unaccountably been translated from our infernal world into an unreachable supernal one. Mallarmé's devotion to the realms of azure has led very often to his being called a small-p platonist; and, to the extent to which the label applies, the case of Mallarmé supports the assertions of his contemporary Friedrich Nietzsche about the psychopathology of Plato's displacement metaphysics. Mallarmé's platonism was decidedly a matter of missing persons.

In any event, the azure, noun and adjective, became one of Mallarmé's most enduring symbols. It is, first, an image of transparency, simplicity, and tranquillity, remembered from childhood. In his poem "Las de l'amer repos" ("Weary of the Bitter Ease," 1864), the colors blue and azure are associated with a flower "smelled in infancy," and the speaker longs to re-create his "soul's blue filagree" in a poem as "limpid and delicate" as a Chinese porcelain cup:

    . . . I'll choose a landscape young
    Which I will paint again on cups, preoccupied,
    A line of azure, thin and pale, will signify
    A lake, amid the sky of naked porcelain.
                                        (22–25)

By a process of projection, or of sublimation perhaps, the azure also signifies eternity, as in the poem entitled "L'Azur" ("The Azure," 1867), which begins: "The eternal azure's serene irony/Overwhelms . . ." The azure (noun) is a dimension beyond petty time and petty space; the adjective signifies the color of childhood innocence; both have associations with the sky and with departed souls. It would appear that the azure is heaven. But Mallarmé determined early that eternity was the province of art rather than religion—though in childhood he had hoped he might one day be made a bishop—for transcendence is "the artifice of eternity": these are the words of Mallarmé's disciple the Irish poet W. B. Yeats. The relation of eternity to our inferior world is signified by absence, by the intuited displacement of everything that could be called ultimate or absolute. Mallarmé's verse endeavors to give the absence presence. Verse has this power because the poet's soul is a "blue angelus," the color of absolute azure ("The Azure")—and because "virgin verse" is a "Nothing," a "blank concern" like "the cup," the empty vessel of reality, which poetry exists "to designate" ["Salut," 1893]. The poet is an apparatus equipped to see absence, and the poem is the absence that he sees.

If poetry and the absolute are related by similarity, then poetry and the world on earth can be related only by contrast. This, at least, was the conclusion toward which the romantic tradition would encourage Mallarmé. The contrast—the opposition—between artists and conventional citizens was an ingrained reflex by Mallarmé's time:

> An exhibition said to be of painting has just opened at the gallery of Durand-Ruel. The harmless passer-by, attracted by the flags which decorate the façade, goes in and is confronted by a cruel spectacle. Five or six lunatics, one of them a woman, an unfortunate group struck by the mania of ambition, have met there to exhibit their works. Some people split their sides with laughter when they see these things, but I feel heartbroken. These so-called artists call themselves *"intransigeants,"* "Impressionists." They take the canvas, paints and brushes, fling something on at random and hope for the best.
>
> (Albert Wolff, review of impressionist exhibition of 1876, quoted in F. Haskell, "Enemies of Modern Art," *The New York Review of Books,* June 30, 1983, p. 19)

This mid-century review exemplifies a strikingly novel situation in the social history of the fine arts. As one cultural historian writes:

> In the nineteenth century, for the very first time ever, in England, in France, and elsewhere in Europe, an extraordinary number of great artists . . . *did*—usually in the early stages of their careers at least—meet with a degree of incomprehension and often savage hatred that is to us astonishing.
>
> (Haskell, "Enemies of Modern Art")

The hatred was mutual. It would be difficult to say whether public hostility to romantic writers preceded or followed the emergence of the *poète-maudit* (accursed poet) cult, but Charles Baudelaire's pursuit of Satanism and sexual license certainly was not calculated to aid the bourgeoisie to achieve comprehension.

Mallarmé was classed as a *poète maudit*—by the reading public and even by Paul Verlaine, when he prepared his famous study of Baudelaire's colleagues—though Mallarmé's history scarcely merited the epithet. His home life was utterly bourgeois (not excluding an extramarital flirtation in middle age); his employment was standard (he was an unsatisfied and unsatisfactory teacher of English); his meanderings were strictly limited (he took European vacations and lived outside France only briefly, in London); and he accepted readily all proffered distinctions (membership in the French Academy, election as Prince of Poets, engagements to lecture at Oxford and Cambridge). Furthermore, Mallarmé publicly abominated Arthur Rimbaud's dissolute behavior, and his own refusal to elaborate on the more unusual events of his past may have been partly in order to dissociate himself from the romantics' celebration of outrageous personality. Mallarmé placed himself, historically, "after the painful vigil of the romantic period," and his work is characterized by a conflict between romantic and counter-romantic elements. He was psychologically predisposed toward platonist metaphysics and romantic sociology: the world of Forms versus the world of shadows, the avant-garde versus the philistines. The extreme difficulty and the intentional obscurity of his poems, the unimaginable hauteur of his critical essays ("It will be said, I suppose, that I am attempting to flabbergast the mob with a lofty statement. That is true" [as translated in *Selected Poetry and Prose,* p. 84]), and his forthright hatred of the middle class, to which he belonged—all these derive from his inheritance of romantic sociology.

Even in his early poems, however, Mallarmé resists his native romanticism. In the sonnet "Le pitre châtié (The Clown Chastized, 1864), the speaker rebukes himself for striking ready-made poses that imply the holding of unwholesome beliefs:

Eyes, lakes with my simple rapture to be reborn
Other than the actor [*l'histrion*], who with a
    gesture evokes
As a quill the ignoble soot of stage lights,
I have pierced in the canvas wall a window.

Limpid-traitor swimmer, with my legs and arms
In multiple bounds, denying the bad
Hamlet! it's as if in the wave I invented

A thousand sepulchers in which to virgin
   disappear.

Hilarious gold of cymbal fists have irritated,
Suddenly the sun strikes the nudity, pure,
Which exhaled itself from my pearl-like coolness,

Rancid night of the skin when you swept over me,
Not knowing, ingrate! that this was my whole
   consecration,
This greasepaint drowned in perfidious glacier
   water.

The clown involves himself with an array of romantic odds and ends: Hamletic histrionics; *maudit* deathiness, staleness, and treachery; platonic dogmatism, escapism, coolness, and virginity. He has one simple passion, to be reborn other than an "histrion" (actor, bad actor, mountebank; possibly, as a pun, historian)—and he wishes to escape, like the futilitarian Hamlet, from the circus of history. Believing he has pierced a window in the canvas tent, he claims to see through the circus-universe into a better one outside. The quill ("plume") of line 3 may associate this clown with poetry and, if he is an artist, he is a type by this time well known in Paris: the Baudelairean poet who gestures with distaste at "the ignoble soot" of the contemporary scene. But this artist's visions are self-deceptive: they are not windows opening onto a new world; they are tombs in which to place the dead. The artist/clown is chastized for believing himself above, below, or beyond the circus, without which, after all, a clown has no significance. In counterpoint to the circus vocabulary there is an apparently unrelated imagery of glacial waters. An overwhelming, wavelike occurrence has swept over our protagonist and at once his circus-hatred appears to him puny and even rancid. The pure, pearllike coolness that he has cherished in himself has been revealed, in the aftermath of the event, for what it is: perfidious frigidity, a lack of personal warmth. He recognizes that his withdrawal from experience has been an ungrateful response to the "greasepaint" that—as clown,

as artist, and as man—is his whole consecration.

The window of escape is invoked to less subtle effect in the poem entitled "Les fenêtres" ("The Windows," 1863). There, the speaker, dying in a hospital bed, clings "to all the window frames/Whence one can turn his back on life in scorn," and the window image is defined for us in a jussive clause: "—Let the window be art, be mystic state—." The speaker wants to escape into aesthetics or mysticism because he is

. . . filled with disgust for the man of callous soul
Sprawled in comfort where his only appetites
Feed, stubborn in searching out this ordure
To offer the wife who suckles his little ones.
                                                  (21–24)

The choice Mallarmé offers is between *la Beauté* (beauty) and *la Bêtise* (stupidity)—or, to use the metaphors of the poem, between angels and pigs—yet there can be in the end no escape from stupidity into splendor: "the world below is master." This poem is among the most extreme expressions of platonism in the Mallarmé canon—he describes it in a letter to Henri Cazalis as "a little poem" for "the unfortunates whom the earth disgusts" (3 June 1863)—but even here the speaker questions whether his flight from conventionality might not be a mere Icarus venture:

Is this a way, O Self who knows gall stings,
To burst the crystal, by the monster insulted
And take flight, on my two unfeathered wings
—At the risk of falling for eternity?
                                                  (37–40)

The only important works in which this sociopathology goes unquestioned are the late *tombeaux* (tombs) and *hommages* that Mallarmé wrote in memory of fellow artists: Edgar Allan Poe (1875–1876), Richard Wagner (1886), Puvis de Chavannes (1895), Baudelaire (1895), Verlaine (1897). In composing these, the poet had to confront a sequence of lives rendered more or less miserable by public harassment or incomprehension, and, in consequence, they resemble a pile of rocks that a gutsy psalmist has prepared to hurl against the philistine. Only one of the *tombeaux* stands on its own as art, and that is "Le tombeau d'Edgar Poe" ("The Tomb of Edgar Poe"). The following is Mallarmé's own translation:

Such as into himself at last Eternity changes him,
The Poet arouses with a naked hymn
His century overawed not to have known
That death extolled itself in this strange voice:

But, in a vile writhing of an hydra once hearing
the Angel
To give too pure a meaning to the words of the
tribe
They thought the spell drunk
In the honorless flood of some dark mixture.

Of the soil and the ether, enemies, O struggle!
If with it my idea does not carve a bas-relief
Of which Poe's dazzling tomb be adorned,

Stern block here fallen from a mysterious
disaster,
Let this granite at least show forever their bound
To the old flights of Blasphemy spread in the
future.

Henry James said that anyone who liked Poe had not given the matter much attention, but the French have always had their unique taste in American writers. Baudelaire's translation of Poe's tales had made Poe a cult figure in France by Mallarmé's time, and, beginning in 1875, Mallarmé undertook to translate Poe's "nonsense" poems, which exemplified his own notion of *poésie pure*. Poe remained for Mallarmé, throughout his career, "the absolute case of literature" ("le cas littéraire absolu"): Mallarmé even rechristened him Poë, as in *poëte*. Yet the sole artistic quality attributed to Poe in the memorial sonnet is his capacity—in T. S. Eliot's translation—"to purify the dialect of the tribe." The bulk of Mallarmé's tribute concerns Poe's awful relations with his American readers: the innuendoes of intoxication ("flights of Blasphemy"), the almost sexual attraction ("arouses with a naked hymn") and almost sexual revulsion ("vile writhing of an hydra").

Poe qualifies as a great artist because of his social heroism. Like the angel Saint Michael, Poe has defeated the vile dragon of incomprehension, and so Mallarmé, the Prince of Poets, has awarded him a verbal tomb and a measure of divinity. (In the French original, the "Lui-même"—Himself—of the first line is capitalized, much as in the *tombeau* and *hommage* respective to each Baudelaire is compared to the god Anubis and the master of Bayreuth is called "The god Richard Wagner.") These late poems are apotheoses of romanticism's martyrs, but Mallarmé desired neither to die their death nor to live their life. The sonnet with which we began, "Victorieusement fui le suicide beau," marks Mallarmé's determination not to join his romantic predecessors and colleagues as a casualty of nineteenth-century social, political, or military history. That sonnet, in fact, may be an anti-*tombeau* in which the life of Stéphane Mallarmé will not be placed: laughter accompanies the solemnities at this empty sepulcher ("my absent tomb"), and the laughter may well be Mallarmé's own. As with all symbolist symbols, the valence of Mallarmé's tomb is equivocal. In the *tombeau* poems, a tomb marks in two senses the end of the poet's persecution: the poet's death is the logical end of his public revilement, and the ornate tomb, the collected works into which "at last Eternity changes" the poet, is also a token of posthumous acceptance and cultural immortality. In the suicide sonnet, the poet escapes from both this agony and this ecstasy; more characteristically, in "Le pitre châtié," the artist discovers too late that his creations have been "sepulchers in which to virgin disappear."

In all of these poems, the artist who begins by dividing himself from conventional life, or by permitting others to isolate him, concludes as the famous occupant of a famous sepulcher. Only once did Mallarmé dare to look inside the aesthete's—the romantic's—tomb, and the sonnet that resulted speaks with vivid authenticity:

The virgin, the alive and the beautiful today
Will it rend for us with a wild wing-beat
This hard lake, forgotten, haunted under the frost
By the transparent glaciers of flights untaken!

A swan of long ago remembers it is he,
Magnificent but without hope, who is delivered
  up
For having failed to sing the realm of life
When the ennui of sterile winter glittered.

All his neck will shake off that white agony
By space inflicted upon the bird which denies it,
But not the horror of the sun where the plumage
  is entrapped.

Phantom by pure brilliance assigned to this place,
Self-immobilized in the cold dream of scorn
Which in his unuseful exile clothes the Swan.
  ("Le vierge, le vivace et le bel aujourd'hui," 1885)

A frozen swan is a peculiarly painful image: the swan is a cultural emblem of beauty, elegance, movement, and (considering its fairy-tale connotations) transcendence. The swan is a type of the artist. But this sonnet is not a parable of the failed artist—not a Wordsworthian worry-poem about poetic sterility and poetic impotence. It is a portrait of the failed human being who takes refuge in art. In Mallarmé's revision of hell, the artist is assigned not to the first circle but to the last. The swan is embedded in ice as a traitor against materiality, contemporaneity, and "the realm of life." Denial of space, of physical existence, can lead only to the frightful discovery that transcendence is a tomb, a trap. There is no transcendence in negation. Platonic scorn for "the beautiful today" is a mere disguise that clothes a hellish condition of deprivation and cowardice. The bird is afraid of flying and terrified that the sun, which shines on every creature, will melt his disdain for the world that every creature shares.

Mallarmé may be a textbook example of the aesthete, of an artist who lived for art, but a poem such as "Le vierge, le vivace et le bel aujourd'hui" must make us qualify this judgment, or else rethink what we mean by aestheticism. Mallarmé's critical essays have been mis- and under-read. There is, for instance, his well-known statement "Everything in the world exists in order to end in a book." Certainly Mallarmé believed that literature, taken as a whole, was moving toward one great work that would encapsulate the world (for several years he thought that he would be its author), and certainly he cannot be accused of underestimating the value of art. The opening for misinterpretation has been what Mallarmé intended by his term *le Livre*. Like "dance," "music," "mathematics," and "game," "book" was among Mallarmé's customary analogies when essaying to define the nature of reality. What these phenomena have in common is their apparent arbitrariness or artificiality: each is a system or, better, a context of terms or signs that may be said to have "meaning" only in relation to one another and to a set of implicit conventions or explicit rules. Such a system is, in the jargon of the moment, "foundationless"—which is to say that the "terms," the gestures, of a system like the ballet are not referential and make no claim to describe or represent "truth" or "reality" or even, for the most part, the physical world. What Mallarmé approved in dance was its essential "nothingness," its "visions no sooner known than scattered." A dancer's movements exemplified, for Mallarmé, "the will of fictions" to comprise atmospheric realities and yet, for all that, to remain transparently fictive. The same was true of mime, which Mallarmé defined as "a medium, a pure medium of fiction" and as "the artifice of a notation of sentiments." In either context, the performer must "comprehend the rules" that alone prevent a performance from disappearing into the void over which it extends.

Such remarks have been hugely influential—for example, via Serge Diaghilev and Igor Stravinsky on the theory and practice of choreography and composition—but Mallarmé had no expertise in any of these extra-literary matters. His critical essays have little to say about their ostensible subjects. At the time Mallarmé wrote his historic piece "Richard Wagner, rêverie d'un poète français" ("Richard Wagner, a French Poet's Reverie," 1885), he had not witnessed a single Wagner opera. Even his criticism of British and American poets makes no contribution to our understanding of those writers; indeed, as T. S. Eliot observed in *To Criticize the Critic* (1965), this English teacher's command of the English language was questionable:

> As for Mallarmé, he taught English and . . . committed himself to writing a kind of guide to the use of the language. An examination of this curious treatise [*English Words*, 1878], and the strange phrases which he gives under the impression that they are familiar English proverbs, should dispel any rumour of Mallarmé's English scholarship.
>
> ("From Poe to Valéry")

But, as Eliot realized, to read Mallarmé's essays for scholarship or information would be an act of misprision. Wagnerian operas, Paris mime shows, impressionist exhibitions, Loïe Fuller dance recitals—these are metaphors that serve only to illustrate the poet's theoretical point. Metaphors of artifice, context, and system were particularly valuable to Mallarmé because, as analogies for the human universe, they demonstrate the possibility of a foundationless world; respectively, they epiphanize the world as Theater or as Book or as Game.

Mallarmé's most revealing analogy is also his best informed and most ignored. Between September and December 1874, Mallarmé published eight issues of a women's fashion journal called *La dernière mode* (The Latest Thing), and the humble analogy of fashion comes closer than music or dance to locating his theoretical position. As in the case of ballet, Mallarmé's prime interest seems to have been in the distinction between reality and artificiality: "One could say of these ladies that

they have the fingers of the roses of morning, but of an artificial morning that makes cloth calyxes and pistils bloom"—this was Mallarmé's description of the artificial flowers on a ladies' hat. It appears at first to be a simple conceit; the cloth flowers are compared with real ones. But the phrase "fingers of the roses of morning" recalls the rosy-fingered dawn of Homer, and so the artificial roses are compared not with real flowers but with conventional, literary ones. Mallarmé's little phrase proves to be less conceit than labyrinth. The "artificial morning" would appear to be Homer's—Homer's association of dawn, roses, and fingers is as artificial as Mallarmé's association of Homer with a flowered hat—and thus our fashion reporter has compared, in anatomical detail, a cloth rose designed to resemble a natural one with a linguistic rose invented some 2,500 years before as a convention for describing the dawn. Worse: these flowers bloom. Mallarmé would have us believe that artificial flowers bloom on artificial mornings by the light, no doubt, of an artificial sun—as of course they do, given the proper context. In Homeric epics, rivers speak, men visit the underworld, and the dawn has rosy fingers. Or, in the language of fashion, the style of the moment is definitive ("résultat définitif"). An accredited style is by definition "true," the most adequate gesture that can be made in a given context, even if it be absurd ("false") in all other contexts. "Fact" and "fiction," "reality" and "artificiality" are defined by the conventions of the context in which they are invoked—this is perhaps what is meant by social correctness—and the human world is an infinitely complex web of imperfectly discrete contexts.

The argument that reality is conventionally defined, defined especially by conventions of language use, is a familiar one in the late twentieth century. We are by now accustomed to the notion that our facts may be presuppositions, and that our statements of fact may be "meta-statements," which, because we know no reality outside of such statements, may only be bits of diction and syntax about other bits of syntax and diction. One hundred years ago this position was so unusual as to be virtually incomprehensible. None of the reigning philosophical orthodoxies could accommodate the symbolist perspective. French positivism, the school of Auguste Comte and Hippolyte Taine, held that language was a useful tool for naming things, expressing ideas, and representing reality; and to this school symbolist aesthetics arose in specific opposition. German idealism, or what was left of it, had been introduced into France before the 1820's, and, while a symbolist would admire any critique of pure reason, the idealist epistemologies were for a symbolist too concerned with defining the objects of knowledge; idealists still supposed that knowledge had objects. Neither did symbolist theory have many allies among the orthodox literati. No dyed-in-the-wool romantic could make peace with the notion that reality is defined by convention, and Leo Tolstoy, on behalf of literary realism, condemned Mallarmé's theoretical position as obscurantist (*Revue blanche*, Feb. 15, 1898).

Mallarmé's aesthetic and linguistic theory "far transcends the nineteenth century's arsenal of terms and definitions" (Lehmann, p. 64), but Mallarmé was not cut out for the pioneer role he in fact played. As a result, the leader of the symbolists came to emphasize in his criticism the literature of the future, and his own formulation of symbolist doctrine was from the first antithetical in nature—his theory was, in other words, erratic, inconsistent, and piecemeal. The major symbolists (Mallarmé, Tristan Corbière, Jules de Gaultier, Remy de Gourmont, Jules Laforgue, Camille Mauclair, Arthur Rimbaud) were raised in the romantic tradition, but there is in symbolist ideology a strong postromantic tug and even an unrecognized affinity with the more sociable tenets of realism. Symbolist "conventionalism" implies a modification of romantic sociology, according to which society is split between avant-garde and philistines, while symbolist "contextualism" implies a rejection

of platonic metaphysics, according to which Truth exists outside and above every human context. But Mallarmé belonged, by both preference and inertia, to the Left Bank counterculture of his time, and his psyche was possessed by a platonic mechanism about which his peculiar biography left him little choice. Mallarmé responded to these conflicting pressures in two ways. The first was confusion—his desire to posit "a doctrine at the same time as its contrary" seems less a principle than a subterfuge—and the second was the elaboration of a poetics that both crowns the romantic tradition and puts in place the machinery of modernism.

Poetry at once manufactures truth and shows how truth is manufactured: to Mallarmé, the former is a poem's metaphysical purpose and the latter its social function. The major difficulty for the poet is that verse is made of words, of sounds, while the Word (*Logos*, truth) is tacit: absent. Yet if the Word could be spoken, there would be no poem, no truth, for "verse makes up for what languages lack." The Word depends for its existence on words. This exposition—given by Mallarmé in his essay "Crise de vers" ("Crisis of Verse," 1886–1896)—has been compared, even by Mallarmé himself, with various forms of mysticism. But his position was, methodologically at least, the opposite of mystical. For if there are two means of achieving the tacit truth, the one to extinguish complexity and the other to maximize it, then mystical procedure must be of the first type and symbolist procedure of the second. A "pure poem" purifies the words of the tribe by arranging their numberless connotations into an incomparably intricate constellation, of which the blank spaces may be said to embody the silence of truth. And the symbolist poet, unlike the mystic, does not indicate, reach for, or merge with ultimate reality—his poem is as ultimate as reality gets:

I say: a flower! and outside the oblivion to which my voice relegates any shape, insofar as it is something other than the calyx, there arises musically, as the very idea and delicate the one absent from every bouquet.

(*Oeuvres complètes,* Paris, 1951, H. Mondor ed., p. 368)

This enigmatic statement by Mallarmé has much in common with his description of the flowered hat in *La dernière mode.* The flower absent from every bouquet, like the Homeric rose of the ladies' hat, is the word "flower," spoken by the poet in a context the poet has assembled. But this sentiment, almost Wittgensteinian in its "equation" of language and reality, is couched in a vocabulary that is neoplatonic. Hence the sentence has been construed to mean that a poem will describe not physical flowers but their essence, not actuality but the Ideal. Yet the poet's flowers are linguistic, and of his own creation. Yeats puts the matter with an explicitness that might have shocked Mallarmé: "And I declare my faith:/I mock Plotinus' thought/And cry in Plato's teeth,/Death and life were not/Till man made up the whole,/Made lock, stock and barrel/Out of his bitter soul" ("The Tower," 3).

This linguistic metaphysics made its first appearance in 1865, in Mallarmé's poem "Sainte":

> At the window ledge concealing
> The ancient sandalwood gold-flaking
> Of her viol dimly twinkling
> Long ago with flute or mandore,
>
> Stands the pallid Saint displaying
> The ancient missal page unfolding
> At the Magnificat outpouring
> Long ago for vesper and compline:
>
> At that monstrance glazing lightly
> Brushed now by a harp the Angel
> Fashioned in his evening flight
> Just for the delicate finger
>
> Tip which, lacking the ancient missal
> Or ancient sandalwood, she poises
> On the instrumental plumage,
> Musician of silence.
>
> (Hubert Creekmore trans.)

It is fitting that this new metaphysics should be divulged by an iconography of Annunciation and that the good news should be proclaimed by silence. The four instruments mentioned create no sound, and the viol is in disrepair (the gilt is peeling). By implication, all the assembled vehicles of the Word—viol, missal, stained-glass window, angel, pallid saint—are quaint and perhaps obsolete. The "ancient missal" is "lacking," and the Christian order, it would seem, has passed into history. The nineteenth and twentieth centuries have produced a number of poems that enact the cataclysmic passage from the Christian metaphysics and cultural milieu to a new one—Shelley's "Ode to the West Wind," Tennyson's *In Memoriam,* Eliot's *The Waste Land*—but this poem is not quite of their company. Its perfect peace (there is only one main verb) bespeaks an expectation less kinetic and historicist. Mallarmé has chosen to paint an apocalypse in miniature.

To begin again: This poem is a verbal portrait of a painting of a stained-glass window. In front of the window, in the painting, stands a Christian muse, the patroness of music: "Sainte Cécile jouant sur l'aile d'un chérubin" (Saint Cecilia playing on the wing of a cherub) was Mallarmé's original title. Her body blocks our view of much of the window, but we can see an angel's harplike wing upon which Saint Cecilia appears, by a quirk of medieval perspective, to be playing. The harp is unreal, an optical illusion; the absent flute and mandore were real once, but in the past; and the angel, that ombudsman of the Ideal, exists merely in stained glass, merely in a work of art. But then, both the saint and her accoutrements are objets d'art as well: they exist only in the painting that Mallarmé describes, and, of course, the patroness, the viol, and the book all represent genres of art. What, then, in this poem is real? Either nothing, or—everything. For saints, angels are real; past, present, and future are real for more ordinary mortals; and the poet believes his poem as real as its subject and reader. We should not be surprised to find that every item conjured by this poem is artificial, for that is true of every poem without exception. The difference between this poem and most other uses of literary language is that Mallarmé faces his trompe l'oeil with unutterable calm, with a silent blessing. He raises none of the questions, ontological and epistemological, that haunt other authors of the play-within-a-play or tale-within-a-tale. In a context where reality should be the question, reality is not at issue. What our words make out of the silence is what the world is, was, and forever shall be. A less simple view would be naive. As we come to expect, Mallarmé makes his point—philosophical, historical, psychological, or political—by making none.

Yet this is art with a social function. A poem such as "Sainte" exists, Mallarmé wrote, "to reveal . . . accords and significations" that otherwise would go unnoticed. The poet's best work exposes the complex of rules by which ordinary language invents reality. Mallarmé has been called a Nonsense poet (he died in the same year as Lewis Carroll), and his verse does seem intended to break down the distinction between nonsensical and sensical uses of language. Sense takes Nonsense to be a mere word game and defines itself as the not-game. But Nonsense also takes Sense to be a game, that game which defines itself (as a part of its rules) as the not-game; Nonsense regards both itself and Sense as serious games upon which much depends. Our perception of the world is at stake, and Nonsense epistemology holds that there is little practical distinction between the world and our perception of it. Sense—language that pretends to correspond to a "foundational" reality beyond itself—is even more nonsensical than Nonsense, which acknowledges the limits of language and perception. Mallarmé would show us that every use of language, and not simply the symbolist poem, is a "jeu littéraire," a language game. In drawing attention to its own artificial and conventional aspects, a Mallarmé poem is not self-referential,

if we mean by that solipsistic, nor is it aestheticist, if we mean by that asocial. Artistic self-consciousness and Nonsense construction comprise the technique—analogy—by which the symbolist poem proposes to redeem the mind that reads it from foolish beliefs about how one "sees the world."

This poetic theory guaranteed that Mallarmé could have his cake and eat it: in pursuit of a rigorous conventionalism, he could write poems that dismay the conventional reader. This double impulse—against established conventions and practices, yet toward the conventional in theory—helps explain the appeal of fascism to the first postsymbolist generation. (Ezra Pound, for instance, rejected the current order, but on behalf of a new and more orderly one.) In Mallarmé's case, the problematic resolved itself in a kind of humanism, or even philanthropy. The reader is the poet's charge. Citizens of Paris, the ennui capital of the world, had been warned, at least since Jean Jacques Rousseau's day, that they had lost all sense of the peculiarity and the incomprehensibility of existence, and Mallarmé's peculiar, incomprehensible verse aimed to restore some of it to them. When, in his collections of myths, *Contes indiens* (Indian Tales, 1927), *L'Étoile des fées* (Fairies' Star, 1881), and *Les dieux antiques* (*The Ancient Gods*, 1880), Mallarmé set out to portray worlds marked by their awareness that reality is makeshift, his customary allusiveness, obscurity, and sleight-of-hand vanished: primitives, children, and ancients do not require the assistance of symbolist poets. The commonplace, Mallarmé said, is inhabited by the occult, and it is the poet's function to revive the mystery wherever sophistication and familiarity have rendered it insensible. Poetry, he wrote, "is the expression by means of human language, restored to its essential rhythm, of the mysterious sense of the components of existence: it endows our sojourn with authenticity and constitutes the sole spiritual task (*Message poétique du symbolisme*, G. Michaud ed., vol. 2, p. 321). This was, for Mallarmé, a cardinal principle. His experimentation with prose poems, for instance, was determined by it: if the Ideal can be found in the commonplace, then should not *poésie pure* be possible in the medium of newsprint? He argued the inferiority of music to verse on precisely these grounds—that music, unlike poetry, has nothing prosaic to overcome and redeem. The Ideal, for Mallarmé, is created by the poet in a cooperative struggle with his culture and its language.

This process was complicated by the fact that, in nineteenth-century France, the poet had two cultures with which to deal—the bourgeois and the romantic—and it is significant that Mallarmé seems most himself in poems that seek to purify the tribal dialect of the avant-garde. The perception that the romantic counterculture had become as ossified as the social order it opposed may have been Mallarmé's most original, and it is all the more impressive considering where he began. His sonnet "Angoisse" ("Anguish"), written in his twenty-second year, could have been the work of any *poète maudit*:

I come not to vanquish your body tonight, O beast
In whom the sins of a people take root, nor to stir
  up
In your impure hair a sad tempest
Under the incurable ennui which my kiss pours
  forth:

I ask of your bed the heavy dreamless sleep
Hovering under the curtains innocent of regrets,
And which you can taste after your black lies,
You who upon the void know more than the dead.

For Vice, gnawing at my native nobility
Has marked me like you with its sterility,
But whereas your breast of stone is inhabited

By a heart which the tooth of no crime can
  wound,
I flee, pale, defeated, haunted by my shroud,
Fearing death whilst I lie alone.

This poem is all pose and no substance. The monster Vice was Baudelaire's bête noire, not

Mallarmé's, and the emotion expressed, a combination of anguish and boredom, was a romantic specialty about which several books and dissertations have been written.

On its own this poem is not particularly interesting, but it is crucial to observe what Mallarmé made of its *maudit* conventions in his later verse. The following is Mallarmé's last sonnet (1887), and the bedchamber in this poem is rather different from that of two decades before:

A lace self-abolishes
In the doubt of the supreme Game
To half-reveal like a blasphemy
Only an eternal absence of bed.

This unanimous blank conflict
Of a garland with the same,
Fled against the sallow glass
Floats more than it encloses.

But, in whoever's place one gilds oneself with
  dream
There sadly sleeps a mandore
With the hollow musician nothingness

Such that toward some window
Pertaining to no belly but its own
Filial something could have been born.
           ("Une dentelle s'abolit . . . ")

This poem—any intellectual venture—is a bit of lace, an intricate dialectical pattern in filial relation to the void. It is delicate and can exist only until its gambit is questioned, at which point it will disappear, revealing that the reality it veiled was foundationless. In the sonnet "Anguish," the bed is an icon of moral and psychological agony, but the bedroom in this later poem is of high ontological moment: we are inside the boudoir of the Absolute. Behind the veil, in the early poem, there is a beast, a myth of the subhuman to counter the Christian mythology of superhumanity, and the void where the beast lives is an analogue of hell. In "Une dentelle s'abolit," behind the veil there is no bed and never has been one, and "the hollow musician nothingness" is barely a metaphor, let alone a myth. The romantics were notorious for the attempt to supplant one mythology by another or to concoct syncretic myths, but Mallarmé was pursuing a rarer literary achievement, to suggest a metaphysics without a concomitant mythology. While retaining the romantics' obsessive vocabulary and symbolic structures, Mallarmé thus drained them of romanticism.

Mallarmé was aware of the "doubleness" in his thinking, and in his longer works, he exploited the incongruity as a mode of organization and as a theme. In *Igitur* (1867–1870) and *Un coup de dés* (A Throw of the Dice, 1897), the works that set forth most comprehensively his protomodernist metaphysics, the ambience seems intentionally inapt. The shadowy figure in *Igitur* comes to us straight from the House of Usher, and the dice game in Mallarmé's last work is interwoven with a Sturm und Drang shipwreck. The effect is not unlike some of Franz Kafka's, but Mallarmé is never funny. It is as if Wittgenstein had been translated by Poe and illustrated by Delacroix.

The sharpest delineation of immiscible milieux appeared at the commencement of his career, in two dramatic pieces that he composed as a pair for his volume *Other Poems.* *Hérodiade* (1864 ff.), on which Mallarmé continued to work all his life, and *L'Après-midi d'un faune* (1865, 1876) were conceived as undiluted opposites, and each embodies half of the poet's sensibility. *Hérodiade,* the story of Salomé and the beheading of Saint John, is historical in subject; apocalyptic in tone; superhuman, female, and platonic in viewpoint. *L'Après-midi d'un faune* is a pastoral tale about a woodland creature and two nymphs— it is timeless and understated, human, male, and skeptical. This pair of poems seem as far apart as Wagner and Diaghilev: one would not think it possible that the same man could have written both. However, *Hérodiade* and *L'Après-midi d'un faune* are thematically linked. Their heroine and hero ponder the problem of mind versus body, and face the fact that sex is the crux between spirit and matter.

Hérodiade loves "the horror of being virgin," while the faun only wonders at "the secret terror of the flesh"—but neither piece affords the consummation devoutly to be wished.

Oddly enough, both of these highly modern poems follow the basic conventions of the troubadour *tradition de refus.* Mallarmé's most significant accomplishment within the context of French literature may have been to transform the medieval/Renaissance poem of love scorned, which was the foundation of most subsequent lyric verse in France, into a form that is momentous and modern. "Autre évantail/de *Mademoiselle Mallarmé*" (Another Fan/of *Mademoiselle Mallarmé's*, 1884) evidences the personal intensity that Mallarmé reinfused into this moribund convention. The Mademoiselle of the poem is at once Mallarmé's daughter, Geneviève, and his deceased sister, Maria—the title indicates both another fan and another Miss Mallarmé—and the poet is finding something of the latter in the former. He compares his daughter's smile to "a buried laugh" and the *refus* of this lyric seems to be the denial of female love (Maria's, Harriet's, his mother's) that death had brought to pass. The imagery is inappropriately sexual, however, in a poem about one's daughter or sister: the speaker yearns to find some outlet for a desire "like one great kiss/Which, wild to be born for no person/ Can neither break forth nor rest." In psychoanalytic terms, there has been a failure of projection. The speaker cannot transfer his childhood affections because he has not learned the "subtle lie" by which men transmute their Oedipal desire (for the progenitress or the female twin) into a mature desire for "the other." In Mallarmé's prose poem "Le nénuphur blanc" ("The White Water-Lily," 1885), the refusal is presented with self-conscious medievalism—the woman is addressed as "Meditative lady, my Haughty, my Cruel"— but the *refus* has been completely psychologized. The male refused and the female refusing seem internal to the androgynous speaker, and the male rejects every candidate for projection; he expresses platonic contempt for "transparent resemblance." The sonnet "M'introduire dans ton histoire" (To introduce myself into your story, 1886) extends the theme of *refus* from sexual psychology into sexual metaphysics. Confronted by his cool mistress, the speaker feels as if he were Achilles taking on a glacier and, Marvell-like or Donne-like, he explains to her with boyish enthusiasm that the resolution, through sexual love, of twoness into oneness is a victory for the cosmos.

Hérodiade is the extreme case of *refus*, metaphysical, historical, and sexual. The daughter of King Herod of Judea—Salomé, or Hérodiade—costs her soulmate his head and in the process refuses Christianity, modern history, and human love. That John the Baptist is Hérodiade's male counterpart and ideal mate is obvious. She may maneuver to execute Christ's herald, but in the poem she is associated with Jesus' nativity, with Daniel's redemption from the lion's den, and with a set of Christ-like characteristics (chastity, self-sacrifice, and, it appears, divinity). Mallarmé did not take Salomé's story as an excuse for exoticism or eroticism, as did Oscar Wilde and other interpreters of the New Testament, because it was not the refusal of material existence that Mallarmé objected to in Christianity. Nietzsche and D. H. Lawrence may confront us with a pagan-Christian either/or choice, but in *Hérodiade,* as in "Une dentelle s'abolit," Mallarmé presents instead the "unanimous blank conflict/Of a garland with the same." Saint John—or rather, at the conclusion of the poem, his chanting head—appreciates the "clean break" that "suppresses or cuts off/The ancient discords/With the body." Hérodiade's ax serves to obviate John's mind-body problem, and this ultimate act of *refus* becomes almost a gesture of sibling love; just as in "The White Water-Lily" the male character finds much to love in the painful refusal of his female counterpart.

Actually there is no such poem as *Hérodiade,* though Mallarmé intended that there should be. The three pieces printed together in current collections were published individually during the poet's lifetime. The first, the "Ancient Overture of Hérodiade," is an operatic recitative spoken by the princess' nurse. The second part, composed first, is entitled "Scene," and is a melodramatic dialogue between the nurse and Hérodiade. The "Canticle of St. John," a sprightly dirge for the severed head, was composed last and is third in the narrative sequence. The overture predictably sets the terms, atmospheric and allegorical, for the ensuing action: a Manichaean imagery of darkness versus light predominates. The sun is in eclipse and the nurse believes her solo will be the swan song of the earth:

Abolished, and its horrific wing in the tears
Of the basin, abolished, which mirrors the
   alarms,
Of the naked gold whipping the space crimson,
A Dawn has—heraldic plumage—chosen
Our tower, cinerary and sacrificial,
Heavy tomb which a lovely bird has fled, solitary
Caprice of dawn in vain black plumage. . . .
Ah! of countries dejected and sad this manor-
   house!
No slapping of water! The mournful water resigns
   itself,
To be slapped no more by the feather nor by the
   unforgettable
Swan: the water reflects the abandon
Of the autumn extinguishing in it its firebrand:
Of the swan when amidst the pale mausoleum
Or [when] its feather submerges its head,
   desolated
By the pure diamond of some star, but
Anterior, which scintellated never.
Crime! Funeral pyre! Ancient dawn! Torture!
Purple of heaven! Pond, accomplice to the purple!
And on these rose tints, wide open, this stained-
   glass window.

The world will not soon end, but we learn why this nurse thinks it will. In the allegory of the piece, she stands for the church: she lives in a house of stained-glass windows, in the paid service of a father-king who "does not know" that her "ancient and dried breast" can no longer nourish. The room in which she takes her stand, yet another deserted bedchamber, is filled with allegorical relics. A shroud of stiffened lace is elevated like the eucharistic host; a baptismal "water of ancient basins grows resigned"; and the bed itself, in which Hérodiade has refused to sleep, is portrayed as a Scripture so overinterpreted that it has lost all mystery and authority:

> the bed with vellum pages,
> Such, useless and so claustral, is not linen!
> Which no longer has the dear obscure writings of
>   dreams
> in its folds.

The temporal setting of this piece is at once pre- and post-Christian, and Hérodiade herself represents both the proud order of antiquity and the brave new world of modernity. The nurse belongs to the epoch that comes between, and in the dialogue "Scene," Hérodiade rejects the nurse's values utterly. The nurse offers Hérodiade "holy water," but the princess abhors both her sacraments and her paradise ("and I, I detest the beautiful azure"). This exchange resembles the closet scenes in Jean Racine's tragedy *Phèdre* between Phèdre and her nurse—though the priggish Hippolyte appears here in the role of a woman—and Hérodiade argues with her nurse about the necessity of marriage. Hérodiade recoils repeatedly from any hint of physicality, and she proffers her own version of Christ's *noli me tangere*. She insists that she will be married only to herself, and the nurse fears a consequent reversion to pre-Christian horrors. She fears that her princess will become the new Fury of a new paganism. On the other hand, in the final section, Saint John appears to accept the new order, which, in its stern beauty, so resembles the old: his falling head "bows a salute" to "the same/Principle which elected me." He welcomes the eternal, eternally changing World Spirit in its new *Zeit*-guise.

The goat-man of *L'Après-midi d'un faune* would not understand this melodrama, and it is possible that Mallarmé, who during more than thirty years was unable to finish the piece, could not understand it either. *Hérodiade* embodies all of the psychological dilemmas that determined Mallarmé's life, and it seems he wrote *L'Après-midi d'un faune* in part to expose that unconscious darkness to the light of midday. In eclipse for Hérodiade, the sun glistens for Mallarmé's faun. The atmosphere is languorous, with "the silence of an afternoon of music," but something is not quite right. The faun feels the "pain of being two" and wishes to become one with some nymph, yet the two nymphs at hand seem inexplicably in love with one another and want no part of him. A faun should not need to ponder the issues of psychology, but this one even faces a philosophical dilemma. He is not certain in retrospect that his nymphs existed, and lacking a sure love object, his erotic meditation reads like an epistemologist's Song of Songs. In *Hérodiade*, Mallarmé expresses his psychic knot to us as it expressed itself to him, not as a problem but as a way of seeing. The piece is a comprehensive *refus*: it dismisses men, sex, matter, social institutions, and even life in favor of a higher order that is heroic, severe, narcissistic, and female. Hérodiade cavils only once, in an aside at the end of part 2, when she admits that her ferocity may be no more than "the sobs, supreme and wounded,/ Of a childhood." *L'Après-midi d'un faune* extends this question and returns to the poet's past for a look at the source of his own "Hérodiadisme." Psychoanalytic critics have enjoyed pointing out that the two nymphs—the "chaster one" and "the other one, all sighs"; the one "inhuman" and the other "timid" but "humid"—are dead ringers for Maria and Harriet. Their refusal to pay attention to the faun and their mysterious disappearance are said, in this interpretation, to replicate the boyhood trauma of seeing two loved girls go off together and never return.

This reading would not command much interest unless, as seems more than likely, Mallarmé knew awfully well what he was doing:

> Did I love a dream?
> My doubt, accumulation of ancient night, ends
> In many a subtle branch, which, remaining the
>   real
> Woods themselves, proves, alas! that the only
>   thing I offered to myself
> For triumph was the ideal absence of roses.
> Let us reflect . . .
>
>   or if the women you gloss
> Configurate a wish of your fabulous senses! . . .
>
> O Sicilian banks of a calm marsh
> That my vanity plunders like the suns,
> Tacit under the flowers of sparks, RECOUNT. . . .
>   (5–10, 26–28)

The faun upon his own couch demonstrates how epistemology turns, inevitably, into psychoanalysis and psychoanalysis into art. Epistemology is by definition a naive science, and the faun begins naively. He assumes a clearcut distinction between the real and the imaginary, and he proposes to categorize his afternoon's experience as one or the other. He will make this judgment by reflection, by storytelling, and by "gloss": he takes his afternoon as a text and, using the techniques of literary criticism (and of what will become dream analysis), he hopes to interpret it. His first observation about the nymphs is that "Their light [is] flesh colored," and with this curious remark he introduces a major obsession of the epistemological tradition. Because what our eyes see is not physical objects in themselves but only the light refracted by them, our knowledge of the physical world in large part depends on our discrimination of colored light. The faun defines his nymphs as an "incarnation" of flesh-colored light and, in fact, this whole afternoon has been a creation of sunlight: the sun has made its dreamy weather, its deceptive shadows, its illusion of antiquity. The sun is "wine's effectual star"— it nourishes the vine—and Mallarmé's tipsy

philosopher acknowledges that he sees the world as through a wineskin, darkly:

> Thus, when I have sucked from grapes their
>   clarity,
> To banish a regret by my ruse put aside,
> Laughing, I raise to the summer sky the empty
>   cluster
> And, blowing in its luminous skins, avid
> For drunkenness, until evening I look through
>   them.
>   (85–89)

The poem seems counter-Solomonic: there are no "things" at all under the sun. Symbolist theorists have been accused of solipsism, of taking nothing outside the individual mind to be objectively real, but Mallarmé was too skeptical even to be a solipsist. He simply declined to believe that illusion should be identified with error. Appearance versus reality may not be a valid philosophical distinction, and for aesthetics, it is clearly not a useful one: art is a *beau mensonge*, a beautiful and mimetic lie. And the faun, for all his doubts about what has transpired, bears the physical evidence of a love bite:

> Other than this sweet nothing rumored by their
>   lips,
> The kiss, which quietly assures of the perfidious
>   ones,
> My chest, virgin of proof, attests a bite,
> Mysterious, due to some august tooth. . . .
>   (42–45)

This is the stigmatum of a postepistemological art. What we dream, what we invent, what we write: our illusions exist—they are *real illusions*—and as such they are facts. But *L'Après-midi d'un faune* does not seek to tell us this datum (Mallarmé thought that "telling" was vulgar); the poem demonstrates its verity. The faun recounts his dream ("CONTEZ," instructs *himself*: to make a *conte*, a story, of), and he thus creates fictitious reality. The faun is an artist—he plays the panpipes—and the poem begins and ends with the confident assertion that, physically extant or not, his nymphs will possess, in his retelling, a permanent reality:

These nymphs, I want to perpetuate them. . . .

Couple, adieu: I'll see the shadow that you've
    become.

But human reality is not created out of nothing, and the faun is aware from the first that his nymphs—his poem—may "configurate a wish." At the climax of his adventure, the faun discovers that his erotic attraction is not to a specific love object but to a projection from the psyche:

So much the worse! towards happiness others will
    pull me
By their tresses knotted to the horns of my
    forehead:
You know, my passion, that, purple and already
    ripe,
Each pomegranate bursts and murmurs with bees;
And our blood, smitten with whoever will take it,
Flows for all the eternal swarm of desire.
                                        (121–126)

And he discovers, more crucially, the root of all such projections:

At the hour when this wood with gold and ashes
    is tinted
A festival is excited in the extinguished foliage:
Etna! It is amid you, visited by Venus
On your lava posing her ingenuous heels,
When a sad sleep thunders or the flame exhausts
    itself.
I hold the queen!
        O sure punishment . . .
                                        (127–133)

The object of male sexual desire—the "hymen desired by the one who seeks the *la*"—is at its source maternal. Mallarmé beat history by half a century when, in this poem, he defined man as the satyr with an Oedipus complex.

Guilt ("O sure punishment") is the cause of robust projection—at least, guilt that is unconscious. A healthy faun is a forgetful faun:

O sure punishment . . .

                        No, but the soul
Empty of words and this heavy body
Succumb late to the proud silence of noon:
Without any more ado we must sleep in
    forgetfulness of the blasphemy. . . .
                                        (133–137)

The failure to forget, to repress, will engender dubious projections, like the one in this poem. Yet consciousness "of the blasphemy" will engender in addition poems like this one. The faun sets out "to perpetuate," to make art of his projections, precisely because his projections have failed him.

A refusal to participate in the natural round of life—a *refus*, like Hérodiade's—is one possible result of too much knowledge of human nature. But obsessive contemplation of nature is also what we mean by culture (and it may be, more or less, what Sigmund Freud meant by sublimation). The faun's libido is aroused, but it does not seem to be the nymphs who have got his goat. Nature calls and culture answers:

But no! [the breeze] . . .
Murmurs not at all of water but what my flute
    pours
On the grove sprinkled with chords; and the only
    wind . . .
Is, on the horizon unstirred by a wrinkle,
The visible and serene artificial breath
Of inspiration, which regains the heaven.
                                (17, 19–20, 23–25)

"The visible and . . . artificial breath/Of inspiration" is a good definition for a line of poetry, just as it is in fact a line in a poem. *L'Après-midi d'un faune* seems oddly tautological, but at the same time that it makes itself unnecessary it becomes an object with which we cannot part. The faun's doubt about his experience becomes itself an experience, both for him and for countless eavesdroppers. And as if to prove Mallarmé's point, the poem has become a consequential artifact of our culture; its postpublication history is virtually a part of the poem. Mallarmé's eclogue was intended from the start for the theater, though the poet had little hope of its production. He was somewhat surprised and a bit disturbed when Claude Debussy premiered his musical version, *Prelude à l'après-midi d'un faune,* in 1894: "I thought that I had already put it to music," the poet told the composer. Considering Mallarmé's attachment to the ballet, it is probable that he would have been more pleased when, in 1912, Waslaw Nijinski choreographed and danced the *Faune* with the Ballets Russes in Paris. Mallarmé was happy with Manet's illustration of 1876, and Matisse followed suit with five illustrations in 1932. Paul Valéry thought *L'Après-midi d'un faune* the most beautiful poem in French literature, and to dissent would be imprudent: certainly it is the European poem of the nineteenth century most honored by European artists of the twentieth.

Mallarmé's fame dates from the publication in 1884 of J. K. Huysmans' novel *À rebours (Against the Grain),* in which *L'Après-midi d'un faune* is elaborately praised, and Mallarmé responded in the same year with his longish poem "Prose," dedicated to Huysmans' hero, the aesthete des Esseintes. Mallarmé's "Prose" complements and completes the effort of his *Faune.* The poems are similar structurally: each establishes a theoretical issue in the first few lines (the two opening stanzas in "Prose") and then moves backward to narrate the experience that originated the question. In both, that experience is in doubt, though in *Faune* it is the speaker who questions it and in "Prose" it is an unnamed and unfriendly "They." Moreover "Prose," like *Faune,* is in the *tradition de refus.* There is a woman, whom the speaker calls his "sister, sensible and tender," and she cools with a smile his ardor and "long desire." "They"—

the judgmental outsiders—doubt that this woman existed, but the speaker insists upon it: "We were two, I maintain this." However, the existence of the female character is not so important in this poem as in *Faune,* and in any case the speaker understands that he and she comprise a "double/Unconscious." "Prose" centers on the existence of an island (not unlike Lewis Carroll's wonderland) where the couple claim to have seen a magic garden of enormous and fast-growing lilies, irises, and gladiola. The first word of "Prose" is a vocative exclamation of the rhetorical term "hyperbole":

> Hyperbole: from my memory
> Triumphally can you not
> Arise, today gramarye
> Cloaked in a book of iron:

—and the central metaphor of the poem is certainly hyperbolic. So too are its vocabulary, syntax, and overrich rhyme scheme:

> *Hyperbole: de ma mémoire*
> *Triomphalement ne sais-tu*
> *Te lever, aujourd'hui grimoire*
> *Dans un livre de fer vêtu:*

The outsize rhetoric and the technical extremism, we are advised from the start, are deployed to liberate the *grimoire,* the volume of occult spells, from the "book of iron" in which it is latent: to make the poetry emerge out of "Prose."

The key to this untoward poem, this *grimoire,* is in the last two stanzas. The speaker has just informed the "They" that he saw the island lilies enlarge beyond all reason, "And not as the river weeps,/When its monotone game lies/In wishing that amplitude should arrive." The poem concludes:

> The child abdicates its ecstasy
> And already learned in paths
> She speaks the word: Anastase!
> Born for eternal parchments,

STÉPHANE MALLARMÉ

Before a sepulcher laugh
Under any clime, its ancestor,
At carrying this name: Pulchérie!
Hidden by the too grand gladiola.

"And not as the river weeps" preempts a cliché. The "monotone game" of cliché is played by language-users in effect to prevent "amplitude" (or hyperbole). In his treatise *On the Sublime,* Longinus, the classical rhetorician, laments the tendency of hyperbolic language to "turn into its opposite," to become a cliché that obscures the outrageous reality it was coined to reveal. "The river weeps" is no longer (but doubtless once was) an original, sublime, and hyperbolic expression, an evocation of the "island" where all men have been and that no poet will let us forget. Likewise "Pulchérie"—a Gallicization of the Latin *pulcheria,* or beauty—no longer means as much as it once did. The concept Beauty must be replaced by a new term of "amplitude": *Anastase.* This word is both a name, with exotic connections to the Byzantine and papal courts, and a derivative of the Greek *anastasis,* which means "raising up." The speaker, in the first stanza, asks Hyperbole to arise from its leaden casing and here, as if in reply, a hyperbolic infant term rises up from the tomb of its "ancestor." In the cemetery of spent and wilted words, Mallarmé's monster gladiola are in bloom.

Many of Mallarmé's shorter poems take poetic creation as a self-conscious analogue for the unconscious means by which Everyman creates every-reality out of words. *L'Après-midi d'un faune* adds to this notion the sense that poetry is both a result of and a solution to the psychic trauma of living in a world where reality is the creature of language. In "Prose/ for des Esseintes," the issue is both more and less linguistic. "Prose" has been called Mallarmé's *ars poetica* and its thrust is oddly practical: it suggests that the poet's role is to maintain "the dialect of the tribe" as an effective means of comprehension. This would seem to imply a positivist moral, that language is a tool of thought—but no positivist would have written and no positivist could accept this poem. Or "Prose" might be said to teach a platonic lesson, that words correspond to static things and static ideas. Critics have made a strong case for the poem's Platonism: there is, after all, a transcendent island where grow unique flora of which the flowers in our world are poor shadows. But Mallarmé's island *is our planet*—he called earth "a festive star," an "unprecedented mystery"—and poetry is for him its instrument of self-revelation. The Real is litotes, the Ideal hyperbole; and the distinction between realms of being may consist in no more than a tone of voice and a nuance of punctuation. It is in this sense that poetry may be said to "create" the Ideal. Hence poetic creations are analogous not merely to the makeshift realities of Everyman; they are parallel to the unique Reality of the Creator God. These two propositions seem contradictory—one tending to relativism or even nihilism, the other to absolutism or even mysticism. Mallarmé spent his career and lived his life trying to hold these impulses together, and the climactic result was less a contradictory aesthetics than a paradoxical theology. In matters of aesthetics, James Joyce's Stephen Dedalus can speak for Stéphane Mallarmé: "The mystery of esthetic like that of material creation is accomplished. The artist, like the God of the creation, remains within or behind or beyond or above his handiwork, invisible, refined out of existence, indifferent, paring his fingernails" (*A Portrait of the Artist as a Young Man,* New York, 1969, p. 215). A creator is both absent from and present in his creation, though the reason for this is not aesthetic, it is theological: the Creator God is at once infinite vacancy and absolute plenitude.

This theology informed Mallarmé's most experimental—most modernist—work, and its formulation was hard won. It evolved during the "nights of Tournon," in the period of the 1860's when Mallarmé taught at the lycée in that provincial town and faced down a long psychological crisis. Mallarmé's letters form the best record of this experience. He called his condition "hysteria" or "permanent insomnia," and its physical manifestation, he said, was the incapacity to hold a pen: his correspondence ceased when palpitations began to occur even during dictation. He felt overcome by "a matchless Nothingness" until, in 1867, he announced that he had died and been reborn—indeed that he had "struggled with that creature of ancient and evil plumage—God—whom I fortunately defeated and threw to earth" (letter of 14 May 1867 to Henri Cazalis). Despite the rhetoric, Mallarmé emerged from his theogony not as the self-deified Caligula of literature but as its righteous prophet Jacob, its Israel. He said he had become "an aptitude of the spiritual universe for seeing and developing itself," and he began, like certain Hebrew prophets, to see in his personal history a parallel to the unfolding of the divine personality through time. Such ideas have precedents, and there has been considerable dispute about how well read Mallarmé was in the Cabala, Buddhist theology, and the Hegelian philosophy of history.

In any event, the poet drew up a plan for a "Great Work" through which the World Spirit, which had been Nonbeing in its original state, would at last achieve its latent fullness of Being. Of this work, he wrote that he would "need twenty years for the five volumes . . . one of them a perfect absolute called 'Beauty,'" and another "a personal work called 'Sumptuous Allegories of Nothingness.'" He projected that the work would consist of "three verse poems, with *Hérodiade* as the overture . . . and four prose poems on the spiritual idea of Nothingness." Instead, as an act of exorcism, a form of cure, Mallarmé wrote a long (unfinished) prose poem, *Igitur.* He seems to have thought its chief use was medical: he read it to a pair of literary friends in 1870 and then filed it away. His son-in-law discovered the manuscript in 1900, but it did not see print until 1925, more than a half-century after its composition. That was just as well; almost no one would have been prepared

for *Igitur* until the era that produced Kafka's *The Castle* and Samuel Beckett's *The Unnameable.* The project, as Mallarmé put it in a late essay, was "to observe with the eyes of the divinity." The title appears to be biblical, though critics are not unanimous about its source. The postpositive conjunction *igitur* appears in the second chapter of the Vulgate Genesis—"Thus [*igitur*] the heavens and the earth were finished"—and, while the word generally means "as a consequence," Mallarmé uses it as a name. He may have learned the cabalistic technique of biblical misreading and so construed this verse to say: Igitur (or Consequence) finished the heavens and the earth. His subtitle, *The Madness of Elbehnon,* supports this interpretation, since *El behnon* could be Mallarmé's version of a Hebrew mystical term that connotes the creative attribute of divinity.

Whatever we make of the title, the work itself concerns Creation in the biblical sense and traces, eon by eon, the history of the Creator's "motives," "feelings," and developing "self-consciousness." This postapocryphal history is divided, like the biblical Creation, into seven stages: a preamble ("IN AN ANCIENT STUDY") and an argument ("FOUR PIECES"), a three-sentence apocalypse ("HE LIES DOWN IN THE TOMB"), and four major, intervening divisions: "MIDNIGHT," "HE LEAVES THE ROOM AND IS LOST ON THE STAIRS (instead of sliding down the banister)," "IGITUR'S LIFE (*Schema*)," and "THE DICE-THROW IN THE TOMB (*Schema*)." Portentous self-irony is the dominant key throughout, and the technical innovations of *Igitur*—including the peculiar comments Mallarmé has placed in the borders surrounding the text—all seem designed to generate an impression of uncomfortable, unaccustomed, unaccountable duality. In *Igitur,* Mallarmé's insistent theme of *refus* takes on theological significance. The creation (*ex nihilo*) of an "Other" by "The One" is problematic, to say the least—and the accommodation of Oneness to the existence of a Second could bring about, temporarily, a repulsion and withdrawal; in other words, a *refus.* This is an ancient theological question—Saint Augustine gives the issue its classic theoretical exposition; the Book of Job treats it in the form of a moral parable—but Mallarmé sets its ramifications forth in modern and personal terms, as a gothic psychodrama.

In the introduction, in the ancient study, the child Igitur and his "ancestors" are gathered in shadow to set the theurgic tone; in part one, at "Midnight," the Big Bang is presented in a blend of biblical cosmogony ("constellations and the sea are separated") and Hegelian exegesis ("a permanent form . . . produced by its own apparition in the mirroring of obscurity"). A more familiar world materializes in the middle sections, though it is seen from the unfamiliar perspective of a disgruntled Absolute, embroiled—as if by chance—in the confusions of relativity. Out of this discomfort emerge, paragraph by paragraph, all of the traditional distinctions and antinomies of Western metaphysics: Ideal and Real, Creator and Created, the Absolute and the Void. As he comes at last to self-consciousness, Igitur finds that he is the Ideal Uncreated Absolute, and he views both this novel dualism and his role in it as the results of a *refus:* "The infinite at last escapes the family, which has suffered from it—old space—no chance. It was right to deny him—its life—so that he may have been the Absolute" (M. A. Caws trans.). The pathos of the cosmos, its "profitable madness," is the pathos of Mallarmé's own life. And Igitur's uneasiness with duality and distinction may suggest the poet's growing dissatisfaction with the dogmatic antinomies—transcendence/immanence, avant-garde/bourgeoisie, poetry/prose —that were the product of biographical separations. Mallarmé traces the path of Igitur down symbolic staircases and through sparsely furnished rooms to the place of his discovery that the unramified Absolute is an unlivable concept ("My certainty disturbs me; everything is overly clear"). Preferring the old ambiguities, weary of "the sick-

ness of the Ideal," Igitur determines that the Absolute is a process dependent on chance and "simply shakes the dice—a motion before going to rejoin the ashes, the atoms of his ancestors." Both Nothingness and the Absolute disappear—at least as concepts—and, in this Sabbath of history, "the poor character" Igitur is restored to his family. The concluding section of the piece is worth reproducing whole:

> HE LIES DOWN IN THE TOMB
> Upon the ashes of stars, the undivided ones of the family, lay the poor character, after having drunk the drop of nothingness lacking to the sea. (The empty flask, madness, all that remains of the castle?) Nothingness having departed, there remains the castle of purity.
> (*Selected Poetry and Prose,* M. A. Caws trans., p. 101)
> *or the dice-*
> *chance ab-*
> *sorbed*

For his last work, a half-life after *Igitur,* Mallarmé returned to the metaphor of dice, the theme of chance, the atmosphere of theogony, and the note of intense poignancy. Unlike *Igitur,* however, *Un coup de dés jamais n'abolira le hasard* (*A Throw of the Dice Never Will Abolish Chance,* 1897) is not presented "from the Absolute point of view" alone. For the career of Mallarmé, that would have been too easy a crown. This long poem is written from two perspectives at once: the Absolute and the conventional, the divine and the human. One "plot," its imagery drawn from biblical cosmogony and pagan theogonies, consists in a toss of cosmic dice. The second "plot," a harrowing shipwreck, draws upon the flood, sea, and storm imagery of Homer, Vergil, Dante, Delacroix, and the Noah chapters of Genesis. Mallarmé is able to sustain this simultaneity by an unprecedented radicalism of technique. That technique is virtually indescribable; it must be seen. Mallarmé says in his preface that the basic unit of this poem is "some simultaneous vision of the Page"; and what follows are the fifteenth and sixteenth pages, which, in the text as here, are meant to face one another:

IT WAS
born of stars

THE NUMBER

DID IT EXIST
otherwise than scattered hallucination of agony

DID IT BEGIN AND DID IT CEASE
welling up when denied and shut when shown
at last
in some outpouring rarely spread

MIGHT IT FIGURE ITSELF

evidence of the sun however little one

IT WOULD BE
worse
no
more nor less
indifferently but as much

DID IT ILLUMINE

CHANCE

Drops
the quill
rhythmical suspending of the sinister
to entomb itself
in the original sprays
whence long ago sprang their frenzy as far as a peak
tarnished
by the identical neutrality of the gulf

The variations in type size and type face are crucial: different sizes and faces may be read as belonging to different syntactic structures and narrative fragments. The word "CHANCE," for instance, belongs to a sentence that is dispersed across the entire poem and that repeats its title. Some of these sentences and clauses belong to one "plot" or the other, but as in the columns above the two are made to criss-cross, overlap, and eventually merge: "the original sprays" and "the gulf," for example, evoke both the mariners' cemetery and the watery abyss of Creation. The typography and spacing have also a mimetic function. When Mallarmé showed him this poem, Valéry said he felt for the first time that thought or doubt could occupy space, and in fact the poem's last line is "All Thought expresses a Throw of the Dice." Moreover, the spray of black ideograms, tossed across an expanse of white space, replicates this poetic score's insistent melody: "NOTHING . . . WILL HAVE TAKEN PLACE . . . EXCEPT PLACE . . . EXCEPTED . . . PERHAPS . . . A CONSTELLATION." Nothing finally exists, in this poem or outside it, but the pattern of inconceivable coming and unpredictable going that existence is.

Un coup de dés is a poem about syntax: its message is that reality (whatever that word means, or can be made to mean) is far too complicated, too qualified, too riddled, too thick a congeries of phenomena, however impressive the various ideas about it may be, to permit its expression in the simple structures either of conversational or of theoretical language. On this issue the forefather of modernist verse and the forefather of modernist prose are agreed. Squeeze the blank spaces from the conclusion of Mallarmé's *Dice*, add a modicum of reductive punctuation—and you will have a sentence by Henry James:

> In these latitudes of the vague, in which all reality dissolves itself (excepted at the summit perhaps, as far as one place fuses with "the beyond")—outside the interest, for its part signaled in general, by such obliquity on such declivity—by fires, toward what ought to be the Septentrion (also North: a constellation), cold from forgetfulness and disuse, not so much as not to enumerate on some vacant and superior surface the successive shock, sidereally, of a total count in the making—waking, doubting, rolling, shining and meditating, before stopping at some last point that sanctifies it—all thought expresses a throw of the dice.

One could say that this is what happens, or must happen, to syntax and the structures of thought in a world that lacks metaphysical foundations; but that would be an insufficiently complex explanation. "Local" explanations of reality are impossible, and explanatory sentences or other bits of syntax ought to be impossibly intricate, precisely because the metaphysical foundations of our universe are in constant flux—they consist of a process still in process, with its outcome to be determined by chance. The Creation of the universe was and remains a game of risk, and the existence of Existence makes irremediably necessary the rule of chance over its affairs. If this were not so, "the Other" would be identical with "The One," the relative and imperfect Creation with the Absolute and perfect Creator, and thus no Other would exist at all. Chance, relativity, change, pain, imperfection, and shipwreck are all implied in the Creator's throw of the dice.

Furthermore — cabalistically speaking — the Absolute would not exist, as Absolute, unless the not-Absolute also existed. And the Absolute would not, as it were, *exist* at all unless *Existence* had been created, unless the dice had been cast. Before Creation (if it be possible to speak chronologically), the Creator was not-Existence and, even after Creation, is an absent presence in relation to Existence. This simultaneous absence and presence Mallarmé represents with a symbol: a white feather or quill ("plume") that is left behind by "some wing/its own/be-/forehand fallen back from incapacity to trim the flight." Like the numeral zero, this "plume" is a sovereign placeholder. As feather, the remnant of an angelic wing, and as quill, the instrument of human intellectual creation, this symbol drifts across the poem, irradiating significance. At the climax of its voyage through poetic space, the "plume" "encounters or grazes" a floating toque and the two, for an instant in tandem, become the thinking cap of the universe— though to wear it would be a mixed honor. The feathered cap is absurd and "derisible," "irresistible" and "heroic": the products of intelligence by nature "scintillate" with a "virginal trace" of Creation, yet all evaporate "in mist" for attempting to impose "a limit on infinity." The absolutist and the nihilist are both correct, every system of understanding is true and every system false. The great surprise, though, is that the Absolute is not an absolutist. As the inventor of the game creation, the Absolute is the ultimate relativist since, from a creator's perspective, a creation is no creation if it is not other-than-the-creator. The doctrine of authorial impersonality is at base metaphysical or even theological, and this "aestheticist's" final poem is not simply an art work about art but a Theodicy of the

Creator God. In it, every creator is defended on the grounds that he remains implicated in, and even dependent upon, the consequences of his creation.

Un coup de dés was received, during the last year of Mallarmé's life, with a nervous cough. The poem was republished in 1914 in the *Nouvelle revue française*, the chief organ of French modernism, and it began a new career in the era of Eliot and Pound, when Mallarmé's influence reached its zenith. But his influence was vast even during his lifetime. Valéry wrote of youthful days with his mentor:

> I said sometimes to Mallarmé: "There are some who blame you, and some who despise you. It has become an easy thing for reporters to amuse the people at your expense, while your friends shake their heads. . . . But do you not know, do you not feel, that there is, in every city in France, a youth who would let himself be cut into pieces for your verses and for you? You are his pride, his craft, his vice. He cuts himself off from everyone by his love of, faith in, your work, hard to find, to understand and to defend.
>
> ("Je disaís quelquefois à Stéphane Mallarmé, *Variété* 3, 1936)

It is said that the greatest privilege a writer or painter or composer or critic could receive in the late nineteenth century was an invitation to attend a "Tuesday" *chez* Mallarmé. The *mardis* commenced in 1878 when the Mallarmé family lived in the rue de Moscou, but the more celebrated occasions occurred at 87 rue de Rome, beginning in 1884. Invitations were written in rhymed verse and the Prince of Poets, a slight man with a shawl and clay pipe, greeted each guest at the door. Inside, guests were welcomed by the family pets: Clair de Lune the screech-owl, the black cat Lilith, a pair of greyhounds named Saladin and Isolde, some small green parakeets, and a bluebird from Bengal. What ensued was not a salon but a lecture. Mallarmé would stand, his guests seated around the dining table, and—beneath the impressionist paintings and drawings—the Sphinx, as Leconte de Lisle called him, would hold forth. Valéry saw him in this pose as a Mosaic aesthetics-giver ("this revealed truth," he called one of Mallarmé's pronouncements); Degas professed boredom, but attended anyway. And two generations of guests were marked for life by the experience; among them, the principal Parnassian poets and the principal symbolists, Gide, Claudel, Pater, Swinburne, Wilde, Yeats, Gauguin, Manet, Rodin, Whistler, and Debussy.

Mallarmé would have been especially pleased with the part he played posthumously in the modernist movement. His reach extends astonishingly—to every art form, to modernist and postmodernist aesthetics (where his effect has been pervasive, if sometimes pernicious), and to the line of language theorists, behavioral scientists, and philosophers that leads from Ferdinand de Saussure to Claude Lévi-Strauss and Jacques Derrida. As for verse, he published only one major collection (*Poésies*, 1884), yet Valéry wrote that Mallarmé reinvented language and compared his poetic "discoveries" with the invention of algebra. In his critical essays, Mallarmé often looked with fondness and expectation to the future. Of his never-executed "Great Work" he wrote, three years before his death in 1898:

> It terrifies me to think of the qualities (among them, genius certainly) which the author of such a work will have to possess. I am one of the unpossessed. We will let that pass. . . . What, then, will the work itself be? I answer: a hymn, all harmony and joy; an immaculate grouping of universal relationships come together for some miraculous and glittering occasion. Man's duty is to observe with the eyes of the divinity; for if his connection with that divinity is to be made clear, it can be expressed only by the pages of the open book in front of him.
>
> ("The Book: A Spiritual Instrument," B. Cook trans., *Selected Prose Poems, Essays, & Letters*, p. 24)

This is the author of *Un coup de dés* imagining the author of *Finnegans Wake*, a cathedral of

Mallarméen prose poetry bearing atop its towers gargoyles meant for the eyes of God alone. Small wonder that, while the heritage of most nineteenth-century figures in the modernist period was rejection ("Kill the nineteenth century dead!" was Gertrude Stein's battle cry), Mallarmé's was indebtedness. He died in middle age on the threshold of the twentieth century, but given his proud ambivalence about his life and times he might, had he lived to ripeness, have approved the modernists' assessment: that Stéphane Mallarmé was the greatest poet of a transitional century.

Selected Bibliography

EDITIONS

FIRST EDITIONS
Poésies. Paris, 1884.

MODERN EDITIONS
La cheveleure vol d'une flamme. Edited by Austin Gill. Glasgow, 1971.
Un coup de dés jamais n'abolira le hasard. Edited by Claude Roulet. Neuchâtel, 1960.
La dernière mode: Gazette du monde et de la famille. Paris, 1978.
Les dieux antiques: Nouvelle mythologie d'après. Paris, 1925.
Divagations. Paris, 1949.
Documents Stéphane Mallarmé. Paris, 1968–.
Les "Gossips" de Mallarmé, Athenaeum, 1875–1876. Edited by Henri Mondor and Lloyd James Austin. Paris, 1962.
Igitur ou la folie d'Elbehnon. Edited by Edmond Bonniot. Paris, 1952.
Les noces d'Hérodiade, mystère. Edited by Gardner Davies. Paris, 1959.
Pages choisies. Edited by Guy Delfel. Paris, 1954.
Prélude à l'après-midi d'un faune: An Authoritative Score. Edited by William Austin. New York, 1970.
Poésies. Edited by Pierre Beausire. Lausanne, 1945.
————— Edited by Jean-Paul Sartre. Paris, 1966.
Pour un tombeau d'Anatole. Edited by Jean-Pierre Richard. Paris, 1961.

COLLECTED WORKS
Oeuvres complètes. Edited by Henri Mondor and G. Jean-Aubry. Paris, 1965.

TRANSLATIONS

Herodias. Translated by Clark Mills. Prairie City, Ill., 1940.
Mallarmé. Edited by Anthony Hartley. Baltimore, 1965.
The Poems of Mallarmé. Translated by Roger Fry, with commentary by Charles Mauron. New York, 1957.
Selected Poems. Translated by C. F. MacIntrye. Berkeley, Calif., 1959.
Selected Poetry and Prose. Edited by Mary Ann Caws. New York, 1982.
Selected Prose Poems, Essays, & Letters. Translated by Bradford Cook. Baltimore, 1956.
A Tomb for Anatole. Translated by Paul Austen. San Francisco, 1984.

LETTERS

Correspondance, 1862–1871. Edited by Henri Mondor and Jean-Pierre Richard. Paris, 1959.
Correspondance II, 1871–1885. Edited by Henri Mondor and Lloyd James Austin. Paris, 1965.

BIOGRAPHICAL AND CRITICAL STUDIES

BOOKS
Beausire, Pierre. *Mallarmé: Poésie et poétique.* Paris, 1974.
Bernard, Suzanne. *Mallarmé et la musique.* Paris, 1959.
Bersani, Leo. *The Death of Stéphane Mallarmé.* Cambridge, 1982.
Bird, Edward A. *L'Univers poétique de Stéphane Mallarmé.* Paris, 1962.
Blanchot, Maurice. *L'Espace littéraire.* Paris, 1955.
—————. "Le mythe de Mallarmé." In *La part du feu.* Paris, 1949.
Block, Haskell M. *Mallarmé and the Symbolist Drama.* Detroit, 1963.
Boulay, Daniel. *L'Obscurité esthétique de Mallarmé et "La prose pour des Esseintes."* Paris, 1973.
Bowie, Malcolm. *Mallarmé and the Art of Being Difficult.* Cambridge, 1978.

STÉPHANE MALLARMÉ

Burnshaw, Stanley, ed. *The Poem Itself.* New York, 1960. Includes exegeses by Burnshaw and Henri Peyre.

Chadwick, Charles. *Mallarmé, sa pensée dans sa poésie.* Paris, 1962.

Chiari, Joseph. *Symbolisme from Poe to Mallarmé.* Foreword by T. S. Eliot. New York, 1970.

Claudel, Paul. *Positions et propositions, I.* Paris, 1928.

Cohn, Robert G. *Mallarmé's "Un coup de dés."* New Haven, 1949.

————. *Toward the Poems of Mallarmé.* Berkeley, Calif., 1980.

Cooperman, Hayse. *The Aesthetics of Stéphane Mallarmé.* New York, 1933.

Delfiel, Guy. *L'Esthétique de Stéphane Mallarmé.* Paris, 1951.

De Man, Paul. "Mallarmé, Yeats and the Post-Romantic Predicament." Ph.D. dissertation, Harvard University, 1961.

Dujardin, Edouard. *Mallarmé par un des siens.* Paris, 1938.

Erwin, John Francis. "Mallarmé and Claudel." Ph.D. dissertation, Columbia University, 1971.

Faure, Gabriel. *Mallarmé à Tournon.* Paris, 1946.

Fowlie, Wallace. *Mallarmé.* Chicago, 1970.

Gengoux, Jacques. *Le symbolisme de Mallarmé.* Paris, 1950.

Gill, Austin. *The Early Mallarmé.* Oxford, 1979.

Giroux, Robert. *Désir du synthèse chez Mallarmé.* Sherbrooke, Quebec, 1978.

Hayman, David. *Joyce et Mallarmé.* Paris, 1956.

Huot, Sylviane. *Le mythe d'Hérodiade chez Mallarmé.* Paris, 1977.

Joseph, Lawrence A. *Henri Cazalis: Sa vie, son oeuvre, son amitié avec Mallarmé.* Paris, 1972.

Kravis, Judy. *The Prose of Mallarmé.* Cambridge, 1976.

Kristeva, Julia. *La révolution du langage poétique.* Paris, 1974.

Lafleche, Guy. *Grammaire générative des "Contes indiens."* Montreal, 1975.

Lehmann, A. G. *The Symbolist Aesthetic in France, 1885–1895.* Oxford, 1968.

Les mardis: Stéphane Mallarmé and the Artists of His Circle. Lawrence, Kans., 1966. Exhibition catalog.

Lewis, Paula Gilbert. *The Aesthetics of Stéphane Mallarmé in Relation to His Public.* Rutherford, N.J., 1976.

Mauron, Charles. *Introduction to the Psychoanalysis of Mallarmé.* Translated by A. Henderson and W. McLendon. Berkeley, Calif., 1969.

Michaud, Guy. *Mallarmé.* Translated by M. Collins and B. Humez. New York, 1965.

Michon, Jacques. *Mallarmé et les mots anglais.* Montreal, 1978.

Mondor, Henri. *Autres précisions sur Mallarmé et inédits.* Paris, 1961.

————. *L'Hereuse rencontre de Valéry et Mallarmé.* Lausanne, 1947.

————. *Histoire d'un faune.* Paris, 1948.

————. *Mallarmé, documents iconographiques.* Geneva, 1947.

————. *Mallarmé lycéen.* Paris, 1954.

Morris, Drewry Hampton, ed. *Stéphane Mallarmé: Twentieth-Century Criticism, 1901–1971.* University, Miss., 1977.

Nicolas, Henry. *Mallarmé et la symbolisme.* Paris, 1965.

Noulet, Émilie. *Études littéraires.* Mexico, 1944.

————. *L'Oeuvre poétique de Stéphane Mallarmé.* Brussels, 1974.

————. *Études littéraires: Exégèse de trois sonnets de Stéphane Mallarmé.* Paris, 1967.

Paxton, Norman. *The Development of Mallarmé's Prose Style.* Geneva, 1968.

Poulet, Georges. *The Interior Distance.* Translated by Elliott Coleman. Ann Arbor, Mich., 1964.

Richard, Jean-Pierre. *L'Univers imaginaire de Mallarmé.* Paris, 1961.

Royere, Jean. *Mallarmé.* Paris, 1931. Preface by Paul Valéry.

Ruchon, François. *L'Amitié de Stéphane Mallarmé et de Georges Rodenbach.* Geneva, 1959.

Scherer, Jacques. *L'Expression littéraire dans l'oeuvre de Mallarmé.* Paris, 1947.

————. *Grammaire de Mallarmé.* Paris, 1977.

————. *Le "livre" de Mallarmé.* Paris, 1957.

St. Aubyn, Frederic Chase. *Stéphane Mallarmé.* New York, 1969.

Symons, Arthur. *The Symbolist Movement in France.* London, 1899.

Thibaudet, Albert. *La poésie de Stéphane Mallarmé.* Paris, 1959.

Valéry, Paul. *Écrits divers sur Stéphane Mallarmé.* Paris, 1950.

Verlaine, Paul. *Les poètes maudits.* Paris, 1884.

Williams, Thomas A. *Mallarmé and the Language of Mysticism.* Athens, Ga., 1970.

STÉPHANE MALLARMÉ

PERIODICALS AND ARTICLES

Austin, L. J. "Mallarmé and the 'Prose pour des Esseintes.'" *Forum for Modern Language Studies* 2:206–208 (1966).

Cahiers du sud 43 (1964). "Autour de Mallarmé" issue.

Cassedy, S. "Mallarmé and Andrej Belyj: Mathematics and the Phenomenality of the Literary Object." *MLN* 97:1066–1083 (1981).

Caws, Mary Ann. "Joyce in Partial Perspective: A Re-reading of Figures." *Comparative Literature Studies* 19:132–134 (1982).

Cohn, Robert G. "The Mallarmé Century." *Stanford French Review* 2:431–449 (1978).

——————. "Mallarmé contre Genette." *Tel quel* 69:51–54 (1977).

——————. "New Approaches to Hérodiade." *Romanic Review* 72:472–481 (1981).

——————. "O quel lointain: Memory in Mallarmé." *Romanic Review* 70:133–145 (1979).

——————. "Stevens and Mallarmé." *Comparative Literature Studies* 16:344–353 (1979).

——————. "Wherefore Igitur?" *Romanic Review* 60:174–177 (1969).

D'Evelyn, T. "Brink of Darkness: Mallarmé and Winters." *Southern Review*, 17:877–906 (1981).

Franklin, U. "Re-examination of Mallarmé's 'Le démon de l'analogie.'" *Romanic Review* 65:266–277 (1974).

Gill, Austin. "Mallarmé's Use of Christian Imagery for Post-Christian Concepts." *In Order and Adventure in Post-Romantic French Poetry*, edited by E. M. Beaumont et al. Oxford, 1979.

Greet, A. H. "Edouard Manet and His Poets." *Il Symposium* 34:311–332 (Winter 1980–1981).

Gronquist, R. "Ravel's *Trois poèmes de Stéphane Mallarmé*. *Musical Quarterly* 64:507–523 (1978).

Jackson, T. H. "Positivism and Modern Poetics: Yeats, Mallarmé, and Williams." *ELH* 56:509–540 (1979).

Les lettres 3 (1948). Mallarmé issue.

Parker, P. "Mallarmé's *Toast funèbre:* Some Contexts and a Reading." *Romanic Review* 71:167–182 (1980).

Le point 5 (February–April 1944). Mallarmé issue.

Riffaterre, Michael. "On Deciphering Mallarmé." *Georgia Review* 29:75–91 (1975).

Sonnenfeld, Albert. "Elaboration secondaire du grimoire: Mallarmé et le poète-critique." *Romanic Review* 64:72–89 (1978).

Walker, S. F. "Mallarmé's Symbolist Eclogue: The *Faune* as Pastoral." *PMLA* 93:106–117 (1978).

Weightman, J. "Stéphane Mallarmé and the Language Obsession." *Encounter* 51:96–109 (1978).

Yale French Studies 54 (1977). Mallarmé issue.

York, R. A. "Sonnefoy and Mallarmé: Aspects of Intertextuality." *Romanic Review* 71:307–318 (1980).

JEFFREY M. PERL

BENITO PÉREZ GALDÓS

(1843–1920)

IN HIS OLD age, having completed most of his life's work—thirty-four novels, twenty-four plays, and forty-six *episodios nacionales* (historical novelettes about nineteenth-century Spain divided into five series)— Benito Pérez Galdós undertook, in 1916, the composition of his memoirs. It was one of the most difficult tasks he had ever attempted—so much so that he never completed it. The title of what amounts to a random collection of autobiographical fragments (published ten years after his death) indicates the problem: *Memorias de un desmemoriado* (Memoirs of a Man Without Memory). Throughout his life Galdós was almost obsessively concerned with preserving his privacy. Those matters about which we would most like to know—childhood experiences, love affairs, personal triumphs and disappointments—were precisely what he, like his admired Cervantes in the first sentence of *Don Quixote,* "did not wish to remember." But even more telling was his inability to reconstruct his own life. He calls out in desperation: "Come, memory of mine, solicitous companion of my thought, why have you deserted me? Are you sleeping? Are you distraught?" Here is how his memory answers:

You're the one who is distraught. Scarcely have you finished one novel than you begin another. You live in an imaginary world . . . and I who am only nourished on reality must confess that I am bored to death in the shadowy cavern of your mind inhabited by phantasms, and I escape whenever I find an exit.

(*Memorias,* "Pereda y yo," 1)

Galdós had poured so much of himself into his fiction, into characters who were for him (and for his avid public) more real than men and women of flesh and blood, that his own existence had become shadowy. His was an advanced case of what Sir Walter Scott, in his preface of 1829 to *Waverley,* had termed the "delitescency" ("the condition of lying hidden") characteristic of novelists in general.

There are, however, two interrelated experiences that Galdós did remember vividly and that have been of crucial importance to his biographers. Although they did not occur until he was in his early twenties, their significance will be clearer after a brief look at what is known about his youth. Galdós was born on 10 May 1843 in Las Palmas, the provincial capital of the Canary Islands. As the youngest of ten children born to a moderately wealthy family (models for the bureaucrats, army officers, and ecclesiastics who were later to populate many of his novels), he was educated privately and given that familiarity with the Latin classics that was to be as useful to him as it was to other novelists of his century. In addition to being—as he remembered ironically—a "good little student," he was fond of music, read voraciously, and filled the margins of his textbooks with surprisingly skilled caricatures. Later he decorated his manuscripts in the same fashion, and the gift for quick delineation was equally evident in his vivid presentation of characters. In an early attempt at creative writing in prose entitled "Un viage redondo por el bachiller Sansón Carrasco" (1861), a pastiche of *Don Quixote* (much of which he could recite from memory), the conjunction of visual and verbal humor is manifest. "Viage redondo" translated into English is literally a "round" trip.

At the age of nineteen, Galdós, like many young Spaniards of his background and station, was virtually condemned to the study of law. It was a discipline he found immensely boring. In the first paragraph of one of his major novels, *Fortunata y Jacinta* (1886–1887), the narrator remembers whispering during lectures, drawing caricatures, and even frying eggs: the former teacher's pet had turned into a quasi-delinquent. Galdós' great consolation, however, was that he was sent to the University of Madrid: the transition from his provincial birthplace to the nation's capital was, in contrast to his academic subjection to rote learning, immensely stimulating. Back in Las Palmas, the only burning issues that had attracted his adolescent attention were the poor quality of itinerant opera singers, the planned location of a municipal theater, and the foibles of his schoolmates. Now he was immersed in the pulsating life of the metropolis, the setting and subject of many future novels. In spite of occasional experiments with rural and provincial locales, Madrid was to be for him what London was for Charles Dickens and Paris for Honoré de Balzac. These writers were his first mentors. Their fascination with the city as a uniquely human phenomenon was contagious, but admiration aside, what Galdós learned from them above all was how to understand the city as a locus of historical change.

In Madrid, history was first of all an oral experience. The city was growing and changing rapidly, and the emigrants who arrived from all points of the national compass—Andalusia, Valencia, Extremadura, Galicia, the country of the Basques—imported the past into the present in their traditional intonations and accents, which had remained unchanged through centuries. Galdós, who had been accustomed to the soft and relatively homogeneous Spanish of his island home, was now exposed to the language of the slums, of parliamentary oratory, of middle-class pretension, and of every kind of profession. Manual laborers, housewives, beggars, salesmen, usurers, waiters, apprentices, and politicians fascinated him with the variety in their intonations, accents, and vocabulary. Madrid's social barriers were particularly osmotic; the colloquialisms of one group's speech soon became part of another's oral expression, and so moved rapidly and easily from class to class. Galdós used this intertwining of slang and affected "rhetoric" in his writing as a means of inducing his readers to confront their social selves, and so to question their personal identities. In this sense, both Gustave Flaubert and Émile Zola should be added not as mentors (Galdós had not yet read them) but as precursors. All three found in spoken language the raw material for literary creation. But in Galdós' case, a melancholy postscript must be appended: in meeting this primary challenge to all nineteenth-century novelists, the peculiarly colloquial, time-bound, and socially conditioned nature of his Spanish prose make its translation exceedingly difficult.

History was also reflected in the daily press. In the Madrid of the 1860's, there were no fewer than eighteen journals that supported the cause of liberalism, and at least as many others in violent opposition. After the death of Fernando VII in 1833, the accession of the child Isabel II to the throne had at first been considered a triumph for the liberal cause. The reactionaries of the time had supported her uncle, the first Carlos of the *carlistas*. However, in later years, her reign became increasingly shaky and repressive, and change was in the air. Galdós, who was a lighthearted and enthusiastic liberal in his student days, recalls in his memoirs his initial political fervor with a certain nostalgia: "In the days prior to the revolution of '68, our disputes were passionate and formidable, since the aim was to change radically the whole of the political organism" (*Las cartas desconocidas de Galdós en "La Prensa" de Buenos Aires,* W. H. Shoemaker ed., p. 520). The "new ideas of our times"—he thought—must and would prevail. It was the turn of the Spaniards to take their place in man's destined ascent to liberty, equality, and fraternity.

Ideas for political reform in nineteenth-century Spain necessarily derived from the French Revolution. Activity was concentrated above all in the streets, and Galdós himself took part in a student riot that occurred in April 1865, after Queen Isabel dismissed the liberal rector of the university, Emilio Castelar. With the passage of time two novelties that had first been given political significance by the upheavals in Paris, newspapers and informal gatherings in cafés for the exchange of ideas, had acquired institutional status in Madrid. In this milieu of political activism the newly arrived law student found himself at home. Neglecting his studies, he began to write for the newspapers and—being characteristically silent—to listen avidly to discussions in the cafés. His ebullience and commitment to the liberal cause were evident in his sarcastic journalistic account of the aforementioned student riot: "The government taking the role of schoolmaster and violating whatever article of the Code of Public Instruction it is that forbids corporal punishment has put a stop to student impudence with the gentle remedy of bullets." Later, friends would remember the young reporter emerging from his lodgings and inviting them with mingled anticipation and irony to go out and take a look at the history of Spain.

On 22 June 1865, Galdós witnessed events so appalling that the experience marked a turning point in his life, a psychic revolution of much greater significance to his future than the April riot. A mutiny of the artillery sergeants stationed at the barracks of San Gil in Madrid was bloodily suppressed by troops loyal to the regime:

> From my boarding house on Olivo Street where I and friends were living, I witnessed the tremendous casualties of that mournful occasion. The roar of the cannon was stupefying, and from nearby streets we heard the cries of the wounded, enraged curses, the intonations of hatred. Madrid was an Inferno. At the end of the afternoon, when we were able to get outdoors, we saw the resultant wreckage and the bloody vestiges of the stillborn revolution. And then afterward I must mention as the saddest spectacle of all—the most tragic and sinister I have ever seen in my life—the passing by along Alcalá Street of the sergeants seated two by two in carriages on their way to be executed by a firing squad against the wall of the old bullring. Overcome with pity and grief, we watched them pass by. I had not the courage to follow the frightful procession to the place of execution, so I hurried home hoping to find some consolation in my beloved books.
>
> (*Memorias,* "Mi llegada a la corte," 2)

History had suddenly exhibited the nightmarish quality with which inhabitants of our own century are only too familiar. It was now that Galdós began to ask himself the questions that were to obsess him for the rest of his life. In what kind of country, with what kind of past, could such atrocities occur? How could the events he had witnessed be comprehended as human phenomena? And what possible spiritual recourse from such a nightmare could be found?

For Galdós, the dilemma of being a citizen of an endemically regressive, mercilessly violent, and hopelessly poverty-stricken nation in a century ostensibly dedicated to progress, prosperity, and the brotherhood of man became far more acute as the result of a second vividly recalled experience. Worried about their youngest son's health, his increasing tendency to withdraw into the world of imagination, and his bohemian existence, Galdós' family decided in 1868 to send him to Paris for a change of scene. The contrast between the monumental grandeur of that city and the vestigial village that still lay behind the metropolitan facade of Madrid could not help but entrance and depress him. Even more: one of those international expositions or world fairs by means of which "Western civilization" periodically celebrates its own importance was being held in the French capital at the time. Along with the Hall of Machines and the various national pavilions (Spain's was quite modest and folkloric), there was an unprecedented exhibit that was a landmark in the exploration of prehistory: a display of primitive artifacts designed to illustrate the "Law of the Progress of Humanity." Did the execution of the sergeants (which Galdós had experienced as a climax to the ferocious and pointless turmoil of post-Napoleonic Spain) mean that the "law" was inapplicable to his own country?

If the visit to Paris had the effect of sharpening Galdós' national self-consciousness, it also provided him with a new means for exploring it. As he remembered inaccurately (a recently discovered list of his early book purchases reveals that he had previously bought works by Balzac) but nonetheless significantly:

> Devoured by feverish curiosity, I spent every day going up and down streets with a map in my hand. . . . I made frequent stops in the bookstalls which there take the form of wooden boxes exhibiting their wares on the *quais* along the Seine. The first book I bought was a little volume of the works of Balzac—one franc, Librairie Nouvelle. With the reading of that little book, *Eugénie Grandet*, I breakfasted on the great French novelist, and during that trip to Paris and on later ones I completed the collection of more than 80 volumes, which I still have and guard with religious veneration.
>
> (*Memorias*, "Mi llegada a la corte," 3)

What Balzac's work taught him was how to experience history in a meaningful way rather than merely record it—how to convert the novel from an adventure story or an analysis of feelings into a medium for historical understanding. Or, as Maurice Merleau-Ponty phrased it, the underlying theme of the whole of Balzac's *Comédie humaine* is "the mystery of history as the appearance of sense within the randomness of events" (*Sens et non-sens*, Paris, 1948, p. 49). Galdós felt that if he could do for Spain what Balzac had done for France, he would serve his country well and might even contribute to its salvation.

Galdós' earliest novel, *La fontana de oro* (1870), is accordingly historical in nature and didactic in purpose. Written in 1868 just prior to the liberal revolution known both ironically and nostalgically as *la gloriosa*, it takes its title from the name of a well-known political café of the period. Sensing the tide of coming events, liberal journals in 1865 had already issued a joint proclamation asking their readers to maintain order and at all costs to avoid reacting violently to provocations from the right. Support from the moderate center had to be preserved. This was precisely the message that Galdós proposed to communicate novelistically. Aside from Scott, his major source was Balzac's *Splendeurs et misères des courtisanes* (1843), a section of which deals with agents provocateurs who after the Bourbon Restoration were assigned to infiltrate a liberal café in order to spy on and discredit opponents of Louis XVIII. As an inveterate reader of both novels and history, the novice author perceived a resemblance of this portion of Balzac's plot to events that had taken place some fifty years before during an abortive and cruelly suppressed experiment with constitutional government known as the *trienio liberal* (the three liberal years from 1820 to 1823). This is the period in which the novel is set. Its characters are a flaming young liberal, Lázaro (Lazarus, or Spain restored to life), a spy, Coletilla (a minion of Fernando VII presented as a caricature of reaction), and Coletilla's ward, Clara (the supposedly docile Spanish people). The significance of this trio is clear. Clara lives in a state of virtual slavery (Spain as an imprisoned heroine is a recurrent allegory in Galdós' early novels), but she may be rescued—liberated—by eloping with Lázaro.

The setting of the novel is the liberal café in which Lázaro and the other young liberal firebrands gather nightly to practice their incendiary oratory. And it is indeed curious to note how this novelistic lesson for Galdós' own times (don't repeat the mistakes of the past) incorporates the two institutions that had captivated him on his arrival in Madrid: the oral language of the café and the printed language of journalism. The latter appears not as a part of the story (what little journalism there was during the *trienio* had not advanced beyond the stage of pamphleteering), but in the structure and variety of styles Galdós had mastered during his apprenticeship as a reporter and columnist. Indeed, *La fontana* is composed of a series of sketches on customs, social types, and manners (ultimately derived from Joseph Addison and Richard Steele) of the immensely popular sort that contributed to the advent of realism in England and France. (*The Pickwick Papers* and the first novel of the *Comédie humaine, La maison du chat-qui-pelote,* are also newspaper novels in this sense.) In addition, slashing verbal caricatures, political editorials, and reportorial observation of events current "fifty years before" contribute to the kind of presentation once assigned in secondary schools: "Describe the execution of Marie Antoinette as if you were writing for *The Times.*"

Galdós' prose, as a result, was from the beginning immediate, vivid, and eminently readable. Yet there was a crucial flaw in the fictional lesson, a flaw that makes itself apparent in the alternate endings to be found in the manuscript and the early editions. In the "happy" version, Clara and Lázaro escape from the persecution of Coletilla and retire to a rustic and peaceful married life—with the implication that freedom might eventually be achieved by their offspring. But in the "tragic" version, the hopelessly naive young hero is ensnared and murdered. The first reflects Galdós' optimistic hope that by 1868 those readers who shared his commitment to political reform might have learned to skirt the pitfalls that had been fatal five decades before. The second clearly predicts that *la gloriosa* too would fail (as indeed it did) because of the quixotic idealism and foolish impulsiveness of its inexperienced partisans. Within the novel, political fable and political prophecy are no more permeable than oil and water.

Ultimately, the composition of *La fontana* was to be more of a lesson to Galdós himself than to his readers. What he learned from writing it is that history is not identical to politics and that fictional analysis of the latter does not necessarily lead to an understanding of the former. As Stendhal had pointed out on several occasions, the introduction of politics into a novel "is like a pistol shot during a concert." In *La fontana,* the staccato movement of the two opposing forces—liberalism and reaction—constantly disrupts and restructures the narrative flow as the reader advances from one static episode to another in a series of short hops. History, on the contrary, as Galdós came to understand it after reflecting on this novel, is a dynamic and quasi-biological continuity: " . . . the continual gestation of events in the womb of others is what History is, daughter of Yesterday, sister of Today, mother of Tomorrow."

Unlike other Europeans who, as a result of the cataclysmic changes that occurred after 1789, quickly began to think of themselves as historical creatures ("children of the century" and no longer of God), Spaniards—Galdós realized—had reached no such self-awareness. The Napoleonic invasion of their peninsula had taught them only politics of the violent and elementary sort depicted in *La fontana:* the sterile confrontation of those who believed that they still lived in those "most happy times" of absolutism with those who believed in the quick utopian fix of constitutional reform. If only the novel could teach his compatriots history (understood as Galdós now understood it), they might at last realize who and *when* they were. And they could then (unlike the hapless Lázaros of the past) proceed into the future prudently, tolerantly, and confidently. But how to go about the task of writing such novels and of creating a public for them out of a mass of politically fervent newspaper addicts?

Galdós proposed to take advantage of the vogue for historical novels (originally imported to Spain via translations from Scott but by the 1870's circulating as debased serials written by native hacks) as a means of re-creating Spain's War of Independence against Napoleonic France. Instead of just remembering those years vaguely as a time of patriotic zeal when almost everybody fought the invaders righteously until their expulsion in 1814 (and then split into liberal and reactionary camps and continued to fight each other mindlessly), the reader would now be led to experience for himself how it felt to exist at such a time. As defined by the critic Américo Castro, "The novel does not just tell what happens but more importantly how it feels to exist within the happening." And especially Galdós intended to explore the meaning of the events of the period to those who had lived through them, and to see how they had contributed to the making of his own society and times.

This was the manifest intention of the ten-volume "first series" of *episodios nacionales* (national episodes). The series begins with the battle of Trafalgar (1805), in which the French and Spanish fleets were defeated by the English under Nelson, and ends with the land battle of Los Arapiles (1812), in which Wellington, with the help of Spanish and Portuguese "regulars," gained a decisive victory. The symmetrical reversal of alliances is obvious, but it is also likely that Galdós wished to contrast the monumental style of warfare under Spain's lost empire with the more ferocious grass-roots variety with which Spaniards responded to invasion. In addition, while Galdós rejected Scott's worship of the dead past, he was aware that Trafalgar was still alive in the consciousness of the nation. In 1870 the Madrid press devoted much attention to a commemorative mass held for the admiral who had commanded the Spanish fleet at that battle, and a number of survivors attended. Galdós believed his *episodios* described the "living roots" of the Spain of his day and saw Trafalgar as the living root of the War of Independence.

Along with an awareness of the organic or biological nature of history (history as the "life" of the nation), Galdós realized that in the nineteenth century, history had become generational. When that "child of the century" Alfred de Musset described himself as a member of "an ardent, pale, and nervous generation" born "during the wars of the Empire" (*Mémoires d'un enfant du siècle*, 1835), it was in tacit recognition of the nineteenth-century coincidence of historical and biographical time. History was just entering the phase of acceleration that so preoccupied Henry Adams and Alfred North Whitehead and that today far exceeds our capacities for personal experience. But if the pace of change is vertiginous now, for little more than a hundred years lives and events marched side by side. And if novelists in the seventeenth and eighteenth centuries had written works that played comically with history (*Don Quixote, Tristram Shandy, Jacques le fataliste*), they now found unexpected seriousness and new prestige in their capacity to describe men as historical beings, as members of successive historical generations. *Waverley*, published in 1814 but with an eponymous hero who belongs to an anachronistic "generation of 1745," was the precursor of the new historical novel. Galdós did not just study "generationality" as a phenomenon (as did Ivan Turgenev in *Fathers and Sons* [1862] or Gustave Flaubert in *L'Éducation sentimentale* [1874]), but instead sought to instill generational—as opposed to political—consciousness in his young and impressionable readers. The public he visualized, the public he wrote for, was not now to be composed of veteran newspaper readers and café addicts; it was the young generation of Spaniards who would shape the future of the country.

Galdós' revised purpose in writing historical fiction is reflected in the design of the ten-volume series he now embarked on, an ongoing narrative in the first person. The narrator, Gabriel Araceli, a retired veteran, presents himself as a member of the generation of the War of Independence who wants to communicate (presumably to a circle of young listeners) his experience of the major events of that tumultuous period. His underlying purpose might very well be formulated in the question: "If this is what we were and could do, who are you, and what can you learn from us in fulfilling your historical mission?" His story is also a lesson in growing up. Gabriel is a naive fourteen-year-old orphan of unknown parentage when, as an officer's servant, he takes part in Spain's naval catastrophe in 1805; and the next seven years of hardship and warfare are to furnish him with his identity, in this case neither Spanish worship of sheer virility *(machismo)*, nor Spanish admiration for commanding human presence *(hombría)*. Gabriel is as brave as he has to be, but he never flaunts or provokes; he is always close to the center of events, but as a reliable witness and not as a charismatic leader. Although he is profoundly patriotic, he is harshly critical of the pride and irrationality of his fellow countrymen. Surrounded by quixotic fanatics and virulent despots on the right and hate-filled revolutionaries on the left, his manly youth grows in clarity of vision, reasonableness, reliability, sound common sense, and above all tolerance. He is a model war correspondent, and a sterling example of the attitude young Spaniards of the generation of *la gloriosa* should adopt to the historical events in which they were immersed.

In spite of a valedictory paragraph at the end of the last novel of the series, in which the narrator presents himself as a model for successful living, these *episodios* do not fall into the category of Bildungsroman, or novel of spiritual education. The reader is supposed not just to learn from Gabriel's example but, far more important, to identify with him. He is expected to read with the same fervor and loss of self that transforms Alonso Quijano into Don Quixote de la Mancha. To that end Galdós was careful to pack his volumes with color and adventure, and also to include an ongoing love intrigue designed to maintain suspense from episode to episode. Gabriel is in love with Inés (like Clara a captive of a tyrannical family), and their chance encounters and separations recur with any number of surprising variations. Not only here in the first series but in all five, Galdós (like sixteenth-century writers of romances of chivalry) took full advantage of one of the oldest plotting devices in the world, derived from the Byzantine tale. But his redesigned historical novel was meant not to induce escapism but to lead the reader to a recognition of himself (in the words of Wilhelm Dilthey) as a "living cell of history."

Moreover, in Spain, unlike in France and England, there was no post-Napoleonic generation that could define itself as such, no common awareness of a group identity. There were parties, *juntas*, lodges, bands of guerrillas, and committees of all sorts, but no realization that the invasion was more than an interruption of absolutist continuity, or that it might present a breach in which overnight political reform could take place. What had happened had not changed the Spaniard's fundamental concept of himself and his possibilities. Here, as in all of Galdós' novels and dramas, there is a juxtaposition between history as it was and history as it should be. Thus, even within his epic celebration of the besieged inhabitants of Zaragoza, the writer expresses grave doubts about the military acumen of the commanding general, and, with few exceptions, ineffective leadership is contrasted ruefully with popular heroism. But even more dismaying is the gradual realization on the part of both author and reader that

that heroism itself is the obverse of fanaticism and cruelty. Gabriel is very much alone in his tolerance, prudence, and generosity.

What followed, therefore, was a second series (1875–1879) that—as was typical of Galdós—turns right about-face and directly confronts the way things had really been. Beginning in 1813 with the ignominious and chaotic retreat of the French across the Pyrenees, passing through the relentless oppression of 1824 that followed the *trienio liberal,* and ending in 1833 just after the death of Fernando VII, the new *episodios* replace the relative optimism of the preceding series with the bleakest pessimism. No longer told in the first person and no longer intended primarily for juvenile readers, they demonstrate a marked improvement in novelistic skill. Galdós had clearly finished his apprenticeship and had abandoned the inhibiting mediation of an amateur raconteur. He could now write unequivocally and directly about the tyranny, torture, executions, massacres, civil war, and treachery of the times. His protagonist is appropriately a traitor—at least in the eyes of his fellow countrymen. He belongs to the small minority of *afrancesados* (quislings), who in the name of progress and reason collaborated with the French during the occupation. In exile from his homeland, his surreptitious returns, his loneliness, his bitterness, his disguises, his conspiracies, his love affairs, his rivalry with his brother (an archreactionary), and his increasing disillusionment with his own cause all distinguish Salvador Monsalud from Gabriel Araceli. Equally honorable and passionate, he is nonetheless afflicted by the self-doubts, temptations, feelings of guilt, and dejected contemplation of ambiguities that come with maturity. The atrocious Goyaesque historical moment is reflected in somber scenes with livid highlights through the eyes of a man capable of feeling and expressing the anguish and the resignation such a moment imposes. Instead of captivating the young with adventure, Galdós is now concerned with telling the bitter truth of experience to his own generation: this is who we were and who we may become again.

Galdós does not quite reach the point of saying "a plague on both your houses." The portraits of Fernando VII and his minions and the caustic description of the future *carlistas* conspiring together establish their indisputable leadership in national villainy. Instead of the self-delusion of the idealistic liberals portrayed in *La fontana,* in his second portrayal of the *trienio,* cowardice, self-service, and fanaticism are clearly in charge. In Galdós' own words: "Despotism lies in the heart of Spain and flows through its veins. That is its character; that is its humor, a leprosy inherited from past centuries, which can be cured only by the medicine of future centuries" (*Los apostólicos* 26). And again later on: "In this country there is nothing but absolutism in its pure form, in all classes and in all regions. The majority of liberals speak and think of revolution, but their hearts, without their being aware of it, overflow with despotism" (*La segunda casaca* 22). Such pronouncements abound, but their editorial cast does not make for a moving representation of the people and their times. Galdós could report vividly and accurately all the appalling things that occurred during those two decades and he could interpret them with despairing generalizations, but he could not enter lives that—from his point of view—were distorted and alien. A different approach was necessary.

The first hint of a change in approach comes in a passing remark in the third *episodio* of this series, *La segunda casaca* (The Turncoat, 1876). The time is 1820; Fernando VII, compelled by the army, has just accepted a more or less liberal constitution, and all Madrid has erupted into the streets to celebrate its newfound freedom. The "turncoat," previously a courtier of Fernando VII, and now an enthusiastic liberal, questions the hero fatuously:

"What do you think of the beautiful and exemplary spectacle represented by Madrid and by the whole nation? Our people are models of good sense. Don't tell me now that we don't know how to act as free men."

"The first day [he answered] it's always fraternity and jubilation. I don't mean to say that that is not good. I am glad to see it at last, and the spectacle does fill my heart with satisfaction."

"And doesn't that eliminate your ridiculous doubts?"

"Oh, no. I'm still as skeptical as ever. Everything that is happening has an official quality that destroys its spontaneity. I've lived in villages and towns where you see the nation as naked as the day it was born acting according to its own impulses, and from what I have witnessed I have come to certain conclusions that all your flag-waving cannot shake."

(25)

Galdós now turned his attention away from civil wars and Madrid with its febrile history to write a sociological novel about a provincial town in which readers could see the "naked nation" at its worst, and from which they would be compelled to draw lessons about its behavior and to comtemplate their own reactions.

That novel, published late in 1876, is *Doña Perfecta,* and its success was immediate. It is also—unfortunately—the novel most often associated with an author who was later to penetrate far more profoundly into human nature. In the Soviet Union it has gone into many editions for ideological reasons, and in other countries, because of its combination of narrative power and thematic simplicity, it has been a favorite text for advanced Spanish courses. The story is set in Galdós' own time, yet it is nonetheless "historical" insofar as its characters are fatally flawed by their cultural heritage. The setting is an imaginary provincial capital, Orbajosa—a name with two etymologies. On the one hand it is derived majestically and pretentiously from the Latin *Urbs Augusta,* and on the other it is related by the local illiterates to the region's most noteworthy agricultural product, *ajo,* or garlic. "Garlictown" is a human ruin, a locus of stag-

nation. Like its crumbling cathedral, it is a degenerate effigy of its supposedly "august" origins.

The sensation caused by the publication of *Doña Perfecta* is partially explicable by the reading preferences of the Madrid public. Like Balzac's Paris, the capital of Spain was replete with emigrants from the provinces who doted on nostalgic literary evocations of the timeless idyllic existence of a rural childhood. Remembered landscapes, traditional customs and costumes, regional dishes, typical occupations, all were combined in stories and novels designed to palliate their rudimentary *mal du siècle*, to relieve their sense of spatial and temporal alienation. And now Galdós dared to tell them not that they could not go home again (which, of course, they already knew), but that should they attempt to do so, it would be devastating: home was empty; home was ingrown; home was closed to outsiders; home was murderous.

The plot is modeled on the Balzacian *scène de province* that Galdós remembered devouring with avidity, *Eugénie Grandet.* A young university-trained engineer visits an aunt in his family's native town in order to claim an inheritance. He is initially shocked by the contrast of boundless local pride and self-righteousness with the barrenness and stagnation of local existence. And then, as he and the town (presented as a kind of collective fatality) react to each other, things go from bad to worse. His inherited estate is encroached on by squatters and tied up with litigation, and, due to certain imprudent remarks about progress, his relationship with his father's sister, Doña Perfecta, and her circle of confessors, hangers-on, friends, and relations becomes increasingly antagonistic. Their perception of the outsider resembles that of antibodies confronted with a transplanted organ. The climax occurs when it is discovered that the hero and a cousin have fallen in love and are about to elope. At that point, Doña Perfecta, who, as her name implies, is the reigning matron of the town and the incarnation of its traditional values, gets the local political boss and professional bully to kill her nephew. As if seen through a microscope, here was a single representative cell of the endemic madness of the nineteenth-century civil wars that Galdós had re-created in the second series of *episodios.*

What did Galdós and his readers learn from this melodramatic tragedy? Most obviously they realized that the heroes and saints of their century were not knightly experts in violence or monastic experts in self-flagellation; rather, they were engineers, scientists, builders, physicians—all those concerned with the technical amelioration of human life. More profoundly, however, Galdós revealed that the roles and values that his compatriots had inherited from the past were obsolete and historically empty. Lacking genuine inner faith, their inquisitorial zeal becomes all the more ostentatious and fervent. Neither politics as such (the opposing views of parties) nor economic determinism (the desire to acquire and defend family property) matter ultimately. The new heretics who have to be exterminated are those whose very identities threaten one's own. Political beliefs and economic interests are so radically personalized that the elopement of the urban liberal with his rural cousin is as intolerable as an alliance between Christian and converted Jew would have been centuries before. Ideological contamination had been substituted structurally for caste (racial and religious) contamination.

A twentieth-century historian and philosopher, Pedro Laín Entralgoz, preoccupied with the peculiar hatefulness of Spain's nineteenth century as well as with the continuation of Hispanic political violence in our own day, has pointed out that ever since the popular pogroms of the 1930's and the institutionalized pogrom founded by Ferdinand and Isabella (the Inquisition), the annals of his people have never been properly historical, mired as they are in caste antagonism (*¿A qué llamamos España?*, Madrid, 1972, p. 144). In his opinion the adjective "conflictive" better describes the events narrated in the second se-

ries of *episodios* and the single fictional event contemplated in menacing sociological slow motion in *Doña Perfecta.* Galdós, however, was a novelist, and he thought novelistically. What he asked himself was most likely this: If for Balzac the avarice of old Grandet is the prevailing vice of French provincial existence, what is its Spanish counterpart? The answer was obvious: Galdós' provincial compatriots, proudly generous with their wine and roast piglets, were fanatically intolerant. This question could well be followed by another: Why focus solely on a particular rural Castilian variety of communal life when all of Spain is equally guilty? The answer was two more contemporary novels about intolerance: *Gloria* (1876–1877), set on the less ingrown northern coast, and *La familia de León Roch* (1878), set in Madrid. In the former, a marriage is forbidden because of racial prejudice, and in the latter, a marriage is destroyed through ecclesiastical interference. Orbajosa, as Galdós was later to insist, was not merely an imaginary locality: It existed, at least potentially, inside all Spaniards.

At this point in his career, Galdós found himself at an impasse. He had mastered the art of narrating history as fiction, but, as an intellectual friend of Galdós', Francisco Giner de los Rios, pointed out, "It is natural that history, understood as a mere narrative of what occurred in the past, cannot enable us to comprehend its essential nature." He had also learned how to construct more or less static social models and family situations that illuminated the devastating social ills and political conflicts of nineteenth-century Spain. What he did not yet know was what Leo Tolstoy knew: how to integrate the two—fictitious individuals and the "essential nature" of history—how to depict human lives within "the continual gestation of events in the womb of others." But it was not with Tolstoy that he was to engage in novelistic dialogue (that would come later), but rather with the most scandalous novelist of the decade, Émile Zola. Galdós began to read his work in French in 1878, and by 1880 two translations of *L'Assommoir* (1877) and one of *Nana* (1880) had appeared in Spain, with the result that both he and the Spanish reading public were prepared for the naturalistic integration of self with milieu—that is, social determinism in the dynamic historical moment. In Zola's documentary novels the members of the genetically flawed Rougon-Macquart family accompany—generation after generation—the rise and fall of Napoleon III's historically flawed Second Empire. The relation is not symbolic (as in the case of Orbajosa) but rather organic. The family is a living constituent of that moment in history. Zola, in other words, appeared on Galdós' horizon at exactly the right moment. As he remembered later, he quickly and without hesitation "joined the procession of naturalism," and by 1881 he had transformed what he had learned into a major two-volume novel, *La desheredada* (*The Disinherited Lady*).

Spanish critics anxious to defend Galdós against charges of having slavishly followed the latest French literary fashion have pointed out that the notion of naturalism was neither the invention nor the private property of Zola and his disciples. The great classics of Spanish literature—*La Celestina, Lazarillo de Tormes*, the picaresque tradition they inspired, and, above all, *Don Quixote*—represent a native naturalism that, because of its healthy strain of humor, avoids the exaggerated morbidity and sordidness of, say, *L'Assommoir*. This may be true, but it is a theory that blurs the very real influence of Zola's work not only on the writing of Galdós but also on that of his major contemporaries, Clarín, Emilia Pardo Bazán, and Vicente Blasco Ibáñez. In the case of *La desheredada*, however, the influence of Cervantes is so patent and pervasive that the book has frequently been interpreted as a hybrid attempt to reconcile the two forms of naturalism. Instead of a genetically impaired family penetrating and corrupting the various social milieux of France, Galdós presents a genealogy of deluded, quixotic individuals from La Mancha

culminating in the protagonist, Isidora Rufete, who, deceived by spurious documents, believes herself to be the disinherited granddaughter of a noble family. The novel tells the story of her vain attempts to reclaim what she believes to be her birthright in a Madrid that, thanks to Galdós' reading of Zola, is now a fully developed urban organism. And it ends not only with final disillusionment (as in *Don Quixote*) but also with a final descent into the lowest depths of prostitution (as in *L'Assommoir*).

In order to understand Galdós' audacious new creative direction, it is necessary to take into account Spain's equally abrupt historical change of course. *La gloriosa* had destroyed itself (as well as Galdós' youthful liberal illusions) in the act of replaying in accelerated tempo the deplorable "politics" of the past: guerrilla warfare, assassination, venal parliamentary maneuvers, ephemeral regimes, regional rebellion, conspiracies, and so forth. Spain was exhausted, and it welcomed the 1874 Bourbon Restoration engineered by the politician of the hour, the pragmatically able but unscrupulous Antonio Cánovas del Castillo. The therapy that he proposed and instituted for the nation's ills was not only the coronation of an attractive young monarch, Alfonso XII, but also a whole new political system designed to import the two presiding values of the late nineteenth century: order and progress. Spain's model was constitutional England (Alfonso had been sent to Sandhurst), but with a difference: Spain's democratic procedures were to be fraudulent. Two parties would alternate through elections rigged by a network of local political bosses. It was, as Galdós described it, "a theatrical affair composed of white lies that, affecting only the surface, would make no profound changes, and, with appropriate slogans, would arrange for a reasonable and fair interchange of candidates" (*La segunda casaca* 22). In other words, Spain would be true to her many centuries of unmitigated injustice and social repression (*la cuestión social* was a laughable commonplace in the bourgeois theater) while at the same time adopting the facade of a modern European nation.

Galdós appropriately opens *La desheredada* in an insane asylum, where order restrains a population of madmen and progress is represented by a map of the nation hung in the anteroom and decorated with such emblems as locomotives, steamships, cogwheels, and factory chimneys. Yet it is Isidora, the daughter of a dying inmate and as winning and attractive at the beginning as any Dickensian heroine-victim, who is the vehicle for the novel's most corrosive criticism of the new epoch. In the past, in spite of the horrors, fanatical Spaniards had at least been willing to sacrifice themselves for what they believed. But now, puffed-up patriotism, get-rich-quick schemes, pervasive corruption, social and colonial exploitation, empty oratory, reckless extravagance, parade-mentality militarism, and addiction to sham all add up to the one accusation that could not be leveled against Doña Perfecta: absence of self-knowledge. Isidora, swollen with delusions of grandeur, coincides with the new Spanish nation: her reckless, irrational, and compelling urge to pretend to be what she is not reflects the vices of the Restoration. Galdós was not just experimenting with a mélange of naturalism culled from Cervantes and Zola; he hoped to teach his compatriots that quixotic self-delusion in its debased nineteenth-century form was a national disease, as fatal to Spanish civilization as the alcoholism, debauchery, and sheer degenerate savagery depicted by Zola were to French civilization.

Although *La desheredada* is by no means Galdós' greatest novel, it is an important one, since it adds a new dimension to his previous tormented interrogation of the Spanish past. In view of Spain's contemporary social and political behavior, what was to be its collective future? His initial, hopeless answer was similar to Zola's (who saw in the death of the courtesan Nana a "prefiguration" of the downfall of the Second Empire): a gradual and unwitting perversion of values leading to ultimate national prostitution. Zola's work had taught Galdós first to represent a life organically joined with its milieu (his great series of metropolitan novels would now appear one after another) and then to visualize the shape of things to come. It was this enlarged vision of the possibilities of his art that led him to classify *La desheredada* as the first of his mature *novelas españolas contemporáneas* (contemporary Spanish novels). He remarked in a personal letter that after the historical gossip of the *episodios* and the historical determinism of the three novels of intolerance, here was "initiated his second or third period." Galdós went on posing questions about the future of Spain in different novelistic contexts and emerged with answers that were to be increasingly profound and, in some instances, less hopeless.

A second distinction between his previous fiction and the novels he now set about writing is Galdós' new ability to make stylistic use of his phenomenal ear for the spoken language. Previously he had leavened his prose with fragments of overheard conversation between caricatured individuals. Aunt Polly talking to Mrs. Harper during the "drowning" episode in Mark Twain's *Tom Sawyer* is a comparable American example. Or he would insert short anecdotes and comic monologues told in a local dialect, much as in Twain's story "The Celebrated Jumping Frog." In *La desheredada* he began to assimilate Zola's acute awareness that speech is an integral element of any social milieu. This includes not only the language men and women hear and repeat but also the language they "think": "'If the weather was right, she would leave tomorrow,' Isidora thought." How the characters talk to others and silently to themselves becomes the measure of who they are. Zola had set out to break through conventional, academic French prose by making a study of slang both in dictionaries and in the streets, in order to convert the natural self-expression of his countrymen into a creative medium. Galdós, however, was himself a "natural," and required no deliberate self-application to follow in Zola's footsteps once he realized what the French author had accomplished. All the colloquial richness of speech that had fascinated him on his arrival in Madrid seemed to write itself in his novels. And as we read, we sense the ironic self-satisfaction of the author in his role as secretary to his society. But unlike his grimly serious mentor, Zola, Galdós juxtaposed all levels of spoken and written style in the tradition of Cervantes to create an essential comic basis for his mature narrative prose.

On the flyleaf, *La desheredada* is ironically dedicated to the exemplary educators who could have taught Isidora the "arithmetic, logic, moral and common sense" that she so badly needed to learn. It is not surprising, then, that the novel that followed, *El amigo Manso* (My Friend Manso, 1882), was the fictional autobiography of an idealistic philosopher-teacher as gentle and goodhearted *(manso)* as his name indicates. This personage was partly modeled on Francisco Giner de los Ríos, whose contribution to the future of Spain was the foundation of La Institución Libre de Enseñanza, a school designed to produce dedicated teachers who would pass on to younger generations moral as well as intellectual principles. Galdós admired Giner and his vocation enormously, but as a novelist he found a certain wry amusement in his character's problematic relationships with the people around him. Manso's best and most affectionate student turns into one more overblown political orator; speech-making was much admired at the time, but it was a talent the author disdained. Galdós was fascinated by the difficulty of being a man like Manso in the Spain of Isidora, where the very nature of the character is inherently at odds with his surroundings.

However, Galdós found in Manso's difficulty in being himself a possible solution to the aspect of Zola's naturalism that most distressed him, the determinism imposed on human identity by heredity and environment.

He eliminates the authorial voice through his choice of autobiographical genre, in which the character who relates his life is literally created by himself, not his environment or, ostensibly, the author. Manso is so selfless that his first words are "I do not exist," and if he then goes on to exist in the intractable Madrid within which he is incarnated, it is always with a sense (inherent in the nature of pure intellect) of irreality. In other words, Manso is an autonomous character whose aspirations, decisions, preferences, and disappointments are self-generated and who in the end can be saved from the difficulties of living only by returning to limbo. All of this is, of course, an entertaining game of solitaire on the part of Galdós, and not really a genuine rebuttal to Zola. Purely intellectual autonomy is not the same as the fully human freedom that was to be the achievement of later characters. Nor did *El amigo Manso* answer the pressing questions about Spain's parlous condition posed in *La desheredada*—except to express a certain skepticism concerning even the best education as a national cure-all.

With the next four novels Galdós therefore returned to the naturalistic mode. *El doctor Centeno* (1883) again examines the problem of education, but in terms of the way instruction was brutally conducted in the parochial schools of the time. In doing so, it puts Manso clearly on the side of the angels. *Tormento* (1884) combines a representation of the intimate repressiveness and pretenses of bourgeois domesticity with a favorite naturalistic subject, clerical celibacy and the "torment" it produces in both the observance and the breach. Like Dickens, Galdós was a veritable connoisseur of pain—spiritual and physical—and in this novel he depicts scenes and episodes of wrenching verisimilitude. The third novel in this trilogy (held together by Galdós' use of reappearing characters) is *La de Bringas* (The Bringas Woman, 1884). This personage, whose corsets symbolize the rigid bourgeois self-righteousness that conceals her moral corruption, is as despicable and shrewd as poor Isidora had been lovable and pitifully naive. And when she too ends as a prostitute, the reader feels neither regret nor sympathy. The society she represents has been exposed for what it is beneath all its hypocritical pretenses.

Galdós was thus little by little falling into a temptation inherent in the naturalistic vision of life—the equation of sexual misconduct with social evil. Or, as J. K. Huysmans expressed it in a moment of disillusion, the literary movement of which he had been a part only too often limited itself to explaining "why Mr. Somebody-or-Other did or did not commit adultery with Mrs. Somebody-Else" (preface to À rebours, 1903). It is a criticism especially applicable to Galdós' last naturalistic novel, *Lo prohibido* (That Which Is Prohibited, 1884–1885). Feeling (from considerable personal experience) that he had been unfair in depicting the corruption of the body politic only in the persons of weak and venal women, he set out to write the confessions of a nineteenth-century dandy who exploits inherited wealth in order to seduce his first cousins. The whole family, with a single exception, is venal and susceptible to various forms of hereditary eccentricity. That exception is the youngest cousin, who is happily married and blessed with such physical and spiritual health that she literally cannot understand the narrator's addiction to "escapades all the more savory in their very abnormality" (1.8). By the end, it is not her resistance to his increasingly desperate advances that brings about his crippling cerebral hemorrhage, but her sheer lack of comprehension of his feelings.

Galdós himself did not think much of *Lo prohibido,* and even before he had finished it, he wrote to his friend and fellow novelist José María de Pereda:

> Why the devil did I get involved in such fancy affairs? I'm up to my neck in "goo." And it isn't working out. There are boudoir scenes naturally but no problems . . . that is to say, only the kind of problems that adultery and other such trifles create.
>
> (C. Bravo Villasante, "28 Cartas de Galdós a Pereda," *Cuadernos hispanoamericanos,* 1970–1971, p. 27)

He was surprised and pleased, however, by the chorus of critical admiration for his characterization—"half virtue, half immunity"—of the invincible cousin. Here was objective support for a decision he had already taken by the end of part 2: he would abandon naturalistic exploration of hopelessly diseased private lives (though, of course, not the narrative techniques he had learned from Zola) in favor of a full-scale novelistic exploration of human freedom and healthy resistance to perversion.

The result was the longest (four volumes) and, for many readers, the greatest of his works, *Fortunata y Jacinta.* Of all the abrupt changes in narrative course typical of Galdós, it represents the sharpest and the most decisive. From this point on, he dedicated his creative attention to what he paradoxically formulated as *naturalismo espiritual.*

If he was to produce a work in such a vein, Galdós realized, his approach would have to be circuitous and deliberate. To begin with, the determining forces of Spanish Restoration history, economic as well as social, had to be studied in far more intimate detail than he had yet attempted. They could not be represented by a Spanish counterpart to Madame Bovary or Nana; rather, they must be explored on every social level, from slum to bourgeois drawing room. Furthermore, for Galdós' present purposes the overtly polemical approach of a literary prosecuting attorney (Zola's "I accuse") would have converted the end of the novel into a foregone conclusion in which the heroine would have to be a helpless victim rather than an autonomous being capable of finding spiritual salvation. The solution Galdós devised for *Fortunata y Jacinta* was to invent the persona of a narrator, an endlessly gossipy reporter in sympathy with the values and behavior of the world in which he lives, and which he minutely depicts in the first volume. The reader's task is to see through the ironic disguise and come to his own—and Galdós'—conclusions.

The result is a complete documentary presentation of the way people of all classes in Madrid provided themselves with the three necessities of life: food, clothing, and shelter. However, within this global naturalistic enterprise, the narrator pays special attention to the second category, the way people dressed. Spaniards were and are characteristically concerned with how they look (el aparentar); honra (honor) depends on the opinion of others and must be preserved by keeping up appearances. In a time when the awareness of fashion had only recently crossed the Pyrenees, clothes had become an obsession for both those who could afford expensive wardrobes and those who could not. Preoccupation with dress was a sign of the superficiality of the times, and the narrator revels in what he terms with unwitting sarcasm "the glorious history of modern tailoring" and exhaustively chronicles the commercial rise of dry goods in Madrid.

Intertwined with all this is the national obsession with genealogy—an obsession that Galdós detested and that, although originating in the medieval worship of noble lineage, had become thoroughly entrenched in the course of the denunciations and investigations of the Inquisition. In an 1865 newspaper article, Galdós had remarked sardonically that a new mercantile class was fast gaining the sort of prestige that had previously attached solely to the aristocracy. Like a servile courtier in former centuries, the narrator of Fortunata y Jacinta lavishes his adulation on a parvenu dynasty of wealthy cloth merchants. Their sumptuous dwelling, their domestic bliss, their admirable habits and tastes, their powerful and socially desirable friends and relations, the pseudodemocracy of their dinner invitations, their prudent charities—these are the summit of his hierarchy of values. It is all so sincerely set forth that we are almost convinced that this family is a perfect human example of order and progress.

At this point, the story proper—too long and complex to be summarized—begins. Juanito Santa Cruz, the scion or "crown prince" of the family, is what is known in Spanish as a typical señorito, a combination of the French fils à papa (father's favorite) and the English dandy, a young man without any vocation and with no other occupation than dressing elegantly, showing himself off in proper circles, and engaging in surreptitious love affairs. He is irresistibly handsome and a brilliant conversationalist, and when he meets by chance a physically superb "daughter of the people," he is captivated (as are many others in the novel, along with generations of readers) by her sheer primitivism. In the terms of naturalism the conclusion is foregone: seduction, pregnancy, abandonment, death of the baby, and subsequent descent into prostitution. Yet unlike Isidora in La desheredada, with whom she is intentionally contrasted, the victim emerges from these experiences unsoiled and still passionately in love with her pseudoprince.

According to his most informed biographer, H. C. Berkowitz, Galdós had actually met and become fascinated by a living model of this character, who had borne the same commonplace misfortunes without succumbing to them. In the novel, Galdós names her Fortunata, and the intensity of his observations about that "child of fortune" (her only genealogy, in contrast to her seducer, who is liberally supplied with ancestors) confirms the impression that she is someone Galdós knew well. She is never described directly, but how she combs her hair, wrinkles her nose, walks, speaks, becomes enraged, looks in the mirror, all endow her with an authenticity that is quite foreign to most literary characterization. She is not "lifelike," but a life in the process of being lived. The novel makes love to her from the moment she is introduced (sucking a raw or "undressed" egg on the stairs of a tenement) until she is last glimpsed lying milk-white in her coffin. It is as if Galdós had known and admired her in her full humanity, unlike her fictional seducer (a civilized animal), who is alternately attracted and repelled by what he conceives to be her wildness.

With his real-life model in mind, Galdós was now novelistically on his own, and he proceeded to invent a biographical context for Fortunata. This includes an impotent, physically grotesque, and quixotic husband who seeks to redeem her; his marginally bourgeois family; a wise protector (an ironic portrait of the future artist as an old man?); and the heartless lover who entangles her in further seductions and desertions. These people (particularly her lover's adorable and barren wife, Jacinta, whom she both admires and envies) affect Fortunata profoundly, and the narrative becomes an account of the growth of her consciousness. This is evidenced first in her growing capacity for assimilating experience (the Madrid we see through her eyes and hear through her ears is as vivid as Dickens' London) and second in her rejection of socially imposed values. When just after her marriage she deserts her husband for her lover, she declares her willingness "to go to Hell." This negative assertion of independence becomes positive much later when Fortunata decides (the role reversal is crucial) to seduce her seducer and bear him a second child. Within her new hierarchy of vital values, she maintains that childbearing is the only true marriage sacrament.

If Galdós began by writing about men and for future generations of men, in his maturity his feminine characters are far more interesting and profound than those of his own sex. This lifelong bachelor seems to have had a special affinity for the problems, reactions, and aspirations of women. In any case, Fortunata, whose only concern had once been the comings and goings of the man in her life, wins salvation on her deathbed when she empathizes with the sufferings of Jacinta and wills to her rival her own infant. There have been several interpretations of this consummate act of generosity. The one most frequently proposed is that only the natural vigor of the Spanish people, as represented by Fortunata, can save the future of the nation from bourgeois sterility. More recently Marxists have condemned the ending as a sellout of the revolution on the part of Galdós. Each interpretation is partly true. However, bearing in mind that the author hoped to transcend the limitations of naturalism, it seems more reasonable to propose that he was primarily interested in the sheer spontaneity and freedom of the decision. Historical inevitability and social determinism were like the windmill-giants that stood in the way of Don Quixote, with the difference that if they could not be vanquished, for a healthy and full-grown consciousness they could at least be successfully defied. It was a question not of altruism or the innate goodness of human nature, but of an unconditional, freely chosen act that makes final sense out of otherwise futile and haphazard experience. Many years later, in 1904, Galdós voiced the hope that Spanish society could yet be redeemed by "an impulse that might spring from its heart." If a single hapless woman could find her way to personal salvation, why not the collectivity of her nation?

In *Fortunata y Jacinta,* the dilemma of being Spanish in the nineteenth century had been transformed into the dilemma of being human in any historical moment and social circumstance. In his next, very short novel, *Miau* (1888), Galdós reacted against the meager yet somehow moving possibility of hope offered by Fortunata with the bleakest metaphysical pessimism. As we know from manuscript versions of his novels, an ending that Galdós had contemplated for both Isidora and Fortunata was suicide; *Miau* is precisely a study of the justification and necessity of self-destruction. There followed in 1888 and 1889 two experimental novels—one a conventional narrative (*La incognita*) and the other composed entirely of dialogue (*Realidad*)—both dealing with the same characters and events. The theme is once again adultery—not as naturalistic corruption, but as an ambiguous event the truth or "reality" of which is difficult to pin down. By its very nature narration is distorted by the suppositions of the narrator and may lead to false conclusions, but speech is unmediated, and it inevitably reveals the speaker. Galdós had taken his cue from Fernando de Rojas' *La Celestina* (1499), a novel in dialogue form that is Spain's second greatest classic.

The attentive reader of *Fortunata y Jacinta* will sense the sudden creative acceleration that accompanies the transition from the painstaking semidocumentary diorama of the first part to the passionate biography of the heroine in part 2. From the writing of this volume until roughly 1911 Galdós' production of novels and plays was prodigious. At the end of the second series of his historical *episodios*, he had vowed to abandon the genre because the years following the change of regime were so close to him that he lacked a clear perspective on them and, at the same time, they were so freshly painful as to inhibit objectivity. Nevertheless, in 1898, beset by financial difficulties, Galdós returned to that best-selling genre and within fourteen years he published no fewer than twenty-six new episodes. The last are particularly interesting in that they deal with events he himself had witnessed. We are privileged to observe the mature Galdós in the act of contemplating his younger self "taking a look at the History of Spain."

The same self-observation is found in the two novels that followed *Realidad: Angel Guerra* (1890–1891) and *Tristana* (1892). The first is a three-volume spiritual "autobiography" or novelistic confession with a somewhat disconcerting cast of allegorical female characters. The second is an ironic meditation on feminine liberation and servitude. It was written at least on one level as a lover's reproach to Doña Emilia Pardo Bazán, at the time Spain's foremost woman novelist and intellectual. At mid-life, when Galdós was just short of fifty, he turned his attention, tempo-rarily at least, from the problems of Spain to those of his personal life. When he did so, like Stendhal in his *Life of Henri Brulard* (1890), he drew on a series of relationships with enchanting members of the opposite sex. Unlike his predecessor, however, Galdós, insofar as he may be represented by his fictional alter egos, was never quite free from guilt and rueful self-reproach in his love affairs.

Two other groups of novels representing Galdós at the height of his creative power remain to be discussed. The first is generally referred to as the Torquemada series. Unlike Balzac, who after creating a character often recalled him for cameo roles, Galdós grew increasingly interested in minor characters and subsequently converted them into the protagonists of later novels. The development of Francisco de Torquemada is an arresting example of the process. He first appears during Galdós' naturalistic period as the grotesquely comic caricature of an urban moneylender, who, like the infamous inquisitor for whom he is named (ironic historical nomenclature is frequent with Galdós), specializes in torture, having a ready-made supply of victims in his impoverished and pretentious bourgeois clientele. We meet him later in *Fortunata y Jacinta*, dressed in the ill-fitting clothes of the *señoritos* upon whom he preys. But then in a long short story, *Torquemada en la hoguera* (Torquemada at the Stake, 1889), Galdós decided to turn the tables on Torquemada and observe his suffering during the sickness and death of the one being he cherishes, his son. The language of pain (always an effective source of Galdosian realism) and the growth of consciousness merge and result in one of Galdós' most intense and probing explorations of human experience in extremis.

After absorbing *Torquemada en la hoguera*, we are left in doubt. Will the usurer be reformed and purified by his martyrdom? The answer is no. But he *is* changed and enlarged and given greater complexity in the course of three full-length novels that present society's decadence and financial corruption with a far greater mastery of technique than in Galdós' earlier naturalistic experiments. In the course of these novels (*Torquemada en la cruz*, 1893; *Torquemada en el purgatorio*, 1894; and *Torquemada y San Pedro*, 1895) we accompany Torquemada—not without a certain sympathy—during his intimately painful and partly unwilling rise from the sordid milieu he began by exploiting to the status of unscrupulous investment banker, ruthless profiteer, corrupt member of parliament, and immensely wealthy pseudoaristocrat. In contrast to *Doña Perfecta*, with its black-and-white confrontation, and *La de Bringas*, with its bleak social exposé, these novels, like *Fortunata y Jacinta*, are centered on the growth of consciousness. And, as a result, the reader reacts with ambivalence and human concern. Like Don Quixote, the caricature—without ceasing to be one—has become a person. Torquemada's speech at his climactic testimonial banquet and his death from indigestion after nostalgically gorging himself on the tavern fare of his early days are thus at once grotesquely comic and somehow pathetic.

The second group of late novels consists of three so-called *novelas de santidad* (novels of sanctity) in which many critics have sensed the subliminal presence of both Leo Tolstoy and Feodor Dostoevsky. Doña Emilia Pardo Bazán had introduced the Russian novel (read in French translation) to the Spanish intellectual public in a series of lectures (published in 1887 as *La revolución y la novela en Rusia*) that Galdós had assiduously attended. He was not slow to acquire copies of the Russian classics, among them Tolstoy's *War and Peace* and Turgenev's *Fathers and Sons*. The influence of the Russian writers is unmistakable, but transmuted by Spanish experience. Unlike Dostoevsky's Prince Myshkin of *The Idiot*, who is naively unaware of any spiritual difference between himself and others, the protagonist of *Nazarín* (the first volume of the series, written in 1895) is a deliberate imitator of Christ whose favorite authors are not romancers of chivalry but Thomas à Kempis and the four Evangelists. He sets out to reenact the Savior's life, wandering and preaching along the prosaic roads of the corrupt rural Spain Galdós had so often depicted. The ambivalent reactions produced by the Torquemada novels are intentionally reversed. If the reader in spite of himself feels a degree of empathy with the wicked and physically disgusting usurer, here he laughs at and is even repelled by the grotesque failures, the needless suffering, the sordid existence (Nazarín's "disciples" are a pair of devoted prostitutes from the lowest echelons of the profession), and mock miracles of a supremely admirable latter-day saint. Like Don Quixote, most of the time Nazarín does himself and others more harm than good.

The sequel to *Nazarín* is *Halma*, written in the same year, and in it the same ambivalence is apparent. Halma, too, is an idealistic, self-conscious Christian who suffers unbearably from sheltering the ungrateful downtrodden. Images from the seventeenth century—Velazquez's dwarfs, stylized gatherings of *pícaros*, and, above all, the stoning of Don Quixote and Sancho Panza by the galley slaves—are ever present in the two novels. The sheer brutality of the narratives is mercifully distanced through the awareness that their realism is historically derived and conventionally grotesque rather than taken from immediate life. Even so, reading them can have a devastating effect on the sensitive reader.

In *Misericordia* (Charity, 1897), however, there is no such distancing. There the poverty-stricken underside of Madrid, which Galdós had depicted tangentially in such novels as *Fortunata y Jacinta* and *Torquemada en la hoguera*, is confronted directly in all its immense, inexcusable misery. Hunger, sickness, and the resultant deformity of body and mind are not glossed over; Galdós documents them thoroughly in both close-up and wide-angle panorama. We do not walk through the shantytowns; we live in them. The force of the novel emerges from the fact that it is an account of a ministry not *to* the poor but *among* the poor. The elderly heroine-saint—she can be described in no other way—Benina, is a picaresque servant of many mistresses who over the years has systematically pocketed and saved a percentage of all the shopping money that has passed through her hands. (The Spanish verb for this practice is *sisar,* and it epitomizes a common self-defense of the poor against the rich.) Benina's last mistress, however, has come down in the world. As a result of past folly, she is completely indigent and without the experience to cope with her poverty. Without knowing it, she is living off Benina's savings; when they are exhausted, the servant secretly enlists in the immense army of Madrid's mendicants, and the two survive on the few pennies she brings home. The title has an ironic resonance in that the penurious and self-righteous ''charity'' of the rich is contrasted with the total and instinctive charity of Benina.

This outline cannot do justice to the treasures of experience and the intricate texture of *Misericordia.* But it does indicate one significant difference between the heroine of this final masterpiece and those of many of the novels that precede it. When Galdós, after years of partisan controversy, was in 1897 finally made a member of the conservative Royal Academy of the Spanish Language, his inaugural address was appropriately concerned with ''present society as novelistic raw material.'' In it he agrees with Balzac in his preface to the *Comédie humaine:* in a century of social change and erosion of class distinctions, the problem of identity (as contrasted to role, which had always been central to the novel) was no longer comic (as in *Don Quixote* and Henry Fielding's *Tom Jones,* for example), but a matter of utmost gravity in the eyes of both a novel's characters and its readers. Who am I? Fortunata and Isidora ask themselves. How can I account for myself as a person in society? Or, more abstractly paraphrased, How can I overcome the social fatality of the past (both the person I used to be and the person others were brought up to think I am) to become the person I aspire to be? At the

end, one finds an answer and the other does not, but Benina is unique in that she does not ask the questions. Not to do so, Galdós implies, if not indicative of sanctity itself, is at least a prerequisite for it.

After the publication of *Misericordia,* Galdós' career took a new turn: he became a dramatist. His abandonment of the novel suggests that Benina, his last fully realized character in this genre, was the answer to the novelistic question that had stimulated and disturbed him for so many years: how to convert being Spanish into a worthy way of being human. *Misericordia* had, as it were, taken him as far as the genre could on the quest that had begun so long before with *La fontana de oro.* The only long narrative he wrote thereafter was anything but a traditional novel. Entitled *El caballero encantado* (The Enchanted Knight, 1909), it is an extended fantasy, an allegorical farewell to the problem of Spain and its ills. In all of Galdós, reality is surrounded by a nimbus of dream, and this is an old man's dream of national salvation surrounded by a nimbus of reality. On the one hand, it recalls fantastic short stories Galdós had written in his youth, and, on the other, it anticipates—for all its narrative awkwardness and cloying sentimentality—such modern works as Gabriel García Márquez's *One Hundred Years of Solitude.* Excluding the *episodios* (which were his bread and butter) and this single isolated experiment, after 1897 Galdós' had completed the transition from novelist to dramatist.

The first step in this direction was not *Realidad* but the brief parody of a romantic drama with which *Tormento* begins. Again in *La desheredada,* Galdós inserted chapters of melodramatic dialogue to illustrate his opinion that Spanish politics were ''no better than a bad play performed by mediocre actors'' (*Las cartas . . . ,* p. 43). But except for these minor fragments, Galdós' five experiments with the mixed genre of the ''dialogue novel'' were due (aside from the notion expressed in *Realidad* that narration tends to distort the truth of consciousness) to the absolutely correct conviction that his novelistic dialogue, with its naturalness and mastery of the vernacular, was infinitely superior to that of the dramatists of the time. In Galdós' opinion, all that contemporary drama had to offer, in contrast to the great theater of the past, was "abbreviated conventional rhetoric without genuine human passion." Even worse, it had nothing to say about the "elemental and primary urgencies" of human life. How better to show himself off, and to show up the vacuity of the contemporary stage, than to write novels without narrative interruption and with scenes and acts in place of chapters: perhaps his readers, who were also avid theatergoers, would realize what they were missing.

The logical next step was to write a play. As is well known, the nineteenth century was not only the great period of the novel but was also prolific in works for the stage. Whatever the merits of the plays, going to the theater was an indispensable form of social communion. And for Spaniards, who had never lost their avid seventeenth-century appetite for sheer spectacle, theater was almost a national mania. Galdós had slowly acquired and educated a considerable literate public who eagerly awaited the publication of each of his novels and, if we can judge by contemporary reviews, understood their innovations. But he had not yet reached out to the mass of his compatriots with drama. Here was the challenge Galdós faced: Could he elevate the drama to the heights of his novels? Could he influence a very different public, a collective audience susceptible only to emphatic declamation, thrilling coups de theatre, sentimental effusion, and reiteration of commonplace values?

On the whole, the answer was disappointing. As a novelist, Galdós was blessed with the extended "time vision" characteristic of his métier, and such a perception of time is by its very nature alien to immediate theatrical timing. His plays are inevitably too long; each act far surpasses the customary forty minutes; and his dialogue, usually crisp in his novels, seems doughy and underdone, as if his char-

acters are repetitiously trying to explain themselves not to each other but to an inattentive or unintelligent audience. As Galdós says in his memoirs, the stage version of *Realidad* (1892) "did not teach me to calculate the dimensions of drama." Many of his plays are adaptations of his previous works, and an author who could visualize "the gestation of events" found the task of cutting anguishing. Detailed comparison of the original novels with their dramatic counterparts reveals his stubborn reluctance to obey "the harsh law of brevity."

Nevertheless, Galdós did have a number of successes, including a controversial hit, *Electra* (1901), which excited all sectors of the audience because of its attack on Catholic fanaticism. Also, his very rupture of the absurd dramatic conventions of his time helped prepare the way for the rebirth of Spanish theater in the twentieth century. During Galdós' last years, increasing blindness slowed but did not halt his urge to create. As the last three *episodios* demonstrate, the necessity of dictation did not alter a narrative style that was in any case profoundly oral. It was only when he tried to hear himself through the ears of an anonymous audience that he floundered.

After his death Galdós' literary reputation suffered a decline that lasted for at least two generations. The year before he died a statue of him was unveiled in the Retiro (Madrid's Central Park). To become a momument is to become old-fashioned. New schools of self-consciously exquisite, young writers found Galdós garrulous and vulgar, an easy target for attack and consequent self-assertion. There were exceptions, of course. Vicente Aleixandre, the Nobel Prize–winning Spanish poet, recalls a café conversation with Federico García Lorca (who later wrote that Galdós possessed "the truest and most profound voice in all Spain") in which the two confessed with surprise to each other that they both were his "passionate admirers."

However, after the catastrophe of the Civil War (1936–1939), which Galdós as a novelist-prophet had predicted with uncanny accuracy both in the second series of *episodios* and in *La desheredada*, opinion about his work changed. One major Hispanic critic after another took on the task of reevaluation, and the curve has been rising almost vertically ever since. Only in other languages and cultures has the formidable difficulty of translating Galdós' colloquial idiom prevented his due recognition. Yet there, too, there are hopeful signs. The stark and sensitive films of Luis Buñuel drawn from Galdós' novels (*Tristana*, *Nazarín*, and *Viridiana*) have attracted international attention. "Who on earth," a French colleague once asked the present writer, "was the author whose work was the source for those extraordinary scripts?" And in English, aside from academic studies, in recent essays the authoritative and impartial voices of V. S. Pritchett and C. P. Snow have elevated Galdós to his proper place in the pantheon of the great novelists of the nineteenth century.

Selected Bibliography

EDITIONS

INDIVIDUAL WORKS
La fontana de oro. Madrid, 1870.
First series of *episodios nacionales.* 10 vols. Madrid, 1873–1875.
Second series of *episodios nacionales.* 10 vols. Madrid, 1875–1879.
Doña Perfecta. Madrid, 1876.
Gloria. Madrid, 1876–1877.
La familia de León Roch. Madrid, 1878.
La desheredada. Madrid, 1881.
El amigo Manso. Madrid, 1882.
El doctor Centeno. Madrid, 1883.
Tormento. Madrid, 1884.
La de Bringas. Madrid, 1884.
Lo prohibido. Madrid, 1884–1885.
Fortunata y Jacinta. Madrid, 1886–1887.
Miau. Madrid, 1888.
La incógnita. Madrid, 1888–1889.
Realidad. Madrid, 1889.
Torquemada en la hoguera. Madrid, 1889.
Angel Guerra. Madrid, 1890–1891.

Tristana. Madrid, 1892.
Torquemada en la cruz. Madrid, 1893.
Torquemada en el purgatorio. Madrid, 1894.
Torquemada y San Pedro. Madrid, 1895.
Nazarín. Madrid, 1895.
Halma. Madrid, 1895.
Misericordia. Madrid, 1897.
Third series of *episodios nacionales.* 10 vols. Madrid, 1898–1900.
Fourth series of *episodios nacionales.* 10 vols. Madrid, 1902–1907.
Fifth series of *episodios nacionales.* 6 vols. Madrid, 1908–1912.
El caballero encantado. Madrid, 1909.
Memorias de un desmemoriado. Madrid, 1930. First published as a series of articles in *La esfera*, March–November, 1916.

COLLECTED WORKS
Obras completas. 4th ed. Madrid, 1961.
Las cartas desconocidas de Galdós en "La Prensa" de Buenos Aires. Edited by W. H. Shoemaker. Madrid, 1973.

TRANSLATIONS
Compassion (Misericordia). Translated by Tony Talbert. New York, 1962.
The Court of Carlos IV (La corte de Carlos IV). Translated by Clara Bell. New York, 1888. Vol. 2 of the first series of *episodios.*
The Disinherited Lady. Translated by G. E. Smith. New York, 1957.
Doña Perfecta. Translated by Mary J. Serrano. With an introduction by W. D. Howells. New York, 1896.
Electra. Translator anon. In *Modern Continental Plays*, edited by S. Marion Tucker. New York, 1929.
Fortunata and Jacinta. Translated by Lester J. Clark. Harmondsworth, 1973.
Gloria. Translated by Clara Bell. New York, 1882. 2nd ed. New York, 1974.
Leon Roch (La familia de León Roch). Translated by Clara Bell. New York, 1888. 2nd ed. New York, 1974.
Saragossa (Zaragoza). Translated by Minna Caroline Smith. Boston, 1899. Vol. 6 of the first series of *episodios.*
Trafalgar. Translated by Clara Bell. New York, 1884. Vol. 1 of the first series of *episodios.*

Tristana. Translated by R. Selden Rose. Peterborough, N. H., 1961.

BIOGRAPHICAL AND CRITICAL STUDIES

Alonso, Amado. "Lo español y lo universal en la obra de Galdós." In *Materia y forma en poesía.* Madrid, 1955. Pp. 230–256.

Berkowitz, H. Chonon. *Benito Pérez Galdós: Spanish Liberal Crusader.* Madison, Wis., 1948.

Bly, Peter. *Galdós' Novel of the Historical Imagination.* Liverpool, 1983.

Bravo Villasante, Carmen. *Galdós por si mismo.* Madrid, 1970.

Brenan, Gerald. *The Literature of the Spanish People.* Cambridge, 1951.

Casalduero, Joaquín. *Vida y obra de Galdós.* Madrid, 1951.

Clavería, Carlos. *El pensamiento historico de Galdós. Revista nacional de Colombia* 19:170–177 (1957).

Engler, Kay. *The Structure of Realism: The "Novelas contemporáneas" of Benito Pérez Galdós.* Chapel Hill, N.C., 1977.

Eoff, Sherman H. *The Novels of Pérez Galdós: The Concept of Life as Dynamic Process.* St. Louis, 1954.

Gillet, J. E. "The Autonomous Character in Spanish and European Literature." *Hispanic Review* 24:179–190 (1956).

Gilman, Stephen. *Galdós and the Art of the European Novel: 1867–1887.* Princeton, N.J., 1981.

Gullón, Ricardo. *Galdós, novelista moderno.* Madrid, 1960.

Hafter, Monroe. "Ironic Reprise in Galdós' Novels." *PMLA* 86:233–239 (1961).

Howells, W. D. *Criticism and Fiction and Other Essays.* New York, 1959.

de Madariaga, Salvador. *The Genius of Spain.* Oxford, 1930. Pp. 46–63.

Montesinos, José F. *Galdós.* 3 vols. Madrid, 1968–1970.

Navarro Tomás, Tomás. "La lengua de Galdós." *Revista Hispánica Moderna* 9:289–313 (1943).

Nimetz, Michael. *Humor in Galdós: A Study of the "Novelas contemporáneas."* New Haven, Conn., and London, 1968.

de Onís, Federico. "Valor de Galdós." In *España en America.* Madrid, 1955. Pp. 389–398.

Pritchett, V. S. *The Mythmakers.* New York, 1979.

Reyes, Alfonso. *Obras completas.* Vol. 6. Mexico City, 1957. Pp. 332–337.

Shoemaker, W. H. *The Novelistic Art of Galdós.* Valencia, 1980.

Snow, C. P. *The Realists: Eight Portraits.* New York, 1978.

Urey, Diane S. *Galdós and the Irony of Language.* Cambridge, 1982.

BIBLIOGRAPHIES

Note: In addition to the usual sources, the *Anales Galdosianos* publishes an ongoing bibliography of the most recent studies.

Hernández Suárez, M. *Bibliografía de Galdós.* Vol. 1. Las Palmas, 1973. Includes all known editions of the works and minor writings.

Sackett, Theodore. *Pérez Galdós: An Annotated Bibliography.* Albuquerque, N.M., 1968.

Woodbridge, Hensley. *Benito Pérez Galdós: A Selective Annotated Bibliography.* Metuchen, N.J., 1975.

STEPHEN GILMAN

PAUL VERLAINE
(1844–1896)

LIKE MOST FRENCH writers, Paul Verlaine lived the greater part of his life in Paris; and like many Parisians, he was originally from the provinces, having been born in Metz on 30 March 1844. His father was Captain Nicolas-Auguste Verlaine, a career officer in the army corps of engineers, and his mother was Elisa-Josèphe-Stéphanie Dehée. Captain Verlaine's family was from what is now Belgium, but in 1798 his native village of Bertrix was part of France. The Dehée family were oil merchants at Arras in northern France; they moved to the nearby village of Fampoux, where his mother was born. In the course of his life Verlaine spent many a vacation in the northern communities of Fampoux, Arras, Lécluse, and Jéhonville. Metz is near the German border in the province of Lorraine, which became German territory as a result of the Franco-Prussian War. As in the case of his father before him, the fortunes of war conferred dual citizenship on Verlaine, so that as an adult he had to opt for French citizenship.

Much significance has been attached to Verlaine's northern origins. French literature has traditionally been a Latin one that regarded the clear precision of classical Greece and Rome as its source. Verlaine, on the contrary, was resolutely a northerner, and his poetry is blurred and shrouded like the mist-draped northern landscapes. Of his brief childhood sojourns in the south of France, he complained that the sun gave him a headache.

His northern origins, his connections with Belgium, and his long stays in England suggest a comparison with several symbolist poets who were Belgian or American, or who wrote French as a second language.

Coming from solid bourgeois stock, the Verlaines were well off: their fortune has been estimated at four hundred thousand francs, a substantial sum at that time. It took Verlaine forty-two years to squander this inheritance. A number of French writers in the course of the nineteenth century enjoyed personal incomes, and others held posts in government ministries, where their duties were apparently less than onerous. This sort of financial independence enabled them to disdain public acceptance of their works and to write according to their own insights for a coterie of fellow writers and enlightened critics. As a result, French literature of the second half of the century is a sort of permanent avant-garde, more advanced in its techniques than other Western literatures.

At the poet's birth his father was forty-six and his mother thirty-five, and after thirteen years of matrimony Paul was their first and only child. His mother had suffered three miscarriages before bearing him, and in a morbid expression of her intense yearning for motherhood, she kept the three fetuses preserved in alcohol for the rest of her days. We hear little of Captain Verlaine's imposing stern discipline on his son, although anecdotes abound of his weak mother's coddling him and indulging his every wish. She was almost constantly at his side until her death when he was forty-two. Popular "wisdom" sees this situation as the source of homosexuality, and indeed Verlaine became a practicing homosexual while in his teens. A cliché of Verlaine biography has it that he was too ugly to be attractive to women; contemporary photographs do not appear to confirm this thesis, but the important thing is that Verlaine believed it and that he never formed a lasting romantic relationship with a woman.

By the time he was a teenager, he was already drinking heavily and frequenting brothels. As a young man he displayed homicidal rages. Joanna Richardson and A. E. Carter point out that for five generations of Verlaine males, from the poet's great-grandfather to his son, his father was the only one not to experience alcoholism, episodes of violence, and brushes with the law. That his father died in 1865, leaving Paul with his permissive mother, did not bode well for the character of a young man who was both weak and rashly irresponsible. Verlaine himself was aware of his weakness and consistently sought the shelter of a stronger personality; in a line from *Poèmes saturniens* (Saturnian Poems, 1866) he describes himself as "a poor orphan without an older sister" ("Voeu"; "Wish"), and in *La bonne chanson* (*The Good Song*, 1870)—surely one of the more original collections of love poetry—he confesses his faults and entrusts himself to the "Being of radiance" who was to guide him through life. Alas! He married an affected and not very bright young woman of seventeen.

When Verlaine was seven the family's private income permitted his father to resign his commission and move his family to Paris. In October 1853 the Verlaines enrolled their son as a boarder at the Institution Landry, a private school. At the end of the first day, dismayed at boarding-school life, young Paul fled and returned home. After an affectionate welcome and with bribes of cakes, his family returned him to school the next morning; but it is significant that for the rest of his life Verlaine would deal with stressful situations by running away. Landry students were taken to classes at the Lycée Bonaparte (today, the Lycée Condorcet, one of the several lycées in Paris that traditionally have formed members of the establishment), where he met Edmund Lepelletier, his lifelong friend and subsequent biographer, and where he received his baccalaureate on 16 August 1862. As seems almost traditional with French writers, Verlaine enrolled in law school, but left after a short time. After a brief period with an insurance company, in March 1864 he entered the Paris city administration as a clerk.

Among Verlaine's colleagues at the hôtel de ville were the poets Léon Valade and Albert Mérat; they would all leave their desks and repair to a nearby café to discuss literature, while Verlaine left his hat at the office to attest to his presence at his post. Toward the end of the year he met the poet Catulle Mendès, through whom he met other poets as well. The previous year he had begun frequenting the soirees of the Marquise Louis Xavier de Ricard, where he met Théodore de Banville, François Coppée, José-María de Heredia, Auguste de Villiers de L'Isle-Adam, Anatole France, and the composer Emmanuel Chabrier. In 1868 he began to frequent the soirees of Nina de Villard, where the tone was less conventional but nonetheless literary. Some French people still have their *soir*, the evening of the week when they are at home to their friends. In the nineteenth century the soirees of literary figures—such as those of Charles Nodier at his apartment in the Arsenal library, of Charles Leconte de Lisle, of Stéphane Mallarmé in the rue de Rome—where young writers met the master, received his advice and encouragement, met other writers, and generally exchanged ideas, were an important feature of Parisian literary life.

Largely as a result of attending the soirees,

the young Verlaine had at least an acquaintance with most of the writers and intellectuals of his day. Since school days he had been reading widely, especially among contemporary poets. When he was only fourteen he sent his first poem to the great Victor Hugo, and he continued to compose poetry. By 1866 he had accumulated enough poems to publish his first collection of verse, *Poèmes saturniens.*

The poems are quite disparate, reflecting their author's readings and affirming his originality. The title and introductory poem, with their allusion to the planet Saturn, refer to a passage in *Les fleurs du mal (The Flowers of Evil,* 1857) by Charles Baudelaire, the poet whose influence is most widespread in Verlaine's book. The prologue and epilogue state Verlaine's adherence to the goals of the poets who published, as he did, too, in the *Parnasse contemporain:* perfection of form, devotion to the ideal of beauty, objective description. The *Parnasse contemporain* was a series of three anthologies of verse: the first published in 1866; a second, prepared in 1868 but whose publication was delayed by the Franco-Prussian War until 1871; and the third in 1876. The first two volumes especially are characterized by the qualities enumerated above. With so many different contributors, of course, not all the poems conform equally closely to these ideals; it is nevertheless such poetry—objective in attitude, visually descriptive, and correct in poetic form—that is designated by the term "Parnassian" and that is typical of Théodore de Banville, Théophile de Gautier, José María de Heredia, and Charles Leconte de Lisle, the leader of the Parnassian group. The second poem, titled "Nevermore" (both the French and English versions bear this title) could have been written by Baudelaire himself; elsewhere there are Parnassian themes, and in the language are echoes of Hugo, Baudelaire, Leconte de Lisle, and others. Some announce the Verlaine to come: the first "Nevermore" (there are two poems bearing this title), "Mon rêve familier" ("My Familiar Dream"), "Soleils couchants" (Setting Suns), and "Chanson d'automne" ("Autumn Song"). What these poems have in common that is typical of Verlaine's best work throughout his career is a studied imprecision in the descriptions (the descriptions are not vague: rather, there is a careful blending of blurred forms and of precise detail, the effect of which is almost tantalizing); visual descriptions; verbal music created by repetitions of words and phrases and by plays on the sounds of words; a gentle sadness the cause of which is not stated. Above all, it is normally impossible to paraphrase the "content" of a poem: what it "says" is an expression of the poet's mood. It is not an exaggeration to observe that Verlaine is probably the only poet in French literature whose thought or ideas have never been discussed by scholars. In the dream mistress of "Nevermore" and "Mon rêve familier" Jacques-Henry Bornecque believes he has found a poignant personal situation, which sheds light on these poems and on several in *Fêtes galantes* (Gallant Festival, 1869). As a teenager Verlaine was in love with his cousin Elisa Moncomble, eight years older than he (she, incidentally, paid for the publication of *Poèmes saturniens*). Never suspecting the depth of her cousin's affection, she contracted a marriage, perhaps of convenience, with a sugar-beet grower from Fampoux. When in 1867 she died in childbirth, Verlaine drowned his grief in a three-day drinking episode.

Also there is a pronounced visual aspect to these poems: several describe landscapes as the poet sees them, and "César Borgia" describes a painting by Raphael. This description of a painting, and "Nuit du Walpurgis classique" ("Classical Walpurgis Night") and "Chanson des ingénues" ("Song of the Ingenues"), which depicts a scene and a situation from eighteenth-century French painting, foreshadow his next collection of verse.

In *Fêtes galantes* Verlaine has found his own voice, although there are still echoes of

Baudelaire and of other poets. While in *Poèmes saturniens* the imitations of earlier poets outnumber poems that are distinctly Verlaine's, in *Fêtes galantes* this proportion is reversed: despite his debt to his predecessors and the fact that his work was part of a vogue for poems on Watteau's paintings, in *Fêtes galantes* Verlaine adapts the material to an original expression of his own attitudes and psychological concerns. The notion of transposing the paintings of Antoine Watteau into poetry was not uncommon: Hugo, Banville, Gautier, and Baudelaire had all done so. Some of Verlaine's readers regard *Fêtes galantes* as one of his major achievements. Since, therefore, discussion of the importance of this collection is best deferred until we examine Verlaine's poetry, we return to the chronology of his life. In 1869 he met a sixteen-year-old named Mathilde Mauté de Fleurville, fell in love with her, and promptly asked for her hand in marriage. After some delay—her youth, Verlaine's drinking, and the possibility of a more suitable match for her caused her family to hesitate—they were married on 11 August 1870, in the midst of the Franco-Prussian War, indeed at the very moment that the French army was suffering disastrous defeats. During their courtship Verlaine had composed poems for her, which he published as *La bonne chanson.* Although the book was announced in December 1870, it was not placed on sale until 1872. As love poetry it was somewhat out of the ordinary: no cruel mistresses, no singing of the lady's charms. Verlaine celebrates the incidents of their courtship, declares his impatience at having to wait, and anticipates their future bliss. More revealingly, he mentions his unsettled life and entrusts himself to the guidance of "la radieuse pensée / Qui m'a pris l'âme l'autre été," ("the radiant thought / That stole my soul last summer," 15).

The bride and groom set up housekeeping on the rue du Cardinal-Lemoine in the Latin Quarter, and Verlaine continued his clerical duties at the hôtel de ville. He had evoked the forthcoming idyl of matrimony in *La bonne chanson:*

> *Le foyer, la lueur étroite de la lampe;*
> *La rêverie avec le doigt contre la tempe*
> *Et les yeux se perdant parmi les yeux aimés;*
> *L'heure du thé fumant et des livres fermés;*
> *La douceur de sentir la fin de la soirée;*
>
> (14)

The hearth, the narrow beam of the lamp; / Dreaming with a finger against my temple / And our eyes losing themselves in those we love; / The hour of steaming tea and of books that have been closed; / The sweetness of feeling the end of the evening.

National catastrophe and Verlaine's own destiny, however, would destroy this dream of middle-class wedded bliss. Within days of their wedding the French army was crushed at Sedan, the emperor Napoleon III abdicated, and Prussian troops surrounded Paris. The newlyweds would spend their first year of marriage in a city under siege, a city bombarded by Prussian heavy artillery; as did other Parisian housewives, Mathilde would purchase cuts of meat at the butcher shop that turned out to be cat, dog, and slaughtered animals from the Paris zoo.

On 4 September the people of Paris proclaimed a republic. The young couple welcomed the new government, and Paul enlisted in the *Garde nationale*, a citizens' militia formed to reinforce the sadly depleted ranks of the regular army for the defense of Paris. During his tours of sentry duty, he unfortunately resumed his drinking. The following year Mathilde became pregnant.

Early in 1871, when the French government concluded an armistice with the Prussians, the people of Paris broke with the official government of France, which moved to Versailles, and proclaimed a Commune, an autonomous government of the city of Paris. Verlaine sided with this regime and was assigned to its press office. At the end of May the Versailles government retook Paris from its own citizens and inflicted bloody reprisals. Verlaine's role in the Commune had apparently been a minor one, but anyone could be denounced as a former communard; so Paul and Mathilde prudently spent the summer of 1871 at Fampoux. In August they returned to Paris, but Paul, again out of prudence, did not return to his post at the hôtel de ville. His parents had consistently found him jobs in order to help him avoid the opportunities for dissipation that idleness provided; now he was idle again, just when the most effectual danger to his marriage and to a respectable life was about to appear.

In August 1870 a sixteen-year-old schoolboy at Charleville, near the Luxembourg border, had written to his former schoolmaster praising Verlaine's *Fêtes galantes*. The boy was Arthur Rimbaud (see the essay "Rimbaud") who, if he is not one of France's greatest poets, at least in three precocious years, between the ages of sixteen and nineteen, revolutionized French poetry and became an important influence on French symbolism and, to some degree, on modern Western poetry. Rimbaud was brilliant and driven by a seemingly demonic urge. In drastic reaction to a dour, severe mother and to the oppressiveness of a small country village, he proposed that the poet should become a seer by "un immense dérèglement de tous les sens" (an immense disordering of all the senses). Rimbaud "disordered his senses" by drinking and by any other behavior-altering mode he could devise. His personal obnoxiousness and truant life were expressions of his literary theory. He also was homosexual, and what he appears to have perceived in Verlaine's verse were Verlaine's homosexuality and effort to evade, through poetry, the constrictions of reality.

The Verlaines had scarcely returned to Paris when Paul received a letter from Rimbaud asking to come to Paris and enclosing some of his poems. A second letter followed, and Verlaine replied with a fervent invitation to stay with his family and with money for the train ticket. Rimbaud's arrival at the home of Mathilde's family on 10 September 1871 was inauspicious. He was a raw peasant youth, roughly clad in garments he had outgrown, and speaking with a thick Ardennais accent. He was tired from the trip, and the pretentious Mauté household (it is significant that the family name was simply "Mauté"; there was no factual basis for adding the aristocratic "de Fleurville," which in French denotes nobility) embodied the traditional bourgeois values that he so despised. He ate dinner without speaking and asked to go to bed. At the end of two weeks the Mauté family firmly advised Verlaine that Rimbaud could no longer stay with them, and for the rest of the winter Rimbaud was alternately maintained by Verlaine or various other writers or lived from day to day by his wits.

Rimbaud's stay in Paris was disastrous. Because of his boorish, hostile manners he quickly alienated everyone. His actions were incredible: at a café he poured sulfuric acid into his neighbor's glass of wine; again, he asked a companion to lay his hand on the table, then attempted to stab the hand with his pocketknife. The nature of his relations with Verlaine became known; even newspapers commented on a performance at the Théâtre Français during which Verlaine strolled arm-in-arm during intermission with the disheveled, dirty "mademoiselle Rimbaud." (An important reservation is in order. It is generally accepted that Verlaine was homosexual, and biographers consistently treat the Rimbaud affair as such a liaison. Nevertheless, to the end of his life Verlaine always denied that his relationship with Rimbaud was actually homosexual.) As for Verlaine, he had resumed drinking, and Rimbaud was a more interesting companion than Mathilde. Finally, returning home drunk in the evenings, he committed a series of physical assaults on his wife and newborn son. By January 1872 he left Mathilde to stay with his mother. Monsieur Mauté instituted separation proceedings against his son-in-law and took Mathilde and the baby to Perigueux in the south for their own safety. She returned to Paris in March 1872.

This period epitomizes the contrast between the effects of Verlaine's emotional problems and the beauty of his poetry. In May 1872, the same month that he tried to set Mathilde's hair on fire (they had attempted a reconciliation), he was writing the superb series of poems, "Ariettes oubliées," that appeared in his next collection of verse, *Romances sans paroles* (*Songs Without Words,* 1874), and Rimbaud was composing "Fêtes de la patience," which Suzanne Bernard has called the high point of his poetic artistry. Rimbaud drastically influenced Verlaine's verse at this time, and he was the inspiration that Verlaine needed after a period of poetic mediocrity and silence; the stimulation was reciprocal, and Verlaine contributed more to Rimbaud's art than has often been recognized.

The attempted reconciliation that brought Verlaine back to the Mauté home and to Mathilde ended on 7 July 1872. Mathilde was ill, Verlaine went out to fetch a doctor, and, apparently by prearrangement, met Rimbaud in the street. Both boarded a train for Belgium. Although Verlaine would see Mathilde again later in the month in another abortive attempt at reconciliation, their marriage was finished.

The following year, almost to the day, is significant for the development of French poetry in the last quarter of the nineteenth century. As the two poets wandered about together, they shared their ideas concerning poetry, and Rimbaud told Verlaine about his extensive readings in the Charleville public library. The exchange of ideas affected the poetry of both men—poetry that, in turn, was a fertile source of inspiration for the symbolist poets fifteen years later.

Verlaine and Rimbaud spent the next months in Brussels or tramping about Belgium. Place names like "Walcourt," "Charleroi," "Bruxelles," and "Malines" in *Songs Without Words* evoke Verlaine's impressions of their travels. In September they embarked for Dover, England, and spent the autumn in London. In November the poets separated, but by the end of May 1873 they were together again and off to England. The mutual poetic inspiration that had united them in Paris continued unabated although marred by quarrels, and both poets produced some of their finest work during and shortly after this period. On 7 July 1873, after a particularly bitter quarrel, Verlaine abandoned Rimbaud and departed for Brussels, leaving the piteous Rimbaud literally stranded on the dockside as the ship pulled out. Verlaine had had enough and was going to return to his wife. In Brussels his mother and Rimbaud both rejoined him, and after more quarreling, this time it was Rimbaud who abandoned the lachrymose Verlaine. But Verlaine had purchased a revolver, ostensibly to use on himself, and he shot Rimbaud twice, wounding him slightly in the wrist. When he threatened to fire again, Rimbaud sought the protection of a Brussels policeman, who duly arrested Verlaine. As with Mathilde, Verlaine would see Rimbaud once again in a fruitless reconciliation effort, but his arrest ended their companionship.

Since Rimbaud refused to prefer charges, the charge against Verlaine was reduced to criminal assault. However, a medical examination determined that he had recently practiced sodomy (examination of the subject's private parts is no longer considered a reliable index of recent homosexual activity), and unfavorable reports concerning Verlaine's political activities during the Commune had arrived from Paris. The judge therefore imposed the maximum sentence: two years at hard labor and a fine of two hundred francs. Verlaine was transferred to the penitentiary at Mons to serve his time. He continued writing poetry; indeed, some of his best and most moving poems, pieces like "Un grand sommeil noir" (A Great Black Sleep) and "Le ciel est, par-dessus le toit" ("The Sky Above the Roof") (*Sagesse,* 3.5 and 3.6; *Wisdom;* 1881) were composed at the Brussels jail or at Mons, and he considered bringing out a collection of prison poems to be called "Cellulairement" (Cellularly).

Meanwhile the Mauté family had been pursuing separation proceedings. On 24 April the separation was granted, and the next month the warden of the penitentiary communicated the decree to Verlaine in his prison cell. Crushed by the news, Verlaine sat in his cell and wept, then fell on his knees before the crucifix in his cell. Shortly after, he asked for a catechism and the prison chaplain. In due time he made his confession and received Holy Communion.

Like most French children of his time (and many today), Verlaine attended religious classes, made his first communion, and then promptly fell away from religious practice. During his youth, his family did know some priests as friends. So it was not altogether unexpected for him to compose some religious poems after the disaster of being sentenced to prison. But upon his conversion he became a Catholic poet: he wrote about God's role in his own life; he treated his sins, remorse, faith, and hope as literary themes. The splendid sonnet sequence in *Sagesse*, "Mon Dieu m'a dit . . . ," relates the emotional experience of a sinner discovering God.

The theme of an unbeliever's discovery of God in a time of despair was relatively new in French literature, but by no means unique. The Catholic writer Jules Barbey d'Aurevilly wrote of Joris Karl Huysmans that, after having composed so despairing a novel as *À rebours* (*Against the Grain*, 1884), his only remaining choice was between the muzzle of a revolver and the foot of the cross. Huysmans, in fact, did turn to Catholicism and wrote about his newfound faith. In Paul Bourget's *Le disciple* (*The Disciple*, 1889), an atheistic professor returns to his childhood faith after learning that a student had committed a murder in the name of his teachings. The theme of such dramatic conversions is continued today in the work of modern writers such as Paul

Claudel, François Mauriac, and Georges Bernanos. Verlaine continued to compose religious verse for the rest of his life.

Verlaine had entered prison leaving unpublished the superb poems written during his association with Rimbaud. While at Mons therefore he entrusted his friend Lepelletier with finding a publisher for them. The task was not easy, for Verlaine was banned from literary circles because of the scandal of the Rimbaud affair. Lepelletier found a publisher at Sens who had previously published a radical newspaper during the Commune, and early in 1874 *Romances sans paroles* was published.

In January 1875 Verlaine was released from prison and rejoined his mother at Fampoux. About a month later he met Rimbaud at Stuttgart, ostensibly to convert him. Instead, the two men made the rounds of local bars and ended with a drunken fistfight on the banks of the Neckar. They never saw each other again. At the end of March Verlaine returned to London and obtained a teaching position at a private school in Stickney operated by a Mr. Andrews. Except for holiday trips to France, he remained there until the spring of 1876. He spent the school year 1876–1877 in Saint Aloysius College, Bournemouth, under a Mr. Remington. After another period in Stickney, in September 1877, he succeeded his friend Ernest Delahaye at the college of Notre-Dame at Rethel, near the Belgian border, where he remained until July 1879.

In Rethel, Verlaine befriended one of his students, a youth of nineteen named Lucien Létinois. Lucien was the same age as Rimbaud had been in 1872, and like Rimbaud he came from the Ardennes. Despite the intensity of and the obvious basis for his attachment to the young man, their relationship does not appear to have been homosexual, and Verlaine habitually described Létinois as his adopted son (the separation decree of 1874 had awarded Mathilde custody of their son, and Verlaine saw him only a few times after that). In any case, Verlaine and Lucien became inseparable. When Lucien failed his *bachot* (the French equivalent of a baccalaureate degree) in 1879, Verlaine obtained a post for him in Stickney while he taught at Solent Collegiate School at Lymington. When Lucien proved unsuccessful as a teacher, the two returned to France. From March 1880 until the beginning of 1882 Verlaine joined the Létinois family in operating a farm he had bought for them in Juniville. While Lucien did his military service in Rheims, Verlaine went along and supported himself as a monitor in a local college. In July 1882, if not a little sooner, Verlaine returned to Paris with Lucien. After another attempt at teaching school, Lucien got a factory job at Ivry. There he died of typhoid fever in April 1883. Verlaine's friendship with Lucien ranks with his love for his wife and his attachment to Rimbaud as one of the major sentimental episodes of his life. He commemorated Lucien in a series of twenty-five poems in the collection *Amour* (Love, 1888).

Verlaine had continued writing devotional verse after his release from prison. He abandoned the idea of "Cellulairement" in favor of a collection of poems dealing with his conversion, a few composed shortly after his arrest and others consisting of Christian meditations. They were published in 1881 as *Sagesse*.

Verlaine's wanderings with Rimbaud, his imprisonment, and his various teaching positions constituted a ten-year exile from Paris and its literary circles, broken only by brief visits. July 1882 marks his definitive return to Paris and the resumption of his literary activities. These last thirteen and a half years of his life are crucial, but to appreciate them we must first look more closely at his poetry.

So far we have mentioned five collections of verse: *Poèmes saturniens, Fêtes galantes, La bonne chanson, Romances sans paroles,* and *Sagesse.* We now include a sixth, *Jadis et naguère* (Recently and Formerly, 1884). As the title suggests, *Jadis et naguère* contains poems of disparate dates, ranging from 1867 to 1883. For this collection, his first publication after

returning to Paris, Verlaine simply assembled all his poems, leftovers from earlier times and recent compositions, into one book, as he had done for *Poèmes saturniens* in 1866. His only books to consist of poems composed during one period around a single theme are *Fêtes galantes, La bonne chanson,* and *Romances sans paroles.* All his other collections are made up of poems composed over a long period of time and only brought together when he wanted to publish a new book. Of course, by the time of his last collections, he had few earlier poems left. To place an individual poem in the larger context of his work, therefore, it is necessary to know the poem's date of composition or of first publication in a periodical.

There are also three clandestine collections of pornographic poems: *Les amies* (Friends, 1867), signed "Pablo de Herlagnez," *Femmes* (Women, 1890), and *Hombres* (Men, n.d. but ca. 1903). The six sonnets of *Les amies* on lesbian love appear in *Parallèlement* (In a Parallel Manner, 1889), and various appendices for a new edition include some poems from *Femmes* and *Hombres.*

Verlaine was to publish thirteen more collections of verse during his lifetime, as well as a *Choix de poésies* (Choice of Poetry, 1891) and an edition of the play *Les uns et les autres* (The Ones and the Others), composed in 1871 and first published in *Jadis et naguère.* The late books of verse have relatively little poetic interest; they are more important as biographical markers during his years of poverty and fame. The prose—fiction, *Les confessiones* (Confessions of a Poet, 1895), criticism, and the like—is of interest chiefly to Verlaine specialists, who read them primarily as biography. Collections of his correspondence continue to appear as private collectors make letters available for publication.

There are several reasons for the distinctly poorer quality of the last collections. Between *Poèmes saturniens* in 1866 (actually somewhat earlier, as apparently he had been composing poetry since 1858) and *Jadis et naguère* in 1884, Verlaine composed thirty-one percent of the some 862 poems that appear in modern editions of his collected works (such as the Pléiade *Oeuvres poétiques complètes* or the Club du meilleur livre *Oeuvres complètes*); in the twelve years until his death in 1896 he compiled the remaining sixty-nine percent, as well as most of his prose. He suddenly began writing much faster: after all, he was producing poems in order to earn a living, instead of creating patiently as the inspiration came to him. Furthermore, by the time he was fifty the years of alcoholism had taken their toll, and Verlaine's mind was no longer as alert as it had been. In any case, after 1884 there is no longer the evolution in his style or the innovations that distinguish his earlier work. Verlaine's later poems all resemble each other or the weaker of his earlier poems.

With his weak and malleable personality, in his poetry as in his life Verlaine was always strongly influenced by the people around him; he apparently needed the stimulation of other creative artists to put his own creative faculties into motion. Paradoxically, he did his most original work while in close association with other poets. It was the intense intellectual milieu of Paris of the 1860's that inspired *Poèmes saturniens* and *Fêtes galantes*. Rimbaud was responsible for the daring of *Romances sans paroles*. After that, he was alone: first the ten years of exile, then Paris of the 1880's and 1890's. While it was, to be sure, a stimulating milieu, only the rare older poet is influenced by younger poets who imitate his early poems, or by new poetic trends that, as in Verlaine's case, he does not understand.

Fêtes galantes is a collection of twenty-two poems, most of them twelve or sixteen lines long (inspired, as we have said, by Verlaine's perception of French painting of the preceding century). Some describe scenes, presumably in the garden at Versailles. Pierrot, Harlequin, and similar figures from the Italian commedia dell'arte theater appear, as well as characters with names from seventeenth-century French novels; several poems consist of dialogue between two persons. Thus there is a theatrical as well as a painterly aspect. Moreover, there is a changing tonality, alternately gay and melancholy, that tends to link the poems as a sustained expression of mood.

The collection deserves attention because of the way Verlaine projects his own emotions and erotic anxiety into a fictive world based on eighteenth-century French painting and on the commedia dell'arte theater. For this enterprise he had numerous literary sources: poems by Gautier, Banville, his friend Albert Glatigny, and Hugo's "La fête chez Thérèse" ("The Party at Therese's") in *Les contemplations* (Contemplations, 1856). The more one looks for sources, the more one finds, since the emotion of Watteau paintings and the gracious world they depict appealed to romantic nostalgia, dreams, and eroticism. During the 1830's there was a *cénacle du Doyenné*, a group of romantic poets who cherished the art of Watteau. The mood continued during the century. Significantly, *Fêtes galantes* was Verlaine's first book of verse to be sold out; his first poem to be imitated recognizably by a younger poet was "La chanson des ingénues," and there was a renewal of interest in the themes of *Fêtes galantes* during the symbolist period.

Another important source for *Fêtes galantes* was the brothers Jules and Edmond de Goncourt. These brothers are among the most interesting figures in nineteenth-century literature: they were successful and highly esteemed novelists; their *Journals* (9 vols., 1887–1896) are a useful source of historical information; and as art critics they had an immense influence on French taste during the latter half of the century. It was their *L'Art du XVIIIme siècle* (Art of the Eighteenth Century, 1857–1858) and *La femme au XVIIIme siècle* (Woman in the Eighteenth Century, 1862) that served as a source for *Fêtes galantes*. Actually, it appears that the Watteau paintings now in the Louvre had not yet been hung by the time Verlaine was composing his *Fêtes galantes*, so that he depended on the Goncourts' descriptions of the paintings and on those of Charles Blanc in *Les peintres des fêtes galantes: Watteau, Lancret, Pater, Boucher* (The Painters of the *Fêtes galantes,* 1864).

Between Verlaine's working from secondary sources and his adapting the mood of Watteau's paintings to his own expressive needs, the atmosphere of Verlaine's *Fêtes galantes* becomes rather different from that of Watteau. One variant is illustrative. In the original version of "Clair de lune" (Moonlight), the ninth line read, "Au calme clair de lune de Watteau," (With the calm moonlight of Watteau); since most of Watteau's paintings take place in daylight, this verse provoked so much criticism that Verlaine was obliged to change it to, "Au calme clair de lune triste et beau," (With the calm moonlight, sad and beautiful). The change is significant; for Watteau's bright, if sometimes introspective, scenes, Verlaine substitutes the romantic moonlight of melancholy and of dream.

In Italy the commedia dell'arte was a theater, usually composed of itinerant troupes of players, in which each actor always had the same name and costume, played the same role, and wore a mask. There was no script; the actors made up their lines extemporaneously on the basis of a plot loosely based on the stereotyped characters. This theater has a long history, reaching back to classical antiquity. In the seventeenth century Molière succeeded as a comic playwright only after having spent some years with companies of commedia dell'arte players in Italy. The form again became popular in France in the eighteenth century (hence the *Théâtre des Italiens* and the *rue* [street] *des Italiens* today) and, as an entertainment of the royal court at Versailles, entered into the world painted by Watteau and his contemporaries. The figures of Gilles, Harlequin, and Pierrot in Watteau paintings come from the commedia dell'arte. What must have intrigued Verlaine is the tension between the stereotyped character represented by the mask and the real person behind the mask who played the role, for that tension echoes the one between the carefree world of *Fêtes galantes* and his own anxieties.

Verlaine underlines the theatrical aspect of eighteenth-century paintings. In "Clair de lune," the collection opens with a landscape of masks dancing an Italian dance *("bergamasque")* to the music of the lute; "Pantomime" describes the actions of Pierrot, Clitandre, Cassandre, Harlequin, and Colombine, characters from the commedia dell'arte. "Sur l'herbe" ("On the Grass") consists entirely of dialogue; "Fantoches" ("Puppets") and "Colombine" continue this theatrical effect. In "Puppets" we see two players silhouetted against the moon:

> Scaramouche et Pulcinella
> Qu'un mauvais dessein rassembla
> Gesticulent, noirs sur la lune.

Scaramouche and Pulcinella / Whom an evil design gathered / Gesticulate, black against the moon.

"Mandoline" and "Les indolents" (The Indolent Ones) rely on dialogue and on narrations of the characters' actions in an essentially theatrical presentation. In poems where there is no dialogue, Verlaine seems to speak to a listener. Many of the poems have an exterior quality, so that we watch characters as from a distance or hear them speak without participating in their emotions. In painting, such an organization of the picture, with figures placed in dramatic relationship to each other, is called dramatic space.

The world of eighteenth-century painting, with characters like Tircis, Clitandre, and Damis, was one of flirtation and gallantry. One thinks of Watteau's *L'Embarquement pour l'île de Cythère* (1717), the embarking for Cythera, the island sacred to Venus. In their *La femme au XVIIIme siècle* the Goncourt brothers draw attention to the sexual freedom of this society. For Verlaine a world of voluptuousness and easy love must have indeed been attractive; there are erotic allusions here and there, and constant references to flirtation. But flirtation is not the same as satisfaction, and if the lady in "Cortège" ("Cortege") is ogled insolently by her black page and her pet monkey; if, as in "En patinant," (While Skating) "Un vent de lourde volupté / Investit nos âmes surprises" (A wind heavy with voluptuousness / Besieged our astonished souls), the souls are surprised that this voluptuous mood should intrude, and the passage concludes with a precious ridiculing of love:

> Nous cédâmes à tout cela,
> Et ce fut un bien ridicule
> Vertigo qui nous affola
> Tant que dura la canicule.
> ("En patinant")

We yielded to all that, / And it was a quite ridiculous / Dizziness that drove us crazy / As long as the dog days lasted.

Somehow, in this licentious society love is never gratified. In "Les ingénus" (The Youths) the young men following their mistresses in the gathering dusk, "un soir équivoque d'automne" (an equivocal autumn evening), although aroused by the sight of a pretty ankle or a bare neck, are awed by the nearness of love: "Notre âme, depuis ce temps, tremble et s'étonne" (our soul, since that time, has been trembling and astonished). As here or in "Pantomime," there is a constant tension between the gaiety, the opportunities of this fictive world, and characters who are suddenly surprised to find that they feel genuine emotion:

> Colombine rêve, surprise
> De sentir un coeur dans la brise
> Et d'entendre en son coeur des voix

Colombine dreams, surprised / To feel a heart in the breeze / And to hear in her heart voices.

In "Clair de lune," the figures are "almost sad under their fantastic disguises"; "they don't seem to believe in their happiness"; the fountains in the garden "sob with ecstasy." Thus there is an unresolved tension between joy and sadness, between flirtation and gratification of desire; amid all this gallantry the characters are surprised that emotion even exists. While the situation around them is erotic, they are only players in a situation comedy.

The lightheartedness of flirtation is the enemy of sincere affection, just as ridicule is the foil to physical desire, and while the characters themselves make light of the hopelessness of their courtship of obdurate mistresses—as in "Dans la grotte" (In the Grotto), "En patinant," "Lettre" (Letter), "Les indolents"—there is a continuing and increasing note of despair. After opening on the uncertain tone of "Clair de lune," the poems of *Fêtes galantes* alternate between carefree gaiety and increasing melancholy. In "Le faune" ("Faun"), a terra cotta statue of an old faun laughs, doubtlessly prophesying an unhappy end to this lighthearted gallantry, and the couple are characterized as "melancholy pilgrims." In "L'Amour par terre," (translated as "Cupid Fallen"), a storm the previous night has overturned the statue of Cupid; the man is saddened by the sight, while the woman frivolously watches a fluttering butterfly. In "Les indolents," the suitor facetiously proposes to his partner that they die together, and that their game is a joke: "—Hi! hi! hi! quel amant bizarre!" (Hee! hee! hee! What a strange lover!). But this poem foreshadows the far more sinister "Colloque sentimental" ("Sentimental Conversation"), which ends the series. "Dans le vieux parc solitaire et glacé, / Deux formes ont tout à l'heure passé" (In the old, lonely, and frozen park / Two forms have just now passed by). They are the ghosts of two lovers. The suitor pleads with the woman to remember and relive their past love; she replies with indifference, because it no longer matters to her. Her callousness is a particularly wounding rebuff to the lover's desperate longing: "—Qu'il était bleu, le ciel, et grand, l'espoir! / —L'espoir a fui, vaincu, vers le ciel noir" (How blue was the sky, and how great our hope!/Hope has fled, defeated, toward the black sky). The poignancy of these poems is heightened by J.-H. Bornecque's theory that the two figures are the young Verlaine and his dead cousin, Elisa Moncomble, who, married to an older man, could not understand her kinsman's yearning for her.

In "Mandoline" the observations that shadows are blue ("Et leurs molles ombres bleues" [And their soft blue shadows]) and that the moon changes color ("D'une lune rose et grise" [Of a pink and gray moon]) as it rises in the sky, point to the impressionists, whose canvases deeply influenced Verlaine's poetry. An illustration of impressionism in "Art poétique" ("The Art of Poetry," in *Jadis et naguère*) indicates the value Verlaine attached to this manner of perceiving and rendering the outside world:

> *Rien de plus cher que la chanson grise*
> *Où l'Indécis au Précis se joint.*
>
> *C'est des beaux yeux derrière des*
> *voiles,*
> *C'est le grand jour tremblant de midi,*
> *C'est, par un ciel d'automne attiédi,*
> *Le bleu fouillis des claires étoiles!*

Nothing dearer than the gray song / In which Vagueness is joined to Preciseness. / It's beautiful eyes behind veils, / It's the broad daylight trembling at noon, / It is, under a mild autumn sky, / The blue backdrop of bright stars!

The notion of the transposition of the arts—reproducing in one art form the effects of another—has a long history in French poetry. In the eighteenth century, French poets described landscape gardens in a manner borrowed from Italian painters. Hugo was an amateur artist, who reproduced in his poetry, as in *Les rayons et les ombres* (Lights and Shadows, 1840), the chiaroscuro effects of light and dark that characterize his drawings. The Parnassian poets likened their strict observance of the rules of versification to the hard outlines of sculpture, as in Gautier's "L'Art" (Art, 1857). Gautier was a painter; both he and Baudelaire wrote art criticism. The latter's poem "Les phares" (The Lighthouses, 1857) treats the work of great painters. And we have seen how, in *Fêtes galantes*, Verlaine, like others before and after him, transposed Watteau's paintings into verse. Today one thinks of Pablo Picasso's friendship with the poets Pierre Reverdy, Max Jacob, Jean Cocteau, and Paul Éluard.

The brothers Jules and Edmond de Goncourt appear again as a source for literary impressionism, in their novel *Manette Salamon* (1867). The novel has to do with outdoor landscape painters; its descriptions resemble paintings, and its style—*écriture artiste* (artist writing) or *style Goncourt*—seeks to reproduce the effects of painting as practiced by artists of the impressionist school: Claude Monet, Édouard Manet, Auguste Renoir, Alfred Sisley, Camille Pissarro, and others. The impressionists first began to exhibit during the 1880's, while Verlaine was composing his *Poèmes saturniens*; furthermore, the publication of the Goncourts' novel and the impressionists' first group show in 1874 bracket the period when he was writing in his most impressionist manner.

To summarize impressionism very roughly (and not altogether accurately, for current research has altered our conception of the impressionist manner, contradicted the impressionists' favorite legends about themselves, and sharpened the distinctions between individual painters), they worked out of doors, doing chiefly landscapes and scenes of contemporary life. Their goal was to capture the effects of light on their subject, especially in the sense of freezing an instant in time—hence their interest in changing subjects like sky, clouds, and water. They used conspicuously brighter colors than their predecessors (partly as a result of recent chemical discoveries that made possible new pigments) and—this is the trait of impressionism that first comes to mind, but it was used by only a few of the painters—they sought to render the effects of reflected sunlight by a technique called divisionism or pointillism: small dabs or brush strokes of different colors that, viewed from a distance, blended optically into a single vivid hue.

The Goncourts sought to translate these procedures into language by a series of stylistic devices. Modifiers, especially of color, come before the noun, so that the impression precedes what produces it (a notable change in French, where the rule is that adjectives of color follow their nouns). The style is essentially nominal: nouns are listed in asyndeton—enumerated one after the other without grammatical connectors, more like a shopping list than a grammatical sentence. Verbs are omitted, replaced by the weakest verb, "to be" (usually "c'est" in French), or replaced by verbal nouns ("the rustle" or "rustling" instead of "to rustle"). Sentence structure is disrupted by separating grammatically paired words such as subject and verb, verb and object, and preposition and object by other groups of words.

In Verlaine's work we in fact find the blue and green shadows of impressionist paintings: "et que le clair de lune fait / Opalines parmi l'ombre verte des branches," (and that the moonlight makes / Opaline in the green shadow of the branches: "Nuit du Walpurgis classique," Poèmes saturniens); "L'ombre des bas tilleuls . . . / Nous parvient bleue et mourante à dessein." (The shadow of the low linden trees . . . / Reaches us blue and dying on purpose: "À la promenade," Fêtes galantes).

Landscapes are as ubiquitous in Verlaine's poetry as in impressionist painting. His descriptions of changing skies or water are impressionist. His references to grimy industrial sites ("Charleroi," Romances sans paroles) or to the holiday recreation of the working classes ("Bruxelles: Chevaux de bois" ["Brussels: Wooden Horses"], Romances sans paroles) echo Édouard Manet's and Edgar Degas's interest in social realism.

We usually, and correctly, think of impressionist landscapes as bright and sunny, but the blurring of contours in much impressionist painting is a form of atmospheric perspective; where the painters do not perceive a landscape through a veil of atmosphere, they often render it in snow or fog. Verlaine preferred subdued lighting, as in the moonlit poems of Fêtes galantes; rain, as in "Il pleure dans mon coeur" ("It Weeps in My Heart"); or cloudy skies:

Il fait un de ces temps ainsi que je les aime,
Ni brume ni soleil! le soleil deviné,
Pressenti, du brouillard mourant dansant à
    même
Le ciel très haut qui tourne et fuit, rose de crème;
L'atmosphère est de perle et la mer d'or fané.
                              ("Bournemouth," Amour)

It's the kind of weather I love, / Neither fog nor sun! the sun guessed at, / Like a foreboding, fog dancing as high as / The sky very high that whirls and flees, cream-pink; / The atmosphere is of pearl and the sea of faded gold.

"L'Heure du berger" (translated as "Dusk") in Poèmes saturniens, with its foggy sunset, and the "aube affaiblie" (weakened dawn) of "Soleils couchants" recall the indistinct effects of Claude Monet's Impression, Sunrise (1874). In "L'Amour par terre" (Fêtes galantes), the artist's name on the pedestal of the statue is barely visible in the shadow. In Sagesse we read "La neige tombe à longs traits de charpie / À travers le couchant sanguinolent," (Snow falls in long wisps of lint / Before the blood-tinged sunset, 3.9). And in a harvest scene the poet sees the wheatfield as if bathed in light: "dans un bain / De lumière si blanc que les ombres sont roses" (In a bath / Of light so white that the shadows are rose-colored, 3.21). The image reminds us of Monet's paintings of Rouen cathedral (1894), in which the facade of the cathedral is almost dissolved in a pastel light. The essence of impressionist theory is that forms are modified by the effects of light; moreover, the painters followed recently discovered optical theories, such as the one that states that shadow colors are the complement of the color of the object that casts them. Verlaine seeks to reproduce this phenomenon by having "white light" cast "rose-colored" shadows (daylight is actually cool, tinted blue from the sky—shadows, then, appear warm, or rose-colored).

Examples of the *style Goncourt* abound in Verlaine's verse. Already in *Poèmes saturniens* he writes, "Sous l'oeil clignotan des bleus becs de gaz" (Under the blinking eye of the gas jets, blue: "Croquis parisien" ["Parisian Sketch"]). In French, adjectives of color follow the noun, while the *style Goncourt* places them *before* the noun so as to stress the impression of color at the expense of what causes it. "Effet de nuit" ("Night Effect") has a typical combination of nouns and incomplete sentences listed in asyndeton. "Walcourt" (*Romances sans paroles*) consists entirely of noun phrases without connectors; there is not a single verb in the poem. In "Ariettes oubliées, 2" ("Songs Forgotten, 2") we read: "une espèce d'oeil double / Où tremblote à travers un jour trouble / L'ariette, hélas! de toutes lyres!" (a sort of double eye / In which trembles through a muddied light / The song, alas! of all lyres!). The normal word order, in French as in English, would be: "in which the song of all lyres trembles through a muddied light, alas!" Verlaine has altered the word order so as to present a series of impressions in this sequence: trembling, a muddied light, a song, "alas!" and finally, the musical instrument that plays the song.

Thus the *style Goncourt* presents sense impressions in the order they reach us, with the impression always coming before the thing that produces it. The goal of such a style is to record impressions at the expense of logical interpretation. In a normal sentence, the grammatical hierarchy of subject, verb, object, modifiers, and coordinate and subordinate clauses forces the words (and their impressions) into an intellectual hierarchy of values; but the impressionist style abolishes sentence structure, claiming that all sense impressions are of equal importance. This sacrifice of rational comprehension for the freshness of the immediate impression corresponds to Verlaine's disdain for ideas and to the absence of intellectual content (as opposed to expression of emotion) in his poetry.

Impressionist painters sought to record not the permanent features of a scene but its appearance at a given moment in a given light. Verlaine too stresses the evanescence of sense impressions, often questioning their nature and their very existence. In one poem he even qualifies his own perception: "In the interminable / Boredom of the plain / The uncertain snow / Glows like sand / The sky is of copper / Without any light. / One would think he sees the moon / Living and dying." ("Ariettes oubliées, 8"). The snow is "uncertain" and resembles another substance; watching the moon emerge and disappear seems unreal. In "Charleroi" he questions the nature of what he perceives: "Quoi donc se sent?" "On sent donc quoi?" (What is felt? What do you feel?) "Parfums sinistres! / Qu'est-ce que c'est? / Quoi bruissait / Comme des sistres?" (Sinister perfumes! / What is it? / What rustled / Like sistras [ancient Egyptian tambourines]?).

In another poem, a piano glimmers vaguely in the pink and gray light of evening, while the tune played on it, "Un air bien vieux, bien faible et bien charmant" (A very old, very weak, and very charming tune) still hovers discreetly in the next room, which for a long time was perfumed by the presence of the poet's wife. Both the tune and the perfume survive the disappearance of what originally caused them. Verlaine then asks them: "What is this sudden cradle / That slowly rocks my poor being? / What would you want of me, gently playful song?" And the song is soon going to die, as it drifts slowly through the partly open window ("Ariettes oubliées, 5"). This subtlety of perception is reinforced by the verbal music: "Qu'as-tu voulu, fin refrain in-

certain / Qui vas tantôt mourir vers la fenêtre''
(What did you want, fine uncertain refrain, /
Who is going to die toward the window?)
Against this background of fading sense
impressions, the language is piercing and strident. The cacophony of the explosives ''Qu'as-
tu'' and of the strident vowels *u* and *-ain* are
in contrast to the dying tune.

Verlaine calls this tension between the
vagueness, the evanescence, of his sense
impressions and the various kinds of stri-
dency that keep them alive an instance of ''la
chanson grise / Où l'Indécis au Précis se
joint'' (the gray song / In which Vagueness
and Preciseness are joined). As style makes
impressions more important than their
causes, and as Verlaine perceives the impressions so remote from their sources in nature
as to be on the point of fading, sense impressions acquire an autonomous existence; they
exist apart from their point of origin. Distant
from the poet who perceives them, their existence reinforced by the music of language,
they occupy a middle ground where poet and
reader meet. Verlaine's most impressionist
poems are also his most musical, for music is
the common denominator of sensation and
emotion.

So, as Jean-Pierre Richard concludes, Verlaine's achievement in his impressionist
poems is a closer mode of communication
than that achieved by other poets, for sense
impressions associated with an emotional experience become substitutes for that experience. In ''Ariettes oubliées, 1'' a personal experience of Verlaine's is equated with sense
impressions that the reader can share:

> C'est l'extase langoureuse,
> C'est la fatigue amoureuse,
> C'est tous les frissons des bois
> Parmi l'étreinte des brises,
> C'est, vers les ramures grises,
> Le choeur des petites voix.
>
> Ô le frêle et frais murmure!
> Cela gazouille et susurre,

> Cela ressemble au cri doux
> Que l'herbe agitée expire . . .
> Tu dirais, sous l'eau qui vire,
> Le roulis sourd des cailloux.
>
> Cette âme qui se lamente
> En cette plainte dormante
> C'est la nôtre, n'est-ce pas?
> La mienne, dis, et la tienne,
> Dont s'exhale l'humble antienne
> Par ce tiède sour, tout bas?

It's the langorous ecstasy, / It's the amorous fatigue, / It's all the shudderings of the woods, /
Among the embrace of the breezes, / It is, among
the gray boughs, / The chorus of little voices. /
Oh, the frail and fresh murmur / That twitters
and whispers, / That resembles the soft cry /
That rustled grass breathes out . . . / You might
say, under the water that swirls, / The dull rolling of pebbles. / That soul that complains / In
that sleeping lament / It's ours, is it not? Mine,
now, and yours, / Whose humble refrain is
breathed out / On this tepid evening, quite low?

The first two lines posit the central experience: the afterglow of physical love. There follow immediately other sensory experiences:
the shuddering of trees in the wind, the chorus of little voices in the tree boughs, descriptions of these, the gentle cry of rustling grass,
and, finally, the rolling of pebbles in running
water. The sense impressions are metaphors,
or equivalents, of the initial sexual experience; by simply listing one *c'est*-phrase after
another in asyndeton, Verlaine avoids differentiating between direct statement and comparison. A metaphor, after all, is only an implied comparison. In the third stanza, the
personal interpretation, ''Cette âme qui se la-
mente . . . C'est la nôtre, n'est-ce pas?'' (That
soul that complains . . . it's ours, is it not?) is
introduced by the demonstratives ''cette'' and
''c'est,'' as were the previous sense impressions; and it is accompanied by other sense
impressions, so that again an emotional state
is equated with a sense perception. In this
way, as Octave Nadal and J.-P. Richard both

point out, sense perceptions become the equivalents ("équivalences sensorielles") of emotions, and in such an impersonal expression of intimate emotion Verlaine achieves his most direct communication with his reader.

What the reader commonly first notices in Verlaine's poetry, and the quality for which his verse is famous, is his music. Composers have set a number of his poems to music, and Verlaine himself advised aspiring poets, "De la musique avant toute chose" (Music before all else: "Art poétique," *Jadis et naguère*). It goes without saying that poetry is the musical form of literature, and that Verlaine, like all poets, uses rhyme, assonance, and alliteration; that he is careful to choose words for their euphony. It is also true that by the middle of the nineteenth century, French poets were particularly interested in the expressive capacity of verbal music. For some listeners French is more musical than other languages. Without the regular beat of a tonic accent, it flows more smoothly and vowels are more resonant. (In English, the tonic accent is the stress that occurs in words like "todáy" or "to-mórrow." Moreover, English speakers tend to swallow unstressed syllables, while French places equal weight on all syllables.) As anyone who has taken a course in French phonetics knows, French possesses a rich gamut of variations on vowels: there are nasal and vocal vowels, open and closed, long and short versions of the same vowel. In French versification, arbitrary rules for counting the number of syllables in a line require that sometimes a mute e that is silent in spoken prose be pronounced as a full syllable; this practice creates a sort of limping rhythm. French poets have traditionally exploited all these resources of their language.

What, then, distinguishes Verlaine's poetry from that of other French poets? Most likely it is the subtlety of his methods and the stark simplicity of his most musical poems. Instead of the refrains of folk songs or the repetitions of anaphora (starting each verse or stanza with the same word or expression), Verlaine alternates between repetitions of entire lines or sentences, repetitions of words or phrases, and repetitions of individual sounds or vocables. (Baudelaire made effective use of refrains and repetitions, and Verlaine further developed Baudelaire's techniques.) Sometimes these repetitions are foreseeable, as in end rhyme or interior rhyme; often they seem to occur at random. He repeats and contrasts subtle variations of the same sound. Certainly he had a wonderful ear. There is an anecdote that he was so fascinated by the sounds of words that when he heard a new word he would say it over and over again, testing its resonances and variations. Most French poets are adept at making their verses sing, but Verlaine's most musical poems are the simplest, those that seem the most artless when reduced to a prose translation. In such poems music takes over from the sense of the words, for the poem has no "meaning"; and vocables, used like the notes of music, acquire an autonomy of their own, much as his impressionist sensations seem to exist independently of their sources in nature.

A well-known example of his music, a poem that students in phonetics classes are often required to learn by heart, is the "Ariette oubliée, 3":

> *Il pleure dans mon coeur*
> *Comme il pleut sur la ville;*
> *Quelle est cette langueur*
> *Qui pénètre mon coeur?*
>
> *Ô bruit doux de la pluie*
> *Par terre et sur les toits!*
> *Pour un coeur qui s'ennuie*
> *Ô le chant de la pluie!*
>
> *Il pleure sans raison*
> *Dans ce coeur qui s'écoeure.*
> *Quoi! nulle trahison? . . .*
> *Ce deuil est sans raison.*
>
> *C'est bien la pire peine*
> *De ne savoir pourquoi*
> *Sans amour et sans haine*
> *Mon coeur a tant de peine!*

Tears fall in my heart / As rain upon the city; / What is this languor / That pierces my heart? / Oh, the gentle sound of the rain / By land and on the roofs! / For a heart that is empty / Oh, the song of the rain! Tears fall without reason / In this heart that is disheartened. / What? No betrayal? . . . / This grief is without reason. It is indeed the worst pain / Not to know why / Without love and without hatred / My heart suffers so much pain!

In contrast to the deceptive simplicity of the language, there is a complex pattern of sounds. In the first stanza, "pleure," "coeur," and "langueur" all rhyme; "pleut" is the "closed" form of the vowel that is "open" in the rhyme words (in French an "open" vowel is pronounced with the mouth more open and the muscles of the mouth more relaxed than in the "closed" version of the same vowel; this difference in enunciation causes an audible difference in sound). In line three, the vowels of "quelle est cette . . . " are all open e's, while "pénètre" in line four opposes a closed e (as in English "pay") to an open one (as in English "let"). There are alliterations of k ("comme," "quelle," "qui," "coeur") as well as of e and r. Thus there is an abundance of repeated sounds. Meanwhile, the rules of prosody require that the final, "mute" e of "pleure," "cette," and "pénètre" all be counted as syllables, although they are silent in conversational French; hence a third variety of e, another assonance, and the peculiar sort of weak rhythm we have described. The i of "ville" is picked up as part of the rhyme of the second stanza, while "sur" contains the u sound of "bruit," "pluie," and "s'ennuie."

In the second stanza, "par terre et sur . . . " and "pour un coeur . . . " introduce a different and subtler repetition: r is regularly preceded by the combination consonant-plus-vowel; all the vowels are different, but the p is repeated. The -eur vocable of the first stanza is repeated by "pour un coeur" in the second, then it recurs three times in the third stanza (where the closed vowel of "deuil" echoes it), and finally

again in the last line. Thus the vocable -eur that dominated the first stanza, recurring in a pattern of retreat and reemergence, serves to unify the whole poem. In spite of these intricate sound patterns, the diction is perfectly natural and unaffected, with no feeling of having been forced in order to yield the choice and pattern of sounds.

Verlaine's reputation as a musician and as the liberator of French versification is based on his poem "Art poétique," which attracted much attention during the 1880's. He begins by advocating music:

> De la musique avant toute chose.
> Et pour cela préfère l'Impair
> Plus vague et plus soluble dans l'air,
> Sans rien en lui qui pèse ou qui pose.

Music before all else, / and for that favor the uneven line [with an odd number of syllables] / More vague and more soluble in the air / With nothing in it that's heavy or pompous.

In two stanzas he warns against the evils of rhyme:

> Prends l'éloquence et tords-lui son cou!
> Tu feras bien, en train d'énergie,
> De rendre un peu la Rime assagie.
> Si l'on n'y veille, elle ira jusqu'où?

> Ô qui dira les torts de la Rime?
> Quel enfant sourd ou quel nègre fou
> Nous a forgé ce bijou d'un sou
> Qui sonne creux et faux sous la lime?

Take eloquence and twist its neck! / While you are at it, you will do well / To make Rhyme a bit better-behaved. / If you don't watch out, how far will it go! / Oh, who will tell the faults of Rhyme? / What deaf child or crazy black / Forged for us this penny jewel / That sounds hollow and false when you file it?

As Verlaine became respected as the leader and guide of a younger generation of poets, those who were interested in free verse cited these stanzas as justification for their endeavors. Verlaine protested in vain that he did not intend the interpretations that were attributed to him. To appreciate his own poetic practices, it is necessary to look more closely at what he actually did.

Without a tonic accent falling on alternate syllables, French versification counts the number of syllables in a line, using some arbitrary rules for including or excluding the mute *e.* Since the fifteenth century, three-quarters of French verse has been written in a twelve-syllable line called the alexandrine. The romantic revolt in the nineteenth century involved changes in the rhythm of the classical alexandrine, and Verlaine wrote some alexandrines that do not fit the prescribed canons of where the stresses and caesuras (pauses) should fall. His usage, however, is not so different from that of his contemporaries as to constitute a liberation of the verse form. There are other verse-lengths in French, usually with an even number of syllables. A line with an odd number of syllables, *le vers impair,* has been infrequently used and has always been regarded as difficult for poets to handle. French people are thought naturally to speak in alexandrines (unrhymed, of course), just as English speech is supposed to fall naturally into iambic pentameter.

What attracted the most attention and imitation in "Art poétique" was Verlaine's attack on rhyme and his recommendation of "l'impair." Blank verse has never been successful in French; apparently rhyme is necessary to supplement the weak stresses of the language. What counts is the kind of rhyme, determined by the number of phonetic elements the two rhyme-words have in common. Rhyme-words must share at least the final two sounds; *tonneau* and *rouleau* do not rhyme because although the *eau* sound (as in English "ō") is the same, the *n* and *l* are different, while *rouleau* and *boulot* do share two phonetic elements, *l* and the final vowel *o* (spelled either "eau" or "ot" in French). In reaction to the romantics' efforts to free versification, the Parnassians sought strict adherence to the traditional rules, so that in Verlaine's time *rime riche* (three phonetic elements shared by the rhyming words, as in *rouleau–boulot* above) was much discussed and admired. When Verlaine in his "Art poétique" warned poets against the excesses of rhyme, he most likely had in mind the *rime riche* of the Parnassians. He himself always rhymed. Where he does weaken the effect of rhyme is in his use of repetitions and refrains. The purpose of rhyme, inherited from the days when poetry was declaimed aloud, is to indicate the end of a line by the regular recurrence of the same sound. When, as in "Mon rêve familier" (*Poèmes saturniens*), Verlaine repeats the rhyming vowel and consonant combination, or even the rhyme word, within the line, and also on different lines, the effect is to confuse the reader as to where the line ends. To be sure, he uses rhyme, and his rhymes are correct (*suffisantes*), but since they do not always serve as end markers for the line of verse, their traditional role is diminished.

Although *vers impairs* have always been used, Verlaine was particularly fond of them, and this different rhythm in the Frenchman's usual penchant for an even number of syllables would therefore be disproportionately important. He even wrote some verses of thirteen syllables (for example, "Sonnet boiteux" [Limping Sonnet], *Jadis et naguère*), and this final syllable in addition to the normal breath group seems particularly disturbing. French rhymes must alternate between "masculine" and "feminine": a feminine rhyme is one that ends in a spelled mute *e* and a masculine rhyme does not have the *e.* It has nothing to do with gender. *Achille* is a feminine rhyme and *satin* masculine, even though both words are of masculine gender. Contrary to this rule, Verlaine uses successive pairs of feminine rhymes. The final mute *e* never counts as a syllable; it is never pronounced. But when Verlaine ends a *vers impair* with a feminine rhyme, there is a tendency to compensate for the lacking syllable by pronouncing the mute *e.* (The rule for alternating masculine and feminine rhymes dates back to the twelfth century, when the e was in fact pronounced.) This tendency is apparent in "Chanson d'automne" *(Poèmes saturniens),* with its four-syllable lines in masculine rhymes and the three-syllable ones in feminine rhymes:

> *Les sanglots longs*
> *Des violons*
> > *De l'automne*
> *Blessent mon coeur*
> *D'une langueur*
> > *Monotone.*

The long sobs / of the violins / Of autumn / Wound my heart / With a monotonous / Languor.

More important than the preceding discussion is the question of stanza form. Much nineteenth-century French poetry was written in quatrains, sonnets, or couplets, with lines of the same length. Every poet, however, creates his own stanza forms with lines of different lengths and with their own rhyme schemes. The Parnassians in particular liked to display their virtuosity by inventing stanzas of long and short lines (short lines are difficult because they call oftener for a rhyme). In the course of two or three stanzas the reader becomes accustomed to the new form and accepts it as regular. What is interesting in Verlaine's case is the number of different stanza forms he devised, and how often he varies them. Pierre Martino has observed that for the forty poems of *Poèmes saturniens,* Verlaine has twenty different stanza forms, a relationship that Martino expresses as an index of fifty percent. In *Fêtes galantes* this index rises to over sixty-five percent; in *La bonne chanson* it goes to sixty percent, but in *Romances sans paroles,* where Verlaine was most influenced by Rimbaud and most inclined to experiment with new forms of verse, every poem has a different stanza form: one hundred percent. In *Sagesse* the index reverts to sixty-five percent. Insofar as these books were published over a period of fifteen years and sold poorly or were not even offered for sale, the index for each collection is merely a statistic. When, however, Verlaine became popular, and when people read each book through from cover to cover, and when they read several in succession, the effect for readers who had literally been schooled in a tradition of alexandrine paragraphs must have been one of much variety and of constantly changing meter. (*Vers libres* has a double meaning in French. One is what we call "free verse" in English, or unrhymed lines of various lengths. The other designates the form of Jean de La Fontaine's *Fables* [1668], where each fable, like each poem of Verlaine's, has its own characteristic stanza form.)

It appears, then, that what Verlaine did to weaken traditional rhythms and to render verse suppler and less regular is not any single procedure, like abandoning rhyme, so much as a combination of various techniques, the whole effect of which is greater than the sum of its parts. In "Ariette oubliée, 3", "Il pleure dans mon coeur," the stanza form is highly original, although Verlaine did not invent it; he borrowed it from the romantic poet Marceline Desbordes-Valmore, who first used it in 1839. The six-syllable lines can be read as *hémistiches,* or half-alexandrines, so that the quatrains can be said to consist of two alexandrines (in French much free verse consists, in fact, of measurable fragments of alexandrines). The rhymes are all *suffisantes,* or correct. It is the rhyme scheme *axaa, bybb,* and so on, that is unusual: the second line does not rhyme, and the first and fourth lines end in the same word, a pairing that does not count as a rhyme. Thus the two alexandrines rhyme in the middle of the line rather than at the end. Rhymes do occur, but in an unorthodox position, while a quite different pattern of recurring sounds serves as the structure of the poem. So a combination of traditional and novel patterns results in one of the freest poems Verlaine wrote, yet one that stops short of unrhymed free verse.

To turn now from Verlaine's poetry to the

events of the last years of his life, we recall that he returned to Paris in July 1882 with the intention of living by his pen. It was a courageous, hopeful, and altogether unrealistic project; Verlaine had always published at his own expense small (350–500 copies) editions that never sold well. Few people had read his poetry, and after ten years of absence he was unknown to a younger generation of writers. As for those of his own generation, because of his scandalous past he was ostracized by editors, publishers, and reviewers, who refused to mention his name. Only the faithful Lepelletier stood by him, turning over to Verlaine his own newspaper column, with its remuneration. Yet at this point in Verlaine's fortunes, it seemed as if where merit and fairness had failed, coincidence was about to correct a longstanding injustice.

Through Lepelletier's influence, in July and November Verlaine published a half-dozen poems in a new review, *Paris-moderne*, recently founded by a bookseller-publisher who had only just turned to publishing literature. One of the poems was "Art poétique," composed in 1874. In reply to a review of one of the few press copies of *Romances sans paroles* to be sent out, "Art poétique" sets forth the aesthetic principles to be deduced from what Verlaine had been writing during the previous two years: "De la musique avant toute chose, / Et pour cela préfère l'Impair" (Music before all else, / And for that favor the odd-syllable line), a description of his impressionism, a denunciation of eloquence and especially of rhyme: "Et tout le reste est littérature" (And all the rest is literature [as opposed to poetry]).

In the fourth issue of a newly founded literary magazine, *La nouvelle Rive Gauche*, Charles Morice sharply criticized the poem and Verlaine's theories. Verlaine wrote to him in reply, met Morice, converted him to Verlaine's conception of poetry, and became a regular contributor to the new magazine, as well as the warm friend of Morice (just as Léon Vanier, of *Paris-moderne*, became Ver-

laine's publisher and lifelong friend). In May 1883 *Le chat noir* published some of his poems, including "Langueur" ("Apathy," republished in *Jadis et naguère*): "Je suis l'Empire à la fin de la décadence" (I am the [Roman] Empire at the end of the decadence), and this poem, too, attracted much attention. In September *Lutèce* (as *La nouvelle Rive Gauche* was now designated) published the first (to our knowledge) poem clearly imitating Verlaine. None of this brought in any money, but it indicates how in a little over a year Verlaine had progressed from obscurity to relative prominence and how younger poets admired him to the point of imitation.

Meanwhile, his companion Lucien Létinois had died, and as usual, Verlaine responded to the emotional trauma by almost literally fleeing. In July 1893 his mother bought the Létinois farm at Coulomnes, and mother and son went there to operate the farm. Although he did keep in touch with literary events in Paris, corresponding with friends and sending manuscripts to Vanier and to magazines, for Verlaine this sojourn at Coulomnes and another absence from Paris was a low point. Totally inept at farming and emotionally disoriented, he abandoned himself to a life of drunkenness and debauchery, sending to Paris for boys, buying expensive presents for his lovers, and being robbed by tramps he met in local taverns. The expense of these debauches, as well as that of selling the farm at a loss, seriously reduced what was left of his private means. As a final degradation, he spent a month in jail for having threatened his mother in a drunken rage. After some weeks of drunken vagabondage, in June 1885 he returned to Paris and settled with his mother in a hotel frequented by prostitutes and their pimps. In January 1886 his mother died. Divorce had been made legal, so Mathilde divorced him; to satisfy the alimony judgment, Verlaine handed over to a bailiff literally the last of his badly depleted fortune. He was penniless and alone in a house of ill repute, although his literary reputation was rapidly growing: such was to be Verlaine's situation for the last ten years of his life.

After Morice's unfavorable article on "Art poétique," "Jean Mario" (three different staff members wrote under this pen name) published in *La nouvelle Rive Gauche* an article that surveyed and analyzed Verlaine's work sympathetically and with understanding. In May 1884 Huysmans published his novel *À rebours*, which has to do with a world-weary, neurotic young man who shuts himself up in his house to devote himself to the indulgence of his aesthetic pleasures. One of his favorite poets is Verlaine, so that Huysmans gives several pages of the novel to a discussion of Verlaine's poetry. Because the novel was a popular and controversial success, it brought Verlaine to the notice of a wider public than had the articles in small literary magazines (translated into English as *Against the Grain* and with a preface by Oscar Wilde, the novel also carried the Parisian literary scene to English readers). In July 1884 Louis Desprès published an article on Verlaine in *La revue indépendante;* in November and December Maurice Barrès discussed Verlaine in an article on Baudelaire and his followers in *Les taches d'encre.* These were all literary reviews, small in circulation and addressed to a specialized audience of writers, their friends, and those interested in avant-garde literature. Then in 1885 Paul Grandet wrote an article on Verlaine in *Le cri du peuple* and Paul Bourget in *Les débats,* both periodicals with large circulations directed to the general public: they not only discussed Verlaine's work, they described him as the leader of a literary school and as much admired by younger poets. In three years, then, Verlaine's literary fortunes had enjoyed a complete turnabout, from obscurity to general recognition.

Verlaine's official acclamation can be said to occur with the article "Paul Verlaine et les poètes symbolistes et décadents," (Paul Verlaine and the symbolist and decadent poets), by the academic critic Jules Lemaître writing in the prestigious *Revue bleue* for 7 January 1888. The article is a turning point in another way, as well. Previous articles had discussed the subtlety and the music of Verlaine's verse, his ability to suggest delicate nuances of emotion, his impressionism. Lemaître omitted *Romances sans paroles* from his study, emphasized *Sagesse,* described Verlaine as a sort of primitive who wrote poetry by instinct rather than by design, and stressed the colorful aspects of the repentant but fallen Catholic poet. Thus Lemaître initiates an emphasis on Verlaine's biography and legend that was to dominate Verlaine studies for the next half-century.

During this period, besides publishing poems in reviews and bringing out *Jadis et naguère,* Verlaine wrote three critical essays on Tristan Corbière, Arthur Rimbaud, and Stéphane Mallarmé under the title *Les poètes maudits (The Damned* [or *Maligned*] *Poets,* 1884). The essays first began to appear serially in *Lutèce* in August 1883 and appeared in book form early in 1884. Vanier published it in an edition of 253 copies that sold well, a fact that encouraged him to continue publishing Verlaine, although the latter still had to pay the expenses of *Jadis et naguère.* By the end of 1884 Vanier had become Verlaine's publisher, and his advertisements for Verlaine's work appeared regularly in *Lutèce* and other literary reviews. Of Verlaine's previous work, only *Fêtes galantes* had been sold out; *Romances sans paroles* and *Sagesse* were still in storage at their respective publishers. For all of Verlaine's previous books, then, Vanier simply bought up the unsold copies and put on his own covers.

As for *Les poètes maudits,* again coincidence appears to resemble providence more than random chance. Until then, Verlaine's prose had never been important, nor his criticism distinguished. By contrast, his first *Poètes maudits* filled a need at just the right time. Tristan Corbière was an eccentric young Breton who published a collection of rather strange poetry, *Les amours jaunes* (Yellow Loves), in 1873, before dying of tuberculosis.

The work would have gone totally unnoticed had not his nephew, himself a poet, migrated to Paris and fallen in with a countryman, Léo Trézenik, editor of *Lutèce*. He and Charles Morice showed the poems to Verlaine, who was so favorably impressed that he devoted his first article to Corbière. It has taken a long time for Corbière to be appreciated in France, but, thanks to Verlaine's article, his work was still discussed in literary circles at the turn of the century when the young Ezra Pound and T. S. Eliot arrived in Paris. They drew heavily on his techniques of word play and his use of references to literary works in order to evoke a mood or an historical period. Consequently, for many years Corbière was probably better known to American readers than to French.

As for Rimbaud, immediately after leaving Verlaine he completed *Les illuminations* (Illuminations), then renounced poetry completely, destroying much of his work and leaving Europe to spend the rest of his life as a trader in Ethiopia. Consequently, not only was he completely unknown, but texts of his poetry were unavailable. In his articles Verlaine quoted extensively from his poets, including complete poems, and in his Rimbaud articles, he called on anyone possessing copies of Rimbaud's poems to send them to him. In 1886 the review *La vogue* published the complete text of *Les illuminations.* Thanks to Verlaine's resurrection of his work, Rimbaud became an important influence on the development of symbolist poetry.

Stéphane Mallarmé was approximately Verlaine's age and had been active as a poet for as long as he. In 1883 he was less well known than Verlaine, so that he did benefit from Verlaine's article. He soon became acknowledged, along with Verlaine, as one of the leaders of the young generation of poets, and subsequently he has come to be considered a major poet and to be regarded more highly than Verlaine.

In a second series of *Les poètes maudits* (1888) Verlaine wrote essays on Marceline Desbordes-Valmore (it was Rimbaud who made known her work to Verlaine); "Pauvre Lélian," an anagram of his own name; and Villiers de L'Isle-Adam. They were less influential than his first series.

Verlaine's rehabilitation and success need to be placed in the context of the literary scene of the 1880's, a scene dominated by the tardy recognition of Baudelaire and by the literary movements of decadence and symbolism.

Baudelaire's *Les fleurs du mal* is perhaps the most seminal individual work of poetry to appear in nineteenth-century France. (The reader is urged to consult the essay devoted to him in this series.) In these poems he perfects, if he himself does not develop, those procedures of suggestion, evocation, and indirect expression that separate modern from traditional poetry. In his own lifetime he was much better known than Verlaine, and his was the most pronounced influence on *Poèmes saturniens.* But with his death in 1867 his name suffered an eclipse.

However, during the 1870's, as French poetry remained in a sort of void, dominated by older men like Hugo (born in 1802!) and Leconte de Lisle, critics began to recall Baudelaire's work in increasingly favorable terms, and young poets turned to him as a model; so that by 1880 it was he who most strongly influenced the emerging generation of young poets. On reading the early issues of *Le chat noir* and *La nouvelle Rive Gauche*, both of which began publication during 1882, one is impressed at the extent of Baudelaire's influence. Leconte de Lisle and Hugo trail him by a substantial distance. As far ahead of his time as innovative artists usually are, Baudelaire had to wait two decades before readers were ready to appreciate him. It was in part their appreciation of Baudelaire that enabled the same readers to accept, in their turn, Verlaine and Mallarmé.

The only edition of *Les fleurs du mal* available until 1930 was a posthumous one of 1868, with a preface by Gautier that characterizes Baudelaire as a poet of the decadence.

Decadence is a complex and contradictory notion that developed in the course of the century. At its inception, some French historians and social thinkers felt that as a nation France was declining, and a reactionary critic made a derogatory comparison of romantic poetry to that of the Silver Age of Latin poetry. The collapse of France in 1870 before invading hordes of Teutons, after the glories and the corruption of Napoleon III's Second Empire, strengthened this conception of history as well as the comparison of modern France to decadent Rome. In a perverse and confused sort of way, French writers were fascinated by the corruption of Rome at the end of the Empire, and they came to think of themselves, like the writers of late Latin, as the last members of a decaying civilization. Baudelaire included a poem in vernacular Latin in *Les fleurs du mal.* In this way, as Jacques Lethève observes, a pessimistic philosophy of history became a literary style.

During the 1880's literary decadence embraced a wide range of expression, from minor writers who celebrated the more lurid aspects of sexual perversion and of the Paris underworld in barely comprehensible latinate French, to more responsible writers like Verlaine, Mallarmé, Gustave Flaubert, and Émile Zola, who echo these themes without compromising their own literary manner. So young poets welcomed two aspects in the work of Baudelaire, Verlaine, and Mallarmé: their decadence (as in Verlaine's poem "Langueur," composed to suit the mood of the time) and their procedures for suggesting and recreating emotion by indirect modes of expression.

Huysmans' *À rebours* is the case history of a decadent aesthete who prizes the decadent qualities in the verse of Baudelaire, Verlaine, and Mallarmé. In 1885 both Verlaine and Mallarmé were identified in *Les délisquescences* of "Adoré Floupette," a parody of decadent verse that drew considerable attention.

Except for a few minor poets who never did desist, these extreme forms of decadence were succeeded around the middle of the 1880's by symbolism. A common occurrence was for a poet to publish a first collection of decadent verse and subsequently to compose poems in the symbolist manner. French symbolism is a complex and multifaceted movement that has been the subject of many studies in its own right and that is outside the scope of this article. To oversimplify again, it is an effort to recreate experience for the reader by means of indirect expression: suggestion, evocation, music, and allusion. Part of Verlaine's achievement is to have been a precursor of symbolism (British scholars, in fact, include Baudelaire, Verlaine, and Rimbaud among the "symbolists").

Verlaine's relations with the young decadents and symbolists were ambiguous. He was an increasingly popular figure, holding court in the literary cafés and receiving the homage of young poets and even of visitors from abroad. He was generous with his friendship and counsel. But although his literary success and livelihood depended on his popularity with the younger generation, he was dubious about being acclaimed the leader of the various poetic schools. Much decadent poetry was ephemeral and downright silly, and in terms of his permanent reputation Verlaine did not wish to be associated with an eccentric group. As symbolist poets turned to free verse, they referred to "Art poétique" as their authority, yet Verlaine disclaimed any responsibility for their innovations. He utterly eschewed literary theory, and this in connection with a movement that tended to produce more statements of poetic theory than poems. Some of his replies to interviewers who sought his opinion for press articles were blunt indeed: "Symbolism? . . . Don't understand. . . . That must be a German word, eh? What can that mean? What's more, me, I don't give a damn." It was Mallarmé, who was at home to friends every Tuesday evening at his apartment in the rue de Rome, who became the leader of the symbolists.

Yet Verlaine's fame grew; he made lecture and reading tours of Belgium and England. He was befriended by the English poets Ernest Dowson, George Moore, Edmund Gosse, and Arthur Symons. The latter's *The Symbolist Movement in Literature* (1899), which discusses Verlaine's work, was important for English literature because it introduced the exciting events happening in Paris to English writers who were dissatisfied with the staid dullness of late Victorian literature. They communicated their enthusiasm for the new developments in French literature to young Americans just arriving in London and Paris. From this exchange of ideas arose the imagist movement in Anglo-American poetry.

During all this activity, Verlaine's material fortunes remained precarious. He had no money and depended on his writings and lecture tours for his livelihood, although eventually his friends and even the Ministry of Education established a fund for his support. After the debauch at Coulomnes, drunkenness and whoring became his daily life, celebrated in his poems. Since his vices were part of the ''Pauvre Lélian'' legend that he himself perpetuated, he made no effort to gloss over them. Yet his attachment to the solid bourgeois atmosphere of his youth remained. No matter how shabbily he was obliged to dress, he always affected a top hat or felt hat, a scarf, and his macfarlane overcoat. He narrowed his amorous attentions to two middle-aged female prostitutes, and, alternating between them according to frequent quarrels, set up housekeeping with each in turn. His joy was to obtain enough money to entertain friends at lunch in his middle-class household. As his health deteriorated (he was constantly plagued by a bad knee), he was treated in public charity hospitals. The doctors liked him, admired his poetry, and did favors for him, like allowing him to write after bedtime, ordering him admitted for treatment, or sending him to Aix-les-Bains for a water cure. These sojourns in the hospital provided him with a place to live, a nourishing diet, and enforced sobriety. On 8 January 1896 he died in another hotel whose guests were mostly prostitutes and their pimps. He was buried in the church of Saint-Étienne du Mont in the Latin Quarter. The priest who heard his deathbed confession characterized him as a Christian.

Selected Bibliography

Unless otherwise stated, all French books are published in Paris.

ORIGINAL EDITIONS

Poèmes saturniens. 1866.
Les amies. Sonnets par le licencié Pablo de Herlagnez. Brussels, 1867.
Fêtes galantes. 1869.
La bonne chanson. 1870.
Romances sans paroles. 1874.
Sagesse. 1881.
Jadis et naguère. 1884.
Les poètes maudits. 1884.
Les poètes maudits. 1888. New series of essays.
Amour. 1888.
Parallèlement. 1889.
Femmes. 1890. Published clandestinely and not for sale.
Dédicaces. 1890.
Choix de poésies. 1891.
Bonheur. 1891.
Les uns et les autres. 1891.
Chansons pour elle. 1891.
Liturgies intimes. 1892.
Odes en son honneur. 1893.
Elégies. 1893.
Dans les limbes. 1894.
Épigrammes. 1894.
Les confessiones. 1895.
Conseil (Sonnet). 1895.
Chair. 1896.
Invectives. 1896.
Oeuvres posthumes. 3 vols. 1903, 1911, 1929.
Hombres (Hommes). No date. Published clandestinely and not for sale. *ca.* 1903.
Biblio-Sonnets, poèmes inédits. 1913.
Oeuvres oubliées. Edited by M. Monda. Vol. 1, 1926. Vol. 2, 1929.

PAUL VERLAINE

COLLECTED WORKS

Correspondance de Paul Verlaine, publiée sur les manuscrits originaux. Edited by A. van Bever. 3 vols. 1922–1929.

Lettres inédits à Charles Morice. Edited by G. Zayed. Geneva and Paris, 1964.

Lettres inédites à Cazals. Edited by G. Zayed. Geneva, 1957.

Oeuvres complètes. Introduction by O. Nadal. Studies and notes by J. Borel. Text edited by H. de Bouillane de Lacoste and J. Borel. 2 vols. 1959 and 1960. Le Club du meilleur livre edition. Best and most complete critical edition.

Oeuvres en prose complètes. Edited by J. Borel. 1972. Pléiade edition.

Oeuvres libres de Paul Verlaine (Les amies, Femmes, Hombres). Preface by E. d'Etiemble. 1961.

Oeuvres poétiques. Edited by J. Robichez. 1969. Classiques Garnier edition. Contains poetry from *Poèmes saturniens* through *Parallèlement*, a chronology, critical apparatus, and a good bibliography of critical works in French.

Oeuvres poétiques complètes. Text edited and annotated by G.-Y. Le Dantec and J. Borel. 1962. Revised by J. Borel, 1978. Pléiade edition. These Pléiade editions are excellent and readily available.

TRANSLATIONS

Confessions of a Poet. Introduction by P. Quennell. Translated by J. Richardson. London, 1950. New York and London, 1971.

Forty Poems. Translated by R. Grant and C. Archer. London, 1948.

Penguin Book of French Verse. Rev. ed. Edited by B. Woledge et al. New York and Harmondsworth, 1975. Contains some poems by Verlaine, with English prose translations.

Poems. Selected with an introduction by A. Wingate. London, 1904.

Poems. Translated by J. Leclerq. Westport, Conn., 1977.

Poems and Translations. Selected and translated by R. D. Norton. London, 1929. Includes translations of the poems of Verlaine.

Selected Poems. Translated by C. F. MacIntyre. Berkeley, Calif., 1948. French and English on opposite pages.

The Sky Above the Roof: Fifty-Six Poems. Introduced and translated by B. Hill. London, 1957.

BIOGRAPHICAL AND CRITICAL STUDIES

The Verlaine bibliography is enormous, and unfortunately much of it is of sparse value. The introductions and studies by Octave Nadal and Jacques Borel in both editions of the *Oeuvres complètes* are excellent.

Adam, Antoine. *The Art of Paul Verlaine.* New York, 1963. Translation of *Verlaine*, Paris, 1955.

Bornecque, Jacques-Henry. *Les* Poèmes saturniens *de Paul Verlaine.* Paris, 1952.

————. *Lumières sur les* Fêtes galantes *de Paul Verlaine, avec le text critique de* Fêtes galantes. Paris, 1969.

Carter, A. E. *Verlaine: A Study in Parallels.* Toronto, 1969. University of Toronto Romance Series 14.

————. *Paul Verlaine.* New York, 1971.

Lepelletier, Edmund. *Paul Verlaine, His Life—His Work.* Translated by E. M. Lang. New York, 1970. Translation of *Paul Verlaine, sa vie—son oeuvre.* Paris, 1907.

Martino, Pierre. *Paul Verlaine.* Paris, 1924; 1944. Dated, but still one of the best studies of Verlaine.

Nadal, Octave. *Paul Verlaine.* Paris, 1961.

Richard, Jean-Pierre. "Fadeur de Verlaine." In *Poésie et profoundeur.* Paris, 1955. Pp. 165–185.

Richardson, Joanna. *Verlaine.* New York and London, 1971.

Symons, Arthur. *The Symbolist Movement in Literature.* London, 1899. Rev. ed., 1908; 1919; New York, 1958.

PHILIP STEPHAN

FRIEDRICH NIETZSCHE
(1844–1900)

IT WAS IN the parsonage at Röcken, a small town in the Prussian province of Saxony, that Friedrich Nietzsche was born on 15 October 1844. Nietzsche's father, Ludwig (1813–1849), had been Röcken's Lutheran pastor since 1842 and was himself the son of a Lutheran minister known as the author of several edifying religious texts. The religion in Nietzsche's background came also from his mother's side of the family: Franziska Nietzsche (1826–1897) was the daughter of the Lutheran pastor in the neighboring village of Pobles.

It may seem ironic that the philosopher who rejected religion, who coined the phrase "God is dead," and who at the end of his creative life penned *Der Antichrist* (*The Anti-Christ*, written in 1888), should have entered the world in so thoroughly Christian an environment. It can be argued, however, that Nietzsche's integrity, his fearless search for truth, and his passionate desire to undertake the most difficult spiritual and philosophical tasks were rooted precisely in the religious world view he eventually sought to overthrow. "Philosophy, as I have so far understood and lived it," he wrote in his autobiography *Ecce Homo* (written in 1888), "means living voluntarily among ice and high mountains—seeking out everything strange and questionable in existence." These words seem a natural outgrowth of the phrases he used to describe his faith in God when he was thirteen:

"All he gives I will joyfully accept: happiness and unhappiness, poverty and wealth, and boldly look even death in the face" ("Ruck-blick," September 1858).

Honesty, love of truth and of the hard task—these are basic teachings of Lutheran and, indeed, of all varieties of Christianity. In Nietzsche's time as in our own, they seemed for most men to serve as nothing more than conventional pieties. But Nietzsche took these precepts seriously, as seriously as they have ever been taken.

If the source of these values can be located in Nietzsche's early Christian environment, the strength with which they became anchored in his character was the result of the single overwhelming event of his childhood, the death of his father. Nietzsche's earliest memories were almost exclusively of his father, and Nietzsche has left us a portrait of the pastor as a noble, cultured, loving man, honored and beloved by everyone he knew. The accuracy of this recollection is impossible to judge, for Ludwig Nietzsche died of a brain inflammation in July 1849, less than three months before his son's fifth birthday. Yet in *Ecce Homo* Nietzsche wrote that he had been privileged to have had such a father. It was because of his father that "it requires no resolve on my part, but merely biding my time, to enter quite involuntarily into a world of lofty and delicate things."

By any lights this is a strange assertion, and

if we are to understand Nietzsche's character, we must ask how seriously and in what manner it ought to be taken. How could the pastor really have contributed to his son's understanding of "lofty and delicate things" in those few years?

The older Nietzsche was a cultured man who, before becoming pastor, had been tutor to the duke of Saxe-Altenburg's daughters. It was in his father's study that Nietzsche, who did not learn to speak until he was two-and-a-half years old, first sensed the magic of books, although in the normal fashion he was attracted more to their pictures than their words. And Nietzsche may well have inherited his musical talent from his father: both were accomplished pianists, particularly skilled at free improvisation. But Nietzsche had only just begun to show an interest in reading when his father died. Furthermore, Nietzsche repeatedly tells us that his love of music was awakened in his ninth year, and we know that his mother, Franziska, not his father, taught Nietzsche the first rudiments of piano playing after the family had left Röcken.

In fact there was only one way in which Ludwig Nietzsche powerfully and unequivocally affected his son, and that was not by his life, but by his death. The evidence for this is to be found in the numerous autobiographical sketches and essays Nietzsche wrote between the ages of fourteen and twenty-two. In these he repeatedly reworked the story of his father's illness and death, clearly indicating its central position in his thinking about the past. These fragmentary self-portraits were an important proving ground for Nietzsche's developing talent as a writer, and particularly in the earlier examples he often seemed as much concerned with embellishing the sad tale in the most literary manner as with understanding it. Nonetheless, these constant returns to his childhood represent a ceaseless and serious effort to understand how his father's death had marked him.

It was not until he reached his twentieth year that Nietzsche fully articulated what the effect of the shock had been. In an 1864 summary of his past, called simply "Mein Leben" ("My Life"), he wrote:

> I know little of my earliest period of my childhood; what has been told to me about it I would rather not repeat. It is certain that I had excellent parents; and I am convinced that precisely the death of such an excellent father, even as it deprived me, on the one hand, of fatherly help and guidance for later life, planted in my soul, on the other hand, the germ of a serious and reflective person.
>
> (p. 117)

In Nietzsche's own estimation, then, his childhood trauma was a decisive influence on his personality. We can fully comprehend exactly how decisive Nietzsche thought this influence was when we note that by 1864 he had ceased to be a believing Christian. He had abandoned the faith of his father, but he had done so in the course of becoming that "serious and reflective person" that his father's death had determined he would be. Whether or not Nietzsche's understanding of his father's influence was correct—we ignore at our own peril any conclusion reached by this master psychologist—it must have been a source of strength for him to think that his own intellectual labors were somehow linked to the spirit of his dead father.

For the family, the consequence of the pastor's death was to be required to leave the parsonage in order to make room for the new minister. But before they could leave Röcken, tragedy struck again: Nietzsche's infant brother Joseph, born in February 1848, died in January 1850. Joseph's death meant that when the family settled in Naumburg in April 1850, Nietzsche was the only male in a household that included two maiden aunts and his sister Elisabeth, born in July 1846.

There is a temptation to see in this female domination of his home life the root of

Nietzsche's attitude toward women. Particularly because his complete misunderstanding and hatred of women is so irrational, it seems the one aspect of his mature philosophy that can only be explained by its psychological origin. It would be foolish to blame Nietzsche's misogyny on the bare fact that he spent these years surrounded by women. But it remains a fact that the two women who were most important in his life—his mother and sister—had absolutely no understanding of him or his philosophy. Furthermore, amazing as it sounds, Nietzsche's depiction of women as grasping, destructive, cannibalistic, sly, and devious is merely an exaggerated portrait of Elisabeth. Nietzsche always loved his sister, yet her jealous and possessive meddling in his personal life (she helped wreck the only serious relationship Nietzsche ever had with a woman, that with the brilliant Lou Salomé), her tiresome lectures to him about Christian morality, her petty and often acid gossiping about his affairs, her marriage to the anti-Semite Bernhard Förster, all led to strained relations, punctuated by breaks and reconciliations, between them. Elisabeth's worst characteristics were given free play after Nietzsche went mad, when she appointed herself guardian of his philosophy and manipulated both her brother's works and his helpless person for her own aggrandizement. With such a sister, it is hard to see how Nietzsche's ideas about women could have been different.

Naumburg was a bustling city compared to Röcken, and it afforded Nietzsche his first introduction to cultured life. His schooling at a private boys' school and at the cathedral gymnasium was quite conventional for the son of a minister whose family hoped he would follow in his father's footsteps: a little Latin and Greek, an insufficient grounding in German grammar and writing, and much time spent in religion classes. But thanks to his grandmother's connections among Naumburg's successful lawyers, and the friends he made at school, Nietzsche spent time in places that were as cultured as they were well-to-do. In one such house he heard the words of Germany's greatest poet, Johann Wolfgang von Goethe, read aloud for the first time; in another his love of music was awakened. With innocent enthusiasm, Nietzsche wrote countless poems. Even as he began to study the piano, he rushed to try his hand at musical composition. Nietzsche tells us that he was a serious and quiet boy in Naumburg, often teased by his schoolmates for his earnestness; but obviously he was also bursting with a wonderful boyhood creativity, writing plays for his sister and friends to act in, directing mock battle scenes from the Crimean War, already reading and writing until late at night.

In 1857 a Prussian school inspector was so impressed by Nietzsche that the boy was offered a free place at the Pforta school. This was the most famous classical school in Germany, where many of the leading German thinkers and writers of the nineteenth century had been educated. It was a boarding school, remarkable for the rigorous exclusion of outside life from its academic routine—barring a few holidays, visits, and letters. Nietzsche's entrance into Pforta in 1858 marked a real separation from his family.

After six years at Pforta, Nietzsche emerged a changed person. His best subjects were classics, German literature, and theology; he did worst in mathematics and drawing. As Nietzsche described his academic experience:

I found [it] a surrogate for a father's education. . . . But precisely this almost military compulsion, which, because it has to affect the mass, treats coolly and superficially what is individual, made me fall back on my own resources. I rescued my private inclinations and endeavors from the uniform law; I lived a secret cult of certain arts; I tried to break the rigidity of schedules and timetables laid down by the rules, by indulging an overexcited passion for universal knowledge and enjoyment.

(*Selected Letters*, p. 47)

Nietzsche and his friends founded a group called "Germania," to which each month one of them would present for discussion an original work of art or criticism. Nietzsche took Germania very seriously. In addition to the long hours of schoolwork, he was busy preparing musical compositions, poems, or essays.

His best-known contribution is his essay of 1861 on the poet Johann Christian Hölderlin, who had gone mad in 1802 and was almost entirely forgotten by the 1860's. By then Hölderlin's haunting lines depicting the fragmentation and isolation of modern man were out of tune with the German mood, yet in this essay Nietzsche called Hölderlin his favorite poet and likened the prose of the play *Hyperion* (1797–1799) to music: "soft melting sounds interrupted by painful dissonances, finally expiring in dark mysterious funeral songs." Above all, Hölderlin told the Germans "bitter truths that are, unfortunately, only too firmly grounded." The poet loved Germany, "but he hated in Germans the mere specialist, the philistine."

The teacher who graded this essay advised Nietzsche "to stick to a healthier, clearer, more German poet." But Nietzsche's youthful judgment was prescient: today Hölderlin is recognized as one of Germany's greatest poets.

At this same time Nietzsche's belief in God was ebbing. R. J. Hollingdale (in his *Nietzsche*) is probably correct in finding a cause in Nietzsche's love of classical culture: "This profound and 'intuitive' understanding of Greek and Roman civilization must have influenced his Christian beliefs, and could very well have been the instrument which destroyed them, through bringing to life in him a whole world *other than the Christian*." In an essay of 1862 for Germania, Nietzsche called Christianity a "custom and prejudice," a two-thousand-year-old "phantasm."

Nietzsche's public break with religion came in the autumn of 1864 when he went to Bonn to study theology and philology at the university. By Easter 1865 he had abandoned theology. At home for the holidays he refused to go to Easter communion. There was a tearful scene with his mother and then a letter from his sister. Nietzsche's answer is as extraordinary for its self-possession as for its intelligence:

> As for your principle, that the truth is always on the more difficult side, I concede this to you in part. Nonetheless, it is difficult to understand that two times two does not equal four, but does that make it any more true?
>
> On the other hand, is it really so difficult simply to accept everything in which one has been brought up, which has gradually become deeply rooted in oneself, which holds true among relatives and among many good people, which does moreover really comfort and elevate man? Is that more difficult than to take new paths, struggling against habituation, uncertain of one's independent course, amid frequent vacillations of the heart, and even of the conscience, often comfortless, but always pursuing the eternal goal of the true, the beautiful, the good? . . .
>
> Is it not . . . true that for the true searcher the result of his research is of no account at all? Do we, in our investigations, search for tranquility, peace, happiness? No—only for the truth, even if it were to be frightening and ugly. . . .
>
> Here the ways of men divide. If you want peace of mind and happiness, then have faith; if you want to be a disciple of truth, then search.
>
> (*Selected Letters*, 11 June 1865)

This remained his position on religion and truth. By the time he had left Pforta, Nietzsche knew that the truth is usually painful, perhaps, as Hollingdale suggests, because for him the unmasking of the truth—his renunciation of religion—brought with it the renunciation of the heaven where his father awaited him. Perhaps, too, Nietzsche was especially aware of the connection between pain and truth because he himself was often in pain. From early childhood he had suffered from headaches and myopia, which were not helped by his habit of working long hours. In later life he would ignore his symptoms until incapacitated by them.

One can also sense a spiritual malaise, an

ambivalence about the profession he was choosing for himself. Within a few months of entering the university, he was a full-time student of philology, which meant that he was aiming at an academic career. Philology, the study of ancient languages and literature, had become a precise and leading field of scholarship in nineteenth-century Germany. Besides the classical side, Greek and Roman sources, much was being done in comparative philology, a science founded single-handedly by Franz Bopp in 1816 when he demonstrated that Sanskrit, Latin, Greek, Persian, and the Germanic languages all had one common ancestor. That language has since been named "proto-Indo-European." Sanskrit, the classical language of India, particularly fascinated the Germans: the philosopher Friedrich von Schlegel theorized early in the century that all European languages were derived from it; Max Müller later undertook the first large-scale translations of Indian works; and Paul Deussen, one of Nietzsche's boyhood friends, became one of the foremost authorities on Indian philosophy.

Nietzsche had done exceptionally well in classics at Pforta. Yet as he noted in 1868, his choice of philology had been based neither on his natural talent nor on his love of the subject: "The feeling that I should never get to the root of things by encyclopedic studies drove me into the arms of a strict scientific discipline. Then [there was] the longing to be done with rapid changes of feeling in my artistic studies by taking refuge in the haven of objectivity." This passage shows an unmistakable urge toward asceticism and self-denial. Philology is envisioned as a suppression of exactly the intense artistic interests that Nietzsche had so much enjoyed earlier. In 1861 he had written admiringly of Hölderlin's hatred of "the mere specialist," yet this was precisely what he was planning to become. No wonder that in 1868, looking at his fellow philologists, he was overwhelmed with doubts and questioned his own motives.

At the university, despite his doubts, Nietzsche threw himself into his studies with characteristic energy and seriousness. It was then that he first began to be recognized as an extraordinary intellect. When his favorite professor, Friedrich Ritschl, moved to Leipzig University in 1865, Nietzsche followed him and completed his graduate training there. Nietzsche's rigor and confident mastery of the sources so impressed Ritschl that when the professorship of classical philology at the University of Basel became vacant in January 1869, Ritschl recommended Nietzsche though he was only twenty-four, the author of but a few articles, and did not have his doctorate. In what is perhaps the most enthusiastic academic recommendation ever written, Ritschl offered to stake his own reputation on Nietzsche's fitness for the post:

> *Never yet* have I known a young man who was so mature as early and as young as this Nietzsche.... I prophesy that he will one day stand in the front rank of German philology.... You will say, I describe a phenomenon. Well, that is just what he is—and at the same time pleasant and modest.
>
> (Quoted in Walter Kaufmann's "Introduction" to *The Portable Nietzsche*)

Basel hired Nietzsche without the doctorate, and Leipzig granted him the degree without a thesis or examination.

But as we know from the doubts mentioned earlier, Nietzsche, on the threshold of a brilliant career, was predisposed to see the dark side. "Yes, yes! I must be a philistine too," he wrote to a friend in April 1869; but "I still have the guts to break out one day and attempt to live this hazardous life somewhere else and in some other way." In fact, while at Leipzig he had come under two powerful nonacademic influences that served to keep his mind occupied with great matters other than scholarship: the philosophy of Arthur Schopenhauer and the art and personality of Richard Wagner.

FRIEDRICH NIETZSCHE

In the autumn of 1865 Nietzsche read *Die Welt als Wille und Verstellung* (*The World as Will and Representation,* 1818) and immediately proclaimed himself a Schopenhauerian. Schopenhauer, the great German philosopher of pessimism, taught that the universe is neither the creation of a divine intelligence nor rational. Rather it is the expression of a blind, purposeless force that he called "Will." Human beings, too, are creations of the Will, caught up in its continuous, aimless striving for existence, in an endless round of conflict and tension. Schopenhauer's Will should not be confused with what we ordinarily mean when we speak of conscious willing, free will, or willpower. The Will, as Schopenhauer meant it, corresponds to that part of human nature which is universal, what today we would call the unconscious, the involuntary biological and instinctual part of our being. For Schopenhauer, our conscious will is merely a reflection of this underlying Will. He was the first modern philosopher to conjecture that our acts of will often have much deeper and less pleasant motives—all rooted in the Will—than we would ourselves like to admit. "Consciousness," he wrote, "is the mere surface of our mind, of which, as of the earth, we do not know the inside, but only the crust."

Not only is free will an illusion: Schopenhauer goes so far as to assert that individuality itself, our existence as separate beings, is also a sad and painful illusion. The Will shapes us out of itself for a brief moment as its biological tools. The Will in itself is not conscious, and our vaunted individual intelligence is "a mere accident of our being, a function of the brain," a by-product of the Will's dynamic striving.

This view makes a mockery of traditional notions of moral good; the unhappiness and pain that, according to Schopenhauer, are every person's inevitable lot, are in themselves meaningless. Yet consciousness, that "accidental and secondary element," is precisely our noblest quality, for it allows us to understand and, to that extent, to overcome the Will. Thus Schopenhauer posits three types of superior individuals: the ethical person, who recognizes the essential identity of all individuals and, freed from egotism, treats all fellow creatures with sympathy and compassion; the artist, who by virtue of an aesthetic disposition becomes a "pure, will-less subject of knowledge," able through contemplation to discover and to communicate in artistic productions profound truths about the reality that lies behind appearances; finally, the ascetic or mystic, who achieves a release from the Will by detachment from earthly desires—in short, by a denial of all willing. Between the first and last two possibilities there is a difference: though a person can become ethical by self-control, no amount of conscious willing enables one to be an artist or mystic. The artist is born with a certain disposition. The ascetic or mystic gains freedom through a mystical insight; the path to liberation can neither be described nor communicated.

Nietzsche eventually rejected two of Schopenhauer's tenets: the unprovable assumption that one force, the Will, underlies all nature; and the pessimism, which Nietzsche came to see as a denial of life. To Nietzsche the desire to escape the Will is based on a judgment that the Will is evil, and this judgment he felt Schopenhauer had no right to make. But Nietzsche never forgot the teaching that the universe is not rational, and his own psychology is based on Schopenhauer's recognition that human intellect, or consciousness, is the surface aspect of deep unconscious drives. Further, Schopenhauer's unusually clear and forceful German prose helped awaken in Nietzsche the desire to become a writer as well as a thinker.

Above all he was inspired by Schopenhauer's unflinching confrontation with the dark truths of life, already Nietzsche's ideal of philosophical conduct. "To permeate my discipline with this new blood," he wrote to a friend in 1869, "to transmit to my listeners that Schopenhauerian seriousness which is stamped upon the brow of that sublime man, this is my wish, my daring hope; I would like to be something more than a drillmaster for competent philologists."

Of even greater significance than his discovery of Schopenhauer was Nietzsche's meeting with Richard Wagner in November 1868, the beginning of what Nietzsche later called "the most profound and cordial recreation of my life." Wagner was one of the most extraordinary figures of his time, not least because his personality comprised such glaring contradictions. A composer of unquestionable genius, Wagner created operas that carried the romantic evocation of emotion to an unparalleled height. Yet Wagner did not scruple to steal from other composers, consistently lifting themes from (among others) Felix Mendelssohn, whom he virulently pilloried in a murky essay of 1850, *Das Judentum in der Musik* (Judaism in Music), which depicted Jews as clever apes, capable only of imitating the essential Germanic spirit that they lacked. But even while airing this absurd variety of anti-Semitism, Wagner demonstrated in other areas genuine insight as a cultural critic. Thus in 1851, five years before Sigmund Freud was born, Wagner called the story of Oedipus a central myth in Western culture. And Wagner's vast operatic treatment of the Norse-Germanic *Song of the Nibelungs* remains one of the nineteenth century's most powerful metaphors for the deadly conflict between human spontaneity and the crushing demands of social and political power.

At first Wagner believed, like the romantics, that art could bring about the revitalization of the materialistic European society he despised. In two essays, *Das Kunstwerke der Zukunft* (The Art-Work of the Future, 1849) and *Oper und Drama* (Opera and Drama, 1851), he developed an idea already embedded in the romantics' high estimation of art, that of the total artwork (*Gesamtkunstwerk*), a synthesis of music, poetry, and theater that would reestablish Western man's connection with the unconscious emotional wellsprings of human existence. To do this, the new art-

form would take as its subject the one surviving link to the collective unconscious: myth. Following the romantic philosopher Johann Gottfried von Herder, Wagner thought that each people has its own unique culture, which is preserved in purest form in that people's folk myths. Thus, as a German, Wagner naturally turned to the German *Song of the Nibelungs* for the subject of his *Gesamtkunstwerk*. But in the beginning at least, Wagner did not mean his retelling of the saga to be an exclusively German affair. The tale of northern gods and heroes was to reveal cosmic truths.

In the early 1850's Wagner became a disciple of Schopenhauer, whose philosophy admirably suited Wagner's own notion of the artist's exalted role. Schopenhauer had two important effects on Wagner. First, Schopenhauer encouraged a pessimism that had grown in Wagner after his participation in the failed revolution of 1848–1849. In that debacle the forces of political reaction had proved invincible, and now Schopenhauer demonstrated to Wagner the futility of any attempt at social change so long as man was "still fully in servitude to the Will." The only answer was a Schopenhauerian renunciation, "annihilation," as Wagner termed it, of the Will. Thus Wagner quickly lost his optimism that art could regenerate the world, and consequently the symbolic message of his operas shifted. The earliest sketch of the *Ring* cycle, completed in 1848, concluded with a reconciliation symbolizing the solution of society's problems; in its final operatic form the *Ring* ends in total annihilation of the gods and the world.

Schopenhauer's second effect was to make Wagner see music as the supreme element in his art. Schopenhauer taught that music stood closest to ultimate reality: it was the wordless, imageless expression of the Will itself. It is no accident that the least theatrical of Wagner's operas, *Tristan und Isolde (Tristan and Isolde)*—the opera Nietzsche knew best before he met Wagner—was composed in 1857–1859 as Wagner's most serious attempt to realize Schopenhauer's philosophy in his total artwork. But despite Wagner's sincere desire to be the complete Schopenhauerian, all of his operas actually took shape first as epic poems, or partially sketched libretti, with music added later, and this is in fact what gives them their many layers of symbolic meaning.

Nietzsche was already a Wagnerian before his first meeting with the master. Long familiar with Wagner's music, he wrote in October 1868:

> One cannot be astonished enough at the significance that one single artistic disposition has in this man, a disposition which allies indestructible energy with many-sided artistic gifts, whereas "culture," the more various and embracing it is, usually appears with dulled eyes, weak knees, and enfeebled loins.
>
> (*Selected Letters*, no. 10)

When the two men met a month later an immediate sympathy sprang up between them. At fifty-five Wagner was at the height of his powers, engaged in the massive tasks of finishing the *Ring* and establishing a theater worthy of its performance. He dazzled Nietzsche with his exuberant performance of various parts from his operas, his enthusiasm for Schopenhauer, his laughter at the foibles of academic philosophers; and he charmed the younger man by the warmth of his farewell and an invitation "to visit him, in order to make music and talk philosophy."

In turn, Wagner was impressed by the young philologist, sensing from the first that Nietzsche might well become a worthy disciple. An overpowering personality, Wagner saw all the world in terms of his own ambition, taking it for granted that kindred spirits would lay their talents at his feet.

Wagner was then living in Switzerland—in part because he feared arrest in Germany for his revolutionary activities in 1848–1849—at the beautiful Villa Tribschen overlooking Lake Lucerne. Nietzsche's new post at Basel put him within reach, and during the next few years he became an intimate of the Wagner household, an artistic and moral world unto itself. There he met Wagner's mistress (soon to be wife) Cosima von Bülow, the daughter of Franz Liszt, who bore three children by Wagner even though still legally married to the musician Hans von Bülow and, by him, the mother of two daughters. It has often been remarked that Nietzsche came to regard Wagner as a second father, with all the love and rebelliousness that such a relation implies. In addition, Cosima's apparently selfless devotion to her husband, her intellectual intensity, and her sensual charm so powerfully affected Nietzsche that, in a sense, he loved her all his life.

One has only to read Cosima's diaries of the Tribschen years—marred as they are by her mindless adulation of Wagner—to understand why Nietzsche could write in *Ecce Homo*: "I'd let go cheap the whole rest of my human relationships; I should not want to give away out of my life at any price the days of Tribschen—days of trust, of cheerfulness, of sublime accidents, of *profound* moments." Tribschen seemed the center of all that was alive in German culture. Evening conversation might deal with the most important issues of aesthetics, music, and philosophy, after which the assembled group might read from Edward Gibbon, Goethe, or Thomas Carlyle. Even the most personal or familiar of details—the children's education or Nietzsche's surprise announcement that he was thinking of becoming a vegetarian—became matters of significance to be dealt with by a dictum from the Master. Above all, everything and everyone at Tribschen were dedicated to Wagner's historical task, the completion of the *Ring*.

Assessing the importance of Wagner for Nietzsche's development, Walter Kaufmann wrote: "It was Wagner's presence that convinced Nietzsche that greatness and genuine creation were still possible, and it was Wagner who inspired him with the persistent longing to equal and then to outdo his friend." It was

Wagner who urged Nietzsche to move far beyond the realms of teaching and scholarship. But of equal, perhaps of even greater importance for Nietzsche's development was his break with Wagner in 1876: as Kaufmann puts it, a "breach [that] developed gradually as Nietzsche became increasingly aware of the impossibility of serving both Wagner and his own call."

The all-encompassing and one-sided nature of the demands made upon Nietzsche was the first flaw in his friendship with Wagner. Dietrich Fischer-Dieskau has noted: "Nietzsche had to swallow his pride in a thousand different ways merely for the happiness of existing for the sublime couple. The Master would say 'My Nietzsche' to him, and this 'My' was the loftiest dignity he ever bestowed." Between 1869 and the last time they met in 1876, Nietzsche's letters to Wagner are laced with expressions of almost doglike devotion, to which Wagner responded with equally flowery words of affection. Yet both the younger man's mind and body were chafing under the requirements of discipleship. Increasingly he begged off from Christmas and other visits to Tribschen (and later to Bayreuth) either because of the demands of his work, an excuse the Wagners did not accept, or because of illness, which Wagner always suspected was psychological. Indeed, Wagner's suspicions were probably not wide of the mark: the migraine headaches that forced Nietzsche to flee the first Bayreuth Wagner festival in 1876 seem to have been a direct response to the Master's demands.

From the first their relationship had its troubling psychological undercurrents. As one biographer of Wagner, R. W. Gutman, has remarked: "Wagner play[ed] his role of father substitute too realistically"; Nietzsche "began to feel an imperative need to preserve his freedom in the face of Wagner's arrogations." The final break itself has been characterized by Hollingdale as a symbolic "parricide."

But whatever the unconscious forces driving the two men apart, there were equally significant conscious influences that forced Nietzsche to change his opinion of Wagner. At least from Nietzsche's point of view, their break was based on profound disagreements that were the natural outcome of both Nietzsche's intellectual growth and the historical moment in which he and Wagner lived. Perhaps the balance between the unconscious and the conscious in their complicated relationship can best be formulated in this way: Nietzsche's unconscious desire for a father figure led him at the beginning to see only an idealized vision of Wagner; his intellect and his powers of observation gradually corrected that view. However, although understanding led to disenchantment, it did not kill love. As we have seen, in *Ecce Homo* Nietzsche wrote with great tenderness of his days at Tribschen; there, too, he calls Wagner "the great benefactor of my life."

That Nietzsche could achieve the distance necessary for his reassessment of Wagner was due in no small measure to the happy accident of his professorship at the University of Basel. In the early days of his friendship with Wagner, both men seemed to treat the post as a convenient base for Wagnerian sallies; but despite his misgivings about academic life and the jokes at Tribschen about professors, Nietzsche took his strenuous teaching responsibilities very seriously. These included lectures six days a week, seminars, and four days of teaching at a Basel public school. From all accounts he was an excellent teacher. At the very least, the professorship provided Nietzsche with an independent existence away from Wagner—so necessary if he was to sort out his conflicting feelings and impressions about Tribschen and, later, Bayreuth. In addition, his post encouraged him to continue his own lines of research in ancient and modern culture and philosophy.

One important line of research that was at odds with both Wagner and Schopenhauer was Nietzsche's study of modern science, indicated by the large number of scientific texts and histories of science he read in Leipzig and

Basel (see *Selected Letters*, p. 44, note 73). Such an interest was not in itself unusual: more than any other, the nineteenth century believed that scientific materialism could answer all the questions of existence. But Nietzsche's attitude toward science was shaped by Friedrich Lange's *Geschichte des Materialismus . . . (History of Materialism)*, a convincing, if sympathetic, critique of the basic assumptions of nineteenth-century materialistic science, which he read upon its publication in 1866. According to Lange, the materialists were correct when they rejected the metaphysicians who had speculated about matters beyond human experience, but were themselves guilty of the same error when they claimed that science could give us absolute truth or discover the original cause or purpose of existence. Science is merely the way in which we organize our perceptions; it possesses no independent validity. Thus, when we say that science is objective, we can mean only that it is objective within the particular framework we have imposed upon the world.

At first Nietzsche found in Lange's book a vindication of Schopenhauer and Wagner. While supporting the materialistic critique of metaphysics, Lange had said that such transcendental speculations answered a deep human need for the ideal, and he assigned religion and art to a separate, nonscientific realm of human understanding. To Nietzsche this confirmed that Schopenhauer and Wagner, both of whom he termed artists, were beyond the reach of scientific disproof: "Who could refute a phrase by Beethoven, and who would find error in Raphael's *Madonna?*"

Yet it was only a matter of time before Nietzsche realized that Lange's preservation of a separate realm for religion and art was an unsatisfactory compromise. If on the scientific level Schopenhauer's Will has to be rejected as an invalid statement about the ultimate nature of things, there can be no reason for it to endure on any other level of our understanding. Lange's argument that humans need ultimate answers can only be accepted if we accept that humans need to believe in lies. Eventually Nietzsche would turn the force of Lange's critique on Schopenhauer and on the Schopenhauerian underpinnings of Wagner's aesthetic, affirming that our only tool for understanding the world is science, free of any hint of metaphysics.

Throughout most of the 1870's Nietzsche's continuing interest in science remained hidden from those who thought they knew him best. That is one reason why *Menschliches, Allzumenschliches (Human, All-Too-Human)*, published in 1878, with its ruthless critique of the metaphysical notions held dear by Wagner, seemed such a rude and incomprehensible break with what had gone before. But in fact, many of the ideas brilliantly recast in the new aphoristic style of *Human, All-Too-Human* had already been brought to the surface in the rich series of works Nietzsche published previously: *Die Geburt der Tragödie (The Birth of Tragedy,* 1872) and the four *Unzeitgemässe Betrachtungen (Untimely Meditations,* 1873–1876). Nietzsche did not call these works philosophy—the first combined philology with aesthetics and the others were primarily cultural criticism—and they were all written while Nietzsche was still under Wagner's direct influence. But with hindsight we can see how rapidly Nietzsche was transcending Wagner.

To understand these first fruits of Nietzsche's intellectual odyssey, we must place them in the context of the final series of events that pulled Nietzsche and Wagner apart. These events were played out on two levels: the grand historical stage of European politics and the smaller stage of Wagner's personal ambition. In a sense, it was the meshing of these two dramas that was decisive in shaping Nietzsche's final judgments of Wagner, Germany, and indeed of Western culture as a whole.

The greater drama began with the overnight transformation of Germany from a mere geographical designation to a blustering great power, achieved in almost one stroke by the

Franco-Prussian War of 1870–1871. Prussia's humiliating defeat of France was used by the Prussian prime minister Otto von Bismarck to accomplish by force of arms what the liberal revolution of 1848–1849 had failed to achieve: the unification of the Germanies. In January 1871, in the Hall of Mirrors at Versailles, the palace that for nearly two hundred years had symbolized the glory of France, a new German Empire or *Reich* was proclaimed, with the king of Prussia as German emperor and Bismarck as his chancellor. The empire included all the Germanies and the formerly French territory of Alsace-Lorraine. Although unification had been engineered by a ruling aristocratic caste that maintained its iron grip on all effective political and military power, any doubts in Germany about either the method or the result were shouted down in the national mood of wild jubilation.

Above all, victory gave the Germans a new feeling of power and a sense of destiny. They quickly interpreted their military triumph as a triumph of German spirit and culture as well. "What a peace for us Germans!" wrote one observer. "United in one Reich, the greatest, the mightiest, the most feared empire in Europe, great not alone through its physical power, greater still through its culture and through the spirit which permeates its people." Even more, victory was seen as a moral judgment, God's punishment of the decadent, immoral French. Heinrich von Treitschke, an influential historian and ardent German nationalist, railed at the citizens of Alsace-Lorraine for their loyalty to France: "The domination of a German tribe by Frenchmen has always been an unhealthy condition; today it is a crime against the reason of history, a subjugation of free men by half-educated barbarians."

When war broke out in July 1870 Nietzsche rushed to defend his native land, even though he had become a Swiss citizen in order to teach at Basel. "Our culture is at stake!" he wrote to his mother on 19 July. "No sacrifice could be great enough!" (At the time no one knew that Bismarck had in fact manipulated the French into declaring war.) Ineligible for combat duty because of his Swiss citizenship, Nietzsche enlisted as a medical orderly in August. In early September, after nursing six severely wounded men for three days and nights in the enclosed space of a small railroad cattle car on a hospital train, he caught both dysentery and diphtheria. Nietzsche was sent to a hospital, and mid-September found him convalescing at his mother's house in Naumburg.

Despite the seriousness of his illnesses, Nietzsche was back teaching at Basel by the end of October. Because from this moment his physical ailments—migraine headaches, vomiting, worsening eye trouble—increasingly dominated his life, it seems likely that he failed to allow enough time for a full recovery. "I am still not in the best of health," he writes in March 1871, "one night in every two I cannot sleep." Such complaints now recur endlessly in his correspondence.

Physical disease was not all that Nietzsche brought back from the battlefield. He returned heartsick as well, anxious about the fanatical nationalism and the hysterical trumpeting of German superiority that had swiftly become the order of the day. The earliest hints of Nietzsche's disenchantment are found in Cosima Wagner's diaries, brief references to letters subsequently destroyed by her husband after the break with Nietzsche. On 16 September 1870 Cosima recorded a "letter from Prof. Nietzsche, who seems to be deeply upset." The cause of Nietzsche's distress is recorded on 24 October: "Letter from Prof. Nietzsche, who, now recovered, has returned to Basel; he voices his fears that in the coming days militarism and, above all, pietism will make their pressure felt everywhere." Pietism is the general name given to the revivalist movement in German Protestantism that began in the seventeenth century. Neither of the Wagners realized that Nietzsche was equating the new faith in German superiority with the worst excesses of unthinking religious zeal.

The Wagners misunderstood their friend because they had wrapped themselves in the mantle of German nationalism. The Parisian premiere of *Tannhäuser* in 1861 had been disrupted by members of the conservative Jockey Club, and to the self-centered Wagner the present victory over the French seemed the tailor-made instrument of his personal revenge. The capture of the French emperor Louis Napoleon (nephew of Napoleon Bonaparte) at Sedan in September 1870 coincided with the christening of the Wagners' son Siegfried. Wagner exclaimed: "I am fatal to the Napoleons." In May 1871, when there were rumors that revolutionaries in Paris had burned the Louvre, Wagner scoffed at the idea of the French daring to maintain a great art museum: "If you are not capable of painting pictures again, you are not worthy of possessing them." Outdoing her husband, Cosima responded to the reports of horrible conditions in Paris by dismissing all of France as "a dreadful, unprincipled nation."

If Nietzsche admitted to himself the extent to which these views differed from his own, he did not feel confident enough to make his sentiments known. In fact, he was never able to disagree openly with Wagner when they were together. Nonetheless the differences between them began to emerge even in Nietzsche's first book, *The Birth of Tragedy*, despite the fact that the work was generally perceived as wholly dedicated to Wagner's cause. Nietzsche wrote *The Birth of Tragedy* in a highly poetic, elusive style, without scholarly apparatus. Even those academic colleagues who had high hopes for him as a philologist would have found the major part of the book hard to accept in any case. But the depiction of Wagner's operas as the true heirs of Greek tragedy made Nietzsche a laughingstock and almost wrecked his career. After the work's publication, Wagner himself expressed worry that Nietzsche had taken too great a risk, even though it had been at his urging that Nietzsche added ten sections of Wagnerian propaganda to the original manuscript. The Master vigorously defended Nietzsche in an open letter to a major newspaper, but this only

made matters worse: another newspaper dubbed Nietzsche one of "Wagner's literary lackeys."

As for Nietzsche, whatever the brave tone he adopted, the dismal reception of his maiden effort hurt him deeply. He became notorious, and the effect on his scholarly credibility was painfully apparent when no classics students registered for his courses at the start of the winter semester in 1872. Ironically the book that was being simultaneously hailed and denounced as a Wagnerian tract celebrated a view of the power and value of art that was quite different from Wagner's own.

In *The Birth of Tragedy* Nietzsche presented a picture of ancient Greek life quite at odds with the vision of contemplative harmony and moderation that had become standard. On the contrary, Nietzsche portrayed the Greeks as violent and vigorous, jealous and power-hungry, a striving people with an incredible appetite for all sorts of competitions, not only athletic contests like the Olympic Games, but contests between dramatists, debaters, poets, politicians, and, lastly, ceaseless contests for power, like the Peloponnesian Wars. Thus, Greek art, the shining example of aesthetic perfection, grew out of the agonies of monumental conflict. Specifically, Greek tragedy (and, Nietzsche would argue, all true art) was the product of two contending forces that Nietzsche called the "Apollinian" and the "Dionysian," names taken from the Greek gods of the sun and of wine.

The Apollinian is the drive for form, order, and intelligibility; it removes people from the realities of existence by hiding the horrors of life behind its veil of illusion. It creates the dream of individuality, protecting us from the chaotic interrelatedness of all creation. On the other hand, precisely this unity is expressed through the Dionysian, the force ceaselessly striving to break down the illusory barriers between all individuals and nature. In this sense it is the Dionysian that expresses reality: not the reality that we imagine exists in our daily lives or our culture, but the irrational moving power of the universe, Schopenhauer's Will, the primordial oneness. But because this breakdown of illusory barriers is overpowering and because of the possibilities for chaos and darkness in the Dionysian realization, the Apollinian illusions of form and separation are strong. Indeed, only intoxication can for a short time allow the individual to be one with Dionysian reality, as in the bacchanal of ancient mythology. And the forgetfulness that accompanies the end of drunkenness allows the Dionysian initiate to forget how meaningless human life is and how helpless he is against the forces of the Will.

Despite their diametrical opposition, a proper balance between the Apollinian and the Dionysian is essential for healthy life. If we existed solely in the world of Apollinian forms—the everyday world, as Nietzsche calls it—we would lose touch with the energies of life and sink under the deadweight of our exhausted boredom. We need the Dionysian if we are to remain vital, but direct contact with the awful truth of Schopenhauer's Will would paralyze us. "The Dionysian man resembles Hamlet: both have once looked truly into the essence of things, they have *gained knowledge,* and nausea inhibits action; for their action could not change anything in the eternal nature of things. . . . Knowledge kills action; action requires the veils of illusion." Thus, as action is essential to existence, it is the Apollinian illusion that makes human life and civilization possible.

In Nietzsche's account, the Apollinian and Dionysian found their perfect balance in Greek tragedy. As the tragedy unfolded it drew its spectators into a confrontation with the Dionysian truth, the meaningless Will. Simultaneously, the veil of Apollo, present on stage as the visible representations of the drama, protected the Greeks from the loss of their individual illusions. Dionysus appeared in the clear outline of Apollinian imagery. This was Nietzsche's explanation of tragic catharsis, that purification of the emotions which Aristotle identified as essential to tragedy. Tragedy

gave the Greeks a revitalizing glimpse of the life-force, and by protecting them from the deleterious effects of this vision, it allowed them to return, renewed, to everyday reality.

"Oh, those Greeks! They knew how to live," Nietzsche writes in the preface to the second edition of *Die fröhliche Wissenschaft* (*The Gay Science,* 1886). "What is required for that is to stop courageously at the surface, the fold, the skin, to adore appearance, to believe in forms, tones, words, in the whole Olympus of appearance. Those Greeks were superficial— *out of profundity."* Because tragedy allowed them to sense the terror at the heart of formless existence, the Greeks loved with unsurpassed passion the fragile construction we call human life. Thus tragedy, like all true art for Nietzsche, was a justification of life.

It was with his notion that art should redeem and strengthen the life impulse that Nietzsche parted ways with Wagner and Schopenhauer. Although both Schopenhauer and Wagner thought that the artist possessed the unique ability to reveal Dionysian truth, they believed that such knowledge could only result in a denial of the Will, a consummation spectacularly realized in the universal conflagration at the end of Wagner's *Ring.* Nietzsche was not simply being an optimist where the other two had been pessimists. Rather, unlike Schopenhauer and Wagner, Nietzsche concluded that the healthy—and intellectually the most honest—course of action was not to deny the toils of mortal life, but to embrace them. Nietzsche was being consistent with the sentiment he had expressed to his sister six years earlier: "Do we, in our investigations, search for tranquility, peace, happiness? No— only for the truth, even if it were to be frightening and ugly." Schopenhauer argued that the only good was tranquility through renunciation, because life offered no peace. Already Nietzsche had taken the opposite approach, a courageous stance that he would later epitomize in the phrase *"amor fati,"* meaning "love of fate."

The difference between this attitude and

optimism is brought home in that part of *The Birth of Tragedy* in which Nietzsche pits his view of art and life against the philosophic tradition that began with Socrates and the confident optimism of Western science. According to Nietzsche, the delicate synthesis achieved in the tragedies of Aeschylus and Sophocles was supplanted by the overintellectual approach of Euripides, who forsook the Dionysian substance in his effort to encompass the entire tragedy in the spoken dialogue. Euripides' failure—in Nietzsche's opinion at any rate—to create a rational tragedy was a response to a new force in culture, the rise of Socratic man. Socrates' optimistic belief that reason could cure all ills spelled the end of Greek tragedy. As a type, Socratic man spurned the Dionysian element that precedes and goes beyond the rational, convinced that what could not be totally grasped by the human mind was worthless.

Nietzsche called Socrates the "vortex and turning point" of Western civilization. He meant, first of all, that this originator of rational science had destroyed tragedy, but he also thought that Socrates had at the same time saved civilization. Compared to the art of tragedy, science is inadequate because it disregards the Dionysian and rests, therefore, on a falsely optimistic view of reality. Yet precisely the unbounded optimism of science became a comforting illusion. Thus even though Socrates and the rationalists who followed him ignored the Dionysian, their world view still served to protect humanity from the chaos of the primordial influence. Nietzsche envisions human history without the Socratic influence:

> If we imagine that the whole incalculable sum of energy used up for this world tendency had been used *not* in the service of knowledge but for . . . egoistic aims of individuals and peoples, then we realize that . . . universal wars of annihilation and continual migrations of peoples would probably have weakened the instinctive lust for life to such an extent that suicide would have become a general custom.
>
> (*The Birth of Tragedy*, sect. 15)

But Nietzsche had said that ultimately this world could only be justified through art. How heartening, then, to discover that there is inherent in science the tendency to reach the same conclusion:

> Science, spurred by its powerful illusion, speeds irresistibly toward its limits where its optimism, concealed in the essence of logic, suffers shipwreck. For the periphery of the circle of science has an infinite number of points; and while there is no telling how this circle could ever be surveyed completely, noble and gifted men nevertheless reach . . . such boundary points on the periphery from which one gazes into what defies illumination. When they see to their horror how logic coils at these boundaries and finally bites its own tail—suddenly the new form of insight breaks through, *tragic insight* which, merely to be endured, needs art as a protection and remedy.
>
> (*The Birth of Tragedy*, sect. 15)

Nietzsche therefore predicted a new synthesis, a union of our Western theoretical heritage with the Greek aesthetic—a combination Nietzsche personified as an "artistic Socrates," a sign that he did not wish to reject the Socratic tradition, but to transcend it. In 1872 he thought he had found this new synthesis in Wagner's total artworks, and he appealed to the Germans to embrace the Dionysian as revealed in Wagner's art.

Nietzsche used the last lines of *The Birth of Tragedy* to sketch an imaginary dialogue between a modern person carried back to ancient Greece and a citizen of old Athens. When the visitor exclaims at the beauty he finds on all sides, the Athenian, "looking up at him with the sublime eyes of Aeschylus," replies: "But say this, too, curious stranger: how much did this people have to suffer to be able to become so beautiful!" The Athenian's answer sums up Nietzsche's vision of culture. The highest art of the Greeks had been rooted in pain and suffering, for the conflict between Dionysus and Apollo so lyrically described in *The Birth of Tragedy* was envisioned by Nietzsche historically as a series of bloody battles, primitive rites that ended in drunken slaughter, as a constant struggle between the forces of civilization and the dark Dionysian invaders. In Nietzsche's view, all civilization is built upon the cruelest torture—he later referred to it shockingly as "vivisection"—quite literally the extreme pain needed to tame and to discipline the human beast.

What with added sections dedicated to his music, it is easy to see why Wagner praised *The Birth of Tragedy* and overlooked his protégé's new ideas about art. He was far less happy with the first three "untimely meditations," which had little to do with him directly. Nietzsche promised to write a meditation about Wagner, but he put the project off until 1876, the year of the first Bayreuth festival. Nietzsche's reluctance to write the Wagner essay increased as with each of the other meditations he grew closer to finding his own voice. "These reflections are . . . untimely," Nietzsche writes, "because I attempt to understand as a defect, infirmity, and shortcoming of the age, something of which our age is justifiably proud." With Wagner's move to the Bavarian town of Bayreuth and the construction there of a world center for his music, he was rapidly becoming a German cultural monument and, therefore, had to be reckoned increasingly as a "defect, infirmity, and shortcoming." As Nietzsche had originally idealized him, Wagner was profoundly untimely, a hero in proud opposition to his age; Wagner as he actually was, and as Nietzsche came to see him, was "human, all-too-human."

Nietzsche's first "untimely meditation," published in 1873, was a biting critique of German culture entitled *David Strauss, der Bekenner und der Schriftsteller* (*David Strauss, the Confessor and Writer*). A follower of Hegel, Strauss had achieved fame with his first book, *Das Leben Jesu kritisch bearbeitet* (*The Life of Jesus Critically Examined*, 1835–1836), in which he argued that the gospels were not divine, but were human creations that at once recorded the life of the exceptional man Jesus and expressed the universal human desire for transcendence. Attacked from all sides, Strauss was forced from his post as lecturer at the University of Tübingen. He came to symbolize for German liberals the causes of free speech and scientific inquiry. But by the 1870's, even as the liberals had become part of the establishment in Bismarck's new Germany, so Strauss had lost his cutting edge. His last and highly popular work, *Der alte und der neue Glaube* (*The Old Faith and the New*, 1872), was an attempt to reconcile Christian values with the good life promised by late nineteenth-century liberalism and materialism. As Hayden White has observed:

> It was this position that won for him the enmity of both Marx and Nietzsche. To Marx, he was the bourgeois *idéologue* par excellence, who tried to combine Christian sentimental ethics and the practices of capitalism in a single package. For Nietzsche, Strauss represented the German *Bildungsphilister* [philistine of culture] who made a show of intellectual radicalism but always left the conventional morality intact.
>
> (*The Encyclopedia of Philosophy*, 8.26)

Using Strauss as his whipping boy, Nietzsche launched an attack upon German "cultural philistinism" in general. In passages that have since become famous he denounced the smug assumption that the victory over the French had proved the superiority of German culture. "French culture continues to exist as before and we are dependent upon it as before," he writes, and German virtues like "strict war discipline, natural courage and endurance, superiority of the leader, unity and obedience among the led . . . have nothing to do with culture." In a manner reminiscent of Hölderlin, he opposes true culture to the German love of pedantry:

> Culture is above all the unity of the artistic style in all the expressions of the life of a people. Much knowledge and learning is neither a necessary means of culture nor a sign of it and, if

necessary, get along famously with the opposite of culture, barbarism, that is, the lack of style or the chaotic confusion of all styles.

(*David Strauss, der Bekenner und der Schriftsteller*, sect. 1)

The specialist, the technical master of philosophical doctrines, the immensely learned pedant—all these merely manipulate the badges of culture without penetrating to its deep truths. That is why, like Strauss, they can spout Charles Darwin and Christianity in one breath, unaware of the confusion in their thinking. Their superficiality is philistinism: they are barbarians who think they are civilized.

Nietzsche's conception of culture was quite beyond the reach of David Strauss and his ilk. To Nietzsche, late nineteenth-century Germany and indeed all of bourgeois Europe seemed dedicated to the pursuit of material comfort and an easy, often hypocritical, sense of spiritual well-being. As we have seen, Nietzsche believed that culture and comfort were mutually exclusive. Many of his harsher remarks, like his use of the term "vivisection" or his insistence that all great cultures have practiced slavery, should be seen in part as attempts to shock Europe out of its complacency. Believing that a people's culture is born out of its suffering, Nietzsche also insisted that culture is for the very few. There had been but one Aeschylus and one Sophocles, yet these two justified all the pain that had gone before. As he would write in *Jenseits von Gut und Böse* (*Beyond Good and Evil*, 1886): "A people is a detour of nature to get to six or seven great men.—Yes: and then to get around them."

In 1874 Nietzsche published the second of his meditations: *Von Nützen und Nachtheil der Historie für das Leben* (*On the Advantage and Disadvantage of History for Life*), an attack upon what he called the "consuming historical fever" of his day. Today, when history is so taken for granted that we seem to study it less and less, it is often forgotten that the modern "science" of historical scholarship was an invention of the nineteenth century, with German scholars playing an especially important part in shaping the historical consciousness of Europe. But to understand the full import of Nietzsche's essay we must bear in mind that the fascination with history was not limited to the specific field that bore its name. For example, Nietzsche's own specialty, philology, was a historical subject; philosophy, too, had been historically oriented ever since G. W. F. Hegel demonstrated that it developed over time; Marxian socialism, taking its cue from Hegel's philosophy, conceived of social science in historical terms as well; and even in the physical sciences the historical sense had triumphed in geology and evolutionary biology, which showed how the earth and its creatures had evolved during their long histories. Even more than in his first meditation, Nietzsche was pitting himself against the ethos of his age.

Nietzsche's point was that an individual or a culture that concentrates too exclusively on the study of history loses the ability to act. Action requires forgetting: one must dare to act even though any specific action has been undertaken an infinite number of times in the past, each time issuing in countless repercussions that have ended in a mere repetition of the identical act. Nietzsche did not wish to do away with the study of history; in fact he maintained that it is precisely our memory that makes us human. But both "the unhistorical and the historical are equally necessary for the health of an individual, a people and a culture," and of the two, the unhistorical is more basic. It links us to our original, biological nature, providing "the foundation upon which alone something right, healthy and great, something truly human may grow." As in *The Birth of Tragedy*, Nietzsche depicts healthy life as a balance between contending forces: without memory we could never become civilized; but if we lacked the ability to act without thinking about what has gone before, we would lose our force and our creativity. The trick is, in Nietzsche's words, "to forget at the right time as well as to remember at the right time."

Thus when Nietzsche writes that he is in favor of history so long as it serves life, he means that, paradoxically, history has to serve "an unhistorical power." But how was history to accomplish this task?

> History belongs to the living man in three respects: it belongs to him so far as he is active and striving, so far as he preserves and admires, and so far as he suffers and is in need of liberation. To this triplicity of relations corresponds three kinds of history: so far as they can be distinguished, a *monumental,* an *antiquarian,* and a *critical* kind of history.
>
> (sect. 2)

In each case history inspires the living man to action: to the emulation of past models, the preservation of his society for the generations to come, and, finally, to the destruction of that which hinders life. But Nietzsche warned that these healthy emanations of human memory were rapidly being perverted by the nineteenth century's hunger for history.

The person who sees history as an incentive to emulate and surpass the past "must be distressed to see curious tourists or painstaking micrologists climbing around on the pyramids of monumental ages." The one who reveres the past in order to preserve it for the future must face the danger that "the time will finally come when everything old and past which has not totally been lost sight of will simply be taken as equally venerable" while "the new and growing will be rejected and treated with hostility." Then, Nietzsche continues, "you may well witness the repugnant spectacle of a blind lust for collecting, of a restless raking together of all that once had been." Finally, the critical understanding of history is changed into the desire to free ourselves entirely from the past, a yearning that denies nature: "Since we happen to be the results of earlier generations we are also the re-

sults of their aberrations, passions, and errors, even crimes; it is not possible quite to free oneself from this chain."

In each of its perversions, history has come to be pursued for its own sake. Nietzsche warned that if history succeeded in becoming "sovereign," that event "would constitute a kind of final closing out of the accounts of life for mankind."

On the Advantage and Disadvantage of History is of much more than passing interest in our own less historical age because Nietzsche's reflections on the study of history are about the nature of truth itself. As such, they set the stage for all he says on that subject in his later works. In arguing that history can never be sovereign, Nietzsche attacks the pretensions of "scientific objectivity." He asks a very pointed question: Has historical objectivity made modern man better, that is, is modern man more just?

> Consider now the historical virtuoso of the present time: is he the justest man of his age? It is true, he has developed in himself such a delicate and sensitive sensibility that nothing human remains alien to him; the most diverse ages and persons immediately reverberate in familiar sounds on his lyre: he has become a reverberating passivity which with its sounds acts again on other such passivities: until finally the whole atmosphere of an age is filled with a buzzing confusion of such tender and familiar reverberations.
>
> (sect. 6)

Amidst this "buzzing confusion" no one notion of right and wrong seems better than any other; indeed, in his pursuit of objectivity the scientific historian prides himself precisely on his moral detachment from his subject. He points to his toleration as the proof that he is just. Nietzsche disagreed: toleration must not be confused with justice. In the first place, toleration is passive, while justice, for Nietzsche, is the supremely active virtue. It is the just individual who dares to create the value system of his society. Secondly, to be just is, in a profound sense, to be intolerant. Justice cannot tolerate injustice.

According to Nietzsche, we confuse passive toleration with justice because we have mistaken detachment for objectivity. As in *The Birth of Tragedy* he uses the image of the artist, this time to make the important point that we become objective not by distancing ourselves from our subject but by recreating it within us:

> One has in mind that aesthetic phenomenon, that detachment from all personal interest with which the painter sees his inner picture in a stormy landscape amid lightning and thunder or on a rough sea; one has in mind the total absorption in things: yet it is a superstition to believe that the picture which things produce in a man in such a state of mind reproduces the empirical essence of those things.
>
> (sect. 6)

What appears to be artistic detachment, the relentless paring away of personal interests in the search for truth, "the dark tranquillity of the artist's eye, flashing within yet unmoved without," in reality signifies "the most powerful and spontaneous moment of creation in the inner being of the artist, a moment of composition of the highest possible kind." It is this artistic rendering of history that Nietzsche calls "objectivity, but as a positive property."

But having made this point, Nietzsche has brought us up against a confusing philosophical problem. To say that the artist recreates empirical reality is to admit that this artistic creation does not necessarily correspond to anything outside of itself. The "objectivity" of the artist, or of the great historian, may give us "an artistically true portrait but not an historically true one." Nietzsche continues: "One could think of a kind of historical writing which would not contain a drop of common empirical truth and yet be entitled in the highest degree to the predicate 'objectivity.'" The great historian weaves the events of history together, but as in a painting or a Greek tragedy,

the result can only stand for itself. How, then, can we use "objective" historical knowledge in any sense as a touchstone for truth?

Here Nietzsche takes an important step beyond what he said about truth in *The Birth of Tragedy*. There he had written of the artist's unique access to the truth and said more than once that life could only be justified through art. But in *On the Advantage and Disadvantage of History* he distinguishes between the artist's vision and other, possibly more valid truths: "So man spins his web over the past and subdues it, so his impulse to art expresses itself—but not his impulse to truth and justice. Objectivity and justice have nothing to do with each other." We come back again to Nietzsche's concern with justice and discover that it is its own type of truth. In this essay the just man, not the artist, is described as the "most *venerable* exemplar of the species man." Nietzsche writes that "no one has more of a right to our respect than he who possesses the drive and strength to justice." He does not tell us much about the origin of that drive, nor has he yet worked out the effect of the just individual upon the human species, but he has concluded that the answers to such questions cannot be found in the aesthetic realm.

In the final analysis, then, if modern man is mistaken about justice, it is because he has looked for it in the wrong place, in the study of history, which, at its best, can embody aesthetic but not moral values. Nietzsche goes even further: he argues that justice, moral values, and even truth itself, cannot be discovered in the historian's recreation of human development because they are in fact above and independent of the historical process; they are what he terms "superhistorical." From this point of view he argues forcefully in the last sections of the essay that human development cannot be defined as a linear process, or as an evolution that necessarily progresses from lower to higher, from worse to better forms of life. Here he explicitly attacks the Hegelian notion that philosophy and civilization develop through history to perfection and argues implicitly against the equally optimistic Darwinian idea that natural selection will automatically perfect the various species over time.

Nietzsche's disagreement with the Hegelians and the Darwinians rests on an assumption that remains fundamental throughout his philosophy. He believed that a vast, unbridgeable chasm separates the exceptional individual from the mass of human beings. He is quite serious when he writes: "Someone has recently wanted to instruct us that at the age of 82 Goethe was burned out: and yet I would gladly exchange a few years of the 'burned out' Goethe for whole cart loads of fresh ultramodern lives." The point is obvious: Goethe's greatness is unique and unsurpassable. Against the widely held belief that whatever survives is necessarily the best, Nietzsche maintained that success in the struggle for survival, or, for that matter, success of any type, could never be the standard by which to measure worth. "Greatness is not to depend on success," he writes, "and Demosthenes had greatness even though he had no success." The example is apt and also remarkably prophetic of Nietzsche's own future. Demosthenes sought unsuccessfully to rouse the ancient Greeks to resist the invading Macedonians, and his speeches have been admired since antiquity. Similarly, Nietzsche's proclamation of the crisis of Western culture would fall on the deaf ears of his contemporaries. It would be left to future generations to marvel at his insight.

For Nietzsche the great individual not only stands above our standards of judgment, he creates new standards. That is why he so fiercely derided "history from the standpoint of the masses," which sought for "laws which can be derived from the needs of these masses, that is, for the laws of motion of the lowest loam and clay strata of society." Embodying superhistorical values, great individuals mock such laws; in their relation to each other they "constitute a bridge across the wild stream of

becoming." The great personalities "do not continue a process but live in timeless simultaneity . . . [and] the task of history is to be the mediator between them and so again and again provide the occasion for and lend strength to the production of greatness." Nietzsche concludes: "the *goal of humanity* cannot lie at the end but only *in its highest specimens.*"

This view is not without serious problems. In *The Birth of Tragedy*, Nietzsche had described a dynamic process of development from the ancient tragic synthesis, through Socratic culture, to the anticipated rebirth of tragedy. True, the deep truth that all art depends upon the Dionysian-Apollinian synthesis would never change, but its expression would be different at different times. And because the empirical truths uncovered by Socratic science, stimulated by a false optimism, represent a valid, growing body of knowledge, it could also be said that truth evolves. How could Nietzsche reconcile this view with the notion of the superhistorical that he had developed in *On the Advantage and Disadvantage of History?*

Furthermore, the exaltation of the exceptional individual to a superhistorical stature was problematic. Such individuals were themselves the products of specific historical epochs, and Nietzsche was well aware that at different times superior beings had acted differently. Could it not be said that the relationship between such individuals was linear over time? Did not the great individuals themselves constitute an historical process? And if each great individual sought to overcome his predecessors, could we not say that the process would have its goal at its end, in some final realization of truth? In their relation to each other, Nietzsche's superhistorical individuals threaten to bring us right back to the conception of the historical process that he had so vehemently attacked.

When we look at Nietzsche's arguments in this way we quickly discover that *On the Advantage and Disadvantage of History for Life* poses more questions than it can finally answer. But it is precisely this quality that makes it an important book, for the difficulties we find in Nietzsche's arguments are our first taste of a dynamic tension that continues throughout his work. Nietzsche never really satisfies our need to know whether or not he believes history is a process with a final purpose. Similarly he never satisfies our sometimes desperate desire for a definite answer to the question of whether truth is absolute and, therefore, superhistorical. Instead of answering our questions, he increasingly focuses on our need for answers to them; instead of giving us certainty, he asks why we so urgently want it.

Nietzsche's first three works not only set the stage for his mature philosophy by raising important questions about truth, culture, and history. They also made him aware of the path he was on. This becomes clear in the third meditation, *Schopenhauer als Erzieher (Schopenhauer as Educator)*, published, like the second, in 1874. The unsuspecting reader will be surprised that the essay says very little about Schopenhauer. Instead it is a meditation on what it means to be a philosopher and, as such, is Nietzsche's attempt to define his own role.

Here Nietzsche explores the heroic image of the philosopher he had already elaborated in his letters and earlier writings. Like the artist and the just individual, the philosopher has a higher understanding, but he also has the greatest responsibility, that of being a teacher. Like all true teachers, the philosopher's task is not so much to instruct as to challenge others to emulate him by realizing their own potential. As in real teaching, the philosopher does not address everyone but only the special individual who can respond to his challenge and educate himself. This type of teaching is a far cry from the university philosophy classes in which conventional wisdom is chewed and digested. The true philosopher seeks truth that is, by its nature, diametrically opposed to convention: he is supremely untimely. Nietzsche quotes Diogenes' remark when a certain philosopher was praised in his presence: "What great thing does he have to show who has done philosophy for so long and yet has *distressed* no one?"

Schopenhauer as Educator suggests, in Walter Kaufmann's words, "an ethics of self realization" that becomes ever more prominent in Nietzsche's work. This concern with the individual led Nietzsche in this essay to condemn the state as institutionalized conformity. The doctrine that the state is humanity's highest goal—a corruption of Hegel's political philosophy that gained wide currency in the German Empire—he branded as "a relapse not into paganism, but into stupidity."

It was not until a few months before he began writing *Ecce Homo* in 1888 that Nietzsche realized that *Schopenhauer as Educator* had really been about himself. Perhaps this was because, like the essay on history, it raised more questions than it answered, this time questions of a very personal nature. How could Nietzsche reconcile his own conventional academic position with the exalted image of the unconventional and courageous thinker? More important, how could he achieve his own self-realization so long as he was still involved in his last and most demanding apprenticeship, his friendship with Wagner? By 1874 the time had come to take the final steps to freedom.

As a creative artist who had known humiliation at the hands of the public, Wagner found much to like in Nietzsche's denunciation of philistinism. But as the fund raiser for the first Bayreuth festival he could ill afford to insult his fellow Germans, even if they were philistines. In October 1873, two months after the first meditation, Wagner asked Nietzsche to write an "Appeal to the German Nation" that would ask for contributions to the Bayreuth project through local music dealers and bookstores. Nietzsche undertook the assignment reluctantly, and the result was unsuitable for Wagner's purposes. Almost as if he were simply writing a continuation of *David*

Strauss, Nietzsche denounced the Germans for not rushing forward to bring Wagner's project to fruition; he did not ask for contributions, but demanded them, threatening that a failure to respond would "wring from posterity the humiliating confession that in the chase after fortune and pleasure, we Germans lost ourselves, just as we had finally found ourselves again."

Wagner claimed to like what Nietzsche had written, but plainly he feared it might antagonize the very people he wanted to reach. At a Bayreuth meeting of Wagner Society delegates, Nietzsche's appeal was rejected and a more optimistic document issued. In the end the new version had no effect; Nietzsche's more challenging tone might actually have attracted some useful public attention. In his letters, Nietzsche expressed no disappointment that his draft had been rejected, perhaps because of a half-conscious desire to separate himself from the Bayreuth project altogether. "There was an unmistakable odor of Philistinism about Bayreuth's certificates, clubs, jingoism, and antisemitism," one of Wagner's more perceptive biographers—Gutman—has written. As Nietzsche wrote later in *Ecce Homo:* "What did I never forgive Wagner? That he *condescended* to the Germans—that he became *reichsdeutsch* [that is, a loyal supporter of the empire]."

Increasingly Wagner presented his art as a purely German affair, the new art of the new empire. At the same time, largely because of Cosima's influence, his circle was becoming ever more stridently anti-Semitic. In the first blush of their relationship, Nietzsche himself had used some mild, conventional anti-Semitic expressions, but he was utterly out of sympathy with the obsessive hatred of the Jews that was to become the hallmark of Bayreuth.

In August 1874, when Nietzsche made one of his rare visits to Bayreuth, he brought along the score of Johannes Brahms's *Triumphlied* (1870–1871), which he had heard and enjoyed in June. Wagner hated Brahms as he hated all but the most obscure, and therefore the most harmless, of his musical contemporaries. In an act of obvious defiance, Nietzsche left the score of Brahms's composition on Wagner's piano. As Wagner told Elisabeth Nietzsche later, it was as if Nietzsche were taunting him, and the Master flew into a rage. Nietzsche withstood the storm in silence; once a devoted disciple, he had become more an observer than a friend. By this time his notebooks were full of notes he had taken in preparation for the meditation on Wagner, and what he had to say in the privacy of those pages was devastating. Wagner's tyrannical egotism, his hypocritical play-acting, his striving for power and domination were all scathingly examined.

None of this saw print. The fourth and final meditation, *Richard Wagner in Bayreuth,* published in 1876, was only ostensibly about Wagner. Like the essay on Schopenhauer, it was really the celebration of an ideal type, the artist as superior being. Of it, too, Nietzsche would later say that it was about himself. But Wagner was overjoyed when he read it: "Friend! Your book is prodigious!" he wrote in July 1876. "How did you come to know me so well?" Only a few weeks later, in August, Nietzsche sought refuge from the Bayreuth festivities and his headaches in the small town of Klingenbruun, where he began to write his next work. "For Nietzsche," says Gutman, "Bayreuth had turned out to be a 'contemptible' little German affair."

The last time Nietzsche and Wagner met was two months later, in October at Sorrento, where both had come to seek rest. Walking together one evening, Wagner spoke about his newest opera, *Parsifal* (1877–1882), and began to describe the important role that religion had played in his life. Once more Nietzsche listened in silence, but Wagner's newfound religiosity was too much to bear. Without a word or a visible sign, Nietzsche decided that the friendship was over. Wagner did not realize what had happened until he received his copy of *Human, All-Too-Human* in April 1878.

The publication of the first part of *Human, All-Too-Human* in 1878 marked the beginning of the great creative period in Nietzsche's life. *Anhang: Vermischte Meinungen und Sprüche (Mixed Opinions and Maxims)* and *Der Wanderer und sein Schatten (The Wanderer and His Shadow)*—the second and third parts of *Human, All-Too-Human*—followed in 1879 and 1880 respectively. *Morgenröte (Dawn)* was published in 1881, the first four parts of *The Gay Science* in 1882. Between 1883 and 1884 the first three parts of *Also sprach Zarathustra (Thus Spoke Zarathustra)* burst upon the world. (The fourth part of *Zarathustra*, although completed in 1885, had its first public edition in 1891.) What are generally considered his masterpieces appeared in the next four years: *Beyond Good and Evil* (1886), *Zur Genealogie der Moral (On the Genealogy of Morals,* 1887), *Der Fall Wagner (The Case of Wagner,* 1888), and *Die Götterdämmerung (The Twilight of the Idols,* 1889). Included also in this last outpouring of his creative life were the fifth book of *The Gay Science* (1887); *Nietzsche contra Wagner* and *The Anti-Christ,* which were published in 1895, six years after their author went mad; and Nietzsche's autobiography, *Ecce Homo,* which did not appear until 1908.

A few works appeared bearing Nietzsche's name after his death, collections by other people of surviving notes, often lines that Nietzsche had discarded in the process of writing his books. The most notorious is *Der Wille zur Macht (The Will to Power),* first compiled and published in 1901 under his sister's direction. It must be approached with care, its contents vigilantly compared with what Nietzsche said on the same subject in the works he personally brought before the public.

Together the works of Nietzsche's maturity comprise an extended analysis of one central problem, what we would call today the crisis of Western values. Like others of his day—Feodor Dostoevsky is the best example—Nietzsche realized that the moral and philosophical foundations of Western society were crumbling. It was his genius to be the first to understand the full implications of that perception. With the death of God the Western notion of absolute truth also perished, and Nietzsche's works are as much about truth, language, power, and human psychology as they are about religion and morals. Despite his singleness of purpose, Nietzsche's works are not repetitive: each successive book unveils new aspects of the crisis, hammering home in crescendo the message that the history of Western civilization is not a story of progress but of error.

The power of Nietzsche's argument is amplified by his style. *The Birth of Tragedy* and the *"untimely meditations"* were divided into relatively short chapters that, more or less, made a continuous argument. In *Human, All-Too-Human,* the sections had become single numbered paragraphs grouped within major subject divisions. Although the paragraphs in each division were related to each other, they did not always form a logical sequence and were often complete in themselves. With a few exceptions, and allowing for a variation in the length of the numbered sections from one to a few paragraphs, this remained Nietzsche's method of composition.

It is a method of great immediacy and force. But it also has its dangers. By abandoning a more traditional, less discontinuous style, by presenting each step of the argument as a self-contained perception, Nietzsche ran the risk that readers might mistake his works for collections of disconnected aperçus. Further, the clarity and brevity of Nietzsche's prose often disguised the complexity of his insights. What is easy to read is often quite difficult to understand, particularly when taken in isolation. In general, where Nietzsche's words have been quoted in support of viewpoints he would have abhorred, those words have been misunderstood because they have been taken out of context.

Nonetheless, once we realize that Nietzsche's strategy was to challenge his readers, to shock them out of outworn patterns of thought, his style seems perfectly suited to the task. This is clearest in his one- or two-sentence aphorisms, those brilliant flashes that effortlessly yet ruthlessly illuminate whole ranges of hidden truth. Thus in *Human, All-Too-Human* Nietzsche gives a new twist to the gospels: *"Luke 18–14 improved:* He that humbles himself wants to be exalted." And in *Beyond Good and Evil* he drives the point home: "He who despises himself still nonetheless respects himself as one who despises"; and "If one trains one's conscience it will kiss as it bites." These are the jewels of Nietzsche's style.

Two of Nietzsche's most important works, *Thus Spoke Zarathustra* and *On the Genealogy of Morals*, depart from his characteristic method of composition. The former is a poetic evocation of his philosophy. Cast as a series of parables about Zarathustra, a prophet who proclaims the death of God and challenges humankind to face its destiny, the book's inspirational style is apt to strike the modern reader as melodramatic, even bombastic. Yet it contains some of Nietzsche's finest poetry and most striking allegories. In *Zarathustra* Nietzsche articulates his theory that a will to domination, to overcoming, lay behind all human activity; here he first visualizes the "Overman," the superior being who was the goal of human development; and Zarathustra announces Nietzsche's controversial theory of eternal recurrence, the notion that all life has been, and will be, lived in exactly the same manner an infinite number of times.

On the Genealogy of Morals is different only in that the three essays are divided into sections that form a continuous, running argument. Stylistically it is the most accessible of Nietzsche's works, although it is as intellectually demanding as any.

Nietzsche's creativity is especially impressive, the incisive grace of his writing all the more remarkable, when we appreciate how dismal his life became after 1878. In the first place, his books failed utterly to provoke the serious discussion or criticism he hoped for. His growing intellectual isolation was matched by a self-imposed exile from human society. Driven to concentrate all his energies on his work, increasingly convinced that no one could understand either him or his mission, Nietzsche gradually divested himself of all but a very few friendships. Until the early 1880's, his natural desire for companionship erupted sporadically in wildly improbable proposals of marriage.

In 1882 Nietzsche thought he had found the perfect mate in the fascinating Lou Salomé—the precocious Russian who later became a member of Freud's circle—but his sister's moralistic meddling and the intrinsic unsuitability of the match led to yet another broken friendship. In the struggle to overcome his disappointed expectations, Nietzsche began to write *Zarathustra*. The depth of his desolation at the break with Lou can perhaps be gauged by the degree to which *Zarathustra* seems a manic, wildly joyful work. "Unless I discover the alchemical trick of turning this— muck into gold, I am lost," he writes to his friend Franz Overbeck, once it was clear that he and Lou had parted forever. "Here I have the most splendid chance to prove that for me 'all experiences are useful, all days holy and all people divine'" (25 December 1882).

As Nietzsche's solitude grew, the illnesses that had begun to afflict him after 1870 steadily worsened. Ill health forced him to resign his professorship at Basel in 1879, a year in which his letters and notebooks tell us he suffered at least 118 days of migraine headaches. Freed from his academic responsibilities, Nietzsche traveled ceaselessly in search of a bearable climate, dividing his time for the most part between Switzerland and Italy. Alarmingly, in his struggle to wrest precious moments of creativity from his ailments, Nietzsche dosed himself freely with all types of medicines to alleviate his pains.

Precisely because of his suffering, no one was more alive than Nietzsche to the interplay of sickness and philosophy. Using his own life, he looked back upon the outbreaks of illness as signals that he was on the wrong path, as if his instincts were using pain to force him toward his destiny. Disease presaged a break with the old and a new beginning. Thus, his migraine headaches at Bayreuth were harbingers of the break with Wagner, and he came to view the process that led to the abandonment of his academic career as another instance of disease as a signpost in his life:

> It was then that my instinct made its inexorable decision against any longer yielding, going along, confounding myself.... Sickness *detached me slowly* ... [it] gave me the right to change all my habits completely ... it bestowed on me the necessity of lying still, of leisure, of waiting and being patient.—But that means, of thinking.... That nethermost self which had, as it were, been buried and grown silent ... awakened slowly, shyly, dubiously—but eventually it spoke again. Never have I felt happier with myself than in the sickest and most painful periods of my life.
>
> (*Ecce Homo*, "Human, All-Too-Human," sect. 4)

Always seeking to discover general truths about human nature in the data of his own life, Nietzsche derived from such experiences one of his most powerful metaphors, that of sickness as a period of gestation. "There can be no doubt that bad conscience is an illness," he writes in *On the Genealogy of Morals*, "but it is an illness the way pregnancy is an illness." We will see later what exactly he meant by this.

But sickness is first and foremost a mark of decay, and most of all Nietzsche valued his illness for the insight it gave him into the crucial role of decadence in human history. Increasingly Nietzsche came to see the philosophical and moral systems of the past not as chapters in a continuing discourse of ideas, but as expressions of the pathologies of their authors. This is best demonstrated in Nietzsche's sustained treatment of Socrates, against whose philosophical optimism he ar-

gued in nearly all of his works. In *The Birth of Tragedy* Nietzsche found an abnormality in Socrates' character that helped explain his failure to appreciate the Dionysian. This was the "daimonon" or divine voice that came at crucial moments to dissuade Socrates from some proposed action:

> In this utterly abnormal nature, instinctive wisdom appears only in order to *hinder* conscious knowledge occasionally. While in all productive men it is instinct that is the creative-affirmative force, and consciousness acts critically and dissuasively, in Socrates it is instinct that becomes the critic, and consciousness that becomes the creator—truly a monstrosity.
>
> (*The Birth of Tragedy*, sect. 13)

In *The Gay Science* Nietzsche recalled that Socrates' last words were "Crito, I owe Asclepius a rooster." Asclepius was the Greek god of healing to whom sacrifices were offered upon recovery from illness. Thus the dying Socrates once more demonstrated how different he was from a normal individual: he seemed to be saying that life itself is a sickness. In its context in Plato's *Phaedo* Socrates' remark seems to refer to his belief in a more abundant afterlife, and Nietzsche took this as yet another sign of Socrates' fundamental decadence, a proof that Socrates was against life.

Nietzsche carried this line of reasoning to its conclusion in the section entitled "The Problem of Socrates" in the *Twilight of the Idols* (section 1):

> Concerning life, the wisest men of all ages have judged alike: *it is no good.* Always and everywhere one has heard the same sound from their mouths—a sound full of doubt, full of melancholy, full of weariness of life, full of resistance to life.... Even Socrates was tired of it. What does that evidence? ... These wisest men of all ages—they should first be scrutinized closely. Were they all perhaps shaky on their legs? tottery? decadents? Could it be that wisdom appears on earth as a raven, inspired by a little whiff of carrion?

Socrates, whom Nietzsche had described as the "vortex and turning point" of history in *The Birth of Tragedy,* is revealed to be history's greatest decadent.

To be sure, Nietzsche's discovery, "this irreverent thought that the great sages are *types of decline,*" was above all the result of his intellectual insight and not of his own disease. But his understanding of those "types of decline" was sharpened by his own experience of decline. Nietzsche explains this best in the preface to the second edition of *The Gay Science* (1886):

> For a psychologist there are few questions that are as attractive as that concerning the relation of health and philosophy, and if he himself should become ill, he will bring all of his scientific curiosity into his illness. . . . After such self-questioning . . . one acquires a subtler eye for all philosophizing to date; one can infer better than before the involuntary detours, side lanes, resting places, and *sunny* places of thought to which suffering thinkers are led and misled on account of their suffering, for now one knows whither the sick *body* and its needs unconsciously urge, push, and lure the spirit—toward the sun, stillness, mildness, patience, medicine, balm in some sense. Every philosophy that ranks peace above war, every ethic with a negative definition of happiness, every metaphysics and physics that knows some *finale,* some final state of some sort, every predominantly aesthetic or religious craving for some Apart, Beyond, Outside, Above, permits the question whether it was not sickness that inspired the philosopher.

This is what Nietzsche means when he writes: "I doubt that such pain makes us 'better'; but I know that it makes us more *profound.*"

Of course, by making explicit the connection between his maladies and his insights, and more, by speaking of it as almost a causal relation, Nietzsche is asking us also to accept his assertion that his philosophy alone cannot be reduced to a pathology of its author. But if we question this assertion, we very quickly find ourselves in an area of inquiry where personal history and philosophy part ways. Nietzsche's philosophy, like all others, must in the end stand or fall not on the basis of whether its creator was sane or mad, but solely on whether it succeeds as a description and explanation of reality. This may seem a bit too fair to Nietzsche—after all, he made quite free with the symptoms of other thinkers. But the point is that Nietzsche ruthlessly analyzed the character of earlier thinkers in the effort to understand why their philosophies seemed so out of keeping with the truth. It is to Nietzsche's own version of the "truth" that we now turn.

Nietzsche was not a systematic thinker—"The Will to a system," he writes, "is a lack of integrity"—and that makes it difficult to capture all the facets of his thought. Rather than attempt, therefore, to be exhaustive in this brief space, we can achieve some sense of the scope and force of Nietzsche's mature philosophy by exploring four topics: the philosopher and his task; Nietzsche's critique of morality; the implications of this critique for the Western notion of truth; and the source of value and justification in a world without meaning. In addition, as a comment on Nietzsche's influence, we will say a few words about the persistence of religiosity in the Western world. First, however, we must briefly describe the wider cultural context of Nietzsche's thought, the crisis he called "nihilism."

Coined in Russia, the term "nihilism" gained a European-wide currency after the publication of Ivan Turgenev's *Fathers and Sons* in 1861. Turgenev's protagonist, Bazarov, was widely taken to epitomize the nihilist: a young man of the most advanced ideas, Bazarov combined an utter disdain for tradition with a blind faith in reason, a commitment to scientific materialism, and an ardent desire for radical social change. In Russia the fictional character had his real-life counterparts. The most concise statement of the nihilist position came from the Russian critic

Dmitri Pisarev: "Here is the ultimatum of our camp: what can be smashed should be smashed; what will stand the blow is good; what will fly into smithereens is rubbish; at any rate, hit out right and left—there will and can be no harm from it."

Russian nihilism gave birth to a variety of political programs, ranging from a surprisingly mild reformism to a cold-blooded terrorism. But as the term came to be used outside of Russia, it lost its political connotations. By the end of the century nihilism meant two things: first, the philosophical view that all religious beliefs and moral principles had to be rejected as rationally unjustifiable, and second, a general despairing pessimism, a conviction that nothing exists or is knowable and, consequently, that human life is trivial.

For Nietzsche, nihilism in either of its forms was a symptom of the collapse of the mistaken Western belief in absolute truth and a God-given universal system of moral value. Behind Nietzsche's proclamation of the "Death of God" lay his perception that the advances of Western science and the increasing secularization of Western life were undermining religious belief. Western society was itself destroying the faith upon which its cultural and social structure was based. As the "madman" says in a well-known aphorism from *The Gay Science:* "Whither is God? I will tell you. *We have killed him*—you and I." Yet in the face of this development the religious habit of mind persisted, and it was the outworn need for an absolute that led to nihilism.

> The nihilistic question "for what?" is rooted in the old habit of supposing that the goal must be put up, given, demanded *from outside*—by some *superhuman authority.* Having unlearned faith in that, one still follows the old habit and seeks *another* authority that can *speak unconditionally* and *command* goals and tasks. . . . One wants to get around the will, the willing of a goal, the risk of positing a goal *for oneself;* one wants to rid oneself of the responsibility (one would accept fatalism). Finally, happiness [appears as the new authority]—and, with a touch of Tartuffe, the happiness of the *greatest number.*
>
> (*The Will to Power,* sect. 20)

Ultimately, when even happiness fails us as a sure guide for our behavior—as J. S. Mill put it: "better to be Socrates dissatisfied than a fool satisfied"—we give in to despair and deny that there is any meaning or purpose to our existence. This is what Nietzsche has in mind when he says in *On the Genealogy of Morals:* "the human will . . . needs a goal—it will rather will nothingness than not will."

As we have seen, from his earliest writings Nietzsche maintained that the fundamental question to be asked of any viewpoint is whether it affirms life. So long as we seek meaning in the old absolute sense of the word, we will be forced in the end to say "no" to life. As Karl Jaspers explained: "If I falsely presuppose that this world must have some all-encompassing meaning, then, since no honest man can discover it, the result is bound to be the vacuity of a frightful disillusionment." This disillusionment is nihilism.

But what does it mean to say that Nietzsche said yes to life, and the nihilists said no? How can we understand this yes from a man who dedicated his life to the ruthless analysis and destruction of the assumptions of his age, who writes in *Zarathustra:* "That which is falling, one should also push!"? We are already familiar with Nietzsche's notion of the yes to life as revealed in *The Birth of Tragedy.* He summarizes his stance toward existence in the *Twilight of the Idols* in the section "What I Owe to the Ancients":

> The psychology of the orgiastic as an overflowing feeling of life and strength, where even pain still has the effect of a stimulus, gave me the key to the concept of *tragic* feeling, which had been misunderstood by Aristotle and, quite especially, by our modern pessimists. Tragedy is so far from proving anything about the pessimism of the Hellenes, in Schopenhauer's sense, that it may, on the contrary, be considered its decisive repu-

diation and counter-instance. Saying Yes to life even in its strangest and hardest problems, the will to life rejoicing over its own inexhaustibility even in the very sacrifice of its highest types—*that* is what I called Dionysia, *that* is what I guessed to be the bridge to the psychology of the *tragic* poet. *Not* in order to be liberated from terror and pity, not in order to purge oneself of a dangerous affect by its vehement discharge—Aristotle understood it that way—but in order to be oneself, the eternal joy of becoming, beyond all terror and pity—that joy which included even joy in destroying.

This joy of life is expressed most dramatically near the end of the fourth part of *Thus Spoke Zarathustra*:

All joy wants eternal being for all things; it wants honey, the dregs of wine, midnight, tombs, the consolation of tears at the graveside, the gilded glow of evening . . . joy is thirstier, heartier, hungrier, more terrible, more secret than all woe . . . joy wants love, it wants hatred; infinitely rich, joy gives, throws away, begs that someone take, thanks the taker, would like to be hated; so rich is joy that it thirsts for sorrow. . . . For all joy wants itself, therefore it also wants agony.

Here, in its starkest terms, Nietzsche expresses his notion of *amor fati*—his principle that "all experiences are useful, all days holy, all people divine."

If we are to join Nietzsche in this affirmation of life we must first transcend our habitual ways of thinking, and it is the philosopher's task to bring about this "overcoming." In *Schopenhauer as Educator*, Nietzsche depicted the philosopher as an untimely individual, the destroyer of complacency, one whose challenge could be understood only by those who were worthy of it. As his sense of his own destiny grew, Nietzsche stressed increasingly the world-historical nature of that challenge. The philosopher, he tells us in *Beyond Good and Evil,* is "the man of the most comprehensive responsibility who has the conscience for the collective evolution of mankind." He is "*necessarily* a man of tomorrow" who "by laying the knife vivisectionally to the bosom of the *very virtues of the age*" shall reveal "a *new* greatness of man, a new untrodden path to his enlargement." In destroying the hollow idols of our age, the philosopher shall create new values.

In saying this, Nietzsche obviously had in mind his own thoroughgoing critique of the entire structure of Judeo-Christian morality. This analysis was presented in its most complete form in *On the Genealogy of Morals.* Nietzsche argued that two opposing value systems had come naturally into existence at some point in humanity's distant past. The first, which he called the "master morality," was defined by the stronger members of the human race. These natural aristocrats called their own strengths "good" and the characteristics of weakness "bad." Because this valuation was spontaneous and reflected the natural superiority of strength, the "master morality" was a healthy expression of the life force. This is not to say, however, that these ancient nobles would have been attractive to modern tastes. As might be said of the Homeric heroes, "anyone who knew these 'good' ones only as enemies would find them evil enemies indeed." And Nietzsche continues: "We can imagine them returning from an orgy of murder, arson, rape, and torture, jubilant and at peace with themselves as though they had committed a fraternity prank—convinced, moreover, that the poets for a long time to come would have something to sing about and praise."

Even as the "master morality" expressed itself, and in large measure as a response to it, the weaker masses of humanity created a warped mirror image of this scheme of things: the weaknesses that the nobles termed bad, were redefined as "good," and the nobility's strengths became "evil." This "slave morality" was fueled by the resentment of the feeble for the strong, and it was this resentment that turned the "slave morality" into a perverse denial of life. By likening the nobles to birds of prey and the weak to sheep, Nietzsche illustrates how the impotent came to deny life:

> There is nothing very odd about lambs disliking birds of prey, but this is no reason for holding it against large birds of prey that they carry off lambs. And when the lambs whisper among themselves, "These birds of prey are evil, and does not this give us a right to say that whatever is the opposite of a bird of prey must be good?" there is nothing intrinsically wrong with such an argument—though the birds of prey will look somewhat quizzically and say, "*We* have nothing against these good lambs; in fact, we love them; nothing tastes better than a tender lamb."—To expect that strength will not manifest itself as strength, as the desire to overcome, to appropriate, to have enemies, obstacles, and triumphs, is every bit as absurd as to expect that weakness will manifest itself as strength.
>
> (*On the Genealogy of Morals*, first essay, sect. 13)

Yet it was precisely this "absurd" expectation that formed the foundation of the "slave morality": "The repressed and smoldering emotions of vengeance and hatred . . . espouse no belief more ardently than that it is within the discretion of the strong to be weak, of the bird of prey to be a lamb. Thus they assume the right of calling the bird of prey to account for being a bird of prey." And, on the other hand, the weak congratulate themselves on their weakness. This is what Nietzsche terms the "duplicity of impotence"—the belief that "the weakness of the weak, which is after all his essence, his natural way of being, his sole and inevitable reality, was a spontaneous act, a meritorious deed."

Just as in *The Birth of Tragedy* Nietzsche describes the conflict of two forces, the Apollinian and the Dionysian, so in *The Genealogy of Morals* he envisions a "terrible battle on this earth, lasting many millennia" between the "two sets of valuations," the master and the slave moralities. This contest, however, did not result in a delicate and productive equilibrium, but in the triumph of the slave morality, shown in the ascendancy of Christianity. Indeed, when read solely against the backdrop of Nietzsche's description of the genealogy of human morality, the most hallowed phrases of Jesus' Sermon on the Mount—that the meek will inherit the earth or the description of "turning the other cheek"—seem the fruit of impotent resentment. Further, this "revaluation" of the "master morality" had its own hidden agenda of domination: "There can be no doubt that these weaklings, too, want a chance to be strong, to have *their* kingdom come." Thus the weak call themselves the "just," the naturally strong become the "damned," and, in Saint Thomas Aquinas' words, "The blessed in the kingdom of heaven will see the punishments of the damned, in order that their bliss be more delightful to them."

Nietzsche's genealogy of morals turns the traditional scheme of virtue and vice on its head. If Christianity represents the triumph of the "slave morality," then its virtues are nothing more than the life-denying products of resentment. And indeed this had always been Nietzsche's view. As the title of *Human, All-Too-Human* tells us, Nietzsche's goal was to disclose the crude motives that lay at the base of humankind's supposed ideals. "When stepped on, a worm doubles up," he writes in *Twilight of the Idols.* "That is clever. In that way he lessens the probability of being stepped on again. In the language of morality: *humility.*" Behind every altruism there lurks the desire for self-preservation and, even further, the desire to dominate, the universal will to power about which more will be said presently. Perhaps one of Nietzsche's most profound insights was the degree to which the behavior of the weak and impotent can often be explained by a will to power:

> Observe children who weep and wail *in order that* they shall be pitied . . . live among invalids and the mentally afflicted and ask yourself whether their eloquent moaning and complaining, their displaying of misfortune, does not fun-

damentally have the objective of *hurting* those who are with them: the pity which these then express is a consolation for the weak and suffering, inasmuch as it shows them that, all their weakness notwithstanding, they possess at any rate *one power:* the *power to hurt.* In this feeling of superiority of which the demonstration of pity makes him conscious, the unfortunate man gains a sort of pleasure; in the conceit of his imagination he is still of sufficient importance to cause affliction in the world.

(*Human, All-Too-Human*, sect. 50)

To the extent that Christianity seemed to him the product of the vindictive desire of the weak to dominate the world, Nietzsche considers its victory the "supreme disaster in human history," even at times calling it a crime.

By damming up the natural flow of aggressive impulses that had been given full play in the "master morality," Christianity turned man's natural belligerence inward, creating a self-mutilation of the human psyche. But Nietzsche was so keenly aware of the good that has been purchased at the price of this "self-vivisection" that those who think he does not value Christianity's importance have simply misread him. The interiorization of aggression played a major part in the centuries of taming the human beast that were prerequisites to civilization. In the long run it was the turning inward of aggression that created humankind's singular achievement, the inner censor called "bad conscience." Regarded as a product of self-vivisection, bad conscience is the clearest indication that modern man is diseased, his natural psyche crushed by the scar tissue of centuries of repression. But in fact it is to the creation of the inner censor that we owe the evolution of consciousness itself:

All instincts that are not allowed free play turn inward. This is what I call man's interiorization; it alone provides the soil for the growth of what is later called man's *soul.* Man's interior world, originally meager and tenuous, was expanding in every dimension, in proportion as the outward discharge of his feelings was curtailed.

(*Genealogy of Morals*, first essay, sect. 11)

Further, as a preparation for what is to come, bad conscience "is an illness in the way pregnancy is an illness": it has yet to work its final effect upon humanity.

In the second essay of the *Genealogy of Morals* Nietzsche asks what is required "to breed an animal with the right to make promises." This "animal" is Nietzsche's "Overman" or superior human (*Übermensch*)—the being to whom modern man is simply a bridge or a preparation. And he answers, without a trace of irony, "How much blood and horror lies behind all 'good things'!" He writes in *Beyond Good and Evil:*

The strange fact is that all there is or has been on earth of freedom, subtlety, boldness, dance and masterly certainty, whether in thinking itself, or in ruling, or in speaking and persuasion, or in the arts as in morals, has evolved only by virtue of the "tyranny of . . . arbitrary laws."

(sect. 188)

In the end, then, Nietzsche presents a paradoxical vision of human history. On the one hand, the triumph of Christianity was the "supreme disaster in human history"; on the other, Christianity's exaltation of life-negating values made possible the highest form of humanity, the Overman. The point is that once we have understood these two sides of traditional morality, we can jettison those of its aspects that are against life and save those that perhaps should be preserved. That we should do this consciously is the essence of Nietzsche's message, for the triumphs of science and secularization have eroded the faith upon which Christianity was based. Unless we squarely face the challenge of life in a world without God, we shall sink into the quicksand of nihilism.

A word needs to be said about the common confounding of Nietzsche's Overman with the "blond beast," a result of the attempt by some Nazi theorists to link their racist notion of Aryan superiority to Nietzsche's philosophy. Nietzsche does, indeed, refer at one point to the original nobles in Germany as "the blond Teutonic beast[s]," adding immediately that "all racial connection between the old Teutonic tribes and ourselves has been lost" (*Genealogy of Morals,* first essay, section 11). But even without Nietzsche's disclaimer, we have already seen that for all their life-affirming qualities, the original nobles were savages, and Nietzsche never meant us to think that the overcoming of Christianity would lead us back to that sort of barbarism. The "blond beast" stands at the beginning of the process Nietzsche describes; the final result of the centuries of discipline has nothing in common with that ancient forebear:

> If we place ourselves at the terminal point of this great process, where society and custom finally reveal their true aim, we shall find the ripest fruit of that tree to be the sovereign individual, equal only to himself, all moral custom left far behind. This autonomous, more-than-moral individual (the terms *autonomous* and *moral* are mutually exclusive) has developed his own, independent, long-range will, which dares to make promises. . . . Being truly free and possessor of a long-range, pertinacious will, he also possesses a scale of values.
>
> (*Genealogy of Morals,* second essay, sect. 2)

The "terminal point" is, of course, the Overman.

A comment is also in order about the difference between traditional morality and "the scale of values" that Nietzsche describes as the possession of the more-than-moral individual, an opposition characterized above as the contrast between autonomy and morality. Nietzsche's emphasis on the importance of discipline makes it clear that he did not propose anarchy or a meaningless letting go as the alternatives to Christian morality. Rather he sought to move from a "customary" or habitual morality to a self-conscious exercise of

autonomy. The Overman has a scale of values, but it is freely self-imposed. Thus, his behavior is controlled not by the dead hand of empty tradition, but by self-discipline.

But this leaves us with an important question: What is the origin of the values that the Overman imposes on himself? How are these values justified? This inquiry gains in urgency when we realize that by knocking down the ideal of an eternally fixed moral scheme given to humanity by God, Nietzsche has also effectively damaged the Western notion of absolute truth. By revealing the "human, all-too-human" roots of the religious experience, Nietzsche had laid to rest one of humankind's greatest errors, the belief that a "rational" or "real" world exists somehow in opposition to the changing world of appearance in which we live. This, too, was an illusion, the product of "decadence, a symptom of the *decline of life.*" To the human need for a transcendent meaning Nietzsche replies in *The Gay Science:* "The total character of the world is in all eternity chaos—in the sense not of a lack of necessity [i.e., physical causation does exist] but of a lack of order, arrangement, form, beauty, wisdom, and whatever other names there are for our aesthetic anthropomorphisms."

Furthermore, in the chaotic universe things exist not in a state of being, but in a constant process of becoming. Change, not stability, is the rule. Nowhere has our tendency to seek for fixed points of reference done more harm than in our attempts to understand ourselves.

> All philosophers have the common failing of starting out from man as he is now and thinking they can reach their goal through an analysis of him. They automatically think of man as an eternal verity, as something that remains constant in the midst of all flux, as a sure measure of things. But everything the philosopher has declared about man is at bottom no more than a testimony about the man of a *very limited* time. . . . Everything *essential* in the development of mankind took place in primeval times, long before the 4,000 years we more or less know about;

during these years mankind may well not have altered very much. But the philosopher here sees "instincts" in man as he now is and assumes that these belong to the unalterable facts of mankind. . . . But everything has become: there are *no eternal facts,* just as there are no absolute truths.

(*Human, All-Too-Human,* sect. 2)

And in this process of becoming, the "meaning" of reality also undergoes endless flux:

There is no set of maxims more important for a historian than this: that the actual causes of a thing's origin and its eventual uses, the manner of its incorporation into a system of purposes are worlds apart; that everything that exists, no matter what its origin, is periodically reinterpreted by those in power in terms of fresh intentions; that all processes in the organic world are processes of outstripping and overcoming, and that, in turn, all outstripping and overcoming means reinterpretation, rearrangement, in the course of which the earlier meaning and purpose are necessarily either obscured or lost.

(*Genealogy of Morals,* second essay, sect. 12)

What meaning there is in the world is the product of the dominant interpretation, itself fated eventually to be reinterpreted in "terms of fresh intentions."

In Nietzsche's terms, then, values spring from the act of "outstripping and overcoming." One aspect of what Nietzsche means by this is revealed by a line from *The Birth of Tragedy* (section 5): "It is only as an *aesthetic phenomenon* that existence and the world are eternally justified." By saying that the world is justified as a work of art, Nietzsche indicates that it is the act of creating order out of chaos—the artistic disciplining of reality—that gives life its meaning. And this creation of meaning is in the hands of the superior types of humanity whom Nietzsche, paralleling Schopenhauer, defined as the artist, the philosopher, and the ascetic. It should be noted, however, that unlike Schopenhauer's

three superior types, these individuals do not deny life, but celebrate it. Nietzsche's ethical man does not renounce the Will; on the contrary, his control of his own impulses results, as we shall see, from his overabundance of the life-force.

But a critic of Nietzsche might ask at this point, is not this talk of imposing order on the world simply a different way of describing progress? Further, does not the concept of the Overman (who is undoubtedly one of those individuals who can force meaning onto chaotic reality) and the notion that he represents the "endpoint" of a development revive the original error that assigned a transcendent meaning to human events? We may recall here one of the questions raised by Nietzsche's early essay on history, namely, that in their relation to one another the great individuals seem to constitute an evolution over time.

To these questions Nietzsche would have answered that although at any given time the imposition of order does give meaning to history, the error lies in assigning to that meaning any absolute weight. Thus, although the creative action of the world-historical figure seems to justify the historical process, that justification has no value beyond itself. "The Revolution made Napoleon possible," Nietzsche writes in 1887, "that is its justification. . . . Napoleon made nationalism possible: that is its excuse." But there can be no answer to the question of why Napoleon existed during his particular span of time and in no other:

The problem I thus pose is not what shall succeed mankind in the sequence of living beings (man is an end), but what type of man shall be *bred,* shall be willed, for being higher in value, worthier of life, more certain of a future. . . .

Mankind does *not* represent a development toward something better or stronger or higher in the sense accepted today. . . . The European of today is vastly inferior in value to the European of the Renaissance. . . .

In another sense, success in individual cases is constantly encountered in the most widely different places and cultures: here we really do find a *higher type*, which is, in relation to mankind as a whole, a kind of overman. Such fortunate accidents of great success have always been possible and *will* perhaps always be possible.

(sect. 3 and 4)

These words from *The Anti-Christ* make it clear that Nietzsche does not view the Overman in any sense as an end point of a historical evolution. The Overman is a possibility, a moral challenge hurled by Nietzsche at a civilization increasingly bereft of the comforts of unquestioned tradition. *"I teach you the overman,"* says Zarathustra to the people. "Man is something that shall be overcome. What have you done to overcome him?" What, Nietzsche asks his readers, have you done to become autonomous individuals, "more than moral"?

And yet the notion that meaning comes from creation only raises another question. Where does this urge to create order out of chaos come from? Although Nietzsche rejects the idea of a transcendent order in the universe, like all philosophers he seeks for a unity in all the phenomena he observes in life. This unifying element he identifies in *Thus Spoke Zarathustra* as the "will to power." In earlier works Nietzsche depicts civilization and culture as the products of conflict. Now he identifies the cause of conflict, humanity's will to domination, as the foundation of all value:

A tablet of good hangs over every people. Behold, it is the tablet of their overcomings; behold, it is the voice of their will to power.

Praiseworthy is whatever seems difficult to a people: whatever seems indispensable and difficult is called good; and whatever liberates even out of the deepest need, the rarest, the most difficult—that they call holy. . . .

Verily, humanity gave themselves all their good and evil. Verily, they did not take it, they did not find it, nor did it come to them as a voice from heaven. Only man placed values in things to preserve himself—he alone created a meaning for things, a human meaning.

(*Thus Spoke Zarathustra*, "On the Thousand and One Goals")

Morality, humanity's self-vivisection, was created by human beings, a function of their will to power. And "through this self-conquest they became pregnant and heavy with great hopes." The greatness of the Overman will be measured by the extraordinary degree and success of his self-conquest.

Nietzsche viewed the will to power as quite a different thing from the unifying causes or transcendent absolutes that previous philosophers had identified as the ultimate meaning of existence. In the will to power he felt he had found a basis of all value that was a purely natural phenomenon, clearly reflected for all who would see it in the world of nature. One of humanity's most dangerous errors, Nietzsche believed, was that it "placed [itself] in a false order of rank in relation to animals and nature." It is from this point of view that Nietzsche makes his remarks about the necessity of slavery in civilization. The domination of the weak by the strong is the law of nature and the basis of the social order. To Nietzsche, a society that feels powerful and confident enough to ignore this law and adopt a liberal or humanistic policy undermines its own foundation. This is perhaps the most disturbing aspect of his thinking, for it contains within it the seeds of much of twentieth-century fascism and totalitarianism. (Although against those forms of government we can balance his rejection of the modern idealization of the state in *Schopenhauer as Educator*.)

With the will to power Nietzsche had found a universal cause that was morally neutral, a force to which humanity's "aesthetic anthropomorphisms" could not be applied. Unlike Schopenhauer, who in effect judged the Will to be evil, Nietzsche maintained that the will to power could not be ethically judged. On the other hand, also unlike Schopenhauer's Will, one can make sense of the will to power; it is not irrational. Once we accept it, all manner of hitherto incomprehensible events (like the victory of the weak "slave morality" over the strong "master morality") become understandable. Further, with the will to power as its basic assumption, human understanding avoids both the pitfall of belief in absolute truth and the error of nihilism. In the endless variety of its overcoming and reinterpretation, the will to power dashes the idea that one truth, one way of looking at reality, can be valid for all time. But, for all that, life is not meaningless. It is the expression of the will to power.

This last observation may seem to involve us in an alarming circularity of thought, and perhaps it does. Powerfully as Nietzsche argues that there is a natural, scientific proof of the will to power—that it is as neutral and irrefutable as the physical law of entropy—he has given us an absolute reference point in a universe that he insists has none. There is also the possibility that Nietzsche was drawn to the will to power because in his crusade to revalue radically traditional thought and morals it seemed so much the opposite of the accepted explanations of human behavior. We know that it was a very effective tool in revealing the human desires that underlie the conventional virtues.

But if the will to power seems a tailor-made cudgel for demolishing customary Christian morality, it is not alien to all value systems. As Walter Kaufmann points out, a very close parallel to Nietzsche's conception of the Overman can be found in Aristotle's description of "the great-souled man" in the *Nicomachean Ethics* and in sonnet 94 by William Shakespeare. Nietzsche's "animal with the right to make promises" is brought to life by Shakespeare's lines:

> They that have power to hurt and will do none,
> That do not do the thing they most do show,
> Who, moving others, are themselves as stone,

Unmoved, cold, and to temptation slow:
They rightly do inherit heaven's graces
And husband nature's riches from expense,
They are the lords and owners of their faces,
Others, but stewards of their excellence.

Here the will to power has found its noblest form. Indeed, whether or not Nietzsche truly found the single cause of all the phenomena of life, supposing even that such a thing exists, he surely discovered something of the utmost importance in the will to power, in what it tells us about both our basest and our most heroic actions.

Nietzsche showed us that, in the best individuals, virtue is not the result of altruism, but is rather the self-discipline that comes from the voracious, life-affirming desire for conquest. "Both art and virtue are always concerned with what is harder," Aristotle wrote in the *Nicomachean Ethics*, "for even the good is better when it is harder." Increasingly, Nietzsche carried this to an extreme: for him the good became precisely what was most difficult.

It is with this in mind that we can best understand the theory of the "eternal recurrence," Nietzsche's answer to a question he first raised in *The Gay Science:*

> What if some day or night a demon were to steal after you into your loneliest loneliness and say to you: "This life as you now live it and have lived it, you will have to live once more and innumerable times more; and there will be nothing new in it, but every pain and every joy and every thought and sign and everything unutterably small or great in your life will have to return to you, all in the same succession and sequence
>
>   . . .
>
> If this thought gained possession of you, it would change you as you are or perhaps crush you. The question in each and everything, "Do you desire this once more and innumerable times more?" would lie upon your actions as the greatest weight. . . . How well disposed would you have to become to yourself and to life *to crave nothing*

more fervently than this ultimate eternal confirmation and seal?

(sect. 341)

What is posed here is not a philosophical question, but a moral one, and we see that the "eternal recurrence" was not meant by Nietzsche to be a new scientific statement about the universe, but, rather, was the ultimate test of an individual's affirmation of life. As Hollingdale puts it: "The *Übermensch* would rejoice in the idea of eternal recurrence: if I do not, why do I not?"

If sometimes Nietzsche appears to us as a martyr who spent his life shouting uncomfortable truths at those would not listen, we must remember that in his terms this type of martyrdom was the greatest triumph. That in the midst of his pain and solitude he could conceive of the "eternal recurrence" and welcome it was proof that he himself was an Overman.

Nietzsche's influence on later thinkers is enormous. The defenders of traditional morality have had to deal with his attack upon it, whereas others, like the existentialists, have accepted the death of God and have gone on to enunciate a full-fledged theory of self-realization. The development of psychoanalysis is unthinkable without Nietzsche; a recent study has affirmed that Freud, despite his denials, was well acquainted with Nietzsche's works. Nietzsche's influence has been equally decisive in a broad range of more purely philosophical subjects than have been discussed here. This is especially true in the study of logic and language. Nietzsche's insight that language is not a depiction of reality so much as a human interpretation of it, and that even as it helps us, language imprisons us in limited ways of thinking, has found its amplification in the works of Ludwig Wittgenstein and his followers.

But if we turn our attention to the world at large we find that Nietzsche has had little impact. This is most noticeable in the continued vitality of the religious frame of mind, evidenced not only by the persistence of traditional faiths, but in the newer "secular religions." If people today do not believe in God, they believe just as fervently and dogmatically in Marx or in something else. It is perhaps ironic that German fascism and the various forms of twentieth-century totalitarianism, while preaching a pseudo-Nietzschean (or a Marxian) rejection of Christianity, have found it necessary to shore up their authority with religious cults of the state and the leader.

Nietzsche explained the function of religion in two ways. First, he saw it as the refuge of those too exhausted or decadent to face the hard truth: "Weariness that wants to reach the ultimate with one leap, with one fatal leap, a poor ignorant weariness that does not want to want anymore: this created all gods and afterworlds." Elsewhere, most extensively in the third essay of *On the Genealogy of Morals*, he analyzed religion as a system of therapy imposed on the weak masses by Overmen—the ascetic priests—who took upon themselves the task of saving suffering humanity. In this conception religion saved civilization by deflecting into the harmless channels of therapeutic ritual the pent-up neurotic anxieties of the masses: "the main object of religion has been to counteract a certain epidemic malaise due to unreleased tension." In either case—whether a choice of the exhausted individual or imposed to keep us from destroying ourselves—religion obviously represented for Nietzsche humanity's inability to step out of the circle of illusions it had formed through centuries of error.

Looking at the world today, should we simply conclude that Nietzsche's message was always for the very few and that it is not suprising that most people remain untouched? This seems the inevitable consequence of his insistence that a "pathos of distance" separates humanity's highest specimens from its "loam and clay." It is that very conception, however, that modern thought finds least attractive in Nietzsche, for we insist that a philosophy embrace all of humanity. And we might well find our ultimate dissatisfaction with Nietzsche in his failure to provide a social theory that promises something for everybody. That such a theory would be an empty promise was Nietzsche's point, of course, and he would recognize in our utopian dreams yet another example of humanity's attempt to satisfy its inner emptiness with sham absolutes.

Whether or not we can live in the icy solitude of such a way of thinking—whether or not we agree that the hope for progress is a childish dream—Nietzsche remains a challenge to each of us. If in the end his road is not ours it makes no difference, so long as we have pondered honestly and long why we have made our choice and not his.

In January 1889 Nietzsche collapsed on a street in Turin, Italy, and from that moment he rapidly descended into insanity. After a brief period in a mental asylum, he was taken home by his mother, who cared for him until her death in 1897. Thereafter, Elisabeth was his guardian. Her relationship with Nietzsche had been strained ever since her meddling had helped destroy his friendship with Lou Salomé, and things had worsened between them even more when she married an antisemitic activist, Bernhard Förster, in 1885. In a letter the year before, Nietzsche had said of her: "There *can* be no reconciliation between a vindictive anti-Semitic goose and me."

Elisabeth followed her husband to Paraguay, where he had established a so-called "New Germany," a "racially pure" Aryan colony, in 1883. The project ended in disaster: Förster committed suicide in 1889 after evidence came to light that he had swindled his fellow colonists. Elisabeth returned home in 1890. The bright spot in her life was a continuing close friendship with Cosima Wagner and the anti-Nietzschean coterie at Bayreuth.

Even before her mother's death, Elisabeth had come to see herself as the rightful interpreter of her brother's works, especially as they were increasing in popularity with each passing day. As for her comprehension of his philosophy, there is expert testimony that she had none. Her biography of Nietzsche was in large part a work of fiction, and it is only thanks to her reluctance to destroy the original documents that the events of his life have been accurately reconstructed by later writers. She supported herself handsomely on the income from the various editions of Nietzsche's works that she published. Much of Nietzsche scholarship after World War II has been dedicated to undoing the pernicious effects of her stewardship.

An especially offensive aspect of Elisabeth's behavior was her use of the now docile Nietzsche for her own purposes. Most of the familiar photographs of Nietzsche—with gigantic moustache and vacant eyes—were taken after the onset of his illness. They were aimed at a growing turn-of-the-century audience who saw in the mad Nietzsche a seer who had moved to a higher plane of existence. She also dressed him in a white robe and allowed special visitors and journalists to watch Nietzsche asleep. Shortly before his death of a final stroke in 1900, Elisabeth moved Nietzsche to Weimar, probably so that he would die in Goethe's city.

Nietzsche was of course unaware of all this. Throughout his madness he remained comparatively gentle, often able to carry on brief conversations with visitors. But he could not bear the mention of his works, and coherent thought was beyond him. The balance of modern opinion is that he suffered a mental paralysis brought on by syphilis, although it is not known when or where he caught the disease. A recent biographer, Ronald Hayman, reviewing the incoherent but not meaningless scribblings of his last years, has raised the possibility that Nietzsche's breakdown was psychological in origin. This view seems linked, however, to the older, largely discredited notion that Nietzsche's madness was self-willed, a final overcoming.

The debate about Nietzsche's madness will continue. Without question his madness marked a needlessly early end to his creative life. Yet with hindsight it is hard to see what more he could have said. He questioned everything in such ultimate terms that there is nothing left for us to do but try to move beyond him. Whether we will in the end actualize his ideal of individual self-realization, or, as sometimes seems more likely, follow the next "Overman" who, by force of will, erects a new "tablet of good and evil," we will seek until we attain a new synthesis. But this, too, Nietzsche foretold. Liberated by him from our old ways of thinking, we will reinterpret the world "in terms of fresh intentions."

Selected Bibliography

INDIVIDUAL WORKS

Die Geburt der Tragödie aus dem Geiste der Musik (The Birth of Tragedy out of the Spirit of Music). Leipzig, 1872.

Unzeitgemässe Betrachtungen (Untimely Meditations): *David Strauss, der Bekenner und der Schriftsteller* (David Strauss, the Confessor and the Writer). Leipzig, 1873.

Von Nützen und Nachtheil der Historie für das Leben (The Use and Disadvantage of History for Life). Leipzig, 1874.

Schopenhauer als Erzieher (Schopenhauer as Teacher). Chemnitz, 1874.

Richard Wagner in Bayreuth. Chemnitz, 1876.

Menschliches, Allzumenschliches: Ein Buch für freie Geister (Human, All-Too-Human: A Book for Free Spirits). Chemnitz, 1878.

Anhang: Vermischte Meinungen und Sprüche (Mixed Opinions and Sayings). Chemnitz, 1879. Second part of *Human, All-Too-Human.*

Der Wanderer und sein Schatten (The Wanderer and His Shadow). Chemnitz, 1880. Third part of *Human, All-Too-Human.*

Morgenröte: Gedanken über die moralischen Vorurteile (Dawn: Thoughts on Moral Prejudices). Chemnitz, 1881.

Die fröhliche Wissenschaft (The Gay Science). Books 1–4, Chemnitz, 1882; book 5, Leipzig, 1887.

Also sprach Zarathustra: Ein Buch für Alle und Keinen (Thus Spoke Zarathustra: A Book for Everyone and No One). Parts 1 and 2, Chemnitz, 1883; part 3, Chemnitz, 1884; part 4, Chemnitz, 1891.

Jenseits von Gut und Böse: Vorspiel einer Philosophie der Zukunft (Beyond Good and Evil: Prelude to a Philosophy of the Future). Leipzig, 1886.

Zur Genealogie der Moral (On the Genealogy of Morals) Leipzig, 1887.

Der Fall Wagner (The Case of Wagner). Leipzig, 1888.

Die Götterdämmerung; oder, Wie Man mit dem Hammer philosophiert (The Twilight of the Idols; or, How One Philosophizes with a Hammer). Leipzig, 1889.

Der Antichrist (1895). First published in *Gross Oktavausgabe.* Vol. 8, Leipzig, 1899–1904.

Nietzsche contra Wagner (Nietzsche Against Wagner) (1895). First published in *Gross Oktavausgabe.* Vol. 8, Leipzig, 1899–1904.

Der Wille zur Macht (The Will to Power). Leipzig, 1901.

Ecce Homo. Leipzig, 1908.

COLLECTED WORKS

Gesammelte Werke. Edited by Richard Oehler and Max Oehler. 23 vols. Munich, 1920–1929.

Gross Oktavausgabe. 15 vols. Leipzig, 1899–1904.

Musikalische Werke von Friedrich Nietzsche. Vol. 1: *Lieder für eine Singstimme mit Klavierbegleitung.* Edited by Georg Göhler. Leipzig, 1924.

Sämtliche Werke. 12 vols. Stuttgart, 1964–1976.

Werke: Kritische Gesamtausgabe. Edited by Giorgio Colli and Mazzino Montinari. Berlin, 1967–. Most comprehensive edition. 30 vols. planned.

Werke in drei Bändern. Edited by Karl Schlechta. 3 vols. Munich, 1954–1956. The most convenient collected edition.

TRANSLATIONS

The Anti-Christ. Translated by R. J. Hollingdale. 1969.

"Appeal to the German Nation." Translated by C. V. Kerr. In *The Nietzsche-Wagner Correspondence,* edited by Elisabeth Förster-Nietzsche. New York, [1970?].

Basic Writings of Nietzsche. Edited by Walter Kaufmann. New York, 1968. Contains Kaufmann's translations of *Beyond Good and Evil, The Birth of Tragedy, The Case of Wagner, Ecce Homo,* and *On the Genealogy of Morals* (translated with

R. J. Hollingdale). These works have also been published separately in 3 vols., New York, 1966–1968.

Beyond Good and Evil. Translated by R. J. Hollingdale. Baltimore and Harmondsworth, 1973.

The Birth of Tragedy and *The Genealogy of Morals.* Translated by Francis Golffing. Garden City, N.Y., 1956.

The Complete Works of Friedrich Nietzsche. Edited by Oscar Levy. 18 vols. New York, 1909–1911; reissued 1964. Unreliable translations, but the only English versions of *Human, All-Too-Human* and *Dawn.*

The Gay Science. Translated by Walter Kaufmann. New York, 1974.

A Nietzsche Reader. Edited by R. J. Hollingdale. Baltimore and Harmondsworth, 1977.

Nietzsche: A Self-Portrait from His Letters. Edited and translated by P. Fuss and H. Shapiro. Cambridge, Mass., and London, 1971.

On the Advantage and Disadvantage of History for Life. Translated by Peter Preuss. Indianapolis, 1980.

Philosophy in the Tragic Age of the Greeks. Translated by Marianne Cowan. Chicago, 1962.

The Portable Nietzsche. Edited by Walter Kaufmann. New York, 1954. Selections from most of the works, letters, and notes, and complete translations of *Thus Spoke Zarathustra, Twilight of the Idols, The Antichrist,* and *Nietzsche contra Wagner.*

Schopenhauer as Educator. Translated by J. W. Hillesheim and M. R. Simpson. Chicago, 1965.

Selected Letters. Edited and translated by Christopher Middleton. Chicago, 1969.

Thus Spoke Zarathustra. Translated by R. J. Hollingdale. Baltimore and Harmondsworth, 1961.

Twilight of the Idols and *The Antichrist.* Translated by R. J. Hollingdale. Baltimore and Harmondsworth, 1969.

The Will to Power. Translated by Walter Kaufmann and R. J. Hollingdale. New York, 1967.

BIOGRAPHICAL AND CRITICAL STUDIES

Alderman, Harold. *Nietzsche's Gift.* Athens, Ohio, 1977.

Allison, D. B., ed. *The New Nietzsche: Contemporary Styles of Interpretation.* New York, 1977.

Andler, Charles. *Nietzsche: Sa vie et pensée.* Paris, 1920–1931.

Binion, Rudolph. *Frau Lou: Nietzsche's Wayward Disciple.* Princeton, N.J., 1968.

Brinton, Crane. *Nietzsche.* Cambridge, Mass., 1941; New York, 1965.

Dannhauser, W. J. *Nietzsche's View of Socrates.* Ithaca, N.Y., and London, 1974.

Danto, A. C. *Nietzsche as Philosopher.* New York, 1965.

Fischer-Dieskau, Dietrich. *Wagner and Nietzsche.* New York, 1976.

Hayman, Ronald. *Nietzsche: A Critical Life.* London, 1980.

Heller, Erich. *The Artist's Journey into the Interior.* New York, 1965. Includes two essays on Nietzsche.

————. *The Disinherited Mind.* Cambridge and Philadelphia, 1952. Includes three essays on Nietzsche.

Hollingdale, R. J. *Nietzsche: The Man and His Philosophy.* London and Baton Rouge, 1965.

————. *Nietzsche.* London and Boston, 1973.

Janz, C. P. *Friedrich Nietzsche: Biographie.* 3 vols. Munich and Vienna, 1977–1978.

Jaspers, Karl. *Nietzsche: An Introduction to the Understanding of His Philosophical Activity.* Tucson, Ariz., 1965.

Kaufmann, Walter. *Nietzsche: Philosopher, Psychologist, Antichrist.* Princeton, N.J., and London, 1950; rev. and enl. ed., 1968.

Morgan, G. A., Jr. *What Nietzsche Means.* Cambridge, Mass., 1941; New York, 1965.

Podach, E. F. *Nietzsches Zusammenbruch: Beiträge zu einer Biographie auf Grund unveröffentlichter Dokumente.* Heidelberg, 1930. Translated as *The Madness of Nietzsche.* New York and London, 1931.

————. *Gestalten um Nietzsche mit unveröffentlichen Dokumenten zur Geschichte seines Lebens und seines Werkes.* Weimar, 1932.

————. *Der Kranke Nietzsche: Briefe seiner Mutter an Franz Overbeck.* Vienna, 1937.

Solomon, R. C., ed. *Nietzsche: A Collection of Critical Essays.* Garden City, N.Y., 1973.

Stern, J. P. *Nietzsche.* Hassock, Eng., 1978.

Vaihinger, Hans. *The Philosophy of "As if."* New York, 1924; 2nd ed., London, 1965. Contains the chapter "Nietzsche and His Doctrine of Conscious Illusion."

MARTIN J. NEWHOUSE

JOSÉ MARIA EÇA DE QUEIROZ
(1845–1900)

I F I HAD been born on this side of the Pyrenees [France], and published my stories in
the *Petit Journal,* I would be a wealthy man."
With these words, written on 28 January 1890
in a letter to his Portuguese friend Oliveira
Martins, Eça de Queiroz lamented not only his
persistent financial difficulties, but also the
limits imposed on a writer whose literary language was Portuguese, "an argot shared by
two peoples—the Portuguese and the
Brazilians."

Eça, who together with the poets Luís de
Camões (1524?–1580) and Fernando Pessoa
(1888–1935) is considered one of Portugal's
three most important writers, produced a body
of fiction (translated into many Western and
Oriental languages) that continues to this day
to be the focus of much study and debate in
the Portuguese-speaking world.

For most of his life Eça lived outside of his
native country, but he never lost contact with
the Portuguese literary and cultural situation.
He was a controversial figure who absorbed
European artistic trends and adapted them to
his creative needs. In turn, his works had a
major impact on contemporaries and successors; and his influence is still evident in the
works of many of today's Portuguese novelists.

Eça was both a unique Portuguese writer
and an exponent of nineteenth-century European naturalism and realism. The quality and
significance of his fiction have drawn the at-

tention of many distinguished writers, critics,
and intellectuals, among them the Brazilian
Machado de Assis (1839–1908) and the Spaniard Miguel de Unamuno (1864–1936). Nonetheless, he has yet to receive the recognition
he deserves in the non-Portuguese-speaking
world as one of the literary giants of the nineteenth century.

I

José Maria Eça de Queiroz was born out of
wedlock on 25 November 1845 in Póvoa de
Varzim, a village in northern Portugal; the illegitimacy of his birth cast its shadow over
everything that followed. Although his parents belonged to the provincial upper
bourgeoisie—his father became a judge and
his mother was the orphaned daughter of an
infantry commander—for as yet unexplained
reasons they did not marry until 1849.

The Portugal into which Eça was born was
a nation that had suffered through the Napoleonic invasions of the early century, a period
of English domination followed by a stillborn
constitutional monarchy, and a decade of civil
war that ultimately led to the feeble socioeco-
nomic and political system of the 1840's.
Eça's paternal ancestors had not been untouched by the national cataclysms. His
grandfather, Joaquim José de Queiroz e Almeida, had been a judge in Portugal's colony
of Brazil earlier in the century. At that time

Brazil was the seat of the Portuguese colonial empire because King João VI of Bragança had fled there upon the invasion of the Iberian peninsula by Napoleon's troops in 1807. Eça's father was born in Brazil in the early 1810's, just before Brazil's independence from Portugal was declared by King João VI's son, Dom Pedro, in September 1822. Eça's grandfather returned to Portugal about that time. Not long after, a series of bizarre fratricidal civil wars began that pitted Dom Pedro (who gave up his right to the throne of Brazil in 1826 in favor of his grandson, the future Dom Pedro II) against his brother Dom Miguel. Eça's grandfather's support went to Dom Pedro, who represented the liberal philosophies of the French Revolution. The wars lasted until 1833, when Dom Miguel, a rabid absolutist, was finally forced into exile in Vienna and an inefficient liberal bureaucracy was installed.

Because Eça's existence was an embarrassment to his unwed parents, his first years were spent with a nursemaid and, later, with his paternal grandparents. His grandfather had imported slaves from Brazil, who worked the family estate; the proprietor had time on his hands and spent many hours relating his life of adventures to his grandson. After his grandparents' deaths, in the mid-1850's, Eça, a fragile child, was returned to the care of his parents, with whom he lived briefly and lovelessly, barely becoming acquainted with his brothers, before being sent off to boarding school in Oporto. Directly after graduation he went to the University of Coimbra to study law.

Eça was legally recognized by his parents in late 1885, only weeks before his marriage. The circumstances of his birth were revealed to the world at large only after the writer's death. Further, Eça studiously avoided all reference to his family background, although threads of his personal anguish repeatedly surface in his writings in both characterization and plot.

This pariahlike relationship with his family probably accounts for Eça's many lifelong fraternal friendships, some of them with men who would shape the last years of the Portuguese monarchy and the first years of the republic. Among these friendships was the one with Ramalho Ortigão. Ramalho taught at the preparatory school headed by his father in Oporto, where Eça prepared for exams in Latin, French, ethics, and other subjects required for admission to the University of Coimbra. Ramalho was nine years older than Eça and, like an elder brother, led him through the early stages of his intellectual growth.

Ramalho instilled in Eça an appreciation for the Portuguese classical writers and some contemporaries. Ramalho's favorite Portuguese work was the philosophical novel *Viagens na minha terra* (Travels Through My Land, 1845) by the viscount Almeida Garrett. It was a work that also influenced Eça's fiction and literary style. Ramalho, a distinguished writer and journalist in his own right, was a sophisticated provincial, equally at home in Portugal and interested in life abroad. Many of his writings deal with Portugal's backwardness in relation to the rest of Europe. He followed Eça's literary career with great interest, and the two kept up a lifelong correspondence, rich in literary and personal interest.

In 1861 Eça began his studies at Coimbra, Portugal's oldest university. He took an immediate dislike to the academic approach to law, which was based on the memorization of printed class notes and on lectures given in French. Part of his time was spent as a member of the university's theatrical group. Theater brought him into contact with literature in general, and, eventually, with Teófilo Braga. By the early 1860's Braga was a poet of some repute; later he became president of the Portuguese Republic. Braga had been deeply influenced by the German romantics; he set out to do for Portugal what they had done for Germany, investigating the origins of Portuguese culture through an examination of folkloric texts and oral traditions. He was an early, ardent socialist. Among his works is a voluminous history of Portuguese literature that, regrettably, is noteworthy mostly for its lack of critical perspective and narrowmindedness. Eça corresponded regularly with Braga and sought his approval on literary theory and publications. In late 1864 Braga introduced him to Antero de Quental, the most radical of the student socialists at the University of Coimbra. If under Ramalho Eça had become aware of the Portuguese classical writers, under Antero's tutelage a whole new world of literature and social doctrine was opened up to him—particularly French and German writers, and the doctrines of Auguste Comte, Pierre Proudhon, Jules Michelet, and Hippolyte Taine, all of whom played major roles in Eça's discovery of his own fictional orientation.

Antero is indeed one of the foremost thinkers that the Iberian Peninsula has produced. He viewed Portuguese destiny as part of the greater question of the future of the peninsula and Europe. By the time he met Eça, he was busily engaged in formulating critical theories about social conditions and leading all sorts of student protests against "antiquated traditions." His earliest poetry dates from 1859; as early as 1860 he was writing on socialist topics. In the introduction to his *Odes modernas* (Modern Odes, 1865), he proclaimed his social and literary aims: "Modern poetry is the voice of revolution." In that same year he led a consequential literary skirmish—what is known as the "questão Coimbrã" (Coimbra question) or the "bom senso e bom gosto" (good sense and good taste) polemic—against the Portuguese ultraromantic literary establishment.

The deacon of ultraromanticism in Portugal, António Feliciano de Castilho, had praised the work of a mediocre poet, Pinheiro Chagas (a figure who would often appear in Eça's literary life), and attacked the new "philosophical poetry," a veiled reference to the works of Antero and Braga, the "Coimbra School." Antero then published a rather vituperative, personal tirade against Castilho,

which set off a polemic that lasted for several months. Romalho, who called for "clearheadedness" in the dispute, became involved in a friendly mock duel with Antero. The sharp extremes of Portuguese literary thought, which lasted until the end of the century, together with the alignment of their respective representatives were established.

The literary storm clouds soon abated over Coimbra, leaving only a tinge of bitterness in the atmosphere. Antero withdrew to the Azores. Eça, who had shelved his law books to follow the polemic as an ardent observer, returned to his studies and his reading—the French romantics (then very much in vogue in Portugal), Victor Hugo and Gérard de Nerval, and the German romantic poets in French versions, especially Heinrich Heine. Eça's graduation from the university coincided with the publication of his first article in the Lisbon *Gazeta de Portugal.* He soon left Coimbra for Lisbon, where his family had resided since 1862.

Judge Teixeira de Queiroz appears to have been quite proud of his son's professional status and literary endeavors. Although his father helped him to obtain a clerkship, Eça was much more interested in getting to know Lisbon and writing than in pursuing a career at law. His weekly columns in the *Gazeta de Portugal* (collected in the posthumous *Prosas bárbaras* [Barbarous Prose, 1903]) forced him to come to grips with his cultural and social interests. He gradually found new inspiration for his serials, stories, and columns in the writings of Charles Baudelaire, Edgar Allan Poe, and particularly Gustave Flaubert.

As it became increasingly apparent that Eça lacked any inclination for the legal career that was part of the family's tradition, his father and friends urged him to enter a field that would combine his training and talents—political journalism. Eça was packed off to the ancient Roman ruins of Evora, near the Spanish-Portuguese border; there he undertook single-handedly to create a political opposition to the government party through the founding of a newspaper, the *Districto de Evora*, in late 1866. Eça handled all aspects of the paper and as chief writer and editor created columns that dealt mainly with political affairs—international, national, and local—but also with cultural topics, and included some purely literary writing. He was successful in using his knowledge of classical and legal rhetoric to enrage and confound the established politicians of the province. Generally, Eça's method was to make mountains out of molehills. His theme was almost always the same: the reigning government's conspiracy against the nation and the people, particularly the rural folk. Thus, *what* was said was often less interesting than *how* it was said: where facts were unknown, invention and innuendo sufficed. After eight months spent rabble-rousing in Evora, Eça considered that *Districto de Evora* had accomplished its avowed political purpose and closed the paper. Evora was an important formative experience for Eça because he returned to Lisbon an accomplished polemicist, one who seems to have realized the power of well-constructed sentences to convey ideas and to convince.

During the period that followed, Eça worked intermittently at law, wrote mediocre poetry, and pursued a bohemian style of life. He became associated with the Cennacle, an intellectual clique of young men from Coimbra and Lisbon that included another of Eça's close friends, Jaime Batalha Reis, and represented a variety of fields of interest such as history, pedagogy, and anthropology; their motto was "Revolution, Metaphysics, Satanism, Anarchy, and Rabid Bohemianism." The Cennacle drifted along until Antero reappeared in Lisbon in 1869 and became its guiding spirit. Indeed, Antero, who had since his Coimbra years traveled to the United States and been a socialist organizer in France, had radically applied Proudhonian social theory to the problems of Portugal's present and future. The pamphlet *Portugal perante a revolução da Espanha* (Portugal Face to Face with the Spanish Revolution, 1868) was the first of his

works to outline the desperate need for an Iberian union—a confederation of Spain and Portugal for the salvation of both nations. Political, economic, and social differences between Spain and Portugal, in addition to the more emotional issues of each nation's own heritage and identity, prevented any movement on Iberian union; nonetheless, Antero, along with many other Portuguese and Spanish intellectuals, adhered to this hapless program for many years. Although Antero exercised a certain fascination on him during the Cennacle years, Eça maintained his distance from the man he called "Saint Antero." Antero encouraged Eça's initial literary activities (he was partly responsible for the publication of Eça's first novel), but he gradually became disenchanted with his friend's fiction, social goals, and political affiliations.

The most memorable personality of the Cennacle was a literary creation, a persona invented by Eça, Batalha Reis, and Antero in 1869 to satirize the complacent Portuguese bourgeoisie—Carlos Fradique Mendes. This epitome of the dandy, reminiscent of Baudelaire, was a "satanic poet"; his "biography" appeared in several Portuguese papers and endowed him with noble origins, extreme physical beauty, refinement, and an unmatchable knowledge of the world and culture. Fradique Mendes, who represented the dandified aspect of Eça's personality, was resuscitated by Eça in the 1880's and his "correspondence" with leading Portuguese intellectuals and writers was published in 1900 as *A correspondência de Fradique Mendes*.

Just as he was deciding on a diplomatic career, Eça received an invitation to accompany his friend, the count of Resende, on a trip to Egypt for the opening of the Suez Canal and a tour of the Holy Land's shrines. Eça set off in late 1869 with Resende (whose sister he married seventeen years later), and with Nerval's and Flaubert's travel writings on the Mideast as his guides. The posthumously published *O Egipto* (Egypt, 1926) consists of the detailed notes Eça took during his stay in the Holy

Land. He relates crossing paths with Théophile Gautier; describes the stolid magnificence of Alexandria and the Nile; offers insights into Egyptian social conditions in relation to the geography and climate; and includes a description of Cairo, with its bazaars, mysterious women, and Turkish baths. The trip to the "marvelous museum" made him sensitive to the need in narrative art for observing and interpreting detail. The influence of the romantic poets is evident in this early writing:

> On the green side of the Nile, of the water, the Sphinx opens her mysterious eyes, which have seen the colossal adventure of man pass before her. The implacable sun falls directly and mortally over the immense silence of the desert. From all sides, the light, the resplendent and lively blue, is cut up by the flight of the crows and vultures. One feels overcome, and our poor humanity perishes before that sinister eternity of things. What most surprises us about the Pyramids is their mystery. Thus walls, stones, interiors, empty sarcophagi, solitary passages all have a shocking silence and secretness. I feel like hitting those stones to oblige them to reveal their secrets. There are no sculptures or inscriptions: everything there makes fun of human curiosity!

> (pp. 234–235)

Upon his return early in January 1870, Eça was lionized by Lisbon society for his unusual voyage. The Cennacle was thriving; new members included the historian Joaquim Pedro de Oliveira Martins. Although Oliveira Martins had published some historical novels prior to 1870, he would distinguish himself through the 1870's and 1880's as an exemplary social scientist. His *Portugal contemporáneo* (*Contemporary Portugal,* 1881) as well as his studies of Portuguese explorations, finances, and emigration, and of socialism and Iberism, were important for Eça's perspective on the society he portrayed in his fiction. Oliveira Martins eventually became a government minister and was instrumental in Eça's consular appointment to Paris in 1888.

Another new member of the Cennacle was Ramalho Ortigão. By 1870 Ramalho had established himself as a respected journalist in Oporto; he was then appointed to the directorship of the Lisbon Academy of Sciences. Under pressure from Eça, the modest Ramalho also joined the Cennacle. The group was quietly mounting a national assault against the romantic tradition's iron hold on Portuguese culture. Eça and Ramalho fired the opening shots with the publication of a parody of the then very popular genre of romantic mystery novels à la Eugène Sue, written in an epistolary form—*O mistério da estrada de Sintra* (The Mystery of Sintra Road, 1870). This collaborative effort was serialized as though it were the ongoing narration of an actual crime; it stirred much public interest and then, when the literary fraud was admitted, resentment against its perpetrators. The novel (one of whose characters is Fradique Mendes) was published in volume form with revisions in 1884; it is relevant to Eça's artistic evolution, especially with regard to plot elements (mysterious births, adultery, femmes fatales [usually Spanish prostitutes named Carmen or Lola], life in Lisbon's high society), structural features (multiple points of view, technique of characterization), and the realist/naturalist concern with preponderant graphic detail.

Eça was preparing for the diplomatic corps examination at the same time he was engaged in this literary fraud. As a prerequisite for his new career, and through the intervention of a family friend, Eça was appointed administrator of the township of Leiria, north of Lisbon. His return to the countryside was different from the Evora experience. He immersed himself in Portuguese rural life, apparently taking copious notes about customs, human types, and scandals. These observations may have been useful for planning his novels *O crime do Padre Amaro* (*The Sin of Father Amaro,* 1876) and *O primo Basílio* (*Cousin Bazilio,* 1878), which are believed to have been outlined at this time. Although Eça placed first in the diplomatic corps examination of 1870, hostile political forces delayed his appointment until 1872.

During his ten-month administration of Leiria, Eça made frequent trips to Lisbon and remained in the thick of things. Along with Ramalho, once again, he published a series of newspaper articles called *Farpas* (Darts, 1871–1872); these articles attacked the backward social status of Portugal and satirized cultural pretensions. The goal of the writers was to demythify the ''glorious'' traditions of Portuguese life by obliging their compatriots ''a ver verdadeiro''—to see things truthfully. Eça's contributions, collected in *Uma campanha alegre* (A Happy Campaign, 1890), reveal thematic concerns that dominate his fiction over the next twenty years. In the initial Dart, he clamors:

> The Nation has lost its mind and moral awareness. Our customs are vanishing. . . . No one respects anyone else. . . . The people live in misery. . . . This is not an existence, rather it is an expiation. And the certainty of our outcast state has invaded all consciences. Everywhere you hear: ''The Nation is at an end.'' No one has any illusions. And what happens? In conversations and while playing cards, everyone—from North to South—agrees: the Nation's economy, moral and State functions are disorganized—and all they ask for is more brandy!
>
> (1.11–12)

Questions of religious life, education (particularly that given, or more exactly not given, to women), general corruption, and literature are dealt with in a similarly vivid style. It is a style that breaks with traditional, fixed rules of Portuguese syntax and relies on popular speech and scornful satire, which in some instances turned out to be prophetic:

> Why do we have colonies? Boy, we won't have them for long. Pretty soon they'll be appropriated for their usefulness. Europe will think that those immense territories should not be perpetually removed from the movement of civilization just because, lamentably, they belong to Portugal; and by taking them away from our national inertia, they will conquer them for the progress of the universe. We have them chained in our private prison of misery. Europe will soon think about taking them. To avoid that day of humiliation, let's be low-class Shylocks, as befits a nineteenth-century nation—let's sell the colonies!
>
> (1.141)

In 1890, when England seized part of Portugal's African territories, few people remembered Eça's 1871 Dart.

Meanwhile, under the aegis of Antero, the Cennacle continued its cultural revolt. Portugal, Antero proclaimed at every opportunity, was a nation in the backwater of European culture and life. Only drastic measures would assure that it would take its place within the mainstream of nineteenth-century historical development. Conferences on the status of Portuguese culture at the Lisbon Casino in May and June 1871 were organized to bring attention to the national malaise; the ''bom senso e bom gosto'' polemic of 1865 had been nothing more than a mild prelude to the extreme Democratic Conferences of 1871.

Antero led off the Democratic Conferences on 27 May 1871, summarizing their aim: ''Portugal must awake to the new currents shaking all societies.'' A week later Antero delivered the first lecture, entitled ''As causas de decadência dos povos peninsulares'' (The Causes of the Decadence of the Peninsular Peoples), which, on publication, was a crucially influential statement on the future of Iberia for all peninsular intellectuals. Antero pointed out that Spain and Portugal had both fallen into disgrace owing first to the religious tenets of the Council of Trent and the church's entry into secular affairs; second to absolutism, whose aristocratic base was maintained at the expense of the paralysis of the rest of society; and third to the sixteenth-century Portuguese explorations, which were an economic disaster from which the country had never recovered:

> Under the influence of the Catholic spirit, the truths discovered by free thought have continued to be ignored. Owing to so many years of absolutism, there are still gentlemen—the influential aristocrats. Since the explorations, people have looked for easy government jobs (as they previously looked for royal pensions) to free themselves from having to work.
>
> (Antero de Quental, *Prosas sócio-politicas,* p. 269)

He offered a revised conception of Portuguese life, calling for "pacific action" to bring the nation into the nineteenth century: "Revolution," he concluded, "is nothing more than the Christianity of the modern world" (p. 296). The third lecture, "Literatura portuguesa," was given by another Cennacle member, Augusto Soromenho, who denied the existence of a Portuguese literature per se; he stated that the press was incapable of publishing honest criticism and preferred to dwell on scandals.

Soromenho's theme was echoed by Eça in a more critical, although probably more improvised, manner in his speech of 12 June, entitled "O realismo como nova expressão da arte" (Realism as a New Expression of Art). Still seeking a social definition of his literary aims derived from his readings of Flaubert, Taine, and Proudhon, Eça declared that realism must be of its own time and draw its material from contemporary life; and that realism must be based on experience, "on the physiology and the science of temperament and characters." Examples of his understanding of "artistic realism" were taken from the plastic arts—the works of Gustave Courbet—and from Flaubert's *Madame Bovary.*

Eça's speech, known to us only through newspaper accounts, set the romantic literary establishment on its ears. Not only had Eça attacked their literature for its content, but he had also censured their verbose, swollen prose. In particular, Manuel Joaquim Pinheiro Chagas, who had participated in the 1865 polemic over literature, rebutted Eça's theories of fiction and denied the possibility of any positive moral value in the direct presentation of characters' psychology. This was the first of many polemics in which the two men would engage over the next quarter-century. Eça always treated the ultrachauvinistic Pinheiro Chagas with respect, but in arguing with him he moderated his tendency to carry legitimate arguments to absurd lengths.

Yet another lecture of the Democratic Conferences took place several days later. Adolfo Coelho commented on the deplorable state of the Portuguese educational system. Echoing Antero, he placed blame on the church, which he alleged was so conservative it prevented the nation's scientific development. The sixth lecture, at which the Orientalist Salamão Sarragá intended to speak on "Os historiadores de Jesús" (The Historians of Jesus), was prohibited by the government. The secretary of state banned any further meetings. The political climate wrought by the conferences, along with the conservative national reaction to the Paris Commune, suggests that they achieved their aim. Protests against the arbitrary closing of the meetings, which cited the abrogation of free speech guaranteed by the Portuguese liberal constitution, appeared in several newspapers and were the topic of several official letters signed by Antero, Batalha Reis, and Eça to various government ministers.

The high-pitched enthusiasm of the Democratic Conferences simmered down with the beginning of summer, and by late 1871 many Cennacle members had left Lisbon. Antero, however, kept busy organizing and writing. Articles from his pen on the First Socialist International, socialism in action, and class struggle appeared in the Portuguese socialist journal *O pensamento social* in 1872 and 1873. During these years Oliveira Martins also wrote and published his *Portugal e o soci-*

alismo (Portugal and Socialism). Eça continued his biting, jocular attacks on Portuguese life through the Darts. Unsettled by the stalemate in his diplomatic career, he commented on the situation in one article and soon his appointment as consul in Havana, Cuba, was announced. He assumed the office in December 1872.

This first professional post left Eça somewhat emotionally and culturally displaced. In a letter of 1873 to Ramalho, he commented on how much he missed Europe:

> Life here—owing to either its unpleasant Spanish manner or to its strange North American character—is quite different from what I need. I need politics, criticism, literary corruption, humor, style, color, and a palette; here, I am stuck in a hotel, and when I have discussions, they are about exchange rates—and when I think, it's about "coolies."

These coolies were Portuguese Chinese who had emigrated to Cuba from the colony of Macao to work on plantations. Manipulations of the contractual system by rich plantation owners had virtually converted their status into that of slaves. Eça, reflecting the Cennacle's concerns with social justice, was horrified, and he took to his pen to register an official protest with the local authorities and to outline the problem to the Lisbon government. Neither effort met with much success.

Eça's stay in the New World included an official visit to North America to examine the conditions of Portuguese emigrants. Montreal, Chicago, New Orleans, the factories of Pennsylvania were on his itinerary. Many of his personal impressions have been lost, but a letter to Ramalho about New York remains; it indicates that he was both attracted to and repelled by the city. Eça concluded that America was just too large for brief study and observation.

He did not remain long in Havana after returning. In March 1874, Eça was recalled to

Lisbon for reassignment. Between March and November he prepared his official report on the status of Portuguese emigrants to the New World, *A emigração como força civilizadora* (Emigration as a Civilizing Force), which remained unknown until 1979. In that report, he presents a general overview of emigration as a phenomenon of the 1870's. He discusses emigration within Europe, from the Old World to the New, and from Africa and Asia to the Americas, with statistical breakdowns and analyses. It is a document that his Cennacle colleagues might well have admired if they had read it, because Eça astutely evaluates the sociopolitical and economic roots of emigration and its effects on the individual:

> For the proletariat, emigration is the natural solution for misery; for the State, it is the remedy to poverty. There are few European governments that have not taken advantage of emigration as an indirect but effective remedy for the density of population, the growth of poverty or industrial crises. This use of emigration, in my opinion, is inefficient, useless, and antipolitical: emigration does not diminish the population, it does not resolve difficulties, and only very indirectly does it alleviate poverty.... Emigration in the nineteenth century has yet another distinguishing feature: it occurs on an individual basis and it is lonely. The emigrant leaves, either alone or with his family, at his own expense, with his own possessions, without prior contracts or people to depend on; he is free, "self-acting," and he appears in the colonial world isolated or with his only support being his strength and desire.
>
> (p. 35)

Although Eça had stopped collaborating on the Darts in 1872, he did not neglect purely literary activities while in Havana. In late 1873, the inaugural work of his new literary phase appeared, the short story "Singularidades duma rapariga loura" ("Peculiarities of a Fair-Haired Girl," 1873). The tale deals with a then shocking theme—kleptomania. His presentation of the heroine attests to the importance he attached to psychological detail in characterization:

> Luisa's temperament was very odd. Her character was pale like her hair—if one can say that yellow-blond is a weak and faded color. She spoke little, was constantly smiling with her little white teeth, and said, "But yes" to everything; she was quite simple, almost unconcerned, and very compliant. She certainly loved Macario but only with such love as her weak, watered-down, null personality could muster. She was like a sheaf of flax bending with every breeze.
>
> (*The Mandarin and Other Stories*, p. 114)

The story echoes previous works and anticipates future themes and methods of characterization. Eça had also been at work, probably since 1871, on the first version of his first novel, *The Sin of Father Amaro*. While in Lisbon, he gave it to Antero and Batalha Reis for inclusion in their new magazine, *Revista ocidental*.

Eça was off to England in November 1874 and arrived at Newcastle-on-Tyne to assume his consular duties in December. There he began an intensive study of English language and literature. Although he had probably known Shakespeare ("a semi-god") through French translation, he expressed in letters to Ramalho his renewed admiration for Shakespeare's creations, as well as his new fascination with English life as presented by William Makepeace Thackeray ("another semi-god") and Charles Dickens' ("a god and a half, the divine Dickens who wrote *David Copperfield*") technique of psychological characterization. Readers of Eça's novels can notice their influence.

Little is known about his personal and social existence during these years in England; bits of information are found in his correspondence. Eça provided the Portuguese government with another astute official report, "Comércio e indústria no norte da Inglaterra, 1874–1875" (Commerce and Industry in the North of England, 1874–1875), in which he outlines the development of the British steel, chemical, and shipping industries and their significance for the Portuguese, European, and world economies. The years 1875–1880, however, appear to have been the most consequential for his overall literary development. Not only did Eça publish three versions of one novel as well as two other novels, but he also planned a series of fictional works to which he devoted the following decades.

Eça was unpleasantly surprised when he was presented with the version of *The Sin of Father Amaro* he had left with Antero and Batalha Reis for "editing." The time he had spent correcting galleys, rewriting, and adding new chapters had been in vain. Antero had "pruned" the "original draft" of "improper material"—he considered certain sections pornographic—and published it as he saw fit. Eça complained to Ramalho that Antero "knows as much about art as I do about mechanics," and he telegraphed Batalha Reis and Antero to halt further publication—alas, too late. Aggrieved that his art had been "sacrificed," he wrote and published a "transmogrified" version of *The Sin of Father Amaro* in 1876; the publication costs were paid by his father. This version was initially ignored by Portuguese critics, perhaps owing to the graphic narration of the evil deeds of a priest-seducer and the related description of the decline of the Portuguese church, both considered improper subjects in Roman Catholic Portugal. In 1878, however, on the appearance of the novel *Cousin Bazilio*, which deals with the sexual degradation of a middle-class Portuguese woman, a criticism of the two novels was written by the distinguished Brazilian novelist Machado de Assis (1839–1908). This criticism perhaps caused Eça to write yet a third version of *The Sin of Father Amaro* (1880), which is the basis for today's edition. Eça wrote a defense of his two novels, which was intended as a preface to the 1880 version but appeared posthumously as a separate essay entitled "Idealismo e realismo" (Idealism and Realism).

By early 1878 Eça had conceived a Balzacian series of novels to be called "Scenes of Portuguese Life," and he described them to his friends and publisher, as in this letter of 12 March 1878 to Braga:

> My ambition would be to portray Portuguese society just as Constitutionalism since 1830 has made it; I want to show the sad country in a mirror image. That is the aim of the "Scenes of Portuguese Life." It's necessary to prick the official world, the sentimental, the literary and the agricultural worlds, and, with due respect, it's necessary to destroy the "false interpretation and fake achievements" that a rotten society attaches to the "eternal institutions."

Eça wrote two novels of the projected series in 1878 and 1879: *A capital* (The Capital City) and *O conde de Abranhos* (The Count of Abranhos); both remained unfinished at the time of his death and were published by his son in 1925. Owing to the financial difficulties that followed Eça throughout his adult life, he began to contribute articles on English life, attitudes, and important personalities to Portuguese and Brazilian newspapers. These articles were collected in *Cartas de Inglaterra* (*Letters from England*, 1905) and *Crónicas de Londres* (Tales from London, 1944). His financial straits became so dire that on appointment as Portuguese consul in Bristol, his debts prevented him from leaving Newcastle and his creditors. "Debts," he wrote to Ramalho on 8 April 1878, "they say, served to excite the genius of Dickens and Balzac; not finding any genius in me to excite . . . they torture me." In yet another letter to Ramalho on 10 November 1878, he described his intention to "ask" for a bribe from the Portuguese government for him not to publish a "scandalous novel," *A batalha de Caia* (The Battle of Caia), about Portuguese high society and corrupt politics; that novel (which was never finished or published) represented "capital" to him. Ramalho, taken aback when asked to be the bagman, advised Eça to secure an advance on his salary from the ministry. Eça followed Ramalho's counsel.

In 1880 Eça published *O mandarim (The Mandarin)*, a short novel and his first "flight from realism." Eça here compares exotic China with bourgeois Portugal, describing a bureaucrat (like himself), in search of a better life. Late that year and into 1881, Eça was involved in a polemic with Pinheiro Chagas (whom Eça had nicknamed "the fatal man" because at various points in Eça's life Chagas seemed to show up to severely criticize him) over the state of the Portuguese nation. Chagas had defended romanticism in the 1865 Coimbra question polemic and had questioned the literary value of Eça's theory of fiction during the period of the Casino lectures in 1871. In 1880 he wrote several articles about one of Eça's contributions to the Rio *Gazeta de notícias*. Eça had made several illuminating remarks on the relation of Portugal to Brazil, which he described as faltering. Indeed, by this time Eça had publicly adopted a very cynical attitude about Portuguese culture. He had come to realize, as had Antero and Oliveira Martins, that the weight of the past had taken its toll on the nation and had left it a withered shell. Chagas found these comments to be "injurious to Portugal," and wrote a verbose defense of the country's achievements. Eça reacted by showing up Chagas and his arguments as pompous and hollow, writing in the jocular tone that characterized all of Eça's exchanges with the platitudinous poet.

Intermittent but lengthy sojourns in Portugal and briefer ones in France, bad health, and financial difficulties marked his existence during the first part of the 1880's. Although he disliked the English climate, Eça sincerely admired English writers and intellectuals. Letters to Ramalho and others from this period detail his problems with Portuguese publishers and the pirated editions of his works then appearing in Brazil. He was much preoccupied with *Os Maias (The Maias*, which appeared in book form only in 1888). Eça was worried about the length of this novel concerning the decadence of the Portuguese upper classes and wrote Oliveira Martins on 10 May 1884: "It is a vast *machine* of boringly monumental paintings *al fresco,* which are worked in all shades of gray, pompous and vain, which will earn me the name Michelangelo of absurdities." In 1883 Eça was made a corresponding member of the Lisbon Academy of Sciences. In 1884 he became acquainted with Emilia Resende, the sister of his friend the count of Resende. He married her in 1886.

During a brief visit to Paris in 1885, Eça was introduced to Émile Zola. Although Eça admired Zola's fiction and had himself been called (principally by his literary detractors) the Portuguese Zola, it is most improbable that Zola had ever read Eça's novels. Victor Hugo's death in 1885 genuinely saddened Eça; he had often expressed his admiration for Hugo. Literary projects filled his free, nonofficial time. One of these was a collection of Fradique Mendes' letters (purportedly discovered by Eça) to intellectuals, family, and lovers. Although the dilettante Francophile had been engaged on a serious work, the *Teoria da vontade* (Theory of the Will), for many years, he was no less absorbed by more mundane topics. After describing his sensation of national pride whenever he speaks a foreign language badly, he relates his aunt's method of breaking linguistic barriers when traveling abroad:

> I had an admirable aunt who spoke only Portuguese (or rather Portuguese of the northern Minho province) and she traveled throughout all of Europe in ease and comfort. This smiling but dyspeptic lady ate only eggs—which she knew and understood only in the national and vernacular name, "ovos." For her *eggs, huevos, oeufs, das ei,* were sounds of a brutal nature, only slightly different from the croaking of frogs or of wood being split. Well, whenever she went to Berlin, Paris, or Moscow and wanted her eggs— this expeditious lady demanded to see the hotel waiter, stared at him with her explicative, sharp eyes, squatted on the rug, imitated with her skirts a chicken laying an egg, and yelled: qui-qui-ri-qui! có-có-ri-qui! có-ró-có-có! Never in any city of intelligence in the world did my aunt fail to eat her eggs—and extremely fresh ones at that!
>
> (*A correspondência de Fradique Mendes,* p. 157)

At the same time, the mid-1880's, Eça began to plan a literary magazine, the *Revista de Portugal.* He was also working on another "work of fantasy," *A relíquia* (*The Relic,* 1887). The tale is set partly in Jerusalem, "my Jerusalem, not of Jesus, as devotion would require, not of Tiberius, as history would ask, because it really belongs to me, being a product of my imagination. History will always be a great fantasy" (from a letter to Luis de Magalhães on 2 July 1887). Eça submitted *The Relic* for a substantial literary prize offered by the Lisbon Academy of Sciences. Although he had no illusions about winning, he hoped "to get a laugh out of the reaction of the Academy members" (from a letter to Ramalho on 14 June 1887). He did indeed fail to win the prize, instead becoming involved in yet another controversy with the "fatal man," Pinheiro Chagas.

Eça's interest in religious themes resulted in several posthumously published hagiographical works written in the 1890's: *Dicionário de milagres* (Dictionary of Miracles, 1900) and *Lendas de Santos* (Legends of Saints, 1912). The latter work narrates the lives of Saint Christopher and Saint Humphrey, in addition to that of a popular Portuguese saint, Friar Gil. Gil is enticed into a pact with the devil to investigate the "black arts" and other realms of knowledge not accessible to ordinary mortals. He finally repents and redeems himself, achieving sainthood through caring for children, the impoverished, and the infirm.

In 1888 *The Maias,* the "vast *machine*" considered to be Eça's masterpiece, was published and resulted in another debate with

Pinheiro Chagas and the "offended parties," over the questions of characterization and caricature. In this same year the first of Eça's four children was born and he realized one of his chief ambitions—a posting to Paris as Portuguese consul. When Eça heard of the impending removal of the resident consul, he immediately wrote to Oliveira Martins (who was by then a minor government minister) to request his aid in securing the appointment. Eça "modestly" described the value to the Portuguese government of his presence in Paris, a city where "decisions are made more on the basis of cultural contacts than on political ones." He took up residence in Paris in November 1888.

In 1889 Eça was busy supervising every detail of the organization of the *Revista de Portugal:* subscribers, contributions, and daily editorial operations. He also became a corresponding member of the group called "Vencidos da vida" (conquered by life), a circle of Portuguese intellectuals and aristocrats whose life-style and opinions were attuned to progressive Europe rather than conservative Portugal. The group suffered jointly through a disastrous moment of contemporary Portuguese history—the English ultimatum of January 1890. In brief, the English demanded that the Portuguese vacate and cede all their territory in Africa between Angola and Mozambique for the construction of Cecil Rhodes's Cape-to-Cairo railroad. Confronted by English power and the threat of impending invasion, the Portuguese had no option but to endure this assault on their honor and empire: they capitulated to English demands. The national outcry against the English was as fierce as might be expected. In a letter to Oliveira Martins, the Anglo-Portuguese conflict is described by Eça as a "moment like no other, when modern Portugal [is] awake and attentive" to its fate. The humiliation had forced the nation to "see itself as it was in 1890," and Eça believed that this crisis presented a favorable opportunity to usher in a new future. Antero and Oliveira Martins, he thought, could be the necessary

spiritual guides for a reformed Portugal. For his part, he expressed a poignant desire to return to his "homeland," but, unless a suitable (financially rewarding) post could be found for him in government, he would have to remain in Paris.

Neither Antero nor Oliveira Martins was in a position to be the spiritual leader of a new Portugal. Antero, who had spent many years as an ardent socialist organizer and supporter of republican causes, assumed the leadership of the militant Northern Patriotic League that had been formed to fight the British. He soon left it, ill and demoralized, and returned to his native Azores. Increasing physical debility and mental anguish over the growing insanity of his ward (the daughter of a deceased friend) caused him to take his own life on 11 September 1891. By 1890 Oliveira Martins was not only Portugal's most eminent social historian and economist, but also a politician with some influence. He had withdrawn from active socialist organizing in the mid-1880's. The nation's inability to institute the reforms he recommended and its overall emotional and economic depression following the ultimatum disheartened him greatly. But as bankruptcy approached in 1892, he was named minister of the Treasury. After the immediate crisis subsided, he was forced to resign because of establishment fears over his "radical socialist doctrines." Demoralized by what he considered his personal failure, he withdrew completely from public life. He dedicated his last years to fiction and died of tuberculosis in 1894.

The deaths of both Antero and Oliveira Martins were deeply felt by Eça. In 1896 he wrote an admiring tribute to Antero. His free time was spent writing and enjoying the company of his beloved wife and children. His home in Neuilly became a center for visiting Portuguese and Brazilian writers, artists, politicians, and intellectuals, as well as a dyed-in-the-wool dandy, the Brazilian Eduardo Prado. Owing perhaps to a chronic stomach ailment, Eça did not take his place in French society; he came, rather, to consider himself a "petit bourgeois retiré." Summer vacations and other trips to Portugal kept him in contact with the national political and cultural situation—and his roots. There were other attempts at launching literary magazines—the *Revista de Portugal* had failed in 1892, according to Eça, owing to its "high intellectual tastes," which did not find an audience. In 1895 Eça published a first version of his paean to Portuguese life, *A cidade e as serras*, which appeared in modified book form posthumously (*The City and the Mountains*, 1901). Between 1897 and 1899 he published *A ilustre casa de Ramires* (*The Illustrious House of Ramires*, 1900) in installments in a Portuguese review published in Paris, *Revista moderna*. This novel contains reflections on Portugal's response to the English ultimatum and the heavy weight of the nation's past on its present. In a letter of the time, Eça wonders if his joint career as diplomat and novelist was misguided; he takes himself to task for his extended absences from Portugal and his lack of success as a writer and says that he might have been happier as a grocer.

As he had done while in England, in 1893 Eça began to publish in both Portugal and Brazil a series of short articles on French and European life. In addition to specific French topics—statesmen; a tribute to his esteemed Flaubert; Parisian living habits; student rebellions—he dealt with general political topics, such as the Monroe Doctrine, and with pseudoscientific questions, such as "Climate and Culture." These pieces were collected in *Ecos de Paris* (Echoes from Paris, 1905) and *Cartas familiares e bilhetes de Paris* (Family Letters and Parisian Notes, 1907). He also considered a visit to Brazil, where he was well known. Eduardo Prado urged his appointment as Portuguese ambassador to Brazil; but the project was abandoned because of Eça's health, his family situation, and political conflicts that might have developed over his nomination. Eça, his family, and his friends participated vicariously in the Spanish-American War, fa-

voring their peninsular brothers, as well as in the Dreyfus affair.

Indeed, the scandal surrounding the case against Captain Dreyfus shattered Eça's idyllic view of the society that had fostered the European enlightenment. This massive disillusionment with France contributed to Eça's writing what is probably the first Portuguese statement on the question of cultural dependency, "O francesismo" (Francophilia, 1899). From the beginning of his career Eça had been categorized as an "afrancesado," a Frenchified writer; indeed, this is one of the recurrent themes of contemporary critiques of his works. In this article he offers his own life, education, and professional and political development as an instructive example of why Portugal had become "a nation translated into French." Although the exact origin of French influence in Portugal eludes him, Eça tells us:

> I and my generation (with the exception of Antero and Oliveira Martins) had become fatally Frenchified in the midst of a society that was becoming Frenchified and which, in all its functions and individual tastes, had broken with national traditions, eliminating Portuguese dress to adorn itself—in thought, legislation, writing, teaching, living, cooking—with materials arriving from France.

Succumbing to this overwhelming influence, the Portuguese remained ignorant of English, German, and even Spanish culture. He analyzes the temperamental, cultural, and literary differences between the French and the Portuguese and refers to what he considers the decadence of the French novel and poetry, which lacks "soul." The serio-comic nature of the initial part of the essay gives way to a more general attack on French culture. Eça sees himself as having come full circle—from the adoration to the derision of France. Consequently, he arrived at a sharper understanding of the positive values of his homeland.

The year 1900 was full of sadness and illness for the Eça de Queiroz family. Eça's eldest son became very ill, although he eventually recovered, while Eça himself went to Zurich for treatment of his unabating stomach ailment. His condition worsened rapidly and he returned to Paris, where he died on 11 August 1900. His body was returned to Portugal in September, and he was interred in Lisbon's Alto de São João Cemetery.

II

Eça was a slow, delicate writer who constantly reworked and rewrote his fiction; he admitted to being preoccupied with "perfection." Thus, his fictional production is limited to seven completed novels published during his lifetime and some half-dozen uncompleted works that have appeared posthumously, as edited by his children and Eça scholars. As recently as 1979 and 1980 two different versions of a manuscript that Eça had rejected for publication, *A tragédia da Rua das Flores* (The Tragedy of Flores Street), were published.

In the course of his novels, Eça vividly dissects a society lost in past centuries, oblivious to contemporary ideas, whether political, social, or cultural. Initially he censured Portugal's backwardness in thesis novels; these are informed by a confused infusion of the social theories of Proudhon, the religious doctrines of Ernest Renan, and the literary aims of Flaubert. As he discovered and affirmed his own literary persona, these influences became less obtrusive and determinative.

Several thematic and technical interests recur in Eça's voyage from naturalism and realism to a unique personal style independent of literary schools and their conventions. His parentless childhood is often suggested through numerous characters in odd family situations—orphans, wards, widowers, individuals without family—and through the theme of incest. Further, Eça's "presence" in the attributes of his novels' characters appears to be an attempt to examine and resolve the extremes of his own personality: the spirit of a romantic dandy in the mind of a practical realist. Finally, his concern with national identity led him repeatedly to examine Portugal's traditional components: rural life, the Roman Catholic tradition, and the national preoccupation with and glorification of the past.

The depth of the stylistic and thematic revolution effected by Eça on Portuguese fiction can be appreciated through a brief overview of the novel in Portugal prior to his 1871 Casino lecture. The chief influence on narrative style was the historical novel. There was an incipient interest in more realistic aspects of Portuguese life (descriptions of customs, festivities, and types), but only within the romantic context of reaffirmation of national identity. Almeida Garrett's *Viagens na minha terra* (Travels Through My Land) was the most exceptional prose work of the 1840's. It departed from the limited thematic and linguistic norms of the time and presented characters who speak in the contemporary popular idiom. These "realistic concerns" were consequential for the development of Eça's own prose. Inspired by the works of Sir Walter Scott, Garrett had also launched the increasingly popular historical novel. This tradition was carried on by Alexandre Herculano and many secondary writers. Herculano, who was then and is still considered today a major historian of Portugal, also wrote short and long fiction about figures and events drawn from the period of the founding of the nation. His story "O Pároco da Aldeia" (The Village Priest, 1851) is a romantic-realist narrative that recounts a sentimental drama set in a realistic background—contemporary rural Portugal. The subject of the activities of a village priest would be adopted by many contemporaries and successors.

The most popular writer in all Portuguese history was Camilo Castelo Branco. According to his biographers, Camilo's life was the stuff of a novel itself: he was involved in political warfare, adulterous relationships, kidnappings, and other adventures. He wrote *Amor de Perdição* (A Love of Perdition, 1862), a novel of passion; it has been the most cherished and widely read work of all Portuguese fiction. Camilo also wrote mystery fiction (à la Eugène Sue) and, when naturalism became fashionable in Portugal, he produced two novels that he intended as parodies of the school, but that are considered among its masterpieces. The novelist who is recognized as the transitional figure between the romantic and realist movements is Júlio Dinis (1839–1871), pseudonym of Joaquim Guilherme Gomes Coelho. Although Dinis' first novel, *As Pupilas do Senhor Reitor* (The Priest's Wards, 1868) evokes Herculano's rural social scenes and the activities of village priests, his final three works reveal a marked interest, realistically expressed, in urban as well as rural life. His final novel, *Os Fidalgos da Casa Mourisca* (The Fidalgos of Casa Mourisca, 1871), advocates a Comtean positivist goal for the Portuguese countryside and nation.

The style of many of these writers (with the notable exception of the vivid, natural prose of Almeida Garrett and, to a certain extent, Júlio Dinis) consists principally of an infinite number of dependent clauses organized in verbose, paragraph-long sentences replete with archaisms. The author/narrator is omniscient. Characters are cardboard figures and are remarkably similar from one novel to the other.

Eça, who maintained basically good relations with the survivors of the elder generation of novelists—principally Camilo—recognized and resisted the romantic orientation of Portuguese fiction. In his Casino lecture of 1871, he had made his position clear. His first work of fiction, co-authored with Ramalho, *O mistério da estrada de Sintra*, and his first story, "Peculiarities of a Fair-Haired Girl," reflect this interest in realism, although they are given a specifically Portuguese flavor through the use of lively, contemporary language and characters who are plausible enough in context.

The publication of Eça's first major full-length novel was a veritable apprenticeship

for him. One critic noted that *The Sin of Father Amaro* was the only novel that Eça "carried in his womb," and its final delivery took some ten years and at least three different versions. It is understandable that Eça would prefer this novel above all his others, and would lament, even as late as the 1890's, the lack of critical attention it had received.

The events narrated in *The Sin of Father Amaro* are based on a situation that Eça had probably heard about during his Coimbra years. During his tenure as administrator of the village of Leiria, he had taken the opportunity to note minutia, idle rumors, and traits of rural life, all sufficient to whet his aroused social awareness of the underside of Portuguese life, and it was probably during his stay in Havana that he set down the first version.

A brief comparison of the three versions—the first (1875), the "definitive" (1876), and the final revised one (1880)—can provide us with an insight into Eça's approach to and development of this novel. The basic plot of *Father Amaro* does not vary in the three versions: a young priest, Amaro, seduces a country girl, Amelia; their child is given to an "angel maker"—a professional child nurse/murderer—and Amelia dies; the priest moves to another parish. The first version is some 136 pages long, the definitive edition 362 pages, while the "completely new, revised, and rewritten edition" of 1880 totals 674 pages. The almost fivefold increase in size reflects Eça's enrichment and embellishment of psychological and emotional details of characterization, development of plot, and greater attention to social issues.

The characterization of Amaro Vieira undergoes the greatest development. Amaro is an orphan—as Eça felt himself to be—favored by a rich benefactor. In the first version, although attracted to women, he is sexually innocent. He is held in check somewhat by his priestly obligations and fear of exposure:

> He had always been chaste. . . . At times, suddenly, in the early bloom of spring or at night

when he wrapped himself in his cape warming himself at the hearth, certain feelings overcame him from the depth of his being; they caused him to stretch his arms and think fixedly. But those demands of his nerves gradually dissipated. . . . Amaro was timid, fearful, and he had the scruples of a novice priest. He was a priest. Amelia would soon marry. He judged her inaccessible and almost confused her with inanimate things—with statues, lithographs, and varnished saints. But, if only! He would only want to kiss her on the soft whiteness of her neck, just one kiss. . . . But, soon, slowly, those sacred fears came upon him.

(1875 version, ch. 2)

In the final version, Amaro's childhood and seminary life are fully described. He is sexually experienced prior to his arrival in Leiria, and proves to be a calculating, perverse, and bad priest who rationally rejects any guilt for his seduction of Amelia:

Parading around the room, he thought about ways to humiliate her. What! Reject her like a bitch. He would gain influence in the religious society of Leiria . . . make it known that her mother was a prostitute. Bury her! Cover her with mud! . . . He would become ambitious, conspire to improve his position, and, protected by the Countess Ribamar, he would ascend in ecclesiastical ranks; and what would she think when she saw him as Bishop of Leiria? . . . What would she be then? A skinny, wilted being wrapped up in a cheap shawl. . . . And he, the Bishop, on the vast hierarchical stairway that rose to the heavens . . . and the priests of his parish would tremble whenever he creased his brow!

(ch. 13)

Amaro's moral decline is presented in graphic scenes that were censured at the time as blasphemous and pornographic.

The inserted tracts on rural decadence, the celibacy of priests, the immorality of the clergy, and the aimlessness of women's lives, for example, are developed from increasingly varied points of view and through different techniques in each version. For example, Eça's attack on the rural clergy is muted at first, but absolutely permeates the 1880 version. Aside from direct indictments of clerical habits (gluttony, lack of compassion for the poor and unfortunate), there is an implied social criticism in his descriptions of characters: Amelia, whose mother is a priest's mistress, lives in a home surrounded by *beatas*, fawningly fanatic religious women. She yields to Amaro's demands not only because of her innocence and lack of education, but principally because she is caught up in a pseudo-religious delirium that prevents her from distinguishing between morality and religious obligation. Every object around her enforces this confusion until she believes that submission to Amaro's sexual desires is her only sure way to heavenly grace:

She had abandoned herself to him completely, fully, in body, soul, will, and feelings; there was not the smallest hair on her skin or the smallest idea running through her head that did not belong to the Father. That possession of her complete being had not occurred gradually; it was complete from the moment his strong arms held her. It appeared that his kisses had sucked up and withdrawn her soul; she was now an inert dependency on his being. And she did not hide it from him. She delighted in humiliating herself before him, offering herself, feeling herself totally his, a slave; she wanted him to think for her and live for her; she happily unburdened herself on him those responsibilities that weighed upon her; her judgments now came already formed from the Father's mind as naturally as if his blood flowed from his heart into her veins. "Father wants or Father says" was a powerful enough reason for her. She lived with her eyes on him, in an animal's obedience. She need only kneel before him when he spoke or at the moment he began to open her dress.

(1880 version, ch. 17)

Only Father Ferrão (in the 1880 version), Amelia's confessor during her pregnancy, is shown to possess true Christian values. Characterization is thus immediately established as a key element of Eça's fictional process.

After he finished the 1876 version, Eça plunged into his most naturalistic work, *Cousin Bazilio*. Set in upper middle-class Lisbon society, *Cousin Bazilio* was probably written rather hurriedly in 1877. Luiza, a slightly educated woman, lolls about in a world of romantic fantasy and bourgeois complacency. She admires the lives of her "liberated" girlfriends, those who dare to scandalize their society. When her husband, Jorge, goes off on a business trip, she becomes involved in a passionate, degrading affair with her Don Juan-type cousin Bazilio, who has made his fortune in Brazil and is visiting provincial Lisbon from glamorous Paris. Luiza's maid, Juliana, suspects their involvement and discovers several discarded love letters from Luiza to Bazilio. Tempted by the prospect of power, not to mention vengeance for her life of servitude, she decides on blackmail. Luiza is forced to become her maid's slave and defend Juliana's aggressive, tyrannical behavior and demands before her uncomprehending acquaintances. After she is deserted by Bazilio, only Sebastião, her husband's best friend, can save Luiza from total degradation. Juliana dies of a fear-provoked stroke (as she sees Sebastião approach the house with a policeman), and Luiza succumbs to brain fever. As in *Father Amaro*, lurid sexual encounters are described in detail.

True evidence of a growing artistic technique is evident in Eça's marvelous description of Juliana's character and in his use of caricature. Juliana represents the burdened servant class, which blames its unfortunate status on the bourgeoisie it serves. She realizes she is not beautiful, but she does have "a pair of feet such as very few can claim":

> She had never had a lover and was a virgin. She had always been ugly, so no one had ever tempted her. Out of pride and dread of dismissal she had never offered herself as so many had done, either to an employer or a fellow servant.

> The only man who had ever looked on her with desire had been a stable groom, with a filthy, afflicted, and criminal appearance. Juliana's slimness and Sundayfied look had excited the brute who looked at her with the eyes of a bulldog. In Juliana he inspired a feeling of horror mixed with vanity. . . . She performed her duties; nobody could reproach her, and, as she had lost all hope of establishing herself on her own, she no longer subjected herself to the rigors of economy but permitted herself some gulps of wine and bought elegant bootees to satisfy her childish vanity.

> (ch. 3)

Through blackmail her personality acquires a new dimension, a commanding role in the novel:

> Juliana stood in front of her [Luiza] tapping her flat chest convulsively, and saying in a hoarse voice: "I will get out [of this house] . . . only if I wish to. Yes, if I wish to." "Joana," shrieked Luiza. "Joana!" She wished to call the cook, a policeman, a man, anybody! But Juliana stood before her with a terribly distorted face; and with her fist high up in the air, said in a trembling voice, "The Senhora must not make me lose my head! The Senhora must not set me beside myself! Pleasé!" and then in a strangled voice between her clenched teeth she said, "You see, not all those papers went down the drain." Luiza recoiled, and cried, "What's that you say?" "I say that the letters that the Senhora writes to her lover are in here," and she struck her little pocket with savage ferocity. Luiza stared at her for a moment, with distracted eyes, and then fell, with a crash, headlong, in a dead faint, beside the couch.

> (ch. 6)

The use of caricature, which is achieved through the comic exaggeration of physical qualities, became a standard technique of Eça's fiction. Here he produces the inimitable, much-respected Counselor Acácio, a representative of mid-century constitutionalism:

> He was tall, lanky, and dressed completely in black, with his neck squeezed into an upright

collar. His face with the sharply pointed chin rose widening to the bald brows, which were vast and shiny, though flattened on the top; he dyed the few hairs that from the bases of his ears formed a little collar round his nape, and the darkness of the dye by contrast gave more luster to his baldness. But he did not dye his moustache. It was gray, thick, and hung downward from the corners of his mouth. He was very pale. He never doffed his dark spectacles. He had a cleft in his chin and huge ears at right angles to his skull.

(ch. 2)

Finally, Acácio's conversations are punctuated by trite clichés uttered at every opportunity. The use of antithesis as a structural feature is repeatedly achieved in the novel by the indirect comparison of life and mores in Bazilio's Paris and Luiza's Lisbon.

Criticism of the 1876 version of *Father Amaro*, Eça complained to Ramalho, was slow to appear, whereas *Cousin Bazilio* was almost immediately recognized for its technical and thematic debts to Balzac and its overall salaciousness. In April 1878, Machado de Assis published a two-part critique of both novels in which he questioned Eça's approach to realism/naturalism; the essay was crucial to Eça's literary development. Machado found many merits in the books, but objected to two weaknesses. First was Eça's reliance on naturalist doctrine, in particular the graphic descriptions, which, in his opinion, went against Eça's ability and artistic aims; even more seriously in this vein Machado cited what he believed to be Eça's plagiarism of sections of Zola's *La faute de l'Abbé Mouret* (*The Sin of Father Mouret*, 1874). Machado's second objection dealt with the artificiality of the plot in *Cousin Bazilio*, specifically the device of the stolen letters, which he viewed as detrimental to the story:

Take away the theft of the letters, Jorge's house [upon his return] becomes a nook of paradise; without this chance circumstance the novel would end. But the substitution of the principal for the accessory, the actions transplanted from the characters and the feelings to the incident, the fortuitous, is what appeared incongruent and contrary to the laws of art.

(Alberto Machado de Rosa, *Eça*, p. 132)

Machado's criticism caused a small scandal and a brief polemic with Eça's literary supporters in Brazil; thus it was necessary for Machado to explain his position once again:

I repeat that the author of *Cousin Bazilio* has in me an admirer of his talents and an adversary of his doctrines. I hope to see him apply his capacities in a different manner. Although I indeed admire his stylistic abilities, I reject his language; his gift of observation is strong, yet complacent and, above all, superficial.

(p. 138)

Interestingly, Machado recognized in Eça's work what were, in fact, essential features of his own art—strong characterization, use of colloquial Portuguese, and irony. Although the two writers had no direct contact after this period, their artistic means would remain similar, though their aims were different. Eça's view of characterization was colored by a sociological/psychological purpose, while Machado de Assis sought a psychological/metaphysical angle; Eça used irony for comic relief, while in Machado's work it is a tool for enforcing his pessimism and preoccupation with the mysterious causes of human thought and action.

After Machado's criticisms appeared, Eça was said to be "bleeding on the inside." Nonetheless, he wrote a solicitous letter to Machado in late 1878, and, perhaps owing to the criticism, wrote yet another version ("completely revised and rewritten") of *Father Amaro*. How much Machado influenced this version is debated by Eça scholars. Where some critics see Machado's shadow, others see Eça's literary advancement. In addition, Eça wrote a self-serving defense of his novel as a preface to the 1880 version, but included only several paragraphs. It has survived in its entirety as the posthumous essay "Idealismo e realismo" (Idealism and Realism). In this essay Eça invokes his Casino lecture, citing his concern with observation and reality. He admits that the first version of *Father Amaro* demonstrated his lack of "observed knowledge" of Portuguese rural life but says that the later versions are faithful testimonies to it. With regard to the accusations of plagiarism, Eça, deceitfully according to modern critics, muddles his critics' arguments and accuses them of not having read Zola's work: "The coincidental similarity of the titles of the novels led them to this error. With knowledge of the two volumes, only poor eyesight or cynical bad faith could relate [Zola's] beautiful, idyllic allegory . . . to *The Sin of Father Amaro*." Eça denies leadership of a naturalist school in Portugal, and, through a comparison of romantic and realist fiction, he astutely defines his own contribution to the contemporary Portuguese novel—realistic characterization.

Father Amaro in its three versions, *Cousin Bazilio*, and the critical controversy they provoked all drained Eça emotionally and led him to reconsider his literary aims. In the important "A Letter That Should Have Been a Preface" to *The Mandarin* (1880), included with the tale since its fifth edition, Eça describes his "pointless" dedication to realism and his need as an artist to "fazer fantasia" (create fantasy):

> Thus, at least for a single small volume, one no longer accepts the inconvenient submission to truth, the torture of analysis, the impertinent tyranny of reality. One enjoys complete aesthetic liberty. . . . One can gild one's adjectives. One can make sentences march across the white page like processions advancing with cadenced steps among bouquets of roses, across sun-filled plazas; then, the last page written, the last proof corrected, one can leave the street, get back on the sidewalk, and resume the serious study of man and his eternal misery. Happy? No, my dear Sir—resigned.

The moral tale *The Mandarin* and the novel *The Relic* (1887) are two realizations of this creative need.

Fantasy for Eça was nonetheless still rooted in reality—in part his very own. Thus Teodoro, the protagonist of *The Mandarin* (nicknamed "The Jinx," because "I am skinny, I always enter rooms with the right foot, I am afraid of mice, I have at the head of my bed a lithograph of Our Lady of Sorrows that belonged to my mamma—and I am stoop-shouldered" [p. 10]), sounds a lot like Eça himself—a harassed bureaucrat living alone in a mediocre Lisbon pension surrounded by a critical landlady and several nosy, boring co-boarders:

> The humble life has its pleasures. . . . I was never excessively unhappy because I do not have much imagination. . . . I am a positivist. I longed only for the rational, the tangible, for that which had already been attained by others in my neighborhood, and for that which is accessible to Bachelors of Arts. And I lived in a state of resignation.
>
> (pp. 11–12)

He jumps at the chance to change his circumstances when he receives a Faustian offer. If he rings a particular bell, he will cause the death of a far-off mandarin and inherit the latter's wealth. Teodoro "touches the little bell" and soon comes into a windfall. Guilt over the murder of the mandarin is intensified by his nighttime images of the mandarin Ti-Chin-Fu and his parrot. The desire for atonement leads to a picaresque excursion to Peking and Mongolia to attempt to restore the mandarin's fortune to his family. Expiation is unsuccessful and Teodoro, near death, moralizes on his life:

> And now the world seems to me an immense mountain of ruins, in which my lonely soul, like an exile wandering among fallen columns, weeps endlessly. . . . And to you, Mankind, I leave only these words, without comment: Only

that bread tastes good that we earn each day with our own hands. Do not kill the Mandarin!

(p. 89)

No direct social or political themes are dealt with here. Eça seems satisfied with a vivid simplicity. The enhancement of artistic interests is nonetheless evident: a more effective use of antitheses of time and space (nineteenth-century Portugal/time-forgotten China); autobiographical characterization and voice; use of irony and sarcasm and comic relief; growing interest in the power of the adjective to make impressionistic suggestions; use of indirect speech to diminish authorial omniscience. The origin and development of the mandarin theme in Eça's fiction and Portuguese literature generally have been studied in depth by the critic António Coimbra Martins.

The Relic, first serialized in the Rio *Gazeta de notícias,* is yet another flight from "reality," and further consolidates many of Eça's artistic aims, in particular the use of spatial and chronological antitheses: hypocritical late-nineteenth-century Portuguese Catholicism is confronted with the mystical origins of Christianity. Ernesto Guerra DaCal, a major scholar of Eça's works, has linked this book to a broader Iberian literary tradition—the picaresque novel. He cites Eça's narrative techniques and his baudy satire as key elements in this tradition. When the English translation appeared in 1925, the *New York Sun* reviewer called it "the most delicious excursion into amorality written in modern literature."

Aside from the initial and final realistic parts, the central portion of this "triptych" is a dream/excursion by the protagonist, Teodorico Raposo, known to all as Raposão, to the origins of Christianity à la Eça de Queiroz—an "apocryphal New Testament" based on Eça's remembrances of Egypt and his positivistic religious beliefs. As a reward for his "piousness," the libertine Teodorico is sent by his sanctimonious aunt on a pilgrimage to the Holy Land. There, aside from engaging in a se-

ries of love affairs, he is beaten up for playing the peeping Tom, and, accompanied by his cicerone, Topsius, he suffers through a series of comic mishaps. His hopes for inheriting his aunt's estate are ultimately thwarted because Auntie discovers these peccadillos. Upon his return to Lisbon, his aunt opens her gift, which she believed to be the "crown of thorns" she had requested:

Auntie took the parcel, made obeisance to the saints, and placed it on the altar. Then devoutly she untied the knot of red string, and carefully, as one anxious not to injure a body which was divine, she undid one by one the folds of the brown paper. A whiteness of linen appeared. Auntie held it in her fingertips and suddenly shook it, and onto the altar, among the saints, over the camelias, at the foot of the cross fell in its ribands and laces Mary's nightdress. Mary's nightdress! In all its shameless luxury, fold on fold. And pinned upon it, clear in the light of the candles, was the paper offering it to me in a round hand: "To my Theodorico, my valiant little Portuguese, in memory of our past joy." Two initials signed it: M.M. I scarcely know what happened in the flowered oratory. I found myself all in a swoon in the green curtain, with my legs hanging down.

(p. 265)

The moral tone of the novel is highlighted through the comic element; the latter increasingly becomes an essential feature of Eça's fiction. The unceremonious, mocking treatment of religious history was a bone of contention between Eça and his critics.

Although Eça, in a letter to a friend who had praised *The Relic,* declared that the novel had a "defective structure and composition," he was nonetheless incensed when the Lisbon Academy of Sciences award was given to a work he considered "nonrevolutionary." Eça decided to lock horns with the critics and published a letter attacking the judges and their literary standards, especially their knowledge of contemporary literature. It was several months before any response appeared, and when it came it was from the pen of the "fatal man." Chagas had been physically assaulted in February 1888 and was "at death's door"; his response to Eça's charges appeared in June, the same month as the publication of *The Maias.* Chagas, one of the judges, accused Eça of inventing an imaginary plot against *The Relic* because he had not received the award. Eça was barely able to respond to this charge before yet another polemic began, this time over *The Maias.*

The thousand-page novel had appeared in two volumes, and in a letter to Oliveira Martins Eça suggested that the historian only glance through it rather than read it page by page. The polemic concerned questions of characterization and caricature. Fialho de Almeida, another important late-nineteenth-century Portuguese writer, had claimed that Eça's characters were merely types repeated from one novel to the next, while Pinheiro Chagas and Bulhão Pato, an ultraromantic poet, protested the caricature of the latter in the novel. Eça responded to all complaints in his usual satirical manner.

The Maias itself was part of the "Scenes of Portuguese Life" series, which had been planned in the late 1870's, and was the only novel of the series to be published in Eça's lifetime. Eça is quoted as having placed "everything he had in his bag" into this vast social portrait of late-nineteenth-century Portuguese life. This return to realism from fantasy deals with the Portuguese elite—no longer the rural folk, the clergy, or the urban bourgeoisie. The sympathetic yet negative view of upper-class society is again achieved through finely interwoven plots, characterizations, caricatures, and satire, all of which reflect Eça's dismay with the condition of his nation. The obligatory sex scenes and plodding details of the earlier realist novels are absent.

The story develops through two intertwining yet distinctive plots: the incestuous love affair between Carlos da Maia and his sister, a kinship unknown to either of them; and life in Lisbon's decadent high society. The patriarch of the Maia family is Afonso da Maia, a distinguished retired diplomat who represents the best of "old Portugal." His grandson, Carlos, and the society he moves in are the opposite— bored and defeated. Although Carlos has been well trained "in the English tradition," he decides that his medical practice is really unimportant and prefers the life of a rich dandy. His defeat is related not only to his mental "ennui," but also to a "nebulous Portuguese condition":

> It was the Moslem fatalism: to fear nothing and to desire nothing. . . . Never to abandon oneself to a hope—or to a disappointment. To accept everything, whatever comes, whatever eludes you, with the tranquillity with which one accepts the natural changes of weather, the stormy days and the calm ones. And in this state of placidity, to let the scrap of material we call the ego gradually deteriorate and decompose until it reenters and loses itself in the infinite Universe. Above all, have no appetites. And more even than that, no vexations.
>
> (book 2, pp. 631–632)

A cast of equally defeated compatriots and resident foreigners surrounds Carlos. Among them are some of Eça's finest caricatures: the trite, ultraromantic poet Alencar; the Jewish banker; the perfectly correct Englishman:

> Ega threw up his hands. It was absolutely essential to know Craft! Craft was quite the best thing that existed in Portugal. "Isn't he English? Some kind of lunatic?" Ega shrugged. A lunatic! That was the general opinion in Rua dos Fanqueiros, for the native Lisboan in the presence of an originality as marked as Craft's could explain it only as madness. Craft was an extraordinary chap.
>
> (book 1, pp. 97–98)

There is even one of the moralizing voices of Eça himself, the caricature of João da Ega:

> "Well!" exclaimed Ega. "If there aren't any women we'll just have to import them. That's the answer to everything in Portugal. Everything

is imported in this country:... Everything reaches us in packing cases by the mail boat. Civilization costs us very dear by the time the Customs duty's paid. And then it's second-hand. It's not made for us and so it doesn't fit.''

(book 1, p. 99)

Not one of the characters triumphs; rather all are quite tragic failures.

Eça continues to cultivate brief moments of comic relief to reinforce the tragic atmosphere of the novel. For example, some ten years after the death of the venerable Afonso da Maia, owing to the disclosure of the "fatal sin" of incest, Carlos returns to Lisbon from Paris, where he lives in "exile," and decides to visit the family estate, Ramalhete. A "Greek family curse" hangs over the house, whose walls, according to tradition, "were always fatal to the Maias." As he, along with Ega, wanders through the rooms, a sort of melancholic fear sets in. Carlos reaches an excited emotional state and decides to take a last look at his grandfather's study. He forces the door open and suddenly bursts into uncontrollable fits of sneezing, owing not to the expected accumulation of dust, but rather to the mounds of white pepper the butler has piled on all the furniture to protect it.

The theme of incest in Eça's work merits note here. Not only is it central to this novel, but it is also developed in the relationship of Luiza and her cousin Bazilio, and, metaphorically, in the situation of Father Amaro and Amelia; and it appears in the posthumously published *A tragédia da Rua das Flores*, which Eça's family had long suppressed. The origin of the theme has been attributed to Eça's reading of classical literature (Sophocles, Shakespeare) or to contemporary opera (Verdi's *Don Carlo*, Wagner's *Die Walküre*). It has even been linked with Eça's fascination with the life of Lord Byron.

Gonçalo Mendes Ramires, the protagonist of *The Illustrious House of Ramires*, is, like Carlos da Maia, a last scion of ancient Portuguese nobility, and also like Carlos, suffers

from the "ennui" of existence. He lacks the moral energy to do anything whatsoever with his life—even to marry and father a child to carry on the Ramires line ("When the Ramireses die out, so does Portugal"). His life in the country is decadent and aimless. He is encouraged by his friend, the ultrachauvinist J. L. Castanheiro, to enter politics through literature: "Literature leads to everything in Portugal ... little by little you end up in Parliament." To achieve this goal, Gonçalo "adapts" an old epic poem about his heroic family as the basis for his own historical novel, which Eça admirably intertwines in the narration. Lamentably, he also manages to compromise his married sister's honor, "selling" her to André Cavaleiro, her one-time lover, for the price of votes to win the election. The result is a delightful tale in which contrasts of time, space, and characterization attain allegoric proportions as Eça shows the depths of decadence into which Portugal has irrevocably fallen.

Unlike his medieval ancestor Tructecindo Ramires, who valiantly fought against the Moors in the Portuguese reconquest of the Iberian peninsula, Gonçalo is a spineless coward. When confronted by peasants on his rural estates who taunt him, by enraged tenants, or by drunks whose loud voices and threats intimidate him, he flees with "his tail between his legs." Although the Ramires family was not always noble—it counts among its forebears proletarian butchers, assassins, and even horse thieves—its less illustrious members do not enter into the novel or into the family "fado" (a traditional song), written by one of Gonçalo's village acquaintances. Gonçalo is obsessed with the bravery of his "ancestral scarecrows." Eça highlights the depth of his cowardice through a vivid nightmare (dreams have already been effectively used to reveal the distressed states of Amaro, Amélia, and Luiza):

... the Nobleman of the Tower went to sleep. But his room filled with shadowy shapes and there began a dreadful, frightening night . . . it was the awesome dead Ramires from Vila Clara, his bones creaking within his armor, and King Don Afonso II, gnashing sharply pointed wolf's teeth, dragging him off to the Battle of Navas. He resisted, his heels wedged in the paving stones. . . . But Don Afonso gave him such a blow in the kidneys with his iron glove that it sent him from Gago's tavern to the battlefield in the Serra Morena, full of brilliance and excitement with pennants and arms. And immediately his Spanish cousin, Gomes Ramires, Master of Calatrava, bending over his black jennet, tore out the last of his hair to the resounding roars of laughter of all the Saracen host and the wailing of Aunt Louredo, borne there on a pallet on the shoulders of four kings! Finally . . . dawn appearing . . . the Nobleman of the Tower . . . jumped out of bed.

(pp. 43–44)

Eça develops his allegory of national decline through the characterization of Gonçalo and his ancestors, and the juxtaposition of medieval with nineteenth-century history. Once a great, fighting, conquering nation, in Gonçalo's time Portugal has been reduced to total impotence. The Portuguese "defeat" as a result of the English ultimatum of 1890 ("the sale of Lourenço Marques [Mozambique]") is a secondary theme. Gonçalo often jokes with family and friends that he might go off to Africa, which he finally does at the novel's conclusion. Perhaps Eça imagined some ironic quirk of fate at work through which the future of Portugal would be in Africa.

The novel Gonçalo writes about his ancestors is Eça's parody of the popular historical fiction genre, for which, Eça admits, he himself always had a weakness. Gonçalo is convinced that his novel *A Torre de Don Ramires* (The Tower of Don Ramires) will "save Portugal from foreign literature" because of its basis in "patriotism." Nonetheless, he avidly reads the works of Sir Walter Scott as well as those of Alexandre Herculano for inspiration and includes all the obligatory clichés—labyrinthine castles with dungeons, superhuman

heroes, and so forth. The ultrachauvinist J. L. Castanheiro is a compassionate caricature of Pinheiro Chagas, who had died several years earlier. Through Castanheiro's bombastic manner of speech Eça seems to evoke points of contention from their polemics over the Portuguese nation:

The fact is that the worst Portuguese despised their fatherland—and the best did not know it. The remedy? Make Portugal known, make it popular. Yes, dear friend! Organize, with great clamor, propaganda for Portugal, so that everyone should know it—at least as well as James's Chest Syrup is known, eh? Everyone must adopt it—at least as much as they'd adopted Congo soap. Known and adopted, everyone should love it, love its heroes and praiseworthy deeds, and its blameworthy ones too, in all its aspects, even its very paving stones.

(p. 13)

Although the novel ends on a sad note of national and personal failure, Eça lays bare some eternal Portuguese qualities: innocence, goodheartedness, nostalgia for a "missing" past (*saudades*), all structured around a good dollop of laziness ("Procrastinare lusitanium est").

To this list of Portuguese characteristics can be added the rural life, as is evident in *The City and the Mountains*, which was edited by Ramalho and published posthumously. (It had been sketched initially as the short story "Civilização" ["Civilization"].) The antithesis here is between ultramodern Paris and rural Portugal, also reflected in the contrast between the hypercivilized protagonist, Jacinto (perhaps modeled on Eça's Brazilian friend Eduardo Prado), and the detester of urban life Zé Fernandes. Jacinto is a rich, Frenchified dandy who rejects his nation's backwardness because he has heard so many rumors about it. He was born in Paris and has always resided there, in a small palace on the Avenue des Champs-Elysées, number 202. He is surrounded by wonderful works of art, some

30,000 to 50,000 books, and the latest inventions, ranging from electric lights to telephones. He flits from one social engagement to another and lives by a formula: "Absolute Knowledge × Absolute Power = Absolute Happiness." Thus he thrives until his gadgets begin to fail. Initially there are small defects, such as a power outage. But soon the complexities of modern technology become overwhelming. In one of the most comic scenes in fiction, Eça describes how an elegant dinner party given by Jacinto turns into a "fishing expedition" when the main dish—a steaming platter of Dalmatian fish—is trapped in the malfunctioning dumbwaiter. All attempts to rescue the fish are to no avail. Thus sets in Jacinto's final boredom with his supercivilization and his satiety with Parisian luxury:

> Then suddenly as if in revolt against this oppressive disgust, which was enslaving him, he would leap up with the fury of one who was breaking his fetters, and stand erect, darting a hard and imperative glare around him, as if insisting that this, his Number 202, which he had so lavishly crammed with Civilization, should at the very least, in return, even if it were only a moment, furnish him with some transitory interest or fugitive pleasure. But Number 202 remained insensible: not even one electric light intensified its even, dumb lustre to encourage him. Only the windowpanes trembled and rattled in the squalls of wind and rain.
>
> (p. 97)

Zé Fernandes suggests a visit to Jacinto's idyllic Portuguese estate, Tormes (modeled on Eça's wife's family home), for "recovery of the spirit." There, after a haphazard voyage, and much hesitation and complaint, Jacinto adapts to and delights in his newfound "simple" life—although he installs all the latest gadgets in his home. He marries, forgets Paris, and arrives at a new understanding of the word *civilization*. Zé Fernandes describes Jacinto's transformation:

> I definitely realized that Jacinto was a changed man and that a perfect balance had established itself at last in his soul. . . . Yes, that withered shoot from the city, transplanted to the mountains, had taken root and absorbed the rich earth of its ancestral home, growing in strength, its roots sunk deep into the earth, the trunk thickened and its branches burst into flower; strong, serene, prosperous, and noble; it lavished fruit and gave shade and, living securely under this shade, a hundred cottagers blessed it.
>
> (p. 202)

III

A popular French saying in the nineteenth century refers to the Iberian peninsula as part of Africa: "Europe ends at the Pyrenees." It was inspired by belief in the sociopolitical and cultural barbarism of Spain and Portugal. Indeed, Eça refers to this attitude in his last novels; it is espoused not only by foreign characters but also by Portuguese characters who have been abroad. Did Eça (or any other Iberian writer for that matter) view membership in "European literature" as the ultimate goal of his art?

Eça de Queiroz was probably the most European oriented of all peninsular writers of the second half of the nineteenth century. His was a continental figure, both culturally and professionally. At the outset of his literary career his aim was quite evidently "to Europeanize" Portuguese experience. Thus he produced his "thesis novels" (*The Sin of Father Amaro* and *Cousin Bazilio*), in which he emulates the theory and art of Balzac, Flaubert, and Zola. Dismayed by the reaction to his "Portuguese brand of realism," he turned to non-European concerns (China and the Holy Land), making use of a literary tradition that had its roots on the Iberian peninsula—the picaresque novel.

From the mid-1880's, it appears that Eça realized that his ambitions to join the mainstream of "European literature" were deluded. Linguistically, he was isolated. Although the Portuguese language had had a glorious history, it was not then considered by Europeans to have the artistic value of English, French, or German. Thus, Eça's art drew inward, that is, he broke the barriers imposed on him by European literary trends and recognized himself as a Portuguese artist. In his last completed novels (*The Maias, The Illustrious House of Ramires,* and *The City and the Mountains*), he is an independent, original, and self-sufficient writer. He initiates what might be considered a Freudian search not only for self-knowledge but also for a definition of the Portuguese being within the national and European world contexts. Writing becomes a cathartic experience. He brings his own existential concerns to his fiction, through his protagonists and major secondary figures. Through them, he comes to terms with many aspects of his personality—from rejected child to closet dandy. Further, Eça viewed himself as summing up Portuguese man at the end of the nineteenth century: a schizophrenic soul that glows comfortably from past grandeur while confronting the bleak present and an even sadder future. Rarely has a writer so well diagnosed his nation's dilemma. Indeed, the present generation of Portuguese novelists—who still write under the shadow of Eça—have returned to his theme of national soul as a result of the 1974 Portuguese revolution and the final blow—the loss of the African territories. In his masterly revelation and portrayal of his nation, as well as his personal acceptance of the conditions it engendered, rests Eça's true gift to Portuguese and world fiction.

Selected Bibliography

EDITIONS

INDIVIDUAL WORKS

COMPLETED NOVELS

O crime do Padre Amaro. Lisbon, 1875–1876; Oporto, 1880.
O primo Basílio. Oporto, 1878.
O mandarim. Oporto, 1880.
A relíquia. Oporto, 1887.

Os Maias. Oporto, 1888.
A ilustre casa de Ramires. Oporto, 1900.
A cidade e as serras. Oporto, 1901.

MISCELLANEOUS

O mistério da estrada de Sintra. Lisbon, 1870.
Uma campanha alegre. 2 vols. Oporto, 1890.
As minas de Salomão. Oporto, 1891. (Translation of H. Rider Haggard's *King Solomon's Mines,* edited by Eça.)
Dicionário de milagres. Oporto, 1900.
A correspondência de Fradique Mendes. Oporto, 1900.
Contos. Oporto, 1902.
Prosas bárbaras. Oporto, 1903.
Cartas de Inglaterra. Oporto, 1905.
Ecos de Paris. Oporto, 1905.
Cartas familiares e bilhetes de Paris. Oporto, 1907.
Notas contemporáneas. Oporto, 1909.
Últimas páginas. Oporto, 1912. Includes *Lendas de Santos.*
A capital. Oporto, 1925.
O conde de Abranhos. Oporto, 1925.
Alves & Cia. Oporto, 1925.
O Egipto. Oporto, 1926.
Cartas inéditas de Fradique Mendes e mais páginas esquecidas. Oporto, 1926.
Crónicas de Londres. Oporto, 1944.
Prosas esquecidas. 5 vols. Lisbon, 1965–1967.
Folhas soltas. Oporto, 1966.
A emigração como força civilizadora. Lisbon, 1979.
A tragédia da Rua das Flores. Lisbon, 1979 and 1980.

COLLECTED WORKS

Obras de Eça de Queiroz. 15 vols. Oporto, 1945–1952. Deluxe edition.
————. 3 vols. Oporto, 1966.
Obra completa de Eça de Queiroz. 2 vols. Rio, 1970. Very incomplete.

TRANSLATIONS

The City and the Mountains. Translated by Roy Campbell. New York, 1956.
Cousin Bazilio. Translated by Roy Campbell. New York, 1953.
The Illustrious House of Ramires. Translated by Ann Stevens. Athens, Ohio, 1968.
Letters from England. Translated by Ann Stevens. Athens, Ohio, 1970.

The Maias. Translated by Patricia McGowan Pinheiro and Ann Stevens. New York, 1965.

The Mandarin and Other Stories. Translated by Richard Franko Goldman. Athens, Ohio, 1965. Includes "Peculiarities of a Fair-Haired Girl."

The Relic. Translated by Aubrey Fitzgerald Bell. New York, 1925. 1954 edition with an introduction by Francis Steegmuller.

The Sin of Father Amaro. Translated by Nan Flanagan. New York, 1963.

BIOGRAPHICAL AND CRITICAL STUDIES

Coleman, Alexander. *Eça de Queirós and European Realism.* New York, 1980.

DaCal, Ernesto Guerra. *Lengua y estilo de Eça de Queiroz.* Coimbra, 1954.

Demetz, Peter. "Eça de Queiroz as a Literary Critic." *Comparative Literature* 19:289–307 (1967).

Gaspar Simões, João. *Vida e obra de Eça de Queirós.* 3rd ed. Lisbon, 1980.

Hourcade, Pierre. *Eça de Queiroz e a França.* Lisbon, 1973.

Machado de Rosa, Alberto. *Eça, discípulo de Machado?* Rio, 1962.

Medina, João. *Eça político.* Lisbon, 1974.

Sacramento, Mário. *Eça de Queiroz: Uma estética da ironia.* Coimbra, 1945.

Saraiva, Antonio José. *As ideias de Eça de Queiroz.* Lisbon, 1946.

Stevens, James R. "Eça and Flaubert." *Luso-Brazilian Review* 3:49–56 (1966).

BIBLIOGRAPHY

DaCal, Ernesto Guerra. *Bibliografía Queirociana sistemática y anotada e iconografía artística del hombre y la obra.* 5 vols. Coimbra, 1975–1982.

IRWIN STERN

JORIS KARL HUYSMANS
(1848–1907)

HUYSMANS' CAREER COULD have occurred only in late-nineteenth-century
France, but the pattern it followed was timeless and traditional. Dante Alighieri in the
Commedia (*ca.* 1307), imitating Christ's
three-day journey from death to resurrection,
dramatized this pattern as he passed through
the stinking ditch of hell on the way to the exultant clarity of heaven. Huysmans, in both
his life and his work, chose a parallel route.
He began in a meaningless chaos of stench
and disease, moved on through satanic cruel-
ties and occult hatreds, and ended in visionary
prayers to the Virgin Mary and grateful affirmations of faith. Huysmans the novelist was
largely a writer of autobiography; all his books
are bulletins on his spiritual progress. The
greatest novelists of his century found a wider
perspective, but Huysmans wrote with such
remarkable vividness of style and observation
that his fascination and importance are permanently assured. In his time his influence
was decisive—he gave shape to the decadent
movement in both French and English literature—and it was Huysmans' manner and
themes that Marcel Proust later adopted and
made his own.

Huysmans' work divides conveniently into
three phases: naturalist, decadent, and religious. Each of these corresponds to a major
element in French literature at the time.
Huysmans' naturalism adapted the methods
of the Goncourt brothers and Émile Zola, a
vaguely scientific-minded realism that sought
to render the workings of psychology and society in all their mechanical ordinariness, although in Huysmans, as in the Goncourts,
this goal did not preclude a self-conscious artificiality of style. Huysmans' decadent phase,
which produced his masterpiece, *À rebours*
(*Against the Grain*, 1884), was part of a general reaction to the mundane vision of the naturalists. The symbolists and others, Stéphane
Mallarmé and Paul Verlaine, sought to raise
art to the realm where (in Huysmans' phrase)
the senses give no assistance, an attempt to
find symbolic meanings beyond the objective
world and to live at the dangerous edge of sanity and the social order.

Finally, Huysmans' religious phase, in
which he shifted toward divinity the same deliberately irrationalist impulses that moved
him to a literature of decadence, was part of a
larger Catholic revival that also found expression in the work of Léon Bloy and Paul Claudel. Each phase of Huysmans' work tended to
find its own separate audience. *À rebours*,
which has the most enduring literary interest
of all his novels, sold 14,000 copies during
Huysmans' lifetime and some 50,000 more in
the half-century after his death. But *La cathédrale* (*The Cathedral*, 1898), a novel that
amounts to a meditation on Catholic art and a
guide to the cathedral of Chartres, sold 20,000
copies in the year it was published, and almost 170,000 in the fifty years following.

Huysmans' various subjects were united

under the banner of his extraordinary style. Paul Valéry described it as

> a style that was peculiarly suited to his nerves: a language that was always striving after the unexpected and the extreme, overloaded with adjectives perverted from their usual meaning; an elaborate monologue, a curious mixture of rare words, peculiar overtones, trivialities, and lucky poetic finds. He liked doing violence to the order of words, separating the adjective from the noun it qualifies, the complement from the verb, and the preposition from the word expected to follow. He systematically used and abused epithets not implicit in the object but suggested by circumstance: a device that he used constantly, a very seductive, a very powerful device—but a dangerous and short-lived one.
>
> *(Maîtres et amis, 1927)*

It was Valéry who also provided perhaps the best description of Huysmans himself, as a difficult-seeming man who inspired loyalty and admiration:

> He was extremely high-strung, quick to develop violent antipathies, prompt to deliver appalling judgments, prolific in disgust, predisposed to the worst, with an appetite for extremes, unbelievably credulous, swallowing with no trouble every horror that can be imagined about human nature, with a relish for peculiar behavior and the sort of tales you might hear from hell's concierge; yet his hands were unstained and he was sometimes as open-handed as a man on the verge of poverty can be; actively charitable, loyal to friends who had fallen on bad times, steadfast in his admirations, even of men whose persons had become unbearable or repellent to him.
>
> *(Maîtres et amis)*

Huysmans was born on 5 February 1848, in a quiet corner of the Paris Left Bank. He was christened Charles-Marie-Georges Huysmans but later adopted what he took to be the Dutch form of his first names, as a tribute to his Dutch ancestry on his father's side. His father was a painter and printer who had moved to Paris from Holland, one of a family of painters who had been active, occasionally distinguished, since the sixteenth century. His mother was French, from a family consisting mostly of civil servants, although her grandfather had been a sculptor whose work can still be seen on Parisian monuments. Huysmans himself followed both these family traditions: he had an artist's vocation (and became a famous critic of painting), and he earned his living working in a government bureau.

When Huysmans was eight, his father died after a period of debilitating illness. His mother soon remarried a man named Jules Og, who provided somewhat more secure finances—he invested in a bookbindery that Huysmans later inherited—but less affection for his stepson. The boy, meanwhile, was sent off to a nearby boarding school where, like most schoolboys with an artistic bent, he found himself miserable. His shy demeanor and unimposing form led to humiliations from older boys and masters, and these continued when he moved from school to lycée at the age of fourteen. "When I look back upon my youth," one of his fictional self-portraits recalls in the novel *En ménage* (*Living Together*, 1881), "I see only a procession of miseries and insults, refuse carts, depravities." Not that he considered these humiliations an unjust persecution of genius: "I was nothing, I was merely second-rate." Finally he refused to return to the lycée and received a final year of instruction in private from one of the masters who taught there. At eighteen he obtained his baccalaureate, and his regular schooling ended.

At this point Huysmans began a double career as a law student and civil servant, working part of the day at the Ministry of the Interior while also pursuing legal studies at the University of Paris. In the evenings he led the life of a student bohemian, sharing in the customary sexual adventures and aesthetic enthusiasms—although he disdained any interest in the revolutionary politics of the time. At nineteen he took a mistress, a popular singer at a theater favored by students. He met her, after many unsuccessful attempts, by elbowing his way backstage in the guise of a journalist who was willing to puff the current production—which in fact he did, in an obscure, short-lived periodical that ceased publishing with the issue containing Huysmans' review.

Huysmans managed to pass his first-year law exams, but he spent the money intended for his second-year fees on his mistress instead. (His stepfather died at this time, and Huysmans was under little further pressure to continue his studies.) After a period of quiet but mutually unsatisfying domesticity, the woman became pregnant by another man and gave birth to a child. What happened next is unknown, but the affair ended, apparently in some bitterness. Huysmans portrayed his mistress in his first novel, but little else is known about her beyond this fictional portrait and a few remarks he made to friends.

Soon afterward, with the start of the Franco-Prussian War in 1870, Huysmans was drafted into the National Guard and sent off to the front. He never arrived there, having been taken ill with dysentery in camp and left in a country hospital. There a friendly nun gave him his first adult glimpse of the cloistered life he sought again in his later years. As the Prussian army approached Paris, Huysmans was sent back to the city on sick leave and then back to work again at the Ministry of the Interior. (In 1876 he was transferred to a different department in the ministry, the Criminal Investigation Department.)

He wrote a memoir of his war experiences—in which the only note of cheer was his affectionate account of the nun who tended him in the hospital—but temporarily abandoned the memoir to pursue a very different sort of writing, a series of prose poems. These appeared in 1874 as *Le drageoir à épices* (*The Spice Dish*). These highly colored poems, with their exotic vocabulary and twisted diction, borrowed and exaggerated the styles of Charles Baudelaire's prose poems and some of Baudelaire's subjects as well. The

book included tormented celebrations of powerful and perverse women, lush word-pictures of Parisian and provincial scenes—even a richly phrased evocation of a herring.

While his poems slowly made their way into public notice, Huysmans became friendly with some of his fellow authors. One evening he told them the story of his inconclusive service in the National Guard, and also recounted his theatrical romance from his student days. His friends urged him to write both these stories in the form of novels, and Huysmans soon reworked his war memoirs under the title *Sac au dos* (Sack on Back, 1880—the order to soldiers to put on their packs), and began another novel, his first to be published, titled *Marthe, histoire d'une fille* (*Marthe, Story of a Prostitute*, 1876).

Marthe is written in a milder version of the lush style Huysmans used in his poems, but its content is largely that of the naturalist school of novelists then becoming dominant in France. Like most French literary schools, the naturalists were as much the product of publicity as of shared beliefs, but they represented nonetheless a crucial phase of nineteenth-century literature. Extending the "realist" example of Honoré de Balzac and Gustave Flaubert, they focused on the lower and middle strata of society, attempted to provide a documentary portrait of their time, adopted quasi-scientific principles of analysis (loosely suggested by Charles Darwin's theories), and treasured as their true subject the ugliness and disorder of daily life. The idealism of an earlier age was renounced; the fetid odors of the present age were lovingly and accurately described. Zola, the leading theorist and practitioner of naturalism, set out to make a scientific study of all the professions and characters of contemporary France, to perceive human nature not as a product of ideals and aspirations but as the working-out of heredity and instinctual desires.

Huysmans used the royalties from his poems to purchase Zola's novels and was immediately impressed by their range and audacity, by their willingness to explore forbidden and sensational subjects. Zola in effect confirmed the literary taste Huysmans had already developed, in which Edmond de Goncourt served as his ideal. Goncourt, with his brother Jules (who died before Huysmans began writing), wrote novels that carefully documented lower-class existence; he devoted many pages to exact details of the progress of disfiguring diseases; and while Huysmans was at work on *Marthe,* Goncourt was writing his own novel about a prostitute, *La fille Elisa* (*Elisa,*1877). Huysmans' *Marthe* had the further and more specific intent of exposing the romantic fantasies of the novel on which the students of the Left Bank then hoped to model their lives, Henri Murger's *Scènes de la vie de bohème* (*Bohemians of the Latin Quarter,*1845–1849), a book that portrayed carefree students and their even more carefree mistresses.

Marthe and her friend Léo, a talented but frustrated writer and Huysmans' self-portrait, live in constant want. The book, one of Huysmans' briefest, opens with the scene in Marthe's life that Huysmans knew best, the evening when Huysmans went backstage and began persuading his favored soubrette to come home with him; the chapter ends with Huysmans-Léo's success. Without transition, Huysmans immediately turns to Marthe's earlier life, and her first employment in a factory making artificial pearls—a setting that gives Huysmans the opportunity to draw on the documentary tradition of Balzac, Zola, and the Goncourts. All the workers in the pearl factory are women, and "a workshop full of women is merely an antechamber leading to the brothel." Within a few paragraphs Marthe begins a love affair, but "the young man she chose ... was so gentle and respectful that she could not resist making him suffer, and they finally separated by common consent." (Huysmans never portrayed a successful relation between the sexes, and began his fiction with a brief portrayal of the emotional cruelty that he took to be the norm in sexual life.)

Marthe then takes up casual prostitution and soon moves in with a young man looking for an affair. Their life is impoverished and repugnant; the floor of their apartment "with its patches of scarlet varnish reminded one of some hideous skin disease." At this point the story begins to coincide with Huysmans' own memories, as Marthe confesses she is pregnant by another man, gives birth in agony, and sees both her baby and her lover die from exhaustion and cold.

But Marthe recovers and enters a brothel as a licensed prostitute. (Prostitutes were obliged by law to live in brothels, under medical supervision.) Huysmans lavishes on the brothel one of his richest word-portraits: detailed evocations of hair styles, flesh, perfumes, and the specialized language of the trade:

> Then she looked with sudden stupefaction at the strange postures assumed by her companions—brazen beauties and saucy tarts, mannish women and skinny wenches, lying face down with head in hands or squatting dog-like on stools or draped like gaudy rags on the corners of divans.
>
> Their hair was arranged in every conceivable way—waved spirals, crimped curls, sinuous ringlets, gigantic coils studded with pink and white daisies and bound with artificial pearls, and black or yellow manes glistening with pomade or sprinkled with powder.
>
> Their sleeveless dressing-gowns, fastened on the shoulder with pale silk ribbons, fell in ample folds, affording glimpses through the diaphanous material of the appetizing nudity of the bodies beneath.

Marthe eventually escapes from the brothel and goes on the stage, to be discovered there by Léo. At this point, again without transition, the narrative returns to Léo and Marthe as they first approach Léo's rooms. Their affair proves to be a series of frustrations and annoyances, ending with Marthe's departure for an older man who finds it easier than Léo did to pay her expenses. But she develops tender memories of Léo and attempts to return to him, only to find that they have lost their passion for each other. The conclusion is reported by Léo in a letter to a friend, written in a tone of tired irony: Marthe has returned to the brothel, and Léo is marrying a woman in whom he is scarcely interested but who will provide the steady comforts of bourgeois existence. The fates of Marthe and of Léo are implicitly equal in disappointment and defeat.

Marthe is a brief and often sketchy book, but it sets the tone of much of Huysmans' career. Its worldly pessimism, its disgust with the flesh, its extravagance of style, were all to persist into Huysmans' religious works, where none of the original attitudes changed but simply contrasted with a religious hope Huysmans had not entertained in his earlier years. For the moment, when *Marthe* was published, Huysmans began an active discipleship to Zola, whom he met through the intermediary of a friend who had called on the older man to profess admiration and was invited to return with any friends he cared to bring along. Zola was delighted to discover in this way a circle of admirers—including not only Huysmans but also the young and as yet unknown Guy de Maupassant—and encouraged them all to write documentary novels in his own style. Huysmans in turn wrote a series of essays in defense of Zola and his school: "Green pustules and pink flesh are all one to us; we depict both because both exist, because the criminal deserves to be studied as much as the most perfect of men, and because our towns are swarming with prostitutes who have the same civil rights as prudes."

While gaining publicity as a member of Zola's circle, Huysmans worked on his second novel, *Les soeurs Vatard* (*The Vatard Sisters*, 1879), an account of two sisters who work in a bindery like the one Huysmans inherited after his mother's death in 1876. One sister is seduced by Cyprien Tibaille, an artist described as "a man depraved, in love with all the nuances of vice provided they were complex and subtle," a painter concerned, like Zola and his disciples, only with modern sub-jects and modern styles. Cyprien, who is another self-portrait of Huysmans, and his mistress suffer through months of resentful bickering, while the other sister and her lover, a doltish workman, gradually lose interest in each other. All the characters except Cyprien have the narrowness and unsavory odor that Huysmans found throughout the Parisian working class, while Cyprien distinguishes himself by his quirky intellect and morbid sensitivity. Zola was delighted by the book; elsewhere Huysmans was accused of libeling the workers of Paris, and the dispute caused a mild sensation in the press.

The public battle over Huysmans, and, with even greater intensity, over Zola, expanded when a book of stories was published by Zola and his friends in 1880, under the title *Les soirées de Médan* (Evenings at Médan), in honor of Zola's suburban home, where the friends frequently met. All the stories concerned the disastrous period of the Franco-Prussian War (the first title proposed for the book was "L'Invasion comique"—The Ludicrous Invasion—which seemed too offensive to be used). Huysmans' contribution was the final version of *Sac au dos.* The book ignited a burst of hostile comment followed by a smaller but spirited defense. Huysmans' story, with its savage account of conditions in the army and in army hospitals (he had removed the recollections of the gentle nun, which had balanced the tone somewhat in earlier versions), was especially denounced. One of the defenses Huysmans received in the press came from a reviewer who noted that he, like Maupassant in the same volume, wrote in a way that had little to do with Zola's plain style but instead used "rare nouns, curious adjectives, unexpected combinations of words, archaisms, neologisms, mutilated syntax, splashes of color, flares of wit, assonance, and discord" in an account of the drab disorder of war.

A few weeks later Huysmans published some brief pieces in similar styles, *Croquis parisiens* (*Parisian Sketches*, 1880), partly reprinted from *Le drageoir aux épices* and partly new—including among other evocations a prose poem that detailed the various smells of women's armpits. Again Zola defended his disciple from the inevitable attacks, while the majority of reviewers, by denouncing, served to excite public attention.

Huysmans also at this time began to make his name as an art critic, one whose energy in attack and praise surpassed even the critics who wrote about his poems and novels. In splendidly spirited essays, collected in *L'Art moderne* (Modern Art, 1883), he denounced the official academic painting of the time and defended the virtually ignored work of outsiders like Edgar Degas, Camille Pissarro, and Paul Gauguin. These, he wrote, were artists whose subjects and techniques were uncompromisingly modern—like the subjects and techniques of his own school of writers—and who would someday win the admiration of the public despite their present neglect. Huysmans' celebration of the impressionist school was so impassioned and persistent that he came to be regarded as a major champion of the school and virtually the coiner of the term "impressionist" itself. (In fact the term had been used once or twice a few years before Huysmans adopted it.)

Cyprien Tibaille, Huysmans' alter ego in *Les soeurs Vatard,* is an impressionist painter. In Huysmans' next novel, *En ménage,* Cyprien Tibaille reappears, described in terms that amount to a self-criticism of the novelist as a young man:

> He was incapable of producing a great work of art, but at moments he had an extravagance, a curious boldness of painting, often successful, a refinement of daring effect, an offending and cruel note directed mostly toward the prostitute, showing her as she is, with the shameful rottenness of what she is underneath and the opulent corruption of what shows.

Cyprien's appearance also corresponds to that of his creator:

Tall and thin, fair-haired and pale, with a blond beard, long slender fingers, fidgeting hands, piercing gray eyes, some white bristles showing among his shaggy hair. His ankles knocked together when he walked, so that his trousers soon wore out at the ends; these, incidentally, were always too short and too wide for his spindly calves. With his back slightly bent, and his left shoulder higher than the right, he looked sickly and poor. His way of walking down the street was, to say the least, singular. He would move by jumps, marking time for a while, then leaping forward like a grasshopper, proceeded merrily along with his umbrella tucked under his arm like a schoolmaster, and rubbing his hands for no apparent reason.

Cyprien, however, is not at the center of *En ménage* but is an observer whose disillusionments figure in the book mostly in the final pages. The bulk of the book is given over to another partial self-portrait, the writer André Jayant, who shares Cyprien's attachment to "naturalism and modernity," and shares his "melancholy vision of life" and his hatred of bourgeois prejudices. Like Cyprien, he has been "burned by women." (Zola, in his novel *L'Oeuvre* [1886], would later imitate his disciple by dividing his own self-portrait into those of an artist and a writer.) As the book opens, André returns home from an evening walk with Cyprien in which he, André, had praised marriage, to find his wife in bed with another man. There is little drama in this potentially explosive scene: André politely and ironically suggests that the man should depart and then leads the way downstairs. The next day, André moves out, and he eventually moves into bachelor quarters.

The story reverts at this point, in Huysmans' characteristic manner, to the youth of André's wife, Berthe—her stultifyingly bourgeois home, and her acceptance of André's proposal of marriage primarily as a means of escape. Berthe lived with her uncle after the death of her father; this uncle, apparently a portrait of Huysmans' hated stepfather, had "read the flattering platitudes uttered about

America by pedantic theorists, [and] exalted the customs of that horrible country, wished ours could resemble it." (Huysmans always used "American" as a shorthand epithet for everything he found shallowly democratic, optimistic, and unaesthetic.) Berthe proves sexually unresponsive and eventually seeks, through a casual affair, the excitement her women friends had whispered about in youthful conversations. The affair gives her no excitement either, but it leads to the fiasco of the opening scene, and then to Berthe's rejection by her lover and her return to her family.

When André finds lodgings of his own, he furnishes them as something of an aesthete's paradise. In his small rooms, "from ceiling to floor, the walls disappeared under a jumble of potteries, pictures, brasses, fine porcelain, in the midst of which two impressionist watercolors scintillated in their gold frames against the gray background of the wallpaper." This paradise is darkened by the annoying dimwittedness of André's maid, by the spying of his neighbors and concierge, and at last by André's "petticoat crisis"—his inability to live without some means of sexual satisfaction. Huysmans' account of this crisis is one of the first and most detailed in literature: André searches out streetwalkers, makes an arrangement with a higher-class prostitute for regular visits, becomes bored by this arrangement, is visited by an earlier mistress who soon moves in with him again, but who finally moves to England where more money is to be had. (This mistress, Jeanne, the woman who is most affectionately portrayed in the book, is a portrait of Huysmans' mistress of many years, Anna Meunier.) At the end, André's wife returns, and they enter into a life of reduced expectations. So, in his way, does Cyprien, who settles into what Huysmans calls concubinage with a plain, older, uneducated woman, as he gives up his ambitions as a painter to design wallpaper and work as a commercial artist.

Huysmans called En ménage "a song of nihilism, punctuated by bursts of sinister gaiety and expressions of ferocious wit." The ancestry of its neurotic and defeated characters may be traced to the romantic heroism of earlier decades, reduced in this latter-day version to a baffled and declining self-absorption. The psychological process the novel portrays is one that begins in irritated hopelessness and ends in sardonic acceptance; the cure is worse than the disease. André and Cyprien take pleasure only in their aesthetic sensibility, not in the external objects of that sensibility; and, like the more famous characters in Huysmans' later novels, they end by recognizing even the futility of their aesthetic satisfactions. A constant motif in the book—as in much of Huysmans—is André's difficulty in eating and digesting: food in this novel is invariably disgusting, falsely advertised, stale, malodorous, its real nature barely concealed by sharp, spicy sauces. (This motif suggests a comparison between, on the one hand, Huysmans' extravagant style and dismal subject matter and, on the other, a rich sauce and the rotten fare it covers.) The odors of decaying meat and game have their counterparts in the odors of living flesh, odors that, as always in Huysmans, serve either to disgust or to seduce.

After publishing En ménage in 1881, Huysmans spent the summer in the Paris suburb of Fontenay-aux-Roses, although he continued to work at his office in the capital. At Fontenay he wrote a brief novel, À vau-l'eau (Downstream, 1882), the story of a government clerk even more wretched than Huysmans ever was. Jean Folantin begins as a youthful aesthete without the means to satisfy his tastes; grows quickly disillusioned with women (a working-class mistress leaves him with venereal disease); cannot take pleasure in food, since he recognizes even the finest restaurant meals as adulterated and inadequate; finds all his acquaintances wanting; is frustrated even in his dealings with shopkeepers and waiters; and finally sees no other possible course of action than letting himself drift and taking no action at all. He has no money, so his pleasures are limited to walks among the Seine bookstalls and distant contemplation of the religious life, whose harmonious order he admires. This is one of the first statements of the religious theme that grows dominant in Huysmans' later books. At the end Folantin finds himself in an unsatisfactory sexual encounter with a woman who accosts him in an equally unsatisfactory restaurant; he then returns home, meditating, as Huysmans himself did, on the pessimism of Arthur Schopenhauer; he is met by a blast of cold air as he enters his room and concludes with the thought that "the best things never happen to penniless fellows; only the worst ever happens."

Folantin senses that only religion could cure his misery. But he has no religion; nor, at the time, did his creator, who thought it a "consolation only for the feebleminded." But the desire for faith kept intruding into Huysmans' writings, most notoriously at the end of his most exotically sardonic novel, À rebours, the masterpiece by which literary history best remembers him. Certainly Huysmans did not anticipate either the religious conclusion to the book or its fame when he began it. He conceived À rebours as a companion piece to À vau-l'eau (their titles have precisely opposite meanings): a book whose hero would have the same need as Folantin to escape the ordinary world, but whose wealth would provide him with exotic and extravagant means of doing so. His protagonist would delight in artifice, and Huysmans found that the book required researches in the fields of jewelry, perfume, flowers, religious and secular literature, secular music, and Gregorian chant. Instead of a humble clerk, his hero is the duke Jean Floressas des Esseintes, last of a great family, who lives his life in the realm of imagination.

All this was the opposite of Zola's naturalism, and Huysmans, in a preface to a new edition of the book twenty years after its first publication, specifies that he had made a deliberate turn away from his early master. "Naturalism was then at its crest," he recalls, "but that school, which rendered the undeniable service of situating true-to-life characters in true-to-life settings, was condemned to repeat itself, to marching in place." Naturalism, in theory at least, gave little attention to the exceptional; its idea of a lifelike character was one who was as average as possible. Its main interest, Huysmans continued, was the common passion of lust; while the truth of the matter is that pride, not lust, is "the most magnificent of the deadly sins to study." À rebours is one of the strangest and most magnificent studies of pride ever written.

Huysmans' own pride led him to think of his book as fated for a small and select audience, and he wrote in the belief that he was exploring realms where few readers could follow. But many did. À rebours became the bible for the fin-de-siècle generation that styled itself "decadent." Oscar Wilde, in The Picture of Dorian Gray (1891), portrayed a not uncommon reaction:

It was the strangest book that [Dorian] had ever read. It seemed to him that in exquisite raiment, and to the delicate sound of flutes, the sins of the world were passing in dumb show before him. Things that he had dimly dreamed of were suddenly made real to him. Things of which he had never dreamed were gradually revealed.

It was a novel without a plot . . . simply a psychological study of a certain young Parisian . . . loving for their mere artificiality those renunciations that men have unwisely called virtue, as much as those natural rebellions that wise men still call sin. The style in which it was written was that curious jewelled style, vivid and obscure at once, full of argot and of archaisms, of technical expressions and of elaborate paraphrases, that characterizes the work of some of the finest artists of the French school of Symbolistes. There were in it metaphors as monstrous as orchids, and as subtle in colour. . . . It was a poisonous book. . . . The mere cadence of the sentences, the subtle monotony of their music, so full as it was of complex refrains and movements elaborately repeated, produced in the mind . . . a form of reverie, a malady of dreaming.

Like many of Huysmans' books, À rebours opens with a departure, a withdrawal from shared or common life. A prefatory chapter tells the history of the des Esseintes family and the early life of des Esseintes himself: his education among the Jesuits, his disappointments in the company of young men of his own class, among writers and artists, among women. He resolves to remove himself entirely from the tedium of society, and to establish himself in an isolated house not too far from Paris. He chooses the same suburb where Huysmans spent the summer of 1881, Fontenay-aux-Roses. Des Esseintes abruptly dismisses most of his servants, departs from Paris without leaving a forwarding address—and the book begins.

À rebours is not quite a book without a plot. Huysmans does tell a story, but in a characteristically indirect and obscure way. Many chapters open with a very brief statement of des Esseintes's activities or frame of mind in the "present" of the story, then devote much of their length to recollections of des Esseintes's past, and finally conclude with a brief statement of some change that has occurred, as if while the past was being recollected, in the story's present. The first chapter, for example, devotes its opening paragraph to des Esseintes's difficulties in furnishing his new house to his exacting tastes; but Huysmans then turns immediately to the eccentricities of his earlier houses: a boudoir elaborately designed to flatter the complexion of his mistresses; a hall to receive tradesmen that he fitted out like a church and where he preached sermons on dandyism to his tailors and bootmakers; the dining room where he once arranged to serve a meal entirely in black, with black food and black furnishings. Almost imperceptibly, this description now shades into des Esseintes's choices of furnishings for his new house at Fontenay, his preference for colors that seem stronger and clearer by gaslight than daylight, his use of poems by Baudelaire, copied out in illuminated manuscript, as decorations.

A later chapter begins with the delivery at the house of a tortoise whose shell des Esseintes had arranged to be encrusted with precious stones, in order to provide a striking contrast with his new carpet. The chapter is mostly a series of flashbacks: des Esseintes's contemplation of various gems and their associations take up the first few pages. Then, briefly returning to the present, des Esseintes directs his servant to bring the tortoise into his study, but, feeling chilled, decides first to visit his "mouth-organ," a counterpart to the musical organ, a device that dispenses exotic liquors as an organ releases and blends sound. Another few pages describe the history and construction of this instrument, until, as des Esseintes drinks some liquor from it, he is reminded by the odor of a visit to the dentist; and the pain and exhaustion of that visit, in contrast with the luxury of the Fontenay household, are then described for a number of pages. Only in the last paragraph of the chapter does Huysmans return to the tortoise, which is lying motionless on the carpet. When des Esseintes touches it, he finds it has died, no doubt because it was "unable to bear the dazzling luxury imposed on it."

The real point of the chapter is the disappointment of des Esseintes's expectations, a disappointment that is virtually inherent in their extravagance. (In another chapter des Esseintes orders his servant to bring him a certain dish of food, which, by the time it arrives a few pages later, sickens and repels him.) The heroes of romantic literature in an earlier generation had characteristically striven toward sublime accomplishments and had been brought down in the end by the inadequacy of the world to match the grandeur of their visions. In Huysmans this tragic curve is reduced but still evident: instead of sublime aspiration, a desire for ornamental extravagance; instead of a catastrophic defeat, a dead tortoise. But each of des Esseintes's disillusionments brings him closer to his concluding prayer for faith.

Before he makes that prayer he explores every possible source of stimulation for his senses. Among his recollections are hints of perverse sexual pleasures and of delight in the disruption of the ordinary pleasures of others. When he learned that one of his friends wanted to marry and set up house in a modern flat with curved walls, he alone urged his friend on, knowing that the furniture would cost too much, that the marriage would founder on the resulting petty irritations, and that he, des Esseintes, would have the stimulation of "an endless source of ridiculous misfortunes." In a more extreme style, des Esseintes once picked up a young working-class boy, took him to a brothel, and arranged to pay for his pleasures for a fixed term. His plan was that the boy, having grown accustomed to sexual luxury, would be unable to renounce it when the payments stopped, and would rob and eventually murder to get the money required. But des Esseintes is frustrated in this scheme also: he never sees the boy named in the newspaper as an accused murderer and is forced to conclude that something outside his control went wrong. This is a pity, he thinks, since "all I was doing was making a parable of secular instruction, an allegory of universal education," education that, in the view of Huysmans and of des Esseintes, only teaches the poor to envy pleasures they can never legally enjoy. Like the marquis de Sade, des Esseintes proclaims a moral purpose for his cruelty: "The more we try to polish the minds and refine the nerves of the underprivileged, the more we shall develop in their hearts the atrociously active germs of hatred and moral suffering."

Des Esseintes's deliberate interference with others' sex lives is one expression of his distaste for the ordinary course of things. At one point he takes nourishment not by the ordinary means but by the *à rebours* (reverse) method of enemas. He prefers to "substitute the vision of a reality for the reality itself," and, in words that Oscar Wilde would later echo, argues to himself that nature has grown old-fashioned and exhausted: "The time has come for artifice to take the place of nature whenever possible." More beautiful than any human form, he thinks, are two locomotives recently put into service, forms he imagines in terms of powerful, exotically corseted women displaying their prodigious strength. Not that he wants to travel by locomotive: "Travel, indeed, struck him as a waste of time, since he believed that the imagination could provide a more than sufficient substitute for the vulgar reality of actual experience." Late in the book, when "once again . . . the solitude he had longed for so ardently and finally obtained had resulted in appalling unhappiness," des Esseintes forgets his own precept to the point where he starts on a journey to England. But he gets only as far as an English tavern in Paris, where, surrounded by English people, he decides that the trip itself would only bring disappointment. As far as he is concerned, he can travel far enough in his imagination. So he returns home the same night, with all his luggage and equipment, "feeling all the physical weariness and moral fatigue of a man who has come home after a long and perilous journey."

The novelty and strangeness of *À rebours* were as much a matter of des Esseintes's artistic tastes as of his actions. Huysmans devoted a long chapter to des Esseintes's fascination with the late Latin literature of the "decadence"; this gave Huysmans the opportunity to make a great show of obscure classical learning, which he later admitted was lifted from the work of a German historian. Corresponding to this taste is des Esseintes's preference, among modern writers, for Baudelaire, Verlaine, and Mallarmé. The latter two were virtually unknown at this time—Huysmans had to ask Mallarmé to lend him the text of some poems he wanted to quote—and Huysmans' chapter was decisive in establishing their reputations. He honored in them their refusal to join the ordinary world of letters, their preference for "taking pleasure [as Huysmans wrote of Mallarmé] far from society, in the caprices of the mind and the visions of the brain; refining upon thoughts that were already subtle enough, . . . loosely linked by an imperceptible thread." He praised Mallarmé's "unique hermetic language, full of contracted phrases, elliptical constructions, audacious tropes." He celebrated Mallarmé's condensed style, a style in which a single word suggested "at once form, scent, color, quality, and brilliance."

Among the poems of Mallarmé that des Esseintes cherishes is the verse drama *Hérodiade* (1869); the daughter of Herodias was Salome, and des Esseintes owns Gustave Moreau's two watercolors of Salome, symbolist works, products of a mind "altogether modern in its morbid sensibility." What Huysmans especially values in these paintings is their transformation of their materials: "never had the poverty of chemical pigments been able thus to set down on paper such coruscating splendors of precious stones, such glowing hues as of painted windows illuminated by the noonday sun, glories so amazing, so dazzling, of rich garments and glowing flesh tints." The key to the fascination of these paintings is their combined sensual luxury and ethical disgust. Huysmans, in his characteristic misogyny, guessed that Moreau "had been thinking of . . . the mortal woman, the soiled vessel, ultimate cause of every sin and every crime," hateful and exquisite at once.

The one resolution for des Esseintes's contradictory and frustrated feelings is the resolution of religious faith. Throughout the book he has moments of sympathy for those who have shut themselves in monasteries, and other moments when he finds himself in a state almost of belief—until, "after a moment's thought, his longing for faith would vanish, though leaving him perplexed and uneasy." Des Esseintes finds himself drawn to writers like the marquis de Sade and his imitators, but he is convinced that sadism is essentially an aberration of religion: if it did not involve sacrilege, it would have no motive at all. He is increasingly divided between his spiritual pride ("Did he know of a single individual who was as capable as he of appreciating the delicacy of a phrase, the subtlety of

a painting, the quintessence of an idea, or whose soul was sensitive enough to understand Mallarmé and love Verlaine?") and his need for faith and the humility that is the precondition of faith.

His growing illness leads him, in the book's final pages, to abandon his isolated home under doctor's orders, and to return to an almost common life in Paris. And in the final paragraph, as he awaits his departure, he suddenly makes his first prayer: "Lord, take pity on the Christian who doubts, on the unbeliever who would believe, on the galley slave of life who puts out to sea alone, in the night, beneath a firmament no longer lit by the consoling beacon-fires of ancient hope!" A reviewer of the book (and one of the authors praised in it), Jules Barbey d'Aurevilly, wrote: "After such a work, it only remains for the author to choose between the muzzle of a pistol and the foot of the Cross." Huysmans, who had no plans to shoot himself, quoted these words in his preface to the novel twenty years later, and added, "It is done." He had chosen.

Huysmans had a circuitous route remaining on his way to Christianity. On one hand, he saw *À rebours* as the final turning point in his departure from Zola and the soirées of Médan. He maintained his friendship with Zola, and tried to tell him that the book was more a joke than a reflection of his own tastes. But Zola saw through this and told Huysmans he was leading the naturalist school astray and that he should return to his earlier style. Huysmans replied that the novel, as Zola conceived it, now seemed to him "moribund, repetitiously threadbare, and for me, whether Zola liked it or not, without interest." On the other hand, Huysmans' next novel turned back from the extravagance of *À rebours*. *Un dilemme* (*A Dilemma*, published in book form in 1887) was a small work in relatively plain style, detailing the cruel financial calculations of the bourgeoisie. *En rade* (*In Harbor*, 1887), his next novel, had similarly realistic elements, but these were balanced by a strong infusion of nightmare and fantasy, which altered the tone in ways Huysmans seems not to have anticipated when he began writing the book.

En rade is the story of Jacques and Louise Marles, who leave Paris to escape their creditors and take refuge in Jutigny, a village in which Huysmans had spent a rustic summer with his mistress Anna Meunier (they did not live together in Paris) not long before. There Marles descends into an isolated bitterness not unlike des Esseintes's. He becomes the victim of nightmares to which Huysmans devotes three long chapters of extravagant rhetoric and imagery. The book alludes to the mysteries of the cabala and to incubi and succubi, the supernatural beings who enjoy sexual intercourse with the living. But outside these visions, the book follows Huysmans' earlier manner, complete with stomach-curdling accounts of rural ugliness and grim portraits of Louise Marles's diseased condition. Like des Esseintes, Jacques Marles finally returns to Paris, abandoning his private dreamworld in disappointment.

During these years of *À rebours* and afterward, the emphasis of Huysmans' art criticism and essays shifted along with that of his fiction. In 1886 he published *La Bièvre de Saint-Séverin*, a long piece on Paris' minor (and now buried) river; this work appeared in book form in 1890. He valued the river Bièvre not for its appearance but for its value as a symbol. It "represents the most perfect symbol of feminine wretchedness exploited by a big city." It arrives from the provinces innocent and unsoiled, and as it moves toward the center of Paris, it is prostituted to the tasks of industry, and finally abandoned in spoiled corruption. *La Bièvre* shares the nostalgia for a lost past that Huysmans expressed in *À rebours*, but its tone is utterly different, a tone of affection and pity, combining the unblinking observation of Huysmans' naturalist beginnings with the spiritual sympathies of his later years.

Huysmans' essays on painting at this time took on a comparable but more intense manner. In earlier years, in the essays collected in *L'Art moderne*, he had celebrated paintings that looked directly at the conditions of the nineteenth century, and architecture that embraced modern techniques. Now, six years later, in the articles collected in *Certains* (Certainties, 1889), he favored art that rejected the present for a visionary past. Gustave Moreau, as in *À rebours*, provides him with his central examples, images that give "an impression of spiritual onanism, repeated but chastely performed," works that evoke "a woman, self-contained, yet raving and crying out invitations to sacrilege and rape, to torture and murder." Elsewhere in the book Huysmans identifies great artists as those who respond to their environment not with a direct and sympathetic gaze but with "hatred and repulsion," who, "out of disgust for the shameful promiscuities they are forced to suffer, throw themselves into the abyss of the ages, into the tumultuous spaces of dream and nightmare." Huysmans offers special praise for the monstrous and grotesque medieval visions portrayed in the gargoyles of the great cathedrals. And it is through this double fascination, with an escape into the medieval world and into the perverse intensities of sacrilege, that the essays in *Certains* point the direction that Huysmans' novels would follow next.

Another work of this period was an autobiographical pamphlet, *J.-K. Huysmans*, published in 1885 in the series *Les hommes d'aujourd'hui* (Men of Today), which Huysmans whimsically chose to issue under the pseudonym "Anna Meunier."

The phrase he devised for the art he now favored was "supernatural realism." He first used this in reference to Matthias Grünewald's great painting of the Crucifixion in the museum in Cassel, Germany, which Huysmans visited in 1888. The painting combines a mystical intensity of feeling with an intense realism in its portrayal of pain and death. Huysmans' first glimpse of the painting crystallized all his recent thought about the function of art. Afterward, recalling "the cry of admiration wrung from him" as he came upon the Grünewald, he wrote:

> Never before had naturalism transfigured itself by such a conception and execution. Never before had a painter so carnally envisaged divinity nor so brutally dipped his brush into the wounds and running sores and bleeding nail holes of the Savior. Grünewald had surpassed all measure. He was the most uncompromising of realists, but his morgue Redeemer, his sewer Deity, let the observer know that realism could be truly transcendent. A divine light played about that ulcerated head, a superhuman expression illuminated the fermenting skin of the epileptic features. This crucified corpse was a very God, and, without aureole, without nimbus, with none of the stock accouterments except the blood-sprinkled crown of thorns, Jesus appeared in His celestial super-essence.
>
> (*Là-bas*, ch. 1)

The way to discover divinity, then, was through the most extreme ugliness and pain, and Huysmans proceeded to put this lesson into effect.

In 1888 Huysmans met a woman named Henriette Maillat with whom he had a brief affair. (Anna Meunier had been suffering for some years from a debilitating disease; but Huysmans continued to give her financial support from his limited funds throughout her life.) Henriette Maillat told him she was familiar with the supernatural sexual activities of succubi and incubi, beings of whom Huysmans had written in *En rade*. Huysmans had before this taken a bookish interest in the supernatural; he saw in it "some compensation for the horror of daily life, the squalor of existence." But now he began to make contact with active practitioners of the mystic arts.

After the affair with Henriette Maillat ended, Huysmans met a woman who claimed even deeper involvement with black magic and satanism, Berthe Courrière. Before long he had come in contact with a Parisian circle of believers and humbugs who claimed to be deeply immersed in the occult, although like most of their nineteenth- and twentieth-century counterparts, their activities were in fact limited mostly to table turning, sacrilege, and blackmail. Huysmans' fascination increased nonetheless, and in 1889 he learned of someone whose occult activities seemed more substantial, the abbé Louis Van Haecke of Bruges, who turned out to be an acquaintance of Berthe Courrière. His presence had been reported at a black mass, and he was rumored to have "organized a demoniacal clan" whose erotic and sacrilegious activities, if in fact they had occurred, would have been among the most extravagant expressions of modern satanism. Huysmans was never able to learn if the stories told of Van Haecke were true. But he soon learned of another practitioner of the occult arts, whose real actions were more extreme even than those imputed to Van Haecke—although Huysmans, now that he had found the genuine article, for a long time refused to believe it.

The name of this occultist was Joseph-Antoine Boullain. He was a defrocked priest whose unorthodox activities had begun when a nun, Sister Adèle Chevalier, was sent to him for spiritual guidance after she had had a series of mystical visions. The priest and the nun founded an organization they called the Society for the Reparation of Souls, whose real purpose was to give them an excuse for meeting privately and for committing various acts of sacrilege. Eventually Adèle Chevalier bore Boullain's child, whom the parents ritually murdered during a private celebration of the mass. (Boullain confessed this crime in a memoir that was not discovered until after his death.) They also committed the lesser crime of fraud, for which they were tried and imprisoned. Later, after a second prison term in the Vatican, Boullain returned to France, still a priest, and exorcised demons from possessed nuns. In the process he contrived to have sexual relations with the nuns, hypnotizing them

1721

into believing they were having these relations with the mystical bodies of the saints or of Jesus Christ.

Eventually the archbishop of Paris heard enough to discipline Boullain, who then left the church and spent all his time practicing occult magic in Lyons with heretical sects. At some point he too made the acquaintance of Berthe Courrière. Huysmans learned about him in the occult circles of Paris and began a correspondence. Boullain dispatched his housekeeper, Julie Thibault, to confirm Huysmans' trustworthiness or credulity, and then, satisfied with her report, began mailing him great quantities of documentation on satanism, occult rites, succubi and incubi, and similar matters.

Huysmans wanted this material for the novel he had recently begun to write. This novel, *Là-bas* (*Down There*, 1891), put into effect his program of spiritual naturalism. By now Huysmans was convinced that succubi existed, that the devil was ruler of this world, that there were mysteries that Zola's variety of naturalism could never hope to fathom. He wrote in *Là-bas:*

> We must retain the documentary veracity, the precision of detail, the compact and sinewy language of realism, but we must also dig down into the soul and cease trying to explain mystery in terms of our sick senses. If possible the novel ought to be compounded of two elements, that of the soul and that of the body, and these ought to be inextricably bound together as in life. Their interactions, their conflicts, their reconciliation ought to furnish the dramatic interest. In a word, we must follow the road laid out once and for all by Zola, but at the same time we must trace a parallel route in the air by which we may go above and beyond—a spiritual naturalism!
>
> (*Là-bas*, ch.1)

The speaker is the character who was to become Huysmans' most extended and searching self-portrait, the character he named Durtal, after a small French village whose name sounded, to Huysmans' ear, more Dutch than French. Durtal's spiritual odyssey is also Huysmans', and it is an odyssey he accomplishes through writing. In *Là-bas*, Durtal has reached the stage where "he did not believe, and yet he admitted the supernatural." He explores the supernatural realm by writing a history of Gilles de Rais—"Bluebeard"—the fifteenth-century marshal of France who spent much of his career kidnapping and torturing peasant children, and who sought the help of the devil in avoiding the consequences. In *Là-bas* this history exists mostly in the form of notes, which Durtal arranges in his mind, and sometimes on paper, as the book progresses.

Là-bas opens with a debate between Durtal and another writer, des Hermies, also a self-portrait, on the subject of spiritual naturalism. There is not much debate, since both writers reject Zola's naturalism, although only Durtal wishes to retain its attention to reality—in the manner of Grünewald. Durtal, a less extreme version of des Esseintes, has ceased to associate with men of letters, whether bohemian or successful. As des Hermies tells him, "You were fated someday to get away from this Americanized art and attempt to create something less vulgar, less miserably commonplace, and infuse a little spirituality into it."

This history of Gilles de Rais provides Durtal with an escape from the present age, and his discovery of this subject cures the "spiritual disarray" of his recent life: "Thus history had for Durtal supplanted the novel, whose forced banality, conventionality, and tidy structure of plot simply oppressed him." Durtal's subject was "the des Esseintes of the fifteenth century," whose actual career, although different in scale and effect, closely paralleled des Esseintes's fictional one. Gilles was an aesthete in an age of brutes, a lover of fine objects and books, a devotee of church music. But he also indulged in excesses of the cruelest and most spectacular kind, excesses that des Esseintes could only admire in books or imitate indirectly. As Durtal explains: "From lofty mysticism to base satanism there is but one step. In the Beyond all things touch.

Gilles carried his zeal for prayer into the territory of blasphemy." Durtal adds: "The Marquis de Sade is only a timid bourgeois, a mediocre fantasist, beside him." This is Durtal's sincere praise. "Since it is difficult to be a saint, there is nothing for it but to be a satanist. . . . 'Execration of impotence, hatred of the mediocre,' that, perhaps, is one of the more indulgent definitions of diabolism."

Durtal is scarcely prepared to follow Gilles in his special manner of turning away from mediocrity. But a woman among his acquaintance, Mme. de Chantelouve, a portrait of Berthe Courrière, does offer him access to the modern counterparts of Gilles de Rais. First, however, she ensnares him in more mundane ways. After rousing his interest in her through a series of unsigned letters, she reveals herself as their author but refuses to go to bed with him (an interlude that provides Huysmans with an opportunity to recount Durtal's rather comic frustration). At last, after telling him that she too is interested in satanism, she yields—and shows that she is not only the reserved woman she seems in the drawing room and the repressed tease Durtal saw earlier, but also "in bed, completely changed in voice and bearing, a harlot spitting mud, losing all shame." What holds together wife, mistress, and satanist in one person? Durtal has no answer, but it occurs to him that Gilles de Rais is divided into the same three proportions: the brave and honest fighting man, the refined and artistic criminal, and the repentant sinner and mystic. This third element in the character of Gilles is now growing prominent in the parallel history that has been passing through Durtal's mind between his assignations with Mme. de Chantelouve: Gilles de Rais, after committing the sacrileges that finally led to his arrest, made a thorough and sincere repentance, and went to his execution willingly, praying for divine forgiveness.

Mme. de Chantelouve, however, is not ready for forgiveness. After explaining to Durtal her interest in satanism, she agrees to conduct him to a black mass performed by Canon

Docre, a character modeled on the rumors surrounding the abbé Van Haecke. (At the time Huysmans wrote *Là-bas* he had not yet learned of the crimes of the ex-abbé Boullain, and while calumniating the probably innocent Van Haecke as the modern counterpart of Gilles de Rais, he portrayed Boullain as the saintly Dr. Johannès, a mighty enemy of satanism, whose knowledge of demoniacal practices is used only to oppose them.) Huysmans discreetly let it be known that in his research for *Là-bas* he attended a black mass, but it seems to have been a tame affair. The more spectacular mass in the book is based on literary accounts. It begins with Docre's extravagant blasphemies ("Jesus, Artisan of Hoaxes . . . since the day when thou didst issue from the complaisant bowels of a Virgin, thou hast failed all thine engagements, belied all promises. Centuries have wept, awaiting thee, fugitive God, mute God!"), continues with his desecration of the sacramental wafers (naked under his robes, he wipes himself with the wafers), and concludes in a howling orgy. Durtal, horrified, drags Mme. de Chantelouve away, but she entices him into a room where "she seized him, and, with ghoulish fury, dragged him into obscenities of whose existence he had never dreamed." When it is over, he realizes that the bed had been strewn with fragments of sacrificial wafers. Durtal has been initiated into the mysteries of satanism, but he is determined to go no further.

Canon Docre and Mme. de Chantelouve are not the book's only representatives of the world of the beyond. Another figure, the bell ringer Carhaix, who lives with his worthy and generous wife in the church of Saint-Sulpice, combines medievalism of outlook with a character that approaches sanctity. Carhaix mourns the passing of his ancient art, and the end of the coherent religious world view that fostered it. Durtal sympathizes with Carhaix's love of art and admires the goodness of his soul, but although he envies Carhaix's faith he cannot yet follow his example.

In the final chapter Durtal, des Hermies,

Carhaix, and his wife are talking together in the church tower—together with an abbé who tells them about Dr. Johannès—and as Durtal recounts the death and repentance of Gilles de Rais and the forgiveness he received from clergy and peasantry, his talk is interrupted by shouts in the street. The crowds are hailing the election results—specifically, the election of the demagogic radical sympathizer General Georges Boulanger. The contrast between fifteenth-century piety and the mob passions of the nineteenth century leads Durtal and his friends to grave reflections on the future. Durtal murmurs, "What whirlwinds of ordure I see on the horizon." And on this note the novel ends.

It would be four years before Huysmans published another novel. In the meantime, his beliefs and way of life continued the upheaval begun in the satanist explorations of *Là-bas*. Immediately after finishing the book he paid a visit to Joseph Boullain in Lyons, where he was received with great kindness. Boullain taught him, among other things, how to defend himself from the spiritual warfare that he assured him would be waged against him, as a result of his book, by the Rosicrucians and others who were Boullain's opponents in the world of the occult. Huysmans took the advice to heart. He developed sensations he attributed first to nervous disease, then decided were the effects of occult bombardment by powerful enemies. He refused to go to sleep without having performed certain defensive spells and burning a mystical concoction in his fireplace in order to receive the defensive benefit of its fumes. By these means he successfully warded off the enmity of sorcerers.

Boullain was less fortunate; he died two years later, having predicted that he would succumb to a supernatural onslaught. Huysmans was convinced that Boullain was the victim of black magic. Partly out of gratitude to Boullain, he eventually hired Julie Thibault, Boullain's housekeeper, to keep house for him in Paris, and he explained to his friends that his best defense against black magic was the presence of Julie Thibault's "unassailable sanctity." Soon, however, Huysmans had the opportunity to read Boullain's memoir of his crimes. Although he could no longer hold the same opinion of Julie Thibault's sanctity, he continued to employ her, and to regard her with amused affection. She served as the model for a recurring comic character in his later novels, a Mme. Bavoil, who formerly had frequent visionary conversations with the Virgin Mary, and believes the visions stopped only because she was too proud of them.

In *Là-bas* Durtal states his conviction that the supernatural exists. Satanism, "gross as it is, seems a sure thing. And if it is," he continues, "and one is consistent, one must also grant Catholicism." When des Hermies replies, "All right, believe," Durtal answers: "I can't. There are so many discouraging and revolting dogmas in Christianity." Yet in the winter of 1890–1891, even before *Là-bas* was published, Huysmans began to visit various churches on the Left Bank. He was still not ready to make his confession or take communion, but his churchgoing continued. Eventually he was ready to seek the advice of a spiritual director. Berthe Courrière, whose acquaintances included pious clergymen as well as impious satanists, put him in touch with the abbé Arthur Mugnier, who became Huysmans' friend for life.

At the same time that Huysmans was receiving another kind of spiritual advice from the ex-abbé Boullain, he began to take guidance from the abbé Mugnier, guidance that led him to make pilgrimages to various monasteries in France. In the summer of 1891 Huysmans combined his two sources of spiritual guidance when he traveled to Lyons to join Boullain and Julie Thibault on a pilgrimage to the Alpine shrine of La Salette (where, thirty-five years before, the monks had advised Adèle Chevalier to place herself under Boullain's care). Huysmans found the church and its furnishings repellent, but he found the religious significance of the shrine deeply compelling.

The Virgin Mary had appeared, weeping, to two children at the site a few decades earlier, and its fame rapidly increased as it became the scene of miraculous cures. Now Huysmans watched the peasants make the difficult climb to the church, where they wept with religious joy. The impression made by this scene was a lasting one, and Huysmans wrote about La Salette in a book he left unfinished, but which he intended, he said, as a spiritual "à-rebours" to *Là-bas.* Logically enough, he gave it the title *Là-haut* (Up There; not published until 1965), although he also experimented with the title "La bataille charnelle," by which he meant "the battle between piety and the flesh."

The first half of *Là-haut* traces Durtal's experiences in Paris churches; the second brings him to La Salette. But the solitude of monastic cells did not yet content Huysmans, and when he returned to Paris at the end of the summer, his carnal battle continued. (In *Là-bas,* and later in *En route* [1895], Durtal finds irresistible the special techniques used by a certain prostitute whom he visits, despite his feelings of self-disgust, within hours of some of his religious observances.)

In the summer of 1892 Huysmans was ready, he said, to "knock at God's door." He asked the abbé Mugnier to suggest a monastery outside Paris where he could make his first confession and was given the name of the Trappist monastery at Notre-Dame d'Igny. There, after some hesitation, Huysmans went on a retreat. It did not begin especially well. Huysmans went to the monastery to give himself strength for a chaste life; the first night there he was subject to terrifying sexual nightmares that reminded him, when he awoke, of the stories of succubi. The next day he attempted to make a confession but failed almost at the start. Only on the day after did he succeed, and then wept from sheer happiness. Still he felt rather unsettled at the monastery, and alternated between moods of happiness and torpor. After nine days he returned to Paris, then traveled to Lyons for a last visit

with Boullain, whose occult practices were beginning to seem more like eccentricities than signs of wisdom. Huysmans still believed in the occult, but his conversion was complete.

"How had he again become a Catholic" he asked, in the guise of Durtal, near the opening of his next novel, *En route,* a book based in large part on *Là-haut.* He answered his own question in this way:

> I cannot tell; all that I know is that, having been for years an unbeliever, I suddenly believe.
>
> Let us see, let us try at least to consider if, however great the obscurity of such a subject, there be not common sense in it.
>
> After all, my surprise depends on preconceived ideas of conversions. I have heard of sudden and violent crises of the soul, of a thunderbolt, or even of faith exploding at last in ground slowly and cleverly mined. It is quite evident that conversions may happen in one or other of these two ways, for God acts as may seem good to Him, but there must also be a third means, and this no doubt the most usual, which the Savior has used in my case. And I know not in what this consists; it is something analogous to digestion in a stomach, which works though we do not feel it [an entirely characteristic metaphor for Huysmans to employ; although in nonreligious contexts digestion is usually a process he feels quite painfully]. There has been no road to Damascus, no events to bring about a crisis; nothing has happened; we awake some fine morning, and, without knowing how or why, the thing is done.
>
> Yes, but in fact this maneuver is very like that of the mine that explodes only after it has been deeply dug. Yet not so, for in that case the operations are material, the objections in the way are resolved; I might have reasoned, followed the course of the spark along the thread, but in this case, no! I sprang unexpectedly, without warning, without even having suspected that I was so carefully sapped. Nor was it a clap of thunder, unless I admit that a clap of thunder can be occult and silent, strange and gentle. And this again would be untrue, for sudden disorder of the soul almost always follows a misfortune or a crime, an act of which we are aware.
>
> No, the one thing that seems certain, in my

case, is that there has been divine impulse, grace.

But, he continues, there were three causes that "after a life of indifference, have brought me into the harbors of the Church, made me wander about her borders, and finally gave me a shove from behind to bring me in." The first was "the atavism of an old and pious family, scattered among the monasteries," along with childhood memories of cousins and aunts in convent parlors. The second and third, only briefly mentioned, are "his disgust for life, and his passion for art."

En route, as all this suggests, is largely a didactic novel, in which Huysmans hoped to set an example for nonbelievers who were, like him, intellectual and artistic, and might be persuaded by the example of one of their number who came to accept a faith he had formerly held in contempt. A constant theme of the book is the superiority of church art, a superiority that Durtal sees as sufficient proof of the truth of Catholicism: "Finally Durtal had been brought back to religion by art. More even than his disgust for life, art had been the irresistible magnet that drew him to God." And so *En route,* like Huysmans' later Catholic works, has little to say about religious philosophy, little about the intellectual as opposed to the symbolic significance of church dogma, and little about the logic of theology. All these matters Huysmans found unsympathetic, preferring to give his aesthetic assent to the purest and least worldly art of the church (he repeatedly states his preference for medieval plainchant over the operatic and symphonic church music of his own day), and to the most mystical and heterodox doctrines of some of its clergy.

The central element of Huysmans' theology was the medieval doctrine of mystical substitution, a doctrine at the outer edges of Christian orthodoxy. It holds that the suffering of the innocent—not only the sufferings of plagues and catastrophes but also the chosen suffering of martyrs and the chosen hardships of monks and nuns—is a means of preserving humanity from the wrath of God. That is, for all sins, there must be restitution; and if the sinner will not make restitution himself, someone innocent must make it for him, willingly or not. In *En route* Huysmans maintains that the contemplative monastic orders are "the lightning rods of society. They draw on themselves the demoniacal fluid, they absorb temptations to vice . . . they appease the wrath of the Most High that he may not place the earth under an interdict." Should the French republic ever dissolve the monasteries, an event that seemed increasingly possible, national catastrophe would inevitably follow.

Huysmans found his most inspiring examples of mystical substitution in the lives of certain martyred women of the Middle Ages, particularly the Blessed Lydwine of Schiedam, whose prayers for ever more wounds and ever more sores were invariably granted. In *En route,* and later in *La cathédrale,* Durtal hopes to write an account of her life, and in fact Huysmans published such a book, *Sainte Lydwine de Schiedam* (1901). The title takes a more exalted view of Lydwine than the church did; she was not officially recognized as a saint. Like all who voluntarily suffer, in Huysmans' view, Lydwine was Christ's representative, expiating the sins of her fellow human beings.

Huysmans developed the theory that there was a continuing and unbroken succession of expiatory victims, that Lydwine was born in the year that her predecessor, Saint Catherine of Siena, died, and that this succession continues, perhaps in secret, to the present day. One effect of this doctrine, and of Huysmans' adoration of the Virgin Mary, was an inversion of his attitude toward women. In his earlier books women were the sexually enthralling carriers of misery and corruption; in *Là-bas* they were literally instruments of the devil. But in later books, although Huysmans regarded women in equally exotic terms, he took an exactly opposite tone. Now the women he wrote most about were nuns, vessels of suffering and purity. In *En route* Durtal hears a convent chorus, and thinks:

> How poor and yet how exquisite are those nuns' voices, which seem nonsexual and mellow! God knows how I hate the voice of a woman in a holy place, for it still remains unclean. I think woman always brings with her the lasting miasma of her indispositions and she turns the psalms sour. . . . Yet in convents of women, that is changed; it is certain that prayer, communion, abstinence, and vows purify the body and soul, as well as the vocal odor that proceeds from them.

(Huysmans combined these attitudes with a temperament essentially heterosexual. Once, in an experimental mood, he spent some days in homosexual circles, "before it was discovered that I was not a true homosexual—and then I was lucky to get away with my life.") At the time he was writing *En route*, Anna Meunier was in the late stages of her fatal disease, and the intensity of her suffering was one of the contributing factors in Huysmans' search for the meaning of pain; she died, deeply mourned by Huysmans, in 1895, a few days after the publication of *En route*.

The first half of *En route*, like that of *Là-haut*, records Durtal's conversion and describes his variously unsatisfactory or incomplete experiences in Paris churches. The second half takes him to the Trappist monastery at Igny and records his shift in mood from disquiet to joy and back again. The book abandons all attempt at a fictional plot—and Huysmans would make no attempt to recover this aspect of the novel in his later work. Although his earlier books, *À rebours* especially, were precursors of Proust in that much of their action was the psychological "action" of memory and contemplation, none of those books so directly took their shape from the sequence of Huysmans' own experience.

En route is a work of a self-revelation and self-analysis—intertwined with a treatise on church music, liturgy, and similar matters.

Huysmans eliminated all his other partial self-portraits early in its pages; des Hermies and Carhaix are reported to have died before the action begins, and Durtal stands alone as Huysmans' representative. None of this implies that Huysmans simply gave up his writing to a slavish imitation of the incidents of his life. In fact, to some extent he made his life imitate his art. *En route*, he explained to a journalist soon after publication, was to be the first volume of a trilogy; the second and third volumes, to be titled *La cathédrale* and *L'Oblat (The Oblate)*, were to follow Durtal on the next stages of his spiritual progress. Durtal learned penance and purgation in the first of the three books; he was to be educated in the full symbolic meaning of Christianity in the second; and in the third he was to combine his way of life and his knowledge by joining a monastery as an oblate, or lay brother, one who lives within the walls but does not take monastic vows and does not obey all the laws of the order. When Huysmans explained this plan he did not intend to follow the same path as his fictional representative. As it turned out, he eventually followed it quite closely.

In *La cathédrale* (1898) Durtal, along with his friend the abbé Gévresin—a combined fictional portrait of Arthur Mugnier and, in a very idealized way, Joseph Boullain—moves to Chartres. Huysmans did not make the same move, but he visited the cathedral often and devoted himself to understanding the vast encyclopedia of faith he found in its decoration and architecture. "What I have done for sacred music in *En route*," he said, "I want to do for the religious architecture, painting, and sculpture of the Middle Ages in *La cathédrale*." This book, as Huysmans recognized, is a shapeless and sprawling work that is nonetheless a glory of style and detail. Valéry called it "an extraordinary network of modern metaphors in which we catch, as though in its entirety, the tremor of the vast and exact alphabet of symbols bequeathed by the Middle Ages."

The book has received greater fame as an

idiosyncratic guide to the cathedral than as a novel. As in Huysmans' other Catholic books, much of the contents is a series of disquisitions thinly disguised as dialogue between Durtal and one priest or another—and punctuated by the comically naive remarks of Mme. Bavoil—on the symbolism of colors, jewels, smells, flowers, and so on. The book ends with Durtal's decision to move to the abbey of Solesmes, famous for its preservation of medieval plainchant, and with his sustained meditation on the culminating symbolic meaning of the cathedral as a whole as a shrine to the Virgin.

Durtal's plan for a visit to Solesmes was one phase of his hope to settle in a monastery in which the worship of God would be accomplished through art. All during the 1890's Huysmans felt that "a craving for the cloister had been incessantly permeating his being." But when he actually visited monasteries for a few days or weeks, he found himself still unsatisfied. What he hoped to find was some "merciful order, devoted to liturgies and adoring art," where he could live as a friar. In 1894 he met a young monk named Dom Jean-Martial Besse who was engaged in restoring a ruined monastery at Saint-Wandrille, and whose ideas about monastic life were very much like Huysmans' own. But Dom Besse's community of monks had too little practical sense to put any of his plans into effect, and Huysmans began to look elsewhere. As he had predicted in *En route* in 1895, he visited Solesmes in 1896 and 1897, but he was again disillusioned. This pattern continued in other monasteries until 1898, when Huysmans retired from the security office and had no compelling reason to remain in Paris, whose modern architecture and manners he found increasingly unendurable.

Only a few weeks after his retirement, Huysmans found a monastery that met his standards in almost every way. This was the abbey of Saint-Martin de Ligugé, where Dom Besse had gone after the failure of his plans for Saint-Wandrille, and where the monks were friendly and the atmosphere cordial. Dom Besse pointed out to Huysmans that Durtal was destined, in the trilogy, to live as an oblate; now Huysmans himself, he argued, should take a house near the monastery and begin his novitiate as an oblate in real life. Huysmans lost little time in purchasing a plot of land very near the abbey, on which he had a house built for himself and for a bourgeois couple, the Leclaires, who had somewhat improbably become his closest friends in Paris. In 1899, having pensioned off Julie Thibault, whose satanist past made her somewhat unsuitable for life just outside a monastery, Huysmans and the Leclaires moved to Ligugé, and Huysmans, taking the religious name of Brother Jean, became an oblate.

Ironically enough, Huysmans' stay in this one satisfactory setting was cut short after only two years, and not as the result of any change of heart in Huysmans himself. In 1901, as an aftermath of the Dreyfus affair, the National Assembly passed the Law on Associations, whose key provisions affected religious "congregations." The French republic, to consolidate its victory over the anti-Dreyfus forces in the church and elsewhere, decreed that new congregations could not be formed without passage of a law defining their specific scope and activities, and that any existing congregation that failed to receive similar authorization from the assembly must be dissolved. Recent parliamentary elections had shown that monasteries would have very little chance of receiving authorizing legislation; and so the monks at Ligugé, like many throughout France, chose not even to ask for it but simply to leave the country and reestablish their community elsewhere. During the summer of 1901 the monastery was abandoned. In order to keep the liturgical cycle unbroken, Huysmans and one or two others stayed on at Ligugé for a few days, maintaining the church calendar until word arrived that the community was in place in Belgium. Then Huysmans returned, most reluctantly, to Paris.

There, living first in a convent annex, and later in various apartments, he wrote *L'Oblat* (1903). The book begins with Durtal's brief excursion to Solesmes, then brings him quickly to Ligugé. Much of the book is, once again, a series of dramatized essays on liturgy, on the fate of the monasteries, and above all on the meaning of suffering, which Huysmans had decided was the center of Christian experience. Christ, Durtal argues, was the betrothed of the allegorical figure of Suffering, who "for Him . . . reserved her passion" and who by Him was "ratified and ennobled, and henceforth . . . comprehensible to Christians." At the end of the book, as Durtal leaves Ligugé and takes the express to Paris, he looks forward to the divine chastisement that must await him and the nation.

Huysmans called *L'Oblat* "a mongrel and a hybrid" and admitted that its few novelistic elements were present mostly for the sake of sweetening its polemical and didactic pill. *L'Oblat* was the last of his novels. He wrote one more book, *Les foules de Lourdes* (*The Crowds of Lourdes*, 1906), in which he portrayed the physical ugliness and spiritual profundity of the famous shrine, and he also wrote a number of shorter pieces, but he made no further attempts at imaginative literature.

Soon he was unable to write at all. For some time he had been suffering from an intense pain in his jaw, which proved to be the result of cancer. By early in 1907 he recognized that he was near death. He spent his last months in accordance with his beliefs about suffering and refused injections of morphine, so that he might feel "the sufferings of God" rather than "the evil pleasures of earth." He died on 12 May 1907. "No one," he said on his deathbed, "has put more of himself into his books than I."

Selected Bibliography

INDIVIDUAL WORKS

Le drageoir à épices. Paris, 1874. As *Le drageoir aux épices.* Paris, 1875. Edited by H. Juin. Paris, 1975.

Marthe, histoire d'une fille. Brussels, 1876. Edited by P. Cogny. Paris, 1955. Edited by H. Juin. Paris, 1975.

Les soeurs Vatard. Paris, 1879. Edited by H. Juin. Paris, 1975.

Croquis parisiens. Paris, 1880; enlarged ed. 1886. Edited by H. Juin. Paris, 1976.

Sac au dos. Paris, 1880. In *Les Soirées de Médan.* Paris, 1881.

En ménage. Paris, 1881. Edited by H. Juin. Paris, 1975.

À vau-l'eau. Brussels, 1882. Edited by H. Juin. Paris, 1975.

L'Art moderne. Paris, 1883. Edited by H. Juin. Paris, 1975.

À rebours. Paris, 1884. New preface, 1903. Edited by H. Juin. Paris, 1975. Edited by M. Fumaroli. Paris, 1977. Edited by P. Waldner. Paris, 1978.

J.-K. Huysmans, by "Anna Meunier." Paris, 1885.

Un dilemme. Paris, 1887. Edited by H. Juin. Paris, 1976.

En rade. Paris , 1887. Edited by H. Juin. Paris, 1976.

La Bièvre de Saint-Séverin. Paris, 1890.

Là-bas. Paris, 1891. Edited by P. Cogny. Paris, 1978.

En route. Paris, 1895.

La cathédrale. Paris, 1898.

Sainte Lydwine de Schiedam. Paris, 1901.

De tout. Paris, 1902.

Esquisse biographique sur Don Bosco. Paris, 1903.

L'Oblat. Paris, 1903.

Le quartier Notre-Dame. Paris, 1905.

Trois primitifs. Paris, 1905.

Les foules de Lourdes. Paris, 1906. Edited by P. Lambert. Paris, 1958.

Trois églises et trois primitifs. Paris, 1908.

Le retraite de Monsieur Bougran. Paris, 1964.

Là-haut. Edited by P. Cogny. Paris, 1965.

COLLECTED WORKS

Oeuvres complètes. 18 vols. Paris, 1928–1935. Reprinted, 9 vols., Geneva, 1972.

TRANSLATIONS

Against Nature (*À rebours*). Translated by Robert Baldick. Harmondsworth, 1959.

Against the Grain. (*À rebours*). Translated by John Howard (pseud.). New York, 1922.

The Cathedral. Translated by Clara Bell. London, 1898.

Down Stream (À vau-l'eau) and Other Works, including Marthe, A Dish of Spices, Critical Papers. Translated by Samuel Putnam. Chicago, 1927. Reprinted New York, 1975.

Downstream (À vau-l'eau). Translated by Robert Baldick. London, 1952.

Down There (Là-bas). Translated by Keene Wallis. New York, 1924.

En Route. Translated by C. Kegan Paul. London, 1896.

Living Together (En ménage). Translated by J. W. G. Sandiford-Pellé. London, 1969.

Marthe. Translated by Robert Baldick. London, 1958.

The Oblate. Translated by Edward Perceval. London, 1924. Reprinted New York, 1978.

Parisian Sketches (Croquis parisiens). Translated by Richard Griffiths. London, 1962.

Saint Lydwine of Schiedam. Translated by Agnes Hasting. London, 1923.

BIOGRAPHICAL AND CRITICAL STUDIES

Aimery, Christiane (pseud.). *Huysmans.* Paris, 1944.

————. *Joris-Karl Huysmans.* Paris, 1956.

Bachelin, Henri. *J.-K. Huysmans.* Paris, 1926.

Baldick, Robert. *The Life of J.-K. Huysmans.* Oxford, 1955. The standard biography.

Belval, M. M. *Des ténèbres à la lumière: Étapes de la pensée mystique de J.-K. Huysmans.* Paris, 1968.

Billy, André. *Huysmans et cie.* Paris, 1963.

Blandin, Henri. *J.-K. Huysmans.* Paris, 1912.

Brandreth, H. R. T. *Huysmans.* New York and London, 1963.

Brunner, H., and J.-L. de Coninck. *En marge d' "À rebours" de J.-K. Huysmans.* Paris, 1931.

Chastel, Guy. *J.-K. Huysmans et ses amis.* Paris, 1957.

Cogny, Pierre. *J.-K. Huysmans à la recherche de l'unité.* Paris, 1953.

Cressot, Marcel. *La phrase et le vocabulaire de J-K. Huysmans.* Paris, 1946.

Deffoux, Léon. *J.-K. Huysmans sous divers aspects.* Paris, 1927; new ed. 1942.

————, and Émile Zavie. *Le groupe de Médan.* Paris, 1920.

Duployé, Pie. *Huysmans.* Paris and Brussels, 1968.

Issaharoff, Michael. *J.-K. Huysmans devant la critique en France (1874–1960).* Paris, 1970.

Laver, James. *The First Decadent.* London, 1954.

Lefèvre, Frédéric. *Entretiens sur J.-K. Huysmans.* Paris, 1931.

Livi, François. *J.-K. Huysmans' "À rebours" et l'esprit décadent.* Brussels, 1972.

Lobet, Marcel. *J.-K. Huysmans, ou le témoin écorché.* Lyons, 1960.

Maignon, Charles. *L'Universe artistique de J.-K. Huysmans.* Paris, 1970, 1977.

Meslanges Pierre Lambert consacrés à Huysmans. New York, 1968.

Ridge, G. R. *Joris-Karl Huysmans.* New York, 1968.

Seillière, Ernest. *J.-K. Huysmans.* Paris, 1931.

Trudgian, Helen. *L'Esthétique de J.-K. Huysmans.* Paris, 1934; Geneva, 1970.

Valéry, Paul. *Maîtres et amis.* Paris, 1927.

Zayed, Fernande. *Huysmans, peintre de son époque.* Paris, 1973.

BIBLIOGRAPHIES

Bulletin de la société J.-K. Huysmans, 1928– . Contains bibliographical and much other material.

Cevasco, G. A. *J.-K. Huysmans: A Reference Guide.* Boston, 1980.

See also the list of bibliographical studies in Baldick, *The Life of J.-K. Huysmans,* listed above.

EDWARD MENDELSON

AUGUST STRINDBERG
(1849–1912)

AUGUST STRINDBERG SOMETIMES presented himself as a victim of superstition. This playwright, novelist, linguist, essayist, painter, chemist, alchemist, botanist, cultural historian, theologian, astrologer, mythologist, and student of the occult plumbed for significance in every fluke and coincidence he encountered. He would look at a landscape he had never seen before and claim that he recognized it from a dream or a premonition or from a pattern inscribed by iron oxide on the inner surface of a zinc basin used in one of his experiments. His beloved daughter, aged two and a half, reminded him, he once wrote, of "the greatest mass murderer of the century" because of a lock of hair over her forehead. He might read faces in flowers, rocks, house fronts, cracks in a sidewalk, fallen twigs, cloud formations, a crumpled pillow. And from the cast of the "features" he could deduce reproaches, warnings, or encouragement that might have come from God or from the Devil or from unspecified "forces," which, he asserted, made him their plaything.

Books he picked up somehow opened to passages that threw light—or subtle shadows—on whatever was troubling him at that moment. According to his diaries and books, he kept meeting people who were look-alikes, even doubles, of himself and others; he liked to speculate on what such resemblances might mean. He glared at a painting or photograph of a person he disliked, recalling some harm done to him in the past, and, as if by black magic, he said, the person was stricken by a disease, or committed a crime and was imprisoned for it, or lost a child, a wife, money, a job. In much the same way, after he suffered some misfortune he wondered in print whether an enemy had bewitched him from a distance. What else could be the significance of mysterious, painful radiations he occasionally felt, like stabs of electricity?

Yet Strindberg, a rigorously purposeful man with formidable gifts of observation and intuition, trained himself to exploit every sliver of chance in his life. He wrote about that life with a frankness that appalled many readers, and he seems to have relished the manufacturing of public portraits of himself: it is impossible to know which of them, if any, to believe in. The difficulty is compounded by his staggering output. So prolific was he and so varied were his writings that when he died in 1912 at the age of sixty-three it was as if he had experienced several lives, fulfilled almost all his scholarly and artistic opportunities, and used himself up—to the height of his powers.

Those powers had proved to be unmatched. In the drama Strindberg ranks with the preeminent late-nineteenth-century exponents of realism (Henrik Ibsen, Henry Becque, Gerhart Hauptmann, Leo Tolstoy, Anton Chekhov, and G. B. Shaw). He also wrote plays that are the precursors of expressionism, dada, and surrealism; capital essays on the theory and practice of theater; a sequence of novels and stories, some autobiographical in part, that are among the most relentless self-explorations, the most authoritative fiction, and the most poetically suggestive documents in literature. Practically all innovative writers and painters of the twentieth century came under his sway, were unable to escape his legacy, whether or not they knew his work at first hand. The Russian-born Frenchman Arthur Adamov said, "It was Strindberg, or more exactly, *A Dream Play*, that incited me to write for the theater." In his journal Franz Kafka wrote:

> I feel better because I have read Strindberg. I don't read him in order to read him, but to press myself against his breast. He carries me like an infant on his left arm. I sit there like a man on a statue. Ten times I am in danger of falling but the eleventh time I'm solidly installed, confident, with a wide perspective before me.

The image of trying to remain close to Strindberg's heart in order to share its palpitations and feel reassured by them signifies a filial warmth toward Strindberg. So does Bertolt Brecht's characterizing of him as "one of the great educators of modern Europe." Eugene O'Neill once said he wished that "immortality were a fact, for then some day I would meet Strindberg."

The first volume of Strindberg's "autobiographical novels," *Tjänstekvinnans son (The Son of a Servant)*, appeared in 1886, when he was thirty-seven. It had not been recollected in tranquillity. He was living in Switzerland and quarreling with his first wife, Siri, whom he had once called his "queen with the sunlit forehead." He had recently outraged Sweden with the collection of short stories *Giftas (Getting Married, 1884–1885)*, which attacked the upper classes, the church, and birth control, and brought him to public trial—at which he was acquitted, but nar-

rowly. He had debts and three children to keep. He considered himself "dead, physically, morally, and financially." Nevertheless, he completed the record of his first eighteen years, almost 100,000 words, in two months, dashed off a succeeding volume in less than a month, and, in the following years, wrote his three most celebrated realistic plays, *Fadren (The Father*, 1887), *Fröken Julie (Miss Julie*, 1888), and *Fordringsägare (Creditors*, 1888). A realistic artist at this time, according to his own statements, he was already toying with theories of the occult and mystical beliefs, going so far as to aver that he had inherited the soul of Edgar Allan Poe, who had died the year he was born, 1849.

The Son of a Servant, Strindberg's account of his origins as a man and a mind, displays a flock of Strindbergs taking cover in one body and one spirit, and performs an admirably thorough, pre-Freudian analysis of them. It also assists our understanding of this author's urge to write and of the nature of his sources, without explaining away his abilities as neuroses. According to an imaginary interview that prefaces the book, he set out to produce not a novel, not a confession ("I have no intention of asking for forgiveness"), but "an attempt at the literature of the future," meaning no doubt fiction drawn from experience and rendered with Zola-like "scientific" detachment, and also stories in which the author associates himself closely with his protagonist. The book's subtitle is "The Evolution of a Human Being, 1849–1867," to which Strindberg adds, "There's only one person's life we really know and that one is our own. And the great advantage of telling one's own life is that one is dealing with a sympathetic and interesting person."

This autobiographical and documentary novel is no whitewash. The author is more callous with himself than a conventional biographer would be. One can only marvel at the quality of the raw pieces Strindberg cut out of his life to make his art. One feels he deliberately created as fascinating a life as he could in order to be able to describe it so well without having to tell lies or embellish. All the same, in this, as in his succeeding autobiographical novels, Strindberg does sometimes remember wrong, according to his American translator and editor, Evert Sprinchorn, who questions certain factual errors and misleading statements: for instance, that he was conceived out of wedlock. He could not always cope with his life as he lived it. Day by day it dizzied him. Yet in retrospect he saw it with a clarity that must have terrified him. Perhaps the act of writing about it at frantic speed served to free him from his worst memories. The relief, in any case, was only temporary. He kept immersing himself in his past until, later, he had to go directly into his unconscious for surcease and inspiration, and, almost by accident, to invent automatic writing (and painting) and thus give rise to a new kind of self-prompted, typically twentieth-century art. This technique sounds suspiciously close to literary masturbation, a fertilizing of oneself. Very likely it was. At fifteen, Strindberg tells us, he read Dr. Kapff's *Warning by a Friend of Youth Against the Most Dangerous Enemy of Youth* and discovered that he had only ten years to live:

> His spinal marrow and his brain would rot, his face would turn into a death's head, his hair would fall out. . . . And the cure? Christ! But Jesus could not heal the body, only the soul. The body was condemned to death at twenty-five; the only thing left was to save the soul from everlasting damnation.
>
> (*The Son of a Servant*, ch. 5)

Strindberg was of a temperament that courts the forbidden. As he grew older, he persisted in defying phenomena and ideas that frightened him—such as the occult, marriage, and the nature of fear itself—by investigating them.

His immediate objective at fifteen, though, was to rescue his soul. He became a Pietist and says he talked of a career as a clergyman (if he did live beyond twenty-five), maybe an iron-nerved Brand: he was sixteen when Ibsen's epic play of the minister who believed in "all or nothing" was published. Still, he might just as well have become a soldier, a biologist, a musician, a chemist, a physicist, a teacher, or a librarian, if the range of his activities at the time meant anything. Subsequently he would practice medicine, journalism, sinology, and acting before and while he wrote his first plays. So many false starts— and some of them would go on into middle age: in 1912, shortly before his death, he willed to his third wife, Harriet, his "formula" for making gold.

During these early years in his native Stockholm he could not get on the right footing with his mother, father, or brothers. He was the fourth of eight children, and yearned for more of his mother's time and affection than she could give. He condemns her unjustness and violence, her making him confess to drinking some wine he had not drunk, her egging his father on to punish the children, and her small-mindedness: she is the servant of the book's title: "But since the children received food and comfort from her, they loved her." She died when he was thirteen; and Strindberg felt like a Hamlet when her place as mistress of the home was taken by the housekeeper, an attractive young woman whom his father shortly married.

His relationship with his father was equally—one might say "classically"—ambivalent. Strindberg calls his father, a shipping agent, "a stranger, more an enemy than a friend," then hops into the paternal shoes for an instant, recalling the time when he is writing and has his own family, and remarks, "That is the thankless position of the father in the family—the provider for all, the enemy of all." The family, he concludes, is the "home of all social evils, a charitable institution for indolent women, a prison workshop for family breadwinners, and a hell for children."

Other themes from Strindberg's writings bud at this stage, such as his noticing poverty among school friends; his detestation of teaching by rote and cruelty; his view of life as a "struggle from beginning to end"; the rudiments of his vulnerable systems of ideas; his facing of the question that recurs to the unorthodox artist: How can I know I am right? But the book's quietly obsessive undercurrent is the forming of his attitude toward women. The sister of his second wife was to write that Strindberg "can be savage with men, but he does not even contradict a girl." This is the man whom people have frequently cast as an inveterate woman-hater.

Strindberg's three marriages began with over-rich expectations. Women must be cushiony wife-mothers, confidantes, tolerant, able to release vast, balmy quantities of consolation. They must also be vibrant young creatures, perfect instruments of lovemaking, and at the same time chaste, inhuman figures to be simultaneously owned and worshiped, private goddesses, exclusive muses. This three-sided vision suggests every man's dream of femininity, his three private, cherished graces—and Strindberg knew that. He pointed out that most marriages of his time were defective, if not doomed, because "under present conditions" men went into matrimony idealizing their wives while becoming enslaved by those wives' bodies. And what, then, would he prescribe for a happy marriage? Well, the husband and wife must be equals as far as was possible, sharers, perhaps as in his short story "An Attempt at Reform."

If Strindberg has often been attacked for the wrong reasons, the misunderstandings may have resulted from the access of power that rose in him when he took up a pen. Timid in person, he found combativeness, as well as relief, in the act of writing. His hard-won ferocity allowed him to articulate man's longing for woman as she ought to be, his unjustified, ungentlemanly disappointment with her as she is, and his awareness that men behave unreasonably over women. In a letter to his older brother, written not long after *The Son of a Servant* had loosed widespread outrage at his

apparent misogyny, he remarked that his dislike of women was "only theoretical; I could never live without the company of a woman." But he did, sometimes for long spells, between and after his marriages. Unluckily for Strindberg, he married women who wanted professional careers, two as actresses, one as a journalist. All three tried more or less to become sharers, his equals. Or was it bad luck? Some lure drew him toward ambition in the opposite sex, not toward the hearty domesticity he envisaged in the ideal wife.

Another autobiographical novel, *Le plaidoyer d'un fou* (*A Madman's Defense*, 1888), written in France—and in French—picks up and fictionalizes Strindberg's story as of 1875, several years after he had left the university at Uppsala without bothering to graduate. He had become a diligent employee, specializing in Chinese studies, at the Royal Library in Stockholm, an eligible bachelor of twenty-six, a careful dresser, and a bit of a man-about-town. That year he was introduced to "the baroness," Siri (née) von Essen: "Her little face was framed by roguish curls, golden as a cornfield. She had the shoulders of a princess and a supple, willowy figure." Siri, a lady of his own age from an aristocratic Finnish family, was the wife of Baron Wrangel and the mother of a three-year-old girl.

A Madman's Defense is, according to its closing lines, an act of revenge on Siri. Its tone is impassioned and strident by comparison with that of the earlier book. In *The Son of a Servant* Strindberg, recapitulating a fairly remote childhood and youth, calls the hero "he." *A Madman's Defense*, which deals with events and people still very much a part of his life, is told in the first person. Possibly to introduce a note of objectivity and to temper the near-hysteria that colors his narrative ("She made a practice of anticipating my wishes so as to thwart them; she said Yes whenever I said No, and vice versa. She hated me with an absolute loathing"), he now calls the hero Axel, his brother's name, instead of Johan, his own first given name, and calls the heroine

Marie, the name of one of Siri's supposed lovers whom Strindberg took to be a lesbian. *Defense* details Axel's infatuation; his misgivings over "stealing" the wife of his friend the baron (even though the baron is conducting a hot affair with a teenaged cousin and goes out of his way to encourage Axel's advances to Marie); the baron's divorce; Axel's marriage after several backings-off; a series of ugly confrontations between Marie and Axel, followed by ecstatic reconciliations; his jealousy over her friendships with people in the theater; and his supicions that, supported by a conspiracy of feminists and lesbians, she is trying to have him certified insane.

The marriage to Siri lasted from 1877 to 1891. In those fourteen years they moved constantly, sometimes together, sometimes apart. Strindberg shuttled between France, Italy, Switzerland, Bavaria, Denmark, with intermittent returns to Sweden. He claims in *Defense* that he wrote plays for her to act in, *Herr Bengts Husfru* (*Herr Bengt's Wife,* 1882) and presumably *Lycko-Pers resa* (*Lucky Per's Journey,* 1881), *Miss Julie,* and *Creditors.* But producers cast her only infrequently, and he implies that she had little aptitude for the stage. However, in 1889 he set up a short-lived acting company with her in Copenhagen, where she played Julie, among several roles, and was derided in the reviews. He also gave her writing lessons, but she didn't really wish to become a writer. None of his attempts at being a companion, adviser, and household god improved the marriage. Nor did the arrival of children. She bore him three daughters and a son, although one daughter died soon after birth. He loved the children and says he protected them from her spasms of anger; but at the divorce proceedings Siri won custody.

By this time Strindberg, a notorious figure in Sweden, regarded as a sensational self-publicist and foe of women, had a few fervent admirers, but many detractors. In 1892 he took off for Berlin, where *The Father* and *Miss Julie* had their first showings outside Scandinavia, at the Freie Bühne. As one of Europe's important new independent theaters, modeled on Antoine's Théâtre-Libre in Paris, the Freie Bühne welcomed controversial plays, and from Strindberg it got them. *Miss Julie* aroused such a storm of protest that it closed after its opening night.

In Berlin Strindberg caroused and had a hyperactive night life with a group of much younger expatriate writers, painters, and artistic pretenders, some from Scandinavia, among them the Norwegian painter Edvard Munch. In this colony of aesthetic rebels he met the attractive Viennese journalist Frida Uhl. He was forty-four, Frida only twenty-two; but she decided he needed a business manager-cum-agent, took his manuscripts around to publishers, and shamelessly promoted Strindberg and his works. In part because of her efforts, more of his plays and novels were printed in German. In 1893 she married him. They separated within a matter of months.

After 1892, a year in which Strindberg completed seven plays—some short and some long—more than half a decade elapsed before he went back to writing for the theater. His biographers and critics have put forward a number of sometimes conflicting explanations for this gap in his theatrical output. Was he depressed by the swift failure of his second marriage? Disgusted by the debaucheries of his stay in Berlin? Written out for the time being? Did he choose to turn away from literature and art in order to devote himself to alchemy and science, to a search for the philosopher's stone, the secret of gold, and for proof that sulphur was not an element but a compound of carbon? Had he started to undergo a conversion from an agnosticism that bordered on atheism to a new, personal creed of mysticism? Was he so troubled of soul, so obsessed with the fear of persecution or of divine punishment, pursued, like Francis Thompson, by the hound of heaven, that he almost lost his sanity? Or did he willfully flirt with—even induce—madness as a means of investigating its characteristics and consequences, playing at being penitent and confessor at the same time? If so, had he abandoned his mostly realistic and naturalistic drama in favor of a new type of dramaturgy based on promptings from the unconscious? Any or all of these questions can be adduced from a reading of either his tortured account of this period in his next autobiographical novel, *Inferno* (1897), or the more laconic treatment in a novel, *Klostret (The Cloister)*, written the following year (1898).

Strindberg's most richly textured, rewarding, and contradictory document, *Inferno* juts up out of nineteenth-century literature, a grand monadnock that invites comparison with Friedrich Nietzsche's *Thus Spake Zarathustra* (1886), Søren Kierkegaard's *Either/Or* (1843), and Thomas Carlyle's *Sartor Resartus* (1835). It is a poem in prose, recording the author's flight from—and yet toward—himself. It throbs with denials and affirmations. And it loops back on his earlier themes while it anticipates and provides material for the later ones, portraying him as a disciple of a new internationalism and interculturalism in the arts, an antifeminist who could be enthralled by women, a retiring, harassed neurasthenic who aggravated the turmoil in himself so that he might serve as his own crucible, and the very personification of romanticism.

Strindberg forsook Berlin in August 1894 for Paris. He was still married to Frida; and she left their child in Austria to rejoin him. At this time Strindberg had to endure celebrity status, thanks to the French premieres of *Miss Julie*, staged by Antoine, and *Creditors* and *The Father*, staged by Lugné-Poë. Less than two months after her arrival, and about a month before *The Father* opened, Frida went back to Austria on learning that their child, Kerstin, was ill. Some acrimonious letters passed back and forth between Frida and Strindberg—he seemed to be trying to shake her off—and eventually led to an unofficial dissolution of the marriage, although they were not legally divorced until a couple of years later: "I loved her, she loved me, and we hated one another with a ferocious love-hate

that was only intensified by the distance that separated us."

Meanwhile, he took up quarters on the Left Bank, near the Sorbonne, the original locale of Henri Murger's *La vie de bohème*. He sold some of his own paintings to a charlatan, who signed and resold them at a profit. He persisted with his laboratory experiments in whatever hotel room he happened to be living in. Staying in the Saint-Louis Hospital for treatment of psoriasis of his hands, he sat at a table for lunch with "a macabre company. The faces were those of dead and dying men. One had a nose missing, another an eye, yet another had a lip hanging loose, another a rotting cheek." This experience can be regarded as a prelude to the ordeal of happenstance, delusions, and apparitions Strindberg recounts in *Inferno*, probably with lurid embellishments to fascinate and astound his readers.

He saw his initials on a hanging sign. He came across an old book that more or less confirmed his theory about sulphur; the author's name was Orfila, and, to Strindberg's amazement, Orfila was the name of a hotel nearby, whereupon he decided to move there. Having settled in and enjoyed the view of buildings from his window, he discovered that one of them had "innumerable" water closets from which flushing noises proceeded at all hours. He almost bumped into a young man who resembled Frida. From a room below his he caught the tinkling of a Schumann melody on a piano and felt convinced it was being played by a friend who had turned against him in Berlin and had come to Paris to kill him. A roomer next door kept moving his chair every time Strindberg moved his; but worse, this man somehow transferred himself into the room flanking Strindberg's on the other side: "He must be in two rooms simultaneously." At two o'clock one morning "I rose from my bed as though sucked up by a vacuum that was trying to tear my heart from my body. . . . A shower of electricity fell upon my neck and pressed me down onto the floor."

From poltergeists, noises, electrical assaults, and other torments that may have been self-induced but struck Strindberg as all too real, he fled to people he knew in Dieppe. They told him he looked "like an exhumed corpse." But his "unknown opponents" would not let up on him: "Everywhere, everywhere, the furies found me out." He determined to go back to Sweden in case he was suffering from "a nervous disease." The friend he consulted at Ystad, a Dr. Eliasson, tried to treat Strindberg with rest, cold water immersions, and warm advice, but Strindberg quickly concluded without evidence that the doctor was in the pay of those mysterious persecutors: "Everything concurred to make me suspect and incriminate my good friend." We can notice exaggerations like "everything" in this last sentence, and "everywhere, everywhere" in the one above, and ask, as Strindberg kept asking himself, whether he was in the grip of a "persecution mania" or dramatizing his plight as he wrote it up afterward. He says he took *Inferno* directly out of his diaries, but he also admitted at different times that he was, after all, a novelist and playwright.

When "the good doctor's malevolent intentions" became too much for him—after about one month in Ystad—Strindberg, who must have been dashing off pitiful letters to friends and relatives, received an invitation to visit Frida's mother in Darnach in the Danube valley. Hoping to find peace, and sleep, he went to Austria by way of Berlin. There a cab drive through the city "seemed to me like a trip through a hedge of thorns, so deeply did all the memories embodied in the city pierce my heart." His mother-in-law and her sister put themselves to some pains to make him comfortable and to offer him spiritual consolation. He also rejoiced—at first—in the affection of Kerstin, now two and a half, whom he had not seen since she was six weeks old.

Austria's peaks, vales, and villages failed to soothe Strindberg. Craggy vistas that delighted his eyes gave him bad dreams. Dogs, a sawmill, a forge, a miller's ovens stamped ugly images on his brain, although he would later overcome by sublimation the fears they had evoked in him when he came to write his trilogy, *Till Damaskus* (*To Damascus*, 1898). The two motherly ladies tried to convert him to Catholicism; he felt bound to resist their ministrations. Kerstin, his "little angel," insisted on accompanying and distracting him on his regular morning walk, in the course of which he liked to order his thoughts and charge himself up for the day's writing or experimenting. Frida's old grandmother had a grudge against him, he believed; when she fell sick he felt responsible. Putting up in the room where Frida "spent the two years of our separation," he grew remorseful: "Poor, poor woman!" He regretted "the crime we had committed in treating love too lightly." (Frida was away at this time, living in Munich with the outstanding Swiss-German playwright Frank Wedekind, by whom she had a child. It takes something like genius to consort with genius not once, but twice.)

Poring over the Old Testament and Emanuel Swedenborg's visions of hell (in *De coelo et ejus mirabilibus et de inferno*); associating himself spiritually at times with Robert le Diable, an eleventh-century Norman aristocrat whose mother reportedly sold him to the Devil, with Napoleon and Julius Caesar, with Jacob, who wrestled with God, and with Job, "the perfect and upright man" who bowed to God's unprovoked punishments; certain that a Swedish philanthropist who had given him money and then tried to win him over to the tenets of theosophy had turned into "an avenging demon"; keeping the household up at night with the noises, shocks, and hallucinations he was subjected to, Strindberg now regarded himself as "a damned soul" who must set off on a "pilgrimage toward expiation."

Once again he went north to Sweden, this time to the tranquil university town of Lund. A fuller edition of Swedenborg, the *Arcana coelestia*, told him that "the attacks of pain (angina pectoris), the constrictions of the chest, the palpitation of my heart, the tightening band that I call the electric girdle'' were not so much physical symptoms of illness as they were the agonies of ''devastàtio,'' that is, ''a process of spiritual purification known to Saint Paul,'' a preparatory cleansing of the soul before a conceptual rebirth.

In Lund, ''imprisoned in this little town of the Muses, without any hope of escape, I joined in fearful battle against the enemy—myself.'' Slowly he pulled himself out of his ''inferno crisis.'' By the following year, 1897, he had triumphed over his hesitations and conceived of a form for the book *Inferno*. He completed its 60,000-odd words in seven weeks, and in French, expecting that it would not easily find a Swedish publisher; but it did.

Like the earlier autobiographical novels, *Inferno* is a kind of subjective case study in that it supplies a chronology of its author's thoughts and feelings, sometimes intricate, sometimes patchy, an idiosyncratic travelogue. It fuses fact and extravagation, preaching, self-contempt, and self-propulsion toward a new state of being and a new outlook. For a time he could shed his guilt and reassure himself that he wasn't responsible for his plight. God had made a laughingstock of him, had chastised him for his pride; but it was God who had created him proud in the first place, and then had held him up as an exemplary figure, a warning, as He had once done with Lucifer.

Despite his spiritual malaise, Strindberg's five years preceding the composition of *Inferno* had not been fallow ones. A compulsive writer, he had produced *Antibarbus* (1894), a collection of papers on chemistry and alchemy that he vainly hoped would ensure his fame as a scientist and secure him a chair in some distinguished university, and *Sylva sylvanum* (1896), which proposed a unifying theory of organic and inorganic matter. That half-decade has also given us the voluminous correspondence and some penetrating essays, most notably the reflective *Études funèbres* (*Graveyard Reveries*, 1896) and *Des arts nouveaux! ou Le hasard dans la production artistique* (The New Arts; or, The Role of Chance in Artistic Creation, 1894), which reads like a premature plea for surrealism.

Strindberg's last two autobiographical books, *Légendes* (*Legends*, 1897–1898) and *Ensam* (*Alone*, 1903), make less of a pretense of being novels. He had entered a new phase of life, although not even a reborn artist discards more than a thin skin of his former self; and the guilt he had tried to unload returned to harry him as he looked back, not only on his sins of commission and omission, but also on sins merely contemplated—malicious and profane thoughts he had harbored in the past. *Legends* tries to validate the author's ''inferno'' pains and distress by recounting similar experiences undergone by others. Its final, unfinished portion, entitled ''Jacob Wrestles,'' represents his futile search during a last stay in Paris for a satisfying religious faith that might drive out his devils of doubt and anxiety; he tells how he twice met the silent, cloaked figure of God in the Luxembourg Gardens at a twilight hour and railed at Him, without quite managing to say what was on his mind. In case you run into God, Strindberg implies, have your complaints rehearsed and orchestrated, or you will give yourself cause for reproach afterward at having spoiled an opportunity.

Alone describes the chosen solitude of an author in Stockholm during late middle age; he is, one might say, a spin-off of Strindberg, not quite the man himself, and he leads a life that is not quite Strindberg's, even if he comes into contact with Strindberg's old friends and acquaintances, with whom he finds it hard to make conversation. He prefers his own company on solo walks every day; he views people and happenings around him with studied nonchalance; and he cherishes the privacy of his desk, where he talks ''through the mouths of children, of women, of old men. I am king and pauper. I am the highest of the high—the tyrant—and I am the lowest and most despised—the persecuted hater of tyrants. I share all opinions, I confess all religions, I live in all ages, and I myself have ceased to exist. In this state I am indescribably happy."

After the visit to Paris during which he wrestled in one-sided debate with the Almighty, he took root again in Sweden, in the Stockholm of *Alone,* for his remaining twelve years. Not, however to retire; far from it. After his fiftieth birthday he wrote thirty-four plays, more than half his life's total. And these exclude parts 1 and 2 of *To Damascus* and the play *Advent* (1898), which he wrote while he was still forty-nine. *To Damascus, Drömspelet* (*A Dream Play,* 1901), and *Spöksonaten* (*The Ghost Sonata,* 1907) would by themselves have conferred landmark honors on Strindberg for their contributions to remaking the modern drama. But he also revived his realistic mode with telling effect in *Brott och brott* (*Crimes and Crimes,* 1899) and the two parts of *Dödsdansen* (*The Dance of Death,* 1902); and he contrived to dramatize events in the lives of Martin Luther, Moses, Socrates, Christ, and a dozen rulers and other political figures out of Sweden's past. (Rouben Mamoulian's 1933 film *Queen Christina,* starring Greta Garbo, is a kind of response to, and flattening of, Strindberg's portrait of Christina.) After founding the Intimate Theater, together with the director August Falck, in 1907, he created a series of medium-length chamber plays. He wrote six novels and novellas, in addition to *Alone;* a quantity of short stories; nonfiction dealing with history, religion, politics, and the evolution of languages. *The Blue Book,* intended to sum up his life's work, consisted of four volumes of essays, dialogues, reminiscences, and ruminations.

For the Norwegian-born actress Harriet Bosse, whom he met in 1900 and married a year later, Strindberg wrote the plays *Påsk* (*Easter,* 1901), *Kronbruden* (*The Bridal Crown,* 1901), and *Svanevit* (*Swanwhite,* 1901). He had given her a leading role in *To Damascus,* for which she proved unsuited, but he had been smitten by her porcelain beauty, youthfulness, and modesty. This third marriage did not last, either. Harriet and he remained on speaking and writing terms, if not exactly friendly, after their divorce in 1904 and her resumption of an independent acting career. Strindberg kept with him the child of that marriage, Anne-Marie, until Harriet's remarriage several years after. In 1908 he fell in love with another young actress, Fanny Falkner, the daughter of his landlady and a member of his and Falck's troupe.

On his sixtieth birthday Strindberg was publicly feted. His plays had found their way into repertories at home and abroad, but mostly for one-night showings. He was far from wealthy, although he sent a thousand Swedish crowns to the relief fund for Swedish writers in Paris, which in his impoverished days had helped him out with a gift. Ever the egalitarian, he wrote more condemnations of the monarchy and the privileged, still considering aristocrats to be a fragile, doomed species, like etiolated plants. In early 1912 there were even more demonstrative celebrations for his sixty-third birthday; he had become a national treasure of sorts. But by then he had contracted stomach cancer. In late April he grieved on hearing of the death of Siri von Essen. He died three weeks after her, on May 14. About five years before, in a letter to a German translator, he had written, "I long for the light, always have done, but I've never found it." Yet he never stopped looking.

Although Strindberg made himself into a Renaissance man in at least two senses—he underwent artistic rebirths or rejuvenations and became a scholar and practitioner of the plastic as well as the written arts—and although he is rightly thought of today as having been, and having *wanted* to be, primarily a dramatist, nevertheless his accomplishments in fiction stand in the forefront of modern novels and short stories. To the Swedish public of the 1880's he was known as the author of the short stories in *Getting Married,* which precipitated his trial on a charge of blasphemy (he was exonerated), of *The Son of a Servant,* and of the novels *Röda rummet* (*The Red*

Room, 1879) and *Hemsöborna* (*The People of Hemsö*, 1887).

Some of his short stories he wrote for the sheer pleasure of exploring the medium; others arose from financial necessity at those times when he teetered on the rim of poverty. But he maintained so conscientious a level of craftsmanship that one cannot distinguish the pleasure-giving stories from the income-providing ones. *Getting Married*, written and initially published in two parts, each with a provocative preface, charts the delights and afflictions, the hopes, clashes, regrets, money worries, adjustments, and resignation in thirty marriages between suited and mismatched partners, who welcome or resist the incursions of children and in-laws. In five or six pages Strindberg can vividly sketch and intertwine two lives and their surroundings, keeping his comic distance, yet, when he wants to, making us feel the sorrows and chagrin of his couples. In "The Phoenix" he requires fewer than 2,500 words to tell hauntingly of a man's engagement and loyal marriage to a girl who, through illness, has lost the good looks that first excited him; of his adoration of their daughter, who grows up to resemble his wife as she was in her youth but who dies in adolescence; and of his second marriage to an eighteen-year-old who reminds him of the dead wife and daughter. This tale of the pursuit of an image of beauty, as much as any other story—and there are memorable others, especially "Autumn" and "Natural Obstacles"—gives the lie firmly to rumors that Strindberg held a grudge against women.

In *The Red Room* painters, sculptors, actors, journalists, merchants, financiers, an evangelist, and a prostitute dart into and out of the rapid action, which reaches across two years in the overlapping worlds of Stockholm's arts and business. Strindberg's young radicals tear up the floorboards of their rented rooms to keep their inner and outer fires burning. They scribble reckless numbers of promissory notes in order to eat. At such late-night hangouts as the Red Room they talk aesthetics and metaphysics. One commits suicide, others achieve fleeting successes, two of them sell out, and all of them rely for recognition on the whims of newspaper critics. Meanwhile, the businessmen manipulate credit, incorporations, and bankruptcies, all of which turn them a profit and ruin others. In these worlds it is nigh on impossible to make an honest living that allows both subsistence and self-respect.

Eight years later, in *The People of Hemsö*, Strindberg chose a setting that contrasts with the city: an island, a skerry, where the community lives off fishing, sporadic hunting, and ill-planned farming. A homeless man in his thirties named Carlsson, something of an operator but also a thoughtful and industrious worker, takes over as manager of some island property belonging to a middle-aged widow. He gets the farm into good shape against opposition from the widow's son, rationalizes the fishing, attracts summer residents and a mining operation, and eventually marries the widow. Then, when he's ready to luxuriate in his proprietary triumphs, luck turns against him and he dies in a blizzard. Even more than in *The Red Room* Strindberg brings into play his gifts of minute observation and interpretation of landscapes and life—the seasonal plants, the behavior of animals, the dynamics of human psychology, details of dress, stature, and complexion. Most of his chapters take place during spring and summer, the times of growth and ripening, but the novel culminates in winter bleakness, and Carlsson's death is all the more affecting for being described in prose as cold and pure as snow. This novel would prove to be Strindberg's most enduringly popular work in Sweden.

Both novels contain scene after scene combining comedy, pathos, and grotesqueries that resound in one's memory: the funeral of a child too young to have received a name, followed by a riotous drinking party; a crowd of people occupying a small boat in which a tar barrel is leaking; a wedding ceremony from which the drunken pastor departs to crawl, with his boots still on, into the bridal bed—from there he has to be removed unobtrusively and lowered out of a window.

In his later fiction, such as *Tschandala* (1888), *En häxa (A Witch)* and *I havsbandet (By the Open Sea)* (both 1890), *Svarta fanor* (Black Banners), *Taklagsöl (The Roofing Feast)*, and *Syndaboken (The Scapegoat)* (all 1907), Strindberg experimented with more openly symbolic and expressionistic prose techniques that would, within a couple of decades, characterize some of the more venturesome literature of the twentieth century.

By the Open Sea, a work complementary to *The People of Hemsö*, also deals with the arrival of a stranger in a small island community, only this time he is a cool-mannered, uncommonly intelligent government inspector; and, instead of sacrificing him to a natural catastrophe, Strindberg shows us his psychological collapse under the strains of loneliness and unrequited love, in a manner reminiscent of Joseph Conrad's ten or fifteen years later. In *The Roofing Feast* an injured man's evocation in a hospital bed of apparently disconnected memories from his past has a musical treatment, employing themes and variations rather in the manner of the author's chamber plays. In its string of monologues it anticipates the method used much later in both novels and plays by Samuel Beckett.

For English readers Strindberg is a creator of fiction whose time has not yet come. His theater has overshadowed his other bountiful writings—not surprisingly, for his dramatic output is awesomely large. He wrote his first play, *Den Fredlöse (The Freethinker*, 1881) at the age of twenty, his last, *Stora landsvägen (The Great Highway*, 1909), at sixty; and averaged a play and a half per year in the intervening time. The range of his settings, historical eras, characterizations, and dramatic structures has exceptional breadth, like the range of his committed interests. Critics usu-

ally divide his work into distinct periods. He kept coming back to the theater with new ideas and new resolutions, so that his early false starts can also be seen as fresh starts. It is convenient up to a point to say that his plays of the 1880's, especially *The Father*, *Miss Julie*, and *Creditors*, are naturalistic; that *To Damascus*, *Oväder (Storm Weather*, 1907), and *Pelikanen (The Pelican*, 1907), are expressionistic; and that *A Dream Play*, *Brända tomten (The Burned House*, 1907), and *The Ghost Sonata* are surrealistic. But elements of naturalism, surrealism, and expressionism often collide and join forces in his work. In his later years he picks up and follows threads or entire patterns he laid down as a younger man. He remained tempted by certain themes and kinds of personality clashes, and his plays ring ingenious changes on these Strindbergian fundamentals.

We can notice several examples of his continuity. First, naturalism: Naturalism is analytical; it works back by a sort of detection from effects to causes. It fastens onto a dramatic situation, such as Miss Julie's aggressively coquettish behavior toward her father's valet, Jean, and his alternations of reluctance and eagerness, leading up to a seduction, and then to regrets on both sides, and finally to her suicide. While observing details or outward effects coolly, even scientifically, naturalism traces their causes: Julie's lonely, aristocratic upbringing; her mother and father's treatment of her as a boy, not a girl; her mother's mannishness; the setting in the servants' quarters, which for a time makes Julie feel reckless; the intoxicating scent of cut flowers and juniper twigs, and the even more intoxicating wine; the festive, anything-goes atmosphere of Midsummer Eve; Jean's yearning since his childhood to be on a par with the upper classes, which results, as Strindberg says in his famous preface to the play, in a character that "is unformed and divided. He wavers between an admiration of high positions and a hatred of the men who occupy them." And there are other causes that Strindberg adduces. But this type of searching analysis, which builds up to an unmasking, the revelation of painful or horrifying truths, occurs also in *To Damascus* and *A Dream Play.*

Second, expressionism: The distinguishing marks of Strindberg's expressionist drama are already visible in the earlier plays of the 1880's. Characters with generic titles rather than names appear in *The Father* (the Captain, the Doctor, the Pastor); so does a typically expressionist hero whom the world considers mad but who considers himself the only sane figure in an insane world; and so do the hero's other distorted perceptions of his surroundings, as when the Captain believes himself surrounded by enemies in his own house.

Third, symbolism: Strindberg's earlier plays, like Ibsen's, Shaw's, and Chekhov's plays, may seem realistic when compared with many commercial or fanciful plays that came before and after them, but their action and dialogue carry a symbolic freight.

Fourth, musicality: Those same plays often develop musically, using themes and variations, leitmotifs, and "instrumental solos" or arias for individual voices, much as do the later, more explicitly musical chamber plays.

Finally, myth: Allusions to Scandinavian, Greek, Hebrew, and Oriental myths abound in Strindberg's early writings, as well as his later ones. He makes plentiful use of mythically evocative names, stories, and encounters, as Harry G. Carlson has demonstrated in *Strindberg and the Poetry of Myth.* In other words, Strindberg, like all outstanding theater artists—actors as well as playwrights—combines drama with lyricism. A lyrical play like *Easter* has its moments of high drama, whereas in, say, *Creditors* and *The Dance of Death* the concentrated dramatic tension is occasionally relieved by a stretch of lyrical writing.

The image of Strindberg presented here is not that of a dilettante flying off the handle, going in whichever direction his impulses sweep him, but of an intrepid craftsman advancing on several fronts, testing memories and styles and hypotheses, sometimes over and over until he believes he has exhausted their possibilities. For he was—and deserves to be remembered as—the most resolute experimenter in the drama since Shakespeare. His scientific studies may not have borne the fruit he wished for, but they sharpened certain of his aptitudes; and there is in his art the amalgam of persistence and daring that we associate with the labors of the inventors, the discoverers, the pathbreakers of science.

If we view his drama as a heterogeneous whole, instead of the works of separate periods each with its own artistic personality, we can take note of similarities and differences among several aspects of his plays: the conflicts, the structures, the staging effects, the characters, and the themes.

The conflicts are often said to arise from trials of strength, partly because his characters themselves declare that they are stronger or weaker than their opponents. The notion of strength has a special connotation here. Obviously it is not brute physical strength, nor is it conventional spiritual strength. Strindberg's men and women, according to a number of critics, are locked in Nietzschean battles of the will; but that is not quite right, either, although Strindberg admired and for about three years corresponded with Nietzsche, counting him as a friend. The stronger character in Strindberg is the one who can more easily shake off the weight of guilt in his past, in order to attack with fewer encumbrances and reservations. Strindberg proclaimed the crippling consequences of guilt more than a decade before Sigmund Freud, although like Freud he met with bitter resistance and condemnation.

Who engages in these conflicts? They commonly erupt between wife and husband, parent(s) and child(ren), sexual rivals, either men or women, and siblings; but they may be complicated by secondary conflicts if the antagonists come from different social classes, or have different standards of morality, or if one is an intellectual and the other not. That is, the complications have to do not only with what the characters *want,* but with what they are. Almost all the conflicts are also colored by self-dissatisfaction; that is, they are seconded by internal conflicts in the characters themselves, who seem unsure about both what they want and what they are.

The conflict between the Captain and his wife, Laura, in *The Father* has chafed them for some twenty years, almost since the start of their marriage. As the situation stands in the play, it has become inflamed because of their disagreement over whether their daughter, Bertha, aged seventeen, shall stay at home and become an artist, as Laura wishes, or move away and train to become a teacher, as the Captain wishes. But the dispute strikes much deeper than an argument over Bertha's future. The Captain is plagued by doubts about whether he actually is Bertha's father; Laura sharpens those doubts, makes them one of her weapons in the matrimonial battle. He works at scientific experiments; Laura believes these to be futile and thinks he should attend more to his military duties. She feels unprovided for and fears poverty for Bertha and herself if anything untoward happens to him; he aggravates her fears by threatening to commit suicide and so deprive her of an insurance claim. Laura seems willing at first to be a partner in the marriage, whereas her husband has resolved to act as "the father" in everything: to manage his scholarly pursuits in his own way, to manage their property, and to manage their child, leaving Laura no more than the management of the household chores. But the conflict's outward manifestations disguise the one-sidedness of the union. For all his ferocity toward her, the Captain has always loved Laura; she has never loved him. He has done everything in his power to assert himself, to become admirable and masterful and, therefore, as he feels, lovable, and he has not succeeded.

Strindberg works a variation on this conflict and gives it a comic slant in his one-act play *Första varningen* (*The First Warning,* 1892). Axel and Olga Brunner, a couple in their late thirties, are about to split up, or rather, he is going to leave her, because he gets jealous when men pay attention to her, including one man referred to, peculiarly enough, as "the Captain." On the other hand, she is incapable of feeling any jealousy about him. Incapable, that is, until a sexy fifteen-year-old girl teases him, and Olga notices and misunderstands. The marriage is then patched up. As another variation of the marital conflict, the double play *The Dance of Death* locks into a game of reciprocal cruelty played out between a retired artillery officer (yet another captain) named Edgar and his wife, Alice, in the obsolete island fortress where they live. A male rival also figures in the action but less as a threat to the marriage than as a pretext for Edgar and Alice to bludgeon each other verbally with a hatred they have refined into something like a source of joy, a reason for living.

An example of the simple conflict between parent and child, or what is often called generation-gap drama, occurs in *Moderskärlek* (*Motherlove,* 1892), a one-act play in which a middle-aged former prostitute has guarded her twenty-year-old daughter, an aspiring actress, so closely that when the daughter has the opportunity to leave her mother, she is unable to break away. (This mother offers a fascinating contrast to Shaw's Mrs. Warren, who is reckless enough to let her daughter study mathematics at Cambridge, grow independent, and finally strike out on her own.)

The old widower Durand, the central figure in the short tragedy *Inför döden* (*In the Face of Death,* 1892), has failed at running a boarding house in Switzerland since his wife died, and clashes with his daughters over their personal and financial affairs. He sets fire to the house and drinks poison, partly in order to let them collect the insurance benefits and partly because he sees himself as a fugitive from life.

1743

A third example of parent-child conflict, *The Pelican,* also involves arson. A brother and sister, whose mother has denied them food and warmth (both heating and parental love) and has driven their father to his grave, burn down their home. In an astonishing last scene the young people cling to each other, choosing to stay there and be incinerated, but like the Little Match Girl they see ecstatic visions as they expire.

The sexual triangle is a staple of Strindberg's drama, whether the third side of the triangle is real or delusory. In *Creditors* a painter's wife has been married previously to a teacher; he catches up with her, almost contrives to reconcile himself with her, and taunts the painter until the latter goes into an epileptic fit and dies. The wife collapses on his body, begging his forgiveness as she swears she loves him. *Den starkare* (*The Stronger,* 1889) is a triangle, so to speak, with the hypotenuse missing, one of the most famous monologues ever written, and a favorite audition piece for actresses. Two ladies sit at a table in a cafe. Miss Y drinks ale, flips through magazines, and says nothing, while Mrs. X drinks hot chocolate and talks nonstop. She mentions that she once modeled herself on Miss Y, adopted her taste in colors and clothes. She then modulates into suspicions that Miss Y has always been after her husband. But she ends up congratulating herself on having a husband and children to love, while Miss Y has none. For the latter Strindberg supplies only a few laconic stage directions. She neither affirms nor denies what Mrs. X says, and we have no idea how much, if any, of the monologue is true. Some directors have played *The Stronger* through twice in succession, with the actresses switching roles in order to contrast their interpretations of the two characters and to hint at the play's wealth of subtext.

In *Crimes and Crimes* the rivals are men. Maurice, a playwright, steals the glamorous cocotte Henriette from his friend and abandons his own mistress, Jeanne. After Jeanne's child dies, Maurice believes he has committed a psychic murder and gives up Henriette. It is a mark of Strindberg's superiority to a boulevard playwright, who might have used such a basic story, that he avoids a conventional reconciliation scene between Maurice and Jeanne as well as a conventional barrage of insults flying between Maurice and his friend.

A conflict between brothers in *The Burned House* also turns on arson and insurance, only in this case the man who burned down his own house, leaving a clue to suggest that it was done by one of his tenants, doesn't collect: the final insurance payment was handed in too late. The house owner's brother, who has been abroad for years, reveals to his sibling, and to us, that the contents of the house were worth little, anyway; he also gives us enough of his family's history to confirm that his brother, a dyer by profession (that is, a disguiser), had the habit even as a child of blaming his misbehavior on others. The brothers in *Debit och Kredit* (*Debit and Credit,* 1892) are a celebrated scholar and a humble gardener; the scholar has borrowed so heavily from the gardener and his wife that they are forced to sell their home.

These four principal types of conflict by no means exhaust all the combinations treated by Strindberg. In *Paria* (*Pariah,* 1890) two men try to find crimes in each other's past based on information they have exchanged. The duel proceeds in an almost abstract fashion, with the characters aptly known, once again, only as algebraic signs, X and Y. Even more abstract and complex is the conflict in *The Ghost Sonata,* between the avaricious old businessman Hummel and the heroic young student Arkenholz. *Bandet* (*The Bond,* 1891–1892) takes place in a rural law court where a husband and wife have applied for a divorce. They have agreed on the terms of a settlement that include the wife's taking custody of their child. But the legal proceedings force them to reopen old wounds and revert to accusations they thought were behind them. It is the law that generates the conflict here and becomes the antagonist of them both. In *Samum* (*Simoom*, 1888) a French soldier in colonial Algeria has hallucinations induced by an Arab girl he thought was in love with him, and also by the onset of the searing simoom wind.

To pass from conflicts to structures: In Strindberg's longer plays the structures depend on whether the action has a late point of attack—whether the curtain goes up only days or hours before the climax—in which case the play is concentrated; or whether it has an early point of attack, in which case the structure is "epic," more diffused, and may consist of many scenes. In this second type of structure the play may not even have a climax in the usual sense, or the climax may not crop up near the end of the play.

In certain of Strindberg's concentrated dramas, among them *Miss Julie*, *The Stronger*, *Pariah*, and *The Pelican*, the stage time corresponds to actual time in the auditorium. In its compactness *Miss Julie* is reminiscent of the successful wooing by Richard III of Anne at the end of the funeral for her father and husband, both of whom Richard has murdered. Jean and Julie start out as virtual strangers. Within forty minutes or less he has lured her out of sight into his bedroom while on stage a group of peasants cavort in a midsummer fertility ritual. After this interlude Jean and Julie emerge from the bedroom and the throes of lovemaking. In another half hour they have vented enough recriminations and insults to send Julie outside in order to kill herself and her shame. Yet so fluent and so well-paced is their dialogue that the lengthy one-act play does not give the impression of being rushed.

Another masterpiece of compactness, *The Father*, reaches across some twenty-four hours of stage time, but the play's actual passage of time, some two hours, delineates in its three tightly packed acts not only the mounting rancor of the contest for supremacy between Laura and the Captain, and his decline into madness and death, but also the critical events in their twenty-year marriage.

The three acts of *Easter* do not constitute a religious drama, although they take place on successive days of Holy Week, Maundy Thursday, Good Friday (known in Sweden as Long Friday), and Saturday, the eve of Easter Sunday. This ingenious construction enwraps a play that has one memorable character in it but lacks the tautness and gathering speed of *The Father*. A family fearful about being evicted goes through two and a half days of travail, but its principal creditor behaves with the sort of Christian mercy that Shakespeare's Portia preaches without practicing, and their Sunday will be a time of rejoicing.

Strindberg was also adept in his use of the early point of attack, which creates the epic or chronicle structure, spread out over time. He chose this form for his history plays dealing with Master Olof (Olaus Petri), a churchman and politician, and such Swedish monarchs as Gustav Vasa, Erik the Fourteenth, Queen Christina, and Charles the Twelfth. Time and again he drew inspiration from Shakespeare's chronicle histories in an attempt to convey an entire life by looking in close-up at a selected span of years, and, further, to write a portrait of an age, not merely of one man or woman. His scenes encompass public and private life. They are set in a castle chamber, a throne room, a church, a royal park, but also in a tavern, on a beach, in the street, or in a business office. They unroll a canvas of swarming figures and multiple intrigues.

Strindberg did not restrict the epic structure to his history plays. One of the structural sources for Shakespeare was the medieval mystery play, sometimes running to as many as forty separate settings, which together could depict a biblical history of mankind from Creation to the Day of Judgment. In some medieval play cycles Christ's passion was presented as episodes at stations of the cross. Strindberg, taking Christ's suffering as exemplary for all men, transports his epic protagonists from one "station" to the next in a parable, a pilgrimage that brings the characters through pain—if not to redemption—at least to a sense of ennoblement or a truce struck with themselves.

His earliest epic, *Lucky Per's Journey*, may have owed something to medieval drama, but it probably owed more to Ibsen's earlier revival of the epic form, especially *Peer Gynt* (1867). *Lucky Per*, a fairy tale laid in the Middle Ages, has seven scenes. Strindberg repeated this mystic number with *Himmelrikets nycklar* (*The Keys to the Kingdom of Heaven*, 1892) and *The Great Highway*, his last play. The three parts of another epic, *To Damascus*, contain respectively seventeen, nine, and eight scenes. Part 1, the best-known and most venturesome of the trilogy, is divided into five acts, but these overlie the pattern of scenes, which makes a symmetrical round trip to madness, a free adaptation of his "inferno crisis" with Frida's family in Austria.

The hero of *To Damascus* has a title instead of a name. In Swedish he is called *den Ökände*, which means the Unknown and has been translated as the Stranger, since he is an unknown quantity, a stranger to himself as well as to others. The Stranger stops off at nine different locations, eight of them of the kind any traveler through life might meet with, such as a hotel room, a beach, a mountain road, a ravine, a country kitchen. The one unorthodox stopover, an insane asylum, is his outward limit on the journey. From there he retraces his steps. The play's seventeen scenes, in all of which the Stranger appears, might be represented diagrammatically as a ladder. Rung by rung he descends to the asylum, his Damascus or Inferno. Here he submits to a spiritual crisis, a conversion—approximately speaking—from Saul-the-seeker to Paul-the-believer. Having "seen the light," he ascends the same eight rungs, concluding at the street corner where he started.

What impels the Stranger? He seems to advance haphazardly, yet each stage, each rung, has its meaning for him. Only gradually are the meanings unveiled so that we see he is being driven onward by a dream, and that the dream may prove to be his salvation from madness. He undertakes the dreamlike journey in a quest for self-knowledge. If he can only fathom the dream he may come to fathom himself, for the dream is the master key to his life. The dream conjures up his past, but warped by memory and his indignation at having felt a victim. The Wordsworthian search for the child who is father to the man may never end. To preserve his sanity this latter-day Paul must unremittingly sift memories from fantasies, dead events from the dreams that bring them back to life twisted.

A Dream Play also consists of a pilgrimage, this time in sixteen scenes, which are not formally marked off from one another. Indra's Daughter, a Christ-like figure, comes down from celestial space to live as a human being, marries a lawyer (the dream of many earthbound young women), has a child by him, and discovers that Earth is also Heaven and Hell. One of the advantages of the epic structure for this piece of stage poetry is that it enables the playwright to avoid laborious transitions, indeed, to eschew transitions altogether. Strindberg used stage magic—the scenery, machinery, and lighting—to transform one setting into the next and to imitate the flux of a dream, its "disconnected but apparently logical form," so that "everything is possible and probable. Time and space do not exist." The play flashes forward and back in time. A character's hair turns gray; he is middle-aged, then old, then restored to his youth. Indra's Daughter is nimbler in space than Puck. She is at one moment at a resort on the Mediterranean, then in Fingal's Cave off the coast of Scotland, then outside an opera house. Two or more subscenes run simultaneously on one set. A castle grows taller, like a flower—literally so, for its uppermost tower is a bud that "bursts into a giant chrysanthemum" to end the play spectacularly.

One other structure worth noticing is that of the enigmatic chamber play *The Ghost So-*

nata, which closes on a different floral note. It too comprises a journey, but in miniature, in three scenes. The hero, young Arkenholz, meets Hummel outside the latter's house. In scene 2 he enters the house and meets its array of weird occupants in "the Round Room." The third scene takes him into the adjoining "Hyacinth Room," where Hummel's daughter sits and guards her secret. The journey of the play is thus a penetration of the house and its secrets. The last of these, the innermost one, the identity of Hummel's daughter, is as open to interpretation as is the secret in the heart of the poet Marchbanks in Shaw's *Candida.* However, if one can judge from hints in the play, it seems that the girl is not a girl at all, but one of that rare and fragile species, a hermaphrodite, perhaps like the mythical Hyacinthus, that "frail youth," according to Ovid, beloved by Apollo, who accidentally slew him and memorialized him as a flower.

As for Strindberg's staging effects, these sometimes result in tableaux that are much more than a convenient, explanatory, or pleasing arrangement of sets and people. They illustrate the overlapped meanings of a scene or even of the whole play for a few instants, and then dissolve—but not before they have stamped themselves on the spectator's eyes and mind. Such tableaux combine intricately with the plays' structures, since they consummate a scene, an act, or, in the case of the tower that blooms into a chrysanthemum, the play itself. When the Captain flings a lighted lamp at Laura, the impulsive gesture sums up his anger and helplessness; he is hurling away all that remains sane in him; the streak of light, if we could imagine it arrested by a camera, speaks eloquently of his inability to make Laura *see* his plight.

As a playwright, Strindberg is a great stage painter. His visual artistry demonstrates for succeeding generations the force of theatrical wonder, so that we take in his tableaux with the awe we might feel on climbing a mountain and watching a mightly landscape unfold or being present at an accident that happens so swiftly that we cannot absorb all that has occurred.

In *Swanwhite* the wicked Stepmother "opens her mouth as if pouring out venom," and live peacocks and doves that decorate the heroine's chamber fall dead. The Stepmother swells: "her clothes become inflated until they hide her head and shoulders; then they seem to be on fire, flaming in a pattern of snakes and branches. The sun begins to rise. The ceiling sinks slowly into the room. Smoke and flame pour from the hearth." The moods of the characters in *Storm Weather* heighten as high winds approach; then thunder and summer lightning strike and the rain washes down. The elements relent, having rinsed the play emotionally clean, and leave the characters in peace, looking forward to a calm, mellow fall.

The "hell scene" of *To Damascus* discovers the Stranger alone at a table in an old cloister converted into an asylum, while at another table sit people who appear to have been summoned out of his past: relatives, foes, and the woman he loves: "All are dressed in white but over their white gowns they are wearing gauze costumes in various colors. Their faces are waxen and deathly white. Their whole appearance and all their gestures are ghostlike." On one wall there hangs a painting of Saint Michael slaying the dragon, as if to remind the Stranger that he will have to "slay the dragons" of memory that oppress him, in other words, liberate himself from disabling fear and guilt that have accumulated since his boyhood. Scene 1 of *The Burned House* takes place in front of a gutted, one-story building. The second and closing scene shows the remaining walls of the house removed to reveal a garden blazing with flowers and fruit trees in blossom.

Stage pictures are, of course, transitory. They alter from one production "concept" to the next, and sometimes, if the actors move around freely, from one performance to the next of the same production. But the very *notion* of using a stage to make a visual statement, and not merely for pretty display—not, that is, to elicit admiring gasps from an audience as the curtain or lights go up—passed on from Strindberg to dramatists and directors of the twentieth century. That final scene of *A Dream Play*, when the castle bursts into flame and then into flower, incorporates a "wall of human faces, questioning, mourning, despairing," which anticipates the massing of actors found later in the drama of Georg Kaiser (the *Gas* trilogy; *From Morn to Midnight*) and Ernst Toller *(Man and the Masses; Hoppla, We're Alive!)*, in the productions of directors like Max Reinhardt and Leopold Jessner, and in the seething imagery of crowds in the films of Fritz Lang *(Metropolis; M)*. Strindberg's precise and yet poetic use of color in interior views may, in much the same way, have been borrowed by Federico García Lorca in the staging requirements for his tragedies.

Strindberg's staging effects are auditory, as well as visual; he is one of the modern pioneers of the sound effect. If he occasionally showed how to use human bodies as scenery, he also called on human voices as sound, and not only as transmitters of dialogue: sound that expressed collective yearnings. With that sound he might combine folk songs or formal music by Beethoven, Mendelssohn, Haydn, or other composers. In our time music has become a crude tool for hammering into us the emotional content of a scene, especially the scores that accompany most films. Strindberg's incidental music, by contrast, is discreet; it enhances, rather than creates or enforces, the dominant mood.

The next aspect of Strindberg's theater, his characterizations, baffled many of his contemporaries because, unlike the figures they were used to and therefore expected and even insisted on, his characters have mixed motives. His men and women are usually uncertain of what they seek in life. If they decide on some goal, they are not certain how to attain it. If, by chance, they attain it, they are not convinced that it was what they wanted in the first place. Happiness, for instance, whatever

that is: in the rare moments when his characters feel it, they feel it slipping away. Maurice, in the second act of *Crimes and Crimes*, has spent the night with Henriette, who infatuates him, and to cap his joy his newly opened play is a hit. His rapturous conversation quickly gives way to disquiet: "The world is mine, and that's why it's beautiful! Oh, how I wish I had wings for us both, to get away from here and fly far, far away, before someone spoils my happiness, before envy and jealousy wake me from my dream—because it probably is just a dream!"

A newlywed husband in *A Dream Play* tells his bride: "My happiness is so complete that I wish to die. . . . In the midst of happiness grows a seed of unhappiness. Happiness consumes itself like a flame . . . and the presentiment of its end destroys it at its very peak. . . . I fear happiness, the deceiver." As we see in these lines, the character cannot get free of his self-consciousness. He is aware of the Yes and the No at odds within him. The positive and negative feelings cancel each other out and lead to either an emotional seesawing or an emotional paralysis.

Given their mixed motives, Strindberg's most striking characters appear at times to have no will power. They surrender to fate (to the future) and its random bestowals, dreading the worst, just in case it does alight on them, because they believe more in bad luck than in good, but mouthing their fearfulness as if by superstition, to ward off dangers and avoid having to do battle with their "dragons."

And when they do act? "If you do something good, someone else is sure to think it is bad; if you are kind to one person, you're sure to harm another." Here a mother speaks in *A Dream Play*, but she articulates a dread familiar to many of Strindberg's characters—that action of any kind defeats its own ends. Yet these mixed emotions are what make Strindberg's characters real, lifelike, and discussible. They gave rise to resentment among his early critics and spectators because they were stage creations who resembled people, including the critics and spectators in their unguarded moments, much as Ibsen's, Shaw's, and Chekhov's characters did. They hit home with discomfiting jolts that were all the harder to bear after decades of characters who had one dominant motive and were not imitations of life but imitations of imitations. New and not-quite-decipherable characters were competing with the established "types," only they were not really new at all. In characterization, as in structure, the model was Shakespeare. Strindberg said appreciatively of Hamlet that he was evil and good, cynical and enthusiastic, cruel and lenient: "a human being, different at every moment, as human beings are."

Strindberg's realism in the imagining of personality extends to his fantasies and mythologizing; it isn't limited to his overtly realistic theater. That realism, that verisimilitude, are what keep Strindberg's fantasies alive today, whereas those of other writers of his time now seem whimsical, precious, or simply stale.

Among the male characters in Strindberg's drama we find a generous assortment of temperaments: the mixing of motives opens up an almost infinite range of combinations. Among them are few, if any, average or ordinary folk. The Captain in *The Father*, who lives in extremis, on the brink of madness, becomes incensed whenever Laura thwarts him and is a pathological case. So is that other Captain, Edgar in *The Dance of Death*, who perversely thrives on marital discord, who lives only to fight another day. But both of them are far more than case studies. Rather they are modernized, domesticated figures out of heroic myths, all the more frustrated because they must spend their days keeping accounts, paying debts, earning bread, acquitting themselves as mercenaries of bourgeois survival. They will never find the time or the additional effort to conquer a Troy, capture a golden fleece, or pursue a Minotaur. The daily round depletes them. Like Shakespeare's Bolingbroke, they will keep finding reasons not to

lead a crusade. And yet they never cease wishing to try.

Near the lower end of the social scale Jean hopes to marry Julie, the daughter of a count—he has always aspired to a highborn wife—and unshackle himself from his position as a menial. He will become the proprietor of an inn in Switzerland. He has prepared himself; has acquired a taste for fine food and wine and for the theater; has learned some French; knows how to talk and conduct himself like a gentleman. He speaks of purchasing a title and joining the ruling classes. But when Julie's father pulls a hand bell to be waited on, Jean freezes and cannot escape from his servitude. His future loses out to his past, that regimen of obsequious habit.

Even Master Olof, Strindberg's first male character of consequence, is described by his author as being full of contradictions: "ambitious and weak-willed . . . great self-confidence mixed with profound dejection; reasonable and unreasonable; hard and soft." Olof wants to supplant the Catholic church in sixteenth-century Sweden with the teachings of Luther and later to defy the king. But the king beats Olof to the draw, and, when offered the choice of recanting or dying a martyr, Olof recants. Göran Persson, the adviser to Erik XIV, takes command of the government as masterfully as a top White House aide and runs the country with pitiless efficiency. He covers up or dilutes Erik's frequent blunders for a time. Then, almost unaccountably, he loses confidence in his control—as though a tightrope walker were to start thinking about how he keeps his balance—and this self-consciousness incapacitates him.

It should be added that, although Strindberg's male characters share some of his opinions and echo them here and there, without necessarily parroting them, and although he injects his own life into his plays occasionally, those characters are no more duplicates of the Strindberg persona than are the heroes of his autobiographical novels, and probably less, for anything like a fully fleshed Strindberg could not be cramped into "the two hours' traffic of our stage." Unfriendly critics sometimes liken remarks made about women by Strindberg's male characters to remarks made by Strindberg himself. Such detractions suggest that he could not conceive of characters who are autonomous; he could only reinvent himself. Still, reinventing oneself is no straightforward task. Some of his men do share with him fractions of his disposition, irritations, and views of women. But so do some of his women. To elaborate in general on the attitudes of his men toward women would require a wall-sized chart made up of little boxes, male on one axis (husbands, brothers, sons, fathers, grandfathers, lovers, various degrees of in-laws, acquaintances, storekeepers, and so on) and female on the other axis (correspondences from wives to customers), and even that ambitious undertaking might not be all-inclusive.

Broadly speaking, the husband in Strindberg's plays looks on his wife as an inveterate flirt, if not an outright seducer. (She seduced him to start with, didn't she?) This woman, he feels, exerts almost effortless spells, consciously or unconsciously, over every man who glances her way. The plays, on the other hand, make it clear that the wives for the most part are anything but femmes fatales, and if they glance back coyly at another man on occasion, they do so to strike fire in their husbands. However, the Strindbergian single man is apt to idealize the women he meets, especially married women, and most of all, older married women. If he comes to know any of them fairly well he graduates to the view of the married man: they are flirts, promiscuously amorous. Such attitudes are naive, and Strindberg makes them appear so. They are also lifelike.

Miss Julie does behave like a tease. Jean and the maid, Kristin, who both have a peasant unbringing, consider her brazen and unmannerly at first. She brushes up against Jean's shoulder, tickles a speck of dust out of his eye with her scented handkerchief, and urges him to dance with her, even though he is unofficially betrothed to Kristin. In the majestic movie of *Miss Julie* directed by Alf Sjöberg they do dance together; she leans back against his arm and fixes him with her gaze, mesmerizing him. But in the later part of the play, after he has taken her, she frantically tries to think of a way to repair her honor. She has given herself to somebody of lesser breeding. We also assume that she has engaged in a sexual act for the first time in her twenty-five years. The opposed motives then come into play, and she is all shame. She can restore her honor (in her own mind, at least) only by doing away with herself. The equation here between sex and death is horrifying to contemplate and returns us to what we have learned of Julie's past with a new understanding of Strindberg's depths of sympathy for this misbegotten girl.

Kristina (Queen Christina), written thirteen years later, introduces another heroine who is ambivalent about men. Like Julie, she has been raised, says Strindberg, "to be a man, contending for her selfhood, and against her own femininity, and yielding to it. . . . So thoroughly a woman that she is a hater of women." (This quotation comes from his written comments to the cast of the Intimate Theater, which contain abundant and shrewd appreciation of the art of acting.) Christina, by turns a spoiled brat ruling over her "doll house," an awesomely regal beauty, a wheedler, and a coquette; stern and unapproachable to some people, kittenish toward the man who was her regent, hopelessly indulgent to the baron with whom she's smitten, and helplessly prodigal with the national purse—this queen is a Julie who can rock the country with her quirkiness and her passion. She would like to be Prometheus, the bringer of light and learning to mankind, but she ends as Pandora, letting mischiefs loose on the world.

The irradiating sexuality of Julie and Christina contrasts with the sedateness of Laura in *The Father.* The Captain alludes to the spell she cast on him when they were courting, and he still craves her approval, if not her love. But he has tried to put her on a pedestal that she refuses to occupy and knows she is unsuited for. Their daughter, Bertha, has absorbed her lovingness, and now he wants to separate her from Bertha. Often nominated by critics for the hall of women's infamy because of her cruel wiles, Laura is actually unimaginative, housewifely, and defensive. If she sounds sarcastic at times, she has learned her sarcasm from her husband. If she seems ferocious, she is counterpunching, mimicking his exaggerated manner of complaining. When it comes to a quarrel she borrows from his armory and so infuriates him all the more. But since he is on the verge of insanity, his are the very weapons she should not use. All she does is aggravate his condition and finally drive him into a stroke. As his pale reflection, she is the monster he unintentionally created during their twenty years of marriage. As if to spite himself, the Captain picked marriage material that was highly unpromising for him. She becomes most appealing when she candidly informs him that she has never been able to love him as a wife should have done. He would have enjoyed a tranquil marriage only with a saint or a masochist. Laura is not definitive enough to be either. She is Strindberg's most explicit evocation of a woman who could never live up to—not even come near—an ideal.

In *To Damascus* Strindberg attempted to sketch in an outline of that ideal. The Lady, who joins the Stranger for most of his journey to his personal hell and back, is a counterpart to Laura. She fulfills the play's need for a patient listener, a sounding board, the other side of a one-sided dialogue. If the Stranger is an Adam, she is an Eve, the name by which he addresses her. (Her given name is Ingeborg.) For his sake she leaves her husband, and, apart from one lapse into disobedience, when she reads a book of his that he has forbidden her to look at (nibbles at the apple), she remains as subservient to him as if she had just emerged from his rib cage.

When he blasphemes she may chide him ("A haughty spirit goeth before a fall"), and when he is pessimistic she may agree with him ("Our consciences crush us; there's no one to help us carry them"). But her own conscience seldom obtrudes. She personifies an idea of the perfect traveling companion through life. She plays the Stranger's confidante and lover; she comforts him like a mother or a daughter (an Antigone to his fiftyish Oedipus); and when she conducts him to her home she becomes his guide, a Jungian "anima figure." She is thirty-four and unmistakably desirable because she was married and worth stealing from her husband. As they move forward through the play's seventeen scenes she sits and crochets. We never learn whether she's working on a scarf, a nightcap, a hip-high sock, or what, but it must be growing noticeably longer; he points out that she is busy with it "all the time." Perhaps it is best regarded as a lengthening tapestry of the journey. And perhaps she is best regarded as being, in her variety of roles, the senior of the three Fates who weave the fabric of destiny, Klotho. Alternatively she might be what Robert Graves calls "the White Goddess, the Muse, the Mother of All Living." In any event, she is passive throughout, and serves as a false antagonist, a device for bringing the Stranger's self-conflict into the open. Her sympathetic common sense offsets his erratic ways.

Two further, quite distinctive versions of an ideal woman, Eleonora and Indra's Daughter, have unearthly qualities otherwise reserved by Strindberg for his fairy tales. Eleonora, the sixteen-year-old in *Easter*, may well have inspired the captivating young women created three decades later by Jean Giraudoux, including the water sprite Ondine. Eleonora really does commune with nature and talk to birds and animals. She feels that there is animation in inert substances: the telephone wires "wail" when people speak ill of one another, and her clock, which has measured her life, knows all about her. She adores flowers (as

Strindberg himself did; he would buy flowers, said his sister-in-law, even when he could not afford food). She quotes feelingly from the Scriptures, and is attuned to the resurrectionary meanings of Easter—might, indeed, be considered a harbinger of summer, for she brings hope to a family that is about to be broken up, and the hope proves justified. Even this saintly character, though, has her moments of doubt, her lapses of faith, when she believes herself abandoned by God. She has more reason to be depressed than to be cheerful. Once she was certified insane and put away in an asylum. Incarceration of this sort, Strindberg implies, is our unthinking response to those few originals who have a sixth, possibly a seventh, sense.

As if to assert that Strindberg's reputation for detesting women had been due to public attitudinizing on his part, prompted by his own tempestuous relations with them, he made the protagonist of *A Dream Play* a marvel of forbearance and magnanimity, a Desdemona. On earth Indra's Daughter takes the name Agnes, which means "chaste," though she marries a struggling lawyer, has his child, and learns the tribulations of poverty. Her mission, not unlike that of a junketing congressman, is to investigate conditions in the lands she visits and report back on whether the plaints arising from earth are warranted. She finds that they are. The poor, the weak, the ugly have lives of monotonous desperation and, as the generations go forward, virtually the same injustices persist, the same misery reigns. Yet this is anything but a protest play of a political stripe. Indra's Daughter speaks of the disappointments that attend life, of its "discord and uncertainty." She has pity for human beings. (Pity is an emotion, as Strindberg pointed out a number of times in his writings, that puts the object of the pity in an inferior position; but Indra's Daughter, being superhuman, can look down on human beings with no trace of disdain.) At last, before her return to the heavenly realm, she enters the growing castle, which is on fire. From out of

the muck of earth springs life. From out of cracks in cement grass and weeds poke up. Through the degenerating mortar of a brick wall ivy drives its shoots. From out of the fiery building sprouts a chrysanthemum to dwarf all others. The flower is an affirmation: it announces the magic and blessing of growth.

The themes in Strindberg's drama are as various as the conflicts, structures, and characterizations to which they belong. The antagonisms between the sexes, between classes, age groups, and standpoints suggest the aloneness of every human being, survival interpreted as a struggle, even in the short term of a single life. The manipulations of one character by another with the aid of threats, persuasion, love, the casting of spells, and symbolic vampirism (the draining away of others' strength) can be seen as efforts to overcome that aloneness by self-assertion. The quests for identity and for a truth that transcends appearances are part of an insatiable curiosity on the part of Strindberg's characters about the meaning, the point, of life. The attempts to expel the poison of guilt, to come to grips with the past by unsealing closet doors and looking skeletons right in the eye sockets—these, like the act of writing about them, are intended to be therapeutic, that is, cleansing and self-purifying.

Strindberg acknowledges the force of chance, which may turn out to be destiny; the persistence of superstition, which may turn out to be a higher, instinctual form of intelligence; and the likelihood of repetitions and recurrences, which may turn out to be part of a cyclical pattern as life staggers on, world without end. In his plays there is the anguish of being alive but also the anguish of dependence on others for company and comfort, sharpened sometimes by the fearful realization of how simple, how tempting, it would be to die. As Albert Camus declared much later, the fundamental decision everybody makes, over and over, is whether or not to commit suicide.

Such themes were like way stations to

Strindberg's ultimate conviction, implicit in the later plays, that oppositions of all kinds, differences of all kinds, are swallowed up in the oneness of life. He may not have joined any religion or cult as a wholehearted subscriber, but he became essentially a mystic in his search for an overriding principle of unification. The Stranger in *To Damascus* surrenders to a sense of this oneness as he stands on an open stretch of beach:

> I'm everywhere now, in the sea which is my blood, in the hills which are my bones, in the trees, in the flowers. My head reaches as high as the heavens and I look out over the whole universe, which is all me, and I feel all the strength and power of the creator in me, for he and I are one. I want to take it all into my hands and knead it into something more nearly perfect, more enduring, more beautiful. I want to see it all created anew and every created being happy—born without pain, living without sorrow, dying in silent contentment.
>
> (Act 2.2)

In case such a cursory restatement of Strindberg's dramatic themes leaves an impression of empty generality, it is worth remembering, first, that a restatement in synoptic form of the ideas of even the most sophisticated metaphysician reduces those ideas to banalities, and second, that Strindberg was not a metaphysician. Perhaps he could have been one, but he chose instead to pursue half a dozen other vocations, and supremely, the writing of plays. His themes, often discussed at length and brought forward in the judgments of his plays, to the disadvantage of his accomplishments as a playwright, are in the end of small consequence by comparison with the drama itself in which he clothed them.

Scholars have tracked down many of the sources of Strindberg's themes, the influences on him, and have come up with a list of philosophers that ranges from Plato and Lucretius to Swedenberg, Arthur Schopenhauer, Eduard von Hartmann, Nietzsche, Kierkegaard, and Auguste Comte; a list of scientists and social scientists that includes Charles Darwin, a batch of pre-Freudian psychologists (Jean Martin Charcot and Théodule-Armand Ribot among them), Ernst Haeckel the evolutionist, as well as a diversified collection of novelists, playwrights, and men of letters—Charles Dickens, Gustave Flaubert, Honoré de Balzac, Victor Hugo, Émile Zola, Maurice Maeterlinck, and Georg Brandes, one of the nineteenth century's most discerning critics. At different times Strindberg paid tribute to all of these authors; with some of them he also kept up correspondence.

One writer to whom he paid only grudging tribute, and rarely, and whom he more frequently attacked, was that other "giant of the north," Henrik Ibsen. Ibsen's influence on Strindberg may have been more negative than positive, for the unmistakable scope, ambitiousness, and dramatically revolutionary qualities of the Norwegian's plays seemed to spur on the Swede, who was twenty years younger, to become a worthy rival. Thus, *Herr Bengt's Wife*, written three years after *A Doll's House*, and the parody *Kamraterna* (*Comrades*, 1888) and a story actually called "A Doll House" (1886), constituted in Strindberg's view effective retorts to Ibsen's dramatization of a husband's treatment of his wife as a sheltered child and plaything. It may well be that this "influence" also eventually worked in reverse. Ibsen's last play, *When We Dead Awaken* (1899), although evolving obviously from the plays that immediately preceded it and from such earlier plays as *Brand*, has several features in common with the first part of *To Damascus*, written the year before.

Inferring influences can be fascinating, but as a rule it is inconclusive and may lead to dead-end questions, such as: Should we say a play that satirizes another play, or publicly answers it, is *influenced* by it? Looking back today we are likely to decide that Strindberg was bent on differentiating himself, on competing, rather than on disclosing any debt he might have incurred to Ibsen, which would automatically have put him in the older playwright's shadow.

This much is certain: Ibsen and Strindberg form the commanding portals to the theater we call modern and both had formative effects on their native languages. But Ibsen, the dramatic logician, tinkered with draft after draft and would not let a script out of his hands until he had worked it through for at least two full years. Strindberg, the conjuror who discovered new tricks while performing, got the text out of his brain as fast as he could, while it was still fresh. Later he might revise or even thoroughly rewrite it *(Master Olof, Comrades)*, but he could complete several plays in a matter of months and between other activities.

Ibsen was the starting point for a new classicism. On the surface his work is spare, businesslike, never indulgent; only after prolonged study does one grow aware of the sheer compression he achieves. Strindberg, at the junction of older and new romanticism, flails out; his writing has an air of disconnectedness, abandon; only after prolonged study does one perceive the steely reticulation of governing ideas that clamps together its parts. Ibsen leads to Chekhov, Bertolt Brecht, Samuel Beckett, Harold Pinter, Peter Handke; Strindberg leads to Michel de Ghelderode, Arthur Adamov, Boris Vian, Eugene Ionesco, Peter Barnes. And Shaw, Luigi Pirandello, and Eugene O'Neill owe much to both. The two master dramatists have more comedy in their work—comedy that is sardonic, rather than broad—than many directors, actors, and audiences give them credit for; they are anything but the dour Viking moralists that newspaper reviewers once misread in them. If they endure it is because the plays of both remain enigmatic. Despite the Ibsen industry and the Strindberg industry among scholars, these are two dramatic poets who still defy final explication.

And yet, as Evert Sprinchorn remarks in the introduction to his translation of *The Son of a Servant*, the taciturn Ibsen "seems like an open book compared to the embarrassingly candid Strindberg who tells all, who strips himself naked before our eyes, and who becomes more elusive, more mysterious . . . as he does so." A unique personality bursts, like a great new species of chrysanthemum, out of *The Son of a Servant*. His false starts were to be the prologue to a badly navigated, tempest-tossed voyage of self-exploration in poetry, prose, and drama that took poor, suffering, sublime Strindberg farther than anyone else has ever been.

Selected Bibliography

FIRST EDITIONS

PLAYS

Den fredlöse (The Freethinker). Stockholm, 1881. Performed 1871.

Mäster Olof. Stockholm, 1872. Performed 1890.

Lycko-Pers resa (Lucky Per's Travels). Stockholm, 1881. Performed 1883.

Herr Bengts Husfru (Herr Bengt's Wife). Stockholm, 1882.

Fadren. (The Father). Stockholm, 1887.

Fröken Julie (Miss Julie). Stockholm, 1888. Performed 1889.

Kamraterna (Comrades). Stockholm, 1888. Performed 1905.

Fordringsägare (Creditors). Stockholm, 1888.

Paria (Pariah). Stockholm, 1890. Performed 1889.

Advent. Stockholm, 1898.

Brott och brott (Crimes and Crimes). Stockholm, 1899.

Erik IV. Stockholm, 1899.

Folkungasagan (The Saga of the Folkungs). Stockholm, 1899. Performed 1901.

Gustav Vasa. Stockholm, 1899.

Drömspelet (A Dream Play). Stockholm, 1901. Performed 1907.

Kronbruden (The Bridal Crown). Stockholm, 1901. Performed 1906.

Påsk (Easter). Stockholm, 1901.

Svanevit (Swanwhite). Stockholm, 1901.

Till Damaskus (To Damascus). Parts 1 and 2—Stockholm, 1898–1901; performed 1900. Part 3—Stockholm, 1904; performed 1916.

Dödsdansen (The Dance of Death). Stockholm, 1902. Performed 1905.

Brända tomten (The Burned House). Stockholm, 1907.

Spöksonaten (The Ghost [or Spook] Sonata). Stockholm, 1907. Performed 1908.

Stora landsvägen (The Great Highway). Stockholm, 1909. Performed 1910.

PROSE

Röda rummet (The Red Room). Stockholm, 1879. Novel.

Det nya riket (The New Kingdom). Stockholm, 1882. Satiric pamphlet.

Giftas (Getting Married). 2 vols. Stockholm, 1884–1885. Stories.

Tjänstekvinnans son (Son of a Servant). Stockholm, 1886. Autobiographical fiction.

Hemsöborna (The People of Hemsö). Stockholm, 1887. Novel.

Le plaidoyer d'un fou (The Confessions of a Fool). Stockholm, 1888; enl. ed., 1893. Autobiographical fiction.

Tschandala. Stockholm, 1888. Novel.

En häxa (A Witch). Stockholm, 1890. Novel.

I havsbandet (By the Open Sea). Stockholm, 1890. Novel.

Antibarbus. Stockholm, 1894. Scientific essays.

Des arts nouveaux! ou Le hasard dans la production artistique (The New Arts; or, The Role of Chance in Artistic Creation). Paris, 1894. Essay.

Études funèbres (Graveyard Reveries). Paris, 1896. Essay.

Sylva sylvanum. Stockholm, 1896. Scientific essays.

Inferno. Stockholm, 1897. Autobiographical fiction.

Legender. Stockholm, 1897–1898. Originally published in French as *Légendes.* Autobiographical fiction.

Klostret (The Cloister). Stockholm, 1898. Novel.

Ensam (Alone). Stockholm, 1903. Autobiographical fiction.

Sagor (Tales). Stockholm, 1903. Stories.

Enblå bok (Zones of the Spirit). Stockholm, 1907–1912. Philosophy.

Svarta fanor (Black Banners). Stockholm, 1907. Stories.

Syndabocken (The Scapegoat). Stockholm, 1907. Novel.

Taklagsöl (The Roofing Feast). Stockholm, 1907. Novel.

Fagervik och skamsund (Fair Haven and Foul Strand). Stockholm, 1913. Stories.

COLLECTED WORKS

Dramer (Dramas). Edited by C. R. Smedmark. Stockholm, 1962–. Now discontinued and incomplete.

Samlade skrifter (Collected Writings). 55 vols. Edited by John Landquist. Stockholm, 1912–1926.

CORRESPONDENCE

Brev (Letters). 15 vols. Edited by T. Eklund. Stockholm, 1943–.

TRANSLATIONS

DRAMAS

The Chamber Plays. Translated by Evert Sprinchorn and Seabury Quinn, Jr. New York, 1962. 2nd ed., Minneapolis, 1981, with K. Petersen. Contains *Storm Weather, The Burned House, The Ghost Sonata,* and *The Pelican,* with "Notes to the Members of the Intimate Theatre."

Eight Expressionist Plays by August Strindberg. Translated by Arvid Paulson. New York, 1972. Contains *Lucky Per's Journey, The Keys of Heaven, To Damascus,* parts 1, 2, and 3, *A Dream Play, The Great Highway, The Ghost Sonata.*

The Father and A Dream Play. Translated by Valborg Anderson. New York, 1964.

Five Plays of Strindberg. Translated by Elizabeth Sprigge. Garden City, N.Y., 1960. Contains *Creditors, Crime and Crime, The Dance of Death, Swanwhite, The Great Highway.*

The Genius of the Scandinavian Theater. Edited and translated by Evert Sprinchorn. New York, 1964. Includes *To Damacus,* part 1, and *Crimes and Crimes.*

Plays of Strindberg. Translated by Michael Meyer. New York, 1964. Contains *The Father, Miss Julie, Creditors, The Stronger, Playing with Fire, Erik the Fourteenth, Storm, The Ghost Sonata.*

Seven Plays by August Strindberg. Translated by Arvid Paulson. New York, 1960. Contains *The Father, Miss Julie, Comrades, The Stronger, The Bond, Crime and Crime, Easter.*

Six Plays of Strindberg. Translated by Elizabeth

Sprigge. Garden City, N.Y., 1955. Contains *The Father, Miss Julie, The Stronger, Easter, A Dream Play, The Ghost Sonata.*

Strindberg: Eight Famous Plays. Translated by Edwin Björkman and N. Erichsen. New York, 1949; London, 1968. Contains *The Link, The Father, Miss Julie, The Stronger, There Are Crimes and Crimes, Gustavus Vasa, The Dance of Death, The Spook Sonata.*

Strindberg: Five Plays. Translated by Harry G. Carlson. Berkeley Calif., and Los Angeles, 1983. Contains *The Father, Miss Julie, The Dance of Death,* part I, *The Dance of Death,* part II, *A Dream Play, The Ghost Sonata.*

Strindberg: Selected Plays and Prose. Translated by N. Erichsen, Evert Sprinchorn, and Robert Brustein. New York, 1964. Contains *The Father, Miss Julie, A Dream Play,* with extracts from *Inferno.*

Three Plays by August Strindberg. Translated by Peter Watts. London and Baltimore, 1953. Contains *The Father, Miss Julie, Easter.*

To Damascus, a Trilogy. Translated by Graham Rawson. New York, 1960.

World Historical Plays. Translated by Arvid Paulson. New York, 1970. Contains *The Nightingale of Wittenberg, or Luther; Through Deserts to Ancestral Lands, or Moses; Hellas, or Socrates; The Lamb and the Beast, or Christ.*

Other (Swedish) History Plays. 5 vols. Translated by Walter Johnson. Seattle, 1955–1959. Vol. 1: *Queen Christina, Charles XII, Gustav III;* Vol. 2: *The Last of the Knights, The Regent, Earl Birger of Bjälbo;* Vol. 3: *Gustav Adolf;* Vol. 4: *The Vasa Trilogy: Master Olof, Gustav Vasa, Erik XIV;* Vol. 5: *The Saga of the Folkungs, Engelbrekt.*

PROSE

By the Open Sea. Translated by Ellie Schleussner. London, 1913.

From an Occult Diary. Translated by Mary Sandbach. New York, 1965.

Getting Married. Translated by Mary Sandbach. New York, 1972.

Inferno, Alone, and Other Writings. Edited by Evert Sprinchorn and translated by E. Sprinchorn, D. Coltman, D. Scanlan, and A. Bermel. Garden City, N.Y., 1968. Includes ''The New Arts,'' *Graveyard Reveries,* and ''Jacob Wrestles.''

Letters of Strindberg to Harriet Bosse. Edited and translated by Arvid Paulson. New York, 1959.

A Madman's Defense. Translated by E. Sprinchorn. Garden City, N.Y., 1967.

The Natives of Hemsö. Translated by Arvid Paulson. New York, 1965.

Open Letters to the Intimate Theater. Translated by Walter Johnson. Seattle, 1966.

The People of Hemsö. Translated by E. H. Schubert. London, 1959.

The Red Room. Translated by Elizabeth Sprigge. New York, 1967.

The Scapegoat. Translated by Arvid Paulson. New York, 1967.

The Son of a Servant: The Story of the Evolution of a Human Being, 1849–1867. Translated by Evert Sprinchorn. Garden City, N.Y., 1966.

BIOGRAPHICAL AND CRITICAL STUDIES

Bentley, Eric. *The Playwright as Thinker.* New York, 1946, 1955.

Bermel, Albert. *Contradictory Characters.* New York, 1973.

Brandell, Gunnar. *Strindberg in Inferno.* Cambridge, Mass., 1974.

Brustein, Robert. *The Theatre of Revolt.* Boston, 1964.

Bulman, Joan. *Strindberg and Shakespeare.* London, 1933.

Carlson, Harry G. *Strindberg and the Poetry of Myth.* Berkeley, Calif., and Los Angeles, 1982.

Dahlström, Carl. *Strindberg's Dramatic Expressionism.* 2nd ed. New York, 1965.

Gustavson, Alrik. ''Strindberg and the Realistic Breakthrough.'' In *A History of Swedish Literature.* Minneapolis, 1961. Pp. 243–275.

Johannesson, E. O. *The Novels of August Strindberg.* Berkeley, Calif., 1968.

Johnson, Walter. *Strindberg and the Historical Drama.* Seattle, 1963.

Lagercrantz, Olof. *August Strindberg.* Translated by Anselm Hollo. New York, 1984.

Lamm, Martin. *August Strindberg.* Translated and edited by Harry G. Carlson. New York, 1971.

McGill, V. J. *August Strindberg: the Bedeviled Viking.* New York, 1930, 1965.

Mortensen, Brita, and Brian Downs. *Strindberg: An Introduction to His Life and Work.* Cambridge, 1949, 1965.

Ollén, Gunnar. *August Strindberg.* Translated by Peter Tirner. New York, 1972.

Palmblad, H. V. E. *Strindberg's Conception of History.* New York, 1927.

Smedmark, C. R., ed. *Essays on Strindberg.* Stockholm, 1966.

Sprigge, Elizabeth. *The Strange Life of August Strindberg.* New York, 1949.

Sprinchorn, Evert. *Strindberg as Dramatist.* New Haven, Conn., 1982.

————. "Brandes and Strindberg." In *The Activist Critic: A Symposium on Georg Brandes.* Copenhagen, 1980.

————. "The Zola of the Occult: Strindberg's Experimental Method." *Modern Drama:* 109–126 (September 1975).

Steen, Birgitta. *August Strindberg.* Atlantic Highlands, N.J., 1982.

Strindberg, Frida. *Marriage with Genius.* London, 1937.

Valency, Maurice. *The Flower and the Castle.* New York, 1963.

Ward, John. *The Social and Religious Plays of Strindberg.* London, 1980.

BIBLIOGRAPHIES

Bryer, Jackson. "Strindberg 1951–1962: A Bibliography." *Modern Drama* 5:269–275 (December 1962).

Gustafson, Alrik. "A Bibliographical Guide." In *A History of Swedish Literature.* Minneapolis, 1961. Pp. 601–610.

Also see *Scandinavian Studies* for bibliographical, biographical, and critical studies.

ALBERT BERMEL

GUY DE MAUPASSANT
(1850–1893)

ACCORDING TO HIS mother, Henri-René-Albert Guy de Maupassant was born on 5 August 1850 in the eighteenth-century château de Miromesnil, an imposing mansion near the village of Tourville-sur-Arques, five miles inland from Dieppe on the Normandy coast. In fact, he was born in a modest apartment in his maternal grandmother's small house at Fécamp, on the coast thirty miles away. Apparently, his parents had rented the château at Miromesnil as a summer residence so that their child might be born in aristocratic surroundings, but the baby arrived early. He was, however, christened on 23 August in the château's Renaissance chapel, and his mother always claimed her son had been born inside the château's western turret. She wrote after his death that "it was eight o'clock in the morning when Guy de Maupassant was born and the most brilliant summer sunshine seemed to bid welcome to him who was to die so young, but not without having achieved some glory" (Lerner, *Maupassant*, p. 17). Such anxiety about social appearances and Laure de Maupassant's lingering self-delusion about the past are recurring themes in much of her son's fiction. Just as the Norman countryside and its peasants, priests, and landowners provide crucial material for a good many of Maupassant's stories, so the strained domestic life and uncertain social and financial circumstances of his family form the autobiographical background of what seems objective, coolly detached storytelling.

Both of Maupassant's parents were members of the Norman upper bourgeoisie of Rouen. The son of a gentleman farmer who had revived the aristocratic *de* in the family name, Gustave de Maupassant was something of a dandy, an amateur painter, a gambler, and a womanizer. Laure Le Poittevin came from an artistic family, and her talented brother, Alfred, had married Gustave's sister, Louise de Maupassant. Their father, Paul Le Poittevin, owned spinning mills in Caux and was a close friend of another important member of the Rouen bourgeoisie, Dr. Achille-Cléophas Flaubert, head of the Hotel-Dieu hospital and father of a daughter, Caroline, and two sons, Achille and Gustave. Alfred Le Poittevin and Gustave Flaubert were close friends, sensitive youths who read philosophy together and planned to be artists until parental pressure turned them (Gustave only temporarily) into law students. As a young girl, Laure moved in their orbit; she was a highly emotional person whose imagination was stirred by their literary and philosophical ambitions. Alfred, however, became a successful lawyer, married, and died at the age of thirty-two in 1848, with Flaubert at his bedside.

The Maupassants had another son, Hervé, in 1856; when they separated at the end of 1860, Gustave remained in Paris, where he eventually became a stockbroker with the firm of Stoltz. Laure moved back with the boys to the Normandy coast, to Étretat, where the family had spent summers. The separation seems to have resulted from a combination of Gustave's promiscuity and what some biographers conjecture was Laure's frigidity and neurotic possessiveness. Whatever the causes, the marriage was unhappy and left its mark on Guy, as is apparent from certain recurring themes of his fiction. He and his brother spent time in Paris with their father, but his mother was the stronger and more formative influence in his childhood.

His formal education began in 1859 at the Lycée Impérial Napoléon in Paris, but in 1863 he was sent to the institution ecclésiastique at Yvetot, not far from Étretat. He was a fairly good student (better at Latin than mathematics), well-behaved and diligent according to school records. In 1868 he wrote to his cousin that his school was a place ''dominated by priests, hypocrisy, and boredom'' (*Correspondance*, Jacques Suffel ed., 1.12).[1] That same year he was abruptly expelled for improper behavior (he wrote an indecent poem and a burlesque of one of the priests' lectures), and his mother sent him to the lycée in Rouen. Even so, life had not been all scholastic discipline. Étretat was a popular sea resort, and Maupassant's great pleasures as a boy and throughout his life were boating and swimming, at both of which he excelled. He is said to have rescued the poet Swinburne from drowning during the summer of 1866. He later recalled visiting the decadent Swinburne and his host for lunch at their cottage and being shown various pornographic photographs and macabre objects, among them a hanged man's severed hand, which he later used in one of his early horror stories, ''La main d'écorché'' (''The Dead Hand,'' 1875).

Rouen marked a change for Maupassant: from a small resort town he moved to France's third-largest city and an important industrial port. His mother returned to Rouen while her son was at school, reestablishing contact with Flaubert, who lived nearby at Croisset. Laure had sent her son to visit Flaubert's mother in

1867, and Guy came to know both Gustave and his closest friend, the poet Louis Bouilhet. Guy had read Bouilhet's poetry with fervent admiration, and the older man was the first to teach him about literary craftsmanship. Bouilhet read and corrected the poems Guy had begun to write as a teenager, and Maupassant later recalled his advice:

> [Bouilhet] made me understand how steady work and complete mastery of one's craft make it possible, on a day of special lucidity, a day of special energy and drive, when you're lucky enough to find the subject in tune with your mind, to produce a piece of work that is a unique distillation, as nearly perfect as possible.
>
> (From preface to *Pierre et Jean* in *Oeuvres complètes de Guy de Maupassant*, xxii)[2]

The first of several substitute fathers and literary mentors in Maupassant's career, Bouilhet died in 1869, just a few days before Guy received his baccalaureate.

That autumn Maupassant began to study law in Paris, living with his father. But the outbreak of the Franco-Prussian War in July 1870 put an end to his studies, and he served for a time in the field with a poorly equipped regiment in Normandy that fled in disarray from the advancing Prussians. The Prussians overran France with humiliating speed, and the war was over by January 1871. Maupassant's father arranged his posting to the quartermaster corps in Rouen, where he was demobilized in September 1871. The failure of his grandfather's business, however, prevented Guy from resuming his law studies. His father had to reduce his son's allowance, but in 1872 he managed to secure a minor post for him at the Naval Ministry in Paris. During the next eight years, until the publication of ''Boule de Suif'' (Roly-poly or Ball of Fat) in 1880, Maupassant served his apprenticeship in literature under Flaubert and other

---

[1]All further references in the text to Maupassant's letters are to this edition.

[2]The volumes in this edition are unnumbered. All further references in the text to Maupassant's full-length novels are to the separate volumes that contain them in this edition.

masters, making various false starts as a dramatist and literary journalist and absorbing the teeming life of Paris. Maupassant loathed the tedious existence of a minor bureaucrat, but he immersed himself when he could in the pleasures of the city, cafés, women, and boating on the Seine.

Although he was a conscientious worker, Maupassant advanced slowly in the bureaucracy, moving in 1873 to the Ministry for the Colonies and in 1878, with a recommendation from Flaubert, to the Ministry of Education. His writing had to be done at home after work. That was difficult and dispiriting. Until 1876 he lived in a small ground-floor room in the same building as his father on the rue Moncey in Montmartre; he then moved into two rooms with a kitchen on the rue Clauzel in the same district, a somewhat disreputable area where many of his neighbors were prostitutes. He suffered from loneliness and frustration, and in 1878, on the verge of literary success, he wrote to Flaubert that his post at the ministry was driving him to despair—so much so that

> I cannot work . . . my mind is barren, worn-out by the calculations that I do from morn till night. . . . I become only too aware at certain moments of the futility of everything, the unconscious malevolence of Creation, the void in my future (whatever it may be), I feel coming over me a total indifference for everything and a desire to remain quietly in a corner without any hopes or irritations.
>
> (1.165)

That pessimism, echoed again and again in his stories, alternated throughout most of Maupassant's short but varied life with high spirits and a manic intensity of work and the pursuit of pleasure. Émile Zola met him in 1874 at Flaubert's apartment in Paris and described him as a hard-working and self-effacing disciple of the master. Maupassant impressed Zola and others who met him by his physical presence and prowess:

> Of medium height, sturdily built, muscular and ruddy, he was at that time a terrific oarsman,

able to row fifty miles on the Seine in one day for pleasure. Besides, he was a proud he-man, and told us dumbfounding stories about women, amorous swaggerings that sent Flaubert into roars of laughter.

(Steegmuller, p. 64)

Broad-shouldered, athletic, and attractive, Maupassant seems to have been a compulsive womanizer. By 1876, at twenty-six, he had contracted syphilis from one of the many prostitutes he patronized. He complained of heart pains; his hair fell out; he developed a skin eruption. The next year he spent two months undergoing a cure in a Swiss sanatorium. Doctors assured him (erroneously, it now seems likely) that it was not syphilis but "constitutional rheumatism." His health seemed to improve, but Flaubert warned him to stick to the straight and narrow, worried that his young friend was losing his commitment to writing:

> You *must*—do you hear me?—you *must* work more than you do. I've come to suspect you of being something of a loafer. Too many whores! Too much rowing! Too much exercise! . . . You were born to write poetry: write it! *All the rest is futile*—beginning with your pleasures and your health: get that into your head.
>
> (*Correspondance*, 9 vols., 8.135)[3]

In the early 1870's Flaubert spent a good deal of time in Paris and, partly at Laure de Maupassant's urging, came to take a deep interest in her son, who reminded him in some ways of his old friend Alfred Le Poittevin. At first Flaubert was cautious in predicting a literary future for the young man; he wrote Laure in 1873 that her son was "a bit of an idler and only mediocre in his application to literary work" (7.9). Flaubert hoped to instill in his young pupil his own artistic credo, in which as he described it to Laure, "the main thing in this life is to maintain one's soul on some higher level, far away from the bourgeois filth

---

[3]All further references in the text to Flaubert's letters are to this edition.

and democracy'' (7.10). Years later, he offered the same advice to Maupassant when he was depressed and needed prodding: "What you lack are *principles*. . . . For an artist, there's really just one: sacrifice everything to Art. The artist must see life as just the means to that end, nothing more, and the first person to be got out of the way is himself" (8.136).

Maupassant himself recalled in 1887 in "Essay on the Novel" ("Le roman") that Flaubert had urged, above all, patience and hard work. Flaubert sought to instill in Maupassant an attentiveness to the actual, an originality of perception earned by single-minded concentration. "Talent is a matter of looking so long and intensely at your subject that you discover some aspect of it that no one else has ever seen or expressed" (*Pierre et Jean*, xxiii). Flaubert asked his pupil to "describe in a few sentences some person or object, in such a way as to define it exactly, and distinguish it from every object of the same race or kind" (xxiv). This theory of the uniqueness of particulars carried with it exhaustive devotion to a matching exactness of style. "Whatever it may be we wish to say," in Maupassant's paraphrase of the lesson, "there is but one word that can express it, one word to make it live, one adjective to modify it. We must search until we have discovered this word, this verb or adjective, and never be satisfied with approximations" (xxiv–xxv).

Perhaps not even Flaubert himself lived up to these standards or solved the opposition between an almost self-sufficient purity of style and a demanding objectivity and particularity of observation. Maupassant developed in a few years a clear and simple style and brought a keen eye to the scenes and experiences he wrote about, but he lacked the leisure and the income to cultivate the artistic purity Flaubert demanded. Even as he submitted poems and stories to the master, Maupassant was striving to break into the world of popular literary journalism. Skeptical about the religion of art that Flaubert preached, far more sensual than his austere and self-denying mentor, pressed by economic necessity, hungering for material success and the pleasures it could bring, Maupassant in time struck out on his own, becoming a thoroughly professional popular writer and also within the limits of his genre a more spontaneous and personal writer, even though less original and profound. He is often crude, cynical, and superficial, but also wonderfully human, appealing in his breadth, variety, and sympathy.

According to Laure de Maupassant, it was Flaubert who encouraged her son to try writing short stories; they had become an increasingly popular form in the 1860's, printed in newspapers as *contes* or short tales and later published in collections by such well-known authors as Alphonse Daudet, whose *Contes du lundi* (*Monday's Tales*, 1873), Maupassant told his mother, he was set on imitating. In 1875 his first story, "The Dead Hand," appeared in a provincial newspaper under the pseudonym Joseph Prunier. A horror story in the manner of Edgar Allan Poe and E. T. A. Hoffmann, based on a recollection of the hideous hand Swinburne had shown him at Étretat, it combines the supernatural—or at least inexplicable—with the psychological. A young man is attacked by the severed hand of an executed criminal, which he has acquired at a country auction and treated as a grisly joke with his friends. The young man survives the attack but goes mad and eventually dies, raving. His friend, the narrator, accompanies the body to the cemetery, where the grave diggers unearth a coffin containing a skeleton, next to which is a severed hand.

That same year, Maupassant was working on another story of this sort, "Le Docteur Héraclius Gloss" ("Doctor Heraclius Gloss," unpublished until 1921), in which the eccentric professor of the title discovers a manuscript explaining the secrets of metempsychosis. The high point of this long tale comes when he sees a figure bent over his manuscript at his desk and imagines it is his double (it turns out to be his pet monkey). Like the hapless young man in "The Dead Hand," Gloss goes mad. Neither of these stories is more than a conventional exercise in horror, but together they announce certain persistent and, as it turns out, deeply personal themes in Maupassant's work that sadly predict his own end. Both stories are about the destructive other self or demonic double, a motif in Poe's and Hoffmann's stories but also a feature of Maupassant's troubled personality.

During these apprentice years, Maupassant continued to write verse and also tried his hand at drama. In 1875 he had written a one-act comedy in verse. "Une répétition" ("A Rehearsal"), which the Vaudeville Theater refused, and in 1876–1877 he wrote a three-act historical verse drama set in fourteenth-century Brittany, "La trahison de la comtesse de Rhune" ("The Treason of the Countess of Rhune"). Flaubert and Zola recommended the piece in 1878 to Sarah Bernhardt, but she declined it, and it was also rejected by the Théâtre Français. Discouraged only briefly, Maupassant wrote another play in 1878, a one-act verse comedy, "Histoire du vieux temps" ("A Story of the Old Days"), which had a short run as a curtain raiser and enjoyed a certain critical success. But even this small triumph brought no financial reward, since Maupassant had to pay the prompter and the director as well as fees for a claque. His most memorable play was written entirely for fun, an obscene farce cooked up in 1875 with his friend, the playwright Robert Pinchon, to amuse their literary friends. "A la Feuille de Rose, Maison Turque" ("At the Rose Leaf, Turkish Brothel") (the title taken from the name of a house of prostitution in Flaubert's L'éducation sentimentale [1869]) concerns an innocent provincial mayor and his wife who wander into the brothel, thinking it a hotel. With Flaubert, Zola, Alphonse Daudet, Ivan Turgenev, and Edmond de Goncourt, among others, in attendance, Maupassant and his friends performed this piece in private, some of them playing the female roles in grotesque costumes that simulated female nudity with huge painted genitals. Flaubert was tremendously amused; Turgenev somewhat shocked by the crudity; and Goncourt found it disgusting.

A rather more decorous eroticism characterizes some of Maupassant's poetry, which he collected and published in 1880 in the volume, Des vers (Some Poems). One of these poems, "Au bord de l'eau" ("By the Edge of the Stream"), is about a young couple who die from the effects of too much lovemaking. Maupassant was threatened with public prosecution when it appeared in a magazine, but the suit was dropped after Flaubert published a letter in its defense. Maupassant wondered at first whether a trial (which could have cost him his post at the ministry) might not advance his literary career, Flaubert having recalled that Madame Bovary (1857) owed much of its success to the public scandal and prosecution it provoked.

Through Flaubert's circle, in 1875 Maupassant had come to know Émile Zola, the most successful literary man of his time and the proponent of a theory of fiction called "naturalism." Maupassant began going to Zola's house every Thursday evening with other aspiring young literary men. With four of them, J. K. Huysmans, Henry Céard, Léon Hennique, and Paul Alexis, Zola and Maupassant planned a volume of stories dealing with the disastrous Franco-Prussian War of 1870, antiwar in emphasis and intended to counteract what they saw as the foolish chauvinism prevailing in France. Part of the planned effect was to shock bourgeois complacency. As Maupassant described it to Flaubert in a letter early in 1880, they set out not to be antipatriotic "but simply accurate. . . . Our integrity in assessing military facts gives the whole volume a shocking and strange appearance, and our deliberate detachment about these matters, into which everyone unconsciously brings his own passions, will exasperate the bourgeois a thousand times more than a frontal attack" (1.253).

Les soirées de Médan (Evenings at Médan), named after the village on the Seine where Zola had a country house, appeared in April

1880. The authors, who purposely gave the book an unrevealing title, apparently hoped to capitalize on Zola's fame, and his story came first in the book, Maupassant's second. Maupassant told Flaubert, in fact, that he hoped the publicity would help sell his collection of poems, *Des vers,* which was shortly to appear. But the success of "Boule de Suif" turned him away from verse writing for good and ended his long period of apprenticeship. Some critics responded to the volume by attacking the naturalism Zola espoused in the preface, but Maupassant's story was singled out for praise by his fellow writers. Turgenev thought it very fine, and Flaubert wrote immediately (on 1 February 1880) to tell his young friend that he considered "Boule de Suif" a "masterpiece": "Nothing more, nothing less. It is the work of a master. It is original in conception, well constructed from beginning to end, and written in excellent style" (8.364). And to his niece, Caroline, he wrote the same day that "'Boule de suif,' the story by my disciple, which I read in proof this morning, is a masterpiece. I repeat the word, a masterpiece of writing, of comedy, and of observation" (8.362). The reading public agreed. The volume was reprinted eight times within two weeks.

Despite Flaubert's enthusiasm, Maupassant was no longer his disciple, nor was he really a naturalist like Zola. Maupassant was the least theoretical of writers and all his life disliked labels and literary programs, refusing interviews in which he would be asked to theorize about his work. As he confessed to one of his fellow writers when the *Médan* volume was being planned. "I believe in naturalism no more than in realism or romanticism" (1.112). Naturalism, as practiced and theorized about by Zola, made the novelist a sort of scientist, who by the discipline of meticulous observation and scrupulous documentation could describe not character and moral action but biological inevitability at work in the human organism. Zola wished to shock the bourgeoisie out of what he conceived as its moral complacency. He therefore treated the characters in his books as animals subject to certain irresistible laws. His novels stress the sexual drives behind behavior, but they study as well the social, economic, and historical factors that combine to produce human destiny. *L'Assommoir* (1877) treats the urban working classes with a graphic insistence on sexual violence and drunkenness, and an authenticity of language and setting that gained tremendous notoriety for the book and its author, making Zola a rich man.

Maupassant admired Zola and his work, prized his powerful intellect, and had a deep sympathy with the biological energies depicted in his books. In 1875 after reading Zola's *La faute de l'abbé Mouret (Father Mouret's Sin),* in which an inexperienced priest falls in love with a young girl, he wrote to Zola of the book's powerful effect on him:

> Even as I imagined what you were describing, I breathed it in; it came up from the page with a strong, persistent odor. You make us feel the earth, the trees; all that fermentation and germination is so vivid that we are plunged into an orgy of copulation and grow dizzy.
>
> (1.77)

In other words, Maupassant responded primarily to the sensuous immediacy in Zola's work, the involving epic sweep of his rendition of natural process. Toward naturalism as a scientific theory and as the basis of a political program he was skeptical, even ironical. In 1879 he wrote to Flaubert:

> What do you think of Zola? I think he is completely crazy. Have you read his article on Hugo? His article on contemporary poets? And his pamphlet, *La république et la littérature?* "The republic will be naturalist or it will not continue to exist." "I am only a scientist." (Nothing but that! Such modesty!)
>
> (1.218)

As "Boule de Suif" makes clear, Maupassant was not a novelist with a theory about life like Zola, nor a novelist with a theory about literature like Flaubert. He was essentially a popular storyteller with a talent for vivid and immediate narration, an eye for detail, and a sympathy (rather than an explanation) for certain characters. The story draws on Maupassant's intimate knowledge of Normandy; it describes a trip from Rouen to Dieppe during the Franco-Prussian War and is said to have been based on an anecdote told by his stepuncle, Charles Cord'homme, who is portrayed in the story as Cornudet, a democrat. According to the anecdote, Adrienne Legay, a Rouen prostitute, was forced to sleep with a Prussian officer while trying to smuggle food and messages to her lover and his friends in Le Havre. The plump prostitute of the story, Boule de Suif, is traveling by stagecoach from Rouen to Dieppe with a group of eminently respectable persons. She alone has thought to bring provisions for the trip, and when she offers to share her repast (lovingly described), the others find their moral scruples overcome by their hunger. When they reach a country inn for the night, a Prussian officer refuses to let them continue their trip unless Boule de suif sleeps with him. Patriotically indignant, she refuses, and the other passengers applaud her decision. But after a delay of several days, they urge her to comply, and she gives in eventually under a barrage of persuasion. While she sleeps with the officer, the other passengers celebrate with champagne. The next day no one speaks to her. At midday when the party pauses to eat, she is without food, and no one offers to share with her. The story ends with Boule de Suif weeping in a corner of the coach while Cornudet sarcastically whistles the "Marseillaise."

The story (actually a novella, or *nouvelle*, of about 13,000 words and much longer than the 2,500 to 3,000 word short stories, or *contes*, Maupassant came to specialize in) is neither an objective rendering of personality in the Flaubertian sense nor a social document in the manner of Zola. Rather, it is a social and moral satire, recalling the profound national humiliation of the war and indicting the moral weakness and hypocrisy Maupassant found illustrated in that conflict. The passengers represent a cross section of society: Count and Countess de Bréville of the aristocracy; Monsieur and Madame Carée-Lamadon of the upper bourgeoisie, owners of textile mills; Monsieur and Madame Loiseau, slightly vulgar, petit bourgeois wine merchants; two silent nuns; Cornudet, an ineffectual republican; and finally, Boule de suif, on the margins of society.

Like so many of Maupassant's stories, "Boule de Suif" turns on an ironic reversal, since it is the prostitute who embodies the values society claims to honor and her traveling companions claim noisily to possess: patriotism, courage, generosity, and moral integrity. When the story begins and the scene is set, we learn that the inhabitants of Rouen have found it prudent to cooperate with their conquerors: "it was surely allowed to be on polite terms in private with the foreign soldiers provided one was not familiar in public with them" (*Contes et nouvelles*, edited by L. Forestier, 1.85).[4] Resistance is led by citizen-officers, "formerly cloth merchants or grain dealers, retired soap-boilers or lard refiners, temporary heroes, made officers because of their wealth or the length of their mustaches" (1.83). But these heroes, "the sole support of France in her death agony," are "terrified of their own soldiers, thieves and murderers, often brave to the point of foolhardiness but fond of pillage and debauchery" (1.83). Maupassant the storyteller finds the inevitable human pattern of self-serving weakness in every prevailing historical context. Ingratitude and prudery conspire against poor Boule de Suif; self-satisfied bourgeois hypocrisy is comically inevitable here, as in so much of Maupassant's work. What makes the narrative a triumph are the compactness and ironic symmetry that reveal this hypocrisy. As the story ends and Boule de Suif sits in a corner of

---

[4]All further references in the text to Maupassant's short stories and novellas are to this edition.

the coach trying to stifle her sobs and ignored by the others while they eat their ample lunch, the countess nudges her husband: ''He shrugged his shoulders as if to say, 'What can you expect? It is not my fault.' Madame Loiseau gave a silent chuckle of triumph and murmured, 'She is crying over her shame.' The two nuns had resumed their devotions after carefully wrapping up what was left of their sausages'' (1.120).

A month after the *Médan* volume appeared, Flaubert died suddenly, and Maupassant helped bury and mourn him, dedicating the third edition of *Des vers* to his memory. He also stopped working at the ministry, taking a leave of absence from which he never returned. He contracted with the editor of a newspaper, the *Gaulois,* to produce a series of sketches, announced as ''*Les dimanches d'un bourgeois de Paris* [*A Parisian's Sundays*], by M. Guy de Maupassant, the young writer Flaubert considered his successor.'' He also began to write for another daily newspaper, the *Gil-Blas.* These sketches (*chroniques*) or impressions of Parisian life were supplemented by book reviews, literary anecdotes, and travel and political pieces. Only a few have survived, but they gradually became more and more anecdotal, a bridge to the short stories Maupassant soon began to publish, mainly in these two newspapers, and for which he is best known.

During the rest of his life, Maupassant became a sort of writing machine, publishing over 200 short sketches for newspapers and magazines and over 300 short stories, in addition to six novels, various travel essays, and several dramatic adaptations. He wrote every morning, from 6:30 or 7 till noon, and read proofs late into the night. It has been estimated that he wrote six pages a day, 1,500 or so every year. From 1880 to 1890 he published an average of three volumes a year, four in 1884 and five in 1885. Most of these writings did double duty, appearing first in newspapers or periodicals and then collected in book form. Maupassant's work was soon translated into English, Russian, and other languages, and that brought further profit.

Very quickly, Maupassant's life changed radically. He moved in 1884 to an elaborate and expensive apartment; he built a villa for himself at Étretat, ''La Guillette'' (Little Guy); and he bought a house for his mother in Antibes and a farm for his brother. He moved in fashionable circles and entertained lavishly in Paris and in the country; he traveled to Corsica, Italy, and North Africa, rented villas at Cannes and Antibes, bought a yacht (the *Louisette*), and kept numerous mistresses. All these changes and pleasures required incessant literary production. In 1884 he wrote to Zola apologizing for not corresponding. ''I have had to produce so much material to pay for my house at Étretat that I really have not had two hours to myself.''

Such a prodigious output demanded strength of body as well as talent, and Maupassant appeared to be a robust, vigorous man. However, in the early 1880's his health had already begun to fail. His eyes troubled him after long periods of writing; he suffered from migraine headaches and became addicted to ether, enjoying both its narcotic effects and the pleasant hallucinations it brought. He fled from the harsh Paris winters to the Côte d'Azur, struggling not only with his infirmities but with recurring depression. Even at the height of his success and in the midst of his triumphs, Maupassant was essentially a tragic pessimist, at times a nihilist. He wrote to Flaubert's niece in January 1881 that he suffered terribly from neuralgia in his head and eyes. That same month he wrote from Étretat to his mother, enthusiastically describing a story he was writing, but also evoking his grim mood:

> I am chilled more by the loneliness of life itself than by the solitude of the house. I sense that all human beings are totally bewildered. I sense the force of the void. And amid this vanishing of everyone and everything, my brain still functions lucidly and exactly.

(2.19)

The story he was working on was "La maison Tellier" ("Madame Tellier's Establishment"), a cheerful, comic evocation of a Rouen brothel whose inhabitants go off to the country to attend the first communion of the madame's niece. Neither sentimental nor melodramatic in its treatment of prostitutes, Maupassant's story exemplifies the lucidity he described to his mother. For the canny Norman peasants in this story, prostitution is simply another profession; and for Maupassant himself the peasant prostitutes represent an honesty and authenticity he clearly admired and found lacking in the urban bourgeoisie. While "Boule de Suif" is social satire, "La maison Tellier" is a farcical folk tale, a series of comic episodes in which the whores on holiday become giggling schoolgirls and afterward, in church at the communion scene, women recalling their own innocence. Maupassant's control of tone, his effortless modulation from social observation to farce to pathos, is remarkable. For example, one of the whores, Rose la Rosse, is a jolly "little roll of fat" who sang songs from morning till night, "alternately indecent or sentimental, in a harsh voice, told silly, interminable tales, and only stopped talking in order to eat, and left off eating in order to talk." Her laugh, "a torrent of shrill cries, resounded here and there, ceaselessly, in a bedroom, in the attic, in the café, everywhere, and about nothing" (1.259). But during the ceremony, Rose remembers her own first communion and begins to cry, her sobs infecting the other whores and then the whole congregation:

> Throughout the church, here and there, a wife, a mother, a sister, seized by the strange sympathy of poignant emotions, and agitated by those handsome ladies on their knees, who were shaken by their shivers and sobs, was moistening her checked cotton handkerchief, and pressing her beating heart with her left hand.
>
> (1.274)

The paragraph that concludes this scene is both moving and ironic, the priest and congregation caught in a moment of human communion whose incongruities Maupassant allows his readers to savor:

> Suddenly a species of madness seemed to pervade the church, the noise of a crowd in a state of frenzy, a tempest of sobs and stifled cries. It passed through them like gusts of wind that bow the trees in a forest; and the priest remained standing, motionless, the host in his hand, paralyzed by emotion, saying: "It is God, it is God, it is God, who is amongst us, manifesting his presence. He is descending upon his kneeling people in reply to my prayers." He stammered out incoherent prayers, without finding words, prayers of the soul, when it soars toward heaven.
>
> (1.274)

In Maupassant's delicate rendering, the priest and his congregation are genuinely transported. The reader is touched but also kept mindful of the circumstances that soon return the story to comic farce. After the communion dinner, Madame Tellier's brother drunkenly tries "to violate Rose, who was dying with laughter." The other whores urge him on, "writhing and holding their sides with laughter, and they uttered shrill cries at every useless attempt that the drunken fellow made" (1.277). The prostitutes return to Rouen, rescuing their regular middle-class customers from boredom by a grand party for which Madame Tellier charges nothing, except for the champagne, six francs a bottle instead of the usual ten. "We don't have a holiday every day," explains the beaming Madame Tellier (1.283). Her generosity, like her piety, is part of a comically represented humanity and its daily concerns.

Like "Boule de Suif," "La maison Tellier" was not written for a newspaper; it was the title story of Maupassant's first collection, which appeared in May 1881. The length of these *nouvelles* (and this is perhaps true of a good many of his longer stories) allows a variety of scene and incident and a corresponding complexity impossible in the shorter stories written initially for the newspapers. "En famille" ("A Family Affair") is nearly as long as "La maison Tellier." First published in *La nouvelle revue* in 1881, it features the incongruity and cruel ironic twist generally associated with Maupassant's stories. And like many of his shorter stories, it centers on a single and surprising incident in a circumscribed, sharply rendered setting. In this case, the milieu is one Maupassant knew all too well and hated—the world of minor civil servants and of unvarying, gray, lower-middle-class domesticity. Monsieur Caravan, a clerk at the Naval Ministry, has done the same things for thirty years: taken the tram and "met the same men going to business at the same time and nearly on the same spot, returned every evening the same way, and again met the same faces, which he had seen growing old" (1.194). Monsieur Caravan's mind, we are told, is "in a state of atrophy from his depressing daily work" (1.194). He "knew nothing more about Paris than a blind man could know, who was led to the same spot by his dog every day" (1.195).

Satire here edges over into crude misanthropic railing, a recurring failure in Maupassant's work, where hatred tends to overcome artful storytelling. Monsieur Caravan is dull and limited; his wife is an ugly, shrewish monster, nagging him incessantly about his ninety-year-old mother who lives with them and is herself avaricious and grotesque. The old lady is pronounced dead by a local doctor of dubious competence as she lies motionless and rigid on her bed. Stricken not so much with grief as with a "mental torpor that prevented him from suffering," Caravan wonders what to do, until his wife takes charge. The body is undressed, washed, and laid out; arrangements are made with an undertaker and a lawyer. Since the old lady has not made a will, the Caravans remove a coveted bureau and gilt clock from her room before the other members of the family arrive. But the busy house of mourning is upset when the children inform their startled parents that the old lady has suddenly awakened. Putting on her clothes, she wonders what has happened to her furniture. As she prepares to come downstairs, Caravan rushes in and embraces her, tears in his eyes, while his wife repeats "in a hypocritical voice: 'Oh, what happiness! Oh, what happiness'" (1.215).

The story is one example of Maupassant's attack on the lower-middle-class existence he narrowly escaped. Lacking the practiced hypocrisy of the provincial bourgeoisie in "Boule de Suif," the characters in "En famille" are conventional in their emptiness and narrowness; the plot is an excuse to make them suffer for our entertainment. Maupassant's stories about the urban petite bourgeoisie, like the famous "La parure" ("The Necklace," 1884), feature individuals locked into an environment where one incident, one disruption of their deadening routine, can change or shape a life. Of course, a short story of about 2,500 to 3,000 words (the length required for newspaper publication) demanded a limited focus; the format is especially suited to lives imagined as so impoverished that there is only room for one interesting (or disastrous) moment. Madame Loisel in "La parure" is married to a minor bureaucrat, but like Flaubert's Emma Bovary she dreams of a glamorous life, of "vast saloons hung with antique silks, exquisite pieces of furniture supporting priceless ornaments, and small, charming perfumed rooms, created just for little parties of intimate friends, men who were famous and sought after, whose homage roused every other woman's envious longings" (1.1198–1199). When an invitation to a ball arrives from the minister of education, she makes her husband buy her an expensive dress and borrows a diamond necklace from a wealthy friend. The ball is a complete "victory so dear to female hearts" (1.1202), but upon returning home Madame Loisel finds she has lost the necklace. Using his life's savings and borrowing the rest, her husband manages to buy a replacement, and the two spend the next ten years drudging and scrimping to pay off the debt. Madame Loisel becomes "like all the other strong, hard, coarse women of poor households" (1.1205). The story ends on the Champs-Élysées where she meets her rich friend, "still young, still beautiful, still attractive" (1.1205). The dreadful, painfully ironic twist comes in the very last line of the story when Madame Loisel learns that the original necklace was paste.

The simplicity of the plot of this famous story distracts readers from its basic implausibility. Like many of Maupassant's stories about the lower middle classes, "La parure" depends upon certain assumptions about them. Maupassant was no naturalist in Zola's scientific sense, but his view of characters drawn from this group depended upon the inevitability of their natures and circumstances. The Loisels are not so much honest as foolishly proud and simpleminded, unable to imagine an alternative to replacing the necklace or confessing its loss. For Maupassant, Madame Loisel is a freak of nature, a beauty born into a family of clerks and thereby doomed to be unhappy and frustrated. Women, says the narrator at the beginning, "have no caste or class, their beauty, grace, and charm" serve them for birth and family (1.1198). Intelligence and judgment have no place in this world of mindless routine, and pretty women deprived of social opportunity to exercise their gifts are subject to the ironic twists of Maupassant's plots. The role of narrator in the stories is unobtrusive but crucial; he is worldly-wise, objective, detached, sometimes amused, with a privileged viewpoint—untouched by the necessity and inevitability he describes.

Some women of Madame Loisel's class are more fortunate, as in the 1883 story "Les bijoux" ("The Jewels"), but only at the price of making fools of their husbands. Monsieur Lantin, another minor bureaucrat, is "unspeakably happy" with his wife; she

was a perfect type of the virtuous woman to whom every sensible young man dreams of one day entrusting his life. Her simple beauty had

the charm of angelic modesty, and the imperceptible smile that never left her lips seemed to be the reflection of her soul.

(1.764)

Her only faults are her love of the theater (where she always goes with a friend since Monsieur Lantin is too tired to accompany her after a day's drudgery at the office) and her fondness for costume jewelry, of which she has a great collection. But one day she catches a chill at the opera and dies a few days later. The grief-stricken widower now finds his income, formerly managed by his wife, insufficient. Pursued by debtors, he resolves to sell one of her necklaces, which he thinks will bring six or seven francs as a fine paste imitation. The jeweler recognizes it as one he sold for 25,000 francs and offers him 18,000. In due course, Monsieur Lantin sells all her jewels for 200,000 francs, overcoming his chagrin at his wife's deception. He resigns his post and marries again. "His second wife was a very virtuous woman but a great scold. She made him suffer a great deal" (1.771). These last sentences tie up the ironies, and we can hear the knowing chuckles of the narrator at this cautionary tale of a contented cuckold. The comic inevitabilities in such stories are as old as the hills, and there are similar situations in Boccaccio and Chaucer. But the comedy is also of the sort associated with a certain kind of naughty French wit; these are male smoking-room stories told at the expense of dull clerks and their cunningly unfaithful wives.

The demands of literary production naturally made Maupassant a repetitive writer; many of his stories are written according to various successful formulas and deal with themes his audience found appealing: satires of the petite bourgeoisie, witty accounts of adultery among wealthy and bored Parisians, stories spun out of news items and bits of scandal—amusing but brittle and often deliberately trivial. "Sauvée" ("Saved," 1885) is a high-society rendering of what could be a trick in a folk tale. To get a divorce, the marquise de Rennedon obtains a photo of her husband's mistress, and hires a woman who resembles the mistress to pose as the maid. An experienced operative (this is her eighth divorce), the maid has no trouble arranging the exact moment to be caught *in flagrante delicto* with the husband. The marquise is there, with her mother and father, an uncle, and a judge. Afterward she dances a little jig of liberation in front of the friend to whom she relates the story, the baronne de Grangerie, who murmurs "in a voice full of dreamy disappointment: 'Why didn't you invite me to see it?'" (2.656). The special wit here lies in the comeuppance of a powerful male through the machinations of women, who comically manipulate male passion the same way that men in other stories cynically exploit female sexuality.

But Maupassant was capable of grander effects and deeper resonances. Scattered among his hundreds of stories are a few small masterpieces in which his facility and technical virtuosity serve more subtle and delicate themes, and where he evokes the lives of ordinary people with a moving simplicity. "Deux amis" ("Two Friends," 1883) is another story that underlines the absurdity of the Franco-Prussian War. Monsieur Morissot, a watchmaker, and Monsieur Sauvage, a draper, meet in a blockaded and famished Paris and recall their weekly Sunday fishing excursions. They resolve to go again, in spite of the war. As they fish and listen to the guns booming, they reflect on the idiocy of war. Captured suddenly by the Prussians, they are shot as spies when they refuse to reveal a password that they do not know. As the soldiers raise their rifles, Morissot "glanced by chance on the net full of gudgeons lying on the grass a few paces from him. The sunshine was falling on that glittering heap of fishes, still full of life" (1.737). As the officer who gave the order watches their weighted bodies sink in the river where they are thrown, he notices

the net full of fish and throws them to his cook. "Get these little things fried at once while they're still alive. They will be delicious" (1.738). The irrepressible simplicity and camaraderie of the two friends, that precious humanity of daily life and small pleasures, are set graphically, in Maupassant's restrained account, against the huge, absurd backdrop of history represented by the war. The unified effect of the short story dealing with a single incident reduces these large, easily mawkish themes to a scale on which they can be grasped—the more implicit or understated, the more powerful they become. The basket of fish is not a symbol of the two friends' futility and absurdity, but a sign of their almost noble persistence in leading a normal life in the face of public disaster.

Not all of Maupassant's best stories are so tightly constructed; one of his finest, "Miss Harriet" (1883), is as psychologically subtle and evocative of mood as Chekhov. The narrator is an old painter who recalls "the most lamentable love affair of my life" (1.877). Wandering in the Norman countryside as a young man, he stays for a time at a farmhouse where he meets a fellow guest, the pious English spinster of the title. In general Maupassant seems to have found the English ridiculous, prudish, and cold; and he later wrote an amusing satire of pious English vacationers, "Nos anglais" ("Our Friends, the English," 1885). "Miss Harriet" could easily have been a satirical rendering of a ridiculous woman, like the English old maids the narrator describes wittily who "carry everywhere their bizarre manias, their petrified vestal manners, their indescribable toilettes, and a certain odor of india rubber, which makes one believe that at night they slip themselves into a case of that material" (1.881). The story, however, is as much about the narrator as it is about Miss Harriet, for he comes to see something touching and strangely powerful in this potential caricature of English prudery.

Miss Harriet, he tells us, gives out "Protestant propaganda'' (even to the local parish priest) and sometimes, without any preliminaries, remarks to their bewildered landlady: ''I love the Saviour above all; I worship him in all creation; I adore him in all nature; I carry him always in my heart'' (1.881). As he paints by the shore, the narrator sees her on the edge of a cliff, gazing ''passionately at the vast sea, glittering in the sunlight, and the boundless sky empurpled with fire'' (1.883). He is ''mysteriously'' attracted and sees in her ''an inward and profound happiness'' (1.886). She comes to watch him paint—sitting for hours, marveling at his work, and talking to him about God. When the painter gives her a small sketch, she is moved to tears, and he feels a shiver in her touch as he reassures her. With the practiced sense of a man who knows women, he realizes she is in love with him and resolves to move on.

That night Miss Harriet happens to see him kissing a servant girl; the next day it is discovered that the spinster has drowned herself in the well. In the last pages of the story, the weakest in their explicit sentimentality, the narrator watches over the corpse and muses on her lonely life and her return as a decaying physical organism to the nature she loved. But before these passages, there is a moment when Maupassant might better have concluded the story, as the narrator recalls washing the corpse, plaiting her hair, arranging ''on her forehead a new and singular coiffure. Then I took off her dripping wet garments, baring with shame, as though I had been guilty of some profanation, her shoulders and her chest, and her long arms, slim as the twigs of branches'' (1.893). The narrator's belated tenderness is exactly right, expressing guilty sorrow for the love he has thoughtlessly inspired. The meagerness of Miss Harriet's life, the frustrated sexuality expressed in her awkward love of nature, and the hopeless intensity of her passion for the painter are contained in this scene without any need for explanatory commentary. Like the net full of

gudgeons in ''Two Friends'' this tender examination of Miss Harriet's corpse is a summarizing image, a flash of insight into the meaning of another person's life.

In ''Miss Harriet,'' Maupassant escapes the provinciality of much of his fiction, its restriction to the particular realities of French life during the Third Republic, to touch on the broadly conceived human issues of love and loneliness. Understanding and pity temper his customary facile ironies, and his technique is effectively unobtrusive. Miss Harriet's melodramatic suicide provokes the narrator's uneasy self-doubt—a very different attitude from the wry and wary sophistication with which many of his tale tellers conclude.

Like many of Maupassant's stories, ''Miss Harriet'' begins with a preliminary scene or framework (cadre is the French term) to provide a narrative occasion for the tale. In ''Miss Harriet'' the frame is the narrator's carriage trip through the Norman countryside from Étretat to visit some ruins. The story is told by the old painter, Léon Chenal, at the request of his gay and aristocratic companions, who want to be amused as they travel. This is one of the oldest, most traditional of storytelling devices, evident in collections of tales like Giovanni Boccaccio's *Decameron* (1353) and Geoffrey Chaucer's *Canterbury Tales* (1400) and used by Maupassant's contemporaries. In the best examples the cadre establishes an interaction between the story and the teller, enriching the narrative situation by involving us, as in ''Miss Harriet,'' with both teller and tale.

Another, particularly good example of this interaction occurs in ''Un soir'' (''One Evening,'' 1889). Set in North Africa, where Maupassant had traveled extensively, the beginning of the story finds the narrator about to leave Bougie (in northwestern Algeria) to go back to Paris, ''that city of futile gossip, of commonplace preoccupations'' (2.1069). He is, however, reluctant to leave a scene where he is ''drunk with light, with wide, fantastic horizons'' (2.1069). By chance he meets an old schoolmate, Trémoulin, who has settled in Bougie and who invites him for a visit. One night, Trémoulin takes him fishing, and the narrator watches, horrified, as his host spears fish with a *fouine*, a sharp, three-pronged fork, and holds them wriggling over the fire that lights their way in the boat. At length, he catches an octopus and holds it to the fire, ''rubbing the thin fleshy ends of its arms against the red-hot bars of the brazier. They crackled as the heat of the fire twisted and contorted them, and I ached all over at the idea of how the hideous beast must be suffering'' (2.1075). Later that night, Trémoulin tells the narrator how he came to settle in Algeria, and we begin to understand the sources of his obsessive cruelty as a spear fisherman. His story is a commonplace one of betrayal and adultery. He and his wife owned a bookshop in Marseilles, and he suspected that one of the frequenters of their literary salon, a young, handsome man, was her lover. After agonies of suspicion, he surprised her instead in the arms of a retired general, sixty-six years old, paunchy and wrinkled but distinguished. The disgust Trémoulin describes extends from his wife to all women, ''prostitutes with hearts of filth'' who give themselves for money or, as he puts it, are ''bought by the glamour of greatness'' (2.1084).

We are, of course, surprised to find that the primary story is the tale of adultery and all that precedes it is the *cadre*. Trémoulin's raging misogyny clarifies the extended *cadre* on the fishing boat, whose relevance we only now understand. The story is not about adultery but sadistic obsession, violent emotions in an otherwise ordinary man. The narrator's concluding insight is typical of Maupassant's best tales: ''Certain chance meetings, certain inexplicable combinations of events, contain—without any outward appearance of the unusual—a greater amount of the secret quintessence of life than is spread over the ordinary course of life'' (2.1085). Maupassant's stories extract that quintessence, finding a moment of revelation or insight into events that appear at first insignificant. The *cadre* creates an ordinary situation in which the extraordinary makes its unexpected appearance.

In other stories it is Maupassant's purpose to show repetition and inevitability in lives in which nothing extraordinary happens. That pattern is evident in Maupassant's tales of Norman peasant life (''La maison Tellier'' is an example). Peasants tend to be authentic primitive beings in Maupassant's work, free of the bourgeois hypocrisy he hated. Even though they are self-serving, avaricious, and lustful in often monstrous ways, and sometimes as brutish as the animals they live with, they are honest and at home in the natural world. The narrow-mindedness he satirizes in minor bureaucrats becomes a touching, frightening, but heroic humanity in his peasants.

''Histoire d'une fille de ferme'' (''Story of a Farm Girl,'' 1881) begins with a compelling rural scene. Rose the servant girl feels herself caressed by the light of the sun, ''her heart was filled with sweetness and a feeling of well-being ran through her body'' (1.226). She watches the hens and the barnyard cock copulate, is almost ''dazzled at the sight of the apple trees in blossom,'' and sees a colt ''full of life and friskiness'' gallop past (1.226). This world of benign, invigorating natural process is an ironic prelude for the story, since what unfolds for Rose is the brutality and pain of life within that natural world. She is seduced and betrayed by a fellow servant and goes home to have her baby. Her widowed mother dies, and Rose leaves the child with neighbors to return to the farm, where she works hard to support the child no one there knows she has. When her master proposes marriage, she is confused, then desperate, and tries to drown herself. Eventually, he rapes her and after a time marries her, turning abusive when they have no children. In the end she tells her husband about her son, and he declares himself happy to adopt the child.

Through all this, Rose is the bewildered but patient victim of natural process and of male tyranny, once narrowly escaping murder as her husband kneels on her stomach, beating her "with clenched teeth and mad with rage" (1.242). She is saved by her husband's practicality, the same peasant characteristic that leads to murderous rage at her infertility and expresses itself earlier in the story in his remark: "When a cow has no calves, she's not worth anything, and when a woman has no children, she's not worth anything either" (1.241). Rose is the heroine because, quite simply, she endures without complaining, with a dogged animal persistence that seems to justify her husband's brutal view of women.

Although there is a terrible bleakness in Maupassant's peasant stories, there is also occasionally a triumph and resilient wit in the tenacity of their characters. Rose is like the heroine of "Rosalie Prudent" (1886), a middle-class couple's peasant maid who is tried for infanticide. Maupassant uses an effective storytelling device in this story. He describes the case in the objective manner of a court reporter: "The girl Prudent (Rosalie), a maid employed by the Varambat family of Nantes, became pregnant unknown to her employers, was brought to bed during the night in her attic bedroom. She killed and buried her child in the garden" (2.699). And he balances that official and unsentimental account with Rosalie's pathetic, halting rendering of her seduction by her employers' nephew and then of her solitary birth-giving, lying "down on the floor, on the boards, so I shouldn't soil my bed" (2.701). The surprise here, for the court and the reader, is that Rosalie had twins that night and killed them out of a crude calculation of the impossibility of supporting both: "One, yes, could be managed, with scraping and saving, but not two. It made my head go round. I didn't know what I was doing, I didn't. And do you think I could choose one rather than the other?" (2.702). With the jury in tears, the judge asks her where she buried the other

one. The exchange is a surprisingly comic moment in the midst of pathos and potential mawkishness, evidence of Rosalie's peasant practicality:

"Which did you find?" she asked.
"Well . . . the one . . . the one who was in the artichokes."
"Oh, then! The other one is under the strawberries—at the edge of the well."

(2.702)

Rosalie is acquitted, but happy endings are rare in these stories. Peasant stolidity is more often shocking, brutally inevitable rather than comic or pathetic. Notable in this regard is "La mère Sauvage" ("Mother Savage," 1884), one of a number of memorable tales about the Franco-Prussian War. The upper-class narrator revisits the idyllic countryside around his friend's château, which was destroyed by the Prussians and is now rebuilt. As he hunts in the woods with his friend and remembers the "heavenly happiness" of fishing in its streams, "which ran through the ground like veins carrying blood to the earth," he comes upon a ruined cottage where he had received a glass of wine from an old woman in 1869 (1.1217). Her dead husband, he recalls, was an old poacher, her son a tall, wiry fellow, and their family name, "Savage." "Was it a name or a nickname?" he wonders (1.1218). Then his friend tells the story: the son had gone off to the war, and four young Prussians were billeted on Mother Savage. In her simple way, she thinks they may know something about her son, asks them about him, and comes to treat them as his replacements. They chop wood for her and do chores; she cooks for them and feels no hatred for them as enemies. "Peasants," Maupassant explains, "have no patriotic hatreds; that is the privilege of the upper classes" (1.1219). But after a letter comes with news of her son's death, she carefully packs the sleeping loft with straw and burns down the cottage with the Prussians in it. She instructs an officer to write to their parents "that it was me that did it. Victoire Simon, the Savage woman! Don't forget" (1.1223). She is shot on the spot, and the local château is burned in reprisal. The privileged narrator's country idyll is transformed by the grim reminder of the recurrent moral idiocy of war in this story of an old woman's terrible and exact justice.

Some of the stories about the war tell of simple heroism and feature courageous peasants who defy the hated Prussians, such as the old hero of "Le père Milon" ("Old Milon," 1883), who dresses in Prussian uniform and murders enemy scouts at night in retaliation for his slaughtered cow and sheep and ruined forage, as well as for his father, killed in the Napoleonic wars, and his son, killed in this war. "Eight for my father, eight for my son, we're quits," old Milon declares, spitting twice in the Prussian colonel's face as he offers to spare him. The directness and simplicity of Maupassant's narrative method, his disdain for psychological analysis, and his sharp focus on specifics is particularly appropriate for these stories of peasant heroism.

Maupassant's rigorously externalized, objective-looking narrative method is evident in other stories, about clerks, club men, country squires, and prostitutes. Personality is summed up in a few telling details, accurate and artistically economical but also often the means of dramatizing and satirizing shallow, predictable personalities. Yet Maupassant could also explore psychological depths. Building on his interest in fear and hallucination and complicating the tradition of the horror tale by focusing on the effects of terrifying experience rather than its mysterious or supernatural causes, Maupassant wrote a number of intensely introspective stories that fall into two categories. In the first a narrator discovers the emptiness and nothingness of life in a moment of revelation. The second category contains veritable case studies of mad-

ness, some told by a detached observer, others by the madman himself in the process of losing his mind or within the obsessional intensity of his fixation. The first group reflects Maupassant's temperamental pessimism, which was strengthened by his enthusiastic reading of philosophers like Herbert Spencer and, especially, Arthur Schopenhauer, "the greatest destroyer of dreams," as a character in "Auprès d'un mort" ("Beside a Dead Man," 1883) calls him (1.728).

"Promenade" ("A Walk," 1884) seems at first to be another satiric rendering of the emptiness of the life of a clerk: "For forty years the old bachelor M. Levas had been arriving at this prison at eight o' clock each morning, and staying there till seven at night, bent over his ledgers, writing with the concentration of a good workman" (2.127). But one day he takes a walk in the Bois de Boulogne, sees lovers all around him, and, as he thinks of his life, his empty room, he hears "around him, above him, everywhere, a confused, immense, continuous roar, made up of innumerable different noises, a dull roar, near and distant, a vast vague quivering of life: the breath of Paris, breathing like a colossal being" (2.132). A couple walking in the park the next morning find him dead, hanged by his braces. Death, says the last line of the story, "was attributed to suicide from a cause unknown. Possibly temporary insanity?" (2.132). In fact, the irony here is with those who think it *was* insanity, since the suicide represents the old man's deliberate and measured reaction to the discovery of his own emptiness and separation from the frightening and vital energies of life. In that moment, he is a sort of hero for Maupassant.

A similar if rather more destructive and comprehensive mad heroism is granted to the schoolmaster in "Moiron" (1887), who is condemned to death for murdering seven of his pupils by feeding them sweets mixed with glass fragments and broken needles. The story is told by the public prosecutor in the case, who is convinced of his innocence by Moiron's confessor, and petitions the emperor for a commutation of the sentence to life imprisonment. Years later, the prosecutor finds Moiron on his deathbed and himself listens to his confession. He killed the children, he admits, because it came to him after his own children died that God is a monster, a murderer who "gives life only to take it away!" and who has invented suffering, disease, and death to divert himself (2.989). He killed the children to play a trick on this monstrous deity. "Now it's all over. I can no longer escape Him. But I have no fear of Him, Monsieur, I despise him too much" (2.989–990).

For Maupassant in his grimmer moods, God and Nature, God's surrogate, are the enemies of mankind. Thus, in "L'Inutile beauté" ("Useless Beauty," 1890) the countess de Mascaret after eleven years of marriage and seven children refuses to sleep with her husband anymore so that she may preserve her beauty. To take her revenge when he tries to force her, she tells him one of the children is not his, but she refuses to say which one. As the story advances six years, two elegant friends at the Opéra look over at the countess, marveling at her beauty and her age—thirty-six! This leads one of them to condemn nature, "our enemy," which makes a beautiful woman into "a mere reproductive machine" (2.1216). Maupassant's men-about-town are for the moment moralizing intellectuals disgusted by a natural order in which, as one of them puts it, God is "a monstrous creative organ unknown to us, who sows millions of worlds through space as a single fish lays eggs in the sea" (2.1217). God is, in Maupassant's Darwinian rendering, a blind force, "ignorant of what he does, senselessly prolific, unconscious of the multitudinous combinations produced by his scattered germs" (2.1220).

Civilization, as Maupassant's spokesmen define it, is summarized in the idealization of a beautiful woman like the countess. Providence gives us a brutal life instinct, bent on reproduction, but "everything that belongs to the imagination comes from us" (2.1223).

The story ends with the countess swearing to her husband that her story was a trick to avoid more childbearing. As the count looks at his wife, he sees her as a woman destined for more than animal reproduction, the embodiment of "a mystic beauty half-seen and intangible," adorned "with all the poetry, the romantic luxury, the conceits, and the aesthetic charm that civilization has gathered around woman, this statue of flesh that engenders as many fevers of the senses as immaterial appetites" (2.1223).

In a reverse treatment of the same theme, "La tombe" ("The Tomb," 1884), a lover is obsessed by his dead mistress, disinters her body, and embraces her decaying corpse. Mortality and the bewildering finality of death clearly fascinated Maupassant, and these stories dramatize intense revulsion and insane attraction as opposing obsessions with physical decay. The preoccupation reappears in "Un fou" ("A Madman," 1885). A manuscript is found among the papers of a lately deceased, distinguished judge in which he describes his homicidal mania based on a crazed vision of the world in which "killing is the glorious law thrust by nature deep into our hearts" (2.542). In part, this story is satirical, for the judge's insanity begins in a coldly rational analysis, rather like that of the marquis de Sade's heroes, of the legalized murder the state sanctions in war and judicial procedure. Maupassant's disgust is as much with society as with nature; the judge's criminal insanity is meant to expose the false rationality of military slaughter and legal execution.

A less contrived and more authentic sort of madness is the subject of "Lui?" ("He?" 1883), in which loneliness leads to vivid hallucinations about a double. The narrator announces to a friend that he is going to marry, in spite of his inability to love one woman, because he can no longer stand living alone. "I am afraid of myself, afraid of that horrible sensation of incomprehensible fear, afraid of the spasms of my terrified mind" (1.870). Behind that fear is the story; he arrives home one cold, wretched evening from a lonely walk to find someone sitting asleep in his armchair by the fire. As he goes to touch him, he realizes with a shock that there is no one there. He is haunted by that hallucination, even though he is aware that it is just that. "I know that he does not exist except in my cowardly imagination, in my fears, and in my anguish!" (1.875). The story surprises us by its swing from a club man's cynical analysis of marriage and women ("I look upon all legalized cohabitation as utterly stupid, for I am certain that nine husbands out of ten are cuckolds") to a study of obsession leading to near madness (1.869). Many critics consider this psychological contradiction as the key to Maupassant's personality. Like the narrator of "He?" he was a compulsive womanizer whose pursuit of pleasure may have masked a deep fear and self-loathing.

The most memorable and extended rendition of this psychological pattern occurs in "Le horla" (first published in 1886, rewritten and expanded in 1887). The title is an invented word (from *hors*, without or outside, and *là*, there); "le horla" is "the thing out there." In part, Maupassant's subject was a result of his shrewd response to the literary marketplace. Similar obsessive hallucinations and mysterious phenomena were part of the enormously popular works of Eugène Sue, author of *The Mysteries of Paris* (1842–1843) and *The Wandering Jew* (1844–1845). Moreover, mental illness was a topic of current interest in the 1880's in France; hypnotism, obsession, hysteria, and neuroses were fashionable topics, and they also represented the beginnings of modern psychiatry. As soon became tragically evident, there were obvious affinities between the madness Maupassant wrote about and his own mental deterioration. The lucidity with which he renders the gradual complications of madness in "Le horla" is a tribute to his powers of introspection for an artistic purpose.

In the first version of the story, the narrator is the patient of a psychiatrist who invites him to tell his story to a select audience. The longer and more effective final version is a diary kept by a man who becomes obsessed by an invisible creature. Unlike the hallucination in "Lui?" this specter seems to leave traces; he turns the pages of books and drinks milk and water the diarist leaves about. The "horla" is, indeed, a projection of the diarist's madness, a nightmare figure, a vampire like Dracula "whose crushing weight lies on my chest as he presses his mouth on mine and drinks my life" (2.823). The narrator later verifies the reality of such a creature—he is a demonic alien who arrived in France on a Brazilian ship. The story breaks off after the narrator burns his house down, hoping to destroy the horla, and kills his servants in the process. Maupassant balances the obsessive and destructive intensity of the character against the clarity and rationality with which he investigates fantastic and inexplicable phenomena.

In the longer version of "Le horla," allowances are made for the slow elaboration of madness and the exploration of the ambiguity surrounding the phenomena that cause it. Some of Maupassant's best stories are after psychological effects that demand the length of *nouvelles* rather than the brevity of *contes*. Along with the full-length novels he wrote, the *nouvelles* mark a division in his fiction between the sharply rendered simple anecdote, the tale or *conte* that focuses on a few sharply rendered significant moments that summarize a character or encapsulate a life, and the longer narrative that explores the development of personality and dwells on the gradual movement of psychological process. The longest of his *nouvelles* is "Yvette" (1884), in which a young, innocent girl discovers that her mother is a courtesan and that her future holds the same fate. Fiction like this is defined by a slow unraveling, a progressive development that sympathetically involves the reader, rather than a moment of illumination or ironic insight and the accompanying detachment of the shorter narratives. "Yvette" and others such as "La petite Roque" ("Little

Roque," 1885), "Monsieur Parent" (1885), and "Le champ d'oliviers" ("The Olive Grove," 1890) are strong psychological studies that extend and deepen Maupassant's characteristic themes of self-discovery.

In "Monsieur Parent," for example, Maupassant characterizes the naive cuckold of the title as a tortured rather than comic figure, tormented not only by his wife's infidelity but by doubt about the paternity of their son. After a violent confrontation with his wife and her lover, his wife tells him the child is not his, and he throws them out, thrusting the terrified child into her hands. Maupassant's biographers note the parallels between this separation and others in his stories and the marital strife he must have witnessed as a child. The narrator of the short story "Garçon, un bock!" ("Waiter, a Beer!" 1884) is an idler and alcoholic who traces his unhappiness to the childhood trauma he suffered when he saw his father beating his mother.

Twenty years after Monsieur Parent's quarrel, he again sees the son and his mother and demands in a frenzy to know the truth. In his rage he finally realizes that she doesn't really know the answer, since she slept with both him and her lover. Biographers have found the roots of this theme of dubious paternity in Maupassant's deep ambivalence toward his father, his perhaps subconscious desire for another father or a grounded suspicion that he was not his father's son. In "Le père" ("The Father," 1883) a father reappears after ten years and begs to see his son, whom he covers with "extravagant kisses" before fleeing "like a thief" (1.1079).

In one of the short stories, "Duchoux" (1887), Baron Mordiane feels the onset of mortality and decides to seek out his natural son, a Monsieur Duchoux, whom the baron had sent as an infant to be brought up near Marseilles. His son turns out to be a pompous provincial architect, vulgar and garlicky, resembling the woman the baron had loved "as a monkey resembles a man" (2.1001). His identity unrevealed to his son, the baron flees

back to Paris, imagining he hears "a metallic, shrill, repellent voice, crying: 'Father!' much as one shouts: 'Stop him!' when a thief is in flight" (2.1002). Guilty fathers recur, but so do lamentable sons. In "Un fils" ("A Son," 1882) an old man, a member of the French Academy, describes the brutish stable boy he engendered in his rape of a peasant girl. Now, every year, unidentified, he watches "this larva of the stables" and feels an intolerable desire to embrace him (1.424). "But I have never even touched his dirty hand" (1.425).

Maupassant lacks complete artistic control of this recurring, clearly obsessive theme in some of these pieces, which are melodramatic and cynical by turns. But the narrative length provided by the *nouvelle* makes "The Olive Grove" a triumphant rendering of tragic paternity. The abbé Vilbois is an aristocrat who becomes a priest after an unhappy love affair with an actress. Confronted with her infidelity, the actress tells him the child she is pregnant with is her lover's, and the baron leaves and turns to the church to forget. Years later, at fifty-eight, he is robust, vigorous, and narrow-minded, but kind to his flock—"a religious leader with a soldier's temperament, a guide who led the sinner by force into the straight and narrow" (2.1184). Piety, a narrow but intense intelligence and moral will, and physical vigor—together they form a complex humanity Maupassant rarely conveys. His picture of the abbé is objective but without any condescension, compassionate without the melodrama and pathos he so often settles for elsewhere. Maupassant beautifully arranges the gradual introduction into the atmosphere of the story of an "unknown individual," a young man of twenty-five, prematurely withered and balding, "a sign of fatigue and early debauchery" (2.1186–1187). The abbé, we have been told at the beginning of the story, has a square-cut brow, "straight, white hair cut short—more the brow of an officer than of a priest" (2.1180). We hardly need to be told that the intruder is the abbé's son; to prove it, he carries a crumpled photograph of the abbé as a young man. This son is a demonic double of the abbé, a flabby devil brutalized by his life with his mother and stepfather—for the shocked priest he is a terrible revelation of "that sewer of moral filth that works as a deadly poison on certain beings" (2.1192).

Maupassant's handling of character is delicate in this tale. Moral melodrama is balanced with human details. As the abbé eats dinner with this "outcast," he savors the fish (caught that morning) and remarks with pride on its freshness, then orders his servant to bring two bottles of good white wine, "for when he offered wine to a guest—an unusual pleasure—he always offered himself a bottle too" (2.1193). Gradually the greedy expectations of his son lead to a quarrel. The son, drunk by now, reaches for a knife, and the abbé knocks him down, upsetting the lamp and plunging the room into darkness. In the dark, the abbé's anger drains out of him and "other ideas took their place, black and sad as the darkness around him" (2.1202). An hour later, the servant hears the gong summoning her: "It rang as if struck by a single hard stroke, sharp and loud, followed by a curious noise of something dropping and of an overturned chair" (2.1202). She finds the abbé dead and the tramp asleep, too drunk, the police later assume, to run away. "It never occurred to anyone that Abbé Vilbois might have caused his own death" (2.1204). This last sentence is no cheap irony; rather, it underlines the insight the story offers. Bewildered by the twistings of fate, which he sees summed up in the mocking image of a long-lost son, the abbé is driven to suicide in that desperate hour of darkness.

"The Olive Grove" is one of Maupassant's last works and differs in mood and intensity from most of the longer works of his frantic decade of literary life, the 1880's. "Yvette" is set in the Paris that Maupassant called "the artist's dunghill" where he "can come to fullest flower." Growth and corruption are intertwined in that witty remark, and Maupassant often fled like some of his characters from the

whirl of city life. Nevertheless, he captured the sights and sounds of Paris as few other writers of his time could. The gay, high life of the boulevards, cafés, and river front that he depicts resembles in its light, color, and variety the world of a painter such as Manet.

Some of Maupassant's most memorable writings are renditions of the Parisian scene he knew as a young man, looking for sport and women along the banks of the Seine. The pleasure-loving crowds in the vulgar restaurant by the side of the river in "La femme de Paul" ("Paul's Wife," 1881) are the center of an exciting, disreputable, slightly menacing world that Maupassant knew how to evoke with a painter's eye for form, color, and composition:

> Women and girls with their yellow hair and breasts developed beyond all probability, with exaggerated hips, their complexions plastered with rouge, their eyes outlined with charcoal, their lips blood-red, laced up, rigged out in outrageous dresses, trailed the crying bad taste of their toilettes over the fresh green sward; while beside them young men posed in their fashion-plate garments with light gloves, patent leather boots, canes the size of a thread, and single eyeglasses emphasizing the insipidity of their smiles.
>
> (1.293–294)

There is a sense of corruption about these women and a dandyish weakness in the young men that predict the outcome of the story. Paul's wife merges with the grotesque crowd and is seduced by some aggressive lesbians. Surrounded by the feverish sensuality of the riverside scene that seems to mock and exclude him, maddened by jealousy and self-pity, Paul drowns himself. In "Yvette" and other larger works, descriptive passages are not connected so tightly to plot and theme; atmosphere invokes a set of social conditions and possibilities without pointing to a particular outcome for the story.

For example, here is a scene at the opening of "Yvette":

A restless crowd swarmed on the boulevard, the crowd that on summer nights is always to be seen there, contented and merry, walking, drinking, and talking, streaming past like a river. Here and there a café flung a brilliant splash of light onto the group that sat outside, drinking at round little tables loaded with bottles and glasses, and obstructing the hurrying crowd of passers-by. And in the road the cabs, with their red, blue, and green eyes, passed swiftly across the harsh glare of the lighted front, and for a moment revealed the thin, trotting silhouette of the horse, the profile of the driver on the box, and the dark, square body of the vehicle. The cabs of the Urbaine Company gleamed as the light caught their yellow panels.

(2.234)

Although "Yvette" is a fine story about the romantic young heroine's acquisition of self-knowledge, it is also about the world so well evoked in this description. The two young men who walk arm in arm through this scene and on whom Maupassant focuses in the next paragraph are at the center of the world that contains Yvette's fate as a courtesan. In evening dress, smoking cigars, "their hats a little on one side, with the nonchalance of men who have dined well and find the breeze warm," Jean de Servigny and Léon Saval and other elegant idlers rule this world of pleasure and social privilege (2.234). Without any illusions to lose, they preside over the Parisian scene Maupassant describes. Yvette will learn in the story that she exists to serve them, that for her they are an irresistible predatory force.

This is how Yvette's mother, the marquise Obardi (a fake title, as everyone knows), tells her the truth.

Yes, I am a harlot. What then? If I weren't a harlot, you'd be a kitchen maid today, as I was once . . . . There's no two ways about it for women, no two ways, d'you hear, when you're a servant! We can't make fortunes on the stock exchange or at high finance. We've nothing but our bodies, nothing but our bodies.

(2.287)

Yvette has to learn this painfully. She tries to commit suicide, but with a beautifully rendered self-preserving inefficiency that allows her to be revived by Servigny, who will be her first lover, she realizes, as the story ends.

Bel-ami (1885) was written two years after Maupassant's second full-length novel, *Une vie*, and is about that same world of Parisian pleasure and social privilege. *Bel-ami* is rather like a series of *nouvelles* like "Yvette," told from the point of view of a male adventurer who has the freedom and opportunity denied to women. Georges Duroy is an opportunistic cad who rises in the newspaper world Maupassant knew so well by a mixture of luck, cunning, and the exploitation of his physical attractiveness to women. Many of the people Maupassant knew recognized themselves in the book, and critics have seen that topicality as its chief virtue. Perhaps deliberately superficial in characterization, presenting people as social masks and compounds of inevitable vices and ambitions, *Bel-ami* is a convincing panorama of the corrupt world of the Parisian upper bourgeoisie in the 1880's, full of adventurers and nouveaux riches.

Thanks to various women, Georges Duroy rises from assistant to a gossip columnist for *La vie française (French Life)* to editor, whose Jewish, nouveau riche owner's wife he seduces. Her husband's inside information helps him make a fortune on the stock exchange, and at length he elopes with his mistress's daughter and becomes a millionaire. They are married in the Madeleine, all of society in attendance, the bishop of Tanger presiding. As they emerge from the church, Duroy sees the Chamber of Deputies across the Place de la Concorde, and he imagines himself as a politician with even greater power.

Bel-ami is a panorama of the 1880's but also a satire of the superficiality of a world where mediocrity and shallowness can thrive. Georges Duroy's moment of self-discovery comes when he sees himself in a full-length mirror and doesn't recognize himself—he wonders for a moment who that elegant chap could be. Having only a small shaving mirror in his shabby room, he is startled by his full-length reflection, dressed as he is for the first time in his life in formal clothing: "And now, looking at himself with care, he recognized that actually the overall effect was quite satisfactory" (p. 30). His rise in society is a series of new postures, carefully arranged and self-consciously opportunistic images. The mirror image is skillfully repeated through the book as Duroy learns that his shallow self-seeking is the way of the world, that high society is precisely on his own low level.

A Life had been an entirely different exercise, the depiction of the painful, extended awakening of a provincial woman to the tragedy and emptiness of her life. In *Bel-ami* the hero's rise provides a measure of continuity, but *A Life* is a series of short-story incidents, a collection of fragments meant to add up to a life. The principle is one of accretion rather than progression. Jeanne Le Perthius des Vauds, daughter of a noble Norman family of modest means, comes home from her convent school and marries a local squire, Julien de la Mare. Disillusionment and disaster follow steadily in a series of vignettes: her husband has an affair with her maid, then with a neighbor; after her mother's death, she finds letters that prove her mother was unfaithful in her youth; Julien and his mistress are killed by the mistress's husband; Jeanne devotes herself to her child, Paul, who eventually runs off and gets into debt; and finally she is forced to sell her château and move in with the maid her husband had seduced, now grown into a grasping Norman peasant woman who dominates her. All this is pitilessly presented in Maupassant's best objective manner, for Jeanne is largely passive and bewildered by experience until the end of the story. The book is rich in observation of the Norman country-side and populated with colorful characters drawn from the locale, but the narrative method makes it a set of fragments rather than a novel.

Maupassant turned from short stories to novels to consolidate his reputation and to acquire the artistic prestige associated with the longer form. His novels brought him attention from literary critics, whereas his collections of tales had been barely noticed by them. Moreover, his novels sold better than the volumes of collected stories. But he had difficulty making transitions between sharply realized scenes and establishing the complexity and depth of theme and character the novel requires. His third novel, *Mont-Oriol* (1887), suffers from an uncertainty of tone, wavering between satire and romantic sentimentality, with touches of peasant life and Parisian cynicism added for good measure. *Mont-Oriol* is based on Maupassant's own experience of health spas and concerns the efforts of a wealthy Jewish businessman, Andermatt, to develop a fashionable health resort around a newly discovered spring. The major subplot deals with his wife's love affair with a feckless young man, Paul Brétigny, who deserts her in disgust when she becomes pregnant. The backdrop for these events is life at the health spa, full of quack doctors, eccentric guests with all manner of hypochondriacal complaints, and fortune hunters.

The sentimental love story gave Maupassant the most trouble, and the book was finished with great difficulty after a year and a half of work. He achieved novelistic unity and psychological penetration, however, in his next novel, *Pierre et Jean* (1888), generally regarded as his best. "A faultless production," Henry James called it the year it appeared, because he found Pierre Roland, the hero, an "operative character," virtually unique, said James, among Maupassant's thousands of characters in his "capacity for reflection . . . addressed to anything higher than the gratification of an instinct."

Pierre and Jean Roland are brothers, sons of a retired jeweler from Paris, who are living in Le Havre. Pierre, the older son, has recently qualified as a doctor and is ready to begin practice; Jean has just completed his law degree. The plot turns on an unexpected legacy to Jean from Léon Maréchal, an old friend of the family's who has died. In due course, Pierre begins to suspect that Maréchal was Jean's father, and he eventually wrings the truth from his mother. Baldly summarized, the plot is familiar to any reader of Maupassant: the obsession with secret paternity and the suspicion of women. Maupassant's delicate skill for suggesting character and predicting conflict with atmosphere and detail is also evident.

The book begins with a Roland family outing where Pierre and Jean childishly vie to outdo each other at rowing. But Maupassant extends his technique past this summary rendering of character in finely observed incidents by focusing on Pierre's troubled mind rather than moving out to a larger social scene as in *Bel-ami* and *Mont-Oriol*.

Maupassant claimed in the preface to the book ("Le roman" ["Essay on the Novel"]) that writing the psychological novel was impossible, since no one could penetrate another's mind, but in *Pierre et Jean* he manages to do just that. To be sure, psychological probing is accomplished only partly—by analysis and paraphrase of Pierre's thoughts—and Maupassant's narrative finds physical, external details that surround, provoke, and dramatize his hero's inner life. The most important of these is the background of the harbor at Le Havre—the fog, ships' lights, and other seascape sights and sounds. The fog (a "brume nocturne") accompanies and symbolizes Pierre's confusion. Out sailing, happy on "the dancing waters," guiding the boat "as if it were a swift and docile winged creature," Pierre is forced back to land by "a gray shadow, deep and swift, blotting out the sky and covering the sea, rushing toward them like a cloud fallen from above" (p. 88).

Pierre's meditations lead him reluctantly to certain troubling insights, and this may be what James had in mind when he praised him as a genuinely reflective character. His mother, Pierre comes to realize,

had been young, with all the poetic weaknesses which agitate the heart of a young creature. Shut up, imprisoned in the shop, by the side of a vulgar husband, who always talked about business, she had dreamed of moonlight nights, of voyages, of kisses exchanged in the evening shadows.

(p. 106)

Pierre thus gains a deep awareness of the circumstances affecting human action, which mold personality and shape lives. Bel-ami is a lucky manipulator, the poor heroine of *A Life* a pure victim, but Pierre experiences and comes to appreciate how human destiny is determined by social and psychological forces beyond individual control.

Pierre bluntly tells Jean of his suspicions, and when he confronts his mother, Madame Roland confesses her guilt. Pierre is stricken with remorse, while Jean, the shallower of the brothers, finds reasons to keep the inheritance and is glad that the loutish Monsieur Roland is not his father. Emotionally agile and resilient, Jean grows closer to his mother in their shared secret, while Pierre grows melancholy, troubled by his emotions and distanced from his family. At the end, he takes a job as a ship's doctor on a passenger liner. The novel ends with his family watching the ship sail away as the symbolic mist reappears. Madame Roland casts a final look out to sea, "but she could see nothing now but a puff of gray smoke, so far away, so faint, that it looked like a bit of fog" (p. 242).

In *Pierre et Jean*, Maupassant avoids the moral melodrama at the heart of his plot by insisting on the emotional ambiguity symbolized by the mist. His last two novels, *Fort comme la mort* (*Strong as Death*, 1889) and *Notre coeur* (*A Woman's Heart*, 1890), lack the convincing psychological intensity and clear focus of *Pierre et Jean*, partly because they deal with the upper class, which Maupassant could only approach satirically. He knew the peasants and the petite bourgeoisie and, sympathizing with them, could write convincingly about their lives. He was led by his friend, the novelist Paul Bourget, to attempt psychological studies of the upper class, though he understood these people only superficially. (Bourget specialized in this subject.) Some critics, too, had complained from the beginning of Maupassant's career of the vulgarity of his subjects and had urged him to depict a better class of people. After reading "La maison Tellier," the influential critic Hippolyte Taine urged him "to increase the range" of his observation. "Some day," he wrote, "you will doubtless portray the cultivated classes, the upper bourgeoisie, engineers, physicians, professors, big industrialists, and men of business" (Steegmuller, p. 288).

The main interest of *Strong as Death* does not lie in its rendering of upper-class life, which is thoroughly dull. In a way, this is a deeply personal book, directly relevant to Maupassant's last dark years. The hero, Olivier Bertin, is an aging and successful artist who falls in love with the daughter of his mistress of many years. He is reminded, poignantly, of his lost vigor both as lover and artist. A sentence from the opening pages suggests how closely Maupassant may have identified with his hero: "After the triumph of his debut, the desire to please, of which he was scarcely aware, had always been at the center of his work, had secretly turned him from his goals and weakened his convictions." Bertin is also haunted by age and terrified of death, which arrives for him as a revolting surprise: "If one saw it, if one dreamed about it, if one was not distracted, amused, blinded by all that passes in front of us, one could not go on living. The spectacle of this endless massacre would drive us mad" (p. 166).

The last years of his life were increasingly painful for Maupassant. Writing became difficult; physical exercise like rowing, the delight of his life since childhood, became exhausting. His eyes, he wrote to his publisher in September 1888, were so bad, his headaches so powerful, that he had been unable to write for months. He went to health spas and traveled in North Africa, but he had to return to writing to maintain his extravagant way of life. He also had to maintain his invalid mother. Further expense and a great shock came in 1887 when his brother, Hervé, became seriously ill and showed signs of the syphilitic madness that killed him in 1889.

Throughout those last years, Maupassant managed to write as much as an ordinary healthy man; one of his best *nouvelles*, the powerful "The Olive Grove," was published in 1890. But the progressive effects of the tertiary phase of syphilis, in which the infection affects the brain, grew worse. When he attempted another novel, *L'angélus*, he managed only about fifty pages. He sought relief in the sun on the Côte d'Azur and on his yacht, but the disease attacked his spine and then, manifestly, his brain. After an unsuccessful suicide attempt in January 1892, he was brought back to a Paris clinic in a straitjacket. By late 1892 his condition had further deteriorated and was marked by megalomania and paranoid delusions that alternated with periods of utter weakness when he could hardly stand. A series of violent convulsions led to death on 6 July 1893, a month before his forty-third birthday.

Maupassant remains one of the world's best-known writers, a born storyteller with enduring popular appeal.[5] He wrote much too quickly to be a great artist like his master, Flaubert; and his vision was perhaps too narrow, his intelligence too limited to make him a powerful writer of the rank of Balzac or Zola. But within the genre of the short story, he was a writer of enormous technical brilliance whose control of image and scene have never been surpassed. And when he allowed himself the expansiveness and more leisurely pace of

[5]During his lifetime and after, unscrupulous publishers brought out stories under Maupassant's name that were in fact imitations written by hacks. For a list of these, see Steegmuller, pp. 353–360.

the *nouvelle*, he produced several stories that are among the most moving in nineteenth-century European literature.

Selected Bibliography

EDITIONS

COLLECTIONS OF SHORT STORIES, POETRY, AND NOVELLAS

Des vers. Paris, 1880.
La maison Tellier. Paris, 1881.
Mademoiselle Fifi. Paris, 1882.
Clair de lune. Paris, 1883.
Contes de la Bécasse. Paris, 1883.
Miss Harriet. Paris, 1884.
Les soeurs Rondoli. Paris, 1884.
Yvette. Paris, 1884.
Contes du jour et de la nuit. Paris, 1885.
Monsieur Parent. Paris, 1885.
Toine. Paris, 1886.
La petite Roque. Paris, 1886.
Le horla. Paris, 1887.
Le rosier de Mme. Husson. Paris, 1888.
La main gauche. Paris, 1889.
L'Inutile beauté. Paris, 1890.

NOVELS

Une vie. Paris, 1883.
Bel-ami. Paris, 1885.
Mont-Oriol. Paris, 1887.
Pierre et Jean. Paris, 1888.
Fort comme la mort. Paris, 1889.
Notre coeur. Paris, 1890.

COLLECTED WORKS

Contes et nouvelles. Edited by Albert-Marie Schmidt. 2 vols. Paris, 1964–1967.
————. Edited by Louis Forestier. 2 vols. Paris, 1979.
Oeuvres complètes de Guy de Maupassant. 29 vols. Paris, 1908–1910.
Oeuvres complètes illustrées de Guy de Maupassant. Preface by René Dumesnil. 15 vols. Paris. 1934–1938.
Oeuvres complètes illustrées. Edited by Gilbert Sigaux. 16 vols. Lausanne, 1961–1962.

TRANSLATIONS

The Collected Novels and Stories of Guy de Maupassant. Translated and edited by Ernest Boyd. 18 vols. New York, 1922–1928.
The Works of Guy de Maupassant. Translated by Albert M. C. McMaster, A. E. Henderson, et al. 10 vols. New York, 1911.
Works of Guy de Maupassant. Critical preface by Paul Bourget and an introduction by Robert Arnot. 17 vols. Akron, Ohio, 1903.

CORRESPONDENCE

Correspondance. 9 vols. Paris, 1926–1933.
Correspondance. Edited by Jacques Suffel. 3 vols. Evreux, 1973.

BIOGRAPHICAL AND CRITICAL STUDIES

Borel, Pierre. *Le destin tragique de Guy de Maupassant.* Paris, 1927.
————. *Le vrai Maupassant.* Geneva, 1951.
Boyd, Ernest. *Guy de Maupassant.* New York, 1926.
Cogny, Pierre. *Maupassant: L'homme sans Dieu.* Brussels, 1968.
Coulter, Stephen. *Damned Shall Be Desire, The Passionate Life of Guy de Maupassant.* London, 1958.
Dubosc, Georges. *Trois Normands.* Rouen, 1917.
Dumesnil, René. *Guy de Maupassant.* Paris, 1933.
Greimas, A. J. *Maupassant. La sémiotique du texte: exercises pratiques.* Paris, 1976.
Ignotus, Paul. *The Paradox of Maupassant.* London, 1966.
Jackson, Stanley. *Guy de Maupassant.* London, 1938.
James, Henry. "Guy de Maupassant." In *The Art of Fiction and Other Essays.* Introduction by Morris Roberts. New York, 1948.
Kirkbridge, R. de L. *The Private Life of Guy de Maupassant.* London, 1961.
Lanoux, Armand. *Maupassant le Bel-ami.* Paris, 1967.
Lerner, Michael G. *Maupassant.* London, 1975.
Maynial, Edouard. *La vie et l'oeuvre de Guy de Maupassant.* Paris, 1906.
Morand, Pierre. *Vie de Guy de Maupassant.* Paris, 1942–1943.

Normandy, Georges. *La fin de Maupassant.* Paris, 1927.

Schmidt, A.–M. *Maupassant par lui-même.* Paris, 1962.

Steegmuller, Francis. *Maupassant: A Lion in the Path.* New York, 1949.

Sullivan, Edward. *Maupassant the Novelist.* Princeton, N.J., 1954.

————. *Maupassant, the Short Stories.* London, 1962.

Vial, André. *Guy de Maupassant et l'art du roman.* Paris, 1954.

Wallace, Albert H. *Maupassant.* New York, 1974.

Williams, Roger L. *The Horror of Life.* Chicago, 1980.

JOHN RICHETTI

ARTHUR RIMBAUD

(1854–1891)

INTRODUCTION

BETWEEN 1854 AND 1891, Rimbaud's life came and went with something of the "terrifying celerity" he exalted in art and experience. In those years, the Franco-Prussian War raged, and the French republic fell; the Paris Commune was established and collapsed; Karl Marx wrote *Das Kapital;* and in only six years, between the ages of fifteen and twenty-one, Rimbaud produced a corpus of work designed to tear down the entire cultural and literary edifice of his age. He then stopped writing abruptly and absolutely in 1875, except for a handful of distinctly unliterary letters dashed off fitfully during the years that he ran coffee, skins, and guns around North Africa and the Middle East as a trader and self-imposed exile on the margin of legality and of European life. At seventeen, in a letter to a friend, he projected one of the most radical literary and biographical experiments in modern culture. During the next three years, Rimbaud lived, as the critic J.-M. Carré remarked, "through the evolution of literature into the modern age." His literary output was small and often impenetrably difficult, and it represents what Stéphane Mallarmé called an adventure "unique in the history of art." It comprises under a hundred poems proper (written for the most part before 1872); some forty prose poems, *Les illuminations* (1872–1875?); the short, intricate, and agonizing autobiographical self-critique *Une saison en enfer* (*A Season in Hell,* 1873); and a few even shorter prose works, mainly fragmentary. Upon this surprisingly slender oeuvre has risen Rimbaud's reputation as the supreme poet-outcast, or *poète maudit,* as Paul Verlaine called him, and one of the two or three greatest modern French poets.

At the center of Rimbaud's revolt was a *bouleversement,* a repudiation, not only of the religious and bourgeois traditions he found intolerably stifling, but of the literary, linguistic, and epistemological structures that accompanied them. Rimbaud refused to be stifled; his work was planned as a staunch resistance to what he took to be the easy assimilations and sly complicities of tradition and culture.

The main force of that resistance was Rimbaud's fierce will to innovate. "Let us ask the poet," he wrote in a letter, "for the *new— ideas and forms.*" And, indeed, Rimbaud's work reflected the general turbulence of French culture. During the period 1848–1875 in France, the forms of political and social representation—in government, journalism, and the arts—underwent numerous and, as Marx saw it, farcically repetitive cycles of change and revolution. We might call this turbulence "the crisis of the new."

Three related phenomena stood behind this crisis: the great material success of the middle class and the political upheavals it engendered; the relative decline in aristocratic and religious ways of thinking; and the astonishing technological successes of science and industry. The latter in particular gave direct rise to an ideology of progress itself, through very visible and continual advances in medicine and technology. Novelty, change, and revolution—indeed the very idea of modernity itself—became a standard in intellectual life and the arts, and with this came a new emphasis on the "contemporary" and the "original" as hallmarks of superiority. For writers of the avant garde like Charles Baudelaire and later Rimbaud himself, contemporaneity and newness almost entirely supplanted older canons of "harmony," "perfection," and "order" in art. As Rimbaud wrote, "Il faut être absolument moderne"—one must be absolutely modern. The historian Eric Hobsbawm put it this way:

> If the pleasure of representing the present comes not only from its possible beauty, but also from its "essential character of being the present," then each succeeding "present" must find its specific form of expression, since no other could express it adequately, if at all. . . . The ways of apprehending all the pasts must inevitably give way to those of apprehending our time, which were better just because they were contemporary. The arts must constantly renew themselves. And in doing so, inevitably, each succession of innovators would—at least temporarily—lose the mass of the traditionalists, the philistines, those who lacked what the young Arthur Rimbaud—who formulated so much of elements of this future for the arts—called "the vision."
>
> *(The Age of Capital, 1848–1875)*

At issue was not simply what one presented in art, but how one represented it, and indeed what the idea of representation itself entailed. Thus a middle-class and scientific ethos of progress, when applied to the arts, caused the collapse of what had been the aesthetic and intellectual ideal of the generation before 1848: the ideal, that is, of an art and culture congruent with the circumstances of the bourgeois society in which it was produced. Realism, the first aesthetic impulse of progress, gave way to new "progressivisms"; and increasingly after the political upheavals of 1848 there arose a bohemian counterculture devoted to the principles of the avant garde and opposed to the society that first formulated them. If, as for Rimbaud, the "new" in art was a way of combating the cramping repetitiveness of culture, the contradiction remained that this program too, albeit in a different fashion, could succumb to the same repetition. Precisely contemporary with the Paris Commune, Rimbaud's work was part of a general movement that heralded, in the words of the critic J.-L. Baudry, "the destruction of an economic, political, and ideological system it was helping to disintegrate." Within the context of the repeatedly failed social and political revolts of the time, we may begin to understand the motif of escape, revolt, and innovation that characterizes Rimbaud's work as well. The contradictions are stark: Rimbaud's society and his writing were both forever beginning anew, if only to reproduce the discrepancies—in value, in form, in meaning—that engendered them.

Rimbaud's entire career was a ceaseless attempt to displace the legacies of culture. "I recognize myself," he wrote, "only today." In his writing and his life, he moved almost continuously. Verlaine, who loved him and who in a fit of lover's despair once shot him in the arm, called him "l'homme aux semelles du vent"—the man with feet of wind. Incessant new beginnings are central to Rimbaud's project and to the stance he sought to adopt with respect to self and culture. The importance and difficulty of his career are that it presents the fascinating case of a man, or adolescent, taking the form of his own rejection of tradition as a model for a new program of vision and understanding. Value and meaning in Rimbaud's work are no longer tied to transcendental design, to the categories of reason and science, or to the gatherings of tradition. Regarding all truths with what he called an "atrocious skepticism," Rimbaud thought of meaning not as a given, but rather as a kind of perpetual innovation in reality. This was his profound moral commitment, and from it emerge the central preoccupations of his work: the search for and production of visions of the unknown; the imperative "changer la vie" (change life); the commitment to radical freedom in art and life. Perhaps in the form of a necessary failure, Rimbaud's work testifies to a distinctively modern faith, what Wallace Stevens once called "belief in an immaculate beginning." There are religious undertones in such a phrase, but Rimbaud like Stevens transposed his notion of immaculate beginnings from the authority of a divine origin to the freedom of human agency in the present. "Poetry," he wrote in a letter later to become known as one of the *lettres du voyant*, "will not lend its rhythms to action, it *will be in advance*." He meant that writing, in a kind of negation of circumstance, should no longer superintend the institutions and habits of a present dominated by the past, but rather attend to the manifold possibilities of a future forever beginning.

To achieve this meant shattering every formal constraint, in life and in art. Rimbaud experimented with free verse ten years before Jules Laforgue, completely transformed the prose poem, and violated almost every social norm. His name is virtually synonymous with iconoclasm, and the revolution he imagined was to be a revolution of both society and self. Recalling Rameau's nephew in the climax of Denis Diderot's great masterpiece *Le neveu de Rameau*, Rimbaud presented the self as a polyphonic musical process, what he termed an "opera fabuleux" and a "suave concert spirituel": "I am present at the birth of my thought: I watch it and listen to it: I draw a stroke of the bow: the symphony begins to stir in the depths, or comes on stage in a single leap" (*lettres du voyant*). Anticipating the insights of psychoanalysis and surrealism, Rimbaud conceived the self quite literally to be scored by diverse forces—social, sexual, and linguistic. He sought in his writing not so much to represent these relations—for representation implies an ability to know and deliver meaning as an achieved and completed given—as to *produce* them theatrically in the process of their complex and changing invention.

Astute critics have said of Rimbaud that he sought to replace the expressive function of poetry by the productive function of the text and language. During the short and brilliant period of his commitment to it, Rimbaud directly identified the combinations of language—including its lapses, discontinuities, and instabilities—with the creative processes of life itself. Before long, he abandoned language as he abandoned almost everything, although the mystery of that renunciation has perhaps been exaggerated by critics. For reality itself to Rimbaud was a kind of unremitting abandonment: "La vraie vie est absente," he remarks in *A Season in Hell;* the true life is absent. In the course of his life, he confronted that absence ferociously: as a vagabond and delinquent, as a poet and seer, finally as a man of action committed to the less exalted, but ineradicably real, world of material goods and trade.

LIFE AND EARLY WORKS

Second son of an infantry captain and a strict, narrow-minded farm woman, Jean Arthur Rimbaud was raised in the Ardennes city of Charleville in northern France. His father left the family when Rimbaud was six, and he grew up thereafter under the unyielding Catholic discipline of his mother. Vitalie Cuif was by all accounts an almost perfect personification of the bourgeois parsimony and niggling class-envy Rimbaud came to despise. She had, as he later wrote in "Les poètes de sept ans" ("Seven-Year-Old Poets"), the "blue glance— that lies." The sketch of her effect on Rimbaud in this poem of 1871 gives an idea of the way his personality was formed in secret negation to the cramped moral circumstances of home life:

And the Mother, closing the exercise book,
Went off satisfied and very proud, without seeing,
In the blue eyes and under his brow covered with
  bumps,
The soul of her child give over to repugnance.

All day he sweated obedience; very
Intelligent; yet dark twitchings, a few traits,
Seemed to testify in him to bitter hypocrisy.
In the shadow of the corridors with their moldy
  hangings,
Passing through he stuck out his tongue, his two
  fists
In his groin, and in his closed eyes he saw spots.

(1–10)

These verses illustrate not only his angry resistance to authority, but how the physical functions of the body formed a part of that resistance. They also suggest—"in his closed eyes he saw spots"—the induced vision of an alternative and private reality, again linked to the workings of the body:

In the summer,
Especially, overcome, stupefied he was bent
On shutting himself up in the coolness of the
  outhouse:
There he meditated, peacefully, opening his
  nostrils.

(13–16)

Rimbaud was always *en avant*. A precocious student, he attended schools in Charleville, where he skipped grades, learned Latin and Greek, and began writing at an early age. His first known literary effort, a prose composition written when he was ten, characteristically shows an impatience with the regimen of school life and with the irrelevance of classical training and the standard curriculum. He nevertheless went on to become top scholar at the Collège de Charleville, winning first prize for a poem in Latin, "Jurgurtha," in 1869.

His first poetic efforts in French, "Les étrennes des orphelins" ("The Orphans' Gifts") and "Première soirée" ("First Evening") appeared in January of 1870 in a journal to which his mother subscribed, *La revue pour tous*. These demonstrate an extraordinary, if by no means original, virtuosity in a fifteen-year-old. Around this time Georges Izambard came to the school as a teacher, recognized Rimbaud's genius, and became his first mentor. With Izambard's encouragement, Rimbaud composed a spate of poems during his last year at school, including "Le forgeron" ("The Blacksmith"), "Bal des pendus" ("Dance of the Hanged Men"), "A la musique" ("To Music"), and others. These show a widening mastery of genre, prosody, and form as well as a continuing obedience to the regnant principles of academic and Parnassian poetry, which in response to earlier romantic excess stipulated classical or conventionally exotic subject matter, rigid exactitude of form, and emotional detachment. Rimbaud sent three of these—"Sensation," "Ophélie," and "Credo in unam" (later called "Soleil et chair," "Sun and Flesh")—to Théodore de Banville in Paris under a somewhat fawning cover letter pledging fidelity to the Parnassians. Banville replied, but did not publish the poems in the prestigious series *Le Parnasse contemporain*, as Rimbaud had wished.

The summer of 1870 and the year that followed mark the first of two great watersheds in Rimbaud's career. The Franco-Prussian War broke out in July, much to Rimbaud's fierce and antipatriotic delight. The effects of war were vivid in the countryside and foreshadowed the fall of Napoleon III and the French republic. At his graduation in August, Rimbaud took top prizes in nearly every discipline and seemed certain to realize his mother's ambition that he go on to win distinction as an academician and a writer. The former was not to be and the latter only in a manner she could never have imagined. On 29 August, Rimbaud excused himself from a family stroll and boarded a train for Paris without a penny in his pocket. In Paris, which attracted Rimbaud as the center of political and literary life, he was arrested for being unable to pay the fare. Izambard bailed him out, and eventually he was returned to Charleville. So far as is known, in the next nine months Rimbaud fled home at least three times and succeeded at least once in reaching Paris. During the spring of 1871, between truancies and flights from home, Rimbaud immersed himself in the library at Charleville (where, as he wrote to Izambard, "everything is dead"). His readings there—in alchemy, philosophy, literature, and history—came to fruition in a radical poetic project expressed in two letters now known as the *lettres du voyant* because of their visionary poetic insights. He may have returned to Paris in the late spring of 1871, before or during the Paris Commune, and it is probably during this period that he had the sordid homosexual initiation that "Le coeur supplicié" ("The Tortured Heart") seems to commemorate. Though he returned home periodically throughout his life, the final escape from Charleville came in the fall of 1871 when Paul Verlaine, replying to a letter Rimbaud had sent him at the behest of his Charleville friend and fellow poet Charles Bretagne, invited him to come to Paris. Verlaine plainly thought him a mature man of letters; in fact he was just seventeen.

During this first phase of his career—stretching from the early poetic efforts of 1869 through the radically experimental verse innovations produced after he went to Paris in 1871—Rimbaud's writing underwent an important transformation. Circumstance and temperament had inclined him from the first to oppose the culture around him. Now, from what we might call his nascent ideological opposition to the banal content of society, Rimbaud cultivated an ethical and philosophical opposition to its every form. Concomitant with this was his increasing dissatisfaction with the available forms of poetic expression, and it is this twofold revolt that we will examine in some detail.

EARLY POETRY

Rimbaud's ideological opposition to society was patent from the start. "My native town,"

he wrote to Izambard in August 1870, "is a supremely stupid provincial town." It astonished him to see, as the town mobilized for war, "all the fat-bellied dignitaries with rifles over their hearts. . . . My country is rising up! . . . I prefer to see it seated." He found the habits and callow, strutting postures of his hometown revolting, especially now in the pell-mell rush to defend the corrupt regime of Napoleon III. In this he was perhaps only following the fashion of angry young men of his day, but he did so from the start with a great deal more savagery and vehemence. In "To Music," he travestied the vapidity of what passed for provincial culture:

On the square, cut into measly plots of grass,
The square where everything is right, trees and
    flowers,
All the wheezy bourgeois, choked by the heat,
Bring on Thursday evenings their jealous
    stupidities.

The military band, in the middle of the garden,
Swing their shakos in the *Waltz of the Fifes:*
Around them, in the first rows, struts the dandy;
The notary hangs from his monogrammed watch-
    charm.
                     (1–8)

As always, it was the meaningless order, the senseless attachments of society that repelled him. Into that order, against its hypocrisy and materialism, Rimbaud insinuated a picture of himself—sly, voyeuristic, and desiring, voluptuously following the "lively girls":

Soon I have revealed the boot, the stocking, . . .
—Burning with fine fevers, I reconstruct the
    bodies,
They find me silly and speak together in low
    voices, . . .
—And my fierce desires fasten on their lips.
                   (37–40)

Part of this desire is ritual: to outrage the bourgeois. But what is striking about the lasciviousness here is not only its calculated sensuality, but the way desire itself—its objects, aims, trajectory—is staged as a process of central significance. In the attention to physical detail, in the ironic notation of the way bodies, desires, and social arrangements are always indiscreetly in excess of the neat categories to which bourgeois conceptions would confine them, Rimbaud was beginning to find formulations for his sense of the powerful latent forces operating beyond the horizons of conventional sensibility. In any event, he knew well that it was the notary who hung from the monogrammed watch-charm, and not the watch-charm from the notary, if he was not yet prepared to articulate exactly why this was so. This reversal of the normal relation of cause to effect, of conscious design to material reality, anticipates his later discoveries.

Every institution of society, every aspect of civil life, came in for Rimbaud's contempt at this time. He lambasted war in "Le mal" ("The Evil," 1870) and "L'Éclatante victoire" ("The Striking Victory," 1870); hypocrisy in "Le châtiment de Tartufe" ("Tartufe's Punishment," 1870) and "L'Homme juste" ("The Just Man," 1871); the conventions of romance and love in "Les reparties de Nina" ("Nina's Replies," 1870) and "Mes petites amoureuses" ("My Little Lovers," 1871); the treatment of the poor in "Les éffarés" ("The Intimidated," 1870); and customs officials in "Les douaniers" ("The Customs Men," 1871). In "Les assis" ("The Men Who Sit," 1871), Rimbaud launches a characteristically scabrous attack on the librarians of Charleville, satirizing the old men who brought him books. He does this by fragmenting the organic unity of the old men's bodies, creating an irrational and comically grotesque orchestration of body parts—eyes, swollen fingers, penises, buttocks, teeth, shoulder blades, eyelids, tonsils, fists, feet, chins, bones—working in concentrated unison with the material objects and the unconscious routines of work. What emerges is a hilarious sexual animation of objects and organs, a bizarre dalliance of buttocks and seats, "ink flowers spitting pollen commas." A common tactic in these poems is to confront sham respectability—that is, *all* respectability—with scatological obscenity, to sketch a "Venus Anadyomene" with an "ulcer on the anus" or catch Brother Milotus in "Accroupissements" ("Squattings," 1871) crouching over his chamber pot. In so doing, Rimbaud is imparting more than just impertinence and outrage to his verse, for with these come new rhythms and sounds, a new kind of lyricism—harsh, physical, but nevertheless supple and deft. When Rimbaud was not pouring scorn on social conventions, he was celebrating the life of physical freedom and vagabondage in "Ma bohème" ("My Bohemian Life," 1870) and "Au Cabaret-Vert" ("At the Cabaret-Vert," 1870).

The same irreverence and eccentric attention to physical detail are apparent in Rimbaud's attacks on the political traditions and structures of France. "The Blacksmith" is an imagined confrontation between a blacksmith and Louis XVI in August 1792: a mob mills about the Tuileries as the blacksmith recounts the centuries of meek submission the peasants and workers are now throwing off ("Oh! the people are no longer whores"). The poem, some ninety alexandrine couplets, eulogizes the mob—"le crapule," the scum—oppressed and exploited by the nobility. Like many of the poems written in this period, "The Blacksmith" is largely a pastiche and derives much from Victor Hugo and Jules Michelet. Nevertheless, it emphasizes the significance to Rimbaud of communal reality and shared history. In it, he juxtaposes the pseudoindividuality and unreal autonomy of the king, in truth parasitic on the political body of the people, to the higher collective reality of the "terrible mob," seething and rising up, "howling like a bitch, howling like the sea." In the political sonnet "Morts de quatre-vingts-douze" ("Dead of '92," 1870), Rimbaud bitterly invokes the memory of the French Revolution traduced by posterity: "We let you sleep with the Republic, / We, crouching under kings as under cudgels."

But if these memories weighed heavily on the present, it was the general weight of European Christian history that Rimbaud most deplored. We touch here on a particularly problematic aspect of Rimbaud's work—the degree to which he attributed the flaws of reality to social and historical forces (and hence to causes susceptible to human intervention and change); or, conversely, how much he conceived those flaws to be built—ontologically, metaphysically—into the very structure of reality itself (hence forming part of the irreducible nature of human experience). So far, I have stressed the kinds of social and political authority against which Rimbaud chafed, and to a degree Rimbaud grouped Christianity with these. Thus in "Les pauvres à l'èglise" ("The Poor in Church," 1871), the hypocritical ideals and rituals of Christianity are shown to be the main props to a way of thinking that falsely naturalizes the humanly constructed and miserable condition of the poor. Christianity, so conceived, is an authoritarian artifice that literally holds the poor in place. Elsewhere, however, Rimbaud's unhappiness with religion seems to be part of a deeper dissatisfaction and touches on the more philosophically radical intuition that experience is intrinsically—and not just socially or historically—built on frustration and denial.

Both elements of this ambivalent response to Christianity, the historical and the metaphysical, were first expressed in "Sun and Flesh," which voices a naive pantheism and a secondhand romantic rejection of the present in favor of the fullness of a ritual association with a bygone classical age. The poem is a pastiche of borrowings from Alfred de Musset, Hugo, Baudelaire, and others. Nonetheless while much of the regret for a "time when the world's sap . . . / Put a universe into the veins of Pan" is borrowed, the sensuality and the critique of Christianity is not:

I believe in you! I believe in you! Divine mother, Aphrodite of the sea!—Oh! the way is bitter

Since the other God harnessed us to his cross; Flesh, Marble, Flower, Venus, I believe in you!

(2.1–4)

Writing with Lucretius' materialist doctrines in mind, Rimbaud constructs a myth of divine origins significantly different from the generally accepted Christian model. It is the fall from Venus, not from God, that generates man's separation from initial perfection. In one central Christian tradition, aboriginal wholeness of being is the function of Logos, the Word, whose perfect equilibration with reality is celebrated in the myth of the Garden of Eden. That myth was revived as far as Rimbaud was concerned by the Enlightenment, in the form of a belief that reason—man's new Word—could progressively reachieve equilibrium with the world man inhabits. Rimbaud rejected all this, Christ ("eternal thief of energy," as he later wrote) and science alike. For all form what he calls in "Sun and Flesh" the great "cloak of ignorance and narrow chimeras" of modern belief—even "pale reason hides the infinite from us." Fullness of being was instead connected by Rimbaud to an infinite, fluid, and distinctly androgynous sensuality. It is the loss of an earth "big with sap and rays of light, / The vast swarming of all embryos," that afflicts the contemporary world.

Now whether this loss could be replaced—whether, that is, it is an invention of man or of God—is a question that continually arises in Rimbaud's poetry. It is a question, I think, about which Rimbaud was fundamentally undecided. On the one hand, "Sun and Flesh" identifies a distinctly historical origin for man's ills: "the way is bitter / Since the other God harnessed us to his cross." The advent of the Christian, the *other*, God, is historicized here in a manner that implies the possibility of his human supercession. On the other hand, what Venus is said to have provided is a kind of wholeness that Rimbaud expresses in distinctly—if rather scandalously sexualized—religious terms. Thus the degree of human access to such wholeness; the role of human or indeed poetic invention in re-creating it; its historical, as opposed to divine, provenance: these are uncertainties constantly invigorating, and vexing, Rimbaud's work from within. It might be said that if Rimbaud's radical desire for wholeness of being shows his work's residually religious motivation, his steadfast refusal to accept ready religious satisfactions shows the profoundly secular tendency of it. One could go further and say that Rimbaud's obsession with sensuality and the human body—an obsession that rose almost to a discipline of license—reflects an attempt to transfer the locus of man's religious quest from the spirit to the flesh. Certainly his sexual life, at once febrile and ascetic, showed the mark of a religious obsession projected on the body's desires.

But this is jumping ahead. Derivative and formally conventional, Rimbaud's poems of 1870 were nevertheless motivated by a handful of related themes central to his work as it was shortly to develop: the desire for physical freedom and the search for sensation; the vituperative rejection of almost every social convention; the sense of political and religious tradition as a burden on the present. Indeed the crux around which almost all of Rimbaud's early poetry may be said to turn, uniting his political, sexual, metaphysical, and poetic concerns, is the paradox of desire. This paradox is, in a sense, the problem his entire work mediates, and understanding it sheds light on the motives of his early poetry and on the direction his work soon took.

We might put the problem this way: The occasion of Rimbaud's writing was characteristically a lack, a need, an insufficiency in reality. A poem arose out of the desire for political justice, which the institutions of Europe denied the people; or the desire for sexual abandonment, which bourgeois culture inhibits; and so on. Poetry, motivated by such desires, was put forward to secure their satisfaction.

Now at the same time, and whether he is addressing political, social, or sexual themes, Rimbaud's ambition *within* a poem is typically, as we have seen, to reachieve a state in which desire is at once excited and satisfied within a single gesture, transpiring simultaneously in a single event. (Indeed, desire itself is typically predicated on there being a delay between its inception and satisfaction.) It is this simultaneity that "Sun and Flesh" both celebrates and mourns; and the image in which this coexistence of desire and fulfillment is projected appears over and over again in Rimbaud's work. This is the image of sun on water; it celebrates a special union of light and fluidity—a vision of liquid reflection—that is reducible to neither sun nor sea, but that is rather the unique, always new and brilliant, creation of both. As he writes in "L'Éternité" in 1872: "It has been found again. / What has?—*Eternity.* / It is the sea gone off with the sun." This image is the emblem of a conceivable simultaneity of cause and effect, desire and satisfaction; and as such it figures a kind of suspension in which the before and after of time are annulled. In this respect especially, the image adumbrates the importance of *voyance*—vision—as Rimbaud was beginning to formulate it. Because of its absolute singularity as an event, reducible to no one of the elements that comprise it, vision of this kind embodied for Rimbaud the possibility of originality, creativity, immediacy, and novelty in experience. Vision, in this sense, would be the way man could create in his own world the unity, wholeness, and eternity of God. Rimbaud addressed this theme in "The Blacksmith," where the goal is a society in which "Man will forge from morning to night, / A hunter of great effects, a hunter of great causes." The aim in poetry, politics, and life is to find a way of forging so that labor will be coeval with what it produces.

But if the goal is a state of perfect coexistence between desire and fulfillment, reality presents an obstacle to this simultaneity. Reality as it currently exists confronts man with the separation, not the simultaneity, of desire and satisfaction. This indeed forms the intellectual, and even physical, center of Rimbaud's antipathy to the contemporary world. As he wrote in "Les soeurs de charité" ("Sisters of Charity"):

The young man, facing the ugliness of this world,
Shudders in his heart deeply irritated,
And, filled with the eternal inner wound,
Begins to desire his sister of charity.

(9–12)

The almost Baudelairean fatalism of these lines echoes the mood of metaphysical despair—as opposed to historical hope—to which Rimbaud was ambivalently disposed. The "eternal inner wound" is an absence, a concavity in man's soul that excites and frustrates desire at one and the same time. It is the sign that in reality man's desires are removed from his satisfactions, and that reality is a perpetual resurgence of unrequited desire. Two years later Rimbaud wrote in *A Season in Hell*, "While still a child, I admired the obdurate convict on whom the prison gates always close." The image highlights the ironic intimacy of desire and constraint, emphasizing as well the paradox that desire, which is for freedom and novelty, arises intrinsically as a kind of repetition. For inasmuch as one desires at all, one confirms the loss of original and immediate satisfactions. This paradox is the central subject of "Sisters of Charity." The "eternal inner wound" is the dialectical opposite and companion to the image of sun on sea— the irreducibly new and harmonious event— to which Rimbaud aspired in his poetry.

Let us put to one side Rimbaud's uncertainty as to whether the paradox of desire is historical or metaphysical in origin. In either case, these vexed circumstances came to symbolize for him the problems of want and need in the social and political order at large. It was his initial hope in his earliest poetic efforts that these contradictions of desire, this temporality by which human want is afflicted, could be resolved or at least ameliorated in poetry itself, or rather in the tradition of poetic

language as Rimbaud might adapt, master, and belong to it. The literary tradition would be the place where the repetitiveness of desire would cease, ceding place to new and full satisfaction. Such a belief was perfectly in keeping with the ethos of "ideal beauty" that the poetic tradition had itself upheld for generations, and on which Rimbaud had waxed lyrical in his letter of May 1870 to Théodore de Banville. The lyric poem is characteristically the place where the discrepancies of reality find resolution in the ideal realm. But what Rimbaud began now to discover was that the poetic tradition itself, the very nature of a received poetic language, together with the inescapable relation of any new poet to his predecessors, recapitulated the same problem of desire. For by depending on the poetic diction and institutionalized methods of his precursors, Rimbaud was tacitly taking part in a temporality of succession, repetition, and replacement it was the aim of his poetry to annul. To the extent that his poetry was pastiche, then—to the extent, that is, that it borrowed the style of well-known and admired literary models—so did it repeat and seem to naturalize, as Baudry has put it, the authority of a previous writer. Appealing to poetic tradition as an access to novelty, originality, and satisfaction, Rimbaud found himself reproducing repetition, derivativeness, and frustration.

From the spring of 1871, then, Rimbaud's attitude toward poetry and the poetic tradition began radically to change. His researches into the method of poetic vision culminated in May in the form of the two letters previously mentioned, one to Izambard and a second longer and more important one to Paul Démeny, in which he outlined a dramatic new project for poetry. We shall examine his letters in more detail later in relation to the *Illuminations*, where the plan outlined in them finds its most complete expression. In these letters, and in the poems he was now writing, Rimbaud firmly rejected the protocols of poetry as they had been practiced for generations. The poet, he wrote, should not just give the "formulation of his thought''; he should be a true ''multiplier of Progress,'' a constant medium of the new. Indeed, so absolute was his rejection of tradition that in June he ordered Démeny to burn the poems he had sent him the year before; they seemed to him now so much banal pastiche and complicity with tradition. Démeny, fortunately, did not burn the poems.

Despite the call for dramatically new forms in the *lettres du voyant,* Rimbaud's poetry remained for some time, in certain outward respects, within the formal traditions of academic poetry. Like the earlier poems, most were written in alexandrine lines; many were sonnets or clung to the procedures of narrative and ballad verse; all followed the classical alternation of masculine and feminine endings. But as he continued to experiment with muscular assonances and novel alliterations in the sound of his poetry, and as he increasingly exploited new idioms—exotic, colloquial, scientific, and perverse—Rimbaud also began to parody, as opposed to borrow from, the traditional styles and ruling masters of poetic form. His work now formed a kind of alembic, in which the uses of poetic language were analyzed, broken down, criticized, and dissolved—to be recast in the fresh forms of his later writing. The most important poems of 1871 constitute a kind of extended parodic critique of the accepted methods of poetic composition and a continued reflection on the problems of desire, novelty, and repetition. They call into question the nature of poetic authority and poetic representation, and of the historical and sexual determinations that lie behind them. If the early poetry suggests his opposition to the religious and social conventions of his culture, the work from May 1871 onward proposes an active resistance to every aspect of it: linguistic, perceptual, cognitive, and literary. At the center was Rimbaud's constant appetite for the new.

In the first of the two letters of May 1871, that to Izambard, Rimbaud included ''The Tortured Heart,'' later entitled ''Le coeur de pitre'' (''Heart of a Clown'') and finally ''Le coeur volé'' (''The Stolen Heart''). The poem provides most of our reason for thinking Rimbaud had an initial homosexual experience during the spring of 1871, although this point is debated. It matters little whether or not he did; he certainly knew of the experience to which the poem unmistakably alludes. It was at this time that Rimbaud began on the conscious program he calls in both letters the ''systematic derangement of all the senses.'' As he first conceived it, this program was to be a campaign for radical self-transformation. He drank to excess, refused to wash or cut his hair, and would idle about the center of Charleville, shouting at the shopkeepers, ''Beware! Your hour is at hand! Order is vanquished!''

''The Tortured Heart'' reflects this transformation in the way it questions the nature of sexuality and sexual identity. The poem, Rimbaud wrote to Izambard, is ''fantasy. . . . It means nothing.'' Nonetheless, it relates disconcertingly unpleasant happenings in the intricate rhymes and capricious sing-song of a triolet, the only one Rimbaud was to write:

> My sad heart drools at the poop,
> My heart covered with tobacco-spit:
> they spew streams of soup at it,
> My sad heart drools at the poop:
> Under the jeering of the soldiers
> Who break out laughing,
> My sad heart drools at the poop,
> My heart covered with tobacco-spit.
>
> (1–8)

From the start, it is somewhat unclear precisely what experience he has undergone, although references in the second and final stanzas to erect phalluses, retching, and so on, make the meaning fairly obvious. What *is* clear is the ambiguous coincidence of opposites that surround the experience; by the poem's end, the heart has been successively associated with anal/oral, passive/active, purifying/degrading, swallowing/retching, incorporative/incorporated, expelling/expelled attributes or functions. The incantatory rhythm of the triolet itself makes a wavering between fascination and aversion its central tone. This ambivalence extends to its teasing allusiveness, to the discrepancies between a clear connotative sense (homoerotic sex) and an oblique manner of speaking at the denotative level. Both linguistically and sexually, the poem is constructed as a fetish: that is, the aims and means of desire and sense are displaced across a series of objects, sensation moving ambiguously from orifice to orifice just as sense moves ambiguously between denotative and connotative levels. In the process, both meaning and pleasure—sexual identity—are explicitly associated with the *transport,* and not the fixity, of sense. It is in movement, oscillation, and transformation that desire in poetry and sexuality is shown to emerge. Perhaps greater than the scandal of what the poem seems to depict is the fact that it does so by blurring the distinctions between the bodily functions associated with sex and sexual identity, thus serving to suggest that sexuality is a collusion of mixed or different identities.

Baver is the French verb "to drool," and the word appears frequently in Rimbaud's poetry in a variety of forms. As in "The Tortured Heart," where the sad heart drools at the poop, hearts drool; plants drool; hypocrites, idiots, and virgins drool; shadows drool in the twilit wood; and so on. There is a general emphasis on the fluid secretions of the body, often metaphorized ingeniously: for example, the child "sweated obedience" in "Seven-Year-Old Poets." This emphasis is related in turn to an interest in the body's apertures, both natural and man-made (wounds). In the often anthologized sonnet "Le dormeur du val" ("The Sleeper in the Valley," 1871), Rimbaud lyrically evokes a young soldier, "his mouth open," recumbent in a meadow. The poem moves gracefully to its last line, where it is revealed "there are two red holes in his right side"—the soldier is not sleeping but dead. The image punctuates the sonnet, just as the holes punctuate the soldier's body, establishing the point of the poem and also finishing it.

Rimbaud's attention is often focused on what might be called the function of perforation: holes; wounds; apertures; windows; orifices that establish, but then also partly abolish, the boundaries between inside—usually of the body—and outside. Hence his interest in what facilitates or undergoes transmission from one to the other: drooling lips, bleeding wounds, ulcerating sores, sweating children, defecating monks, vomit, tears, blood, saliva, and so on. Put abstractly, this is a recurrent interest in what simultaneously opens and closes the frontiers separating fundamental human categories: self and other, life and death, man and nature, body and soul, exteriority and interiority, art and life. Rimbaud's imagination was characteristically pitched at those extreme points where limits and barriers are established and transgressed.

In "L'Orgie parisienne, ou Paris se repeuple" ("Parisian Orgy or Paris Repopulated," May 1871), Rimbaud condemns those Parisians who streamed back into the city once the Commune had fallen: "Drink! When light comes intense and mad, / Piercing at your side the streaming luxuries, / Are you not going to drool, with no gesture, with no word, / Into your glasses, your eyes lost in the white distances?" (17–20). Political motion—the force that joins the individual to the body politic—is conveyed through a series of images (piercing, streaming, drooling, eyes lost) that suggest a breaking down of the barriers that divide self and society, subject and object. Rimbaud is suggesting that the desires that merge the individual with the body politic are both cause and effect of this piercing of difference between the subject (metaphorized in this poem as "your eyes": the perceiving self) and object (the society surrounding the self, here metaphorized as "white distances" in which subjective vision or selfhood is lost). Real social and individual motion is thus depicted as a force that cuts across the boundaries conventionally thought of as defining human reality; indeed that force is characterized as arising from the very abolition of such distinctions. Rimbaud's purpose was to engage the multiple and productive forces that traverse the human body and the body politic; his method of doing so emerges in a poetry that itself mitigates what he considered to be the false limits of language and self. As always, the aim is to engage human reality as it is created or invented anew.

Without stretching the point, we might say that drooling served Rimbaud as a kind of perverse metaphor for what true poetic language and writing should be. Like drooling, language for him is material ("smells, sounds, colors, thought holding on to thought and pulling," as he wrote in *A Season in Hell*); it is related to the body; it is occasioned by desire, which it signals; and it is ideally fluid, scandalizing, and perverse.

And indeed Rimbaud signed the poem "Ce qu'on dit au poète à propos de fleurs" ("What Is Said to the Poet Concerning Flowers") "ALCIDE BAVA": Alcide, a Latin name for Hercules, perhaps because, as many critics have suggested, Rimbaud likened his task of renovating French poetry to that of Hercules' cleaning out the Augean stables; and Bava, of course, because it is a form of *baver*: to drool. Rimbaud, the poet and Herculean drooler.

The poem, which Rimbaud sent to Banville in August 1871, is dated 14 July, Bastille Day, in honor of the French Revolution. In parodic quatrains of eight-syllable lines, Rimbaud attacks the idealist aesthetics and mannerisms of the Parnassians. Rimbaud was, of course, particularly rude about Banville himself, whose penchant for flower imagery elicited his untempered scorn. This was the kind of arrogant and uncompromising behavior that throughout Rimbaud's career did little to endear him to his contemporaries. More important, "What Is Said to the Poet" is a major example of Rimbaud's revised technique; and a brief comparison of the poem's method with the stylistic servilities of "Ophélie" and "Sun and Flesh," which he had sent to Banville the year before, reveals the astonishing transformation that had meanwhile taken place. Along with poems like "Les mains de Jeanne Marie" ("The Hands of Jeanne Marie"), in which he parodies what he felt was the effete hand fetishism of Théophile Gautier's "Études de mains," 1852, and Albert Mérat's "Tes mains," 1866, it summarizes Rimbaud's newly acute perception of the way literary tradition itself colludes with the social arrangements to which it only seems to offer an alternative. The poem has two main polemical targets: the descriptive ethos of Parnassian poetry and the cult of elite "literariness" such poetry upheld. It thus identifies and deliberately affronts two kinds of poetic authority: that of the thing represented over the forms representing it; and that of a literary tradition, a school, a prestigious style, over its practitioners.

> Thus always, toward the black azure,
> Where shimmers the sea of topazes,
> The Lilies, clysters of ecstasy,
> Will function in your evening.
>
> (1–4)

The key word here is "function": Rimbaud is concerned chiefly with the function lilies play in poetic discourse, over and above anything they may seem to stand for. "In our age," he writes, "plants work hard"; they displace or absorb, for example, the disgust that "religious Prose" might otherwise elicit. Throughout, Rimbaud sarcastically shows what flowers as linguistic emblems enable or disbar in poetic performance; what ritual associations they invoke, or are invoked by; what possibilities of sense are licensed or proscribed by them, and so on. To understand the true function of poetical elements like flowers (or hands, orphans, hanged men: all clichés of Parnassian poetry), one must first interrupt the circuit of existential reference they seem to establish:

> Dear Fellow, Art no longer consists, now,
> —It is the truth—in permitting

The amazing Eucalyptus
Boa constrictors a hexameter long!

There! . . . As if Mahogany
Served, even in our Guianas,
Only as swings for monkeys
In the heavy maze of creepers!

(3.9–16)

The connection between poetic form and reality is not governed by the relation between a word and the thing it seems to stand for: Rimbaud attacks just these mimetic assumptions of descriptive poetry:

Concerning your forest and meadows,
O very peaceful photographs!
The Flora is nearly as diverse,
As stoppers on decanters!

(2.9–12)

Poetic form to Rimbaud was connected to nonlinguistic reality via the cognate conventions both deploy. Thus the line "Love lets only Lilacs pass your customs" suggests the way language allows only certain transitions and combinations, just as a country's frontiers are controlled and regulated institutionally. Mimetic poetry is innocent of this higher political force of language, masking even as it conveys the productive processes of social and linguistic reality. What is needed, Rimbaud writes, is a poetry attuned through its own inventiveness to the constitutive processes of all reality:

You, enliven in our torpor
Hysteria by means of perfumes;
Exalt us toward whiteness
More pure than Marys!

Merchant! colonial! medium!
Your Rhyme will rise up, rose, or white,
Like a ray of sodium,
Like a bleeding rubber-tree!

(5.5–12)

What any translation will diminish is the dazzling verbal inventiveness of these lines, as well as the extent to which the diction and metaphor are dictated by the arbitrary requirements of meter, rhyme, and sound. Even these features serve Rimbaud's main intention: to highlight the productive transactions of language and culture, as against repetitive and mimetic ones. Hence the jarring but finally very suitable coexistence of almost hallucinatory poetic inventions with insistent social, political, and economic exhortations: telegraph poles, the monarchist Monsieur Kerdrel, the potato blight, all find their way into the poem. Such widely disparate terms of reference cohere in the ethos of productiveness and invention that they share, which is poised against what Rimbaud felt was the tyranny of mere representation.

In September 1871, when his first and only real literary break came with the invitation from Verlaine, Rimbaud went to Paris armed with "Le bateau ivre" ("The Drunken Boat"), possibly his most famous poem. Arranged in twenty-five quatrains of classically measured alexandrine lines and alternating masculine and feminine rhymes, the poem is in fact formally stricter and more rationally organized than many just preceding it in composition. Numerous sources have been adduced for it, including works by Hugo, Edgar Allan Poe, Jules Verne, and many others. Indeed the setting of the poem—a barque set loose on strange seas—is a recurrent theme in nineteenth-century literature. Arthur Schopenhauer used the image as a way of describing the tragic separation of ego from environment, and there is evidence that Rimbaud was familiar with these writings. But "The Drunken Boat" is most closely related to Charles Baudelaire's "Le voyage" (1857), to which it is in part a kind of extended gloss or reply. In the *lettre du voyant* to Démeny, Rimbaud had praised Baudelaire above all other poets as the "first seer, a king of poets, *a real god.*" But even Baudelaire "lived in too artistic a world; and the form so highly praised in him is trivial. Inventions of the unknown call for new forms." Although "The Drunken Boat" is neither intrinsically a satirical piece nor formally very experimental, it nevertheless represents a more sophisticated stage in Rimbaud's critical and parodic stance toward the literary tradition. In this poem, written explicitly for "les gens de Paris"—the established literary names—Rimbaud extended his exploration into the conditions of poetic vision. The poem represents one kind of "systematic derangement" and is perhaps Rimbaud's most extreme exploration of the possibilities of novelty in language within traditional poetic form.

Baudelaire's "The Voyage" is crucial to an understanding of the advance Rimbaud hoped to achieve in his own poem. For Baudelaire it was the new that held the promise of meaning in existence; but the thrust of "The Voyage" is to show that man cannot experience novelty. In expressing this, Baudelaire connects the nature of representation to the discrepancies dividing self and circumstance in a fallen world, and especially to the repetitive desires to which man is prey. The poem is a retrospective narrative of a search for novelty in experience, which, the poet concludes, is available in neither life nor poetic expression. For since "satisfaction adds more force to desire," travel begets the desire for more novelty until the "finite seas" have been exhausted; and it is apparent that only the repetition of desire is infinite. Novelty is available only outside life and language, in death; for only death abolishes the distinctions on which man's life is predicated: distinctions between desire and satisfaction, guilt and innocence, Hell and Heaven, repetition and novelty, the known and the unknown, representation and reality. The poem closes with an invocation to Death:

Pour us your poison [Death] that it may console
    us!
We would plunge, so much does the fire burn our
    brain,
To the bottom of the abyss, it matters not whether
    to Hell or Heaven,
To the depths of the Unknown in order to find the
    new!

The perception that novelty and the unknown are available only outside language and life in death is intimately related to Baudelaire's sense of the ironic nature of language. It is on this ground that the significant differences between Baudelaire and Rimbaud emerge. In the first place, and whether we take it to be realistic or allegorical, Baudelaire purported to make statements about, or to refer to, a reality outside the poem itself. "Le voyage" the poem, in other words, is distinct from the voyage narrated. Moreover, instead of directly relating the voyage, third parties (the voyagers) recount it retrospectively to a group of interlocutors, all of whom are more or less distinct from the superintendent poetic voice. Together, such features serve to emphasize the distance separating the event of the voyage from its retelling in language. By forcefully presenting in this way not so much the voyage as its verbal repetition in language, Baudelaire highlights the representational and narrative frame of poetry and borrows as insight a contradiction seemingly central to it: the actual absence in representation of the experience represented. Just as the new, the desire for which motivates travel, is shown to fall outside the compass of any voyage except that of death, so the voyage itself falls outside the compass of poetic expression. The poem is trapped within a duplicitous world of representation that reflects as such the duplicitous condition of man's life. An image for this situation occurs in the opening lines of the poem. Like the "maps and prints and stamps" that excite in children an appetite that experience cannot finally satisfy, so the poem as a representation excites desire for a reality it is incapable of delivering.

Baudelaire thus uses the distance between "The Voyage" as a poem and the voyage it represents to sum up a series of insurmountable "distances" central to the poem's point: the distance separating satisfaction from desire, novelty from repetition, meaning from absurdity, all of which in turn recapitulate the distance dividing death and real meaning from life. Baudelaire first severs language from reality and then identifies its separation with the nature of man's condition. The poem's symbolic system thus constitutes the state of affairs it expresses: separation, repetition, and so on. These are the penalties, in life as in language, man pays for "l'immortal peche," original sin.

It is this system, together with the distance it establishes between art and reality, language and experience, novel creation and banal repetition, that Rimbaud seeks to abolish from the outset in "The Drunken Boat." Baudelaire's first mistake, according to Rimbaud, had been to separate the voyage from the process of poetry itself. Baudelaire's world was thus, as Rimbaud had said, "too artistic"—but then also not artistic enough. Adhering to a notion of language as symbol, representation, and allegory, Baudelaire perpetuated a set of invidious distinctions between the orders of life and art. For Rimbaud, poetry no longer represents a state of affairs; it is one.

Thus in Rimbaud's poem the persona is no longer split by language between past and present, self and other, experience and representation; for the persona of the poem is now the boat itself as it undergoes the voyage. This serves emblematically to identify both the creative and the created personae with the vehicle of expression—language. The boat is at once subject and object of the voyage, at once the voyager and the means of voyage; and by making it the first person of the poem, Rimbaud constructs a tight analogy between the *boat* as a wayward vehicle of discovery and *its* poetic vehicle—language. All of this is part of Rimbaud's general intention in the poem to reduce almost to zero the difference between language and reality, and thereby to relocate novelty and the unknown, not in death and silence, but in language and life.

The poem, like the boat, begins by throwing off all impediments to motion:

As I was going down impassive Rivers,
I no longer felt myself guided by the haulers!
Shouting Red Indians had taken them for targets,
And had nailed them naked to colored stakes.

The bearer of Flemish wheat and English cotton,
I was indifferent to all crews;
When the uproar, with my haulers, had ceased,
The Rivers let me go where I wanted.

Into the furious lashing of the tides,
More heedless than children's brains, I
The other winter, ran; and Peninsulas let loose
Have not submitted to a more triumphant
  confusion.

The boat sheds the instruments of organized motion with the symbols of civilization as customary order is left behind and the distinctions of rationality are subdued: the difference between inside and outside ("green water penetrated my hull"); between past and present (the poem moves steadily from a present perfect to a series of timeless present participles); between passivity and activity (motion becomes almost entirely relative as the boat is swept along, now passing, now being passed by drifting, dreamlike figures). In the sixth stanza, the distinction between language and reality itself is annulled, or at least rendered irrelevant: "From then on I bathed in the Poem / Of the Sea, infused with stars and lactescent." The identity of poem with the sea is thus provisionally established, and thence begins a sequence of tremendous and brilliant visions as the boat wanders across and under exotic seas.

We might say that where the experience of Baudelaire's poem rests on a consciousness of the ever-widening gap separating language and reality, desire and satisfaction, the experience of Rimbaud's poem rests on an intention to close this distance. The importance of vision and language to Baudelaire is that they more or less constantly advert to a Christian order of reality they are incapable of directly presenting. Vision and language, for Baudelaire, are intrinsically *ironic*, for they can only allude to a past and future reality from which the present is debarred. By contrast, the importance of Rimbaud's words and images consists in the sheer difficulty they impose on any attempt to make them conform—even ironically—to an order outside the poem, allegorical or realistic. Rimbaud is not representing a voyage so much as trying to foment one in language, and this involves a different protocol of motion, another method of elaborating images and sense, from that dictated by the proprieties of symbol, representation, and allegory.

The order and logic of the poem may be said to arise mainly from Rimbaud's sustained impulse to countervail the conventions of symbolic and mimetic language. Now if the logic of symbols supports a distinction between language and reality, so too may it be said to underwrite the very notions of "distinctness" and "separation" themselves. "The Drunken Boat" is largely given over to a language of dissolution and merging, of change and interpenetration, a tendency as apparent in the progression of tenses noted above as in the choice of words: "infused," "penetrated," "dying," "fermenting," "mingling," and so on. Quite apart from the local situations in which they occur, the reiterated stress on such words contributes to a cumulative diminution of limits of all kinds. Connected to this is Rimbaud's constant use of participles: "bathing," "devouring," "staining," "illuminating," "rising," "awakening," "rolling," "descending." Like the poem's abrupt commencement after the action has begun, this language serves to put in the foreground the process as opposed to the perfection of the actions presented, thereby diminishing verbal distinctions in time in favor of an ongoing verbal presence. By the same token, the boat's fantastic itinerary—"I struck unbelievable Floridas"—annuls habitual notions of contiguity in space. Asserting its own spatial and temporal coordinates, the poem seeks to displace the customary logic of symbolic sequence. Later events are not adumbrated by earlier ones as they are in Baudelaire's poem; Rimbaud

tended to avoid such prefigural and, as he saw it, latently Christian modes of coordinating past and present events irreversibly. Instead of prefiguration, the sequence of images follows what might be called the logic of *emergence:*

I know the skies bursting with lightning, and the
  waterspouts,
And the surf and the currents; I know the
  evening,
And the dawn, exalted like a nation of doves,
And I have sometimes seen what man believed he
  saw!

(35–38)

Both the kinds of images Rimbaud produces and the sequence he produces them in emphasize the moment of an event's becoming, the vividness of its emergence as a vision. This emphasis is not, as is sometimes claimed, a mere reveling in the randomness of images haphazardly ordered. Visions arise in the poem in a carefully arranged inconsequence intended to loosen the hold of everything that diminishes the status of a word or image as a pure event. Such an intention is the main motive behind Rimbaud's insistent use of participles. The aim is to coax language toward an ever more explicit (re)presentation of itself as an event in its own right. Thus, in turn, poetic awareness might penetrate to what was for Rimbaud the most meaningful aspect of poetry: the existentially irreducible moment of its creation in language. Series of adjacent images in "The Drunken Boat"— such as "yellow and blue awakening of singing phosphorus"—stress this sudden incipience of the event.

Rimbaud had remarked in his second *lettre du voyant* that the poet must be "present at the birth of his own thought." It is this presence that Rimbaud was trying to achieve in "The Drunken Boat." The emergent moments of vision unite the perceiving self (the poem's created persona) to the perceived object (the poem's created images) in the single, differentiated event of created language. Attempting to mime, tautologically, the process of its own creation, language approaches the unknown and the new.

The first-person pronoun, repeated some twenty-four times in a series of statements largely without hierarchical relations—"I bathed," "I have known," "I have dreamed," "I have followed," and so on—at once sustains and dissipates its identity across the surface of the changing poetic images with which it is identified. It is as if in presenting the poem Rimbaud refused to be excluded as a presence from the poetical process he created, and thus was willing to reduce the space and time of personality to the quicksilver slashes of a changing linguistic event. Historical depth, which the retrospective frame of Baudelaire's poem had accorded its persona and which had tacitly acknowledged the actual absence of the author's presence in the work, is here abolished: there is very little distance between the events recorded and the person recording them. Subjectivity is presented as a kind of mobile and mercurial surface, the scene no longer of disillusioned self-possession, but of rapidly changing visions and transformations.

Rimbaud refused to force his images to mean anything but what they were; the aim was to achieve a coincidence of meaning and being. If these images are signs of the new, the fact that their novelty abates is simply a contingent, if very difficult, condition of life in history. It is not, as it was for Baudelaire, the proof and penalty of man's moral turpitude. This attitude in Rimbaud gives proof of an abundance of what Keats called negative capability: the ability to abide paradox and uncertainty without retreating into pessimism or the cynical security of forgone conclusions. At the end of "The Drunken Boat," when Rimbaud is called back from ecstatic vision to his sole self, the voyage is simply finished for a time. As the poem nears its conclusion, the intense immediacy of the boat's experiences subsides, and distance—"hearing at fifty leagues off"—begins to reappear in its percep-

tions. As it does, the poem becomes more conscious of itself as an artifact rather than an experience freely undergone; more conscious, that is, of the central contradiction besetting the poem. For while it is the poet's intention to present spontaneous, novel, and unmediated events, these appear inevitably in the form of an achieved construct in language. The very fact that vision is made to endure in language mitigates the novelty and immediacy it is its purpose to embody. The voyage in poetry can itself only fleetingly engage the constantly fomented effervescence of the new—"these bottomless nights," these "million golden birds"—which is a "Future Vigor" forever breaking upon the shores of the present. When Rimbaud writes in the third stanza from the end, "O let my keel burst! O let me go into the sea!" it is not so much Baudelaire's lament that the unknown and the new are unavailable in life, but a recognition that life itself is always in excess of the poetic form that diminishes, even as it celebrates, it. It is the "keel" of fixed linguistic form that Rimbaud would break, the better to burst forth into the sea of visionary experience. In this Rimbaud was already beginning to orient himself toward the much more radical experiments in form that he makes in the *Illuminations*.

The end of the poem comes like the "ancient parapets" of Europe that the boat begins to regret: both are reminders of culture's obdurate persistence as form and distinction, as a limit on the freedom of experience:

If I want a water of Europe, it is the black
Cold puddle where in the sweet-smelling twilight
A squatting child full of sadness releases
A boat as fragile as a May butterfly.

No longer can I, bathed in your langour, O waves,
Follow in the wake of the cotton boats,
Nor cross through the pride of flags and flames,
Nor swim under the terrible eyes of prison ships.

Distance, perspective, frame, loss, separation, memory: these replace vision, as the poem closes with the recognition that such are the conditions of culture; conditions to which the poem itself had proposed a brief intermission but that cannot for all that be so easily, let alone permanently, cast off. They can be resisted, however; and even in the last stanza Rimbaud sets himself against the standards, the incarcerations, and the authority of culture. "Nor swim under the terrible eyes of prison ships": in highly compressed form, the final line voices Rimbaud's refusal to submit his vision to the tyrannical gaze of an official culture governed by commerce and law.

Rimbaud, in "The Drunken Boat," converts language—the great "Poem of the Sea"—into a theater on whose stage the problematic drama of vision unfolds. Language could lend itself to this drama because, as Rimbaud conceived it, its presence embodies an ambiguous conflict between the past, which appears in it as memory, and the future, whose possibilities arise in it as vision. In two other poems, "Voyelles" ("Vowels"), written just before or after Rimbaud left for Paris, and "Mémoire" ("Memory"), written in early 1872, Rimbaud extended his exploration into the problems of memory, vision, and language.

"Memory" takes its point of departure in a sense from the cold black puddle that appears as a memory at the end of "The Drunken Boat." Where the latter concerns the transient freedom from memory to which vision may be incited in language, "Memory" reverses the perspective: it is concentrated on the fatal fixity in which memory (and the past) hold vision. It is a negative image of "The Drunken Boat," a nightmare to the earlier poem's dream. The sustained present tense and specificity of image in "The Drunken Boat" give way to dreamlike timelessness and strange lack of definition in "Memory." While retaining stanzaic and alexandrine form, "Memory" works subtle rhythmic changes in the use of enjambment, internal rhyme, and exclusively feminine endings. More important, statements and images are arranged, not narratively, but thematically, by groups and asso-

ciations of sense and sound; in this respect the poem represents an experimental advance over the "The Drunken Boat."

At once vividly sensual and difficult to construe, the poem is built around an interplay of clarity and obscurity. Commencing with an image of "clear water" and closing on the question "in what mud?" it defines memory as the way the past persists in the present as a reminder of visions permanently gone:

Clear water; like the salt of tears in childhood,
the assault in the sun of the whiteness of
  women's bodies;
the silk, in masses and of lilies pure, of banners
under the walls which once a maid defended;

the play of angels;—No . . . the golden current's
  motion
moves its arms, black and heavy, above all cool,
  with grass. She,
dark, having the blue Sky for canopy, calls
for curtain the shade of the hill and arch.

                         (1–8)

Despite uncertainties of reference, the poem establishes a relation—we have seen this before—between water, sexualized as a woman, and light, sexualized as a man. This relation is expressed initially as an equilibrium of surfaces and depths, a supple mesh of light and water, vision and volume, energy and matter, whose most perfect expression is "clear water" itself, a volume of infinitely superimposed transparent surfaces. As the poem continues, allusions to maidenhood and incipient sexuality lend the lines an epithalamic tone: "The wet surface extends its clear broth" and "the water fills with pale unfathomable gold the ready beds." But more striking than this story of union allegorized as the mating of sun and river is the way the process of vision itself is made an inextricable part of the drama. When a marsh marigold is described as the "yellow and warm eyelid" of the river, it is apparent that the surface of the poem, the perspective that it adopts, is the surface of an eye, metaphorized as the surface of a river. There is no superintending point of view in the poem distinct from the surface of this watery eye. The vantage of memory is thus given as a phantasmic film extending like the wet surface of water, neither sunlight nor water itself, but a tenuous shimmering surface, the locale of an undulating paradoxical conjugation of water and light, above and below, man and woman, present and past:

More pure than a sovereign, yellow and warm eyelid
the marsh marigold—your conjugal faith, O Spouse!—
at midday prompt, from its dull mirror, envies
in the sky gray with heat the rose and dear Sphere.

(2.5–8)

Under the baffling surface of the poem, an almost ritual pastoral comedy transpires in which the arousal and satisfaction of desire are identified with the casting and reflection of images on the surface of the water/eye. All of this in turn serves as an analogy for the way the before and after of passing time is merged in the fixing of a memory not yet separate from the act of perception itself.

But forthwith such separation commences. The poem's progression of female personae advances: first a maid, then a spouse, "She" is "Madame" by the fourth stanza. The syntactical and intelligible surface of the poem becomes more fragmented, and as this occurs the harmony of light and water is sundered:

He, like,
a thousand white angels separating on the road
departs beyond the mountain; She, all
cold and black, runs! after the man's departure!

(3.5–8)

The surface of the water is abandoned by the male and female principles that had animated it. It is thus as if the visual, verbal, and thematic integrity of the poem's surface is, like a child, first engendered and then cast off in the poem's symbolic action. The marriage of light and water is annulled, and language is dimmed from pure vision to memory:

After, there is the surface, without reflection, without springs, gray:
an old man, dredging, toils in his motionless boat.

Toy of this sad eye of water, I cannot pluck,
O motionless boat! O arms too short! Neither this
nor the other flower: neither the yellow one which troubles me
there, nor the blue one, friend to the ash-colored water.

Ah! the dust of willows shaken by the wing!
The roses of the reeds devoured long ago!
My boat, still fixed; and its chain drawn
to the bottom of this rimless eye of water,—to what mud?

(4.7–8; 5.1–8)

As the poem moves from childhood to old age, from union to separation, from timelessness to memory, vision is transformed from a mirroring principle of unity and integration to a colorless surface, "without reflection." The verbal surface of the poem, where once the "play of angels" had danced like light on the surface of water, holds at the end only the image of the anchor chain, obscurely connecting a diminished present cut off from a receding past, unable to reach either. Memory, the poem shows, is the calling forth into language not only of what is no longer present but of the progression through which presence itself is banished from the real. Reality is expressed in memory as a kind of permanent discrepancy between a past that cannot be repeated and a tantalizing present that can never be fully seized.

"Memory" for Rimbaud is thus the repetition of the past as a kind of absence just as vision is the novel incipience of the future as full presence. Language is the scene of a titanic struggle, a fierce alternation, between the poetic power to create—which comes as a negation of history—and the insistent return of history itself in the form of negation and

1803

loss. Language is the place where memory and vision are arbitrated on the occasion of any particular attempt to seize reality and make it one's own, to borrow Charles Maurras's description of Rimbaud's art. It was between these radical and extreme possibilities of failure and success in language that Rimbaud's imagination came increasingly to operate.

Language itself, as the scene of the production of sense in poetry, is the subject of "Vowels," probably the last of the sonnets Rimbaud wrote in 1871, and certainly one of his most famous poems. It was published initially by Verlaine in the journal *Lutèce* in 1883 and appeared again the following year in Verlaine's notorious collection of essays, *Les poètes maudits*. Apart from anything else, the poem is famous for the hermeneutic fervor it has inspired in critics attempting to affix some definite sense to its engimatic statements:

A black, E white, I red, U green, O blue: vowels,
I will tell one day your latent birth:
A, black hairy corset of sparkling flies
Which buzz about the cruel stench,

Gulfs of shadow; E, whiteness of vapors and tents,
Lances of proud glaciers, white kings, shiver of
   umbels;
I, purple, spit blood, laughter of beautiful lips
In anger or penitent bliss;

U, cycles, divine vibrations of verdant seas,
Peace of pastures seeded with animals, peace of
   furrows
That alchemy imprints upon broad studious
   brows;

O, supreme Clarion full of strange stridor,
Silences traversed by Worlds and Angels:
—O the Omega, violet beam from His Eyes!

Paradoxically, as one French critic has noted, this sonnet has most often been interpreted according to the order of representation that it refuses. Virtually every possible key has been provided for unlocking its sense: alchemical, psychological, magical, psychoanalytic, optical, religious, and so on. To attempt such interpretations, however, is to obscure the point

that language in "Vowels" is meant no longer to be judged in relation to "another sense," but rather very consciously in relation to itself and to Rimbaud's fierce will to make it mean what he wants.

Of all the "codes" mentioned, it is perhaps alchemy that has the greatest claim to validity, although not because the poem's difficulties can be resolved by translating them into the meanings of alchemical science. It is rather that poetry and alchemy share an intention to create value through transformation; the one to derive sense from circumstances where before there was none, the other to derive gold from base metals. To accomplish this, language in "Vowels" doubles back on itself; words refer to words, and the text is posited as its own representation. Language does not follow from sense, but sense from language; and in this Rimbaud's method recalls Mallarmé's edict to "cede initiative to words and to the force of their mobilized inequality." Rimbaud differs from Mallarmé, however, insofar as for him the poet thereby brings to the fore, not some abstract purity of language, but the supreme initiative of poetic invention. As he later wrote in *A Season in Hell:* "I invented the color of the vowels! . . . I regulated the form and movement of each consonant, and with instinctive rhythms I prided myself on inventing a poetic language accessible some day to all the senses. I reserved translation rights" ("Délires II: Alchimie du verbe"). Although he was to reconsider the audacity of this project, his comments make clear that it is the will of poetic intention alone that forces an identification of sense and sensation, color and language: "A black, E white," et cetera. In regulating this movement—in reserving to himself translation rights, and not forfeiting them to, for example, a notion of the relation between words and things—Rimbaud hoped to bring poetry into a new and immediate relation to "all the senses." In this manner, poetic will attempts at once to be *and* to represent itself in an act of invention inseparable from the gesture that brings it to expression.

Certain symbolic sequences stand out in the sonnet: for example, the way it moves from death (black/cruel stench), through life (red/blood, green/plants), to spiritual ascendance (blue/sky/Angel). But this trajectory mimics the movement from a zero degree or "death" of meaning to fully significant vision ("His Eyes"). The aim is not to vindicate any set of rules for transposing vowels into visions, as if some natural relation obtained between the orders of language and reality. The two intersect "naturally" only in the constant and diversely sensual processes of human invention that characterize both.

Rimbaud's commitment to language in "Vowels" was thus a way of resisting the authority of any order of significance posited outside the precincts of poetic creation. In saying this, we begin to describe the peculiarly political motivations invigorating what seems, after all, to be an idiosyncratically private kind of poetic vision. For if "Vowels" mimes creation in a parody of God, it does so not to affirm the divine power of the artist; rather it asserts the artist's oppositional ability to reappropriate creative powers intrinsic to the production of all meaning, but systematically parasitized by the established institutions of culture (especially religious institutions: we recall Rimbaud's depiction of Christ as the "eternal thief of energy"). Not for nothing did Rimbaud find an ideal figure for the poet's vocation in the image of Prometheus, stealer of fire from the gods.

To come this far, however, is to see how the "new" in poetry involved for Rimbaud an irreconcilable contradiction. As we have seen in "Vowels" and elsewhere, the new was to be a departure from the mimetic traditions of poetry; but at the same time it was to fashion a kind of higher mimesis by participating in the productive forces of reality. Put another way, visionary language is at once a response to the inventive nature of reality and inventiveness itself; and in this manner, the poet's activity reduces to zero the difference between the presence of reality and the representation of

language. But this in turn presents a whole series of related and fundamental ambivalences central to Rimbaud's work. It is impossible to determine, for example, whether the poet's language is entirely disciplined by the nature of the reality the poet sees, or whether reality itself is being forcibly coerced into the poet's visionary forms. Parallel to this is the uncertainty in Rimbaud's writing as to whether the poet is the passive occasion or the active agency of meaning in language. On the one hand, Rimbaud represents the poet in this passage from the first *lettre du voyant* as the instrument of other forces: "I is another. It is too bad for the wood which finds itself a violin." The poet is thus in no simple sense the autonomous author of the meanings to which he gives rise: other forces, social, sexual, linguistic, coincide to constitute those diverse meanings. On the other hand, the poet, precisely in order to engage these forces, cedes his authority to no other agency or tradition; as Rimbaud remarked, "I prided myself on inventing a poetic language." This ambivalence is apparent elsewhere in Rimbaud's writing, in the severe juxtaposition, for example, of the private and the social, the ascetic and the sexual. It arises in Rimbaud's very formulation of poetic method itself, for the "systematic derangement of all the senses" is the commitment of an intransigent will to its own dissolution. Perhaps most important, what all of these uncertainties reveal is the way poetic invention involved for Rimbaud a fine equivocation between novelty and repetition, creation and destruction. For one can no longer distinguish in his poetic practice whether the will to invention generates novelty or simply repeats an unchanging disposition to do so; or whether the poetic act radically negates form or provides an absolute access to it.

The shape and trajectory of Rimbaud's rapid career emerge from the interplay of these contradictions. If form and the invention of form itself are indistinguishable, then poetic creation will consist in a continual invention, destruction, and reinvention of forms. What began as a discrepancy *within* Rimbaud's earliest poetry—the discrepancy between novelty and repetition that the problem of poetic form itself posed—pushed him to exhaust traditional forms until he exploded, in the *Illuminations,* the boundaries of poetic form altogether. There, the contradictions of novel creativity—which appear at the level of form as the inseparability of form and formal invention, and at the level of poetic agency as the poet's ambivalent power over and subservience to the creative principle—arise no longer as discrepancies *inside* poetic form, as they do in "The Drunken Boat," where the intention to deliver novelty collides with the form of the poem itself. In Rimbaud's later writing, the contradiction besetting the poet's intention to create novelty is projected instead across a series of fragmentary, changing prose-poetic constructs—constructs that in their very form refer outward to a world of constantly changing visionary experience in which form itself undergoes constant revolution. The discrepancies underlying Rimbaud's project do not so much find resolution in the new forms of the *Illuminations* as achieve a maximum of violent and unreconciled opposition. Looking ahead, *A Season in Hell* is in this respect a kind of meditation on the fact of such unreconcilability. We might note as well that if all these contradictions remain permanently unresolved in Rimbaud's writing, this is perhaps partly because it was his intention to confront reality with the blatant contradictions of the new, rather than with what he took to be the spurious resolutions of the old.

RIMBAUD AND VERLAINE

Except perhaps to Verlaine, Rimbaud was not a pretty sight when he arrived in Paris in September 1871. His systematic program of deranging all the senses was already beginning to tell in his appearance; tramping in the Ardennes countryside, months of drinking, and a steadfast refusal to wash, dress, or behave hygienically combined to make Rimbaud an unlikely and even fearful apparition in the staid Verlaine ménage. Verlaine's wife recognized him instantly for the enemy he was of every domestic value. Verlaine himself was surprised to find Rimbaud not the flower of provincial poetic sensitivity he had expected, but a painfully adolescent, willful, and wild-looking youth. He immediately fell in love with him, and thence began a stormy romance that has attracted more literary gossip, more vituperative claims and counterclaims, than can easily be alluded to. There is no question that they were lovers. Their debauches, which involved most imaginable excesses—sex, drugs, alcohol, absinthe, violence—were notorious. This did little to endear Rimbaud to Verlaine's family, who viewed him as a satanic force of depravity in Verlaine's life. Indeed Rimbaud seems to have been constitutionally incapable of ingratiating himself to anyone, and he only redoubled his efforts to outrage Parisian literary society when it became clear that his comportment was far from acceptable to it. His behavior, like his poetry, affronted virtually every standard of value, and he did nothing to disguise his contempt for the mores and writing of his contemporaries, whom he took to be reactionary, passé, and hypocritical time-servers. Before long, Rimbaud and Verlaine, who took his *enfant terrible* everywhere, were being ostracized in many of the literary circles they frequented. One memorable evening at the exclusive literary supper club *Les vilains bonshommes,* Rimbaud drank himself into an aggressive stupor and began heaping abuse in a chorus of loud "merdes" upon Jean Aicard, who was reading a selection of his poems that evening. When the increasingly infuriated company finally called him to order, Rimbaud exploded, grabbed Verlaine's sword cane, and attacked one of the guests. After being disarmed, he passed out, and thereafter was forbidden permanently to attend the society's dinners.

ARTHUR RIMBAUD

From the beginning, Verlaine and Rimbaud were co-conspirators in dissipation, inciting each other to ever greater acts of abandonment and dissolution. But Verlaine, ten years Rimbaud's senior and apparently the weaker and more dependent of the two, was less completely committed to a life of outrage. Debauchery for him was perhaps more a symptom of unhappiness, an intermittent alternative to a more conventional life; for Rimbaud it was fully congruent with his political, moral, and philosophical outlook, an integral part of his program for transforming self and society.

In any event, their *folie à deux* lasted some two years. Each made attempts to leave the other, and their families often intervened to try to put an end to their unholy doings. Rimbaud, who had no reputation to lose, soon established himself as a dangerous wild man, and then sank for the most part out of social purview. Verlaine, after much vacillation, finally succeeded in alienating his wife entirely, and they were divorced.

During the winter of 1871–1872, Rimbaud and Verlaine were members of the *Cercle zutique,* a group of Parisian artists devoted to thumbing its nose at middle-class values. The group's output, mainly parodies of established writers, obscene sketches, and other attempts to outrage, were recorded in a short volume entitled *Album zutique.* A number of Rimbaud's most obscene and scatological poems were included, which besides their wit and scandal are interesting for the light they shed on his sexuality, especially on the role fathers play in his sexual fantasy and identity. Meanwhile, the obsessive sexual attachment between Verlaine and Rimbaud waned and waxed, producing frequent and violent quarrels. Rimbaud returned to Charleville for a few months in the late winter and early spring of 1872, where he worked on the relatively tranquil poems sometimes grouped by early editors under the headings *Vers nouveaux et chansons,* or *Derniers vers.* He returned to Verlaine in May; in July they traveled to Belgium and then to London, where they settled until Rimbaud left again in December. Peregrinations continued until July 1873, when events—including suicide threats from Verlaine and hysterical quarrels and reconciliations—came to a head in Belgium. Verlaine, who had decided to go off to fight in Spain, summoned Rimbaud to Brussels for a last farewell; but upon his arrival Verlaine abruptly abandoned his plans and begged Rimbaud to resume their relationship once more. Rimbaud refused; whereupon Verlaine, very distressed, went out, purchased a revolver, returned to their hotel room, and shot Rimbaud, wounding him slightly in the wrist. This did not persuade Rimbaud to stay, and after the wound was dressed at a nearby hospital, he left for the railway station to return to France. Verlaine, still distraught, followed Rimbaud to the station and may—the evidence is unclear—have attempted to shoot Rimbaud again. In any case Rimbaud now summoned the police for his own protection and had Verlaine arrested. Despite Rimbaud's attempts to have the charges against his lover dismissed, Verlaine was tried and given a stiff sentence of two years in prison—the severe sentence stemming, it has been suggested, from the moral opprobrium attached at the time to Verlaine's evident homosexual liaison with Rimbaud. Verlaine went to prison, and Rimbaud back to France, where he continued work on *A Season in Hell.*

This was Rimbaud's last, or nearly last, literary endeavor, and as he himself put it in a letter to his mother in 1873, "My fate depends upon this book." In it Rimbaud reflects on the delusions of his poetic project and the bitter lessons of his relationship with Verlaine. Both had been the subject of intense and cryptic celebration in what Rimbaud once called "these few fragments in prose": the *Illuminations.* It is to these, as well as to the nature of the visionary project motivating them, that we shall now turn.

ARTHUR RIMBAUD

THE ILLUMINATIONS

The most reasonable if a very cautious hypothesis as to when Rimbaud wrote the *Illuminations* is that they were composed, as C. A. Hackett concludes, "sporadically during the period from 1872 to 1875, the majority before, a few after, *Une saison en enfer.*" This is not very satisfying if one wishes to understand the latter as a dramatic swan song to poetic vision, a theory held by many over the years, and one rendered problematic by the possibility that Rimbaud composed at least some of the visionary *Illuminations* after it. The evidence on this matter is equivocal and has been the subject of hundreds of pages of debate. It is perhaps as well then to agree with Albert Camus, as the scholar C. A. Hackett does, that "the order in which his two great works were produced is of no importance. . . . If he wrote them one after the other, he agonized over them simultaneously." Such a view at least has the advantage of being supported by the nature of Rimbaud's work, which as we have seen always acknowledges the cohabitation of failure and success, affirmation and denial.

The order of the prose poems provides another dilemma, and editions vary dramatically in the way the sections are arranged. There is some agreement: "Génie" ("Genius") is typically placed last, while "Après le deluge" ("After the Deluge") is invariably set at the beginning (Félix Fénéon's first and very incomplete edition adopted this order). All arrangements inevitably reflect the interpretive predilections of an editor, and in lieu of any more certain sense of how Rimbaud would himself have ordered them—if indeed he cared—there is little more to go on. Readers must bear in mind this uncertainty of sequence, and in any case understanding the *Illuminations* need in no sense depend on any given organization.

Everything that has so far been said of Rimbaud's work—the problems of desire, the intention to break with form and tradition, the effort to engage the future in language—comes to an intense and idiosyncratic focus in the *Illuminations.* Rimbaud's experiments in poetic form became even more radical after he met Verlaine, whose own experiments with looser rhythms and weak endings had a marked impact on Rimbaud's work. In "Fêtes de la patience" ("Festivals of Patience"), he explored mixed patterns of meter and rhyme, and, as in "Memory," he began to use intentionally imperfect kinds of versification. More than ever before he refused to cede authority to canons of literary propriety. Finally, in two poems now usually included in the *Illuminations,* "Marine" and "Mouvement" ("Movement"), he abandoned meter altogether, and many critics believe these to be the first systematically free verse efforts in French. But it was in the prose form itself that Rimbaud found the freedom his program necessitated.

Rimbaud did not invent the prose poem: Gérard de Nerval, Aloysius Bertrand, Charles Cros, and Baudelaire had all experimented in the form before him. But Rimbaud was the first to realize completely the possibilities of a poetic prose, the first to jettison from it all anecdotal and straightforwardly biographical detail. In the second *lettre du voyant,* Rimbaud had written that the poet "will have to have his inventions smelt, felt, and heard; if what he brings back from *down there* has form, he gives it form; if it is formless, he gives formlessness." It was the complete mobility that the prose poem allowed, the possibilities of sudden shifts in tone, diction, image, reference, and rhythm, that appealed to Rimbaud's desire to find a style and an embodiment for the subtle superimpositions, rapid convergences and deviations of his new poetic vision. Previously, moving from the repetition of poetic tradition in pastiche to its critique in parody, Rimbaud had achieved an access to novelty in formal poetic structure. Now he was to abandon formal poetic structure altogether for the fluid forms his new poetic vision both required and made possible. The complex intentions informing this vision were first laid out in the letters of May 1871, and these shed light both on what we have seen Rimbaud to have achieved up to then and on what he hoped to attain in his new art.

In the longer letter, to Paul Démeny, Rimbaud expresses an acute awareness of the problematic conditions that history imposes on life and human understanding. It has done so since the ancient Greeks, for whom, Rimbaud suggests, things were somewhat better. Then, "verses and lyres" gave "rhythms to action," and this special congruence of words and reality yielded "la poésie Greque: Vie harmonieuse," harmonious life. Since then, however, poetry, language, and life have been falling off, the "game, degradation, and glory of countless idiotic generations." Rimbaud's analysis of this situation, however daring, jubilant, and brilliant it may be, is also rambling, at times naive, and certainly unmethodical. It can fairly be said, however—though with a deal more system than Rimbaud himself uses—that the degradation of life and language derived for him from three related delusions to which culture adhered: the myth of the autonomous "subjective" author; the myth of history as a single, continuous process; and the myth that language somehow freely represents reality. Indeed, these three delusions indulge in different ways a single misapprehension: the belief that the forms of human reality issue from, or are produced in relation to, a self-sufficient origin or source, which gives rise to them in a stable, unified, and progressive manner. The forms of language, within what Rimbaud calls this "moldy game," are made to stand for a world they putatively signify, as an author's creation to the author himself, or as the manifestations of history to the "source" from which they are supposed to spring—that is, as copies of some great model, repetitions struck from an original pattern. In this dispensation, life, and with it poetry, are caused to appear as the expression of a prior order; reality is subdued to the notion of representation itself.

Such a view was for Rimbaud the aesthetic and philosophical correlative of tyranny in the political order. Tradition and the past conceived in this way implacably dominate the present, forcing their false meanings, their "millions of skeletons," on contemporary existence. For Rimbaud, as for his contemporary Friedrich Nietzsche, history tyrannizes life by imposing on it false generalities of language, habit, and custom. To submit to history is thus to suffer false idols, like the myths of bourgeois religion and morality and their representatives in the individual self, the "false meanings of the Ego": "If old imbeciles had not discovered only the false meanings of the Ego," as Rimbaud puts it in his second *lettre du voyant*, "we would not have to sweep away those millions of skeletons which, from time immemorial, have accumulated the results of their one-eyed intellects by claiming to be authors." This statement forms the center of Rimbaud's objections to what he calls the "subjective poetry" of his contemporaries. In arrogating to themselves a false authority in their writing, poets have enslaved man's apprehension of reality, and hence reality itself, to a regime of mere accumulation. So enslaved, history unfolds as the institutionalized repetition of a prior orginality.

Now all of Rimbaud's intuitions told him that life, and the poet, must "give more—than just the formulation of [this] march toward Progress"; and hence the poet, rather than expressing a prior order, should "define the amount of the unknown awakening in his time in the universal soul" (second *lettre du voyant*). This is not as cryptic an insight as it may at first seem. Rimbaud starts from the perception that life and reality are always "more," as he says, than merely the sum of events and words as these are inertly (or *additively*) recorded by tradition. Life cannot be summarized by the patterns tradition imposes on it; nor do words exhaustively summarize reality, or works of art the artists who make them. To think so is to submerge the "more" of true reality—all that Rimbaud calls the "unknown"—beneath the generalizations of language and culture.

Against tradition, then, conceived as the domination of the general—the persistent, the repetitive, the nameable, all that is known—Rimbaud set his visionary practice of poetry, conceived as the freedom of the particular, the innovative, the *inouie* and the *inconnu:* the ineffable and the unknown. Against the banal accumulations of culture, the poet—"truly the thief of Fire"—appropriates the power to create the *"new—ideas and forms."* This power, and the multiple forms and determinations it uncovers, are the true meanings of the ego, which tradition has hitherto disguised. The truth and life that the poet gives rise to will thus no longer issue dynastically from an originating center (the author, reality, history) to an expressive appearance (the ego, the word, the event). It is the break with the sovereignty of the ego that the celebrated phrase from the *lettres du voyant*—"JE est un autre"; *I* is another—conveys. The poetic self is not a cause or *primum mobile* from which masterful effects emanate. Rather the forms of the self are themselves the effects of other processes, historical, linguistic, material. It is thus "wrong to say: I think. One ought to say: I am thought." It is the plurality inhabiting the seeming integration of the self that the poet tries to elicit. Hence the "truth" of personality is no longer a particular content, but rather a specific disposition toward the many forms that constitute it: either a collusion with those forms, and this yields the "false meanings of the Ego"; or a willful resistance to them, which uncovers the dense multiplicity of their true nature. As he later wrote in *A Season in Hell*, "It seemed to me that to each being several *other* lives were due." It is such intuitions that underlie many of the cryptic statements in the *Illuminations*, as when Rimbaud writes in "Enfance" ("Childhood"): "I am the saint . . . I am the scholar . . . I am the wanderer . . . I might have been the child"; or when he remarks in *A Season in Hell:* "I have known the eldest son of every family" ("Mauvais sang"). The true poet always resists the alleged unity of personality to make common cause with the real collectivity that is history.

One consequence of all this is that a different kind of attention is required from the reader to make sense of Rimbaud's later work. If we are to take him at his word, his writings do not in any simple sense represent a state of affairs. Rather, they are intended to be part of a transformation in reality itself; the *Illuminations* are best read then as a series of statements and reflections on the nature of that transformation; not so much an expression of it as a guide to it, an imperative toward it, at best perhaps even an embodiment of it. Rimbaud's writing as a whole tends to resist either isolated "readings" of individual pieces or single-minded summations about what in its totality it is about. Rather, his work is a constant cross-referential self-commentary, in which Rimbaud forever objects, adds, contradicts, qualifies, and transforms what he has said elsewhere, to arrive—perhaps on another occasion—at a more precise approximation of his vision of reality as pure creation. The very form of his work as it progresses can be taken as a resistance to the false unities of artistic form, so that the poet can make common cause with the real processes of creativity.

As they are created continually anew, "ideas and forms" transact a metamorphosis of past and present into future, partly engaging, partly constituting the incipient edge of that future. The short section "Departure" sketches this contraposition of past and future in a vivid way:

Seen enough. The vision appeared in every kind
  of air.
Had enough. Noises of cities in the evening, in
  sunlight, and forever.
Known enough. The haltings of life.—Oh! Noises
  and Visions!
Departure into new affection and new sound.

Rimbaud's poetic intention is to incite the moment of sudden discontinuity the self is able to assert between the constraints of history, on the one hand, and itself as a form of absolute novelty, on the other. The poet ends the repetitions of history by instituting a sudden departure into the new.

This poetic project was to be part of a larger movement of social liberation. It would break the "endless servitude of women"; institute an ethos of constant progress; allow new forms of justice and equality. Such ideas about the radical social function of art were not original to Rimbaud. Charles Fourier, Saint-Simon, Hugo, Pierre Proudhon, and others had formulated versions of it before him, although none so radically nor with such fierce commitment to what might be called the epistemology of freedom. Lautréamont, among Rimbaud's contemporaries, had conceived a poetry "made by all, not by one." From Jules Michelet Rimbaud borrowed the historian's opposition to the fetters of tradition, and it was partly by extending the ideas of Giovanni Battista Vico, whose *Scienza nuova* Michelet had translated into French, that Rimbaud found a format for his own nascent sense of the material, as opposed to the spiritual, basis of human history.

Rimbaud's radical conception of the *voyant*, or seer, if it owed much to arcane alchemical research, owed even more to Baudelaire: especially the emphasis on discipline and self-sacrifice and the importance of (often drug-induced) visions of the new. But where Baudelaire appealed, however ironically, to a spiritual realm as a way of resolving the contradictions of reality, for Rimbaud there was no such supervening spiritual resolution. "I shall be free," he wrote in *A Season of Hell*, "to possess truth in one body and one soul." He meant that truth is available there, and nowhere else.

To attain that truth, the poet

> makes himself a *seer* by a long, gigantic and rational *derangement* of *all the senses*. All forms of love, suffering, madness. He searches himself. He exhausts all poisons in himself and keeps only their quintessences. Unspeakable torture where he needs all his faith, all his superhuman strength, where he becomes among all men the great patient, the great criminal, the one accursed—the supreme Scholar!—Because he reaches the *unknown*.

In this climactic passage from the second *lettre du voyant*, Rimbaud makes clear that only so radical and extreme a discipline of derangement can unbuckle the severe constraints of tradition. As for Nietzsche, with whose writing this and many passages in Rimbaud show such a marked affinity, real knowledge for Rimbaud was an antimemory, in which tradition and experience are absorbed and exhausted in a process of relentless introspection. As he wrote in "Jeunesse" ("Youth"), in the *Illuminations:* "Your memory and your sense will only serve to feed your creative desires. Nothing, in any case, will remain of what is now visible." The result of this exhaustion, the "quintessence" attained in this radical process of negation and creation, is the unknown. This is Rimbaud's expression for that extreme poetic experience in which life and knowledge of it coincide in a moment of flashing insight, a veritable illumination of the ground on which reality and man's apprehension of it simultaneously emerge. This is knowledge and life seized, not in the romantic mode as recollection but as a methodical pruning away, a progressive elimination of all abstract and reified forms of life and thought so as to arrive at the irreducible event, life and knowledge together, which is reality itself. This event, for Rimbaud, arcane though it may be, is not a moment of transcendence in the religious sense; it does not establish the enduring identity of life and thought, matter and mind, real and ideal. It is rather the emergence of both, body and soul, as an instance of irreducible and unique novelty.

It is the advent of this supreme and living knowledge that all the poems in the *Illuminations* try to achieve, and it is particularly vivid in "Matinée d'ivresse" ("Morning of Intoxication"):

> *My* story of the Good and the Beautiful! Terrible fanfare of music where I never lose step!

Magical rack! Hurrah for the miraculous work and for the marvelous body, for the first time! It all began with the laughter of children and will end there. This poison will still be in my veins even when the fanfare dies away and I return to the earlier discord. And now that I am so worthy of this torture, let me fervently gather in the superhuman promise made to my created body and soul. This promise, this madness! Elegance, science, violence! They promised me they would bury in the darkness the tree of good and evil, and deport tyrannical codes of honesty so that I may bring forward my very pure love. It all began with feelings of disgust and it ended—since I could not seize its eternity on the spot—it ended with a riot of perfumes.

Laughter of children, discretion of slaves, coldness of virgins, horror of figures and objects from here, be consecrated by the memory of that night. It began in slyness and it came to an end with angels of fire and ice.

Brief night of intoxication, holy night! even if it was only for the mask you bequeathed to us. We assert you, method! I am not forgetting that yesterday you glorified each of our ages. I believe in that poison. I can give all of my existence each day.

Behold the time of the ASSASSINS.

Rimbaud's ecstatic and almost total self-absorption in this vision is alarming indeed, but this should not deter us from recognizing the brilliant integrity of his visionary experience even in its egomaniacal extremes. The poem must be read as a series of statements composed around an event of vision that, precisely because it is an event of novelty itself—a vision, we might say, of difference, vision *as* difference—cannot be represented. For representation implies just that ability to appear again, to be "re-present," which it is the point of the vision to subvert. As the drug-induced hallucinations subside, Rimbaud reflects on his "method": intoxication, the derangement of thought and sense. This promise, this madness, a whole new violent and elegant science, shatters the hold of tradition on perception, instituting a new temporality, which Rimbaud defined precisely by its difference from the sequentiality of usual time. On the one hand, there is the circumstance that events seem to have beginnings and ends; on the other, the visions themselves invoke a time not susceptible to the before and after of the clock. For this reason, Rimbaud is scrupulous to record how his visions begin and end, the better to distinguish them from just such an order. What is more, this new temporality carries with it the realization that all the antitheses of normal moral, aesthetic, and cognitive judgment depend on what Rimbaud considered to be the chimerical antitheses of before/after, past/present, desire/satisfaction—of historical time as it is routinely perceived. Thus as the "poison" dissolves distinctions of time, so does it abolish received Christian ideas of the distinction between good and evil, truth and falsehood, beauty and ugliness, all of which are buried in the darkness. Intoxication is truly "the time of the ASSASSINS" because it violently murders the notion of the past itself, along with the traditions and "codes" it imposes.

Few people will be comfortable with this doctrine, even if it makes exhilarating reading. This is mainly, I think, because Rimbaud was using a rationale and a method to undercut and destroy the moral categories we normally think of as supporting a rationale or making a method meaningful. (Likewise, Nietzsche himself once said, "It is not the victory of science that distinguishes our nineteenth century, but the victory of scientific method over science.") Looking back on these experiences in a more critical mood in *A Season in Hell*, Rimbaud describes how he had grown

accustomed to pure hallucination: I saw quite frankly a mosque in place of a factory, a school of drummers made up of angels, carriages on roads in the sky, a parlor at the bottom of the lake: monsters, mysteries. . . .

Then I explained my magic sophisms with the hallucination of words!

> At the end I looked on the disorder of mind as sacred.
>
> ("Délires II: Alchimie du verbe")

So committed was Rimbaud at this time to the possibilities of freedom, invention, and change that distinctions themselves between the imaginary and the real had to be abandoned as falsely limiting. We might hesitate to go as far as Rimbaud in seeking to extirpate the roots of oppression at their imagined source in primary categories of consciousness and perception. We can nevertheless appreciate the principled and uncompromising vision that beckoned him to do so himself.

The price of this discipline of derangement was the almost certain eclipse of intelligibility for the poet. As Rimbaud wrote in the second *lettre du voyant:*

> He reaches the unknown and when, bewildered, he ends by losing the intelligence of his visions, he has at least seen them. Let him die as he leaps through unheard of and unnameable things: other horrible workers will come; they will begin from the horizons where the other has collapsed.

The poet deliberately poised himself at the brink of his culture's condition of rationality in order to break the tyranny that condition imposed. The risk is meaninglessness, but it was taken in the service of a rational impulse to freedom and change.

It was for this commitment to modes of experience outside the categories of normal consciousness that Rimbaud was exalted—first by the symbolists and later by surrealism and psychoanalysis—as the explorer par excellence of unknown and subconscious psychic states. The emphasis in this regard has been perhaps somewhat misplaced, for if Rimbaud sought the irrational, it was always in the interests of a severely rational discipline of discovery.

To create a new discourse and orient it toward the freedom of the future, Rimbaud sought to accomplish in his writing what Roland Barthes called "so pure a present in its language that the whole of discourse is identified with the act of delivery." We have seen this ethos of a "pure present" in "The Drunken Boat" and "Vowels," where meaning is tied to novelty and novelty itself to the purest possible present tense that verse can provide. But the *Illuminations* take this program further still, and that brings to the fore questions of context and form central to the composition (and to the interpretation) of Rimbaud's later work.

The problem as we saw with "The Drunken Boat" is that the context of poetic form diminishes the poem's ability to participate in novelty. To circumvent this difficulty, in the *Illuminations* Rimbaud intentionally shrugs off the conventional contexts—narrative, historical, biographical and literary—through which meaning is customarily extracted from language. Many of the headings in the *Illuminations* make this point themselves: "Anguish," "Story," "Scenes," "Lives," "Phrases," "Cities," "Movement," "Sale." The environment of an *Illumination* is typically its own sudden and stark presentation, sometimes as a hallucinatory landscape, sometimes as a brief parable, often only as a fragment or a phrase emerging out of nowhere. The difficulty this format presents—a kind of deliberate decontextualization—must be understood not as an obstacle to interpretation, but as a large part of the meaning of Rimbaud's most complex work. The temptation is strong in reading Rimbaud to restore his writings to some context, a temptation evidenced by the many critical efforts to determine the specific biographical experiences that "lie behind" the *Illuminations.* Such interpretation is useful to a degree; but when we consider how radically Rimbaud's writing is itself a meditation on the relation between experience and its recurrence in language, the matter becomes more complex.

The following passage from "Childhood," for example, is explicitly concerned with the relation between "childhood" and language.

Whatever experience underlies the images is far less important than the clear intention to render it into the purely present tense of poetic vision:

> In the woods there's a bird whose singing stops you and makes you blush.
> There's a clock which doesn't strike.
> There's a clay-pit with a nest of white animals.
> There's a cathedral coming down and a lake going up.
> There's a little carriage abandoned in the woods or rolling down the path, with ribbons all over it.
> There's a troupe of child actors, in costume, whom you can see on the road through the edge of the woods.
> And then there's someone who chases you off when you're hungry and thirsty.
>
> (3)

Critics have often, and with reasonable success, made shift to ascribe events in Rimbaud's childhood to these images. But the more important point is that language—the "hallucination of words"—is being called on to establish an order precisely indifferent to the modality of time that separates Rimbaud from such childhood events as he writes. The paradoxical intimacy of opposites—the strange coincidence of an event that both arrests and incites motion, of a time that is timeless, of impossible ascents and descents, of objects that exist in two places at once—testifies to the way poetic vision licenses antinomies in time that "biographical experience" does not. The incantatory rhythm—"There's a clock"; "There's a clay-pit"; "There's a cathedral"—highlights the way language alone is where the fact of an event and its expression concur perfectly, a concurrence precisely debarred in the relation between a past experience and its representation in words. If such an emphasis occurs characteristically on the occasion of a remembered desire and its frustration—"There's someone who chases you off when you're hungry and

thirsty"—this serves to show how the reality of language presents the possibility of a more satisfying relation than reality itself.

What the fluid and novel form of the *Illuminations* allows is a presentation of language stripped as much as possible of all preconditioning contexts. Open to every kind of syntactical attack, lyrical intrusion, insistent repetition, and abruptly disjunctive contrast, each fragment arises as a novel intervention, a ferocious resistance to any context other than those mandated by Rimbaud. At the same time, what most of the fragments are in some sense "about" is precisely the nature of this intervention and resistance and especially the new possibilities of sense and sensation they allow.

It is of these possibilities that Rimbaud writes in "Conte" ("Story"):

> A prince was tired of merely spending his time perfecting conventional impulses. . . . He wanted to see the truth and the time of full desire and satisfaction. He wanted this, even if it was a misuse of piety. At least he possessed a large reserve of human power.

In the opening, Rimbaud concocts a hasty mock parable to describe the aims and techniques of his project. A large reserve of human power is required to institute these aims, which involve absolute acts of destruction and re-creation. The place where this ambivalent gesture occurs is language (here, a "story"); for in language loss and renewal, destruction and creation coexist. Thus the parable relates fantastic feats of rejuvenation through annihilation in which wives, comrades, servants, and animals are slaughtered by the prince, and yet miraculously survive:

> He took delight in cutting the throats of the pet animals. He set fire to the palaces. He fell on the servants and hacked them to pieces.—The servants, the gold roofs, the splendid animals were still there.

The union of destruction and rejuvenation comes to a climax when the prince meets a genie of "unspeakable, unmentionable beauty." They kill "one another probably in the prime of life": "But this Prince passed away, in his palace, at a normal age. The Prince was the Genie. The Genie was the Prince." Visionary language is where love—those "huge reserves of human power"—activate its aims, for in it every distinction that hinders "truth and the time of full satisfactions" is abolished. "La musique savante manque à notre désir": Language is that "cunning music," as Rimbaud writes, where the contradictions of desire are temporarily resolved.

Rimbaud was thus not interested in integrating the "real" past with the present—bourgeois culture, after all, accomplishes this all too successfully in the repetitions it imposes. Whether the separation between "real past" and language is experienced as loss (as in "Memory") or creation (as in "Vowels"), language for Rimbaud institutes a radically different order of time and perception. As he writes in "Genie": "Down with these superstitions, these old bodies, these couples, these ages. This is the time that has gone under!" Poetic vision involves the abolition of all customary arrangements, especially those of time and desire.

It might be said that form and sense in the *Illuminations* are tied to the ascetically irreducible minimum of formal recognition in language, that is, to the patterns of repetition and difference that word, sound, rhythm, and image present. Indeed, repetition and variation might be said to substitute for all the other contexts that Rimbaud's prose poems eschew, a point borne out in this section from "Phrases": "I stretched out ropes from spire to spire; garlands from window to window; golden chains from star to star; and I dance." Working with the bare elements of language, Rimbaud causes a certain interplay between repetition (spire/spire, window/window, star/star) and variation (ropes, garlands, golden chains) to take place. In so doing he enacts a process in which repetition begets change, change begets renewal, and all are fused in the present tense of poetic production: "I dance."

Such passages evoke the catalytic agency of the poet himself in the creative process. This emphasis should not obscure the related fact that poetic agency is reduced here to the ascetic minimum of causing repetition and variation to appear in language. This indeed is a reflection in form of the central ambivalence inhabiting Rimbaud's poetic intention, where rage, negation, destruction, and formlessness coincide with form, love, affirmation, and invention. It is within these polarities that most of the *Illuminations* are conceived. Rimbaud's work, as he wrote in "War," is a "dream of War, of justice and power, of unsuspected logic. It is as simple as a musical phrase."

Apocalyptic annihilation and creation are the central themes of "After the Deluge," whose action is poised between catastrophe and creation at the liminal moment after "the idea of the Flood has subsided." This *Illumination* has an emblematic importance in that it typically comes first in editions of Rimbaud's prose poems. The world that arises here is precipitously and ironically bourgeois, mercantile, and Christian, as if no sooner had creation occurred than the degradations of custom, repetition, and persistence had set in. Accordingly, the section ends just as precipitously with a second apocalypse:

> —Gush forth, waters of the pond. Foam, pour over the bridge and over the woods. Black shrouds and organs, lightning and thunder, rise up and spread everywhere. Waters and sorrows rise up and bring back the Floods.
>
> For ever since they have gone—oh! the precious stones buried and the opened flowers!—we have been bored! The Queen, the Witch lighting her coal in the earthen pot, will never tell us what she knows and what we do not.

The forms of a created world, precisely by persisting, abate the novelty of their founding moment—and hence must be annihilated anew so as to make possible the opening of flowers once more. Language is the place where this rapid cycle of creation, boredom, and destruction repetitively occurs.

The *Illuminations,* together with the poems contemporary with them, are founded on this ambivalence: the absolute will to create new form and the absolute rage against form itself. As Wallace Fowlie has said of "After the Deluge," it "represents its own emergence from chaos, and the final triumph of chaos as the poem precipitates itself into its original pristine absence of form." The furious will to shatter form, and the poignant recognition that form will persist, are the subject of "Qu'est-ce pour nous?" ("What Does It Matter?"), written in 1872: "Industrialists, princes, senates: / Perish! power, justice, history: down with you! . . . / Europe, Asia, America—disappear!" The poem comes to a climax as the "earth melts"; but in an italicized postscript, Rimbaud notes: "It is nothing: I am here; I am still here."

The range of subject matter in the *Illuminations,* like the mode of presentation, is wide, covering childhood and the time of Rimbaud's (relative) maturity; nature and metropolitan life; hallucinations and tranquil visions of the countryside; fairy tale; agony; movement; dawn; and life itself. But in another sense, as W. M. Frohock has noted, the range of themes in his work is extremely narrow and constantly returns to novelty, creation, destruction, and repetition. In "Genie," which closes most editions of the *Illuminations,* Rimbaud gives perhaps his most vivid expression to the paradoxical creative and transfiguring principle he perceived to inhabit reality:

> He is affection and the present moment because he has thrown open the house to the snow foam of winter and to the noises of summer, he who purified drinking water and food, who is the enchantment of fleeing places and the superhuman delight of resting places. He is affection and future, the strength and love which we, erect in rage and boredom, see pass by in the sky of storms and the flags of ecstasy.
>
> He is love, perfect and reinvented measure, miraculous, unforeseen reason, and eternity: machine loved for its qualities of fate.

His body "is the dreamed-of liberation, the collapse of grace joined with new violence. All that he sees! all the ancient kneelings and the penalties canceled as he passes by." Every principle of movement, commencement, contrariety that we have so far noted is here: "Genie" is the abolition of distinction, the penetration of barriers, the future constantly fomenting into the present. He is the cessation of all antitheses, moral, perceptual, mental; he is the future endlessly inventing itself anew, a violent agency of change, multiplicity, revolution, the "terrifying celerity of forms and action when they are perfect." In the climactic final paragraph, Rimbaud invokes his "genie" as a great polymorphous body in which all vision, sensuality, and desire are summarized, destroyed, and recreated:

> He knew us and loved us. May we, this winter night, from cape to cape, from the noisy pole to the castle, from the crowd to the beach, from vision to vision, our strength and our feelings tired, hail him and see him and send him away, and under tides and on the summit of snow deserts follow his eyes, his breathing, his body, his day.

In these pulsing periods, carrying forward phrase after phrase whose incantation expands to incorporate all reality, Rimbaud celebrates novel and visionary experience in a manner he was never to surpass. "Genie" is a vivid and moving apotheosis of formal invention embodying and transfiguring itself in the hallucinated vision of words, so rapidly, so often, and with such constant novelty that the contradiction of "constant novelty" itself recedes—if only for a time—into the distance of an infinitely accelerated creativity. Couched in the quasireligious vernacular of a hymn to

God, "Genie" is a eulogy to the sensual and material supercession of all religion, the Christian God overwhelmed by the body of poetic vision: his eyes, his body, his day. This was as close as Rimbaud was to come without religion itself to a vision of redemption in a secular world.

It is not surprising that this vision could not be sustained.

A SEASON IN HELL

A Season in Hell is a freak in the history of prose narrative: part autobiography, part self-critique, part hallucinatory self-parody, and a dramatic if logical revision of the visionary project Rimbaud had been pursuing for two years. The obsessions of his other work carry over into this strange prose concoction: the antitheses of history, the dualities of desire, the problems of cultural inheritance, and the impulse to find a form equal to the circumstances of the modern world. But *A Season in Hell* was written from the standpoint not of literary innovation or poetic vision but of experience itself. It embodies a recognition that language and vision even as Rimbaud had conceived of them at their most innovative are not in themselves sufficient to effect the changes he had once hoped were possible.

Begun in April 1873 and finished in August after the shooting episode in Brussels, *A Season in Hell* was composed during a period of extreme inner turmoil and crisis for Rimbaud. If it represents the final parturition of his thought from the bourgeois and idealist traditions he so despised, it remains to be seen why this fulfillment of his project took the form, ironically enough, of a complete rejection of the visionary methods he had so fervently expounded and pursued.

The book is perhaps the only sequel one can imagine to the *Illuminations* (if, indeed, it is entirely a sequel), and this is so not despite but because of its difference in so many respects from his other works. Apart from any-

thing else, it stands out for the great care he devoted to its editing, organization, and publication. The early and later verse, like the *Illuminations,* was for the most part collected and arranged by others, in many cases only after Rimbaud's death and once, as in the case of five illuminations published in the magazine *La vogue* in 1886, by editors laboring under the misbelief that he was dead. (By then he might as well have been, as far as the literary world was concerned. In the ten years that had passed since he quit writing in 1875, Rimbaud had wandered all over Europe, the Middle East, and Africa, where by 1886 he had settled into the lonely and adventurous life of a trader and sometime gunrunner for Menelik, King of Shoa, in Abyssinia.)

Thus in contrast to the lofty arrogance with which he dispatched his other works into the world (having little time and less concern for their place in a culture he was determined to leave behind), there is something emblematic about the attention he lavished on *A Season in Hell*—"little stories in prose," as he wrote his friend Ernest Delahaye in May 1873, when he had finished three of the projected nine sections. All of Rimbaud's work shows the mark of painstaking craftmanship; but surviving drafts of three sections of *A Season in Hell,* the letter to Delahaye, and Rimbaud's own assertion—"my fate depends on this work"—testify to the importance he ascribed to it and the great deliberation with which he crafted it. Everything about the book reveals that Rimbaud was no longer viewing history from the standpoint of vision, nor identifying life with the rapid transformations of formal invention. The world, to be sure, was still a place of form and change; what had changed was Rimbaud's faith in his visionary vocation within it.

A Season in Hell is constructed in nine prose sections. Part of the difficulty in interpretation concerns the fact that, while it encompasses the entirety of Rimbaud's career, much of the narrative proceeds in the present tense, or in ventriloquially shifting perspectives that ironically distort distinctions in time for polemical effect. Nevertheless, it has a discernible beginning, middle, and end, and is clearly planned as a form of confession, analytic retrospect, and spiritual autobiography. The work, he wrote his mother in 1873, "means exactly what I've said, literally and completely, in all respects." This autobiographical literalism complements his pragmatic attention to the work's publication; both signal a new acceptance of what Rimbaud had previously striven so hard to overcome: the inescapable circumstances of a biographical and historical milieu.

A recurrent theme as he reviews his career in this work is the constant effort he had made to circumvent or resolve the contradictions he felt stigmatized European culture. But where in his other work he had hoped to cancel the contradictions of culture, to render unto history a renovated vision of itself whole, undivided, and equal unto itself, *A Season in Hell* is Rimbaud's reluctant and very agonized return to history conceived as *inevitably* discrepant with his visions of renovation. This return is parallel in the book to Rimbaud's shift from escape to acceptance, from ecstatic vision to rational understanding. "Am I escaping?" he asks himself at one point; and answers: "I am explaining." The work in this sense represents a return of the repressed dualities—between self and other, present and past, language and life—which in his other work he had attacked so strongly. *A Season in Hell* is a kind of severe and ascetic acceptance that language and vision cannot put these dualities to rest. As he wrote on a draft page of one section of the manuscript: "Now I can say that art is a stupidity."

Thus where his other work is visionary and poetic, *A Season in Hell* is steadfastly discursive. If his previous writing was a constant incitement to image and vision, the only images that appear in the *Season* arise in the context of Rimbaud's ironic citation and criticism of his earlier work. Its frenzied, intensely variegated, and embattled prose shows the same fierce energy and resistance apparent in all his writing; but the energy is no longer in the service of a visionary poetic experience bent on outstripping, in the interests of renovated life, the difference between life and vision itself. "Truth" is no longer, as it was in the work from "The Drunken Boat" through the *Illuminations,* the function of a vision that cancels all "differences" and all "times." As he writes at the end of the work, "I shall be free to possess truth in one body and one soul." In one sense, this statement repudiates the will (which his previous work had embodied) to go beyond the dualities of time, desire, and thought. But to the degree that Rimbaud's critique of the dualities of time and desire had been based on an intensely secular and unswerving commitment to reality, the statement represents a logical outcome of his development. Whether the experience of division gave rise to the critique of history, or whether history gave rise to division, Rimbaud in *A Season in Hell* is sure of one thing: *voyance* may have diagnosed the sickness of self and society; it cannot in itself heal them. "Truth" shall no longer be the frantic visionary will to cancel division; it shall reside, instead, in "one body and one soul."

The working title of the book—"Pagan Book, or Negro Book"—recalls Rimbaud's attempt to find in a kind of imaginary pre-Christian culture modes of perception that do not invoke the Christian discrepancies of desire and of history. This attempt, however, is now viewed ironically as an understandable but nevertheless deluded response to the inadequacies of Christian culture. Indeed the great power of *A Season in Hell* consists in the way it comprises Rimbaud's longing for innocence (that time of "full desire and satisfaction") and a conviction of his inescapable complicity with Christian culture.

A Season in Hell represents the final realization of what Rimbaud had already foreseen in the second *lettre du voyant,* that "the future will be materialistic." Then, however, it had been visionary poetic practice that would engage this material future: "Always filled with *Number* and *Harmony*," he wrote in 1871, "these poems will be made to endure.—Fundamentally, it would be Greek poetry again." Now, in *A Season in Hell*, the same intuitions as to the material basis of history persist, but the vanguard role of poetic vision has been stripped away. For far from engaging the future, that project seemed now to Rimbaud to have been a "deleterious instinct," yet another false "vision of purity." But "without knowing how to explain this without pagan words," and no longer believing in his vision of a pagan escape from the Christian present, Rimbaud "prefers to be silent." Poetic vision was not an end in itself but merely a station along the way, something to be abandoned once it had accomplished the necessary break from the old superstitions.

In the opening section of the work, Rimbaud evokes the time, "long ago, if my memory serves me," when "life was a banquet where everyone's heart was generous, and where all wines flowed." But pulling "Beauty" down on his knee, he had "found her bitter," as indeed he had found experience and even the poetic tradition of beauty itself debased and unsatisfactory. For these reasons, he had "taken arms against justice," hoping to expel "all human hope" from his vision of reality, the better to arrive at a renewed vision of it. He recounts in summary form his effort to derange all the senses: "Disaster was my god. I stretched out in mud. I dried myself in criminal air. I played clever tricks on insanity. . . . Spring brought me the idiot's terrifying laugh." Then he continues: "But recently, on the verge of my last croak, I thought of looking for the key to the ancient banquet where I might possibly recover my appetite." *A Season in Hell* is Rimbaud's attempt, not to displace the old contradictions of desire, but to find again and come to terms with the longings that had motivated his project to begin with. The aim is no longer to dissolve the con-

tradictions of history and personality in visions of the new, but to understand the inevitable conditions under which those contradictions have arisen.

In the next section, "Mauvais sang" ("Bad Blood"), Rimbaud reviews his bourgeois French inheritance, especially his loathing for Christianity. That hatred is founded on its hypocritical inability to deliver the "freedom and nobility" Christ had promised, but which Christian history has in fact endlessly deferred. The appeal of paganism, which he now sardonically recalls, had been precisely its promise of a time untainted by Christianity, by the advent of the "eternal inner wound" and the divisions of desire and satisfaction. But while Rimbaud "had never been a Christian," he is yet unable to "remember farther back than this land and Christianity," and thus is a "slave to my baptism." Caught between the desire for "pagan blood" and an inescapable Christian legacy, Rimbaud summons his strength to confront this impasse with a cold eye. Appealing no longer to pagan rites and orgies of sin, setting aside all "rage, debauchery, madness," he sets out dispassionately—if with great anguish—to "evaluate" the "extent of my innocence." Innocence here is Rimbaud's word for the freedom, the unity of desire and satisfaction, he had felt was his due, and which in love, madness, drugs, and poetic vision he had struggled to achieve. The balance of the book, accordingly, evaluates these methods and, one by one, leaves them behind.

In the section "Nuit de l'enfer" ("Night in Hell"), Rimbaud ironically reinvokes the visionary hallucinations, the better to understand the delusions they had entailed. As he swallows in memory the "monstrous mouthful of poison" again, "countless hallucinations" rise up. He adopts the present tense, but now with an irony that abates the old immediacy of vision drugs had induced: "I intend to unveil all mysteries: religious mysteries or those of nature, death, birth, the future, the past, cosmogony, the void.'' Rimbaud means to include here the "mystery" of vision and the "hallucination of words" themselves, which need now to be unveiled and discarded. Rimbaud is no longer drawn up into his visions as he recounts them; rather, through juxtaposition and antithesis of assertion and counterassertion, he creates a constant ironic equilibrium in which his previous uncritical enthusiasms are suspended.

In "Délires I: Vierge folle/L'Époux infernal" ("Delirium I: The Foolish Virgin/The Infernal Bridegroom"), Rimbaud adopts the voice of Verlaine in order to recount his own attempt to find through love and sensuality the time of full desire and satisfaction and the eradication of all differences. The interpenetration of their souls had been not a fullness but a mingling of two voids or absences set off against each other. Thus the "foolish virgin" (Verlaine) is made to say; "I was in his soul as in a palace that had been emptied in order not to see so mean a person as myself.'' The manner in which Rimbaud puts words into Verlaine's mouth poignantly emphasizes the way their love had confirmed their separate individualities. In "Délires II: Alchimie du verbe" ("Delirium II: Alchemy of the Word''), Rimbaud reviews his own poetic project. The section is interspersed with slightly altered versions of six of his poems, which, as Wallace Fowlie has noted, creates a "subtle interplay between the time when the poems were written (a recent past, but treated as remote), the tenses used in them (mainly the present), and the tenses in the prose text, which, though obviously more recent, are almost entirely in the past.'' This device serves to distance and make more ironic Rimbaud's visionary project, which is now anatomized and dismantled. "Damned by the rainbow,'' the visionary crusade had failed, each episode of intoxication or flight of vision ending repetitively in a return to the everyday world, thus begetting the need for more visions, more intoxication, as Rimbaud led himself ever deeper into madness, disaffection, cynicism, and ill health.

For all the attempts to escape from reality and institute a new order, Rimbaud had never "thought of the pleasure of escaping from today's suffering.'' This is the subject of the next section, "L'Impossible":

> I did not have in mind the bastard wisdom of the Koran.—But is there not real torture in the fact that, since the declaration of science and Christianity, man deludes himself, proving obvious truth, puffing up with the pleasure of repeating his proofs, and living only this way? A subtle, ridiculous torture; source of my spiritual wanderings.

In spite of his desire to escape the banalities of culture, Rimbaud never abandoned, as A *Season in Hell* makes plain, the rational will to truth, no matter how difficult or unpleasant that truth might be. The excesses had never been an attempt simply to escape truth, to "cultivate fog'' and subside into easy alternatives. The aim had always been to arrive at truth and knowledge—in whose pursuit "science is too slow,'' while Christianity is at a kind of permanent standstill ("Gluttonously, I wait for God''). Visionary knowledge had moved too fast, always outstripping the life it was meant to revitalize.

In this manner re-experiencing, anatomizing, and exhausting all the delusions of his project in an ironic rendition of the introspective process described in the second *lettre du voyant*, Rimbaud leaves them all behind in the final section, "Adieu":

> I have created all celebrations, all triumphs, all dramas. I have tried to invent new flowers, new stars, new flesh, new tongues. I believed I had acquired supernatural powers. Well! I have to bury my imagination and my memories! A fine reputation of an artist and a story-teller lost sight of!

From life seen in the perspective of vision, Rimbaud now sees vision in the perspective of life; and thus is he "thrown back to the earth, with a duty to find, and rough reality to embrace." The escape from history and the pursuit of the new have brought him full circle. The labor of poetic vision has shown him finally the insufficiency of words and hallucination to change reality, indeed that a "writer's hand is no better than a ploughman's," as he remarks in "Bad Blood."

A Season in Hell shows Rimbaud as committed as ever to the new; as he declares in this final section, "We must be absolutely modern." But this no longer means the creation in poetry of the new, but rather the confrontation of the "harsh new hour" of reality itself. Perhaps, "armed with ardent patience, we will enter magnificent cities." In the meantime, Rimbaud concludes, he shall be free *"to possess truth in one body and one soul."* If all of Rimbaud's work had been produced in response to the divisions he experienced so sharply between self and other, mind and body, present and past, language and reality, this final statement in *A Season in Hell* represents not so much a response to these divisions as an assumption, once and for all, of the burden they inescapably entail. As René Étiemble—Rimbaud's great bibliographer and a staunch enemy of the myriad myths in which posterity has wrapped his work—has written, *A Season in Hell* represents the triumph of realism finally corrupting every idealism.

With meteoric speed and brilliance, Rimbaud's inspiration burnt itself out as quickly as it had ignited. After the lukewarm reception of *A Season in Hell,* he was to do little, if any, serious writing. He lived the rest of his short life in relative obscurity, wandering and working in foreign lands. He worked hard as an engineer and then as a trader-merchant; he curbed completely the wild debauchery of his literary years; but he never really established any lasting relationships, nor did he succeed in business very brilliantly. In 1890 a tumor

on his knee was removed, but not before metastasizing, and in 1891 he died a painful death from cancer. Perhaps ironically, he was brought to God on his deathbed, asking for extreme unction at the very end. His final conversion means little, however, beside the enormous labor of questioning that his work embodies and continues to embody.

Selected Bibliography

FIRST EDITIONS

Les stupra. Paris, 1871.
Une saison en enfer. Brussels, 1873.
Les illuminations. Introduction by Paul Verlaine. Paris, 1886.
Reliquaire, poésies. Preface by Rodolphe Darzens. Paris, 1891.
Poèmes, Les illuminations, Une saison en enfer. Preface by Paul Verlaine. Paris, 1891.
Poésies complètes. Edited by M. Vanier, preface by Paul Verlaine. Paris, 1895.
Oeuvres. Edited by Paterne Berrichon and Ernest Delahaye. Paris, 1898.
Oeuvres (vers et proses). Edited and annotated by Paterne Berrichon, preface by Paul Claudel. Paris, 1912.

MODERN EDITIONS

Album zutique. Introduction, notes, and commentary by Pascal Pia. Paris, 1962.
Ce qu'on dit au poète à propos de fleurs. Edited by Agnes Rosenfeld. Paris, 1981.
Les illuminations. Edited by H. de Bouillane de Lacoste. Paris, 1949.
————. Edited by Albert Py. Geneva, 1967–1969. Standard text with annotation, commentary, introduction, index of themes, and bibliography.
————. Edited by André Guyaux. Neuchâtel, 1984.
Lettres du voyant. Edited by Gérald Schaeffer. Geneva, 1975. Introductory study by Marc Eigeldinger, "La voyance avant Rimbaud."
Oeuvres complètes. Introduction and bibliographical notes by Pascal Pia. Maestricht, 1931.

─────. Edited by R. de Renéville and J. Mouquet. Paris, 1946, 1954, 1963. For years the most authoritative edition, now superseded by the edition of Antoine Adam, below.

─────. 2 vols. Preface by Tristan Tzara. Lausanne, 1948.

─────. Edited by H. de Bouillane de Lacoste. Paris, 1950.

Oeuvres. Edited by Antoine Adam. Paris, 1957. Reprinted 1972.

─────. Edited by Paul Hartmann. Paris, 1957.

─────. Edited by Suzanne Bernard. Paris, 1960. Reprinted 1970.

─────. Edited by Suzanne Bernard and André Guyaux. Paris, 1981.

Poésies. Edited by H. de Bouillane de Lacoste. Paris, 1939. Reprinted 1947.

─────. Edited by Marcel A. Ruff. Paris, 1978.

Poésies, Derniers vers, Une saison en enfer, Illuminations. Edited by Louis Forestier, preface by René Char. Paris, 1973.

Poésies et table de concordances rythmique et syntaxique. Edited by Frédéric Eigeldinger and Gérald Schaeffer. Neuchâtel, 1981.

Ressources. Foreword by Roger Pierrot. Slatkine, 1979. Reprint of 1873 edition of Une saison en enfer and 1886 edition of Les illuminations.

Une saison en enfer. Edited by H. de Bouillane de Lacoste. Paris, 1941.

CORRESPONDENCE

Lettres de la vie littéraire d'Arthur Rimbaud (1870–1875). Edited by J.-M. Carré. Paris, 1931.

TRANSLATIONS

Arthur Rimbaud: Complete Works. Translated by Paul Schmidt. New York, 1975.

The Illuminations, Coloured Plates. Translated by Nick Osmond. London, 1976. Bilingual edition.

Prose Poems from Les Illuminations. Translated by Helen Rootham, introduction by Edith Sitwell. London, 1932.

─────. Translated by Louise Varèse. New York, 1946.

Rimbaud: Complete Works, Selected Letters. Translated with introduction and notes by Wallace Fowlie. Chicago, 1966. Bilingual edition.

Rimbaud's Illuminations. Translated by Bertrand Mathieu, foreword by Henry Miller. Brockport, N.Y., 1979.

A Season in Hell. Translated by Delmore Schwartz. Norfolk, Conn., 1939.

─────. Translated with introduction by George Frederic Lees. London, 1932. Reprinted 1949.

─────. Translated by Norman Cameron, drawings by Keith Vaughan. London, 1950. Includes original French text.

A Season in Hell and The Drunken Boat. Translated by Louise Varèse. New York, 1945.

A Season in Hell. The Illuminations. Translated by Enid Rhodes Peschel, foreword by Henri Peyre. Oxford, 1973.

Selected Verse Poems of Arthur Rimbaud. Translated by Norman Cameron. London, 1942.

BIOGRAPHICAL AND CRITICAL STUDIES

ARTICLES

Adam, Antoine. "L'Énigme des Illuminations." Revue des sciences humaines, nouvelle série 60:221–224 (1950).

Baudry, J.-L. "Le texte de Rimbaud." Tel quel 35:46–63 (1968).

─────. "Le texte de Rimbaud." Tel quel 36:33–53 (1969).

Bernard, Suzanne. "Rimbaud et la création d'une nouvelle langue poétique." In Le poème en prose de Baudelaire jusqu'à nos jours. Paris, 1959. Pp. 151–211.

Blanchard, J. Marc. "Sur mythe poétique: Essai d'une sémiostylistique rimbaudienne." Sémiotica 16:67–86 (1976).

Chisholm, A. R. "Sources and Structure of Rimbaud's 'Bateau Ivre.'" The French Quarterly 12:41–52 (1930).

Hough, Graham. "The Modernist Lyric." In Modernism 1890–1930, edited by Malcolm Bradbury and James W. McFarlane. Atlantic Highlands, N.J., 1978. Pp. 312–322.

Lawler, J. R. "Rimbaud as Rhetorician." In The Language of French Symbolism. Princeton, N.J., 1969. Pp. 71–111.

Little, R. "Rimbaud: Au seuil de l'illumination." In Revue des lettres modernes: Arthur Rimbaud. Vol. 2. Paris, 1973. Pp. 81–105.

Porter, Laurence M. "Artistic Self-Consciousness in Rimbaud's Poetry." In Pre-Text/Text/Context: Essays on Nineteenth Century French Literature, edited by Robert L. Mitchel. Columbus, Ohio, 1980. Pp. 159–171.

Richard, J.-P. "Rimbaud ou la poésie du devenir. In *Poésie et profondeur*. Paris, 1955. Pp. 187–250.

Thibaudet, Jean. "Mallarmé et Rimbaud." *La nouvelle revue française* 18:199–206 (1922).

Todorov, T. "Une complication de texte: *Les illuminations.*" *Poétique* 34:241–253 (1978).

Weinberg, B. "'Le Bateau Ivre,' or the Limits of Symbolism." *PMLA* 72:165–193 (1957).

BOOKS

Balakian, Anna. *The Symbolist Movement: A Critical Appraisal.* New York, 1967.

Beaumont, E. M., et al., eds. *Order and Adventure in Post-Romantic French Poetry: Essays Presented to C. A. Hackett.* New York, 1973.

Bonnefoy, Yves. *Rimbaud par lui-méme.* Paris, 1961.

Bouillane de Lacoste, H. *Rimbaud et le problème des "Illuminations."* Paris, 1949.

Breton, A. *Flagrant délit.* Paris, 1949.

Brunel, Pierre. *Rimbaud, ou l'éclatant désastre.* Paris, 1978.

————. *Rimbaud, projets et réalisation.* Paris, 1983.

Camus, Albert. *L'Homme révolté.* Paris, 1951.

Carré, J.-M. *Les deux Rimbauds.* Paris, 1928.

————. *La vie aventureuse de Rimbaud.* Paris, 1926.

————. *La vie de Rimbaud.* Paris, 1939.

Cartier, M. *Sa vie, son oeuvre.* Paris, 1957.

Chadwick, C. *Études sur Rimbaud.* Paris, 1960.

————. *Rimbaud.* London, 1979.

Chisholm, A. R. *The Art of Arthur Rimbaud.* Melbourne, 1930.

Clarke, M. *Rimbaud and Quinet.* New York, 1946.

Clauzel, R. *"Une saison en enfer."* Paris, 1931.

Cohn, Robert G. *The Poetry of Rimbaud.* Princeton, N.J., 1973.

Coulon, M. *Le problème de Rimbaud, poète maudit.* Nîmes, 1923.

Davies, Margaret. *"Une saison en enfer": Analyse du texte.* Paris, 1975.

Debray, Pierre. *Rimbaud le magicien désabusé.* Paris, 1949.

de Graaf, Daniel A. *Arthur Rimbaud: Sa vie, son oeuvre.* Paris, 1960.

Delahaye, Ernest. *Rimbaud.* Paris, 1923.

————. *Souvenirs familiers.* Paris, 1925.

de Renéville, Rolland. *Rimbaud le voyant.* Paris, 1947.

Dhôtel, André. *Rimbaud et la révolte moderne.* Paris, 1952.

Dubois, Daniel, ed. *Rimbaud.* Paris, 1976.

Eigeldinger, M. *Rimbaud et le mythe solaire.* Geneva, 1964.

————. *La voyance avant Rimbaud.* Geneva, 1975.

Étiemble, René. *Le mythe de Rimbaud.* 3 vols. Paris, 1952–1961. Vol. 1: *La genèse du mythe.* Vol. 2: *La structure du mythe.* Vol. 3: *L'Année du centenaire.*

Étiemble, René, and Y. Glauclere. *Rimbaud.* Paris, 1936. Reprinted 1950.

Fondane, Benjamin. *Rimbaud le voyou.* Paris, 1933.

Fowlie, Wallace. *Climate of Violence: The French Literary Tradition from Baudelaire to the Present.* New York, 1976.

————. *Rimbaud: The Myth of Childhood.* London, 1946.

Frohock, W. M. *Rimbaud's Poetic Practice.* Cambridge, 1963.

Gengoux, J. *La symbolique de Rimbaud.* Paris, 1947.

————. *La pensée poétique de Rimbaud.* Paris, 1950.

Gilman, Margaret. *The Idea of Poetry in France.* Cambridge, 1958.

Godchot, Col. *La voyance de Rimbaud.* Paris, 1934.

Hackett, C. A. *Rimbaud l'enfant.* Paris, 1949.

————. *Autour de Rimbaud.* Paris, 1967.

————. *Rimbaud: A Critical Introduction.* Cambridge, 1981.

Hobsbawm, Eric. *The Age of Capital, 1848–1875.* London, 1975.

Houston, J. P. *The Design of Rimbaud's Poetry.* New Haven, Conn., 1963.

Izambard, Georges. *Rimbaud tel que je l'ai connu.* Paris, 1946.

Kahn, Gustave. *Symbolistes et décadents.* Paris, 1902.

————. *Les origines du symbolisme.* Paris, 1936.

Kittang, A. *Discours et jeu: Essai d'analyse des textes d'Arthur Rimbaud.* Oslo and Grenoble, 1975.

Macé, Gérard. *Ex libris: Nerval, Corbière, Rimbaud, Mallarmé, Segalen.* Paris, 1980.

Mallarmé, Stéphane. *Oeuvres complètes.* Edited by

Henri Mondor and G. Jean-Aubry. Paris, 1945. Reprinted 1956.

Matarasso, Henri, and Pierre Petitfils. *Vie de Arthur Rimbaud.* Paris, 1962.

Maurras, Charles. *Barbarie et poésie.* Paris, 1925.

Michaud, Guy, ed. *La doctrine symboliste.* Paris, 1947. Excerpts from original writings of the symbolists.

————. *Le message poétique du symbolisme.* Paris, 1947.

Miller, Henry. *The Time of the Assassins.* New York, 1956.

Morrissette, Bruce. *The Great Rimbaud Forgery.* St. Louis, 1956.

Mouquet, Jules, ed. *Rimbaud raconté par Paul Verlaine.* Paris, 1934.

Noulet, Émilie. *Le premier visage de Rimbaud.* Brussels, 1953.

Peschel, Enid Rhodes. *Flux and Reflux: Ambivalence in the Poems of Arthur Rimbaud.* Geneva, 1977.

Plessen, J. *Promenade et poésie: L'Expérience de la marche et du mouvement dans l'oeuvre de Rimbaud.* The Hague and Paris, 1967.

Pound, Ezra. *Make It New.* New Haven, Conn., 1935.

Quennell, Peter. *Baudelaire and the Symbolists: Five Essays.* London, 1929.

Raymond, Marcel. *From Baudelaire to Surrealism.* London, 1957.

Richard, Noel. *A l'aube du symbolisme; hydropathes, fumistes et décadents.* Paris, 1961.

Rivière, Jacques. *Rimbaud.* Paris, 1930. Reprinted 1977.

————. *Rimbaud. Dossier, 1901–1925.* Paris, 1977.

Ruff, M. *Rimbaud.* Paris, 1968.

Starkie, Enid. *Rimbaud.* London, 1961.

Symons, Arthur. *The Symbolist Movement in Literature.* New York, 1919.

Verlaine, Paul. *Rimbaud raconté par Paul Verlaine.* Paris, 1934.

Wilson, Edmund. *Axel's Castle: A Study in the Imaginative Literature of 1870–1930.* New York, 1969.

Wing, Nathaniel. *Present Appearances: Aspects of Poetic Structure in Rimbaud's "Illuminations."* University, Miss., 1974.

BIBLIOGRAPHIES

Étiemble, René. *Le mythe de Rimbaud.* Vol. 1: *La genèse du mythe.* Paris, 1954. Includes bibliography.

Matarasso, H., and P. Petitfils. *Album Rimbaud.* Paris, 1967.

Petitfils, P. *L'Oeuvre et le visage d'Arthur Rimbaud: Essai de bibliographie et d'iconographie.* Paris, 1949.

Bernard, Suzanne. "État présent des études sur Rimbaud." *L'Information littéraire* 2–3 (1962).

ERIC BURNS

GIOVANNI PASCOLI
(1855–1912)

ROM HIS EARLIEST publications, Giovanni Pascoli succeeded as a popular poet in Italy. His striking treatment of scenes and sounds from the Italian countryside and his autobiographical family tragedy won him a wide if not always discriminating audience. Only in the last thirty years has the dust begun to settle from the critical polemics waged over Pascoli's succession of lyric collections; and he has emerged as the undisputed father of a major line of twentieth-century lyrics.

This change in critical opinion derives partly from a more widespread change in aesthetic perspective—from a basically classical and, thanks to Benedetto Croce, idealistic view of artistic representation, with its insistence that precise poetic intuitions fuse with images most obviously apt to express them, to a new awareness of the fragmentary, uncertain quality of human consciousness and a new interest in language itself as a source of meaning. Recent poets and critics have been struck by the way Pascoli's lyrics conjure a chain of sensuous images out of a lexicon with none of the usual respect for proper "levels" of language—he is as apt to enlist a word from local dialect as from classical tradition. They have marveled at his ability to set a haunting, almost metaphysical background behind precise, often realistic, images. They have admitted that although Pascoli's texts often offer little traditional coherence, they nonetheless excite the mind powerfully, as so many sparks

shot from a single flame. But as one might expect, these qualities gained widespread acclaim in Italian criticism only after the lessons of the symbolists, surrealists, and futurists had been fully learned; after the classical measure had been cataloged as just one among many, and a different set of critical standards had emerged to judge a text according to its calculated revolt against a previous tradition rather than its adherence to it.

The earliest reviews of Pascoli's poetry often stumbled against a range of diction more problematic than that of his contemporaries. Domenico Gnoli, for instance, complained in an 1897 review of *Poemetti* in *L'Italia* that he found everywhere "the preoccupations of someone who fears to make himself understood, of one who has a horror of the beaten path." But the most intransigent and most powerful criticism of Pascoli's work came from Benedetto Croce, who spoke of him as a "little great poet," and who formulated the familiar *odi et amo* (love–hate) motif that has dogged several decades of Pascoli criticism. In an essay (20 January 1906) he writes: "I read some of the most celebrated poems of Giovanni Pascoli, and I get a strange impression. Do I like them? Do I dislike them? Yes, no: I don't know. . . . No matter how often I reread, the strange perplexity recurs." In a series of articles, Croce taxes Pascoli with mixing rhetoric and lyric, with concentrating on realistic detail to the detriment of lyric intuition, and with employing a verse structure that more often than not works against the grain of the poetic sentiments it is meant to express. Above all, Croce and his followers perceived in Pascoli an anticlassicist, the source of the decadent and futurist schools they heartily disliked for political as well as aesthetic reasons.

If critical opinion constrained by the methodological limits of Croce's work or of classicism in general was often hostile to Pascoli, important voices outside official channels—such as Giosue Carducci and Gabriele D'Annunzio—were enthusiastic, as was Renato Serra, who in a justly famous essay early described what he called the ''pure music'' of Pascoli's poetry. But the tide of criticism did not turn fully in Pascoli's favor until the 1950's, after Gianfranco Contini wrote a groundbreaking essay on the language of Pascoli, exploring his formal and structural innovations with heightened insight. In a tightening focus on his language and a broadened awareness of his historical position, recent critics have asserted Pascoli's revolutionary power, acclaimed his drive against the grain of Italian classicism, and explored his fascination with what modern linguistics calls the signifier (the sound image rather than the concept conveyed by a given word). Pascoli has, in short, become the herald of Italian—and, for some, even European—modernism. Ottavio Giannangeli discusses his experiments with space and time; Giacomo Debenedetti has categorized Pascoli's effects as approaching those of impressionism; and Gian Luigi Beccaria has written of his poetics of the signifier. Comparisons tie Pascoli's literary ''revolution'' to those of Paul Verlaine, Stéphane Mallarmé, and Edgar Allan Poe. To write about Pascoli today is to write as much about the problems of the modern lyric as about the poet himself.

Pascoli has perhaps been distorted to serve this larger myth of modernism, though it is equally true that earlier critics often treated him harshly. The present is probably a favorable moment for an informed assessment. The past thirty years have provided the essential apparatus and the certainty that, no matter what polemics surrounded it before, Pascoli's poetry has endured and has provided a leavening influence on generations of modern poets.

LIFE

Pascoli was born on the last day of 1855 in San Mauro, now renamed San Mauro Pascoli, in Romagna. His father, Ruggiero, was known for miles around as the honest and industrious administrator of a large feudal holding; his mother, Caterina, was totally devoted to the happiness of her ten children. Unfortunately, Pascoli was to spend only a few years in the warmth and protection of his family circle, but his memories of his parents and siblings were later an important source of poetic inspiration. As we shall see, they were memories made particularly precious by a series of painful misfortunes.

Pascoli received his earliest education from a maternal cousin and, somewhat later, from the public school in Savignano, a nearby town. When he was seven, his father took him—along with his two older brothers—to the well-respected Collegio Raffaello at Urbino. For five peaceful years, Pascoli studied under the guidance of his teachers, excelling in all his subjects. Summers and vacations were spent at home; at the end of the school term, the boys always eagerly awaited the sound of their father's carriage coming to take them back to their large and loving family.

At the age of twelve, an event occurred that completely altered Pascoli's life. His father was returning to his family from official business at the nearby town of Cesena when he was shot and killed. Then, within the same year, Pascoli's older sister died of typhus and his mother died too, of heart failure. Not long afterward, financial problems put an end to Pascoli's schooling at the collegio, but before he left he was also to lose his brother and favorite childhood companion, Luigi, who died, at only seventeen, of spinal meningitis.

For a few years the Pascoli orphans lived under the compassionate eyes of the oldest brother, Giacomo; thanks to his care and encouragement, Pascoli managed to finish his studies at secondary schools in Rimini, Florence, and finally Cesena in 1873. Then, on the advice of his "little father," Giacomo, Pascoli entered a competition for scholarships offered by the University of Bologna. In the essay, "Ricordi di un vecchio scolaro" (Memoirs of an Old Pupil), Pascoli later recalled the examination committee, which included, among others, the impressive poet Giosue Carducci. At the moment the scholarships were announced, Pascoli recounted:

> The examiners were all there: the proud head of the poet was turned to the side, as if indifferent. . . . The first name sounded in the silence of the room. . . . It was his [Pascoli's]. At that moment, the poor boy saw a smile flash. Yes, the poet's face had lighted with a smile soon extinguished.

Pascoli's university studies began auspiciously but were unexpectedly interrupted in his second year, when misfortune struck again: Giacomo died of typhus, leaving Giovanni, now the oldest son, responsible for what was left of the Pascoli family. In this darkest, most tumultuous moment of his life, Pascoli rebelled. No doubt he was reacting to the dire injustice of his family's fate, and with reason could blame destiny itself. But in this case there was more to offend his sensibilities: the identity of his father's assassin was widely known by the townspeople and by the Pascolis themselves, but he had never been apprehended and punished. All of the poet's efforts to forward the cause of justice were repelled by the police, who evidently had political motives for ignoring the case. Later in Pascoli's career the personal experience of evil and social injustice led him to a humanitarian socialism and a solemn attentiveness to the suffering of the poor and the innocent. But at the age of twenty-four, Pascoli let his indignation take an activist turn. He joined the anarchist movement then gaining adherents in Romagna and contributed "La morte del ricco" (The Death of the Rich Man) to *Il nettuno,* a revolutionary journal.

This period of defiance came to an abrupt halt in 1879, when Pascoli was arrested at an anarchist demonstration; he was imprisoned for more than three months before being acquitted for lack of evidence. During these months he had much opportunity to ruminate—both on his tragic past and his future possibilities. As he tells us in one of his poems, "La voce" (The Voice), he seriously considered suicide, but turned finally in a more fruitful direction. No doubt he realized that the often violent anarchist position was less congenial to his nature than a more tolerant, humanitarian viewpoint—a political commitment associated with the socialists, but without their Marxist insistence on class conflict. He became aware too that he could have some effect on others through his gifts as a teacher and writer. Pascoli determined to return to school, finish his degree, begin an academic career, and write.

In the first period of Pascoli's life, poetry was not a major concern, although he published several poems in its course. Only in the years around 1880, after the critical months spent in prison, did he begin to compose the lyrics that would eventually find their place in his first major book. Poems of the simple life in Romagna, reminiscences of his childhood, poems about the poet's role, these small but secure affinities offered some sort of anchor for his storm-tossed life.

When Pascoli received his Doctor of Letters degree in 1882, he was sent to teach Latin and Greek in secondary schools, first at Matera, later in Massa and Livorno. Not long after, he called his two younger sisters, Ida and Maria, from the convent to which they had been sent after their mother's death, and set up a household with them, a mere remnant of the large and happy family that haunted Pascoli's imagination, but nevertheless an effort to retrieve something of its atmosphere. The poems Pascoli wrote during these years appeared first in journals, but in 1891 a first edition of *Myricae* (Tamarisks) was published. The title is drawn from Vergil's description of his first songs, and a passage from the beginning of the Fourth Eclogue serves as an epigraph: "Arbusta iuvant humilesque myricae" (saplings and humble tamarisks are pleasing).

The motto suggests both the theme of the poems and the classical inspiration that informed these and literally all of Pascoli's Italian writings. Not only was he trained as a classical scholar, teaching Greek and Latin texts to his young students, he was also expert at composing in Latin and wrote it every bit as well as his native Italian. In fact, shortly after *Myricae* was published, Pascoli distinguished himself by winning the Hoeufft medal for Latin poetry from the Royal Academy of Amsterdam with his ode "Veianius," a triumph he would repeat twelve more times in the course of his life.

Honors and new friendships—such as those with the critic Adolfo De Bosis and the poet Gabriele D'Annunzio—followed in the wake of these publications, as did an appointment in 1895 as assistant professor of classics at the University of Bologna. In these years, after the marriage of Ida, Pascoli and Maria were able to secure a new home in the serene, pastoral surroundings of Barga. He rented and later purchased what would be known in his poetry simply as Castelvecchio. It was a lovely villa surrounded by gardens, a beautiful retreat in which memories could be cultivated and country life observed. In his study, Pascoli placed three desks: one for his work in Italian poetry, one for his Latin poetry, and one for his Dante criticism. These three desks correspond to the three fields to which Pascoli contributed so richly in the years to come.

The Italian poems *Canti di Castelvecchio* (Songs of Castelvecchio, 1903) testify to the inward reach of memory, as Pascoli sought, with the help of Maria, to relive and to some degree explain the tragic events that haunted his past. More optimistic are the *Poemetti* (Short Narrative Poems, 1897), reflecting in a different way the humble life at Castelvecchio. This collection of poems, later expanded into the *Primi poemetti* (First Short Narrative Poems, 1904) and *Nuovi poemetti* (New Short Narrative Poems, 1909), is georgic in nature, a meditation on country life and the peasants with whom Pascoli always felt at ease and whose colorful language he loved. Not only did Castelvecchio inspire his Italian works, it also offered themes for his Latin poetry, especially for "Castanea" (The Chestnut).

The muse that had been muffled and intermittent in Pascoli's early life could not be silenced now. In fact, the assignment to Bologna, though it certainly meant a new, more distinguished phase in Pascoli's career, did not wholly please him, worried as he was that he would not have enough time for writing. He was already involved in other projects: two anthologies of Latin poetry, *Lyra* (Lyric Poetry, 1895) and *Epos* (Epic Poetry, 1897); a continuation of his collection *Myricae;* and the first of the three book-length studies of Dante that would occupy a central place in his critical work.

Pascoli's academic career was a restless one. In the years between 1879 and 1903, he moved from Bologna to Messina, then dissatisfied, to Pisa. These years were marred by difficult relations with his colleagues and by severe criticism of both his poetry and his Dante studies, but his productivity continued unabated. Always, Castelvecchio remained "home," the villa, garden, and vistas shared with Maria and, from time to time, with friends and colleagues. It was here he spent his holidays and accomplished most of his writing. Other lyrics, including the collection *Poemi conviviali* (Convivial Poems, 1904), followed in quick succession, as did his controversial books on Dante.

Of the various moves Pascoli made from

one university to another, the last was by far the most significant. In December 1904, when Carducci retired from the chair of Italian Literature at the University of Bologna, students and professors clamored for Pascoli to replace him. Since this popular demand was as much as to say that Pascoli was next in line as Italy's greatest poet, it is little wonder that he received the call to Bologna with a mixture of joy and trepidation. Was he worthy of the post? Could he satisfy the high expectations that would greet him? More out of a sense of duty than of ambition—duty to his family, to his beginnings in Romagna, to those who remembered the Pascoli family—he decided to go. So in 1905 he returned in triumph to the university he had left as an obscure youth many years before.

While there Pascoli published his last works—among them the *Odi e inni* (Odes and Hymns, 1906) and *Poemi italici* (Italian Poems, 1911). Political events also drew his attention. He wrote his famous discourse, "La grande proletaria si è mossa" (The Great Proletariat Has Stirred), in which he honored the dead and wounded of the Italo-Turkish War, and he sent a poem called "La notte di Natale" (Christmas Night) to the Italian soldiers and marines fighting in Tripoli. His best Latin poem, "Thallusa" (Tallusa), belongs to these final years, as well as a number of Italian political poems, including the beginnings of the posthumously published *Poemi del Risorgimento* (Poems of the Risorgimento, 1913).

From 1908 on, Pascoli's health began to fail. A condition first diagnosed in 1911 as cirrhosis of the liver was in time identified as a cancer of the stomach. Although neither Pascoli nor his sister knew until the very end that his condition was fatal, his suffering soon caused him to discontinue work. In 1912 his doctors decided to move him from Castelvecchio to Bologna, where he could receive better medical attention. This journey, first by automobile, then by train, was crowded with well-wishers at every stop, giving the tormented and suffering poet a loving, admiring farewell.

After less than a month in Bologna, he died. The date was 6 April 1912. The poet was fifty-six years old, the same age as Dante at his death.

WORDS AND THINGS

The poetry that made Pascoli famous sets before the reader's eyes images of simple things from country life. Rejecting the illustrious world of aristocratic figures, of abstract metaphysical themes, and even of great historical subjects, Pascoli kept his lyrics close to home and down to earth (as he himself suggests in his titles). The trees, bushes, and plants native to Romagna, brief sketches of domestic life—the frugal country meal, the child's lullaby—provide Pascoli's major themes. This choice of subject matter was itself a step away from the Italian lyric tradition that had begun with Petrarch and culminated in the works of Giacomo Leopardi and Pascoli's own teacher, Carducci. True, by turning to humble things Pascoli took up some of the lessons inherent in the prose of Alessandro Manzoni, and of the young Giovanni Verga, then writing his early works. And Charles Baudelaire in France had certainly rejected the rhetorical and illustrious in *Les fleurs du mal* (1857). But nothing matching the intensity of Pascoli's feeling for individual elements of nature had yet emerged in the Italian lyric or, perhaps, in the lyric of any other country.

But if Pascoli had merely given the world an accomplished body of nature poetry, it is doubtful whether his work would have elicited as much interest as it has in the twentieth century. There is another side to his verse that lends it more depth than brilliance and leads critics to claim it for modernism. Pascoli's simple scenes, so striking in their graphic detail, stand out against a background filled with wonder, complexity, sometimes even fear. Take, for instance, the poem "Nebbia" ("Fog"):

Nascondi le cose lontane,
tu nebbia impalpabile e scialba,
tu fumo che ancora rampolli,
   su l'alba,
da' lampi notturni e da' crolli
   d'aeree frane!

Nascondi le cose lontane,
nascondimi quello ch'è morto!
Ch'io veda soltanto la siepe
   dell'orto,
la mura ch'ha piene le crepe
   di valerïane.

Nascondi le cose lontane:
le cose son ebbre di pianto!
Ch'io veda i due peschi, i due meli,
   soltanto,
che dànno i soavi lor mieli
   pel nero mio pane.

Nascondi le cose lontane
che vogliono ch'ami e che vada!
Ch'io veda là solo quel bianco
   di strada,
che un giorno ho da fare tra stanco
   don don di capane . . .

Nascondi le cose lontane,
nascondile, involale al volo
del cuore! Ch'io veda il cipresso
   là, solo,
qui, solo quest'orto, cui presso
   sonnecchia il mio cane.

Hide the faraway things,
you impalpable, pale fog,
you vapor that still springs up
   with the dawn,
from night's flashing lights and from the
   fall of airy landslides!

Hide the faraway things,
hide from me what is dead!
That I may see only the
   garden hedge,
the wall that has its cracks
   filled with valerian bloom.

Hide the faraway things:
the things are drunk with tears!
So I see only two peach trees,
   two apple trees,
that give their sweet honeys
   for my crust of bread.

Hide the faraway things
that want me to love and roam!
So I see only that white of
   the road there
that I must one day take midst a tired
   dong dong of tolling bells . . .

Hide the faraway things,
hide them, steal them from the flight
of my heart! So I see the cypress
   only, there,
and here, only this garden, near which
   my dog lies dozing.

Allowing the immediate scene—with its hedge and wall, its peach, apple, and cypress trees—to float, suspended in what might be called a metaphysical space, Pascoli here presents a discomfiting, mysterious glimpse of life that might well be considered emblematic of his work.

This technique can be traced in part to the intellectual climate of the time. Unlike Manzoni, who wrote some fifty years earlier, Pascoli and his contemporaries were no longer sustained by the certainties of religion and a belief in scientific laws of history. Religious questioning was the order of the day and scientific positivism had showed its limits. In the wake of thinkers such as Herbert Spencer, Charles Darwin, and Henri Bergson, it was difficult to conceive of certainty of any sort. Rather than an eternal law, only an eternal questioning seemed to lie behind the visible world. Pascoli at times addresses these questions directly (as in the poem, "Alla cometa di Haley" [To Haley's Comet, 1910]), but more frequently he raises them indirectly, through the diffuse and uncertain background of the scenes he depicts.

Closely related to this general concern is the more personal, existential mystery that Pascoli had experienced so deeply in his youth—the sorrow and perplexity arising from the shadow of death and human suffering. Why does death strike? How does it come? What, if anything, is there beyond life—perhaps only memories of it? What, in the light of death, homelessness, poverty, can make for happiness or at least for serenity? It is this human mystery that suffuses so many of Pascoli's arresting images, such as the portrait of two young cousins, one of whom dies, in "I due cugini" (The Two Cousins, 1896) and the recollection of his family's dislocation after his father's death, in "Il nido di 'farlotti'" (The Nest of "Shrikes," 1903).

Although most critics would agree that it is next to impossible to penetrate fully the sense of mystery at the heart of Pascoli's verse, the techniques most frequently used to create it—depersonalization, "the objective correlative," the fragment—are extremely familiar to students of twentieth-century verse. More than any previous Italian poetry, Pascoli's seems to speak through the voice of things and creatures observed. Imagery is often "objective," presenting objects directly rather than filtering them through an authorial point of view. In this world of objects, the human self becomes merely one thing among others, or resolves its emotional charge into what T. S. Eliot later called the objective correlative, describing it in "Hamlet and His Problems" as a "set of objects, a situation, a chain of events" that acts as the formula of an emotion, rather than the direct expression of it.

It is easy to see how a poetry such as this can be troubling, especially when a literary tradition is unprepared for it. Without a clear point of reference in the human *io*—the I or self—our sense of history dissolves, as does the security of customary hierarchies that subject objects to people, and inanimate to animate objects. Add to this Pascoli's aptitude for illuminating the humble detail through short, often apparently fragmentary, poems. At times, individual lyrics seem to exceed their boundaries, to merge into some great open book of verse. Devices for achieving these effects are complex. Perhaps the best way of coming to grips with them is briefly to take the microscopic approach so common in contemporary criticism. Gianfranco Contini, for instance, rightly insists on Pascoli's lexical "democracy," his tendency to include the names of all things in his vocabulary, regardless of their "place" in the traditional literary scheme. In this, Pascoli not only takes a full step away from the Italian lyric tradition; he goes so far as to challenge the Italian language as an institution. He integrates words from specialized languages—above all from Italian dialects—and frequently heightens the specificity of his imagery through the use of proper names.

It is true that the technique reaches back at least to Dante, and Pascoli had several immediate precursors versed in its use. His contemporary D'Annunzio, for instance, was expert at enriching the usual Italian vocabulary with the rare word, the exotic place name. Moreover, the French symbolists (whom Pascoli probably did not know, or at least not in any detail) had done something of the same a few years before. Mallarmé's "Je t'apporte l'enfant d'une nuit d'Idumée!" (I Bring You the Child of an Idumean Night) from "Don du poeme" ("Gift of the Poem") does not seem to be too different in spirit. In fact, what makes Pascoli unique is not so much linguistic exoticism as his tendency to combine esoteric vocabulary with words drawn from a sphere that linguists would classify as pregrammatical (Contini), perhaps even prelinguistic. The onomatopoeia so startling to Pascoli's early critics belongs in this category. In "Ov'è" ("Where?"), for instance, Pascoli imitates the cry of a baby; in other poems, such as "Dialogo" (Dialogue) and "L'Usignolo e i suoi rivali" (The Nightingale and His Rivals), the sounds of birds. Croce spoke harshly of these phonic effects. But in fact it is this effort to suppress the barrier between grammaticality and the evocativeness of language that announces the modernity of Pascoli's work and lends it much of its complexity. It stands behind the experience of the dadaists and surrealists, as well as their predecessors, the futurists, whose major figure, Filippo Tommaso Marinetti, was, even as a young poet, eager to approve and imitate Pascoli's innovations.

Through stylistic techniques such as these, Pascoli achieved one of the effects most sought out by modern poetry and most clearly articulated by Paul Valéry in his 1939 lecture "Poetry and Abstract Thought." He developed what Valéry recognized as a distinctive poetic language within the linguistic institution. The arbitrary connections between words and things, which grow with language as a social institution, are transcended in the intentional musicality of a poem, so that there develops a primordial, seemingly "natural" link between text and what it represents.

In a poetic sphere like this, in which words seem to take on a profound and revolutionary contact with things themselves, individual images strike the eye and the ear with a specificity unknown to previous generations of Italian poets. By naming with new names, by sounding evocative effects, Pascoli brought words into new prominence and, with the words, the humble things they evoke.

But Pascoli does not simply strike the reader with the peculiar presence of his imagery. He juxtaposes lexical elements in a syntax that deftly disorients and fragments. In the process, he effectively opens these images to poetic mystery. Situated in a syntax that avoids the usual logical development of thought in favor of looser forms, Pascoli's cinematic precision becomes a compendium of effects to break down the literary walls responsible for the "purity" associated with classical art. It brings with it instead a catalog of uncertainties.

One of Pascoli's preferred methods simply abandons the complex, hypotactic sentence, with its clear hierarchization of thought and its ultimate subjection to a governing "io" or "I." In its place, he offers paratactic structures that present "things" in all their power, as if freed from the judgment of a speaking self and from the logical certainty that the human element, through its subordinating effects of syntax, tacitly ascribes to the world. Consider, for instance, "Temporale" ("Thunderstorm"):

> *Un bubbolìo lontano . . .*
>
> *Rosseggia l'orizzonte,*
> *come affocato, a mare;*
> *nero di pece, a monte,*
> *stracci di nubi chiare:*
> *tra il nero un casolare:*
> *un'ala di gabbiano.*

In the distance the thunder's rumbling . . .

The horizon shows red,
as if afire, on the sea,
pitch black, on the mountain,
vestiges of light clouds:
mid the black a farmhouse:
a sea gull's wing.

Far from the Ciceronian period so common in the Italian lyric, Pascoli's text develops as a series of fragments. Suppressing the logical "when . . . then" structure of the sentence, Pascoli uses typography to set the initial clause aside, indicating through suspension points and a blank space that results are to follow. When the phrases of the result clause appear, they depend as so many observable fragments from the single verb of line 2 (*rosseggia*, shows red). This strategy imitates with wondrous ease human perception as it glances at a scene briefly lit by lightning, quickly gathering in particulars before darkness closes in on it again. But it must be admitted that the technique is about as comforting as a lightning bolt for those born and bred in the strict classical, or even romantic, canon. The poem halts and starts, its string of noun phrases having no explanation but those the reader's mind can provide as he or she looks back retrospectively on the whole.

Of course, what often replaces logical continuities in Pascoli's poetry is sound. Here, the rhyme scheme (*abcbcca*) is particularly effective in drawing images together, soldering fragments into phonic unities. Rhymes manage to remind us that the six seven-syllable lines belong very firmly with the opening eight-syllable line. As the final rhyme ties the last line back to the first, its image completes the poet's perceptions.

Through just such arresting plays of language, repeated in a large number of texts, Pascoli creates the paradoxical precision and mystery that combine in his verse as complementary facets of a single whole. It is a poetry that in fact has little like it in the preceding Italian tradition. But it does have some theoretical bases in a poetics that Pascoli presented through the image of *il fanciullino,* the little child.

POETICS OF "IL FANCIULLINO"

Efforts to categorize the spirit of Pascoli's work by associating it with a specific late-nineteenth-century or postromantic school—be it decadence, naturalism, symbolism, or impressionism—invariably fail. Pascoli's verse is decadent in its choice of melancholy themes, naturalist in its eye for the small, seemingly ordinary detail, symbolist in its reliance on sound and mystery, and impressionist in its preference for fragmentary structures. But as a whole, his work transcends any single school, Italian or European. Built on romantic bases, it extends its reach in several distinctly modern directions. And his theory of poetry, presented through the image of *il fanciullino* offers some insight into a poetry that more than once has been called the most difficult in the Italian language. The theory, like the concrete poetics of his lyrics, simply brings together a number of contrasting tendencies.

In his most famous essay (the first chapters of which were published in 1897 and the entire essay in 1903), entitled, precisely, "Il fanciullino," Pascoli flatly renounces traditional rhetoric and conventional themes in favor of a spontaneous "pure poetry" calculated to bring the world rather than the poet into close focus. The artist ought to be a mere medium through which a world is newly spoken. And the poetry he writes belongs to no specific time and place, but rather addresses that primitive, childlike capacity for joy, wonder, and vision that, though frequently hidden under the mantle of material concerns and the sheer weight of adult responsibility, belongs to all peoples of all ages.

But Pascoli does not simply announce a new spontaneity. He builds his theory as a poet would, drawing out to the fullest the central analogy between childhood and poetry, poet and child. A little child—like the poet, alive to the childlike voice within him—can see, hear, and feel things that escape the notice of the ordinary adult, and can convey perceptions with a directness and simplicity that bring objects to the mind's eye with startling clarity. The little child is "still in the presence of a new world and in order to signify it uses the new word." Precisely this vision and this search for the new word stand behind Pascoli's poetry, whose often startling language derives from the intense effort to reproduce a fresh, literarily innocent contact with life. In fact, though the sort of intuition Pascoli sought would never have appealed to Croce's taste, since it rested ultimately on a belief in objective things rather than on the "idea," it is indeed ironic that the great critic never realized how much Pascoli's work prefigured his own conclusions about intuition, expression, and the difference between poetry and oratory.

The poet's task, as Pascoli conceived it, could never be easy; he is only too aware that the direct attention to detail he prizes is particularly difficult to achieve in a tradition like the Italian, which always sets before it revered models from the past. Too often poets lapse into traditional, generic terms that lack the spontaneity and precision Pascoli thought necessary to poetry. Even writers whom Pascoli admired, such as Leopardi, often fall away from the purest poetry. Pascoli complained at one point that Leopardi's famous phrase "un mazzolin di rose e di viole" (a small bouquet of roses and violets) is nothing but an old trope meaning simply "flowers." Why fall into dead metaphors to describe a living world? Pascoli asks. Why not instead name precisely what one sees and in this act revivify it? This, according to Pascoli, is the poet's true mission.

To judge by all this, one might think that Pascoli's poetics of "Il fanciullino" could support only a very naturalistic sort of verse. In fact, both his theory and the concrete poetics worked out in his poems are of a piece: if the vision of the *fanciullino* is precise and fresh, it is also filled with wonder at the world and its ultimate mystery. Although the adult may be hardened to life, too committed to the well-trodden path of responsibilities to accord the world any sense of the marvelous, Pascoli reminds us that a child—and the childlike voice in every poet—sees mystery everywhere. The little child is

> he who fears the dark, because he sees things there or believes he does; he who dreams in broad daylight or who seems to do so, remembering things he's never seen; he who speaks to the beasts, to the trees, to the stones, to the clouds, to the stars; he who peoples the shadows with phantasms and the sky with gods.

It is just such mystery that pervades the true poet's work.

According to Pascoli, it haunts the epic as well as the lyric poem. Even Homer's great sagas grew from the blind seer's ability to hear and record a child's marveling voice. And it is the fascination with the mystery of human existence that explains for Pascoli one of the major appeals of the *Divina commedia.* In a short footnote to "Il fanciullino" that tells as much about Pascoli's poetry as about his life-long involvement with Dante, Pascoli explains the eternal fascination of Dante's great epic: "Nothing is more proper to the childhood of our soul than the contemplation of the invisible, the journey through mystery, the conversing, weeping, the getting angry and rejoicing with the dead." Thus joining the

child's fresh vision with his underlying sense of wonder, Pascoli uses the persona of the child–poet to describe his own aspirations with great liveliness and candor.

It is not unlikely that Pascoli's very choice of the image of childhood is directly related to his biography. Critics of a psychoanalytic bent in fact find Pascoli's case a perfect example of psychic regression. According to this reading, Pascoli chose the image of the child to represent the poet for the same reasons that he chose to avoid the most typical adult experiences in favor of a protected life in a country villa. Here was a man who wrote much of his poetry about the family yet never founded one himself, who turned away from conjugal ties to reestablish a remnant of his childhood home with his sister. Here too was a man of great goodness, often fired with ideas of social justice, who in fact retired from the real world and from active political commitment to cultivate his flowers and his poems in an idyllic country retreat.

Though there may be truth to these speculations, Pascoli surely had literary as well as biographical reasons to choose the motif of the child. The image is standard in romantic literature. Novalis had taken the persona of the child in his own discussions of poetry and at least one critic, Alfredo Galletti, names Novalis as one of Pascoli's likely sources. But, as Albert Valentin points out, Pascoli did not have to venture beyond his own native tradition. Leopardi himself spoke in *Scritti vari inediti* of true poetry as intuition, one depending on a childlike ability to see the world anew:

> What the ancients were, we have all been, and what the world was for several centuries, we have been for several years; it is when we were children and took part in this ignorance and these fears and these joys and these beliefs and this limitless activity of the imagination . . .

Though Leopardi doubtless influenced Pascoli's poetics, he never made the image of the child the cornerstone of his own poetics. Nor did he develop its possibilities in the same way as Pascoli. Whereas Leopardi paints the poet's childlike sensitivity in order to glorify the poet, Pascoli describes the child–poet's intuiting voice without, however, celebrating it. Like Victor Hugo before him, who speaks of the poet as a *crystal sonore*, reflecting the things of the world itself, Pascoli favors a poetry that resonates with the world around it. His attempt to make his poetry itself objective lends the romantic image of the "fanciullino" a distinctly modern cast.

Long before T. S. Eliot spoke of the objective correlative, Pascoli's "Il fanciullino" was urging the poet's essential self-renunciation. The poet, Pascoli writes, has no other goal than to "melt back into the nature from which he came, leaving in it an accent, a ray, a new, eternal 'throb' of his own." Seeing, hearing, and naming constitute the poet's task, and to accomplish it he must continually deny his egotistical desires, which subtract from what he can say rather than add to it. Instead of offering the world a portrait of his own richness of language, he must put egoism aside to portray the world.

Although one or two of the turn-of-the-century schools with which Pascoli has been associated might lay claim to an objective poetry, and though as many might speak of poetry's source in intuition, few have joined these elements into a single whole, and none through the persona of the child. There is another way, too, in which Pascoli's poetics point to his uniqueness. More than most who espoused an objective poetry, and more than those others who glorified the poet's intuition, Pascoli claims a social purpose for poetry. Not that he meant for poetry to function as a political or historical statement. On the contrary. Poetry ought simply to awaken us to the world, allow us to consider it anew. Though the task seems small, the results can be surprisingly grand. By making us look again at our surroundings and find beauty in the everyday, poetry ultimately teaches comfort and contentment. Viewed this way, poetry is an absolute necessity for modern man. It is a saving gesture of generosity in a world increasingly busy, increasingly filled with chronic discontent.

To describe pure poetry's social function, Pascoli draws on a variety of images and examples. Equating the good with the poetic, the bad with the unpoetic, he speaks, for instance, of Vergil's rejection of slavery as a proper theme for poetry. At another point, he employs a standard romantic image for poetry, the burning lamp. But unlike the earlier romantics, who stressed the lamp's intrinsic fire, Pascoli emphasizes its power to shed light for others. In "La poesia" (Poetry, 1897), an effective distillation of the theme, Pascoli describes a lamp hung in the vestibule for all who live in the house and for those who pass by to see. This is precisely the poet's lamp of pure poetry, shedding its light on all who approach:

> Io sono la lampada ch'arde
> soave!
> nell'ore più tarde,
> nell 'ombra più mesta, più grave
> più buona, o fratello!
>
> Ch'io penda sul capo a fanciulla
> che pensa,
> su madre che prega, su culla
> che piange, su garrula mensa,
> su tacito avello;
>
> lontano risplende l'ardore
> mio casto all'errante che trita
> notturno, piangendo nel cuore,
> la pallida via della vita:
> s'arresta: ma vede il mio raggio,
> che gli arde nell'anima blando:
> riprende l'oscuro vïaggio
> cantando.

> I am the lamp that burns with radiant
> sweetness
> in the latest hours,
> in shadows that are saddest, gravest,
> most good, O my brother!
>
> Whether I hang over a young girl
> who's thinking,

a mother who prays, over the cradle
that cries, over the convivial table,
   over the silent tomb;

my chaste ardent light shines far away
on the wanderer who makes his way
on the pallid roadway of life,
in the night, with tears in his heart.
He stops; but he sees my shining light
that warms his spirit benignly:
now he takes up his dark voyage
   with singing.

MYRICAE

When asked to name Pascoli's most influential work, critics typically point to his first lyric collection, *Myricae*. Certainly it was the critical acclaim garnered in this slowly maturing work that first made Giovanni Pascoli a name to reckon with in Italian literary history. Written during the years that the poet was writing "Il fanciullino," it puts the essay's most important ideas into practice.

Like many lyric collections, *Myricae* grew in stages. First published in 1891 when the poet was thirty-five, it went through four more editions before achieving its final form in 1900. At each phase, Pascoli added poems, some already published, some newly written, and reorganized the whole to better fit the architectural design—and poetic ideal—gradually taking shape in his mind. Given his constant rearrangements of the whole, the actual chronology of the poems yields in importance to thematic and stylistic concerns. But just what are Pascoli's themes? And how do they manifest themselves in this sequence of short, often disjunctive poems?

Beginning with the second edition, Pascoli introduced autobiographical motifs in the collection. Its preface opens with a dedication to his father, Ruggiero: "May these poems remain, may they remain on the tomb of my father!" And the first and final poems reflect autobiographically on the inner lyrics they bracket. The first poem, "Il giorno dei morti" (The Day of the Dead), is a long ode that gives voice both to the poet's dead family and to his own guilt and sorrow. Although this opening might portend a strictly autobiographical series of poems, it actually serves a more far-reaching purpose. It introduces the theme of a poetic redemption of the past, the poet's ability to relive through his words a past now destroyed. In the last poem of the collection, "Ultimo sogno" (The Last Dream), again about the poet's relation to his dead, Pascoli takes up this redemptive theme directly. We see at once that a transformation has occurred. The poet's very choice to write of death has worked an expiation of sorts. Revivifying through poetry those loved ones definitively lost, the poet has liberated himself—at least in part—from the burden of their death.

It is just this inspiration that stands behind *Myricae*, guiding Pascoli's linguistic efforts and determining its characteristic themes: the home, the family—present or, more often, absent in death—the homeland. The poet returns in memory to the past, attempting to recuperate all that time, nature, and human evil have destroyed.

As we might expect, frankly pathetic themes abound. Some poems, with their wrenching descriptions of abandoned, sick, or dying children, perhaps reveal too directly the poet's experience or his efforts to elicit a sympathetic response. "L'Orfano" ("The Orphan"), for instance, is a lovely poem, but its title (changed from "Fides" [Faith] to "Neve" [Snow], then finally to "L'Orfano" in the later editions) plays blatantly on the reader's emotions:

> *Lenta la neve fiocca, fiocca, fiocca.*
> *Senti: una zana dondola pian piano.*
> *Un bimbo piange, il piccol dito in bocca;*
> *canta una vecchia, il mento sulla mano.*
> *La vecchia canta: Intorno al tuo lettino*
> *c'è rose e gigli, tutto un bel giardino.*
> *Nel bel giardino il bimbo s'addormenta.*
> *La neve fiocca lenta, lenta, lenta . . .*

Slowly the snow falls flake by flake by flake.
Listen: a cradle rocks softly, softly.
A baby cries, his wee thumb in his mouth;
an old woman sings, her chin in her hand.
Sings the old woman: Round your little bed
are roses, lilies, all a fine garden.
In the fine garden, baby falls asleep.
The snow falls slowly, slowly, slowly . . .

Yet in spite of occasionally awkward titles or overly melodramatic themes, Pascoli's visions of abandoned childhood often ultimately succeed—as this one does—through their ability to evoke childhood's innocence subtly and profoundly.

But Pascoli does more in this collection than capture the universal emotions of childhood and family life. Memory ranges beyond the home to the surrounding countryside. Plants, trees, birds, farm animals flourish in *Myricae*; and from the first, Pascoli's striking imagery brought him enormous critical acclaim—and controversy. "Sera d'ottobre" ("October Evening"), with its traditional rhyme scheme and brief development is a lyric generally applauded:

> Lungo la strada vedi su la siepe
> ridere a mazzi le vermiglie bacche:
> nei campi arati tornano al presepe
>   tarde le vacche.
>
> Vien per la strada un povero che il lento
> passo tra foglie stridule trascina:
> nei campi intuona una fanciulla al vento:
>   Fiore di spina! . . .

Along the road you see the red berries
laughing in bunches on the hedge:
the cows return slowly to the crib in
          the plowed fields.

Down the road comes a poor fellow whose slow
step drags along through the shrill-sounding
     leaves:
in the fields a girl strikes a song to the wind:
          Flowers with thorns! . . .

"L'Assiuolo" ("The Horn Owl"), experimental through its evocation of the sound of birds, has only more recently acquired a critical following:

> Dov'era la luna? ché il cielo
> notava in un'alba di perla,
> ed ergersi il mandorlo e il melo
> parevano a meglio vederla.
> Venivano soffi di lampi
> da un nero di nubi laggiù;
> veniva una voce dai campi:
> chiù . . .
>
> Le stelle lucevano rare
> tra mezzo alla nebbia di latte:
> sentivo il cullare del mare,
> sentivo un fru fru tra le fratte;
> sentivo nel cuore un sussulto,
> com'eco d'un grido che fu.
> Sonava lontano il singulto:
> chiù . . .
>
> Su tutte le lucide vette
> tremava un sospiro di vento;
> squassavano le cavallette
> finissimi sistri d'argento
> (tintinni a invisibili porte
> che forse non s'aprono più? . . .);
> e c'era quel pianto di morte . . .
> chiù . . .

Where was the moon? the heavens
were swimming in a dawn of pearl,
the almond and the apple trees
seemed to rise to see it better.
Puffs of flashing light were coming
from a distant blackness of fog;
a voice was coming from the fields:
whoo . . .

The stars were shining here and there
in the midst of the clouds of milk:
I heard the rocking of the sea,
I heard a rustling in the scrub;
I felt my heart pound suddenly
as in echo to a cry that was.
From afar the sob was sounding:
whoo . . .

Upon all the shining summits
A breath of wind was trembling;
the grasshoppers moved restlessly
the subtlest of silver sistra
(jingling at invisible doors
that perhaps no longer open? . . .);
and there was that deathly weeping . . .
whoo . . .

Whatever their imagery or variations on a theme, almost all the *Myricae* are, however, short poems like this, fragmentary in quality. Each offers a brief illumination, an almost imagistic insight discontinuous with all else. Deprived of logical or chronological continuities, Pascoli's fragmentary lyrics acquire a compensatory depth. The particulars he revivifies in poetry, giving them thus strange new life, act synecdochically to draw forth entire scenes or states of mind. Language itself, reborn in Pascoli's hands to imitate a childlike perception of the real, acquires a new potency. Such striking glimpses of things, events, persons, even words, offer more than the remarkable immediacy of poetic vision sought out by the poet of "Il fanciullino." They seem to suggest that the fragment is all we, as human beings, can have of the universe. Reality is mutable, continually in motion, and to be embraced only in fleeting particulars. Pascoli at times dramatizes this awareness, as in "Notte dolorosa" (Sorrowful Night), a poem that portrays, in the miniature dimensions of a child's world, nature's constant mutability and ultimate indifference to human suffering:

Si muove il cielo, tacito e lontano:

la terra dorme, e non la vuol destare;
dormono l'acque, i monti, le brughiere.
Ma no, ché sente sospirare il mare,
gemere sente le capanne nere:
v'è dentro un bimbo che non può dormire:
piange; e le stelle passano pian piano.

Heaven moves, silent and far away:

earth sleeps, and he does not want to wake her:
the waters sleep, the mountains, and the heaths.
But no, because he hears the sea whisper
and he hears the black hovels moaning:
inside there lies a child who cannot sleep:
the child cries, and the stars pass slowly by.

For all its uncertainty and sorrow, the image of life Pascoli gives us in *Myricae* does not entirely lack hope. Not only does it bring a forgotten past rushing forward, enhanced by the recognition that language can thus—almost miraculously—confer a second life. It also works isolated fragments into loose architectural frameworks that attempt to redeem the endless parade of particulars through larger, humanly meaningful forms.

Unlike most lyric collections of the romantic period, which range their poems one after another, *Myricae*, the better to simulate the poet's spontaneity, organizes its fragments into sections, each subtitled. From "Dall'alba al tramonto" (From Dawn to Dusk) to "Tristezze" (Sorrows), "L'Ultima passeggiata" (The Last Promenade), "In campagna" (In the Country), "Primavera," (Spring), "Tramonti" ("Sunsets"), and "Alberi e fiori" (Trees and Flowers), Pascoli supports his fragmentary portrait of human existence with larger, if always loose and merely suggestive formal structures. Baudelaire's *Fleurs du mal* readily comes to mind as a lyric collection that attempts something of the same sort.

But the enterprise is not an easy one, and Pascoli's efforts to weave *epos* into *lyros* are only moderately successful. If we strain to do so, we can imagine that *Myricae* figures in all its parts a single mythic day. The introductory section, "Dall'alba al tramonto," and the later "Sunsets" suggest as much. And viewing the whole as a liberally illustrated diary of a day in the countryside lends some coherence to it, as does the awareness that this day offers, symbolically, the aspect of a lifetime, punctuated with the many small voices of nature, great seasonal patterns, and the span from childhood to death. But this structure strains and breaks down at many points, giving place once again to the fragment, the particular. Pascoli's most continuous structures are to be found, if anywhere, in the subsections of the book rather than in its entirety.

Of all these carefully worked poetic cycles, "L'Ultima passeggiata" has most impressed the critics. Renato Serra and Emilio Cecchi have even discovered in it the genesis of Pascoli's most original, most characteristic verse. Though it is impossible in a short essay to consider the section in detail, its structure warrants a brief analysis, since it is in many ways exemplary of Pascoli's early lyric art.

The section in fact originated as a wedding present for a friend and fellow student at Bologna, Severino Ferrari. Published first in 1886 as a series of eight madrigals, it took final shape only after growing to twice that size. Through it all, it maintained its vivid character and underlying melancholy, as much a statement about the poet's exclusion from happiness as a celebration of life.

Here, as frequently in Pascoli's work, the reader is faced with brief insights, signs of a precarious and indeterminate world, but a world full of beauty and contemplated with love. The poet dwells on concrete, expressive particulars that, even in their poetic settings, lose nothing of their impact. If anything, they gain by this placement. Moreover, even though most of the events and sights Pascoli evokes could belong to any epoch, he is not entirely forgetful of his own historical place. The agricultural era is coming to a close and his poetry exhibits a certain historical consciousness when the image of the railway ("La via ferrata") is added to surrounding rural images, almost as if to suggest that the pastoral world of which Pascoli speaks is a dislocated one, one no longer, or not much longer, viable. Part of his past, it will soon be part of Italy's past too. Pascoli does not belabor this motif. But it does intensify the modern sense of anxiety that touches nearly every poem. Gone is the serenity of the past, usurped by a world itself in constant change

and a psyche hopelessly seeking its truth in events already elapsed.

The first poem of "L'Ultima passeggiata," "Arano" ("Plowing"), is a lyrical still life whose precision details simple events. Its separate elements may be dramatically unimportant, yet from the briefly turned images of vegetation, birds, and anonymous laborers derives a sense of unusual expanse and mystery:

> Al campo, dove roggio nel filare
> qualche pampano brilla, e dalla fratte
> sembra la nebbia mattinal fumare,
>
> arano: a lente grida, uno le lente
> vacche spinge; altri semina; un
>   ribatte
> le porche con sua marra paziente;
>
> ché il passero saputo in cor già gode,
> e il tutto spia dai rami irti del moro;
> e il pettirosso: nelle siepi s'ode
> il suo sottil tintinno come d'oro.

In the fields, where a few vine leaves gleam fiery red in a row, where the dawn fog seems to send up its mist from the brush wood,

they are plowing: with slow callings, one man drives
the slow-moving ox; another sows; one turns over again the ridge with his patient hoe:

for the knowing sparrow already rejoices and spies all from the mulberry's bristly branches;
and the robin redbreast: from the hedges one hears
the thin note of his call, almost like gold.

As in so many of his works, the effects here draw primarily on Pascoli's ability to offer brilliant imagery and fracture it by a syntax that breaks the temporal flow, that stymies the reader, slowing the perception and widening the microscopic vision into something much larger, more mysterious. Consider, for instance, the second stanza, where the pace of each line creates an expressive counterpart to syntactic divisions, spacing the three exemplary figures—"uno (one) . . . altri (another) . . . un (one)"—and their actions in the broad and mysterious territory of the reader's imagination. Punctuation marks the end of each laborer's act, while the end of each line halts the flow of clauses midstream. Predicates are stripped to the barest essentials and ranged in a historical present that seems to seal the scene in a static place, stilled for contemplation.

But the genius of "L'Ultima passeggiata" lies not simply in the intensely drawn scene. It derives to some extent from the careful interweaving of its sixteen texts. On the most obvious level, "Plowing" shares with several other poems the common Pascolian motif of "nebbia," or fog. More important, all share the temporal present of the poet's imagination. A happening, an event from the past, stands before the reader's eyes almost as a vision:

> La lodola perduta nell'aurora
> si spazia . . .
>> ("Di lassù")

> Al cader delle foglie, alla massaia
> non piange il vecchio cor . . .
>> ("Galline")

> Nel campo mezzo grigio e mezzo nero
> resta un aratro senza buoi . . .
>> ("Lavandare")

> I due bimbi si rizzano . . .
>> ("I due bimbi")

> Tra gli argini sui cui mucche tranquillamente pascono, bruna si defila la via
> ferrata . . .
>> ("La via ferrata")

> The lark, lost in the dawn,
> roams . . .
>> (From on High)

> At the falling of leaves, the housewife's
> weary heart does not weep . . .
>> (The Hens)

> In the half gray and half black field
> lies a plow without oxen . . .
>> (The Laundresses)

> The two children stand up . . .
>> (The Two Children)

> Between the embankments where cows graze
> tranquilly, the railway—all brown—
> goes straight . . .
>> (The Railway)

Above all, the poems enjoy a formal continuity. Each madrigal builds through two tercets followed by a quatrain of alternating rhyme (aba cbc dede), creating a formal pattern that balances the highly individual character of each piece, so one is aware that the fragmentation is subject to human control. Rhyme and meter thus contribute, if at times only subliminally, to the impression of a narrative poem, an impression all the more consciously conveyed by the final poem. Here, the thematic closure of the section derives added impact from the rhyming couplet at its end:

> —O vano sogno! Quando
> nella macchia fiorisce il pan porcino,
> lo scolaro i suoi divi ozi lasciando
> spolvera il badïale calepino:

> chioccola il merlo, fischia il beccaccino;
> anch'io torno a cantare in mio latino.

> —O empty dream! When
> in the brush wood the cyclamen blooms,
> the scholar, leaving his rich idleness,
> dusts off his huge Latin dictionary:

> the blackbird whistles and the snipe chirps;
> I too return to sing in my idiom.

As the reader reaches the final madrigal, he is thus asked to reconsider the whole, now from the perspective of the poet's memory and desire.

Such poetry as "L'Ultima passeggiata" makes *Myricae* a remarkable first book, even considering the poet's mature age at its date of publication. Here was a poet whose originality, with its insistence on the childlike, untraditional vision, was already evident and whose greatness could be predicted. But if *Myricae* is remarkable for anything in Pascoli's entire oeuvre, it is perhaps for its tendency to contain so many of his characteristic themes and techniques. Pascoli once spoke of his desire to make of his various lyric collections one grand book. That this was more than a passing fancy is clear enough to anyone who reads the epigraphs of Pascoli's six lyric collections. All are ordered by Latin phrases drawn from the first verses of Vergil's Fourth Eclogue: *Myricae* (1) and *Canti di Castelvecchio* (4) carry the same motto: "Arbusta iuvant humilesque myricae"; the *Primi poemetti* (2) and the *Nuovi poemetti* (3) use the phrase "paulo maiora" (somewhat greater); the *Odi e inni* (5) recall Vergil's "canamus" (let us sing); and the *Poemi conviviali* (6) the "non omnis arbusta iuvant" (not to all are saplings pleasing).

The best of Pascoli's later works, turning back to the same humble stock first evident in *Myricae*, are not so much new directions as new perspectives on the same subjects. They may not all weld the Pascolian elements together in the same way. Nor may they meet so fully the expectations set forth in "Il fanciullino." But the poetry for which Pascoli is remembered grows organically out of this initial statement.

THE LATER ITALIAN POEMS

Where critical controversy about Pascoli's gifts still rages, the works published after the 1892 edition of *Myricae* and with the loosest thematic ties to that work are the ones most often attacked. During the years that Pascoli was preparing later versions of the book, he was also composing and editing poetry of a very different character. True, *Poemetti* and *Canti di Castelvecchio* both depend for many of their effects on the poetics of "Il fanciullino" and, of the later works, are most warmly received by Pascoli's critics. *Poemi conviviali*, *Odi e inni*, and the several books dating from Pascoli's final years depart dramatically from the poetry of *Myricae* to focus on classical themes and sociopolitical purposes. Though the last works are generally considered Pascoli's least successful, they are nonetheless important for understanding the unusual range of a poet often mistakenly associated only with the country vignette.

The *Poemetti*, later expanded into two volumes called *Primi* and *Nuovi poemetti*, blend epic and lyric as *Myricae* had attempted in a few of its sections. But the balance and scale have changed dramatically. In *Poemetti*, one encounters a strong determination to subsume the brilliant, fragmentary insight into an epic narrative. If the Vergilian epigraph and the terza rima stanzas (*aba bcb cdc*) reminiscent of Dante lend these poems the outward trappings of epic verse, a narrative nucleus recounting the meeting, love, and marriage of two young peasants, Rosa and Rigo, provides them with a substantial inner shape.

Add to all this an evident social purpose. As Pascoli makes clear in a letter to his artist friend Anthony De Witt, in which he describes his newest works, he firmly believed that the best remedy for the evils of modern Italian life was a return to agrarian society. And it was precisely the beauty and serenity of country life he intended to portray through the main narrative line of his *Poemetti*. If this theme was common enough to the classics, especially Vergil and Horace, it raised a particularly pressing issue for the Italy of Pascoli's day, when the emigration of workers was sapping so much of the country's strength. This commitment to a strong agricultural society is no doubt what led the poet to close *Primi poemetti* with the poem "Italy," which vividly portrays—with appropriate Italo-American speech patterns—emigrants returning to the homeland after some years in the United States. And the final poem of *Nuovi poemetti*, "Pietole," completes the ideological framework, celebrating a nation (Italy) redeemed through its return to agrarian pursuits. Building in this way on the rural impulse already well established in *Myricae*, Pascoli alternately presents in each of the two volumes the humble epos of love, marriage, and family life, and poetic cycles more meditative and descriptive in nature.

Parts of the narrative nucleus charm by their innocence and simplicity. Take, for instance, the beginning of "La canzone del bucato" (The Washing Song) from *Primi poemetti*:

> Quel tintinno diceva:—Era l'estate:
> le cicale cantavano sui meli:
> bianca famiglia, voi dove eravate?
> Certo nei campi: lunghi e verdi steli
> col fiore in cima: ondoleggiando allora
> non pensavate a diventar dei teli.

> That jingling announced:—it was
>   summer:
> cicadas sang in the apple trees:
> family of white, where were you?

> In the fields, surely, long and green stele
> with a flower at the top: swaying then
> you did not think of turning into cloth.

But the narrative impulse of the book all too frequently loses its energy. Though beautiful in parts, the story generally lacks the immediacy that Pascoli so delightfully conveys in *Myricae*, and depends for its effect on a weak blend of allegory and innovative attempts to incorporate proverbs and everyday speech. To make the narrative yet more problematic, the plot too readily breaks down into descriptive sections with seemingly little connection to the whole.

Held in higher esteem today are those parts of *Primi* and *Nuovi poemetti* that stand fully outside its narrative structure. These meditations on human suffering, on cosmic questions, on the inscrutability of the universe and the mystery of life add an essential counterpoint to the happy love affair drawn in the epic sections of the work. They also support Pascoli's belief that Italy should build its future on an agrarian society, where all could find satisfaction in a life close to nature, filled with simple pleasures and duties, but also with awe-inspiring mystery. A poem such as "L'Aquilone" (The Kite), for instance, with its remembrance of the death of a fellow student, recalls the nostalgic return to childhood so fundamental to the inspiration of *Myricae*. "Digitale purpurea" (The Purple Foxglove), "Suor Virginia" (Sister Virginia), "Nella nebbia" (In the Fog), and "Il transito" (The Transit), on the other hand, strike a more novel note. Here, the mystery and ambiguity of life weigh far more heavily than the immediacy of impression typical of Pascoli's earlier collection, and come closer to a symbolist ideal than any of the *Myricae* texts. "Digitale purpurea," for instance, offers a striking narrative of two young women, Rachel and Maria, meeting and reminiscing about their adolescence in a convent. The poem contains recognizable Pascolian motifs. The imagery is fresh and brilliant. Syntax halts—and then rushes forward meaningfully. And the past of memory transforms itself rapidly into the present as the poet sets before us images of the cloister and the young girls dressed in a white appropriate to their innocence. But in the garden of the convent stands the purple foxglove whose ghastly appearance—as of a human hand drenched in blood—and sweet, attractive odor paradoxically symbolize death. In the youthful confession of Rachel to Maria that ends the lyric, Pascoli portrays the flower's fatal attraction for the girl:

> Maria, ricordo quella grave sera.
> L'aria soffiava luce di baleni
> silenzïosi. M'inoltrai leggiera,

cauta, su per i molli terrapieni
erbosi. I piedi mi tenea la folta
erba. Sorridi? E dirmi sentia: Vieni!

Vieni! E fu molta la dolcezza! molta!
tanta, che, vedi . . . (l'altra lo stupore
alza degli occhi, e vede ora, ed ascolta

con un suo lungo brivido . . .) si
   muore!

Maria, I remember that solemn eve.
The breezes blew forth silent flashes of
lightning. I walked forward with a light step,

cautiously, the way up the moist grassy
embankments. The thick grass held on to my feet.
You smile? And I felt it say to me: Come!

Come! And the sweetness was enormous! So
   much!
so much that, you see . . . (the other raises
her eyes in amazement, sees now, and listens

with a long shudder of her own . . .) I am dying!

Critics marveling at the poem's beauty but struggling with its sense have tried to specify what its final words—"si muore"—mean. Is Pascoli asking us to imagine Rachel actually dying, as in the closing scene of a melodrama? Is he referring to a druglike effect of the flower? Is it sexual knowledge that the flower, with its phallic shape, is meant to figure? Or is it a spiritual death of some kind that Pascoli portrays, and does the flower's presence in the garden reveal the ubiquitous presence of error, sorrow, and death in human life? Though most readers today would probably choose the last interpretation, the poem lives precisely through its disparate suggestions, the impossibility of offering a determinate solution to its closely developed imagery.

Pascoli would doubtless be surprised to know that of all the *Poemetti*, poems such as this, rather than his narrative nucleus of agrarian peace, have had the greatest impact on the public. But if the epic framework of *Poemetti* has not left a lasting impression, it is

an important intervening step toward the civic and patriotic themes that appear in Pascoli's later years.

Yet between *Poemetti* and Pascoli's attempts at taking on the role of the civic muse, there stands an important monument to his individual experience and the poetic vein already explored in *Myricae*. Pascoli doubtless meant *Canti di Castelvecchio* to be taken as an equal partner to his early, very successful work. Not only does the same epigraph grace both collections, the preface to *Canti* complements the moving dedication of *Myricae:* "And may these other songs remain on the tomb of my mother—these too, the song of birds." Like *Myricae*, *Canti* includes, on the one hand, realistic poems inspired by the countryside and by simple rural life—this time, though, the scene is usually Barga, the area surrounding Castelvecchio—and, on the other hand, poems in which autobiographical motifs dominate. As before, the thought of death is transformative. As Pascoli puts it in his preface, "Life without the thought of death, that is, without religion, is a delirium, intermittent or continuous, solid or tragic." In *Canti*, Pascoli portrays with unusual power the suffering that joins all members of the human family as they face what is perhaps their sole common reality, death. But since his poems evince a boundless love for even the smallest living creatures, and find beauty in all things, including death and destruction, they offer as a whole more than a new insight into human suffering. They express an underlying joy in life.

Though *Canti* may be compared neatly to *Myricae* in all these ways, it would be wrong to view it as merely a continuation. It gained much through the experience of *Poemetti*. Whereas *Myricae* uses visual and phonic impressions to engage the reader, *Canti* most often entrances with a haunting mystery. And if *Canti* is more frankly autobiographical, it is also stylistically more complex and more solidly structured.

True, an occasional poem may strike the

reader as too slick, too pathetic, or too preachy. But many others must be numbered among Pascoli's best. "Il ricordo" (The Memory), "Il ritratto" (The Portrait), "Il nido di 'farlotti,'" (The Nest of "Shrikes"), "La cavalla storna" ("The Grey Mare"), and "La voce" (The Voice) gain warmth and resonance from the poet's personal experience of tragedy. Though these poems immediately gripped the hearts of Italian readers when they first appeared in print, and are frequently anthologized today, more appealing to critics are such haunting pieces as "Il gelsomino notturno" ("The Night Jasmine") and the cycle "Il ritorno a San Mauro" (The Return to San Mauro). One or two of these poems deserve a closer look.

Originally written as a wedding gift to a friend, Gabriele Briganti, "The Night Jasmine" develops the theme of the mystery of life, renewing itself even at the very moment when all is immersed in the quiet of night:

> E s'aprono i fiori notturni,
> nell'ora che penso a' miei cari.
> > Sono apparse in mezzo ai viburni
> > le farfalle crepuscolari.
>
> Da un pezzo si tacquero i gridi:
> lá sola una casa bisbiglia,
> > Sotto l'ali dormono i nidi,
> > come gli occhi sotto le ciglia.
>
> Dai calici aperti si esala
> l'odore di fragole rosse.
> > Splende un lume là nella sala.
> > Nasce l'erba sopra le fosse.
>
> Un'ape tardiva sussurra
> trovando già prese le celle.
> > La Chioccetta per l'aia azzurra
> > va col suo pigolìo di stelle.
>
> Per tutta la notte s'esala
> l'odore che passa col vento.
> > Passa il lume su per la scala;
> > brilla al primo piano: s'è spento . . .
>
> > È l'alba: si chiudono i petali
> > un poco gualciti; si cova,
> > dentro l'urna molle e segreta,
> > non so che felicità nuova.

And the flowers of night are opening
at the hour when I think of my dear ones.
> From the midst of the viburnum trees
> the twilight butterflies have appeared.

For a while now the shouts have been
silenced:
one lone house is still whispering there.
> Nests are sleeping underneath wings
> like eyes sleep under their eyelids.

Out of the open calyx rises
the odor of crimson strawberries.
> A light is shining there in the hall.
> Grass is being born on top of the graves.

A belated bee is buzzing,
finding the cells already taken.
> The Pleiad hen moves through the heaven-
> blue
> threshing floor with her starlike chirping.

Throughout the night the perfume that
passes on the wind rises up.

> The light passes up the staircase;
> it shines on the second floor: it goes
> out . . .

It is dawn: the petals, somewhat crumpled,
are closing; within a moist and secret
> vessel there is already brooding
> no one knows what sort of new happiness.

The first line of the poem is particularly effective (and notably Pascolian) with its conjunction "e" gesturing to the mysterious realm of thought and memory that precedes the poem itself. But as one reads this text, one senses that the mystery shrouding its first line is all pervasive. The pulsating life force continues into the nocturnal silence, but brings with its reassuring power inevitable suffering to the human heart. As Giorgio Petrocchi puts it with particular clarity in *Storia della poesia di Giovanni Pascoli*, through a play of images, Pascoli evokes "the sorrowful accord between life and suffering, joy and death, things near and far, between present emotions and memory." Pascoli does so through a concise use of alternating couplets—evoking first the contemplating poet communing with his dead ("miei cari"), and then a nuptual scene, by reference to a light traveling up the stairs of a house and finally going out. The closing image of the "urna" of the flower, a moist and secret place that will produce a "new happiness," completes the brief epithalamium. As in so many of Pascoli's earlier still lifes, this poem invites the reader to join the fragments and conjure up the proper imagined space. But the efforts required are, if anything, greater here than in *Myricae*, because real-life images are more fully detached from one another and from any recognizable setting.

This poem, a veritable series of suggestions, contrasts strongly with the apparently more realistic emphasis of the cycle "Il ritorno a San Mauro" Since this nine-poem cycle clearly evokes "L'Ultima passeggiata" of *Myricae* through its similar setting in the village of Pascoli's youth, it allows us to gauge the maturing of the poet's gifts. The opening poem, "Le rane" ("The Frogs"), begins, for instance, as a still life not unlike "Plowing." The imagery is fresh and seemingly spontaneous. But, as we can see from the first three stanzas, the mystery is more intense and the role of the persona more pronounced:

> Ho visto inondata di rosso
> la terra dal fior di trifoglio;
> ho visto nel soffice fosso
> le siepi di pruno in rigoglio;
> e i pioppi a mezz'aria man mano
> distendere un penero verde
> lunghesso la via che si perdè
> lontano.
>
> Qual è questa via senza fine
> che all'alba è sì tremula d'ali?
> chi chiamano le canapine
> coi lunghi lor gemiti uguali?
> Tra i rami giallicci del moro
> chi squilla il suo tinnulo invito?
> chi svolge dal cielo i gomitoli
> d'oro?
>
> Io sento gracchiare le rane
> dai borri dell'acque piovane
> nell'umida serenità.

> E fanno nel lume sereno
> lo strepere nero d'un treno
> che va . . .

I have seen the earth flooded
with red from the clover flowers;
I have seen in the soft ditch
the thorn bush hedges in bloom;
and poplars in midair slowly
stretch out a green festoon by
that road vanishing in the
distance.

What is this road without end
that from dawn so trembles with wings?
Who do the warblers call with their
long and equal sounding moans?
From yellow limbs of the mulberry
who rings his resonant call?
who unwinds the balls of gold
from the sky?

I hear the frogs who are croaking
from the ditches of rainwater
in the damp serenity.
And within the serene light
they sound the din of a train
that passes . . .

Rather than presenting an "objective" scene of country life, this poem speaks directly from the poet's past. Not only does the poet dramatize his voice repeatedly—"Ho visto" (I have seen)—he also includes clearly subjective perceptions, such as the comparison between the sounds of the frogs and of a far-off train. Though this would seem contrary to the poetics of "Il fanciullino," it is above all a development of the sense of mystery always considered essential to pure poetry and practiced frequently in *Poemetti*. In this particular poem, the poetic persona's entrance does not so much detract from the scene as add layers of meaning to it. His voice questions the sensory world and gives it a responsive voice of its own. The questioning, the pauses in thought, are inscribed in the poem's repetitive syntax and in the short, nine-syllable lines that issue harmoniously from the poet's perspective. The frogs, their evening noises,

1845

make no pretense of existing in their own right. They are the voices of memory that inundate the poet and conjure a visionary present. Pascoli here is the poet of the dream vision, a guise in which he appears with some frequency in his later poems, but which was already foreshadowed by *Myricae* and *Poemetti.*

At this point in his career, Pascoli was equally successful with the short narrative poem. "La tessitrice" ("The Weaver"), another text from "Il ritorno a San Mauro," takes up a seldom heard theme in Pascoli's repertoire: love. Here remembrance blends rapidly into the present of dialogue. But this particular dialogue fades into a realization that it is made of one solitary voice—the poet's, imagining. The woman is actually dead. Or better, she lives only in the poet's heart.

As is evident in these two poems, more holds this cycle together than the geography of San Mauro. It is the role San Mauro plays in the poet's psyche, and the effort he makes to memorialize it, that gives the cycle its emotional and narrative charge. The image in "The Frogs" of a continual seeking for something never there pervades all nine poems and finds meaning only in the poet's redemptive mission. The last poem of the group puts it succinctly, as the voice of Pascoli's father speaks from the tomb about the animating power of his son's verse:

> io là sarò, col figlio mio sepolto,
> che mi ridona ciò che gli donai
> che m'ha ridato ciò che tu m'hai tolto.

I will be there, entombed there with my son,
who gives me back again that which I gave,
who has given me what you [assassin] have taken.

In *Poemi conviviali* and *Odi e inni,* Pascoli relinquishes autobiography in favor of classical and patriotic themes. But at the same time, his sense of the poet's mission, developed in all three previous collections, gathers strength. *Poemi conviviali* takes its title from the literary journal *Convito,* explicitly dedicated to "rescuing a bit of beauty and the ideal from the wave of vulgarity that is submerging [Italy]" (Preface to *Poemi conviviali*). Here, Pascoli had earlier published three poems from the collection—"Gog e Magog," ("Gog and Magog"), "Alexandros," and "Solon." As the titles of these poems suggest, *Poemi conviviali* does not strive to reproduce the immediacy of a sensory impression or a memory. These poems offer specifically literary reminiscences. For the first time, Pascoli consciously writes poetry about poetry, and the expert classicist who had been developing apace in his Latin poems makes his presence felt.

The classical model is the Greek epic, as the collection outlines an ideal history of ancient civilization from its beginnings in Greece to the triumph of Christianity. Like the epic poet described in "Il fanciullino," Pascoli throughout "speaks at great length, telling the particulars one by one, not leaving any out" ("Il fanciullino"). He also incorporates classical meter into Italian verse. For this use of "unnatural" rhyme schemes and classical phrasing, Pascoli has often been criticized. But at his best, he does much more than vividly recall a classical past. He imbues the myths with a distinctly modern spirit. "Solon," for instance, weaves classical allusions to Sappho into an entirely modern statement on the worth of poetry. And in the best-known piece from the collection, "L'Ultimo viaggio" ("The Last Voyage"), he completely recasts the story of Ulysses. Drawing here on a particularly rich literary tradition—not only Homer's brief reference to Ulysses' last voyage, but the later elaborations of Dante, Alfred Lord Tennyson, and Arturo Graf—Pascoli reshapes the legend according to his own lights. As he presents it, Ulysses' last voyage is neither a search for knowledge nor a final attempt at heroism. It is a journey back through time to dreams of youth and a Hamlet-like quest for self-knowledge. When grafted elegantly onto the original Homeric elements, this Pascolian theme grows into a vigorously modern branch of a classical legend.

At moments in the collection, Pascoli still takes on the guise of the poet of mystery who had asserted himself with increasing fervor in works published after *Myricae*. Symbols accumulate, some releasing their meaning easily, almost at first reading, as in "La cetra d'Achille" ("The Cithara of Achilles"). Others are more resistant, such as in "Gog and Magog," a synthetic reworking of the biblical legend of captive barbarians finally overrunning the civilized world. If there is no question that Pascoli here intends to describe the decline of the classical world that began with the invasion of the barbarians, the historical climate in which he was writing—with its socialist uprisings and Marxist thought—and the purpose of the journal that the collection commemorates make one wonder just how far Pascoli meant this legend to allegorize the predicament of his own age.

The poem, which fascinated critics from the first, is instructive, for the collection as a whole is best appreciated when its aestheticizing impulse is understood as more than merely a humanistic exercise. Rather it is an attempt to revivify and memorialize Italy's cultural past and so protect it from all that threatens it in the modern world. In this respect, this often beautiful, frequently moving collection joins *Poemetti* in its poetic mission to build a better Italy.

Ever since Dante, civic poetry has occupied an important place in the Italian literary tradition. With the Risorgimento and the patriotic verse of Giosue Carducci, the notion of a patriotic muse had only gained fresh ground. Considering that Pascoli, in his last years, was teaching from Carducci's chair, with a tempest of political questions in the air, it is hardly any wonder that he began writing lyrics of an ever more patriotic cast. The collec-

tion called *Odi e inni,* which he continued to revise until the last year of his life, gives fullest expression to his consciousness of his age and its social ferment.

Dedicated to the youth of Italy, the book intends to preserve through poetry the ideals that Pascoli saw crumbling about him. Poems about heroism—such as "Al Re Umberto" (To King Umberto) and "Al duca degli Abruzzi e ai suio compagni" (To the Duke of the Abruzzi and His Comrades)—and about the supreme moral laws of duty, goodness, and love stand out against the background of meditations on death and sorrow, such as "Il cane notturno" (The Night Dog) and "Il vecchio" (The Old Man). Questions of class conflict, crises of a capitalist society, problems of emigration and hopes for colonial expansion all find their way into these lyric poems. Some texts are intriguing, such as "Pace" (Peace), which recalls the poet's youthful ideals of a life redeemed by work and lived in peace and justice, and "Alle batterie siciliane" (To the Sicilian Batteries), in which Pascoli evokes his earlier life in Messina. But most of these poems have never acquired—and probably do not merit—the readership of the earlier books. Too much in them is frankly oratorical. It is nonetheless certain that the *Odi e inni* reveals an essential element in Pascoli's lyric impulse. They also prepare the ground for his last works: *Poemi italici* (1911), "Le canzoni di Re Enzio" (1908–1909, incomplete), and finally the *Poemi del Risorgimento* (published posthumously in 1913), which Pascoli intended as his "supreme tribute to his country and to the heroes and martyrs of the Risorgimento."

Of these final lyric—and epic—efforts, not much need be said. They continue the patriotic themes more originally broached in the often revolutionary prose that Pascoli was writing at the time and the humanistic vein more vividly alive in his Latin works. Some passing mention should perhaps be made of the often discussed poem of *Poemi italici,* "Paolo Uccello," in which Pascoli, in an extended flight of imagination, uses the historical figure of the painter to affirm symbolically a view of art as that which possesses a soul freed from material needs and to portray once again the intense love of nature that inspires many of his earliest—and best—poems.

It is by now a critical axiom that Pascoli, like so many poets before and after, declined in his later works. All we may say here is that these final collections—indicative of the poet's patriotic as well as poetic commitment—are essential to our understanding of him. They come near to giving us a lyric map of the classical and patriotic side of Pascoli's intellect, too often left completely out of the picture. They also lead us into a brief consideration of Pascoli's prose and his Latin poetry. As we shall see, the poet did not so much lose his lyric impulse in his later years as displace it—to some extent into his prose writings and significantly into his Latin poems.

THE DANTE CRITICISM AND THE POLITICAL ESSAYS

Though his reputation lies elsewhere, Pascoli wrote a great many essays and three long books in prose. These works range widely and include, in addition to his theory of poetry, his voluminous Dante criticism and several illuminating political statements. If these do not retain as much intrinsic interest for us today as do the lyrics, the more important among them amplify some of the issues raised in the poems.

Pascoli's efforts as a Dante critic were especially intense, and as he labored at his "Dante" desk at Castelvecchio, he had the highest hopes that his work would be greeted with critical acclaim. In his view, at least, he had done nothing less than discover the key to Dante's poetic universe:

And I, I am telling you the truth, I have seen it! Yes: I had reached the pole of Dante's world, of that world that all the learned investigated as if it were the work of another God! I had discovered, in a certain way, the laws of gravity of this other nature; the whole meaning of the universe was about to reveal itself!

(Minerva oscura)

Discovering the underlying laws of the *Divina commedia* entailed a profound investigation into its allegories. Its results appeared in an impressive series of books and articles that Pascoli published under the titles *Minerva oscura* (Dark Minerva, 1898), *Sotto il velame* (Under the Veil, 1900), *La mirabile visione* (The Admirable Vision, 1902), and the incomplete "La poesia del mistero dantesco" (The Poetry of Dante's Mystery), traces of which appear in the collected *Conferenze e studi danteschi* (Dante Lectures and Studies, 1915). However, for all Pascoli's optimistic enthusiasm, his scrutiny of the world of the *Divina commedia* never received the welcome he expected. Intent on exploring the allegorical levels of the poem, Pascoli's symbolist, almost mystical approach failed to impress his contemporaries. His interpretations seemed needlessly esoteric, far afield from the central poetic interest of the work. Only very recently have Pascoli's contributions begun to attract serious attention for their ability to relate the symbolic values of the *Commedia* to the writings of medieval mystics and theologians. In this way, Pascoli brings Dante's poem into particularly close touch with medieval ideas about the world and the human soul, and so sheds an important historical light on the spiritual structure of the poem.

To connoisseurs of Pascoli's lyrics, the Dante studies hold an equally strong, if somewhat different appeal. So closely interwoven are all of Pascoli's writings, so fully dependent on a central spiritual mainspring, that in Pascoli's "discoveries" about Dante's poem, we find confirmation for the very "laws of gravity" governing Pascoli's own verse. The painstaking analysis of Dante's allegories, for instance, displays the same overpowering desire to probe the mystery of existence that animates the bulk of Pascoli's own poems, just as his careful attention to the intricate interplay of personal destiny and social justice in the *Commedia* reveals his more general tendency to ascribe a social role to poetry and a humanitarian mission to the poet.

Pascoli's political writings even more strongly underscore his belief in the poet's social function as they help to clarify his political views. "Una sagra" (A Feast, 1900) and "L'Avvento" (The Accession, 1901), for instance, set forth his position as a "patriotic socialist" and confirm the broadly humanitarian role of the poet. The class conflict emerging in Pascoli's day filled him with considerable anxiety, and in "Una sagra" he briefly imagines an apocalyptic scene of mounting tension:

> *Che sarà di noi? . . . Questa. Le ricchezze gravitano a trovarsi insieme nel medesimo tesoro. Il campicello è assorbito dal campo, il campo dalla tenuta, la tenuta dal latifondo, e via via. Intere nazioni, sto per dire sono espropriate della loro proprieta fondiaria.*

> What will become of us? . . . This. Riches will gravitate to one and the same treasury. The small field will be absorbed by the large, the large field by the ranch, the ranch by the large landed estate, and so on. I am saying that the landed property of entire nations will be expropriated.

He concludes that, as in economic conflicts where the poor rise up against the rich, so must small nations (like Italy) seek justice against growing empires. Raising the Marxist concept of class struggle to the level of international conflict, Pascoli purposefully leaves the ranks of what he can only call a "blind Marxist socialism" to espouse beliefs more hospitable to his patriotism and especially to his concern for the problem of Italian emigration. In "L'Avvento," Pascoli notes a growing compassion in mankind. Calling for a new era of sentiment to replace the outworn epoch of reason, he advocates a universal humanitarian faith that would nonetheless accommodate a sense of patriotism.

Pascoli's "patriotic socialism," it has often been said, was destined, despite its being anchored in belief in a superior law of human goodness, to encourage an aggressive nationalism. It does so most explicitly in the 1911 essay "La grande proletaria si è mossa," in which he assumes the role of poet–prophet more indirectly found in his verse. Building on his familiar concern for the problem of Italian emigration, Pascoli here justifies the current Italian policy of colonial expansion. He does so by transforming the Italian nation into the proletarian class with a right to impose its power where it can:

> *Ma la grande Proletaria ha trovato luogo per loro: una vasta regione bagnata dal nostro mare, verso la quale guardono, come sentinelle avanzate, piccole isole nostre; verso la quale si protende impaziente la nostra isola grande; una vasta regione che gia per opera dei nostri progenitori fu abbondevole d'acque e di messi, e verdeggiante d'alberi e giardini; e ora, da un pezzo, per l'inerzia di popolazioni nomadi e neghittose, è per gran parte un deserto.*
>
> *Là i lavoratori saranno, non l'opre, mal pagate mal pregiate mal nomate, degli stranieri, ma nel senso più alto e forte delle parole, agricoltori sul suo, sul terreno della Patria . . .*
>
> *Anche là è Roma.*
>
> *E Rumi saranno chiamati. Il che sia augurio buono e promesso certa. Sì: Romani. Sì: fare e soffrire da forti. E sopra tutto ai popoli che non usano se non la forza, imporre, come non si puo fare altrimenti, mediante la guerra, la pace.*

But the great Proletariat has found a place for itself. It is a vast region bathed by our seas, toward which our little islands—like advanced sentinels—look, and toward which our great island stretches out impatiently. It is a vast region that already, through the work of our ancestors, abounded in waters and crops, and was verdant with trees and gardens; and that now, for some time, through the inertia of nomadic and slothful populations, is largely a desert.

There the workers will not be hired hands, poorly paid, undervalued, and demeaned by foreigners. Rather they will be—and this in the highest and strongest sense of the word—farmers *on their own land,* on the soil of the fatherland.

There too is Rome.

And they will be called *Rumi.* Which will be a good omen and a sure promise. Yes: Romans. Yes: *to act and suffer like the strong.* And above all, to impose peace by means of war (since we cannot do otherwise) on all the peoples who use nothing but force themselves.

This famous and, in Italy, well-received defense of colonialism reveals little of the revolutionary spark associated with Marxist socialism. It advocates standards responsive above all to the political climate of the day and the particular needs of the nation. In short, although the word "socialist" graces the pages of these political essays, Pascoli's views can fairly be described as conservative.

If anything here strikes a revolutionary note, it is only Pascoli's prose style. His expressive syntax, with its frequent parataxis and countless interjections, recalls the syntactic experiments of the early lyrics and goes some way to revealing the poet's fascination not only with the world but with language's power to enliven it. Though Contini may exaggerate when he speaks of Pascoli's prose as in fact more revolutionary than his verse, it is certainly true that in his later years, prose writings such as "La grande proletaria si è mossa" ring with greater immediacy and power than almost any of his late poems.

CARMINA

Of the many fronts on which Pascoli worked a subtle literary revolution, one of the most distinctive was Latin verse. Ever since his youth, Pascoli had been writing Latin poems. He had learned Latin and Greek at the Collegio Raffaello in Urbino and excelled from the first in translations. As he grew to maturity, he developed an amazing facility with this second language—one probably unmatched in modern times. And his career as a Latin poet stretched over the entire arc of his Italian writings. The thirteen medals Pascoli won for the Latin verse at the Royal Academy of Amsterdam date from 1892, the year in which *Myricae* was first published, and continued through the years without major interruptions until the year of his death. Though comparably little has been written about Pascoli's Latin verse, some believe it to be his most continuously successful work. It was certainly his most constant and voluminous.

Generally, Pascoli's Latin poems stay closer than the Italian verse to his original insight into the poetry of the *fanciullino.* In most of them, the same Pascolian sense of mystery persists, as does the same search for a childlike freshness of vision and the same efforts toward a more vivid and responsive language. If anything, his later years bring him nearer to this original inspiration. It is as if in the Latin works—from which he could expect little by way of public response—he was better able to pursue his deepest poetic instincts. In fact, when one considers the evolution of Pascoli's Latin verse, its themes seem to develop in a direction opposite to his Italian work. The early Latin poems begin with historical and political themes, as in "Gladiatores" (Gladiators), later capture a bucolic mood in "Myrmedon" and "Pecudes" (The Herd), then wax historical again with "Jugurtha"; but they finally deliver their civic burden to the Italian collections *Poemi conviviali* and *Odi e inni.* Conversely, as the historical and patriotic vein was deepening in Pascoli's Italian verse, the poetry of intuitive insight and natural description, which had grown through *Myricae* and *Canti di Castelvecchio,* began to seek out the Latin language, and there flourished anew in poems such as "Fanum vacunae" (The Temple of Vacuna) and "Thallusa."

Though in one or two of his Latin poems— "Catullocalvos" (The Clash Between Catullus and Calvus), for instance—Pascoli ap-

GIOVANNI PASCOLI

proaches the art of the *Myricae;* in the "Fanum vacunae" (1910) he transcends it. Composed as a series of fragments, the separate sections of the Latin text resemble the earlier Italian collection in theme as well as form. But though the familiar motifs of the poet's retreat into nature, compassion for human suffering, the sense of life's transience, and the eternalizing power of poetry are the same, the autobiographical is now treated with a new composure, and the contemplation of natural life with an intensified awareness of its mutability. Take, for instance, the poet's address to the river in "Digentia" (The Digenzia):

O utinam, similis plane tibi, laberer, manerem!
  et unda frondes ferret atque flores,

non vocem, non hoc murmur leve, quod viator
    edo,
  non quae mei pars maior est et omni,
non cantum, quem, rive fugax, canis, ut cano
    fatigans
  ad saxa fluctuslabilemque vitam.

                                    (253–258)

O if I too, just like you, could pass yet remain!
  and the waves carry leaves and flowers,

but not the voice, not this slight murmur that I,
    pilgrimlike, utter,
  not the part of me that is greater even than all,
not the song that you, runaway river, sing, as I
    sing,
  tiring the flow of fleeting life on the stones.

Cesare Goffis aptly points out that such well-chiseled fragments bring together a host of poetic associations from elsewhere in Pascoli's verse, as they join in a unity of musical as well as semantic echoes virtually unmatched in Pascoli's Italian works. But not unmatched among his Latin compositions. The very year after completing the "Fanum vacunae," Pascoli wrote "Thallusa" and entered it in the Amsterdam competition. Less than a month before he died, he received a telegram from the academy advising him that, by unanimous vote, he had just received his thirteenth gold medal for Latin verse.

Unlike many of Pascoli's lyric poems, "Thallusa" is not a series of fragments, but rather a narrative piece about Tallusa, a Christian slave and nursemaid to a pagan family. Alone with her master's children, Tallusa recalls her unhappy lot: a husband who has been killed and a tiny infant who has been taken from her. But just as she relives her past in anger and tears, her master's baby cries. And as Tallusa rocks him in his cradle and sings the song she once sang to her own child, the baby smiles for the first time, as if recognizing her as his mother. At this, Tallusa feels great joy, re-creating a moment of maternal happiness by giving all her love to the infant. But as we know from the first section of the poem, Tallusa has already been sold. She will not be able to enjoy even this surrogate love for more than the moment.

Though Pascoli did historical research to prepare the poem, the reader is not made to feel the distance of history but rather the universality of the themes of motherhood and social injustice. And though Pascoli searched his dictionaries and encyclopedias to discover proper Latin names for the children's toys that color the opening lines of the text, he juxtaposes the arcane terms with diminutives and colloquialisms, until the poem conveys less of the esoteric than of the humble and the everyday. The setting of "Thallusa" may be classical and its language Latin, but its poetry comes to us fresh and new. Precisely in this, Pascoli shows the greatness of his Latin poetry. Its closing stanza is one of the most remarkable in all Pascoli's works:

Flet Thallusa canens, aeque memor, immemor
    aeque.
Ecce puer leni pacatus momine cymbae
et dolci cantu, iam cessat flere nec idem
singultit: tranquillus hiat patulisque canentem
sub tremula lychni flamma miratur ocellis.
Tum stupet in varia, quae lumine lampadis icta
labilis a cilio Thallusae pendet et ardet,
lacrimula. Tandem crispatur buccula. Ridet.
"Ridet!" ait Thallusa furens, oblita sui, nil
percipiens oculis aliud, nil auribus, omnis

in puero, risum lacrimans, deperdita "Ride!
Coepisti tandem risu cognoscere matrem!"

Mater adest sed vera redux auditque loquentem.
"I cubitum: primo cras surgas mane necesse est."
Primo mane domo servam novus emptor abegit.

Tallusa cries while singing, both mindful and
    forgetting.
But the baby, calmed by the gentle rocking of his
    cradle
and by the sweet song, stops his crying and no
    longer
sobs: he remains quiet with his mouth open
and, open-eyed, looks at her who sings
under the trembling flame of the lamp.
And then a rainbow colored tear, that in the
    lamplight
sparkles briefly on the eyelash of Tallusa,
    enchants him.
His little mouth curves, wrinkles up. He laughs.
"He laughs!" cries Tallusa, raving, beside herself,
seeing and hearing nothing else, all absorbed
in the child, crying and smiling, nearly mad,
    "You laugh!"
"Finally, with your laugh, you begin to know your
    mother!"

But the mother, the real one, has returned and
    hears her speak.
"Go to bed: tomorrow you must get up at dawn."
    And at dawn the new buyer took the slave
    away.

With consummate art, Pascoli paces the climax of the poem—Tallusa's moment of maternal happiness and our knowledge of its proximate end. And he touches the reader all the more strongly by so thoroughly revivifying the dead language in which he writes. More than a pastiche of classical quotations, this is Latin as used by a thoroughly bilingual twentieth-century poet. His unique touch manifests itself in lines such as "Flet Thallusa canens, aeque memor, immemor aeque" (Tallusa cries while singing, both mindful and forgetting), in which a fluid uncertainty lends a modern psychological interest to the story of a Roman slave. The music created by its repetitive, chiasmic close is reminiscent of

no classical author, but of Giovanni Pascoli alone.

Admitting all this, one might still rightly ask, just why did Pascoli turn to Latin so frequently in his career, and why did he create in its seldom used forms some of his greatest works? More likely than not, he felt drawn to this dead language as he felt drawn to all beautiful things now past. It lent itself as well as Italian—sometimes even better—to a lyric impulse that found inspiration in a desire to revivify and memorialize the past, the invisible, the dead. In one of his earliest, unpublished writings, Pascoli states:

I consider my conception [of poetry] great in this, that I do not deny to humanity even the dead, and that I gather their ashes religiously, to place them in cinerary urns sculptured with a fine chisel in the luminous alabaster of art.

In his maturity, he again declares:

Poetry is reliving what was, reliving it spontaneously and fully, before a temple whose columns have fallen to the earth, before a poem whose language is ancient and obsolete, lifting up those gigantic columns suddenly with the lever of dream and re-creating with the inspiration of thought, that immense world.

(*Scritti danteschi*)

Poetry manifested itself in the great Latin lyrics of Pascoli's final years as it had earlier in *Myricae* and *Canti di Castelvecchio*—as an effort to re-create the past, to make it live again, to redeem it. This fascination with the past, with the memories of a race, led the poet to resurrect an entire language, just as memories of his departed family inspired him to revitalize traditional Italian verse. It has taken more than a half century to come to terms with such fundamental innovations. But it can never be regretted that our changing values have allowed the poet to take his proper place among late-nineteenth-century writers; and his redemptive, if antitraditional, power of language to take its place in the history of poetry as the first development in a new line of verse we associate with the modern.

Selected Bibliography

EDITIONS

ITALIAN POETRY

Myricae. Livorno, 1891; Bologna, 1906 (definitive edition).

Poemetti. Florence, 1897; Milan, 1968 (most recent edition). Later divided into *Primi poemetti* (Bologna, 1904) and *Nuovi poemetti* (Bologna, 1909).

Canti di Castelvecchio. Bologna, 1903; 1907 (definitive edition).

Poemi conviviali. Bologna, 1904; Milan, 1964 (most recent edition).

Odi e inni. Bologna, 1906; 1953 (most recent edition).

Poesie varie. Bologna, 1912 and 1913.

Poemi italici. Bologna, 1911; 1914 (together with "Le canzoni di Re Enzio"); 1954 (most recent edition).

Poemi del Risorgimento. Bologna, 1913; Milan, 1955 (most recent edition).

ESSAYS

Minerva oscura. Prolegomeni: La construzione morale del poema di Dante. Livorno, 1898; 2nd ed., 1917.

Sotto il velame: Saggio di un'interpretazione generale del poema sacro. Messina, 1900; 3rd ed., 1923.

La mirabile visione: Abbozzo di una storia della Divina commedia. Messina, 1902; 3rd ed., 1923.

Pensieri e discorsi. Bologna, 1907; 3rd ed., 1920. Contains "Il fanciullino."

Patria e umanità. Bologna, 1914.

Conferenze e studi danteschi. Bologna, 1915.

LATIN POEMS, TRANSLATIONS, AND ANTHOLOGIES

Lyra. Livorno, 1895; Florence, 1956. Latin anthology.

Epos. Livorno, 1897 and 1938. Latin anthology.

Traduzioni e riduzioni. Bologna, 1913 and 1954.

Carmina (1885–1911). 2 vols. Bologna, 1914, edited by E. Pistelli; 1930, edited by A. Gandiglio.
———. Edited by M. Valgimigli. Milan, 1951.

COLLECTED WORKS

Poesie. Edited by Arnoldo Mondadori. 4 vols. Milan, 1968. Contains two introductory essays by Gianfranco Contini: "Profilo di Giovanni Pascoli" and "Il linguaggio del Pascoli."

Tutte le opere di Giovanni Pascoli. 5 vols. *Poesie,* vols. 1 and 2, edited by A. Baldini; *Prose,* vols. 1 and 2, edited by A. Vacinelli; and *Carmina,* edited by M. Valgimigli.

Opere. Edited by Maurizio Perugi. 2 vols. Milan, 1980–.

TRANSLATIONS

Convivial Poems. Text, translation, introduction, and critical notes by Egidio Lunardi and Robert Nugent. Painesville, Ohio, 1979.

Giovanni Pascoli, Selected Poems. Cambridge, 1938. Reprinted 1957. Poems in Italian with English notes and lexicon by G. S. Purkis.
———. Edited with English notes and vocabulary by P. R. Horne. Manchester, 1983.

Poems of Giovanni Pascoli. Translated by Arletta Abbott. New York, 1927.
———. Translated by E. Stein. New Haven, 1923.

BIOGRAPHICAL AND CRITICAL STUDIES

Barberi Squaretti, Giorgio. *Simboli e strutture della poesia del Pascoli.* Messina, 1966.

Beccaria, Gian Luigi. *L'Autonomia del significante: Figure del ritmo e della sintassi di Dante, Pascoli, D'Annunzio.* Turin, 1975.

Benedetti, Natalia. *La formazione della poesia pascoliana.* Milan, 1955.

Binni, Walter. *La poesia del decadentismo italiano.* Florence, 1936.

Cecchi, Emilio. *La poesia di Giovanni Pascoli.* Milan, 1968.

Contini, Gianfranco. "Il linguaggio del Pascoli." In *Studi Pascoliani.* Bologna, 1958. Later published in *Poesie,* cited above.

Croce, Benedetto. *Giovanni Pascoli, studio critico.* Bari, 1920.

Debenedetti, Giacomo. *Pascoli: La rivoluzione inconsapevole.* Milan, 1979.

Del Serra, Maura. *Giovanni Pascoli*. Florence, 1976.

Felcini, Furio. *Bibliografia della critica pascoliana* (1887–1954). Florence, 1957.

————. *Indagini e proposte per una storia delle Myricae: Alle origni del linguaggio pascoliano*. Rome, 1976.

Ferri, Teresa. *Pascoli, il labirinto del segno: per una semantica del linguaggio poetico delle Myricae*. Rome, 1976.

Flora, Francesco. *La poesia di Giovanni Pascoli*. Bologna, 1959.

Galletti, Alfredo. *La poesia e l'arte di Giovanni Pascoli*. Rome, 1918.

Giannangeli, Ottavio. *Pascoli e lo spazio*. Bologna, 1975.

Getto, Giovanni. *Carducci e Pascoli*. Naples, 1965.

Goffis, Cesare. *Pascoli, antico e nuovo*. Brescia, 1969.

Gramsci, Antonio. *Il Risorgimento*. Turin, 1969.

Luzi, Mario, "Giovanni Pascoli." In *Storia della letteratura italiana*, edited by Emilio Cecchi and Natalino Sapeano. vol. 8. Milan, 1968.

Momigliano, Attilio. "Giovanni Pascoli." In *Storia della letteratura italiana*. Milan, 1936.

Pascoli, Maria. *Lungo la vita di Giovanni Pascoli*. Milan, 1961.

Pasolini, Pier Paolo. "Pascoli e Montale." In *Passione e ideologia*. Milan, 1960.

Petrocchi, Giorgio. *Storia della poesia di Giovanni Pascoli*. Rome, 1975.

Ragusa, Olga. "Giovanni Pascoli." In *Columbia Dictionary of Modern European Literature*, edited by Jean-Albert Bédé and William Edgerton. 2nd ed. New York, 1980.

Salinari, Carlo. *Miti e coscienza del decadentismo italiano*. Milan, 1960.

Savoca, Guiseppe, and Mario Tropea. *Pascoli, Gozzano e i crepuscolari*. No. 59 in *Letteratura italiana Laterza*, edited by Carlo Muscetta. Rome, 1976.

Schiaffini, Alfredo. "Forma e rivoluzione poetica di Giovanni Pascoli." In *Siculorum Gymnasium* (July–December, 1955). Pp. 509 ff.

————. "Antilirismo nel linguaggio poetico di cento anni." In *Cento anni di lingua italiana*, by G. Devoto, B. Migliorini, and A. Schiaffini. Milan, 1962.

Scuderi, Ermanno. *Pascoli senza pascolismo*. Catania, 1974.

Serra, Renato. "Giovanni Pascoli." In *Scritti critici*, edited by G. De Robertis and A. Grilli. Florence, 1938.

Sozzi, Giuseppe. *Giovanni Pascoli nella vita, nell'arte e nella storia della critica*. Florence, 1962.

Traina, Alfonso. *Il latino del Pascoli—Saggio sul bilinguismo poetico*. Florence, 1971.

Trombatore, Gaetano. *Memoria e simbolo nella poesia di Giovanni Pascoli*. Reggio Calabria, 1975.

Valentin, Albert. *Giovanni Pascoli, poète lyrique*. Grenoble, 1925.

Valgimigli, Manara. *Pascoli*. Florence, 1956.

Varese, Claudio. *Pascoli decadente*. Florence, 1964.

SANDRA BERMANN

ANTON CHEKHOV
(1860–1904)

ANTON PAVLOVICH CHEKHOV is recognized today as perhaps the most important short-story writer of all time. His formal and thematic innovations in the art of narration have altered literary conventions. Although the bulk of his work is in the form of prose narrative, he was also a master of the art of the drama. His plays, first produced by Constantine Stanislavsky at his Moscow Art Theater, have had an equally radical influence; together with the plays of August Strindberg, they have laid the basis of modern dramaturgy, and the development of the Western version of Stanislavsky's dramatic method, called in America simply the "Method," owes a good deal to the acting techniques realized in their production.

LIFE

Chekhov was born on 17 January 1860[1] in the town of Taganrog in southern Russia, on the Sea of Azov. His paternal grandfather was a serf on the estate of Count A. D. Chertkov (the father of one of Leo Tolstoy's most ardent disciples) who had been able to buy his free-dom. Chekhov's father, Pavel Egorovich, ran a grocery store in Taganrog, but he was more interested in music than in business, to the detriment of his fortunes. He was a severe and intensely religious man who forced his children to attend interminable church services and sing in the choir he had organized, as well as to work long hours in the small family store, which was freezing cold in winter. Chekhov said later that in his childhood he had had no childhood at all. He recalled that his father was as "hard as flint . . . you could not make him budge an inch" (letter to his brother Alexander, February 1883).

Chekhov's studies began at the Greek school in Taganrog, a town that had a large and prosperous Greek population, and only when he was eight years old did he enroll in the local Russian secondary school. Here he showed a marked interest in literature and wrote for the school newspaper. At this time his passion for the theater revealed itself: he organized amateur theater performances and acted out little sketches of his own invention at home.

In 1876, the family store failed, and Chekhov's parents were forced to move to Moscow in order to escape debtors' prison. Anton remained in Taganrog for two more years to complete his secondary schooling. He then enrolled in the medical school of the University of Moscow, from which he received his degree of Doctor of Medicine in 1884. Al-

---

[1]All dates are marked according to the Julian calendar (Old Style), used in Russia until 1917. In Chekhov's lifetime, the Julian calendar was twelve days behind the Gregorian (New Style) calendar used in the West and used in Russia since 1917. Thus January 17 (OS) would be January 29 (NS).

though he never seriously pursued a medical career, he did practice intermittently, and his scientific training and interest are noticeable in his writings. He used to say of his two fields of activity that medicine was his wife, whereas literature was his mistress.

Soon after arriving in Moscow, Chekhov began his professional literary career in earnest, contributing brief sketches to popular humor magazines under the name Antosha Chekhonte. His quick mind and gift for words enabled him to turn out quantities of jokes, anecdotes, and potboilers of all kinds, thus providing much-needed income for his impoverished family, who were living in a wretched basement apartment in a Moscow slum. At the same time, he also composed more complex anecdotes, several literary parodies, and his first serious prose works.

In 1884, the first collection of Chekhov's short stories appeared in book form, under the title *Skazki Mel'pomene* (Tales of Melpomene). Two years later, he contributed his first piece to a serious journal, the conservative Moscow daily *Novoe vremya* (New Times), whose editor, the writer Aleksey S. Suvorin, was to become one of Chekhov's closest friends. The friendship continued, in spite of their political differences (Chekhov was becoming increasingly liberal, while Suvorin was ultraconservative), until 1897, when Chekhov's open defense of Captain Alfred Dreyfus and support of Émile Zola's contribution to the case brought him into sharp conflict with Suvorin, who took part in the anti-Semitic wave that accompanied the Dreyfus affair not only in France but also in Russia. Chekhov's letters to Suvorin are of great interest; they contain some of his most penetrating remarks on literature and politics. The break with Suvorin marked the beginning of Chekhov's friendship with several writers of the radical left, including Maxim Gorky. When, in 1902, the Russian Academy of Sciences, ceding to government pressure, canceled Gorky's membership, Chekhov resigned in protest.

We can divide Chekhov's career, somewhat arbitrarily, into three main periods. During the first period, 1880 to 1887, Chekhov wrote primarily for humor magazines and produced a great number of short prose pieces at a rapid pace. During the second period (1888–1893), Chekhov no longer contributed to the humor journals and paced his writings in a more leisurely fashion. In 1888, there appeared the long prose narrative "Step" ("The Steppe"), which introduced his experimentation with a lyrical prose style. From this period on, much of his work is dominated by the theme of contrast between, on the one hand, beauty, sensitivity, and life, and, on the other, ugliness, banality, and death. As in later stories and plays, isolation also becomes a dominant theme. Other stories from these years reveal Chekhov's search for a coherent world view, a concern that led him to a sympathetic study of Tolstoy's philosophy of nonresistance. Dependence on Tolstoy's ethics came to a halt in 1889, after Chekhov—already ill with the pulmonary tuberculosis that caused his death—traveled to the penal colony of Sakhalin in the northern Pacific, the Russian Devil's Island. The injustice and cruelty Chekhov observed during this expedition, set down in his long sociological monograph *Ostrov Sakhalin* (*The Island: A Journey to Sakhalin*, 1891–1894), changed Chekhov's attitude to Tolstoyanism fundamentally. In several stories of this period, such as "Ward No. 6" (1892), the Tolstoyan doctrine of nonresistance to evil is satirized.

In general, this second creative period is marked by increased concern with social and psychological problems: the oppressed position of the peasants ("Peasant Wives," 1891), the hypocrisy of the upper classes ("The Wife," 1892), the life of missed opportunities ("The Teacher of Literature," 1889–1894), and narcissism ("The Princess," 1889, as well as "The Grasshopper," 1892).

The last period of Chekhov's creative life, from 1894 to his death in 1904, is marked by the appearance of his most complex stories;

they have little external action, and lyrical-musical elements predominate. It is during these years that Chekhov became active in the theater and wrote his four great plays, *The Seagull* (1896), *Uncle Vanya* (1899), *The Three Sisters* (1901), and *The Cherry Orchard* (1904). This burst of dramatic writing was related to an important event, Chekhov's association with Stanislavsky's Moscow Art Theater, which began in 1898 with a production of *The Seagull* and continued until Chekhov's death. The stylized image of a seagull adorns the curtain of the Moscow Art Theater even now to commemorate the theater's production of Chekhov's first great play, which catapulted both the play and the theater to fame.

In May 1901, Chekhov married Olga Knipper, a leading actress in Stanislavsky's company. It was a happy marriage, but it came at a time when both knew that he was marked by death. Chekhov's life was marred by persistent ill health. Even in the late 1880's, when he was not yet thirty, there were the first warnings of the disease that was to blight his remaining years. From 1887 until his death, illness forced him to live either in the mild climate of the Crimea or at German and French spas; and, except for few and rare intervals, he was no longer able to live in Moscow or Saint Petersburg, cities he loved. He died on the night of 2 July 1904 at the German spa of Badenweiler, with Olga Knipper at his side. His body was transferred to Moscow and was buried in the cemetery of the Novo-Devichy monastery, in the section reserved for artists, writers, and musicians.

Chekhov's career comes at the end of the last generation of writers contributing to the great age of Russian literature, the generation of Tolstoy and Feodor Dostoevsky. When Chekhov began working for the humor journals, Tolstoy had already rejected his own major novels as frivolous and was turning to religious-didactic writing. Dostoevsky died in 1881, shortly after Chekhov had begun writing his short humorous sketches; and Ivan Turgenev died in 1883. Chekhov's artistic life thus spans the end of the so-called Golden Age of Russian letters, the age of the great novelists, and the threshold of its Silver Age, associated with the Russian symbolist movement. Clearly, Chekhov's prose evolved from the "realistic" prose tradition, and was influenced by the lyrical and somewhat melancholy work of Turgenev. But Chekhov went on to create fundamentally new forms; for example, the plotless short story. In the western European tradition, Chekhov's closest kinship is with the short stories of Guy de Maupassant, from whom he learned the art of brevity and of the surprise ending. But the poetry and symbolic weight of his stories are Chekhov's own creation, and the new literary forms he created anticipate in many ways the contemporary short story. Many Russian writers of the turn of the century, including such diverse figures as Ivan Bunin, Alexander Kuprin, and even Gorky, can be looked on as his disciples. Today, there is hardly a more popular prose writer and dramatist in Russia than Chekhov; his plays are constantly in the repertory of the Moscow Art Theater and other Soviet theaters. A definitive and fully annotated edition of his complete works and letters in thirty volumes has been published by the Soviet Academy of Sciences (1974–1982), and a somewhat smaller edition, in twenty volumes, appeared between 1944 and 1951; individual works and collections are continually being republished. Some of his stories and plays have been made into films in the Soviet Union.

In Western literature, Chekhov's influence has never abated. Of writers in the English language, Katherine Mansfield is probably the most strikingly indebted to Chekhov's prose. In both theme and form, Chekhov also influenced Franz Kafka, Albert Camus, and the creation of the French *nouveau roman* (new novel). Themes that are taken up by later writers include the fate of the little man, the phenomena of absurdly wasted lives and social isolation, and the failure of communication, together with ineffectuality. Chekhov's plays find echoes in the actionless dramas of such writers as Samuel Beckett.

Thus Chekhov has clearly influenced much of modern prose and dramaturgy, and indirectly modern theater production. At the same time, Chekhov's art resists classification and cannot be fitted neatly into any traditional school or movement; for it was revolutionary in ways that still demand analysis. For example, a frequently discussed problem is the nature of Chekhov's relation to impressionist art. No historical data yet found support the view that Chekhov was directly acquainted with the works of the Western impressionist painters. Furthermore, impressionism never existed as an organized school in Russia; only Chekhov's friend the painter Isaac Levitan exhibited some of the qualities of impressionist painting, but he did not take part in the theoretical development of the French school. While some characteristics of Chekhov's prose and dramaturgy suggest the impressionist movement, these resemblances remain diffuse and difficult to pinpoint. There was a general current in the air by the end of the century: the fresh and immediate approach to color and situations and the depiction of the everyday mediocre rather than the ideal or dramatically poignant marked both the visual and verbal arts.

We shall now turn directly to Chekhov's works, examining first the boisterous humor stories of his youth and then his increasingly mature prose and his plays.

EARLY PROSE

Humor Stories

From 1883 to 1886, most of Chekhov's stories were published in the important Saint Petersburg popular humor magazine *Oskolki* (Fragments). During this period, Chekhov wrote great quantities of stories at prodigious speed. In 1883 alone, he published more than one hundred stories. In 1886, the novelist Dmitry V. Grigorovich, who had read and praised Chekhov's tale "Eger" ("The Huntsman," 1885), wrote to implore him to write in a more serious and leisurely fashion. It was only then that Chekhov abandoned the breakneck speed of his writing and resolved to go more slowly, in order to escape the limitations of the humor magazines. In fact, 1884 was the last year in which Chekhov wrote stories that are predominately humorous.

Even in his earliest anecdotal pieces, we find Chekhov testing the limits of literary norms and conventions. It is particularly with Turgenev, from whom Chekhov learned so much, that Chekhov took issue in his works. The formal structure of the Turgenev short story, with its lengthy introduction, elaborate prologue, digressions elucidating the past of the characters, apostrophes to the reader, and epilogues, is not found even in Chekhov's earliest works. Rather, Chekhov favored terse introductions, impressionistic characterization by significant details, internal rather than external action, and unexpected endings.

Two techniques for endings are characteristic of Chekhov's early stories. The first, closing by means of a surprise, was well known from the prose of Maupassant; but the second, closing by means of what the Russian critic Viktor Shklovsky has called a "zero ending," is a Chekhovian innovation. In the first, the story line anticipates a certain denouement but veers off from it in an unexpected direction. Thus in Chekhov's "Orden" ("The Decoration," 1884), the teacher Pustyakov wears a borrowed government decoration to cut a better figure at a dinner, only to find himself seated opposite a colleague who knows that he does not have the right to wear this decoration. Throughout the dinner, the terrified teacher eats and drinks using only one hand, so he can hide the decoration on his chest with the other. The story builds up to a dramatic climax when Pustyakov, who is standing with a glass in his hand waiting for a toast, is asked to pass another glass. Now he must remove his shielding hand and reveal his fraud. But the expected catastrophe is replaced by a farcical outcome: the other teacher is equally guilty—he also wears a borrowed decoration. Two more surprises follow: the other teacher's borrowed decoration is a higher one than Pustyakov's; and Pustyakov, far from being chastened by this experience, only regrets that he was not clever enough to borrow an even higher order to outshine his colleague.

In the zero ending, the conflict of the story leads us to expect a dramatic denouement, but the story ends instead in a seemingly unmotivated relaxation of tension, without a climax. The most interesting early story of this type is "Mstitel" ("The Avenger," 1887). A man who has surprised his wife with a lover enters a gunsmith shop to buy a pistol for his revenge. However, as the salesman describes the murderous capacities of the various models, the husband's fury begins to give way to an uneasy embarrassment. Finally, instead of a pistol, he buys a net for bird catching and retreats sheepishly from the shop. Not only does the dramatic denouement for which the story prepares the reader not occur, but the story line is inverted. The thoughts of the cuckolded husband are played in diminuendo against the crescendo fervor in the salesman's talk. Both the surprise and the zero ending play on the tension between the expected and the actual. It is, of course, the zero ending, which relies less directly on external action, that is of particular importance in Chekhov's mature prose and in his plays as well. In the early stories, the relation of the conclusion to the body of the story is sometimes contrived. In the later stories, conclusions become an organic part of the story's inner action and frequently contribute to the lyrical inner rhythms and equivalences of the work.

Other characteristics of the early anecdotes that suggest some of the innovations important in Chekhov's later style include terse introductions, contrasting, for example, with Turgenev's leisurely openings. Thus the story "Ekzamen na chin" ("Examination for Advancement," 1884) opens abruptly with a terse internal monologue: "The geography teacher Galkin does not like me and I shall fail his part of the examination today." The speaker is identified only by the ensuing dialogue and action.

Chekhov's compact style also affects his characterizations: the traditional leisurely revelations familiar from Turgenev's writings are replaced by a few significant details of external description. Such details in the later stories often connote general moods and atmosphere, whereas in the early stories the use of such elements is more specific and frequently serves as a means of caricature.

Thematically, the early stories assault social traditions and values, just as in their formal innovations they run counter to prevailing literary conventions. Many of the early narratives are social satires, assailing consciousness of rank, the Russian police state, the vulgarity of the press, and the mistrust of education. It is not surprising that the young Chekhov, who delighted in taking issue with existing social and artistic conventions, would find parody appealing. His early parodies are not often attacks on serious belles-lettres, but rather attack the periphery of literature, such as the comic sketches of the humor magazines, the Gothic tale, the crime thriller, and the like. Examples are "Tysyacha i odna strast, ili strashnaya noch, roman v odnoy chasti s epilogom (Posvyashchaetsya Viktoru Gyugo)" ("One Thousand and One Passions; or, A Terrible Night [A Novel in One Part with an Epilogue, Dedicated to Victor Hugo]," 1880). Gothic horror stories are parodied in "Krivoe zerkalo" ("The Crooked Mirror," 1883), "Strashnaya noch'" ("A Terrible Night," 1884), and "Bespokoyny" ("The Restless Guest," 1886).

In two of Chekhov's best-known parodies, "Svedskaya spichka" ("The Swedish Match," 1883) and "Drama na okhote" ("The Shooting Party," 1884), the object of ridicule is the popular whodunit. Elaborate complications and misleading clues caricature the traditional devices of this genre and are followed by a surprise ending: in "The Swedish Match," the victim turns out to be alive and well; in "The Shooting Party," the murderer turns out to be the narrator.

Serious Stories

The early Chekhov was not only a humorist, however; some of his early works are serious in tone and begin to suggest the transition to be effected by the end of the 1880's, when Chekhov dropped Antosha Chekhonte to become Anton Chekhov, the creator of the significant stories and plays on which his fame rests today. The first serious stories, "Barynya" ("The Lady of the Manor") and "Tsvety zapozdalye" ("Late-Blooming Flowers"), appeared in 1882, just two years after Chekhov had begun his career as a professional writer. Both these pieces, while still conventional in many ways, anticipate some of the themes and story-telling devices of the later works. "The Lady of the Manor" initiated a series of stories about peasant life that was to culminate in "Muzhiki" ("The Peasants," 1897). It is a rather traditional treatment of the conflict between peasant values and those of the aristocracy, and the resulting disintegration of a peasant family. "Late-Blooming Flowers," while traditional in form, anticipates Chekhov's later theme of the life of missed opportunities and presents a foretaste of the many characters in the stories and plays who fail to act to attain their goals.

An important group of serious early stories are told from the point of view of a child, a technique that Tolstoy had used earlier in his *Childhood* (1852). Many of these "children stories" are satires of the adult world, as seen through the distorting prism of the child's perspective. The most significant of these is "Spat khochetsya" ("Sleepy," 1888), the protagonist of which is an exploited child forced to watch nightly over her employers' baby; in her exhaustion she strangles the infant and then falls asleep, relieved of her burden. The story contains a masterly treatment of a child's dreams.

One of the few early stories that Chekhov later included in his first collected works, and perhaps the most significant of the early serious narrations, is "The Huntsman." In a brief dramatic sketch two contrasting characters are presented: a freedom-loving huntsman and his placid peasant wife, whom the huntsman married while he was drunk. The focus of the story is the tragedy of two individuals who cannot communicate with each other. It is limited to a brief description of their meeting in an open field, and of their parting, with their differences unresolved. (This lack of resolution becomes ever more frequently the conclusion of Chekhov's stories.) "The Huntsman" is distinguished by a marked syncretism, as nature is depicted almost in painterly fashion with a few blotches of color. But, unlike the works of Turgenev, in which nature is simply presented as an accompaniment to the action, in "The Huntsman" it is part of the total instrumentation of the story: nature themes, much like musical motifs, are woven through the action and characterization. Nature is a part of the conversation of the two protagonists, not only as a topic, but also as its background, and it is depicted both in colors and in sounds ("Again, silence. From the harvested fields a quiet song rises, only to be broken off at the very beginning. It is too hot to sing . . . "). As we shall see, this intermingling of elements of color and of music with the verbal material will become ever more pronounced in Chekhov's mature years.

1888–1893

"The Steppe"

In 1888, Chekhov's "The Steppe" was accepted by *Severnye vestnik* (The Northern Messenger), then one of Russia's principal intellectual journals. It is one of Chekhov's longest works and his first truly important story. We shall therefore analyze it in some detail.

Superficially, "The Steppe" is modeled on the traditional tale of the adventures and observations of a traveling hero. Unlike the traditional model, however, it is almost completely devoid of external action. Rather, it presents an inner symbolic action expressed through the interplay of themes and counterthemes, motifs and countermotifs.

"The Steppe" recounts the journey of a young boy, Egor, through the steppe country of southern Russia. But unlike the hero of the usual travel tale, Egor is not an active participant in the adventure. His role is passive; he travels across the steppe in spiritual and psychological isolation from his environment. Even his arrival at his destination, where he is to remain in boarding school, does not alter his condition; he remains as lonely as he was when the carriage set out on the long journey. The multiple meanings of "The Steppe," as well as its construction, give a foretaste of Chekhov's later prose and plays. A recurring motif is the contrast between art, beauty, and sensitivity and the vulgarity, ugliness, and banality that Russians sum up in the word *poshlost,* a fundamental conflict in Chekhov's mature work. On a philosophical level, this opposition is expressed as the struggle between the forces of life and death in the steppe, the latter always gaining on the former. There is the melancholy song heard during the travelers' noonday rest, in which nature appears to brood over the realization that nature soon will have to die unsung and unnoticed because of the dry heat. In another passage, nature utters one last desperate shout: "A singer, a singer!"; but no one hears nature's forlorn cry of death. The stifling heat, a graveyard, distant funeral mounds function as images of death against which the hope of the morning's freshness, the pleasantly warming sunlight, the shimmering of a distant hill struggle in vain as forces of life. As the carriage rumbles through the monotonous landscape, impressionistic pictures continue to play upon the theme of futility and death: a kite flies aimlessly overhead "and suddenly stops in mid-air, as though reflecting on the dullness of life"; a young girl lies on top of a passing wagon laden with grain, "sleepy and exhausted by the heat"; a lonely poplar appears on the horizon, "but who planted it there and why it is there, no one knows"; the carriage passes a group of reapers whom the heat seems to be suffocating; wild dogs hurl themselves against the carriage and Egor fears that he will be torn apart by their teeth; a sad song sounds; a birdlike child appears from nowhere, its belly swollen from hunger; animals kill animals, human beings kill animals. Against these images of death, there is one detail that stands throughout the narrative as a symbol of vitality: Egor's bright red shirt, which is blown about by the steppe winds and fascinates those whom the boy meets.

"The Steppe" is still marked by signs of artistic immaturity, such as the frequent interpolation of authorial comment, but it suggests major concerns of the mature Chekhov. A technique that becomes increasingly important is the use of recurrent sound motifs, which symbolically signify the song echoing through the steppe, doors creaking, drivers shouting to the horses, and many instances of onomatopoeia.

With the completion of "The Steppe," Chekhov reached a turning point: he never again returned to the short, hurriedly written, humorous story. "The Steppe" is distinguished from the later works, however, not only by its length (there is only one other story quite as long, "The Duel," 1891) but also by its marked allegorical character.

Chekhov and Tolstoy

It was during this period that Chekhov briefly came under the influence of Tolstoyanism. Examples of the influence of Tolstoy's "postconversion" views can be found in some stories of the 1880's; for example, "Pripadok" ("The Nervous Breakdown," 1888), which depicts the debasing nature of prostitution. For a brief time, Chekhov seems to have been swayed by Tolstoy's doctrine of nonresistance to evil, as evidenced by such stories as "Khoroshie lyudi" ("Good People," 1886), which contains an extended discussion of Tolstoy's doctrine. This moralizing story praises, in Tolstoy's terms, nonresistance to evil and the moral beauty of humble labor; it differs markedly in tone from Chekhov's later work. Fifteen years after its publication, Chekhov revised "Good People" for his collected works of 1901 by eliminating part of the debate and by weakening the Tolstoyan emphasis. Other works, notably "Nepriyatnost" ("An Unpleasantness," 1888) and "Vragi" ("Enemies," 1887), are sympathetic to Tolstoy's injunction against giving vent to anger. In the latter story, a doctor whose child has just died answers an emergency call to the house of a rich neighbor; there he discovers that the neighbor's wife, whose life-threatening illness was given as the reason for the call, has only pretended illness in order to facilitate her elopement with a lover. There ensues an angry verbal duel between the cuckolded husband and the enraged doctor, but the story ends on a Tolstoyan note: the immorality and futility of violent thoughts and actions.

After 1890, Chekhov wrote no further stories influenced by Tolstoy's religious and ethical views. As he explained in a letter to his editor, Suvorin, with typical facetiousness:

> Maybe it is because I no longer smoke that Tolstoy's teachings have ceased to move me. In the depths of my soul, I feel hostile to them and that is plainly unjust. In my veins courses peasant blood, and no one can impress me with examples of peasant virtues. . . . Yet, Tolstoy's philosophy touched me strongly . . . for some six to seven years. I was influenced not so much by Tolstoy's basic positions . . . as by the Tolstoyan manner of expressing himself, by his wisdom and probably by some kind of hypnotism. Now something in me protests; prudence and justice tell me that there is more love for humanity in electricity and steam than in chastity and vege-

tarianism. War is an evil; law courts are evil; but this does not mean that I must walk around in bast shoes and sleep on the stove with the workmen. But the question is not whether I am "for" or "against" Tolstoy, but that somehow Tolstoy has become remote from me, that he is no longer in my soul.

(27 March 1894)

But Chekhov never stopped admiring Tolstoy's art. It is clear from the diaries of Tolstoy and Chekhov that the two men exerted a magnetic influence on each other. Chekhov's own letters express this admiration: "In my entire life I have never respected a single man so profoundly, I might even say so extremely, as [Tolstoy]" (9 November 1889). And on 28 January 1900, apropos of Tolstoy's illness: "I am afraid of Tolstoy's death. If he should die, there would be a huge void in my life. . . . Without him, [the world of literature] would be a flock without a shepherd."

Tolstoy's mysticism and rejection of science and medicine never attracted Chekhov, even in his brief period of discipleship. Many of Chekhov's most positive characters are scientists. Science, to him, was an indispensable adjunct to art, although he was later to take issue with those who worshiped science uncritically. His medical training undoubtedly affected his artistic outlook. His almost anatomical dissection of character and his conciseness clearly are part and parcel of a scientific method that he acquired through his professional schooling. Nor could Chekhov ever agree with Tolstoy's renunciation of art as sinful. Concerning Tolstoy's *What Is Art?*, which contains the essence of his attack on art, Chekhov wrote that it

> represents nothing of interest. All this is old hat. To say of art that it has become enfeebled and has entered a cul-de-sac, that it is not what it should be, is like saying that the desire to eat and drink has become old-fashioned and that it is no longer what it should be. Of course, hunger is an old phenomenon, and in our desire to eat we

have come to a cul-de-sac; yet to eat is necessary, and we shall continue to eat no matter what the gentlemen philosophers tell us.

(letter to Suvorin, 4 January 1898)

In the 1890's, Chekhov began to take direct issue with Tolstoy's philosophy. Certain of his protagonists, for example Gromov in "Palata No. 6" ("Ward No. 6," 1892), strongly attack the doctrine of nonresistance to evil. Chekhov's attitude toward the old master was tempered by his own scientific and artistic skepticism, yet remained complex, so that even after 1890 certain characters continue to be presented in something like the Tolstoyan spirit.

Hypocrisy and Narcissism

A persistent Chekhovian theme—self-admiration to the point of self-deception—has a significant beginning in the period under discussion. Two stories stand out here, "Knyaginya" ("The Princess," 1889) and "Poprygunya" ("The Grasshopper," 1892).

In "The Princess," the picture of a hypocritical and sentimental woman is achieved by a skillful manipulation of the point of view. While the voice of the story is that of the omniscient author, the work develops a many-faceted picture by presenting her as others see her and as she sees herself.

The most significant among the stories that develop the theme of the narcissistic woman is "The Grasshopper," which makes further use of the multiple point of view. This novella contrasts an idealized physician, Osip Ivanovich Dymov, with his shallow and pretentious wife, Olga, who imagines herself to possess great artistic talent. When Dymov discovers that his wife is having an affair with a mediocre painter, he allows himself to become infected by one of his patients in an act of self-sacrifice that causes his death.

The story opens at the wedding of Dymov and Olga, presented initially from Olga's point of view:

"Look at him: it is true, isn't it, that there is something in him?" she said to her friends, nodding toward her husband as though wishing to explain why she had married such a simple, very ordinary, in no way distinguished man.

This description of Dymov is clearly Olga's disdainful view of her husband; what follows is an authorial objective view, contrasting with the negative estimate just expressed:

Her husband, Osip Ivanovich Dymov, was a physician with the rank of Titular Councillor. He worked in two hospitals: in one, as a visiting physician, in the other, as a pathologist. Daily, from nine in the morning until noon, he saw patients and made rounds in the wards; and in the afternoon, he took a horse tram to the other hospital, where he dissected bodies. His private practice was small and earned him only some five hundred rubles a year. That was all. What else could be said about him?

Here, again, the objective authorial tone is modified by a phrase of reported speech, representing Olga's point of view ("That was all"). And so it continues, with one perspective qualified or contradicted by its opposite. As the Soviet critic Alexander Chudakov has pointed out, the insincere value words and attitudes of the heroine are continually juxtaposed with the neutral tone of the objective observer. So are the details that characterize her: the fake artiness that mixes a Renaissance lamp with a pair of peasant bast shoes, a medieval halberd with a sickle; the clichés in which she speaks. All these are given side by side with the authorial voice that describes Olga and her actions in objective tones.

Olga Ivanovna in her narcissism is a prototype of Chekhov's many men and women who, like Madame Ranevskaya in *The Cherry Orchard* and Professor Serebryakov in *Uncle Vanya*, have a falsely exalted view of themselves.

Early Social Stories

As a result of his sociological research trip to Sakhalin Chekhov not only rejected Tolstoy's religious doctrine, but also experienced an increase in social awareness that aligned him with the liberal camp in Russia. The only stories of 1890, "Vory" ("Thieves") and "Gusev," both completed after his return from Sakhalin, as well as "Baby" ("Peasant Wives," 1891), "Zhena" ("The Wife," 1892), and "V ssylke" ("In Exile," 1892), reflect this strengthened social awareness.

"Thieves" depicts a group of horse thieves. Suvorin, for whose journal the story was written, criticized it for failing to distinguish clearly between good and evil. Chekhov's letter of reply is a manifesto of method that is as close to the ideology of Zola's naturalism as Chekhov was ever to come:

> You criticize me for objectivity, calling it indifference to good and evil, absence of ideals and ideas and so on. You wish that when I depict horse thieves, I should say that horse stealing is bad. But this has been known for a long time, even without me. Let the jurors pass judgment on this; my task is only to show what horse thieves are like. I write: you are dealing with horse thieves, so you should know that they are not beggars, but well-fed people, that they are people of conviction, and that horse stealing is not only thievery, but a passion. Certainly, it would be nice to combine art with preaching, but for myself personally this is extremely difficult, and almost impossible because of problems of technique. In order to show horse thieves in seven hundred lines, I always have to speak and think in their tone, and feel in their spirit, otherwise—if I added subjectivity—my images would become diluted and the tale would not be as compact as a short tale must be. When I write, I put all my faith in the reader, presuming that the subjective elements lacking in my tale will be supplied by him.
>
> (March 1889)

"Peasant Wives" is a study of hypocrisy and oppression; its chief protagonist is a trader, one of whose victims is a peasant woman. With its treatment of the oppression of women in patriarchal peasant society, "Peasant Wives" anticipates many of Chekhov's later stories that depict the cruel treatment of women, such as "The Peasants" and "V ovrage" ("In the Ravine," 1900).

In 1889, Chekhov took an active part in famine relief. He worked in a program organized to buy up the horses that peasants were forced to sell for lack of food and fodder, so as to return the animals to the peasants in time for spring ploughing. He collected money for this project and helped to publish a volume of articles and belles-lettres in aid of the famine victims. "The Wife," published in January 1891, deals with the famine. It depicts the indifference of the landowners to the lot of the peasants and satirizes the ineffectiveness of aristocratic philanthropy. This is contrasted with the harsh realities of peasant life, naturalistically conveyed through the tone and mood characteristic of Chekhov's later peasant stories. But "The Wife" is marred by heavy-handed didacticism and a black-and-white presentation.

A work also concerned with broad social problems but more subtly drawn is "In Exile," inspired by Chekhov's observations in Sakhalin. It treats the exiles in Siberia, to whom human dignity is denied. The protagonists are two men of different social background, a young Tatar who is ill and yearns for his warm land and his wife, and an old aristocrat, deserted by his wife, who desperately searches for a doctor to cure his hopelessly ill daughter.

The Quest for a World View: 1889–1894

Simultaneous with Chekhov's concern with social problems and his estrangement from Tolstoy's ideology is his search for a coherent world view of his own. One cannot say that Chekhov ever evolved a unified philosophy. He was, after all, an artist and not a philosopher. But search he did, and this quest is expressed in a series of stories that deal more directly than his other works with specific philosophical questions. These stories are: "Skuchnaya istoriya" ("A Dreary Story," 1889) "Duel'" ("The Duel," 1891), "Gusev," "Ward No. 6," "Chorny monakh" ("The Black Monk," written in 1893 and published in 1894). After "The Black Monk" Chekhov never again showed so intense an interest in philosophical ideas. Subsequent to this story questions of moral philosophy are never posed directly; rather, they are suggested obliquely by the inner movement of the work.

One of the most important themes in the "philosophical stories" is man's dedication to intellect and science; as Chekhov was himself a man of science, this is not surprising. It has become almost a cliché to depict Chekhov as a man dedicated to the scientific point of view. His clinical probing of character, his lack of moralizing (with a few exceptions), and his objective approach to the problems his heroes face frequently bring Chekhov close to the method of Zola, whom he greatly admired, although this influence must not be exaggerated. Chekhov was intimately acquainted with Zola's *Le roman expérimental* (The Experimental Novel, 1880), as well as with Claude Bernard's *Introduction à l'étude de la médecine expérimentale* (Introduction to the Study of Experimental Medicine, 1865), which strongly influenced Zola's literary theories. The sympathetic portraits of medical men, who in Chekhov frequently represent the humane point of view in the conflict between beauty and vulgarity, have struck many readers. Yet it would be oversimplifying to say that Chekhov's identification with the scientific outlook was unqualified. While he was clearly inclined toward the spirit of empiricism, positivism, and scientific optimism that reigned at the end of the century, he was skeptical about the *scientistic* attitude, also very strong in his day, which tended to place science above man. This conflict between science and traditional humanistic values is reflected in the stories we have labeled "searching."

In "A Dreary Story," an exaggerated dedication to scientism by a capable scientist is one of the causes of his isolation and unhappiness; in "Gusev," the superiority of intellect is satirized; in "The Duel," belief in a scientific superman is voiced by a cold Nietzschean scientist; in "Ward No. 6," the idea of the overpowering importance of the intellect serves to justify submission to evil; and in "The Black Monk," a scientist hallucinates the phantasmal figure of a monk who persuades the former that he is a superman, made all-powerful by the strength of his scientifically trained mind.

"A Dreary Story" portrays a noted professor of medicine who realizes in his old age that, in spite of his scientific accomplishments, his life has been a failure. His search for a unifying world view has proved unsuccessful; his fame has brought him moral and philosophical isolation. Perhaps the underlying error is the professor's total commitment to the scientism of the age. Although realized at the highest level, this dedication proves in the end to be inadequate. The professor vaguely feels the imperfection of his science and faintly yearns for beauty and art; he cannot experience life as an integrated whole. In "A Dreary Story," as in all the "searching" stories, the philosophical perspective is tied to the psychological one, as the narratives examine man's search for life as wholeness, the elusiveness of this unity, and the individual's consequent isolation.

"Gusev" combines elements of social protest with some of the same philosophical considerations. It is set in the squalid ward of a military hospital ship and unfolds through the conversation of two moribund patients: the simple peasant Gusev, who accepts his illness and impending death stoically, and the intellectual Pavel Ivanych, who opposes Gusev's humility and its Tolstoyan implications with a powerful assertion of intellectual protest.

"The Duel" is Chekhov's longest prose work, longer even than "The Steppe," from which it is distinguished by its greater dependence on action and dramatic conflict. It pursues the theme of overcommitment to science in the character of a young natural scientist, von Koren, who is contrasted with an uncommitted, drifting intellectual, Laevsky. The conflict of the story lies in the philosophical and personal antagonism of these two. In opposition to the lackadaisical but sensitive Laevsky, cursed by indecisiveness, is the young scientist, a puritanical fanatic who believes that Charles Darwin's theory of the survival of the fittest justifies the destruction, in the name of humanity, of all those who do not make a material contribution to mankind, including Laevsky. Von Koren speaks of his desire to destroy Laevsky, and his opportunity arises when the latter challenges him to a duel. This duel, presented as a parody of all the duels in Russian romantic literature, leads to a quite unmotivated reconciliation between the two: Laevsky can now set to work and von Koren is chastened. "The Duel" is the only one of the "searching" stories in which Chekhov attempted to resolve the philosophical conflict within the context of the story; and this attempt, as well as the story's uncharacteristically wordy conclusion, constitute its weakness.

The clinical naturalism of "Ward No. 6" extends the mood of "Gusev," and a treatment of Tolstoyan issues relates it to "The Duel." "Ward No. 6" also continues the search for a unifying idea and studies the consequences of a heightened intellectualism. But the main issue is the doctrine of nonresistance to evil. We are shown two individuals of differing, though not quite opposite, temperaments: Ivan Gromov, a patient in the psychiatric ward of a provincial hospital, and Dr. Andrey Ragin, a physician in the same hospital. Gromov, an intelligent and sensitive man, will not acquiesce in the brutality and injustice he sees around him, and he continues to yearn for the fullness of life that escapes him. In contrast to Gromov's sincere, though sterile, idealism is the hypocrisy of the satirically drawn administrator of the disorderly hospital, Dr. Ragin.

He too is repelled by conditions in the hospital, but he withdraws from all conflict. His attitude leads him into an isolation even more profound than that of the protesting Gromov. Ragin meekly accepts evil; but unlike the submissive Tolstoyan type whom he emulates, he makes of his humility an intellectual justification for moral impotence and sterility. He loves "deep" books, but his manner of reading them betrays his dilettantism.

> He does not read as rapidly and passionately as Gromov. He reads slowly, frequently stopping over a passage which seems to him particularly pleasing or incomprehensible. He always has a decanter of vodka next to his book, and a salted pickle or a pickled apple always lies before him, directly on the tablecloth, without a plate. Every half hour, without taking his eyes from the book, he pours himself a glass of vodka and drinks it. Then, without looking, he gropes for the pickle and bites off a little piece.

Ragin's idealism, at odds with his untidy pickle-eating reading habits, emerges in his discussions with Gromov, to whom he attempts to justify his passivity by preaching his version of the stoic philosophy of Marcus Aurelius: we only imagine pain, he tells Gromov; the pain will disappear if we do not complain. Again, if you can find inner happiness, it does not matter if you are not physically free. Gromov rejects the doctor's defense of submissiveness with an appeal to the overwhelming importance of sensation. He who does not react to pain with protest no longer lives, Gromov asserts. Christ himself "reacted to reality by smiling, by sadness, by anger, and even by melancholy. He did not meet his suffering with a smile on his lips; on the contrary, he prayed in the garden of Gethsemane that this cup might pass him by." In a final ironic twist, Ragin's close association with Gromov leads to his also being considered insane by the society that has passed judgment on Gromov. He too is locked in the cruel Sixth Ward, and in the face of his own suffering he protests and, implicitly, renounces his Tolstoyan submission.

In 1894, Chekhov completed the last of the philosophical stories begun in 1889, "The Black Monk," which he had worked on during the summer of 1893. While in his later works philosophical questions are no longer treated as directly as they are in the stories we have called "searching," they continue to be posed and are increasingly integrated into the psychological and dramatic action. This trend is already evident in "The Black Monk."

The protagonist of "The Black Monk" is a mediocre and ineffective scientist, Kovrin, who begins to have visions in which a black-robed monk tells him that he is an intellectual superman. The belief in a scientific and intellectual superman, already posed in "The Duel," is now explored through the hallucinations of a most ordinary man. The monk talks beguilingly of Kovrin's mission to lead mankind to immortality and eternal truth; but the charm the monk casts by his eloquence is broken when he fails to answer Kovrin's question about the nature of that "eternal truth." At this point, the monk falters and disappears.

"The Black Monk" is probably the least successfully analyzed of all of Chekhov's stories, for it is often read in an oversimplified manner. Some critics have attempted to find a single key to the story, or have tried to find Chekhov's "answer" to the problems posed in the work. But Chekhov never meant to "solve" the problems he posed; rather, he followed the method he had explained to Suvorin, "to pose a question correctly, as a judge should," and to leave it to the readers, as the jury, "to make up their own minds, each according to his taste."

As to the phantom monk himself, one cannot agree with those critics who have claimed that the monk's views are rejected by the story. While it destroys the monk's premise, belief in the intellectual superman, one cannot say that all the monk's beliefs are shown as delusions. When the monk speaks of "the great and brilliant future" of mankind in the wake of science humanely conceived, he echos the hopes of Chekhov's most positive heroes, although these hopes are never presented without some irony.

In Chekhov's mature work, the conflict between the exceptional person and a venal and vulgar environment recurs frequently; but in "The Black Monk," this theme acquires a new and bitter twist. Kovrin's wish to recapture his hallucination is both pathetic and ironic. The pathos of a life without illusions, be they even delusions, which must be Kovrin's as he is treated with sedatives, leads to an almost tragic conclusion; he has lost both his illusions and his sanity. But Chekhov's Kovrin is not a tragic hero; he is only a little man, the victim of a sensitivity that does not allow him to accept his mediocrity. Interesting parallels to the theme of "The Black Monk" can be found in Henry James, another writer whose characters perpetually search for the elusive meaning of life. Thus in James's early story "The Madonna of the Future" (1873), a mediocre artist believes himself to be an especially sensitive and intelligent interpreter of art and philosophy, and the creator of a great masterpiece. He dies when he is made aware of his illusion. In "The Beast in the Jungle" (1903), the mediocre Marcher, who lives in total isolation and uncertainty, is sustained only by his obsession that his life is reserved for some strange, momentous, and perhaps terrible purpose. Only after the death of Mary Bartram, who personifies his ideal vision, does he realize that his fate was to have no passion at all; he is the man to whom nothing was ever to happen.

MATURE STORIES (1894–1904)

The Bourgeoisie and the Village

In the 1890's, Chekhov's notebooks and letters begin to express his growing interest in the various strata of society in Russia. This interest is reflected in several stories of the

1890's in which a realistic depiction of the Russian social scene is of the first importance. These stories bear on the growth of Russian industry, the new bourgeoisie, industrial labor, and life in the villages, where the emancipation of the serfs in 1861 had not served to relieve the peasants' misery. In these stories, the sources of human frustration are related to flaws in a social order that forced a majority of Russians to live in deprivation while, as Chekhov indicated, giving no satisfaction to the ruling group either. It is in these stories that we find Chekhov's closest approach to Zola's naturalism. Written between 1894 and 1900, they form a cohesive series; Edmund Wilson, struck by their unity, was reminded of Balzac when he referred to them as a miniature *Comédie humaine,* but this claim seems excessive. Social facts, although fundamental to these stories, are subordinate to Chekhov's main preoccupation—the isolation of people because of their inability to communicate.

Three of these stories depict the new bourgeoisie: "Babe tsarstvo" ("A Woman's Kingdom," 1894), "Tri goda" ("Three Years," 1895), and "Sluchay iz praktiki" ("A Doctor's Visit," 1898). Stories dealing with the social order and the village are "Dom s mezoninom" ("The House with a Mezzanine," 1896; also translated as "An Artist's Story"), "Moya zhizn'" ("My Life," 1896), "The Peasants," "Na podvode" ("A Journey by Cart," 1897; in Constance Garnett's translation, "The School Mistress"), "Novaya dacha" ("The New Villa," 1899), and "In the Ravine."

"A Woman's Kingdom" tells of the frustrated life of a factory owner, Anna Akimovna, who lives in a provincial industrial town. Here, the familiar Chekhovian theme of human isolation is played out against a social background that contributes to the heroine's unhappiness.

Chekhov was not to return to the problem of the industrial proletariat or the new bourgeoisie until 1898, when he published "A Doctor's Visit," a story set in a provincial town that examines the baneful influence of the local factory owners. But in 1895, the story "Three Years" appeared. A long work set in Moscow's milieu of rich merchants, it evokes the atmosphere of emptiness and cruelty associated with this new class. The merchant milieu had already been forcefully depicted in the plays of Alexander Ostrovsky. We are often reminded in Chekhov's story of Ostrovsky's tyrannical patriarchs *(samodury),* as well as the playwright's recurrent theme of the impossibility of love and happiness in these merchant households. But whereas Ekaterina, the heroine of Ostrovksy's tragedy *Groza (The Storm,* 1860), is driven to suicide by the cruelty of her relatives, there is no such dramatically stated consequence in Chekhov's more oblique depiction of the degeneration of this class. On the contrary, all external conditions appear to be positive and business prospers.

The publication of "The House with a Mezzanine" and "My Life" in 1896 marks the beginning of the group of stories focusing on the Russian peasant. It is clear from his earlier works that Chekhov knew and understood the peasant milieu better than he did the world of factory and trade. The rural characters in these early stories—"The Huntsman," "Agafya," "At the Mill," "The Steppe," "Gusev," "Peasant Wives"—are excellently drawn. In the first two stories of the later cycle, Chekhov examines certain intellectual attitudes. In "The House with a Mezzanine," he explores the view of the Russian populists *(narodniki)* that the peasants could be saved by education and hygiene, and in "My Life," the Tolstoyan tenet of "simplification." Both solutions to social evils are found wanting. In the peasant cycle's subsequent stories, naturalistic pictures of village life overshadow social issues.

The April 1897 issue of the journal *Russkaya mysl* (Russian Thought) contained Chekhov's story "The Peasants." Though a few passages were deleted by the censor, Chekhov was able to reinstate them in the first edition in book form, published in the same year. Books were not subject to the same stringent censorship laws as periodicals. The story concentrates on the members of one peasant family, the Chikildeevs. Each member of this family has his own tragic fate, caused by poverty and the resulting degradation, drunkenness, and brutality. It is through the eyes of Nikolay Chikildeev, a Moscow waiter who falls ill and decides to return to his native village, that we see the life of these peasants who drink and beg, the men beating their wives and children. Through Chikildeev's wife and children we also see how and why these creatures live like animals—crowded in a filthy hut, tortured by lice, cold, and stench. These peasants, just like those of Zola in *La bête humaine* and *La terre*, are stripped of the slightest trace of idealization. Only the sexual violence of Zola's peasants is lacking. The naturalistic approach is also evident in the objectivity and lack of sympathy for the characters, which is carried here to an extreme unusual for Chekhov.

In sharp contrast to "The Peasants" is Chekhov's longest story of the cycle, "In the Ravine," published in 1900 in the Marxist journal *Zhizn* (Life). Chekhov had written it at the urging of Gorky, and he himself called it "a strange story" (letter to Olga Knipper, 2 January 1900). We may agree with this estimate, for in the characterization of its protagonists Chekhov has sacrificed realism and produced figures in the spirit of Dostoevsky's philosophical heroes and of the late works of Tolstoy—symbols of ideas. The creation of an atmosphere of power and cruelty is the most striking effect of the story, whose conflict, rather simplified and exaggerated for Chekhov, is essentially that between natural labor and materialistic greed.

"In the Ravine" describes a family of rich peasants, the Tsybukins, who live in a village that has been reached by industrialization. They have abandoned farming and keep a store in which they secretly sell vodka. The picture of commercial greed connects this work to "Three Years," but the Tsybukins, who have remained peasants, are not only hypocritical and greedy, they are also very

cruel, and recall the peasants in Tolstoy's play *The Power of Darkness* (1889).

As the story opens, we are introduced to the Tsybukin world. The patriarch of the family hates the other peasants. He rides through the streets on an expensive horse to show that he is better than them. His oldest son is a police informer, as well as a counterfeiter.

The stark juxtaposition of two sets of characters—like those of the medieval mystery play—can be seen to epitomize the conflict between the kingdom of darkness and the kingdom of light. The world of darkness is composed of the Tsybukins and various factory owners. To the world of light belong all those who live by the labor of their hands, not by exploiting others. "In the Ravine" expresses more clearly than any other of Chekhov's peasant stories his theme of beauty and sensitivity stifled by vulgarity, banality, and a "purely businesslike relation among people," to use a phrase from "The Steppe." Beauty belongs to those who perform useful labor. This idea, treated satirically by Chekhov in the early peasant stories, where it is related to the hypocritical adoption of Tolstoyan simplification, is treated sympathetically in many of his later works. Its spokesman in this work is the laborer Kostyl (The Crutch), whose remarks function as a kind of chorus to the main action. His saying "He who works and suffers is better" could be taken as an epigraph for this late work. Vanya in the play *Uncle Vanya* and Tuzenbakh in *The Three Sisters* make similar statements. "In the Ravine" concludes Chekhov's peasant cycle. Its moralism and romanticism set it apart; it is not surprising that Tolstoy, who had criticized "The Peasants" for its objectivity, was enthusiastic about "In the Ravine."

"Rothschild's Fiddle"

In "Skripka Rotshilda" ("Rothschild's Fiddle," 1894), a story of premature death, we find the opposition of life and death expressed in the contrast between music and what Chekhov had called earlier "a purely businesslike attitude." This conflict is embodied in Yakov the coffin maker, who plays the violin beautifully but sees everything as an aspect of his business—and the business is death at that. He accepts orders for children's coffins only grudgingly, since they are smaller and cheaper; he grumbles that people die out of town, thus depriving him of business; he takes his wife's measure for her coffin while she is still alive, builds it in the room where she lies dying, and then enters it in his account book in the debit column.

This story, like "The Steppe," is based on a musiclike interplay of several motifs and images. In the opening of the story, the theme of Yakov's greed is introduced in a passage the neutral tone of which is modified by a subtext that points to the narrow outlook of the coffin maker: "The little town was small, worse than a village and inhabited almost only by old people who died so rarely that it was even annoying. In the hospital and the prison few coffins were ordered. In a word, business was miserable."

Many details convey Yakov's narrowness and materialism, and the omnipresence of death. He is surrounded by coffins and hates Jews. He is cold to his wife and subservient to the medical assistant who examines her when she is dying. The metonymic detail that indicates Yakov's crassness becomes a leitmotif; it is the word "deficit" (ubytok); he views life as a persistent struggle against "deficits," and this view leads him to a final absurdity, for when he is himself dying, he finds death to be the most rational and economical state: "Since man lies in his little grave not one year, but hundreds, thousands of years, one must figure that there really is a tremendous profit." Yakov concludes with logical consistency: "Life brings only deficit, but death brings profit."

Played against the motifs of ugliness and death are the notes of life, beauty, and art, represented by music. When Yakov lies sleeplessly in bed, thinking of deficits, he is comforted by touching the strings of his violin. When his wife is dying, she reminds Yakov of the willow tree under which they used to sing when they were young; and Yakov's violin playing moves those around him.

The opposing themes have their complexities and contradictions. Motifs of banality, greed, and death may deform those of beauty and life. Even music may be so deformed; it is first stated in terms of the profit it brings Yakov. The stifling atmosphere of the Jewish orchestra in which Yakov plays occasionally, at weddings, to earn extra money, is seen from Yakov's point of view, in a picture that points only to his hate: "When Bronza [Yakov's nickname] sat in the orchestra, his face was sweaty and red. It was hot, there was a choking smell of garlic. The fiddle was screaming, the double bass sounded hoarsely in his right ear; in his left ear, the flute was weeping."

Here, synesthetic images transform the scene of harmony into one of dissonance and ugliness; and these images are strengthened by the sound orchestration of the verbal material, which, in the Russian original, through assonance and alliteration, achieves a pejorative onomatopoeia. "Rothschild's Fiddle" is the first major story of the last period in which the technique of zero ending is extended from the formal to the ideological. Chekhov's hero has posed a question: "Shall one live a life in which the struggle against 'deficit' predominates? Can a life in which beauty and art prevail extinguish the battle for profit and the struggle of man against man?" The story does not provide an answer; the problem persists even after Yakov's death—in the life of Rothschild, the Jewish fiddler to whom Yakov bequeathes his instrument. The story contains, albeit in a somewhat simple fashion, many of the elements that characterize Chekhov's mature prose and also his plays: the thematic indeterminacy, the syncretic character, and the "musical" construction that replace external action, in which nothing really happens and nothing is resolved.

"The Teacher of Literature"

"Uchitel slovesnosti" ("The Teacher of Literature," 1889–1894) suggests parallels to "Rothschild's Fiddle" in the treatment of the conflict between beauty and vulgarity. It is the story of the love of the young teacher Nikitin for Masha Shelestova, the daughter of a prominent member of the society of a provincial town, and depicts the gradual disillusionment of Nikitin. The central theme is the contrast between Nikitin's idealized vision of Masha and her family and the stagnation and pretense of their lives. In each of the story's two chapters motifs of banality and vulgarity on the one hand, and of beauty on the other, are interwoven; the center of emphasis gradually shifts from expressions of beauty and happiness to manifestations of materialistic crassness.

The first chapter opens on an idyllic note, though subtly infused with ugliness. Nikitin and Masha are on a romantic horseback ride; Nikitin dreams of his love for an idealized Masha. A beautiful atmosphere is described:

> Here the acacias and the lilac no longer smelled, music was no longer heard; instead, the smell was of fields; young rye and wheat stood green, marmots were whistling, crows were crowing. Wherever your eyes fell, there was green.

But it is tempered by an antistrophe immediately following:

> . . . only somewhere there could be seen the blackness of melon fields, and far on the left, at the graveyard, one could see the white of apple trees whose blossoms were beginning to wilt.
>
> They passed the slaughterhouse and then the beer brewery.

And so the story continues, always playing images of life and death against each other. The balance gradually shifts toward the death motifs when Nikitin and Masha marry and Nikitin's disillusionment grows. At the end Nikitin has lost all his dreams, and the motifs of banality and vulgarity are all-pervasive.

The Little Trilogy

In 1898, *Russkaya mysl* published three stories by Chekhov that, because of their close formal and romantic relationship, can be considered a trilogy. They are all part of a frame story. These stories are "Chelovek v futlyare" ("The Man in a Shell"), "Kryzhovnik" ("Gooseberries"), and "O lyubvi" ("About Love"). All three are exemplary tales, each illustrating a particular kind of constricted life in which a person "encases" himself, as it were, in a shell to avoid contact and communication with others. This, of course, is one of the central problems of Chekhov's protagonists. The characters of these stories suffer from isolation and the inability to participate in life. The theme of dedication to an excessively narrow segment of life, one of the unifying themes of the "searching" stories, can now be seen as only one aspect of the general problem of man's inescapable limitation of spirit. Perhaps a phrase from "Gooseberries"—in turn a reference to Tolstoy's moral tale "How Much Land Does a Man Need?"—states the theme of the trilogy most succinctly: "Man needs not six feet of soil, not a farm, but the whole earth, all of nature, where, unhindered, he can display all his abilities and the properties of his free spirit." The protagonists of all three stories are constrained by a shell, a mental-psychological-moral "six feet of soil" that prevents them from living full or satisfying lives.

The frame that unites the three stories is a familiar one. After a day's hunting, three huntsmen pass the time in the barn where they have settled for the night by telling each other stories. The theme of the trilogy is presented in the introductory frame story: two of the huntsmen, the teacher Burkin and the veterinary surgeon Ivan Ivanych Chimsha-Gimalaysky, the narrators of the first two stories, are talking about Mavra, the wife of the village elder who owns the barn. She has never been beyond the confines of her village and for ten years has left her house only at night. Burkin remarks that he does not find that surprising; after all, there are many people "who try to withdraw into a shell like a hermit crab," a thought that launches him on the story of his colleague, the secondary-school teacher Belikov, who is the "man in a shell" of the story of that title. The story elaborates the theme of withdrawal suggested by Mavra's behavior, investing it with the broadest symbolic import, in which a man so fears life beyond its outward forms that he goes to excessive lengths to protect himself with various types of "shells." This story leads to the next, "Gooseberries," in which a different kind of narrowness is exemplified in the yearning of the hero for his own plot of land (his "six feet of soil"). When he gets his wish, its achievement makes him even smaller and more selfish. Finally, in "About Love," deadening conventionalism and emotional paralysis prevent the realization of a love affair.

In "The Man in a Shell" the teacher Belikov tyrannizes an entire town in his self-appointed role as the guardian of the "proper" forms of life. When he becomes engaged to Varenka, a pretty, vivacious girl, the results are disastrous, for his outlook on life clashes with that of his fun-loving fiancée. After a violent argument, Varenka's brother throws Belikov down the stairs. Belikov's fragile self is shattered; he locks himself in his room and dies.

Belikov is insulated from life's content by form, the shell: "Any infringement of the rules, any deviation from them, plunges him into gloom." Belikov's estrangement from life, his inability to live, are expressed by the trivialities behind which he hides his soul and by the external barriers with which he shields himself. He speaks only in clichés; he is never without dark glasses; he wears galoshes and a quilted coat even when the weather is fine; his face is always hidden by a high collar; his ears are stuffed with cotton plugs. At home, he wraps himself in a dressing gown and covers his head with a nightcap; the curtains and shutters of his room are always kept closed, the doors and windows securely bolted; he will not ride in an open carriage; his umbrella, his pocket knife, and his watch are protected by cloth covers; and his thoughts are of the past rather than of the present:

> Actuality irritated and frightened him, kept him in constant anxiety; and perhaps to justify his timidity, his aversion for reality, he would always praise the past and things that had never existed. And the ancient languages he taught were actually for him the same galoshes and umbrella behind which he sought protection from the realities of life.

Belikov's compulsive attachment to forms of behavior destroys his marriage plans and leads to his death. He withdraws to his bed behind curtains, covered by a heavy quilt, hiding himself beneath several protective layers as he prepares to die. Only when he lies in his coffin, shielded forever from the perils of contact with life, does he appear happy: "His expression was meek, pleasant, even happy, as though he were glad at last to have been placed in a shell which he would never leave again. Yes, he had achieved his ideal."

"Gooseberries" is the story of the narrator's brother, who, obsessed with the desire to own his own "estate," scrimps and saves, denying himself all the pleasures of life, even food. The idyllic life of retirement on the land is symbolized for him by a gooseberry bush from which he can eat "his own" berries. When he finally realizes his dream, the narrator visits him and finds that he has grown old and fat, and that the homegrown gooseberries are hard and sour. The narrator realizes the futility of the achievement, and is appalled at the price in humanity with which it was bought.

In "About Love," the third narrator, Alekhin, tells of his love for Anna, the beautiful wife of a judge; he feels himself unworthy of her. While Belikov is destroyed by fear and the

1872

owner of the gooseberry bush by the pettiness of his aims, Alekhin's limitations are more elusive. Unlike the earlier protagonists, he is vaguely aware of a failing; but he is prevented from taking action by inertia. Only when it is too late does he realize that inertia has ruined his chances for happiness.

A New Mood

During the last six years of Chekhov's life, a change in his point of view can be noted. After the trilogy and "Ionich," which represent the fullest expression of Chekhov's concern with man's destruction by venality and vulgarity, we find a somewhat less pessimistic tone; some stories written after 1898, as well as the major plays (all written after 1896), express a slight hope, albeit strongly qualified, that perhaps man can find a measure of happiness. The three stories that express most clearly the mood of Chekhov's later years are "Dushechka" ("The Darling," 1898), "Dama s sobachkoy" ("The Lady with a Dog," 1899), and "Nevesta" ("The Betrothed," 1903).

"The Darling" is the story of Olenka, a young woman who can exist only in total submission to a love object. She cannot live without love and remarries every time she is widowed. Her husband's world becomes totally hers; she speaks in his clichés and is interested only in his work. When she is married to the manager of an open-air theater, she can talk only of the lack of culture of the audience. When, after her first husband's death, she marries the manager of a lumberyard, she talks only about the price of lumber and the taxes that threaten to ruin her husband. After the death of the lumber dealer, she becomes friends with an army veterinarian. Although they are not married, everybody knows what the situation is when Olenka suddenly begins to complain about the danger of animal epidemics. When her lover is transferred, she is left alone:

> And above all, and worst of all, she no longer had any opinions whatever. She saw objects around her and understood what was going on, but she could not form an opinion about anything and did not know what to talk about. And how terrible it is not to have any opinions! You see, for instance, a bottle, or the rain, or a peasant driving a cart, but what the bottle is for, or the rain, or the peasant, what is their meaning, you cannot tell, and you could not, even if they paid you a thousand rubles. When Kukin was around, or Pustovalov, or, later, the veterinarian, Olenka could explain it all and give her opinion about anything you liked, but now there was the same emptiness in her head and in her heart as in her courtyard.

In the end, Olenka finds a new love in the veterinarian's schoolboy son, whom she mothers. Now she can have opinions again—about teachers, school textbooks, the burdensome character of homework.

The picture of Olenka, devoid of a personality of her own, is of course partly satirical. But "The Darling" is not just the story of an empty woman. Tolstoy liked "The Darling" better than any other work by Chekhov, and he called Olenka a "wonderfully holy being"; whether one agrees or disagrees with Tolstoy's view, his interpretation cannot be ignored. While it appears at first that Olenka may become one of Chekhov's typical figures of emptiness and hypocrisy, that she is capable of love, albeit so submissive and possessive a love, distinguishes her from the many of Chekhov's lonely protagonists. Yet Tolstoy's view that in elevating the submissive Olenka Chekhov had—at least subconsciously—rejected his earlier ideas on women's emancipation is not justified, for Olenka's absurdity cannot be overlooked. The satire in the depiction of Olenka is strengthened if we consider, as did Renato Poggioli, the relation of Chekhov's story to the myth of Eros and Psyche. Poggioli saw "The Darling" as a modern version of the ancient myth. He noted that Chekhov's heroine is called by the Russian nickname *dushechka*, an endearing expression close to the English "darling," which is also the title of the story. *Dushechka* is also the affectionate diminutive form of the Russian word *dusha,* "soul," which also has the meaning of the Greek *psychē.* Poggioli saw the similarity of Olenka and Psyche as Chekhov's "furtive hint that even in the profane prose of life, there may lie hidden poetry's sacred spark." But he did not note the ironic implication of the parallel with the myth. Psyche breaks Eros' command not to look at him during their lovemaking. When she disobeys, the god vanishes. Like Psyche, Olenka loves blindly; but she is satisfied to love unseeingly and never attempts to "inspect" the object of her love. And those whom Olenka loves successively are but absurd shadows of the god of love; it is their prosaic qualities and their insignificance, not their godlike characteristics, that cannot stand up to inspection. Thus Olenka and her lovers are lower versions of the personages in the myth; and its echo, rather than indicating a romantic interpretation of Olenka's unquestioning love, implies that Chekhov's heroine, who retains her illusions, is too naive and weak to see or bear the ensuing doubt.

In "The Lady with a Dog," written one year after "The Darling," the note of gentle sympathy becomes more pronounced and the story ends on a note of qualified—though highly muted—hope. The plot can be summarized as follows: In a Black Sea resort town, Gurov, a married, cynical ladies' man, meets Anna, a young married woman, and lightly enters into an affair with her. But he is transformed by a love that transcends the casual summer affair. Many of the stories we have discussed depict the ruin of love by banality and vulgarity. "The Lady with a Dog" suggests that banality and vulgarity can be conquered by love.

This story has some points in common with Tolstoy's novel *Anna Karenina* (1875–1877). But while much in the story—the first name of the heroine, the opening situation, the initial behavior of Gurov—parallels the details of Tolstoy's novel, Chekhov's story reverses the traditional romantic-realistic adultery theme of which *Anna Karenina* is the classic

example; it contains none of Tolstoy's dramatic turns of action, nor is there a tragic denouement.

"The Lady with a Dog" evolves along parallel lines. There is the simple linear story that evolves in a manner typical of traditional plot development: Gurov meets Anna, they start an affair; the lovers suppose the affair is over when they leave the resort to return to their respective spouses. But they discover that they are attached to each other with a new and profound kind of love. Behind this linear plot, where event follows event, there evolves another text, with other meanings that cast light on the conflict between two ways of living and loving: the conventional way, which permits superficial affairs but strictly circumscribes them; and a life and love free from artifice and falsehood. These two story lines intertwine, forming a network of harmonies and contrasts; and it is these parallelisms that determine the story's lyricism and govern its poetic rhythms.

In December 1903, only seven months before Chekhov's death, there appeared in *Zhurnal dlya vsekh* (Journal for All) his last story, "Nevesta" ("The Betrothed"), a work pervaded by the tone of melancholy optimism that we have noted in this late group. In many respects, "The Betrothed" represents the apotheosis of the innovation Chekhov brought to the art of the short story. And it is the work that best demonstrates the revolutionary character of his narrative art. In its treatment of time and space, in its inner lyricism, in its high degree of syncretism, "The Betrothed" is the culmination of Chekhov's striking out in new directions. We have already noted the frequently nonlinear character of time in Chekhov's work. The usual relation of forward movement *in* space *through* time—in short, directionality— is in fact suspended, and a heightened artistic tension results from the interplay between the temporal and the atemporal, the directional and the nondirectional. Thus, for example, in "Arkhierey" ("The Bishop," 1902), the action is based on the motif of the coming and going of the bishop from home to church, to home, to church, repeatedly, until he returns home to die. Similarly, in "The Darling," the movement of the heroine from one dependent love relationship to another remains in the end directionless. She has moved in a circle, and her apparent cause-and-effect relations are all without consequence.

"The Betrothed" concerns Nadya, a young girl who lives in a provincial town with her widowed mother and her loud and coarse grandmother. She is engaged to the handsome but dull Andrey, the son of the local priest. The artist Sasha, a protégé of the grandmother, awakens in Nadya a sense of futility about her life. Responding to his plea, she leaves her home to study in Saint Petersburg, thus breaking off her engagement. On her way back home for a visit, she stops briefly at Sasha's quarters in Moscow, realizes that he is not a liberator, and sees that he lives poorly and is ill. Once home, she sees her environment with new eyes, and leaves again. The story ends with the phrase: " . . . she left the town—as she supposed, forever."

The underlying meaning of the story concerns Nadya's attempt to free herself from what is first depicted as the stifling environment of her grandmother's household, her shallow mother, and her fiancé. Nadya's soul is torn between the banality of her home and a vague idea of freedom, the most extreme form of which is the utopia preached by Sasha. Psychological space is molded by actual dimensions, ranging from the most circumscribed (Nadya's bedroom; the house) to the most unbounded (Russia; all of nature). But the ambiguity of this opposition is realized later, when the bedroom becomes an infantile haven, nature becomes hostile, and Nadya can no longer see them in their pristine opposition. While there is a value relation, the outside being marked as positive and the inside as negative, this relation is fluid and never fixed; it is not always as fluid as this in Chekhov's work. The theme of opposition between ugliness and beauty, banality and art, epitomized in Nadya's revolt, is played out through her changing perceptions.

The story has evoked considerable debate over the question of its optimism. Does Chekhov imply Nadya's liberation as she is awakened to a new life and rejects the old one? This is the common interpretation of the story, and clearly, there is in the ending a melancholy optimism, also characteristic of Chekhov's later plays: Nadya has returned to her home, which she sees with a new maturity: "And it seemed to her that . . . everything was merely waiting—waiting not so much for the end as for the beginning of something young and fresh."

But the wistful remarks that follow—"Oh, if only this new clear life would arrive more quickly" and "Such a life would come sooner or later"—disturb the hopeful tone, as does the modifier in the phrase that ends the story: "The next morning, lively and gay, she left the town—*as she supposed*, forever" (emphasis added). Thus while the story ends on a positive note (there is a new life), it is contradicted by a multitude of signs implying that nothing has really changed. The question raised in the critical debate as to the optimism or pessimism of the story therefore seems misplaced, since the very essence of the artistic form of "The Betrothed" is that it consists of two interpenetrating, contrapuntal voices. Chekhov has not only asked a question; he has also shown that in life there are no simple answers.

CHEKHOV THE DRAMATIST

The bulk of Chekhov's literary output was narrative prose, and one might well argue that he was first and foremost a writer of short stories who revolutionized this genre. But his dramaturgy was equally revolutionary, and in many ways similar in development and artistic innovation. Chekhov's dramatic production is usually divided into two categories: (1)

traditional-action plays, in which the action takes place onstage in full view of the audience; and (2) indirect-action plays, with little external action onstage: Only the results of action, which takes place elsewhere, are shown. To the latter category belong Chekhov's four major plays, *Chayka* (*The Seagull*, 1896), *Dyadya Vanya* (*Uncle Vanya*, 1899), *Tri sestry* (*The Three Sisters*, 1900–1901), and *Vishnevy sad* (*The Cherry Orchard*, 1904).

Chekhov began writing plays later than stories. His first play, *Ivanov*, was written in 1887, during the time when he was writing "The Steppe." Most of his early works are one-act comedies, very similar to his early anecdotes—some, in fact, are adaptations of these sketches. Others are serious, even tragic. Ronald Hingley called two of them, *On the High Road* (1885) and *Swan Song* (1887–1888), "tearjerkers." But Chekhov's early farces have significance because they anticipate some of the revolutionary techniques of his later plays. These farces, *Medved* (*The Bear*, 1888), *Predlozhenie* (*The Marriage Proposal*, 1888–1889), *Tragik po nevole* (*A Tragic Role*, 1889–1890), *Svadba* (*The Wedding*, 1889–1890), *Yubeley* (*The Anniversary*, 1891), and *O vrede tabaka* (*The Evils of Tobacco*, worked on for sixteen years and finally published in 1902), are not so much situation comedies as comedies of character, each character individualized through idiosyncratic speech patterns and gestures. The farces have little intrigue: the dramatic tension is determined by the characters and their interrelations.

Chekhov's first full-length play, *Ivanov* (1887–1889), contains elements of traditional dramatic action, with situations strongly reminiscent of the one-act farces. Many characters show the influence of the traditional "humors," that is, they are characterized by a single predominant trait: stinginess, ignorance, and so forth. Of the more complex characterization, much also is traditional: the characters "introduce" themselves in soliloquies in which they reveal their essence. But

the use of subtext, often evoked by nonverbal sounds (for example, the repeated hooting of the owl) and running counter to the text; the use of silences; the idiosyncratic language of the characters; the importance given to intonation, for which stage directions are provided ("through tears," "happily," "calmly," "jokingly")—all presage the masterpieces to come.

It is with *The Seagull* that Chekhov begins his search for new dramatic forms. The play revolves around the question of the nature of art and love, and the relations of the characters are expressed in terms of both love and art. The action reflects the debate of Chekhov's day about art—especially the so-called decadent art of the symbolists—and about the role of the artist in society. The dramatic construction is innovative. There is practically no overt action onstage. What is important takes place outside the play and is merely talked about onstage. Even the suicide of Treplev, the young playwright, which might have been a dramatic climax, takes place offstage and is reported with remarkable understatement by another character. Indeed, the play is devoid of the traditional kind of conflict between characters; all conflicts are primarily inner conflicts. This means that dramatic tension is created by new means, no longer by opposition but by the unresolved difficulties within each character and secondarily in their mutual relations. Therefore there are no dramatic climaxes expressed in action or dialogue. The most important events are referred to only in passing.

Chekhov's next play, *Uncle Vanya*, carries forward the style and technique of *The Seagull*. Again, the play lacks a single "hero" and a dynamic action plot; the external action is minimal; and there are no real positive heroes or any real villains. And again, Chekhov's method does not rest on the action on the stage, for that is trivial and ineffective (even a shot fired does not kill and remains without result). Rather, the play is informed by a general mood that cannot be verbalized and might perhaps best be compared to the manner in which music touches our sensibilities. The definition of character, the qualities of the dialogue, the lyrical composition of the endings of the acts—all develop directly out of the lyrical conception of *The Seagull.*

The success of *The Seagull* and *Uncle Vanya* on the stage of the Moscow Art Theater impelled Chekhov to write his next two (and last) plays with an orientation derived from the principles of stagecraft of Stanislavsky's theater—his subtle and profound psychological realism and his fanatical attention to the minutiae of stage business and stage effects. This effort first produced his masterpiece, *The Three Sisters.* Again the movement of the acts is lyrical, the onstage action derived from emotional developments occurring offstage and presented to the audience usually in moments of crisis. The expressive speech of the characters is frequently commented on by a choruslike second "action" on the stage, and consists of pauses and literary allusions. Thus, for example, *The Three Sisters* opens with a lyrical conversation among the sisters, Olga, Irina, and Masha, reminiscing on the occasion of Irina's name day, their lyrical mood brought on by the beautiful spring morning and their dreams of Moscow. But the lyrical, somewhat sentimental, tone of the sisters' conversation is abruptly disturbed by the remarks and laughter of Chebutykin, Tuzenbakh, and Solyony, who have been standing at the back of the stage and acting out a kind of pantomime. Thus:

CHEBUTYKIN: The hell you say!
TUZENBAKH: Of course, it's all nonsense.

Tuzenbakh's and Chebutykin's remarks are, we are given to understand, a part of their private conversation and overtly have no connection with the conversation of the three sisters stage front. But the import is clear to the audience; they comment indirectly, in choruslike fashion, on the sisters' words. And later in the same act, Solyony suddenly quotes two lines from Krylov's fable *The Peasant and the Farm Laborer:*

> Before he had time to let out a yell,
> The Bear was squeezing him to hell.

This is also a multifaceted chorus statement. It comments not only on the energetic way Masha has counterattacked against Solyony, but also on Protopopov, who has just been mentioned and is to be responsible for evicting the three sisters from their home. Chekhov makes this connection even clearer by having Masha flounder for Protopopov's name and patronymic, at one point calling him Mikhail Potapych, the humorous name given to bears by Russian peasants. Plays on this name and on the Krylov quotation are woven, together with other literary quotations, throughout the dramatic action, where they act as subtle subtexts. Again, the play ends not in a tragic denouement (although we learn that one of the characters has been shot in a duel and one of the sisters must part from her lover), but in a lyrical ebbing away, similar to the zero ending of the mature stories. Perhaps a subdued optimism sounds the last note.

The Cherry Orchard has probably been Chekhov's most consistently misunderstood play, both in Russia and abroad. From the very beginning, Chekhov insisted that the play was a comedy, not a tragedy, and that it should be played as a comedy. In fact, the play is subtitled "A Comedy in Four Acts." The insistence of Stanislavsky and Vladimir Nemirovich-Danchenko, the literary director of the theater, on producing the play as a symbolic tragedy almost led to a serious rift between Chekhov and the Moscow Art Theater.

The subject of *The Cherry Orchard* is the forced sale of an estate. Again, what occurs onstage is ancillary action derived from events that take place offstage and are not dramatized. The result is a patchwork of almost static pictures, the cause of Chekhov's reputation as the author of actionless plays. The characters are conceived in absurdly comical poses, many of them broad caricatures. Sometimes the action is reminiscent of the early farces, as, for instance, when Lopakhin, who is later to buy the estate, suddenly sticks his head in a room where a serious conversation is taking place and imitates the lowing of a cow. But here the absurd interruption does not just serve the cause of farce; it also acts as a choruslike commentary, admonishing the audience not to take the earnest talk too seriously. At times, the speeches are of less importance than the nonverbal means the characters use to communicate with each other: pauses, silences, guitar-strumming, and the sound of an ax chopping down trees. All these are of great semantic import, as are intonations, for which there are detailed instructions in the text, more so in *The Cherry Orchard* than in the preceding plays—it contains about 175 directions for delivering lines. Speeches often have no clear denotative meaning; the meaning must be sought in the connotations that hide behind the spoken words. Thus in the final act Varya and Lopakhin meet when others are not present. The preceding speeches have hinted that Lopakhin entertains romantic feelings for Varya, and Madame Ranevskaya, who has just sold the estate, hopes for an understanding and a proposal. But the dialogue that ensues is disconcerting. Lopakhin is alone onstage, having been left by Madame Ranevskaya, who has suggested that he propose to her ward; Varya enters, also at Madame Ranevskaya's insistence:

> VARYA: *(Examines the luggage for a long time)* It's strange, I just can't seem to find . . .
> LOPAKHIN: What are you looking for?
> VARYA: I packed it all myself, and I can't remember. *(Pause)*
> LOPAKHIN: Where are you going now, Varvara Mikhaylovna?
> VARYA: Me? To the Ragulins. . . . I've agreed to look after their place . . . as the housekeeper. At least, that's the impression I get.

> LOPAKHIN: That's at Yashnevo, isn't it? About twenty versts from here. *(Pause)* And so life is over and done with in this house. . . .
> VARYA: *(Examining the luggage)* Where on earth could it . . . Or maybe I packed it in the trunk. . . . Yes, life in this house is over and done with. . . . It will never come back here anymore. . . .
> LOPAKHIN: And I am just now on my way to Kharkov . . . on the next train, you see. I've got plenty to do. I am leaving Yepikhodov here to look after the work outside. I've hired him.
> VARYA: Well, hmm!
> LOPAKHIN: Last year at this time we already had snow on the ground, if you recall, but now it is pretty quiet with plenty of sunshine. It's just cold, that's all. . . . About three degrees of frost.
> VARYA: I haven't looked. *(Pause)* Besides, our thermometer is broken. . . . *(Pause)*
> *A voice from outside is heard calling through the door: "Yermolay Alekseich!"*
> LOPAKHIN: *(As if he had been waiting a long time for this summons)* Coming! *(Quickly goes out)*
> *Varya sits on the floor, lays her head on a bundle of clothing, and quietly sobs.*

Clearly, what is important here is *how* the words are spoken; nothing else will tell the audience the meaning behind them.

Another example is the nonverbal "dialogue" in the third act of *The Three Sisters* between Masha and Vershinin, who have become lovers:

> MASHA: Tram-tam-tam . . .
> VERSHININ: Tram-tam . . .
> MASHA: Tra-ra-ta . . .
> VERSHININ: Tra-ra-ta . . .

This conversation is repeated a second time:

> VERSHININ: Tram-tam-tam . . .
> MASHA: Tram-tam . . .

The conversation takes place a third time, as Vershinin's voice is heard offstage:

> VERSHININ: Tram-tam-tam . . .
> MASHA: *(Getting up, in a loud voice)* Tra-ta-ta . . .

It is clear, as was pointed out by Nils Åke Nilsson, that these nonsense words form a love dialogue of mutual understanding between the two—in fact, as Nilsson called it, a love duet.

There is no climactic ending in *The Cherry Orchard*. The estate is sold; the buyer is the former serf Lopakhin; the owners of the estate must now leave. Thus the material of a great tragic climax is provided, but it never occurs; it is avoided by understatement and by the inappropriate reactions of the owners, who go off to new, totally unsuited occupations. Instead of the tragic denouement we are led to expect, we are given a zero ending: not words, but sounds. The last words of the play do not belong to any character; they are stage directions:

A distant sound is heard. It seems to come from the sky, the sound of a breaking string mournfully dying away. Then, all is silent once again, and nothing is heard but the sound of the ax on a tree far away in the orchard.

All four plays end on a symbolic, nonverbal note. In *The Seagull*, it is the noise of the suicide shot of Treplev, sounding offstage and perhaps coming closest to a true dramatic climax. *Uncle Vanya* ends with this scene:

SONYA: . . . *(Through tears)* You have never known happiness in your life, but wait, Uncle Vanya, wait a little while. . . . We shall rest. . . . *(Embraces him)* We shall rest! *(The watchman taps. Telegin quietly plays the guitar. Maria Vasilevna writes on the margin of her pamphlet. Marina knits a stocking.)* We shall rest!

And *The Three Sisters* ends as follows:

OLGA: *(Embraces both her sisters)* Listen, listen to the band play so joyfully, so happily, you want to live! Oh, dear God in Heaven! Time will pass, and we shall be gone forever. We won't be remembered, they will forget what we looked like, forget our voices and how many of us there were.

But our sufferings can turn to joy for those who live after us. In time, happiness and peace will come to this earth, and people will remember and speak kindly and bless those of us who live now. Oh, my dear sisters, our life is not over yet. We shall live, we shall! The band plays so joyfully, so happily, and it seems that in a little while we shall know the reason we live, the reason we suffer. . . . If only we knew, if only we knew!

(The band plays more and more softly; Kulygin, happily, smiling, brings the hat and the cape; Andrey pushes the baby carriage, in which Bobik is sitting.)

CHEBUTYKIN: *(Hums quietly)* "Ta-ra-ra boom-di-yay, sitting on a curb today . . . " *(Reads newspaper)* It doesn't matter! It doesn't matter!

OLGA: If only we knew, if only we knew!

Selected Bibliography

EDITIONS

Polnoe sobranie sochinenii. 23 vols. Edited by A. F. Marks. Saint Petersburg, 1903–1918.

Polnoe sobranie sochinenii i pisem. 20 vols. Edited by S. D. Balukhatii. Moscow, 1944–1955.

Sobranie sochinenii. Edited by V. V. Ermilov. Moscow, 1960–1964.

Polnoe sobranie sochinenii i pisem. 30 vols. Edited by N. F. Belchikov. Moscow, 1974–1982.

TRANSLATIONS

Anton Chekhov: Peasants and Other Stories. Translated by Edmund Wilson. New York, 1956.

Anton Chekhov's Plays. Translated by Eugene K. Bristow. New York, 1977.

Chekhov: The Major Plays. Translated by Ann Dunnigan. New York, 1964.

Chekhov: Plays. Translated by Elisaveta Fen. Harmondsworth, 1951.

Chekhov: Selected Stories. Translated by Ann Dunnigan. New York, 1965.

The Island: A Journey to Sakhalin. Translated by Luba and Michael Terpau. New York, 1967.

Lady with a Lapdog and Other Stories. Translated by David Magarshack. Harmondsworth, 1964.

Letters of Anton Chekhov. Translated by Michael Henry Heim in collaboration with Simon Karlinsky. London, 1973.

Letters of Anton Chekhov. Selected and edited by Avrahm Yarmolinsky. New York, 1973.

Letters on the Short Story, the Drama and Other Literary Topics by Anton Chekhov. Selected and edited by Louis Friedland. New York, 1964.

Notebook of Anton Chekhov. Translated by S. S. Koteliansky and Leonard Woolf. New York, 1921.

The Oxford Chekhov. Translated by Ronald Hingley. Oxford, 1961–.

Plays of Tchehov. Translated by Constance Garnett. London, 1923–1924.

The Portable Chekhov. Translated by Avrahm Yarmolinsky. New York, 1965.

Six Plays of Chekhov. Translated by Robert W. Corrigan. New York, 1962.

The Tales of Tchehov. Translated by Constance Garnett. London, 1916–1922.

Tchekov's Plays and Stories. Translated by S. S. Koteliansky. London, 1937.

BIOGRAPHICAL AND CRITICAL STUDIES

ENGLISH

Bruford, W. H. *Anton Chekhov.* New Haven, 1957.
———. *Chekhov and His Russia.* Hamden, Conn., 1971.

Chudakov, A. P. *Chekhov's Poetics.* Translated by E. J. Cruise and D. Dragt. Ann Arbor, Mich., 1983.

Eekman, T., ed. *Anton Čexov, 1860–1960.* Leiden, 1960. Essays by N. A. Nillson, T. A. Eekman, V. Markov, Z. Papernyj, Gleb Struve, D. Tschiżewski, T. G. Winner, and others.

Elton, Oliver. *Chekhov.* Oxford, 1929.

Garnett, Edward. *Chekhov and His Art.* London, 1929.

Gerhardi, William. *Anton Chekhov: A Critical Study.* New York, 1923.

Gilles, Daniel. *Chekhov: Observer Without Illusion.* New York, 1968.

Gorky, Maxim. *Literary Portraits.* Translated by Ivy Litvinov. Moscow, n.d. Pp. 134–168.

Hahn, Beverly. *Chekhov: A Study of the Major Stories and Plays.* New York, 1977.

Hingley, Ronald. *Chekhov: A Biographical and Critical Study.* London, 1966.
———. *A New Life of Anton Chekhov.* New York, 1976.

Jackson, Robert Louis, ed. *Chekhov: A Collection of Critical Essays.* Englewood Cliffs, N.J., 1967.

Kirk, Irina, *Chekhov.* Boston, 1981.

Kramer, Karl. *The Chameleon and the Dream.* The Hague, 1970.

Llewellyn-Smith, Virginia. *Anton Chekhov and the Lady with the Little Dog.* Oxford, 1978.

Magarshack, David. *Chekhov: A Life.* New York, 1955.
———. *Chekhov the Dramatist.* London, 1952.
———. *The Real Chekhov.* London, 1972.

Pitcher, Harvey. *The Chekhov Play: A New Interpretation.* New York, 1973.

Poggioli, Renato. *The Phoenix and the Spider.* Cambridge, Mass., 1957.

Rayfield, Donald. *Chekhov: The Evolution of His Art.* London, 1975.

Simmons, Ernest J. *Chekhov: A Biography.* Chicago, 1970.

Styan, J. L. *Chekhov in Performance.* Cambridge, 1971.

Toumanova, Nina Andronikova. *Anton Chekhov: The Voice of Twilight in Russia.* New York, 1937.

Valency, Maurice. *The Breaking String.* New York, 1966.

Winner, Thomas G. *Chekhov and His Prose.* New York, 1966.

RUSSIAN

Belichikov, M. P. *Chekhov i ego sreda.* Leningrad, 1930.

Berdnikov, G. *A. P. Chekhov.* Moscow and Leningrad, 1961.

Bicilli, P. *Tvorchestvo Chekhova: Opyt stilisticheskovo analiza.* Sofia, 1942.

Bunin, I. *O Chekhove.* New York, 1955.

Chudakov, A. P. *Poetika Chekhova.* Moscow, 1971.

Derman, A. *Anton Pavlovich Chekhov: Kritiko-biograficheskii ocherk.* Moscow, 1939.
———. *O masterstve Chekhova.* Moscow, 1959.
———. *Tvorcheskii portret Chekhova.* Moscow, 1929.

Ehrenburg, Ilya. *Perechityvaya Chekhova.* Moscow, 1960.

Ermilov, V. *Anton Pavlovich Chekhov: 1860–1904.* Moscow, 1953.

Gushchin, M. *Tvorchestvo A. P. Chekhova.* Kharkov, 1954.

Grossman, Leonid. "Naturalizm u Chekhova." *Vestnik Evropu* 7:218–247 (1914).

Papernyi, Z. *A. P. Chekhov: Ocherk tvorchestva.* Moscow, 1960.

Roskin, A. *A. P. Chekhov.* Moscow, 1959.

Shklovsky, Viktor. *Khod konya.* Moscow and Berlin, 1923.

Sobolev, Yu. *Chekhov.* Moscow, 1930.

Trofimov, I. I. *Tvorchestvo Chekhova: Sbornik statey.* Moscow, 1956.

Vinogradov, V. V. *Literaturnoe nasledstvo: Chekhov.* Moscow, 1960.

Zaytsev, B. *Chekhov: Literaturnaya biografiya.* New York, 1954.

BIBLIOGRAPHIES

Magarshack, David. "Biographical Index of the Complete Works of Anton Chekhov." In his *Chekhov: A Life,* New York, 1955. Pp. 393–423. Gives Russian titles and titles of English translations.

THOMAS G. WINNER

JULES LAFORGUE
(1860–1887)

J ULES LAFORGUE PRESENTS an interesting case of international understanding and national misunderstanding. Although traces of his influence can be found in French poetry around 1900, and two very gifted younger writers, Charles-Louis Philippe and Alain Fournier, were among Laforgue's admirers, he can hardly be said to have attracted much interest in France in the past, nor does he inspire much today, apart from the attention of three or four editors. Competent editions of some of his work have come out only recently, two of them published in the English-speaking world, where, moreover, the best biographical studies of Laforgue have appeared. The reason behind Laforgue's drifting into the culture of English speakers, although he virtually disappeared from French letters, would, on the surface, seem to lie in his influence on T. S. Eliot, which the latter defined as ''a sort of possession by a stronger personality.''

Laforgue's effect on Eliot can be succinctly described as the revelation of modernism: the sense of a break with artworks of the past, the notion that radically new techniques are necessary if art is to survive at all. In its most extreme form, modernism may seem to deny even the validity of previous art. There are, however, various ways of effecting a break, various new techniques, and various ways of criticizing the past. This essay on Laforgue constitutes, to a large extent, an exploration of

such ideas. Moreover, T. S. Eliot is not the only English-speaking poet whose work is, if not dependent on, at least noticeably related to that of Laforgue. When we look closely, we find Laforgue's version of modernism relevant to other major American poets: Ezra Pound, Wallace Stevens, Hart Crane. They were less directly and obviously possessed by Laforgue than Eliot, but we can see Laforgue as the archetypical modernist behind them. Where the French would consider Arthur Rimbaud or Stéphane Mallarmé as the central figure in late-nineteenth-century poetry, for a long time Laforgue also fulfilled that role for creative minds among American poets as opposed to mere readers.

Jules Laforgue was born in 1860 in Montevideo, Uruguay, the son of French immigrants who eventually returned to France, where he received his schooling at the lycée in Tarbes, a small town near the Pyrenees. Laforgue's relations with his family seem not to have been stormy, unlike those of other poets such as Baudelaire and Rimbaud, but one thing that may have influenced his philosophical horror of reproduction was his mother's death in childbirth after many pregnancies. Laforgue was an average student at the lycée, but when he later came to Paris with his family, he began a regimen of reading at the national library that made of him a highly if fitfully erudite poet.

Laforgue stayed on in Paris after his family

returned to the south. Even after he became employed, at a quite decent wage, as secretary and assistant to a rich art collector and historian, he gave the impression in letters that he was very poor. But his poverty, like so much in Laforgue's life, was more a sentiment than a fact, a function of philosophical pessimism and the feeling of marginal existence experienced by many modern artists. One constantly receives the image of someone sad, lonely, and downtrodden in reading Laforgue, even in those poems written when he lived in opulence; for Laforgue knew life at one of the most powerful courts in Europe.

Laforgue's well-connected Paris friends, always on the lookout for ways to improve his financial situation, found him a position at the court of Augusta, queen of Prussia and empress of Germany. The empress continued the old German tradition of cultural francophilia: she could not do without a French reader to bring some authenticity to the French that was regularly spoken around her and to daily select and read aloud interesting items from the French press. The task was complicated by the fact that anti-German remarks had to be spotted and deftly censored; however, the official duties were more monotonous than onerous. Laforgue spent the years 1881–1886 with the empress, following the court in its round of palaces and watering places, such as Baden-Baden, and returning to France for his vacations. During these years he profited from the Berlin musical scene (Richard Wagner, for example, was scarcely to be heard in France), from Berlin low life, which amused him, and from whatever Germany offered in the visual arts, for he had become deeply interested in the idea of modernism in painting.

No one at court knew that Laforgue was a poet; few people in Paris were aware of it; and possibly no one at all realized that during the early 1880's he was becoming the most technically accomplished young poet in the French language and perhaps the most original anywhere at that moment. By late 1881, before his departure for Germany, Laforgue was already accumulating what he later called *vers philo*, that is, philosophical verse. However, *philo* was also the name of the final year in a lycée, where young Frenchmen were invited to ponder, no matter how immaturely, the great problems in thought. There is a distinctly juvenile quality in this early verse, which was to have appeared under the title "Le sanglot de la terre" (The Earth's Sob). Laforgue's muse was a scientific and pessimistic one; he drew on both contemporary views of the decay of the universe and the framework of ideas constructed by Arthur Schopenhauer, who was then only beginning to be much talked about in France.

These often talented poems, which survive in manuscript, help one to define, by contrast, how Laforgue broke with the main line of French poetry, which they in many ways represent. Here are some characteristic lines, scarcely more valuable poetically in French than in translation: "Yes, I want to know! Speak! Why are things as they are?" "Who drew the universe out of the night?" "I could die this evening! . . . without having been among the stars!" "Certainly I am a genius, for I have exhausted life's anguish!" "How alone we are on our earth . . . alone in the universal frenzy of the heavens!"

One might say that the point of these lines lies as much in their excited punctuation as in what they say. Laforgue declaims quite without irony. At the end of his life, writing of Victor Hugo's posthumous *La fin de Satan* (*The End of Satan*, 1886, written 1854–1860), Laforgue comments: "The boredom of those great stones regularly rolling down from Mount Sinai as usual. . . . There is never any reason for it to end." Such is exactly the problem with Laforgue's early verse: there is too much manufactured grandeur; it could be divided up and sold by the stanza or by the canto, it scarcely matters. And as for Moses-Hugo on the mountain, Laforgue admitted that at the time of his philosophical verse his shapeless nocturnal meditations took place in a "Sinaic atmosphere."

JULES LAFORGUE

Yet during the period of his early verse Laforgue seems already to have had in mind a different kind of poem. He proposed, in a note, to make of his verse "the diary of a Parisian of the year 1880," who reaches philosophical nihilism within the realistic surroundings of the city, its river, its sunsets and rain, and its muck underfoot. A diary suggests an intimacy of tone, a syntax of jottings, and the urban setting recalls the work of the newer novelists of the day: Émile Zola, Joris Karl Huysmans, and other realists. Indeed, the novel, having been a far more flourishing genre than poetry in the late 1870's and early 1880's, would particularly appeal to one in quest of the modern. Zola and Huysmans had also written art criticism in defense of the impressionists, whose freedom in subject matter they admired. A painter in Huysmans' *En ménage* (*Living Together*, 1881), which Laforgue esteemed, sets forth an aesthetic of the smokestack, of the industrialized modern city.

For a young man like Laforgue, the contrast was less between poetry and prose than between officially sponsored academic painting and well-reviewed, prize-winning books, on the one hand, and impressionism and the new literature—prose or verse—on the other. Thus, new currents in the visual arts and in fiction reinforced each other. Complex ideas of style that had emerged in the novel with Gustave Flaubert made prose fiction as self-conscious an art form as verse. It is not surprising, then, that Laforgue himself toyed with the idea of writing a novel, one that would have a single main character, a painter, just as Huysmans' *À rebours* (*Against the Grain*, 1884) was to have a single figure, the aesthete des Esseintes, as its focus.

By 1882 Laforgue was writing from Germany about a new collection of verse he was planning, having realized the inadequacy of the projected earlier volume. This time the title was a provocation, *Les complaintes* (*Street Ballads*, 1885), which, with its single noun, was intended to put a gulf between Laforgue's work and the rather decorous middle-class idea of poetry that prevailed among those whose taste was generally agreed to be of the best. The plebeian-sounding *complainte* even suggests the irregular prosody of songs, something completely foreign to the whole edifice of French poetry since the beginning of the seventeenth century. Laforgue actually stated that the notion of *Les complaintes* came to him while he mingled in a proletarian crowd on a holiday and listened to the street singers. The title of his volume was in some ways more audacious than its contents: only a few poems imitate popular songs, although there are snatches of song or allusions to street ballads elsewhere.

If the title of *Les complaintes* seems to promise overmuch in the line of plebeian entertainments, other aspects of the volume are considerably more revolutionary than anything a mere title could convey. A good place to start is the "Complainte des pianos qu'on entend dans les quartiers aisés" ("The Lament of the Pianos You Hear in Rich Neighborhoods"), since we know it dates from the spring of 1883, not long after Laforgue first spoke of his *Complaintes*. The title introduces a sociological dimension to verse quite undreamed of before and suggestive of the analyses of upper-middle-class life Zola had been making, most notably in *Pot-Bouille (Routine)* of the preceding year. The opening lines of the poem,* devoid of the usual complement of verbs, resemble jottings or the stream of consciousness of the much read and excessively sensitive young man in whose mind we find ourselves placed:

Menez l'âme que les Lettres ont bien nourrie,
Les pianos, les pianos, dans les quartiers aisés!
Premiers soirs, sans pardessus, chaste flânerie,
Aux complaintes des nerfs incompris ou brisés.

Ces enfants, à quoi rêvent-elles,
Dans les ennuis des ritournelles?

---

*Extracts throughout this article are taken from the Pascal Pia editions of *Les complaintes et les premiers poèmes* and *L'Imitation de Notre-Dame la Lune, Des fleurs de bonne volonté, Derniers vers.*

Lead your soul well nourished on literature— the pianos, the pianos, in the rich neighborhoods! First spring evenings, without a coat, a chaste stroll, with the laments of your misunderstood and shattered nerves. Those girls, of what do they dream, amid the boredom of refrains?

Sex is on the mind of both the shy boy and the girls in whose heads swim sentimental songs. As he hears the sound of the pianos drifting through the open French windows onto balconies, he can imagine the scene of comfort and boredom within. Suddenly we have a stylized rendering of the girls' consciousness:

> — *Préaux des soirs,*
> *Christs des dortoirs!*
>
> *"Tu t'en vas et tu nous laisses,*
> *Tu nous laiss's et tu t'en vas,*
> *Défaire et refaire ses tresses,*
> *Broder d'éternels canevas."*

Convent gardens in the evenings, Christs of the dormitories! "You are going and leaving us, you are leaving us and going, to do and undo our hair, to embroider on endless hoops."

First we have the setting of the girls' lives, the school where the nuns teach them to be accomplished and mindless young ladies; then comes the refrain of the sugary romance, which is written in the prosody of songs (with three unpronounced e's) rather than of French poetry.

The young man tries to imagine what kind of girls these could actually be, behind the conformist surface of proper upbringing; he is especially curious as to how they react to men:

Jolie ou vague? triste ou sage? encore pure?
O jours, tout m'est égal? ou, monde, moi je veux?
Et si vierge, du moins, de la bonne blessure,
Sachant quels gras couchants ont les plus blancs
>   *aveux?*

> *Mon Dieu, à quoi donc rêvent-elles,*
> *A des Roland, à des dentelles?*

Pretty or vapid? sad or good? still pure? Is she indifferent to everything or always saying "Give me." And if she is virgin at least in body, does she know the voluptuousness of sunsets and of virginal confessions in the evening? My God, what are they dreaming about: of Rolands? of lace?

He surmises that the girls' minds are divided between their idle preoccupation with clothes and a perfectly unreal conception of men as heroes. We learn more about the young man in his angry reaction: "Allez, stériles ritournelles!/La vie est vraie et criminelle!" (Stop, empty songs! Life is real and criminal!). He has read Schopenhauer and knows that the life force or Will impelling us in our endless cravings and strivings is essentially evil and painful; there are no Rolands coming to solve things and take young ladies into an ideal world away from their pianos and embroidery hoops.

At the same time, the young man cannot help but imagine how he, un-Roland-like as he is, would appear in the girls' eyes. He could be someone's hero but realizes it is unlikely he would be recognized as such (this section of the poem is highly elliptical and needs close reading):

Il viendra! Vous serez les pauvres coeurs en faute,
Fiancés au remords comme aux essais sans fond,
Et les suffisants coeurs cossus, n'ayant d'autre
>   *hôte*
Qu'un train-train pavoisé d'estime et de chiffons.

He will come! But your poor hearts will be at fault in not recognizing him; betrothed to remorse and to baseless attempts to escape their fate: you have smug, rich hearts occupied with nothing more than your routine enhanced with self-esteem and new clothes.

After this outburst, when he realizes that he can offer the girl who would choose him little more than philosophy, he calms down and thinks more realistically about the situation:

1886

"Peut-être brodent-elles,/Pour un oncle à dot,/des bretelles?" (Perhaps they are embroidering suspenders for the bachelor uncle who will supply the dowry?) This uncle is a familiar figure in nineteenth-century fiction: he is pardoned any debauchery provided he does not marry, keeps his capital intact, and contributes to his nieces' marriage settlements. Finally, the young man reflects that despite all that Schopenhauer has to teach us, the life force wins out, first in silly fantasies about ideal males, then in the concreteness of marriage:

> Et c'est vrai! l'Idéal les fait divaguer toutes;
> Vigne bohéme, méme en ces quartiers aisés.
> La vie est là; le pur flacon des vives gouttes
> Sera, comme il convient, d'eau propre baptisé.
>
> Aussi, bientôt, se joueront-elles
> De plus exactes ritournelles.

And it's true, the Ideal has them all gushing, like some wild bohemian weed, even in these rich neighborhoods. But life is there. The pure flagon of their living essence will be *properly* baptized with clean water. Soon, therefore, they will be playing more knowledgeable songs.

Laforgue's metaphor of baptism for sexual initiation is not unlike his often devious-seeming figurative language. However, the word "flagon," as in "stay me with flagons," recalls the Song of Solomon, and we realize that the abundant references to pure water in the biblical text constitute the prototype of Laforgue's lines. Finally, we have a last glimpse of the girls languishing in adolescent vapors and laments while awaiting Roland:

> "—Seul oreiller!
> Mur familier!
> Tu t'en vas et tu nous laisses,
> Tu nous laiss's et tu t'en vas,
> Que ne suis-je morte à la messe!
> Ô mois, ô linges, ô repas!"

"Single pillow, wall I know too well! You are going and leaving us, you are leaving us and going. Why didn't I drop dead at mass? O time, o trousseau, o meals!"

The form of this *complainte* obviously has nothing to do with street ballads; it is a highly imaginative fictional sketch of a kind no novelist was to think of until the establishment of stream-of-consciousness techniques with James Joyce and Virginia Woolf. Essentially, we have the young man's thoughts rendered and interspersed with stylized, typical fragments of rich girls' notions and daydreams. Whereas in Laforgue's earlier philosophical verse a traditional poet-figure had merely declaimed with solemnity, here we have an ironic interplay of voices, a form that reaches resolution and an appropriate ending, while also permitting philosophical attitudes to be expressed elliptically as part of the young man's character. Syntax is sometimes reduced to a juxtaposition of nouns in accordance with what was to be a widespread modernist tendency: the meaning of the poem lies in the interweaving of the elliptical thoughts of the young man and the girls, not in a fully articulated definitive statement. Moreover, the modern novel in France, such as Huysmans' *En ménage,* was tending toward plotlessness or at least toward an extreme reduction in the amount of plot interest, as atmosphere and mood more and more constituted the principal unity of fiction. Such a mood could entail the use, at least to some degree, of nonliterary language. Flaubert had been the first to exploit fully the essential role that clichés, stupid thoughts, and banalities could play in suggesting his characters' world; thus language of no aesthetic value in itself becomes a means employed by the artist toward a higher end. In the "Lament of the Pianos," the idiotic, doggerel refrain ("You are going and leaving us, you are leaving us and going") is a form of trashy feeling and expression redeemed by its place in the general design of the poem. One of the most famous subsequent examples in English of Laforguean doggerel employed in modern poetry is T. S. Eliot's couplet in "The Love Song of J. Alfred Prufrock" (1917): "In the room the women come and go/Talking of Michelangelo." Eliot's silly rhyme conveys the inanity of the conversation.

The contrastive form of the "Lament of the Pianos" permits the poem to display an almost novelistic sense of social classes rare among traditional poetic statements. The marginal figure of the young philosopher is played off against one of the most vapid manifestations of middle-class life: daughters raised to be foolish, sentimental, unrealistic, and totally absorbed in the idea of marriage. Not only do novels of the period show the sociological connection between Laforgue's poem and fiction, but Zola devoted a lecture precisely to the rearing of girls among the bourgeoisie and its unfortunate results (included in *Une campagne* [*A Campaign,* 1881]).

Aside from the social dimension of his poetry, Laforgue was aware of another bond between the naturalist novel and his work: he wrote many little prose sketches that read like scenic excerpts from fiction. In them he shows an eye for the details of modern life that he prided himself on sharing with the impressionists. However, surface realism was not his ultimate goal: he wanted his poems to be "bathed in dreaminess" and devised ineffably delicate stanzas employing rare combinations of line lengths, as in the "Complainte de l'automne monotone" ("Lament of Monotonous Autumn"):

> Automne, automne, adieux de l'Adieu!
> La tisane bout, noyant mon fue;
> Le vent s'époumonne
> A reverdir la bûche où mon grand coeur tisonne.
> Est-il de vrais yeux?
> Nulle ne songe à m'aimer un peu.

> Milieux aptères,
> Ou sans divans;

> Regards levants,
> Deuils solitaires,
> Vers des Sectaires!

> Le vent, la pluie, oh! le vent, la pluie!
> Antigone, écartez mon rideau;
> Cet ex-ciel tout suie,
> Fond-il decrescendo, statu quo, crescendo?
> Le vent qui s'ennuie,
> Retourne-t-il bien les parapluies?

Autumn, autumn, farewells of the definitive Farewell. My tea water boils over and puts out my fire. The wind grows hoarse trying to make the log unburnable that my great heart is stirring with the poker. Are there true eyes? No woman thinks of loving me a bit. Milieus without wings or divans. Rising eyes, solitary mourning, schismatic verse! Wind, rain, oh! wind, rain! Antigone, open my curtains. This ex-sky, all soot, is it melting *decrescendo, statu quo, crescendo*? Is the bored wind really turning the umbrellas inside out?

Among the more immediate observations about tea water, logs in the fire, the wind, and umbrellas, we find Laforgue's elliptic expressions such as the mention of eyes—for him highly sexual and suggestive of the whole woman—and pure symbols such as Antigone, whose lamenting figure Laforgue associated with his favorite season. But the most problematic language is to be found in the short lines, which form not so much a contrasting voice as the poet's compressed vision of his inspiration: his surroundings do not suggest to him the winged flights of traditional lyricism ("divan" is an old Persian word for poetry). "Rising eyes" are the dawn of some woman's presence in his life, which he can only imagine. "Mourning" and "schismatic verse" refer to his dissident philosophical pessimism. These are the subjects that haunt his creative mind as he sits before the fire. In a later short-line stanza, we move from a preceding vision of the dying sun, standing for scientific pessimism, to a mysterious revelation:

Nuits sous-marines!
Pourpres forêts,
Torrents de frais,
Bancs en gésines,
Tout s'illumine!

Underwater nights! Purple forests, cool water currents, fish schools spawning, everything lights up!

This is the imagery of the unconscious, in the somewhat special sense of the term Laforgue borrowed from a favorite book, Eduard von Hartmann's *Philosophy of the Unconscious* (1870). Hartmann was much concerned with the life force, the Will of Schopenhauer's philosophy, but he took a rather less pessimistic view of it. For him this force, which he called the Unconscious, was a source of art and intuitions of the divine as well as a cause of sexual frustration and ceaseless agitation. Hartmann bolstered his views by much reference to contemporary social and natural science, an erudite approach that Laforgue appreciated and that permitted him at times a less gloomy vision of the world than he commonly expressed in his Schopenhauerian moods.

It is of course only reasonable that someone so creative and so aware of all the manifestations of modernism as Laforgue should be unable to identify himself completely with Schopenhauer's life-denying pessimism. It is especially interesting in this *complainte* that the sky imagery of Laforgue's philosophical poems on the death of the universe should be opposed to the underwater world of the Unconscious, where light, reproduction, and organic growth prevail. One of T. S. Eliot's most notable borrowings from Laforgue is to be found in the submarine imagery at the end of "The Love Song of J. Alfred Prufrock," where it contrasts with effete terrestrial life.

The psychological patterns we have seen in the "Lament of the Pianos" and the "Lament of Monotonous Autumn" represent just one side of Laforgue's remarkable inventiveness. They anticipate the dramatic monologues of twentieth-century poetry, but beside them we also find bizarre fables, which, resembling at times some strange joke, anticipate rather certain of Wallace Stevens' poems on fanciful figures like "Don Joost," "The Comedian as the Letter C," or the strange creature called "Chieftain Iffucan of Azcan in Caftan of Tan" (1923). The exploitation of allusion, so frequent in Laforgue and modern poets, is nicely illustrated by the "Complainte du roi de Thulé" ("The Ballad of the King of Thulé"). The poem by Goethe about the king of Thule (which Laforgue may have known by way of Gounod's *Faust*, 1859) tells an exemplary story of a king's faithfulness to the memory of his dead mistress. Laforgue's version, which has the same opening line, presents a king of Thule who abhors the life force or Will represented by sex:

Il était un roi de Thulé,
  Immaculé,
Qui, loin des jupes et des choses,
Pleurait sur la métempsychose
  Des lys en roses,
  Et quel palais!

There once was a king of Thule, immaculate, who, far from skirts and material life, wept over the transformation of [virgin] lilies into [voluptuary] roses, and what a palace he had!

The word "immaculate," as in "Immaculate Conception," is just the first of a series of references to Catholic tradition in the poem. Not only does the king deplore nubility in his flowers, he sets off to console the sun, who must gaze all day on "the viviparous holocausts of the cult they name Love," that is, the endless chain of birth and death brought about by sex and the life force. The veil (reminiscent of Veronica's Veil), or the Holy Shroud the king has woven for the dying, setting sun, is bestowed on the latter in the king's self-sacrificial plunge into the sun's palace below the horizon. Obviously, the sun is, as in tradition, a type of Christ, but here of the dying Christ, a "soleil crevant" rather

1889

than the more conventional "soleil levant," or rising sun. This is not a precise allegory such as earlier centuries would have produced, but it is sufficiently rich in associations to convey the general idea of an ascetic, holy retreat from all sexuality.

The justification for this perfectly bizarre-sounding ballad is to be sought in Schopenhauer's interpretation of Christianity. The philosopher made Christianity acceptable to atheist pessimism by deciding that original sin and asceticism constituted its true core and that all the rest was merely idle accretion. This view was congenial to Laforgue, who retained from his Catholic upbringing a taste for liturgical color and the more extreme manifestations of religion, but little else. The king of Thule performs a kind of imitation of the Christ-sun, as he dies with it in the "fairy church" of the bleeding sunset. Of course, Schopenhauer would not have understood Laforgue's poem in the slightest. He was a man of the earlier, romantic nineteenth century and felt, with his contemporaries, that high seriousness was requisite in a work of art. The ironic poem, going so far sometimes as to seem a joke, is a characteristic feature of modernism, which may reject traditional seriousness on the grounds that it is hollow.

Laforgue's favorite among his strange symbolic characters was evidently "Lord Pierrot," to judge from the number of poems about him. There is even a play on Lord Pierrot's marriage, and we see here an analogy with T. S. Eliot's character Apeneck Sweeney, who figures not only in poems but in the drama fragment *Sweeney Agonistes* (1930). The peculiarity of Lord Pierrot is that we see him always in his relations with women. The "Autre complainte de Lord Pierrot" ("Another Lament of Lord Pierrot") opens:

Celle qui doit me mettre au courant de la Femme!
Nous lui dirons d'abord, de mon air le moins
    froid:
"La somme des angles d'un triangle, chère âme,
    Est égale à deux droits."

She who is destined to familiarize me with Woman! First we shall say to her, in my least cold manner: "The sum of the angles of a triangle, dear love, is equal to two right angles."

This Pierrot's clowning has nothing to do with the circus: he is trying to keep his self-composure in this momentous encounter. The representative Woman opens with passionate rhetoric, while he takes refuge in clichés:

Et si ce cri lui part: "Dieu de Dieu! que je t'aime!"
—"Dieu reconnaîtra les siens." Ou piquée au vif:
—"Mes claviers ont du coeur, tu seras mon seul
    thème."
Moi: "Tout est relatif."

And if this cry bursts from her: "Oh God, how I love you!" I respond: "God will reward his own." Or if she's stung to the quick and says: "My keyboards are rich and resonant; you'll be my only theme." I reply: "Everything is relative."

This little moral fable illustrates a phenomenon of which Laforgue could have studied technical analyses in Hartmann, but with which he surely had practical experience: the structure of the male and female minds—or their Unconscious, as Hartmann would have said—may be so different, depending on social circumstances, that they can scarcely make any sense at all to each other:

De tous ses yeux, alors! se sentant trop banale:
"Ah! tu ne m'aimes pas; tant d'autres sont jaloux!"
Et moit, d'un oeil qui vers l'Inconscient s'emballe:
    "Merci, pas mal; et vous?"

—"Jouons au plus fidèle!"—"A quoi bon, ô
    Nature!
"Autant à qui perd gagne." Alors, autre couplet:
—"Ah! tu te lasseras le premier, j'en suis
    sûre . . ."
    —"Après vous, s'il vous plaît."

Gazing passionately, feeling too banal, she may say: "You don't love me; many other men are jealous." With a glance, het up by the Unconscious, I answer: "Quite well, thanks. And you?" She: "Let's play who can be more faithful." I:

"What's the point, O human nature! Might as well play 'he who loses wins!'" Then she sings another tune. "Ah, you will be the first to grow weary, I'm sure." I: "After you, if you please."

She is of course banal in her female way, while Pierrot's excitement at what might happen expresses itself only by a progressive drop in tone. At the end, in accents Eliot echoed in "Portrait of a Lady" (1917), though on a more realistic social plane, she dies:

Enfin, si, par un soir, elle meurt dans mes livres,
Douce; feignant de n'en pas croire encor mes
    yeux,
J'aurai un: "Ah çà, mais nous avions De Quoi
    vivre!
"C'était donc sérieux?"

And what if she should die some evening, in my books, gently? Pretending not yet to believe my eyes, I will exclaim, "Fancy that! But we had what it takes to live! Was she really in earnest?"

But naturally, as she dies in Lord Pierrot's books, she had no reality; we remember the suppositional and future verbs of the opening of the poem. It has all been a projection of his psyche; he has failed in his encounter with sex before even meeting a real woman.

In the commedia dell'arte farce *Pierrot fumiste (Pierrot the Dabbler,* 1892), Laforgue's figure once again faces Woman, and though this posthumously published little piece is not in *Les complaintes,* I mention it here to show how Pierrot, "a very lyric poet," is used in various ways to illustrate the dilemma of sexual relations among the bourgeoisie of the nineteenth century. The farce is written mostly in silly clichés startlingly put together to form an unexpected whole, much in the fashion of Eugene Ionesco's plays. It concerns Pierrot's marriage with Colombinette, which he does not consummate, first to her relief and then to her bewilderment. Given that Pierrot will not discuss the matter medically or otherwise, after two months of this "white" union Co-

lombinette's family begins legal proceedings for an annulment. On the last night before their legal separation Pierrot exercises his conjugal rights "like a bull" and then leaves for Cairo, assured that now Colombinette is an "unremarriable widow."

This playlet about a poet of superior sensibility, whom "no one understands," like so many of Laforgue's symbolic figures, is best read as a dirty trick that philosophy plays on the life force. Pierrot wishes to remain virgin in order to break the chain of marriage, sex, birth, and death, as Schopenhauer's analysis of life would urge on one. However, the Will or life force has erected an elaborate system of laws and institutions, such as marital sexuality, to channel its energies and protect and further itself, so that a purely spiritual union becomes impossible in wedlock. Nonetheless Pierrot demonstrates that a philosopher and lyric poet is not without cunning: he makes sure that, by the bourgeois conventions of the day, Colombinette will be unacceptable as a wife to anyone else and so breaks the sexual and reproductive chain, in this specific case at least.

Pierrot the Dabbler is not, I think, to be interpreted as an antifeminine play, although it is not difficult to see in Schopenhauer's philosophy the heritage of the old misogynist position—common, for example, in Elizabethan literature—that women are sexually draining and that men are destined for higher things than eroticism. Converted into nineteenth-century middle-class terms, this means that marriage and children become part of the female entrapment of men: the sorceress Armida turns wife. Interpreted according to Schopenhauer's philosophy, the social institution of marriage can be seen as a legalized justification for the evil Will or life force; it is something a philosophic soul should avoid. Laforgue, however, had a more historical view of women, as many notes collected in the volume called *Mélanges posthumes* (1903) interestingly show.

Laforgue, whom Simone de Beauvoir had

occasion to refer to in *The Second Sex* (1949), identified something in the society of his day that he called "féminiculture" and that has a certain coincidence with what is now termed the "feminine mystique":

> As women have been left in slavery and idleness, with no other occupation and weapon than their sexuality, they have magnified it and have become the Eternal Feminine with their fashionable dresses, jewels, bustles . . . novels . . . packets of letters on scented stationery, and honeymoons. We have allowed women to become vast exaggerations of themselves, a whole world for us, which, however, is identified with sex, and, since sex lasts only thirty minutes, women have been obliged, to fill up the empty time, to become a separate human race. . . . With women we have, up to now, merely played dolls.
>
> (*Mélanges posthumes*, p. 52)

As we read the words about dolls, we of course remember Ibsen's *A Doll's House* (1879), along with other images from realist novels and plays. It would seem that, for various social reasons, the late nineteenth century was a high point in the history of making toys of women. Laforgue's solution to the problem was not unlike that of the romantic theorizers of women's emancipation; he thought women should simply resemble men, be "intimate brothers" with men, shake hands with them as equals:

> You have to kill them off because you can't understand them or else reassure them, reform them, get them over their infatuation with jewelry, make them our equal fellows, our intimate friends . . . dress them differently, cut their hair, tell them everything.
>
> (*Mélanges posthumes*, p. 48)

The great variety of positions taken by the modern authors of feminist writings show that Laforgue's notions are rather schematic and simplistic. He denies a bit quickly the existence of various psychological and biological realities.

It is obvious that Laforgue, being an artist and not a polemicist, treats the relations between men and women variously, as the form of his poems evolved or diversified. In the "Lament of the Pianos" we see adolescent girls dreaming in sentimental images, the boy at once fascinated and repelled by them. The "Ballad of the King of Thule" embodies a strict and dogmatic opposition between sexuality and an ascetic ideal, but the whole poem is conceived as an ironic fable that might be read in opposing ways, as is so often the case with highly ironic works. Another much-admired poem on relations between the sexes, the "Lament of Nostalgia for the Prehistoric," takes the initial form of an after-dinner fantasy:

> La nuit bruine sur les villes.
> Mal repu des gains machinals,
> On dîne; et, gonflé d'idéal,
> Chacun sirote son idylle,
> Ou furtive, ou facile.
>
> Echos des grands soirs primitifs!
> Couchants aux flambantes usines,
> Rude paix des sols en gésine,
> Cri jailli là-bas d'un massif,
> Violuptés à vif!

Night drizzles on cities. Unsatisfied by material gains, each man dines. Then, puffed up by images of the ideal, each man sips at his idyll, be it furtive or facile.

Echoes of great primeval evenings! Sunsets like factories in flames! Harsh peace of the earth giving birth! Screams from a nearby thicket! Raw and voluptuous ravishings!

Suddenly there is a narrative voice representing a male stumbling down into a poppy-filled valley where a "bestial" girl is smacking her lips over ripe apricots. The pair cover each other with apricot juice and lick it off while wrestling. The scene concludes with peaceful copulation in the twilight. What is especially notable here is the absence of any suggestion of seducer and seduced, of conqueror and conquest, or any of the other common terms of sexual exploitation. The total image is in accord with Laforgue's general view of the necessary relations between the sexes. This poem is, of course, at a great remove from the Schopenhauerian pessimism in the "Ballad of the King of Thule." Laforgue was not a prisoner of any system of thought, although he loved to develop the theses of the most negative German philosophy. However, in the last stanza of "Nostalgia for the Prehistoric" we see how for Laforgue pessimism was clearly linked to upper-middle-class habits of his time:

> La nuit bruine sur les villes:
> Se raser le masque, s'orner
> D'un frac deuil, avec art dîner,
> Puis, parmi des vierges débiles,
> Prendre un air imbécile.

Night drizzles on cities. Shave your mask; dress in a mourning tailcoat; dine expertly. Then, among the sickly virgins, put on one's silly look.

The motion of putting on "a face to meet the faces that you meet," as Eliot later had it in "Prufrock," the sheer outward show and inner poverty are the signs of a late and decadent age rather than arising from the permanent and essential structure of the mind. It is worth remembering, in reading this *complainte,* that Laforgue was considered charming at the court of the empress Augusta and came to loathe the invitations that he received in quantities.

The juxtaposition of very different kinds of imagery, which we see in the "Lament of Nostalgia for the Prehistoric," is perhaps the single most striking feature running through the volume *Les complaintes.* However, these effects of contrast are far from mechanical devices, since they are put together of such diverse materials: the picture of the autumn sky and the underwater Unconscious in the "Lament of Monotonous Autumn," for example, is quite unlike the opposing images of primitive days and nineteenth-century effeteness in the "Lament of Nostalgia for the Prehistoric."

One is implicit and elliptical, the other sharp, explicit, and ironic. Laforgue draws at times on quite extravagant antitheses of style.

Besides what we might identify as his straight lyric manner (say, the copulating primitives of prehistory), Laforgue sometimes resorts to a superpoetic, parodically poetic manner, as in the "Complainte du pauvre chevalier-errant" ("Lament of the Poor Knight Errant"), where a highly literary and imaginative young man makes the following offer to any girl who will accept it:

> Jupes des quinze ans, aurores de femmes,
> Qui veut, enfin, des palais de mon âme?
> Perron d'oeillets blancs, escaliers de flamme,
> Labyrinthes alanguis,
> Edens qui
> Sonneront, sous vos pas reconnus, des airs
> reconquis.

Skirts of girls of fifteen, dawns of women, who, in short, is interested in the palaces of my soul? Outer staircases of white carnations, inner ones of fire, languorous labyrinths, Edens that, recognizing your step, will play reconquered melodies.

It happens often in Laforgue that images that at first seem quite fanciful have a very concrete and often quite erotic sense. The double entwining white staircases (the *perron* of neoclassical architecture) are the boy's arms seen from the outside; the fiery staircases are the image of the sensation he has in his inner arms in an embrace. The grandiose metaphor of the young man's spiritual and sexual treasures is then developed to the point where he is not only a palace or castle but the surrounding domain as well, with its exotic fauna; in other words he is the Eden as well as the Adam, an Eden "reconquered" by intensity of feeling:

> Oui, sans bruit, vous écarterez mes branches,
> Et verrez comme, à votre mine franche,
> Viendront à vous mes biches les plus blanches,

Mes ibis sacrés, mes chats,
  Et, rachats!
Ma Vipère de Lettre aux bien effaçables crachats.

Yes, soundlessly, you will push aside my branches; and you will see how, at the sight of your candid face, my whitest does will come to you, my sacred ibises, my cats, and, for its redemption, my literary viper whose venomous spittle is quite easily wiped off.

All this imagery, poured out so excitedly as to suggest the young man's enthusiasm and inexperience, derives from traditional poetic sources, from the Bible and from the poetry to which Genesis gave rise. Even the snake is included; it stands for the young man's complicated and somewhat ironic literary gifts. A Renaissance poet would have understood the principle of such an allegory and would not have stinted on the detail. The speaker is, of course, identified in the title of the poem as a knight errant, of the kind who roamed in search of chivalrous deeds to perform, so that the poeticalness of the lines is thoroughly self-conscious—he is assuming a character. Laforgue also understood the use of sexual imagery in older allegories and creates a vision of the knight's senses invading the chapel, which is made of the fabric of a girl's dress:

Puis, frêle mise au monde! ô Toute Fine,
O ma Tout-universelle orpheline,
Au fond de chapelles de mousseline
  Pâle, ou jonquille à pois noirs,
    Dans les soirs,
Feu-d'artificeront envers vous mes sens
  encensoirs!

Then, like a fragile birth, O all-subtle one, O my cosmic orphan, in the depths of pale muslin chapels—or yellow with black dots—in the evening, like fireworks, my censer-senses will rise toward you!

Naturally the ironic note lies in the reference to such very modern materials as the fluffy muslin and the polka-dotted fabrics of La-

forgue's day. Laforgue has a truly impressive way of creating in these stanzas an ambiguous effect: we perceive and are charmed by the lyricism of the young knight's words, while recognizing that they are modeled in part on an allegorical convention that was worn out long ago and is distinctly overdone according to more recent criteria of taste. The last stanza quoted is especially interesting in that a great erotic intensity is conveyed while we are aware, at the same time, of the disparity between late-nineteenth-century feminine clothing and the idealizing vision of the young man, which, for all its sexual explicitness, belongs to a grand conception like the Song of Songs.

It is worth lingering over the various ways one feels and interprets, if unconsciously, the language of a poem like this, for Laforgue was a great master of the many shades of irony and lyricism. Impatient readers have tended to miss the extraordinary craft in the building of a poem like this one. When we have savored the stanzas where the young man's mood and character are so deftly projected, we are prepared for the sudden drop at the end of the poem:

—Mais j'ai beau parader, toutes s'en fichent!
Et je repars avec ma folle affiche,
Boniment incompris, piteux sandwiche:
  Au Bon Chevalier-Errant,
    Restaurant,
Hôtel meublé, Cabinets de lecture, prix
  courants.

But I strut in vain, no girl gives a damn. And I set off again with my crazy sign, my come-on misunderstood, a pitiful sandwich man: At the Sign of the Good Knight Errant. Restaurant. Furnished Rooms. Lending Library. Competitive Prices.

The last eight words or expressions in this stanza quite possibly had never before been used in a serious work of French verse ("quite possibly" because of a few forgotten experiments in "realist" poetry). Although some of

1894

the shock they may once have had is dissipated, the violent contrast with what precedes still affects us. These are words that do not belong to literature of the nineteenth century except in the framework of a novel by Balzac and his imitators; their appearance in verse is almost as startling as if the stanza were written in Danish or Portuguese. The cheap residential hotel that the "palaces of my soul" have become imparts a whole set of images of dirty urban streets, bad food, idle sessions of bored reading, and crude advertising.

The "Lament of the Poor Knight Errant" doubtless owes its origin to a stylistic idea; there is much less of a subject here than in the other *complaintes* we have examined, which can be said to express certain social, psychological, or even philosophical ideas. Naturally we can find here, in an implied form, the customary distinction between the sexes in Laforgue: the male is imaginative and idealistic, the female practical and adjusted to the realities of life. However, that theme became something of a convenience, a pretext for ironic and imagistic developments, as Laforgue elaborated the collection *Les complaintes.* And that leads us to the differences of opinion about the value of the volume.

Some have found *Les complaintes* scrappy, repetitive, and uneven, a repository of every passing inspiration Laforgue entertained. To my mind, however, it is a work of dazzling richness and diversity. There is no poem, even among the relatively slight ones, that does not have profoundly original touches of style, the kind of inventiveness several lesser poets could have based long careers upon. There is, however, a stylistic premise that must be understood if we are to arrive at Laforgue's intentions and the value of his work.

In France there has been, since the seventeenth century, a quite clear idea of what literary classicism is—and therefore also of all that it is not. Essentially, classical style consists of a unified texture of words, of a polished surface in which words are felt to fit together rather than standing out from one another by some remarkable effect of individuality. In various genres and at various levels of style, the same basic notion of classicism was elaborated: we find in French literature such examples as the classical tragedies and comedies by Jean Racine and Molière, the classical fables and novels by Jean de La Fontaine and Madame de Lafayette, the classical odes and mock epics by Nicolas Boileau-Despréaux and Voltaire, and the classical maxims and essays on society by François de La Rochefoucauld and Jean Jacques Rousseau. Each work sets its own limits in vocabulary, sentence structure, or sound patterns; each work is based on a quite plain and unambiguous idea of unity of effect. In English literature, there is not a sufficiently varied number of works of classicizing tendency—even Alexander Pope became radically unclassical in *The Dunciad*—for us to feel the general validity of this idea of style.

There are various terms one could apply to the opposite of a classicizing style, that is, to a style filled with surprises and brilliant sui generis inventions. In France both "romantic" and "decadent" often imply something of the sort. In Laforgue's day, "decadent" especially expressed the notion of a style falling apart through the showiness of its individual parts. Some writers, like Flaubert, had attempted to forge a new unity of style, but the overall impression given by nineteenth-century French literature is one of exploration of the antiunitarian idea.

Here, however, we must note that educated French and English speakers perceive matters of style in quite different ways. Because of the dominance of classicism in earlier French literature, plus the tendency to use examples of the classic ideal as pedagogical devices, classicism has become a norm in France to which anticlassicism is always a peculiar exception. In English literature there are no large polarities of style to which the notions of "desirable" and "undesirable" can easily be attached. In fact, by following a strict, "French" classic interpretation of stylistic phenomena, we find English literature full of brilliant decadent works: certainly *Hamlet,* with its mosaic of styles, and *Moby Dick,* one of the most ambitious pieces of prose in American literature, would be emphatically decadent according to French conceptions. When we see this difference in the perception of style between French and English speakers, it becomes possible to understand why, for many in France, Laforgue represents merely some small, odd vagary of late-nineteenth-century style, whereas for such Americans as T. S. Eliot and Ezra Pound, Laforgue's work was one of the great phenomena of modern literature.

Behind the sense of modernism in the English-speaking world, there is also a particular idea of experience that Laforgue's poetry illustrates. The notion that in recent times we are aware of disparateness and fragmentation in experience and ideas is fundamental to Eliot's and Pound's way of writing, with their abrupt juxtapositions of varied materials and frequent absence of transitions. This is scarcely the place for deciding whether such a notion is generally valid, but we can note that by Laforgue's day there was certainly no unity in the perception of what was art: the academic and the modernist had gone in different directions, and among the modernists, a truly startling multiplicity of styles was to be found. A distinction between the sentimental or sensational literature for mass consumption and a more serious art for the reflective reader had set in.

Laforgue's writing of *complaintes* in popular versification and in quite rare forms as well can be seen as characteristic of the disintegration of the traditional French definitions of art. Another such manifestation can be found in the "Complainte de l'orgue de Barbarie" ("Lament of the Hurdy-Gurdy"), where the hurdy-gurdy plays snatches of banal songs that add up to nothing coherent in any normal sense: the sentimental detail and the obscure total form of the poem present a startling contrast.

We have seen how Laforgue juxtaposes nouns in a kind of loose, verbless syntax, which produces either disparity or ellipticalness. Something of the same occurs in the stanzas of the "Lament of Nostalgia for the Prehistoric," where he uses infinitives rather than finite verbs. This gives a curious immediacy, uncommon in poetry, which Eliot imitated with second-persons and imperatives: "Wipe your hand across your mouth, and laugh." Mingling two words ("violupté," composed of *viol,* "rape," and *volupté,* "sensual pleasure") or shifting a part of speech (the verb "feu-d'artificieront") likewise creates the sense of a newly invented, nonce language. In the total form of the poem, allusion—as to the king of Thule or to Antigone's state of mind—or the general method of leaping from one notion to another sustains the effect of compression. All this is profoundly anticlassical, since, much as classicists value succinctness, they preserve normal syntactic structures.

In the years 1885 and 1886 there was what may be seen as a rejuvenation of French poetry, revealed by works appearing in little magazines or slim volumes. Of all the "decadents," however, Laforgue was by far the most gifted, and in the last two years of his life he produced some truly splendid work. *Les complaintes,* published in 1885, was one of the first works by a radically new poet, and it was followed the next year by *L'Imitation de Notre-Dame la Lune selon Jules Laforgue (The Imitation of Our Lady the Moon According to Jules Laforgue),* the result of a sudden burst of inspiration while correcting the proofs of *Les complaintes.* Meanwhile the tales called *Moralités légendaires* (Legendary Fables) were being written. The spring of 1886 saw the founding of *La vogue,* a periodical that published Rimbaud's *Illuminations* (1886), some writings by Mallarmé, and finally Laforgue's last poetry, his free verse work referred to today as the *Derniers vers (Last Poems).*

Laforgue's private life was as full as his poetic activity: he asked Leah Lee, the English girl from whom he took English lessons in

Berlin, to marry him, and by the end of the year, newly married, he left Germany for good. The great artistic event of 1886 in Laforgue's life was his decision not to publish the poems of the spring called *Des fleurs de bonne volonté (Flowers of Good Will)*, but to rework the material, first into a little play, *Le concile féerique (The Fairy Council)*, which *La vogue* published in July 1886, then into free verse, of which the first piece appeared in August 1886. With the latter, Laforgue found himself more than ever in the vanguard of French poetry. It is unfortunate to record that after this great burst of creativity, Laforgue grew increasingly ill, from the beginning of 1887 until his death from tuberculosis in August of the same year. Leah Laforgue took care to put his vast number of papers into the hands of literary friends and then left Paris, dying shortly afterward herself from tuberculosis.

The Imitation of Our Lady the Moon has never attracted the critical attention accorded to *Les complaintes* or the last verse, although its many Pierrots are among the most charming of such images in French. The clown, representing a radically stylized and expressionistic form of art, is a figure we find increasingly frequently in French literature since the mid-nineteenth century. All those circus figures in Picasso's early work were well established in literary sources by the time he came to paint them. The attractiveness of Laforgue's Pierrots, however, does not stand out quite enough from the rest of the clown literature of the day for *The Imitation* to achieve the same kind of distinction as his other work. However, one aspect of the style of certain poems addressed to the moon demands a word. Laforgue invented a kind of mock-heroic diction that we find again in Wallace Stevens (as in "On the Manner of Addressing Clouds") or in Hart Crane (in parts of *The Bridge*):

> *Lune, Pape abortif à l'amiable, Pape*
> *Des Mormons pour l'art, dans la jalouse Paphos*
> *Où l'Etat tient gratis les fils de la soupape*
> *D'échappement des apoplectiques Cosmos!*
> ("La lune est stérile")

Moon, amicably abortive pope, pope of art's Mormons in jealous Paphos, where free of charge the State controls the safety valve of apoplectic universes!

The old rhetorical syntax of apostrophes and periphrases is used, but in conjunction with such astonishing vocabulary as to be at first unrecognizable. Baroque literature had brought the periphrasis to a high point of surprise and pomp, and here the figure recaptures, in a zany way, its old quality of amazement, the *admiratio* of the rhetoricians.

For such a sizable output of verse in such a short lifespan, the general quality of Laforgue's verse is high, in the sense that there are authentic new notions of style everywhere; even *Flowers of Good Will*, which Laforgue saw fit not to publish, contains remarkable amounts of fine verse—which we omit here only because the splendid and substantial sequence of the free verse awaits us.

Before we examine the *Last Poems* as a whole, some words are necessary about free verse and its theory. The old kind of neoclassical free verse tended to work in groups of lines of standard lengths, such as eight, ten, or twelve syllables, and was always rhymed. It produced a sense of the irregular within the context of seventeenth- and eighteenth-century literature, but its usually regular components corresponded to the generally recognized materials of French poetry of the time. The brief episode of Rimbaud's free verse (mostly in the "last verse poems") represents more a series of experiments than a coherent, widely applicable, new prosody.

The major source of ideas about free verse before Laforgue is to be found in Walt Whitman, and the fact that Laforgue translated some Whitman for *La vogue* has given rise, among those who do not have a thorough knowledge of French and French prosody, to the mistaken notion that Whitman's free verse somehow influenced Laforgue's. The two aesthetics of free verse could not be more distant from one another. Here is the opening of "Song of Myself" (1855):

I celebrate myself, and sing myself,
And what I assume you shall assume,
For every atom belonging to me as good belongs
   to you.

I loafe and invite my soul,
I lean and loafe at my ease observing a spear of
   summer grass.

My tongue, every atom of my blood, form'd from
   this soil, this air,
Born here of parents born here from parents the
   same, and their parents the same,
I, now thirty-seven years old in perfect health
   begin,
Hoping to cease not till death.

The main characteristic is the patterning repetition of words: the rhythmic structure is that of cadenced prose. The parallelisms obviously relate this to the English Bible, whose traditional typography is a kind of half-prose, half-verse.

   Laforgue's notion of free verse is entirely different. It often adheres to traditional verse-line lengths, but syllables are counted as they might be spoken rather than with the fixed regularity traditionally observed in the literary language. Here is the opening of "L'Hiver qui vient" ("The Coming of Winter"), first of the twelve free-verse poems. The number of syllables, calculated according to Laforgue's method, is noted, and the uncounted e's are marked:

Blocus sentimental! [6] *Messagéries du Levant!* . . .
   [6]
Oh, tombée de la pluie! [6] *Oh, tombée de la nuit!*
   [6]
   [6 + 6 = 12 in both lines]
Oh, le vent! . . . [3]
La Toussaint [3], *La Noël* [3] *et la Nouvelle*

Année, [6]

   [3 + 3 + 6 = 12]
Oh dans les bruines [5], *toutes mes cheminées!*
   . . . [5]
D'usines . . . [2]
   [5 + 5 + 2 = 12]

Sentimental blockade! Wind deliveries from the East! Oh, the falling rain! Oh, the falling night! Oh, the wind! All Saints' Day, Christmas, and the New Year, Oh, in the drizzle, all my factory chimneys!

We see alexandrines, that is, lines of twelve syllables, divided in the traditional 6/6 and 3/3/6. The brief lines of three syllables punctuate the forward movement, whereas the second short line, that of two syllables, forms a late-nineteenth-century alexandrine (5/7) by enjambment from the preceding line.

   When the alexandrine assumes a traditional sequential form, the line is jangling and doggerel-like:

On ne peut plus s'asseoir, tous les bancs sont
   mouillés;
Crois-moi, c'est bien fini jusqu'à l'année
   prochaine,
Tant les bancs sont mouillés, tant les bois sont
   rouillés,
Et tant les cors ont fait ton ton, ont fait ton
   taine! . . .

You can't sit down anymore, all the benches are wet. Believe me, everything is finished until next year. The benches are so wet, the woods so rusted, and the hunting horns have blown so much.

Sometimes Laforgue exploits the slightly off effect of joining an alexandrine with a line of eleven or thirteen syllables (uncounted e's are marked):

Ah, nuées accourues des côtes de la Manche,
Vous nous avez gâté notre dernier dimanche.

1898

Ah, storm clouds gathered from the Channel coast, you have spoiled our last Sunday.

An exceptionally long line of fourteen syllables may resolve itself into part of a series, as here:

Soleils plénipotentiaires des travaux en blonds Pactoles

Des spectacles agricoles,

Où étes-vous ensevelis?

[7 + 7 = 14; + 7 + 7]

Fully empowered suns presiding over the farming display of rivers of gold, where have you gone?

Thus many traditional verse lines and the phenomenon of rhyme, but both in a slightly distorted form, are commonly found in Laforgue's free verse, which could rarely be confused with prose. The distortion of iambic pentameter in the Elizabethan and Jacobean playwrights, whom Eliot studied as well as Laforgue, offers perhaps some distant analogy: it is the same case of a standard prosodic system being twisted and wrenched a bit in the hope of expressiveness. Whitman's usage could not be more remote.

For later practitioners of free verse in France, the aesthetic principles are not always the same, any more than Pound's free verse is Whitman's. Each poet can interpret the idea of free verse as he wishes. Laforgue's free verse, in any case, was used for the creation of a long poem, monologic or dialogic by implication at times, based on a fiction about a young man and women.

The existence of a woman is most delicately hinted at in "The Coming of Winter" by the use of an unexplained "we" and "us" (*nous* and *on*), but the burden of this young man's poem is that life retreats from the countryside to a hard, cold, poverty-stricken, death-haunted winter city:

C'est la saison, c'est la saison, adieu vendanges! . . .
Voici venir les pluies d'une patience d'ange,
Adieu vendanges, et adieu tous les paniers,
Tous les paniers Watteau des bourrées sous les maronniers,
C'est la toux dans les dortoirs du lycée qui rentre,
C'est la tisane sans le foyer,
La phtisie pulmonaire attristant le quartier,
Et toute la misère des grands centres.

It's the season, it's the season, farewell grape harvest! Here come the rains patient as angels. Farewell grape harvest and farewell grape baskets, the Watteau panniers dancing bourrées under the chestnut trees. It's the cough returning to the lycée dormitories, it's herb tea with no home to drink it in, tuberculosis making the neighborhood dismal, and all the wretchedness of urban life.

We should pause here to reflect once again on the fact that before the last months of 1887, Laforgue had never known real poverty or really poor neighborhoods. What we have here is an authorial voice of poverty, not a real one; Zola, for example, assumes the point of view of the poor in his novel *L'Assommoir* (1877). Laforgue is not writing a lyrical autobiography either here or in the episodes that follow. Indeed, at the end of the poem the speaker announces that he is the "chorus" setting the tone for what follows.

The second poem, "Le Mystère des trois cors" ("The Mystery of Three Horns"), consists of an "immoral" fable about a triangle of hunting horns who commit suicide after contemplating the sunset. The imagery of the death of the sun has various connotations in Laforgue; the one relevant here is that of unsatisfied sexual desire. The significance of the poem can only be seized by rereading the whole of the last poems, where we can see that Laforgue is building up contrasting symbols of chastity and eroticism.

The main monologue then begins in "Dimanches" ("Sundays") quite abruptly, with memories of a fiancée lost like a rose at sunset, with an autumn windstorm on the night commemorating their break, and a sudden vision of a calm Sunday morning on which chaste girls in white dresses pass by on their way to church. The technique of juxtaposition becomes noticeable here: we must supply the connections, and so, after the girls in white, we must realize that the next lines are an obsessive recollection of the lost fiancée:

> Oh! voilà que ton piano
> Me recommence, si natal maintenant!
> Et ton coeur qui s'ignore s'y ânonne
> En ritournelles de bastringues à tout venant,
> Et ta pauvre chair s'y fait mal! . . .

Oh! how the sound of your piano begins to echo in me again like something inborn! And your heart, which scarcely understands its own self, drones on in these tavern refrains addressed to any passerby, and your flesh aches as you play them.

Here the imagery of "The Lament of the Pianos" has become debased into something more frankly erotic and the poet addresses the fiancée in a more savage way than the young man of the *complainte*:

Ah! que je te les tordrais avec plaisir,
Ce corps bijou, ce coeur à tenor,
Et te dirais leur fait, et puis encore
La manière de s'en servir
De s'en servir à deux.
Si tu voulais seulement m'approfondir ensuite un
    peu!

> How I could twist them in two, your perfect body and your tenor-loving heart—and then tell you what is wrong with them—and then, even, how to use them—how a man and a woman should use them. If afterwards you just would look into me a bit further!

The sudden shift of tone from the violent to a mingling of insinuation and the irony of familiar language is typical of the way passages modulate in these free-verse poems. Quickly the poet recalls and rejects his idea of a fraternal relation with women, and at the end Edenic imagery suggests a more "prehistoric" relation between the sexes, one that repeats what we have seen in *Les complaintes*. The conception of women in these poems can abruptly shift from the white and virginal girl to a sexually stirred and possibly promiscuous woman or to an Eve-like creature whose eroticism brings no threat of jealousy. We might, for the time being, identify these as the three myths of the female. The first two recur more frequently in the last verses, but there are interesting interreactions among them and the generation of yet one or two further female types.

Memory, obsessive and blotting out the present, as it occurs in the first "Sundays," is balanced by a present tense of deceptive implications. In the second "Sundays," the first marriage poem, we move, with the same present reference, in a progressive pattern of what seems to be the narrator's dialogue with one of the white Sunday girls. We hear only what the narrator says, but the girl's part is understood, as when he says: "What's that I hear about your being anemic? Come tell your troubles to your old friend." Their relation appears to deepen or become something apart from the purely sexual when the poet says: "I am not interested in seductions but in metaphysics." Meanwhile the girl has eyes that reflect the Unconscious in its sexual-reproductive sense and contains within her the whole "mortal womb of being." This particular virgin is dangerous not because of erotic weakness but because of her potential fecundity, which goes against the poet's pessimist philosophy. His idea of their union is expressed in the imagery of a nuptial mass:

> Oh! puissions-nous quitter la vie
> Ensemble dès cette Grand'Messe,
> Ecoeurés de notre espèce
> Qui bâille assouvie
> Dès le parvis! . . .

Oh! would that we could die together at this high mass revolted by the human race, which is yawning, sated, at the threshold!

Their union lies in the joint suicide that their "first great evening" will consist of. Whether the girl involved accepts this or not we do not know, and in fact it does not matter. The wish of the last sentence suggests that the dialogue is purely a monologue and, moreover, fantasy on the poet's part: the poet is obviously not dead, and we have experienced, in the present tense, a daydream growing more and more intense until some linguistic detail reveals its inauthenticity.

The fifth poem, "Pétition" ("Petition"), is not a monologue but a meditation on the "historical slaves" that women are and with whom love is "simple and faithless as a shake of the hand." The divine rose-window of love has grown dim at a time when matches or marriages are "delivered by the gross." Essentially the poem is concerned with the destruction of the feminine mystique, which is called the "Ideal," as in the "Lament of the Pianos," that is to say, absolute and unreal notions about the relations between men and women:

> Mon Dieu, que l'Idéal
> La dépouillât de ce rôle d'ange!
> Qu'elle adoptât l'homme comme égal
> Oh, que ses yeux ne parlent plus d'Idéal,
> Mais simplement d'humains échanges
> En frères et soeurs par le coeur,
> Et fiancés par le passé
> Et puis unis par l'Infini!

My God, if only the Ideal of life would relieve her of this role of angel! If only she would take man as an equal. If only her eyes would speak no more of the Ideal, but simply of human relations, of brothers and sisters through their heart's choice, and betrothed by their past, and finally joined by the Infinite!

There is a great deal of subtle implication here that we should not pass over simply because the style is not brilliantly imagistic. "Be-

trothed by their past" refers to the Edenic notion of man and woman; "brothers and sisters through their heart's choice" reflects the new romantic social ideology of equality of the sexes, and "finally joined by the Infinite" alludes to the even newer notion of the Unconscious. The last image is one of a couple at sunset who hear a hunting horn and drink to the past years, "which have left no regrets." The sunsets and horns are introduced in quiet, scarcely imagistic or elaborated form, as befits their contrasted appearance: up to now, as well as later in these poems, sunset and horns stand for frustrated eroticism, so that here we have what might be called the converse or readjustment of a normal symbolic connotation. This is horn and sunset without gusts of emotional turbulence.

"Simple agonie" ("Simple Death Throes") is another meditation, but one fortified by the examples of Hugo and Rimbaud, to whom allusions are made. The opening is in the self-doubting Laforgue-Eliot style: "You know perfectly well, outcast, that what you say is not it at all." The poem goes on to show what the ideas and feelings are that hide the real "it." A fantasy of revolution—"It will be barbaric," as Rimbaud might have said—follows, in which ill-treated animals are revenged—a Hugoesque motif—and can be summed up by "Smash everything!" The details are nicely worked out in this turning from the personal to the social, but the effect that gives the poem its perfect structure is the abrupt change to the third person at the end:

> Il prit froid l'autre automne,
> S'étant attardé vers les peines des cors,
> Sur la fin d'un beau jour.
> Oh! ce fut pour vos cors, et ce fut pour l'automne,
> Qu'il nous montra Qu' "on meurt d'amour!"

He caught cold last fall when he lingered to hear the horns drone their sorrow at the end of a beautiful day. Oh, it was for your horns and for autumn that he showed us that "you can die of love."

The real subject of the poem is eroticism, the frustrations of which are falsely masked by social concerns. Here we find the classic Laforguean symbols of unsatisfied desire: autumn, hunting horns, sunset.

"Moon Solo," which follows "Simple Death Throes," again shows Laforgue's care in varying the "chapters" of the long poem. The time is suddenly July; the poet is smoking on the roof deck of a coach in the night; the road runs through a pine forest; and the moon has risen. Thoughts of the fiancée, the one of the first "Sundays," fill his mind, and we find typical Laforguean themes. He is an Ariel; she is the prey of sexual temptations. They are "crazy for happiness" but have not succeeded in falling on their knees "together" in mutual frankness. We see the characteristic views of male and female here, but the poem has, despite the lyrical setting in the countryside, a good deal of hard realism:

> Donc, que ferons-nous? Moi de mon âme,
> Elle de sa faillible jeunesse?
> O neillissante pécheresse,
> Oh! que de soirs je vais me rendre infâme
> En ton honneur!

What shall we do then? I with my soul, she with her vulnerable youth? O woman aging in sin, how many evenings will I sully myself in your honor!

The future evenings the poet refers to are those spent in brothels. The poet honors his fiancée by going to a bordello because thoughts of her inspire sexual desire and because—this is an implied meaning that becomes clear only later in these poems—her erotic compulsions may have led her to cross the line of respectability and become some sort of bought creature. This fiancée figure has, of course, not the slightest autobiographical reference. She is part of the novel of the Last Poems.

As usual there are wonderful stylistic details in "Moon Solo," such as the line: "Je n'ai que l'amitié des chambres d'hôtel" (Hotel-

room friendships are all I know). There are colloquialisms like "Y a pas de port" (postage-free). The cross-references of the free-verse poems are most perceptible at the end of this one: the poet wishes he could preserve somehow the starry night to enjoy it still in the coming autumn. Autumn then brings on its connotation of sickness, and he worries about the ex-fiancée's constant cough. The end of "The Coming of Winter" has formed an image in our minds of urban misery and tuberculosis, so that Laforgue need only briefly refer to it here in order to summon up the whole picture in our minds.

"Légende" ("Legend"), which follows "Moon Solo," is exclusively autumnal and deals with a "woman with a past"—exactly what the fiancée of "Moon Solo" has become. The two women even share the same dry cough. However, they are not the same: in these complexly ordered poems the characters reflect each other and thematically become each other, yet the identification is not literal. Eliot's comment on how the characters in The Wasteland melt into one another and finally into Tiresias is the best observation, from a poet himself, we could find on this technique.

The structure of "Legend" is a good example of Laforgue's use of two or more textures and conventions. In the opening scene a woman wandering along the deserted shore engages the poet in dialogue. Her checkered past is revealed in an amusing sort of language applicable to a legend:

> "Il vint le premier; j'étais seul près de l'âtre;
> Son cheval attaché à la grille
> Hennissait en désespéré . . . "

"He was the first to come; I was alone by the hearth. His horse, tied to the gate, neighed desperately."

Emotional life has its fantasies, which are absurd when contrasted with the language of reality. Yet the suggestion of knight and maiden, as well as a medieval image or two, conveys the characters' way of seeing themselves. The poet observes that the life of watering places is at an end:

> "Remarquez que dès l'automne, l'automne!
> "Les casinos,
> "Qu'on abandonne
> "Remisent leur piano;
> "Hier l'orchestre attaqua
> "Sa dernière polka,
> "Hier, la dernière fanfare
> "Sanglotait vers les gares . . . "

"Notice, as soon as autumn comes, the deserted casinos put their pianos in storage; yesterday the orchestra struck up its last polka; yesterday the last fanfare sobbed toward the railway stations."

The detached "remarquez" (notice) is the language of reality, the real autumn where the equivalent of casinos closing is the sickness and dreariness of the city in "The Coming of Winter." It is important to see the limits of exchange between the two characters; the poet makes indifferent observations, like Lord Pierrot telling his destined girl about geometry. Laforgue introduces the turnabout, typical of his monologue-dialogues, with the words "Voici que l'on compte enfin avec moi" ("Ah! now she's taking me into account finally!"). This summarizing remark replaces a multitude of conversational exchanges. It functions as a transition to the end of the poem, where we find, as opposed to the unemotional "remarquez," the Edenic reference, which is the highest view of sexual relations in Laforgue:

> . . . moi pétri du plus pur limon de
>   Cybèle!
> Moi qui lui eusse été dans tout l'art des Adams
> Des Édens aussi hyperboliquement fidèle
> Que l'est le Soleil chaque soir envers
>   l'Occident! . . .

I am molded of Cybele's purest clay, I, who would have been, with the whole of Adam's art in Eden, as faithful as the sun is to the west in the evening, when it describes its hyperbola as it descends.

Adam and Eve run throughout Laforgue's work; they are in their prelapsarian state and represent ideal sexual-psychological relations. They constitute perhaps the major anti-Schopenhauerian element in the last poems.

The metaphoric style, such as we see it in the last poem, tends to be superficially obscure in these poems. For example, "Petition" opens with this amazing couplet in 10/12 syllables:

> Amour absolu, carrefour sans fontaine;
> Mais, à tous les bouts, d'étourdissantes fêtes
>   foraines.

Absolute love, crossroad without a fountain; but, in every direction, deafening circuses.

Fountains have a long symbolic history beginning with that of the water of life in Eden; the absence of fountain at the crossroad, however, suggests the "fountain sealed," the woman, in the Song of Songs. The traditional symbol is contrasted with the distinctly modern one of circuses: in other words, the poet glimpses the possibility of absolute love in a contemporary setting. Much of Laforgue's elaborate imagery involves this use of elements with disparate associations.

In general we note two styles in the *Last Poems;* one is imagistic and sometimes obscure-seeming; the other exploits colloquial language, even clichés. The ninth poem deals almost entirely with a fantasy in which a girl comes to tell the poet of her love for him in often gushy terms. She is seen arriving at his threshold and rolling on the doormat, "which I put for that purpose in front of my door." The tenth poem, a fantasy of marriage, continues the thematic material of the ninth; its monologue evolves as the "daily little woman," the *petite quotidienne,* changes from an object of admiring contemplation, as she moves in society, to someone with whom to quarrel, and finally to a complete hindrance to the poet's rather quixotic impulses. In the last lines the poet uses the future perfect tense to striking effect, summing up his life as a whole, seen from its end:

> J'aurai passé ma vie le long des quais
> A faillir m'embarquer
> Dans de bien funestes histoires,
> Tout cela pour l'amour
> De mon coeur fou de la gloire d'amour.
>
> Oh, qu'ils sont pittoresques les trains
>   manqués! . . .
>
> Oh, qu'ils sont "À bientôt! à bientôt!"
> Les bateaux
> Du bout de la jetée! . . .
>
> De la jetée bien charpentée
> Contre la mer,
> Comme ma chair
> Contre l'amour.

I will have spent my life on railroad platforms, almost setting off on deplorable adventures. And all for the love of my heart crazy for the glory of love. How picturesque, the trains we miss! How "See you soon!" are the boats at the end of the pier! The well-built pier against the sea, as is my flesh against love.

We pass from the fantasy that the whole marriage episode has represented to a sober self-realization: the poet is constantly afraid of experience, which accounts for all the conditional tenses in the preceding sections as he fantasizes on and on. We see that the rift of poet and fiancée in the first "Sundays" and in "Moon Solo," while cryptic-seeming at first, depends completely on his elusiveness. The dream of a marriage in the second "Sundays," in which poet and virgin would die in a high-mass–love-death, is a philosophical justification for his temperament.

A brief penultimate poem, of lesser poetic interest than the others, introduces some episode of jealousy in the past, which may or may not be hypothetical. The last poem, however, deals with material that is very present and real. And with its confrontation between the fiancée figure and the girl in white, it refers back in a pronounced way to both of the "Sundays" and to "Moon Solo." The opening winter scene is a fitting conclusion to the anticipation of winter in "The Coming of Winter":

> Noire bise, averse glapissante,
> Et fleuve noir, et maisons closes,
> Et quartiers sinistres comme des Morgues,
> Et l'Attardé qui à la remorque traîne
> Toute la misère du coeur et des choses,
> Et la souillure des innocentes qui traînent,
> Et crie à l'averse. "Oh, arrose, arrose
> "Mon coeur si brûlant, ma chair si intéressante!"
>
> Oh, elle, mon coeur et ma chair, que fait-elle? . . .

Black northwind, howling downpour, and black river, and brothels, and neighborhoods sinister as morgues, and the belated passerby who drags in his wake all the wretchedness of the heart and of things, and sullied innocence, crying to the storm. "Oh drench my burning heart, my so interesting flesh!" And she, *my* heart and *my* flesh, what is she doing?

The sight of the prostitute brings to mind the lost fiancée, looking for "happiness at any cost." The epitaph from *Hamlet* ("Get thee to a nunnery") provides a transition:

> Nuit noire, maisons closes, grand vent,
> Oh, dans un couvent, dans un couvent!

Black night, brothels, heavy winds, oh get thee to a nunnery, to a nunnery go!

Hamlet's familiar use of "nunnery" for "brothel" is here turned into a literal convent, and a vision of provincial nuns in their rounds follows. The fiancée is urged to follow their example. The contrast between the absolutes and extremes of chastity and lust is at its most pronounced here. For the man, there is no "daily little woman," much less an Eve, in life, only virgins and prostitutes. Naturally this fits the Schopenhauerian notion of surrendering to sex and the Will or resisting them utterly. The poet imagines the fiancée soliciting at a window as the symbol of sunset as erotic longing recurs:

Oh! ce ne fut pas et ce ne peut étre,
Oh! tu n'es pas comme les autres,
Crispées aux rideaux de leur fenétre
Devant le soleil couchant qui dans son sang se
vautre!

Oh! it was not the case and it cannot be. Oh, you are not like the others, clutching the window curtains and watching the setting sun wallow in its own blood.

Marriage is rejected:

La nuit est à jamais noire,
Le vent est grandement triste,
Tout dit la vieille histoire
Qu'il faut étre deux au coin du feu,
Tout bâcle un hymne fataliste,
Mais toi, il ne faut pas que tu t'abandonnes,
A ces vilains jeux! . . .

Night is forever black. The wind is terribly sad. Everything repeats the old story that there have to be two of you by the fireplace. Everything blurts out the same thoughtless fatalistic hymn. But you mustn't give in to those ugly mating games!

There appears to be no escape from the pessimistic dualism of the poem, which repeats all the other unsolvable situations in the series, for the impossibility of the union of the sexes is the basic theme of which all the other themes are reflections. At this point, however, a familiar interjection introduces the reconciliation of poet and fiancée:

Eh bien, pour aimer ce qu'il y a d'histoires
Derrière ces beaux yeux d'orpheline héroïne,
O Nature, donne-moi la force et le courage
De me croire en âge.

And so, that I may appreciate the complications behind the beautiful eyes of this orphan heroine, O Nature, give me the strength and courage to believe myself old enough to accept them.

The reference to age is a way of seeing the whole novel of the free-verse poems as an extended bout of youthful, even adolescent emotion. The exaggerated philosophical borrowings in the poems are perhaps the most striking example of immaturity of thought, along with the intense fantasy life on the poet's part. At this point, we see how elaborate and controlled Laforgue's fictional design is: the adolescent reactions and daydreams grow steadily stronger until the breaking point is reached with the "Eh bien" of the above passage. When there seems nothing left to invoke in this prolonged monologue of youth, maturity occurs as the one solution to all the poet's dualisms. And the last line of the poem ("Since, sooner or later, we shall die") gives the decisive argument, for it sees the end of life as justifying the ordinary desire for satisfaction. The notion of this conclusion, however, probably came to Laforgue from a philosophical source: in his *Philosophy of the Unconscious*, Hartmann reaches the final idea that consciousness and the Unconscious must be reconciled, that pessimism and optimism are equally impossible, and that the concern for life outweighs all purely abstract considerations.

The echoes in the last words of this last poem suggest also the complicated cross-references of Laforgue's final work. The fiancée's eyes are the symbol of her Unconscious, as in "Sundays" and "Petition." She is called an orphan, a recurrent term in Laforgue, stressing the total solitude and lack of usual attachments characterizing a girl who can live only for the poet. The reference to death recalls the way the poet sees his life as a whole in the future perfect tense of the tenth poem; there a rejection of marriage is the burden ("I will have spent my life . . . "). Death also brings to mind the ending of "The Coming of Winter," as do the allusions to coughs and respiratory ailments in a poem like "Moon Solo." However, we also see a contrast with the various fantasy figures of women who have preceded:

the fiancée is no longer Eve or the girl filled with sexual desires, the virgin in white or the "daily little woman." The emergence from daydream to reality is the movement of the *Last Poems*. There is a parallel movement from theory or Schopenhauerian pessimism to actual relationship.

Laforgue's *Last Poems* can be seen as a kind of stream-of-consciousness novel in which we are situated so intimately in the main character's mind that we often cannot easily distinguish fact from fantasy, past from present, real speech from imagined dialogue. Curiously enough, the novel that James Joyce pointed out as the first stream-of-consciousness piece of fiction, Édouard Dujardin's *Les lauriers sont coupés* (*We'll to the Woods No More*), is almost contemporary with Laforgue's last work. However, Dujardin's novel concerns the thoughts of a character in the course of a few hours, with very little of the depth of memory or play of daydream that we find in Laforgue. The latter's elliptic technique and scrambling of planes of reference is actually much closer to a work like Virginia Woolf's *The Waves* (1931) or William Faulkner's *The Sound and the Fury* (1929). However, this analogy with the novel should not make us forget the equally important one with modern poetry.

One of the most interesting notions in nineteenth-century poetic theory is Edgar Allan Poe's rejection of the long poem, which was taken up by Charles Baudelaire and subsequent French poets. Poe saw the long poem as a series of lyrics with transitional fillers lacking in poetic intensity in themselves. Although Laforgue apparently did not think of his work in relation to Poe's caveat, he nonetheless set about devising a modern kind of long poem, which would not be open to Poe's objection. The *Last Poems* may be seen as the first of a series of long poems, including Paul Valéry's *La jeune parque* (*The Young Fate*, 1917), Pound's *Cantos* (1930), and Eliot's *The Wasteland* (1922), through which the modern poet reaffirms the poet's right to treat complex thematic and psychological material in extended fashion. The basis of this kind of poem is dramatic monologue rather than narrative. The technique of the monologue often includes free verse, elliptical syntax, colloquial and formal speech mingling or alternating, a lack of transitions or articulations, shifting identities in regard to the speaker and the other characters, and a structure of recurrent words, images, and themes. Musical analogies have been common in criticism for describing such works, though they usually reflect little sound technical knowledge of music on the part of the critic.

Juxtaposition of contrasting styles might be pointed out as the most obvious *literary* aspect of the modern long poem. Such juxtapositions allow colloquial language or clichés, which have little inherent poetic value, to assume considerable power exactly because of their effect of contrast. Thus various types of language are salvaged and redeemed for poetry, whereas the earlier kind of long poem, with its more unified style, fell easily into a monotonous movement, its words losing force by their sameness. The criticism that Laforgue made of Hugo's epic *The End of Satan*, quoted at the beginning of this essay, is an excellent example of the modernist poet's examination and rejection of the earlier form of the long poem with its magnificent tedium.

It remains for us to speak briefly of Laforgue's *Moralités légendaires* (*Moral Tales*), the series of prose stories he worked on in 1885 and 1886. These are literary or mythological narratives, such as "Hamlet," "Salome," "Lohengrin," and "Perseus and Andromeda," retold with appropriate changes to make of them philosophical tales in a burlesque genre. There is something in them of the peculiar kind of French joke called a *canular*, a put-on devised by students, frequently of a literary or pseudo-erudite character. Laforgue's tales were to have well-known and brilliant continuations in such modern retellings of myth as Jean Giraudoux's play on the Trojan War (*Tiger at the Gates*, 1935) and Jean-Paul Sartre's version of the Electra myth (*The Flies*, 1943). Seen in this perspective, the *Moral Tales* have capital importance for a certain strain in more recent French literature. It would be difficult to translate any of the more spectacular passages from the *Moral Tales* because of their bizarre stylistic mixture: we find the colloquial mingled with abstruse terms, set expressions and allusions deformed in ironic fashion, and oddities of syntax. Allusions are dense and fanciful, as at the beginning of "Lohengrin," where Elsa, a Vestal Virgin, is being "stripped of her rank" on the square in front of the Church of Our Lady the Moon, to the accompaniment of the "Nox irae." The crowd next "ululates" as an "expurgated version" of Palestrina's "Stabat Mater" is intoned. All manner of religious ceremonies from various times and places are referred to. The burden of the story concerns Elsa and Lohengrin's wedding night, when, predictably, Lohengrin is repelled by the idea of sexual intercourse and is carried off by his white pillow, which metamorphoses into a swan boat.

As is obvious, the *Moral Tales*, like *Les complaintes* and the *Last Poems*, replace the traditional high seriousness of literature with another kind of seriousness that can accommodate jokes and parodies and other ironic devices. Laforgue's other great innovation, the presentation of the voice of intimate consciousness, is also in its way a refusal of the formalized, rhetorical language of high seriousness. And if we examine the shape and style of Laforgue's major poems, it becomes evident that the numerous and varied original details to be found in them—such as free verse—can be said to derive from the twin principles of poetry as irony and poetry as the most intimate inner voice. Therein lies the essence of Laforgue's modernism and his special contribution to the literary ideas of subsequent generations.

Selected Bibliography

EDITIONS

INDIVIDUAL WORKS
Les complaintes. Paris, 1885.

L'Imitation de Notre-Dame la Lune selon Jules Laforgue. Paris, 1886.

Le concile féerique. Paris, 1886.

Moralités légendaires. Paris, 1887.

Des fleurs de bonne volonté. Paris, 1888.

Les derniers vers. Edited by Édouard Dujardin. Paris, 1890. Includes *Le concile féerique, Des fleurs de bonne volonté,* and *Derniers vers.*

Pierrot fumiste. Paris, 1892.

Lettres à un ami. 3rd ed. Paris, 1941.

Derniers vers. Edited by Michael Collie and J. M. L'Heureux. Toronto, 1965.

Les complaintes et les premiers poèmes. Edited by Pascal Pia. Paris, 1970; 2nd ed., 1979.

L'Imitation de Notre-Dame la Lune, Des fleurs de bonne volonté, Derniers vers. Edited by Pascal Pia. Paris, 1970; 2nd ed., 1979.

Les complaintes. Edited by Michael Collie. London, 1977.

Moralités légendaires. Edited by Daniel Grojnowski. Geneva, 1980.

COLLECTED WORKS
Oeuvres complètes. 3 vols. Paris, 1901–1903. Vol. 1: *Moralités légendaires;* Vol. 2: *Poésies;* Vol. 3: *Mélanges posthumes.*

———. 6 vols. Paris, 1922–1930. Vols. 1 and 2: *Poésies;* Vol. 3: *Moralités légendaires;* Vols. 4 and 5: *Lettres;* Vol. 6: *En Allemagne.* Both of the foregoing editions are very incomplete.

TRANSLATIONS

French Symbolist Poetry: An Anthology. Edited and translated by J. P. Houston and M. T. Houston. Bloomington, Ind., 1980.

Laforgue: Poems. Translated by Patricia Terry. Berkeley, Calif., 1958.

Laforgue: Selected Writings. Edited and translated by W. J. Smith. New York, 1956.

BIOGRAPHICAL AND CRITICAL STUDIES

Arkell, David. *Looking for Laforgue: An Informal Biography.* Manchester, 1979.

JULES LAFORGUE

Collie, Michael. *Jules Laforgue.* London, 1977.

Debauve, Jean-Louis. *Laforgue en son temps.* Neuchâtel, 1972.

Hiddleston, J. A. *Essai sur Laforgue et les "Derniers vers."* Lexington, Ky., 1980.

Ramsey, Warren. *Jules Laforgue and the Ironic Inheritance.* New York, 1953.

————, ed. *Jules Laforgue: Essays on a Poet's Life and Work.* Carbondale, Ill., 1969.

JOHN PORTER HOUSTON

THE WELL-MADE PLAY

THE DEFEAT OF Napoleon at Waterloo in 1815 was a turning point in the history of France. The political and social turmoil of the French Revolution and the heroic years of the First Empire under Napoleon had caused profound and irreversible changes in the structure of French society. The aristocracy had been dispossessed, and the bourgeoisie became the economically dominant class; later they would assume political power too. The decades of the Restoration (1815–1830) and the Second Empire (1852–1870) saw an unprecedented commercial and industrial boom that established France as a leading economic power in Europe. The bourgeoisie who accomplished this transformation were a class whose fashions and tastes came to be emulated by the bourgeoisie of other European countries when they in turn rose to power later in the century.

Such radical changes in the power structure of French society were bound to have far-reaching effects on the cultural life of the country, and nowhere was this so instantly apparent as in that most socially determined of all arts, the theater. Until the Revolution, theater in France had been centered mainly in Paris; it had been confined either to the Comédie Française, whose principal mission was to sustain the classical tradition in tragedy and comedy; to the Opéra and the Théâtre Italien; or to the rather informal mixed entertainments of song, pantomime, dance, and unpolished farce performed for the general populace at fairs and markets. In the latter half of the eighteenth century, this popular theater found a regular home in the rather disreputable premises lining the boulevard du Temple. Here, during the Napoleonic years, the melodrama, which appealed largely to illiterate audiences, held sway. But post-Napoleonic theater saw a significant increase in the audiences of the Théâtre Français, the Opéra, and the boulevard theaters of the newly prosperous bourgeoisie. Audiences in these theaters came to be composed substantially of the families of bankers, financiers, lawyers, and businessmen—people whose energies were devoted to creating their own and France's fortunes—and of the petite bourgeoisie, such as shopkeepers, clerks, tailors, and others who benefited from the new distribution of wealth.

The theatrical fare required by these audiences was different from the staid neoclassical tragedy and sophisticated high comedy that had retained their hold on the regular stage throughout the previous century. In the popular theater, such audiences found to their taste the turbulent and extravagant melodramas of Guilbert de Pixérécourt, but they were not particularly inclined to appreciate drama that aroused in them confusing and often contradictory passions. Consequently, the fine romantic dramas of Victor Hugo and Alexandre Dumas *père* enjoyed only a brief vogue during the 1830's. The new audiences were out for entertainment rather than enlightenment or powerful and disturbing experiences. What they expected from the theater were plays that reassured rather than questioned their beliefs,

1909

that provided them with enjoyment and refreshment after a hard day's work.

The theater in Paris during the first half of the nineteenth century can properly be seen as the first phase of our modern commercial theater. Plays were not written and produced to challenge the assumptions of the audience; neither were they intended to provide an artistic experience that would transform, however briefly, the lives of those who watched them. At the Comédie Française, even though the plays of Jean-Baptiste Molière and Jean Racine continued to be performed, the modern dramas that came into the repertoire were no longer decorous imitations of classical drama intended to awaken in the audience an awareness of a grand national heritage. Instead, both at the Comédie and on the boulevards, theater was intended to please, and, as the fledgling capitalist world of Paris quickly discovered, a lot of money could be made out of giving such pleasure. Entertainment offered in the Parisian theaters became, as Arnold Hauser has observed, more overtly a consumer commodity than before, and those who sold it could, if they were lucky, make as large a fortune from writing or producing plays as they could from investing in the stock market. All they had to do was to discover what people wanted.

At this critical point in its development, the Parisian theater had at its disposal the talents and energies of one of the most successful dramatists ever to have written (Augustin) Eugène Scribe (1791–1861). Scribe was born into a solid bourgeois family that was doing well in the Parisian silk trade. Like many young men of his class, he was educated to enter the legal profession; but from childhood on he had demonstrated unusual facility as a writer, and while he was at school, it became increasingly apparent that the proper outlet for his gifts would be the theater. He began by writing *comédie-vaudevilles*, one-act plays with songs, lightly satirizing the life of the ordinary French citizen, a form that had flourished on the stages of the eighteenth-century fairs and continued to thrive on the boulevard du Temple. Scribe did not meet with instant success, but in November 1815, five months after the fall of Napoleon, his comedy *Une nuit de la Garde Nationale* (A Night with the National Guard) was a great hit at the Théâtre du Vaudeville. Audiences were delighted by his portrayal of the popular civilian militia, by the comparative realism of the dialogue and characterization, by the warm atmosphere of good humor, and above all by the slight and ingenious plot, which involved a series of deftly managed disguises and misunderstandings.

After this initial success, Scribe's rise to prominence in the theaters of Paris was slow but effortless. Whatever theatrical form he turned his hand to, he seemed virtually guaranteed to win popular applause. Although he continued throughout his life to produce *comédie-vaudevilles*—over two hundred in all—for the boulevard theaters, these generally slight works were soon overshadowed by his achievements in the city's more prestigious theaters. Despite a false start at the Comédie Française with *Valérie* in 1822 and his five-act comedy of manners *Le mariage d'argent* (Marriage for Money) in 1827, he eventually became the company's leading playwright. His first full-length comedies, beginning with *Bertrand et Raton* (Bertrand and Raton) in 1833 and including *L'Ambitieux* (The Ambitious Man, 1834), *La camaraderie* (The Coterie, 1837), *La calomnie* (Slander, 1840), *Le verre d'eau* (The Glass of Water*, 1840), *Une chaîne* (A Chain, 1841), and *Adrienne Lecouvreur* (1849), formed the basis for the Comédie's modern repertoire.

But Scribe was not content to write solely for the legitimate theater. He was also a prolific opera librettist, especially for Giacomo Meyerbeer, whose collaborations with Scribe—*Robert le Diable* (*Robert the Devil*, 1831), *Les Huguenots* (The Huguenots, 1836), *Le prophète* (*The Prophet*, 1849), and, posthumously, *L'Africaine* (The African Girl,

1865)—were among the most successful of all grand operas in an age when opera had reached its zenith of development. All in all, Scribe was responsible for over four hundred theater pieces, which makes him, along with Lope de Vega and the early French tragedian Alexandre Hardy, one of the most prolific dramatists ever. When he died he was worth over two million francs, the largest fortune until that time that had been made by a playwright.

Scribe's prodigious output had, of course, a method behind it. No single man could produce so many plays and libretti if each work were to be unique in its conception and execution. In order to provide the theaters of Paris with a constant stream of plays, Scribe rarely worked on his own. He used collaborators, some of whom, such as Jean Bayard, Vernoy de Saint-Georges, and Ernest Legouvé, were respectable dramatists in their own right. The collaborators generally provided Scribe with ideas for plays, wrote some of the scenes, or developed scenarios, although Scribe, who freely acknowledged the help he received, was nearly always responsible for the finished product. But the main reason for his productivity was his constant repetition of a model that, as experience proved, was precisely what audiences wanted. Although Scribe never defined this model exactly, so many of his plays, from the one-act vaudevilles to the five-act comedies and dramas, exhibit similarities in structure that we can establish the prototype from which he worked. It has been called the *pièce bien faite,* or the "well-made play."

The well-made play takes to extreme limits Aristotle's dictum that plot, "the structure of events," is the most important single feature of drama, with its corollary that this plot must have a beginning, a middle, and an end. Scribe was scrupulous in observing these principles; nearly all his plays follow the same pattern. After a brief introductory scene to set the action, Scribe's characters embark on a formal exposition, a description of the events that have occurred before the play begins. The length and complexity of the exposition de-

pends on the length of the play. It is brief and simple in a one-act vaudeville, and in a long three- or five-act play most of the first act will be devoted to an explanation of the complicated series of incidents and intrigues that, at the moment the play begins—called "the late point of attack"—has created a crisis. The complication and working out of the crisis is the action of the play itself. This action consists of a succession of scenes, each of which is a logical consequence of the previous scene. In these scenes, characters form alliances and intrigue against the interests of another character or group of characters. As the play progresses, action tends to increase in tempo until it reaches the climax, the *scène à faire,* or "obligatory scene," which the audience has eagerly been anticipating from the very start, and in which hostility between the warring parties is openly declared. In this *scène à faire,* the hero, who usually has been at a severe disadvantage for most of the play, emerges victorious; after which follows the denouement, or "unraveling," in which he receives his just rewards. Meanwhile the less sympathetic characters go down in defeat. Thus the four constant structural features of the well-made play are exposition, complication, *scène à faire,* and denouement.

Most of Scribe's well-made plays also include extensive use of the *quiproquo,* or "misunderstanding," in which some characters fail to recognize the identity of other characters, or are ignorant of crucial information about them. This information is often contained in documents or letters, which are the most frequent hand props in the well-made play. But while characters may be hampered in the intrigue by their ignorance, no secrets are kept from the audience, who can therefore observe the action with Olympian comprehension. This superiority of viewpoint allows the audience to follow the workings of cause and effect and to anticipate the denouement, even though they are not quite sure how it will be achieved. Scribe's ability to surprise his audience through the ingenuity of the denouement was one of the prime sources of his appeal, and it was crucial to the success of his plays that it appear to be a logical outcome of all that had gone before. When the members of the audience left the theater, they were satisfied they had seen a complicated puzzle ingeniously solved. So vital was this need that Scribe would often begin work on a play at the *scène à faire* and denouement, and plot it in reverse. Once this had been done to his satisfaction, all that was needed was the relatively unimportant task of writing the dialogue.

Scribe's method of constructing a play was not entirely novel. The four structural features of the well-made play had been current in European drama for centuries, from the plays of Menander and Plautus to the comedy of the eighteenth century. Moreover, the use of intrigue and the exploitation of tension aroused by it to hold the audience's attention was also entirely familiar; Pierre Augustin de Beaumarchais in *Le mariage de Figaro* (*The Marriage of Figaro,* 1784) had produced a masterpiece of intrigue comedy. What was new with Scribe was his systematic use of these features. His plays work like machines, in which aspects of structure are more important than characters. Scribe's characters have little individual life; they are largely instruments of the plot, revealing no wayward ambitions or desires that might threaten to disturb its smooth working. Scribe's is a comedy of situation, not character.

A good machine registers a continuous hum when it is running well; if the hum is interrupted or varies in pitch, something is wrong with the mechanism. Scribe's plays have no such disturbing interruptions or variations; they are notable for the consistency of their appeal to the audience, a consistency described by the late nineteenth-century critic Françisque Sarcey, who coined many of the terms to describe the well-made play, as "unity of impression." Sarcey, who admired Scribe even though he had few opportunities to see his plays, argued that while the play in

performance must appear to be a reflection of life, it must not affect the spectator in the way life does. Instead it must enthrall him. The spectator's constitution must not be shocked by sudden transitions of mood on stage. Hence even though in everyday life the spectator is used to experiencing joy and pain together, such a mixed condition is not suitable for the theater. In witnessing a play, "the human soul is not flexible enough," wrote Sarcey, "to pass readily from one extreme of sensation to the contrary one. These sudden jolts overwhelm it with painful confusion." The unity of impression guarantees against this confusion, and Scribe was a master at sustaining it. Although the mood may change as the play progresses, its shifts are gradual, almost imperceptible. Even if the play moves, as many of Scribe's do, from a credible to an incredible situation, the relentless logic of the plot and consistent unity of impression create the illusion that everything happening on stage is possible. In this way reality is transformed into fantasy. Scribe's drama could thus be marvelously escapist and highly pleasing.

Salient characteristics of the well-made play, then, are uniformity of structure, a rigorously logical plot in which the workings of cause and effect are made utterly clear, and unity of impression. A fourth distinctive feature of the well-made play is the general avoidance of controversial issues and ideas. This blandness, combined with the rational view of the world implied by the plot structure, is another of the chief reasons for Scribe's appeal to the Parisian bourgeoisie. His most frequent theme was marriage, money, and the interdependence of the two. Now while most playwrights dealing with such material favor the cause of youth against age, of marriage for love against marriage for money, Scribe takes a more practical view of romantic matters. He denies his characters that energy which threatens to overthrow the orderly life of a well-established household or institution. For example, in his two-act vaudeville *Le mariage de raison* (The Reasonable Marriage, 1826), the pretty orphan Suzette is persuaded to marry a one-legged army veteran some years older than she, to put off the philandering son of the local count. Despite temptations and tribulations, by the end of the play it is apparent she has found happiness, not in the arms of wanton youth, but at the hearthside with age and experience.

Le mariage de raison was a tremendous success, as was *Le mariage d'inclination* (Marriage from Inclination, 1828), in which Scribe demonstrates the dangers of entering into a marriage not sanctioned by parental approval. He would not, however, deny entirely the claims of the heart, so long as they have been tempered by prudence. In *Le mariage d'argent,* the adventurer Poligini is obviously headed for a life of marital discord with the empty-headed Hortense, a fitting punishment since he has married her solely for her fortune. Meanwhile the penniless artist Olivier marries the newly widowed Madame de Brienne, rejected by Poligini, as a reward for his faithful devotion to her. Essentially, the attitude expressed by Scribe toward personal relationships in this play and elsewhere is an inheritance from the sentimentalist ideas of the eighteenth century, ideas that were common to the bourgeoisie of both the previous century and his own. Relationships should be based neither on sexual attraction nor the desire for money. Instead, they should be formed and tested over time; happiness should be the result of moral rectitude and demonstrated fidelity. Money, of course, is necessary for comfort, so prudent attention to one's material needs to protect the relationship from strain is highly advised. In all his plays on marriage, Scribe's moralizing on the middle way is light and unemphatic; but when he dramatizes the breaking of the bonds of marriage, as he does in *Dix ans de la vie d'une femme* (Ten Years in the Life of a Woman, 1832), he reveals a vindictive streak toward the individual who resists accepted conventions, showing poverty

and a miserable death as the inevitable consequences of adultery and the denial of the virtues of the bourgeois home.

The plays of Scribe are therefore examples of a mechanism that is well constructed, well oiled by the unity of impression, and well tuned to the partialities of his audience. Not surprisingly in a city where high art was prized, Scribe and his drama had many detractors—in fact these critics comprised a considerable portion of the intellectual and artistic community. Artists associated with the romantic movement especially disliked Scribe's facility of composition and the slick, seamless quality of his plays; they were enraged when he spoke for bourgeois philistinism and satirized them, the romantic artists, in *Le charlatanisme* (Charlatanism, 1825) and *La camaraderie.* He was regarded as an enemy of the art that challenged orthodox assumptions or that might transport the reader or spectator to new levels of awareness. Even the younger generation of bourgeois dramatists who, as we shall see later, owed much to Scribe, considered him an entertaining trifler whose work was unredeemed by social concerns.

The most extended attack on Scribe was conducted by the romantic poet, novelist, and critic Théophile Gautier, who for well over twenty years wrote on theater in the journal *La presse.* Gautier, who at seventeen had been a prominent demonstrator at the first night of Victor Hugo's *Hernani* at the Comédie Française in 1830, continued to serve as the standard-bearer for the romantic cause in theater well into the middle of the century. For Gautier, theater should be unfettered in expression, articulating "high anger" and "sublime indignation" at the paltry compromises of life. Because it should be devoted to a realization of the ideal, it should also be steeped in poetry. But Scribe had, according to Gautier, an "antipoetic nature par excellence." Although Scribe's technical ingenuity ensured a species of entertainment, Gautier found him to be nothing but a mediocrity: "His ideas are those of the crowd, he loves what it loves, he does not dominate it and he is not inferior to it; he is neither in front nor behind, so everyone understands him, except the poets and the artists" (*L'Histoire de l'art dramatique,* vol. 2, p. 236).

The mediocre was clothed, moreover, in distinctly unattractive trappings. Gautier persistently berated Scribe for his utter lack of style; for his dialogue, which "resembles a familiar conversation among people who do not talk very well"; for his cold and prosaic characters, who are the "enemies of youth and love"; and for the absence in his plays of any idealism, passion, enthusiasm, or love of nature. Scribe was acceptable fare, Gautier felt, for those theaters that aimed to provide nothing but entertainment; he should never have been allowed to enter the august portals of the Théâtre Français, where theater should remain a high art. His plays on that stage were dismissed by Gautier as nothing more than a string of vaudevilles, whose only appeal to the audience was to keep it guessing about what happened at the end. Scribe was the antithesis of all that was romanticist.

Gautier's criticisms of Scribe have been echoed by scholars and historians of the theater ever since; indeed few playwrights have had a press as consistently bad as Scribe's, once the novelty of his works had worn off. Today he still strikes us as an irredeemably limited and dated writer. Because his characters are lacking in individuality and life, because their function is solely to fulfill the requirements of plot, their destinies do not interest us and we forget them quickly. Moreover, they are too much figures of their time and place—Paris after the Restoration—even in the plays that have historical settings. We also find it difficult to accept Scribe's philosophy, which appealed to his contemporaries, that the great crises and movements in life have their origins in trivial causes. Scribe scales down history so that even the grandest of events is shown to be the result of petty ambition, and the most powerful of rulers is rep-

resented as having interests as narrow as those of the obscurest shopkeeper.

At times this scaling down works, as in *Bertrand et Raton,* Scribe's most successful study of political intrigue and one of the few of his plays that could stand revival today. It demonstrates acutely how an unscrupulous politician can exploit for his own ends popular discontent and the vanity of his fellow plotters. This politician, Bertrand Rantzau, is also one of a handful of characters created by Scribe who has those faintly superhuman dimensions that make a dramatic figure memorable. At times Scribe actually seems to rebel against the triviality that crimps the spirit and offends the dignity of the individual. His protest is clear in *La calomnie,* a fine play showing how a person's happinesss can be ruined by malicious gossip.

But all too often Scribe assents to triviality. He frequently chooses expansive subjects for his plays. *The Glass of Water,* set at the court of the English Queen Anne, has for its background nothing less than the English struggle for hegemony in Europe. But throughout the play, Scribe reduces history to a fairy tale by his insistence on demonstrating the truth of his intriguer Bolingbroke's claim that "great effects are produced by small causes"; even wars are represented as being determined by the commonplace passions of those in power. The outcome of the War of the Spanish Succession is therefore shown as an effect of the rivalry of two jealous women for the affections of a young captain. Ultimately our response to the play is anger that so much promising material has been sacrificed to such little effect. We feel suffocated by triviality rather than enlightened by insight into a world different from our own.

How little substance there is in many plays by Scribe becomes abundantly clear when we examine a work such as *Adrienne Lecouvreur,* where his usual skill at constructing an interesting plot fails him. *Adrienne Lecouvreur* was widely performed in the second half of the nineteenth century, primarily because the romantic allure of the eponymous heroine, one of the legendary actresses of the eighteenth century, made it an ideal vehicle for many stars. But there is little life in the play. We are not moved by the lovers Adrienne and Maurice, for they never express convincing passion for each other. Scribe and his collaborator, Legouvé, were obviously aware of their inability to conjure up such feelings, for they avoided extended love scenes between the two protagonists and concentrated instead on a stupefyingly complex intrigue, at times very poorly plotted, that includes long, irrelevant passages on political events in Poland. The lovers eventually come to grief, not because of a crisis in their relationship or because of an inexorable series of events that drives them apart; they are parted through the transparently contrived circumstance of Adrienne's dying after sniffing a bouquet of poisoned violets, which had been introduced in the first act but conveniently forgotten afterward to make way for the hurly-burly of the plot. Without an effectively worked-out intrigue, without characters full of life or a well-planned denouement, Scribe's drama descends easily into bathos.

Nevertheless, reservations about the quality of Scribe's drama must not obscure his immense importance to the theater of his time. Between 1820 and 1850 Scribe was by far the most widely performed playwright in Paris, and even in Europe. Gautier himself, after he had retired from *La presse*, was forced to admit Scribe's "marvelous fecundity, his rare understanding of the stage, his extreme skill in handling difficult situations, and finally a continuity of successes that is not obtained without real merit." In a rare moment of democratic generosity, Gautier concluded that "the public cannot be mistaken in its pleasures for forty-five years." What, then, were the strengths of Scribe's plays?

For a start, Gautier was wrong to describe the full-length plays as just a string of vaudevilles. They are not; rather they are enlarged vaudevilles, showing an acute sense of form,

which audiences delighted to see repeated in different permutations. Moreover, these audiences were, at a possibly subliminal level, reassured by the illusion created in the plays that there is meaning and progress in time. From the artistic point of view, Scribe's devotion to form and his sense of economy, which prompted him never to use unnecessary characters or to include superfluous material, had a valuable corrective influence on the popular theater, in which the formal extravagances of melodrama and the loose episodic structures of vaudeville were, until his time, the rule. Further, Scribe restored to the French theater its traditional concern for neatness, balance, and harmony in the structure of its drama, even if he did not stick rigidly to the three neoclassical unities, which until the nineteenth century had been de rigueur in the writing of serious drama; the ingenuity Scribe used to compress the most complicated plot material into a regular form earned him eulogies even from his enemies and can still impress today.

If Gautier was right when he said that Scribe had no style, we can now—using the wisdom of hindsight—regard that as a virtue. He rescued dramatic dialogue from the portentous raving of melodrama and substituted for it conversation that sounded realistic. In this way he prepared the ground for the later naturalist dramatists, who would use such dialogue to probe effectively into the psychology of their characters. Scribe's pared-down language and his frequent use of the pause and of sentences broken off halfway also allowed for a freer style of acting, prompting performers to move away from the formal attitudinizing that had always been one of the hallmarks of French acting. On the whole, Scribe laid the foundations for a theater that, in the words of Émile Zola, himself no lover of Scribe, allowed for a "study of reality." In an age when realism was becoming the dominant literary mode, Scribe was a key figure in bringing it into the theater.

But realism presupposes fully drawn and individually distinct characters, and no one can claim that Scribe created these. Even Legouvé, his most eloquent apologist, admitted that Scribe "lacked the gift of individualizing," that his characters "are only the men and women of [the] situation. They fill it adequately but never go beyond it." Yet even in his approach to character, Scribe rectified an imbalance brought about by the melodrama. While most figures in melodrama are little more than mouthpieces for the moral polarities of the play and are therefore to be judged morally, Scribe presented a range of types, lightly sketched admittedly, in which negative traits of character are credible and even sympathetic. This means that while the world he painted was grayer than in the more colorful melodrama, in many if not all of his plays he represented a conflict that did not seem solely aimed at eliciting a moral response from the audience. Scribe's world may well be lacking in idealism and poetry, but it is one in which conflicts between people whose claims have equal legitimacy can begin to develop.

In the final years of his life, Scribe's plays were less frequently performed in Paris than they had been earlier, and after his death in 1861 his work went into a sudden and irreversible decline. For the remainder of the century only a few of his plays stayed in the repertoire of the Comédie Française, and these were not received with much warmth. His influence was far from exhausted, however, for a host of playwrights both at the Comédie and on the boulevards continued to turn out plays that followed his structural principles. Of these the most successful, both in France and internationally, was Victorien Sardou (1831–1908).

Sardou ended his life even richer than his mentor Scribe, but his early years were less successful. Only after several years of near starvation attempting to make a living in the theater did Sardou finally strike gold when his farce *Les pattes de mouche* (*The Scrap of Paper*) was produced at the Théâtre du Gymnase in May 1860. Scribe, who was present at this first night, acknowledged the young playwright's talents, clearly because Sardou dem-

onstrated as highly developed a sense of dramatic structure as his own. Sardou had learned his technique, he claimed, by reading only the first act of a play by Scribe and then sitting down and plotting out the rest of it using only the information provided in that act. After some practice, Sardou found that he could accurately predict complication, *scène à faire,* and denouement. Like Scribe, moreover, he was a master at judging what his audiences wanted. The more than seventy plays and libretti he wrote were intended to reflect passing fashions and tastes and the leading issues of the day: *Rabagas* (1872) reflects the political turmoil of the Paris Commune; *Daniel Rochat* (1880) presents the conflict between atheistic and Christian thought; while *Divorçons!* (*Let's Get a Divorce!*, 1880), the most durable of all his plays, is a farce about the new divorce laws. But Sardou never examined his issues in depth or asked his audience to come to conclusions about them. Instead he used such issues merely to give a topical, occasionally sensational appeal to his drama, and as an excuse to exhibit his flamboyant and adroit flair for situation. In some respects he wrote for a theater technically more sophisticated than Scribe's, so he became adept at exploiting the potential for stage spectacle. His historical plays—from *Patrie!* (*Fatherland,* 1869) through the extravaganzas he wrote for Sarah Bernhardt such as *Fédora* (1884), *La Tosca* (1887), *Cléopâtre* (1890), and *La sorcière* (*The Sorceress,* 1903)—all required grand and sumptuous staging on an operatic scale. In all his work Sardou stuck to the formula of the well-made play, but his plots were never as complicated as Scribe's. And unlike other practitioners of the well-made play, he tended to revert to melodrama, so that the appeal of many of his situations depends more on their raw theatricality than on their demonstration of the rules of cause and effect.

One of the reasons for Scribe's decline in popularity toward the end of his life can be attributed to a radical shift in the moral sensibilities of the public for which he wrote. During the Second Empire the Parisian bourgeoisie indulged in extravagant displays of wealth. The court of Napoleon III was notorious for its elaborate balls and their general aura of dissipation. The values that had created the bourgeoisie came to be seriously eroded, the elegant courtesan became a very popular figure in a pleasure-loving society, and Paris acquired its spicy reputation as the capital of European fashion, frivolity, and vice. This spirit was most completely captured in the music of Jacques Offenbach, "the king of the boulevards," whose operettas were the hottest commodities in town.

Needless to say there were some who spoke out against what they considered to be a disastrous decline in moral standards. In the theater this responsibility fell mainly to Alexandre Dumas *fils* (1824–1895) and Émile Augier (1820–1889). Both Dumas and Augier had little respect for Scribe. They found him to be not only a trifler but an egotist, lacking in any firm moral sense; his plays advocated an ethos of unscrupulous self-seeking. Furthermore, they felt he turned a blind eye to the most potent threat to the social and moral welfare of French society, the decline of the family. In orthodox Christian fashion, Dumas and Augier understood social stability to depend on fidelity between husband and wife and loyalty between parents and children. But the widespread license of the time and the habit of contracting marriages for financial reasons or for reasons of social prestige was seriously threatening the durability of the family unit. Dumas's vision of moral decay was almost apocalyptic. If "the Beast" that was the adulteress and courtesan was not contained, he warned, then social collapse and chaos would result. Indeed he attributed the downfall of the Second Empire in the Franco-Prussian War of 1870 to moral laxity in the nation's capital.

At first it appeared that Dumas was at one with the moral drift of his time. His first successful play, *La dame aux camélias* (*The Lady of the Camelias*, 1852), one of the most celebrated plays of the century, appeared to invite sympathy for the courtesan, Marguerite Gautier. She is painted in the most delicate of colors, and, in the moving final scene, when she dies of consumption, is elevated to a status of semi-sainthood. But Dumas soon abjured such extravagance. His later plays, beginning with *Le demi-monde* (*The Demi-Monde*, 1855), all express bitter discontent with the sexual degeneracy of the time. *The Demi-Monde*, perhaps Dumas's most substantial work, attacks a stratum of society composed of adulteresses, adventuresses, and others bent on sexual pleasure, all of whom strive to maintain a veneer of social respectability and elegance. Dumas also dramatized problems suggested by his own background as an illegitimate child in *Le fils naturel* (The Natural Son, 1858) and, tangentially, *Un père prodigue* (A Prodigal Father, 1859); and he dealt with the ubiquitous problem of the fallen woman, sometimes with sympathy as in *Les idées de Madame Aubray* (The Ideas of Madame Aubray, 1867), sometimes with immense venom, as in *La femme de Claude* (*Claude's Wife*, 1873). Adultery and its attendant miseries are his constant theme; and in plays like *La Princesse Georges* (Princess George, 1871), *L'Étrangère* (The Foreign Woman, 1876), and *Françillon* (1887) he attacks not only the siren who tempts husbands away from the strait-and-narrow way, but also the double standard of morality that discriminates against women. All Dumas's plays are informed by a missionary zeal. They are "useful" theater, directing attention toward hypocrisy, injustice, and promiscuity and animated by the purpose of promoting reform and repentance.

Dumas's writing has a shrillness that is absent in Augier, despite similarities in the two men's views. Augier's early verse play *Gabrielle* (1849), which shows a wife saved from an adulterer's arms by a loving, forgiving husband, won him the French Academy prize for virtue and established him in the eyes of the public as a leader of "l'école du bon sens" (the school of good sense)—a group of writers whose works were considered to represent a return to balance and moderation after the excesses of the romantic movement. The play's famous final line, "O père de famille! o poète, je t'aime!" (O father of the family! O poet, I love you!) became the byword for the drama of moral regeneration. Augier's insistence on images of respectability meant that he was initially opposed to Dumas. *Le mariage d'Olympe* (*Olympe's Marriage,* 1855) was written as a rebuttal of Dumas's alleged idealization of the courtesan in *The Lady of the Camelias.* But Dumas's change of heart brought the two men closer together. In *L'Aventurière* (*The Adventuress,* 1848), *Les lionnes pauvres* (The Poor Women of Fashion, 1858), *La contagion* (The Infection, 1866), and his final play, *Les Fourchambault* (*The House of Fourchambault,* 1878), Augier mounted an attack on illicit love in all its forms. But his most impressive work is broader in scope than Dumas's. Augier was deeply disturbed by the current mania to acquire wealth at any cost: his finest play, *Le gendre de M. Poirier* (*M. Poirier's Son-in-Law,* 1854), examines how the ideals of marriage are violated when husband and wife marry for money or title; while the trilogy *Les effrontés* (The Shameless Ones, 1861), *Le fils de Giboyer* (*Giboyer's Son,* 1862), and *Lions et renards* (Lions and Foxes, 1869), demonstrates how political loyalties are prostituted to an individual's desire to gain wealth and power. Augier concentrated especially on class conflict, on the impoverished aristocrat who marries into or politically aligns himself with the bourgeoisie to regain his fortune, and on the bourgeois obsession to possess an aristocratic title. The world of his plays is brutally materialistic: everything is for sale, and people act mainly from motives of greed and snobbery.

Yet despite their faint respect for Scribe, Dumas and Augier represent in their work a development of the well-made play in the direction of social criticism. Their values, those of Augier especially, are an extension of Scribe's, although they are articulated with greater clarity. Technically Scribe also remained a powerful influence on them. In both playwrights, the opening act is normally devoted to a long exposition, followed by complication as intrigue develops, involving a fairly frequent use of the *quiproquo.* The intrigue leads to a *scène à faire,* in which the issues at the heart of the play are discussed fully. The denouement then resolves the action—occasionally, as in *Olympe's Marriage* or *Claude's Wife,* with suddenness and violence. The plots are usually constructed on the logical principles of cause and effect, although Dumas's plays occasionally fall short here, despite his claim that his denouements are the rigorously logical outcome of his actions. In other respects Dumas and Augier were very different kinds of dramatist.

Dumas innovated a type of drama that has come to be known as the *pièce à thèse,* or "thesis play." In *The Lady of the Camelias,* as Marguerite is persuaded to abandon her idyllic life with Armand and return to being a courtesan in Paris, she delivers a solemn speech: "And so, whatever she may do, the woman, once she has fallen, can never rise again. God may forgive her, the world never." The sudden lucidity with which Marguerite speaks, her momentary ability to rise above her predicament, seems to give her speech the status of a "thesis," that is, an idea about a social problem, the truth of which will be demonstrated in the subsequent action. Unfortunately in *The Lady of the Camelias* it is not; Dumas avoids joining issue with the idea by having Marguerite die beatifically. But in later plays his plots are more deliberately constructed to prove the thesis. Although Dumas's first full-fledged thesis play is usually considered to be *Le fils naturel,* we can already see a thesis being worked out in *The Demi-Monde,* in which the plot demonstrates, not always with conviction, the impossibility of a member of the demimonde's achieving social respectability and financial security through marriage. In *Le fils naturel* the injustice of the social ostracism of illegitimate children is argued; in *Les idées de Madame Aubray* the possibility of pardoning the fallen woman is examined; in *L'Étrangère* a pseudoscientific theory about unhealthy particles in society—"vibrios"—is put to the test. In almost all cases the thesis is worked out through a plot of considerable complexity.

Augier was less ruled than Dumas by the desire to prove something. In the banal *Olympe's Marriage* he shows how women who have led dissipated lives will always be dominated by their "nostalgia for the mud"; and in the more liberated *Mme. Caverlet* (1876) he argues in favor of divorce. Yet with Augier the thesis play is the exception rather than the rule; instead, he gradually leads us to draw our own moral at the conclusion of the action: do not sacrifice personal conviction for political gain *(Giboyer's Son)*; do not seduce and abandon defenseless young women *(The House of Fourchambault)*. Action is dominant in Augier, while in Dumas it is subordinate to thesis. This leads to a radical difference in the characters the two playwrights created.

Dumas's plays are saved from dryness by his acute powers of observation and his ability to create striking stage figures: Suzanne d'Ange in *The Demi-Monde*, Charles Sternay in *Le fils naturel,* and the bizarre Mistress Clarkson in *L'Étrangère* are only a few. But as we read a play by Dumas, we often have the sense that these characters are out of place, because while they have a life of their own, the characters around them are primarily there in the service of the thesis. Dumas's plays are intended to suggest an ideal for life rather than to represent life as it is. As a result his more realistic characters are forced eventually—sometimes against their very nature—to submit to the demands of the thesis. Those characters who serve the thesis are, like Scribe's, unmemorable: they are merely counters in a game; others, like Olivier de Jardin in *The Demi-Monde* or Aristide Fressard in *Le fils naturel,* are mouthpieces for the playwright; they slip uneasily from being charac-

ters within the plot to being spokesmen above it. Dumas's penchant for preaching through these characters often holds the action up interminably, with a resulting loss in the momentum necessary to a successful well-made play. All his characters, even the living ones, are arranged to realize a moral scheme. They are clearly aligned with the forces of either good or evil and are ultimately possessed of little will of their own. Scribe's characters, too, have little will, but they are more neutral. After Scribe had labored to save the theater from the simplicities of melodrama, Dumas seemed bent on returning it to them. Only in *The Lady of the Camelias* and in his fine last play, *Françillon*, does he offer conflicts in which the darker side is presented with some degree of sympathy and a response is required of the audience that is more complex and less rigidly moral than with the earlier plays.

In Augier characters appear to have greater autonomy than in Dumas, and a figure such as the unfortunate Olympe Taverny, who is condemned by the thesis she represents, is comparatively rare. While it is difficult for us to echo the opinions of Augier's contemporaries, who saw him as a second Molière, comparing his plays to *Tartuffe* (1664) or *Le misanthrope* (1666), he did have a developed sense of character and of the way in which it can determine action. In comparison with Dumas, he was adept at creating convincingly realistic, seemingly "normal" people, and given the fact that both wrote dialogue as close to the speech of everyday Parisians as possible, such realism can be considered a positive asset. Augier's characters are flexible beings: they grow and change in the course of the action. In *M. Poirier's Son-in-Law* the feckless Gaston de Presles comes to learn the value of bourgeois ways through the unexpected growth of affection for his wife and the recognition of her capacity for self-sacrifice. In other words, the main theme of the play, that it is better to work than to live off others, emerges through Gaston's experience and consequently strikes us with greater force than it would in an overt thesis play. Poirier himself is also an arresting character. Stalwart of the bourgeoisie that he is, he is fully aware of all the personal qualities needed to make a fortune. But he is torn between his good sense and his desire to gain, through Gaston's influence at court, a useless aristocratic title. Augier created other inwardly divided characters, like Giboyer in *Les effrontés* and *Giboyer's Son,* a writer who sells his talents to the highest bidder in the political arena rather than use them according to his personal convictions; in this way he can buy for his illegitimate son an education needed for advancement in the world. Giboyer's dilemma is as human as it is moral, even though the conclusion of the second play clearly expresses Augier's disapproval of Giboyer's corruptibility. But despite touches of moralizing, in Augier's plays character is allowed to determine action more freely than in other works in the well-made play mold. His characters are human beings who can, partly at least, exercise their own wills. Augier, like Scribe, follows the logic of cause and effect strictly, but because his plots are invariably less complex than Scribe's, he leaves himself more room for character study.

By now Dumas and Augier have dated. Their plays give us penetrating insights into the life of the Parisian upper bourgeoisie, but the issues they address no longer have point. We do not now view sexual activity outside marriage with the same horror Dumas did, and we are unlikely to be appalled by one or even several deviations from conventional nineteenth-century moral norms. To today's more emancipated tastes, in fact, several of Dumas's judgments on woman and her place in society strike us as sexist. Finally, Dumas's often tortuous plots lose much of their credibility as we see character twisted in support of thesis.

Augier's work may seem closer to us. His dislike of a society in which everything is for sale is relevant to our own world, which is no less materialistic than his was. But his concentration on class and his frequent exploitation of specific political issues tend to rob his plays of immediate relevance. Despite his superior abilities at character creation, he was not capable, as some of his more enthusiastic admirers have claimed, of forming characters as rich as Sancho Panza, Falstaff, or Tartuffe. Neither could he trace as subtly as later naturalist dramatists were to do psychological shifts and fluctuations in his characters. Consequently he was a forerunner of things to come rather than a playwright whose work retains an importance in itself.

Dumas and Augier did not, as has been unfairly said of them, "do trivial things grandly, and grand things trivially," though the criticism can be leveled against Scribe. But even though they were opposed to the prevalent moral trends of their time, they did not challenge their audiences to think deeply about themselves. In fact whatever the excesses of contemporary society, they affirmed conventional morality and failed to ask questions of broad human interest. They are interesting minor writers.

Still less important were those dramatists who continued the tradition of the well-made play. There was Henri Meilhac (1831–1897), known mainly for his libretti for Offenbach and for Georges Bizet (*Carmen,* 1875), and who also produced, generally with collaborators, a number of delightful light comedies, including the play on which Franz Lehár's operetta *Die lustige Witwe* (*The Merry Widow,* 1905) is based. Édouard Pailleron (1834–1899) was noted for his satire on artistic fashions of the time, *Le monde où l'on s'ennuie* (*The Art of Being Bored,* 1881), which held the stage in Paris for years, while Théodore Barrière (1823–1877) was known for his thesis plays. All playwrights worked from the Scribe model, though few were capable of producing plots as detailed and ingenious as Scribe's.

Toward the end of the century such playwrights became concerned, almost to the point of tedium, with the question of sex both inside and outside marriage. Most notable in this respect were Paul Hervieu (1857–1915) and Eugène Brieux (1858–1932), whose solemn, generally humorless plays reflect an increasing liberalism in public attitudes toward sex. Hervieu remains tied to the well-made play, both the simplicity of his plots and the autonomy of his characters reflecting developments achieved by Augier. Hervieu develops intrigue minimally and uses the *quiproquo* hardly at all. Instead, in a play such as *Le dédale* (The Maze, 1903), in which a woman is torn between two husbands, one of whom she has divorced, the plot is composed mainly of a series of *scènes à faire,* which increase in intensity up to the joint climax-denouement, when the two men, while locked in physical combat, topple over a precipice into a whirlpool below. Despite occasional sensationalism like this, Hervieu could be a graceful writer, creating characters with whom we can sympathize even though the barriers standing between them and their happiness seem to us now to be rather absurd.

Brieux was cruder. Everything in his plays is subjected to the thesis, which he hammers home with monotonous regularity. He lacks the sense of structure possessed by his predecessors and, with the possible exception of his diatribe against corruption in the French judicial system in *La robe rouge* (*The Red Robe,* 1900), it is difficult to place him in the well-made play tradition. His most powerful work, *Les avariés* (*Damaged Goods,* 1903), has virtually no plot at all. Taking the undeveloped situation of a syphilitic father passing his disease on to his child, Brieux uses most of the play to lecture through his spokesman, a doctor, on the dangers of unchecked venereal disease. Although its setting is realistic, the play's concern with hard fact anticipates later developments in documentary drama and a totally new phase of theater. But Brieux's lack of a sophisticated dramatic technique makes it difficult for us now to understand Bernard Shaw's extravagant claim that he was "incomparably the greatest writer France has produced since Molière."

If the general evolution of the well-made play after Scribe represents a simplification of his original model, there was one group of playwrights who delighted in his intricacy of plot and took it to even further extremes. These were the great farceurs, especially Eugène Labiche (1815–1888) and Georges Feydeau (1862–1921), whose plays, along with the best farces of Sardou, represent a high point in the history of the well-made play.

Labiche, after several years as a vaudeville writer, had his first hit with the famous *Un chapeau de paille d'Italie (An Italian Straw Hat)* in 1851. For the next twenty-five years his farces, ridiculing aspects of bourgeois life, remained a constant favorite with Parisian audiences. The most notable are *Le voyage de M. Perrichon (Perrichon's Journey,* 1860), *Célimare le bien-aimé* (Celimare the Beloved, 1863), *La cagnotte* (The Money Pool, 1864), and *Le plus heureux des trois (The Happiest of the Three,* 1870). On his retirement in 1876, Labiche was considered to have been little more than a successful commercial dramatist. But when in 1879 Augier persuaded him to publish 59 of his 179 plays, Labiche suddenly found himself acclaimed as one of the greatest comic writers in the language: once again comparisons were made with Molière.

Similar comparisons have been made with respect to the work of Feydeau. Feydeau's first success came when he was twenty-five, with his breathtakingly hectic marital farce, *Tailleur pour dames* (Ladies' Tailor) in 1887. After some years of modest acclaim and two years of silence in which he perfected his technique, Feydeau began producing a series of farces that are among the most complicated well-made plays ever written and that provided the prototype for one of the most popular of modern dramatic forms, the "bedroom farce." Among these are *Un fil à la patte* (*Chain and Ball,* 1894), *L'Hôtel du libre-échange (Hotel Paradiso,* 1894), *Le dindon* (The Turkeycock, 1896), *La dame de chez Maxim (The Girl from Maxim's,* 1899), *La puce à l'oreille* (*A Flea in Her Ear*, 1907), and *Occupe-toi d'Amélie!* (*Keep an Eye on Amélie*, 1908). The furious pace that is characteristic of these farces becomes less physical and more psychological in the one-act plays that constitute the final phase of Feydeau's work. Here, in pieces such as *On purge bébé* (*Purging Baby*, 1910) and *Mais n'te promène donc pas toute nue!* (Don't Walk Around in the Nude, 1911), the farce turns darker, as the plays offer a view of marriage as bitter as any in the modern theater. These final plays both reflect Feydeau's own domestic problems and anticipate the breakdown he was to suffer in 1919. He died two years later in a mental asylum.

The French farceurs succeeded partly because what was weakest about Scribe's well-made play became a source of great strength in their own plays. Scribe had frequently been criticized for making his characters little more than "pawns in a game of chess." Such is often the case with Dumas as well, but this tendency is not in itself an automatic failing. The real problem in Scribe and Dumas is that we feel their characters *should* be fully drawn people, unconstrained by the demands of plot or thesis, that there is just enough sense of independent life in them to allow us to demand a less doctrinaire or mechanical approach to organizing the action of the play. With the farceurs there is no such problem. Their characters are frankly presented as cogs in the plot, which itself is developed in an almost inhumanly logical sequence of action.

The way in which these characters are controlled by the machinery of plot is best described by Henri Bergson in his classic essay *Le rire* ("Laughter," 1900). Laughter both in life and on stage is occasioned, Bergson argues, by the sight of an individual's spontaneous movement being halted by something inert. A comic effect results when we see "automatism in contrast with free activity." We laugh when we see a man slip on a banana peel because his freedom of action suddenly becomes subject to laws of gravity: in seconds he changes from a self-determining person to one who is determined. Similarly we laugh when a person's behavior is determined by traits of character—greed, vanity, or absent-mindedness—of which he is either unaware or which he denies. While he assumes he is autonomous, we see him as a marionette, with his vices or shortcomings as the controlling strings. He displays "a kind of automatism that makes us laugh," and we feel "a comic character . . . generally comic in proportion to his ignorance of himself." It is through ignorance of themselves and others that the characters of Labiche, Feydeau, and Sardou become part of the complex mechanism of farce.

The means of triggering this mechanism into action is borrowed, once again, from Scribe. A trivial cause gives rise to massive effects. In *An Italian Straw Hat*, for example, Fadinard is about to marry Hélène; but because of a quite fortuitous and absurd set of circumstances, he is forced to go chasing about Paris in search of a very specific style of straw hat made only in Florence. Whether his marriage takes place or not depends, of course, on the outcome of his search. Naturally he cannot go alone. He is accompanied by the whole wedding party, who, since they are up from the country, know little of life in Paris. Because Fadinard cannot admit what he is doing, at each stage of the hunt he tries to convince the party that they are at a certain point in the wedding ceremonies. Complications ensue, *quiproquos* accumulate with bewildering rapidity, while the denouement, involving a clash with the National Guard, unravels the play marvelously. At the end harmony is restored and happiness promised to Fadinard and Hélène. The comedy of the play lies in the paradoxical distance between trivial cause and momentous effect, as it does in Sardou's *Scrap of Paper*. In this play the fortunes of people at a country-house party depend upon information written on a scrap of paper—a love letter from years past—which is unwittingly passed from hand to hand and used for varying purposes. Trivia are glorified: the more trivial the cause, the louder our laughter. While Scribe believed in the importance of trivia, the farceurs found in it a source of humor.

Even richer comic effects are achieved when characters are seen as marionettes activated by their own shortcomings. In Labiche's *Perrichon's Journey* a suitor for the hand of Perrichon's daughter, Henriette, manages, after many complications, to win her father's consent to their marriage by playing on the old man's absurd hatred of being indebted to anyone. In *La cagnotte* a party of country folk, in Paris for the day, fall prey to their ignorance of life in the city.

Labiche's farces are generally constructed in a series of episodes that, while causally related, are discrete entities. He does not develop separate lines of action—"series of coincidences," Bergson called them—which, as the play progresses, become so entangled that when the playwright unravels them all in the denouement, the solution strikes the audience as a masterpiece of inventive reasoning. That was the peculiar genius of Feydeau.

It is impossible, Marcel Achard claims in his introduction to Feydeau's complete works, to summarize satisfactorily the plot of a Feydeau farce. It resembles a "well-oiled machine" in which "unexpected *coups de théâtre* superabound, follow upon one another, and frequently become entangled," yet each incident has its logical place, and each is a necessary stage in the "infallible geometry that marks the point of departure and traces the graph of the action." Achard compares Feydeau to a clockmaker who produces "the comic poetry of a logarithmic table." His farces are supremely well made; not a word can be cut, not a stage direction ignored.

Feydeau's characters all have vices, usually sexual, which, in the interests of maintaining peace at home, they strive to conceal. Wives and husbands construct labyrinthine schemes to hide from each other the existence of their lovers, but they are always thwarted. Feydeau's most important principle was: "when two of my characters should under no circum-

stances encounter one another, I throw them together as quickly as possible." Thus, in *Chain and Ball*, as Bois d'Enghien is frantically trying to conceal his impending marriage from his doting mistress, Lucette, a nightclub singer, the mother of his bride-to-be is inviting Lucette to sing at the betrothal party. The resulting fracas, the ever more desperate attempts of Bois d'Enghien to be fiancé to one lady and lover to the other, complicated by attentions paid to Lucette by a bullish South American general, lead to a climactic *scène à faire* in which all is revealed.

The mechanism of a Feydeau farce is usually set in motion by the collision of characters as they attempt to satisfy their desires and yet hide from all but their guilty partner the fact that they are doing so. The action culminates, often in a hotel bedroom (*Le dindon*) or series of bedrooms (*Hotel Paradiso*) in which everyone becomes partnered with someone else, and *quiproquo*s proliferate until each character is in a state of utter confusion as to the identity of the others. It is a madhouse atmosphere, yet the strength of Feydeau's farces is that he shows us this madness created by totally logical means. It is, of course, a logic only the audience can follow. A Feydeau character is invariably obtuse. He can see only one course of action and will follow it come what may, however much it goes against common sense. In the first act of *Le mariage de Barillon* (Barillon's Marriage, 1890), for example, Barillon is about to marry Virginie. Unfortunately, because of the error of a drunken clerk, he marries her mother instead. Common sense naturally says that such a formal slip can be remedied, but not in a Feydeau farce. The subsequent turmoil, in which the first husband of the mother, long thought drowned at sea, returns hungry to claim his marital rights, is strictly ruled by the blind adherence of everyone to the situation created by the first error. The logic of such farce leads close to the brink of chaos, while the laughter it causes comes from our recognition of the distance between Feydeau's reasoning and that of common sense. Indeed, while Scribe and later practitioners of the well-made play held fast to the logic of common sense, Feydeau disregarded it for a more absurd, though equally stringent logic.

At times such logic could be used for bitingly satirical purposes. One of Feydeau's most successful farces, *Champignol malgré lui* (*Champignol in Spite of Himself,* 1892), involves, predictably, a wife who tries to hide from her husband, Champignol, the existence of a lover. Due to a series of improbable circumstances, which Feydeau makes entirely probable, the lover ends up doing military service for the husband. But the husband himself also enlists, so the army camp he enrolls in has two gentlemen, both going by the name "Champignol." Feydeau exploits the situation with his customary resourcefulness, and in so doing manages a number of telling strokes against the military mentality: the obsession with uniform that substitutes dress for the man—a failing Feydeau often fastens on; the rigid obligation of subordinates to obey an order, whatever the consequences; and the soldier's incapacity to understand any situation that cannot be accounted for by the supposed rationalities of the regulation book. Eventually such rationalities appear to be as absurd as the logic of the farce they help to create, and stalwart French officers are reduced from the eminence of command to the status of cogs in the improbable Feydeau machine.

The audience that laughed at Feydeau came from the same society that acclaimed Scribe. But by the turn of the century it no longer needed to be assured of the values supposedly enshrined in its domestic and professional life. Nevertheless, Feydeau never went so far as to challenge those values. Eric Bentley has written that "farce . . . wishes to damage the family, to desecrate the household gods." This is not entirely true, at least not in Feydeau's plays. Feydeau wishes *almost* "to damage the family," but not quite. Farce, like tragedy, has its own catharsis, which is achieved by having the audience witness on stage the fulfillment of its "most treasured unmentionable wishes," or rather their near-fulfillment. Wives and husbands may be perilously close to breaking their marital vows, but they never quite reach that point. Force of circumstance, created by the mechanism of the plot, always saves them at the eleventh hour, and the play ends with marital harmony restored, at least temporarily. Even in the one-act farces, where the strings that manipulate husband and wife are their own hatred for and boredom with each other, the plays end with an uneasy truce. Feydeau never quite let them spill over into the disturbing area of "tragic farce," as later playwrights have done. To the end, he maintained what Sarcey, one of his greatest admirers, called "the unity of impression."

The most widespread influences on the develoment of drama in nineteenth-century Europe originated in Paris. First Pixérécourt provided Europe with the prototype for the melodrama; then Scribe presented the equally widely adopted prototype of the well-made play. Few playwrights have been as frequently performed in their lifetime, both in and out of their country, as Scribe. Gautier sardonically remarked:

> At this moment in Timbuctoo there are actors busy learning a vaudeville by M. Scribe, and . . . a young negress of Dumanhour is studying the affected roles of Mme. Leontine Volys [an actress who appeared in many of Scribe's vaudevilles] in front of her mirror of polished brass. The Papuans of the South Seas, when playing social comedy, always choose *The Reasonable Marriage* or *Michael and Christine* [one of Scribe's most popular and frequently adapted vaudevilles]. The Chinese themselves, with their faces like pots with two handles and their physiognomy like a folding screen, are translating and playing the vaudevilles of M. Scribe in their theaters of bamboo, so that afterward sinologists will retranslate them into French and we will consider them to be compositions of the dynasty of Hang or Hing.
>
> (*L'Histoire de l'art dramatique*, vol. 2, p. 67)

Gautier was sardonic, but it was astonishing how rapidly Scribe became part of international culture, at least in Europe. Because international copyright laws did not exist at the time, his plays were adapted by both skilled and hack dramatists to suit the tastes of local audiences far and wide. In London over a hundred of his works were seen on stage in the course of the century, with some of the more popular plays, like *Adrienne Lecouvreur*, and operas, like *Le domino noir* (The Black Domino, 1837), going through several adaptations. In Germany, where the native popular repertoire was comparatively underdeveloped, the appetite for Scribe was enormous, and we read of adaptors setting to work on the first acts of his comedies before the final ones had even arrived in the mail. Toward the middle of the century, Scribe's plays were as popular in Germany as were the plays of Auguste von Kotzebue and August Wilhelm Iffland. Meanwhile in Vienna, for most of the century the theatrical capital of the German-speaking world, one theater alone, the Burgtheater, staged over 1,800 performances of about 70 vaudevilles and comedies by Scribe. He was a European, if not a world, phenomenon; before the middle of the century his plays composed a substantial part of the Spanish, Italian, Slavic, Scandinavian, German, and Anglo-American repertoires.

Strangely enough it is not always easy to trace Scribe's actual influence on contemporary and later dramatists. Some of the principles of the well-made play were eminently imitable. Playwrights were able to develop briskly paced action, unity of impression, and realistic dialogue. They were also strongly influenced by Scribe's concern for neatness and regularly employed the main structural features of his plotting. But few were capable of creating the extraordinarily detailed and convoluted situations Scribe specialized in. His influence on European drama was therefore similar to his influence on the French: toning down the excesses, both linguistic and emotional, that had marred all but the best romantic plays and rescuing the theater from the simplistic morality of melodrama. But in place of his complexity, European dramatists, like most of the French, provided simpler plot lines, allowing for a more ample development of character and often for a study of life in the society for which the plays were written.

Take, for example, the work of Eduard von Bauernfeld (1802–1890), who, from 1831 for upward of forty years was one of the most prolific and popular of Viennese playwrights. Bauernfeld specialized in light comedies of intrigue reflecting the life of his city, most notably during the Biedermeier era (1815–1848). One of his best plays, regularly revived throughout the century, was *Bürgerlich und Romantisch* (Bourgeois and Romantic, 1835), a delightful comedy in which two pairs of lovers, one expressing bourgeois attitudes toward love, the other aristocratic-romantic attitudes, go through a series of misunderstandings before they are finally united. The play is mild in tone, the *quiproquos* cause no convulsive crises, and the simple plot allows for an affectionate satire on contemporary artistic tastes. All in all, it is a neatly organized study of manners, employing the contours if not the complexity of Scribe's pattern.

A more assiduous disciple of Scribe's was the Silesian Heinrich Laube (1806–1884), who, as director of the Burgtheater between 1849 and 1865, produced innumerable well-made plays translated or adapted from the French; he even went to the extreme of regularizing Shakespeare in the Scribean manner. Laube was no mean playwright himself, and his historical works, especially the comedy *Rokoko* (1842) and the tragedy *Struensee* (1847), which uses the same material as *Bertrand et Raton*, come closer to the densely plotted well-made play than most German drama of the period.

Practitioners of the well-made play elsewhere in Germany were numerous. Karl Gutzkow (1811–1878), one of Laube's early associates, wrote historical intrigue comedies such as *Zopf und Schwert* (Pigtail and Sword, 1844) and *Das Urbild des Tartuffe* (Tartuffe's Original, 1847), which represent aristocrats of the past as contemporary bourgeois. Especially popular in the nineteenth-century German theater were the plays of Charlotte Birsch-Pfeiffer (1800–1868), who often worked from French originals. But perhaps the most distinguished of these writers in the well-made play tradition was Gustav Freytag (1816–1895), whose important theoretical work, *Die Technik des Dramas* (*The Technique of the Drama*, 1863), is the century's most thoroughgoing examination of well-made dramatic structure. Freytag drew broadly, and not always accurately, on plays from the world repertoire in order to construct his famous model of the play as a pyramid with four component parts: the "introduction," corresponding to the exposition; the "rising action," which is set in motion by an "exciting force"; the "climax" at the apex of the pyramid, corresponding to the *scène à faire*; and the "catastrophe," corresponding to the denouement. Freytag's theory, despite the many pages he used to expound it, was essentially a simplification of the French well-made play structure, and it became standard reading for aspiring dramatists in Germany and elsewhere until well into the twentieth century. Freytag was, however, less successful as a dramatist. The only one of his plays still occasionally revived is *Die Journalisten* (*The Journalists*, 1854), a good-humored comedy of intrigue in which the political and romantic aspirations of the central characters conflict. The play is pyramidal in structure, with the climax—a local election—coming at the start of the third and penultimate act rather than later, where Scribe would have placed it. *The Journalists* reflects the familiar, solid belief in bourgeois values that was characteristic of almost all well-made plays.

In England, too, the well-made play underwent a process of simplification. Tom Robertson (1829–1871), who has been described as the pioneer of realism on the English stage, had early in his career translated one of Scribe's most enduring international successes, *Bataille des dames* (*The Ladies' Battle*, 1852). But Robertson's mature plays, especially *Society* (1865), *Caste* (1867), and *M.P.* (1870) are, at best, modified Scribean structures in which thesis rather than action is the most important consideration. *Caste*, for example, has a distinctly reformist bent. While not radically challenging the status quo, the play is intended to question the assumption that the "laws of caste"—that is, of social class—should be allowed to determine whom a person marries. The plot, which traces the varying fortunes in the marriage of the young aristocrat D'Alroy to the working-class actress Esther, has little complication beyond D'Alroy's briefly hiding from his mother the fact of his marriage; and it has but one contrived circumstance, everyone thinking that D'Alroy has been killed while on military duty in India. The only fully drawn character is Esther, whose responses to the situations in which she finds herself are believable. Other characters remain social types reminiscent of the melodrama. The aristocrats are mouthpieces for attitudes commonly attributed to them, while the working-class characters are rather pale imitations of those of Charles Dickens. This means that the happy denouement, which demands a radical conversion to democratic ideas by D'Alroy's mother, who until that time has been insufferably blue-blooded, seems contrived to prove the thesis, rather than emerging as the inevitable outcome of the action.

The preeminence of thesis is also characteristic of many plays by Henry Arthur Jones (1851–1929). After some years of writing melodrama, Jones turned his attention to social problems, especially those in which sexual laxity runs foul of religious or social orthodoxy. Jones's rather puritan mentality often caused him to overemphasize his thesis, a tendency that weakens the impact of his psychologically complex characters; they are often forced to submit to a pattern of action that, as in Dumas, we sense is not right for them. Only in *Mrs. Dane's Defence* (1900), a subtle study of the so-called woman with a past, does he create a play in which action is consistently a consequence of character, and the thesis, the predictable one that a woman who has once fallen can never rise again, is communicated naturally and with pathos.

One of the most consistent advocates in England of careful dramatic structure was the critic William Archer, whose very readable manual *Play-making* (1912) is heavily indebted to Freytag's work. Archer was no friend of the French "play of elaborate and ingenious intrigue," which he considered to be "ill made," in that vast preparations were used to serve very little effect. For Archer, the dramatist should observe and portray human character working itself out through a series of crises that are logically related through the behavior of the characters. Character rather than action is therefore the unifying force of the drama. But this preference for character, a familiar English trait, must not obscure Archer's many shared tastes with French theorists and practitioners. Like Sarcey, for example, he appreciated unity of impression—"the most destructive fault a dramatist can commit . . . is to pass, in the same work, from one plane of convention to another"—while he admired the qualities of harmony and proportion in a play, and felt that all should be "complex yet clear, ingenious yet natural."

For Archer, the model English playwright was Arthur Wing Pinero (1855–1934). Pinero, over the course of his long playwriting career, which lasted for exactly fifty years, managed in some degree to free himself of the artifices associated with the well-made play. In his best works, written in the 1890's and 1900's, the plots do not depend on an extremely late point of attack, nor do they involve complex intrigues; consequently, exposition can be brief and natural. Plays such as *The Second Mrs. Tanqueray* (1893) and *The Benefit of the Doubt* (1895) have technically proficient introductory acts in which the minimal information needed to launch the plot is

conveyed without recourse to a contrived situation and while forwarding the action. As with other late practitioners of the well-made play, Pinero develops action that is generally uncomplicated and makes little use of secrets or *quiproquos*, which, when they are introduced, seem obtrusive. John Russell Taylor, an enthusiastic admirer of Pinero, has argued that when such occurrences take place as Ellean Tanqueray's discovery that her fiancé, Ardale, is her stepmother's former lover, or the revelation of a bundle of incriminating letters in *His House in Order* (1905), they are justified, as they could happen in real life. But this judgment is inadequate. The texture of Pinero's drama, in contrast to that of some of his predecessors, is seamless; such moments are false, and when they obtrude we hear briefly the grinding machinery of the French well-made play, by now grown worn and rusty.

The strength of Pinero's art is his naturalness, which is due to his constant endeavor to mask the component parts of his play. It is also aided by his seeming disinclination to argue a thesis. Although Pinero was clearly aware of class conflict, of changing sexual mores, and of the pressures these imposed upon individuals, he did not, like Dumas, use the drama to argue the case for one side at the expense of the other. As a result his world is in some ways more limited than Dumas's. His characters often appear to represent little more than themselves. This would have been fine had Pinero been able to create complex and interesting people; unfortunately he lacked the ability to penetrate personalities, to discover what Bernard Shaw called their "inner clue"; so he failed ultimately to diagnose either the cause or the consequence of patterns of social, marital, and familial change. For example, his most serious play, *Mid-Channel* (1909), effectively details the breakup of a fourteen-year-old marriage, and at the same time presents in a peculiarly unattractive light the alternatives open to the estranged spouses. Zoe and Theodore Blundell, when presented with the possibility, are unable to come together again. At this point Pinero would seem to be set for a penetrating analysis of the components of personality that prevent their reunion. Instead he unexpectedly and disappointingly falls back on a thesis—the argument that their marriage was doomed from the start because they had determined they would have no children to be free to pursue single-mindedly their passion for money and social status. This might have been fair enough reasoning had the previous action centered on this specific flaw in their relationship; but it had not. At the point where Pinero might have genuinely startled and disturbed his audience by revealing the gaps between his characters' aspirations and their reality, he deflected the issue and retreated to a well-worn and comfortable thesis. Even though some of his dramas, like *Mid-Channel,* end with the death of the protagonist, fundamentally middle-class family values are upheld. Like Scribe, Pinero did not wish to disconcert his audiences unduly.

Only one playwright in the European theater successfully exploited the well-made play in order to disturb radically the sensibilities of the world that had produced it: the Norwegian Henrik Ibsen (1828–1906). Ibsen's early career, from 1851 to 1862, was spent as a director in the national theaters of Bergen and Christiania, where a substantial portion of the repertoire was composed of plays by Scribe and others of his French school. Not surprisingly this experience influenced his own playwriting. One of his first significant works, *Fru Inger til Østraat (Lady Inger of Ostraat,* 1855), is a classic intrigue play à la Scribe, although its gloomy atmosphere is far distant from Scribe's generally bright world. But Ibsen's mind was much too independent for him to cultivate a single form, especially when that form was associated with a man who, to his mind, was singularly lacking in serious concern for the quality of life and art. Ibsen's first major plays were in fact written in forms more closely akin to romantic verse drama. But when he turned his attention to the problems of living in the nineteenth century, he looked once more to Scribe. His first major realistic dramas—*De unges Forbund (The League of Youth,* 1869), *Samfundets støtter (Pillars of Society,* 1877), *Ett Dukkehjem (A Doll's House,* 1879), and *Gengångere (Ghosts,* 1881)—are all, to a greater or lesser degree, well-made plays.

Of the four, *Pillars of Society* is the most like Scribe in structure, pace, and complexity; indeed it is one of the very few well-made plays from the nineteenth century that still has a regular place in the repertoire today. *Pillars of Society* is about Karsten Bernick, a wealthy small-town Norwegian businessman who is forced to admit publicly the sexual and financial misdemeanors of his past. In long scenes of exposition, which last well beyond the opening act, scandalous events are unfolded, initially from the point of view of a society that looks upon Bernick as a paragon of moral rectitude, later in scenes between the main participants in those events, when Bernick's true role becomes clear. For years, it appears, he has been prepared to shift the blame for breaking a marriage and for irregularities in his company's books onto the shoulders of his young brother-in-law, Johan Tønneson, who is safely away in America. It is Johan's return, along with his half-sister, Lona Hessel, who was once in love with Bernick and was betrayed by him, that provides the "exciting action" for the unmasking of the hypocrite.

With consummate artistry Ibsen develops a series of parallel plots—Bernick's present business ventures, labor troubles in his shipyards, problems at home with his wife and son, and Johan's growing attachment to Dina Dorf, an orphan who is engaged to an insufferably pietistic schoolmaster, Rørlund—all of which reach climactic points at the same time, at the ends of the two middle acts. As pressure relentlessly grows on Bernick, he is forced to expose more and more of his past, while his present business appears to be ever more shady. During these middle sections, exposition and action proceed hand in hand; in fact, the action appears to speed up the more the truth of the past is revealed. Yet if this is one variation on the Scribean model, toward the end of the play Ibsen invents an even more important one when he separates the play's climax from the *scène à faire*. Disaster is about to strike when it appears that Johan, Dina, and Bernick's young son, Olaf, are all about to drown aboard an unseaworthy ship that Bernick has allowed, for his own ends, to set sail. At the climax, circumstances save all the potential victims, and then, after Bernick has suddenly been freed of all that encumbered him, he admits his culpability in the presence of a group of admiring citizens. In other words, his confession, the *scène à faire*, is not forced from him by events, but is given by him freely. It therefore seems to be a conversion to honesty. But the crucial point is that we listen to him at the end not because we are interested in the consequences of his confession, which are very anticlimactic, but because of what he has to say and the way in which it throws light on the issues at the heart of the play. At the conclusion it is the thesis that "the spirit of truth and the spirit of freedom . . . are the pillars of society" that wins out.

Pillars of Society is an exhilarating play. Its action is precisely timed; it is unabashed in its theatricality; its different plots are superbly balanced, and its optimistic thesis is clearly demonstrated. The thesis is, as in all well-made plays, one it is easy to assent to, while the characters are also appropriate to the form, as they are more elements in the play's moral landscape or mouthpieces for social attitudes than they are fully sentient beings. But this cannot be said of Ibsen's subsequent dramas.

A Doll's House is, as many have observed, full of Scribean business. Nora's secret about working to pay off her debt is kept from her husband, Torvald, until the climax. This extended *quiproquo* creates ever increasing tension, and to support it there is much use of documents and letters. But the plot is far simpler than that of *Pillars of Society*, so Ibsen

has more time to explore his characters. Once again, at the end of the play, he separates climax and *scène à faire*, making the *scène à faire* the denouement so that we can listen to a discussion of the play's issues without any concern for plot. The play appears to end on a note of firm resolution, as all good well-made plays should, even though Nora's departure into the outside world is a far cry from the reassuring conclusions presented by Scribe and his followers. But there is something even less reassuring about this ending; we are not quite sure how to take it; we question the apparent note of finality. Nora's conduct during her discussion with Torvald is inconsistent with her past behavior, and we are uncertain how to interpret her decision: Does it signify a new condition of awareness within her or is she just playing another role with her husband? Although we have Ibsen's word that Nora should be taken seriously, the thesislike pronouncements coming from her mouth, however plausible they may sound, are difficult to take at face value. We cannot entirely trust her as the carrier of the play's message, for a *quiproquo* might still be in the offing; despite her confident tones, Nora may not, we feel, understand herself fully. Therefore we view her ironically, sensing a distance between the woman we have known during the play and the words she is now speaking. It is this distance, the gap between overt statement and hidden meaning, that Ibsen explores in his later work.

At this point we leave the well-made play proper, for certainty and unanimity in audience response was one of its key aspects. Nevertheless, Ibsen continued to exploit the salient structural features of the well-made play, though he shifted the plane of action from external event to the inner experience of his characters. Exposition increases in complexity and length until it comes to take up most of the stage time. This allows characters to reveal both to themselves and to others that they are different people from what they originally thought they were, that they are flexible and changeable beings rather than monoliths.

In recalling the past and the discovery of inner rather than external truths, the *quiproquo* is constantly in operation, but not in a mechanical way. Rather it is used to show how characters have misidentified themselves, have attributed to themselves and often others personalities that do not in fact exist. Some of these characters, such as Rosmer in *Rosmersholm* (1886) or Allmers in *Lille Eyolf* (*Little Eyolf*, 1894), initially deliver speeches that sound unambiguously like theses, and they have programs of reform they wish to pursue with vigor. But the actions of the plays serve to reveal that such speeches are little more than covers for lack of inward strength, and that the pursuit of truth can never take place on an external plane, as in *Pillars of Society*, but only within the minds of the characters. Ultimately Ibsen denies the basic philosophy of the well-made play, that there is meaning and progress in time, and that all human beings are rational creatures, subject to the reassuring process of cause and effect.

Despite this denial, Ibsen never fully escaped from the well-made play. Even his later works are structured with carefully contrived climaxes and often spectacular denouements. Given the elusive nature of his material, a firm sense of dramatic structure was fortunate if he were not to lose his audience entirely. But such firmness could be deceptive. In *Rosmersholm*, for example, the logical progress of the action gives the impression that Rosmer and his partner, Rebekka West, are advancing toward some positive goal; in fact the impression turns out to be merely an ironic counterpoint to the steady growth of their realization that suicide is the only solution to their lives, which in fact have no meaning. It is at moments like this that the clarity and lack of ambiguity that were so strong a cause for the well-made play's appeal are totally abandoned. Ambiguity and paradox take their place, and these become expressed not only through conflicting lines of inner action but also through Ibsen's famous symbols, which ultimately take upon themselves the full meaning of the play and deprive action, the soul of the well-made play, of prime significance. It is here that Ibsen goes far beyond any drama that could have been conceived by Scribe, or even Scribe's mentor, Aristotle. For Ibsen, Scribe was a starting point only, and the well-made play was of significance to him mainly as the springboard for a drama that extended far beyond the limits of the surface world, limits within which Scribe and most playwrights who followed him were happy to be confined.

The well-made play has not enjoyed a good reputation in recent years. Like "melodrama," the phrase has become a term of abuse rather than of praise. Although many scholars have argued recently that we should accord the form greater respect, there are good historical reasons for our suspicion of it today. By the end of the nineteenth century, the well-made play and the popular commercial theater were almost synonymous conceptions, at least in the eyes of those who wanted to create an alternative to the Parisian boulevards or the London West End. Our own theater, or at least the influential experimental work in it, has consistently followed the reactions of those pioneers.

The first phase in the development of an alternative to the commercial theater began in 1887, when André Antoine founded the Théâtre Libre in Paris. Antoine, along with Émile Zola, advocated naturalism in the theater, rejecting the contrived situations of the well-made play, claiming that too much attention was being paid to form and not enough to recreating on stage the conditions of everyday life. Though some playwrights staged by Antoine—Brieux and Ibsen among them—had clearly been influenced by the well-made play, the main purpose of his theater became, partly against his will, to present "slices of life," plays that were virtually formless and were intended to arouse in his audiences an awareness of how life was lived outside the drawing room. The themes of such plays naturally threatened rather than confirmed the beliefs of the well-heeled audiences who patronized the commercial theaters. So Antoine's theater, even though it was influential in inspiring similar enterprises elsewhere, remained a minority taste. In Paris the companion movement to naturalism, symbolism—most notably in the plays of Maurice Maeterlinck under the direction of Aurélien Lugné-Poë—and neoromanticism in Germany, Austria, and Russia, were devoted to creating an awareness of extraterrestrial forces, to reinstilling into the theater a poetry that, it was claimed, had been lost because of the theater's obsession with the well-made play.

Each subsequent movement in European theater contradicted the basic assumptions of the well-made play. George Bernard Shaw, who while he was a critic had bestowed on the form the dubious accolade of "Sardoodledom," cultivated as a playwright a drama in which the discussion of ideas was the center of interest, even though his work owed a considerable debt to the popular drama he claimed to despise. The German expressionists were violently opposed to the well-made, well-bred theater. In their plays, plots based on cause and effect were abandoned, while unity of impression was constantly violated by their disconcerting and occasionally powerful changes of style in the middle of the play. Their work was influenced by one of the most widely performed of all early avant-garde dramatists, August Strindberg, who, from early in his playwriting career, worked constantly to undermine the hold of the well-made play. Bertolt Brecht campaigned against a theater in which the audience's attention was engaged by suspense alone. He also wished to destroy the illusion of reality that had always been an element of the well-made play. Instead he exposed the mechanism of the theater and used the stage as a platform from which to change the ideas of his audiences. In Paris meanwhile, in the years between the wars, experimentation in styles of poetic theater, ranging from the austere productions of Jacques Co-

peau to the nihilistic visions of Antonin Artaud, were all aimed at destroying the theater of the well-made play substituting for it a stage on which people were seen not solely as social beings, but as part of a greater natural, even supernatural, world.

Our theater today is far more varied than it was at the end of the nineteenth century. In Europe and America there is now a vigorous noncommercial theater that has often been abrasive, iconoclastic, offensive, ecstatic, tasteless, violent, and occasionally obscure to the point of perversity. It is a theater that has little concern for the niceties of balance and structure, and it does not ask for a mute, passive audience. It wants to do what Scribe never did, to disturb and challenge. This has often been an exhilarating theater. Because it has at times been startlingly original, naturally we tend to pay more attention to it than we do to the more quotidian activities of the commercial theater. But that too, despite the assaults made on it since Antoine's time, is even today, for good or ill, alive. Alive with it is the well-made play.

A hundred and fifty years ago, Scribe did not suddenly invent a new form of drama. Instead, by finding the right combination of a number of dramatic elements that had been used since drama began, he discovered how to tell a story in a way that catered with remarkable precision to the tastes of his audience. In later years, playwrights modified his formula, but the fundamental elements and their linear relationships were maintained. Even today, if one wishes to tell a story and hold an audience's breathless attention, Scribe's formula is inescapable. Thus, while we do not see on Broadway or the West End the plays of Scribe, Dumas, Augier, or Robertson, and all too rarely see Labiche, Feydeau, or Pinero, the well-made play is still with us. Noel Coward, Terence Rattigan, even Harold Pinter and other important contemporary dramatists, have constructed their plays with Scribe's formula in mind, even when they may not recognize their source. The same is true of popu-

1931

lar dramatists in America, Neil Simon being an excellent case in point.

Now, of course, the well-made play is not only seen on stage. In the massive outpouring of acted drama demanded by television, scriptwriters, like Scribe in the early nineteenth century, have no freedom, leisure, or incentive to produce works of art that are painstakingly written or carefully crafted. Instead they constantly fall back on well-tried situations, stock characters, and a familiar formula. Turn on any episode in a soap opera, a comedy, or a thriller series, and ninety-nine times out of a hundred you will see the old arrangement of exposition, complication, *scène à faire*, and denouement. As you watch that episode, spare a thought for the patron saint of it all, Eugène Scribe, and wish that more writers today had even a modicum of the resourcefulness, ingenuity, and sheer sense of theater that distinguish his plays and those of his successors.

Selected Bibliography

COLLECTED WORKS

Augier, Émile. *Théâtre complet.* 7 vols. Paris, 1889.

Bauernfeld, Eduard von. *Gesammelte Schriften.* 12 vols. Vienna, 1871–1873.

Brieux, Eugène. *Théâtre complet.* 9 vols. Paris, 1921–1930.

Dumas fils, Alexandre. *Théâtre complet avec préfaces inédites.* 8 vols. Paris, 1890–1898.

Feydeau, Georges. *Théâtre complet.* 5 vols. Introduced by Marcel Achard. Paris, 1948–1951.

Freytag, Gustav. *Dramatische Werke.* 2 vols. Leipzig, 1868.

Gutzkow, Karl. *Dramatische Werke.* 4 vols. Jena, 1881.

Hervieu, Paul. *Théâtre complet.* 3 vols. Paris, [ca. 1910].

Ibsen, Henrik. *Samlede verker.* 21 vols. Oslo, 1928–1957. Centenary edition.

Labiche, Eugène. *Théâtre complet.* 10 vols. Introduced by Émile Augier. Paris, 1878–1898.

————. *Le Théâtre de Labiche.* 4 vols. Edited by Pierre-Aimé Touchard and Gilbert Sigaux. Paris, 1970.

Laube, Heinrich. *Dramatische Werke.* 12 vols. Leipzig, 1886–1900.

Meilhac, Henri, and Ludwig Halévy. *Théâtre.* 15 vols. Paris, 1859–1882.

Pinero, Sir Arthur Wing. *The Plays of Arthur W. Pinero.* 25 vols. London, 1891–1915.

Robertson, Thomas W. *Principal Dramatic Works of Thomas William Robertson, with a Memoir by His Son.* 2 vols. London, 1889.

Sardou, Victorien. *Théâtre complet.* 15 vols. Paris, 1934–1961.

Scribe, Eugène. *Oeuvres complètes.* 5 vols. Paris, 1840–1841.

————. *Oeuvres complètes.* 16 vols. Paris, 1854.

TRANSLATIONS

Augier, Émile. *Four Plays by Augier.* Translated by Barrett H. Clark. New York, 1915. Includes *M. Poirier's Son-in-Law, Olympe's Marriage, The House of Fourchambault, The Post-Script.*

Bentley, Eric, ed. *Let's Get a Divorce! and Other Plays.* New York, 1958. Includes Labiche, *A Trip Abroad (Le voyage de M. Perrichon), Célimare;* Feydeau, *Keep an Eye on Amélie.* Essays by Bentley on "The Psychology of Farce" and Marcel Achard on "Georges Feydeau."

Bermel, Albert, trans. *Three Popular French Comedies.* New York, 1975. Includes Labiche, *Pots of Money (La cagnotte).*

Brieux, Eugène. *Three Plays by Brieux.* Translated by Mrs. [George] Bernard Shaw, St. John Hankin, and John Pollack. Preface by George Bernard Shaw. London, 1911. Includes *Maternity, The Three Daughters of M. Dupont,* and *Damaged Goods.*

————. *Woman on Her Own, False Gods, and The Red Robe.* Translated by Mrs. [George] Bernard Shaw, J. F. Fagan, and A. Bernard Miall. Preface by Eugène Brieux. London, 1917.

Clark, Barrett, ed. *World Drama: An Anthology.* 2 vols. New York, 1933. Includes Augier, *M. Poirier's Son-in-Law,* translated by Barrett H. Clark; and Dumas fils, *The Demi-Monde,* translated by Harold Harper.

Davies, Frederick, ed. and trans. *Three French Farces.* Harmondsworth, 1971. Includes Labiche, *The Happiest of the Three;* Sardou, *Let's Get a Divorce!;* Feydeau, *Get Out of My Hair (Un fil à la patte).*

Feydeau, Georges. *Better Late (Feu la mère de Madame)*. Translated by Peter Meyer. New York and London, 1976.

————. *First to Last: Eight One-Act Comedies.* Translated and introduced by Norman Shapiro. Ithaca, N.Y., and London, 1982. Includes *Ladies' Man (Notre futur); Wooed and Viewed (Par la fenétre); Romance in a Flat (Amour et piano); Fit to be Tried; or, Stepbrothers in Crime (Gibrier de potence); Mixed Doubles (C'est une femme du monde); The Boor Hug (Les paves de l'ours); Caught with His Trance Down (Dormez, je le veux); Tooth and Consequences; or, Hortense said: "No Skin off My Ass!" (Hortense a dit: "Je m'en fous!").*

————. *Fitting for Ladies (Tailleurs pour Dames)*. Translated by Peter Meyer. London, 1974.

————. *Four Farces.* Translated and introduced by Norman Shapiro. Chicago and London, 1970. Includes *Wooed and Wed; On the Merry-go-Wrong (Le marriage de Barillon); Not by Bed Alone (Un fil à la patte); Gone to Pot (On purge bébé).*

————. *A Flea in Her Ear.* Translated by John Mortimer. London, 1960.

————. *Hotel Paradiso.* Translated by Peter Glenville. New York, 1957.

————. *Sauce for the Goose (Le dindon).* Translated by Peter Meyer. London, 1974.

————. *A Close Shave (Champignol malgré lui).* Translated by Peter Meyer. London, 1974.

Hervieu, Paul. *The Labyrinth.* Translated by Barrett H. Clark and Lander MacClintock. New York, 1913.

Ibsen, Henrik. *The Oxford Ibsen.* 8 vols. Edited and translated by James W. McFarlane. London, 1961–1977.

Labiche, Eugène. *The Italian Straw Hat and The Spelling Mistake.* Translated and adapted by Frederick Davies. London, 1967.

Pailleron, Édouard. *The Art of Being Bored.* Translated by Barrett H. Clark. New York, 1914.

Scribe, Eugéne.*The Queen's Gambit (Bataille des dames).* Translated and adapted by Maurice Valency. New York, 1956.

Stanton, Stephen S., ed. *Camille and Other Plays.* New York, 1957. Includes Scribe and J. F. A. Bayard, *A Peculiar Position;* Scribe, *The Glass of Water;* Dumas fils, *Camille; ou, La Dame aux camélias;* Augier, *Olympe's Marriage;* Sardou, *A Scrap of Paper.* Also includes bibliography of all ascertainable adaptations and translations of the plays of Scribe, Dumas fils, Augier, and Sardou.

BIOGRAPHICAL AND CRITICAL STUDIES

CONTEMPORARY THEATER AND CRITICISM

Archer, William. *Play-making: A Manual of Craftsmanship.* London, 1912.

Bergson, Henri, *Le rire: Essai sur la signification du comique.* Paris, 1900. Translated as "Laughter" by Wylie Sypher in his edition *Comedy.* New York, 1956. Pp. 61–190.

Freytag, Gustav. *Die Technik des Dramas.* Leipzig, 1890. 6th ed. Translated by Elias J. MacEwan as *Technique of the Drama.* Chicago, 1894.

Gautier, Théophile. *Histoire de l'art dramatique.* 6 vols. Paris, 1858–1859.

Matthews, Brander, ed. *Papers on Playmaking.* New York, 1957. Includes papers on playwriting by Dumas fils, Labiche, Sardou, Sarcey, and Augier, as well as Ernest Legouvé's essay on Scribe.

Sarcey, Françiscque. *Quarante ans de théâtre.* 4 vols. Paris, 1900–1902.

Shaw, George Bernard. *Our Theatres in the Nineties.* 3 vols. London, 1932.

GENERAL

Bentley, Eric. "Farce." In his *The Life of the Drama.* New York, 1964.

Hauser, Arnold. "The Generation of 1830" and "The Second Empire." In his *The Social History of Art,* vol. 4. Translated by Stanley Goldman. New York, n.d. Pp. 3–105.

Lamm, Martin. *Modern Drama.* Translated by Karin Elliott. Oxford, 1952.

Matthews, Brander. *French Dramatists of the Nineteenth Century.* 5th ed. New York, 1914.

Montague, C. E. "The Well-Made Play." In his *Dramatic Values.* New York, 1911. Pp. 63–74.

Nicoll, Allardyce. *A History of Early Nineteenth Century Drama, 1800–1850.* 2 vols. Cambridge, 1930.

————. *A History of Late Nineteenth Century Drama, 1850–1900.* 2 vols. Cambridge, 1946.

————. *World Drama from Aeschylus to Anouilh.* New York [1950?]. Pp. 485–518.

Simon, Elliott M. *The Problem Play in the English Drama, 1890–1914.* Salzburg Studies in English Literature. Salzburg, 1978.

Smith, Hugh A. *Main Currents of Modern French Drama.* New York, 1925.

Stanton, Stephen S. "Introduction" to *Camille and Other Plays.* New York, 1957.

Taylor, John Russell. *The Rise and Fall of the Well-Made Play.* New York, 1967.

ALEXANDRE DUMAS *FILS*

Schwarz, Stanley H. *Alexandre Dumas* fils, *Dramatist.* New York, 1927.

Taylor, Frank A. *The Theatre of Alexandre Dumas fils.* Oxford, 1937.

GEORGES FEYDEAU

Baker, Stuart E. *Georges Feydeau and the Aesthetics of Farce.* Ann Arbor, Mich., 1981.

Pronko, Leonard C. *Georges Feydeau.* New York, 1975.

Shapiro, Norman. "Suffering and Punishment in the Theatre of Georges Feydeau." *Tulane Drama Review* 5:117–126 (1960).

Steiner, Roger J. "The Perennial Georges Feydeau." *Symposium* 15:49–54 (1961).

ARTHUR WING PINERO

Lazenby, Walter. *Arthur Wing Pinero.* New York, 1972.

Leggatt, Alexander. "Pinero: From Farce to Social Drama." *Modern Drama* 17:329–344 (1974).

Miner, Edmund D. "The Limited Naturalism of Arthur Pinero." *Modern Drama* 19:147–159 (1976).

THOMAS W. ROBERTSON

Durbach, Erroll. "Remembering Tom Robertson (1829–1871)." *Educational Theatre Journal* 24:284–288 (1972).

Savin, Maynard. *Thomas William Robertson: His Plays and Stagecraft.* Brown University Studies 13. Providence, R.I., 1950.

VICTORIEN SARDOU

Hart, Jerome A. *Sardou and the Sardou Plays.* Philadelphia, 1913.

EUGÈNE SCRIBE

Arvin, Neil, C. *Eugène Scribe and the French Theatre, 1815–60.* Cambridge, Mass., 1924.

Bentley, Eric. "Homage to Scribe." In his *What Is Theatre? A Query in Chronicle Form.* Boston, 1956. Pp. 64–67.

Gillespie, Patti. "Plays: Well-Complicated." *Speech Monographs* 42:20–28 (1975).

————. "Plays: Well-Constructed and Well-Made." *Quarterly Journal of Speech* 58:313–321 (1972).

Koon, Helene, and Richard Switzer. *Eugène Scribe.* Boston, 1980.

Raafat, Z. "Scribe's Plays and Their English Versions in the Nineteenth Century." *Révue de Littérature Comparée* 45:237–255 (1971).

Stanton, Stephen S. "Ibsen, Gilbert, and Scribe's *Bataille de Dames.*" *Educational Theatre Journal* 17:24–30 (1965).

SIMON WILLIAMS